CRITICAL COMPANION TO

William Shakespeare

*A Literary Reference to
His Life and Work*

VOLUME I

CRITICAL COMPANION TO

William Shakespeare

A Literary Reference to His Life and Work

VOLUME I

CHARLES BOYCE

Facts On File, Inc.

Critical Companion to William Shakespeare:
A Literary Reference to His Life and Work

Facts On File, Inc.
132 West 31st Street
New York NY 10001

Library of Congress Cataloging-in-Publication Data
Boyce, Charles
Critical companion to William Shakespeare: a literary reference to his life and work / Charles Boyce.—Rev. ed.
p. cm.
Rev. ed. of: Shakespeare A to Z. 1990.
Includes bibliographical references and index.
ISBN 0-8160-5373-1 (hc: alk. paper)
1. Shakespeare, William 1564–1616—Dictionaries. 2. Dramatists, English—Early modern,
1500–1700—Biography—Dictionaries. I. Boyce, Charles. Shakespeare A to Z. II. Title.
PR2892.B69 2005
822.3'3—dc22   2004025769

Facts On File books are available at special discounts when purchased in
bulk quantities for businesses, associations, institutions, or sales promotions.
Please call our Special Sales Department in New York at
(212) 967-8800 or (800) 322-8755.

You can find Facts On File on the World Wide Web at
http://www.factsonfile.com

Text design by Joan M. Toro
Adapted by Erika K. Arroyo
Cover design by Cathy Rincon

Printed in the United States of America

VB Hermitage 10 9 8 7 6 5 4 3 2 1

This book is printed on acid-free paper.

Contents

PREFACE

In the 14 years since the first edition of this book was published, study of the playwright and his works has proceeded apace, though with the usual healthy amount of dissent the field seems always to stimulate: A new play, *Edward III,* has been admitted to the panoply of the works; another *Cardenio,* has been published as such but generally rejected; two poems—*A FUNERAL ELEGY* and "SHALL I DIE?"— much under discussion in 1990 as possibly Shakespeare's, have been assigned elsewhere; and our constantly coursing curiosity about the man and his works has continued to spur inquiry, including recent investigations into his possible Catholicism and his probable collaboration with other playwrights. And of course Shakespeare provides, as always, grist for the various mills of literary theory, though these tedious machines are not dealt with here.

Indeed, it is worth remarking again that this book is not meant as scholarship; my intention has been to assemble conveniently a body of lore for the information and entertainment of the student and general reader. I have not studded the book with references to the scholarship of others that underlies it, for I have assumed that most readers will have little interest in knowing, say, who first suggested that Brian ANNESLEY was a living model for King Lear's madness. I make no claim to having discovered this possibility, though I do not name the scholar who did. It is enough that someone did, and that the discovery came to my attention, so that I can bring it to yours.

How to Use This Book

Part I of this book contains a brief biography of Shakespeare. Part II contains entries on all of Shakespeare's known works. Furthermore, each entry on a play contains subentries on all the characters appearing in that play. Many characters appear in more than one play but are fully entered at only one to avoid pointless duplication. In this case cross-references are provided in the other corresponding plays. Part III contains entries on related places, terms, documents, references, works, and people, including collaborators, actors, scholars, relatives, and more. Part IV contains the appendices: a collection of quotations, a Shakespearean time line, a suggested reading list, and a list of the entries in this book divided into categories.

Reference to any name or term that appears as an entry in Part III: Related Entries is printed on first appearance in SMALL CAPITALS.

A NOTE ON CITATIONS

Line citations used in this book are taken from the *New Arden Shakespeare* (Methuen, 1951–84), except in the case of two plays not included in the *New Arden* canon. For *The Two Noble Kinsmen,* citations are from the New Penguin edition (Penguin Books, 1977), and for *Edward III,* from the New Cambridge edition (Cambridge University Press, 1998).

Part I

Biography

Shakespeare, William
(1564–1616)

The few available facts about Shakespeare's life are mostly mundane details, reflecting the ordinary existence of an Englishman of his day and social position. He exemplified the enterprising yeoman advancing to gentleman status, a common phenomenon in his day. Like many ambitious early modern Englishmen, he was attracted to LONDON without surrendering his roots in the countryside. In terms of day-to-day life, the only unusual feature was that he was a part of the theatrical world. In Shakespeare's day, actors, playwrights, and theatrical entrepreneurs were only just emerging from an era in which they were stigmatized by both law and custom (see ELIZA-BETHAN THEATER). Though in the course of Shakespeare's lifetime, the courts of Queen Elizabeth I (see Elizabeth I in *Henry VIII*) and King JAMES I gave prestige to acting, and a few theater people—including Shakespeare—got rich, protest against drama and acting was still very strong in England. The fascination with theatrical lives that resulted in memoirs and biographies in later periods did not yet exist. Nevertheless, the broad outlines of Shakespeare's life can be discerned.

Shakespeare's life falls into three main periods. His first 20 years were spent in STRATFORD, where his father was a member of the local establishment. His career as an actor and playwright in London lasted about 25 years. Finally, he retired to Stratford, where for about five years before his death he was a moderately wealthy member of the local gentry. The first two periods are linked by several years about which we know absolutely nothing—the so-called dark years—and the transition between the last two was gradual and cannot be precisely dated.

William Shakespeare was baptized on April 25, 1564, and since the normal lag between birth and baptism was several days, his birthday is conventionally regarded as April 23—also the date of his death 52 years later. The infant Shakespeare survived an episode of plague that swept Stratford in the summer and fall of 1564, killing about one-eighth of its inhabitants. His father, John SHAKESPEARE, was the son of a farmer who lived near Stratford. A member of the yeoman class, John became a tradesman and moved to the town. He prospered and became one of the leading figures of Stratford's establishment, only to encounter serious financial difficulties, for unknown reasons. These began during Shakespeare's adolescence and were only resolved 20 years later, with the money Shakespeare earned in the theater. However, the family was evidently never impoverished, for the family home (see BIRTHPLACE) was never sold, and John's status in the community was probably not seriously diminished. Shakespeare's mother, Mary Arden SHAKESPEARE, was a member of the gentry, the next higher social class. Her father, Robert ARDEN, was an owner of inherited property that he both farmed himself and leased to other farmers. The boundary between the gentry and yeoman classes was notably permeable in the 16th century, and John Shakespeare's rise in status through marriage was quite typical.

No record of Shakespeare's education has survived, but he doubtless attended the excellent Stratford Grammar School, which was appropriate to his family's status and free of charge, since his father was an official of the town. Under the guidance of a series of schoolmasters—Simon HUNT, Thomas JENKINS (the most important in terms of time spent with Shakespeare), John COTTOM, and possibly Walter ROCHE and Alexander ASPINALL—Shakespeare studied mostly Latin literature, in Latin. Fragments of the standard textbook of the day, William LILY's *Latin Grammar*, appear in the plays, most amusingly in the famous "Latin scene" (4.1) of *The Merry Wives of Windsor*. Also, the Latin authors he studied, such as OVID, LIVY, and VIRGIL, are echoed, quoted, and occasionally mentioned in the plays.

Shakespeare probably left school at the normal age, about 15, in 1579. It seems likely, particularly in view of his father's financial problems, that young William took a job of some sort at this point. A number of possibilities have been envisioned—based on various traditions and on references in the plays that imply familiarity with certain occupations—including assistant schoolmaster, law clerk, gardener, and, perhaps the most natural supposition, assistant to his father, who was a glover and dealer in commodities. In any case, John Shakespeare's business activities left the playwright with specialized knowledge that he was later to put to good use—for instance, when the Clown in *The Winter's Tale* puzzles over the market price of wool in 4.3.32–34, or when a beard is described as "round . . . like a glover's paring-knife" (*Merry Wives*, 1.4.18–19). Recollections of life in the countryside around Stratford are also frequently found in the plays (see, e.g., HAMLETT, KATHERINE; PERKES, CLEMENT; VISOR, WILLIAM), especially in the INDUCTION to the early *Taming of the Shrew* (see SLY, CHRISTOPHER). The town life he knew in Stratford itself is not often appropriate to his dramas, but it too is convincingly portrayed in *The Merry Wives of Windsor*.

Within a few years after leaving school, Shakespeare had an affair with Anne HATHAWAY, which led to her pregnancy and a hasty marriage, late in 1582 (see RICHARDSON, JOHN; SANDELLS, FULK; TEMPLE GRAFTON; WHITGIFT, JOHN). Anne, eight years older than her 18-year-old husband, was the daughter of a farmer in a nearby village. In May 1583 their first child, Susanna SHAKESPEARE, was born; twins, Hamnet and Judith SHAKESPEARE, soon followed. The christening of the twins in February 1585 provides assurance that Shakespeare was in Stratford nine months earlier, but no record of his activities between then and 1592 has survived. That period, utterly opaque to modern investigation, constitutes the "dark years."

Scholarly speculation has not been wanting, of course. Most notoriously, there was a local tradition—first published in the 18th century—that Shakespeare had been caught poaching by a local nobleman, Sir Thomas LUCY, and had thus departed for London as a fugitive. Modern scholarship finds both story and conclusion highly dubious, and attention has instead focused on Shakespeare's likely occupation during the dark years. In addition to the various possibilities already outlined, suggestions have included a term as a soldier—in the Netherlands under Robert Dudley, Earl of LEICESTER, or as part of the defense forces assembled against the Spanish Armada in 1588—or a job in the London publishing industry, perhaps with his fellow Stratfordian, the printer Richard FIELD.

A 17th-century writer established a tradition that Shakespeare had been a butcher during this period, reporting that young Will had been known to "kill a calf" in uproarious spirits. His conclusion was based on a misunderstanding: to "kill a calf" was Elizabethan theatrical slang for a particular comic routine, the details of which are lost. Nevertheless, the anecdote points to the only certain fact about the dark years: at some point Shakespeare became involved with a theatrical company. Many traveling companies played at Stratford, an important provincial town, during Shakespeare's youth, and LEICESTER'S MEN were there in 1586, followed by the QUEEN'S MEN (who possibly had a vacancy [see KNELL, WILLIAM]) in 1587. However, there is no evidence that such troupes ever recruited on the road, and Shakespeare probably had to go to London to begin his career.

A recent theory has focused on the possibility that the young Shakespeare was a secret Catholic, and that during the dark years he was in Lancashire training to be a priest. (The most salient piece of evidence suggesting Shakespeare's Catholicism is the SPIRITUAL TESTAMENT OF JOHN SHAKESPEARE, though this speaks more to the religion of Shakespeare's father than to his own, and it is unfortunately true that on the subject of Shakespeare's own religion, virtually no hard evidence exists.) Stratford was a center of secret Catholicism, in a period when overt Catholicism was considered by the English government to be treason against the newly Protestant state and was subject to severe punishment (including, for priests, death), and several of Shakespeare's teachers, were probably Catholic activists. In fact, John Cottam was connected with a Lancashire nobleman named Alexander Hoghton, who harbored a clandestine training center intended to prepare young men for a career as Jesuit priests, and it is hypothesized that Cottam may have recruited Shakespeare into this program.

In 1581 Hoghton wrote his will, in which he asked a neighbor to "be friendly unto" two young men he employed, either hiring them himself or finding them "some good master." These men were named Fulke Gillam and William Shakeshafte; the latter's suggestive name has sparked a train of speculation: Gillam is known to have been an actor and therefore Shakeshafte may have been one, too. Hoghton was apparently acquainted with

Ferdinando Stanley, Lord STRANGE, and therefore Shakeshafte may have been placed with STRANGE'S MEN, who are believed to have employed the young Shakespeare. The government uncovered the Catholic center in Lancashire and destroyed it—eventually executing several participants, including Cottam's brother—just at the time William Shakeshafte would have left the Hoghton household. Disguised or at least employed as a player, Shakeshafte may have found his way to London.

However, this chain of suppositions—which further supposes that a young Catholic activist, perhaps destined for the priesthood, would have responded to the interruption of his training by joining a theatrical troupe, a decidedly secular enterprise, *and* by beginning or resuming his illicit affair with Anne Hathaway—is more suggestive than conclusive. It involves very little actual evidence and is not widely accepted among scholars.

By whatever roads he may have traveled, Shakespeare was probably in London no later than about 1589, for he was established as an actor and playwright by 1592, when the scurrilous criticism of Robert GREENE makes it clear that he was well known. The response by Henry CHETTLE makes it just as clear that he was respected and admired. Several of the plays were already popular—*3 Henry VI* is quoted from by Greene—and while the earliest plays are notoriously difficult to date, it seems likely that they included *The Comedy of Errors, Titus Andronicus,* the three *Henry VI* plays, *Richard III, Edward III,* and *The Taming of the Shrew.* In recent years, scholars have established that many plays of ELIZABETHAN DRAMA were written collaboratively, sometimes by teams of several playwrights. Moreover, it seems clear that, especially in his early years, Shakespeare was a member of such teams—paying his dues, as it were, by contributing to other people's projects, before he was assigned his own—and a number of the earliest plays are now considered to have been written collaboratively. Most certainly determined (though some commentators disagree on any given point): George PEELE was very probably a coauthor of *Titus* and possibly of *Edward III,* and while no collaborator in *1 Henry VI* can be surely named, it was certainly written by a pair or group that included the young Shakespeare.

Several of these plays were performed by an acting company called PEMBROKE'S MEN, and it seems likely that early in his career Shakespeare wrote and acted for them. Similar considerations also suggest links with the ADMIRAL'S MEN, SUSSEX'S MEN, and Strange's Men. The latter seems especially likely, because the earliest sure evidence of his employment is a document of 1594, in which he is listed as a principal member of Strange's Men's successor, the CHAMBERLAIN'S MEN.

In the meantime his career was affected by a plague outbreak that closed the theaters in London for about two years, beginning in 1592. Shakespeare may have toured the provinces with a company under William ALLEYN, but he may have left the theater for a period. He turned his attention to a purely literary endeavor, the writing of book-length poems. His virtues as a writer had by now been established, and the theater was not regarded as the best career for a serious literary artist in the 16th century. The likeliest avenue to fame and fortune was to write major works of poetry or prose. Writers offered their works as tokens of esteem to wealthy nobles, who, if they were pleased, might respond with a gift of money or even some extended financial support. It was the aristocracy that supported the literary world, for the most part, with publishing playing only a small role. A writer might live quite comfortably with a generous patron, and it is evident that Shakespeare attempted to tap this market during the long layoff due to the plague. He wrote his two long poems, *Venus and Adonis* (1593) and *The Rape of Lucrece* (1594), during this period and dedicated them to Henry Wriothesley, Earl of SOUTHAMPTON. Some scholars believe he lived at Southampton's estate for some part of the time. The first of his dedications, in 1593, is an ordinary approach to a potential patron, conventionally flattering and self-deprecating, while the second suggests a warm friendship and makes it clear that the earl had responded positively to the young poet's work. In fact, that the two men were friends is one of the few undocumented aspects of Shakespeare's life that virtually all scholars accept. In addition to their success with Southampton, the two poems were immediately popular with the reading public, as well, as we know from the published remarks of Richard BARNFIELD, Gabriel HARVEY, and William COVELL.

However—whether out of concern for his independence or from love of the theater or in view of some unknown factor—Shakespeare returned to the stage in 1594. Strange's Men were reorganized as the Chamberlain's Men in June of that year, and the playwright is assumed to have joined them then or shortly thereafter, since he was a prominent member of the company in December, when he was a representative of the troupe at court. He was to remain with this company for the rest of his career. During his first few years with them, he wrote a long string of successful plays, probably including (though dates continue to be uncertain) *Love's Labour's Lost, Romeo and Juliet, Richard II, A Midsummer Night's Dream,* and *King John.* An earlier play, *Richard III,* was extremely popular as performed by the Chamberlain's Men; later tradition had it that it established both Shakespeare and its leading man, Richard BURBAGE, as important figures in the London theater world. They became subjects of gossip, at least, for the only surviving personal anecdote of Shakespeare that can be certainly dated to his lifetime concerns Burbage and a female admirer during a production of *Richard III* (see MANNINGHAM, JOHN).

Tax assessments and the records of an obscure lawsuit (see GARDINER, WILLIAM) reveal some of Shakespeare's residences during this period. He apparently moved across the city when the Chamberlain's Men moved from the THEATRE, in a northern suburb, to the SWAN THEATRE, in southern SOUTHWARK. Some scholars believe that his tax bill in the first of these homes was too large for a single man's dwelling, suggesting that his wife and children spent time with him in London. There is no further evidence to confirm this, however.

Throughout the 1590s, and perhaps somewhat later, Shakespeare wrote his *Sonnets,* a complex sequence of love poems that is one of the masterpieces of English poetry. These poems are often taken to reflect a real love for a man and a woman, but they probably represent merely Shakespeare's pursuit of a fashionable genre. In any case, if they are autobiographical they are deliberately obscure and can contribute little to our knowledge of his life; they recount no events or incidents, and they offer little concrete information about the persons depicted. Shakespeare also composed an allegorical poem, "The Phoenix and Turtle," written for *LOVE'S MARTYR* (1601), an anthology of poems celebrating an aristocratic marriage. In addition, a number of brief EPITAPHS are sometimes ascribed to Shakespeare by various scholars.

Shakespeare continued to turn out plays at a great rate, probably completing the following between 1596 and the death of Queen Elizabeth in 1603: *The Merchant of Venice,* the two *Henry IV* plays, *The Merry Wives of Windsor, Henry V, Much Ado About Nothing, Julius Caesar, As You Like It, Hamlet, Twelfth Night,* and *Troilus and Cressida.* In 1598 an edition of *Love's Labour's Lost* was the first publication to have Shakespeare's name on it, as booksellers realized the value of his growing fame. In the same year Francis MERES cited him as among England's best playwrights for both COMEDY and TRAGEDY and compared his poetry to the greatest of the ancients.

In 1596, after the first years of Shakespeare's theatrical success, John Shakespeare was awarded a COAT OF ARMS. Such tokens of gentlemanly status were nominally awarded for a family's services to the nation, but they were in fact bought, and it is assumed that the playwright paid the fees for the Shakespeare escutcheon. Such a public assertion of his family's recovery from their earlier troubles must have been satisfying to Shakespeare, especially when it was confirmed by the purchase of a grand Stratford mansion, NEW PLACE, in 1597. However, Shakespeare's triumphs were not unalloyed, for in 1596 his son Hamnet died at the age of 11. Shakespeare presumably returned to Stratford for Hamnet's burial, though his appearance went unrecorded; the earliest surviving documents indicating his presence in the town after 1584 are those recording the sale of New Place. The absence of any certain association of Shakespeare and Stratford for 13 years has sparked suggestions that the playwright had turned his back on his home, perhaps because of an unhappy marriage. However, the grant of arms, the purchase of New Place, and Shakespeare's continuing close involvement with Stratford thereafter constitute so firm a commitment to the town as to imply a strong earlier involvement as well. Later tradition recorded that he had all along returned frequently, and there is no reason to doubt it. That only the later visits can be substantiated merely points up the impact of wealth, for it is Shakespeare's money matters that are mostly recorded. He was soon a force in Stratford, being recorded in 1598 as a leading owner of grain and figuring several times in the correspondence of Richard QUINEY as a man of business. His father died in 1601, and Shakespeare inherited the birthplace, in half of which his family continued to live, while the other half—formerly his father's shop—was leased as an inn. New investments were made in Stratford in 1602 (see COMBE, JOHN; CHAPEL LANE COTTAGE) and land was added to the property surrounding New Place.

In London in 1599, Shakespeare became one of the partners in the new GLOBE THEATRE, a successful enterprise that furthered his prosperity. Most Elizabethan playwrights only wrote, and of the few who also acted—such as Thomas HEYWOOD and Nathan FIELD—Shakespeare alone was a partner in an acting company, deriving his income from the long-term success of the enterprise, rather than merely from the production of single plays. After the accession of King James in 1603, the company was part of the royal household—the number of courtly performances per year more than doubled—and in the first five years of the new regime, Shakespeare produced an astonishing sequence of major plays: *Othello, Measure for Measure, All's Well That Ends Well, King Lear, Macbeth, Coriolanus, Antony and Cleopatra,* and possibly *Pericles,* plus the unfinished *Timon of Athens.* Similarly, when, in 1608, the company acquired the BLACKFRIARS THEATRE, with its unusual new scenic capabilities and its sophisticated clientele, Shakespeare responded with plays in a new genre, the ROMANCES. These, with *Henry VIII, The Two Noble Kinsmen,* and the lost play *Cardenio,* comprise his final period.

Late in his career, Shakespeare was acquainted with the young Christopher BEESTON, whose son, retelling his father's reminiscences years later, left us one of the few glimpses we have of the living playwright. Beeston described Shakespeare as "a handsome well shap't man—very good company, and of a very readie and pleasant smooth Witt." Beeston also said that the playwright "understood Latine pretty well, for he had been in his younger yeares a Schoolmaster in the Countrey" (the earliest such statement), and added that he was "the more to be admired that he was not a company keeper [i.e., a partygoer] and he wouldn't be debauched."

In late 1603 Shakespeare appeared in a play by Ben JONSON; this may have been his last appearance on stage, for he does not appear on later cast lists. His career as an actor is obscure. He certainly began as one—Robert Greene complained in 1592 that it was presumptuous of him, as an actor, to write plays—and he appears in the cast lists of several plays put on by the Chamberlain's Men. We do not, however, know of any role he played or even that he ever appeared in one of his own works (though as a member of the company he probably did). He may have played the title character in George PEELE's *Edward I* (ca. 1593), for another character, referring to the king, says, "Shake thy spears in honour of his name." Several contemporary references seem to associate him with kingship (see, e.g., DAVIES, JOHN), and scholars have supposed that he played Duncan, Henry IV, or Henry VI (the great kingly protagonists such as Richard III and Lear were played by Burbage, however). Later traditions ascribed to Shakespeare the roles of Adam in *As You Like It* and the Ghost in *Hamlet.* From all this it seems likely that he specialized in roles of older, dignified men, but that his contribution as an actor was not a great one.

Late in his career, semiretired, Shakespeare again collaborated with other playwrights: possibly (a little earlier) with Thomas MIDDLETON on *Timon of Athens;* probably with George WILKINS on *Pericles;* and certainly with John FLETCHER, on *The Two Noble Kinsmen, Henry VIII,* and the lost *Cardenio.* This almost surely reflects Shakespeare's retirement to Stratford; he was certainly in residence there by 1612 (when he visited London to testify in a lawsuit [see MOUNTJOY]), and some scholars believe he may have made the move as early as 1610, writing *The Tempest* in the country. He presumably visited the city to confer with Fletcher and others on the late plays.

In 1607 his older daughter, Susanna, married a prominent Stratford physician, Dr. John HALL, who seems to have become Shakespeare's friend if he was not already, and in 1608 the couple had a child,

Elizabeth HALL. As the master of New Place, Shakespeare was one of the social leaders of the town; when visiting preachers came for high holy days, they stayed at Shakespeare's home. He continued to invest in Stratford real estate, and he may have planted the first mulberry tree in the town (though this idea, not published until 1790, was first reported by a neighbor born after Shakespeare's death), perhaps in response to King James's published desire (in 1609) that England introduce the cultivation of silkworms and attempt to compete with the ancient Chinese silk industry. The tree in question was long a local landmark. In 1605 Shakespeare bought a share of the tax revenues of some agricultural land (a purchasable commodity in those days), was involved in a lawsuit about it in 1611, and astutely managed the investment during the enclosure controversy of 1614 (see WELCOMBE). Also, in 1613 he bought an investment property in London, the BLACKFRIARS GATEHOUSE.

In January 1616 Shakespeare's lawyer, Francis COLLINS, prepared a draft of the playwright's last will and testament. In February his younger daughter Judith married the scandalous Thomas QUINEY, and Shakespeare rewrote his will to protect her portion from her husband, signing it on the 25th of March. On April 23 he died. We do not know the cause; a later tradition that he caught a chill drinking with his fellow playwrights Ben Jonson and Michael DRAYTON is almost certainly apocryphal. On April 25 he was buried—52 years to the day after his baptism—in the chancel of Holy Trinity Church. Sometime before 1622, the chancel wall received a memorial relief featuring a portrait bust by Gheerart JANSSEN, presumably commissioned by his family.

Shakespeare's gravestone bears the following epitaph (its archaic spelling modernized): "Good friend for Jesus' sake forbear / To dig the dust enclosed here. / Blessed be the man that spares these stones, / and cursed be he that moves my bones." (The moldering stone was replaced sometime around 1820, but an earlier record establishes that the epitaph was properly transmitted.) These lines have often been attributed to the playwright himself, but they are known on unrelated graves elsewhere and are probably a 17th-century cliché,

possibly not even a reflection of Shakespeare's taste, let alone his pen; they were not attributed to him until 40 years after his death. Oddly, the stone, set in the church floor, bears no name. Now in a prominent central location within the church, which may not have been the original burial site, it may have been damaged in being moved. Or it may originally have been placed below Janssen's memorial, where no name would have been needed. However, it is generally accepted as Shakespeare's; it lies with the other Shakespeare family stones, and its epitaph was well known as his since not long after his death.

This bald recitation of facts is as much as we can know about Shakespeare's life, unless further evidence is uncovered. Over the centuries speculative scholars and fantasizing enthusiasts have added a great variety of suppositions, extrapolating from the plays to make a more fully motivated, psychologically credible human being—or perhaps simply a more interesting person—than the simple documents allow. This is most easily done by assuming that the opinions expressed by the major characters in the plays—and by the persona of the poet in the *Sonnets*—are those of the author. However, efforts to interpret the works as fragments of autobiography are generally mistaken; the characters are imaginary, and because they must occupy all the niches of various fictional worlds, they naturally hold a wide range of attitudes and opinions. Even very broad interpretations are highly problematic. For instance, some critics have seen *The Winter's Tale*, in which unjust jealousy is followed by reconciliation, as an autobiographical rendering of the playwright's relationship with his wife. Though the story is in the play's source material, it is argued that Shakespeare must have been driven to choose that source by some similar experience of his own. However, in the absence of evidence, such a hypothesis remains untestable, and it certainly seems unnecessary. A writer who could produce almost two plays a year for 20 years and make real such diverse characters as, say, Falstaff, Hamlet, Volumnia, and the Nurse in *Romeo and Juliet*, can have had no serious problem finding material outside his own life. To argue that specific experiences are necessary for Shakespeare's art suggests that, on the evidence of *Hamlet,* he must have suffered from writer's block.

Nevertheless, if considered with care, Shakespeare's works can help us to a fuller comprehension of the man. Repeated motifs and concepts in the plays permit us to draw a few conclusions, however tentatively, about Shakespeare's sensibility and his general ideas on certain subjects. The HISTORY PLAYS and ROMAN PLAYS reflect a political conservatism—in the sense of resistance to changes in the existing system of social organization—that we might expect of a man of his time and social position. The late 16th and early 17th centuries were an anxious period in England, for the newly Protestant country was at odds with the Catholic powers of continental Europe—to the point of repelling an attempted invasion—and internal strife bubbled up in such episodes as the rebellion led by Robert Devereux, Earl of ESSEX. Indeed, civil war was regarded as a serious prospect during the last years of Elizabeth's reign (and after a brief respite it became reality, not long after Shakespeare's death). On a more personal level, the playwright's social position was newly achieved and, as his father's experience had demonstrated, precarious.

In these circumstances Shakespeare's politics were naturally conservative. For instance, the plays clearly demonstrate that he places a high value on the preservation of social order and distrusts the disorder that he sees in popular political assertiveness. From Jack Cade, through the Plebeians who kill the wrong man in *Julius Caesar* and the shifty Junius Brutus of *Coriolanus,* to *The Tempest*'s rebellious Caliban, the common man in his political aspect is generally a villain, though the playwright's fondness for the common people of England is evident in his many sympathetic characterizations, from the very early Dromios to the very late Boatswain. Still, the violent and fickle common man is only a secondary villain. In both the history and Roman dramas, popular disorder is seen as a *symptom* of moral sickness rather than a cause. The rulers of the state are the major focus, as aristocratic shortsightedness, greed, and ambition lead to usurpations and civil war. Shakespeare clearly found the greatest threat to society in disruption of the system at the top. Perhaps for this reason, he is

sometimes interpreted as representing a proto-revolutionary strain of thought; however, his notions actually reflect the political orthodoxy of the TUDOR DYNASTY, which naturally feared the threat of an opposing aristocratic faction, having come to power as one itself. Shakespeare's work and life considered together do not show us a member of the rising bourgeoisie who is nervous about the crown's overweening power—the proto-revolutionary image—but rather the unmistakable lineaments of a country gentleman and a social conservative.

An interpretation of Shakespeare's life from his work that sparks great controversy is the suggestion that the *Sonnets* indicate Shakespeare was a homosexual. However, the love for a man expressed in the *Sonnets* is not sexual (as is specified in Sonnet 20), though sexuality is important in the world of the poems. SONNET sequences were a fashionable vehicle for comments on love, and they conventionally took unrequited passion as their topic. The love triangle implicit in the *Sonnets* is probably such a convention—albeit more complex and involving than most (as we might expect of Shakespeare)—and so more convincing. In any case it almost certainly does not involve a homosexual relationship. Here, seeming biographical data have been forged from nothing, by applying modern values to premodern materials. As Stephen Booth, a modern editor of the *Sonnets,* has observed, "William Shakespeare was almost certainly homosexual, bisexual, or heterosexual. The sonnets provide no evidence on the matter."

Moreover, the plays repeatedly focus on heterosexual love and its culmination in marriage. Shakespeare's heroines are frankly interested in sex. Juliet longs for her wedding night and its "amorous rites" (*Romeo and Juliet* 3.2.8); Rosalind envisions Orlando, whom she has just met, as "my child's father" (*As You Like It* 1.3.11); and Perdita describes Florizel's body as "like a bank, for love to lie and play on" (*The Winter's Tale* 4.4.130). Throughout the plays, Shakespeare celebrates sexuality in marriage, and he plainly sees marriage as a vehicle for the fulfillment of humanity's place in the natural order of things. Nothing that can be seen of his own marriage suggests that he regarded it in any different light, and there seem no compelling grounds for the idea that he was not a conventional husband with a conventional sex life.

Propositions based on the work are necessarily speculative, but a few elements from the plays do seem related to what we know of Shakespeare's life. For instance, we have seen that Stratford is reflected in the early plays, and the playwright's love of country life is evident throughout his work. English rustics reappear in such unlikely settings as ATHENS (in both *A Midsummer Night's Dream* and *The Two Noble Kinsmen*), DENMARK (*Hamlet*), and BOHEMIA (*The Winter's Tale*). More personal concerns may also emerge. Looking at Shakespeare's remarkably similar doomed boys, the Son of Macduff in *Macbeth* and Mamillius in *The Winter's Tale,* both charming and intelligent lads seen in touching conversation with their mothers, it is easy to suppose that the playwright was remembering Hamnet. Also, we can surmise that Shakespeare's consciousness of his own increasing age is reflected in his remarkable sequence of tragic lovers. Romeo and Juliet (created ca. 1595, when Shakespeare was around 30) are virtually children, powerless in the face of adult society; Troilus and Cressida (1602) are young adults and have roles in their societies, but those roles are themselves oppressive and help undo their love; Othello and Desdemona (ca. 1604) are fully adult, married, and entirely in control of their positions in the world, though not of themselves; Antony and Cleopatra (ca. 1608, when Shakespeare was 44) are quite mature and have had adult lives full of incident and accomplishment. Shakespeare seems to have identified himself with different age groups as he grew older; this is of course natural, and in observing it we are not learning about Shakespeare's life through the plays but rather confirming our awareness that he made his plays out of life.

PART II

Works
A–S

All Is True

Alternative title for *Henry VIII*. The play is called *All Is True* in a contemporary account of its performance the day the GLOBE THEATRE burned down. This was probably a subtitle—perhaps to imply a contrast to another play about Henry VIII, the blatantly fictitious *When You See Me, You Know Me* (1605) by Samuel ROWLEY. Some scholars, however, contend that *All Is True* was Shakespeare's original title, which was altered in the FIRST FOLIO (1623) to go with the other HISTORY PLAYS, all named for kings.

All's Well That Ends Well
SYNOPSIS

Act 1, Scene 1

The Countess of Rossillion's son Bertram is leaving for the court of the King of France. The Countess and Lord Lafew discuss the King's poor health; she regrets that the father of her ward, Helena, has died, because he was a great physician. The Countess bids Bertram farewell and departs, and Bertram, after a cursory farewell to Helena, leaves with Lafew. Helena soliloquizes on her seemingly hopeless love for Bertram. Bertram's friend Parolles arrives and engages Helena in an exchange of witticisms on virginity. Parolles leaves, and Helena decides that she must act if her love is to be rewarded. She sees an opportunity in the King's illness.

Act 1, Scene 2

The King discusses the war between FLORENCE and Siena, stating that he has decided to permit noblemen of FRANCE to fight in the conflict if they wish. Bertram arrives and is welcomed warmly by the King. The King remarks on his ill health and regrets the death of the famed doctor who had served in the court at ROSSILLION.

Act 1, Scene 3

The Countess's jester, the Clown, requests permission to marry, making obscene jokes and singing songs. The Steward wishes to speak about Helena, and the Countess sends the Clown to get her. The Countess remarks on her fondness for Helena, and

the Steward confides that he has overheard the young woman musing on her love for Bertram. As the Steward leaves, Helena arrives, and the Countess elicits from her a confession of her love for Bertram and of her intention to go to Paris. Helena asserts that she has secret prescriptions of her father's that she is convinced will cure the King, and the Countess agrees to help her travel to Paris to try them.

Act 2, Scene 1

The King bids farewell to the First and Second Lords (1) and other young noblemen leaving to fight in Italy. Bertram regrets that he is commanded to remain at court. Lafew appears and introduces Helena as a young woman who can cure the King's illness. Helena convinces the King to try her medicine, offering to wager her life that it will work within 24 hours. In return, she asks the King to approve her marriage to the man of her choice.

Act 2, Scene 2

The Clown jests about life at the King's court, and the Countess gives him a message to take to Helena.

Act 2, Scene 3

Lafew, interrupted repeatedly by Parolles, tells of the King's return to health. The King arrives with Helena, who is to choose from among the young gentlemen of the court. She selects Bertram, but he refuses to marry her, saying that her social rank is too low. However, the King orders him to accept, and he acquiesces. Parolles puts on airs, and Lafew disdains him with elaborate insults. Lafew leaves, and Bertram reappears, declaring that he will run away to the wars in Italy before he will consummate his marriage to Helena. He plans to send Helena back to the Countess alone.

Act 2, Scene 4

Parolles conveys Bertram's instructions to Helena.

Act 2, Scene 5

Lafew warns Bertram not to rely on Parolles. Helena tells Bertram she is ready to leave; he pointedly avoids a farewell kiss. She departs, and Bertram and Parolles leave for Italy.

Act 3, Scene 1

The Duke of Florence receives the First and Second Lords (1).

Act 3, Scene 2

The Countess reads Bertram's letter declaring that he has run away from his new wife, as Helena appears with the First and Second Lords (1), who are on leave from Florence. She reads aloud a letter from Bertram: he will not acknowledge her as his wife until she wears his ring and bears his child, which, he insists, will never happen. In a soliloquy, Helena decides that she must leave France and become a wanderer so that her husband may live unhindered by an unwanted wife.

Act 3, Scene 3

The Duke of Florence makes Bertram his general of cavalry. Bertram rejoices to be engaged in war, not love.

Act 3, Scene 4

The Steward reads a letter from Helena stating that she has become a pilgrim. The dismayed Countess orders him to write Bertram, asking him to return, hoping that Helena will eventually come back as well.

Act 3, Scene 5

The Widow Capilet, a landlady of Florence, her daughter Diana, and their neighbor Mariana remark that the new French general, Bertram, has attempted to seduce Diana, sending Parolles as his intermediary. Helena appears, identifying herself as a French pilgrim, and she is told about the general, whom the ladies have heard has rejected his wife. Helena agrees to lodge with the Widow.

Act 3, Scene 6

The two Lords (1) propose to prove to Bertram that Parolles is a coward. They will kidnap him and make him believe he has been captured by the enemy; they are sure that he will betray his comrades out of fear while Bertram overhears his interrogation. Parolles enters and brags that he will retrieve a captured regimental drum, a prized emblem. He leaves, and the First Lord follows to prepare the plan; Bertram invites the Second Lord to visit Diana with him.

Act 3, Scene 7

Helena has told the Widow that she is Bertram's wife, and she proposes a plot: if Diana pretends to accept Bertram as a lover, Helena will substitute for the young woman in bed; Bertram will not recognize her in the dark. The Widow agrees.

Act 4, Scene 1

The First Lord (1) instructs his men to pose as foreign mercenaries, pretending to speak in an exotic language to Parolles, and a Soldier volunteers to act as their "interpreter." Parolles appears, wondering what excuse he can offer for returning without the drum. He is captured and immediately promises, through the "interpreter," to reveal military secrets if his life is spared.

Act 4, Scene 2

Bertram attempts to talk Diana into sleeping with him. She demands that he give her his ring, a family heirloom, and also asks him to promise not to speak to her when they meet later that night. He agrees.

Act 4, Scene 3

The First and Second Lords (1) discuss Bertram's disgrace for having left his wife, noting also that he has seduced a young woman by giving her his family ring. They have heard that his wife has died, and they regret that he is probably pleased by this. Bertram arrives, and the blindfolded Parolles is brought in to be "interrogated." He reveals military secrets, disparaging both Bertram and the Lords as he does so. The blindfold is removed, and Parolles sees who has exposed him. The Lords, Bertram, and the Soldiers bid him a sardonic farewell and leave for France, the war being over. Alone, Parolles declares that having been proven a fool, he will simply have to become a professional FOOL, or jester.

Act 4, Scene 4

Helena intends to take the Widow and Diana to the King's court at MARSEILLES, where she can get an escort to Rossillion and arrive ahead of Bertram.

Act 4, Scene 5

In Rossillion, Lafew, the Countess, and the Clown mourn Helena. Lafew proposes that Bertram marry his daughter, and the Countess agrees. Lafew has learned that the King will visit Rossillion shortly. The Clown reports Bertram's approach.

Act 5, Scene 1

In Marseilles, Helena and her companions encounter a Gentleman who informs them that the King has gone on to Rossillion.

Act 5, Scene 2

In Rossillion, Parolles, now in rags, is teased by the Clown. Lafew appears, and Parolles begs him for assistance. After chastising him for having earned his misfortune through knavery, Lafew promises him a position in his household.

Act 5, Scene 3

The King pardons Bertram for his part in Helena's death and tells him of his prospective marriage to Lafew's daughter. Bertram offers Lafew a ring to give his daughter. The King recognizes it as the one he had given Helena, but Bertram claims that it came from an admirer in Florence. The unbelieving King orders him arrested. Diana arrives and asserts that Bertram cannot deny that he took her virginity. She produces his family ring and says that Parolles can testify to her relationship with him. Bertram insists that she seduced him and then demanded his ring; he equates the gift with payment to a prostitute. Parolles appears and states that Bertram's infatuation with Diana extended to promising marriage. Helena appears and claims Bertram as her husband, reminding him that he had said he would accept her when she wore his ring and bore his child. She says these things are done and tells of her impersonation in Diana's bed. The delighted King promises Diana a dowry if she wants to marry. He speaks an EPILOGUE to the audience, asking for applause.

COMMENTARY

All's Well That Ends Well presents the customary material of COMEDY—the triumph of love over obstacles—in a grotesque and ambivalent light, and this has led most scholars to place it with *Measure for Measure* and *Troilus and Cressida* among the so-called PROBLEM PLAYS. Like its fellows, *All's Well* centers on sex and social relations and offers no sure and convincing resolution at its conclusion, leading its audiences to recognize the inadequacy of humanity to live up to the grand ideals and happy endings of literary romance. Nevertheless, *All's Well* is humorous, and it does in the end offer the traditional comedic resolution, albeit in muted form.

Though love is the play's most prominent subject, there is a marked absence of the mutual joy of earlier Shakespearean lovers—as in, say, *Much Ado*

About Nothing. Helena is obsessed with a clearly inferior man whose response to her is wholly negative until his grudging and heavily qualified acceptance at the close, and she wins him only through the rather sordid "bed trick." The comments of the Lords, the Clown, and other characters deflate the main plot even further. However, although the play supports negative interpretations, it is clear that Shakespeare did not intend such views to predominate. They are effectively countered by the positive attitudes of the Countess, the King, and Lafew. The playwright is careful to build his lovers up and to minimize the vileness of the bed trick, and he provides the traditional reconciliation scene at the close of the play. Moreover, in Helena's persistent pursuit of Bertram despite his manifest unworthiness, some commentators have seen an allegory of Christian grace, though others disagree. In any case, many critics see an artistic failure in the playwright's attempt to force his naturalistic presentation of Bertram's snobbery and Helena's manipulation into the traditional mold of reconciliation comedy. That *All's Well* is weaker than many other Shakespearean dramas is widely conceded, but it remains of considerable interest precisely because of its conflict between naturalism and romantic fantasy. Though somewhat unsatisfying in its own terms, the play constitutes a step toward the ROMANCES, where a different approach to the same conflict yields more successful results.

All's Well centers on Helena. Though she is sometimes seen by critics as a satirical portrait of a possessive woman, this view seems contrary to Shakespeare's intentions, for he presents her in the most flattering of lights. She is the subject of highly complimentary remarks by the Countess and Lafew at the play's outset, and the King also admires her, both before and after the success of her medicine. In restoring a dying monarch to health, she resembles a heroine of age-old legends, and she takes on an appropriate aura of undoubted goodness. Later, the Widow and Diana welcome her into their lives enthusiastically, and upon her return to those who believe her dead, in 5.3, she is received with the awe due a goddess. Moreover, her immediate resolution of all problems seems to justify this reverence; she is a virtual deus ex machina.

The only cause for Bertram's rejection of Helena is her nonaristocratic status. In this respect she becomes an emblem of the play's point: true nobility resides in the spirit of an individual, not in his or her rank in the social hierarchy. This idea is expounded by the King when he chastises Bertram's snobbery, observing that "From lowest place when virtuous things proceed, / The place is dignified by th' doer's deed" (2.3.125–126). Significantly, Helena's inferior social status was invented by Shakespeare for this purpose. In his source, both lovers were aristocrats of equal rank.

Given Helena's highly positive characteristics, the bed trick places her in less disrepute than it otherwise might. It may be seen as a symbol rather than a realistic maneuver, a mere plot device that fulfils our expectation that Helena will get her man. In the source, the bed trick results in the presentation of twin sons to the unwary father, but the playwright purposefully muted this outcome to an almost unnoticeable implication that Helena is pregnant in 5.3.307. Moreover, the extreme artificiality of the device, combined with its familiarity to Shakespeare's audience as an element of traditional folklore, help to distance its squalor from Helena's nobility of spirit. Lastly, its importance is further minimized by the prominence given to the exposure of Parolles while it is taking place. Helena is established as a heroine in the first half of the play, and thereafter—when her actions might not seem heroic—she plays a relatively minor role, becoming a central figure again only in the play's last moments.

Bertram, too, is favorably presented in the first half of the play. The Countess and the King both praise him, the Duke of Florence grants him high command despite his youth, and the First and Second Lords, while deploring his morals, recognize his potential worth and hope that their exposure of Parolles will cause the young count to "take a measure of his own judgements" (4.3.31–32). Though his faults are plainly evident, Shakespeare's unmistakable position is that Bertram has underlying merit. The possibility that the young man will mature and reform is present throughout the play, helping us to accept his folly.

The nearest character to a villain in All's Well is Parolles. He is a braggart and a coward, and the depths of his ignobility are exposed when he proves willing to betray his comrades to save his life. Parolles offers another example of the moral that nobility is a matter of spirit, not rank: Although a gentleman, apparently on a par with Bertram, he is presented from the outset as an unworthy man. Much of the blame we might otherwise attach to Bertram is placed on Parolles, who encourages his young friend in his errors and who precedes him in suffering humiliation and downfall. However, Parolles's very villainy makes him an appropriate object of redemption, and his response to his humiliation is telling, for he is resilient; he accepts his own nature and vows to go on as best he can, espousing the highly sympathetic sentiment that "There's place and means for every man alive" (4.3.328). In this spirit, he falls within range of the play's reconciliation, finding a new career as jester to his old enemy, Lafew.

The basic developments of All's Well were provided by the play's source material, but Shakespeare inserted some significant details. Several new characters present distinctive slants on the action. As we have seen, Parolles deflects unfavorable attention from Bertram, while Lafew, the Countess, and the King (who appears in the source material but is much less prominent) are entirely wise and generous, in contrast to the more problematic major characters. They are elderly and are concerned with thoughts of death and fond recollections of their own youth, but, unlike the older characters in standard comedies of the day, they are not the opposition who must be defeated for love to triumph. Instead they are benign figures who offer understanding and support for the lovers, thus establishing a context that muffles the unpleasant aspects of the story.

We have seen that Shakespeare intended his lovers to be well regarded, and the final reconciliation is in no way rendered impossible by the moral defects of the characters, as it seems to be in Troilus and Cressida. Helena is a paragon of virtue, despite the machinations to which she is driven, and Bertram, who is admittedly sinful, is also forgivable. Nevertheless, the ambiguous nature of the lovers' relations puts a strain on the play's conclusion, and Shakespeare tightens this strain to an almost unbearable pitch as he postpones Helena's reappearance. Bertram disgraces himself ever more fully with lies and evasions, and even Diana is duplicitous in not revealing Helena's presence. The emotional tension that this generates is made evident even as it is relaxed, when Lafew admits that his "eyes smell onions" (5.3.314) and borrows Parolles's handkerchief. This moment also clinches Lafew's acceptance of Parolles, and thus the two most corrupt characters—Parolles and Bertram—are forgiven. The scene's complex emotional tone reflects the reality of its world: as in life, happiness in *All's Well That Ends Well* is unpredictable and emerges, if at all, only through "The web of our life [which] is of a mingled yarn, good and ill together" (4.3.68–69). Yet in the play's final line, the King fully expresses the spirit of traditional comedic resolution: "The bitter past, more welcome is the sweet" (5.3.328).

Nonetheless, though the play's title—a proverb used twice by Helena, in 4.4.35 and 5.1.25—refers plainly to the conventionally happy ending of romantic comedy, Helena's happiness is just as clearly precarious. When she finally asks for Bertram's acceptance, he replies only to the King and only conditionally, in 5.3.309–310. Fittingly, the King's remark in the play's next-to-last line—wittily playing on the title—is ambiguous: "All yet seems well" (5.3.327) is as far as he can go. Bertram and Helena's marital bliss is doubtful.

The naturalism of the play—its well-drawn characters and credible social milieu—leads us to expect a more plausible denouement, and we emerge dissatisfied. The romance of an adventurous maiden who can cure kings is unsuccessfully integrated with the more realistic tale of sexual intrigue, and the two components of which the play is made—a psychologically real world versus a conventionally comic one—merge at the end only at a considerable cost in dramatic power.

The conclusion of *All's Well* unquestionably lessens its effectiveness, but if the play is considered in light of Shakespeare's development, its failings seem less significant and its ending less arbitrary. The problem plays are similar to the romances in a number of ways: Both depend on unrealistic stories, and both emphasize the power of noble spirituality over circumstances. Particularly in their conclusions, both favor symbolism and ritual over psychological realism. However, in *All's Well* (as in *Measure for Measure*, especially), the latter element still has great power, and the balance between the two is uncomfortable, barring a firm sense that spiritual values have indeed triumphed, despite the play's assertion that they have. *Cymbeline* and *The Winter's Tale*, like *All's Well*, have endings that tax belief and that depend on the evocation of supernatural powers while maintaining the underlying assumption that naturalistic causes have in fact been operating. However, whereas the contradictions of *All's Well* generate an atmosphere of conflict and stress, similar polarities in the later plays yield a pleasurable sense of life's many aspects. In *All's Well That Ends Well*, Shakespeare had not yet developed the capacity to sublimate reality without denying it, but his instincts were leading him in that direction.

SOURCES OF THE PLAY

The main plot of *All's Well That Ends Well*, the story of Bertram and Helena, comes from the *Decameron* (1353) of Giovanni BOCCACCIO, who apparently invented it. Shakespeare used the translation by William PAINTER of Boccaccio's tale in *The Palace of Pleasures* (probably in the third edition, 1575), supplemented by the French translation by Antoine LE MAÇON, which Painter also used. Lord Lafew, the Countess of Rossillion, and the SUBPLOT concerning Parolles were Shakespeare's inventions, though the last may have been influenced by an episode in *The Unfortunate Traveller* (1594) by Thomas NASHE.

TEXT OF THE PLAY

All's Well was probably written ca. 1604. However, no mention of the play prior to its publication in 1623 has survived, and its date of composition has troubled scholars. In the 18th century it was believed to be the mysterious *Love's Labour's Won*, cited as Shakespearean by Francis MERES in 1598; it was accordingly presumed to have been written before that year. However, *All's Well*'s obvious similarities to *Hamlet*, *Troilus and Cressida*, and *Measure for Measure* were soon recognized, and Samuel Taylor COLERIDGE introduced another hypothesis: he held that an early version of the play was indeed

Love's Labour's Won but that Shakespeare rewrote and retitled it between 1604 and 1606. This suggestion was felt to account for perceivable differences in style within the play (as, e.g., the use of a SONNET in 3.4.4–17 and rhymed couplets in several passages). This theory was widely accepted until fairly recently. However, modern scholarship is more inclined to find stylistic variation normal in Shakespeare's plays and to suppose that *All's Well* was a single creation. There is no clear internal evidence to indicate a date for his composition, and estimates have ranged from 1599 to after 1608. However, scholars generally rely on *All's Well's* close resemblance to the securely datable *Measure for Measure*—in its plot, its heroine, even in its vocabulary—and assign it the same date, 1604.

The play was first published in 1623, in the FIRST FOLIO. The Folio text is believed to have been printed from Shakespeare's own manuscript, or FOUL PAPERS, for several reasons, most notably its vague and inconsistent speech headings and stage directions and the existence of Violenta, a GHOST CHARACTER. The Folio text, though somewhat flawed, is necessarily the basis of all subsequent editions.

THEATRICAL HISTORY OF THE PLAY

No production of *All's Well* is known before a single performance of 1740, although several references suggest that it had been performed in the early 17th century. The play was popular in the 1740s—Theophilus CIBBER was a popular Parolles, and Peg WOFFINGTON played Helena—but was revived only occasionally during the rest of the century. In the early 19th century a 1794 adaptation by John Philip KEMBLE, heavily abridged and censored, was performed from time to time, and this version was also put on by other producers, including Samuel PHELPS. However, the play was not frequently staged in any version.

Only in the second half of the 20th century did *All's Well* become more popular. Among noteworthy productions have been those of Robert ATKINS (1949), Tyrone GUTHRIE (1953 and 1959, in Stratford, Ontario, and STRATFORD, England), and John BARTON (1967, Stratford, England). Guthrie's presentation—which in 1959 starred Zoë CALDWELL as

Helena and Edith EVANS as the Countess—was highly controversial; it freely abridged Shakespeare's text (the Clown was eliminated entirely) and treated the play as a farce, adding much comic stage business involving such modern props as a radio microphone. The scenes in Paris and Rossillion were set in an Edwardian world, while the Italian wars were startlingly represented by modern desert legionnaires. It was extremely popular at both Stratfords. Another production that evoked the punctilious society of the Edwardian era was Trevor NUNN's (1981–83), which starred Peggy ASHCROFT as the Countess and moved from Stratford to London to Broadway. Sir Peter HALL directed the play for the ROYAL SHAKESPEARE COMPANY in 1992. Never a movie, *All's Well* has been produced several times for TELEVISION. Mario CASTELNUOVO-TEDESCO, who composed numerous works based on Shakespearean texts, wrote an OPERA based on Shakespeare's play in the mid-1920s, but it was suppressed by the Fascist government of Italy because the composer was a Jew. It was not performed until 1958.

CHARACTERS

Bertram (Count of Rossillion) Character in *All's Well That Ends Well*, a young French nobleman, the errant husband of Helena. Bertram is an imperfect man whose decline from callous self-absorption to more serious sin is arrested only by Helena's forceful entrapment. That his peccadilloes make him seem unworthy of Helena's love is one of the play's most bothersome features; as Samuel JOHNSON complained, Bertram is "dismissed into happiness" that he clearly does not deserve. Moreover, his highly qualified acceptance of Helena in the play's final scene does much to dilute any sense of resolution. This is one of the aspects of *All's Well* that places it among the PROBLEM PLAYS.

Helena persuades the King of France to make Bertram marry her as her reward for curing the monarch. Under the influence of the foppish coward Parolles, Bertram defies the King and abandons Helena, an act that the other characters uniformly deplore, and he departs from her with casual cruelty in 2.5. Bertram then declines into further immorality as he attempts to seduce the virginal Diana. As his mother, the Countess of Rossillion, remarks, he "cannot thrive" (3.4.26) without Helena's influence.

Our attitude toward this undeniably dubious figure must color our sense of the play as a whole, and many commentators have felt that he is important evidence that *All's Well* is a bitter satire. However, we can see that Shakespeare took considerable pains to mitigate Bertram's failings: The playwright altered his source, a tale by BOCCACCIO, in Bertram's favor, and he emphasized his youth, by way of excuse for his misdeeds, and his virtues, by way of compensation for them. In Boccaccio, the character corresponding to Bertram goes to the wars expressly to avoid his wife, while Shakespeare's young man displays an earlier desire to leave, a noble urge to distinguish himself in battle. His unwelcome marriage makes flight all the more alluring, and Parolles encourages him in this rebellion. Parolles is himself an addition to the tale, and although Bertram's unthinking acceptance of Parolles's advice reveals his own shallowness, it is also clear that Parolles's chief function is to deflect blame from Bertram. Not only does he encourage Bertram's flight, but he is also the go-between who furthers his seduction of Diana. Other characters, particularly the First Lord and the Countess, explicitly hold Parolles responsible for corrupting Bertram.

Bertram's youth, another plausible excuse for his folly, is repeatedly referred to. He is in his "minority" (4.5.69), a ward of the King, who feels he is too young be a soldier. Lord Lafew is asked to advise him for he is "unseason'd" (1.1.67). When he rejects Helena, the King calls him a "proud, scornful boy" (2.3.151), and when his mother learns of his flight, she calls him a "rash and unbridled boy" (3.2.27). Even Parolles describes him as "a foolish idle boy," "a dangerous and lascivious boy," "that lascivious young boy" (4.3.207, 212, 290). In 5.3 the Countess asks the King to forgive Bertram his "natural rebellion done i' th' blade of youth" (5.3.6), and he himself confesses to having seduced Diana "i' th' wanton way of youth" (5.3.210).

Not only is Bertram excused for his youth, but he is also aggrandized for his virtues. The Duke of Florence appoints him a cavalry commander despite his age, and he triumphs, being reported "high in fame" (5.3.31). (In Boccaccio, his counterpart was merely an officer.) He receives the praise of both the Countess and the King, as well as the intense approval of Helena. Even the First and Second Lords, though they deplore his morals, nonetheless recognize that "he contrives against his own nobility" (4.3.23–24). Further, Bertram is linked with the virtues of his late father by both the Countess and the King in 1.1 and 1.2. The hope that Bertram will grow into nobility does much to enhance our acceptance of his youthful faults.

In 5.3 Bertram is exposed as a moral coward and a liar, falsely maligning Diana and retreating ignominiously before the King's interrogation. His disgrace is complete. Then suddenly he is rescued by Helena's return. Bertram's wickedness is stressed mercilessly just before he is restored to favor, in order to emphasize the power of his redemption through Helena's love. His central position in the reconciliation that closes the play elevates him to Helena's level of goodness.

However, Bertram's ignominy cannot be completely ignored, and Shakespeare acknowledges the truth of the situation by keeping Bertram in character to the end. His initial response to Helena's arrival is ambiguous: His "O pardon!" (5.3.302) has been seen as genuine repentance but also as a self-serving effort to lessen his disgrace, for when Helena asks him to acknowledge that he is truly her husband, he does not reply to her but speaks only to the King and only with a qualification: "If she, my liege, can make me know this clearly / I'll love her dearly, ever, ever dearly" (5.3.309–310). We can hardly fail to doubt the prospects for Bertram and Helena's happiness; even the King, closing the play, can only venture that "All yet seems well . . ." (5.3.327).

Shakespeare tried to merge the traditional happy ending demanded by comedy with the psychological realism of Bertram's portrayal as a callow, thoughtless youth. The attempt is generally regarded as a failure; that Bertram is all too human is part of the problematic nature of *All's Well That Ends Well*. However, the portrait is an absorbing effort to adapt moral mediocrity to a romantic framework; figures such as Posthumus of *Cymbeline* and Leontes of *The Winter's Tale* owe something of their development to this less successful predecessor.

Clown (Lavatch, Lavach) Character in *All's Well That Ends Well*, court jester to the Countess of Rossillion. The Clown comments on aspects of the play, both through parody and by direct references. He professes to be a rustic (as his designation as a CLOWN suggests), "a woodland fellow" (4.5.44) who enjoys ridiculing the royal court, but he is clearly a sophisticated professional FOOL. His somewhat cynical worldliness adds an element of realism that counters the improbabilities of the play.

Sometimes the Clown is overtly contemptuous, as in his insults to Parolles in 2.4 and his disparagement of Bertram in 3.2, but usually his function is more indirectly carried out; his concerns parallel those of the main plot, drawing our attention to it in odd ways. For instance, he expounds upon his proposed marriage to "Isbel the woman" (1.3.16) just after we have been introduced to Helena and Bertram. He goes on to equate Helena with Helen of TROY, a digression that suggests the sexual conflict emerging in the main story line. Later, in 3.2, he rejects Isbel, apparently out of sexual exhaustion, just as the Countess is reading the letter in which Bertram tells of his rejection of Helena. The Clown's parody of courtly manners in 2.2 immediately precedes Parolles's assumption of gentlemanly airs in 2.3 and is itself a commentary on the vanity of social rank, a theme of the play. In his final lines, in which he asserts exuberantly that Parolles smells bad, he not only emphasizes Parolles's loss of status, but the rankness of his "similes of comfort" (5.2.24–25) seems to sum up the play's obnoxious developments to this point, At the same time, he offers some sympathy for Parolles, declaring, "I do pity his distress" (5.2.24), thus maintaining our hope of a milder outcome, which is indeed about to develop.

The Clown is an oddly melancholy jester, with his low-key parodies of theology and his claim to be in the service of "the black prince . . . alias the devil" (4.5.39–40). He is sometimes somewhat nasty, as when he rejects Isbel, and he can be overly wordy, as Lafew reminds us when he tells him, "Go thy ways; I begin to be aweary of thee" (4.5.53). However, the Countess clearly enjoys him, though she recognizes that he is, as Lafew says, a "shrewd knave and an unhappy" (4.5.60). He reminds her of her late husband, "who made himself much sport out of him" (4.5.61–62). The pleasant relationship between the Countess and her jester contributes to our sense of her household as a source of generosity and kindness that helps to offset the unpleasant aspects of the play.

It is presumed that the Clown's part was intended for Robert ARMIN, the actor who specialized in jesters for the KING'S MEN. His name, Lavatch (sometimes rendered Lavache), is not mentioned until 5.2.1. The name is usually regarded as a corruption of the French *la vache* ("the cow"), though some scholars believe it represents the French *lavage* or the Italian *lavaggio* ("washing, cleansing").

Countess of Rossillion Character in *All's Well That Ends Well*, the mother of Bertram and guardian of Helena. The Countess comments on the main action of the play, overseeing from her estate at ROSSILLION the relationship between her son and her ward. Loving Helena, she promotes their marriage; loving Bertram, she rues his foolishness in abandoning his bride, and she is present to see them reconciled at the play's close. With Lord Lafew and the King, the Countess helps to create a world of kindness and generosity that counters the play's unpleasant aspects.

One of her most important functions is to guide the audience's responses to the major characters through her own, exalting Helena and forgiving Bertram. Her love for Helena is as generous as her affection for her son is natural. Her sympathy for Helena's love, based on her "remembrances of days foregone" (1.3.129), is touching, and her collaboration with Helena serves to start the heroine on her way. She is also aware of Bertram's defects while at the same time remaining willing to make allowances and forgive. The Countess loves her son, but when he abandons Helena, she recognizes that he is a "rash and unbridled boy" (3.2.27) and sends letters that she hopes will bring him to his senses. The Countess is an especially sympathetic character in a play full of moral ambiguity. George Bernard SHAW called hers "the most beautiful old woman's part ever written."

Diana Character in *All's Well That Ends Well*, young woman of FLORENCE who assists Helena to entrap her runaway husband, Bertram. The lustful

Bertram wishes to seduce Diana, who is respected in Florence for "a most chaste renown" (4.3.14). She, honorably determined to remain a virgin, resists his advances until in 4.2, as part of Helena's plot, she agrees to sleep with him (though Helena will in fact occupy her bed). She is demure and pliant in making this arrangement, but she expresses herself zestily after Bertram's departure, brusquely critiquing male morals and declaring, ". . . in this disguise, I think't no sin / To cozen him that would unjustly win" (4.2.75–76). In 5.3 she confronts Bertram in the presence of the King and accuses him of violating his promise to marry her. She is denounced as a whore, and then, when she claims to be a virgin although Bertram has seduced her, she is further subjected to the irritated King's threat of imprisonment before Helena appears and resolves matters. The King thereupon grants her a sumptuous dowry as part of the final reconciliation that closes the play.

Diana has little real personality, being a stereotype of the virginal maiden, but her symbolic importance is considerable. As the object of Bertram's attempts at seduction, she serves by contrast to emphasize his evil nature; as the long-suffering complainant of 5.3, she exemplifies victimization, making the final outcome more dramatically satisfying.

Duke of Florence Character in *All's Well That Ends Well*, the ruler of FLORENCE. In 3.1 the Duke welcomes the French noblemen who have come to fight for him against Siena, and in 3.3 he appoints Bertram to command his cavalry. The Duke is merely an example of a courtly ruler, offering a contrast with the less chivalrous behavior of Bertram and Parolles.

Gentleman Minor character in *All's Well That Ends Well*, a nobleman who helps Helena. In 5.1 the Gentleman tells Helena that the King has left MARSEILLES. He takes her message to the King, appearing in 5.3 with the letter that entraps Bertram at the play's climax. The Gentleman is merely a stereotypical courtier and a pawn of plot development.

Helena (Helen) Character in *All's Well That Ends Well*, the lover of Bertram. Helena's pursuit of Bertram constitutes the main plot of *All's Well*, and

his lack of interest, combined with her use of the vulgar "bed trick"—substituting herself for another woman in bed and thus inducing him to father her child—help to give the work the dark and troubling quality that places it among the so-called PROBLEM PLAYS. The central figure in the play, Helena is subject to quite contradictory interpretations, depending largely on one's view of the play as a whole.

Some commentators have found Helena wholly good. Samuel Taylor COLERIDGE called her Shakespeare's "loveliest character," and her persistent efforts to win Bertram despite his feelings have been seen as an allegorical representation of Christian grace, chiefly on the strength of a remark by the Countess. Bertram's mother, that her son "cannot thrive, / Unless her prayers, whom heaven delights to hear / And loves to grant, reprieve him from the wrath / Of greatest justice" (3.4.26–29). However, other critics have seen in Helena a satirical portrait of an ambitious, possessive woman, intent on marrying a man who does not love her and unscrupulous in using her body to deceive him.

In 1.1 Helena is introduced as a young woman of great energy and determination. She is first seen dressed in mourning, with the elderly Countess and Lafew. They discuss the late Count's death and then her own father's and the seemingly terminal illness of the King. Helena is especially depressed because her secret love, Bertram, is leaving, and, as she puts it, "there is no living, none, / If Bertram be away" (1.1.82–83), and she prepares to "sanctify his relics" (1.1.96). Then Parolles, the play's comic villain, appears, and his cynical banter about virginity makes Helena realize that she must fear the influence of such worldly wisdom on Bertram: "The court's a learning-place," she reflects, "and he is one—" (1.1.173); she suppresses the observation that Bertram is likely to be an apt pupil. More important, Parolles's vitality stimulates a similar energy in Helena. He leaves, and in the ensuing soliloquy (1.1.212–225), written in formal couplets intended to suggest her elevated mood, she firmly decides to pursue Bertram.

Thus the main plot opens with the establishment of Helena's initiative. But whether she is an admirably plucky young woman or an ambitious schemer remains a matter of interpretation. This unresolved question is often considered part of the play's larger failure to combine naturalistic elements with the scheme of reconciliation and love that COMEDY traditionally demands. To some extent, the contradictory points of view may be taken to represent different aspects of the same personality, and, as so often in Shakespeare, the resulting paradox offers us a rewarding sense of the complexity of human nature.

However, there are numerous clues that Shakespeare intended Helena as a virtuous and spunky heroine. Most significantly, the play's final resolution is accomplished only by a highly dramatic, carefully planned appearance by Helena late in the closing scene, in which she disentangles the plot's complications in a few lines, like a deus ex machina. A satirical figure used in this manner could only inspire sardonic reflections on the hypocrisy of happy endings, and nothing in the dialogue suggests any such intent on the playwright's part. Further, the fairy-tale motif of the maiden who cures the King is presented in the solemn music of rhymed couplets and mystical language that would be utterly inappropriate to a satirical purpose. Similarly, Helena has several other striking and lyrical speeches, such as her declaration of love in 1.3.186–212 and her dramatic renunciation in 3.2.99–129, whose evident sincerity tends to enforce a view of her as an admirable heroine.

In addition, Shakespeare altered the story that he took from his source, a tale by BOCCACCIO, and some of his changes were plainly designed to elevate the moral character of the heroine. For instance, he added such sympathetic characters as the elderly Countess and her friend Lord Lafew, whose chief purpose is to shape our opinions of the major characters. They convincingly inform us of Helena's virtues, as does the King. Shakespeare also added another theme to the tale, in which Helena is clearly a heroine: the King, responding to Bertram's rejection of her as a commoner, defends her as an illustration of the value of an individual's spiritual nature regardless of his or her rank in society. In Boccaccio, the pursuer and pursued are aristocrats of equal status, and no social question is raised.

When Boccaccio's protagonist triumphs at the end, she presents her reluctant husband with twin sons. In *All's Well*, only the merest mention is made of Helena's pregnancy, in 5.3.307; Shakespeare plainly wished to de-emphasize the physical aspect of the bed trick because this ruse is clearly the most embarrassing episode of Helena's story. In another significant departure from his source, Shakespeare altered the circumstances of Helena's appearance in FLORENCE. In Boccaccio, she hears of her husband's attempt at seduction, devises the bed trick, and goes to Italy to perform it. In *All's Well*, she wanders to Florence as a pilgrim and must be informed by the Widow of Bertram's presence. Thus the bed trick seems a product of fortunate happenstance, rather than a calculated ploy.

Shakespeare also used dramatic structure to mitigate the bed trick's bad impression and maintain Helena's heroic stature. After 3.2 Helena is much less frequently onstage than before. She appears in only four brief scenes and has no important speeches before returning 30 lines from the end of the play. We remember her in the highly positive light in which she was presented in the first half of the play, and we are influenced by the Countess's observations on the efficacy of Helena's prayers, the similarly complimentary remarks of the two Lords in 4.3, and the loving regrets of the Countess's household when they believe her dead; even the cynical Clown is moved to call her "the sweet-marjoram of the sallet" (4.5.15). Shakespeare therefore establishes Helena as a heroine early in the play, and later, when her actions seem less heroic, he downplays her, permitting only brief and positive glimpses.

Thus Helena seems intended as a delightful romantic heroine. Lafew says she can "quicken a rock, and make you dance canary / With sprightly fire and motion" (2.1.73–74)—and her infatuation with Bertram's "arched brows, his hawking eye, his curls" (1.1.92) is no less endearing for her healthy interest in sex. In this light she seems to be a lively, virtuous young woman to whom divine favor offers opportunity and then success. And in the second half of the play, the possibly manipulative exploiter of sex is more properly regarded as a contrite, self-sacrificing wife whom fortune has led to a happy resolution of her problems. At the play's conclusion she is received with the awe due a goddess, and her summation of the play's final statement of reconciliation suggests that she deserves this treatment. Indeed, Helena's role is an exalted one: In the course of capturing and keeping a husband, she has saved the King's life, preserved Bertram from a life of idle sin, and brought new life, in the form of their child, into the world. The absorption in death with which the play opened has been dispelled.

King of France Character in *All's Well That Ends Well*, the ruler of FRANCE. The dying King recovers his health through the ministrations of Helena. He rewards her with marriage to the unwilling Bertram. Bertram's disdain for a commoner sparks the King's most important speech, a lecture on the value of individual virtues over social rank (2.3.117–141), a trenchant summary of one of the play's important themes. In 5.3 he forgives Bertram's flight from Helena, but he then presides over the exposure of the young man's perfidy toward Diana and his justice is as stern as his forgiveness had been yielding. When Helena finally unravels the plot and the final reconciliation takes place, the King behaves with great magnanimity, granting a dowry to Diana and offering a final statement that, although qualified, insists on the traditional happy ending of COMEDY: "All yet seems well, and if it end so meet, / The bitter past, more welcome is the sweet" (5.3.327–328).

With the Countess and Lord Lafew, the King helps provide an atmosphere of generosity and wisdom that offsets the play's unpleasant aspects. His gracious welcome of Bertram in 1.2 stimulates in the audience a sense that the young man, despite his faults, is basically worthy. Similarly, his immediate appreciation of Helena in 2.1 helps to establish her virtue. The King is himself a wholly sympathetic figure, a stereotypically "good" ruler: wise and moderate in deciding not to go to war while still permitting his young noblemen to distinguish themselves on campaign in Italy; touching in his nostalgic remembrance of Bertram's father; and generous in friendship and forgiveness to the young people.

Lafew, Lord (Lord Lafeu) Character in *All's Well That Ends Well*, friend of the Countess of Rossillion. Lafew is an elderly gentleman who comments on the main action. He also introduces Helena to the King

of France, whom she cures, thereby winning Bertram as her husband. Lafew counsels Bertram, the Countess's son, to accept marriage to Helena and to reject the friendship of Parolles, but Bertram ignores him. Lafew is most prominent in 2.3.184–260, where he mercilessly insults Parolles, recognizing that the foppish, boastful courtier lacks the nerve to fight. Lafew's temper justifies his name, the French for "fire." The episode clinches our recognition that Parolles is a coward and blusterer, though Bertram does not see this until later in the play. In 5.3 Lafew accepts the thoroughly defeated Parolles into his household as a FOOL, or jester, a generous action that exemplifies the play's spirit of reconciliation. Thus Lafew demonstrates the wisdom to be found in the courtly world of honor and patronage, both by exposing Parolles as a scoundrel and by sympathizing with him later. Throughout the play, Lafew, with the Countess and the King, represents a world of wisdom and generosity that stands in contrast to the less pleasant major plot.

Lord (1) Either of two characters in *All's Well That Ends Well*, French noblemen. Though distinguished as the First Lord and the Second Lord, these two characters are very similar and serve the same dramatic purpose. Reappearing throughout the play, they offer a distinct viewpoint on its developments, especially on the progress of Bertram and Parolles, and they help to mold the audience's opinions. Recognizing the dishonorable cowardice of Parolles, they devise a plan to expose him to Bertram. They recognize Bertram's moral weakness, but they believe in his capacity for improvement, thereby offsetting our possible distaste for him. In addition, their fond admiration of the King of France in 1.2 and 2.1 stimulates our appreciation of him, which in turn influences our opinions of Bertram and Helena when the King shows affection for them. The Lords encourage our positive response to Helena when they sympathize with her abandonment by Bertram in 3.2, while at the same time they downplay Bertram's guilt by blaming Parolles for his behavior.

The Lords are stereotypes of noble courtiers, and they lack individual personalities. Their parts differ slightly only once, when, at the end of 3.6, the First Lord assumes the job of capturing Parolles while the Second Lord leaves with Bertram for an offstage visit to Diana, thus enabling him to report on Bertram's attempted seduction when the two Lords critique the young count in 4.3.

In the FIRST FOLIO text of the play, the First and Second Lords are, respectively, designated "G" and "E" in speech headings and stage directions. These initials are presumed to refer to actors in the KING'S MEN who played the parts, probably William ECCLESTONE and Samuel GILBURNE or Robert GOUGH.

Lord (2) Any of four minor characters in *All's Well That Ends Well*, young noblemen whom Helena rejects as possible husbands. In 2.3, having recovered his health through Helena's treatment, the King of France offers her the agreed-upon reward: her choice of a husband from among the young men of his court. She speaks to several of the Lords before choosing Bertram, as she had intended all along. The rejected Lords merely comprise a tableau of knightly personages; they speak only three lines among them.

Mariana Minor character in *All's Well That Ends Well*, a neighbor of the Widow Capilet, a Florentine innkeeper. In 3.5.16–28 Mariana roundly condemns Parolles and Bertram as unscrupulous womanizers, thus helping to establish the situation when Helena arrives in Florence. She has no personality beyond that of a stereotypical gossip.

Messenger Minor character in *All's Well That Ends Well*, a servant of Bertram. In 4.3 the Messenger tells two gentlemen that his master will soon be returning to FRANCE. His single brief speech separates two elements of a long scene: the Lords' (1) critique of Bertram's morality and Bertram's arrival for the interrogation of Parolles.

Page Minor character in *All's Well That Ends Well*, a servant of the Countess of Rossillion. In 1.1.183 the Page summons Parolles for Bertram, then exits. He evokes the world of an aristocratic household but is otherwise of no consequence.

Parolles (Paroles) Character in *All's Well That Ends Well*, a cowardly follower of Bertram. As his name, the French for "words," suggests, Parolles is a blusterer who pretends to be a warrior and nobleman but whose deeds cannot match his boasts. Shallow and thoughtless, he influences Bertram to follow his worst instincts. Parolles aggravates Bertram's tendencies to self-indulgence, and he encourages him to disobey the King of France and run away to the wars in ITALY. After Parolles's humiliation in 2.5.14–48 by Lord Lafew, who has seen through his pretensions to gentlemanly status, he is ready to leave the court; he sees his chance in Bertram's wish to abandon Helena, whom the King has made him marry. "A young man married is a man that's marr'd. / Therefore away" (2.3.294–295), he urges. Once in Italy, Parolles again supports Bertram's inclinations to vice, serving as a go-between in the young man's attempt to seduce the virginal Diana. Bertram's friends, led by the First Lord, then "capture" Parolles and expose his cowardice and treachery in 4.3.

Parolles's defects have been recognized all along by everyone around Bertram. Upon his first appearance, Helena calls him "a notorious liar . . . a great way fool, solely a coward" (1.1.98–99), and the Lords agree with Bertram's mother, the Countess, that her son has been corrupted by Parolles, who is a "very tainted fellow, and full of wickedness" (3.2.87). Parolles thus serves an important dramatic function, deflecting the negative image that might otherwise be attached to Bertram, whose stature must not sink too low, lest the central element of the plot—the determination of Helena to marry him—become ludicrous.

In his evil influence on Bertram, Parolles is most nearly the play's villain. However, after his exposure as a charlatan, Parolles shows a striking resilience. Though his self-promoted career as a noble warrior is over, he will make the most of his new situation. "Simply the thing I am / Shall make me live" (4.3.322–323), he observes, realizing that he can, "being fool'd, by fool'ry thrive" (4.3.327). He resolves to become a jester, or FOOL, among the French lords, a role well suited to his nature. In a line that is richly suggestive of Shakespeare's generous vision of humanity, he declares that "There's place and means for every man alive" (4.3.328). In becoming a fool and acknowledging his defects,

Parolles shows himself wiser than Bertram, preceding him in self-knowledge, just as he has preceded him in delinquency. His acceptance of life on any terms demonstrates a tremendous vitality, and he is certainly the most dynamic character in the play, with the possible exception of Helena.

Significantly, Parolles sparks Helena's energy in 1.1. In this scene Helena is understandably depressed; the household is in mourning for both Bertram's father and her own, and Bertram, her secret love, is leaving. Then Parolles appears, and his broadly humorous exercise in fashionable cynicism about virginity has a twofold effect on the heroine. First, she sees that the courtly life that Parolles represents will offer sexual opportunities for Bertram, which she fears he will accept. Second, Parolles's vitality inspires Helena to declare, "Our remedies oft in ourselves do lie" (1.1.212), and to decide to pursue Bertram. Thus Parolles's energy pervades *All's Well*, infusing the spirits of both major characters for good and evil alike. Finally, in becoming the jester for his old enemy Lafew at the close of the play, Parolles accepts—unconditionally, in contrast to Bertram—the reconciliation that is at the heart of Shakespearean COMEDY.

Although he has a distinct and credible personality, Parolles is descended from an ancient comic character type, the MILES GLORIOSUS of ancient Roman drama and the braggart soldier of Italian COMMEDIA DELL'ARTE; he shares his ancestry with several other Shakespearean characters, most notably Falstaff.

Soldier Any of several characters in *All's Well That Ends Well*, troops in the army of FLORENCE. The First Soldier is the pretended interpreter during the interrogation of Parolles. In 4.1 and 4.3 Parolles is captured by the First Lord, who proposes to demonstrate the foppish courtiers's cowardice and treachery to his deluded friend, Bertram. The captors pretend to speak a foreign language so that their victim will not realize that they are French, and the First Soldier pretends to interpret between the Lord and the prisoner. Parolles treasonably discloses secrets, and the First Soldier induces him to insult the Lords and Bertram, which maintains a humorous tone to the scene. The Second Soldier is

a messenger who is sent in 4.1 to tell Bertram of Parolles's capture. His submission to orders helps suggest the strength and efficiency of the military, which is contrasted with the cowardice and treason of Parolles.

Steward (Rynaldo, Rinaldo, Reynaldo) Minor character in *All's Well That Ends Well*, the chief officer of the household of the Countess of Rossillion. The Steward twice offers information about Helena. In 1.3 he reports having overheard her musing on her love for Bertram, stimulating the Countess to assist Helena's plan to pursue Bertram. In 3.4 he reads aloud Helena's letter to the Countess telling of her departure from Rossillion so that Bertram, now her unwilling husband, may live there in peace. This letter touchingly reveals the wretchedness of Helena's position.

The Steward's name—rendered by different editors as Rynaldo, Rinaldo, and Reynaldo—is mentioned only after his role is almost complete (in 3.4.19, 29). Many commentators think that this offers a glimpse of Shakespeare's creative processes, for he appears to have been continually developing even this minor character as he wrote.

Violenta Character named but not present in *All's Well That Ends Well*. Violenta appears in the FIRST FOLIO in the stage direction that opens 3.5. It reads, "Enter old Widow of Florence, her daughter, Violenta, and Mariana . . ." Violenta could be the daughter's name, set off by commas, but Diana is certainly the Widow's daughter. Shakespeare may have originally named Diana differently, or he could have intended a fourth character whom he did not in fact use, in which case Violenta is a GHOST CHARACTER. In either case, the name survived in the text through an error on the part of the printer.

Widow Capilet Character in *All's Well That Ends Well*, a landlady of Florence who befriends Helena and is the mother of Diana. The Widow permits Diana to make a sexual assignation with Bertram, Helena's runaway husband, though Helena will occupy Diana's bed. When she first appears, in 3.5, the Widow has charm as a stereotypical gossip, and she shrewdly recognizes Bertram for the cad he is, but thereafter she serves merely as a pawn of the plot.

Antony and Cleopatra
SYNOPSIS

Act 1, Scene 1
In ALEXANDRIA the Roman Philo laments to Demetrius that their leader, Antony, is involved with the Egyptian queen, Cleopatra, and neglects his military duties. Cleopatra and Antony appear as news from ROME arrives, and she taunts him and accuses him of subservience to his wife and the Roman senate. He therefore refuses to hear the messages.

Act 1, Scene 2
An Egyptian Soothsayer predicts that Cleopatra's waiting woman Charmian shall outlive her mistress, and adds that she has seen better times in the past than she shall in future. He sees an identical fortune for another waiting woman, Iras. The two women laugh over these predictions with their fellow servant Alexas. Cleopatra arrives and declares that she will not speak with Antony, who is approaching, and then leaves with her servants. Antony arrives accompanied by a Messenger (1) who bears the news that Antony's feuding wife and brother had united to fight against Octavius Caesar but were defeated. The Messenger also states that a renegade Roman general has led the Parthians in a conquest of Roman territory. Antony is angry with himself, for the conquered lands were lost while he was dallying with Cleopatra. More news arrives: Antony's wife has died. Antony dismisses the Messengers and reflects that he had wished his wife dead and now regrets it; he now wishes he could break away from Cleopatra. He summons his lieutenant, Enobarbus, who makes bawdy jokes about Antony's affair with the queen until Antony sternly orders preparations for a return to Rome where he is needed to aid Caesar against a rebel, Pompey.

Act 1, Scene 3
Charmian advises Cleopatra to accommodate Antony in every way if she wants him to love her, but the queen rejects this idea. Antony appears and announces his departure; Cleopatra taunts him, but he remains determined, and she finally wishes him well. He assures her of his love.

Act 1, Scene 4
In Rome Caesar disgustedly tells Lepidus of Antony's debauchery with Cleopatra. News arrives of the rebel Pompey, aided by the pirates Menecrates and Menas. Caesar hopes that Antony will return to the soldierly ways he was once famous for.

Act 1, Scene 5
In Alexandria Cleopatra grieves over Antony's absence and praises him enthusiastically. Charmian teasingly reminds her that she had once felt the same about Julius Caesar when he was in Egypt years earlier.

Act 2, Scene 1
In MESSINA Pompey confers with Menas and Menecrates. He states that his chances of defeating Caesar and Lepidus are good since Antony, their ally, dallies in Egypt. News arrives that Antony is about to rejoin his friends; Pompey worries but continues to hope for the best.

Act 2, Scene 2
Lepidus entreats Enobarbus to encourage in Antony a peaceful attitude toward Caesar, but Enobarbus declares that Antony's honor comes first. Antony and Caesar arrive to negotiate. Antony denies any part in the rebellion of his wife and brother. He apologizes for not having assisted Caesar against it and admits that he has been too decadent in Egypt. The two leaders agree to put the issue aside and fight together against Pompey, and to further their alliance Antony shall marry Caesar's sister Octavia. The leaders leave together while their followers remain, and Enobarbus tells Maecenas and Agrippa about the gorgeous Cleopatra. He predicts that Antony will never leave her for good.

Act 2, Scene 3
Antony, married to Octavia, promises faithfulness. He consults the Soothsayer who has come to Rome with him. The seer advises him to return to Egypt because Caesar's presence diminishes his prospects for success. Antony decides to follow this advice.

Act 2, Scene 4

Lepidus, Maecenas, and Agrippa prepare to leave Rome; they will meet Antony on campaign against Pompey.

Act 2, Scene 5

In Alexandria Cleopatra receives word that Antony has married Octavia. Raging, she threatens the Messenger (3) with death; calming, she sinks into depression.

Act 2, Scene 6

Pompey agrees to a truce with Antony, Caesar, and Lepidus. The leaders leave to attend a celebratory feast aboard Pompey's ship. Enobarbus and Menas stay behind and gossip; they agree that Pompey should have maintained his rebellion while he could. Enobarbus predicts that Antony will abandon Octavia for Cleopatra.

Act 2, Scene 7

At the banquet the drunken Lepidus is teased by the other leaders. Menas takes Pompey aside and suggests that they kill all three Roman leaders, leaving Pompey the sole ruler of the empire, but Pompey declares that while he could approve such an action after it was done, he cannot honorably order it ahead of time. To himself, Menas declares that he will desert this foolishly scrupulous master, for Pompey will obviously lose in the political wars. Caesar declares that their drunkenness is wasteful and leaves. The other leaders follow.

Act 3, Scene 1

Antony's general Ventidius, who has defeated a Parthian army, tells his lieutenant Silius that he will not pursue the fleeing enemy. He states that he does not want to succeed too thoroughly lest Antony feel overshadowed and in revenge crush his military career. Silius admires Ventidius's political shrewdness. They go to meet Antony in ATHENS.

Act 3, Scene 2

Antony and his followers prepare to depart from Rome. Caesar and Octavia are deeply moved at the separation; Caesar and Antony exchange tense and suspicious farewells.

Act 3, Scene 3

Cleopatra interrogates the Messenger (3) about Octavia; he tells her that Antony's new wife is an unattractive woman and details her unappealing features. The queen is greatly relieved.

Act 3, Scene 4

In Athens Octavia is upset by the rising enmity between her husband and her brother and begs to be sent as an intermediary between them. Antony agrees, and she prepares to go to Rome.

Act 3, Scene 5

Eros informs Enobarbus that Caesar and Lepidus have defeated Pompey, but that Caesar has arrested Lepidus and sentenced him to death. Enobarbus anticipates war between Antony and Caesar.

Act 3, Scene 6

In Rome Caesar angrily reports that Antony, now in Egypt, has crowned himself and Cleopatra rulers of the eastern empire—a betrayal of both Octavia and Caesar and a virtual act of war against Rome. Octavia arrives to negotiate for Antony, whom she believes is still in Athens.

Act 3, Scene 7

At an army camp near ACTIUM, Enobarbus tells Cleopatra that her presence is a distraction to Antony, but she insists on remaining. Antony appears and remarks that Caesar has made a very rapid advance. He declares he will accept Caesar's challenge to fight a naval battle, despite the objections of his advisers that they are weakest at sea.

Act 3, Scene 8

Caesar warns his general Taurus not to fight on land until after the sea battle.

Act 3, Scene 9

Antony orders Enobarbus to establish a post from which to observe the sea battle.

Act 3, Scene 10

Troops from both sides march past; a sea battle is heard. Enobarbus despairs as he sees Antony's flagship retreat. Scarus reports that just as the battle might have been won by Antony's navy, Cleopatra sailed away from it. Antony followed, and the rest of the fleet followed him. Canidius arrives and confirms the news of defeat. He declares that he will surrender his forces to Caesar.

Act 3, Scene 11

Antony tells his attendants to flee, for he no longer deserves their loyalty. He declares to Cleopatra that though he is filled with despair, his love for her still seems worth all that has been lost.

Act 3, Scene 12

An Ambassador delivers to Caesar Antony's request that he be permitted to live in Egypt or Athens and that Cleopatra continue to rule Egypt. Caesar sends him back with a rejection of Antony's request and an assurance to Cleopatra that she can have whatever she wants if she will kill Antony or drive him from Egypt. Then he sends Thidias to her with the same message, telling him to make her any promises he chooses.

Act 3, Scene 13

Thidias arrives and declares to Cleopatra that Caesar believes she had joined Antony out of fear, not love. The queen accepts Caesar's offer of deliverance from Antony. Antony appears as Thidias kisses Cleopatra's hand in acknowledgment of her alliance with Caesar. Antony has his Servants (2) carry Thidias away and whip him, and he accuses Cleopatra bitterly. When the beaten Thidias is returned, Antony sends him back to Caesar with a defiant message. Cleopatra says that despite her surrender to Caesar, she still loves Antony. He takes heart and declares that he is prepared to carry on the war against Caesar, who has arrived at Alexandria, with the remnants of his forces. He says that they will have a grand banquet that night, as in the past, and he and Cleopatra leave to prepare for it. Enobarbus reflects on Antony's folly and decides that he will desert him.

Act 4, Scene 1

Caesar describes Antony's contemptuous challenges. Maecenas recommends attacking immediately, for Antony's judgment is clearly clouded by anger, and Caesar agrees.

Act 4, Scene 2

At the banquet, Antony declares that he will fight to the end and either win or recover his honor in death. When he bids the Servitors farewell, he suggests that this night might be his last. When the servants and Enobarbus weep, he declares that, on the contrary, they will triumph the next day.

Act 4, Scene 3

A group of Antony's sentries hear strange noises that they take to be a bad omen for the forthcoming battle.

Act 4, Scene 4

Antony lets Cleopatra help him into his armor, and he leaves for the battle in high spirits.

Act 4, Scene 5

Antony learns that Enobarbus has deserted to Caesar, but he is not angry. He recognizes that his own faults have driven his subordinate to despair. He orders Enobarbus's belongings sent to him.

Act 4, Scene 6

At Caesar's headquarters a Soldier (3) brings Enobarbus the belongings sent by Antony, and the deserter is stricken by pangs of conscience. He declares that he will die of a broken heart.

Act 4, Scene 7

Agrippa and his troops retreat before Antony and Scarus's forces. Scarus is wounded but insists on continuing the pursuit.

Act 4, Scene 8

Victorious in the day's fighting, Antony returns to Cleopatra. He praises Scarus for his great bravery and prowess.

Act 4, Scene 9

Outside Caesar's camp, a Sentry and his Watchmen discover the dying Enobarbus, who regrets his disloyalty and grieves for his lost honor.

Act 4, Scene 10

Antony and Scarus prepare for a combined battle on both land and sea.

Act 4, Scene 11

Caesar decides to concentrate on fighting at sea.

Act 4, Scene 12

Scarus muses on bad omens and on Antony's fretful mood. Antony announces that Cleopatra's navy has deserted to Caesar and that the battle is lost.

He sends Scarus to order a general retreat, and he reflects that his desperate condition is the fault of his infatuation with Cleopatra, whom he believes has betrayed him. Cleopatra appears and Antony drives her way with his rage. He declares that he will kill her.

Act 4, Scene 13

Cleopatra flees from Antony and takes refuge in a monument. She sends him word that she has committed suicide, speaking his name as she died.

Act 4, Scene 14

As Antony contemplates suicide, he is brought word that Cleopatra has killed herself, and he decides to do so, too. He orders Eros to kill him, but Eros kills himself instead. Antony then attempts to fall on his sword but succeeds only in wounding himself. Decretas appears and takes Antony's sword to Caesar to ingratiate himself with the conqueror. Diomedes brings word from Cleopatra. Realizing that Antony might kill himself, she reveals her lie and summons him. Antony orders himself carried to her on a litter.

Act 4, Scene 15

Antony, on his litter, is hoisted up to Cleopatra's hiding place in the monument. He tells Cleopatra that she should trust only Proculeius among Caesar's court. He proudly states that in killing himself he has prevented Caesar from killing him, and he dies. Cleopatra declares that she too will die in the proud Roman fashion.

Act 5, Scene 1

Caesar sends Dolabella to demand that Antony surrender. Decretas arrives with Antony's sword and word of his suicide. Caesar and his friends mourn the death of a great man even though he was their enemy. An Egyptian appears, sent by Cleopatra to receive Caesar's orders. Caesar sends him back with assurances that he offers mercy to the queen; he sends Proculeius and Gallus to Cleopatra to confirm the message.

Act 5, Scene 2

Cleopatra says that she is content to die. Proculeius arrives and assures her that Caesar will give Egypt to her son. Gallus appears with soldiers to guard Cleopatra. When she sees this, she attempts to stab herself but is disarmed by Proculeius. Dolabella arrives to replace Proculeius; moved by Cleopatra's elegy for Antony, he confides that Caesar intends to parade her ignominiously through the streets of Rome. Caesar arrives and generously offers mercy to Cleopatra, who submits, giving him a list of all her possessions. However, her treasurer Seleucus asserts that the list is incomplete. Cleopatra rages at him, but Caesar assures her that it does not matter for she can keep whatever she wants. He leaves, and Cleopatra sends Charmian on a secret errand as Dolabella returns to tell the queen that Caesar intends to transport her to Rome in three days. Charmian returns, and a Clown arrives with poisonous snakes. After he leaves, Cleopatra prepares to die. Iras dies, brokenhearted, as Cleopatra applies two asps to herself and dies when they bite her; Charmian does the same. Dolabella and Caesar return, and Caesar declares that Cleopatra shall be buried with Antony after a grand funeral celebrating the nobility of their love.

COMMENTARY

The opening scenes of *Antony and Cleopatra* establish the basic conflict of the play. Soldierly duty is squarely placed opposite the satisfactions—both physical and emotional—of sexual involvement. The Roman soldiers see Antony as "a strumpet's fool" (1.1.13), but Antony envisions finding a "new heaven, new earth" (1.1.17) in the experience of love. Antony refuses to acknowledge the call of duty represented by messages from Rome and stresses the conflict of the play when he declares, "Now for the love of Love, and her soft hours, / Let's not confound the time with conference harsh" (1.1.44–45). But when he learns, in 1.2, of a successful revolt against the Roman power he is supposed to be defending, Antony realizes that his honor demands that he "must from this enchanting queen break off" (1.2.125). He returns to Rome, but he can leave Cleopatra only with difficulty. He compromises his sense of duty by telling her he is her "soldier, servant, making peace or war, / As thou affects" (1.3.70–71), before he wrenches himself away. In 1.4 a purely Roman view of the situation is presented as Caesar and Lepidus regret Antony's neglect of his duty, even as he is returning to Rome.

Thus Shakespeare efficiently establishes the dramatic action of Acts 1–4 of the play: Antony wavers between his Roman heritage of military rigor and his attraction to the "soft hours" of indolence and lust. The emotional center of the work therefore fluctuates between the too-demanding rigors of Roman power and the too-seductive delights of Egyptian luxury, finally escaping to an immortal world created in the imaginations of the lovers—a paradise "Where souls do couch on flowers" (4.14.51). In Act 5, after Antony's death, Cleopatra, in a striking transformation that constitutes one of Shakespeare's greatest climaxes, raises the lovers' relationship to the level of transcendent love. But the focus returns to Rome's "great solemnity" (5.2.364), in the play's final words. Even as love triumphs, the final victory of Rome is affirmed in Caesar's closing speech as he translates the tale into a mundane memorial. Shakespeare does not permit the basic conflict, which extends throughout the play, to be overridden by a clearly stated declaration of values.

The fine balance achieved between the values of Rome and Egypt has led to differing interpretations of Shakespeare's play. *Antony and Cleopatra* has been seen on one hand as a romance on the transcendence of love over the mundane, and on the other as a lesson against neglect of duty; as an exaltation of love and as a rejection of lust. Antony has been seen as a sordid politician who is transfigured by the love of Cleopatra, a courtesan who is similarly transformed. He has also been seen as a fool who sacrifices his nobility to sensual gratification—in more modern terms, a weak individual who indulges in pleasure to escape reality. The play seems to offer no definite conclusion as to the priority of duty or sensuality. This ambiguity has sometimes led to the classification of *Antony and Cleopatra* among the PROBLEM PLAYS, works with disturbingly unresolved attitudes toward issues of love and sex in public contexts.

However, Shakespeare does provide a resolution; it is simply twofold. Social discipline and order—as seen in the order of Caesar's Rome—is presented as a necessary element for society's health and spiritual development. On the other hand, the lovers' fate—paralleled by that of Enobarbus—brings about an awareness of a different level of fulfillment: for the individual, love is more important than political or material success. When love is opposed by the forces of conventional society, as here, its pursuit can result in an intense realization of self, which is what happens to Cleopatra in Act 5. Thus, the transfiguration of Cleopatra is not invalidated by Caesar's final triumph, because the two climaxes exist in different worlds and point to equally potent but separate resolutions.

After Antony's death in Act 4, the conflict is seen in the opposition of Cleopatra and Caesar—Egypt and Rome, love and duty—and Caesar's victory is stressed in the play's final lines. The virtue of his triumph is made quite plain: Caesar declares as his victory approaches "The time of universal peace is near" (4.6.5), a statement that unmistakably refers—though the character is unaware of it—to the imminent coming of Christ. As Shakespeare's original audiences were completely aware, Caesar will found the Roman Empire, which was seen in the 17th century as not only a highlight of history but as a secular manifestation of the will of God, provided as preparation for the coming of the Messiah.

Although Caesar's victory is thus clearly intended as a genuine resolution and a statement that the tragedy has not been a waste of human potential, his triumph cannot be total. The world of conflicting values that undid the lovers—the world in which Caesar operates—is clearly transcended in Cleopatra's final moments. The lovers, with their jealous quarrels and seeming betrayals, their separations and deceptions, are distinctly of the "dungy earth" that Antony contrasts to "the nobleness of life" (1.1.35, 36), but they have the capacity to transcend themselves. Cleopatra's extraordinary vitality leads them beyond death to the "new heaven, new earth" (1.1.17) that Antony has envisioned. So there are two triumphs: that of Rome, which requires personal sacrifice in the name of the greater good of the world; and that of the lovers, in which individual happiness—particularly as expressed in sexual love—takes precedence over the demands of society.

Cleopatra's ultimate transfiguration cannot be dominated by Caesar's soldiers, and thus the final triumph is that of the individual's aspiration toward transcendence. Cleopatra's vision of reunion with

Antony in death is sheer poetry; as such, it can have no effect on the practical, prosaic world of empire building. Her seeming defeat is actually a triumphant assertion of the continuing value of what might have been and what should be. She can, indeed, "show the cinders of [her] spirits / Through the ashes of [her] chance" (5.2.172–173). The superiority of the individual imagination over the power of government is stressed, even as the necessities of society maintain their dominance in the real world.

The contrasting elements—power and politics versus pleasure and passion—are mingled and opposed throughout the drama. The political and military developments—first Pompey's rebellion against the Triumvirate and then Caesar's push for sole power—point up the fact that whatever the lovers do has repercussions in the great world, and, conversely, events in the political realm determine their fate. One of the ways in which Shakespeare maintains an even balance between these different worlds is by suppressing the more spectacular aspects of the military situation. The play's two battles occur almost entirely offstage—necessarily so in the case of Actium, a naval battle, but also in Act 4's ground combat—with only glimpses of marching soldiers provided. In fact the play's only violence is the two suicides. Thus, the love affair is not overwhelmed by the spectacle of clashing powers dividing the known world.

Cleopatra and Antony are not in any sense public figures victimized by the loss of private happiness; their love depends on the political situation that finally destroys them. They value their positions as world figures, and their affection is grounded in this appreciation. Antony promises Cleopatra that he will provide "Her opulent throne with kingdoms" (1.5.46), and she envisions him as "an Emperor Antony" (5.2.76). In fact, on his return to Egypt, his gift to her is a political act; as Caesar—who regards the act as a cause of war—observes, Antony "gave [her] the stablishment of Egypt, made her / Of Lower Syria, Cyprus, Lydia, / Absolute queen" (3.6.9–11). Antony knows that Cleopatra loves power, and he delights in giving it to her. But love influences politics as much as politics influences love, and Antony places his power in jeopardy by using it in this way.

The merciless entanglements of power and politics are thus contrasted with the possibility of private withdrawal into sensual pleasure. The aggressive manipulation of society as represented by the armies and ethics of martial Rome has always served an evident social purpose. The nurturing of the individual is an equally pervasive need; it is illustrated extravagantly in the luxuriant court of the Egyptian queen. Antony is absolutely human in his need for both aspects of life; he stands between two principles, and he cannot fully reject either. In this lies his grandeur as a tragic hero.

Just as the political world of Rome is both potentially good and a source of tragedy, so love has two aspects, being a manifestation of the life force but also a stimulus toward self-destruction. In the latter mode, love demands the renunciation of life, but in the former it glories in life. In this respect, though *Antony and Cleopatra* is unquestionably a TRAGEDY, it displays some of the features of a COMEDY. The structure of the play resembles that of traditional comedy, with Rome and Egypt being similar to the court and the forest of *As You Like It* and *A Midsummer Night's Dream*, or to VENICE and BELMONT in *The Merchant of Venice*. Moreover, comedy traditionally ended in a marriage, typically arranged through the wiles of the leading female character, and *Antony and Cleopatra* closes on a significant reference when Cleopatra, about to die, cries out "Husband, I come" (5.2.286). Not for nothing are the asps provided by the Clown, a traditional comic rustic.

Further, the comedy of the Clown is only one instance of a feature displayed elsewhere in the play: *Antony and Cleopatra* is often quite funny. In 1.1 Cleopatra's baiting of Antony is humorous, as is her anecdote of dressing her drunken lover in her clothes, in 2.5.19–23. Indeed, in one aspect Antony and Cleopatra embody another ancient comic tradition, that of the infatuated old man enthralled by a scheming young woman. In 1.2 we see an example of the hilarity of Egyptian court pastimes, and in 1.5 the queen jests about the sexlessness of her eunuch, Mardian. Cleopatra's mistreatment of the hapless Messenger (2.5.61–74, 106) may not strike modern audiences as particularly amusing, but such treatment of servants was another traditional comic routine, at least as old as

Roman drama (compare its use by Shakespeare in *The Comedy of Errors*). The bluff old soldier Enobarbus is at times a quite comical figure, especially when he mocks Lepidus in 2.7 and 3.2. In the former scene Lepidus also assumes a conventional comic role, that of the foolish drunk—a character type in Shakespeare's time that is still seen today. After 3.2, as the political plot comes to fruition and Antony goes down to defeat, the comedy disappears; its reemergence in 5.2 in the person of the Clown is all the more effective.

The comic aspects of the play point to *Antony and Cleopatra*'s place in the evolution of Shakespeare's work, for the tragic vision of *King Lear, Othello,* and *Macbeth* is here modified by elements from the earlier romantic comedies. The comedies always displayed a potential for tragedy—in the possible success of evil—that was forestalled by the forces of love. In *Antony and Cleopatra* this situation is reversed; tragedy is in the forefront, and the romantic comedy of love amid the Egyptian court remains in a distinctly secondary position. However, the spirit of comedy does recur at the close in support of the final transfiguration of Cleopatra. This treatment foreshadows the magical transcendence that is at the heart of the later ROMANCES.

The mingling of love and politics, lust and strategy, triumph and defeat characterizes *Antony and Cleopatra*. In its fusion of the mundane and the exalted—the "dungy earth" (1.1.35) versus "fire, and air" (5.2.288)—*Antony and Cleopatra* is one of the most complex and rewarding of Shakespeare's plays.

SOURCES OF THE PLAY

By far the most important source for *Antony and Cleopatra* was the "Life of Marcus Antonius" in Sir Thomas NORTH's *Lives of the Noble Greeks and Romans* (1579), which was a translation of Jacques AMYOT's French version (1559–65) of PLUTARCH's original Greek (ca. A.D. 125). The playwright followed Plutarch's historical account fairly closely, though he gave different emphasis to its incidents. An earlier play on the subject, Samuel DANIEL's *Cleopatra* (1594), apparently influenced Shakespeare in these variations, especially in his treatment of Cleopatra's suicide. Shakespeare's descriptions of

Egypt, particularly in 2.7, probably derive from LEO AFRICANUS as translated by John PORY in *A Geographical History of Africa* (1600).

TEXT OF THE PLAY

Antony and Cleopatra was written before the spring of 1608, when it was registered with the STATIONERS' COMPANY by Edward BLOUNT. Samuel Daniel's *Cleopatra* was altered between its editions of 1605 and 1607 in ways that reflect the influence of *Antony and Cleopatra*, which may therefore have been written as early as 1606. Barnabe BARNES's play *The Devil's Charter* contains an apparent echo of *Antony and Cleopatra*; it was performed in February 1607, then revised and published in October, suggesting that Shakespeare's play had been performed in 1607 or 1606. That it was not written earlier than 1606 is clear in light of the unaltered 1605 version of Daniel's work, as well as on stylistic grounds.

Antony and Cleopatra was registered for publication in 1608, but if a printed book was indeed actually produced, no copy of it has survived, and the earliest known text is that published in the FIRST FOLIO (1623). The Folio text was apparently derived from Shakespeare's own manuscript, as is indicated by a number of distinctive misspellings and abbreviations, along with elaborate stage directions, often precise yet impractical, unlikely to have been used in a PROMPTBOOK. As the only authoritative version of the play, the Folio has been the basis for all subsequent editions.

THEATRICAL HISTORY OF THE PLAY

No early performances of *Antony and Cleopatra* are recorded, but a production of ca. 1606—presumably the initial staging—is probable in view of the 1607 alterations made to Samuel Daniel's *Cleopatra*. (see "Text"). Richard BURBAGE is presumed to have originated the role of Antony. No other production is recorded for a century and a half, though John DRYDEN wrote a play about the lovers—*All for Love, or the World Well Lost* (1678)—that was influenced somewhat by Shakespeare's play. Its popularity was so great that it eclipsed *Antony and Cleopatra* until 1759, when David GARRICK staged a version of Shakespeare's text prepared by the noted scholar Edward CAPELL. Though it featured grandiose sets and elaborate costumes and starred Garrick and Mary Ann YATES, two of the most popular players of the day, the production was a failure, closing after a week; the public preferred *All for Love*, which continued to be revived.

In 1813 J. P. KEMBLE presented *Antony and Cleopatra*—using an abridged text that was amply supplemented with Dryden's lines—that starred Helen FAUCIT. Following the taste of the times, this production featured spectacular effects, including a sea battle and a grand funeral for the title characters, but it was as poorly received as Garrick's. In 1833 William Charles MACREADY starred in his version of the play, likewise spectacular, likewise mixed with Dryden, and likewise unsuccessful. Only in 1849 was Shakespeare's original play produced by Samuel PHELPS, who played Antony opposite Isabel GLYN, though it, too, was a commercial failure.

In the second half of the 19th century *Antony and Cleopatra* increased in popularity, and several productions were ventured, including those of Charles CALVERT (1866), F. B. CHATTERTON (1873), and Ben GREET (1897). Beerbohm TREE's production of 1907 continued the 19th-century tradition of dazzling spectacle requiring many extra players.

In the 20th century *Antony and Cleopatra* was more widely appreciated, and numerous productions were staged. The simply staged, textually accurate 1905 presentation of F. R. BENSON was notable for its rejection of the taste for spectacle. This modern tendency was furthered in the 1922 OLD VIC staging by Robert ATKINS, presented on a bare stage. This production starred Edith EVANS, who also played Cleopatra in several later productions. In 1936 Theodore KOMISARJEVSKY staged a controversial STRATFORD production starring Donald WOLFIT. Godfrey TEARLE and Katherine CORNELL were acclaimed as the lovers in New York in 1947; Laurence OLIVIER and Vivien LEIGH took the parts in London in 1951; Michael REDGRAVE and Peggy ASHCROFT played them in London and Stratford in a 1953 staging by Glen Byam SHAW; and in 1967 Zoë CALDWELL and Christopher PLUMMER triumphed at Stratford, Ontario. In 1972 Trevor NUNN staged all of the ROMAN PLAYS at Stratford, England.

Gian Francesco MALIPIERO composed an OPERA, *Antony and Cleopatra* (1938), based on the play.

The American composer Samuel BARBER also did so, but its initial production (staged by Franco ZEFFERELLI in 1966) was a failure. However, Barber revised his *Antony and Cleopatra*, and restaged by Gian Carlo Menotti (b. 1911) in 1975, it has found a place in the modern operatic repertoire.

As a FILM, *Antony and Cleopatra* has yielded six movies, three of them silent films. The best-known film version is that directed by and starring Charlton Heston (1972); the fabled flop *Cleopatra* (1962), starring Elizabeth Taylor and Richard Burton, was not derived from Shakespeare's play. *Antony and Cleopatra* was part of THE SPREAD OF THE EAGLE (1963), a TELEVISION series of the Roman plays, and Trevor Nunn's theatrical production was taped for the small screen in 1974. The play was also directed for television in 1981 by Jonathan MILLER.

CHARACTERS

Agrippa, M. Vipsanius (63–12 B.C.) Historical figure and character in *Antony and Cleopatra*, a follower of Octavius Caesar. In 2.2 Agrippa displays considerable influence when he suggests the marriage between Antony and Octavia, and in 4.6 and 4.7 he is in command of Caesar's army. For much of the remainder of the play he serves as an opposite to Antony's Enobarbus, with whom he exchanges remarks on the principal characters; he displays the demeanor of a gruff veteran soldier.

Shakespeare's character does not reflect the importance of the historical Agrippa, who was probably the most important figure—after Caesar himself—in the defeat of Antony and the subsequent establishment of the Roman Empire. Along with Maecenas, he was one of Caesar's few close friends and advisers. His origins are entirely obscure; even his contemporaries knew nothing of his family or homeland, although he was believed to have been Caesar's schoolmate in Athens before accompanying the future emperor on his return to Italy after the assassination of Julius Caesar in 44 B.C. (Agrippa does not appear in Shakespeare's *Julius Caesar*.) He was a prominent general throughout the civil wars. He put down revolts in Italy and Gaul and created and commanded the fleets that defeated Pompey in Sicily and Antony at ACTIUM. After Antony's defeat, Agrippa was Caesar's right-hand man in governing

Rome. In 23 B.C. Caesar nearly died of an illness, and he apparently intended that Agrippa would succeed him as ruler. In 21 B.C. Agrippa married Caesar's daughter. He served as a general and administrator in various parts of the empire until the year of his death.

Alexas (Alexas Laodician) (active ca. 32 B.C.) Historical figure and minor character in *Antony and Cleopatra*, an attendant to Cleopatra. Alexas is a cheerful fellow who jests with Charmian and Iras in 1.2. He brings Cleopatra a message from Antony in 1.5 and attends her—almost without speaking—in 2.5, 3.3, and 4.2. However, Alexas's desertion to Octavius Caesar, after the battle of ACTIUM, is reported in 4.6, and he appears to be a more important figure than his earlier role would suggest. Enobarbus reflects that Alexas had been sent by Antony to "jewry" (4.6.12), where he persuaded the ruler, Herod, to join Caesar. He goes on to remark that Caesar, shocked by this treachery, had executed Alexas. The account elaborates on the important Act 4 theme of Antony's fall as many of his onetime followers are seen to have deserted him.

Shakespeare took his account of Alexas Laodician from his source, PLUTARCH's *Lives*, where the Greek servant's promotion to diplomatic status is said to have resulted from the friendship that developed between him and Antony through his job as Cleopatra's message bearer. His surname—found in Plutarch—suggests that he was from the important ancient city of Laodicia, in Asia Minor, but otherwise Alexas is not found in history.

Ambassador Minor character in *Antony and Cleopatra*, a representative of Antony. In 3.12 the Ambassador carries his master's formal surrender to Octavius Caesar after the battle of ACTIUM, and in 3.13, after he has reported that Caesar refuses Antony's request for his life but offers leniency to Cleopatra if she will abandon Antony, Antony sends him back to Caesar with a challenge of hand-to-hand combat. Antony identifies the Ambassador as the "schoolmaster" (3.11.71) of his and Cleopatra's children. In 3.12 Dolabella observes that the use of the schoolmaster as an emissary indicates the totality of Antony's defeat. This schoolmaster is identified

by Shakespeare's source, PLUTARCH, as one Euphronius, presumably a Greek scholar but otherwise unknown in history. This name is sometimes used in modern editions of the play, following its introduction in the 18th century by Edward CAPELL. Plutarch adds that his diplomatic employment was necessary because of the earlier abandonment of Cleopatra by her attendant, Alexas.

Antony, Mark (Marcus Antonius) (ca. 82–30 B.C.) Historical figure, character in *Julius Caesar* and title character in *Antony and Cleopatra*. In the former play Antony leads the forces opposing the assassins of Julius Caesar, led by Marcus Brutus. In the latter, his love for Cleopatra leads to his downfall and the triumph of Octavius Caesar.

In *Julius Caesar*, Antony is a courageous but crafty schemer whose political skill brings about a civil war. He helps demonstrate the social harm done by the powerful when they pursue their political ends. On the other hand, Antony, a strong personality, is an emotionally honest man and a much more sympathetic character than the virtuous, but cold and domineering, Brutus. Thus, Antony is both a positive and a negative figure who contributes greatly to the moral uncertainty that is at the heart of the play.

Part of Antony's power in *Julius Caesar* comes from Shakespeare's careful presentation of him. In the first two acts he is an unimportant figure who speaks only 33 words, but other characters refer to him numerous times and acknowledge his potential greatness. Most significant, Cassius desires that Antony be killed along with Caesar (2.1.155–161). He calls him a "shrewd contriver" and accurately predicts that if he lives he will be a difficult opponent.

These references prepare us for Antony's sudden dominance of the play in Act 3. Even before he appears, the message he sends to Caesar's assassins (3.1.126–137) establishes his strong personal style; a confident and powerful tone, both rhetorical and emotional. He soon arrives in person, and his initial response to the sight of Caesar's corpse is direct, uncalculated, heartfelt grief. Even in the presence of the murderers he does not hide his initial outburst. But he quickly turns to the future and takes control when he arranges to speak at Caesar's funeral.

His boldness and fervor are both powerful and charming, but Antony disqualifies himself for our moral sympathy with the long soliloquy (3.1.254–275) in which he proposes to provoke a ghastly civil war—he describes the bloody slaughter of innocent people in detail—in order to avenge Caesar's death. Antony's fine human qualities—his courage and intelligence—bring about tragic consequences.

Our ambivalence about Antony is furthered by his magnificent funeral oration (3.2.75–254), one of Shakespeare's most renowned passages. The speech's virtues—its bold rhetoric, its manipulative presentation of evidence, its appeal to pathos—seem to be clever but cheap effects intended to exploit the passions of the unthinking multitude. Certainly the speech has this effect, as Antony knew it would. But one realizes that Antony does not seek to advance himself personally, and that he does not resort to slander against Brutus, or downright dishonesty. Antony is genuinely grieved by Caesar's death, and his expression of it, while extremely inflammatory, is not false. He actually feels the way he brings his audience to feel. And we too are moved to share his emotion, even as we are aware of Brutus's virtues in contrast with the mayhem Antony intends.

In 4.1, in an episode invented by Shakespeare to intensify our response to Antony, he bargains away the life of his nephew Publius. In contrast with Brutus's refusal to kill Antony, this action seems particularly detestable. Moreover, Antony also proposes to loot Caesar's bequest to the people, and his attitude to his ally Lepidus, whom he regards as no more than a tool, reinforces a sense that he is a cynical politician. As we approach the play's climax at the battle of PHILIPPI, we are inclined to favor Antony's foes, Brutus and Cassius.

However, at the close of the play, when Antony delivers his famous eulogy of Brutus (5.5.68–75), he is very generous, and the balance of our sympathy is somewhat restored. Antony not only acknowledges Brutus's noble motive in killing Caesar, he also observes that Brutus was unable to recognize the true nature of his fellow conspirators. Thus, Antony emphasizes once more the play's chief theme: that evil can attend good intentions when established rulers are unseated.

In *Antony and Cleopatra*, written about seven years later, Antony again contributes much to the ambivalence that characterizes the work. He is both a major political figure and the protagonist of a love story. As a result of his love, his position in the world undergoes great change. Initially he wields immense power, ruling half the known world—a status that Shakespeare emphasizes with a persistent stream of political references and events. However, he willfully throws this position away for the sake of his passion—a passion whose self-indulgence is stressed by repeated descriptions of the opulent luxury of Cleopatra's court.

As a soldier, Antony has proven himself a model of Roman military virtues—the Romans are dissatisfied with his conduct in Egypt precisely because they value his earlier record as a "mate in empire, / Friend and companion in the front of war" (5.1.43–44), whose "goodly eyes . . . Have glow'd like plated Mars" (1.1.2–4). His earlier successes enacted in *Julius Caesar* are referred to several times, as in 3.2.54–56. Antony values himself for the same reasons and regrets his "blemishes in the world's report" (2.3.5), but he is trapped in another role by his intense attraction to Cleopatra. Under her influence he has become a voluptuary; he has abandoned his duty for the "love of Love, and her soft hours" (1.1.44) in Alexandria.

As a lover, Antony offers us a glimpse of the transcendent nature of passion, a theme that Cleopatra will triumphantly present—in Antony's name—after his death. In 1.1, when Cleopatra, as the wily courtesan, demands that he declare how much he loves her, Antony states that love cannot be totaled, for lovers must "find out new heaven, new earth" (1.1.17). Thus, it is he who introduces the theme of transcendence through love, and this desire is emphasized by hints of the book of Revelation that frame his story in the play. Indeed, "new heaven, new earth" is very close to the biblical text (cf. Rev. 21:1)—much more familiar to 17th-century audiences than it is to today's—and the imagery that marks his death confirms the association: "The star is fall'n. / And time is at his period" (4.14.106–107 [cf. Rev. 8:10; 10:6]).

Although Cleopatra disrupts Antony's loyalty to Rome, he is not totally committed to her either.

Though he only tears himself from her with difficulty, in 1.3 he returns to Rome and makes a political marriage to Octavia. Further, his love for Cleopatra is mingled with distrust—with considerable justification, for the Egyptian queen transcends the behavior of a courtesan only after Antony's death—and he dies presuming she will strike a bargain with his conqueror, Caesar. Moreover, he dies not as a tragically committed lover but rather more like a clever Roman politician—albeit a loving one—when he offers Cleopatra advice on the politics of Caesar's court. Antony demonstrates that the ideals of love and power are both insufficient, thus manifesting the duality presented by the play as a whole.

Shakespeare followed his source—PLUTARCH's *Lives*—fairly closely in his account of the historical career of Marcus Antonius, with two exceptions. As already noted, the playwright invented Antony's callous sacrifice of a nephew in *Julius Caesar*, and in *Antony and Cleopatra* he placed Antony's involvement with Cleopatra earlier in the sequence of events; in Plutarch the love affair did not actually begin until after Antony's marriage to Octavia. Thus Shakespeare's Antony seems indecisive about his loyalties, if not actually disloyal to Cleopatra as well as to Octavia. However, the change may simply have been motivated by dramatic strategy, for it is obviously better to begin the play with the love affair than to introduce it in the middle, after the political situation has evolved.

In *Antony and Cleopatra* Shakespeare departed from the general impression of Antony left by Plutarch. For the ancient historian, Antony was simply a moral failure, a man who threw away his life because he was unable to control his appetites. Antony's catastrophic moral collapse justified Caesar's war against him, and his defeat was entirely for the good. Shakespeare, however, made certain we would see that Antony's vices contained germs of virtue, and that his passion was firmly bound to a noble if ill-defined idea of love.

Plutarch depended on pro-Caesar sources (see, e.g., MESSALA) since the victorious Caesar permitted no others to survive, and thus his account is unfairly biased against Antony in the opinion of modern scholars. The debauchery indulged in by

Marcus Antonius was rather ordinary among the powerful Roman aristocrats of the time, and we cannot be certain that the political concessions he made to Cleopatra were in fact made at all, nor that they were as foolish as they seem in the sources. In any case, modern scholars generally agree that it was not his affair with Cleopatra that ruined Antonius but rather his political and military failings: Had he been more clever and ruthless, he might have enforced the maintenance of the joint rule that Caesar upset, or he might have triumphed himself and ruled Rome.

Attendant   Any of several minor characters in *Antony and Cleopatra*, servants of Mark Antony. In 1.1 an Attendant brings word that news has arrived from ROME, though Antony refuses to hear it. In 3.11 a group of Attendants declare their loyalty following Antony's defeat at ACTIUM, though he grandly insists they should flee, his fortunes being obviously on the decline. The Attendants' function is to demonstrate the grandness of Antony's household and the loyalty that his magnanimous leadership inspires. The Attendant in 1.1 is designated a Messenger in some editions.

Boy   Minor character in *Antony and Cleopatra*, a singer. Some modern editions include a stage direction specifying that a Boy sings the SONG that accompanies the dance led by Enobarbus (2.7.111–116) because Enobarbus stipulates that "the boy shall sing" (2.7.108), although the authoritative FIRST FOLIO text does not include a specific mention of the Boy.

Caesar, Octavius   (63 B.C.–A.D. 14)   Character in *Antony and Cleopatra*, the successful rival of Mark Antony for control of the government of ROME. (The same figure appears in *Julius Caesar* as Octavius.) Caesar is to some extent a foil for Antony. He is a coldly ambitious, dispassionate, and manipulative political and military leader whose triumph points up Antony's opposite traits: passion, generosity, and misjudgment. Caesar typically regrets drinking wine at a celebratory banquet, saying "our graver business / Frowns at this levity" (2.7.118–119). In consequence he is superior to his rivals in action; in war, as Canidius remarks before the battle of ACTIUM, "this speed of Caesar's / Carries beyond belief" (3.7.74–75). Less attractively, Caesar breaks his treaty with Pompey and betrays Lepidus, while Antony, in contrast, magnanimously forgives Enobarbus for deserting. But whatever else Caesar may be, he is successful. At the outset of *Antony and Cleopatra,* Caesar shares power with Antony and Lepidus in the Triumvirate, but in the course of the action he defeats each of them in separate civil wars, and before the play's climax he assumes sole power over Rome's vast territories.

However, Caesar's greatest importance comes in Act 5, after Antony's death, when he is powerfully contrasted with Cleopatra. His Roman dedication to power stands in opposition to her vivid appeal to passion as the justification for life. Caesar schemes to prevent Cleopatra's suicide. He treacherously assures her of his goodwill, when in fact he intends to exhibit her in a parade of triumph in Rome and subject her to the ultimate humiliation in order to demonstrate Rome's relentless power and his own strength. Though Cleopatra achieves transcendence in death, Caesar commands the stage at the close of the play and Rome's triumph is finally asserted.

However, Caesar is not simply a villain; he clearly cares for his sister Octavia—though he also uses her as a political pawn when he marries her to Antony—and he is capable of appreciating Antony's virtues. In his first lines, opening 1.4, he declares his admiration for his rival, and in his final tribute to the "pair so famous" (5.2.358) he recognizes the "strong toil of grace" (5.2.346) that Cleopatra has shown in her noble death. Nevertheless, Caesar is a ruler whose actions are not governed by his emotions; he can understand his opponents sympathetically, but he makes them his victims all the same.

As the representative of the growing Roman power, Caesar has a significance that is quite independent of his personal qualities. He declares that his victory will usher in a "time of universal peace" (4.6.5). In a stroke of dramatic irony, Caesar cannot recognize the implications of this remark, but for the playwright and his original audiences its meaning was both profound and obvious. It refers to the imminent coming of Christ, for Caesar went on to found the Roman Empire, whose establishment of political unity in the Mediterranean world—the *pax romana*—was seen in the 17th century as a manifestation of the will of God, the period of peace that ushered in the coming of the Messiah. Thus, Caesar displays a dignity and majesty that seem to reach beyond the world of the play.

Shakespeare's cold and ambitious ruler seems to correspond fairly closely to the historical Octavius Caesar—who took the title Augustus upon becoming emperor—though it is difficult to be certain as Octavius is known in history from only a few biased accounts, one of which is Shakespeare's source, PLUTARCH's *Lives.* However, it is noteworthy that the playwright significantly altered the story he read in Plutarch. Shakespeare's Caesar has failings—particularly moral ones—but is nonetheless a singularly potent figure who personally dominates the political and military worlds of the play. However, though undeniably a great leader, Octavius Caesar was highly dependent on his subordinates. Only the most notable of these—Agrippa, in the military realm, and Maecenas, as a diplomat— have even minor roles in *Antony and Cleopatra.* The triumphant warrior of the play was in fact a weak and sickly campaigner; this is alluded to by the embittered Antony in 3.11.35–40, but little is made of it. Shakespeare's aggrandizement of an already grand figure reinforces our sense of Caesar's dignity and majesty.

Canidius (Camidius, Publius Canidius Crassus)

(d. 30 B.C.) Historical figure and character in *Antony and Cleopatra,* a general in Antony's army. Canidius appears only briefly, in 3.7, where he objects to Antony's decision to fight Caesar at sea; and in 3.10, where he declares that he will surrender his troops to Caesar after Antony has lost the battle of ACTIUM. Antony's power and authority waned due to the influence of Cleopatra, and his followers lost their faith in his success. The character Canidius demonstrates this.

The historical Canidius was in fact the only major figure among Antony's followers to stay with him to the bitter end. He fled after Actium and made his way back to ALEXANDRIA, where he was captured and executed upon his leader's final defeat and death. Shakespeare's source, PLUTARCH's *Lives,* was based on an anti-Antony source (see MESSALA), and modern scholars believe that Canidius's impressive record as a hardy and loyal officer makes Plutarch's interpretation of his actions unlikely.

Captain   Minor character in *Antony and Cleopatra,* an officer in Antony's army. In 4.4 the Captain greets Antony cheerfully on the morning of a battle, listens to his leader's parting remarks to Cleopatra, and leaves with him. His function is to add a note of martial bustle to the scene. In the first edition of the play, in the FIRST FOLIO, this character was designated as Alexas, but this reflects an error—probably Shakespeare's—for in 4.6.12–16 we learn of Alexas's earlier treason and execution. Nicholas ROWE altered the designation and assigned the Captain his rank in the 1709 edition of the plays, and all subsequent editors have accepted the change.

Charmian   Character in *Antony and Cleopatra,* an attendant of Cleopatra. In 1.2 Charmian is pleasantly humorous as she banters with her friends Alexas and Iras over the predictions of the Soothsayer, and one can understand Cleopatra's obvious fondness for her. The queen addresses Charmian more intimately and much more often than she does her other servants. She confides in her and permits her to offer advice, even if she usually rejects it. In 2.5.15–18 Charmian reminisces with her mistress about fishing expeditions she took with Antony; she also boldly attempts to restrain the queen's temper when she says, "Good madam, keep yourself within yourself" (2.5.75), and she teases her about her past affair with Julius Caesar in 1.5.67–73. Charmian is a spirited, attractive young woman of a type that Shakespeare often depicted.

In 4.13, however, it is Charmian who makes the ill-fated suggestion that Cleopatra let Antony believe she has committed suicide. This is perhaps a device whereby Shakespeare intended to remove blame from the queen, whose transition from courtesan to transcendent lover is about to take place. Charmian herself undergoes such a change along with her mistress, fulfilling the Soothsayer's prediction that she "shall be yet far fairer" (1.2.16) than she already is. Her loyalty takes on a grandeur as she accompanies her mistress's grave poetry with cries of grief—"Dissolve, thick cloud, and rain, that

I may say, / The gods themselves do weep" (5.2.298–299)—and she cries out to the queen with almost religious intensity, "O eastern star!" (5.2.307). When Cleopatra dies, Charmian touchingly straightens her mistress's crown before she kills herself in the same way. As she dies, she proudly declares to a Roman soldier that Cleopatra's suicide "is well done, and fitting for a princess / Descended of so many royal kings" (5.2.325–326). Her coda to Cleopatra's grand declaration of ultimate love adds an echo of ecstasy before the final triumph of Octavius Caesar.

Shakespeare adapted Charmian from a mere mention in his source, PLUTARCH's *Lives,* and developed the character greatly. Plutarch states that Cleopatra was attended at her death by a serving woman named Charmian, but this person is otherwise unknown in history.

Cleopatra, Queen of Egypt (68–30 B.C.)   Historical figure and title character of *Antony and Cleopatra,* the Queen of Egypt and the lover of the Roman general Mark Antony. Throughout Acts 1–4 Cleopatra displays the powerful charms of an experienced and thoroughly professional courtesan. She attempts to control her lover with a strategy of alternate taunts and insults and seductive sexuality. Then in Act 5, after Antony is dead, Cleopatra acknowledges the depth of her true feelings for her lover and dedicates her suicide to their joint love. She thereby transcends her earlier nature through the power of passion.

Many commentators who admire Cleopatra's ultimate nobility do not accept the reality of her earlier role as the exploiter of Antony's sexuality. But Shakespeare's Cleopatra is clearly representative of a familiar dramatic character type: the scheming courtesan. From her first appearance she ridicules Antony, makes outrageous demands for his exclusive affection, declares that his love is insufficient—all classic techniques of emotional domination—and is oblivious to Antony's more romantic interpretation of love. She even uses his devotion against him when she declares that his lack of affection for his wife is evidence that he will eventually desert her as well.

Cleopatra also has great charm, and she richly deserves the famous tribute from Enobarbus, "Age cannot wither her, nor custom stale / Her infinite variety" (2.2.235–236). She is witty even in the direst extremity. As the dying Antony is hoisted to her hideout she can jest (4.15.32). In fact, some critics consider her one of the great comic figures in Shakespeare, comparable to Falstaff. She has a pleasing delight in mischief; Enobarbus accompanies his description of her magnificence with an account of when she put aside regal dignity and hopped gaily through the streets. Her beauty is enrapturing, and she has in abundance the intoxicating sexuality essential to the successful courtesan; as Enobarbus puts it, "vilest things / Become themselves in her" (2.2.238–239).

She also has genuine affection for Antony, but even as she reveals her fondness for him—in his absence—she discloses her past history as a courtesan. She speaks in 1.5.29–34 of her earlier affairs with Julius Caesar and Pompey the Great (father of the play's Pompey). Her hurt and anger at the news of Antony's marriage to Octavia are certainly genuine, but when she learns of Octavia's unattractive physical features her spirits are restored, for, courtesan-like, her confidence in her sexual allure assures her that she will win her lover back. She does, but when her flight from the battle of ACTIUM brings about Antony's disgrace, she once again displays her essentially selfish nature, in 3.13, when she accepts the alliance offered by Octavius Caesar. She coolly waits out Antony's rage—"I must stay his time" (3.13.155)—and resumes the role of docile and playful lover. However, when her sailors again betray Antony and his rage drives her away, she resorts to an extremely cynical ploy, the pretended suicide that sparks Antony's real one. Falsely assumed emotion—the favorite weapon of the courtesan—remains Cleopatra's most characteristic resource.

However, in the end she is transformed through her noble response to the death of her lover. In 4.15.25–26 she first mentions the idea of suicide simply as a way to foil Caesar's potential humiliations, but after Antony's death she refers to it as a noble ideal on the model Antony himself has offered, "the high Roman fashion" (4.15.87). In refusing to be humiliated, Cleopatra finds herself at one with Antony in the Roman ideal of honorable

suicide. Seleucus's revelation that she has withheld treasure from Caesar is sometimes taken as evidence that Cleopatra reverts briefly to ideas of survival, though another interpretation is that she chose to deceive Caesar as to her intentions so that he would not prevent them. However, even if we suppose that she does waver, she also returns to the idea of a noble death, and her focus remains on Antony—rather than on Caesar—as she approaches the deed.

Cleopatra accepts death because it is the only end equal to her newly awakened love for Antony. It is in her ecstatic appraisal of him as "an Emperor Antony . . ." (5.2.76–100) that she first finds the exalted note of commitment to the memory of her lover that carries her through to the end. When she cries, "Husband, I come" (5.2.286), she completes her transformation into "fire, and air; my other elements / I give to baser life" (5.2.288–289). When she abandons her actual, earthly relationship with Antony for an eternal union, Cleopatra transcends the mortal world of politics and courtesanship where she and Antony had come to grief.

Cleopatra's personality does not change with her final ecstasy—Shakespeare was too good a writer to exchange one sort of portrayal for another at the close of the play. Cleopatra dies, but she makes her death a luxurious and hedonistic one. She combines the splendor of grand costume—"Give me my robe, put on my crown" (5.2.279)—with an almost sexual surrender to death at the end, when she cries, "As sweet as balm, as soft as air, as gentle. / O Antony!" (5.2.310–311). Her theatrical nature provides the grandeur that elevates the tragedy provoked by her earlier conduct. Thus we can see Cleopatra's moral defects—her selfishness as a lover and her practice of the courtesan's wiles—in a new light, as inextricable elements of a personality powerful enough to generate the mysterious grace that she brings to her final gesture. Through this grace and power, Cleopatra's vision of reunion with Antony after death is a triumphant affirmation of love and life. Even in seeming defeat she embodies the imagination of the individual and the value of what could have been over what wordly power has insisted on. She knows that compared to her, Caesar is "but Fortune's knave" (5.2.3), for the conqueror, with his limited vision, can suppose only that "her life in Rome / Would be eternal in our triumph" (5.1.65–66). But Cleopatra's death is the true triumph celebrated by the play.

The historical Cleopatra bore little resemblance to Shakespeare's character. She was not particularly beautiful—Shakespeare's source, PLUTARCH's *Lives*, attributes her magnetism to her conversation. Nor, in all probability, did she die for the sake of love but rather for the more practical end of avoiding a horrible captivity, and she only killed herself after she attempted to win Caesar with a promise to betray Antony. She was descended from one of the Greek successors of Alexander the Great and was entirely of Greek ancestry, not African in any degree, despite the modern tendency to classify her among Shakespeare's black characters. Cleopatra inherited the throne of Egypt in 51 B.C., at the age of 17. Deposed by an aristocratic clique in 49 B.C., she was restored with the assistance of Julius Caesar a year later.

She became Caesar's mistress, and she later filled the same function for Pompey the Great and Antony; unlike in the play, however, she did not become Antony's mistress until after his marriage to Octavia. In all three cases her motive is clear; she needed the political support of the forces of ROME present in the eastern Mediterranean, and thus she ingratiated herself with whoever commanded them. Modern scholars think it unlikely that she influenced the policies of any of her protectors, who simply used her as a means of extracting wealth from Egypt. Antony's gifts to her of kingdoms and power that Octavius Caesar complains of in the play were merely ordinary applications of Roman policy by which administrative jurisdictions in conquered lands were consolidated under a client ruler. The arrangement inspired no mistrust at the time. Cleopatra, who was reportedly greedy for even the trappings of power, persistently requested more such titular kingdoms, but Antony refused her.

When Antony found himself at war with Caesar, he naturally made use of the Egyptian kingdom that he governed through Cleopatra, but the unreliability of Egyptian forces at Actium and afterward—as recounted in the play—cannot be attributed to her influence. It is uncertain whether Antony and Cleopatra were married, but she bore three children by him; the two boys were killed after Caesar's victory, and the girl later became a pawn of Roman politics and was married to a Numidian king.

Clown   Minor character in *Antony and Cleopatra*, the pretended fig seller who provides Cleopatra with the poisonous snakes with which she kills herself. The Clown, summoned by Charmian in 5.2, is a CLOWN in the literary meaning of the term. He is a conventional comic figure, the ludicrously naive country bumpkin who had figured in COMEDY from ancient times. He comically warns Cleopatra that poisonous snakes are dangerous. Solemnly, he states, ". . . his biting is immortal: those that do die of it, do seldom or never recover" (5.2.245–247). Clowns are usually talkative, and he goes on to tell of "a very honest woman, but something given to lie" (5.2.250–251) who has reported on her own death by snakebite. He further expounds on the tendency of women to be corrupted by the devil—another medieval comic routine—before Cleopatra can get him to leave.

With Antony dead and Cleopatra about to kill herself, this episode comes at an agonizing point in the play's climax. The scene shatters the fascinated horror of the audience while at the same time heightening it by the inane and excruciating postponement of the plot's development. Further, the play's sudden comic tone at this crucial moment highlights the triumphant, celebratory aspect of Cleopatra's suicide; the traditional ending of a romantic comedy is evoked, and the transcendence of Cleopatra's total commitment to love is emphasized.

Decretas (Decretus, Dercetas, Dercetaeus, Dercetus) (active 30 B.C.)   Historical figure and minor character in *Antony and Cleopatra*, a member of Antony's personal guard. In 4.14 Antony stabs himself with his sword, and Decretas, seeing that his master's defeat is now complete, takes Antony's sword to Caesar, where he hopes to ingratiate himself with the conqueror by being the first to tell him of his enemy's death. In 5.1.5–26 he makes his presentation to Caesar and praises Antony eloquently, after which he disappears from the play.

He demonstrates, by his flight to Caesar, the collapse of loyalty around Antony, and then—somewhat incongruously—he bears witness to the nobility of the hero's end, a major theme of Act 5.

Shakespeare took the name of this minor figure—unknown in history outside this anecdote—from his source, PLUTARCH's *Lives*, and it has been variously rendered. In Plutarch and in Sir Thomas NORTH's English translation his name is Dercetaeus. Shakespeare—or someone else associated with early productions of the play—simplified this spelling, and it appears in the FIRST FOLIO (1623) as "Decretas" (twice, plus several abbreviations beginning "Dec") and "Dercetus" (once). In 1725 Alexander POPE compromised and introduced a new variant, "Dercetas," and subsequent editors have chosen from among these possibilities.

Demetrius Minor character in *Antony and Cleopatra*, a follower of Antony. In 1.1 Demetrius and his friend Philo discuss Antony's neglect of his military duties while he dallies with the Queen of Egypt, Cleopatra. The episode establishes a disapproving Roman view of the love affair.

Diomedes (Diomed) (active 30 B.C.) Historical figure and minor character in *Antony and Cleopatra*, a servant of Cleopatra. In 4.14 Diomedes comes to Antony with a message that states that his mistress is alive, despite an earlier report that she had committed suicide, but he arrives too late, for Antony has just stabbed himself. Diomedes accompanies the soldiers who carry Antony to Cleopatra and announces their arrival in 4.15. Diomedes appears by name in Shakespeare's source, PLUTARCH's *Lives*, but he is otherwise unknown in history.

Dolabella, Cornelius (active 30 B.C.) Historical figure and minor character in *Antony and Cleopatra*, a follower of Octavius Caesar. Dolabella appears as a minor member of Caesar's entourage in 3.12, 4.6, and 5.1; in the third of these scenes we see him sent to Antony with a demand for surrender, before it is known that Antony is dead. Attention is brought to this errand later in the scene when Caesar recollects it; thus, the focus is drawn to Antony once again. In 5.2, now delegated to guard Cleopatra, Dolabella succumbs to her charms and reveals to her that Caesar intends to humiliate her in a triumphal parade in ROME. This furthers her decision to commit suicide.

Little is known of the historical Dolabella beyond the anecdote of his brief encounter with Cleopatra, told in Shakespeare's source, PLUTARCH's *Lives*. Modern scholars believe that Caesar was actually maneuvering Cleopatra toward suicide. He wanted her out of the way but found the execution of a woman an undignified proceeding for a Roman ruler, so Dolabella may not have been as charitable—or as charmed—as it seems in Plutarch and Shakespeare. Another Roman writer later reported that Dolabella was an intimate of the Emperor Augustus, as Octavius Caesar became known.

Egyptian Minor character in *Antony and Cleopatra*, a messenger for Cleopatra. The "poor Egyptian," as he describes himself in 5.1.52, appears before Octavius Caesar, who has just defeated the forces of Cleopatra and Mark Antony. He has been sent to learn Caesar's orders to the Egyptian queen; Caesar sends him back with a conciliatory message. This episode demonstrates Cleopatra's changed circumstances; she is no longer mistress of her own fate, a situation that she will find intolerable. The Egyptian's modest mission ushers in the final development of the play.

Enobarbus (Gnaeus Domitius Ahenobarbus) (d. 31 B.C.) Historical figure and character in *Antony and Cleopatra*, Mark Antony's chief lieutenant who later deserts him and joins Octavius Caesar. Antony's closest friend and adviser through Acts 1–3, Enobarbus abandons his leader when he perceives, in 3.13, that Antony's involvement with Cleopatra has led to inevitable defeat. However, when he learns of Antony's sympathetic response to the betrayal, Enobarbus feels terrible pangs of guilt and declares that he will "go seek / Some ditch, wherein to die" (4.6.37–38). In 4.9 a Sentry and his Watchmen listen as Enobarbus praises Antony and prays for death, then they see him collapse and die. Enobarbus realizes that he was wrong to permit good sense to overrule loyalty, for by being prudent he has broken his own heart. The episode foreshadows Cleopatra's final transcendence, and demonstrates that the power of love can invalidate questions of military and political success. In fact, Enobarbus's betrayal is loving, for it is clear that he leaves Antony because he cannot bear to witness his leader's slide into weak-willed failure. Enobarbus thus offers another complex angle on the play's themes of love and power.

Enobarbus is a wise and witty figure before his crisis draws him under. He frequently offers frank, sardonic comments on the other characters and fills some of the functions of a CHORUS. For instance, his mockery of Lepidus, in 3.2, satirizes the dishonesty of Roman politics. On the other hand, his persistent criticism of Antony's love affair helps establish the point of view of the rigorously disciplined ROME, as opposed to the pleasure-oriented world of Cleopatra's court. Enobarbus rises to fine poetry, as in his famous description of the first meeting of Antony and Cleopatra—"The barge she sat in, like a burnish'd throne / Burn'd on the water . . ." (2.2.191 ff.), but he is more often a gruff veteran of the civil wars who jests about the conflict's ups and downs and feels comradeship with his onetime and future enemies. His soldier's humor is well developed and provides a significant portion of the play's comic spirit, an important element in Shakespeare's dramatic strategy.

The historical Domitius Ahenobarbus, as he was called, came from an important Roman political and military family. He fought for Pompey the Great (father of the play's Pompey) against Julius Caesar and was later convicted of participating in Caesar's murder in 44 B.C. He commanded a naval force for Brutus at PHILIPPI in 42 B.C., though he does not appear in *Julius Caesar*. After Philippi, he established himself as a warlord. He controlled the Adriatic Sea with his fleet and issued coins bearing his portrait. In 40 B.C. he allied himself with Antony. He opposed Cleopatra's participation in the war against Caesar, and in 31 B.C. he changed sides, as in the play, but he did it just before the battle of ACTIUM, rather than afterward. Shakespeare knew this from his source, PLUTARCH, but he preferred that his character be a basically loyal subordinate who leaves only when Antony's failings have made defeat inevitable. Ahenobarbus, on the other hand, deserted when his services must still have seemed valuable to his new master. However, he immediately became too sick to command troops, and he died soon after the battle.

Eros Character in *Antony and Cleopatra*, servant of Antony. Eros first appears in 3.5, where he reports to Enobarbus that Octavius Caesar has defeated Pompey and imprisoned Lepidus, news that foreshadows the conflict with Caesar that will prove fatal to Antony. Eros appears thereafter several times—in 3.11, 4.4, 4.5, and 4.7—as an obviously devoted servant; in 4.14 the defeated Antony, believing that Cleopatra has committed suicide, orders Eros to take his sword and kill him, in accordance with a promise made when Antony had freed the servant from slavery, years earlier. However, Eros cannot bring himself to do it and kills himself instead. Antony, declaring Eros "Thrice-nobler than myself" (4.14.95), follows his example and stabs himself. This episode, a familiar dramatic exercise (compare, for example, the death of Marcus Brutus, in 5.5 of *Julius Caesar*), lends pathos to the noble death of Antony.

Gallus, Caius Cornelius (ca. 69–27 B.C.) Historical figure and minor character in *Antony and Cleopatra*, a follower of Octavius Caesar. In 5.1 Gallus wordlessly follows Caesar's order to accompany Proculeius on his mission to offer mercy to Cleopatra, and in 5.2 he arrives at the quarters of the Egyptian queen with a squad of soldiers. Gallus leaves immediately, but his appearance—and his remark, "You see how easily she may be surpris'd" (5.2.35)—makes clear that Cleopatra is now entirely in Caesar's control. She responds by attempting to stab herself, but she is prevented by Proculeius. Gallus reappears as part of Caesar's entourage later in the scene, but he does not speak again.

The historical Gallus was an important Roman poet, regarded as the principal inventor of the Roman love elegy, but only a fragment of a single line of his work survives. He abandoned art for war after an unsuccessful love affair and became a leading member of Caesar's military establishment; historians give him much of the credit for Antony's final defeat. After the war he became the first Roman governor of Egypt. He put down several rebellions and traveled up the Nile into what is now Sudan, where he established relations between Rome and Ethiopia. However, he was a notably poor administrator, and a scandal, the details of which are lost, resulted in his dismissal. He was convicted of treason and punished with exile from Rome, to which he responded by killing himself.

Guardsman (1) Any of several minor characters in *Antony and Cleopatra*, soldiers who serve as Antony's personal guards. In 4.14 three Guardsmen (designated First, Second and Third Guardsman) discover the wounded Antony, who requests that they kill him as he has unsuccessfully attempted suicide. Horrified, they flee from the room. Twenty lines later, when called by Diomedes, several of them return and carry the wounded Antony to Cleopatra. Though dismayed and sorrowful, the Guardsmen have no real personalities; they merely reflect the demoralized state of their leader.

Guardsman (2) Any of several minor characters in *Antony and Cleopatra*, soldiers in the army of Octavius Caesar assigned to guard Cleopatra. In 5.2 they enter with Gallus at 5.2.34, but none of them speak until 5.2.232, when one of them announces the arrival of the Clown, who secretly delivers to Cleopatra the poisonous asps with which she will kill herself. After her death the Guardsmen enter as a group to discover the situation and call an officer, Dolabella. Two of them speak, and they are designated First and Second Guardsman. Their presence emphasizes Cleopatra's captivity and thus helps to justify her suicide.

Iras Character in *Antony and Cleopatra*, an attendant of Cleopatra. In 1.2 Iras is a pleasantly humorous young woman who jests over the predictions of the Soothsayer, but she displays almost no personality thereafter. She is overshadowed by Charmian in the queen's household, as she is on much less intimate terms with her mistress and has a much less developed role. Significantly, the Soothsayer tells Iras only that her fortune will be the same as Charmian's (1.2.52). She appears often with Cleopatra and Charmian but speaks very little. In 5.2 as Cleopatra prepares her suicide, Iras declares

her loyalty and says that she will not see the queen as a Roman prisoner, "for I am sure my nails / Are stronger than mine eyes" (5.2.222–223), but, as elsewhere, she is a faint echo of Charmian. When Cleopatra applies the poisonous asp to herself, Iras falls dead. Perhaps she has used the snake herself, moments earlier, or perhaps she simply dies of grief. In either case, she departs wordlessly. Shakespeare's source, PLUTARCH's *Lives*, states that Cleopatra was attended at her death by a serving-woman named Iras, but she is otherwise unknown in history.

Lamprius Minor character in *Antony and Cleopatra*, an attendant of Enobarbus. Lamprius appears only once and does not speak; he is mentioned only in the opening stage direction of 1.2. Like Rannius and Lucillius who accompany him, he is a GHOST CHARACTER. Some editors assume that Lamprius is the name of the Soothsayer—the stage direction reads "*Enter Enobarbus, Lamprius, a Soothsayer, Rannius . . .*"—though the Soothsayer appears to be an Egyptian in 2.3, and Lamprius is a Roman name. Shakespeare may have found the name in his source, PLUTARCH, who states that his own grandfather was named "Lampryas."

Lepidus, Marcus Aemilius (d. 13 B.C.) Historical figure and character in *Julius Caesar* and *Antony and Cleopatra*. Lepidus is a member of the Triumvirate, the three-man governing committee that consists of Lepidus, Octavius (later Octavius Caesar), and Mark Antony. The Triumvirate rules Rome in the aftermath of the assassination of Julius Caesar. Octavius imprisons Lepidus and then fights Antony for sole control of the Empire. In both plays Lepidus is a markedly weaker figure than his colleagues, and their casual dominance of him helps establish an impression of Roman power politics that is important in each work.

A minor character in *Julius Caesar*, Lepidus appears only once, in 4.1, when the Triumvirs decide on a list of political enemies that must be arrested and executed as part of their campaign against Brutus and Cassius. After a brief exchange, Antony sends Lepidus on an errand and then belittles him to Octavius. He calls him "a slight unmeritable man" (4.1.12) and a "barren-spirited fellow"

(4.1.36), and says he does not deserve a position as ruler. He compares him to an ass or horse, whose usefulness is limited and who will be turned out to pasture when he has fulfilled his role. Lepidus does not reappear in the play, and Antony's opinion of him seems appropriate. This episode may deepen our impression of Antony as a cynical political manipulator, or it may justify his boldness in seizing leadership in a power vacuum. In either view, Lepidus serves as a foil to sharpen our sense of Antony.

In *Antony and Cleopatra* Lepidus is similarly weak, though he plays a more prominent role in affairs. He is dominated by Caesar as the two confer on Antony's absence, in 1.4. In 2.4 he pointlessly urges reconciliation between Antony and Caesar, who are already intent on it, and he has little to say once negotiations are underway. He is again a minor player in the talks with Pompey in 2.6, and at the subsequent banquet he is the butt of a humiliating joke as he has been pressured into drinking too much. He makes a fool of himself and finally must be carried away—in pointed contrast to Caesar, who ends the party with a complaint about the ill effects of wine. The episode is comical, but even a Servant recognizes its significance for Lepidus's position in high politics, saying, "To be called into a huge sphere, and not to be seen to move in't, are the holes where eyes should be . . ." (2.7.14–15). Lepidus disappears from the play at this point, though his fate is later reported: Caesar has accused him of treason and imprisoned him "till death enlarge his confine" (3.5.11–12). Once again, Lepidus provides an example of the necessity for sharp wits and hard morals in the world of power politics, though here the contrast reflects more on Caesar than on Antony.

The historical Lepidus was indeed a lesser figure than his colleagues, though Shakespeare exaggerated this to emphasize the brutal competition of Roman politics. Lepidus was from a traditionally powerful Roman family. He supported Julius Caesar in his rise to power, and in the aftermath of Caesar's assassination in 44 B.C. he naturally allied himself with Antony. By chance he commanded troops in the vicinity of Rome at the time, and he was able to control the city. It was at this point that he probably held as much real power as he ever would. In *Julius*

Caesar, events are telescoped; the Triumvirate only came together after an 18-month period, during which Lepidus was courted by Antony and Octavius, and also by Brutus and Cassius. Upon the formation of the Triumvirate, Lepidus was given control of Italy and Gaul, but soon Caesar took over these important commands, and Lepidus was shifted to Africa, also important but more remote. From this base, Lepidus assisted—though only slightly—in the defeat of Pompey's forces in Sicily by Caesar's general, Agrippa, in 35 B.C., soon after the events of Act 2 of *Antony and Cleopatra*. However, when Lepidus attempted to override Agrippa once the victory was assured, Caesar daringly entered Lepidus's camp, unarmed, and demanded his surrender to arrest. Lepidus was despised for his weakness by his own troops, and they seized him. He was forced to publicly plead for mercy, after which he was formally ousted from the Triumvirate. His treatment was better than is implied in Shakespeare, however. He was permitted to retain his post as Pontifex Maximus—the chief clergyman of the state religion—and was mercifully exiled to a comfortable retreat where he lived out his life.

Lucillius GHOST CHARACTER in *Antony and Cleopatra*, an attendant of Enobarbus. Lucillius appears only once and does not speak; he is mentioned only in the opening stage direction of 1.2, along with Lamprius and Rannius.

Maecenas, Gaius (d. 8 B.C.) Historical figure and minor character in *Antony and Cleopatra*, a follower of Octavius Caesar. Maecenas is a courtier who serves to swell the ranks of Caesar's court. He offers some important advice in 4.1 when he encourages Caesar to advance on Antony and finish him off while he is distracted with rage and humiliation after the battle of ACTIUM. This remark helps signal Antony's approaching end.

The historical Maecenas was far more important to Caesar than the play indicates. He was among the future emperor's earliest allies, and he assisted Caesar's arrival in Italy to claim the inheritance of the assassinated Julius Caesar in 44 B.C. (Maecenas does not appear in Shakespeare's *Julius Caesar*, however.) Along with Agrippa, Maecenas was one of the most trusted friends and advisers of Caesar throughout the civil wars and in the early days of the empire, and he conducted numerous delicate diplomatic missions. He was descended from the ancient kings of Etruria, though his family's fortunes had fallen when his grandfather joined a revolt against Rome. However, Maecenas became one of the highest-ranking and richest men of the early Roman Empire. As such, he was a great patron of Roman literature, the role for which he is now best known. He befriended and supported many poets and writers, including VIRGIL.

Mardian Minor character in *Antony and Cleopatra,* a eunuch in the court of Cleopatra. Mardian is a minor member of the queen's entourage. In 4.14 he performs his only significant act when, on Cleopatra's orders, he delivers to Antony the false message that she has committed suicide. This triggers Antony's suicide attempt. Mardian is the closest thing to a jester, or FOOL, in Cleopatra's court. He is referred to as "saucy" (4.14.25), and he is mildly amusing when he declares that he thinks on "What Venus did with Mars" (1.5.18) when his mistress jests about his sexlessness. He appears to be the court musician, though he never performs as Cleopatra's willfulness leads her to reject his songs before she hears them. Aside from these semiofficial functions, Mardian's function is to swell the ranks of Cleopatra's grand establishment.

Menas (active ca. 40–ca. 35 B.C.) Historical figure and character in *Antony and Cleopatra,* a pirate who fights for Pompey. Menas and Menecrates are called famed buccaneers who make "hot inroads" (1.4.50) on the coast of Italy in support of Pompey's rebellion. In 2.1 Menas confers with Pompey and predicts accurately the future disputes of Antony and Octavius Caesar. In 2.6 he is among his leader's advisers at the signing of the Treaty of MISENUM, though he privately disapproves of it and says, "Pompey doth this day laugh away his fortune" (2.6.103). In 2.7, during the banquet aboard Pompey's ship, Menas proves himself a true pirate and advises Pompey to cut the throats of the Roman leadership—Caesar, Antony, and Lepidus—and seize the state. When Pompey refuses, Menas

decides to abandon him as doomed, for "Who seeks and will not take, when once 'tis offer'd, / Shall never find it more" (2.7.82–83). This shrewdly cynical sailor reveals the mistrust and disloyalty that informs the politics of the play.

The historical Menas is well represented in the play, for he was indeed a notably cynical turncoat. He deserted Pompey at Misenum in 39 B.C. and joined Caesar. Discontented with his rewards, he deserted again and returned to Pompey in time to participate in his defense of Sicily in 36 B.C. Again, however, he disapproved of what he saw as Pompey's lethargy and indecision—an opinion shared by military historians—and he changed sides for a third time and rejoined Caesar. Little more is known of him.

Menecrates (active ca. 40 B.C.) Historical figure and character in *Antony and Cleopatra,* a pirate who fights for Pompey. Mentioned with Menas as one of two "famous pirates" (1.4.48) who support Pompey's rebellion against Rome with "hot inroads" (1.4.50) on the coast of Italy, Menecrates turns out to be a mild buccaneer when he appears, in 2.1. He philosophically recommends that Pompey have patience with the slow pace of his success. He then disappears from the play. He is mentioned with the more important Menas as a "notable pirate" in Shakespeare's source, PLUTARCH's *Lives.*

In the FIRST FOLIO text of the play, all the speeches in 2.1 except Pompey's are designated "Mene" and seem to belong to Menecrates, though Menas is spelled Menes once elsewhere in the Folio. However, since one of these five speeches— 2.1.38–41—clearly belongs to Menas, editors have restored that speech to him and often give him more. In fact, beginning with the 1765 edition of Samuel JOHNSON, some editors give all these lines to Menas, leaving Menecrates mute.

Messenger (1) Any of three minor characters in *Antony and Cleopatra,* bearers of news to Antony. In 1.2 the First Messenger says that Antony's wife and brother have been defeated by Octavius Caesar in the Roman civil wars. He also tells of the conquest of Roman territory in Egypt by a renegade Roman general. A Second Messenger announces the arrival of a Third Messenger, who brings word that Antony's wife has died. The rapid sequence of messages establishes the importance of both the political and the personal situation in which Antony lives. Although he seems unnecessary, the Second Messenger, who speaks only five words, contributes to the atmosphere of crisis. One of the Messengers (or, perhaps, a fourth) reappears in 3.7 at the battle of ACTIUM with word of Caesar's troop movements.

Messenger (2) Either of two minor characters in *Antony and Cleopatra*, bearers of news to Octavius Caesar. In 1.4 the Messengers appear, one after the other, with news of the success of Pompey and of his alliance with the pirates Menecrates and Menas. One of the Messengers (or, possibly, a third) appears in 4.6 with word of Antony's preparations for battle. The Messengers strengthen our sense of Caesar as an informed and decisive leader.

Messenger (3) Minor character in *Antony and Cleopatra*, a servant who brings Cleopatra news of Antony's marriage to Octavia. In 2.5 Cleopatra's rage is so great when she hears of Antony's action that she beats the Messenger and threatens to kill him. He naturally flees. He is coaxed to return and repeat his message to the unwilling queen, and he flees again when she is again angry. In 3.3 he assures Cleopatra that he has seen Octavia and knows her to be an extremely unattractive woman whose defects he details. For this tactful report, Cleopatra rewards him with gold and agrees that he is a "proper man" (3.3.37–38). The episode demonstrates the mercurial nature of the Egyptian queen. The Messenger represents an ancient theatrical stereotype, the comic servant.

Octavia (d. 11 B.C.) Historical figure and character in *Antony and Cleopatra*, the sister of Octavius Caesar and wife of Mark Antony. In 2.2 Octavia's marriage is arranged as part of a treaty; she appears briefly in 2.3 and 3.2 as a dutiful wife. She accompanies Antony to ATHENS, where, in 3.4, she learns of renewed enmity between her husband and brother and volunteers to help negotiate a new truce. However, when she arrives in Rome in 3.6, she is greeted with the news that Antony has

returned to Cleopatra. Once Antony's desertion is established Octavia disappears from the play. Her docile, peaceable nature makes her a suitable victim, while she also serves as a foil both to Caesar, the cynical politician, and to Cleopatra, the irresistible sensualist.

The historical Octavia had a more prominent and complex role in Roman affairs than she does in the play. The most striking difference in Shakespeare's account concerns the timing of her marriage to Antony, which occurred in 40 B.C. This was before he had begun his affair with Cleopatra—he actually had another mistress at the time, in Athens. Also, Shakespeare telescopes events in his play and gives short shrift to Octavia's success as a diplomat. She in fact brought about a treaty between her husband and brother in 37 B.C., and it lasted for several years. After Antony deserted her, Octavia remained loyal to him. Even after he divorced her in 32 B.C., she continued to care for his children by two prior marriages. Her nobility and humanity won her widespread fame as a sympathetic and estimable figure, a reputation that is reflected in Shakespeare's source, PLUTARCH's *Lives* and survives in the "beauty, wisdom, [and] modesty" (2.2.241) of the peaceable if ineffectual woman of the play.

Philo Minor character in *Antony and Cleopatra*, a follower of Antony. In 1.1 Philo and his friend Demetrius discuss Antony's neglect of his military duty due to his infatuation with the queen of Egypt, Cleopatra. Philo's angry complaint opens the play with an emotional flourish. The episode establishes a disapproving Roman view of the love affair.

Pompey (Sextus Pompeius) (d. 35 B.C.) Historical figure and character in *Antony and Cleopatra*, a rebel against the coleaders of ROME, Octavius Caesar, Lepidus, and Mark Antony. Pompey's threat spurs Antony to action when he is luxuriating with Cleopatra in Act 1, but the rebel displays his weakness in Act 2. In 2.6 he negotiates a truce with the Roman leaders, but the remarks of his follower Menas make clear that he is foolish not to continue his rebellion while he is in a strong position. In 2.7 he refuses Menas's suggestion that he murder his opponents during the feast that celebrates the truce. Pompey is unwilling to seem dishonorable and lets the opportunity go by. Menas observes that "Who seeks and will not take, when once 'tis offer'd, / Shall never find it more" (2.7.82–83), and he decides to abandon his alliance with this weak leader. Pompey is not seen again in the play, but we hear of his fate. After being defeated by the forces of Lepidus and Caesar, he retreats to Antony's territory, where he is murdered, as is reported in 3.5. Pompey's career offers a case study in the cold realities of Roman politics and war. He cannot win because he is not unscrupulous enough, and he lacks good sense. No vestiges of the ancient Roman concept of honor survive, and only a cool and unsentimental manipulator can triumph. It is in this context that we must weigh the conduct of Antony and the triumph of Caesar.

Antony surveys the rebel's strength in 1.2 and outlines Pompey's background. He is continuing a rebellion originated by his father—a famous and popular leader of an earlier generation—and he therefore commands a dedicated following. This is an accurate assessment of the historical Sextus Pompeius, whose father, Pompey the Great (106–48 B.C.), was one of the major figures of early Roman history. He was the defeated opponent of Julius Caesar, as is mentioned several times in Shakespeare's *Julius Caesar*. The renown of Pompey the Great was such that Shakespeare could mention him in three non-Roman plays (*Henry V, 2 Henry VI, Love's Labour's Lost*) and name a comic character after him in *Measure for Measure* (Pompey Bum), which assumes that audiences would still know of him after 1,700 years. Pompeius Sextus fought with his father's forces, and after their defeat—and Pompey the Great's murder—in 48 B.C., he reorganized the rebellion around a naval force, which he centered first in Spain and later in Sicily. After Julius Caesar's assassination in 44 B.C., Pompey continued to fight against Caesar's successors, though as part of his policy he briefly supported Antony against Octavius Caesar not long before the period of the play. The peace of Misenum, enacted in 2.6, was negotiated in 39 B.C. but did not last long. Caesar attacked Pompey the next year and totally defeated him in 36 B.C. The loser retreated to Asia Minor

and attempted to reestablish himself, but he was captured and killed by Antony's lieutenant, probably on Antony's orders. Shakespeare, however, protects his hero's honor by having Eros report his distress at the execution, in 3.5.18–19.

Proculeius, Caius (active ca. 40–ca. 20 B.C.) Historical figure and character in *Antony and Cleopatra*, a follower of Octavius Caesar. When he advises Cleopatra to surrender to Caesar, Antony tells her, "None about Caesar trust but Proculeius" (4.15.48). In 5.1 Caesar sends Proculeius to the Egyptian queen with instructions to promise her anything. Caesar wishes to prevent her from committing suicide so that he can triumphantly display her in ROME. In 5.2 Proculeius prevents Cleopatra from stabbing herself. He counsels her to be temperate, and tells her she will receive good treatment from Caesar. Because he has been recommended for his trustworthiness, his lies stress the isolation of Cleopatra in defeat, which helps motivate her suicide.

The historical Proculeius, a military commander, had a reputation as a forthright and honest man. This doubtless accounts for Antony's mistaken assumption (Shakespeare took the entire incident from PLUTARCH's *Lives*), but his loyalty was entirely with Caesar. He was a close personal friend of his leader, and he remained so for many years, though he never attained—or, apparently, aspired to—high office in the empire that Caesar was to found.

Rannius GHOST CHARACTER in *Antony and Cleopatra*, an attendant of Enobarbus. Rannius appears only once and does not speak. He is mentioned in the opening stage directions of 1.2, along with Lamprius and Lucillius.

Scarus Character in *Antony and Cleopatra*, a follower of Antony. Scarus first appears at the battle of ACTIUM, in 3.10; he reports on the catastrophic rout of Antony's forces by the navy of Octavius Caesar. Despite the defeat and the desertion of Canidius, Scarus remains faithful to Antony. He fights bravely in his master's brief victory of 4.7 and makes light of his wounds—"I had a wound here that was like a T, / But now 'tis made an H"

(4.7.7–8)—and Antony praises him to Cleopatra after the battle. He accompanies Antony to final defeat in 4.12, before he disappears from the play. This scarred veteran—his "honour'd gashes" (4.8.11) are cited by Antony—illustrates the courageous conduct in Antony's followers to the last, even after the desertion of Canidius and Enobarbus. Antony's ability to hold such an honorable soldier allows us to see him and his fate as noble.

Scarus's name, which does not appear in Shakespeare's source, PLUTARCH's *Lives*, apparently is a pun referring to his scars, unless it was a misspelling of M. Aemilianus Scaurus (active ca. 40–30 B.C.). Scaurus was a stepbrother of Pompey who joined Antony after his kinsman's final defeat in 36 B.C.—referred to in 3.5.4–12—and remained with him to the end. Scaurus was pardoned by the triumphant Caesar, and though he never held high office in the empire that Caesar established, his son did under the second emperor, Tiberius (ruled A.D. 14–37).

Seleucus (active 30 B.C.) Historical figure and minor character in *Antony and Cleopatra*, Cleopatra's treasurer. In 5.2 Cleopatra calls upon Seleucus to confirm the inventory of her household which she has submitted to the conqueror of Egypt, Octavius Caesar. Instead, he tells Caesar that she has withheld more than she has listed. Caesar, who is amused by Cleopatra's ploy, tells Seleucus to leave as Cleopatra subjects him to a tirade of insults.

This episode has been variously interpreted. It can be seen as evidence of Cleopatra's shallow character. It continues the play's earlier portrayal of a grasping courtesan who here attempts to salvage what she can from the wreck of her and Antony's fortunes. On the other hand, it may actually demonstrate her cool—and, in the play's scheme of things, noble—intention to die rather than live on in humiliating defeat without Antony. Once Caesar has the idea that Cleopatra wishes only to retain a comfortable existence, he leaves her alone, free to arrange her suicide, whereas if her real intention were known, he would prevent her. Shakespeare may have intended Seleucus as the queen's pawn in a successful effort to deceive the conqueror. The playwright's source, PLUTARCH's *Lives*, states that this was her plan, and though Shake-

speare changes many of the details in Plutarch's account of the episode, he may well have included it for the same purpose.

Sentry Minor character in *Antony and Cleopatra*, a soldier in the army of Octavius Caesar. The Sentry and his two underlings, the Watchmen, are guards at Caesar's camp outside ALEXANDRIA. They discover the dying Enobarbus and bring him into the camp. The Sentry demonstrates the intelligence expected of a good noncommissioned officer when he holds the Watchmen back, at first, to discover what Enobarbus will say, in case he should reveal useful information. He helps demonstrate the high morale in Caesar's forces as they approach their final victory. In some editions of the play, the Sentry and the Watchmen are designated as the First, Second, and Third Soldiers.

Servant (1) Any of several minor characters in *Antony and Cleopatra*, workers in the household of Pompey. The servants are waiters at a banquet that celebrates the truce between Pompey and the Roman leaders—Antony, Lepidus, and Octavius Caesar. At the opening of 2.7, two of the Servants—designated the First and Second Servants—gossip about Lepidus's drunkenness at the feast. They observe that Lepidus has weakened himself in relation to the others. Their conversation prepares us for the comic scene of Lepidus's intoxication that follows and points up the treachery that lurks in the world of high policy and warfare, also illustrated in the remainder of the scene.

Servant (2) Any of several minor characters in *Antony and Cleopatra*, workers in the household of the title characters. In 3.13 a Servant announces the arrival of Thidias, an ambassador from Octavius Caesar to Cleopatra; when Antony discovers the ambassador kissing her hand, he summons Servants to whip him. Later, one of them brings Thidias back and declares that he has been punished. The actions of the Servants demonstrate that there is still a remnant of pomp and power available to Antony as he approaches his end.

Servitor Any of several minor characters in *Antony and Cleopatra*, servants of Antony. In 4.2

Antony bids farewell to these attendants while they serve a banquet before his final battle against Octavius Caesar. He announces that their allegiance to him may be at an end, and says, "Perchance to-morrow / You'll serve another master" (4.2.27–28). They respond with tears, and Enobarbus, also weeping, chastises Antony for causing "discomfort" (4.2.34). Antony laughs and declares that he intends to be victorious in the next day's battle. He rousingly calls for the banquet to begin as the scene ends. The episode demonstrates the disturbed state of Antony's mind as the play's climax approaches. The Servitors, who speak only three words in unison, are merely extras who witness this demonstration.

Silius Minor character in *Antony and Cleopatra,* a lieutenant of Ventidius. Ventidius has just defeated a Parthian army in the name of Mark Antony, and in 3.1 he explains to Silius why he will not pursue the fleeing enemy. He does not want to succeed too thoroughly, lest Antony feel overshadowed and in revenge crush his military career. Silius admires Ventidius's political acumen. He has no personality and serves merely as a sounding board for his superior officer.

Soldier (1) Minor character in *Antony and Cleopatra,* a member of Antony's army. In 3.7 the Soldier pleads with Antony not to fight the forthcoming battle against Octavius Caesar at sea, where the opponent has the advantage. However, Antony's pride demands that he accept Caesar's challenge to naval warfare, and he engages in the fatal battle of ACTIUM. The Soldier reappears in 4.5, and Antony acknowledges that he was right. The Soldier then reports that Enobarbus has deserted, an event that signals the utter collapse of Antony's fortunes just before what is to be his final battle. The Soldier thus serves as a measure of Antony's declining destiny.

Soldier (2) Any of several minor characters in *Antony and Cleopatra,* members of Antony's army. In 4.3 a group of Soldiers gather to perform sentry duty. They hear strange, wailing, music-like noises—seemingly under the street—and they interpret this phenomenon as a bad omen that portends the loss of

the next day's battle. Four of them speak and are designated as the First, Second, Third, and Fourth Soldiers. In 4.4 the Soldiers (or perhaps other soldiers) appear the next morning and march to the battle without complaint, but the earlier episode tells us that Antony's end is fast approaching.

Soldier (3) Minor character in *Antony and Cleopatra,* a member of the army of Octavius Caesar. In 4.6 the Soldier brings a message to Enobarbus, who has deserted Mark Antony and joined Caesar; his former master has sent his belongings after him. The Soldier, though busy with his battle preparations, pauses to remark, "Your emperor / Continues still a Jove" (4.6.28–29). This disinterested praise from an enemy confirms the play's image of Antony as a great man while it also furthers the plot, for it plunges Enobarbus into the guilt that will break his heart and kill him in 4.9.

Soothsayer (Lamprius) Minor character in *Antony and Cleopatra,* a seer patronized by Mark Antony. In 1.2 the Soothsayer predicts that Cleopatra's waiting-woman Charmian shall outlive her mistress but will see a worse time in the future than in the past. He adds that he sees an identical fate for another waiting-woman, Iras. He accompanies Antony to ROME, and in 2.3 he recommends that they return to Egypt to get away from Octavius Caesar. He declares that Antony's spirit is bested by Caesar's when the two are together. Antony dismisses the Soothsayer curtly, but he muses to himself on the truth of the man's observation. In both episodes the Soothsayer's remarks prove pertinent, and in hindsight the audience can recollect his words.

In 2.3 the Soothsayer appears to be an Egyptian whom Antony has brought to Rome. Some scholars, however, believe that he may be the otherwise unknown Roman Lamprius, for the stage direction opening 1.2 reads, in part: "*Enter* Enobarbus, Lamprius, *a Soothsayer, . .*" Thus, the Soothsayer can be construed syntactically as being named Lamprius.

Taurus, Titus Statilius (active 36–16 B.C.) Historical figure and minor character in *Antony and Cleopatra,* a general under Octavius Caesar. Taurus appears briefly at the battle of ACTIUM and receives, in 3.8, Caesar's order to maintain his army ashore, without fighting, while the naval battle is fought. He marches wordlessly through 3.10 and avoids contact with Antony's forces under Canidius, which stresses the inconclusive nature of the land fighting. He is a pawn of Caesar's strategy and speaks only two words.

The historical Taurus was a highly successful general, second only to Agrippa among Caesar's military men. His background is unknown, though his name suggests descent from the pre-Roman Lucanians of southern Italy. He is first recorded as an admiral who commanded a unit in the defeat of Sextus Pompeius—the Pompey of the play. He went on to lead numerous other campaigns and governed conquered territories in North Africa and Spain.

Thidias (Thyreus)   Character in *Antony and Cleopatra*, a diplomat who represents Octavius Caesar. In 3.12 Caesar sends Thidias to Cleopatra—in the wake of her and Antony's defeat at the battle of ACTIUM—to promise her whatever she wishes if she will abandon Antony. In 3.13 Thidias receives from Cleopatra a lavish declaration of allegiance to Caesar, but as he kisses her hand as a formal token of this new diplomatic relationship, Antony appears. "I am Antony yet," he says furiously (3.13.93), and he has Thidias taken away to be whipped. A Servant returns to report that Thidias begged for mercy during this punishment. Antony sends him back to Caesar with an angry message of defiance, and tells him that if he wants revenge he should whip one Hipparchus, a freed slave of Antony's now in Caesar's service. The episode demonstrates Antony's continuing vitality, but also the disturbed state of his mind.

In Shakespeare's source, Thomas NORTH's translation of PLUTARCH's *Lives*, Caesar's representative is named Thyreus, and many editions of the play, beginning with that of Lewis THEOBALD (1733), use this name. Presumably, Shakespeare simply misremembered the name of this minor character. (In fact, North himself was mistaken, for the ambassador in Plutarch is named Thyrsus, a figure otherwise unknown in history.)

Varrius   Minor character in *Antony and Cleopatra*, a follower of Pompey. In 2.1 Varrius brings the dis-

quieting news to Pompey, Menas, and Menecrates that Antony has left Egypt to rejoin the coalition against Pompey. Varrius's function is to introduce a development of the plot.

Ventidius, Publius (ca. 90–38 B.C.)   Historical figure and minor character in *Antony and Cleopatra*, a Roman general. In 2.3.40–41 Ventidius is sent by Mark Antony to put down a rebellion in Parthia; in 3.1 he has accomplished his task. He appears with Silius, who encourages him to pursue the fleeing Parthians and conquer all of Mesopotamia. Ventidius replies in 3.1.12–27 with a lesson in military politics: He will not attempt to do as well against the Parthians as he might, for if he does too well, he may seem to show up his superior, Antony, who may seek vengeance and destroy his career. These remarks stress the cynicism demanded by the Roman world of politics, a cool and unemotional calculation that Antony rejects in his infatuation with Cleopatra.

The historical Ventidius was famous in his own day for his extraordinary rise in society amid the chronic turbulence of the time. As an infant he had been enslaved, for his family—from a pre-Roman tribe—had been involved in the last attempted revolt against Roman dominance in Italy. After serving as a Roman soldier, he became a contractor of military supplies. Like many defeated Italians, Ventidius became a backer of Julius Caesar in the Roman civil wars, and he was granted a senate seat as a reward; after Caesar's assassination he allied himself with Antony. However, despite his caution in victory—which Shakespeare took from PLUTARCH's *Lives*—his success against the Parthians ended his career. He returned to Rome, where his triumph was extravagantly celebrated, but Antony discharged him amid rumors of bribes taken from a Mesopotamian ruler, and he died shortly thereafter.

Watchmen   Two minor characters in *Antony and Cleopatra*, soldiers in the army of Octavius Caesar. Commanded by a Sentry, the Watchmen guard the perimeter of Caesar's camp outside ALEXANDRIA, in 4.9. They discover the dying Enobarbus and bring him into the camp. These guards, designated First and Second Watchman, are alert and active soldiers, examples of the higher morale among Caesar's forces after Antony's defeat at ACTIUM, an important development in the play. Some editions follow 18th-century editorial practice and designate the Sentry and the Watchmen as First, Second, and Third Soldiers.

As You Like It
SYNOPSIS

Act 1, Scene 1
Orlando reports that his older brother Oliver has ignored their late father's will, withholding Orlando's inheritance, denying him an education, and treating him like a peasant. Oliver appears and harasses Orlando, finally striking him, at which Orlando seizes his brother and refuses to release him until he vows to reform. Oliver promises and is released, and Orlando leaves. Oliver plots to get rid of Orlando, and the wrestler Charles appears with news from the court: Duke Frederick has usurped his position from Duke Senior, his older brother; Duke Senior now lives in exile in the Forest of ARDEN, although his daughter, Rosalind, remains at court. Charles goes on to say that he worries about injuring Orlando in the wrestling competition soon to be held at court. Oliver asserts that Orlando, being proud and evil, intends to kill Charles if he can and suggests that Charles should do the same to him.

Act 1, Scene 2
Duke Frederick's daughter Celia attempts to cheer her cousin Rosalind, who is depressed over her father's banishment, by promising her own friendship and loyalty. Touchstone, the court jester, or FOOL, arrives and jokes on knightly honor. A foppish courtier, Le Beau, appears and reports that the wrestler Charles has brutally killed several opponents. He says that the matches are to be resumed on the site where they are speaking. The duke's court arrives, accompanied by Charles and Orlando. Rosalind and Celia, taken by Orlando's youth and beauty, attempt to dissuade him from wrestling, but he insists on challenging Charles. They wrestle, and Orlando wins. When Orlando identifies himself, the duke refuses to give him the promised prize because Orlando's father had opposed his usurpation. The duke and his followers leave, but Celia and Rosalind remain and congratulate Orlando. Rosalind is clearly lovestruck, giving Orlando her necklace and attempting to converse further, but the tongue-tied Orlando cannot respond, as he laments once they are gone. Le Beau returns to warn Orlando that the temperamental duke intends evil toward him. Orlando asks him about Rosalind's identity before fleeing.

Act 1, Scene 3
Rosalind tells Celia of her love for Orlando. The Duke announces that Rosalind is banished because her father was his enemy. Celia volunteers to share her cousin's exile, and they decide to join Rosalind's father in the Forest of Arden. Rosalind will disguise herself as a young man, take the name Ganymede, and pose as Celia's brother; they will ask Touchstone to join them.

Act 2, Scene 1
Duke Senior and his noblemen discuss the pleasures of their life in the forest. One Lord describes the amusing sight of the melancholy Jaques lamenting the death of a shot deer.

Act 2, Scene 2
Duke Frederick discovers Celia's absence and mistakenly believes that she and Rosalind are with Orlando. He sends men to arrest Orlando or, if he has fled, Oliver.

Act 2, Scene 3
An old family servant, Adam, meets Orlando to warn him that Oliver intends to kill him. Adam volunteers to flee with Orlando, offering his savings as a means of support.

Act 2, Scene 4
Weary with travel, the disguised Rosalind, Celia, and Touchstone arrive in Arden, where they overhear Corin, an old shepherd, in conversation with Silvius, a young man who bewails his unrequited love for a girl named Phebe. Talking with Corin, they learn that they can buy a house, land, and Corin's sheep, hiring him to tend them.

Act 2, Scene 5
Amiens sings a SONG of the Spartan virtues of woodland life. Jaques parodies it, mocking the affectation of courtiers who take up rural life.

Act 2, Scene 6

Orlando and Adam arrive in Arden, and Adam, exhausted, collapses. Orlando promises to find him something to eat.

Act 2, Scene 7

Duke Senior and his men are eating dinner as Jaques reports his encounter in the forest with a Fool, whose comical dissertation on Time has inspired him. He wishes to be a fool himself, licensed to satirize without fear of punishment. Orlando appears, demanding food at swordpoint. The duke offers him a place at the table, and Orlando apologizes for his thievish conduct, explaining his desperation. He goes to fetch Adam. Jaques moralizes on the stages of human life. Orlando returns with Adam, and the dinner is resumed. Amiens sings of the evils of man and the jolly woodland life, and the duke welcomes Orlando to his court-in-exile.

Act 3, Scene 1

Duke Frederick disbelieves Oliver's protestations that he does not know where Orlando is, dispossesses Oliver of his dukedom, and threatens him with death or banishment if he does not find Orlando within a year.

Act 3, Scene 2

Orlando hangs a love poem to Rosalind on a tree and wanders off, intending to decorate the forest with such declarations. Touchstone baits Corin on his lack of sophistication, but the old shepherd is confident of the virtues of his simple life. Rosalind appears in her disguise as Ganymede, reading a poem she has found that celebrates herself; Touchstone parodies it. Celia arrives with another poem to Rosalind and informs her that she has seen Orlando sleeping nearby. Orlando and Jaques appear, and the women eavesdrop. Orlando rejects the melancholy Jaques, who mocks his love for Rosalind. Jaques departs, and Rosalind, as Ganymede, approaches Orlando and interrogates him about his love. She proposes to cure him of his lovesickness by posing as Rosalind and spurning his courtship; he agrees to call on Ganymede each day and pretend to woo him as if he were Rosalind.

Act 3, Scene 3

Jaques observes Touchstone wooing Audrey, a goatherd; the fool's comical remarks satirize love,

women, and marriage. Nevertheless, he and Audrey have decided to marry, and Sir Oliver Martext, a country parson, arrives to conduct the ceremony. Jaques objects to the irregularity of the rite and escorts the couple away.

Act 3, Scene 4

Rosalind is distressed that Orlando is late for his date with Ganymede, and Celia accuses all men of being dishonest breakers of appointments. Corin arrives and offers to show them the courtship of Silvius and Phebe.

Act 3, Scene 5

Rosalind, Celia, and Corin overhear Phebe rejecting Silvius. Rosalind steps forward and castigates the thankless young woman for disdaining a good lover, being ugly and unlikely to find better; Phebe instantly falls in love with Ganymede. Left alone with Silvius, she is kinder to him, understanding and pitying his passion, and she agrees to permit him to share her company if he will carry her letters to her new beloved.

Act 4, Scene 1

Rosalind berates Jaques for his melancholy and dismisses him. Orlando appears, addressing Ganymede as Rosalind, in accordance with their agreement. She pretends to chastise Orlando for being late and to satirize his talk of love. She asks Celia to perform a mock marriage ceremony between them, after which Orlando announces that he must meet the duke but will return at two o'clock. Rosalind confides to Celia that her passion for Orlando grows more intense.

Act 4, Scene 2

Jaques and some of the duke's lords sing a hunting song.

Act 4, Scene 3

Orlando is late, to Rosalind's dismay. Silvius arrives with a letter from Phebe to Ganymede, which Rosalind mocks. She sends Silvius back to Phebe with the message that Ganymede rejects her. Oliver appears, seeking Ganymede and his sister. He carries a bloody bandage. He explains that Orlando, walking through the forest, had seen a sleeping man being stalked by a lion. He had recognized the man as his evil elder brother and had contemplated letting the lion kill him. Instead, however, he had mercy, drove the lion away, and was wounded in the process. Oliver confesses that he is the brother, though he has reformed his evil ways, and he goes on to tell that Orlando, recovering from his wound, has asked him to bear a message to Ganymede offering the bloody cloth as excuse for his lateness. He offers the bandage to Rosalind, and she faints. Reviving, she insists that her faint was counterfeit and that Oliver must tell Orlando so.

Act 5, Scene 1

Touchstone and Audrey encounter William, who is also a suitor of Audrey; Touchstone poses as a sophisticate and threateningly drives William away.

Act 5, Scene 2

Orlando and Oliver, now reconciled, discuss Oliver's love for Celia, which she has returned; the two are to be married the next day. Oliver asserts that he will surrender all of their father's estate to Orlando and remain with Celia, whom he believes to be a shepherdess. He leaves as Rosalind arrives, still disguised as Ganymede. Orlando declares that his lovesickness for the absent Rosalind is such that he can no longer accept the masquerade of Ganymede as his lover. Ganymede then declares that he knows magic and can summon Rosalind; he promises that Orlando can marry her at Oliver and Celia's wedding the next day. Silvius and Phebe arrive, and Ganymede promises Phebe that, if he will marry any woman, he will marry her, but that if she sees that Ganymede will *not* marry any woman, she must accept Silvius. She agrees.

Act 5, Scene 3

Touchstone and Audrey also plan to marry the next day. Two Pages appear and sing a love song.

Act 5, Scene 4

Orlando tells the duke that he is unsure of Ganymede's promised magic. Rosalind, as Ganymede, appears with Silvius and Phebe; she elicits the duke's assurance that he will permit his daughter, Rosalind, to marry Orlando if he can produce her, and he has Phebe reaffirm her promise to marry Silvius if she must refuse Ganymede. Then Ganymede leaves. Touchstone and Audrey arrive; Touchstone

satirizes dueling and courtly honor. Hymen, the Roman god of marriage, leads a festive MASQUE. Rosalind, appearing as herself, enters and identifies herself as the duke's daughter and Orlando's bride. Phebe sees that she must marry Silvius and agrees with goodwill, as Hymen sings a wedding hymn. Jaques de Boys, a brother of Oliver and Orlando, arrives with the news that Duke Frederick, having come to Arden with the intention of killing Duke Senior, has been reformed by a holy man. He has accordingly restored the duchy to his banished brother and intends to retire to a monastery. The melancholy Jaques decides to join him, preferring a solitary life of contemplation to the festive court. He leaves as the wedding celebration begins with a dance. Rosalind then speaks an EPILOGUE, soliciting applause for the play.

COMMENTARY

As You Like It, as its title asserts, has something to offer every taste. On one level it serves as a stock romantic comedy, with disguised princesses, an unjustly deposed ruler, and a handsome leading couple. But the play also offers food for thought on a traditionally entertaining subject: the assets and drawbacks of country life. The dedicated student of literature can consider the play's relationship to a favorite RENAISSANCE literary mode, the PASTORAL romance, a form of escapist writing with roots in ancient Greece. Further, the play is a sparkling theatrical entertainment, with more songs than any other Shakespearean play and several diverting set pieces: an onstage wrestling match in 1.2, a procession of singing hunters in 4.2 (traditionally carrying a deer's carcass, though a set of antlers has been generally substituted in more modern times), and Hymen's charming masque in 5.4.

These features enliven a work whose plotting is strikingly undramatic. After Act 1 establishes the separate banishments of Duke Senior, Orlando, and Rosalind, Acts 2–4, set in Arden, lack striking change. Adam seems near death in 2.3, but we know that the exiled duke's comfortable establishment is near, and we feel only admiration for Orlando's devotion rather than anxiety for Adam's plight. Orlando invades the Duke's banquet, but we know that he will be graciously received, and we are not chilled by any threat of violence. Oliver's tale of peril and salvation offers no thrilling tension, for we know he survived to tell us about it.

Instead of a plot, the play presents conversations among different combinations of characters. They talk mostly about romantic love, country living, or both. Their remarks weave a shimmering pattern of agreements and contradictions, harmonies and counterpoints, that constitute the substance of Acts 2–4. There emerges from this fabric of ideas an opposition of two points of view: a responsiveness to love and life, represented by Rosalind; and a withdrawal from complexities and commitment, represented by Jaques. The play's climax in Act 5 produces a resolution in favor of the former. Jaques, although no villain, must be defeated if the life-affirming spirit of the lovers is to triumph, for his doctrine of passivity and retreat is ultimately antisocial.

Shakespeare neatly and subtly presents the opposition of Jaques and the lovers by having first Orlando and then Rosalind dismiss the melancholy courtier from the stage with a rebuke, in 3.2.289 and 4.1.31, respectively, before each of the two great wooing scenes. This is a bold instance of the dominant technique in the play; the development of dramatic tension not through plotting, as we have seen, but by juxtaposing encounters among the characters. For the most part, we are not expected to judge the speakers but rather to enjoy their meetings and gradually appreciate their differences.

For instance, the pastoral world of the banished duke in the Forest of Arden is described, even before we see it, as one in which the exiles "fleet the time carelessly as they did in the golden world" (1.1.118–119), a reference to the golden age of ancient mythology, analogous to Eden in the Judeo-Christian tradition. However, once the play's action moves to Arden, this proposition is undermined. The duke's praise of his exiled court's woodland life is followed immediately by an account of Jaques's lament for the wounded deer, which critiques human interference with nature. Jaques's comments also present a cynical, distrustful image of human society, as he "invectively . . . pierceth / The body of country, city, court" (2.1.58–59). In 2.2 Duke Frederick's villainy is once again displayed, supporting Jaques's dark viewpoint but also reaffirming the essential virtue of the exiled Duke Senior's court. Shakespeare establishes Arden as an ideal, pastoral world in which characters criticize the real one, but then other characters criticize *them,* both explicitly and by implication. Further, when Rosalind arrives in Arden with Celia and Touchstone in 2.4, their initial response is humorously unenthusiastic, with Rosalind weary in spirit and Touchstone weary in body; the fool comments that "at home I was in a better place" (2.4.14). Thus we can ponder several points of view without being diverted from the central situation of the drama.

In 2.5 Amiens sings a song that illustrates the Duke's attitude toward the pastoral life, that those "who doth ambition shun" (2.5.35) are happy to have no enemies but the weather, but Jaques responds with a comically insulting parody. In 2.7 Jaques's delightfully expressed desire to be a jester like Touchstone, licensed to satirize everyone, provokes a sharp reprimand from the duke for wishing to correct the world's vices when he has sinned himself. Later in the same scene Jaques's position is again rejected. As the melancholy courtier completes his sardonic account of human life with a morbid description of helpless old age, Orlando bears in Adam, whom the duke, who is entirely unaffected by Jaques's speech, treats with reverence. The scene closes with another instance of such subtle contradiction. Amiens sings a song condemning humanity for ". . . ingratitude" and asserting that "most friendship is feigning, most loving mere folly" (2.7.174–193). Just at that moment, the duke's hospitality is enabling Orlando to express his gratitude for Adam's friendship and loyalty. The bases of the pastoral convention—the idealization of rustic life and an accompanying cynicism toward sophisticated society—are espoused, but they are just as persistently contradicted and undercut.

Most telling in this respect are the play's comparisons of different lovers. The central figures are Rosalind and Orlando. They are flanked by comic variations: the ridiculously conventional Silvius and Phebe on the one hand, and the equally preposterous yet earthy Touchstone and Audrey (with an assist from William) on the other. The lovesick shepherd and the hard-hearted shepherdess who rejects him were standard figures in pastoral literature, and Silvius and Phebe are absurd manifestations of it. Their exaggeration is emphasized by Rosalind's own overstated realism when she advises Phebe, "Sell when you can, you are not for all markets" (3.5.60).

Silvius's sentimentality is countered in Touchstone's attitude to Audrey. So far from adoring Audrey, or being in love with love itself, the jester finds only that "man hath his desires, and as pigeons bill, so wedlock would be nibbling" (3.3.72–73). His detached and resigned submission to human instincts is ironically opposed to the worship of an ideal woman. Touchstone also provides a foil for Rosalind's love for Orlando. When Silvius's plaintive lament reminds the heroine of her seemingly impossible passion (Orlando not yet having arrived in Arden), Touchstone immediately mocks her by saying that his preposterous love for one Jane Smile led him to kiss "the cow's dugs that her pretty chopt hands had milked" (2.4.46–47).

In another repeated theme, different sorts of rustic characters are contrasted. Silvius and Phebe are essentially stereotypical literary lovers, countrified only vaguely by their occupation as shepherds. Audrey and her hapless swain William are typical rustic buffoons, instances of the Shakespearean CLOWN. And Corin is a lifelike peasant, a man who fully understands the realities of extracting a living from the land. In 2.4.73–84 he frankly discusses his poverty and, by implication, the essential falseness and sentimentality of the pastoral convention. At the same time, he does not envy the courtiers their easier but less honest life, and his exchanges with Touchstone in 3.2.11–83 constitute one of the most telling critiques of the pastoral in the play. The country world holds its own against courtly sophistication, yet its hardships and difficulties are clearly stated.

Even the two figures who comment on the activities of the others, Touchstone and Jaques, are pointedly different from each other. They first meet offstage, as we hear in Jaques's enthusiastic report on the "motley fool" (2.7.13). Touchstone's observations on the human tendency to ripen and then rot appeal greatly to the melancholy courtier. However, the jester ridicules everything and has no philosophy, while Jaques is dedicated to a pessimistic view of life and looks to mockery to "cleanse the foul body of th'infected world" (2.7.60). His jaded attitude leads him to withdraw from human society at the play's end, whereas Touchstone enters the play's swirl of courtships with enthusiasm, if also with sarcasm. Touchstone eventually joins the "country copulatives" (5.4.55) and marries, while Jaques departs, declaring himself "for other than for dancing measures" (5.4.192). The contrast reflects the play's two opposing poles, love and withdrawal.

The play's repeated juxtapositions of ideas and temperaments constitute its overall mood and are perhaps referred to in its title. Each character has an opinion about love and the good life, but then another personality presents a viewpoint that contradicts or modifies it. Each idea is qualified, and each has some merit. In the end, with the multiple marriages in 5.4, the dominant theme is the unifying power of love.

Rosalind represents this theme throughout, and perhaps the most telling juxtaposition in the play is that of Rosalind to herself in her disguise as Ganymede. Ganymede insists that Orlando's love is a sickness he can cure. The delightful result is the spectacle of Rosalind, while madly in love with Orlando, telling him that "love is merely a madness" (3.2.388) and then quite hysterically confiding her love to Celia—"O coz, coz, coz . . . that thou didst know how many fathom deep I am in love!" (4.1.195–196). The climax nears in 5.2, when Ganymede's masquerade can no longer suffice. The love between Celia and Oliver is too much for Orlando to witness without pain; he insists that he cannot go on with the pretence that Ganymede is Rosalind. The disguised heroine realizes that her lover has outgrown the conventional attitudes she has been teasing him about, and she prepares to resume her true identity. Her turn to magic—reprised in the appearance of the supernatural Hymen in 5.4—is appropriate to the position she has occupied as the prime manipulator of affairs. Disguised as Ganymede, she has been invisible though entirely in control. She returns accompanied by the solemn magic of Hymen's masque, casting a spell of acceptance and reconciliation; even Jaques, despite his withdrawal, blesses the couples with humor and wisdom.

Hymen's nature is problematic, but whether he is a supernatural being or a costumed human recruited by Rosalind is not as important as his role as a symbol of divine approval for the play's happy ending. This suggestion has been prepared for by various religious references. Some are quite touching evocations of traditional religion, such as Adam's touching prayer, "He that doth the ravens feed, / Yea providently caters for the sparrow, / Be comfort to my age" (2.3.43–45), and Orlando's equation of "better days" with times when "bells have knoll'd to church" (2.7.113–114). Others are more prosaic allusions to biblical episodes. Orlando touches on the parable of the prodigal son in describing his lot under Oliver, in 1.1.37–39; In 2.1.5 Duke Senior likens his exile to the expulsion from the Garden of Eden, and Jaques refers to the plagues of Egypt in 2.5.58. Corin assumes that one may "find the way to heaven / By doing deeds of hospitality" (2.4.79–80). Duke Frederick is converted by "an old religious man" (5.4.159), and Rosalind invents an "old religious uncle" (3.2.336) for Ganymede. The entire episode of Sir Oliver Martext, however ridiculous, raises other issues of churchly doctrine. These references subtly suggest the parallels between Christian ideals of pity and loving kindness and the play's themes of love and reconciliation.

SOURCES OF THE PLAY

Shakespeare's only important source for *As You Like It* was Thomas LODGE's prose romance, *Rosalynde* (1590, 4th ed. 1598). For the tale of a young heir's mistreatment by his older brother, Lodge drew on a medieval English poem, *The Tale of Gamelyn;* he apparently invented the story of Rosalind and Celia as well as the subplot of Corin, Silvius, and Phebe (though Shakespeare changed all of his names except Rosalynde and Phoebe, as Lodge spelled them). Shakespeare added most of the other characters: Jaques, Touchstone, Le Beau, Amiens, Audrey, William, and Martext. Shakespeare also made brothers of the usurped and usurping dukes, providing a parallel to the story of Orlando and Oliver and thus tightening the relationship between the plots. Significantly, the playwright also invented the repentance of Duke Frederick; Lodge's counterpart dies in battle against the denizens of Arden. Shakespeare's atmosphere of reconciliation was to be all-inclusive.

Certain details reflect the playwright's further reading. The name *Orlando* invokes the hero of ARIOSTO's 16th-century romance *Orlando Furioso.* Another famous romance, Jorge de MONTEMAYOR's *Diana Enamorada,* is actually referred to in 4.1.146, and it may have influenced Shakespeare's creation of a network of lovers here, as it did in *A Midsummer Night's Dream.* Also, *As You Like It* contains echoes of several works by John LYLY, who also influenced Lodge's *Rosalynde.* Finally, the name *Corin* probably came from an English play of the 1570s, published in 1599, *Syre Clyomon and Clamydes,* as did, perhaps, hints of the characters Audrey and William.

As You Like It is both an example and a parody of PASTORAL literary conventions, which 16th-century English readers knew well. The most familiar ancient example of pastoral, the *Eclogues* of VIRGIL, were widely read, both in the original Latin and in several English translations, and the ancient Greek originator of the genre, Theocritus (active, third century B.C.), was translated into English in 1588, shortly before Shakespeare wrote his play. In the English Renaissance the pastoral achieved its greatest popularity in Sir Philip SIDNEY's *Arcadia,* a work that the playwright drew on in other plays. Although Shakespeare did not draw directly on any of these pastoral works in composing *As You Like It,* they nevertheless underlie its general nature.

TEXT OF THE PLAY

As You Like It was probably written in 1599, though this date is uncertain. The play was in existence by August 1600, when Shakespeare's CHAMBERLAIN'S MEN registered it with the STATIONERS' COMPANY as a play "to be stayed"—that is, *not* to be published. This was a tactic that theater companies used as a defense against piracy, and it is believed to have applied only to new plays, suggesting that *As You Like It* was a recent work. This theory is supported by circumstantial evidence. The play is not mentioned in Francis MERES's list of Shakespearean plays, published in 1598. More significant, for Meres could accidentally have omitted it, the role of Touchstone, Shakespeare's first professional fool, is thought to have been written for the noted comic Robert ARMIN, who did not join the Chamberlain's Men before early 1599. It is also thought that the company may have intended to profit from a vogue for romantic tales of outlaws, stimulated by two plays about Robin Hood—by Anthony MUNDAY and Henry CHETTLE—presented by the rival ADMIRAL'S MEN in 1598. Duke Senior is compared to the celebrated outlaw in 1.1.116, when his exile is introduced. Further, Jaques's satirical bent and his discussion of humor's purpose in 2.7.44–87 may reflect a dispute on the validity of satire that raged in London in early 1599, culminating in a public book burning in June of that year.

Another theory holds that the play was originally written much earlier, probably in 1593, and reworked later. The strongest evidence in favor of this hypothesis is a pair of references—one certain, one doubtful—to the killing of Christopher MARLOWE on May 30, 1593. Marlowe's death was among the most notorious news items of the year, and some scholars hold that it is alluded to in Touchstone's remark that "when a man's verses cannot be understood, . . . it strikes a man more dead than a great reckoning in a little room" (3.3.9–12), which may refer to the fatal dispute—a brawl over a tavern bill, or "reckoning"—and certainly seems to echo a famous phrase in Marlowe's extremely popular play *The Jew of Malta:* "infinite riches in a little room." If this passage indeed refers to Marlowe's death, it does suggest an early date, for it can have had news value for only a season or two. The other instance, in which a line of Marlowe's *Hero and Leander* is quoted and ascribed to a "dead shepherd" (3.5.81–82) is unquestionably an elegiac reference to Marlowe, though it need not have been made in the wake of his murder. Most scholars still find the earlier dating dubious, and in any case Shakespeare may have cannibalized a lost or unfinished earlier work when writing the surviving text of *As You Like It.*

The play was not published in Shakespeare's lifetime; it first appeared in the FIRST FOLIO (1623). Its text is among the clearest and least disordered in the Folio, and it appears to have been taken from a PROMPTBOOK, with its brief, imperative stage directions and accurate speech headings. The Folio thus provides the only authoritative text of *As You Like It,* and it has remained the basis of all subsequent editions.

THEATRICAL HISTORY OF THE PLAY

As You Like It may have been written expressly for the first season of the GLOBE THEATRE in the autumn of 1599, but no certain record of an early performance exists. However, an effort was made to discourage pirate publication, which suggests that the play was popular. Robert ARMIN originated the role of Jaques, and tradition holds that Shakespeare himself played Adam.

The earliest definitely known production of *As You Like It* was LOVE IN A FOREST (1723), by Charles JOHNSON, a free adaptation eliminating several characters and incorporating elements from several of Shakespeare's other plays. A reasonably faithful version of Shakespeare's text was staged in 1740, with James QUIN as Jaques, Kitty CLIVE as Celia, and Hannah PRITCHARD as Rosalind. This production was a great success, and the play remained popular throughout the 18th century; the part of Rosalind was taken by most of the leading actresses of the period, including Peg WOFFINGTON, Mary Ann YATES, Mary "Perdita" ROBINSON, and Sarah SIDDONS. Dorothy JORDAN was especially successful, playing Rosalind many times between 1787 and 1814. Jaques was played by Colley CIBBER and John HENDERSON, among others. Charles MACKLIN and Richard YATES appeared as Touchstone, but the most famous of the 18th-century jesters was Tom KING. From 1776 to 1817, *As You Like It* was the most performed Shakespearean play at London's Drury Lane Theatre.

In the 19th century Rosalind remained in the repertoire of most leading actresses, notably including Helen FAUCIT, Mary ANDERSON, and Julia NEILSON. J. P. KEMBLE and William Charles MACREADY played Jaques, the latter in his own 1842 production, a careful restoration of Shakespeare's text. In Paris, the French novelist George Sand (1804–76) staged her adaptation of the play (1856), in which Celia marries Jaques instead of Oliver. Late in the century, two important productions were popular in London: Rosalind was played by Neilson in one and by Ada REHAN in the other. *As You Like It* was often staged in the 20th century, being particularly popular in outdoor performances. Notable productions included those of

Oscar ASCHE (1907), Glen Byam SHAW (1957), and a controversial 1967 version at England's National Theatre, with an all-male cast headed by Ronald Pickup as Rosalind. Other notable Rosalinds of the century include Edith EVANS, and Peggy ASHCROFT.

As You Like It was made as a silent FILM three times, but only two modern movie versions have appeared: a 1936 film directed by Paul CZINNER, starring Laurence OLIVIER as Orlando and with a score by William WALTON. A low-budget 1992 effort by director Christine Edzard (b. 1945), set amid slums, failed to attract an audience in Britain and was never released in the United States. The play has been produced on TELEVISION several times.

CHARACTERS

Adam   Character in *As You Like It*, aged servant of Orlando. Adam is a figure of unalloyed goodness, loyalty, and faith. In 2.3 the old man volunteers his life's savings to help Orlando flee the evil intentions of his brother Oliver. Orlando equates Adam's virtue with "the constant service of the antique world, / When service sweat for duty, not for meed" (2.3.57–58). Their flight to ARDEN nearly kills the old man, and Orlando's attempt to steal food for Adam brings him into contact with the exiled court of Duke Senior. Adam is a sentimental, melodramatic archetype of the loyal servant, but he also has a credible personality. Verbose and nostalgic in the manner of the aged, he boasts a touching combination of moral strength and physical frailty.

A tradition dating from the 18th century asserts that Shakespeare himself performed the role of Adam in the original production by the CHAMBERLAIN'S MEN. This theory is supported by evidence that the playwright played old men on other occasions, but it cannot be proven. Shakespeare derived the character from his source, Thomas LODGE's *Rosalynde.* Lodge in turn followed a medieval English poem, *The Tale of Gamelyn,* which features a faithful servant named Adam Spencer (meaning "steward" or "butler"), and the figure seems to be an ancient staple of English folklore.

Aliena   In *As You Like It,* the name Celia takes when she and Rosalind, banished by Duke Freder-

ick, travel in disguise to the Forest of ARDEN. The name suggests her exiled state.

Amiens   Character in *As You Like It,* singer in the court of Duke Senior. Amiens has no distinct personality of his own and functions primarily to affirm the duke's sentiments about his exile in ARDEN. His songs, which he sings in 2.5.1–8, 2.5.35–42, and 2.7.174–193, insist on the virtues of life in the woods, compared to life at court: "Here shall [one] see / No enemy, / But winter and rough weather" (2.5.6–8).

Scholars believe that Amiens may have first been played by Robert ARMIN, a singer/comedian who joined Shakespeare's acting company, the CHAMBERLAIN'S MEN, just before *As You Like It* was written. Armin probably played Touchstone also, but Amiens's SONGs may have been created with his abilities in mind.

Audrey   Character in *As You Like It,* a goatherd loved by Touchstone. Audrey is a Shakespearean CLOWN, a comic caricature of a peasant. She is uneducated to a ridiculous degree—she is unfamiliar with the words "feature" and "poetical"—and she says little, being chiefly a butt for Touchstone's humor. She is, however, charming in her simplicity. She acknowledges her homeliness, saying "and therefore I pray the gods make me honest" (3.3.29–30), and as her marriage to Touchstone approaches, she rejoices tentatively: "I do desire it with all my heart; and I hope it is no dishonest desire, to desire to be a woman of the world" (5.3.3–5).

Though she is a minor and somewhat conventional figure, Audrey is a deftly drawn personality who helps fill out the play's satiric presentation of country life and love. Her passivity contrasts tellingly with Phebe's conventional resistance to Silvius; the two couples parody the lovers of the PASTORAL tradition, each in their own ways. Audrey mocks the pretensions of the literary shepherdesses represented by Phebe by being exaggeratedly down to earth.

Celia   Character in *As You Like It,* Rosalind's cousin and friend, daughter of Duke Frederick. Celia is a secondary but important figure. In 1.3 she defies her tyrannical father when he banishes Rosalind; her spirited loyalty and sense of morality trigger the central action of the play, the two women's flight to the Forest of ARDEN. Thereafter, Celia listens to the disguised Rosalind's professions of love for Orlando, which she cannot otherwise express while disguised as a man. Celia responds skeptically in remarks such as, " . . . the oath of a lover is no stronger than the word of a tapster" (3.4.27–28), which maintain the play's ironic stance toward romance until the climactic resolution.

When Celia herself is betrothed to Oliver in Act 5, the triumph of love is complete. The marriage of the chaste Celia to the once-villainous Oliver has been criticized as unrealistic, unfair to Celia, and unduly generous to Oliver. However, the union is largely symbolic in intent. It serves to confirm the sincerity of Oliver's repentance, and it contributes greatly to the spirit of reconciliation that closes the play.

Charles Minor character in *As You Like It*, a wrestler. Charles is a professional performer who takes on all comers; his patron is the aristocratic Oliver. In 1.1 Oliver's younger brother Orlando proposes to challenge Charles at a forthcoming festival, and Oliver falsely informs Charles that Orlando is by nature an evil man and intends to kill him. He promises Charles that he will not be punished if Orlando dies instead, and the wrestler assures Oliver that this will be the outcome. In 1.2, however, Orlando defeats Charles soundly. This scene helps to establish Orlando as a hero. Charles also introduces a major theme in 1.1, informing us—and Oliver—of the fact that Duke Senior, having been deposed and exiled by his brother, Duke Frederick, has set up a court in the Forest of ARDEN.

Shakespeare derived his wrestler from his source, Thomas LODGE's *Rosalynde,* but toned down the character considerably. The original, an inhumanly strong and cruel villain, takes a bribe to kill Orlando's counterpart, but Charles is led to believe he will be in the right to do so; Lodge's wrestler kills his earlier opponents outright, while Charles's survive. Lodge made much of the contrast between his hero and the gigantic, villainous wrestler; Shakespeare's Charles is a more neutral figure who is simply defeated for the good of the plot.

Corin Character in *As You Like It*, an honest, elderly shepherd. In 2.4 and 3.5 Corin is associated with Silvius, a conventional shepherd who is filled with literary conceits about love; in most PASTORAL literature the countryside was an idealized setting for amorous tales of shepherds and shepherdesses, such as Silvius and his beloved Phebe. Corin, by contrast, is a real shepherd. He describes the economic plight of the shepherd to Rosalind and Celia in 2.4.73–84 while at the same time establishing himself as a representative of traditional rural values, offering such modest hospitality as he can.

In 3.2 Corin expresses his down-to-earth relationship to his world, and he can say, "I am a true labourer: I earn that I eat, get that I wear; owe no man hate, envy no man's happiness . . ." (3.2.71–72). Touchstone wittily derides this simple life, but he cannot upset Corin. The honest shepherd anchors the rustic life of ARDEN in the real world and thus offsets the high-flown sentiment of pastoral tradition.

Corin's name was commonly applied to shepherds in late medieval and Renaissance romantic literature; it may be a masculine form of Corinna (active ca. 500–470 B.C.), an ancient Greek lyric poetess. Shakespeare may have been inspired to use the name by an English play of the 1570s, published in 1599, *Syre Clyomon and Clamydes,* in which a princess disguised as a man serves a shepherd named Corin.

Dennis Minor character in *As You Like It*, servant of Oliver. Dennis appears only to announce the arrival of the wrestler Charles in 1.1.88–92.

Duke Frederick Character in *As You Like It*, younger brother and deposer of Duke Senior. Duke Frederick is the villain of the play. A cardboard character with no real personality, he is a conventional bad man, intended simply to anchor one end of the play's scale of values. He not only exiles his brother to the Forest of ARDEN, but he also banishes his innocent niece Rosalind, thus provoking the flight of his daughter Celia. His hostility toward Rosalind is said to be based "upon no other argument / But that the people praise her for her virtues, / And pity her for her good father's sake" (1.2.269–271). The Duke's reported reformation, after encountering "an old religious man" (5.4.159) while launching an army against Arden, is entirely unbelievable in human terms. However, it symbolizes the play's climactic triumph of harmony and reconciliation.

Duke Senior Character in *As You Like It*, ruler deposed by his brother, Duke Frederick, and exiled to the Forest of ARDEN. The father of Rosalind, Duke Senior is a symbol of authority and wisdom with little distinctive personality. Before we meet him, we are told that he and his followers in exile "fleet the time carelessly as they did in the golden world" (1.1.118–119), a reference to the rustic life idealized in PASTORAL literature. In his first speech the Duke introduces the audience to Arden and firmly establishes the contrast between the woodland world and the realities of politics and power: "Hath not old custom made this life more sweet / Than that of painted pomp? Are not these woods / More free from peril than the envious court?" (2.1.2–4). The Duke makes the best of his exile, finding "tongues in trees, books in the running brooks, / Sermons in stones, and good in everything" (2.1.16–17). Such remarks, like the songs of AMIENS, express the ideal of an escape from the pressures of the real world.

However, the Duke is aware that Arden is no paradise. He acknowledges that he has "seen better days" (2.7.120), and he shares some attitudes with the alienated and melancholy courtier Jaques. In 2.1.22–25 he regrets having to kill deer for food shortly before an elaboration on the thought is attributed to Jaques. In 2.7.136–139 he suggests to Jaques his famous comparison of human life to the action in a drama ("All the world's a stage, / And all the men and women merely players" [2.7.139–140]). Nevertheless, the Duke also opposes this point of view: In 2.7.64–69, he chastises Jaques for wishing to satirize the world when he is himself hardly free from sin, and, in doing so, he sets a limit on the play's tolerance for Jaques's criticisms. Most important, when Duke Frederick's religious conversion and abdication are reported in 5.4, Duke Senior is immediately ready to resume his dukedom, and, as Jaques remarks, his "patience and . . . virtue well deserve it" (5.4.186). The Duke's fondness for the pastoral life

is less powerful than his sense of social responsibility, mirroring Shakespeare's own view that a ruler's duty to his position is paramount.

Ganymede In *As You Like It*, name taken by Rosalind when, banished by Duke Frederick, she travels with Celia to the Forest of ARDEN disguised as a young man. In Greek mythology Zeus, the king of the gods, became infatuated with Ganymede, a beautiful boy, and took the form of an eagle to kidnap him and carry him to Mount Olympus, where the youth became a cupbearer to the gods. The name Ganymede thus came to suggest boyish beauty.

Hymen Minor character in *As You Like It*, the Roman god of marriage. In 5.4.107–145 Hymen is the central figure in the MASQUE that accompanies Rosalind's appearance, undisguised, to resolve the play's complexities. Hymen, after making a formal statement of divine pleasure when earthly confusions are resolved, announces the return of Rosalind. Rosalind in turn declares her true relationship to her father, Duke Senior, to Orlando, and to Phebe, all hitherto hidden by her disguise as a young man. Hymen then solemnly blesses four couples—Rosalind and Orlando, Celia and Oliver, Phebe and Silvius, and Touchstone and Audrey—leads a "wedlock hymn" (5.4.136), which everyone sings. This formal celebration of marriage represents the happy conclusion of the play's various courtships.

It is unclear whether Shakespeare intended Hymen as a human impersonator of a god taking part in a festive tableau arranged by Rosalind or as an actual deity appearing to mortals, as gods do in other Shakespearean plays—e.g., in *Cymbeline*, 5.4, and *The Tempest*, 4.1. In either case, Hymen's function is the same: His masque lends a gracefully solemn air to the play's climax. The part of Hymen is often assigned to Amiens, who is a singer and who is present in this scene, according to the stage direction at 5.4.1, but who has no spoken lines in it.

Jaques Character in *As You Like It*, gloomy follower of Duke Senior who provides a contrast to the play's comic values. Jaques muses on the viciousness of human hypocrisy, affects to dislike music and dancing, and praises only the satire that can expose the sins of the world. When the duke prepares to return to his dukedom at the play's close, accompanied by most of the other characters, Jaques decides to stay in the Forest of ARDEN and pursue a life of contemplation.

Jaques's pessimism and self-imposed isolation place him at odds with the play's central tenet, that love is the most valued element in human life. However, he never seriously threatens this ideal; his position is consistently undercut, in part because Shakespeare envisioned Jaques to some extent as a parody of a fashionable 16th-century affectation of cynicism and melancholy. People who held this attitude doubtless felt that they appeared intellectually superior and penetrating, but others found them amusingly pretentious.

The ineffectuality of Jaques's ideas is repeatedly pointed up by his repudiation by the other major characters. His elaborately melancholy pose is described even before we meet him, when the duke hears of his lament over a slain deer (2.1.26–66). In 2.5, in his first appearance, Jaques satirizes Amiens's song, which mirrors the duke's sentiments about the virtues of life in Arden. Then, in 2.7, having encountered the jester Touchstone, he raves about the opportunities for a FOOL to "cleanse th'infected world" (2.7.60) through satire. However, Jaques is then sternly chastised by the duke for "chiding sin" (2.7.64) when he has been a sinner himself. Even Jaques's most spectacular speech, his cynical depiction of the seven ages of man, beginning, "All the world's a stage, / And all the men and women merely players" (2.7.139–140), is undercut. No character bothers to respond to it, and immediately after Jaques's harrowing description of old age, the ancient Adam is borne on stage and treated as a respected member of the community.

Jaques is most explicitly contrasted with the lovers Rosalind and Orlando. When he first meets Orlando, Jaques declares he would rather be alone, and he disparages Orlando's poetry, his wit, and his lover's name. Jaques has said that he is seeking a fool, meaning Touchstone, but Orlando invites him to look in the brook, where he will see his own reflection. Insulted, Jaques leaves.

Rosalind is similarly dismissive. In 4.1 Jaques asserts that he is melancholy, saying, "I do love it better than laughing" (4.1.4). The heroine fiercely insists that those who are excessive in laughter *or* melancholy are "abominable fellows, and betray themselves to every modern censure, worse than drunkards" (4.1.5–8). Further, when he says that his state of mind has been influenced by his travels, she delivers a standard Elizabethan diatribe on the foolishness of travel. Significantly, these rebukes each occur just before one of the two major courtship scenes between Rosalind and Orlando, 3.2.290–423 and 4.1.40–190. Jaques's negativism must be overcome before the lovers' affirmation can occur.

Touchstone seems to resemble Jaques at first glance; they are both given to satire, wit, and cynicism. However, Touchstone is a professional comic whose statements are usually meant only to be humorous. His comprehension of the world's ways stirs him to amusement rather than despair. Jaques, by contrast, is a philosopher of sorts, and he has a consistently dour viewpoint that opposes sociability; as he remarks, "I am for other than for dancing measures" (5.4.192).

Jaques wishes for a pristine past, before human societies came to Arden to kill deer, before humans existed at all, perhaps. This is an extreme form of the PASTORAL literary conventions, a target of the play's parody. Such extravagantly antisocial desires place Jaques beyond the reach of the celebration of love that closes the play. This is a recurring device that Shakespeare uses in his COMEDIES: Characters whose actions are not motivated by love and whose presence would mar the harmonious resolution of the play—such as Don John of *Much Ado About Nothing* and Malvolio of *Twelfth Night*—are left out of such scenes of reconciliation.

However, Jaques is not a villain, as is Don John. Except in his encounter with Orlando in 3.2, he behaves with civility. In 2.5 he and a group of fellow courtiers listen to music. In 4.2 he sings with others in a ribald interlude celebrating the hunt with jokes about cuckold's horns and deer's antlers (quite forgetful of his distress over the slain deer of 2.1). Even his satire of Amiens's song in 2.5 is good-natured, particularly since the "gross fools" (2.5.53) he criticizes include himself. Also, although he expresses antisocial views, Jaques converses with more different people than any other character. Finally, the blessings that Jaques bestows on the duke and each of the marrying couples in 5.4.185–192 are pleasant and humorous, as well as perceptive.

In fact, Jaques's closing lines reveal that he, too, has been affected by the general awareness of love's power that surrounds him. He knows that he is not destined to be a part of it, but he certainly does not begrudge the lovers their happiness. In fact, his final remarks concern his friends and their prospects; Jaques has become humanized. He remains isolated, but he is no longer a malcontent. He does not disparage the wedding festivities; he simply opts for something else. His reason for remaining in Arden is eminently acceptable: "There is much matter to be heard and learn'd" (5.4.184).

Jaques's final self-acceptance is in keeping with the play's spirit of conciliation, most vividly represented by the multiple marriage in 5.4. Further, his early cynicism, although inappropriate to the world of Arden and therefore countered by the other characters, sharpens the flavor of a play that might otherwise be overly sentimental. Lastly, Jaques's railing reminds us that outside the magical world of Arden, the ways of the world are all too often wicked indeed.

Jaques de Boys Minor character in *As You Like It*, brother of Oliver and Orlando. Jaques is named in 1.1.5, but he does not appear until 5.4, when he suddenly arrives with the news of Duke Frederick's armed march on ARDEN and later conversion to a life of religious contemplation. The episode both provides a place for the villain in the play's ultimate reconciliation and, in its suddenness, intensifies the play's atmosphere of romantic wonder.

The duplication of names with a major character, the pessimistic courtier Jaques, presents a minor difficulty. Jaques de Boys identifies himself only as "the second son of old Sir Rowland" (5.4.151). In the FIRST FOLIO edition of the play, stage directions identify him as "Second Brother," and some modern editions follow this practice, avoiding the issue to some extent, but the mention of his name in 1.1 suggests carelessness on Shakespeare's part. Perhaps the playwright originally intended his melancholy courtier to be Orlando

and Oliver's brother, established his existence with the reference at 1.1.5, and then developed Jaques as a member of the exiled Duke Senior's court, neglecting to remove the earlier reference.

Le Beau Minor character in *As You Like It*, a foppish nobleman in the court of the tyrannous Duke Frederick. Rosalind and Celia mock Le Beau in 1.2.86–114. He is fastidious in his diction but less so in his tastes; his description of brutal wrestling as "good sport" (1.2.92) provokes Touchstone's quite sensible reply: "It is the first time that ever I heard breaking of ribs was sport for ladies" (1.2.128–129). However, Le Beau's affectations and callousness are offset when he warns Orlando of the Duke's evil intentions in 1.2.251–275.

Lord Any of several minor characters in *As You Like It*, noblemen in the court of the exiled Duke Senior. In 2.1 two Lords tell the duke of an encounter with Jaques, and in 2.7 they attend the duke's forest banquet. They also seem likely to be the unspecified "others" of several stage directions—e.g., at the opening of 2.5.

In addition, two other Lords, from the court of the evil Duke Frederick, tell their master in 2.2 that Rosalind, Celia, and Touchstone have fled his court.

Martext, Sir Oliver Minor character in *As You Like It*, a country priest. In 3.3 Touchstone and Audrey meet with Martext, "the vicar of the next village" (3.3.37), to be married. Martext speaks only two lines before the ceremony is broken up by Jaques, who belittles the virtues of a marriage performed by a country bumpkin and leads the couple away.

Martext is a parodic figure with particular relevance to Shakespeare's audiences. The English Reformation—instituted about 50 years before the play was written—had produced a shortage of trained clergy, for not only did many Catholic priests refuse to transfer their allegiance to the Church of England, but the new church did not develop training programs immediately. The quality of the lesser clergy was accordingly poor, even as late as the 17th century, and the illiteracy and ignorance of country priests were subjects of much scandal and humor, of which this scene is an example.

Martext's name not only suggests his incompetence, but it may also be a satirical reference to Martin Marprelate, the central figure in a religious controversy of the late 1580s. Marprelate—a fictitious name with anticlerical overtones—was the supposed author of a series of anonymous tracts advocating radical Puritanism. Their publisher defied the government's CENSORSHIP for several years before being captured and hung. Martext's name may therefore suggest that he is a radical as well as an oaf—thus doubly a target for comic insult. However, Shakespeare's humor on religious subjects is never bitter, and the playwright permits Sir Oliver a dignified response to his rejection: Once alone, Martext says, "'Tis no matter. Ne'er a fantastical knave of them all shall flout me out of my calling" (3.3.97–98).

Oliver   Character in *As You Like It*, older brother of Orlando. Oliver is plainly a villain from the outset. In 1.1 he is seen to have deprived Orlando of his birthright, then he plots to have Orlando killed by the wrestler Charles. His malice derives from envy, as he admits when he observes that Orlando's virtues are so great that he, Oliver, is "altogether misprised" (1.1.168–169). In 3.1 Oliver becomes a victim himself, as the tyrannous Duke Frederick seizes his estate and threatens him with banishment if he does not capture Orlando. Oliver protests, asserting that he "never lov'd my brother in my life" (3.1.14) (to which the Duke replies concisely, "More villain thou" [3.1.15]).

Yet in 4.3 Oliver is a reformed person, a gentleman of sufficient virtue to attract the love of Celia, whom he marries in 5.4. This turnabout has no humanly credible motivation, nor is it meant to; Oliver is a cardboard character, intended to play a purely symbolic role. His villainy serves to heighten the malevolence from which the Forest of ARDEN offers escape, and the change in him testifies to the power of love, as found in this idyllic wood, to defeat evil. However, Oliver's conversion is not simply magical; it is the result of Orlando's humane decision to forswear revenge and save his sleeping brother from the serpent and lioness, as Oliver describes in 4.3.98–132. This unselfish act, undertaken at the risk of Orlando's life, provokes Oliver's utter total repentance. Oliver decides to give his estates to Orlando, and his loving relationship with Celia, incredible though it is in realistic terms, is the ultimate symbolic confirmation of—and reward for—his sincerity.

Orlando   Character in *As You Like It*, the lover of Rosalind. Orlando is first seen as a victim of his older brother, Oliver, who has seized Orlando's rightful inheritance and plots to have him killed by the wrestler Charles. After defeating Charles (and meeting Rosalind) in 1.2, Orlando is warned by his faithful servant, Adam, that Oliver still intends to harm him, and the two flee in 2.3. As they arrive in the Forest of ARDEN, Orlando's noble spirit is stressed as he stoops to robbery in order to find food for the feeble Adam. Fortunately, his efforts lead him to the court-in-exile of Duke Senior, where, in 2.7, he is welcomed as a gentleman. He recalls Rosalind in a juvenile and conventionally romantic way, as he hangs love poems to her from the trees, but he encounters her only in her disguise as Ganymede, who scoffs at his professed love and suggests that he might be cured of it if he pretends to woo "him" and is rebuffed. Orlando is consistent in his avowals, however, though only later does he come to a mature sense of what love means.

The growing power of love in him is demonstrated when he resists the temptation to let a lioness kill his evil brother and instead risks his own life to save him, as Oliver reports in 4.3.98–132. Orlando has become aware of his own need for love and reconciliation in all aspects of his life. His full maturation is triggered by the love that arises between Celia and the reformed Oliver. Faced with the real thing, Orlando tells Ganymede, "I can live no longer by thinking" (5.2.50), and Rosalind realizes that she can now discard her disguise, for Orlando is unquestionably committed to her and not simply to the idea of romantic love. Though Rosalind is the spokesperson for most of the play's position on the nature of love, Orlando's development is a powerful secondary demonstration of love's link to self-knowledge.

Orlando is something of a cardboard character. As a handsome leading man without a very well-developed personality, he contributes to the play's parody of PASTORAL literary conventions. Shakespeare's original audiences will have recognized Orlando as a romantic hero immediately, for reasons that are less evident to modern readers and viewers. His name is a version of Roland, one of the greatest heroes of medieval legend and literature, and an Orlando was also the hero of the most popular and well-known of 16th-century pastoral romances, Ludovico ARIOSTO's *Orlando Furioso* (1516, translated into English by Sir John HARINGTON in 1591). Further, Shakespeare's Orlando is identified with two great heroes of classical legend, Aeneas and Hercules. At 2.7.167 Orlando carries the weak and starving Adam to the Duke's banquet, a tableau that, to a classically educated reader or theatergoer, must have brought to mind the well-known image, from VIRGIL's *Aeneid*, of Aeneas carrying his father to safety during the sack of Troy. And to an Elizabethan audience, Orlando's conquests of Charles and the lioness will have immediately suggested the myths of Hercules wrestling Antaeus—depictions of which were extremely popular throughout RENAISSANCE Europe—and his killing the Nemean lion barehanded. In addition, Shakespeare dropped a broader hint when Rosalind says to Orlando, "Now Hercules be thy speed, young man!" (1.2.198).

Page Either of two minor characters in *As You Like It*, singers in the court of Duke Senior. In 5.3 the Pages sing a parody of a love song for Touchstone and Audrey that provides a brief interlude of pure entertainment before the play reaches its climax.

Phebe (Phoebe) Character in *As You Like It*, shepherdess loved by Silvius. Phebe is a caricature of the cruel shepherdess of the PASTORAL tradition, who rejects the love of the shepherd. In spurning Silvius, Phebe scorns romantic passion and denies that her coldness can wound her wooer. In presenting such a perfect parody of literary lovers, Shakespeare permits his hero and heroine, Rosalind and Orlando, to seem relatively normal and to conduct their own courtship free from the extravagant posturing of traditional romances.

Rosalind, disguised as a young man, Ganymede, chastises Phebe for her attitude, pointing out that, being homely, she would do better to take Silvius than mock him. She advises Phebe, "Sell when you can, you are not for all markets" (3.5.60). This extreme candor parodies the exaggerations of conventional sentiment. Then Phebe falls in love with Ganymede and thus assumes the same role as Silvius—that of the love-struck suitor. When Rosalind eventually discloses her true identity and holds Phebe to her promise to take Silvius if she could not have Ganymede, she points up the lesson of the parody: Love is falsified by an excessive insistence on doting or rejection.

Rosalind Character in *As You Like It*, lover of Orlando and daughter of the exiled Duke Senior. Rosalind is the play's most important character. She symbolizes the love and commitment that finally prevail when her manipulations result in the multiple marriages of 5.4. Both a counselor and a learner about love, she presents many of the play's themes.

Although her banishment by Duke Frederick in 1.3 necessitates her masquerade as Ganymede, Rosalind retains the disguise in the Forest of ARDEN. As a young man she escapes the restrictions that were traditionally placed on women and can control her relationship with Orlando and influence that of Silvius and Phebe, conventional shepherds of PASTORAL literature. Playing the parts of both a man and a woman, both an expert on love and its victim, she simultaneously mocks love and feels it, and she can test Orlando's feelings and her own. The result is both moving and comical, as she finds herself arguing against the conventions of love, saying, "love is merely a madness" (3.3.388), even as she herself feels "many fathoms deep . . . in love!" (4.1.196).

Rosalind is a natural and unpretentious figure who opposes affectation both in Phebe and her own Orlando. She punctures the unworthy Phebe's lofty scorn for Silvius, rebuking her in down-to-earth terms that satirize the conventions of the hard-to-get lover, telling her to ". . . sell when you can, you are not for all markets" (3.5.60). And when Orlando says he will die if Rosalind refuses him, she, speaking as Ganymede, denies it: ". . . men have died from time to time and worms have eaten them, but not for love" (4.1.101–103). Similarly, his conventional assertion that he will love Rosalind "for ever, and a day" (4.1.137) brings her reply, "Say a day, without the ever . . . men are April when they woo, December when they wed. Maids are May when they are maids, but the sky changes when they are wives" (4.1.138–141). This recognition that emotions evolve through time does not deny the virtue of affection or imply a lessening of the intensity of her own love for Orlando. She is herself at a peak of loving good humor as she speaks; she simply wishes to counter the egotistic intensity of love-cults, knowing that a more human approach will yield a truer affection. Our final sense of the love between Rosalind and Orlando is enhanced by this evidence of its freedom from illusion.

Rosalind, in seeking Orlando's love, commits herself to an involvement in life that is directly opposed to the isolation of the melancholy Jaques, the play's other major figure. She criticizes Jaques's excessive pessimism when she lumps him with all other extremists, who are, she says, ". . . abominable fellows, . . . worse than drunkards" (4.1.5–8). Her repudiation of his negativism is emphasized by its juxtaposition to a passage of elated love talk with Orlando, which follows immediately. Similarly, Jaques's earlier rejection by Orlando is followed by Rosalind's initial encounter with her lover in Arden. Rosalind's love replaces Jaques's antisocial reserve repeatedly. Rosalind's opposition to Jaques thus comes across indirectly as well as in explicit dialogue.

When we first meet Rosalind, in 1.2, she is sad because of her father's banishment, but her spirits rise throughout the play, as first she meets Orlando at the wrestling match in the same scene and as she later tests and accepts his love. Her attitude toward love grows more mature as well. In 1.2 she treats love as a lark, saying, "I will . . . devise sports. Let me see, what think you of falling in love?" (1.2.23–24). She is clearly ripe for love, but her attitude is naive.

In Arden, Rosalind acquires a fuller understanding of love. She absorbs the jester Touchstone's bawdy parodies of love in his account of Jane Smile (2.4.43–53) and in his comic love poem "If a hart do lack a hind" (3.2.99–110). As Ganymede, Rosalind acquires a growing sense of what love can be, as her responses to both Orlando and Phebe indicate. Then, when Orlando's own growth makes

him impatient with his "courtship" of Ganymede, in 5.2, Rosalind is ready to reintroduce herself undisguised and claim his love.

Rosalind's association with magic in Act 5—in claiming, as Ganymede, the ability to "do strange things" (5.2.59) and in invoking the blessing of Hymen in the MASQUE in which she appears in 5.4—suits the role she has played among the lovers. Disguised as Ganymede, she has been invisible in a sense and has been able to control the situation entirely, guiding the development of Orlando's love through the playful fantasy of portraying herself, bringing together Silvius and Phebe with her "magical" change of sex, and overseeing the union of Oliver and Celia as the latter's supposed brother. She embodies comic pleasure, and her humorous tricks and deceits result in the play's happy ending centered on marriage.

In the EPILOGUE, Rosalind speaks as a man, saying, "If I were a woman . . ." (5.4.214), referring to the fact that the part was originally played by a boy. This offers a piquant twist to her final manipulations, for we are reminded of the equally magical theatrical illusion that has given us one of Shakespeare's most charming heroines.

Silvius   Character in *As You Like It*, a young shepherd, lover of Phebe. Silvius is a caricature of the ardent lover in the PASTORAL tradition that the play satirizes. Silvius's courtship of Phebe is presented as "a pageant truly played" (3.4.48), and as such it follows well-established traditions. Using a familiar gambit of the Elizabethan sonneteer, Silvius insists that, in rejecting his love, Phebe is harder on him than an executioner. Rosalind calls him "a tame snake" (4.3.70); his weakness, an exaggeration of the stock posture of the unrequited lover, is part of the play's mockery of literary conventions.

Touchstone   Character in *As You Like It*, a professional FOOL and follower of Rosalind. Touchstone is initially in the service of Duke Frederick, but he joins Rosalind and Celia when they flee to the Forest of ARDEN after Act 1. He uses his unbridled humor to satirize all targets. In particular, Touchstone parodies the romances of the other characters in his own courtship of the goatherd Audrey.

A touchstone is a mineral used to test gold and silver alloys; when the alloy is rubbed with a touchstone, a discoloration, whose precise shade indicates the metal's purity, is produced. Similarly, something of the quality of the other characters is revealed through Touchstone's mockery of them. Jesting and mimicking, he tests their approaches to the worlds of PASTORAL love and country life, the themes of the play.

Unlike Jaques, who also mocks the other characters, Touchstone presents no alternatives and has no clear-cut vision of the world. Also unlike Jaques, he is consistently funny; his cynicism is amused, not despairing, and his enthusiastic approach to love and rusticity stands in marked opposition to Jaques's isolation. Significantly, while Jaques withdraws from the world at the play's close, Touchstone marries and is part of the climactic festival of love and reconciliation.

The jester is a courtier, both by inclination and profession, a point he explains satirically when he says, "I have trod a measure, I have flattered a lady, I have been politic with my friend, smooth with mine enemy, I have undone three tailors, I have had four quarrels, and like to have fought one" (5.4.43–47). In 1.2.58–74 his first jest of the play is at the expense of knightly "honour," and he mocks Le Beau's callous enthusiasm for brutal sports in 1.2.127–129. In his encounter with the shepherd Corin in 3.2.11–83 he cannot keep his arguments for the superiority of courtly wit from backfiring upon himself, so extravagant are they. His extraordinary send-up of dueling (5.4.67–102) has lost much of its point for modern readers, but it is a virtuoso satire of the handbooks of gentlemanly combat that flourished in Shakespeare's day.

Touchstone also turns his humor on the supposedly idyllic country life; when he first arrives in Arden, he exclaims, "Ay, now am I in Arden, the more fool I; when I was at home I was in a better place . . ." (2.4.13–14). His feet hurt, and he will not let his discomfort go unnoticed. He mocks the dimness of Audrey's rustic swain, William, in 5.1, and his pursuit of Audrey satirizes peasant life by caricaturing an unconsidered, merely biological mating.

However, Touchstone's courtship of Audrey is most strikingly a comical contrast to the relationship of Silvius and Phebe, who present the literary ideal of pastoral love. Touchstone's forthrightness and Audrey's passivity enable these lovers to achieve a very direct and uncomplicated match, whereas only Rosalind's elaborate machinations can unite the shepherd and shepherdess. Earlier, Touchstone mocks both Silvius and Rosalind, after they remark on the pathos of love, by offering the preposterous example of his own romance with "Jane Smile" (2.4.43–53).

Touchstone's romance is also contrasted with the genuinely moving love between Rosalind and Orlando. In 3.2.99–110 his bawdy parody of Orlando's love poetry is intended to embarrass his mistress. She responds with an apt comparison of the jester and a soft fruit, insinuating that Touchstone will be rotten with age before his mind is ripe. The fool has the last word, however, when he says, "You have said; but whether wisely or no, let the forest judge" (3.2.119—120). Like the forest, Touchstone's indiscriminate comedy is a force of nature, and all manner of things are "judged" by exposure to it.

Significantly, Touchstone's initial encounter with Audrey follows immediately after Orlando's meeting with the disguised Rosalind. Orlando's promise "by the faith of my love" (3.2.416) to demonstrate his passion for the supposedly absent Rosalind is thus juxtaposed with Touchstone's insistence on animal desire as the motive for his own romance. The jester is detached about and resigned to his role as a husband: "As the ox hath his bow . . . so man hath his desires, and as pigeons bill, so wedlock would be nibbling" (3.3.71–73). His assumption that any wife will assuage his physical desire is the opposite extreme to Orlando's proposition that only Rosalind can possibly serve. The idealism of the latter point of view lacks the acknowledgment of instinct that Touchstone offers. As Rosalind and Orlando's relationship evolves, the play moves beyond Touchstone's simplistic position, but first it must also offer this stance as a specimen of pastoral love.

Touchstone is a professional jester, a performer who was expected to make fun of the members of an aristocratic court for their entertainment and as living proof that they did not fear criticism. His profession required a jester to seem incapable of common sense, and he was accordingly excused from ordinary social life. He developed a purposeful detachment from the real lives of the people around him in favor of a concern with the artificialities of wit. Touchstone is seen only in the light of his calling; though delightful, he is not a fully developed person. His amalgam of fast talk and brash earthiness is dazzling, but he is merely doing his job. As such he can parody the rest of the characters, but the play is not at all dependent on him, as it is on Rosalind or Jaques. If he were absent, we would be poorer for not knowing him, but *As You Like It* would still make its key points.

Jesters were familiar figures in the drama and literature of the 16th century, obvious vehicles for parody and satire. It is thought that the part of Touchstone was written for Robert ARMIN, an actor who specialized in these parts and who joined the CHAMBERLAIN'S MEN at about the time when *As You Like It* was written. Touchstone was the first of Shakespeare's jesters, and in Jaques's speeches describing an offstage performance by the "motley fool" (2.7.12–61), one can almost hear the playwright exulting in the potential of this new sort of role.

William Minor character in *As You Like It*, a rustic swain whom Touchstone intimidates into abandoning his courtship of Audrey. Like Audrey, William is a CLOWN, a comic caricature of a peasant as imagined by the London audience for whom he was created. He fancies he has "a pretty wit" (5.1.28), but he is preposterously ill-spoken; the longest word he speaks is his own name, and his longest speech has only seven words. He has no substantial personality; he simply offers a humorous contrast to the courtly ways of the major characters. William's unsophisticated weakness parodies the conventions of love in his own way, as the attitudes of Touchstone and Silvius satirize them in others.

Cardenio

Lost play, possibly written by Shakespeare and John FLETCHER. In 1613 the KING'S MEN twice performed a play recorded as *Cardenno* or *Cardenna*. In 1653 the

manuscript collector and publisher Humphrey MOSELEY claimed the copyright on an old play, *The History of Cardennio*, said to be by Shakespeare and Fletcher, but his copy did not survive. In 1727 Lewis THEOBALD produced a drama titled *Double Falsehood* (published 1728), which he asserted he had adapted from an unpublished play manuscript by Shakespeare. This play derives from a story in Miguel de CERVANTES's *Don Quixote*, whose hero is named Cardenio. Theobald wrote that he owned three manuscript copies of the play, but they subsequently disappeared, and when he published his edition of Shakespeare's plays in 1733, he did not include this one. Moreover, scholars agree that the play, at least in Theobald's version, is very un-Shakespearean. It is speculated that the King's Men's play of 1613 was passed on, in a corrupt form, as far as Theobald, who came to reject its authenticity.

Around 1613 Fletcher and Shakespeare collaborated on *The Two Noble Kinsmen* and possibly *Henry VIII*, so there is nothing unlikely about a third such project. Moreover, a translation of *Don Quixote* was published in 1612. Fletcher used it as a source for later plays, so his hand in the King's Men's play of 1613 seems likely. However, the play's absence from the FIRST FOLIO (1623) suggests that its editors—King's Men themselves—felt it was not by Shakespeare, either because his part in it was too slight to merit mention or simply because he had nothing to do with it at all.

In 1994 Charles Hamilton (1913–97), an autograph dealer, handwriting expert, and amateur Shakespearean scholar, published a manuscript he entitled *Cardenio*, by Shakespeare and Fletcher. This was in fact a play known as *The Second Maiden's Tragedy* (a misnomer based on the MASTER OF REVELS's mistaken assumption that it was a sequel to Francis BEAUMONT and John Fletcher's *Maid's Tragedy* [1610]). Hamilton claimed that the manuscript, dated 1611, was written in Shakespeare's handwriting. Scholars of the period find this highly dubious, observing that the form the manuscript takes is more like a scribal rendering than an author's FOUL COPY, that the play itself has numerous similarities to the work of Thomas MIDDLETON (who is known to have drawn on Cervantes's work, and to whom *The Second Maiden's Tragedy* has long been ascribed), and that Humphrey MOSELEY's 1653 inventory lists both *The Second Maiden's Tragedy* and *Cardenio*. Hamilton's claim remains a subject of controversy, but most authorities do not accept this play in the Shakespearean CANON.

Comedy of Errors, The

SYNOPSIS

Act 1, Scene 1

Duke Solinus of Ephesus informs Egeon, a merchant of Syracuse, that he is subject to the death penalty, prescribed for any citizen of Syracuse found in EPHESUS, unless he can pay an immense ransom. Egeon tells of the long search that has brought him to Ephesus: 23 years earlier, his wife and one of their infant twin sons had been separated from him in a shipwreck. The other son had set forth, at the age of 18, in search of his lost brother. He took with him his servant, who had also been separated from a twin brother in the same shipwreck. Egeon himself had then begun to roam the world for news of either son. The Duke is sympathetic to this tragic tale; he gives the prisoner the rest of the day to beg or borrow ransom money.

Act 1, Scene 2

A local Merchant advises Antipholus of Syracuse, newly arrived, not to reveal his origins, telling of the fate of Egeon. Antipholus instructs his servant, Dromio of Syracuse, to return to their inn and guard their money. In a soliloquy, Antipholus tells of his search for his lost brother, and the audience realizes that he is one of Egeon's sons. Dromio of Ephesus enters and mistakes Antipholus for his own master, Antipholus of Ephesus. Antipholus of Syracuse in turn mistakes this Dromio for his own servant. The presence in the city of the two sets of twins is now known to the audience. Dromio of Ephesus relays his mistress's demand that his master return home. Antipholus of Syracuse asks about the safety of the money, and Dromio denies knowledge of any money. Antipholus beats him, and the mystified servant runs away. Antipholus remarks to himself on the reputation of Ephesus as a center for witchcraft and thievery, and he hurries back to his inn, fearing theft.

Act 2, Scene 1

Adriana, the wife of Antipholus of Ephesus, complains that her husband is late for lunch, thus triggering a disputation on marriage with her sister, Luciana; Luciana holds for wifely obedience in all things, while Adriana asserts her independence. Dromio of Ephesus returns to tell of the beating he has received. Adriana sends him out again to fetch Antipholus home. Adriana asserts that her husband prefers the company of other women to her own, though Luciana rebukes her for unjustified jealousy.

Act 2, Scene 2

Antipholus of Syracuse encounters his own servant, whom he berates for the behavior of the other Dromio and then beats when he declares his innocence. Adriana and Luciana appear, and Adriana, thinking Antipholus of Syracuse to be her husband, chastises him for infidelity. When he responds with natural confusion, he is rebuked by Luciana. The servant also claims ignorance, and the two are jointly condemned by the women. The visitors are mystified and fear that supernatural doings are afoot. However, Antipholus decides to follow the drift of things in the hope of discovering the truth, and he permits himself to be taken to Adriana's home, where Dromio is assigned the gate-guarding duties of his namesake.

Act 3, Scene 1

Antipholus of Ephesus enters with his servant Dromio and two friends, Angelo, a goldsmith, and Balthasar, a merchant. Antipholus invites his friends to come to his house, but they are turned away at the gate by Dromio of Syracuse, who is obeying his orders to keep out all comers. Another servant, Luce, and finally Adriana herself, persist in keeping Antipholus out, believing him to be an imposter. The outraged husband announces that he will pay a visit to a Courtesan he knows and that, moreover, he will give that woman the gold necklace he had commissioned from Angelo as a gift for his wife.

Act 3, Scene 2

Luciana is appalled that Antipholus of Syracuse, whom she believes to be her brother-in-law,

Antipholus of Ephesus, has declared his love for her. She concludes that he is mad and flees, announcing her intention to tell Adriana about this turn of events. Dromio of Syracuse enters and tells of the extravagantly ugly kitchen maid, Nell, who has claimed him as a husband. Antipholus sends him to prepare to depart; as he observes in a soliloquy, they must flee the witchery of the place, especially since he has fallen in love with one of the supernatural creatures—namely, Luciana. Angelo appears with the gold chain commissioned by the other Antipholus and turns it over to this one, despite the latter's bewildered protests.

Act 4, Scene 1

A Merchant demands of Angelo the repayment of a debt, and he is accompanied by an Officer empowered to arrest debtors. Angelo says that he can satisfy the debt as soon as Antipholus pays him for the gold chain. Just then, Antipholus of Ephesus appears with his servant, whom he sends to buy a rope, with which he proposes to whip his wife for having kept him out of his house. When he sees Angelo, he protests that he has not received the chain. Confusion leads to anger, and Antipholus is arrested. At this point, Dromio of Syracuse appears. He announces that he has arranged passage on a ship and bids Antipholus go aboard. For this seeming asininity, and for not having a rope, Antipholus rebukes Dromio and promises him a future beating. The servant is then sent to Adriana for bail money.

Act 4, Scene 2

Luciana and Adriana discuss the apparent infidelity of Antipholus. Dromio of Syracuse enters and tells of the need for bail. The women, who think he is Dromio of Ephesus, send him back with the required funds.

Act 4, Scene 3

Antipholus of Syracuse is wearing the gold chain provided by Angelo. Dromio of Syracuse arrives with the bail money, but of course his master does not know what he is talking about. Antipholus attributes their confusion to the supernatural qualities of Ephesus. Consequently, when the Courtesan appears, asking if his gold chain is the one he has promised her, he responds by asserting that she must

be an agent of the devil. When she demands the return of a ring she had given him, the two Syracusans flee. The Courtesan reflects that Antipholus must surely be mad. She determines to tell Adriana of her husband's state.

Act 4, Scene 4

Antipholus of Ephesus, in the custody of the Officer, sees Dromio of Ephesus and thinks his bail money has arrived. This Dromio, however, has the rope he was sent to purchase. He is struck with it by the furious Antipholus and delivers an elaborate lament on being beaten. Adriana, Luciana, and the Courtesan arrive with Doctor Pinch, whom Adriana entreats to restore Antipholus to sanity. Antipholus, becoming more and more enraged, attempts to strike Adriana, and he and Dromio are restrained and tied up by a group of passersby. Pinch takes the two prisoners to Adriana's house for treatment. Antipholus and Dromio of Syracuse appear; the others flee, believing the two have escaped from Pinch and are bent on revenge.

Act 5, Scene 1

Angelo and the Merchant discuss the strange behavior of Antipholus of Ephesus. Antipholus and Dromio of Syracuse appear; Angelo charges Antipholus with dishonesty, and tempers flare. Antipholus and the Merchant draw their swords. Adriana, Luciana, and the Courtesan reappear, calling for help in capturing Antipholus and Dromio. The two Syracusans flee, taking sanctuary in the PRIORY. The Abbess of the Priory, Emilia, emerges. Adriana demands the return of her husband; the Abbess refuses to permit a violation of the right to sanctuary.

Adriana determines to appeal to the Duke. The Duke appears, with a retinue including the unfortunate Egeon, who is to be beheaded. Antipholus and Dromio of Ephesus arrive, having escaped from Pinch. Antipholus, too, demands justice of the Duke. Charges and countercharges are exchanged by Antipholus, Angelo, Adriana, and the Courtesan. The extent of the confusion overwhelms the Duke, who sends for the abbess. Egeon claims Antipholus of Ephesus as his son, but as it is the wrong Antipholus he addresses, he is repudiated. The abbess reappears with Antipholus and Dromio

"Methinks you are my glass, and not my brother" (*The Comedy of Errors* 5.1.417). The two Dromios, brothers separated at birth, are reunited at the end of the play. *(Courtesy of Culver Pictures, Inc.)*

of Syracuse. All are stunned by the presence, together for the first time, of the two sets of identical twins. The abbess recognizes Egeon and reveals that she is his long-lost wife, Emilia. The identities of the twins are quickly established, and Emilia invites all the company to a feast of celebration in the Priory.

COMMENTARY

The Comedy of Errors is an early work, lacking most of the features we associate with Shakespeare's masterpieces. It contains no brilliant dialogue or poetry, no very impressive characters, and, most strikingly, its plot line is difficult to take at all seriously. Of all Shakespeare's plays, *The Comedy of Errors* most nearly resembles a FARCE, pure and sim-

ple, which the *Oxford English Dictionary* defines as "a dramatic work (usually short) which has for its sole object to excite laughter."

This play is both short and funny, but it is also more than that. Shakespeare's genius lies in his concern with what it is to be human and here he elevates a common farce by means of telling depictions of the human condition. He presents and resolves disruptions and anxieties that invite sympathy and stimulate compassion. In watching or reading *The Comedy of Errors*, we experience an awareness of the value to an individual of relationships to other people. Further, the play presents aspects of the situation of women in Elizabethan society, a matter Shakespeare often dealt with. The redeeming power of love, a profound theme in much of the playwright's later work, is also presented here, in an uncomplicated foreshadowing of subtler renderings.

A traditional opinion among scholars and critics, only lately being revised, is that *The Comedy of Errors* is best regarded as an apprentice work, only marginally related to the greater plays that followed. There is some justification for this point of view. For one thing, the play is very conventional, conforming in staging and general outline to standard Elizabethan ideas, derived from what was known, from ancient Roman drama, of what constituted a proper play. In staging his play, Shakespeare was content to abide by most of the ancient conventions of the form. In accordance with accepted neoclassical doctrine, the action of the play takes place in a single place and in a single day. The setting consists of three buildings—the PHOENIX, the PORCUPINE, and the Priory, each labeled with a sign or emblem—in imitation of Roman stagecraft as it was understood in Shakespeare's time.

Moreover, Shakespeare's play is undeniably farcical in its assembled absurdities. These are simply conventions of farce, as acceptable to a 16th-century audience as those of the Marx Brothers are acceptable today, and no different in kind. In adding the twin servants to the story he received from PLAUTUS (see "Sources," below), Shakespeare doubled the chances for misadventure and created a set of complications that has been likened to a Bach fugue, but the principles of farce remain the same.

Another striking addition Shakespeare made, changing the character of the work in a very important way, is the SUBPLOT featuring Egeon. Egeon's explanation of his family's separation in 1.1 serves as a PROLOGUE to the play, a classical device that Shakespeare used more formally elsewhere. More important, Egeon's pathetic circumstances serve to color the farcical main plot: We cannot wholly forget this poor, unfortunate father to the Antipholus twins. Because this is a humorous play, we of course presume that all will end well, but we know that before it does this potential tragedy will have to be overcome somehow. Indeed, Egeon experiences a moment of extreme despair after his seeming rejection by his long-sought son (5.1.298–322). Thus, the coming reconciliation scene ends a truly important human crisis, as well as resolving the comic confusions of the central tale. Shakespeare, even as a young man at the beginning of his career, felt that a happy ending should not be divorced from an awareness of mortality and human frailty. In this he utterly transcends the genre of farce.

Some critics have charged that this device damages a play that might have been a fine farce but that, in its present form, is neither tragic nor wholly comic. However, modern opinion has generally held that the Egeon subplot is necessary, providing a moral ground for an otherwise unenlightening display of low comedy. In any case, this subplot is an early example of an important aspect of Shakespeare's art—the formulation of more than one point of view, generating different and potentially conflicting responses from the audience.

Chief among the characters involved in the central story of *The Comedy of Errors* is Adriana, one of the earliest of Shakespeare's many attractive heroines. Shakespeare developed Adriana from a stereotype of the contentious, jealous shrew, and she conforms to this image. But she is raised from a type to a real human being through the wit her creator gives her. Further, her evident loyalty to and love for her difficult husband render her quite sympathetic and admirable. She resembles such other Shakespearean women as Katherina in *The Taming of the Shrew* and Beatrice in *Much Ado About Nothing* in being sharp-tongued and independent-minded but ultimately tender and accepting. The playwright could thus present the reality of Elizabethan women whose personal strengths enabled them to temper, if

not overcome, the general subservience of their gender, while at the same time confirming the legitimacy of the system, as his own conservatism inclined him to do. Adriana is contrasted with her sister Luciana, who is a dimmer figure, demure and passive. The debate between the two women on the proper relation of man and wife (2.1.7–42) is a set-piece disputation of a sort often presented on the Elizabethan stage. Although Adriana is a much more interesting and appealing character, Luciana's attitude to marriage seems to prevail at the play's end, in keeping with the common opinion of the day, which most women and Shakespeare shared.

Many of Shakespeare's plays hinge on a basic political question, the nature of the relationships among the citizen, the ruler, and the state. In this early work, the matter is only touched upon, but in a fashion that reveals an attitude that the playwright was to hold all his life. In a brief but telling passage, the Duke of Ephesus refuses to allow any alteration in the laws (1.1.142–148). He is explicit: His personal honor requires this relationship to the state. This is a kingly ideal that is expressed repeatedly, in much greater elaboration, in later plays. That the young Shakespeare found occasion to present it here, without any compelling reason to do so, suggests its early importance for him.

For Shakespeare and his contemporaries, everyone, not just the king, took his or her identity from a relationship with society as a whole. One was not simply a conscious, individual being, but, more important, one occupied a position in the social framework. Shakespeare was to consider this matter of social identity in a number of ways in later plays; it is touched on in this early work. Antipholus of Syracuse is concerned for his lost selfhood when he regrets the loss of his family in a touching soliloquy (1.2.33–40) on his lack of contentment. Also, it is evident that the distress undergone by the four misidentified twins is caused by the loss of their sense of identity; as the people in their world fail to recognize them, they experience a painful uncertainty as to who they are themselves.

Antipholus of Syracuse, in his confusion, seeks to be remade through love, by Luciana. The transforming power of love was always an important theme for Shakespeare; in several later plays, it is a major concern. Here it is overwhelmed by the farce for the most part, but we see it roughly sketched out with reference to romantic love in the depiction of the marriage of Adriana and Antipholus of Ephesus, and in the wooing of Luciana by Antipholus of Syracuse. Familial love triumphs in the reunion at the close of the play. And Emilia, the abbess who provides the resolution when the Duke, for all his power, cannot, represents the strength of Christian grace and mercy, a transcendent form of love.

Shakespeare's interest in the inner and outer worlds of human experience is what makes him great. He writes of the web of relationships, both political and domestic, that make up a society, and his characters have inner lives that we can recognize as realistic. In *The Comedy of Errors*, although it is derivative and rather limited in range, we see his talent already beginning to produce a drama of conflict and resolution in a world of basic human concerns, using themes and materials that would recur in his mature work.

SOURCES OF THE PLAY

Shakespeare's principal source for *The Comedy of Errors* was *The Menaechmi*, a play by the ancient Roman playwright Plautus. The first English translation of *The Menaechmi*, by William WARNER, was not published until 1595, a little later than the date when Shakespeare's play was presumably written, but the playwright may have known the translation in manuscript, as was common at that time, or he might have read it in one of several 16th-century Latin editions. Shakespeare made a number of important changes in the story, as he usually did when using sources. His boldest and best-known alteration was the addition of a second set of misidentified twins, a twist he took from another play by Plautus, *Amphitryon*. A number of other changes result in a general shift in the qualities of the play. For example, a ribald emphasis on a husband's relations with a mistress is elevated to a concern with the virtues of courtship and marriage.

The subplot concerning Egeon may derive from any of a number of sources; the motif of separated and reunited families had been familiar since ancient times. Shakespeare surely knew it from the medieval *Gesta Romanorum*, translated by Richard ROBINSON—later a source for *The Merchant of Venice*—and the *Confessio Amantis*, by John GOWER—later a source for *Pericles*. However, the hostility between cities resulting in a traveler's death penalty comes from George GASCOIGNE's *Supposes* (performed 1566, published 1573), where the situation is invented as part of a ruse; it is used in the same way to dupe the Pedant in *The Taming of the Shrew.*

TEXT OF THE PLAY

The Comedy of Errors is sometimes said to have been the first play that Shakespeare wrote, although this cannot be proven. It was certainly one of his earliest. The play's first recorded performance was held on December 28, 1594, as part of a program of Christmas revels at Gray's Inn (see INNS OF COURT). This private performance, the play's brevity (with fewer than 1,800 lines, it is Shakespeare's shortest), and its resemblance to ancient Roman comedy have prompted some scholars to suggest that the play was commissioned for this presentation to a particularly learned audience. However, most scholarly opinion holds that it was written at an earlier date; estimates have ranged from the late 1580s to 1594.

The play was initially published in the FIRST FOLIO in 1623. This version is believed to have been derived from Shakespeare's FOUL PAPERS. The Folio contains the only early publication of *The Comedy of Errors*, and it has been the basis for all subsequent editions of the play.

THEATRICAL HISTORY OF THE PLAY

The Gray's Inn performance of December 1594 and a performance at the court of King JAMES I in the Christmas season of 1604 are the only known early productions, although various references in contemporary plays and books suggest that there were probably other 16th- and 17th-century stagings. In the 18th century and well into the 19th, all presentations of *The Comedy of Errors*, with the possible exception of a brief run in 1741, were adaptations that varied more or less grossly from the original. The brevity of the play, its esoteric relation to classical drama, and a sense that it was more an "apprentice" piece than a mature work seem to have combined to provide justification for a long series of illegitimate productions by Thomas HULL and others. Among these was a 1786 OPERA by the English composer Stephen STORACE with a libretto by Lorenzo da Ponte (1749–1838), Mozart's favorite librettist. But perhaps the strangest of these offspring was the 1819 opera produced by Frederick REYNOLDS, whose libretto included songs from *As You Like It, Love's Labour's Lost, King Lear,* and *Othello,* plus two of the *Sonnets,* and which used additional dialogue and entire scenes from various sources, only some of them Shakespearean.

Shakespeare's play was first restored to the stage in its proper form by Samuel PHELPS in 1855. It has gradually increased in popularity since then and has often been produced in recent years. Variations on the play continued to be produced in the 20th century; the 1938 musical comedy *The Boys from Syracuse,* by Richard Rodgers and Lorenz Hart, is an example. In 1976 Trevor NUNN made a FILM of *The Comedy of Errors* with Judi DENCH as Adriana, and the play has been made for TELEVISION several times.

CHARACTERS

Adriana Character in *The Comedy of Errors,* the jealous but loving wife of Antipholus of Ephesus. Adriana first appears in 2.1, complaining that Antipholus is late for lunch. She argues with her sister, Luciana, about the proper obedience owed a husband, in a standard disputation on marital relations that was common in Shakespeare's day. While Luciana adopts the position that a man is rightly the master of his wife, Adriana asserts, "There's none but asses will be bridled so" (2.1.14). Later in the scene, she bemoans her husband's attentions to other women, and jealousy is her characteristic trait throughout the play, finally triggering a humorous but acid sermonette by the Abbess, Emilia, in the final scene (5.1.69–86).

The circumstances of confusion and error that create the atmosphere of the play also stimulate Adriana's jealous streak. In 2.2 she accosts Antipholus of Syracuse, thinking him to be her husband, and demands that he come home to eat. Bemused and baffled, he nevertheless goes with her, and there ensues (3.1) the central misidentification of the play; Adriana refuses to admit her real husband to their home, believing him to be an imposter.

In 4.2 Luciana reports to Adriana a declaration of love from the man both believe to be Antipholus of Ephesus; both women thus believe that Adriana's husband is attempting to betray her by courting her own sister. Adriana rails against her husband but concludes: "Ah, but I think him better than I say, . . . / My heart prays for him, though my tongue do curse" (4.2.25–28).

This note of wifely affection grows stronger as the play hurries to its resolution, for Adriana is truly fond of her husband, irascible and domineering though he may be. She tries to aid him, once she has concluded that he is temporarily insane; the confusions of the plot have led her (and others) to this error. She appears in the final scene just as Antipholus of Syracuse is about to fight a duel, and, thinking him her husband, she implores, "Hold, hurt him not for God's sake; he is mad" (5.1.33). Antipholus and his servant flee into the PRIORY. Adriana follows her husband there and demands that the Abbess turn Antipholus over to her. The Abbess refuses, however, and Adriana has recourse to the Duke. His investigation triggers the final resolution of the play's confusions, although Adriana plays no great part in that process.

An interesting tradition has it that Adriana was written as a portrait of Anne HATHAWAY, but modern scholarship debunks this idea. Nevertheless, Adriana was clearly an important creation for Shakespeare, for she is a markedly more fully drawn and consequential figure than her predecessor in his source for the play. She is an early example of a Shakespearean character type that recurs often in the plays (e.g., Katherina, in *The Taming of the Shrew,* and Beatrice, in *Much Ado About Nothing*)—an independent woman whose sharp words and sometimes forbidding manner conceal a tender heart. Adriana's dual nature would come to typify Shakespeare's greatest characters. The playwright insisted on presenting multiple points of view about a character or situation, offering his audience varying and often conflicting impressions, and thus re-creating on the stage the inconsistencies of actual life.

Aegeon See Egeon.

Aemilia See Emilia.

Angelo Minor character in *The Comedy of Errors*, a goldsmith and friend of Antipholus of Ephesus. Angelo makes the gold necklace that figures in the confusions and misunderstandings at the play's heart. His effort to have Antipholus arrested for debt, having failed to pay for the necklace, results in Antipholus of Syracuse retreating into the sanctuary of the PRIORY (5.1.37). This flight triggers the play's final resolution.

Antipholus of Ephesus and Antipholus of Syracuse Characters in *The Comedy of Errors*, long-separated twins who are comically confused with each other and eventually reunited. The twins were parted, each with a different parent, in a shipwreck when they were infants. Twin servants, each called Dromio, were being brought up with the boys, and they too were separated in the wreck, one going with each master. In 1.1 the twins' father, Egeon, explains their history before they appear, so the audience knows of their relationship, though neither they nor any of the other characters do. In adulthood, the twins have both become merchants, each from a different city, but each bearing the same name.

Antipholus of Syracuse arrives in Ephesus, searching the world for his lost brother, for he cannot feel whole until he finds his family. In Ephesus he is mistaken for his twin, a well-known local merchant, and various strangers startle him by knowing his name and assuming he knows them. He finds himself dining in his brother's home, and his brother's wife, Adriana, believes him to be her husband. Misunderstanding and confusion continue to abound until Antipholus of Syracuse is driven to take refuge in a priory.

The two brothers are distinctly different characters. Antipholus of Syracuse is so completely mystified by his curious circumstances that he blindly accepts them. Meanwhile, Antipholus of Ephesus has been subjected to similar difficulties, but his responses are characteristically more angry than bemused. For example, when locked out of his house by servants and wife (who believe him an imposter, for the other Antipholus is dining there), he proposes to force his way in with a crowbar but is dissuaded from this course.

In the end the brothers are reunited, as the Duke of Ephesus attempts to resolve the disorders that the confusion has created. The Dromios are brought back together again as well; Antipholus of Ephesus and Adriana are reconciled; Antipholus of Syracuse is free to woo Luciana; and the twins' parents, Egeon and Emilia, rediscover each other, too. The story of the twins presents in an early work a theme that was to be important in Shakespearean COMEDY: the power of providential happenings to defeat potential evil through a general reconciliation. This theme provides the moral ground beneath the farcical atmosphere of *The Comedy of Errors*.

Balthasar Minor character in *The Comedy of Errors*, a merchant who is a friend of Antipholus of Ephesus. Balthasar is present when, in 3.1, Antipholus is kept out of his own home by his wife and servants, who believe he is an imposter. Balthasar dissuades Antipholus from breaking down the door, on the grounds that such an action would damage his reputation in the neighborhood.

Courtesan Minor character in *The Comedy of Errors*, a "professional entertainer" visited offstage by Antipholus of Ephesus after he is mistakenly rejected by his wife, Adriana. The Courtesan appears later, in 4.3, to claim a necklace Antipholus promised her in exchange for her ring. She mistakenly approaches Antipholus of Syracuse, who rejects her as a sorceress or agent of the devil. She goes to Adriana and accuses her husband of lunacy and of the ring's theft, thus triggering the pursuit that results in Antipholus of Ephesus's treatment for insanity at the hands of Pinch.

Dromio of Ephesus and Dromio of Syracuse Two characters in *The Comedy of Errors*, twin servants to the twin masters Antipholus of Ephesus and Antipholus of Syracuse. The Dromios were separated from each other in infancy, each with a similarly separated master, in a shipwreck. They share with their masters the confusions and errors that mistaken identities lead to. As comic buffoons, the Dromios receive numerous beatings as their masters' affairs become increasingly disordered, and they respond with quips and quibbles, in a tradition of stock humorous servants and slaves that extends back at least to the Roman drama from which Shakespeare took much of the material for the play. The Dromios also share with their masters the joyful reunion at the end of the play.

Shakespeare may have taken the name Dromio from the play *Mother Bombie* by John LYLY (published 1594), who may, in turn, have based it on the name Dromo, frequently used for slaves in the work of the Roman dramatist TERENCE.

Duke Solinus of Ephesus Character in *The Comedy of Errors*, the ruler of the city of Ephesus, where the play takes place. The Duke first appears in 1.1 to condemn Egeon, a wandering merchant from Syracuse who has arrived in Ephesus, unaware of the hostilities between that city and his own, and is sentenced to either death or an immense fine, which he cannot pay. Egeon tells of his separated family and his search for them, and the Duke expresses pity for the old man but says he cannot exempt him from the law.

The sources and use of power are subjects that were important to the playwright, and they are dealt with in a number of the plays. In this early work, the Duke regrets that he cannot act on his pity but explains that the law explicitly limits his range of action, while at the same time it is the implicit source of his authority. His crown and his dignity are equated with his oath, a matter of law. However, the Duke will bend as far as he feels he legally can, out of pity for the aged wanderer, and he gives Egeon a day in which to find some way to raise his ransom money. This day becomes the time in which the play proper takes place.

Neither the Duke nor Egeon reappears until the final scene, when the confusions and mistaken identities that are the chief material of the play have reached a climax. When he reenters, at 5.1.130, the Duke is still sympathetic to Egeon's plight, although the unfortunate victim is escorted by the Headsman and seems fated soon to die. The Duke is immediately swept up in the misunderstandings of the central plot, being requested to rule against the abbess, Emilia, who has granted sanctuary in her PRIORY to Antipholus of Syracuse.

When Antipholus of Ephesus appears, the true complexity of the situation becomes apparent. The Duke, the representative of secular law, is clearly baffled, so he sends for Emilia, who enters with the second Antipholus, bringing the twins together for the first time. Further, Emilia recognizes Egeon as her long-lost husband, and the resolution of the play's complexities begins. The intervention of Christian grace and mercy, represented by Emilia and the Priory, has tempered the insensitive cruelties of secular justice. However, the Duke is quite evidently pleased with the outcome, in keeping with his consistently sympathetic attitude. When Emilia proposes a "gossip feast" or celebratory party, the Duke accepts with enthusiasm and leads the company offstage to close the play.

Shakespeare may have taken the name Solinus (which appears only in 1.1.1) from that of an ancient geographer, Gaius Julius Solinus, who described (ca. A.D. 200) the seaports of the Mediterranean. His work was published in an English translation in 1587, a few years before *The Comedy of Errors* was probably written.

Egeon (Aegeon) Character in *The Comedy of Errors*, the condemned man who proves to be the father of the long-separated twins Antipholus of Ephesus and Antipholus of Syracuse. Egeon's tale is presented only in the first and last scenes of the play, framing the principal plot. A wandering merchant from Syracuse, in Sicily, Egeon comes to Ephesus, on the Aegean coast of Asia Minor, not knowing that hostility has arisen between that city and his home. The penalty of death or a large ransom has been imposed by each city upon any citizen of the other who enters it. Egeon has thus been sentenced to pay a thousand marks of ransom or die.

In 1.1 his situation is revealed in his conversation with Solinus, the Duke of Ephesus. Egeon elaborates on the tragedy that has enveloped his life, beginning when he was separated from his wife and one of his infant twin sons in a shipwreck 23 years before, never to see them again. The other son, at the age of 18, had insisted on setting out to search for his lost brother. Egeon himself has unsuccessfully spent the last five years looking for news of either twin. The Duke, sympathetic though stern, offers Egeon the freedom of the city for the coming day so that he can beg or borrow the money to pay his ransom. These hours become the time of the action of the play.

Egeon does not reappear until well into the final scene of the play, but the audience cannot forget his desperate plight. Although the comic misadventures and errors that follow are chiefly farcical, they are colored by our somber recollection of Egeon's imminent fate.

In the final scene, Egeon is escorted on stage by the Duke, accompanied by the Headsman and seemingly doomed to die. The Duke reminds us of his plight (5.1.130–132) before being sidetracked into attempting to unravel the confusions of the main plot. Amid these complexities, Egeon, upon seeing Antipholus of Ephesus, believes him to be the other Antipholus, the son who left Syracuse five years earlier. He identifies himself to this Antipholus, only to be rejected, of course, for Antipholus of Ephesus does not know him. Egeon's stricken response is rendered in a moving passage (5.1.298–322); the Duke concludes that Egeon's "age and dangers" have driven him mad.

As the confusion and errors are eventually resolved and the play reaches its conclusion, Egeon is a spectator, for the most part; the principals in this denouement are the two sets of twins and Emilia, Egeon's long-lost wife, whose recognition of her husband begins the resolution. Although he has good lines in both 1.1 and 5.1 and is an important figure, Egeon is not so much a fully developed character as he is a vehicle for a simple, secondary plot, an evocation of pathos intended to temper our view of the central wrangle of error and delusion.

Emilia (Aemilia)   Character in *The Comedy of Errors*, the stern and peremptory Abbess of the PRIORY who is revealed to be the long-lost wife of Egeon and mother of the twins Antipholus of Ephesus and Antipholus of Syracuse. She first appears in the final scene (at 5.1.37), after Antipholus and Dromio of Syracuse take refuge in her Priory, a place of legal sanctuary. She determines that Adriana has been jealous of her husband and delivers a short, epigrammatic sermon on the evils of jealous womankind (5.1.69–86). Emilia further declares that the

sanctuary of the Priory may not be violated by the return of the two refugees, and she exits briskly.

Later in the scene, having been sent for by the Duke of Ephesus to help resolve the confusions that have by now come to a head, Emilia returns with Antipholus of Syracuse, placing the twins on stage together for the first time (5.1.329). Ten lines later, she recognizes the condemned Egeon as her lost husband. She relates how kidnappers had stolen away the infants who had survived the shipwreck that separated the family years before. The Duke deduces that these infants are now the adults Antipholus and Dromio of Ephesus. After all is revealed, she invites the company to the Priory for a "gossip's feast" of celebration (5.1.405), to which all depart, ending the play. The term *gossip's feast* refers to a baptismal or christening party, underlining the importance of Emilia as a symbol of Christian mercy, softening the hard authority of the Duke's laws, and embodying the resolution of the play's complexities.

Headsman   Minor character in *The Comedy of Errors*, the ax man prepared to behead Egeon. The Executioner, who does not speak, appears in 5.1 in the entourage of Duke Solinus. His presence attests to Egeon's desperate plight.

Jailor   Minor character in *The Comedy of Errors*, a guard. The attendant assigned to the condemned Egeon in 1.1 speaks only one line and functions to emphasize the power of the state and the extremity of Egeon's predicament.

Luce   Minor character in *The Comedy of Errors*, a servant who, with Adriana, refuses Antipholus of Ephesus entrance to his own home in 3.1, believing him to be an imposter. Luce is often identified with Nell, who is referred to later in the play.

Luciana   Character in *The Comedy of Errors*, the sister-in-law of Antipholus of Ephesus and the beloved of Antipholus of Syracuse. Luciana first appears in an argument with her sister Adriana about marital relations, in a standard disputation of the day. Luciana says that a man is properly the master of his wife and urges: "O, know he is the bridle of your will" (2.1.13).

Luciana's demure pliancy is apparently attractive to Antipholus of Syracuse, for when he finds himself in his brother's house, not knowing himself to be mistaken for his twin, he meets Luciana, falls in love, and attempts to court the object of his affections. Luciana, believing him to be her brother-in-law, is naturally horrified by his advances and chastises him roundly (3.2.1–28). Moreover, she describes this exchange to Adriana, thereby furthering the confusion and misunderstanding at the heart of the play. Luciana's subsequent importance to the action is slight. Even when Antipholus of Syracuse observes at the play's conclusion that the reestablishment of his identity will permit him to court her in earnest, Luciana remains silent.

Luciana represents a type, rather than a fully drawn human being. She is the modest and sub-servient female, whose stipulated position in Elizabethan society served to perpetuate an ideal notion of the family (and, by extension, society at large) as a secure and lasting hierarchy, decreed by God and tradition and undisturbed by change or individual assertion. (Such assertion was of course present among Elizabethan womanhood, as represented by Adriana.) The two sisters together constitute an early attempt by the playwright to achieve a complex portrait of contemporary femininity. While Luciana is thus an incomplete character, she foreshadows aspects of later, more successful Shakespearean heroines, such as Viola in *Twelfth Night* and Imogen in *Cymbeline*.

Merchant Either of two minor characters in *The Comedy of Errors*. Two Merchants appear in this play (they enter first in 1.2 and 4.1, respectively), and, while Shakespeare apparently made no distinction between them by name, they are plainly different people. The first to appear is familiar with the affairs of Ephesus, offering advice to the foreigner Antipholus of Syracuse and warning him not to reveal himself as a Syracusan, lest he be sentenced to death. Having thus reminded the audience of Egeon's desperate plight, this Merchant disappears from the play. He is generally distinguished in modern editions as "First Merchant."

The "Second Merchant," however, seems to be a visitor himself, for he must inquire (5.1.4) about the reputation of Antipholus of Ephesus, a well-known local figure. Attempting to collect a debt owed Angelo by one Antipholus, the Merchant mistakenly challenges Antipholus of Syracuse to a duel, precipitating that twin's flight into the PRIORY, which ultimately leads to the resolution of the play.

Messenger Minor character in *The Comedy of Errors*. In 5.1.168–184 he brings Adriana a frantic account of the escape of Antipholus of Ephesus from the custody of Pinch and comically describes Antipholus's revenge on that pseudo-physician.

Nell Minor character in *The Comedy of Errors*, a servant in Adriana's household. Dromio of Syracuse refers to Nell in his account to his master of the "kitchen wench" (3.2.93) who claims him as her husband. This parallels Adriana's mistaken identification of the master, Antipholus of Syracuse. In a long, broadly comic passage (3.2.71–154), Dromio describes Nell as so grotesquely fat that her other, equally unattractive features are best equated with the continents of the globe.

Though Nell is described here (and in 5.1.414–416) as the kitchen maid, Luce, who appears in 3.1.48–64, is also identified as the kitchen maid (at 4.4.72–73). This has produced confusion; the two are often thought to be the same character. Some editors of the play have gone so far as to rename Luce as Nell in both stage directions and text.

The different names may be the result of an error on Shakespeare's part; such inconsistencies are common throughout the plays. On the other hand, Dromio may be sarcastically using a pointedly common woman's name to refer to Luce, who is, to his mind, a very common woman. Most simply, the playwright may have expected us to conclude that Adriana had more than one kitchen maid. If this is the case, and Luce and Nell are not identical, then Nell never actually appears in the play.

Officer Minor character in *The Comedy of Errors*, an agent empowered to arrest debtors. In 4.1 a Merchant engages the Officer to arrest Angelo, who owes him money. Antipholus of Ephesus owes Angelo enough to cover his debt to the Merchant, so Angelo in turn pays the Officer to arrest Antipholus. In 4.4 the Officer turns Antipholus over to Pinch.

Pinch, Dr.   Character in *The Comedy of Errors,* a quack physician. Dr. Pinch is consulted when Antipholus of Ephesus, as a result of the confusion and mistaken identities that are the chief business of the play, is presumed to be insane. Antipholus later describes him as: ". . . one Pinch, a hungry lean-fac'd villain; / A mere anatomy, a mountebank, / A thread-bare juggler, and a fortune-teller, / A needy-hollow-ey'd-sharp-looking-wretch; / A living dead man. . . ." (5.1.238–242).

Pinch is not a physician in any modern sense; he is merely a man of some learning. He is identified as a "schoolmaster" (in a stage direction in 4.4.38) and as a "conjuror," or exorcist (4.4.45 and 5.1.243). Both references are to the fact that he can speak Latin, which was commonly believed in Shakespeare's day to be the language of spirits and ghosts.

Whatever his appearance or qualifications, Dr Pinch's prescription for a case of lunacy ("They must be bound and laid in some dark room" [4.4.92]) was widespread in the 16th and 17th centuries. Although it now seems inhumane, both insanity and this particular treatment of it were common subjects of humor on the Elizabethan stage. The same regime is meted out to Malvolio, in *Twelfth Night,* for instance. If Pinch seems a brutal doctor to us, no less so seems his fiery, filthy comeuppance (5.1.171–178), though we may be sure the original audience delighted in it, for such abuse was a comic staple. Shakespeare at least keeps it offstage.

Contention, The

Abbreviated title of the first QUARTO edition of *2 Henry VI.* Published in 1594 by Thomas MILLINGTON, the play was originally titled, in the florid manner of the time, *The First part of the Contention betwixt the two famous Houses of Yorke and Lancaster, with the death of the good Duke Humphrey: And the banishment and death of the Duke of Suffolke, and the Tragicall end of the proud Cardinall of Winchester,* *with the notable Rebellion of Iacke Cade: And the Duke of Yorkes first claime unto the Crowne. The Contention,* known as the Q1 edition of *2 Henry VI,* is a shorter, inferior version of the F edition in the FIRST FOLIO, published in 1623. The Q2 edition of *2 Henry VI,* varying very little from Q1, was published by Millington in 1600, also as *The Contention.* Q3, a more heavily edited version, appeared in 1619, combined with a BAD QUARTO edition of *3 Henry VI* in one volume now known as *The Whole Contention.*

The existence of Q1 has generated a number of theories. It has been regarded as an original play, written earlier than *2 Henry VI,* probably by Robert GREENE, George PEELE, Thomas NASHE, Christopher MARLOWE, or possibly Shakespeare himself (or some combination of these in collaboration). Later, according to this theory, Shakespeare revised the play for a new production, creating the F text.

Another theory holds that *The Contention* is a "reported" version of *2 Henry VI,* i.e., a bad quarto that was assembled from the recollections of actors or viewers for purposes of unauthorized publication. It has even been speculated that *The Contention* may be a reported version of yet another play, a lost original *2 Henry VI* would then be a revision of either *The Contention* or of the lost play.

All these theories can be supported in one way or another, and the truth of the matter cannot be ascertained from the existing evidence. However, modern scholarship has generally, though not unanimously, accepted the second of these propositions—that *The Contention* is a reported, or "memorial," text of *2 Henry VI.* It was perhaps created in 1593, at the time of the bankruptcy and temporary collapse of the PEMBROKE'S MEN, the acting company that originally produced the play.

Coriolanus
SYNOPSIS
Act 1, Scene 1

Rioting Romans seek the death of Martius, a leading aristocrat who is known for his pride. Menenius stalls them with a humorous fable that justifies the aristocracy. Martius arrives, and his scathing anger quiets the rioters. He reports that the rioting has resulted in a concession to the commoners: The people have been allowed to elect their own judges, called tribunes, two of whom are Sicinius and Brutus. News arrives that ROME is threatened by a neighboring tribe, the Volscians. A municipal delegation—the generals Cominius and Lartius, some Senators, and the new tribunes—seek Martius's support in repelling the invaders. He agrees, and remarks on his desire to fight the noble Volscian general, Aufidius, who is a former foe. The aristocrats all depart to prepare for war and leave the tribunes, who talk of their hatred of Martius.

Act 1, Scene 2

At CORIOLES, the Volscian Senators meet with Aufidius to plan their campaign. Aufidius will take the field, and the Senators will defend Corioles.

Act 1, Scene 3

Martius's mother, Volumnia, berates his wife, Virgilia, because she is not pleased that he has gone to war. She declares that her son's honorable death would bring her more joy than his birth had. She describes the wounds she hopes her son will receive, which will increase his honor, and she mocks Virgilia's revulsion. Virgilia's friend Valeria appears, and they discuss the son of Martius and Virgilia, who resembles his father. Valeria brings the news that Martius and Cominius have Corioles under siege.

Act 1, Scene 4

At Corioles, a delegation of Volscian Senators defies the Romans, and combat begins. The Romans retreat. Martius curses them and charges alone through the city's gates. The Romans believe he has been killed, but he emerges from Corioles, chased by Volscians, and the Romans rally to his defense.

Act 1, Scene 5

Corioles has been taken, and Martius insists, despite his wounds, that he join Cominius who is fighting Aufidius.

Act 1, Scene 6

Martius arrives as Cominius withdraws against superior forces. Full of enthusiasm for battle, Martius insists that he resume the fight and face Aufidius.

Act 1, Scene 7

Lartius places a Lieutenant (1) in charge of Corioles and goes to join Cominius and Martius.

Act 1, Scene 8

Martius and Aufidius fight. Several Volscians arrive to assist their general, but Martius drives them all away. Aufidius cries out that he has been shamed by their support.

Act 1, Scene 9

Martius modestly objects to hearing his deeds praised amidst the cheers of the soldiers. Cominius proposes that in honor of his courage at Corioles, he shall hereafter be known as Coriolanus.

Act 1, Scene 10

Aufidius rages against Martius, who has now defeated him five times. He swears that next time he will not lose even if he must resort to treachery rather than valor.

Act 2, Scene 1

Menenius berates Sicinius and Brutus for their animosity toward Martius, and he scorns the bad judgment of the common people they represent. Martius, now Coriolanus, returns and is formally welcomed and taken by the aristocrats to the Capitol to receive further honors. The tribunes voice their resentment of Coriolanus, who will now be nominated as consul, the highest office in Rome. However, they reflect that his pride will probably prevent him from displaying his scars to the commoners—as tradition requires—and that as the commoners' representatives, they can then oppose him and keep him from the office.

Act 2, Scene 2

An Officer and his two fellows speculate that Coriolanus's pride will lead to his rejection as consul, though they believe him worthy of the office. Coriolanus is nominated for the consulate, but he asks to be excused from exhibiting himself to the common people. The tribunes refuse to accept the idea, and the aristocrats attempt to persuade Coriolanus to go through with it. Though uneasy, he agrees and goes with them to perform the ceremony.

Act 2, Scene 3

A group of Citizens (1) decide to support Coriolanus if he will formally ask them to. Coriolanus arrives, dressed in the traditional humble garb, and he asks groups of citizens for their support, though in a surly, begrudging manner. They agree to support him, and Menenius and the tribunes confirm his election. Coriolanus and Menenius leave, and the tribunes upbraid the citizens for supporting the proud Coriolanus. They convince them to rescind their approval before Coriolanus's formal installation as consul.

Act 3, Scene 1

Coriolanus hears that Aufidius has expressed a desire to fight with him, and he wishes for a war. The tribunes report that a mob has risen against Coriolanus. Despite the efforts of the aristocrats to calm him, Coriolanus angrily declares the commoners unworthy of a voice in the selection of a consul. The tribunes declare him a traitor to the laws of Rome and summon the mob. The mob follows Sicinius's lead and demands that Coriolanus be killed. Coriolanus draws his sword, but the aristocrats take him away. Brutus and Sicinius continue to raise the mob's fury, but Menenius convinces them to follow legal procedures and try Coriolanus for treason in the tribunes' court. He promises to get the general to attend it.

Act 3, Scene 2

Volumnia helps the other aristocrats convince Coriolanus to swallow his pride and apologize to the commoners as a matter of practical politics. After lengthy argument, he finally agrees.

Act 3, Scene 3

Brutus and Sicinius instruct a subordinate to prepare the crowd to support whatever line they take in the trial of Coriolanus, whom they plan to provoke to anger. Coriolanus and his friends appear, and at first Coriolanus mildly makes the recantation demanded by the tribunes. When Sicinius calls him a traitor, however, he responds wrathfully and rejects the authority of the common people in insulting terms. The tribunes convict him of treasonous hostility to the people's justice and declare him banished from Rome; the mob takes up the cry. Coriolanus replies angrily that he shall be glad to

leave a city controlled by such ignorant commoners, and he departs. The tribunes encourage the mob to follow him out of the gates of the city.

Act 4, Scene 1

Coriolanus bids farewell to his family and friends and departs for exile.

Act 4, Scene 2

Volumnia rages furiously at the victorious tribunes.

Act 4, Scene 3

A Roman (2) gives information to a Volsce, telling him of Coriolanus's banishment. He recommends that the Volscians strike against the city now that it has lost its most illustrious general.

Act 4, Scene 4

Coriolanus, disguised as a poor man, arrives in ANTIUM and is directed to Aufidius's house.

Act 4, Scene 5

Coriolanus finds Aufidius and tells him bitterly of his banishment; he offers to fight for the Volscians against Rome. Aufidius is ecstatic at encountering his great enemy and agrees enthusiastically. Aufidius's servants marvel that their master has accepted a poor wanderer, but when one of them learns the truth they rejoice at the prospects for a successful war.

Act 4, Scene 6

The tribunes refuse to believe the news that the Volscians are again attacking Roman territory, led by Coriolanus. A crowd arrives, and the Citizens (1) declare that they had had misgivings about the banishment all along. The worried tribunes hope that the news will prove untrue.

Act 4, Scene 7

A Volscian Lieutenant (2) worries that Aufidius will be overshadowed by Coriolanus's growing popularity among their soldiers. Aufidius confides that he intends eventually to turn against the Roman.

Act 5, Scene 1

Cominius reports that Coriolanus, whose Volscian army threatens the city, has refused to meet with him. The tribunes convince Menenius to attempt to beg mercy for the city. Cominius declares that

Menenius will also fail, and that their only hope lies in Coriolanus's mother and wife.

Act 5, Scene 2

Volscian guards declare to Menenius that Coriolanus has specifically refused entry to any Roman. When Menenius insists that he is an old friend and will be accepted, they mock him. Coriolanus appears and pointedly rejects Menenius.

Act 5, Scene 3

Volumnia appears, accompanied by Virgilia, Valeria, and a Boy—Coriolanus's son. Coriolanus becomes increasingly upset as he hears and rejects their petitions for mercy. Finally, a long speech by Volumnia convinces him to make peace with Rome. Aufidius, in an aside, observes that he now has the means to get revenge on Coriolanus.

Act 5, Scene 4

Menenius and Sicinius despair for the city, but news arrives of Volumnia's success and the withdrawal of the Volscian forces.

Act 5, Scene 5

The Senators thankfully welcome Volumnia and the other women back to Rome.

Act 5, Scene 6

Aufidius consults with a group of Conspirators. They agree to support his charges of treason against Coriolanus and then to help him kill his enemy. Coriolanus appears, followed by an enthusiastic crowd of Volscians. Coriolanus presents his treaty with Rome as a conquest, but Aufidius accuses him of treachery. He calls him unmanly because he has given up the city in response to a woman's plea. Coriolanus angrily threatens to beat him, but Aufidius turns the crowd against him. When the mob loudly demands that Coriolanus be lynched as an enemy, the Conspirators attack him in a group and kill him. Aufidius defends the killing as motivated by patriotic rage, but he goes on to observe that Coriolanus was a great warrior and stipulates that he should have a noble funeral.

COMMENTARY

Coriolanus is one of the most politically oriented of Shakespeare's plays; it depicts political confrontation between social classes. However, though *Coriolanus* opens with a civil insurrection and features the political manipulations of tribunes and aristocrats, Roman political strife is not the principal subject matter. Rather, it provides a context for the main plot, which is another sort of story. The play is first and foremost a TRAGEDY, the personal story of a great man whose greatness is accompanied by moral and psychological failings that bring about his downfall. As Coriolanus's story unfolds, Roman politics fall away, and the climactic confrontation in 5.3 does not oppose social classes or even political rivals. Rather, it presents an internal conflict within the protagonist, the clash between his pride in himself and his psychological dependence on his mother.

Coriolanus's importance to the plot is immediately established in Act 1, where he is prominently regarded as a brilliant military hero. Moreover, after the tragedy has run its course, the statement that "he shall have a noble memory" (5.6.153) confirms this status for the protagonist. In between, his excessive pride produces catastrophe. Even before Coriolanus appears, his pride is carefully established as a major theme of the play in the remarks of the First Citizen; then it is flagrantly demonstrated with his first entrance. After Menenius has established a truce of sorts with the rioting commoners, Coriolanus appears and destroys it. His first three lines are a burst of anger that immediately creates a gulf between himself and the people that will never be bridged. He has the pride appropriate to a warrior, but he lacks a sense of ordinary social intercourse, let alone of compromise. He does not consider the justice of the commoners' complaints; he is simply offended that they should question aristocratic authority at all. His response is to suggest a massacre: "Hang 'em! . . . I'd make a quarry / With thousands of these quarter'd slaves" (1.1.189–198). From this initial outburst to his final anger at Aufidius's taunt that he is a "boy of tears" (5.6.101), Coriolanus is incapable of flexibility. He has sense enough to see the propriety in other approaches—he understands Volumnia's Machiavellian argument in 3.2, and, too late, he courts the Volscian common people in Act 5—but his pride repeatedly overwhelms his common sense.

The influence of Volumnia is the driving power behind Coriolanus and the play. Well may she boast to her son, "Thou art my warrior: / I help to frame thee" (5.3.62–63), for she has bred in her son the pride that makes him believe that he and his class are incontestably superior. Yet Coriolanus is entirely incapable of dealing with the play's developments. At two crucial moments, Volumnia makes demands of her son that are inconsistent with his sense of his own superiority. After her persuasion in 3.2, he attempts to compromise with the political world, but the tribunes trigger his too-ready anger, and he is banished from Rome. Thus, he loses his only honorable standing—as a Roman

Shakespeare's Coriolanus is a great and noble warrior, but excessive pride leads to his defeat. *(Courtesy of Culver Pictures, Inc.)*

warrior—and he deserts to the Volscians. When his mother comes to plead that he refrain from assaulting the city, in 5.3, he is trapped. If he destroys Rome, he will destroy himself psychologically through his mother's rejection, but by giving in to her he accepts an ignominious death at the hands of Aufidius. His responses are woefully limited, and his inflexibility proves his undoing; he is fragile in his great strength. Yet it was his mother who bred in him the sternly martial pride that brought him to eminence in the first place. This ironic situation demonstrates the basic theme of all Shakespearean tragedy: Great strength is inextricably interwoven with correspondingly great weakness.

The changing world of Rome provides the secondary component of the play, its political plot. The heavy political emphasis of much modern commentary on *Coriolanus* is not misplaced, for the conflicts that spark the tragic hero's downfall are representative of the social clashes that constitute much of political history. The play stresses a theme that was important to Shakespeare when he wrote his earlier English HISTORY PLAYS: the impact of immoral behavior in the ruling class on the peace and prosperity of all of society. As Shakespeare knew from his source, PLUTARCH's *Lives,* the ancient warrior was thought of as a member of peaceful society as well as a leader in war. To maintain his honor, he was obliged to participate in society by submitting to its laws and customs just as did his nonheroic fellow citizens. Coriolanus lacks the moral discipline to honor this social contract; indeed, he would rather abandon the contract altogether and join Rome's enemies than honor it and accept Rome's common people. Not only does he imperil himself, he endangers the city's very existence. Thus, the personality defects of the protagonist have profound political consequences.

The other aristocrats are conscious of the need to compromise with the commoners, and to a certain extent they counteract Coriolanus's ill effects. However, their grudging willingness to accept the need of such an arrangement also corrupts the social contract. Menenius's "belly speech" (1.1.95–153) is politic and mild, but it is accompanied by an undisguised disdain for the common man, the "great toe" (1.1.154) of society. In

3.2.41–86 Volumnia recommends that Coriolanus be hypocritical with the people. This Machiavellian speech betrays a cynical disregard for "th'ignorant" (3.2.76) that flouts the social cooperation that it supposedly furthers. Coriolanus's indignant assumption that Brutus knows nothing of "service" (3.3.84) is typical of the aristocratic rejection of social cooperation, though the tribune is obviously an industrious representative of his constituency. In fact, one may conclude that Brutus provides more useful service to the commoners than the proud warrior does to his own caste. Coriolanus represents the ideal of one sort of virtue: the warrior's single-minded quest for glory as the military hero of his people. This ideal is no longer desirable in a community that acknowledges the demands of all its people. The emergence of the new political morality causes Coriolanus's fall; put another way, the stresses of that emergence are enacted in his catastrophe and death.

These themes are reinforced by a fascinating and bizarre motif, the confusion of normal love, sexual and maternal, with the warrior's enthusiasm for war. Coriolanus embraces a fellow warrior on the battlefield and declares that his delight equals that of his wedding night (1.6.29–32), and later, Aufidius responds to him in similar fashion, in a passage (4.5.107–127) of extraordinary sensuality. When we first see Volumnia, in 1.3, she compares the thrill of giving birth to Coriolanus with that of seeing him as a soldier, and goes on to identify the beauty of a mother's breast with the sight of a head wound. She later attributes Coriolanus's fierceness in combat to her nursing of him, in 3.2.129. In her final manipulation of her son, she equates motherhood with the state in a violent image—". . . assault thy country [and] tread / . . . on thy mother's womb" (5.3.123–124)—that reinforces our sense that she is a horrifyingly abnormal mother. In fact, when Coriolanus attempts to resist Volumnia's influence, he supposes himself outside the procreative process, "as if a man were author of himself" (5.3.36). This recurring theme of emotional misplacement is a strong reminder that the moral world of Coriolanus and Volumnia is an unhealthy one and that their story can only come to a tragic end.

The common people are not the cause of the city's near fall. Their objections to the rule of the aristocracy are given a fair presentation, especially in Act 1, where the First Citizen makes a sensible argument against the unfair distribution of corn that is the cause of the commoners' rebellion. Yet the cynicism of the tribunes, combined with the fickleness of the crowd, supports the aristocratic argument that the common people are not worthy of power. The critical element in Rome's catastrophe is Coriolanus's decision to defect, not simply his banishment, and he would not have defected had he not been driven from Rome by the ungrateful people who were manipulated by the tribunes. Moreover, this issue is reprised in the episode of the Volscian commoners in 5.6, where Coriolanus is again abandoned by a fickle mob.

Thus, the faults of both the aristocracy and the plebeians are exposed. The combination has produced a bewildering range of critical assessments, and *Coriolanus* has been declared to be the vehicle of fascist, conservative, moderate/pragmatic, liberal, and communist sentiments. While Shakespeare certainly displayed a conservative bias in favor of the established, hierarchical society, he was aware of, and wished to present, both sides of the political question. As a playwright he was more interested in dramatic effect than in political science, and in this work he heightened the human foibles that lead to conflicts of the sort that he found in his sources.

The common people as a social and political class are more prominent in *Coriolanus* than in the history plays, which may reflect developments in England just before the play was written. (Also, the ROMAN PLAYS, set in a remote time and place, offered Shakespeare a chance to explore social issues more fully than government CENSORSHIP would have allowed in works dealing with relatively recent English history.) In *Coriolanus*, Shakespeare emphasizes a corn shortage as the cause of plebeian discontent, while in Plutarch it was a relatively minor factor. Scholars connect this alteration with the extensive corn riots—called the Midlands Insurrection—that shook much of rural England in 1607. These demonstrations, which extended to brief losses of governmental control of some areas, raised issues of poverty and powerlessness that had not been publicly considered in generations. As a landowner and agricultural investor, Shakespeare may be presumed to have taken a particular interest in the phenomenon. He may even have witnessed a riot—or at least spoken to witnesses—since disturbances erupted near STRATFORD at a time when he may have been there. Thus, the class warfare we see in *Coriolanus* may reflect events in England, which, though Shakespeare could not know it, was only a generation away from a cataclysmic civil war.

Thus, *Coriolanus* displays the political concerns of the history plays within the more grandiose framework of a tragedy. Shakespeare emphasized the stresses that result from these political concerns, rather than attempting to alleviate them, and *Coriolanus* is a very complex and dynamic play. Its rough, spontaneous poetic style is accompanied by structural devices intended to reinforce our sense of crowded conflict. Surprises in tone startle us at several important points: Volumnia's violent manner of speech in a pointedly domestic setting, in 1.3; the banished Coriolanus's unexpected appearance in Antium in 4.4; and the silence at the close of Volumnia's long, final speech. This is one of Shakespeare's most brilliant *coups de théâtre*, specified in the stage direction, "Holds her by the hand silent" (5.3.182). All of these serve to keep the audience's attention at a peak, aware that the play's developments do not flow predictably.

The inevitability of events is nevertheless made clear through another structural device, the use of many parallel scenes and images. Menenius's "belly speech" of 1.1 is repeatedly invoked with images of food and physiology that stud the play. In 1.3 Coriolanus's son is vividly described as like his father when he kills a butterfly with his teeth, and when Coriolanus marches on Rome with the Volscians, their advance is likened to "boys pursuing summer butterflies" (4.6.95). As we have seen, the Volscian Commoners reenact the Roman mob's change of heart toward Coriolanus in the play's final episode. Aufidius's welcome to Coriolanus in 4.5 echoes the strange mixture of love and war that Coriolanus displayed to Cominius in 1.6. When he calls him a "traitor in the highest degree" (5.6.85), Aufidius tempts Coriolanus into the defiance that results in his death with almost the same insult ("traitor to the

people" [3.3.66]) that Sicinius used to elicit the defiance that resulted in his banishment. Most striking, Volumnia's dramatic final plea echoes her earlier effort to move her son to submit to her instructions, in 3.2. These parallel themes are startling as they are recognized on each occasion and are also cumulatively powerful as Coriolanus's fate inexorably unfolds. The great strength of the play is its complexity, for its similarity to both the history plays and the tragedies make possible its difficult presentation of Coriolanus as a tragic hero in a real society.

SOURCES OF THE PLAY

Shakespeare's principal source for *Coriolanus* was Plutarch's *Lives*, in Thomas NORTH's translation (2nd ed., 1595). The general course of developments is taken from this account, and several important passages—e.g., Volumnia's appeal in 5.3.94–182—follow North's text very closely. Though Shakespeare invented several minor incidents—including all of Volumnia's other appearances—and developed the psychology of his hero, his fidelity to Plutarch was generally quite close in this play as compared to the other Roman plays.

Only one passage strongly reflects other sources. Menenius's comparison of politics and anatomy in 1.1.95–159—very well known since ancient times—was derived from several earlier renderings. In addition to North's version, which he followed fairly closely, Shakespeare also took a number of significant details from William CAMDEN's *Remaines* (1605), where the fable is told by a medieval pope, and from another variant of the Coriolanus story found in LIVY's *Ab urbe condita*, translated by Philemon HOLLAND as *The Romane Historie* (1600).

TEXT OF THE PLAY

It is difficult to determine the date *Coriolanus* was written, and estimates range from 1603 to 1612. However, most scholars favor 1605 to 1609, for several reasons. First, the play must be later than Camden's *Remaines*, which was possibly available to Shakespeare in manuscript as early as 1603, though more probably used after its publication in 1605. Second, there is an apparent allusion to *Coriolanus* in Ben JONSON's play *Epicoene*, which was produced in late 1609 or early 1610. This implies that Shakespeare's play was written and staged somewhat earlier.

Further support, especially for the later part of this range of dates, is provided by other evidence. Applications of the VERSE TEST suggest that the play was roughly contemporary with *Antony and Cleopatra* (ca. 1606), *Pericles* (ca. 1607), *Cymbeline* (ca. 1608–10), and *The Winter's Tale* (ca. 1610–11). Also, some commentators find topical allusions in the text of the play. For example, "fire on the ice" (1.1.172) may refer to the freezing over of the Thames River in the winter of 1607–08; and Coriolanus's metaphor for treachery, "he'll turn your current in a ditch / And make your channel his" (3.1.95–96), may have been inspired by the much-discussed failure of an English canal-building scheme in 1609. Some scholars believe that Shakespeare's treatment of relations between the aristocracy and the plebeians may have been stimulated in part by the Midlands Insurrection of 1607. This featured extensive corn riots suggestive of the similar disturbances that open the play. Further, psychoanalytically minded commentators feel that the prominence of Volumnia may reflect the death of Shakespeare's mother in 1608. Since none of these suggestions can be confirmed or denied, the date of composition of *Coriolanus* remains uncertain, with 1608 as perhaps the best estimate.

The play was initially published in the FIRST FOLIO (1623). The text was probably printed from Shakespeare's own manuscript, or FOUL PAPERS, for it contains elaborate and literary stage directions (e.g., at 1.3.1 and 5.3.183), variable speech headings (*Cor., Corio., Coriol.*), and idiosyncratic spellings (especially Sc for S in Sicinius, a form closely associated with Shakespeare [see MORE, SIR THOMAS]). It also contains other irregularities that would have been omitted or corrected in a copy made by a scribe or in a PROMPTBOOK.

THEATRICAL HISTORY OF THE PLAY

Though no evidence of early productions of *Coriolanus* has survived, an apparent allusion to the play in Jonson's *Epicoene* implies that the work was performed ca. 1609. Richard BURBAGE was probably the original Coriolanus. The lack of contemporary references suggests that it was staged infrequently,

and the play has never been consistently popular. Many productions have been intended primarily as political propaganda, and Shakespeare's text has been persistently altered to serve these ends.

The earliest recorded version of *Coriolanus* is the adaptation by Nahum TATE, *The Ingratitude of a Commonwealth*, which was performed in 1681–82, an uncertain period in English politics. This version stressed the importance of respectful loyalty, and supported Coriolanus's complaints about the commoners of Rome and de-emphasized the hero's faults. Though it retained some of Shakespeare's text, it was virtually a different play, and it included numerous passages of lurid violence. Despite these features, it was a commercial failure. In 1718 John RICH staged a *Coriolanus* that was probably Shakespeare's, but it was immediately followed by another politically motivated adaptation, *The Invader of His Country: or, The Fatal Resentment*, by John DENNIS. This work—largely Dennis's text, with insertions of Shakespeare's—was directed against the 1715 invasion of Britain by the exiled STUART DYNASTY. It starred the popular Barton BOOTH but nevertheless lasted only three performances.

Though Dennis's failure apparently triggered presentations of Shakespeare's play—in some form, at least—in each of the next three years, *Coriolanus* was then ignored for a generation. In 1754 Thomas SHERIDAN combined Shakespeare's play with another *Coriolanus*—an entirely independent work by James Thomson (1700–48)—in an adaptation that was quite popular and was frequently revived for almost 15 years. In 1754 David GARRICK attempted to rival it with an abridged version of Shakespeare's text, but this production lasted only a week.

In the 19th century the play's popularity grew. Between 1789 and 1817 John Philip KEMBLE staged a series of successful versions of Sheridan's adaptation that usually starred himself and his sister, Sarah SIDDONS. In 1819 W. C. MACREADY—and in 1820, Charles KEAN—staged the play with abridged but otherwise genuine Shakespearean texts. Kean's version was a failure, but Macready's was popular, and he revived it frequently for almost 20 years. Samuel PHELPS—who had played Aufidius in one of Macready's productions—put on the play several times in the 1840s and 1850s, but after this the play was again ignored in England for years, though Edwin FORREST scored notable successes in New York. In the 1890s Frank BENSON restored the play to the English stage with several successful productions.

The 20th century's apocalyptic history has prompted a continuing interest in this most political of Shakespeare's plays. In fact, *Coriolanus* played a small part in that history. In the winter of 1933–34 a Paris production—condemned as fascist and briefly closed by the government—provoked pro- and antifascist street demonstrations. The uproar is said to have contributed to the rallying of public support for the French government at a time when it very nearly fell to fascist and royalist conspirators. In Nazi Germany *Coriolanus* was taught in schools. The protagonist was identified with Hitler as a model of firm leadership, and the injustice of his banishment was emphasized. After World War II, the American occupation forces banned the play until 1953.

On the other hand, a 1935 Moscow production of *Coriolanus* stressed the protagonist's treachery and his aristocratic pride. It was acclaimed by Stalin's propagandists as an excellent lesson in the betrayal of the people by an individualistic leader in the Western mode. Perhaps the most notorious modern adaptation of the play is that of the Marxist German playwright Berthold Brecht (1898–1956), who prepared a text for an East German ensemble that cut all hints of approval of Coriolanus or of disapproval toward the common people. This version is a simplified text that unambiguously celebrates the revolution led by the tribunes. The West German writer Günter Grass (b. 1927) was stimulated by this work to write a play called *The Plebeians Rehearse the Uprising* (1970), in which Brecht is ironically seen rehearsing his *Coriolanus* during the 1953 antigovernment riots in East Berlin (though in fact Brecht's play was not produced until after his death in 1963).

In England, Benson continued to produce the play through 1919, and numerous later productions have confirmed the play's popularity. The most significant of these was probably Lewis CASSON's 1938 production that starred Laurence OLIVIER and Sybil THORNDIKE. This version's success firmly established the play in the repertoire of the modern British theater. Other notable productions include those of Glen Byam SHAW (1952, with Anthony QUAYLE in the title role; Peter HALL (1959, with Olivier and Edith EVANS and 1984, with Ian MC-KELLEN); Joseph PAPP (1965, in New York's Central Park); and Trevor NUNN (1973, with Nicol WILLIAMSON). *Coriolanus* has not been produced as a FILM (except for a very loose Italian adaptation of 1964, *Thunder of Battle*), though two versions have been made for TELEVISION, and it is included in *THE SPREAD OF THE EAGLE*, an adaptation of all the Roman plays.

CHARACTERS

Adrian   See Volsce.

Aedile   Any of several minor characters in *Coriolanus*, subordinates of the Roman tribunes Sicinius and Brutus. The Aediles serve chiefly as messengers for the tribunes. They summon the crowds to rally against Coriolanus in 3.1; they announce Coriolanus's approach and are instructed in coaching the crowd in 3.3; and an Aedile brings the tribunes the first report of the Volscians' advance against ROME in 4.6. They demonstrate the institutional power that the tribunes command.

Aufidius, Tullus   Legendary figure and character in *Coriolanus*, the leader of the Volscians and the murderer of Coriolanus. Aufidius is the oft-defeated rival of Coriolanus, and he vows that he will overcome him by dishonorable means, since he cannot win in combat. Therefore, when Coriolanus deserts ROME and joins the Volscians, Aufidius schemes to kill him. After Coriolanus is dissuaded by Volumnia from sacking Rome, Aufidius accuses him of treachery, and the Conspirators stab the Roman to death in the play's final scene.

Shakespeare found Aufidius in his source, PLUTARCH's *Lives*, but from a single brief mention of their rivalry he constructed the charged relationship of the play. The playwright's villain is a warped mirror image of his protagonist. Aufidius focuses directly on Coriolanus throughout the play, and neither man can forget the other for long. Like Coriolanus—

though without his political difficulties—Aufidius is first and foremost a charismatic warrior, motivated by wholly personal, indeed, egotistical drives, and obsessively concerned with his own achievements. When Coriolanus joins the Volscians, the fellowship of warriors leads Aufidius to welcome his rival with the warmth of a lover. "Let me twine / Mine arms about that body" (4.5.107–108), he says, and compares their encounter with his wedding night. The extraordinary sensuality of this passage offers bizarre evidence of the misplaced emotional thrust engendered by warrior culture.

Frustrated, Aufidius decides to defeat Coriolanus dishonorably, and his grandeur becomes that of a villain rather than a great warrior. He undergoes this change in Act 1, after the siege of CORIOLES, and he admits that his effort "Hath not that honour in't it had" (1.10.13). In this respect he is a foil to Coriolanus, whose failing is that his pride will not permit him to sacrifice any aspect of his warrior's persona. Also, when compared with the treachery of Aufidius, Coriolanus's betrayal of Rome seems the lesser villainy. However, after he has killed Coriolanus, Aufidius resumes something of his earlier nobility when he acknowledges his enemy's greatness. He grants him a warrior's funeral and declares, "he shall have a noble memory" (5.6.153), in the play's final statement.

Boy Minor character in *Coriolanus*, the son of the title character. After Coriolanus has been banished, he joins the Volscians and threatens ROME with destruction. His mother and wife go to beg him to desist, and they bring the Boy with them. Coriolanus addresses his son with a brief homily of the warrior's honor that he himself has lost: "The god of soldiers . . . inform / Thy thoughts with nobleness, that thou mayst prove / To shame unvulnerable" (5.3.70–73). The Boy speaks only once. With both courage and good sense, he declares that his father "shall not tread on me. / I'll run away till I am bigger, but then I'll fight" (5.3.127–128). Coriolanus is clearly touched and insists that he must listen no more to his family or he'll give in. Eventually—at the play's climactic turning point—he does indeed surrender to their influence, to which the Boy has added his share.

The Boy is described in 1.3.55–68 as an energetic lad who would rather play at war than go to school and who has a temper like his father's, which leads him to kill a butterfly with his teeth. This image is effectively reprised when Menenius describes the fearful approach of the Volscians—led by Coriolanus—who advance confidently, like "boys pursuing summer butterflies" (4.6.95). The image contributes to the antiwar theme that runs through the play.

Brutus, Junius, and Sicinius Velutus Quasi-historical figures and characters in *Coriolanus*, legendary tribunes of ROME. Brutus shares power with Velutus, and since they are very similar characters who always appear together (except for a brief final appearance by Sicinius Velutus in 5.4), they are both covered here. The tribunes represent the common people's share in political power, and they reject their foe, the aristocratic Roman warrior Coriolanus. By orchestrating mob violence—and aided by Coriolanus's foolish actions—they succeed in having him banished from Rome. They enjoy their triumph, but when the exiled Coriolanus attacks Rome, the tribunes deny their responsibility; "Say not we brought it" (4.6.121), they retort, and insist that the aristocrats resolve the crisis. The tribunes are stereotypes of scurvy politicians and are scarcely distinguishable from each other, but Shakespeare does vary their functions somewhat, with Junius Brutus dominant in the first half of the play.

The shortsightedness of the tribunes' campaign against Coriolanus certainly threatens the city. They are an example of the dangers that result when power is accorded to the common people, an important theme of the play. At the same time, however, they are concerned with the health of the city. Their offices were created as a result of the corn riots that open the play. The riots are attributed to the arrogance of Coriolanus and the other aristocrats in the face of the common people's hunger. As Sicinius observes in the wake of Coriolanus's banishment, Rome enjoys "peace / and quietness" as a result of their victory, while the aristocrats "blush that the world goes well" (4.6.2–3, 5). When Coriolanus contemptuously asks Brutus,

"What do you prate of service?" the tribune replies with dignity, "I talk of that, that know it" (3.3.84–85). Indeed, he seems to attempt more service for his people than does the foolish and treacherous warrior for his fellow aristocrats. Nevertheless, the tribunes have a chiefly negative significance in the play's political world, for in a properly run society—as Shakespeare conceived it—the common people would follow the leadership of their social superiors and have no tribunes. However, Coriolanus's pride has promoted social disruption, of which the tribunes are a result.

The social conflict enacted in *Coriolanus*—taken by Shakespeare from his source, PLUTARCH's *Lives*—is representative of several such episodes that occurred in the late sixth century B.C. as the Roman Republic came into being. Though the story of Coriolanus is entirely legendary, Brutus may have been a real person. He appears as Junius Brutus in Shakespeare's *The Rape of Lucrece*, though as a very different character. Shakespeare followed Thomas NORTH's translation of Plutarch and erroneously transcribed Sicinius's second name as Velutus, which Plutarch renders as Bellutus. In any case, Plutarch's Sicinius is otherwise unknown in Roman legend, unless he is identifiable with Lucius Sicinius Dentatus, who appears in other sources and is said to have represented the plebeians, though at a somewhat later period.

Citizen (1)   Any of several minor but significant characters in *Coriolanus*, residents of ROME. The Citizens, or Plebeians, are chiefly important for their fickleness, as their opinions of Coriolanus change repeatedly under the influence of various other characters. In this they symbolize a political doctrine that Shakespeare espoused in a number of plays: the common people, however sympathetic as individuals, are politically irresponsible as a class.

The Citizens are most distinguishable as individuals in 1.1. Amid a riot, the First Citizen introduces the play's most important motif: the excessive pride of Coriolanus. He recommends killing him, but the Second Citizen opposes this suggestion and points out the great services that Coriolanus has performed as the military genius of Rome. He thereby introduces the counter-theme

and prepares us for the tragedy that will constitute the main plot, as the noble hero falls victim to his own pride. The riot is halted as the Citizens listen to the aristocrat Menenius justify the powers of the aristocracy with a simplistic fable—his famed "belly speech" (1.1.95–153)—and though the First Citizen offers sensible objections, the crowd as a whole is diverted from its original intentions. The arrival of Coriolanus cows them altogether, and they depart, in an initial demonstration of their malleability.

Thereafter the Citizens serve chiefly to further the same point. They are manipulated by the aristocrats, who influence them to vote for Coriolanus in Act 2, and by their own representatives—the tribunes Brutus and Sicinius—who organize them as a mob in Act 3, and bring about the banishment of Coriolanus. Lastly, in 4.6 some Citizens thank the tribunes for getting rid of their enemy, but when word arrives that the banished Coriolanus is marching on Rome with the army of the Volscians, they reappear to declare that they had had misgivings about the banishment all along. With the exception of the First Citizen in 1.1, the Citizens are not portrayed as individuals and serve only as pawns of both the tribunes and the playwright.

Citizen (2)   Minor character in *Coriolanus*, a resident of ANTIUM. In three brief lines the Citizen directs Coriolanus to the home of Aufidius. He serves merely to advance the plot.

Cominius   Legendary figure and character in *Coriolanus*, a Roman general. Cominius is the commander of the Roman troops fighting against the Volscians at CORIOLES, and his friend Martius (later Coriolanus) is a general under him. Cominius is a discreet general who contrasts with the hero. He executes a sensible withdrawal in 1.6, before he is joined by Coriolanus, who goads him on to a successful counterattack. In the same scene we see Cominius as the subject of Martius's bizarre enthusiasm. Excited by the fighting, Martius embraces him with the fervor, he says, of his wedding night. The commander accepts this as normal battlefield comradeship, however, and in 1.9 he praises Martius and proposes that he take the honorable name

Coriolanus. In 2.2 he nominates Coriolanus to the consulate. However, in Act 3 he cannot prevent Coriolanus's obstinate pride from bringing about his own banishment, and in 5.1 he reports that he has been unable to persuade Coriolanus—now fighting for the Volscians—from his campaign against Rome. Cominius is a representative of the ineffectual aristocracy who cannot control events.

Shakespeare took Cominius from his source, PLUTARCH's *Lives,* but added the intimacy of his relationship with Coriolanus, and thereby established him as a foil to the protagonist. As Coriolanus's friend. Cominius helps us see Coriolanus at his problematical best, early in the play. We recognize his value to his fellows while we acknowledge that he is excessive in his enthusiasm for combat.

Commoner Any of several minor characters in *Coriolanus,* citizens of ANTIUM who first support and then turn against Coriolanus. In 5.6 Coriolanus has spared ROME from destruction at the hands of his Volscian troops, and he reports to the Volscian leaders at Antium accompanied by a throng of enthusiastic Commoners. In ironic contrast to his history in Rome, Coriolanus now has the support of the common people for the first time in the play. However, once Aufidius accuses him of treason, they turn against their hero. "Tear him to pieces!" (5.6.120), they cry, in an episode that parallels the fury of the populace in 3.3 that led to Coriolanus's banishment from Rome. Though mostly mute—their three lines are assigned to the whole group—the Commoners' placement in the play's last moments is crucial. They stress again an important theme of the play, one that has been demonstrated repeatedly by their fellows in Rome: The common people, as a group, are susceptible to inflammatory rhetoric and are therefore unreliable participants in political life.

Conspirators Minor characters in *Coriolanus,* followers of Aufidius. In 5.6 the Conspirators affirm that they will help Aufidius take revenge on Coriolanus. They encourage him in his anger and point out that Coriolanus is overshadowing him. When Aufidius accuses his enemy of treason, they lead the mob in demanding Coriolanus's death, a

demand they then fulfill by killing him with their swords. Though the Conspirators are designated First, Second, and Third, they are indistinguishable from each other, and their speeches are divisions of a single voice. The Conspirators help to illuminate one of the play's principal themes: The common people are susceptible to manipulation and are thus an unstable and unreliable component of society. On the other hand, because they encourage—even goad—Aufidius to kill Coriolanus in such an ignominious fashion, they also help demonstrate the inadequacies of the warrior class.

Coriolanus, Martius (Caius Martius) Legendary figure and title character of *Coriolanus,* a famed Roman warrior whose excessive pride leads him to dishonor and death. His pride is part of his sense of himself as a warrior and aristocrat, a self-image that he has acquired from a rigorous upbringing by his extraordinary mother, Volumnia. When the changing political world of ROME—represented by the tribunes Brutus and Sicinius—demands compromises that his pride will not accept, Coriolanus is driven from Rome and joins the city's enemies, the Volscians. Finally, when his mother persuades him to spare Rome, he is killed by the Volscian leader, his archrival Aufidius.

Like Othello and Macbeth, Coriolanus is a successful warrior who finds himself in a situation—here, the political world of Rome—to which he is temperamentally unsuited and in which he can be manipulated by others. Politically unsophisticated and emotionally immature, he can neither strike political deals with the tribunes nor resist his mother's insistence that he do so. He is reduced to blind vengeance, but she blocks him in that direction as well. Under these pressures, his great strength can only destroy him. His fate contains the irony found in all Shakespeare's tragedies: With greatness comes great weakness. Coriolanus's pride makes him great, but it also brings about his downfall.

Coriolanus's relationship with his mother makes him one of the most psychologically interesting of Shakespeare's protagonists. He is entirely Volumnia's creation, and thus Coriolanus is psychologically dependent on her good opinion, as is demonstrated in both of their crucial scenes. In 3.2 she bullies him into political compromise as his resistance collapses under her disdain: "Thy valiantness was mine . . . but owe thy pride thyself" (3.2.129–130). In 5.3 he cannot withstand another personal denial—"This fellow had a Volscian to his mother" (5.3.178)—and he abandons his life rather than suffer his mother's disapproval. She can manipulate him because when she created him she deprived him of all motives but one, his pride, which depends on her continuing approval. Though he avoids the psychological trauma of her rejection and saves his honor as a Roman warrior, by giving in to her he must accept an ignominious death at the hands of his enemy Aufidius.

Nevertheless, Coriolanus is brave and ready to go beyond his duty as a soldier; he is clearly a noble figure. His name reminds us of this: He is known as Martius through the first eight scenes and is renamed in honor of his military exploits at CORI-OLES. The hero's nobility is made clear throughout the play, in the opinions of both the Romans—friends like Menenius all but worship him, and even the tribunes concede that he has "served well for Rome" (3.3.84)—and of his enemy Aufidius, who calls him "all-noble Martius" (4.5.107). Moreover, the play's final statement is that Coriolanus "shall have a noble memory" (5.6.153). However, he lacks a genuine sense of himself, and Volumnia's inflexible creation becomes increasingly dehumanized under the pressure of developments. He is isolated from others—significantly, Shakespeare used the word *alone* more often in this play than in any other. Strikingly, he characterizes himself as a "lonely dragon" (4.1.30). By the time he has joined the Volscians, he is chillingly described as "a kind of nothing, titleless, / Till he had forg'd himself a name o'th'fire / Of burning Rome" (5.1.13–15). He willfully sheds his connection with humanity. "Wife, mother, child, I know not" (5.2.80), he cries. However, he cannot distance his weakness. As he anticipates his fall, he cries out, "I melt, and am not / Of stronger earth than others" (5.3.28–29), and he attempts to find strength by imagining himself to be parentless: "I'll . . . stand / As if a man were author of himself / And knew no other kin" (5.3.34–37).

In the final moments of the play, Shakespeare deftly reminds us of his protagonist's ultimate weakness. Coriolanus protests against being called a "boy of tears" (5.6.101), and he cites his triumph at Corioles. "Alone I did it" (5.6.116) he cries, and this "Alone" only makes clearer the nature of his failure. His perverse dependence on his mother has made him unable to recognize and accept his need for involvement with others—first the people of Rome, and now the Volscians. The result is that his truly noble elements—his bravery and his warrior's achievements—are negated. It is because he has indeed remained a boy, emotionally, that he has been unable to avoid his final calamity.

Shakespeare had long been interested in Cori-olanus's tale, as we know from his use of it as a metaphor for revenge in *Titus Andronicus* 4.4.67–68, but in *Coriolanus* the playwright made a subtle but important change in the character he found in his source, PLUTARCH's *Lives*. The ancient historian stated that Coriolanus's pride was the consequence of his father's early death and his resulting lack of guidance. Shakespeare, however, does not present his hero's failings as a function of neglect, but rather as the product of a Roman aristocratic ideal that is applied excessively. The commentary on the potential harm in this situation is strongly made and is one of the play's important themes. Though both Shakespeare and Plutarch believed Coriolanus's story to be historically accurate, modern historians realize that it was based on a pre-Roman fable, probably Volscian, that may have told originally of the local deity who gave his name to Corioles.

Gentlewoman Minor character in *Coriolanus*, an attendant to Virgilia and Volumnia. In 1.3 the Gentlewoman announces the arrival of Valeria and then escorts her on stage. She speaks only a single line and serves to indicate the prestige and wealth of the ladies she serves.

Herald Minor character in *Coriolanus*. In 2.1 the Herald accompanies the army's return into ROME and formally announces that Caius Martius has been awarded a new name. In honor of his extraordinary bravery in taking the city of CORIOLES, he is to be known henceforth as Coriolanus. The Herald speaks five grandiose lines and concludes with the cry, "Welcome to Rome, renowned Coriolanus!" (2.1.165), which is repeated by the assembled crowd. Shakespeare provided the Herald to lend an air of pomp and circumstance to Coriolanus's reception. This heightens the dramatic irony when this same reception turns ugly later in the same act.

Lartius, Titus Legendary figure and minor character in *Coriolanus*, a Roman general. Lartius is a brave and capable officer who, despite earlier wounds, campaigns with Martius (later Coriolanus) against the town of CORIOLES and leads the forces that join the heroic Martius after he has entered the city alone. After the victory, "busied about decrees" (1.6.34), he commands the occupied town. He delivers a brief elegy when Martius is believed dead, and an even briefer compliment after the hero has triumphed. He is inconsequential thereafter, a minor member of Coriolanus's entourage who disappears entirely after 3.1. Lartius helps establish our sense of the Roman military establishment; he represents the solid virtues of the Roman aristocracy in a play where the weaknesses of the class are more often seen.

Lartius appears at Corioles in Shakespeare's source, PLUTARCH's *Lives*, but much less prominently. Shakespeare invented his praises of Coriolanus and, perhaps to make the praiser a more vivid figure, endowed him with the crutches he uses in 1.1.241. His spirited wager with Martius in 1.4.1–7 is also an addition, probably to the same end. Thus, Lartius offers an interesting example of the playwright's manipulation of a minor figure to develop the play's world.

Lieutenant (1) Minor character in *Coriolanus*, a Roman officer. In 1.7 the Lieutenant receives orders from Lartius to maintain control of CORIOLES, which the Romans have captured from the Volscians. He speaks only half a line in reply, in an episode whose purpose is to tell that the town has been captured.

Lieutenant (2) Minor character in *Coriolanus*, a follower of Aufidius. In 4.7 the Lieutenant tells Aufidius that Coriolanus, who has deserted from the Romans, is growing in popularity among the Volscians. He regrets that Aufidius has permitted Coriolanus to command troops, because Aufidius is becoming overshadowed. The Lieutenant furthers the play's development with these remarks, for they inform us of Coriolanus's successes and spark Aufidius's hostile replies, which foreshadow the play's concluding episode.

Lord Any of several minor characters in *Coriolanus*, noblemen of ANTIUM. In 5.6 Aufidius presents the Lords of the City, as they are designated in the stage directions, with his evidence that Coriolanus has betrayed the Volscian army, which he had joined when he was banished from ROME. Aufidius's inflammatory speech rouses the crowd into a lynch mob, while various Lords—designated as First, Second, and Third Lord—attempt to keep order without effect. Like Menenius in Rome, the Lords are peaceable men whose efforts to control the mob are ineffective when faced with a leader who can manipulate the shifting moods of the common people. Thus they help demonstrate an important point of the play: that the common people are unreliable participants in political life.

Martius, Caius (Marcius) In *Coriolanus*, the name by which Caius Martius Coriolanus is known before 1.9.64, when he receives his new name, his "addition" (1.9.65) of honor for his military exploits in the taking of the city CORIOLES. In the ancient Roman naming system, Martius is a clan name; there is no equivalent in modern Western naming. Shakespeare apparently followed tradition (and his source, Thomas NORTH's translation of PLUTARCH's *Lives*) when he used it as a family name in the sense we understand. However, the names Caius and Martius are mistakenly reversed several times in the play—including at 1.9.64—an example of the numerous minor errors to which Shakespeare was prone throughout his career.

Menenius Agrippa Legendary figure and character in *Coriolanus*, friend and adviser of the title character. Menenius is an elderly aristocrat who is distinguished by his canny political sense in a time of popular discontent in ROME. In 1.1 he defuses a riot with his clever speech, and he establishes a rapport with the people's tribunes, Brutus and Sicinius. Nonetheless, he cannot prevent Coriolanus from destroying himself politically by refusing to compromise his stern aristocratic ideals. In this respect, Menenius's actions are as futile as those of all the aristocrats. Their failure to control Coriolanus is fatal to the hero himself and almost to all of Rome.

Though Menenius's capacity for compromise makes him stand out, and a Citizen calls him "one that hath always loved the people" (1.1.50–51), he nonetheless shares the aristocracy's disdain for the common people. He thereby contributes to the sense of a disturbed society that is one of the play's important themes. He cleverly deflects the mob with his "belly speech" (1.1.95–153), an elaborate comparison of the body politic to the human anatomy that justifies the hierarchy of Roman society. This was an ancient political fable when it appeared in Shakespeare's source, PLUTARCH's *Lives*, and it was still current in the playwright's time. However, Menenius goes on to dismiss the intelligent remarks of the First Citizen. He calls him the "great toe" of society (1.1.154), and he insults the tribunes as "the herdsmen of the beastly plebeians" (2.1.94–95). Like the other aristocrats, Menenius is too proud to contribute to the welfare of the entire city, and instead he contributes to the play's disasters.

After 1.1 Menenius is merely a mildly amusing figure, in his own words a "humorous patrician, and one that loves a cup of hot wine" (2.1.46–47) ("humorous" here meaning "temperamental"). He idolizes the much younger Coriolanus and greets him with "A hundred thousand welcomes. I could weep, / And I could laugh, I am light and heavy. Welcome!" (2.1.182–183). He rejoices girlishly over a letter from his hero, and fumes angrily when the tribunes belittle him. However, after Coriolanus has joined the Volscians and is besieging Rome, he goes to plead with him to spare the city. His rejection yields a moment of genuine pathos and stoic dignity as the elderly gentleman, heartbroken, turns away and says, "He that hath a will to die by himself, fears it not from another" (5.2.102–103).

Menenius Agrippa makes his "belly speech" in Plutarch but is otherwise unimportant. Shakespeare

made him a paternal friend of his protagonist to lend pathos to the story. Despite Menenius's appearance in Plutarch and other ancient histories, modern scholars recognize him to be entirely legendary.

Messenger   Any of several minor characters in *Coriolanus*, bearers of tidings. In 1.1, 1.4, and 1.6, Messengers who are apparently military men (or perhaps the same man each time), bring reports on the advancing Volscians to Coriolanus or Cominius. In 2.1, 4.6, and 5.4, other Messengers who are apparently civilians (or, again, perhaps a single person), bring news of events in ROME to the tribunes, Brutus and Sicinius. The Messengers serve to announce plot developments.

Nicanor   See Roman (2).

Officer   Either of two minor characters in *Coriolanus*, petty officials who prepare for a meeting at which Coriolanus is to be honored. They speak of Coriolanus's nomination to the post of consul and remark on the possibility that the general may be rejected by the commoners of ROME because of his aristocratic disdain for them. As the First Officer puts it, "he's vengeance proud, and loves not the common people" (2.2.5–6). They remark on the fickleness of the crowd and on the obstinacy of Coriolanus, but they agree that the warrior hero's long record of extraordinary service makes him more worthy of the post than the politicians who achieve the office by currying favor with the electorate.

Like a CHORUS, the Officers are anonymous and outside the action of the play. They interrupt the progress of the plot to provide a commentary on the merits and faults of Coriolanus and on the Roman political situation. Their interruption breaks the intensity of the political developments and thereby promotes a more objective attitude in the audience, permitting us to see both sides of the issue.

Patricians   See Senator.

Plebeians   See Citizen (1).

Roman (1)   Any of three minor characters in *Coriolanus*, soldiers in the Roman army. At the opening of 1.5, each soldier—designated as the First, Second, and Third Roman—speaks one brief line about the loot they are carrying away from the battle of CORIOLES. Coriolanus appears and remarks sarcastically, "See here these movers, that do prize their hours / At a crack'd drachma!" (1.5.4–5). These Romans, like the civilians of the city and some of their fellow warriors, serve to demonstrate the unreliability of the common people, a primary theme of the play.

Roman (2) (Nicanor)   Character in *Coriolanus*, a traitor who gives information on the affairs of ROME to a Volsce, whose tribe, the Volscians, is at war with the city. In 4.3 the Roman, named Nicanor, meets the Volsce, named Adrian, to whom he has transferred intelligence before. He tells of the banishment of Coriolanus, and he advises that the Volscians attack Rome at this moment of weakness. His cool treachery is an appropriate preparation for the next scenes, in which Coriolanus joins the Volscians against Rome.

Senator (Patricians)   Any of several characters in *Coriolanus*, lawmakers of ROME. The Senators appear in 1.1 to summon Coriolanus to fight for the city against the Volscians, and in 2.2 they honor him by nominating him to be a consul. In all three scenes of Act 3, they fruitlessly attempt to calm Coriolanus in his encounter with the tribunes, Sicinius and Brutus. After Coriolanus is banished, takes arms against Rome, and is dissuaded from destroying the city by the arguments of his wife and mother, two of the Senators welcome the women back from their successful intercession, in 5.5. These lawmakers are ineffectual aristocrats, and their presence in the play serves to illustrate the weakness of authority in a disordered society.

In the FIRST FOLIO edition of the play, the stage entrance at 2.2.36 designates the Senators as "the Patricians," and speech headings for a Senator at 3.1.252 and 259 specify "Patri." "Nobles" also appears in a stage direction at 3.2.1. Shakespeare knew the terms were not interchangeable—they are used separately in 4.3.14 and 5.4.54—so this minor carelessness simply indicates his awareness that the Roman Senators were aristocrats.

Senator   Any of several minor characters in *Coriolanus*, lawmakers of the Volscians, enemies of ROME. In 1.2 the Senators confer with the general Aufidius; two of them, designated First and Second Senator, do most of the talking. They agree that Aufidius should command the field army, while they govern the besieged CORIOLES, their capital. In 1.4 the Senators ineffectually defy the Romans. The presence of the Senators makes clear that the Volscians have a viable state, rather like that of Rome, and their role as Aufidius's nominal superiors helps establish the general's position as Coriolanus's opposite.

Serving-man   Any of several minor characters in *Coriolanus*, servants of Aufidius. In 4.5 when Coriolanus arrives at Aufidius's home disguised as a poor man, the Serving-men—designated as First, Second, and Third—attempt to throw him out. He beats one of them, who runs out of the room before Aufidius arrives and the other two Serving-men withdraw. At the close of the scene, two of them reappear to discuss the stranger. They pretend to have recognized Coriolanus's worth from the beginning, and, comically, they hesitate to speak before sounding each other's opinion. The Third Serving-man reappears with news of Coriolanus's identity and of his defection to the Volscians, for whom he will fight against ROME. The Serving-men are pleased with the prospect of an easy triumph and welcome the coming war. They make humorously greedy predictions of excitement and loot.

In the opening of 4.5, the Serving-men fill an ancient role of foolish servants who emphasize the nobility of their social betters when they mishandle a situation. The episode may have seemed more humorous to its original audiences than it does today, for the beating of servants was a traditional comic routine, dating back to Roman drama. At the close of the scene the Serving-men's comical nature is more evident. Their pleasure at the prospect of war is a sharp piece of social satire that keeps our attention on the political themes of the play.

Sicinius Velutus   See Brutus, Junius, and Sicinius Velutus.

Soldier (1) Any of several minor characters in *Coriolanus*, members of the Roman army. The Soldiers retreat before the Volscians at the gates of CORIOLES, and they refuse to follow Martius—later given the name Coriolanus—when he enters the city. "Foolhardiness! Not I" (1.4.46) is the reply in the words of the First Soldier, who speaks for the group apart from one line given to a Second Soldier. However, when they observe Martius's return they are inspired to join him and fight their way into the city. Another group of Soldiers accompanies Cominius in 1.6, and they too are inspired by the arrival of the battle-torn Martius. The Soldiers say very little except in unison, and their chief function, much like that of the Citizens, is to demonstrate the changeable nature of the common man, an important theme of the play.

Soldier (2) Any of several minor characters in *Coriolanus*, members of the Volscian army. In 1.10, one of the Soldiers—designated the First Soldier—interjects four single lines into Aufidius's long speech on Coriolanus's recent victory over the Volscians at CORIOLES. The First Soldier is merely a sounding board who provides the occasion for the audience to see his leader's vengefulness and rancor toward Coriolanus.

Usher Minor character in *Coriolanus*, a servant of Valeria. The Usher accompanies the lady he serves when she visits Virgilia and Volumnia, in 1.3. He does not speak and serves merely to indicate the prestige and wealth of his mistress. He is often dropped from productions of the play. In medieval and RENAISSANCE times an usher was a servant whose function was to precede his employer and open doors, prepare seats, and so on.

Valeria Minor character in *Coriolanus*, a friend of Coriolanus's wife, Virgilia. Valeria is a cheerful, but somewhat insensitive young noblewoman who visits Virgilia in 1.3. Her bland acceptance of the Roman aristocratic ideal, combined with her charming vivacity, contrasts forcefully with the melancholy of her friend, who is distressed by the martial fervor of her mother-in-law, Volumnia. Valeria describes the Boy, son of Coriolanus and Virgilia, in 1.3.57–65, and she is not aware that she

presents a disturbing picture of the Boy killing a butterfly with his teeth. She does not speak in the three remaining scenes in which she appears, having served her function as a foil for Virgilia.

Valeria accompanies Volumnia and Virgilia on their crucial mission to dissuade Coriolanus from invading Rome, and though she does not speak, she is described in 5.3.64–67 as a particularly noble Roman woman. This allusion reflects the greater role that Valeria plays in Shakespeare's source, PLUTARCH's *Lives*, where she stirs Volumnia to action. However, the playwright preferred to have Volumnia stand alone, and Valeria's role remains minor.

Velutus, Sicinius See Brutus, Junius, and Sicinius Velutus.

Virgilia Legendary figure and character in *Coriolanus*, the wife of Coriolanus. When we first see her in 1.3, Virgilia makes her strongest impression, as she worries over her husband's return to war. She can only respond feebly to the martial enthusiasm of her powerful mother-in-law, Volumnia, who calls her weak because she fears for her husband's safety. Virgilia has the inner strength, however, to refuse to continue her social life. She speaks very little in the remainder of the play—Coriolanus calls her his "gracious silence" (2.1.174)—but though her role is small, her modesty offers a distinct and significant emotional note that contrasts with and emphasizes the more strident tone of her husband and her mother-in-law.

Virgilia acts as a foil to Volumnia and makes clear that her mother-in-law's war-loving, masculine nature is not the only one possible for a Roman matron. Rather, we see that Volumnia is not normal. Virgilia is also a foil to Coriolanus; in contrast with her, he seems crude. This is especially obvious when he returns from combat in 2.1 and he jokes with her about coffins and death. He is clearly not aware of her sensibilities, which we have been exposed to just a few scenes earlier.

Her presence, also sheds light on her husband in a subtler fashion. He doesn't understand her or perhaps even perceive her clearly, but his recollection of their farewell kiss, "Long as my exile, sweet as my revenge" (5.3.44–45), is touching, if also twisted. That his demure wife inspires such affection suggests to us a softer, undeveloped aspect of Coriolanus's nature, Virgilia stands for a world that might have been, and the latent presence of that world makes the dramatic reality of the tragedy more wrenching.

Volsce (Adrian) Character in *Coriolanus*, a spy who receives information for his tribe, the Volscians, from a Roman. In 4.3 the Volsce, named Adrian, meets the Roman, named Nicanor, from whom he has gathered intelligence before. He learns of the banishment of Coriolanus. The episode emphasizes the atmosphere of intrigue that pervades Coriolanus's world and prepares us for his defection in the next scenes.

Volscians In *Coriolanus*, an Italic tribe that makes war against ROME. Coriolanus receives his name for his bravery when he besieges and takes the Volscian town of CORIOLES. When the Romans banish him, he joins the Volscians and leads them in a successful campaign. Under him the Volscians almost take Rome, but the ex-Roman gives in to the pleas of his mother and spares the city. Though the resulting treaty requires large reparations from Rome, the Volscian leader Aufidius has Coriolanus killed. This brings to a close the tragedy of a leader whose uncontrolled pride, combined with civil disorder, leads to catastrophe for himself and for Rome. Shakespeare employs the Volscians in this tale as he does the Goths in *Titus Andronicus*, FORTINBRAS in *Hamlet*, and the English in *Macbeth*: They are all foreigners who dominate a society once it succumbs to weaknesses that result from the shortcomings and misdeeds of its rulers. Thus, the Volscians are a sort of nemesis, a punishing fate that confirms the evil of selfish ambition or pride among the privileged. This was an important political point for Shakespeare throughout his career.

The historical Volscians were enemies of Rome throughout its early history. The record is obscure, but many hints—including the legends surrounding Coriolanus—imply Volscian successes. They were finally defeated by the Romans during the fourth century B.C., and after 304 B.C.—about 200 years after the time of the play—they were politically incorporated into the Roman state. The Volscians were so thoroughly assimilated that almost all traces of their ancient culture had disappeared before the earliest surviving Roman accounts of them were written.

Volumnia Legendary figure and character in *Coriolanus*, the mother of the title character. Volumnia, an aristocratic Roman matron, has raised her son to be a proud warrior above all else. She dominates her son, for she has so thoroughly bred her own values in him that he is psychologically dependent on her approval and cannot oppose her. As she claims, "There's no man in the world / More bound to's mother" (5.3.158–159). Desiring that Coriolanus receive the consulate, ROME's highest honor, Volumnia bullies him until he agrees to sacrifice his pride and solicit the approval of the common people. This is one of Shakespeare's most Machiavellian passages (3.2.41–86). However, because Coriolanus is what Volumnia has made him, he cannot restrain his proud contempt, with the result that he is banished from Rome. When he joins the Volscians, Rome's enemy, and threatens to sack the city, Volumnia again uses her influence over him with an elaborate appeal in 5.3.94–182, a virtuoso passage that is the high point of the play, dramatically. She convinces him to withdraw his forces, though he knows this means he will be killed by the Volscians.

Volumnia controls her son by withdrawing her approval; in both 3.2 and 5.3 she disdainfully disowns him—"Thy valiantness was mine . . . but owe thy pride thyself" (3.2.129–130), and "This fellow had a Volscian to his mother" (5.3.178). While her advice to him is sound, it is only necessary because her influence has made him incapable of functioning sensibly. Because he has only the rigorous pride she has developed in him, he goes to his destruction. He is a tragic hero precisely because his greatness is mingled with his weakness. He is incapable of being anything except what his mother has made him. The influence of Volumnia is thus central to the play.

Volumnia is correct when she boasts to Coriolanus, "Thou art my warrior: / I holp to frame thee" (5.3.62–63). Her upbringing of him has made him both the charismatic warrior who becomes a great Roman hero and the inflexible aristocrat who sparks the hatred of the Roman people. Her rigorous martial code is revealed on her first appearance, in 1.3, where she delights in Coriolanus's return to combat. She sternly rejects the concern for his safety displayed by his wife, Virgilia, and rejoices in the prospect of her son's wounds, or even his death, for the sufferings of war are badges of honor to her mind.

Volumnia's moral code—and thus that of Coriolanus—is seriously flawed, and this is made clear in Shakespeare's depiction of her warped sense of maternal love. In 1.3 her thirst for glory leads her to equate her joy at Coriolanus's birth with her pleasure in his fighting, and she compares the beauty of a mother's breast to that of a head wound. This obviously pathological attitude helps demonstrate the unhealthiness of the rigorous aristocratic ideal that Volumnia upholds, and it is part of the play's critique of the aristocracy. We are not surprised when the results of Coriolanus's upbringing prove catastrophic.

Shakespeare invented all of Volumnia's appearances save that in 5.3—her dramatic appeal to save Rome—which occurs in the play's source, PLUTARCH's *Lives*. When he devised a powerful mother-son relationship to account for Coriolanus's submission, Shakespeare not only added psychological weight to his protagonist's sudden reversal, he found a basic component of his tragedy.

Watchmen Several minor characters in *Coriolanus*, soldiers in the Volscian army. In 5.2 the Watchmen guard the Volscian camp when it is approached by Menenius. He seeks to persuade Coriolanus, who has deserted ROME and is fighting for the Volscians, not to attack the city. Two of the Watchmen—designated First and Second Watchman—declare that Coriolanus has banned all Roman emissaries, and they mock Menenius when he claims to be an old friend who will be welcomed by the general. When Coriolanus emerges and rejects Menenius, the Watchmen redouble their taunts as the ambassador departs. This episode provides a mildly comic way to portray the depth of Coriolanus's vengeful hatred for Rome, while reserving the protagonist for the climactic scenes that follow.

Cymbeline
SYNOPSIS

Act 1, Scene 1
One Gentleman tells another that King Cymbeline's daughter Imogen has married a poor but worthy nobleman, Posthumus Leonatus, whose father had died—before he was born—in the king's service. However, Posthumus has been banished from Britain because the king had wanted Imogen to marry Cloten, the boorish son of the Queen of Britain. He adds that Imogen is the king's only child, with the exception of two sons who were kidnapped 20 years earlier and never recovered.

Act 1, Scene 2
The Queen affects friendship for Imogen and the departing Posthumus, but Imogen mistrusts her. The Queen warns them that the king may find them, but in an aside she declares that she will send the king their way. As they bid each other farewell, Imogen gives Posthumus a diamond ring, and he gives her a bracelet. The king appears and angrily drives Posthumus away. Posthumus's servant Pisanio reports to Imogen that his master has told him to remain at court and serve her. He adds that Posthumus and Cloten have fought but that Posthumus refrained from hurting his opponent.

Act 1, Scene 3
Cloten boasts to a Lord of his swordplay against Posthumus while a Second Lord mocks him behind his back.

Act 1, Scene 4
Pisanio tells the lovesick Imogen of Posthumus's departure.

Act 1, Scene 5
In ROME the exiled Posthumus meets Iachimo. They speak of a duel that Posthumus had once fought over his claim that Imogen was superior to all other women, both in beauty and virtue, Iachimo declares that Imogen is not so virtuous. He offers to bet his estate against Posthumus's diamond ring that he can seduce her, and the enraged Posthumus accepts the wager.

Act 1, Scene 6
In Britain the Queen assures the physician Cornelius that the poison he has given her is intended only for

experiments on small animals, to further her education in herbal lore. Pisanio arrives, and the Queen muses to herself that she will poison him since he serves Cloten's enemy. In a soliloquy, Cornelius reveals that since he mistrusts the Queen he has substituted a powerful sleeping potion for the poison; a victim will appear dead for a time but will suffer no harm. The Queen tries to recruit Pisanio to convince Imogen to marry Cloten, and as a reward she gives him the poison. She tells him it is a potent restorative.

Act 1, Scene 7

Iachimo arrives at court and meets Imogen. He tells her that Posthumus leads a riotous life in Rome and that he speaks mockingly of his faithful lover at home. He encourages her to seek revenge by sleeping with him. When she angrily dismisses him, he declares that he did not mean it but had merely been testing her virtue to see if Posthumus's praise had been true. Imogen is mollified and agrees to assist Iachimo. She says she will keep a chest containing valuables that are partly owned by Posthumus safe in the most secure possible location—her own bedchamber.

Act 2, Scene 1

Cloten brags of his ill temper over gambling losses and is mocked behind his back by the Second Lord, who sympathizes with Imogen in a soliloquy.

Act 2, Scene 2

In her bedchamber Imogen retires for the night. Iachimo emerges from the chest, which is being kept there as Imogen had agreed. He memorizes the nature of the furnishings and decorations, takes a bracelet from the sleeping Imogen's wrist, notices a mole on her breast, and returns to the chest.

Act 2, Scene 3

Musicians hired by Cloten serenade Imogen, but she does not respond. He accosts her. She tries to turn him away politely, but when he persists she lashes out at him and declares that he is not worth the clothes Posthumus wears. She leaves, and Cloten vows revenge.

Act 2, Scene 4

In Rome, Iachimo has returned from Britain and claims the diamond ring Posthumus had wagered.

He offers a description of Imogen's bedchamber as proof that he has slept with her. When Posthumus refuses to believe him, he displays the bracelet—which Posthumus had given Imogen—and then clinches his case when he tells of the mole on Imogen's breast. Posthumus believes him and, cursing all women, vows to seek revenge on Imogen.

Act 3, Scene 1

In Britain, Lucius, the ambassador from the Roman emperor, informs Cymbeline that Britain owes tribute money to the Romans. Cloten boldly insists that the tribute shall not be paid, and the king agrees. Lucius replies with a declaration of war.

Act 3, Scene 2

Pisanio grieves over a letter from Posthumus that orders him to murder Imogen as punishment for her adultery; he is confident that Posthumus has been tricked. Imogen arrives and Pisanio gives her a letter from Posthumus; it tells her to run away and join him at Milford Haven, a port in WALES. Delighted, she immediately makes plans to do so.

Act 3, Scene 3

Belarius stands outside a cave in Wales and addresses his sons Guiderius and Arviragus. He praises the wilderness life they lead as infinitely superior to life at a king's court. The two young men respectfully declare that they regret the lack of an opportunity to prove themselves in the great world. Belarius argues that his own unjust banishment justifies his remarks. The sons leave to prepare for the day's hunt, and Belarius soliloquizes that their enthusiasm for accomplishment reflects their royal blood. Although they believe him to be their father, they are actually royal princes, the sons of King Cymbeline, kidnapped by Belarius when he was exiled.

Act 3, Scene 4

Near Milford Haven, Pisanio shows Imogen the letter from Posthumus that declares her unfaithfulness and commands her murder. Grief stricken, Imogen raves madly until Pisanio proposes a plan. The deceived Posthumus must be made to believe she is dead until he can learn the truth. Pisanio will claim to Posthumus that he has killed Imogen, and news of her disappearance from court will confirm the account. In the meantime, she should disguise herself as a page boy and take service with Lucius, who is expected in Wales soon. She can then go to Rome and at least maintain contact with Posthumus. She agrees and assumes her disguise. Pisanio gives her the medicine he received from the queen in case she falls ill while alone, and returns to the court.

Act 3, Scene 5

Lucius regrets the end of his friendship with Cymbeline and leaves the court for Milford Haven, where he will sail for Rome. Imogen's absence is reported. Cloten encounters Pisanio and threatens to kill him if he does not tell where Imogen is. He reveals Posthumus's letter to Imogen that tells her to meet him in Wales. Cloten then orders Pisanio to bring him some of Posthumus's clothes. After a soliloquy in which he plans to kill Posthumus in front of Imogen and then rape her, all while wearing the very clothes that she had insultingly compared him with, he sets out for Wales.

Act 3, Scene 6

Imogen, tired and in despair, comes to Belarius's cave. Seeking rest, she calls out; she gets no answer and enters the cave.

Act 3, Scene 7

Belarius, Guiderius, and Arviragus return from the hunt and discover Imogen, disguised as a boy. She identifies herself as "Fidele" and says that she is traveling to join her master at Milford. Struck by "his" courtly manners and almost supernatural beauty, the two young men declare their brotherly love for the stranger. They invite Imogen to stay the night before traveling on.

Act 3, Scene 8

In Rome a Senator issues plans for the invasion of Britain. Lucius is to command a force raised from the gentry of Rome.

Act 4, Scene 1

In Wales, Cloten wears Posthumus's clothes and compliments himself on his appearance. He believes he will soon find his enemy and have his revenge.

Act 4, Scene 2

Imogen, who is ill, takes the medicine Pisanio has given her and retires to the cave. Cloten appears;

Belarius recognizes him and believes he has been sent to arrest them. He and Arviragus go to scout for soldiers, and Guiderius addresses the intruder. After Cloten insults him, the two begin to fight and they skirmish their way off stage. Belarius and Arviragus reappear and meet Guiderius, who returns with Cloten's head. Belarius is afraid of the consequences, but the two young men are happily defiant. Their pleasure collapses when they discover that "Fidele" has apparently died. They sing an elegy for "him" and leave the body with the headless corpse of Cloten while they go to prepare a funeral. Imogen awakes and sees a headless body in Posthumus's clothes. She believes that her lover is dead. Grief stricken, she falls insensate on the body. Lucius appears, on his way to join the troops arriving from Rome. He sees Imogen, who identifies herself again as Fidele and says that her master has been killed by brigands. She is taken into Lucius's service, the Roman orders his men to bury the corpse, and he departs with his new page.

Act 4, Scene 3

Cymbeline is distracted because Imogen is missing and the Queen has been stricken with madness since Cloten is also missing. He threatens Pisanio with torture if he does not reveal Imogen's whereabouts. News arrives of the approaching Roman army, and the king goes with his lords to prepare. Pisanio, in a soliloquy, admits bewilderment, having heard nothing from either Posthumus or Imogen. He puts his hope in providence, for he can do nothing.

Act 4, Scene 4

At their cave, Belarius, Guiderius, and Arviragus hear the battle. Belarius wishes to retreat into the mountains, but the young men insist on fighting. They say that it would be dishonorable not to take the opportunity to prove themselves. They convince him, and the three go to join the British forces.

Act 5, Scene 1

Posthumus is serving as a Roman officer. He contemplates the bloody cloth Pisanio has sent him as proof of Imogen's death, and he is stricken with remorse. He wishes he had died rather than she and decides that he will disguise himself as a peasant and fight for the British until he is killed.

Act 5, Scene 2

The Roman army, which includes Lucius and Iachimo, skirmishes with the British army, which includes Posthumus. Iachimo is disarmed by Posthumus but is left alone as the battle shifts off-stage. He laments that he has blackened Imogen's name and supposes that his burden of guilt has made him inept in battle. The battle continues; Cymbeline is briefly captured by the Romans, but Belarius, Guiderius, and Arviragus, aided by Posthumus, rally the British troops and rescue him.

Act 5, Scene 3

Posthumus tells a fleeing Briton that the British, though nearly defeated, have won the battle thanks to an old man and two handsome young ones, who rallied the British troops. Posthumus regrets that he was not killed in battle and decides to resume his Roman garb and be captured by the British. He hopes that they will avenge the day's slaughter by killing their prisoners. A British Captain (2) appears and talks about the old man and his sons who saved the army, and a Second Captain adds that they were assisted by a British peasant. Posthumus accosts them and is taken prisoner.

Act 5, Scene 4

In jail Posthumus prays for death. He falls asleep and has a vision. His father, Sicilius Leonatus, appears, accompanied by his Mother and Brothers. In solemn rhymes they beseech Jupiter to have mercy on Posthumus, who has suffered enough. The god himself appears, riding an eagle, and declares that Posthumus shall recover and marry Imogen. Posthumus awakes, and a Gaoler arrives to escort him to his execution. However, a summons calls Posthumus to the king.

Act 5, Scene 5

Cymbeline knights Belarius, Guiderius, and Arviragus as the heroes of the battle and regrets that he cannot find the peasant who fought beside them. Cornelius arrives with word of the Queen's death and reports her deathbed confession. She had planned to poison the king and place Cloten on his throne. The Roman prisoners include Lucius, Iachimo, the Soothsayer, Posthumus, and Imogen, who is still disguised as Fidele. Lucius asks mercy for

Fidele; Cymbeline is struck by "his" appearance and offers the "boy" a boon. Imogen demands that Iachimo explain where he got the diamond ring he wears. Iachimo tells of his wager for Posthumus's ring, and Posthumus comes forward, declares himself a gullible fool, and confesses that he had Imogen murdered. This leads to a series of explanations that reveal the play's complications to all. Cymbeline, delighted with the return of his sons, forgives Belarius for kidnapping them and then frees the Roman captives. Iachimo begs for death, as punishment for his wager, but Posthumus pardons him. Cymbeline declares that his happiness makes him desire peace, and he agrees to resume paying the Roman tribute. He commands a celebration of the renewed alliance.

COMMENTARY

With *Cymbeline*, Shakespeare continued to develop the ROMANCES, an experiment with a new genre that began with *Pericles* and culminated in his two late masterpieces, *The Winter's Tale* and *The Tempest*. His attempt to blend the features of TRAGEDY and COMEDY with the magical fantasy of romance, a literary mode familiar from 16th-century prose and poetry, was not yet successful. The play is a veritable anthology of motifs and situations from romantic literature: a wicked stepmother, long-lost children, the discovery of bodily identification marks, a decoded riddle, the appearance of a god, and so on. These motifs appear in a profusion intended to generate a seductive fairy-tale world. However, in *Cymbeline* vestiges of earlier modes remain—from the tragedies, in particular—and the effect of the romantic features is seriously undercut. The realism in character and setting that creates our emotional involvement in the tragedies is not appropriate to the idealization of the new genre, and the domestic pleasantries of comedy are not yet sublimated in the unreal world of romance.

Cymbeline therefore exhibits a jarring set of components that distract from the play's themes. The central message of the play is that order transcends chaos and that, ultimately, despite our human ineffectuality, peace and love can triumph in a grand reconciliation of disordered elements. This idea is present throughout the romances.

Here, marking an advance on *Pericles*, the emphasis falls on forgiveness of others: it is necessary for humans to act with mercy rather than justice, in keeping with the behavior of the gods. However, the potential for catastrophe is too strongly presented in *Cymbeline*, and by the time Jupiter appears to reassure us that all will be well, a state of near chaos has steadily grown, and events appear to be entirely out of control. Iachimo's scheme has succeeded; Imogen believes Posthumus has been killed by Pisanio, who is in fact her only ally; Guiderius and Arviragus remain unrecognized as princes; and Britain is locked in a foolish war against Rome. Most dire of all, perhaps, Posthumus is suicidal because he believes Imogen is dead, a situation appallingly suggestive of *Romeo and Juliet*. The generally romantic context suggests that these problems will be resolved, but the tone is almost as anarchic as that of *Macbeth*. The play's final sequence of revelations and reconciliations therefore seems confusing, if not simply arbitrary, and its message is accordingly weakened.

Nevertheless, the play has many real virtues, one of the greatest being its variety of attractive characters. Imogen's considerable charm, which we shall consider later, heads the list, of course, but several of the other characters are also quite entertaining. For instance, Cloten's offensiveness is of an intriguing sort. His vice and violence are accompanied by great foolishness—he inspires the Second Lord's mockery and is several times referred to as a fool—and he is clearly intended to be a humorous grotesque. He is a predecessor of *The Tempest*'s Caliban. Along with his mother, the archetypal wicked stepmother of fairy tale, Cloten manifests the other-worldliness of romance. The other comic villain of the piece, Iachimo, is a pleasing creation who also helps maintain the play's tone. He is a stock MACHIAVEL and is often downright comic—for example, when he emerges from his trunk like a jack-in-the-box and compares himself vaingloriously to the truly menacing Tarquin. His humorous aspect takes the edge off his villainy and permits us to recognize that Imogen's disgrace can have no lasting consequences in the world of romance. In 5.5 Iachimo's long confession, as boastful as it is apologetic, constitutes a plea for forgiveness and

entitles him to share in the play's final reconciliation. Pisanio is another sort of figure, the loyal and clever servant of tradition who stands firmly for common sense, truth, and resourceful continuance. Finally, however, as the chaos of the plot builds, he throws up his hands and commits himself to providence. "Fortune brings in some boats that are not steer'd" (4.3.46), he declares.

Cymbeline is very exciting to watch on the stage, for the complexities and improbabilities of its plot yield many splendid surprises. The role of the central figure, Imogen, shifts constantly. The plot turns from the theme of separated lovers to that of a wager on the maiden's chastity (and two different, equally repellent, assaults on it) to the maiden's ambivalent journey—she braves the wilderness to find her lover but is actually being ambushed by him—and finally to a traditional comic ploy, the maiden disguised as a boy. In the meantime, two other plots have been introduced, either of which might be central in a more conventional play. One concerns lost princes raised in the wild, and the other offers high politics and war as Britain refuses tribute to Rome.

Particular episodes offer individual surprises as well. Iachimo's first appearance, in 1.5, is entirely unanticipated, and he later startles us again when he emerges from the trunk in Imogen's bedroom. The first presentation of Belarius's cave suddenly introduces a very different SUBPLOT, just as the main plot is growing increasingly complicated. We are shocked (though probably delighted) when Cloten's head is borne onstage by Guiderius, and while we are prepared for Imogen's false death, its conjunction with Cloten's headless corpse is a pleasantly novel complication. Not least, Posthumus's supernatural vision in 5.4 is probably the most spectacular eruption of the unexpected in Shakespeare. Shakespeare's earlier works had occasionally offered surprises—the final episode in *Love's Labour's Lost* is a famous example—but a great emphasis on novelty is distinctive to the romances, and the dramatic excitement produced is strongly felt by audiences.

This emphasis on the playwright's artfulness has inspired many commentators to insist that *Cymbeline* is merely an artistic experiment undertaken for its own sake. However, the play's marked esthetic aspect generates a sense of unreality that is important to the central theme of the romances—humanity's dependence on providence—and to their major motif—magic and the supernatural. We are notified that the play is *not* about real life, and if we permit it, a state of timeless suspension is the result.

The play's complications and surprises also serve another purpose. Tragedy and comedy each enact events that lead toward a conclusion, be it the triumph of love or of disaster. In *Cymbeline,* however, the pattern is so complicated and the turnings of fate so unpredictable that we can only rely on the final surprise of 5.4 (final to us; 5.5 offers a long series of surprises for the characters), the literal deus ex machina of Jupiter's appearance, to resolve the situation. Jupiter's descent is significantly climactic. It follows the battle scene that envelops all the characters, and precedes the all-too-human fumbling that is revealed in the comically complicated final scene. We are reminded of Pisanio's prediction—fortune, not steering, will bring in the boats—and that humanity is dependent on providence.

The play's seeming peculiarities reflect this message. Its variety of characters and tonalities—comic or tragic, realistic or fantastic—all are reconciled in a positive and unifying vision. The comic is never farcical, and the potentially tragic remains merely potential. The realistic does not preclude abstraction, and the elements of romance do not give away to an entirely escapist retreat from reality. *Cymbeline* thus suggests and attempts to demonstrate, in not completely effective fashion, a vision of human weakness transcended. Shakespeare more successfully accomplished this vision in less complicated and more homogeneous plays, *The Winter's Tale* and *The Tempest.* For though its themes are dramatic, *Cymbeline* is nevertheless decidedly flawed. As we have seen, it leans disconcertingly toward tragedy, as if the author's intentions had been uncertain. Similarly, several of the characters seem to reflect too many differing ideas and are inconsistently presented. Iachimo, for instance, while a conventional comic villain, also offers glimpses of tragedy, as when he envisions infidelity in terms of passion and damnation and invokes "all the plagues of hell" (1.7.111). Here, as when he fleetingly iden-

tifies himself with utter evil—"hell is here" (2.2.50)—he sounds more like Othello or Macbeth than the play can bear. Posthumus, likewise, is presented to us as the traditional romantic hero—the "most prais'd, most lov'd" of men (1.1.47)—but when he accepts the wager, believes Iachimo, and finally takes revenge through Pisanio, he is immature and ignoble. He also resembles Othello in his insecurity; he believes that Imogen would find it easy to betray him. His tirade against women, with its vividly bestial image of Imogen and Iachimo, strikes a horrifying note that is as unromantic as Iachimo's earlier evocations of evil. Posthumus's ultimate decision to seek death in battle is also unsuitably grim.

Imogen is subject to similar inconsistencies, and the main plot seems to have caused Shakespeare to revert to familiar modes of creation. The heroine is the traditional, idealized princess, "more goddess-like than wife-like" (3.2.8), and the proper mate to Posthumus's glorious prince. However, in her resourcefulness and wit, Imogen is plainly a typical Shakespearean comic heroine, capable of disguising herself as a man and going in search of her lover. She sharply—and wittily—rejects the unwanted attentions of Cloten; she acknowledges—and overcomes—her feminine fear of swords. She resembles Rosalind of *As You Like It,* Beatrice of *Much Ado,* and Viola of *Twelfth Night,* rather more than she does the passive object of adoration and intrigue that is the central figure in traditional romance. Imogen is enchanting, and her transformations onstage are delightful, but while she captures our affections, the fashion in which she does so is contrary to the general direction of the play.

Further, the presence of differing character types seems similarly disjointed. Fairy-tale figures such as the queen and the lost princes coexist with more psychologically developed figures. The more peripheral characters seem more appropriate to the essentially comic optimism of romance, while the central situation has the potential for tragedy. The play is also disjointed in its setting. No fewer than four distinct worlds are evoked: classical Rome, RENAISSANCE Italy, pagan Britain, and the abstracted countryside of pastoral romance (represented by Wales). The intricate reconciliation of these venues in the final scene requires such extraordinary ingenuity that it has inspired equal measures of praise and ridicule, as perhaps no other scene in Shakespeare has. Another device, the use of comic relief, such as in 2.1 and 5.4.152–192, reflects the need to dilute a mood of growing tragedy that is counter to the play's general thrust.

In *Cymbeline* the seams of Shakespeare's construction show; they don't in *The Winter's Tale* and *The Tempest*. We should not reject the play altogether, however, for as we have seen, it has magic. Samuel JOHNSON complained of the play that "to remark the folly of the fiction, the absurdity . . ., the confusion . . . were to waste criticism upon unresisting imbecility, upon faults too evident for detection. . . ." However, these evident faults also provide, along with folly and confusion, the escapist charms of romantic literature in general and of Imogen's world in particular. They need not be apologized for but merely accepted, and *Cymbeline* may be enjoyed for itself as well as for its place as the immediate predecessor of Shakespeare's last two masterpieces.

SOURCES OF THE PLAY

The main plot of *Cymbeline*—a man wagers on his lover's chastity and is fooled, orders her death, which a good servant prevents, and is finally reunited with her—had been popular for centuries in various forms and in several languages. Shakespeare's version drew on two sources: one, an anonymous English translation of a Dutch tale, *Frederyke of Jennen* (Antwerp, 1518; London, 1520, 1560); and, much better known, a tale in the *Decameron* (1353) of Giovanni BOCCACCIO. Although no English translation of Boccaccio's story appeared before 1620, Shakespeare may have read it in Italian (though his capacity to do so is disputed), or in a French translation such as the very popular version of Antoine LE MAÇON (1545). The same tale was to be a minor source for *The Winter's Tale*. Boccaccio's tale and *Frederyke of Jennen* (i.e., of Genoa) apparently stem from the same medieval Italian source, which is now lost. They both tell essentially the same story, but *Cymbeline* reflects details exclusive to each.

Another source was Raphael HOLINSHED's *Chronicles of England, Scotland, and Ireland* (2nd ed., 1587),

which provided an account of the historical Cymbeline's reign. However, minor details come from at least two other historical sources, Robert FABYAN's *New Chronicle of England and of France* (1516) and A MIRROR FOR MAGISTRATES (1587), a popular collection of biographies. An obscure, anonymous English play, *The Rare Triumphs of Love and Fortune* (performed in 1582, published in 1589), provided Shakespeare with most of the other important components of *Cymbeline*—Posthumus and Imogen's love, Cloten's jealousy, Posthumus's banishment, Imogen's flight to an unjustly banished courtier who lives in a cave—along with various minor details. Some scholars speculate that a nearly contemporary play, *Philaster* by Francis BEAUMONT and John FLETCHER, may have influenced some of the language in *Cymbeline*, but since the dates of both plays are obscure, and since Beaumont and Fletcher were novice playwrights at the time, other scholars believe that the younger men imitated Shakespeare.

TEXT OF THE PLAY

Cymbeline was probably written ca. 1608–10, but firm evidence is lacking. A performance was recorded in the summer of 1611, so the play cannot have been composed later than early in that year. Stylistic evidence makes clear that it was roughly contemporary with the other ROMANCES, especially *The Winter's Tale* (ca. 1610–11), and it seems to represent an advance over *Pericles* (ca. 1607) in the development of the genre. Some scholars believe it was written during the plague-imposed closure of the London theaters from the summer of 1608 to December 1609.

The play was not published in Shakespeare's lifetime, and it appeared first in the FIRST FOLIO (1623). This text was probably printed from a transcription of Shakespeare's FOUL PAPERS, though some scholars believe it was taken from a PROMPTBOOK. As the only early version of the play, the Folio text has been the basis for all subsequent editions.

THEATRICAL HISTORY OF THE PLAY

The earliest known performance of *Cymbeline*—probably at the GLOBE THEATRE—was recorded by Simon FORMAN in the summer of 1611; no other early performances are known. Thomas D'URFEY adapted the play as *The Injured Princess or the Fatal Wager* (1682), a popular version with an elaborate subplot in which Cloten kidnaps a daughter of Pisanio. It was revived periodically for 80 years.

Colley CIBBER produced a version of Shakespeare's play in 1744, and *Cymbeline* was mildly popular for the rest of the 18th century, though only with altered texts. David GARRICK, who staged the play several times beginning in 1761, was especially noted for his Posthumus (opposite Sarah SIDDONS, in the 1780s). In 1767 the play was staged in colonial New York. The 19th century saw few productions of *Cymbeline*, but they were very elaborately staged. The most important of these were the productions of John Philip KEMBLE (1806, 1827). Helen FAUCIT played the heroine a number of times up to the age of 48, with great success, and Adelaide NEILSON was also associated with the role. Ellen TERRY, in Henry IRVING's production of 1896, was widely acclaimed as the century's greatest Imogen. This production was heavily abridged (as most have been); for example, the vision of Jupiter was cut.

Cymbeline was not widely produced in the 20th century, either, though George Bernard SHAW staged his own witty version of Act 5, titled *Cymbeline Refinished*, in 1937. Probably the most notable modern productions of the play were the 1923 modern dress staging by Barry JACKSON—his first such experiment—and the 1957 STRATFORD staging by Peter HALL, starring Peggy ASHCROFT as Imogen. Though *Cymbeline* was twice made into a silent FILM—in the United States (1913) and Germany (1925)—it has not been a movie since. The BBC produced a TELEVISION version starring Claire Bloom in 1984.

CHARACTERS

Arviragus   Character in *Cymbeline,* one of the two kidnapped sons of King Cymbeline. Arviragus and his older brother Guiderius have been raised to be woodsmen and hunters in the wilds of WALES by their foster father Belarius, who kidnapped them in infancy when he was unjustly exiled by Cymbeline. When their sister Imogen, disguised as a young man, happens onto their cave, the boys immediately love "him," although they don't know that they are siblings. Like Guiderius, Arviragus is inherently noble and desires to prove himself in the greater world of kingly courts and warfare. When the Romans invade Britain, the brothers have their chance. After they save the British army they are honored by the king, and then, in the extraordinary sequence of revelations and reconciliations in 5.5, they are reunited with their father.

Both Arviragus and Guiderius are simple fairy-tale figures—lost princes who are eventually discovered and restored to their rightful positions—and they have the princely attributes of courage, sincerity, and high spirits. However, Shakespeare takes care to distinguish them from each other. Arviragus is the more reflective of the two; he also speaks some of the play's best poetry. He responds more strongly to Imogen's beauty, and when Guiderius praises her cooking, the more esthetic Arviragus emphasizes her singing. When they believe her dead, Arviragus expresses their grief in a lyrical passage (4.2.218–229) that compares her beauty to the flowers. Arviragus also offers an intellectually grounded, if simple, denunciation of money, in 3.7.26–28. Belarius has given Arviragus the name Cadwal, and this name is occasionally used in dialogue, but he is designated as Arviragus in speech headings and stage directions.

Attendant   Any of several minor characters in *Cymbeline,* servants of King Cymbeline. In 3.5 an Attendant is sent to find Imogen and returns to report briefly that her chambers are locked and silent. This informs the court of what the audience already knows—that Imogen has fled. The Attendant serves merely as an instrument of communication. Also, a number of Attendants mutely swell the king's retinue when he is informed of the approaching Roman army, in 4.3; their function is purely decorative.

Belarius   Character in *Cymbeline,* the foster father of Guiderius and Arviragus. Belarius was unjustly exiled from the court of King Cymbeline many years before the time of the play, and in revenge he had kidnapped the king's infant sons. He has since raised them in the wilds of WALES. When the Roman army invades Britain, Belarius helps his foster sons save the British army, and the three are honored by the king. However, because Guiderius has killed Prince Cloten, he is threatened with the death sentence prescribed for commoners who kill a prince. Belarius, to save the young man's life, reveals the truth. Though he has exposed himself to capital punishment because he had kidnapped the heir to the throne, Belarius is forgiven by the king in the play's final sequence of mercies and reconciliations. Belarius is a good man, unjustly persecuted, who recovers his position only by accident. He thus embodies an important theme of the play, that man is helpless without the aid of providence.

Belarius has taken the name Morgan, but he is designated Belarius in speech headings and stage directions. His Welsh pseudonym goes well with his comic habit of speaking in moralizing clichés, for he fills the 17th-century English stereotype of the dull Welshman.

Brother Either of two minor characters in *Cymbeline,* the deceased siblings of Posthumus who appear to him as apparitions in 5.4. The Brothers appear with the spirits of their father, Sicilius Leonatus, and their Mother. Led by Sicilius, the group pleads with Jupiter for mercy on Posthumus. The Brothers point out Posthumus's qualities in an elaborate poem; the First Brother speaks two stanzas and the Second Brother one. The Second Brother notes that they had both died, with their father, before Posthumus was born. This fact has been previously mentioned in 1.1.35–40. The episode adds to the romantic strangeness of the play, and the Brothers have the eerie presence of supernatural beings.

Cadwal In *Cymbeline,* the false name under which King Cymbeline's son Arviragus is raised from infancy by his kidnapper and foster father, Belarius.

Captain (1) Minor character in *Cymbeline,* an officer in the Roman army. In 4.2 the Captain reports to Lucius that the army has landed in WALES. His six terse lines serve to convey information that moves the plot to a new stage.

Captain (2) Either of two minor characters in *Cymbeline,* officers in the British army. In 5.3, after the British victory over the Romans that is

described by Posthumus earlier in the scene, the Captains discover Posthumus in his Roman uniform and take him prisoner. They turn him over to King Cymbeline in a DUMB SHOW that ends the scene. With only a few lines between them, the Captains' function is to further the plot. However, they also inform the audience that in addition to the heroes Belarius, Guiderius, and Arviragus—already described by Posthumus—there was a fourth. This leads us to guess that this man was Posthumus himself, which proves to have been the case.

Cloten Character in *Cymbeline,* the uncouth son of the Queen of Britain and the rejected suitor of Imogen, who then plans to rape her and kill her husband Posthumus. Cloten is a comic villain for the most part. He is a stupid and vainglorious man who inspires bemused contempt, though he has his threatening moments and reminds us of the potential for tragedy that underlies the fairy-tale ambience of much of the play. He is finally killed when he happens, entirely by chance, on the lost prince Guiderius, who handily beheads him and then remarks, "This Cloten was a fool, an empty purse" (4.2.113). His function is that of a fairy-tale villain whose fate is to be defeated by the hand of providence.

Cloten's personality and function vary considerably in the course of the play. In Acts 1–2 Cloten is quite simply a boor; a braggart who is mocked by his own companions and by Imogen's Lady. Imogen tells him he is not worth the "mean'st garment" of Posthumus (2.3.132), and complains that she is "sprited with a fool" (2.3.138). In Act 3 Cloten takes on a different, less inane, air as he blusters patriotically and helps to commit Britain to a foolish war against ROME. Finally, in Act 4 he is the villain who schemes to kill Posthumus in front of Imogen before he rapes her and who crassly insults Guiderius for his supposed inferiority.

Such changes make it hard to precisely characterize Cloten's function in the play, and this problem offers a hint of Shakespeare's trouble with the ROMANCES, a new genre in which *Cymbeline* was an experiment. The irregularities in Cloten's personality are similar to those of the play as a whole, and they betray the playwright's difficulty in melding the realistic characters to which he was accustomed with the ethereal figures required by the romances. Cloten seems to be a compound of several types of writing, created as Shakespeare struggled with the task of generating a new type of character, a villain who must convincingly represent evil without being so real as to intrude on a world of fantasy. Though a faulty character, Cloten foreshadows a much more successful figure of this kind, Caliban of *The Tempest.*

Some scholars have speculated that portions of Cloten's role may have been considerably modified by the actor who played the character, probably Robert ARMIN. Armin wrote plays and was famous for improvisation, so he was capable of creating additional dialogue. Moreover, in addition to his Shakespearean roles, he specialized in playing a character type of his own devising, a mentally limited CLOWN who may be reflected in some of Cloten's doltishness. Cloten's speeches are in both prose and verse, and this theory suggests that the prose passages were written—or at least altered in performance, before publication—by Armin. However, though some such alteration could have contaminated the text— if it was based on a PROMPTBOOK—this idea cannot be proven. More probably the evidence reflects the difficulties mentioned above.

Cornelius Character in *Cymbeline,* a physician to the Queen of Britain. In 1.6 Cornelius has provided the Queen with a poison—for experimental purposes, she says—but he informs us in an aside that he distrusts her and has substituted a sleeping potion. Imogen later takes this and is mistaken for dead. Later, in the play's final scene, he recounts the dying Queen's confession (5.5.31–61) and explains again about the poison (5.5.243–258). Cornelius's function is to further the plot and highlight the Queen's evil nature.

Cymbeline (Cunobelinus) (d. ca. A.D. 40) Historical figure and title character of *Cymbeline,* the king of Britain and father of Imogen. Though Cymbeline is the title character, he is not an important one. The title of the play suggests the land he rules, rather than him personally. He is a typical king of fairy-tale and romantic literature. He loses his prosperity when he follows evil advisers, and then recovers it in a traditional happy ending through the workings of a benevolent fate. Influenced by his vicious Queen of Britain and her son Cloten, he proceeds unjustly against his innocent daughter and her husband, Posthumus. He loses Imogen as he once lost his sons, by another unjust action, the banishment of Belarius 20 years earlier. Moreover, still under the influence of his wife and stepson, he commits Britain to a foolish war against ROME. However, fate intervenes, and Cymbeline is eventually freed from evil. The Romans are miraculously defeated by the king's long-lost sons, and Cymbeline recovers his family and survives to be merciful to his enemies at the play's close.

Cymbeline is a passive figure whose competence as a ruler can be restored only by a happy ending brought about by chance, rather than by himself. On the other hand, his crimes are equally not his own; he is only unintentionally cruel, and though wrongheaded, he is quite willing to admit his folly and accept the mercy of providence. He is a figure from traditional lore who is necessary to the plot but does not contribute to it. His character is not fully developed, and what we see is a feeble store of anger in early scenes, a dumbfounded confusion later on, and a mild exaltation at the end.

The historical Cymbeline, generally called Cunobelinus, was a powerful ruler among the Celtic tribes of southeast England, but Shakespeare's figure bears virtually no resemblance to him. Shakespeare's source, HOLINSHED's *Chronicles,* was rather vague and inaccurate regarding Cunobelinus's reign, but the playwright did not follow his source particularly closely in any case. The most striking difference is that Rome's invasion—a successful one that established Roman rule in Britain—came several years after Cunobelinus's death. Cunobelinus was among the most successful of England's tribal kings in terms of conquering his neighbors, but little else is known of his reign.

Dutchman and Spaniard Minor characters in *Cymbeline,* nonspeaking witnesses of the wager between Posthumus and Iachimo. Neither the

Dutchman nor his companion the Spaniard does anything at all; they are mentioned only in the stage directions at 1.5.1. Shakespeare found both figures in one of his sources, *Frederyke of Jennen*, but scholars differ on their function in the play. Each may be a GHOST CHARACTER, considered by the playwright but then abandoned and therefore not actually employed in early productions. Alternatively, lines they spoke, probably brief explanatory ones, may have been lost. Finally, Shakespeare may have intended them as comic caricatures of their nationalities—a popular dramatic feature in his day—and perhaps he intended them to be in a drunken stupor, also popular in comedy.

Fidele   In *Cymbeline*, the name taken by Imogen in her disguise as a young man. Fidele is a French name, and this contributes to the multilingual confusion of the play, a characteristic feature of Shakespeare's ROMANCES.

Frenchman   Minor character in *Cymbeline*, a friend of the Roman gentleman Philario. In 1.5 Posthumus arrives in ROME. He has been exiled from Britain because he married the king's daughter, Imogen, and he meets the Frenchman and Iachimo at Philario's home. The Frenchman has known Posthumus in the past, and he recollects a duel the Briton once fought over the virtues of a woman. This triggers the fateful wager between Posthumus and Iachimo over Imogen's chastity. The Frenchman is a pawn of plot development, and represents the world of gentlemanly duels inhabited by Posthumus and Iachimo.

Gaoler   Either of two minor characters in *Cymbeline*, keepers of the captured Posthumus, who is believed to be a Roman prisoner of war. In 5.4 the First Gaoler is a CLOWN who interrupts the action with humorous remarks on life and death (the Second Gaoler speaks only half a line). He provides comic relief as the plot becomes most troubling. He offers a sardonic philosophy of death as a relief from life, a view that encapsulates Posthumus's depressed state.

The placement of this character is significant. The Gaoler (after a mute appearance in 5.3, and a brief one at the opening of 5.4) arrives to summon Posthumus to his execution, at 5.4.152. This is after Posthumus has had his vision of Sicilius Leonatus and Jupiter—which we recognize as the climax of the play. Thus, the Gaoler's comic approach to the tragic potential of life comes only after an assurance that the play will have a happy ending.

The Gaoler resembles such predecessors as the Porter of *Macbeth* and the Grave-digger of *Hamlet*. Some scholars believe that the First Gaoler's part was written to be performed by the same actor who played Cloten—probably Robert ARMIN. This hypothetical idea is based on the clownishness of the two characters and the possibility of one person playing both, since Cloten dies early in Act 4.

Gentleman   Either of two minor characters in *Cymbeline*, noblemen at King Cymbeline's court. In 1.1 the First Gentleman tells the Second Gentleman about the marriage of the king's daughter, Imogen, to Posthumus, a poor but noble youth who has been banished from Britain because the king had wanted Imogen to marry the boorish Cloten. He adds that Imogen is the king's only child, other than two lost sons, kidnapped 20 years earlier and never recovered. The First Gentleman's excitement is clear in his hurried speech. This stirs interest in the audience, though his companion merely punctuates his monologue with brief questions. The episode, which fills the whole of the play's first scene, establishes the basic situation of the plot.

Guiderius   Character in *Cymbeline*, one of the two kidnapped sons of King Cymbeline. Guiderius and his younger brother Arviragus have been raised as hunters in the wilderness of WALES by their foster father Belarius, who kidnapped them in infancy when he was unjustly exiled by Cymbeline. Guiderius shares with his brother the desire to prove himself in war, which is evidence of his inherently regal courage. Their sister Imogen, who is unknown to them, appears by chance, disguised as a boy, and both young men immediately love "him." This good-hearted response emphasizes their kinship, which is of course already known to the audience, in a classic demonstration of dramatic irony. When the Romans invade Britain, the brothers display their innate capacity for leadership and save the British army. They are honored by the king and then identified and reunited with him, as part of the revelations and reconciliations at the play's close.

Guiderius, like Arviragus, is a simple fairy-tale figure—a lost prince who is restored to his rightful position—and his personality is mostly seen in courage and high spirits. However, Shakespeare takes care to distinguish the brothers from each other. As the future heir to the throne, Guiderius is more forceful and dynamic than his reflective brother Arviragus. When they discuss Imogen's virtues, Guiderius proves more practical when he mentions her cooking, while Arviragus praises her singing. When they believe her dead, Guiderius cuts short his brother's "wench-like words" (4.2.230) and says, "Let us bury him, / And not protract with admiration what / Is now due debt. To th'grave!" (4.2.231–233). At his most striking, Guiderius kills Cloten with soldierly aplomb earlier in the same scene. He brandishes his victim's head while he remarks, "This Cloten was a fool, an empty purse" (4.2.113). Later he declares he will throw the head into the creek "to tell the fishes he's the queen's son" (4.2.153). In 5.5 he manfully acknowledges that he has killed Cloten despite the threat of capital punishment for killing a prince (he is not yet known to be a prince himself). His "I have spoke it, and I did it" (5.5.290) has a kingly simplicity and force. Belarius has given Guiderius the name Polydore, and this name is occasionally used in dialogue, but he is designated as Guiderius in speech headings and stage directions.

Iachimo Character in *Cymbeline*, the villain who pretends to have seduced Posthumus's new wife, Imogen. He thus provokes the murderous jealousy in Posthumus that stimulates much of the action of the play. Motivated only by an irresponsible pleasure in mischief, Iachimo wagers that he can seduce Imogen. When he fails, he resorts to trickery. He secretes himself in her bedroom, steals her bracelet, and then poses as her lover. He flaunts his knowledge of her intimate surroundings and declares the bracelet a gift. His plan accomplished in 2.4, Iachimo pockets the diamond ring he has won from Posthumus and disappears from the play until very

near its close, when he returns to Britain as a member of the Roman army. He proves unsuccessful in combat, and he supposes that his guilt for blackening Imogen's name has weakened him as a warrior. Captured, he confesses to his crime when the disguised Imogen recognizes on his hand the ring he has won. In the aura of reconciliation that closes the play, he is forgiven by Posthumus.

Commentators have often compared Iachimo to Shakespeare's most extraordinary villain, Iago (of *Othello*), whose lies are similar in content. His name, the diminutive of Iago, suggests a similarly evil temperament, but Iachimo is a very different sort of villain. He is closer to the likable Autolycus, the vagabond thief of *The Winter's Tale*. Iachimo is essentially a stock comic figure, the unscrupulous Italian (see ROME). He has no intention of destroying anyone's life, as Iago does; he barely has any intention at all. He is more like a con man than a rapist, though he compares himself to the genuinely fearful Tarquin (of *The Rape of Lucrece*). However, he does so just as he has comically emerged like a jack-in-the-box, from a trunk (2.2) and such a ludicrous villain assures us that Imogen will not be permanently damaged. This aspect of Iachimo is important to the play's generally optimistic tone. We are never in doubt that the world of romance is dominant; Iachimo is merely an instrument of fate, which controls the adventures of Posthumus and Imogen. Even in the humiliation of his final exposure, Iachimo remains comic. Our awareness of his harmlessness is reinforced as he shamelessly embroiders the truth, apparently hoping to make himself seem a pleasingly audacious young gentleman. Both boastful and apologetic, he seems an entirely appropriate object of mercy—an immature fool. Unlike the other villains of the piece, the Queen of Britain and Cloten, mercy is granted to him.

Imogen Character in *Cymbeline*, daughter of King Cymbeline and wife of Posthumus. Imogen, the central character of the play, loses the love of her husband through no fault of her own, is exposed to great danger and wanders in the wilderness, and then is finally restored to happiness. She embodies the play's lesson that while humanity may exhibit courage and an undefeatable spirit of love, our happiness nevertheless depends on providence. Imogen has long been among the favorite heroines in Shakespeare. The Victorian poet SWIN-BURNE extravagantly called her "the woman best beloved in all the world of song and all the tide of time." However, her great charm is also evidence of a failure on the playwright's part as he struggled with a new genre, the ROMANCES.

Imogen is subjected to a harrowing sequence of misfortunes. Her father banishes Posthumus to Italy, and she faces the unwanted courtship of both the boorish Cloten and the oily Iachimo, the latter of whom malevolently convinces Posthumus that she has been unfaithful. Posthumus thereupon arranges for her murder in the wilds of WALES. A faithful servant, Pisanio, warns her and provides her with a disguise as a young man, but she finds herself stranded in the wilderness. After several adventurous episodes during which she comes to believe Posthumus is dead and is herself believed to be dead by others, she returns to her father's court in the guise of a Roman prisoner of war. In the final scene's sequence of reconciliations, her identity is revealed, and she is reunited with both husband and father.

Though Imogen has always enchanted audiences, her resourcefulness and charm suggest one who battles against destiny rather than the helpless victim of fate. In the literature on which Shakespeare's romances were based, the traditional character type corresponding to Imogen was the fairy-tale princess who is adored for her beauty and passive calm, an object of intrigue but not a participant in it. She represents humanity's helplessness and inspires pity in her plight, rather than admiration for her pluck. Imogen is intermittently presented in terms of this ideal. To Pisanio, she is "more goddess-like than wife-like" (3.2.8), and Iachimo compares her to "th'Arabian bird" (1.7.17), the fabled Phoenix who cannot die. She sometimes seems to be a helpless puppet of the plot, as when she immediately accepts Iachimo's transparently false excuse for having proposed adultery with a humble "You make amends" (1.7.168). Moreover, she adopts a purely conventional morality when she refuses to sleep with Posthumus even after they are

married, presumably because she awaits her father's approval of the match.

However, Imogen has another set of qualities as well. In her spunk, her sharp wit, and her willingness to pursue her lover—as well as in her male disguise—Imogen is typical of Shakespeare's earlier comic heroines. In *Cymbeline* the playwright approached a new sort of character but could not divorce himself from habits of characterization that he had used earlier. This happened with several of the characters in the play. Imogen is a transitional figure; Shakespeare would soon create female characters whose ethereal serenity would fulfill the romantic ideal. In Imogen he produced an uneasy conjunction of ideal womanhood—seen in Hermione of *The Winter's Tale* and Miranda of *The Tempest*—and boyish pluck, such as had enlivened Rosalind of *As You Like It*, and Viola of *Twelfth Night*, among others. Imogen, for all her charming virtues, presents an image slightly contrary to the general tone of the play and thus in part contributes to its weakness.

Jupiter Pagan god and minor character in *Cymbeline*. Jupiter, the Roman king of the gods, appears to the desperate Posthumus in a vision where he assures the spirit of Posthumus's father, Sicilius Leonatus, that the young man will be restored to good fortune. He then departs, leaving a tablet with a cryptic message (5.4.138–145) that is interpreted later by the Soothsayer as an allegory of reunion and renewal. Posthumus does not realize that his chaotic drift toward tragedy has ended with the god's appearance, and he is still intent on death. However, the audience is aware that he shall be "happier much by his affliction made" (5.4.108), as the god puts it. Thus, Jupiter embodies the play's moral: that humanity depends on providence for happiness.

Jupiter's style is very formal. He speaks in rhyming verse and old-fashioned language unlike anything else in the play. This signifies his supernatural nature. In performance, his lines are sometimes sung. The stage direction at his entrance reads, "Jupiter descends in thunder and lightning, sitting upon an eagle . . ." (5.4.–92); this makes it clear that either the BLACKFRIARS THEATRE or the GLOBE THEATRE, or both, were equipped with a mechanical apparatus that permitted characters to enter a scene from above by being lowered from the ceiling. As in the present case, this permitted a literal deus ex machina, or "god from the machine," the phrase for a surprise appearance by a god who resolves the situation of a play. The machine was originally a cranelike device used in ancient Greek theater to lower actors portraying deities as though they were descending from heaven.

Some scholars believe Jupiter may have been intended as an allegorical representation of King JAMES I, newly crowned as the first joint monarch of England and Scotland. In this light, the cryptic tablet reads as a tribute to the union of the two countries, a matter that was disputed in the first years of James's reign.

Lady   Any of several minor characters in *Cymbeline*, noblewomen of King Cymbeline's court. Attendants of Imogen or the Queen of Britain, the Ladies serve mostly to signify their mistresses' royal status and to swell the scene at court, though one Lady does offer an amusingly disdainful reception to the boorish Prince Cloten in 2.3.76–84, which helps to characterize the play's comic villain.

Lord   Any of several minor characters in *Cymbeline*, noblemen at the court of King Cymbeline. In 1.3 and 2.1, two of the noblemen are featured as followers of the uncouth Prince Cloten; the First Lord is attentive and flattering, but the Second Lord mocks the obnoxious prince behind his back, which helps to characterize the play's comic villain. In Acts 3–5, the Lords play a smaller part as often-silent figures who swell the scene at Cymbeline's court. A single Lord appears in 5.3 as a soldier who has fled from the battle against the Romans. Though this could possibly be a different person, Posthumus's disdain for him would be appropriate if he were one of Cloten's followers. In any case, this Lord serves to receive information as Posthumus tells him—and the audience—of the battle's outcome.

Lucius   Character in *Cymbeline*, ambassador from ROME to the Britain of King Cymbeline, later the commander of the invading Roman army and the employer of the disguised Imogen. In 3.1 Lucius informs Cymbeline that Rome demands tribute from Britain. When he receives the king's refusal, he transmits his government's declaration of war. However, he adds that he regrets this, for he appreciates the hospitality he has received in Britain. His gentlemanly nature is again evident in 3.5, when he departs from the king's court, and we understand why Pisanio recommends that the disguised Imogen become a page for Lucius. He calls the Roman "honourable, and . . . most holy" (3.4.178–179). In 4.2 Lucius readily offers employment and protection to Imogen. He believes that she is a young man, Fidele, and he takes particular care of "him" when the Romans are defeated in battle in 5.2. Finally, in 5.5 Lucius nobly faces death at the hands of the victorious Cymbeline, before he receives mercy in the play's final aura of reconciliation.

Lucius is a noble person who is unable to influence the course of events in the play. He is contrasted with assorted weak, but not evil, figures like Posthumus and the king, and thus he offers a positive image of humanity's need for the intervention of providence. The ancient tradition that a soldier named Lucius was the first Roman converted to Christianity may be reflected in Shakespeare's choice of name for this positive character. Two of Shakespeare's other characters named Lucius are also right-minded and in the military, so these may well be conscious references to the ancient convert, who was still fairly well known in the 17th century.

Messenger   Minor character in *Cymbeline*, a servant of King Cymbeline. In 2.3 the Messenger announces the arrival of an ambassador, and in 5.4 he summons Posthumus from his pending execution to an audience with the king. The Messenger's function is to advance the plot.

Morgan   In *Cymbeline*, the name taken in exile by the banished courtier Belarius.

Mother   Minor character in *Cymbeline*, the deceased parent of Posthumus who appears to him as an apparition, in 5.4. The Mother appears with other ghosts: her husband, Sicilius Leonatus, and her two sons. Led by Sicilius, they plead with Jupiter for mercy on Posthumus. The Mother's part in this ritualistic solicitation is small; she points out that she died when she gave birth to Posthumus and left him an orphan; because of this, he deserves pity. She is a supernatural presence in an episode whose function is to create an air of eerie romance.

Musicians Minor characters in *Cymbeline*, players who serenade Imogen for Cloten. One of the Musicians sings the song, "Hark, hark, the lark" (2.3.19–25), but otherwise they do not speak and leave as soon as they have completed their performance. The episode offers a musical diversion that is appropriate to a comedy. It also relieves the sense of menace from the previous scene— Iachimo's trespass in Imogen's bedchamber—and from the approach of Cloten. Additionally, it provides time for Imogen to change her costume from nightclothes to daytime garb.

Philario Minor character in *Cymbeline*, Posthumus's host in ROME. In 1.5 the gentlemanly Philario attempts to defuse the argument that leads to Posthumus's fatal wager with Iachimo. In 2.4 when Iachimo claims to have won the bet by seducing Imogen, Philario tries to convince the enraged Posthumus not to believe him. He has no success in either endeavor. He thus represents human virtue, a force that promises good in the world but proves useless in the face of evil. As such, he reinforces the play's theme that humankind is dependent on providence more than on its own efforts.

Pisanio Character in *Cymbeline*, the faithful servant of Posthumus. When his master is exiled for having married Imogen, King Cymbeline's daughter, Pisanio remains at court to serve her. He embodies a well-known figure of folklore and literature: the faithful servant who serves his master best by disobeying him. When Posthumus is deceived by Iachimo and believes that Imogen has betrayed him, he orders Pisanio to murder her. Instead, the servant helps Imogen escape and provides her with a disguise as a page, in which she has further adventures. However, for all his steadfastness and common sense, Pisanio cannot provide further assistance. He loses contact with both Posthumus and Imogen and finds himself under suspicion at court. Fearful and confused, he resigns himself to whatever fate may bring. "The heavens still must work" and "Fortune brings in some boats that are not steer'd" (4.3.41, 46), he says. He thus states neatly the play's central lesson: that humanity is dependent on providence.

Polydore In *Cymbeline*, the false name under which King Cymbeline's son Guiderius is raised from infancy by his kidnapper and foster father Belarius.

Posthumus Leonatus Character in *Cymbeline*, the husband of Imogen. Banished from Britain for secretly marrying the daughter of King Cymbeline, Posthumus goes to ROME. There he boasts of Imogen's virtues and wagers the diamond ring she has given him that the courtier Iachimo cannot seduce her. Iachimo is unsuccessful, but he deceives Posthumus, who foolishly believes him and vows revenge on Imogen. By letter, he instructs his servant, Pisanio, to murder her. Once he has established the situation that faces Imogen in Acts 3–4, Posthumus disappears from the play until, near the end, he reappears, stricken with guilt over the murder he believes has been committed. He seeks death in battle and fights for Britain against ROME, but he is not killed. He then seeks death as a Roman prisoner of war, but while in captivity he dreams of his family and the god Jupiter, who promises that his story shall end happily. Unaware of this when he awakes, Posthumus appears before the king as a Roman captive, but he reveals himself when Iachimo confesses his deception. Posthumus, in his turn, confesses to Imogen's murder before he discovers that she is alive and he is reunited with her. In the aura of reconciliation that closes the play, the king accepts Posthumus as a son-in-law.

In the course of the play, Posthumus's qualities vary enormously from the ideal to the seriously flawed. In this respect he offers clues to the difficulties Shakespeare faced when he wrote the ROMANCES, a new genre of plays in which *Cymbeline* was an experiment. The playwright faced the problem of integrating realistic settings and characters, which he was accustomed to creating, with the ethereal, almost abstract characters of fairy tales and traditional romantic literature on which the romances were based. Posthumus, like other characters in *Cymbeline,* demonstrates that he was not always successful.

As the play opens, Posthumus is praised by a Gentleman who declares, "I do not think / so fair an outward, and such stuff within / Endows a man, but he" (1.1.22–24); here, he is simply a traditional romantic prince and a proper mate for Imogen. However, once on his own in Rome he is ludicrously immature, intent on an inflated idea of masculine honor. In 1.5 he, Iachimo, and the Frenchman almost seem to offer a satire on dueling. His wholly unnecessary defense of Imogen's chastity is no less ridiculous than his readiness to disbelieve in it later, and his response is ignoble when he instructs his servant to murder Imogen in revenge. Nevertheless, he is once again the traditional princely hero when he helps the king's long-lost sons, Guiderius and Arviragus, defeat the Romans, and it is certainly to his credit that he comes to regret his earlier actions and feel guilt. However, the basic problem with his character is most evident here. His elaborate attempts at suicide detract from our appreciation of his real personal distress. On one hand, it is difficult to accept Posthumus as a real figure like the victimized Othello, while on the other, he does not provide a bold allegorical representation of human error, like, say, Leontes, of *The Winter's Tale.* Shakespeare had not yet learned to permit the symbolic to dominate, and Posthumus's human reality interferes with his value as an archetype of jealousy. This makes him a somewhat ridiculous and unsympathetic figure.

The name Posthumus indicates that its owner was born after his father's death. It is so rare today that it seems intended to convey some extra meaning, perhaps comical. However, though unusual (like the phenomenon it commemorates), the name was regularly given in Shakespeare's day (see, e.g., HOBY, SIR THOMAS POSTHUMOUS).

Queen of Britain Character in *Cymbeline,* the wife of King Cymbeline and stepmother of his daughter Imogen. The Queen, one of several villains in the play, is the most purely vicious of them. She had planned that Imogen marry her son, the oafish Cloten, but Imogen eloped with Posthumus

instead. Posthumus is banished, and the Queen directs her malice toward Imogen and Pisanio, Posthumus's servant who has stayed with Imogen. She is the archetypal wicked stepmother, and her villainy is clear from her initial appearance, in 1.2, when she pretends to protect Imogen but reveals her malice in an aside. Imogen is undeceived and notes the Queen's "dissembling courtesy" (1.2.15); thus, the Queen's wickedness is immediately established. In 1.6 the Queen collects poison from the physician Cornelius and offers it to Pisanio as a health-giving potion in the hope that he will take it and die. However, Cornelius "will not trust one of her malice" (1.6.35) and has substituted a sleeping potion for the poison. The Queen is ultimately ineffective, but her evil intent is a prominent element of the first half of the play.

Once her nature is well established, the Queen plays a lesser role. At the play's close we learn of her death from an illness caused by her despair at Cloten's sudden disappearance. Her final confession of sins—including an intent to poison the king himself—prepares for the final sequence of reconciliations in 5.5. The Queen has only been forestalled by the whim of fortune: Cloten has been killed by a chance encounter that is the result of a long series of events that began with the exile of Posthumus. She has therein fulfilled the villain's role in this play, which is to be defeated by the intervention of providence.

Senator Either of two minor characters in *Cymbeline,* Roman legislators. In 3.8 the Senators inform two Tribunes that the emperor has ordered them to raise an army from the gentry of ROME to be sent against King Cymbeline. The First Senator does all the speaking—apart from the Second Senator's single word in 3.8.11—and he serves to convey information to the tribunes and to the audience.

Sicilius Leonatus Minor character in *Cymbeline,* the deceased father of Posthumus who appears as a ghost in 5.4. The spirit of Sicilius is accompanied by those of his wife, Posthumus's Mother, and his two elder sons. Sicilius leads them as they plead to Jupiter on behalf of Posthumus. Sicilius observes that he died before Posthumus was born, a circumstance that earns pity for his son. The family demands that Jupiter show mercy and restore Posthumus to happiness, or else, Sicilius declares, they will appeal to "th' shining synod of the rest" of the gods (5.4.89). Jupiter appears and promises mercy, Sicilius responds with awe and wonder, and all the apparitions disappear.

Sicilius's appearance is foreshadowed at the beginning of the play. In 1.1 a Gentleman tells of Posthumus's parentage. We learn that Sicilius Leonatus gained his surname, which means "lion-like," for his bravery in battle, and that he died fighting for Britain against the Romans. Posthumus inherited the name and the bravery—as he demonstrates in battle in 5.2—so when Sicilius appears, we see him as an emblem of his son's virtues combined with the awesome presence of a supernatural creature. The episode contributes to the bizarre and romantic atmosphere of the play. Sicilius and the other ghosts employ a rhyming, sing-song mode of speech that has encouraged some scholars to speculate that the passage may not have been written by Shakespeare, who was certainly capable of much more elegant poetry. However, the ghosts' language is ritualistic and establishes an eerie air of the occult prior to the appearance of Jupiter.

Soothsayer Minor character in *Cymbeline*, a priestly fortune-teller who serves the Roman army. In 4.2 the Soothsayer tells of his dream of "Jove's bird, the Roman eagle" (4.2.348), which he interprets as an omen of victory for the forthcoming battle against King Cymbeline's British forces. Though he is mistaken—the Britons win—this reference may be recalled by the audience when Jupiter (or Jove) appears to Posthumus, in 5.4. In 5.5 the Soothsayer, who is now a prisoner of war, interprets the text that Jupiter left behind. He offers an interpretation that formulates the play's symbolic values of reunion and renewal. The Soothsayer's name, Philarmonus (5.5.434), suggests the joyful conclusion that he foretells.

Spaniard See Dutchman and Spaniard.

Tribune Either of two minor characters in *Cymbeline*, Roman officials. In 3.8 the Tribunes are informed by a Senator of the emperor's orders: They are to recruit an armed force from among the gentry of ROME that will be sent against King Cymbeline. Only the First Tribune speaks; he asks two brief questions and tersely accepts the orders. These two figures serve as recipients of information intended principally for the audience.

Edward III
SYNOPSIS

Act 1, Scene 1
The Count of Artois, an exile from FRANCE, supports the English king Edward III's claim to the French throne. The Duke of Lorraine arrives with arrogant demands from King John of France. Edward declares he will conquer France and claim his rightful crown. His son the Prince of Wales joins in his defiance, and Lorraine departs. Montague arrives with news that King David of Scotland has broken a truce and is besieging the castle of the Countess, whose husband, Salisbury, is already fighting against France, in a proxy war on Edward's behalf. King Edward orders preparations made for invading France; in the meantime, he will repulse the Scots. The Prince exults in the prospect of battle.

Act 1, Scene 2
The Countess, on the wall of her besieged castle, overhears King David assure Lorraine of his allegiance to France. The King argues with his follower Douglas, claiming possession of the soon-to-be-conquered Countess. Two messengers bring news of the approaching English army, and the Scots flee hastily, taunted by the Countess. King Edward arrives, and at the sight of the Countess he is instantly overcome with love.

Act 2, Scene 1
Lodowick, King Edward's secretary, reflects on his master's obvious infatuation and fears he will abandon the war. The King appears, musing on his love, and he decides to have Lodowick compose a love poem for him to use. He describes the Countess in amusingly extravagant poetic terms, which Lodowick amusingly fails to convert into a poem. The

Countess arrives, and the King confesses his love to her and asks her to demonstrate her love for him. She refuses on moral grounds: Each of them is married. She leaves, and the King vents his frustration, declaring that he must have her sexually, so that his love can find its outlet. His follower Warwick is the Countess's father, and the King decides to make him force his daughter to comply. He tricks Warwick into swearing that he will assist his master before knowing what his errand is, and then he demands that Warwick persuade his daughter to sleep with him, the King. The Countess returns, and the King leaves. The reluctant Warwick fulfills his promise by stating the King's case, but he is relieved when his daughter spurns the idea, declaring that she would rather die than give in.

Act 2, Scene 2

Derby and Audley return from making preparations for the war, only to find the King completely distracted by thoughts of the Countess. The Prince arrives, ready for battle. The King returns guiltily to his proper concerns, but upon the announcement of the Countess's approach, he once again reverts to absorption in his lust for her. She arrives, and after reminding him unavailingly of the immorality of his love, she draws a knife and threatens to kill herself if he will not withdraw his suit. Shocked into shame, he agrees passionately and returns to vigorously planning the proposed invasion of France.

Act 3, Scene 1

Near SLUYS, King John of France and his sons, Charles and Philip, exult over the easy victory they anticipate, although Lorraine counsels caution. Bohemia and a Polonian Captain arrive with reinforcements, increasing the King's extravagant bragging. A Mariner brings news of an approaching English fleet and returns to his vessel. The King disposes his troops on the land nearby. Soon the Mariner returns with a horrifying account of the French loss at sea. A dismayed King John hastens to regroup his forces to meet an English invasion.

Act 3, Scene 2

Several residents of CRÉCY (see Citizen (1); Frenchman; Woman) gather and worriedly exchange news of the approaching English army, observing that

Edward's claims seem just and reporting an ominous prophecy of French defeat. Another Frenchman, panicked, brings news of the French army's defeat, and they all flee.

Act 3, Scene 3

King Edward rewards a Frenchman, Gobin, who has guided his troops across the Somme River. The Prince reports that King John is near. King John appears and insultingly offers Edward a bribe to leave France. The two kings and their followers exchange insults, and each king declares that he will prove his claim to the French crown in combat. The French depart, and Edward ceremonially arms the Prince for his first battle.

Act 3, Scene 4

During the battle, King John and Lorraine despair at the rout of their forces. They leave to try to rally them. King Edward and Audley rest from the fighting, grateful for their apparent victory. Artois arrives, reporting frantically that the Prince is surrounded by French warriors and needs to be rescued. The King, however, declares confidently that his son will prove victorious on his own. Derby, bringing the same message, meets the same response. Audley begs for a relief mission, but the King insists that the Prince will either save himself and gain both stature and self-confidence, or he will die with knightly glory. The noblemen all rue the King's decision, but the Prince appears, victorious and bearing the corpse of Bohemia. The King then formally knights his son. He directs the Prince and Audley to pursue the fleeing French to POITIERS, while he and Derby besiege CALAIS.

Act 4, Scene 1

In BRITTANY, Lord Mountford, restored to his dukedom, thanks Salisbury for his help. Salisbury wants to join the English army at Calais and asks the French prisoner Villiers, a friend of Prince Charles of France, to arrange a safe-conduct for him, in exchange for freedom. Villiers agrees, promising to return to captivity if he fails in this errand.

Act 4, Scene 2

At Calais, King Edward regrets the town's refusal to surrender, necessitating a siege. He grants alms and passage through his army's lines to a group of refugees, including the First Poor Man. Lord Percy brings news that the Scots have been defeated and King David has been captured by John Copland, that Copland has offended Queen Philippa by refusing to turn David over to her, and that the Queen is en route to join the King at Calais. A French Captain (1) emerges from Calais to negotiate a surrender. King Edward declares that, as punishment for the city's earlier intransigence, he will destroy it unless six of its leaders come forth, barely clothed and with nooses around their necks, to be hanged or otherwise punished, as he shall decide.

Act 4, Scene 3

Near Poitiers, Prince Charles of France refuses Villiers's request that he issue a passport for Salisbury. Villiers declares he must then return to captivity. The Prince tells him to violate his oath, but Villiers's conscientious statement of his honor impresses him, and he grants the passport. Villiers leaves to send the document to Salisbury, and King John appears, hurrying to the battle scene and exulting that the English Prince's force has been surrounded and cannot escape, being severely outnumbered. Prince Charles tells of a prophecy he received from a hermit: They should only dread the day that birds make their troops afraid or stones rise up from the ground and put them to flight, and even then they will advance as far in England as the English will in France. The King is pleased to hear this seeming augury of victory.

Act 4, Scene 4

At the battle, the Prince and Lord Audley are surrounded. A French Herald (1) arrives with an offer to spare the English if the Prince and his noblemen will surrender and be held for ransom. The Prince sends him back with a refusal. Another Herald insultingly offers a horse on which to flee; a third brings a religious book with which to prepare for death. Each is sent back with a message of defiance. Audley and the Prince reflect on the inevitability of death and prepare to face it in the battle.

Act 4, Scene 5

King John and Prince Charles receive word of a vast flight of ravens that has darkened the sky and paralyzed the French troops with fear. The King

recalls the prophecy but is certain it can be overridden, and he sends Prince Philip to rally the men. A French Captain (2) arrives, with Salisbury as his captive. Salisbury carries Prince Charles's safe-conduct, but King John orders him hung anyway. Charles pleads for his honor, declaring that his opposite number, the English Prince, would certainly have honored his own word in a similar case. John reluctantly orders Salisbury released and sends a message to King Edward, taunting him on his son's imminent death.

Act 4, Scene 6

On the battlefield, Prince Edward exults over the turn in the battle brought about by the appearance of the ravens. Artois laments that the English have run out of arrows, and the Prince exuberantly declares that they shall fight on with stones. They hurry away to keep fighting, and the French king appears, distressed that the battle is going badly and that the prophecy of the stones seems to be upheld, for the English have unexpectedly begun to use them. Charles and Philip arrive with increasingly bad news: Their army is retreating in confusion. They return to the battle, hoping to fight to the death or reinvigorate their men. Audley, carried by two Esquires, is wounded and dying, but he rejoices in the victory and goes to report it to the Prince.

Act 4, Scene 7

The jubilant Prince, with the captive King John and Prince Charles, greets Artois, who has captured Philip as well. The dying Audley arrives and is eulogized by the Prince, who presents him with a reward, which Audley gives to the two Esquires. The Prince doubles the award and then orders the army to proceed to meet the King at Calais.

Act 5, Scene 1

At Calais, King Edward assures the Queen that he will be properly severe with Copland. The six burghers of Calais appear, each Citizen (2) with a noose around his neck, as the King had commanded. They ask for clemency, but the King, while granting it to the city, as he had promised, condemns them to be tortured and killed. The Queen intercedes to ask mercy for them, and the King accedes to her wish and frees the Citizens. Copland

and his prisoner, King David, arrive. Copland declares that he has felt it proper to deliver so important a prisoner only to the King in person, to whom his loyalty most firmly lies. The King, pleased by this defense, knights Copland on the spot. Salisbury arrives and tells of Mountford's victory. However, he also reports that the Prince was last seen surrounded by French troops and facing certain defeat and death. The King, aggrieved, vows vengeance, but an English Herald (2) arrives to announce the arrival of the Prince with King John and Philip as prisoners. After the King and Queen greet their son with rejoicing, the King informs John that he will be taken as a prisoner to England, and the French king realizes that the final element of the prophecy has been fulfilled. The Prince hopes that his accomplishments will inspire the world's respect for England, and King Edward joyfully proclaims the end of the current war in France.

COMMENTARY

Edward III was not included in the CANON of Shakespeare's plays in the first edition of this book, but trends in scholarship over the intervening years have suggested its inclusion here as a play on which the young Shakespeare probably collaborated. Historians of ELIZABETHAN DRAMA have come to recognize the practice of collaboration in many, perhaps most, plays of the time (including at least three long-acknowledged Shakespearean plays, *1 Henry VI*, *Henry VIII*, and *The Two Noble Kinsmen*), and *Edward III* has been reconsidered in this light. However, though performed and published in Shakespeare's lifetime (see "Theatrical History of the Play" and "Text of the Play"), *Edward III* was not included in the 1623 FIRST FOLIO edition of his works and was for several centuries largely disregarded by both theatrical producers and scholars of Shakespeare.

Edward CAPELL first proposed that *Edward III* might have been written by Shakespeare, and he published an edition of the play in 1760, though he did not include it in his 1768 edition of the plays. However, except in Germany, where Ludwig TIECK translated the play as Shakespeare's, this idea was unsupported for more than a century. In 1874 F. G. FLEAY theorized that Shakespeare had collaborated

on the play, probably writing the first two acts. Two years later John Payne COLLIER (still a respectable commentator, despite his forgeries) wrote an essay declaring Shakespeare the play's sole author, and he republished Capell's text in 1878. But in 1908 C. F. TUCKER BROOKE included *Edward III* in his *Shakespeare Apocrypha* (see APOCRYPHA) attributing it to George PEELE, and with this authoritative opinion the play's exclusion from the canon was set for almost another century.

However, recently developed statistical analyses of language and imagery in Shakespeare and other Elizabethan writers have tended to support the idea of Shakespearean authorship in *Edward III*, particularly in the first two acts. A number of words, phrases, and notions are common to the play and the *Sonnets*, some of which, at least, were probably written at about the same time. (Strikingly, a line from Shakespeare's Sonnet 94—"Lilies that fester smell far worse than weeds"—is repeated exactly in 2.1.452, though as commentators point out, one may suppose the play not Shakespeare's and then ask which author imitated the other, for such borrowing was commonplace among Elizabethan authors.) More important, perhaps, SOLILOQUY, a favorite Shakespearean device, is prominent in the first two acts and virtually nonexistent in the remainder of the play. In addition, in the original published play there have survived a number of idiosyncratic spellings only occurring elsewhere in definitely Shakespearean texts (see "Text of the Play"). In recent years the play has been published three times as Shakespeare's: once (as entirely Shakespearean) by Eric SAMS, in 1996; in 1997, as collaborative effort, in *The Riverside Shakespeare;* and most recently in 1998, again as a collaboration, by the Cambridge University Press. Though its authorship is still a vexed question, a consensus seems to be emerging among scholars that *Edward III* is a work by several writers, one of them Shakespeare. Among the playwrights most frequently nominated as likely collaborators are Christopher MARLOWE, Thomas KYD, Robert GREENE, and George Peele.

Shakespeare's principal contribution to *Edward III*, in the opinion of most scholars who accept his involvement, consists of Acts 1 and 2—containing the story of King Edward and the Countess—

believed to have been added to an already extant script. The absence of Warwick from the initial stage direction of 1.1, though he appears in the scene as part of the establishment of the Countess's importance, suggests that her importance, and his appearance, were only present after Shakespeare had supplemented the existing play with these features. Parts of the original script will have survived in the first pages of the published play. Shakespeare may also have written all or part of 4.4 (a scene that resembles *Henry V*, 1.2). However, most commentators focus on the first two acts, in which the young playwright created a character, the Countess, who anticipates Shakespeare's strong women of later plays. When we first encounter her, she has the wit and nerve to eavesdrop on her enemies, and then the sass to mock them as they retreat in the face of Edward's arrival. She is strong-willed and spirited and absolutely ready to oppose the will of a man, even the most powerful. At the same time, she can be demure and downright statesmanlike. We are not surprised when Edward finds her "As wise as fair" (1.2.162). Later, when Edward commences his suit, she resists him firmly but diplomatically, and when that approach fails, she has the resourcefulness and courage to devise a last resort and draw her knife. We do not doubt that she will use it on herself if Edward does not desist. But desist he does, for her dramatic gesture shocks him into an awareness of his own misuse of power. He gratefully accepts this lesson and declares that he has gained "The power to be ashamed of myself" (2.2.189).

The story of the Countess and King Edward coheres with the blood-and-thunder of the HUNDRED YEARS' WAR better than one might imagine. Both aspects suit the play's place as an example of a popular literary genre of Elizabethan times: tales of the moral education of princes. The maturing of Shakespeare's Prince Hal into his later status as Henry V, in *1* and *2 Henry IV* and *Henry V*, is another fine example. The Countess teaches King Edward a lesson in honorable conduct; variations on this lesson are presented in the course of enacting the King's triumphs in France. Most significantly in the SUBPLOT concerning Salisbury's safe-conduct through the French army's territory, the value of a promise is demonstrated.

Salisbury begins the process by accepting the word of honor of Villiers, one of the detested French. With this act, Salisbury sets in motion a train of effects that parallels the Countess's effect on the King. First, in 4.3 Villiers stands by his oath, insisting to Prince Charles ". . . in an oath we must be well advised / How we do swear, and, when we once have sworn, / Not to infringe it, though we die therefor. / Therefore, my lord, as willing I return [to captivity] / As if I were to fly to paradise" (4.3.40–44). Impressed, the Prince relents. He soon has occasion to exercise his new understanding when, in 4.5, King John wants to ignore the captured Salisbury's safe-conduct and hang him. Charles pleads for the value of his honor: "I hope your highness will not so disgrace me / And dash the virtue of my seal at arms" (that is, his sworn signature; 4.5.73–74). When Charles goes on to declare his certainty that the English monarch would never permit such a disgrace to *his* son, King John reluctantly concedes and frees Salisbury. The King's reluctance may signal Shakespeare's sense of his audience's assumptions about limits to French honor, but nonetheless the episode has presented its idea about proper conduct to higher and higher levels of leadership and prevailed. It is no coincidence that the Countess's husband is the vehicle for this demonstration; the echo of the Salisbury name reminds the audience of the earlier episode, and this reinforces the lesson. Just as King Edward came to see that his immoral behavior toward the Countess of Salisbury was a disgrace to him as a ruler, so has King John had to concede that his initial impulse toward the Earl of Salisbury was disgraceful. Shakespeare was often to write plays demonstrating the harm that immorality among the elite can bring to a society—the HISTORY PLAYS are rife with such demonstrations—and *Edward III* is clearly an early example of the same intention.

Edward III is possibly the earliest of Shakespeare's history plays, and it prefigures some of the concerns dealt with in the later works. The foreshadowing of Prince Hal's career in *1* and *2 Henry IV* and *Henry V* has been mentioned. As do *Richard III* and, especially, *Henry V* (the culminating plays of each of the two main series of history plays [see TETRALOGY]), *Edward III* ends on a note of magnanimity and peacemaking after the turmoil and violence of a battlefield. Also, of course, the reign of King Edward immediately preceded that of King Richard II, so that *Richard II* is in a sense a continuation of *Edward III*. From the point of view of the deposed Richard II, the events enacted in *Edward III* represent a Golden Age whose idealized image is disappearing, overtaken by the brutal politics of Richard's own age. Most important, *Edward III* marks the beginning of Shakespeare's involvement with ideas about the need to resolve conflicts that arise between private emotions and public duty, a theme that resonates through the history plays and much of the rest of Shakespeare's later work, including some of his greatest masterpieces.

Like the other history plays, *Edward III* presented its writer with a set of problems that don't pertain to other sorts of drama: how to make a compelling theatrical presentation of an original story that takes years to elapse, often in many different locales, and involves many more significant people and occasions than can be made into characters and episodes in a play. *Edward III* deploys many of the devices used in the other plays, especially alterations in chronology and the elision of even quite important historical figures and events. In *Edward III*, the first phase of the Hundred Years' War—which occurred, historically, over about 20 years—is compressed into a period that seems at most a few months. The campaign against Scotland that provides the setting for the King's encounter with the Countess, in Acts 1 and 2, actually occurred (without that feature) in 1341, a year after the battle of Sluys, presented in 3.1. And the battle of Crécy seems to spring directly from the victory at Sluys, though it was in fact fought during a different campaign, six years later. Further, though the siege of Calais did indeed follow the English triumph at Crécy, it lasted a year, not the matter of days that seem to pass in the play. Moreover, the play's siege, enacted in 4.2 and 5.1, appears to occur simultaneously with the battle of Poitiers, enacted in 4.4–4.7, though the latter actually took place 10 years later. These alterations, compressing decades, also had the effect of deleting a king of France. The play's King John (Jean II) actually only acceded to the throne in 1350 (after

all of the play's events except Poitiers), but to avoid confusion, the playwrights simply eliminated his father, King Philip VI (ruled 1328–50), though this leaves the play's King John with the odd distinction of representing not only himself, defeated and captured at Poitiers in Acts 4–5, but also his historical father, the French commander at the battles enacted in Act 3. (And his historical son, the play's Prince Charles, does the same, enacting his father's position, as heir and advisor, at Sluys and Crécy).

Numerous other alterations of the historical record were indulged in by the playwrights. Perhaps most importantly, Prince Edward was never in any great danger of defeat at the battle of Poitiers: although badly outnumbered (so much so that before the battle the prince actually attempted to surrender and withdraw from France, though the overconfident French refused to negotiate (an episode that was omitted from the play), once the battle started, the English forces used their superior weaponry—the longbow—and an excellent tactical disposition of their troops to establish an early advantage that they never relinquished. (The elaborate description of the French forces in 4.4.10–39 is fictitious.) Other significant divergences from the historical accounts include the spurious capture of Prince Charles in 4.7; the presence at the end of the play of the French noblemen Artois and Mountford (valuable onstage as examples of French support for Edward), who in fact died years earlier; and the appearance of Queen Philippa at the surrender of Calais, where her plea for mercy was in fact made by Sir Walter de Manny (d. 1372; he is replaced by Salisbury elsewhere in the play). The playwrights' sources differed on the question of the queen's presence (modern scholarship has found she was in England at the time), and they may have wanted her on the scene to provide a feminine element to the play's climax in peace and magnanimity, and perhaps also to balance the Countess's importance at its beginning.

The Countess—largely, at least, Shakespeare's own creation (as opposed to that of a collaborator)—was generated in something like the same way. The playwright's sources (see "Sources of the Play") told of her relationship with Edward and its resulting triumph of virtue, but the story is unconnected to a siege. However, Shakespeare also read of an occasion when a woman was the commander of a besieged castle, but she was not the Countess. And while a woman had been chatelaine at Roxborough Castle during a siege by the Scots (though at a slightly later date), she was not the Countess, either (though she may have been the subject of an attempted seduction by King Edward). These various accounts were all put to use to provide a satisfactory situation for King Edward's temptation and response. (Scholars speculate that this confusing assortment of originals may be the reason that the Countess is never assigned a first name in the play.)

Another aspect *Edward III* shares with some of the other history plays, especially *Henry V,* is that it is expressly and enthusiastically patriotic. Written at a time of national danger and triumph, immediately following England's successful resistance to the Spanish Armada in 1588, the play (especially in those episodes least associated with Shakespeare) has a pronounced patriotic aura. The young Prince of the play (probably a creation of Shakespeare's collaborators, for the most part) grows in military acumen and skill but cannot otherwise be said to develop in the course of the play, though he is the leading figure in the fighting. His dash and courage are pure attitude, suitable to the enactment of military derring-do. The Scots and the French are both satirized as preposterous braggarts and cowards (in the tradition of the MILES GLORIOSUS). A well-known account of the Armada is paraphrased in the Mariner's description of the naval fight at Sluys, and the play's final scene, 5.1, is largely a celebration of England's triumph. And Shakespeare's creation, the Countess, in her courage, chastity, and intelligence, probably reminded—and was meant to remind—16th-century audiences of the patriotic public image of their monarch, Queen Elizabeth (see Elizabeth I in *Henry VIII*), who was known as the Virgin Queen and who had taken a prominent role in the resistance to Spain.

The history plays, as a genre, arose to satisfy an interest in national history sparked by the national conflicts of the period, and Shakespeare and his collaborators were among the first playwrights ever to have attempted to present real historical events, in something like the way they may actually have occurred, on the stage. *Edward III*, which was among the first such plays to be presented, thus provides a sharp sense of the public tastes and concerns of the Elizabethan period.

SOURCES OF THE PLAY

The principal sources for the history presented in *Edward III* were Raphael HOLINSHED's *Chronicles of England, Scotland, and Ireland* and the *Chroniques* of the French historian Jean FROISSART, which Shakespeare will have known in the translation of Lord BERNERS. Holinshed offers a brief account of King Edward's obsession with the Countess of Salisbury, but his is an undramatic version in which the King propositions the Countess, is turned down, and simply lets it go at that. Froissart presents the outlines of the encounter as enacted in the play. However, another version, from *Palace of Pleasure*, an anthology of tales published in 1566–67 by William PAINTER, appears to have had the chief influence on Shakespeare's rendering, providing the presence of Lodowick as a go-between for the King (though the comical poetry-writing scene is Shakespeare's) and the notion of the King pressuring the Countess's father (though Shakespeare contributed the telling detail of Warwick's oath). Painter, in turn, had drawn on the Italian writer Matteo BANDELLO (whom Shakespeare probably knew from other sources as well), who introduced the originals of Lodowick and Warwick. The Second Herald's taunting of the Prince in 4.4 may have been inspired by the similar scene in an earlier play, *The Famous Victories of Henry the Fifth* (see FAMOUS VICTORIES, THE—also the source for the famous "tennis balls" scene in *Henry V*).

Froissart wrote of Queen Philippa's intervention in favor of the Citizens of Calais (modern scholars—and Holinshed—disagree), and his version was followed in Act 5. Another episode in Froissart was adapted to become the subplot involving Salisbury's safe-conduct. A journalistic account of the Spanish Armada's defeat by Petruccio UBALDINO, published by Augustine RYTHER in 1590, provided various details about the war, especially concerning the naval battle of Sluys, recounted in 3.1. (though one passage in that recounting, 3.1.144–184, apparently derives from Thomas Kyd's *Spanish Tragedy*). Lastly, the influence of Christopher Marlowe's *Tamburlaine* is detectable in the rhetoric of King Edward in 5.1.162–175, where the grieving King, believing the Prince has been killed, echoes a similar speech in Marlowe's play, which was then a recent blockbuster of the Elizabethan stage.

TEXT OF THE PLAY

Edward III was written sometime after Ubaldino's 1590 report on the Spanish Armada and sometime before December 1595, when it was registered for publication by Cuthbert BURBY. The possible reference to Shakespeare's *The Rape of Lucrece* in 2.2.194–195, and several resemblances to the language of his *Sonnets*, mostly in 2.1, suggest a date of composition toward the end of this period, in 1594 or 1595. On the other hand, the 1594 publication of a BAD QUARTO of *2 Henry VI*, known as *The Contention*, which was assembled by actors who knew that play, seems to contain traces of knowledge of *Edward III* as well, suggesting an earlier date of composition for the latter, not later than 1593. The question accordingly remains a subject of scholarly inquiry.

The play was first published by Burby, in an edition known as Q1, in 1596. This text, printed by Thomas SCARLET, is rife with errors, irregularities, and omissions, especially in the stage directions and speech headings, perhaps because the printer only received the copy in parts. Acts 1 and 2, as mentioned in the Commentary, above, contain a number of idiosyncratic spellings and punctuation associated with Shakespeare; this is evidence for his authorship, and it also suggests the piecemeal manner in which the copy was assembled. It is thus believed by scholars that the copy from which the printer worked was neither a FOUL COPY (an author's manuscript) nor a scribe-made FAIR COPY, but rather some sort of indefinable set of papers, the consequence of multiple authorship with contributions that were not all made at the same time.

A second edition, Q2, also published by Burby but printed by Simon STAFFORD, appeared in 1599. Stafford corrected Scarlet's most egregious errors, but it is clear that his copy-text was the first edition. Therefore, subsequent editors rely on Q1 as the authoritative text, except with respect to the muddled stage directions and speech headings, which had apparently been edited in Q2 by someone who knew the play, and these amendments are generally adopted by modern editors.

That the play was *not* published in the 1623 First Folio has often been presented as evidence that Shakespeare did not write it, but recent research has suggested that the play may have met with official disapproval, beginning in the 1590s (see "Theatrical History of the Play"), which may have militated against any further publication. In any case, the play was not published again until Capell's 1760 edition.

THEATRICAL HISTORY OF THE PLAY

Both 16th-century editions of *Edward III* (1596, 1599) declare on their title pages that the play "hath been sundry times played about the city of London," presumably before the initial registration of the play for publication in December 1595. That this declaration does not associate the play with a particular theater company suggests to scholars that the play had not been presented lately, perhaps because the company was no longer extant, and the date further indicates that this may have been a consequence of the outbreaks of plague that closed the London theaters for most of the years 1592–94.

No further production of *Edward III* is known before the 20th century. Recent research has revealed that Scottish diplomats informed English officials in the 1590s that they disapproved of an anti-Scottish play that had been presented in London. Scholars find no convincing candidate but *Edward III* in these years; certainly the presentation of King David and his men in 2.1 is quite scurrilous. Official disapproval would of course have continued after the Scottish King JAMES I succeeded Elizabeth I as ruler of England, in 1603. This would account for the play's absence from both the theaters and the First Folio edition of Shakespeare's work.

The first modern presentation of *Edward III* consisted solely of the second act, offered in 1911 by William POEL in a single performance (along with another full-length play) as a demonstration of the likelihood of Shakespearean composition. A fuller (though not complete) version was presented on TELEVISION by the BBC in 1963 (cuts were made to keep the performance time down), and a production of the complete play was only offered in 1986 by the Shakespeare Society of America, not as the work of Shakespeare but rather in a Los Angeles staging of the complete contents of Tucker Brooke's *Apocrypha*. The first modern, professional production of *Edward III* as a play by Shakespeare was presented in 1987 by Theatre Clwyd in Wales. The only later staging (as of mid-2003) was by the ROYAL SHAKESPEARE COMPANY in STRATFORD in 2002–03, as part of a special season of rarely seen Elizabethan plays. Also, several amateur and university programs, responding to the attention given to *Edward III*'s reception into the canon, have presented readings of or excerpts from the play.

CHARACTERS

Artois, Robert de Beaumont-le-Roger, Count of (1287–1343) Historical figure and character in *Edward III*, a French nobleman who sides with King Edward against King John of France. In the first scene of the play, Artois, said to be banished from FRANCE, outlines Edward's claim to the French throne and declares he will support the English ruler. He says as much to the French ambassador, the Duke of Lorraine, and is cursed as a traitor. Though he appears in several other scenes, he has little to say, having made his impact merely by lending legitimacy to Edward's invasion of France.

The historical Artois, an uncle of King John, had fled France after losing out in a contested succession to the earldom of Artois and had been taken up by Edward, filling exactly the function he fills in the play. As Earl of Richmond (a title he is granted in 1.1.4), he accompanied Salisbury to Brittany in his campaign to assist Jean de Montfort, the play's Mountford, and was killed there, years before all the events enacted after Act 2 of the play. Though this was known to Shakespeare from his sources, Artois, like Mountford, is kept alive in order to represent Edward's French support.

Audley, James, Lord (ca. 1316–1369) Historical figure and character in *Edward III*, a follower of King Edward. In the play's opening scenes, Audley is among the noblemen preparing for war with

FRANCE in Act 1, but he only comes into his own at the battle of POITIERS in 4.4. The forces of the Prince of Wales are surrounded and badly outnumbered; Audley outlines the situation in an elaborate description (4.4.10–39), and he and the Prince vow to fight to the finish. Audley's speech in defiance of death (4.4.134–149) draws thanks from the Prince, who says, "Ah, good old man, a thousand thousand armours / These words of thine have buckled on my back" (4.4.150–151). In 4.6 Audley is carried from the battlefield, mortally wounded but exultant at England's victory. In 4.7, taken to the Prince, he magnanimously conveys his master's reward of a great estate in England to his escorts, whereupon the Prince doubles it. In 5.1, mute (and presumably on a litter), he is present for the triumphant finale. Audley is a representative of chivalric England at its best, a grand old man delighted to be dying in the service of his king.

The historical Audley was not an elderly man at the time of Poitiers, but he was a famous soldier, eventually becoming one of the original Knights of the Garter. Shakespeare knew from his principal source, the history of FROISSART, that Audley had astonished witnesses with his sustained bravery and fighting spirit after having been severely wounded at Poitiers. However, he did not die there; he went to the south of France with the Prince and was acting governor of the region when the Prince was campaigning in Spain. When the war with France resumed, Audley commanded an army in the initial campaign, but he contracted an illness and died. Fittingly, his funeral was held in Poitiers.

Bohemia, King of (John of Luxembourg) (1296–1346) Historical figure and character in *Edward III*, an ally of the French at the battle of CRÉCY. Bohemia speaks three lines, at 3.1.40–42, declaring his alliance to King John on the eve of the battle, and he appears with the King, but does not speak, in the encounter with King Edward of England, in 3.2. His tiny part, while derived from the playwright's sources, serves merely to aggrandize the French forces, thereby making greater the English achievement in defeating them in the ensuing battle. He dies at Crécy, and his body is displayed by the victorious English Prince of Wales in 3.4.

The historical king—John, Duke of Luxembourg and King of Bohemia, the son of one Holy Roman Emperor and the father of another—became ruler of BOHEMIA by marriage in 1310. He was an important figure in the international politics of the day and spent much of his reign engaged in warfare throughout Europe. He did indeed die at Crécy, as Shakespeare and his collaborators knew from their sources.

Captain (1)   Minor character in *Edward III*, a defender of CALAIS. The Captain emerges from the besieged city, at 4.2.62, to negotiate a surrender with the English king Edward III. However, the King refuses to negotiate except upon the sacrifice of six of the town's elite, and he departs, leaving the Captain to regret that the town had depended on the unreliable aid of King John of France. This brief episode prepares for the subsequent mercy of King Edward in 5.1.

Captain (2)   Minor character in *Edward III*, an officer in the French army who escorts the captured Lord Salisbury. The Captain delivers Salisbury to King John and Prince Charles and speaks a few lines telling of the capture (4.5.56–60). This completes his small role, whose function is simply to bring Salisbury to the French commanders, which sparks the climax of a subplot. (See also Villiers.)

Charles, Prince of France and Duke of Normandy (later King Charles V) (1337–1380) Historical figure and character in *Edward III*, the son of King John of France. Charles first appears in 3.1 at SLUYS as the French army awaits the English invasion that will open the HUNDRED YEARS' WAR; he contributes briefly (3.1.13–18) to the prevailing air of overconfident, derisive dismissal of their foe. Similarly, in 3.3 he contributes two lines to the exchange of insults between the commanders of the two armies before the battle of CRÉCY, but in 4.3 and 4.5, he takes on greater importance. In 4.3 he is asked by the paroled French prisoner of war Villiers to issue a safe-conduct for the English Earl of Salisbury; his initial response is to refuse—he remarks sensibly, "I wonder, Villiers, thou shouldst importune me / For one that is our deadly enemy" (4.3.1–2)—but when

Villiers declares that if he is refused he must return to captivity, Prince Charles is shamed by the nobleman's sense of honor, and he accedes to his request. In 4.5, at the battle of POITIERS, he is present when Salisbury, a prisoner of the French, produces his safe-conduct only to have King John repudiate it and order the Englishman hanged. Charles, conscious now of his honor, implores his father, "I hope your highness will not so disgrace me" (4.5.73), and upon meeting further resistance, he declares his confidence that had the English Prince, his opposite number, given *his* word, it would have been honored. King John reluctantly concedes, and Salisbury is released. In the remainder of Act 4, Charles is again merely another member of the king's retinue, sharing in the panic of retreat of 4.6 and (mutely) in the ignominy of having been captured in 4.7. His importance in the play lies entirely in the repetition of a lesson in honorable behavior, begun by Salisbury in his trusting Villiers, conveyed by Villiers to Charles, and retransmitted by Charles to his father. The value of a sworn oath is among the lessons in princely propriety that constitute a principal theme of the play.

The historical Charles is poorly represented in *Edward III*, for Shakespeare and his collaborators took manifold liberties with the history they received from their sources, beginning with the basic chronology: the boastful warrior of Act 3 was in fact not present with the army, being only three years old at the time of Sluys and nine at Crécy. Significantly, he was also not yet Duke of Normandy. This title was held by the heir-apparent to the throne of France, who was, until 1350 (after all but the battle of Poitiers, among the events of the play), Charles's father, the play's King John. The episode of the safe-conduct has its origin in events that occurred in 1340, so it was John, not Charles, who actually issued the safe-conduct and defended it against the intransigence of *his* father, King Philip VI. The remaining discrepancy concerning Charles is minor: though he did fight at Poitiers (and was Duke of Normandy by that time), he was not taken prisoner, as in 4.7, but escaped to Paris, where he served as Regent of France during his father's captivity in England. Later he became the father of Charles VI, the French King of Shakespeare's *Henry V,* and grandfather of Charles VII of *1 Henry VI.*

Citizen (1)   Any of several minor characters in *Edward III*, French civilians living near CRÉCY. In 3.2, the Citizens, along with a Woman, declare their intention to flee the invading English army, despite the unconcern of a passing Frenchman. The First Citizen, who does most of the speaking, declares that the French forces will probably lose, since the English King Edward's claim to the French throne is just and will therefore be favored by fate. They all flee when news of a French defeat arrives. The incident furthers the play's military developments while also confirming King Edward's righteousness in invading FRANCE.

Citizen (2)   Any of several minor characters in *Edward III*, residents of CALAIS and prisoners of King Edward when he besieges the town. In 4.2, following his victory at the battle of CRÉCY, the King demands the surrender of Calais and meets with a refusal. He then declares that he will have his army sack the town unless, within two days, six of the richest merchants present themselves as prisoners, with nooses around their necks, prepared to "be afflicted, hanged, or what I please." In 4.1, the six "Burghers of Calais" (as the Citizens have been known ever after) appear, offering their own lives and pleading for mercy on their city. Only two of them have speeches, offering flowery supplications (of seven and five lines) to the King, but he is adamant, and they are ordered to a painful death. However, Queen Philippa pleads with the King for mercy, and he grants it. The Citizens join in unison in a one-line accolade to the King before exiting.

The episode was adapted by Shakespeare or his collaborators from historical accounts, with two alterations: the King initially questions the social status of the Citizens, suggesting that they may not in fact be rich merchants, as specified; this fiction was apparently intended to prolong the tension before the ultimate grant of mercy. Also, Queen Philippa was not in fact present, though one of Shakespeare's sources, Jean FROISSART, provides the play's presentation; the sentiments she expresses in the play were offered in reality by a prominent English knight, Sir Walter de Manny (d. 1372; see Salisbury). Froissart's version provides a feminine presence as part of the play's concluding air of English triumph and magnanimity.

Although their risk was not taken voluntarily and they escaped without harm, the "Burghers of Calais" became a byword for civic devotion and sacrifice. They are probably best remembered today as the subjects of a great series of sculptures bearing that title by the French artist Auguste Rodin (1840–1917).

Copland, John   (active 1346)   Historical figure and minor character in *Edward III*. Copland is an English gentryman who, having captured King David of Scotland in battle, is knighted by King Edward. In 4.2 his feat is reported to the King at the siege of CALAIS, with the news that he has refused to turn his captive over to Queen Philippa, thereby offending her. He is summoned to Calais to explain himself, and King Edward assures the Queen that he shall be severe with the disrespectful commoner. However, when Copland appears, in 5.1, his defense—that he felt it most proper to deliver so important a prisoner only to the king in person, and not to the royal delegate the Queen, for it is to the monarch himself that his loyalty most firmly lies—pleases the King so much that he knights Copland on the spot and grants him a generous annuity.

The historical Copland did indeed capture King David, did withhold him from the queen's custody, and was summoned to Calais and rewarded by the king. His story is faithfully enacted in the play as it appears in Shakespeare's source, the history by FROISSART, except that Queen Philippa was not present. However, nothing more is known about him.

Countess of Salisbury   Character in *Edward III*, the object of the lust of King Edward. The first two acts of the play present King Edward's obsession with the Countess, which distracts him from his duty as king. The Countess has assumed command of ROXBOROUGH CASTLE in the absence of her husband, Salisbury, who is fighting in FRANCE in the first phases of the HUNDRED YEARS' WAR. She is rescued from the besieging forces of King David of Scotland by King Edward and his army. When the Scots flee at King Edward's approach, in 1.2, she mocks them saucily. When Edward arrives, he is smitten by her beauty and intelligence, and in the next scene he demands that she become his lover. When she refuses on moral grounds, pointing out that they are each married, he attempts to trick her father, Warwick, into coercing her. To this the Countess declares boldly, "No, let me die, if his too boist'rous will / Will have it so, before I will consent / to be an actor in his graceless lust." (2.1.428–430). Undeterred, the King seeks to persuade her again in 2.2, going so far as to threaten to kill their respective spouses if concern for them is what stands in her way. At this she draws a knife and threatens to kill herself if he continues to pursue her. Shocked into shame, he withdraws his suit, passionately acclaims her virtue, and returns to his proper concern, the preparations for his forthcoming invasion of France.

The Countess, having thus enlightened the King as to moral decency and the need for mastering his passions, has also illuminated one of the playwright's central themes, the proper conduct of rulers. Edward understands the value that this lesson has for him, "The power to be ashamed of myself" (2.2.189). This accomplished, the Countess disappears from the play, though not before having presented us a fitting predecessor to Shakespeare's later, grander female characters. She has the sassy spirit of Katherina in *The Taming of the Shrew*, the rectitude of *Cymbeline*'s Imogen, and the stately beauty of Olivia in *Twelfth Night*, although, being an apprentice effort, as it were, she is not fully developed in any of these directions.

The story of King Edward's dalliance with the Countess was familiar to Shakespeare from historical sources, but it may have been merely a single encounter, in which the King's impetuous proposition was politely and piously rejected, and the King went on his way. However, the chief source for the play was a tale by William PAINTER, a highly elaborated and largely fictitious account. In all these versions, the story is unconnected to a siege. The Countess's plight at Roxborough appears to have been inspired by an account of a French woman who did lead the resistance to a siege: the Countess of Montfort (historical wife of the play's Lord Mountford). (This was a part of the campaign Salisbury is said to be engaged in at 1.1.133–134.) And while a woman had been chatelaine at Roxborough Castle during a siege by the Scots, she was not the Countess of Salisbury but the wife of the play's Montague, who, as a vassal of Salisbury, was the castle's governor. She took no notable part in the resistance (though she may have been the subject of an attempted seduction by King Edward when he arrived). These different accounts were conflated to provide a satisfactory situation for King Edward's moral lesson.

It is likely that Shakespeare's fictional Countess was also intended to resemble England's popular sovereign, Queen Elizabeth (see Elizabeth I in *Henry VIII*). In her most outstanding qualities—her resolute defiance of a foreign enemy and her honorable insistence on sexual morality—the Countess exhibits the most important features of Elizabeth's public image: the Virgin Queen who boldly leads her country's resistance to its enemies. Like Elizabeth's England in the face of the Spanish Armada's attempt at conquest, the Countess's castle is said to be "begirt with siege" (1.1.137) by an invading power (here Scotland). Created in the wake of the Armada, the Countess probably pleased the patriotic Elizabethan theatergoers in her resemblance to their heroic sovereign.

Danes Minor characters in *Edward III*, nonspeaking members of the French military forces at the battle of CRÉCY. Shakespeare and his collaborators learned from their sources that Danes and Poles (see Polonian Captain) had served as mercenaries in the French forces that opposed Edward's invasion. Mentioned only once (personified as "the warlike Dane" in 3.1.34), the Danish soldiers merely flesh out the massive opposition the English must overcome, making their achievement all the greater.

Derby, Henry of Lancaster, Earl of (d. 1361) Historical figure and character in *Edward III*, a follower of King Edward in his war with FRANCE. In the opening scene, Derby is present at the King's reception of the French ambassador and the King's subsequent council of war, and at 1.1.147 he is ordered on a diplomatic mission, but he does not speak. In 2.2 he speaks several lines when he returns and finds that the King is uninterested in the results of his mission, being infatuated with the Countess. In 3.3 he is again present, without speaking, at the meeting of the French and English commanders before the battle of CRÉCY, though he does intone his six-line piece in the formal initiation of the Prince that follows (3.3.186–191). In 3.4 Derby's four scattered lines reinforce the pleas of Artois and Audley that the King send reinforcements to the Prince, and in 4.2 he again speaks a scant few lines, as a member of the court. In 5.1's grand finale, celebrating the English triumph, he speaks a single line. Some commentators have speculated that Derby's odd, nearly mute ubiquity in the play may reflect the young Shakespeare's professional association with the son of the Earl of Derby at the time *Edward III* was written, Ferdinando Stanley, Lord STRANGE, who was proprietor of the theatrical company called STRANGE'S MEN, known as DERBY'S MEN after 1593, when Strange inherited the title.

Historically, the Earl of Derby presented in *Edward III* was a major figure in the period depicted; he was a principal adviser of King Edward, and he successfully led English armies in France, although the campaigns in which he shone are not enacted in the play. In 1351 he was rewarded by being created the first Duke of Lancaster, a title he passed on to his son-in-law, John of Gaunt; through him, Derby was the ancestor of the Lancastrian kings of England, beginning with his grandson, the Bolinbroke of *Richard II*, later King Henry IV.

Douglas, Sir William (active 1340) Historical figure and minor character in *Edward III*, a follower of King David of Scotland. In 1.2 the besieged English Countess of Salisbury overhears her besieger, King David, argue with Douglas over the possession of what they suppose is the soon-to-be-captured ROXBOROUGH CASTLE. Douglas declares, "I crave the lady, and no more" (1.2.42), but the King claims the Countess for himself. Douglas goes on, "Why then, my liege, let me enjoy her jewels" (1.2.45), but the King denies him these as well. This gentlemanly discussion is interrupted by a Messenger bringing word of the approaching English army, and the Scots panic and flee. This brief episode, in which Douglas speaks only four lines, serves only to present a comic stereotype, the greedy but cowardly Scot.

The historical Douglas, highly renowned as a military tactician in the endless petty warfare of the Scottish borderlands, was of no importance to Shakespeare, who simply took his name from the historical accounts of Edward III's war with David of Scotland.

Edward III, King of England (1312–1377) Historical figure and title character of *Edward III*, the leader of England in the opening phase of the HUNDRED YEARS' WAR. The King is the protagonist of Acts 1 and 2—Shakespeare's major contribution to *Edward III*, a collaborative work—while taking a less prominent role, though still a leading one, in the remainder of the play. The principal theme of the drama is the importance of honor and devotion to duty in a ruler, a concern in much of Shakespeare's work. In the first two acts, the King presents an object lesson in poor leadership, abandoning his kingly duty to lead English forces against FRANCE and instead pursuing a sexual infatuation. In 1.1, as plans for the war take form, King Edward undertakes a campaign to secure England against an incursion by King David of Scotland, who has besieged ROXBOROUGH CASTLE, home of the Countess of Salisbury. However, once he arrives at the castle and the Scots have fled, the King becomes besotted with the Countess. The King's secretary Lodowick observes the King's infatuation and remarks, "Then, Scottish wars, farewell" (2.1.22), as he foresees the King's abandonment of his mission. After a humorous interlude in which the King attempts to instruct Lodowick in the composition of a love letter to the Countess, he proceeds to proposition her directly, an offer she civilly but firmly rejects, on moral grounds.

He recognizes that she is entirely right, but her virtue, added to her beauty and spirit, simply inflames his illicit passion. He proceeds to a less direct and wholly reprehensible approach when he attempts to get her father, Warwick, one of his own followers, to coerce her. He tricks Warwick into vowing to try to talk her into the King's bed, but she rejects the proposition no less firmly when her father presents it, in 2.1.374–460. The King, thoroughly obsessed, goes so far as to declare to the Countess that he will have her husband and his wife murdered. At this she draws a knife and threatens to kill herself if he does not stop dishonoring himself and her with his pursuit. Shocked into self-recognition, he swears by "that power . . . that gives me now / The power to be ashaméd of myself" (2.2.188–189) that he will drop his dishonorable quest and return to his proper activity, and he immediately begins anew the preparations for invading France. In this episode, which occupies fully the first third of the play, King Edward foreshadows such later and greater creations as Angelo of *Measure for Measure* and Prince Hal of *1 and 2 Henry IV*, in enacting the need for those in power to resist temptations to abuse it. However, his lovestruck rhetoric—sometimes comic, sometimes malevolent—is his only distinctive feature, and he gives little hint of the fully developed characters Shakespeare was to achieve in his maturity.

In the remainder of the play, the reformed King leads the English invasion through the battles of SLUYS, CRÉCY, and POITIERS, though the spotlight is increasingly on his son the Prince of Wales, who demonstrates an ideal of chivalric behavior in war; and on a SUBPLOT concerning another lesson in honor, centering on the Duke of Salisbury. The King is not merely a spectator of these developments, however; two further episodes demonstrate his virtues as a ruler. In 4.2 the King has declared that he will have his army destroy the besieged town of CALAIS, which has rejected an initial demand to surrender, unless six of its most prominent citizens will present themselves for any punishment the King chooses. In 5.1 they do so, and he orders them to a painful death. However, Queen Philippa persuades him to grant them mercy, and in doing so he enacts an ideal of kingly behavior: magnanimity toward a defeated enemy. He then (in 5.1.64–96) grants a knighthood and a generous income to the soldier John COPLAND, despite the Queen's disapproval, and demonstrates a praiseworthy generosity to his followers, such as was expected of a ruler.

The historical King Edward III ruled for 50 years, a long reign whose events are only very selectively touched on in the play. Edward was crowned at the age of 14, when his mother—Queen Isabella (ca. 1290–1358), known as "the She-wolf of France"—and her lover, a rebellious English baron, deposed his father, Edward II (1294–1327), and installed him on the throne. For several years the usurpers ruled in Edward's name and were hated for their rapacious and arbitrary abuses of power. But young Edward was no puppet: At 17, he claimed power, sending his mother to (comfortable) exile, while executing her lover. As king, Edward was principally a warrior, leading victorious campaigns against SCOTLAND and France, including those enacted in *Edward III* (though the play's history is faulty in many respects). His infatuation with the Countess, as rendered in Shakespeare's main historical source, was apparently brief and without consequence (although another version of the encounter, unknown to Shakespeare, culminates in a brutal rape, which may more likely reflect the inclinations of a medieval warrior-king).

King Edward's reign closed ingloriously. The war in France resumed in 1369, with losses to the English. After Queen Philippa died in the same year, Edward was dominated by his mistress, leader of a faction favoring one of the king's sons, John of Gaunt, against another, the Prince—and, after the Prince's death, against the supporters of his six-year-old son, soon to be King Richard II. This intramural political squabbling was to last for decades; its eventual repercussions dominate the opening moments of Shakespeare's *Richard II*.

Esquire Either of two minor characters in *Edward III*, attendants to the dying Lord Audley. In 4.6, during the battle of POITIERS, the Esquires solicitously assist the mortally wounded Audley, whom they have rescued from the French. They speak a line and a half between them. He asks them to take him to his commander, the Prince of Wales, anticipating their second, mute, appearance in 4.7. There, Audley, dying in the presence of the Prince, grants to the two Esquires the large annuity with which the Prince has just rewarded him. The Prince promptly doubles the gift.

This episode, which Shakespeare took from Raphael HOLINSHED's account—though Holinshed features four Esquires—emphasizes the noble magnanimity of both the Prince and Audley, in the atmosphere of English triumphalism that pervades the scene, following their victory in battle. The Esquires themselves are little more than extras.

First Poor Man   The spokesman among six minor characters in *Edward III*, refugees from the French city of CALAIS, besieged by King Edward III. In 4.2, the First Poor Man, the only member of his group to speak, reports to the English that they have been expelled by Calais's leaders, who think they are not worth what they might eat of the city's meagre supplies. The King grants them food, alms, and passage through his army's lines, in an episode that magnifies the virtue of the title character.

In the playwrights' sources, the refugees from Calais are said to have numbered some 1,700. Faced with this flow of possible prisoners of war, the English essentially paid them, in food and petty cash, to keep moving, so they would not be an encumbrance to the besieging army.

Frenchman   Any of several minor characters in *Edward III*, civilians who find themselves near the battle of CRÉCY. In 3.2, two Frenchmen meet several residents who are frightened at the approach of the English army. The First Frenchman answers their alarm with skepticism, but then a Third Frenchman appears, panic-stricken, to report a skirmish lost by the French. They all then flee. The incident furthers the military developments in the play, while also offering a variation on a familiar Elizabethan stereotype, the cowardly Frenchman.

Gobin de Grace   (active 1346)   Historical figure and minor character in *Edward III*, a French prisoner of war who has guided the invading English army of King Edward to a river crossing. After the crossing, as the scene (3.3) opens, the King summons the guide, asks him his name, and releases him with a large reward. Gobin speaks only a line and a half before disappearing from the play. His small part serves to emphasize the magnanimity of the King. He is probably not the creation of Shakespeare himself, but rather of a collaborator.

The historical Gobin's service to the English is mentioned in the play's chief sources, the histories of Jean FROISSART and Raphael HOLINGSHED, but no more is known of him. His surname is dubious and may be an epithet. In Froissart he appears as Gobyn a Grace, and in Holingshed he is named once as Gobin de Grace and twice as Gobin Agace (he is mentioned elsewhere as Gobin Agache). The first edition of the play (Q1) denominates him Gobin de Graie (probably a misprint for de Grace), and Q2 changed this to de Grey. Most modern scholars have favored de Grace.

Herald (1)   Any of three minor characters in *Edward III*, messengers from the French commanders to the Prince of Wales during the battle of POITIERS. In 4.4.67–76 the first Herald brings a formal offer of truce from King John of France, including the humiliating conditions of the Prince's surrender, along with 100 of his noblemen. He is sent back with a message of defiance and is immediately followed by the Second Herald, from Charles, Prince of France, who insultingly presents a horse to flee on; and the Third Herald, from Philip, Prince of France, who mockingly offers a book of prayers with which to prepare for death. Each herald is also repudiated and sent back to the French army.

Some commentators believe that these taunting emissaries were Shakespeare's personal contribution to *Edward III*—as opposed to that of his collaborators—because they (especially the Second Herald) resemble the Ambassador in the famous "tennis balls" scene in *Henry V* (1.2), though other scholars point out that they might also have been taken from other accounts of the same famous incident, especially that in *The Famous Victories of Henry the Fifth* (see FAMOUS VICTORIES, THE).

Herald (2)   Any of several minor characters in *Edward III*, English attendants to Edward III. Just before the battle of CRÉCY, King Edward formally initiates his son, the Prince of Wales, as a warrior; the ceremony begins with the arrival of "four Heralds bringing in a coat of armour, a helmet, a lance, and a shield" (S.D. 3.3.178). The Heralds do not speak; their function is simply to furnish an aura of pomp to the scene. Later one of them (or a fifth one) does speak, announcing the arrival of the victorious Prince after the battle of POITIERS (5.1.176–184), though only to a similar, purely ceremonial purpose.

King David of Scotland (ca. 1318–1371) Historical figure and character in *Edward III*, invader of England and besieger of the Countess of Salisbury at ROXBOROUGH CASTLE. In the play's opening scene, King Edward learns that "the treacherous king" David, though nominally an ally of England, has "made invasion of the bordering towns" (1.1.124, 127). Edward vows to break the siege and marches north. In 1.2 David's perfidy is magnified when he confers at Roxborough with the Duke of Lorraine and professes his loyalty to King John of France in his war against England. The besieged Countess then overhears King David argue with his follower, Douglas, over the possession of what they suppose is the soon-to-be-captured Countess. When a Messenger brings word of the approaching English army, the Scots panic and flee, to the derisive taunts of the Countess. This brief episode, filled with such Scotticisms as "our bonny riders" (1.2.26), serves only to present a comic stereotype: the greedy, treacherous, and cowardly Scot. King David's nonspeaking appearance as a prisoner before the triumphant King Edward in 5.1 rounds off his symbolic role as the initial, lesser foe of England and marks the symmetrical structure of the play.

The historical King David is not reflected in the character, who is simply a caricature, though some of the events of his career are presented. Unmentioned by Shakespeare is the fact that David was Edward's brother-in-law, having married the English king's sister upon his own accession to the crown of SCOTLAND, thus establishing the alliance with England. It had, however, been broken and reformed before the invasion of England described in 1.1, and this event actually occurred a decade earlier than the siege of Roxborough Castle. Here, in the events that coincided with the HUNDRED YEARS' WAR, we see the Scottish War of 1341, which actually took place *after* the battle of SLUYS, which is not enacted until 3.1, an aspect of the play's skewed chronology. The play's account of King David's capture by John COPLAND is true, though he was never taken to Calais but was imprisoned in London before Calais had been taken. In any event the historical king was less significant than his role as a stereotype, a feature of the play that may have spurred a diplomatic complaint about it in the 1590s.

King John of France (Jean II) (1319–1364) Historical figure and character in *Edward III*. King John rules FRANCE during Edward III of England's invasion of the country, in the first phase of the HUNDRED YEARS' WAR. On his first appearance, in 3.1, King John is brashly overconfident, but the English naval victory at SLUYS sobers him. In 3.3, meeting the English leaders before the battle of CRÉCY, the King upholds his end of the ritual exchange of challenges and insults traditional in Elizabethan theatrical combats. Early in the next scene, he appears briefly, attempting to rally his fleeing forces. In Act 4, at the battle of POITIERS, the King's role is similarly slight, except in one respect: In 4.5 the captured English Earl of Salisbury is brought before him. Salisbury has a certificate of safe-conduct signed by John's son, Prince Charles, but the King refuses to honor it, until his son implores him not to sully his sworn word. Reluctantly, John gives in and releases the Englishman. Thus, King John participates in the series of lessons on the value of honor that is a chief theme of the play. For the rest, the King goes down with his countrymen at Poitiers: Before the battle, in 4.3, he interprets the prophecy recounted by Charles in a too-optimistic manner. In 4.4 his Herald (1) offers a humiliating truce to the English Prince, which is refused. In 4.6 he is again reduced to trying to rally a defeated army, and in 4.7 he is a prisoner of war, speaking only one line, a whining lament at his luck. In 5.1 he is about to be sent to England, and he briefly curses the prophecy that had obscurely predicted it.

The historical King John is hard to find in the play, and not only because the character is simply a stereotype of a bragging, cowardly Frenchman, who despite his noble rank must be persuaded to honorable behavior. Shakespeare and his collaborators had radically rearranged the chronology of events presented in their sources. To begin with, John was not actually king until after most of the play's events. His father, King Philip VI (1293–1350), ruled France and commanded its armies until his death, which occurred after all the events in the play except Poitiers. Rather than have the title character face two different opponents, Philip in Act 3 and John in Act 4, the playwrights simply adopted the latter for all purposes, while at the same time tightening the progress of events further by treating 16 years of history as though it took a few months. Thus, for all of Act 3, Shakespeare's King John is enacting the history of King Philip, his father. Moreover, his most significant moment in the play is also unhistorical, for the safe-conduct episode is based on events that actually occurred in 1340, long before the battle of Poitiers. In reality, at that time John bore the title Duke of Normandy, traditionally held by the heir-apparent to the throne of France, who is Charles in the play. So it was John, not Charles, who actually issued the safe-conduct and defended it against the intransigence of *his* father. King John was, however, in command at Poitiers, and he was captured and sent to England. So Shakespeare's character plays both his historical self and his historical father.

In the tangle of politically motivated marriages among the royal families of medieval France and England, King John was the ancestor of at least 10 figures in the HISTORY PLAYS, including one of Shakespeare's greatest female characters, the remarkable Margaret of Anjou, who appears in four plays (*1–3 Henry VI* and *Richard III*), as well as her husband, King Henry VI; Henry VI's mother, the Princess Katharine of *Henry V*; and the English Queen Isabel of *Richard II*. John was also grandfather or great-grandfather to six French figures who appear in either or both of *Henry V* and *1 Henry VI*.

Lodowick   Character in *Edward III*, secretary to King Edward. After the King has met and become obsessed with the Countess in the first act of the play, Lodowick opens the second with a wry assessment of the love-struck monarch, concluding with the couplet, "Then, Scottish wars, farewell; I fear 'twill prove / A lingering English siege of peevish love" (2.1.22–23), predicting the King's coming dereliction of duty. Then, in a sparkling piece of comedy (2.1.53–184), Edward attempts to have Lodowick compose a love poem for him to use. He describes the object of his affections in comically extravagant terms, which Lodowick, affecting innocence in such matters, comically fails to render as a suitable poem. Lodowick is dismissed when the Countess herself appears; though he returns briefly

several times as a messenger in 2.2, his role is essentially finished in the previous scene.

Lodowick was drawn from the tale of King Edward's obsession in the *Palace of Pleasure* by William PAINTER, which features a privately disapproving go-between employed by the King, a rather bland figure. But Shakespeare's Lodowick is essentially loyal to the King; he is more worried about his master than he is censorious. This humanizes the monarch and suggests his future reform. Also, Lodowick is one of the first of Shakespeare's ironic straight men, especially in the poetry-composing scene, where his brief remarks and serious demeanor accentuate the King's comical enthusiasm. For instance, 2.1.95, after about 40 lines of Edward's romantic rhetoric, the secretary blankly inquires, "Write I to a woman?" and after 80 more lines he confesses to having composed only two, himself. This scene offers comic relief from the development of the King's rather ugly obsession. It also constitutes an amusing send-up of the Elizabethan craze for SONNETs, and it has been read as a critique of the use of poetry to manipulate people.

Lorraine, Raoul, Duke of (Rudolph, Duke of Lorraine)   (d. 1346)   Historical figure and character in *Edward III*, follower of King John of France. Lorraine serves as FRANCE's ambassador to England's King Edward, in 1.1, bringing King John's disdainful demand for subservience, and he essentially declares war when Edward refuses. He speaks boldly amid the hostility of the English court, even drawing his sword on Artois, whom he regards as a traitor. In 1.2 he visits SCOTLAND and, speaking only two lines, accepts King David's agreement to an alliance with France. Lorraine is next seen in 3.1 among the French commanders before the battle of SLUYS, quietly providing frank and measured assessments of the situation, in comparison with the overconfident braggadocio of the King and Prince Charles. Lorraine accompanies the French court at their meeting with the English prior to the battle of CRÉCY in 3.3, but he does not speak. In 3.4, at the battle, he briefs the king on a setback to French forces and goes with him to rally the troops. At this point Lorraine disappears from the play, having served to lend a note of dignity to the French court.

The historical Lorraine died at Crécy, in fact, though this is not mentioned in the play. The Duchy of Lorraine, now in northeastern France but an independent territory at the time, was a major ally of medieval France, and the Duke was a close adviser of King Philip VI (whose place is taken in the play by King John), as well as his ally in war, but he never served as an ambassador for France.

Mariner Minor character in *Edward III*, a French sailor. In 3.1.62–78, the Mariner informs King John of France that the English invasion fleet is approaching the coast. He returns to his ship, and King John and his entourage hear the sounds of a naval battle (see SLUYS). The Mariner then returns to report the English victory, in 3.1.141–184.

Though his small part in the play serves merely to provide an account of offstage action, the Mariner has 60 lines of quite elaborate and flowery speech. While his diction can sound absurd to modern ears, he would have lent an air of grandeur to the situation for Elizabethan audiences. The playwright, whether Shakespeare or a collaborator, took part of the Mariner's information from Petruccio UBALDINO's report on the Armada, the Spanish fleet that had attempted to invade England not long before the time of the play, as well as from historical accounts of the battle of Sluys.

Messenger Either of two minor characters in *Edward III*, soldiers in the service of King David of Scotland. In 1.2 the Messengers bring news of the approach of English troops (the first Messenger, at 1.2.48) and then of their imminent arrival (the second, at 1.2.67). Their palpable alarm, and the subsequent hasty flight of King David and his men, serve both to advance the plot and to offer the crude humor of an insulting ethnic stereotype—the Scot as coward—dear to the English of Shakespeare's time.

Montague, Sir William (active 1341) Historical figure and minor character in *Edward III*, nephew and emissary of the Countess of Salisbury. In 1.1 Montague brings King Edward a request for aid from the Countess: England's supposed ally, King David of Scotland, has invaded English terri-

tory and has besieged ROXBOUROUGH CASTLE, where the Countess lives without her husband, the Earl of Salisbury, who is fighting in FRANCE. The King agrees to march north and drive off the Scots, and Montague is the first of the English army to reach Roxborough Castle and greet his aunt, in 1.2. His small part serves only to introduce the materials of the SUBPLOT concerning the Countess.

Shakespeare found Montague's role as emissary in the history of the HUNDRED YEARS' WAR by Jean FROISSART, but in a different siege than the one in which the playwright places the Countess. The Scots, in a different incursion, had indeed besieged Roxborough Castle, and Montague, nephew and follower of the Earl of Salisbury, was in charge in Salisbury's absence and had delivered a request for aid to King Edward, but the Countess had not been present. The woman at Roxborough had been Montague's wife, Alice (whom some sources report was herself the object of the King's lust when he raised the siege). The Countess's spirited resistance was modeled on another event (see Mountford, Lord), in which Montague played no part. One 14th-century report says that around 1350 Montague beat Alice to death and was excused from punishment by the king.

Mountford, Lord (Jean IV de Montfort, Duke of Brittany) (1293–1345) Historical figure and character in *Edward III*, an ally of King Edward at the outset of the HUNDRED YEARS' WAR. At 1.1.134 Lord Mountford is mentioned as the French ally for whom the Earl of Salisbury is fighting, but he does not appear in person. In 4.1, having become Duke of Brittany through Salisbury's assistance, he swears eternal allegiance to King Edward, in thanks. Salisbury conveys this pledge to the King in 5.1.99–101. Mountford's brief appearance serves to usher Salisbury into the play.

The historical Montfort actually pledged his allegiance to Edward much earlier, in 1341, after England's first success in the war at SLUYS. He was seeking, and received, English support against the French king's nominee as Duke of Brittany. He was shortly captured by French forces and died in prison a few years later, prior to the time of his appearance in the play. But Montfort's campaign was carried on, with English support, by his wife, Jeanne of Flanders (active 1340s), and only at this point was Salisbury dispatched to aid the cause. (The Comtesse Jeanne served admirably in 1342 as the military commander of a castle besieged by the English, going so far as to don armor and lead sallies against the enemy, as recounted by Jean FROISSART and read by Shakespeare, who assigned her heroic status to the Countess of Salisbury.)

Mountford and his war in Brittany may have been introduced into the play by Shakespeare as part of the insertion of Acts 1 and 2. They provide for Salisbury's absence from England in Acts 1 and 2, while King Edward attempts to seduce his wife. In addition, however, Mountford, like ARTOIS—who is also kept alive beyond his years to attest to English triumphs—represents French support for King Edward's dynastic claims against King John of France.

Percy, Henry, Lord (ca. 1299–1352) Historical figure and minor character in *Edward III*, a follower of King Edward. Lord Percy arrives at the siege of CALAIS, in 4.2, to report to Edward on the victory of English forces in SCOTLAND. In 18 lines, he tells of the capture of King David by John Copland, of Queen Philippa's anger at Copland's refusal to surrender his captive to her custody, and of the Queen herself being on her way to Calais. His message delivered, he disappears from the play, having introduced the Copland subplot, which matures in 5.1.

The historical Percy, a powerful feudal baron of northern England, was co-regent of England during King Edward's absence in FRANCE. He commanded the forces that defeated the historical King David at the battle of Neville's Cross, the victory he reports to the King in the play (without mentioning his role in it, presumably to keep the audience focused on Copland; in historical fact, Percy did not travel to Calais at all). One of his grandsons, another Henry Percy, was the Earl of Northumberland, a character in *Richard II* and *1* and *2 Henry IV*. Another grandson, Thomas Percy, Earl of Worcester, appears in *1 Henry IV*. Through Northumberland, *Edward III*'s Percy was also great-grandfather to the Henry Percy who appears in *Richard II* and, as Hotspur, in *1 Henry IV*; and Hotspur was in turn grandfather to the Northumberland of *3 Henry VI*.

Philip, Prince of France (1341–1404) Historical figure and character in *Edward III*, younger brother of Prince Charles and younger son of King John of FRANCE. Prince Philip is insignificant in the drama's action, but he is presented, in part, as a striking figure. In 3.1 Philip witnesses his brother and father vaingloriously underestimating the approaching English invasion at SLUYS, but he keeps silent until, in 3.1.107–113, he displays a mature judgment of political issues as well as a measured courage. In 3.3, during the ritual exchange of insults between the leaders of the two countries before the battle of CRÉCY, only Philip shows common sense, adjuring his father to "range your battles, prate no more. / These English fain would spend the time in words, / That, night approaching, they might escape unfought" (3.3.137–139). In 4.5–4.7, at the battle of POITIERS, Philip is merely a participant in the defeat of the French. He is unnerved by the startling flight of ravens that panics the French troops, in 4.5; in 4.6 he displays nobility in bravely facing France's catastrophic loss, crying out, "No hope but death, to bury up our shame" (4.6.47), and in 4.7 he is mutely brought in as a prisoner of war.

The historical Philip was known as Philip the Bold for his courage at Poitiers, where he fought at the age of 15. Earlier, at Sluys, he had not been present, being as yet unborn, and he missed Crécy, being five years old at the time; Shakespeare's rearrangement of historical chronology required his presence on the earlier occasions. Philip became the Duke of Burgundy in 1363, after that then-obscure duchy reverted to the French crown. He continued his military career, campaigning extensively for France and Burgundy against, at different times, England and various rebellious Flemish cities. He was renowned for his enlightened government of Burgundy, and he began the process of alliances and marriages that turned it into a major European power of the 15th century. He was a grandfather of the Duke of Burgundy who appears in Shakespeare's *1 Henry VI* and *Henry V*.

Polonian Captain Minor character in *Edward III*, a Polish military officer in the French army at the battle of CRÉCY. The Polonian Captain, a mercenary soldier, reports to King John in 3.1.46, declaring that his troops "willingly will venture in thy cause." His four-line appearance serves merely to aggrandize the English achievement in defeating FRANCE by lending a sense of international scope to French power.

Prince of Wales, Edward (1330–1376) Historical figure and character in *Edward III*, the son of King Edward and a leading participant in the HUNDRED YEARS' WAR against FRANCE. The Prince appears chiefly in the final three acts, which are regarded by scholars as having been written largely by Shakespeare's collaborators and is thus not a creation of the young playwright himself. The Prince is presented as a bold and steadfast warrior. He appears briefly several times in the first two acts of the play as a member of his father's court, but he comes into his own as the English and French forces face each other before the battle of CRÉCY, when his father and other noblemen formally invest him with his knightly armor (3.3.172–228). During the battle, the Prince is reported to be surrounded, "close encompassed with a world of odds" (3.4.33) and facing certain defeat, but the King refuses to send reinforcements, confident in his son's ultimate victory and declaring that in any case, even if defeated and killed, he will have fulfilled a knightly destiny. The Prince returns, of course, victorious and bearing the body of the defeated King of BOHEMIA. His modest but impressive account of the combat inspires his father to grant him a knighthood on the spot.

The Prince reprises this combat history at the battle of POITIERS in Act 4, where he and Lord Audley face certain death in 4.4, and the Prince repudiates three separate, increasingly contemptuous, French demands for surrender. In 4.6, on the battlefield, the Prince exults in an English recovery despite a shortage of arrows, and he declares that they will win even if forced to fight on with stones. At the close of the scene, as first the French leaders and then the dying Audley report, the English have won the day. In 4.7 the Prince magnanimously rewards Audley and his Esquires, before leaving to rejoin the King at the siege of CALAIS. There, in 5.1, the play culminates in a celebration of English triumphs in which the arrival of the victorious Prince is a highlight. As an exemplar of knightly virtue

and battlefield success, the Prince is something of a cardboard character, and he serves chiefly to heighten the patriotic aspects of the play.

The historical Prince was renowned as a brave and resourceful warrior and is enshrined in English history as "the Black Prince," a reference to the color of his armor (though the epithet only came into use three centuries later). As a well-known English hero, he was a natural element in a patriotic HISTORY PLAY. Historically, he was indeed present at Crécy and was the victor at Poitiers, though the playwrights altered the chronology and many details of these battles. The play's account of the insulting French demands for surrender at Poitiers is entirely fictitious (it may have been derived from the same source as the similar "tennis balls" scene in *Henry V*—the anonymous play known as THE FAMOUS VICTORIES). The initiation and knighting of the Prince in 3.3 are equally fictitious and may have been inspired by accounts of his installation as one of the original Knights of the Garter (an English chivalric order established by Edward III); in fact, some scholars believe that prior to Shakespeare's involvement in the collaboration, the play may have been intended as a so-called Garter Play, meant for performance on the grand state occasion of the induction of new members (as was the case for *The Merry Wives of Windsor.*

As a prospective king, the historical Prince Edward was less impressive than he was in combat. After the English victories enacted in *Edward III*, he governed most of southwest France, but he spent much of the province's wealth in fruitless military campaigns in support of a deposed Spanish nobleman. Local discontent with the prince inspired King Charles V of France (the play's Charles, who had by then succeeded the play's King John) to resume the Hundred Years' War, in 1369. However, the prince's health was failing, and he returned to England in 1371, dying five years later, predeceasing his father. (Elizabethan audiences will have recognized King Edward's comments on the Prince's prospective death, in 3.4.34–36 and 3.4.53, as references to the historical prince's early demise.) Prince Edward's son was to become King Richard II, whose fate is presented by Shakespeare in *Richard II.*

Queen Philippa of England (1314–1369)　Historical figure and character in *Edward III*, the wife of Edward III. The Queen is present only in 5.1, the play's last scene, but her appearance is prepared for in 4.2, at the outset of the siege of CALAIS, when Percy brings Edward news that King David of Scotland has been captured in battle by John Copland, that Copland has offended the Queen by refusing to turn his prisoner over to her, and that the Queen is on her way to Calais. Just at this moment, a French Captain (1) arrives to negotiate a surrender. King Edward declares that he will allow his troops to sack the city unless six of its leaders come forth, with nooses around their necks, to be hanged or otherwise punished, as he shall decide.

These two plot elements—the Queen's displeasure with Copland and the possible sacrifice of the six citizens—come together in 5.1. As the scene opens, the Queen has arrived at Calais for the final stage of the siege, and the six citizens emerge. The angry King orders them to a painful death. The Queen intervenes, however, and asks him to "be more mild . . . [for] kings approach the nearest unto God / By giving life and safety unto men" (5.1.39–42). The King concedes, ordering the men released. At this point Copland arrives with King David. Copland explains his belief that he should only surrender his prisoner to the King in person, and though the Queen upbraids him, the King finds his justification sufficient and forgives him. The Queen does not demur and only speaks again to briefly bewail (in five lines) the elaborate account given by Salisbury of the apparent death in battle of her son, the Prince of Wales, and then (in two lines) to express gratitude for his survival when he appears, victorious. Her function, already achieved, has been to establish the quality of reconciliation at the triumphant close of the play, both as seeker of mercy and exemplar of maternal love.

Historically, Queen Philippa was indeed piqued with Copland, and Copland was called to King Edward's presence in Calais to account for himself and was forgiven, but the queen was not there at the time, as Shakespeare probably knew from his sources; he placed her there for her symbolic value. The historical queen was known as Philippa of Hainault, then an independent territory in what is now Belgium, and her marriage to Edward was a maneuver in the complicated dynastic politics of 14th-century Europe; the alliances it produced for England are alluded to in 2.2.204–205 and 3.1.23–24. She bore him 12 children, nine of whom survived; among them, besides the Prince, were three prominent figures in Shakespeare's *Richard II*: John of Gaunt; Edmund, Duke of York; and Thomas, Duke of Gloucester. Through them, she was ancestor to a host of other men depicted in Shakespeare's HISTORY PLAYS, including seven English kings.

In Q1 and Q2, the 16th-century editions of *Edward III*, the Queen's name was spelled "Philip" or "Phillip" and was clearly treated as a two-syllable word, as scanned in the poetry; beginning with Edward CAPELL, modern editors have tended to render her name as "Philippa" (the usual modern spelling of her unusual name) in stage directions and as the two-syllable French version "Philippe" in the text.

Salisbury, Sir William Montague, Earl of (d. 1344)　Historical figure and character in *Edward III*, husband of the Countess, and like her an exemplar of loyalty and chivalric honor. After being mentioned often in the first two acts of the play, while the obsessed King Edward unsuccessfully attempts to seduce the Countess—Salisbury is in Brittany fighting for Lord Mountford and, by proxy, for Edward himself—the earl suddenly appears in 4.1, receiving Mountford's thanks for his victory against FRANCE. Salisbury now decides that his place is with King Edward at the siege of CALAIS, so he commissions a captured French officer, Villiers, to go to the French Prince Charles and get from him, on Salisbury's behalf, a safe-conduct through the French army's lines. Villiers must acquire this document or return to captivity, on his word of honor. The earl declares, "Thus once I mean to try a Frenchman's faith" (4.1.43), thereby countering the play's earlier stereotyping of the French as braggarts and cowards—a bias shared by Shakespeare's audiences in Elizabethan England. Villiers succeeds (in 4.3), and Salisbury next appears at the battle of POITIERS, in 4.5, as a captive of the French. He produces his safe-conduct, but the French King John refuses to accept it and orders Salisbury hanged.

However, Prince Charles is present and insists that his word must be honored, and the King, ashamed of himself, permits Salisbury to travel onward to Calais, though he sends with him a message to Edward that his son the Prince of Wales will soon be dead. In 5.1 Salisbury arrives in Calais to deliver news of both Mountford's victory and Prince Edward's apparent defeat, the latter with an elaborate eyewitness description of the battle, concluding, "Away we turned our wat'ry eyes with sighs / As black as powder fuming into smoke. / And thus, I fear, unhappy, have I told / The most untimely tale of Edward's fall" (5.1.153–156). Salisbury's part is now complete, for the Prince arrives, victorious. The earl does not speak again.

Salisbury's role in the drama is highly symbolic. His loyal wife offered by example and precept a lesson that King Edward needed, at the play's beginning; her husband presents a similar lesson—the value of honor and respect for a sworn oath—as it ends. He offers trust to Villiers. Villiers in turn influences Charles, and Charles influences King John; Salisbury's lesson is pervasive. With his wife, he exemplifies a principal theme of the play, a favorite of Shakespeare's: the need for honor and trust in a society.

The historical Salisbury did indeed fight in Brittany for Jean de Montfort (the historical Mountford), but the episode of the safe-conduct obtained in order to return to the King was actually reported in Shakespeare's sources as the effort of another man, Sir Walter de Manny (d. 1372), a famous warrior of the day. Salisbury was drafted to take his place in order to effect a parallel with his wife's behavior in Acts 1–2. Historically, Salisbury died in 1344, well before the battle of Poitiers and the events enacted late in the play. He was the grandfather of the Earl of Salisbury who appears in *1 Henry VI* and *Henry V*, but the title was held by different families at different times, so he is not related to the other Shakespearean Salisburys.

Villiers   Minor but significant character in *Edward III*, a French nobleman who obtains a safe-conduct for the Earl of Salisbury. In 4.1, Villiers, a prisoner of war, is sent to find the French Prince Charles and solicit a safe-conduct through the French army lines

for Salisbury. He must acquire this document or return to captivity, on his word of honor. Salisbury declares, "Thus once I mean to try a Frenchman's faith" (4.1.43). This rather graceless concession doubtless fed audience sentiment, for *Edward III* was an overtly patriotic play at a time of national danger, and its original audiences may well have been surprised by this presumption of honor in an enemy. But as part of the SUBPLOT's emphasis on knightly honor, Villiers counters the play's earlier stereotyping of the French as braggarts and cowards and demonstrates honorable behavior. In 4.3 Prince Charles refuses Villiers's request, so the nobleman declares he must return to captivity. The prince advises him to violate his oath, but Villiers refuses. His conscientious statement of his honor impresses the prince, who grants the passport. Villiers leaves to send the document to Salisbury and then departs from the play. He has functioned as a conduit for the lesson in honor initiated by Salisbury in accepting Villiers's promise, taught here by example to Charles, and later passed on by him to his father, the French King John, in 4.5.

Shakespeare based this episode on a real one in Jean FROISSART's history, where the real original of Villiers is anonymous. The playwright apparently took his character's name from a French town.

Warwick, Thomas de Beauchamp, Earl of (active 1340)   Historical figure and character in *Edward III*, the father of the Countess of Salisbury and a follower of King Edward. In 2.1 King Edward, obsessed with the Countess, tricks Warwick into swearing an oath that he will try to persuade his daughter to sleep with the King. Warwick reluctantly takes on the task of encouraging his own daughter's dishonor, but he is delighted when she adamantly refuses. His speech at this point, restating the reasons why it is right for her to refuse, offers a prime piece of evidence of Shakespeare's authorship of the play, for it contains a line—"Lilies that fester smell far worse than weeds" (2.1.452)—that also appears in Shakespeare's *Sonnets* (94.14). Warwick appears but does not speak, as part of the King's entourage at the close of 2.2.

The theory that in collaborating on *Edward III*, Shakespeare provided material for an already extant play is also supported by the observation that Warwick, an essential element of the story of Edward's unhealthy obsession, is not provided for in the initial stage direction of 1.1, though he appears in the scene, most significantly as part of the introduction of the Countess theme, at 1.1.131–135. The assumption is that his appearance was first provided for in a supplement to the play's original manuscript, and that part of the original has survived in the first pages of the published work, where Warwick is omitted.

Thomas de Beauchamp, the historical Earl of Warwick in the time of Edward III, was not in fact the father of the Countess of Salisbury. Shakespeare took the error from a source, William PAINTER, who had taken it from his Italian source, Matteo BANDELLO, who had simply assigned the Countess a well-known English figure, Richard Neville, Earl of Warwick (the Warwick of *2* and *3 Henry VI*), as a father. Painter had eliminated any reference to Neville, "the Kingmaker," who was much too well known to Elizabethan readers to pass for anyone else, but retained the ducal title, which Shakespeare, in his turn, also used.

Woman Minor character in *Edward III*, a French civilian living near CRÉCY. In 3.2 the Woman, with two small children and several men (see Citizen [1]), flees the approaching English army. She adds to the group's worries by mentioning an ominous prophecy of French defeat. She then joins the others in flight when word of an initial English victory arrives. The Woman's account prepares the audience for the later, more elaborate prophecy presented in 4.3.

Hamlet

SYNOPSIS

Act 1, Scene 1

On the castle wall in ELSINORE, a sentry, Barnardo, replaces Francisco on guard and is joined by Horatio and Marcellus. Barnardo and Marcellus tell of a supernatural being they have seen. The Ghost of the late king of DENMARK silently appears and with-

draws. The three agree that this visitation seems especially ominous in view of an impending war with Norway. The Ghost reenters but disappears again when a cock crows. Horatio decides that they should tell Prince Hamlet of the appearance of his father's spirit.

Act 1, Scene 2

Claudius, the King of Denmark, speaks of the recent death of the late king, his brother, and of his marriage to Queen Gertrude, his brother's widow and Hamlet's mother. He also tells of an invasion threat from young Prince Fortinbras of Norway, who is acting without the knowledge of his uncle, the Norwegian king. The King therefore sends Cornelius and Voltemand with a letter to the King of Norway advocating restraint. Laertes, the son of the King's adviser Polonius, requests permission to return to his studies in France, which the King grants. The King and Queen urge Hamlet to cease mourning his father's death. The King denies Hamlet permission to return to his own studies at Wittenberg; the Queen adds her wish that he stay in Denmark, and Hamlet agrees to do so. The monarchs and their retinue depart. Hamlet remains and muses mournfully on his mother's hasty and incestuous marriage. Horatio, Marcellus, and Barnardo appear and tell Hamlet about the Ghost. With great excitement, he arranges to meet them on the castle wall that night.

Act 1, Scene 3

Laertes, leaving for France, warns his sister, Ophelia, about Hamlet's affection for her, which he says cannot be permanent in view of the prince's royal status. Polonius arrives and gives Laertes moralizing advice on his conduct abroad. Laertes departs with a last word to Ophelia about Hamlet; this triggers a diatribe from Polonius about the suspect morals of young men, and he forbids Ophelia to see the prince.

Act 1, Scene 4

The Ghost appears to Hamlet, Horatio, and Marcellus, and Hamlet speaks to it. It beckons, and Hamlet follows.

Act 1, Scene 5

The Ghost confirms that it is the spirit of Hamlet's father. It declares that the prince must avenge his murder: The King had poured poison in his ear. The Ghost departs, and Hamlet vows to carry out its wishes. Horatio and Marcellus appear, and Hamlet swears them to secrecy—about the Ghost and about his own intention to feign madness—as the Ghost's disembodied voice demands their oaths.

Act 2, Scene 1

Polonius sends his servant Reynaldo to spy on Laertes in Paris. Ophelia reports that Hamlet has come to her and behaved as if he were insane. Polonius concludes that his separation of Ophelia and Hamlet has driven the prince mad, and he decides to inform the King of this.

Act 2, Scene 2

The King and Queen welcome Rosencrantz and Guildenstern, fellow students of Hamlet, who have been summoned in the hope that the prince will confide in them. They agree to spy on their friend. Voltemand and Cornelius arrive to report that the King of Norway has agreed to redirect Fortinbras's invasion to Poland. Polonius then declares—with comical tediousness—that Hamlet is lovesick, producing a love letter from the prince that he has confiscated from Ophelia. He offers to arrange for the King to eavesdrop on an encounter between Ophelia and Hamlet. Hamlet appears; Polonius advises the King and Queen to leave, and he approaches the prince alone. Hamlet answers him with nonsensical remarks and absurd insults. Polonius interprets these as symptoms of madness and departs, as Rosencrantz and Guildenstern enter. Hamlet greets them with more wild talk, and he badgers them into admitting that they have been sent to observe him. Players from the city arrive, and Hamlet welcomes them enthusiastically, asking the First Player to recite a dramatic monologue describing an episode of revenge from the TROJAN WAR. Hamlet requests that the Players perform THE MURDER OF GONZAGO before the court that night, inserting lines that he will compose. He dismisses the actors and the courtiers and soliloquizes on his delay in avenging the Ghost. He suspects that the spirit may have lied; he will have the Players enact a killing similar to his father's murder, and if Claudius responds guiltily, he will know that the Ghost has spoken the truth.

Act 3, Scene 1

Polonius instructs Ophelia to meet Hamlet while he and the King eavesdrop. The two men hide themselves as Hamlet approaches, meditating on the value of life, and Ophelia greets him. He passionately rejects her with a wild diatribe against women. He leaves her grieving for his apparent madness. The King tells Polonius that he has decided to send Hamlet on a mission to England, accompanied by Rosencrantz and Guildenstern. Polonius suggests further surveillance in the meantime, proposing that his mother summon Hamlet after the performance by the Players; he, Polonius, will spy on their conversation.

Act 3, Scene 2

Hamlet lectures the Players on acting, saying that overacting and improvisation are distractions from a play's purposes. The court assembles, and the Players perform an introductory DUMB SHOW, in which a murderer kills a king by pouring poison in his ear as he sleeps. He then takes the king's crown and exits with the king's wife. The Player King and Player Queen then speak; she asserts that she will never remarry if he dies, but he insists that she will. He then rests, falling asleep. Another Player, in the part of Lucianus, speaks darkly of the evil powers of poison and pours a potion in the ear of the Player King. The real King, distressed, rises and leaves in anger. Hamlet exults in the success of his plan. Rosencrantz and Guildenstern, and then Polonius, deliver the Queen's summons to Hamlet, and he agrees to go to her, but not before ridiculing them. He prepares himself to meet his mother, feeling great anger but reminding himself not to use violence against her.

Act 3, Scene 3

Polonius tells the King that Hamlet is on his way to the Queen's chamber, where he, Polonius, will spy on their meeting. He goes, and the King soliloquizes about his murder of his brother. He says that he has been unable to pray for forgiveness because he is conscious that he is still enjoying the fruits of his crime—his brother's kingdom and his widow. He tries again to pray; Hamlet enters, sees the King on his knees, and contemplates killing him on the spot. He reflects, however, that if the King dies while at prayer, he will probably go to heaven and the revenge will be incomplete. Hamlet decides instead to wait until he finds the King engaged in some sin, however petty, and then kill him, ensuring that his soul will go to hell.

Act 3, Scene 4
Polonius hides behind a curtain in the Queen's chamber. Hamlet arrives; he attempts to make his mother sit down, and she cries for help. Polonius cries out also, and Hamlet stabs him through the drapery, killing him. After expressing regret that his victim was not the King, Hamlet condemns his mother's behavior. He compares the virtues of his father to the vices of his uncle; the distraught Queen's cries for mercy only enrage him more. The Ghost appears. The Queen, unaware of its presence, thinks Hamlet is mad as he speaks with the spirit. The Ghost reminds Hamlet of the vengeance he must exact, urges pity on the Queen, and departs. Less violently than before, Hamlet urges his mother to confess her sins and refuse to have sex with the King. He leaves, dragging the body of Polonius with him.

Act 4, Scene 1
The Queen tells the King that Hamlet has killed Polonius. The King sends Rosencrantz and Guildenstern to recover the body.

Act 4, Scene 2
Rosencrantz and Guildenstern confront Hamlet. He mocks them, refusing to tell them where the body is, but he goes with them to the King.

Act 4, Scene 3
The King tells his courtiers that Hamlet is dangerous, yet, because of the prince's popularity, his exile to England must seem routine. Rosencrantz and Guildenstern return with Hamlet under guard. Hamlet expounds humorously on corpses before revealing where he has put Polonius's body. The King tells Hamlet that he is being sent to England immediately for his own safety. The King's entourage escorts Hamlet to the boat, leaving the King alone to muse on his plot: he is sending letters to the English that threaten war unless they kill Hamlet immediately.

Act 4, Scene 4
Hamlet, accompanied by Rosencrantz and Guildenstern, encounters a Captain from Fortinbras's army, on its way to Poland. The Captain speaks of Fortinbras's war as a fight over a small, insignificant piece of territory. Hamlet compares himself, unable to avenge his father's death, with the 20,000 men who will fight and die for an inconsequential goal. He vows that in the future, he will value only bloody thoughts.

Act 4, Scene 5
A Gentleman tells the Queen that Ophelia is insane, rambling wildly in senseless speeches that yet seem to convey some unhappy truth. Ophelia enters, singing a song about a dead lover. The King arrives, and Ophelia sings of seduction and betrayal. She leaves, speaking distractedly about a burial. A Messenger appears with the news that Laertes has raised a rebellion and is approaching the castle. Laertes and several Followers break down the door and enter. He demands vengeance for his father's death, and the King promises that he shall have it. Ophelia returns, singing about a funeral, and distributes flowers to the King, the Queen, and Laertes. She sings again, about an old man's death, and departs. The King takes Laertes away to plot revenge on Hamlet.

Act 4, Scene 6
A Sailor brings Horatio a letter from Hamlet. It tells of his capture by pirates who have agreed to release him; Rosencrantz and Guildenstern continue to sail to England. Horatio goes with the sailor to meet Hamlet.

Act 4, Scene 7
The King tells Laertes that he cannot act directly against Hamlet, out of consideration for the Queen and because of the prince's popularity. The King proposes a plot: they shall arrange a fencing match between Hamlet and Laertes, in which Hamlet will use a blunted sword intended for sport while Laertes shall secretly have a sharp sword. Laertes agrees and adds that he has a powerful poison that he will apply to his sword point. The King further suggests a poisoned glass of wine to be given Hamlet when the sport has made him thirsty. The

Queen appears with the news that Ophelia has drowned, and Laertes collapses in tears.

Act 5, Scene 1

A Grave-digger who is a CLOWN speaks with his friend, the Other clown, about Ophelia, who has been granted Christian burial although possibly a suicide. He comically misconstrues the law on suicide and jokes about grave-digging. Hamlet and Horatio arrive, and Hamlet meditates on death's leveling of the wealthy and ambitious. He talks with the Grave-digger, who displays a skull that had belonged to Yorick, a court jester whom Hamlet had known. The prince reflects on the inevitability of death. Ophelia's funeral procession arrives, accompanied by Laertes and the King and Queen; the Priest declares her death a suicide. When Hamlet realizes whose funeral he is witnessing, he rushes forth and tries to fight Laertes, challenging his position as chief mourner. Restrained, he departs in a rage. The King assures Laertes that he will get his revenge.

Act 5, Scene 2

Hamlet tells Horatio how he rewrote the King's letter arranging his death, substituting Rosencrantz and Guildenstern's names for his own. He assumes that the two courtiers were killed, but he feels no remorse, since they were schemers. OSRIC, an obsequious and mannered courtier, arrives with the King's request that Hamlet fence with Laertes; the King has wagered that Hamlet can win. Hamlet mocks Osric before sending word that he will fight. He tells Horatio that the proposed match makes him uneasy but says that he is prepared to die. The King and Queen, a group of courtiers, and Laertes arrive for the match. The King pours wine to toast Hamlet's first successful round, and he places a pearl—a congratulatory token, he says—in Hamlet's cup. Hamlet and Laertes fence, but after his first victory Hamlet postpones refreshment and resumes the match. The Queen drinks from his cup, although the King tries to stop her. Laertes wounds Hamlet with the poisoned sword, the two fighters scuffle and accidentally exchange swords, and Hamlet wounds Laertes. The Queen falls, exclaims that she is poisoned, and dies. Laertes, himself poisoned by the exchanged sword, reveals the King's plot.

Hamlet wounds the King with the sword and then forces him to drink the poisoned wine. Hamlet and Laertes forgive each other, and Laertes dies. Horatio starts to drink the poisoned wine, but Hamlet demands that he remain alive to tell his side of the story. Osric announces the return of Fortinbras from Poland; Hamlet declares Fortinbras his successor and dies. Fortinbras arrives and takes command, ordering a stately funeral for Hamlet.

COMMENTARY

Hamlet is the most notoriously problematic of Shakespeare's plays, and questions about it still bedevil commentators after 400 years. Tremendous amounts of energy have gone into considering its possible interpretations, and the range of opinions on them is immense; as Oscar Wilde wittily put it, perhaps the greatest question raised by *Hamlet* is, "Are the critics mad or only pretending to be so?"

Hamlet was classed with the PROBLEM PLAYS when that term was first applied to Shakespeare's works of the early 17th century (see BOAS, FREDERICK S.). Like those dark comedies, this TRAGEDY deals with death and sex and with the psychological and social tensions arising from these basic facts of life. And like the problem plays, *Hamlet* treats these issues without providing clear-cut resolutions, thereby leaving us with complicated, highly emotional responses that cause both satisfaction—at seeing basic elements of our own lives treated dramatically—and pain—at the nagging persistence of these difficulties, as in real life.

It is precisely through such ambiguity, however, that *Hamlet* offers a robust and vital assertion of human worth, for the play is essentially a moral drama whose theme is the existence of both good and evil in human nature, a central concern in Shakespeare's work as a whole. Although it anticipates modern psychological dramas in some respects, *Hamlet* is not itself such a work; the extraordinary presentation of Prince Hamlet's troubled mind is simply the vehicle—albeit a vivid one—for the development of his acceptance of humanity's flawed nature. Shakespeare's great accomplishment in *Hamlet* was to express the philosophy that underlies this realization.

Illustration of the grave-diggers scene in *Hamlet*. "Alas, poor Yorick. I knew him, Horatio" (5.1.178). Hamlet confronts the fact of human mortality. *(Courtesy of Culver Pictures, Inc.)*

Some of the play's many puzzles are interesting but superficial, such as Horatio's status at the Danish court, the identification of Hamlet's inserted lines in *The Murder of Gonzago*, or the determination of the prince's age. These matters chiefly reflect the playwright's lack of concern for minor inconsistencies, a trait seen throughout the plays. Others are deeper matters of plotting and psychology: Is Hamlet's emotional disturbance real or feigned? What is the nature of his relationship to Ophelia? Is King Claudius an unalloyed villain? The "problem of problems," as it has been called, is Hamlet's unnecessary delay in executing the revenge he plainly accepts as his duty.

The basic story—a young man grieves for his father while faced with the duty to avenge his death—came from Shakespeare's source, the UR-HAMLET, and its genre, the REVENGE PLAY, but Shakespeare's attitude toward vengeance is not the traditionally approving one. Hamlet's regret when he says, "The time is out of joint. O cursed spite, / That ever I was born to set it right" (1.5.196–197), testifies to this, as does the existence of a parallel revenge plot, that of Laertes's revenge of *his* father's murder by Hamlet. The hero of one plot, Hamlet is in effect the villain of the other, casting an inescapable doubt upon his heroic role. Hamlet recognizes the ambivalence of his position when he says of Polonius's death, ". . . heaven hath pleas'd it so, / To punish me with this and this with me" (3.4.175–176).

This paradox suggests the essential duality of human nature, which is both noble and wicked, and numerous comparisons throughout the drama stress this point. Several times Hamlet contrasts his murdered father and his uncle—the former an ideal ruler, just and magnanimous; the latter an unscrupulous killer and lustful adulterer. Similarly, Hamlet juxtaposes his father's virtues with his mother's sin in accepting her husband's murderer and having sex with him. Other polarities abound: the chaste Ophelia versus the incestuous Queen; the faithful Horatio versus the treacherous Rosencrantz and Guildenstern; the devious duellist Laertes versus the manly soldier Fortinbras. Each of these contrasts recalls and reinforces the play's basic opposition between good and evil.

Faced with the awareness of evil, Hamlet longs for death and is disgusted with life, especially as it is manifested in sex, which he not only sees as the drive behind his mother's sin but which he abhors as the force that inexorably produces more life and thus more evil. "Why wouldst thou be a breeder of sinners?" (3.1.121–122), he cries to Ophelia, and his rejection of her stems from his rejection of sex. Shakespeare did not intend their relationship as a love story; instead, it is an allegory of the condemnation of life, a point of view whose ultimate rejection is central to the play.

Hamlet's notorious procrastination of his revenge has a similar function. Though he accepts the Ghost's orders, he senses the evil in this duty, sent from "heaven and hell" (2.2.580), and he resists its fulfillment. Though psychologically true to life, Hamlet's delay serves primarily to offer opportunities to stress the duality of human nature:

as avenger, Hamlet is both opposed to and involved in evil. His repeated insistence on postponing his highly ambiguous duty emphasizes his ambivalence and stimulates our own. Emotionally, Hamlet's procrastination produces in him a growing rage that leads to his killing of Polonius in 3.4, an act that provokes the King and Laertes to set in motion the incidents that lead to the bloody climax and that hastens Hamlet's exile and his escape from the King's execution plot. This event, in turn, jars Hamlet from his absorption in his personal tragedy and prepares him to find the "divinity that shapes our ends" (5.2.10).

Both Hamlet and the play undergo a sweeping change before the climax, and this change is well prepared for by the establishment of a dominant tone in the play's language that is later varied to quite dramatic effect. Through Acts 1–4, the pervasiveness of evil and its capacity to corrupt human life are conveyed by an extended use of the imagery of illness, evoking a strong sense of stress and unease. In the play's opening moments, Francisco declares himself "sick at heart" (1.1.9), and Horatio, speaking of evil omens, refers to the moon being "sick almost to doomsday with eclipse" (1.1.123). Hamlet equates evil with bodily disorder when he speaks of a birthmark, "nature's livery" (1.4.32), as the "dram of evil" (1.4.36) that makes a virtuous man seem corrupt and ignoble. He is referring figuratively to the excessive drinking of Danish courtiers, rather than to the more serious evils soon to arise, but he strikes a note of disease, death, and physical corruption that recurs throughout the play.

For instance, Hamlet speaks of the King's prayer as "physic [that] prolongs thy sickly days" (3.3.96) and of resolution as "sicklied o'er" (3.1.85); the King refers to those who tell Laertes of his father's death as ". . . buzzers [who] infect his ear / With pestilent speeches . . ." (4.5.90–91). Strikingly, diseases of the skin, where an inner evil is presumed to be present, are often mentioned, as in Hamlet's reference to a "flattering unction . . . [that] will but skin and film the ulcerous place, / Whiles rank corruption . . . / Infects unseen" (3.4.147–151), or in his image for the outbreak of a pointless war: an abscess "that inward breaks, and shows no cause without / Why the man dies" (4.4.28–29).

Planning to exile Hamlet, the King observes, "Diseases desperate grown / By desperate appliance are reliev'd" (4.3.9–10). He refers not only to the danger he faces from an avenging Hamlet, but he is also thinking of Hamlet's apparent insanity. Hamlet's lunacy seems at times to be real, at least in some respects, such as his hysterical rejection of sex and love, but he himself asserts that it is false on several occasions—e.g., in 3.4.142–146. The question remains one of the play's many enigmas. In any case, Hamlet's insanity, whether feigned or real, is itself a major instance of the imagery of sickness, a constant reminder that "something is rotten in the state of Denmark" (1.4.90).

A particularly vivid example of disease imagery is the Ghost's clinical description of the action of the poison that first thinned his blood and then produced on his skin a "vile and loathsome crust" (1.5.72) before killing him. The poisoning is enacted twice in 3.2, first in the Players' dumb show and then by the Player playing Lucianus. Further, a similar fate awaits the four major characters in 5.2.

An extension of the play's imagery of death is the repeated suggestion of suicide, although it is rejected. Hamlet's first soliloquy regrets the religious "canon 'gainst self-slaughter" (1.2.132). Horatio worries that the Ghost may tempt Hamlet to the "toys of desperation" (1.4.75) on a cliff overlooking the sea. In 5.1 the Grave-digger discusses the law on suicides, and Ophelia's death is declared "doubtful" (5.1.220) by the Priest. In his last moment, Hamlet prevents Horatio from killing himself with the poisoned cup. The prince also discusses the possibility of suicide at length in the soliloquy beginning "To be or not to be . . ." (3.1.56–88) before rejecting the idea. More important, near the crucial midpoint of the play, just before his dramatic rejection of Ophelia and love, Hamlet raises the question of the desirability of life and answers, in effect, that we have no choice but to accept our destiny and live. Thus, while suicide serves as part of the play's imagery of despair, its rejection foreshadows the ultimate acceptance of life and its evils.

Act 5 opens with Hamlet meditating on death in the graveyard, but now death, represented with ghoulish humor by the skulls dug up by the Grave-digger, is not a potential escape, nor is it the fearful introduction to a possibly malign afterlife; it is merely the destined end for all humans. The conversation with the Grave-diggers offers comic relief as the climax draws closer, and Hamlet's recollections of Yorick offer a healthy appreciation of the pleasures of the past as well as a sardonic acceptance of death: "Now get you to my lady's chamber and tell her, . . . to this favour she must come" (5.1.186–188). The prince is no longer in the grip of his grief. Ophelia's funeral and Hamlet's encounter with Laertes bring a final catharsis, and he is able to assert the love for Ophelia that he once denied and to accept his role in life by taking the royal title "the Dane" (5.1.251).

In the first episode of 5.2, we hear of the cause of this change as Hamlet tells of the plot he has foiled by sending Rosencrantz and Guildenstern to their deaths in his place; in impulsively acting to save himself, he has learned, "There's a divinity that shapes our ends, / Rough-hew them how we will . . ." (5.2.10–11). Hamlet finally comes to terms with his duty to exact vengeance, even though he cannot do so without committing the very crime he avenges, murder. In realizing that he must be evil in order to counter evil, Hamlet also accepts his own death; although he senses his end approaching as the King's plot takes form, he remains composed, saying, "There is special providence in the fall of a sparrow. If it be now, 'tis not to come; if it be not to come, it will be now; if it be not now, yet it will come. The readiness is all" (5.2.215–218).

The tragic paradox at the close of *Hamlet* is that the protagonist's psychological liberation comes only with his own death, a death that inspires Horatio's lovely farewell wish to Hamlet that "flights of angels sing thee to thy rest" (5.2.365). The attitude toward death expressed in this elegiac prayer is unlike anything earlier in the play, and its emphatic placement after the climax clearly marks it as the drama's conclusive statement, a confirmation of the benevolence of fate despite the inevitability of evil and death.

SOURCES OF THE PLAY

Shakespeare's basic source for *Hamlet* was the *Ur-Hamlet* (ca. 1588), a play on the same subject that is known to have been popular in London in the 1580s but for which no text survives. This work, believed to have been written by Thomas KYD, was apparently derived from a tale in François BELLEFOREST's collection *Histoires Tragiques* (1580). Although Shakespeare knew Belleforest's work, he adopted a central element of *Hamlet*, the Ghost, from the *Ur-Hamlet*, and this fact, along with the theatrical success of the lost work, suggests that it was Shakespeare's chief source.

Belleforest retold a story from a 12th-century Latin work, the *Historiae Danicae*, by SAXO GRAMMATICUS, first published in 1514. Saxo provides the earliest complete account of a legendary tale—ninth-century fragments are known from the Icelandic sagas—of Amleth, a Danish nobleman who took revenge after his uncle killed his father and married his mother. The name Amleth, from Old Norse, means "dim-witted" or "brutish," in reference to his stratagem of feigning madness after his father's murder. Many other elements of *Hamlet*—including a dramatic encounter between Amleth and his mother, during which he kills a spy; his love affair with a beautiful woman; his exile to England and his escape by replacing the order for his execution with one condemning his escorts—are present in Saxo's account.

Shakespeare doubtless found much of this in the *Ur-Hamlet*, but this work, to judge by its probable companion piece, Kyd's *The Spanish Tragedy* (1588–89), lacked *Hamlet*'s dramatic development and thematic unity; Shakespeare may have found hints of a unified point of view in Belleforest's version. In particular, the French writer develops the contrast between the good king who is murdered and his evil, incestuous killer, a comparison that is prominent in Hamlet's thoughts.

Many scholars believe that *The Spanish Tragedy*, also a revenge play, was itself a source for numerous elements in *Hamlet*. For instance, Kyd's play has a procrastinating protagonist who berates himself for talking instead of acting and who dies as he achieves his revenge; it also features a play within a play, a heroine whose love is opposed by her family, and another woman who becomes insane and commits suicide. However, some commentators feel that Kyd took at least some of these elements from the *Ur-Hamlet*, whether he wrote it or not, and that Shakespeare could have done so as well.

Other sources contributed to *Hamlet* in minor ways. A play that provokes a confession of guilt was a well-established literary motif, but Shakespeare's company had recently staged an anonymous drama, *A Warning for Fair Women* (1599), in which it is used, so this work was probably the immediate stimulus for Hamlet's *Mousetrap* plot. The physician Timothy BRIGHT's *A Treatise of Melancholy* (1586) may have influenced Shakespeare's portrayal of Hamlet's depression. Thomas NASHE's widely popular pamphlet, *Pierce Penniless His Supplication to the Devil* (1592), influenced several passages of the play, especially Hamlet's diatribe on drunkenness in 1.4.17–18. Some of Hamlet's remarks on graves and death in 5.1 echo a popular religious work, *Of Prayer and Meditation,* by the Spanish mystic Luis de GRANADA, which Shakespeare probably read in the translation by Richard HOPKINS. *The Counsellor* (1598), an anonymous translation of a volume on good government by the famed Polish diplomat Laurentius GOSLICIUS, is echoed in several passages, most notably Hamlet's speech beginning, "What a piece of work is a man" (2.2.303).

PLUTARCH's *Lives,* always one of Shakespeare's favorite sources, mentions a Greek tyrant, famed for many cold-blooded murders, who wept at a recital of HECUBA's woes, and this may have inspired the recitation by the First Player in 2.2. However, the playwright also knew the tale of Hecuba from VIRGIL's *Aeneid,* where it first appears, and from *The Tragedy of Dido* (1594), a play by Nashe and Christopher MARLOWE.

Shakespeare could also have read a retelling of Plutarch's Hecuba anecdote in the *Essays* of Michel de MONTAIGNE, either in French (publ. between 1580 and 1595) or in a manuscript of John FLORIO's translation, (publ. 1603). Echoes of Montaigne occur in several key passages—e.g., both Hamlet and the French essayist liken death to a sleep and to a "consummation" (3.1.63).

Some scholars believe that an incident of 1577 at the court of Marguerite de Valois, a French princess married to the King of Navarre, influenced Shakespeare's conception of Ophelia's death. A young woman of the court was reported to have died of love for a young nobleman; he was absent from the court at the time and learned of her death only when he accidentally encountered the funeral procession upon his return. This event was widely reported in England at the time, due to the English support of the Protestant forces, led by Navarre, in the French Wars of Religion. The same event is thought to be referred to in *Love's Labour's Lost.*

A real event also inspired the murder of Hamlet's father by pouring poison in his ear. In 1538 the Duke of Urbino, one of the leading military and political figures of the day, died. His barber-surgeon confessed that he had killed the duke by putting a lotion in his ears, having been hired to do so by one Luigi Gonzaga. Shakespeare gave the name of the plotter to the victim (as *Gonzago* [3.2.233]), but the combination of his name and the unusual method of poisoning point to this actual crime as the stimulus to the playwright's fictional one, although the *Ur-Hamlet* may have used it first.

TEXT OF THE PLAY

Hamlet was probably written in late 1599 or early 1600, though possibly a year later. It followed *Julius Caesar*—performed in September 1599—for it echoes *Caesar* in 1.1.116–118 and alludes to it in 3.2.102–105, and it probably preceded John MARSTON's play *Antonio's Revenge,* staged in late 1600, which recalls *Hamlet* in many places, indicating that Shakespeare's play had been performed by no later than the autumn of 1600.

However, one passage in *Hamlet*—2.2.336–358, describing the competition of the Players with a troupe of child actors—clearly refers to the WAR OF THE THEATERS, a rivalry among acting companies that dominated the London theater in the spring of 1601. If *Hamlet* was written in 1600, then this passage must have been inserted later. Some scholars, however, hold that *Hamlet* was written in its entirety in early 1601 and that either *Antonio's Revenge* was Shakespeare's source rather than the other way around or both Marston and Shakespeare took their common materials from the *Ur-Hamlet.*

Hamlet was first published in 1603 by Nicholas LING and John TRUNDELL in a QUARTO edition (known as Q1) printed by Valentine SIMMES. Q1 is a BAD QUARTO, a mangled version of the text, assembled from the memories of actors who had performed in the play. It was supplanted by Q2

(1604, with some copies dated 1605), printed by John ROBERTS and published by him and Ling. A sound text, Q2 is believed to have been printed from Shakespeare's own manuscript, or FOUL PAPERS, with occasional reference to Q1 where the manuscript was unclear. However, two substantial passages appear to have been deliberately cut from Q2: Hamlet's reflections on Denmark as a prison (2.2.239–269), perhaps thought offensive to the Danish wife of England's new king, JAMES I; and the passage on child actors mentioned above, which may have been cut because James patronized a CHILDREN'S COMPANY or perhaps simply because it was out of date by 1604. In 1607 Ling sold his rights to the play to John SMETHWICK, who published three further quartos, Q3 (1611), Q4 (1622), and Q5 (1637), each of which was printed from its predecessor.

Hamlet was published in the FIRST FOLIO edition of Shakespeare's plays (1623). This text, known as F, derives from Q2 but differs from it significantly. It corrects many small errors and improves on Q2's stage directions, but it also contains its own, more numerous, omissions and errors. F "modernizes" words the editors or printers thought old-fashioned, and some bits of dialogue apparently derive from actors' ad libs, such as a cry of "Oh Vengeance!" in the middle of Hamlet's soliloquy at the end of 2.2. More important, F provides the significant passages cut from Q2. It is thought that the printers of F followed both Q2—probably a copy that had been annotated for production use—and a FAIR COPY, a transcription of Shakespeare's manuscript, with errors and alterations made by a scribe but including the missing material.

Modern editions rely on Q2 because it is plainly closest to Shakespeare's own manuscript, but they turn to F for its restored cuts and for frequent minor improvements. Rarely, Q1 provides a correction of an obvious error in the other two texts or a clarification in stage directions.

THEATRICAL HISTORY OF THE PLAY

From the outset, *Hamlet* has been recognized as one of the greatest works of the English stage, and it has remained the most widely produced of Shakespeare's plays (though most productions—probably including the original one—have used an abridged text). Most leading actors—and some actresses—of every generation have played the title part. The play has also been frequently performed in other languages.

The first production was that of the CHAMBERLAIN'S MEN in 1600 or 1601, referred to in the registration of the play with the STATIONERS' COMPANY in 1602. Contemporary references, along with many echoes of the play in the work of other playwrights, testify to its early popularity. Richard BURBAGE was the first Hamlet; after his death in 1619 the role was taken, to great acclaim, by Joseph TAYLOR. A tradition first recorded by Nicholas ROWE in 1709 reports that Shakespeare played the Ghost in the original production.

"The Grave-Makers," an adaptation of 5.1 of *Hamlet*, was performed as a DROLL during the period of revolutionary government in England (1642–60), when the theaters were legally closed. After the restoration of the monarchy, *Hamlet* was revived by William DAVENANT, though with a much abridged text, in a 1661 production starring Thomas BETTERTON, who was celebrated in the role for the rest of the century.

David GARRICK played Hamlet many times between 1734 and his retirement in 1776. Susannah Maria CIBBER, who often played opposite him, was regarded as the best Ophelia of the day. Garrick's production of 1772 was one of the most severely altered, and is still notorious for its elimination of much of Act 5. Beginning in 1783, John Philip KEMBLE, regarded as one of the greatest Hamlets, played the part often, sometimes opposite his sister, Sarah SIDDONS, as Ophelia.

Siddons herself was the first of many women to play Hamlet, taking the role in 1775. Female Hamlets were most popular in the late 18th and 19th centuries; among the best known were Kitty CLIVE, Charlotte CUSHMAN, Julia GLOVER, and Sarah BERNHARDT. In the 20th century Judith ANDERSON (at the age of 73) and Eva Le Gallienne, among others, also played the prince.

Most of the major theatrical entrepreneurs of the 19th century produced *Hamlet* at least once. Among the most acclaimed Hamlets of the period were Ira ALDRIDGE, William Charles MACREADY, Edwin BOOTH, and Henry IRVING (usually opposite Ellen

TERRY as Ophelia). Irving had his first great Shakespearean success with the play in 1874, later staging an extravagantly scenic and very popular version (1879). William POEL used the Q1 text in 1881.

F. R. BENSON staged Shakespeare's complete text in 1900, confirming that the resulting four- to five-hour performance was feasible. Other noteworthy 20th-century *Hamlet*s included the controversial 1925 Barry JACKSON production, which introduced modern dress to the Shakespearean stage; a New York staging by Margaret WEBSTER, starring Maurice EVANS (1939); and Joseph PAPP's productions of 1972 and 1987, starring Stacy Keach and Kevin Kline, respectively. Several 20th-century actors were especially well known for their portrayals of Hamlet, including John BARRYMORE, John GIELGUD, Laurence OLIVIER, and Evans. *Hamlet* continues to be frequently staged. Among recent productions was an acclaimed presentation by Peter HALL in 1994.

Hamlet has been acted on FILM at least 25 times—far more than any other Shakespeare play—since 1900, when Sarah Bernhardt played the prince in a silent movie. Among the best-known films are Olivier's heavily abridged version of 1948, with music by William WALTON; the Russian Grigori KOZINTSEV's epic presentation of a prose translation by Boris PASTERNAK (1964); and the 1969 film by Tony Richardson (b. 1928), with Nicol WILLIAMSON. More recently, in 1996 Kenneth BRANAGH starred in his own production, in which Derek JACOBI played King Claudius; and director Michael Almereyda (b. 1960) set his very popular version (2000) in midtown Manhattan. An OPERA of *Hamlet* by Ambroise THOMAS was one of the most popular productions of the 19th century and still holds a place in the opera repertoire. *Hamlet* has also been presented on TELEVISION a number of times, perhaps most notably in the 1980 BBC production starring Jacobi in the title role.

CHARACTERS

Ambassador Minor character in *Hamlet*, an emissary from England to DENMARK. The Ambassador arrives at the Danish court, in 5.2, after the deaths of King Claudius, Queen Gertrude, Laertes, and Hamlet. He reports on the execution of Rosencrantz and Guildenstern, thereby completing an unfinished element in the play's plot. With Fortinbras, the Ambassador offers an outsider's shocked view of the bloody collapse of Denmark's monarchy, reinforcing the play's central theme that evil has a corrupting influence that spreads far beyond its immediate consequences.

Barnardo (Bernardo) Minor character in *Hamlet*. Barnardo and Marcellus are the two sentries who have seen the Ghost of Hamlet's father before the play begins. In 1.1 they introduce Hamlet's friend Horatio to the phenomenon. When the three tell Hamlet about the spirit in 1.2, Barnardo barely speaks, and when Hamlet accompanies Horatio and Marcellus to encounter the Ghost in 1.4, Barnardo has disappeared from the play.

Captain Minor character in *Hamlet*, an officer in the Norwegian army of Prince Fortinbras. In 4.4 the Captain tells Hamlet of Fortinbras's march with 20,000 soldiers to conquer a small, valueless parcel of land in Poland. Shakespeare may take an ironical stance toward the folly of war in these brief and straightforward lincs, but Hamlet seems to accept Fortinbras's goal as reasonable, responding to the Captain's account only by comparing his own scruples and hesitations with the unthinking commitment of the soldiers, who will die fighting for so small a prize. Thus the incident emphasizes Hamlet's concern with his failure to avenge his father's death—the central strand of the play's plot—and reminds us of Fortinbras's strength, which will assume greater importance at the end of the play.

Cornelius Minor character in *Hamlet*, ambassador to the King of Norway from the King of Denmark. In 1.2 Cornelius and Voltemand are appointed to carry a message to Norway. The two ambassadors return in 2.2, and Voltemand reports Norway's reply. Cornelius barely speaks and serves only to flesh out the play's presentation of courtly diplomacy.

First Player Character in *Hamlet*, the leading member of the Players, a traveling company of actors who visit ELSINORE and perform before the court of King Claudius. In 2.2 Hamlet greets the Players with enthusiasm and requests that the First

Player recite a speech he remembers hearing him deliver in a play. Hamlet begins the speech, and the First Player takes it up; it is a highly dramatic account of an episode in the TROJAN WAR, the vengeful killing of King Priam (see *Troilus and Cressida*) by Pyrrhus, followed by the grief of Queen Hecuba. The First Player's fine recital is testified to by Polonius, who observes approvingly that he has "turned his colour and has tears in's eyes" (2.2.515–516), effects that were conventionally associated with fine acting in a tradition extending back to Plato. More significantly, his vigorous performance serves to trigger Hamlet's great soliloquy beginning "O what a rogue and peasant slave am I!" (2.2.544), in which he contrasts the player's passion—"Tears in his eyes, distraction in his aspect / . . . And all for nothing! / For Hecuba! / What's Hecuba to him, or he to her, / That he should weep for her?" (2.2.549–554)—with his own vacillation in seeking revenge for his father's death. The First Player receives Hamlet's instructions to stage THE MURDER OF GONZAGO before the court in 2.2.531–536, and he presumably appears as the Player King in the playlet.

Follower   Any of several minor characters in *Hamlet*, rebels led by Laertes. Upset about the killing of his father, Polonius, by Prince Hamlet, Laertes returns to DENMARK from abroad in a fury. When he arrives in 4.5, he and his Followers break down the door to get to King Claudius. However, he immediately dismisses his men, and the King persuades him to seek revenge against Hamlet rather than through revolution. The Followers speak very little and serve primarily to demonstrate the widespread effects of evil, as political rebellion and social disorder arise from the more personal conflict between Hamlet and the King.

Fortinbras   Character in *Hamlet*, Prince of Norway and enemy of DENMARK. Although he does not appear until 4.4, Fortinbras is described in 1.1.98–107 as a hot-blooded young warrior intent on recapturing lands taken from Norway after the combat in which his father, the late king of Norway, was killed by Hamlet's father, the late king of Den-

mark. Thus he is immediately established as a parallel figure to Hamlet, one who is also compelled to avenge his father's death. Fortinbras's brief appearance in 4.4 on his way to an invasion of neighboring Poland energizes Hamlet, who sees in this war, directed at no more than "a little patch of ground . . . this straw . . . an eggshell" (4.4.18, 26, 53), a direct and shaming contrast to his own inaction in taking revenge against his father's murderer, King Claudius. When Hamlet, nearing death at the play's end, learns that Fortinbras is returning from Poland, he proclaims him heir to the crown of Denmark. When he arrives, Fortinbras takes command and orders a military funeral for Hamlet.

While Fortinbras's example inspires Hamlet to fierce declarations—"My thoughts be bloody or be nothing worth" (4.4.66)—Hamlet's rhetoric is an overreaction to a situation that is not in fact analogous to his own. As the play unfolds, Hamlet comes to realize that an acceptance of fate and its evils is the only way to understand human life; within this context, Fortinbras, who works his will in the world and is doubtless uninterested in such philosophical matters, is clearly a lesser figure. Still, his stalwart resolution and military valor—reminiscent of Shakespeare's Henry V—are not only admirable but also stand in important contrast to the evil and debased intrigue of Hamlet's world.

When Fortinbras appears after Hamlet's death in 5.2, he reminds us that he comes as a hostile power, declaring that he will claim his revenge as his "vantage doth invite" (5.2.395), and we realize that Claudius's evil has damaged his kingdom to the extent that an outsider has taken over. Thus Fortinbras symbolizes a lesson in political morality that Shakespeare offered in several plays (e.g., *Titus Andronicus, Macbeth, King Lear*): Personal evil in powerful members of society will weaken the state as a whole, often resulting in a surrender of sovereignty to another country.

Francisco   Minor character in *Hamlet*, a sentry on the walls of the castle at ELSINORE. Francisco is relieved from duty by Barnardo at the opening of 1.1, as the scene's locale is established. He declares himself "sick at heart" (1.1.9), suggesting immediately that something is amiss in the play's world.

Gentleman Minor character in *Hamlet*. In 4.5 the Gentleman brings Queen Gertude news of Ophelia's madness, describing her erratic behavior and confused language, "That carry but half sense . . . [but] would make one think there might be thought . . ." (4.5.7–12). He thus prepares us to understand the meaning in Ophelia's disconnected songs and talk in the rest of the scene.

Ghost Character in *Hamlet*, the spirit of the murdered king of Denmark, Hamlet's late father. The Ghost, which has been silent in its appearances before the play opens and in 1.1 and 1.4, speaks to Hamlet in 1.5, revealing the secret of his death— "Murder most foul" (1.5.27) at the hands of his brother, the present King Claudius—and insisting that Hamlet exact revenge. This demand establishes the stress that disturbs Hamlet throughout the play. The Ghost reappears in 3.4 to remind Hamlet that he has not yet accomplished his revenge, thereby increasing the pressure on the prince.

The Ghost is clearly an awesome presence, as the responses of Barnardo, Marcellus, and Horatio make clear in 1.1 and 1.4, and we are plainly meant to be impressed by Hamlet's bravery in speaking to it. At first Hamlet cannot be sure whether it is "a spirit of health or goblin damn'd" (1.4.40), and his doubts recur when he suspects that its message may be a lie that "Abuses me to damn me" (2.2.599). Only Claudius's reaction to the playlet reenacting the murder makes clear that the Ghost is to be trusted.

The Ghost pushes Hamlet to face the trauma of his father's murder and his mother's acceptance of the murderer. It keeps his anguish sharp. However, the Ghost is absent at the end of the drama. It has represented the emotional demands of Hamlet's grief and despair; when Act 5 offers the play's reconciliation of good and evil, the Ghost has no further function.

Belief in ghosts was common in Shakespeare's world—King JAMES I, who was regarded as a competent writer on religious matters, wrote a treatise on their characteristics—though many educated people regarded such beliefs as unfounded superstition. Shakespeare's own opinion cannot be known, for the only evidence is the attitudes he ascribes to his fictional characters; Hamlet certainly accepts the reality of the spirit, doubting only its purposes for a time. In any case, a ghost was a common feature of the REVENGE PLAY, a popular genre in the early 17th century, and Shakespeare took the Ghost in *Hamlet* from one such work, the UR-HAMLET.

Grave-digger (First Clown, First Grave-digger) Minor character in *Hamlet*, the digger of Ophelia's grave. At the opening of 5.1, the Grave-digger talks with his friend, called the Other, in a comical series of exchanges on suicide, the law, and the profession of grave-digging. Hamlet, meditating with Horatio in the graveyard, speaks with the Grave-digger, who gives flip and enigmatic answers to his questions. In the course of describing the decomposition of corpses, he presents the prince with the skull of the late court jester, Yorick. This plunges Hamlet into another conversation with Horatio, and the Grave-digger does not speak again.

This scene does not further the plot; indeed, it quite distinctly delays development, providing some needed comic relief in the face of the rapidly approaching climax. The Grave-digger also serves as a subtle commentator on the main action, rather like a CHORUS. He frankly suggests the possibility of Ophelia's suicide, and his equally honest and humorous attitude to the world of the aristocrats and "great folk [who] have countenance in this world to drown or hang themselves more than their even-Christen" (5.1.27–29) reminds us of the extent to which intrigue infects Hamlet's world.

Most important, the Grave-digger's remarks and behavior reflect the play's attitude toward death: it is the normal human fate to die. The Grave-digger's job makes this an everyday fact rather than a philosophical observation. At a crucial point in the play, his demeanor, both prosaic and comical, helps to make clear to the audience that Hamlet's meditations on death no longer reflect the depression and grief that characterized him in Acts 1–4 but are rather the healthy recognition that death and decay are parts of life that must be accepted.

The Grave-digger is addressed by his companion as "Goodman Delver" (5.1.14), which may be his surname preceded by the honorific "Goodman" (roughly equivalent to "Mister"), or it may simply refer to his occupation as a digger. In his uneducated but knowing humor, he is a good instance of a character type, the rustic CLOWN and some editions, including the earliest ones, designate him accordingly in stage directions and speech headings.

Guildenstern See Rosencrantz and Guildenstern.

Hamlet Title character of *Hamlet,* the crown prince of DENMARK. Prince Hamlet is required by his murdered father's Ghost to take vengeance on the present monarch, his uncle, King Claudius, who committed the murder and then married the widow of his victim, Hamlet's mother, Queen Gertrude. Hamlet's troubled response to this situation, his disturbed relations with those around him, and his eventual acceptance of his destiny constitute the play.

Hamlet is almost universally considered one of the most remarkable characters in all of literature. His language, extraordinary even in Shakespeare's oeuvre, sweeps us up in a seemingly endless stream of brilliant impressions. He does not often use the similes and metaphors of ordinary speech, instead pouring forth fully fleshed images that convey the excitement of his thought. His psychology is stirringly genuine because it is humanly complex; he is filled with passion and contradiction, and his emotional life develops credibly through the course of the play. His personality, his attitudes and ideas, even his subconscious, have intrigued readers and theatergoers for centuries, and copious commentary on him is still being written. Many writers have supposed that Hamlet's troubled mind reflects a traumatic development in Shakespeare's life, although there is almost no evidence of the playwright's personal life to confirm or refute this theory.

Although Hamlet foreshadows the psychologically realistic characters of modern drama, Shakespeare did not create the prince's emotional life for its own sake but rather as a vehicle for presenting a philosophical attitude. Hamlet's troubled mind demonstrates the development of an acceptance of life despite the existence of human evil, and this is the dominant theme of the play. The critical element in this development is the prince's recognition of evil in himself; in containing both good and evil, he represents the dual nature of humankind.

The reconciliation of humanity with its own flawed nature is a central concern of Shakespeare's work, and in Hamlet an evolution of attitudes leading to this conclusion is displayed in a grand and powerful portrait.

Although he can deal in a practical manner with the world of intrigue that surrounds him, Hamlet is more a thinker than a doer, and he directs our attention often to his own concerns, large issues such as suicide, the virtues and defects of humankind, and the possibility of life after death. Above all, his circumstances demand that he consider the nature of evil.

We first encounter the prince as he struggles to deal with his father's death. In 1.2.76–86 he describes his mournful state; dressed in funereal black, conscious that he looks dejected and can be seen to have been weeping, he nevertheless asserts that this appearance cannot convey the depths of his grief. By focusing on the difference between appearance and reality—a difference that here is merely one of degree since his inner state is at least superficially indicated by his dress and demeanour—Hamlet betrays the confused perception that comes with great emotional trauma. In the early stages of grief, the ordinary aspects of existence seem absurdly thin and weak, inappropriate to the mourner's overwhelming sense of pain and loss.

In this state of mind, Hamlet is strongly offended by his mother's hasty and incestuous remarriage, even before he learns from the Ghost of his father's murder. He sees his father as an ideal man and a great king, an assumption supported by other opinions in the play and by the dignity and grandeur of the Ghost. He is thus appalled by his mother's willingness to accept an inferior man, a libertine and—as is soon revealed—a murderer. Hamlet comes to see his mother as evil and is devastated by the idea. Although he is the son of a godlike father, he is also the son of a mother who readily beds with "a satyr" (1.2.140). Plunged into despondency, he rejects life, saying, "How weary, stale, flat, and unprofitable / Seem to me all the uses of this world! . . . things rank and gross in nature / Possess it merely" (1.2.133–137). This attitude is further expressed in one of literature's most powerful evocations of mental depression, "I have of late . . . lost all my mirth

[and] this goodly frame the earth seems to me a sterile promontory, this most excellent canopy the air . . . appeareth nothing to me but a foul and pestilent congregation of vapours. What a piece of work is a man, . . . and yet, to me, what is this quintessence of dust? Man delights not me—nor woman neither . . ." (2.2.295–309).

He declares that his life is not worth "a pin's fee" (1.4.65); indeed, he longs for death, as he declares more than once, wishing, for instance, ". . . that this too too sullied flesh would melt" (1.2.129) and declaring death ". . . a consummation / Devoutly to be wish'd" (3.1.63–64), though in both of these speeches he also rejects suicide, once because of the religious injunction against it and once out of fear of the afterlife.

His disgust with life turns, therefore, to a revulsion against sex, the mechanism of life's continuance. Not only does sex generate life, with its evils, but the attractions of sex have led his mother to adultery and incest. Though some commentators have supposed that Hamlet unconsciously desires his mother sexually, as in the Oedipus complex hypothesized by Freud, such a theory is unnecessary, for the play's world provides the prince with real, not fantasized, parental conflicts: His father is dead, and he is the enemy of his mother's lover. However, the facts of Hamlet's situation, dire as they are, are less important than the interpretation that he puts upon them. Plainly influenced by his disgust with sex, he is obsessed by the image of his mother's "incestuous sheets" (1.2.157); he virtually ignores the political consequences of his father's murder—the murderer's succession as king—and focuses on the sexual implications, and, most significantly, he transfers his mother's sexual guilt to Ophelia.

Hamlet denies his love for Ophelia in 3.1.117–119, though only after affirming it two lines earlier, and Shakespeare plainly intended us to take Hamlet's courtship of Ophelia before the play begins as having been sincere. Ophelia's shy description in 1.3.110–114, along with her regretful one in 3.1.97–99, make this clear. Moreover, Hamlet's intensity and confusion as he parts from Ophelia—in the strange behavior she recounts in 2.1.77–100 and in his famous insistence that she enter a nunnery in 3.1.121–151—indicate his great

emotional involvement. However, although he apparently loved her earlier, Hamlet does not actually respond to Ophelia as a person in the course of the play. Theirs is not a love story but rather a dramatization of Hamlet's rejection of life, and of love, marriage, and sex. "Why wouldst thou be a breeder of sinners?" he cries in 3.1.121–122, and he immediately goes on to identify himself with the world's evildoers. Hamlet cannot avoid his sexual desire for Ophelia, as his obscene jesting in 3.2.108–119 demonstrates, but this episode is also a plain indication of the disgust he now feels for sex. His attitude symbolizes his condemnation of life, a viewpoint that he overcomes by the end of the play.

Hamlet's delay in seeking revenge may similarly be seen as a psychological trait emphasized to make a philosophical point. The prince's procrastination is not immediately obvious, for not much time seems to pass and only one plain opportunity for revenge presents itself (in the "prayer scene," 3.3), but Hamlet insists upon its importance, berating himself as "a rogue and peasant slave . . . / A dull and muddy-mettled rascal" (2.2.544, 562); his assumption of guilt is clearly excessive. Though committed to the idea that revenge is his duty, Hamlet senses the evil in the obligation, sent from "heaven and hell" (2.2.580), and he resists.

Once the King's guilt is firmly established by his response to the performance of THE MURDER OF GONZAGO, Hamlet falls victim to a pathological rage. This is first shown in his chilling resolution, "'Tis now the very witching time of night, / . . . Now could I drink hot blood . . ." (3.2.379–381). This state of mind persists as he demands eternal damnation for the King, not merely murderous revenge, and therefore avoids killing him at prayer in 3.3. Then in 3.4 he vents his hysterical rage at his mother and kills Polonius with a furious gesture in the process. This crime lacks even the justification of revenge. Whatever his faults, Polonius was innocent of Hamlet's father's murder, and moreover, his death leads to the insanity and subsequent death of Ophelia, whose blamelessness is absolute. Hamlet's avoidance of one evil has thus involved him in another, greater one.

Hamlet's rage and his descent into evil are central to the play, both literally, occurring near its midpoint, and figuratively, for his deeds trigger its climactic development. Polonius's son, Laertes, seeks revenge and eventually kills Hamlet, and more immediately, Polonius's death results in Hamlet's exile, during which he finds his salvation.

In Act 5 we find that Hamlet has changed. He meditates on death in the graveyard in 5.1, but now death is neither welcoming nor fearful; it is merely the normal human destiny and the prince's remarks are satirical thrusts at the living. His memories of Yorick are pleasurable appreciations of the past, as well as occasions for sardonic humor. Ophelia's funeral triggers a last explosion of emotion as Hamlet assaults Laertes, but although this resembles his fury of Act 3, here Hamlet restrains himself and departs. His outburst has been cathartic, producing two significant declarations. As he challenges Laertes, Hamlet proclaims himself "Hamlet the Dane" (5.1.251), at last accepting his role as his father's heir—Denmark, once his "prison" (2.2.243) is now his kingdom—and at the same time implicitly challenging the King. Perhaps given courage or awareness by this pronouncement, he goes on to assert the feelings he had suppressed in his anger and depression, stating "I lov'd Ophelia" (5.1.264). The prince is no longer in the grip of his grief.

In 5.2 Hamlet confides to Horatio the cause of the change in his sense of himself: By impulsively rewriting his death warrant to save himself, he has realized that his hesitations and ponderings had been beside the point. He sees that "Our indiscretion sometime serves us well / When our deep plots do pall. . . . There's a divinity that shapes our ends, / Rough-hew them how we will . . ." (5.2.8–11). He acknowledges that he cannot carry out the revenge called for by the Ghost without committing murder, the very crime he must avenge. He accepts that he must be evil in order to counter evil. He senses a basic truth: the capacity for evil exists in him because he is human.

In accepting his destiny, Hamlet also prepares for his own death. He senses his end approaching, as the King's plot takes form, but he remains composed, saying, "There is special providence in the fall of a sparrow. If it be now, 'tis not to come; if it be not to come, it will be now; if it be not now, yet it will come. The readiness is all. Since no man, of

aught he leaves, knows aught, what is't to leave betimes? Let be" (5.2.215–220). This final remark—since we know so little of the world, it is no great matter to leave it early—reflects the prince's awareness of the futility of his earlier philosophical inquiries. It is more important to live and then to die, coming to terms with one's fate.

Hamlet's salvation—his awareness of his human failings—comes only with his death. However, Horatio's prayer for him, "[May] flights of angels sing thee to thy rest" (5.2.365), offers the hope of an eternal release from the stresses the prince has undergone. The playwright leaves us assured that his tragic hero has finally found peace.

Hecuba Legendary Trojan queen whose famed grief is described dramatically in *Hamlet*. In 2.2 the First Player, at Hamlet's insistence, delivers a monologue telling of Hecuba's response to the killing of her husband, King Priam, by Pyrrhus; her grief is said to have produced tears in ". . . the burning eyes of heaven / and passion in the gods" (2.2.513–514). Her distress is implicitly compared with the short-lived widowhood of Hamlet's mother, the Queen, before she married her husband's murderer, King Claudius. Thus the passage reminds Hamlet and the audience of the central focus of his life and of the play—his need to avenge his murdered father.

Hecuba was well known in Shakespeare's day as one of the great heroines of classical mythology; she appears in HOMER's *Iliad*, where she elaborately mourns the death of her son Hector (an episode alluded to in 5.10.15–21 of *Troilus and Cressida*); in several Greek tragedies; and in VIRGIL's *Aeneid*. PLUTARCH's *Lives*—a favorite Shakespearean source—reports that a Greek tyrant, famed for many cold-blooded murders, once wept at a recital of Hecuba's woes; this may have inspired Hamlet's request for the monologue.

The most famous classical model of the sorrowing woman, Hecuba is often referred to in Shakespeare's plays, most frequently in *Troilus and Cressida*, where she is actually said to be present in 1.2.1—though she does not appear on stage—but also in *Titus Andronicus* (4.1.20–21), *Coriolanus* (1.3.40–43), and *Cymbeline* (4.2.313). Also, in a famous passage in *The Rape of Lucrece* (lines 1464–1491), the woeful Lucrece vents her emotions by acting the part of the grieving Hecuba.

Horatio Character in *Hamlet*, friend and confidant of Prince Hamlet. Horatio is the one person in Hamlet's world whom the prince values and trusts. With Horatio he can speak freely, and in doing so he demonstrates the evolution of his emotions. Further, the presence of Horatio lessens Hamlet's otherwise total alienation and permits relief—for him and for us—from the heightened tension that characterizes his existence.

Horatio is a calm and stoical figure whom Hamlet admires as "A man that Fortune's buffets and rewards / Hast ta'en with equal thanks . . . [a] man / That is not passion's slave" (3.2.67–72). He thus represents a RENAISSANCE ideal—a person with the mental discipline to resist highly emotional responses, which were seen as evidence of humanity's fall from grace. This ideal was considerably influenced by the newly rediscovered Stoic philosophy of the classical world, and Horatio rightly thinks of himself as "more an antique Roman than a Dane" (5.2.346). His restraint makes Horatio one who "in suff'ring all,. . . suffers nothing" (3.2.66), and Hamlet, embattled by his own suffering, envies his friend's relative peace of mind. However, it is precisely his vulnerability that gives Hamlet's emotional odyssey the grandeur that makes it worth recording. Horatio is an admirable figure, but he does not spark our imagination or sympathies.

Horatio knew Hamlet at school, as the prince makes plain in welcoming him from Wittenberg as a "fellow student" (1.2.177), but otherwise his past is unclear. In 1.1 he seems to be an intimate of the Danish court, but at several points—most notably when he must ask if musical accompaniment to drinking toasts is "a custom" (1.4.12)—he appears to be unfamiliar with local ways. Horatio's status in DENMARK—Danish nobleman or foreign visitor—is an example of the many problematic points in *Hamlet* that scholarship cannot resolve. Shakespeare probably simply formulated the character in different lights as he composed the drama and did not concern himself with the minor contradictions that resulted, as was apparently his habit throughout the plays.

King Claudius of Denmark Character in *Hamlet*, murderer of and royal successor of Hamlet's father and husband of his victim's widow, Queen Gertrude, Hamlet's mother. The central issue of the play is the conflict between Hamlet's desire for vengeance against the King—to which he has been sworn by his father's Ghost—and his recognition that revenge would involve him in evil himself.

The King's crime, by his own confession, "is rank, it smells to heaven; It hath the primal eldest curse upon't" (3.3.36–37)—that is, he has followed Cain, the first criminal, in murdering his brother. Cain is referred to several times in the play—e.g., in 1.2.105 and 5.1.76—reminding us of the King's heinous offense.

Hamlet repeatedly compares his father and King Claudius. Although he is surprised when the Ghost tells him of the murder, he is not surprised, a few lines later, to learn the killer's identity, for his "prophetic soul" (1.5.41) had already apprehended his uncle's character. Earlier, in his first soliloquy, he despises the King as an inferior successor to his father, "so excellent a king, that was to this / [as] Hyperion [is] to a satyr" (1.2.139–140). He elaborates on this comparison when he upbraids his mother in 3.4.

In 1.1 an ideal of kingship is established in recollections of the heroic achievements of Hamlet's father and in the sense of dread occasioned by his death; the implicit contrast with Claudius persists throughout the play, as we become aware that the King's crime is the source of the evil that permeates the play's world, the "something . . . rotten in the state of Denmark" (1.4.90). In a telling detail, the King is closely associated with excessive drinking, presented as a characteristically Danish failing. He often proposes toasts, the rowdy behavior of his court is noted, and Hamlet finds it likely that he would be "distempered . . . With drink" (3.2.293–294) or "drunk asleep" (3.3.89). Appropriately, Claudius finally falls victim to his own poisoned wine.

Despite the King's distinctly evil nature, he does have some redeeming features. In fact, some commentators believe that the playwright intended King Claudius as an admirable ruler and man and that Hamlet's contrary opinion is a result of his tragic insanity. Most critics, however, find the King's wicked nature abundantly evident; his good features exemplify Shakespeare's genius for providing fully human portraits. The King is clearly intelligent and quickwitted, particularly in 4.5.120–152 and 199–216, where he defuses the coup by Laertes with smooth talk and converts the rebel into an accomplice. In 1.2, as he disposes of court business, we see that he is a reasonable man, a competent diplomat, and a generally able monarch. The King even reveals, however fleetingly, his bad conscience about his crimes when he compares his "deed to [his] painted word" (3.1.49–54) and when he tries to pray in 3.3. However, as he recognizes, "Words without thoughts never to heaven go" (3.3.98), and, unable to repent sincerely, he continues in his evil ways.

Beginning with his recruitment of Rosencrantz and Guildenstern to spy on Hamlet, the King schemes cruelly against the prince. His two death plots—to have him executed in England and to arrange a rigged fencing match—are particularly vile. The King recruits Laertes after Hamlet escapes from England, but when, at the climax, his follower repents and seeks the prince's forgiveness, the King is left as the sole focus of our sense of evil in the play. When Hamlet kills him, he cries, "Here, thou incestuous, murd'rous, damned Dane" (5.2.330); his villainy is emphatically described and condemned. Horatio leaves us with a final summary of the King's role when he refers to his "carnal, bloody, and unnatural acts" (5.2.386).

Shakespeare may have named Claudius, or the name may have come from his source, the UR-HAMLET, but in either case the King was named for a Roman emperor, Claudius I (10 B.C.–A.D. 54), who was regarded in Shakespeare's day as a prime example of an evil ruler. (His modern reputation is considerably better, in part because of Robert Graves's novel *I, Claudius* [1934].) Upon his accession to the throne in A.D. 41, Claudius married his niece Agrippina, an incestuous relationship that may have influenced the choice of names. Agrippina later poisoned Claudius and was herself murdered by her son, Nero, as Hamlet recollects in 3.2.384–385.

Laertes   Character in *Hamlet*, son of Polonius and brother of Ophelia, who seeks vengeance against

Hamlet for his father's murder. Laertes is placed in direct contrast with Hamlet by the fact that each seeks and finally achieves revenge for his father's murder, although they do so in very different ways. Laertes is distinctly unheroic. He stoops to fraud and poison with no thought for consequences or morality. Yet at the close of the play he regrets his underhandedness, offers forgiveness in place of vengeance, and is himself forgiven.

Laertes is shallow and immature, as shown by the trite moralizing that inspires his insistence in 1.3 that Ophelia distrust Hamlet's love and by his rhetorical and exaggerated responses to his sister's insanity and death in 5.1. As an avenger, he is easily manipulated in 4.5 by King Claudius, who dissuades him from his rebellion with smooth talk about the divine right of kings. He gives no thought to honor as he accepts with grim glee the King's suggestion of a rigged fencing match, adding the idea of poisoning his sword. Moreover, he is thoughtlessly bold, prepared to sacrifice the peace of the country and his own salvation—"To hell, allegiance! Vows to the blackest devil! / Conscience and grace, to the profoundest pit! / I dare damnation" (4.5.131–133), he bellows—to satisfy his rage.

Yet in the end Laertes begs to "exchange forgiveness" (5.2.334) with Hamlet, and he admits that he is "justly kill'd with mine own treachery" (5.2.313). "The King—the King's to blame" (5.2.326), he cries, and, as he renounces his revenge, Laertes shifts the moral balance of the play in its last moments, leaving the King as the sole focus of evil. Laertes and Hamlet each kills his father's killer, while each forgives, and is forgiven by, his own killer. Contrasted earlier in the play—in their differing relationships with Ophelia; in Laertes's return to university while Hamlet is detained; in the contrast of a father's "double blessing" (1.3.53) for Laertes and Hamlet's father's death and reappearance as the Ghost—they come together at its close to represent the conjunction of good and evil in humanity, a fact whose acceptance is the play's major theme.

Lord   Any of several minor characters in *Hamlet*, members of the court of King Claudius of DENMARK. In 4.3 the Lords provide an audience for the King's remarks on the danger of Prince Hamlet's madness.

In 5.1 they attend the funeral of Ophelia and help break up the fight between Hamlet and Laertes. In 5.2 one of the Lords delivers a request from Queen Gertrude that Hamlet make peace with Laertes before their upcoming fencing match, and the Lords are presumably among the crowd of courtiers—"all the State" in the stage direction at 5.2.220—who witness that contest. As anonymous onlookers, the Lords heighten our sense of Hamlet's isolation, and they also contribute to a sense of the stratified social world in which the prince lives.

Lucianus Character in THE MURDER OF GONZAGO, the playlet presented within *Hamlet*. In 3.2.135–255 the Players, following Hamlet's instructions, perform before the court of King Claudius. In their play Lucianus murders the Player King by pouring poison in his ear, paralleling the murder of Hamlet's father by the real King. The play is interrupted by the King's guilty response—according to Hamlet's plan—and Lucianus does not get to complete his role, which would have involved marrying the Player Queen. Significantly, Lucianus is the nephew of the king he kills—not the brother, as a strict analogy with Claudius's crime would require—and thus he presents to the King not only the image of himself as murderer but also that of Hamlet as avenger. Lucianus's only lines—a brief address to his poison "of midnight weeds collected" (3.2.251)—are in a highly rhetorical style that is designed to highlight the artificiality of the play within a play.

Marcellus Minor character in *Hamlet*. Marcellus, with Barnardo, has seen the Ghost of Hamlet's father before the opening of the play. In 1.1 they tell Horatio about the spirit, and in 1.2 Hamlet is informed as well. Marcellus accompanies Hamlet and Horatio when they encounter the Ghost in 1.4; he and Horatio fearfully attempt to dissuade Hamlet from following it, and in 1.5 Hamlet swears them to secrecy. Speculating on the cause of the phenomenon, Marcellus utters the famous observation "Something is rotten in the state of Denmark" (1.4.90). Scholars believe that the BAD QUARTO of *Hamlet* (Q1, 1603) was recorded by an actor who had played Marcellus, since that role is the only one whose dialogue is very accurately rendered there.

Messenger Minor character in *Hamlet*. The Messenger brings King Claudius of DENMARK news that Laertes has raised a rebellion and is approaching. His hysteria emphasizes the degree of disruption that the play's developments have produced. In a calmer mood the Messenger brings the King letters from Hamlet in 4.7.

Ophelia Character in *Hamlet*, lover of Prince Hamlet. In 1.3 Ophelia's brother, Laertes, cautions Ophelia against believing Hamlet's professions of love, and her father, Polonius, forbids her to see him. A demure and obedient daughter, Ophelia returns Hamlet's letters, and, under the pressures of the main plot, Hamlet turns on her with a seemingly

Unable to reconcile her love for her father, Polonius, with her love for her father's murderer, Hamlet, the innocent Ophelia is driven to madness in *Hamlet*. The actress in this early photo wears wildflowers in her hair, a standard device to suggest the disorder of Ophelia's mind. *(Courtesy of Culver Pictures, Inc.)*

insane revulsion against women in general and her in particular. She reports his behavior in 2.1 and encounters it in even more virulent form in 3.1. After her former lover kills her father, Ophelia becomes insane, babbling about funerals and singing scraps of songs in 4.5. Her death by drowning is reported by the Queen in 4.7.163, and her funeral in 5.1—abbreviated by the Priest because the death seems a suicide—triggers an encounter between Hamlet and Laertes that foreshadows the play's climax.

Ophelia's nature is abundantly affectionate; her wounded but faithful love—both for her father and for Hamlet—makes her one of the most touching of Shakespeare's characters. As Laertes observes about Ophelia's lunacy: "where [love] is fine / It sends some precious instance of itself / After the thing it loves" (4.5.161–163). He refers to her love for the dead Polonius, which has caused her to send herself figuratively (and later literally) after him to a world beyond life, but the remark is equally appropriate to her love for Hamlet.

However, the relationship between Hamlet and Ophelia is not a love story, for Hamlet has rejected love. He loved Ophelia before the play opens, as is attested first by her touching recollection of his gifts and the "words of so sweet breath compos'd / As made the things more rich" (3.1.98–99) and then by his admission at her funeral in 5.1.264–266. He remains sexually attracted to her—as is shown by his obscene jesting in 3.2.108–117—but he has displaced on her much of his anger with his mother, the Queen. She has become for him simply a stimulus for his disgust with women and sex, and he no longer really sees her as an actual person. Ophelia's fate is thus an outgrowth of Hamlet's emotional collapse; not only is her life diminished—and ultimately destroyed—by his actions, but she is a measure of what he has lost through his mistaken vision of the world.

Ophelia's insanity is triggered by the crushing of her love for Hamlet and then intensified by the loss of her father to Hamlet's madness. Her pathetic ravings in 4.5 are concerned with lost loves and death, the grim realities that have broken her mind. She cannot absorb the conflict implicit in loving both her father and his murderer. Her bawdy songs reflect the lusts of the outside world, of which she has no experience but that have contributed to her plight. The flowers she obsessively alludes to, themselves symbols of innocence, are poignant emblems of her own youth and inability to deal with the harsh world of the play.

While the Queen's description of Ophelia's drowning in 4.7.165–182 permits us to view it as accidental—a tree branch broke as she fell—she also reports that the victim made no effort to save herself. In 5.1 the Grave-digger and the Priest view her as a suicide, and her death is certainly a result of her madness. But her insanity is the consequence of the actions of others, and Ophelia is unquestionably a victim of the tragic events that beset DENMARK throughout the play.

Some scholars believe that Ophelia's name—which means "succor" in Greek, a seemingly inappropriate designation for so victimized a character—may have been used in error instead of Aphelia, meaning "simplicity" or "innocence." Both names were rare in Shakespeare's time.

Osric Minor character in Hamlet, a foppish nobleman in the court of King Claudius of DENMARK. In 5.2 Osric carries the King's request that Hamlet meet Laertes in a fencing match adding that the King has made a wager on Hamlet. Osric's highly mannered language and behavior inspire Hamlet's amused derision, and the prince mocks the messenger, demonstrating the ease with which the courtier can be made to agree to contradictory assertions and making fun of his high-flown language. Osric later umpires the fencing match, though no further attention is paid to him.

Osric functions as comic relief in the face of the King's rapidly unfolding plot against Hamlet, which hinges on the fencing match. Further, the distraction offered by Osric subtly suggests Hamlet's own detachment from the danger that threatens him. The prince's bemused handling of the silly fop is reminiscent of his healthy appreciation of Yorick in 5.1. He is no longer in the grip of grief, and, newly aware of the importance of providence in human affairs, Hamlet can *enjoy* Osric. Osric is an ancient Anglo-Saxon name that was still used occasionally in Shakespeare's day.

Other (Other Clown, Second Clown, Second Grave-digger) Minor character in *Hamlet*, the Grave-digger's friend. The Other is a straight man whose simple remarks and questions give rise to the ripostes of his companion in 5.1.1–60. Although theatrical tradition dating to the 17th century makes the Other—his designation in early editions of the play—a second grave-digger, some modern editors point out that he seems to belong to another, unspecified profession when he addresses the Grave-digger in 5.1.14. Like the Grave-digger, the Other is a CLOWN, and some editions identify him accordingly in stage directions and speech headings.

Player King Character in THE MURDER OF GON-ZAGO, the playlet presented within *Hamlet*. In 3.2 the Players stage a play in which the Player King anticipates that his wife, the Player Queen, will remarry if he dies, despite her protests to the contrary. Then he is murdered by Lucianus, who pours poison in his ear while he sleeps. This scenario resembles the actual murder of Hamlet's father by King Claudius—as the Ghost has recounted it the prince—and the King reacts to it with great distress, fleeing from the room. Thus, as he had planned, Hamlet is presented with proof that the Ghost had told the truth.

The Player King speaks in a highly rhetorical style that distances the play within a play from the action of the play itself, emphasizing its artificiality. The part of the Player King is presumably taken by the First Player, who demonstrates his dramatic gifts when the Players first arrive at ELSINORE in 2.2.

Player Queen Character in THE MURDER OF GONZAGO, the playlet presented within *Hamlet*. In 3.2 the Players perform before the court of King Claudius. Following Hamlet's instructions, they stage a play in which the Player Queen assures her husband, the Player King, that she will never remarry if he dies before her. He insists that she will; in the next scene he is murdered. The play parallels the murder of Hamlet's father by the King and the remarriage of his mother, the Queen, so it is obvious that the Player Queen's part would include her marriage to the killer. However, the performance is interrupted by the King's guilty reaction, and she never reappears.

The Player Queen is merely a symbolic character. Her highly rhetorical diction helps to emphasize the extreme artificiality of the play within a play.

Players Characters in *Hamlet*, touring actors who are hired by Prince Hamlet to perform a play that he hopes will shock King Claudius into an unconscious revelation of guilt. After commissioning the Players to perform THE MURDER OF GONZAGO, a brief drama that enacts a crime similar to the King's killing of Hamlet's father, the prince makes his famous remark, "The play's the thing / Wherein I'll catch the conscience of the King" (2.2.600–601). The playlet—featuring the Player King, the Player Queen, and Lucianus—achieves the expected result in 3.2.

There are at least three Players, enough to play the three parts in the playlet, with one of them doubling as the speaker of the PROLOGUE and all three participating in the DUMB SHOW that precedes the spoken play. The elaborate stage direction at 3.2.133 calls for extra players in the dumb show, but this requirement may be ignored in production.

The troupe is led by the First Player, who demonstrates his art when he recites a monologue on Pyrrhus and Hecuba in 2.2. He presumably plays the Player King in 3.2, where he also receives Hamlet's opinions on acting—thought to reflect Shakespeare's own—in 2.2.1–45.

In 3.2.330–358 Rosencrantz and Guildenstern report that the Players' popularity has suffered due to the success of a boys' acting company. This incident reflects the WAR OF THE THEATERS, the competition between the professional players and the CHILDREN'S COMPANIES that raged in London in 1601.

Polonius Character in *Hamlet*, a minister of the King Claudius of DENMARK. Polonius, the father of Ophelia and Laertes, loves intrigue and resorts to espionage whenever possible. He volunteers to spy for the King on Hamlet's conversation with his mother, Queen Gertrude, in 3.4, and when Hamlet discovers the intruder, he kills him. The prince stabs through a curtain, so he does not know who his victim is until he is dead, but he feels no remorse for the deed, remarking coolly that his victim has learned that "to be too busy is some danger" (3.4.33). This killing is the central event of the play, hastening Hamlet's exile to England and triggering Laertes' vengeance on the prince.

Polonius's deviousness and dishonesty exemplify the state of moral decay in Denmark. After he offers Laertes his famous advice, "to thine own self be true . . . Thou canst not then be false to any man" (1.3.78–80), his hypocrisy reveals itself, for in 2.1 he sets a spy on Laertes, offering detailed instructions in espionage and duplicity to Reynaldo. He bars Ophelia from any contact with Hamlet, presuming that the prince's professions of love cannot be truthful, perhaps arguing from self-knowledge, and when it appears that he was wrong and that the prince has gone mad from frustrated love, he spies on the lovers himself.

In *Hamlet,* Polonius is a pedantic bore and a hypocrite. These traits may derive from the comical Pantaloon of the Italian commedia dell'arte. *(Courtesy of Culver Pictures, Inc.)*

However, Polonius's murder is not to be taken as justifiable; much of its point depends on our recognition of it as an evil act, leading us to the further awareness that Hamlet is capable of evil. Also, Polonius is not completely without good points, making his killing more reprehensible than it would appear if he were an absolute villain. For example, while his means are deplorable, Polonius clearly cares about his son, and his involvement in his welfare serves to cause Laertes to remain memorable through his long absence from the play (between 1.3 and 4.5); similarly, Polonius is a fool in his handling of Ophelia, but there is no doubt of his paternal concern, even if it can be overlaid with ulterior interests at the same time. Ophelia's evident heartbreak at his death in her "mad scene" (4.5) testifies to his adequacy as a parent.

Polonius is also a comic character at times. Speaking to the King and Queen of Hamlet's alleged madness, he begins by stating an ideal that he proceeds to demolish, asserting " . . . since brevity is the soul of wit, / And tediousness the limbs and outward flourishes, / I will be brief," and then going on to use such verbiage as "Mad call I it, for to define true madness, / What is't but to be nothing else but mad?" (2.2.93–94). When this amusing long-windedness is challenged by the Queen's request for "More matter with less art," Polonius replies with unwitting candor, "Madam, I swear I use no art at all" (2.2.95–96). The passage, in which Polonius repeatedly interrupts himself and loses his train of thought, parodies a popular tendency of the day to overelaborate rhetoric, and it softens the portrait of Hamlet's victim. In creating Polonius, Shakespeare may have been influenced by the Pantaloon, a comically windy moralizer from the Italian COMMEDIA DELL'ARTE.

Polonius has sometimes been seen as a satirical figure (see BURGHLEY, LORD), since Corambis, his equivalent character in Shakespeare's source, the UR-HAMLET, may have been. Most scholars now find this unlikely, however. In fact, though Shakespeare often changed the names in his sources for no particular reason, here he may have wished to avoid using any caricature intended in the *Ur-Hamlet.* However, the name Polonius itself makes a clear reference to Poland, also known as Polonia in Elizabethan England. Scholars believe that the play-wright probably intended an allusion to one of the play's minor sources, a well-known book on good government, *The Counsellor* (1598), an English translation from the Latin work of a Polish states-man, Laurentius GOSLICIUS.

Priest Minor character in *Hamlet,* the officiating clergyman at Ophelia's funeral. In 5.1 the Priest denies Ophelia the full ceremony because her death appears to have been a suicide. He asserts that even an abbreviated service is too much—only "great command" (5.1.221), presumably that of King Claudius, has made it possible—and suggests that, instead of prayers, "shards, flints, and pebbles should be thrown on her" (5.1.224). He insists that the rites for the dead would be profaned if Ophelia received them. This ugly episode heralds the mood of gloom and anger that dominates the conclusion of the play.

In some editions of the play the Priest is called the Doctor of Divinity, based on the speech head-ing "Doct." used for both of his speeches in the Q2 edition (1604). Some scholars conjecture that this makes him a Protestant.

Pyrrhus Legendary Greek warrior whose bloody killing of King Priam of TROY is recalled as an exam-ple of regicide in *Hamlet.* The First Player, at Hamlet's request, recites a dramatic monologue in which this episode from the TROJAN WAR is vividly recounted. Pyrrhus at first hesitates, as "his sword . . . seem'd i'th' air to stick" (2.2.473–475) and he "like a neutral to his will and matter, / Did nothing" (2.2.477–478). This inaction parallels that of Hamlet, who has so far failed to avenge his father's murder by King Claudius. But then Pyrrhus's "aroused vengeance" (2.2.484) impels him to complete his deed, and the recital implicitly stimulates Hamlet to action.

Pyrrhus appears as Neoptolemus in HOMER and other early accounts of Priam's death, but he is Pyrrhus in VIRGIL's *Aeneid,* which was probably more familiar to Shakespeare. He was the son of Achilles, and he is mentioned as such in *Troilus and Cressida* (3.3.208). In one version of his myth, he founded a dynasty of kings, one of whom, also called Pyrrhus, is now much better known than he, as the general who achieved a costly, or Pyrrhic, victory.

Queen Gertrude of Denmark Character in *Ham-let,* Hamlet's mother, who has married the brother, successor, and murderer of the king of DENMARK, her late husband. Hamlet is horrified by the Queen's acceptance, soon after her husband's death, of "incestuous sheets" (1.2.157), and he expostulates, "Frailty, thy name is woman" (1.2.146). His disgust at her behavior is heightened when he learns from the Ghost, in 1.5.42–52, that she had been the lover of the new King Claudius, before he killed Hamlet's father. Hamlet's detestation of his mother's part in these evils is transformed into a revulsion against women in general and against the love—and sex—that they offer, which lead only to the creation of more humanity and thus more wickedness. His own beloved, Ophelia, tragically comes to bear the brunt of the prince's misogyny.

Although the Queen provides an example of the evil that infects Denmark, she herself is a some-what faceless character. She is basically evil through weakness rather than inclination. The Ghost attributes her wickedness to Claudius and tells Hamlet to exclude her from his revenge— "Leave her to heaven" (1.5.86). In her main scene, in which Hamlet repudiates her for her adultery and her acceptance of the King as a husband, she acknowledges her guilt, crying out that her soul is contaminated by ". . . such black and grained spots / As will not leave their tinct" (3.4.90–91). After Hamlet leaves and the King returns in 4.1, the Queen resumes her role as his accomplice. But in 5.2, when the Queen turns on her husband and cries out a warning to Hamlet as she dies, we may suppose that her son has had some effect on her.

Reynaldo Minor character in *Hamlet,* servant of Polonius. In 2.1 Reynaldo is assigned to spy on his master's son, Laertes, who is studying in PARIS, to make sure he is not engaging in "such wanton, wild, and usual slips / As are companions . . . / To youth and liberty" (3.2.22–24). Reynaldo hears out his employer's long-winded instructions and departs, disappearing from the play.

This brief episode humorously illustrates the cor-rupt moral tone of Hamlet's DENMARK, paralleling the later, more sinister use of spies—Rosencrantz and Guildenstern—by King Claudius. It also displays the intrusiveness and love of spying that eventually bring Polonius to his death. Reynaldo is clearly more sensible than his master, hesitating at times over his orders, but he has little real personality.

Rosencrantz and Guildenstern   Two characters in *Hamlet*, courtiers who assist King Claudius of DENMARK in his plots against Hamlet. Only once, and only in some editions, does one appear without the other. (In 4.3.11–15 some editors follow the FIRST FOLIO text and have Guildenstern enter four lines after Rosencrantz.) So familiar as a couple, and so similar to each other are this pair, that they are best dealt with as a unit.

We first encounter Rosencrantz and Guildenstern as the King recruits them to spy on Hamlet in 2.2, where he refers to them as the prince's childhood friends. They respond in the smooth and unctuous language of courtiers, assenting readily and thus establishing themselves immediately as toadies. When they first encounter Hamlet, he sees them as his "excellent good friends" (2.2.224), but they will not "deal justly" (2.2.276) with him about their mission from the King, which he has guessed, and he realizes that he in fact lacks allies, except Horatio. This disappointment triggers his impressive monologue on depression (2.2.295–310). As foils to Horatio, the courtiers point up Hamlet's alienation. As agents of the rottenness that infects the Danish court, they help establish a polarity between the prince and the King.

Hamlet quickly ends friendly relations with the two courtiers, to their eventual doom. When they summon him to a meeting with his mother, he dismisses them by coldly using the royal "we" for the only time in the play (3.2.324–325). He speaks of them to his mother as "my two schoolfellows, / Whom I will trust as I will adders fang'd" (3.4.204–205). His distrust of them leads to his discovery of the documents ordering his execution in England and his plot to send the courtiers to this fate in his stead. Their deaths are bluntly reported in 5.2.376; "Rosencrantz and Guildenstern are dead."

This line was to provide the title for Tom Stoppard's 1967 comedy of existential dread. In *Rosencrantz and Guildenstern Are Dead* the two courtiers are innocent, facing death in a play they know nothing about, and the question of their innocence in *Hamlet* is often raised. Rosencrantz and Guildenstern almost certainly did not know of the King's deadly plot and may thus be seen as innocent victims of Hamlet's counterstroke. However, the two have unquestionably been the willing allies of the King; Hamlet has long recognized them as such and can say: "They are not near my conscience, their defeat / Does by their own insinuation grow" (5.2.58–59). The playwright plainly expects us to see the poetic justice in their end; the fate of Rosencrantz and Guildenstern reflects their involvement in the evil environment of the Danish court.

Guildenstern and Rosencrantz were notable Danish family names of the 16th century; it is recorded that at the Danish royal coronation of 1596, fully one-tenth of the aristocratic participants bore one name or the other. Moreover, several students of each name were enrolled in the university at Wittenberg—the alma mater of both Hamlet and the two courtiers—in the 1590s. Shakespeare was surely as delighted as we are by the faintly comical tone conveyed by the combination of these grand names (see, e.g., 2.2.33–34), but they also help to convey the foreignness of the play's locale.

Sailor   Any of several minor characters in *Hamlet*, bearers of a letter to Horatio. In 4.6 a group of Sailors bring Horatio a message from Prince Hamlet. The First Sailor speaks for them all; he seems to lack sophistication because he delivers the missive and afterward ascertains Horatio's identity. Horatio reads the message aloud, in an aside, and we realize that the Sailors are probably part of the pirate crew mentioned in it. Horatio leaves with them to find the prince. The episode announces Hamlet's return to Denmark and the approach of the play's climax.

Servant   Minor character in *Hamlet*. The Servant tells Horatio that some "seafaring men" (4.6.2) have letters for him. Beginning with the earliest productions of the play this part has often been cut.

Voltemand (Voltimand, Valtemand, Voltemar, Voltumand)   Minor character in *Hamlet*, ambassador to the King of Norway from King Claudius of DENMARK. In 1.2 Voltemand and Cornelius are appointed to deliver the King's message demanding that the Norwegian king's nephew, Fortinbras, who is preparing an invasion of Denmark, be restrained. The two ambassadors return in 2.2, and Voltemand delivers a document of agreement that he summarizes in courtly language. The episode introduces the audience to Fortinbras while demonstrating the state of national crisis in which the play takes place.

This character's name was spelled both Voltemand and Valtemand in the most authoritative early edition of the play (Q2, 1604); Voltumand and Voltemar appear in other early editions. The second FOLIO edition (1632) used Voltimand, and this became the established practice until recently, when a compromise version became popular. In any form it is a corruption of Valdemar, the name of several Danish kings.

Yorick Figure mentioned in *Hamlet*, the deceased court jester (see FOOL) whose bones are dug up by the Grave-digger in 5.1. Yorick's skull sparks a monologue by Prince Hamlet on the inevitability of death. The prince also responds with pleasure to his recollection of Yorick in life, "a fellow of infinite jest, of most excellent fancy" (5.1.178–179). With the Grave-digger's earlier remarks, the passage on Yorick presents the familiar religious theme of earthly vanity: Given the inevitability of death, the things of this life are inconsequential. In fact, Hamlet meditating on the skull of Yorick immediately became a popular symbol of this theme, and it has remained so.

That Hamlet can turn to this doctrine and at the same time indulge in the healthy nostalgia of reminiscing about Yorick, a friendly figure of his youth, reflects his recovery from the racking grief that tortured him in Acts 1–4. Thus Yorick is an emblem of the spirit of acceptance that prevails at the close of the play.

Scholars differ on the etymology of Yorick's unique name. It may be a corruption of Eric, a name appropriate to the play's setting in DENMARK; of Jörg, the Danish equivalent of George; or of Rorik, the name of Hamlet's maternal grandfather in older forms of the tale (Rorique in BELLEFOREST; Roricus in SAXO). (See also COOKE, GEORGE FREDERICK.)

Henry IV, Part 1
SYNOPSIS

Act 1, Scene 1

King Henry IV's plans for a crusade are upset by a report from the Earl of Westmoreland that Welsh rebels under Owen Glendower have defeated and captured Edmund Mortimer. There is better news, however: young Henry Percy, nicknamed Hotspur, has defeated rebellious Scots under the Earl of Douglas and has taken many prisoners. Henry observes that Hotspur's honorable success in war reflects badly on his own son, Prince Hal, who leads a dissolute life in LONDON. However, he goes on to complain of Hotspur's prideful refusal to turn over his prisoners to the king, as is customary. Westmoreland attributes this stubborness to the influence of Hotspur's uncle, Thomas Percy, Earl of Worcester.

Act 1, Scene 2

Prince Hal and Falstaff jest about their debauched life of petty crime, drunkenness, and wenching. Poins arrives with a plan for a highway robbery. At first the Prince does not wish to participate, but after Falstaff leaves, Poins proposes to Hal that they play a joke on Falstaff: They will go to the scene of the crime but avoid taking part; then, after Falstaff and the others have stolen the money, Poins and the Prince can steal it from them; the cowardice of Falstaff and his friends will make this easy. Later they will have the pleasure of listening to Falstaff lie about the episode, followed by the further delight of exposing the old rogue. Hal agrees, and Poins leaves. In a soliloquy the Prince reveals his intention to eventually abandon his life of idle dissolution and become a sound ruler.

Act 1, Scene 3

Hotspur tells the king that he had not refused to surrender his prisoners, as Henry believes, but had merely responded in hasty anger to the arrogant courtier who had presented the king's claim. Unappeased, the king observes that Hotspur not only still holds the prisoners but also insists that Mortimer be ransomed from the Welsh before he turns them over. Henry asserts that Mortimer, who has married Glendower's daughter, has treasonably defected to the Welsh, and he refuses to ransom him. Hotspur defends Mortimer, and the king exits angrily. Hotspur rages against Henry's ingratitude to the Percy family, which helped the king depose Richard II. With difficulty, Worcester calms Hotspur and proposes that Hotspur should release his Scottish prisoners and enlist them in a rebellion against the king while his father, the Earl of Northumberland, recruits the Archbishop of York. Worcester himself will join Glendower when the time is ripe, and the three forces will rise simultaneously.

Act 2, Scene 1

At an inn in ROCHESTER, two Carriers prepare to leave for London. Gadshill, a highwayman, appears and learns from them that they will be accompanied by some gentlemen carrying valuables. The Chamberlain of the inn tells Gadshill of these potential victims in more detail. Gadshill boasts of an accomplice in high places who can get them off if the theft goes wrong.

Act 2, Scene 2

The robbers assemble at GAD'S HILL. Hal arranges an ambush, placing himself and Poins in a reserve position just down the road. The Prince and Poins leave just before the Travellers appear. The thieves rob the Travellers and bundle them offstage; when the thieves return, they are themselves effortlessly robbed by the Prince and Poins.

Act 2, Scene 3

Hotspur reads a letter from a nobleman who makes excuses for not joining the rebellion. Lady Percy appears, and Hotspur announces his imminent departure. She speaks worriedly of his absorption in his plans—he even speaks of military matters in his sleep—and she demands to be told what they are. Hotspur playfully refuses to tell her, claiming military secrecy.

Act 2, Scene 4

At the BOAR'S HEAD TAVERN, Prince Hal teases Francis, a waiter, and he laughingly compares his own good humor with Hotspur's mania for war. Falstaff enters; egged on by Hal and Poins, he tells an elaborate tale of his courage in resisting the brigands who robbed him. After leading Falstaff on to ludicrous exaggerations, the Prince reveals the truth, and Falstaff comically claims to have recognized Hal at the

time and to have fled so as to avoid harming the heir apparent of the realm. A message from King Henry commands Hal's presence in the morning; a rebellion, led by Hotspur, has begun. Falstaff anticipates the king's anger at Hal and suggests that the Prince rehearse his response. Falstaff pretends to be Henry and chastises Hal for the company he keeps, excepting only one commendable man called Falstaff. They change roles, and Hal, as the king, upbraids his "son" for tolerating so bad a man as Falstaff. Falstaff, playing the Prince, defends Falstaff. He is interrupted by the approach of the Sheriff. Falstaff was recognized at Gad's Hill and has been traced to the tavern. Falstaff hides; the Prince assures the Sheriff that the thief is not present and that he, the Prince, will guarantee that any stolen money will be refunded. The Sheriff leaves, and Hal discovers that Falstaff has fallen asleep in his hiding place. The Prince looks forward to the campaign against the rebels.

Act 3, Scene 1

The rebel leaders convene to make a formal alliance, but friction between Glendower and Hotspur threatens to break up the meeting. The discussion turns to the division of the realm after King Henry has been deposed. Hotspur objects that his portion is too small, and his arrogance offends Glendower. They argue again, but the Welshman gives in and a tenuous peace is maintained. Glendower leaves, and Mortimer and Worcester chastise an unapologetic Hotspur for offending a valuable ally. Glendower returns with his daughter, Lady Mortimer, and Lady Percy. Mortimer regrets that he cannot speak Welsh, his wife's only language; Glendower interprets as the couple exchange loving remarks. Lady Mortimer invites her husband to lie in her lap while she sings to him. Hotspur humorously mocks this in conversation with his wife, whom he teases affectionately. After Lady Mortimer's song, the men leave to join their troops.

Act 3, Scene 2

Henry speaks to Prince Hal about his dissipated behavior and doubts his son's loyalty in the coming conflict. Hal apologizes for his debaucheries and assures his father that he intends to conquer Hotspur. News arrives that the rebels have assembled at SHREWSBURY, and the king devises a plan for the campaign; Hal is to command one of the armies.

Act 3, Scene 3

At the Boar's Head, Falstaff speaks of repentance for his ways but goes on to praise bawdiness and merriment. He teases Bardolph about his fiery complexion and banters with the Hostess. The Prince arrives, excited about the coming campaign; he tells Falstaff to meet him the next day to receive his orders. He leaves, and Falstaff turns to his meal, wishing he could conduct his part in the war from the tavern.

Act 4, Scene 1

Hotspur, Worcester, and Douglas, encamped at Shrewsbury, receive word that Mortimer is extremely sick and cannot join them with his forces. Sir Richard Vernon reports the approach of the King's armies and reveals that Glendower's troops cannot come for another two weeks. Although the rebels are seriously outnumbered, Hotspur urges that they fight anyway.

Act 4, Scene 2

Falstaff, marching toward Shrewsbury, soliloquizes on the money he has made selling exemptions from the draft. The Prince and Westmoreland meet him and urge him to hurry, for the battle will soon begin. After they leave, Falstaff remarks to himself that he hopes to arrive just as the battle ends.

Act 4, Scene 3

Hotspur and Douglas argue for an immediate attack on the king's forces, but Vernon and Worcester want to wait for reinforcements. Sir Walter Blunt appears with a message from King Henry offering a negotiated peace. Hotspur condemns Henry's usurpation of the throne and his ingratitude toward those who helped him carry it out. However, he agrees to have Worcester meet with the king the next day.

Act 4, Scene 4

The Archbishop of York speaks of the likely defeat of the rebels at Shrewsbury, and he begins to prepare for further opposition to the king.

Act 5, Scene 1

Worcester and Vernon arrive to negotiate with King Henry. Worcester justifies rebellion by pointing out the King's ingratitude. Prince Hal offers to fight Hotspur in single combat to settle all issues, but Henry rejects the idea, offering the rebels a last chance for surrender with amnesty: if they reject it, the two armies must fight. Worcester and Vernon depart. Falstaff asks the Prince to protect him in the battle; Hal, leaving, responds that he will have to take his chances. Falstaff muses that he will not follow an honorable course in the battle, for honor is a minor matter compared to life.

Act 5, Scene 2

Worcester insists to Vernon that they not tell Hotspur of the king's offer of an amnesty lest he accept it; he believes that Henry cannot be trusted and that, while Hotspur may be forgiven on grounds of youth and high-spiritedness, he, Worcester, would bear the brunt of the king's wrath. Worcester accordingly reports that the king has elected to fight, and he tells of Hal's challenge. Hotspur responds by preparing for battle.

Act 5, Scene 3

During the battle Blunt, disguised as King Henry, is killed by Douglas. Falstaff meets Prince Hal and lies about his courageous combat, but the Prince discovers a bottle of sack in Falstaff's pistol case.

Act 5, Scene 4

During a lull in the battle the king suggests that his sons Prince Hal and Prince John of Lancaster retire from the fighting, but they both refuse. Lancaster rejoins the fray, and Hal lauds his fighting spirit before following him. Douglas appears and fights the king, nearly killing him; the Prince returns and drives Douglas away. The king comments that Hal has proved himself. Henry exits, and Hotspur arrives to exchange challenges and fight with the Prince. Falstaff watches this combat until Douglas enters to fight him; Falstaff feigns death, and Douglas moves on. The Prince kills Hotspur and eulogizes his dead foe. He then sees Falstaff and, believing him dead, pronounces a more casual benediction before leaving. Falstaff rises, stabs Hotspur's corpse with his sword, and declares that he will take credit for killing him. The Prince and Lancaster return and are surprised to see Falstaff alive. Falstaff claims to have killed Hotspur and supposes that the king will reward him; out of friendship, the Prince agrees to corroborate his lie.

Act 5, Scene 5

King Henry sentences the captured Worcester and Vernon to death, while Douglas is to be set free. The king begins to make plans to fight the remaining rebels.

COMMENTARY

Henry IV, Part 1 was a highly innovative work in 1596 for precisely the reasons that make it one of the greatest of Shakespeare's HISTORY PLAYS. It marks an advance both in Shakespeare's development and in the growth of English drama, for by repeatedly shifting its focus between affairs of state and bawdy irreverence, the play presents a composite image of a whole society, something that had never been attempted before. In addition to the quarrels and alliances among the aristocracy, the principal interest of the earlier histories, here Shakespeare offers the scruffy circle of common laborers and petty criminals who frequent the Boar's Head Tavern. Both worlds are more vivid for the contrast, and a dramatic tension is established between them. Groundbreaking in its own day, *1 Henry IV* is still impressive in ours, due to the range of people, events, and language, from the most casual ribaldry to the boldest rhetoric, realistically presented on stage.

Prince Hal belongs to both worlds; surrounding him are such boldly drawn figures as the volatile Hotspur and his charming wife, the talkative Hostess, and the many personalities evoked by Falstaff's parodies and imitations: churchmen and highwaymen, knights and knaves. The Prince's significance lies in the choice he must make between worlds, and his dilemma emphasizes, as in the other history plays, the question of order in society. Both the Falstaffian delinquents of the Boar's Head Tavern and the rebels led by Hotspur have contributed to the decay of the social fabric, and King Henry believes that both groups have been sent by heaven in revenge for his own disturbance of society, the deposition of King Richard II (as enacted in *Richard II*). Hal's choice is indeed pivotal for the future of the realm. Of course, Shakespeare's original audiences knew that Hal went on to become the highly successful King Henry V, so there is no suspense about the Prince's choice; the tension lies instead in the presentation of the alternatives.

Although the SUBPLOT concerning Falstaff is highly diverting, the major concern is Hal's decision to embrace his role as Hotspur's rival, abandoning the life of a barfly for that of a military leader. This central issue is not fully resolved until the end of *2 Henry IV*, when Hal rejects Falstaff, but *Part 1* presents an initial phase of Hal's development: his acceptance of his role as princely hero.

The play's climax is the hand-to-hand combat between Hal and Hotspur at Shrewsbury. Not only does the play build to this climax through a series of episodes depicting the progress of Hotspur's rebellion, but Hal and Hotspur are repeatedly compared, both by the king—as early as 1.1.77–90—and by Hal himself. The king regrets that his own son seems so feckless in comparison to the rebel leader. Hal assures his father that he is not the dissipated playboy he seems and that he will prove superior to Hotspur when the time is ripe. This motif—the potential readiness of the Prince—has already been established in Hal's famous "reformation" speech (1.2.190–212). Shakespeare makes it abundantly clear that the Prince will indeed prove himself in the traditional terms of chivalry, and in the combat at Shrewsbury, an episode devised by the playwright for this purpose, Hal becomes the hero he has promised to be.

Hotspur's defeat attests that chivalry is not an unalloyed virtue, as does his outsized personality, which consists of impatience and an exaggerated sense of honor. Hotspur is a temperamental, driven man who is concerned only about his reputation for bravery in battle. His fixation is as excessive in its way as is Falstaff's licentiousness. This leads to his own destruction, as he cannot bring himself to postpone the battle at Shrewsbury until his side has a better chance.

Hotspur has his redeeming features as well. Hal admits that his military accomplishments are worth aspiring to, and the Prince's eulogy over Hotspur's corpse (5.4.86–100) is genuinely admiring. Moreover, while the rebellious noblemen are certainly self-serving to various degrees, Hotspur's own motive is not personal gain or power; he is driven by an ambition for honorable action that one could admire if it were in better balance in his life. Hotspur's loving marriage to the engaging Lady Percy is presented in 2.3 and 3.1, and we recognize that he is not simply a "wasp-stung and impatient fool," as his father calls him in 1.3.233, but also a husband who credibly inspires affection. His domestic bliss does not in any way negate the problem of his flawed values, but it makes him a multidimensional character.

Falstaff embodies an opposite weakness to Hotspur's, that of an anarchic refusal to accept responsibility. His world of food, women, and wine has no need for "redeeming time"—as Hal vows to do in the "reformation" speech (1.2.190–212)—for time is of no consequence when one refuses to acknowledge any obligations. Falstaff staves off all demands and responsibilities—the stuff of history—with humor, continually devising witticisms and preposterous excuses for his behavior. We are as delighted with his inventive comedy as Hal is in 1.2, but, like the Prince, we can see that a ruler must live a more orderly life. In addition, the fat knight displays a chilling disregard for ordinary values, in an episode that Shakespeare plainly intended as a satire on a military abuse of his own times, when he callously offers the soldiers he has recruited to be "food for powder, food for powder" (4.2.65–66), meaning that they will be quickly consumed by gunpowder, i.e., combat. He later announces coolly that he has abandoned his troops under fire, where "there's not three of my hundred and fifty left alive" (5.3.37). Falstaff's anarchy here has an unpleasant, even evil edge to it. His crimes and misdemeanors may be forgivable in a comedy—and *1 Henry IV* is somewhat comic—but they are unacceptable in the domain of history, where the hard realities of peace and war are at stake.

Just as Hotspur has an unrealistic view of the world, so does Falstaff. Falstaff lives in an immature universe where one's appetites are gratified immediately and the inevitability of age and death is denied. He has been seen as a re-creation of ancient figures of European folklore who traditionally enlivened holiday celebrations by behaving in perversely loose ways that are normally forbidden. These figures, who returned to ordinary behavior after the festival, made a great show of eating and drinking to excess, of flouting authority, and, often, of sexual promiscuity. Thus illicit cravings were acknowledged and vicariously satisfied without disrupting the society. Such customs were prominent in premodern societies and were still well known, if not widely practiced, in Elizabethan England. Falstaff's gluttony, his lechery, and his very fatness are easily associated with such figures.

However, Falstaff is not simply a temptation to be resisted or a negative lesson for Hal. Falstaff's world is also in itself useful for the Prince, offering him an arena in which he can test himself and come to understand the people who will be his subjects when he is king, and learn about himself as well. At the Boar's Head, Hal tries on the roles of robber, of tavern servant, even of king. The other worlds of the play—Hotspur's inflexible, honorbound world or Henry's tense world of political calculation—do not permit the temporary attitudes and stances necessary to learning. The world of comedy thus has virtues that the world of history cannot provide.

Just as Hotspur's happy marriage deepens his characterization, so Falstaff is caught in a revealing moment of uneasiness about his life in 3.3, when he worries that he is wasting away and muses on his long absence from church. When his eventual death is suggested by Bardolph, the fat knight immediately reverts to his more usual comic line, but we have seen that he, too, has a soul and is subject to universal fears.

Both Hotspur and Falstaff are strong figures, and it is not wholly possible to dismiss or accept either of them; with great force of irony, we are made to sympathize with both the impatient firebrand and the irresponsible rogue, even as we recognize the faults of each. When Prince Hal comes fully into his own, it is appropriate that we see him standing between these two extremes; Falstaff lies to one side, rejecting honor by feigning death, and Hotspur lies to the other, dead because he overvalued honor.

Hal's story does not end with this play; *2 Henry IV* is a sequel. Scholars debate whether or not Shakespeare had fully evolved this relationship when he was writing *1 Henry IV,* but the evidence suggests strongly that he had. First, Hal's rejection of Falstaff in *2 Henry IV* hinted at several times in *1 Henry IV*—e.g., in his "reformation" speech; when he portrays his father in the tavern ("I do, I will" [2.4.475]); when he dismisses Falstaff during the battle (5.3.55)—while the play closes with the fat knight at an acme of both wrongdoing and acceptance, boasting that he has killed Hotspur himself (after stabbing the corpse) and finding the Prince generous enough to let his claim stand. This situation prepares us for a continuation of Falstaff's adventures, when his death, with Hotspur's, could have closed the play effectively. Further, Shakespeare invented an important role for John of Lancaster at Shrewsbury, establishing him as a major figure in apparent anticipation of his function in *2 Henry IV.* Moreover, both the rebels and the king are preparing for further action as the play ends. Each of these points may be explained in some other way, but collectively they strongly suggest that *1 Henry IV* was written with *2 Henry IV* in mind. Nevertheless, *1 Henry IV* is a complete drama, with its own plot line that reaches fruition independently of its sequel.

Shakespeare's great achievement in *1 Henry IV* is the establishment of a sense of community between the audience and the fictional world of the play. Structurally he accomplishes this by a continual oscillation between two poles, the aristocratic and the common or the political and the hedonistic. These elements are sometimes parallel—as in 1.1 and 1.2, where preparations for war are followed by preparations for robbery—and sometimes in opposition, as in the comparison of Hal and Hotspur. Some scenes have analogues in *2 Henry IV*—e.g., Hotspur's farewell to his wife in 2.1 is comparable to Falstaff's departure from Doll Tearsheet in 2.4 of the sequel. Such juxtapositions enforce a comprehensive sense of a complex, lifelike fictional world, quite aside from the historical actions of the political plot.

The integration of two genres, comedy and history, permits each to influence the other. The history, presenting issues that impinge on all our lives, is made graver because it affects the lives of the comic figures. The comedy, while providing an ironic slant on social themes, is given sharpness of tone and richness of texture by its proximity to the serious aspects of life. By successfully accommodating two genres, the play—and its implicit tolerance—is made more intense: Although one is made aware of human failing, one may also glory in human possibility.

SOURCES OF THE PLAY

Shakespeare's principal source for the historical material in *1 Henry IV* was Raphael HOLINSHED's *Chronicles of England, Scotland, and Ireland* (2nd ed., 1587), but the playwright was also greatly influenced by Samuel DANIEL's epic poem *The Civil Wars between the Two Houses of York and Lancaster* (1595). In Daniel, the streamlined narrative emphasizes the relation of King Henry's troubles to his deposition of Richard II, and it climaxes with the battle of Shrewsbury, compressing the remainder of Henry's reign into a cursory account. Shakespeare's handling of historical events in *1 Henry IV* closely reflects this approach. Daniel also supplied the inspiration for the hand-to-hand encounter between Hal and Hotspur in 5.4 and for the alteration in Hotspur's age. Daniel, while stating no ages, implies that Hotspur was of Hal's generation; Shakespeare makes this explicit. Historically, however, Hotspur was older than Hal's father.

The anonymous play WOODSTOCK (ca. 1592–95) provided various details for the fictitious highway robbery in 2.2, and, more significantly, featured a story of national politics that is integrated with comical doings by a high-ranking criminal, a possible predecessor of Falstaff. Tales of Prince Hal's misspent youth had been part of English popular lore since his own time; Shakespeare derived his account chiefly from the anonymous play *The Famous Victories of Henry the Fifth* (see FAMOUS VICTORIES, THE), a farce that was acted at least as early as 1588. Most of the episodes of Hal's dissipated existence in EASTCHEAP, and of his later rejection of it, were presented in this work, which in turn drew on several earlier accounts, including the historical works of John STOW. Shakespeare probably consulted these independently, finding there the assertion that Hal refunded the victims of his companions' robberies, along with some additional details.

Other sources, including well-known ballads about the Percy-Douglas feuds and a biography of

Glendower in the popular collection A MIRROR FOR MAGISTRATES (1559), may have provided incidental material. It has also been suggested that this play and *2 Henry IV* may have been derived from an earlier play by Shakespeare on the same subject, but this speculation is unprovable.

TEXT OF THE PLAY

The date of composition of *1 Henry IV* can only be inferred, but with some precision. It seems to follow closely upon *Richard II*; not only does *1 Henry IV* come next in historical sequence, but *Richard II* contains material that seems to point to a sequel. *Richard II* is generally dated to 1595 or 1596; *1 Henry IV* was therefore composed no earlier than 1596. Oldcastle's name was changed to Falstaff as a consequence of protests following performances of the play, and that alteration was apparently made before or during the writing of *The Merry Wives of Windsor*, which was first staged in the spring of 1597. Thus it is likely that *1 Henry IV* was being performed during the winter of 1596–97 and was probably written in early or mid-1596.

Two QUARTO editions of *1 Henry IV* were printed by Peter SHORT for publisher Andrew WISE in 1598. Only four sheets (1.3.199–2.2) survive from the earlier of these, known as Q0; the other, Q1, was printed from Q0 with minor emendations. Four more quartos were published before the FIRST FOLIO of 1623: Q2 (1599), Q3 (1608), Q4 (1613), Q5 (1622). Although Q2's title page claims that it was "newly corrected by W. Shakespeare," it was in fact printed—again with minor changes—from Q1, and each subsequent quarto was derived from its predecessor. The Folio version of *1 Henry IV* was printed from Q5; it also contains many minor alterations, some of which may have come from a PROMPT BOOK. Q0 is thought to have been printed from Shakespeare's manuscript, either in the form of a FAIR COPY or his original FOUL PAPERS. Q1 is thus the basis for most modern editions.

In addition to the published texts, there is a handwritten copy of a play that combines *1* and *2 Henry IV*, the DERING MANUSCRIPT. The material it takes from *1 Henry IV* appears to derive from Q5 and the Folio text and is thus dated 1623–24. Its variations from these texts are not thought to reflect either alterations by the playwright or the practices of early productions, and modern editions do not follow it.

THEATRICAL HISTORY OF THE PLAY

Although no certain records of 16th-century performances of *1 Henry IV* have survived, numerous references in contemporary documents, especially to Hotspur or Falstaff, testify to its popularity. Several actors are said to have played Falstaff during the early 17th century, including John LOWIN, John HEMINGE, and William HART. During the Commonwealth, when the revolutionary Puritan government outlawed the theater, *The Bouncing Knight*, an abbreviated version of *1 Henry IV*, was performed secretly, as a DROLL. After the restoration of the monarchy in 1660, *1 Henry IV* was among the first plays performed in the reopened theaters, and it remained popular: Samuel PEPYS records productions in 1660, 1661, 1667, and 1668. In 1682 Thomas BETTERTON produced an adaptation of the play in which he played Hotspur; this version was so popular that it was still being revived 18 years later, by which time the 65-year-old producer was playing Falstaff. The play was also frequently staged in the 18th century, and most of the leading actors of the day played Hotspur or Falstaff. David GARRICK, among others, played both; he was acclaimed as Hotspur, but the most successful Falstaffs were James QUIN in the first half of the century and John HENDERSON in the second. In the late 18th century producers twice experimented with a woman, once the famed Julia GLOVER, in Falstaff's part.

In the first half of the 19th century a number of productions of the play were popular. William Charles MACREADY and John Philip KEMBLE were notable Hotspurs, and the latter's two brothers, Charles and Stephen KEMBLE, played Falstaff. The leading Falstaff of the time, however, was Charles BARTLEY.

Henry IV, Part 1 declined in popularity in the second half of the 19th century, although it was presented by Samuel PHELPS, F. R. BENSON, and Beerbohm TREE. However, it was often staged in the 20th century. Among the most successful productions was that of Margaret WEBSTER, starring Maurice EVANS as Falstaff, in 1939. Laurence

OLIVIER played Hotspur in 1940 and 1945; Ralph RICHARDSON's Falstaff in the latter production is considered one of his greatest successes. Orson WELLES adapted the two *Henry IV* plays in his 1965 FILM *Chimes at Midnight*, in which he starred as Falstaff. Several cycles of the history plays have presented *1 Henry IV*, notably those at STRATFORD in 1906, 1951 (with Michael REDGRAVE as Hotspur), and 1964. A number of TELEVISION productions of the play have been broadcast since the 1950s. The continuing appeal of the *Henry IV* plays was demonstrated by a 1987 production in London: The two plays and *Henry V* were staged on different nights of the week, and most strikingly, theatergoers responded with enthusiasm to marathon Saturday performances featuring all three works in succession. In 2000 the ROYAL SHAKESPEARE COMPANY again staged both *Henry IV* plays.

CHARACTERS

Archbishop of York, Richard Scroop (d. 1405) Historical figure and character in *1* and *2 Henry IV*, a leader of the rebels against King Henry IV. In *1 Henry IV* the Archbishop appears only briefly, in 4.4, where he confers with his friend Sir Michael. He predicts the defeat of Hotspur at SHREWSBURY and lays his plans for the rebellions to be enacted in *2 Henry IV*. Shakespeare may have intended the episode as a preparation for the later play, or it may simply have served to remind the audience that the battle of Shrewsbury was not to be the last of Henry's troubles.

In *2 Henry IV* the Archbishop leads the continuing revolt, although his cause is doomed by the treacherous withdrawal of the Earl of Northumberland. In 4.1 he states the dilemma of the good man who is provoked into rebellion by poor government but nevertheless believes in the divine right of kings. However, the Earl of Westmoreland firmly asserts the point of view of the play: rebellion is a heinous violation of the natural order, and the gravity of the offense is aggravated when the rebel is a clergyman, for a representative of God should not oppose a divinely appointed king. In 4.2 the Archbishop disbands his army after Prince John of Lancaster promises that his grievances will be considered, and is then arrested for treason and sentenced to death.

The historical archbishop had sided with Henry when he deposed Richard II, although several members of his family supported Richard, including his brother Stephen Scroop, who appears in *Richard II*. (Later, Stephen's son, Henry Scroop, was executed for treason by Henry V, as is enacted in *Henry V*.) The archbishop's cousin William Scroop, Earl of Wiltshire, was one of Richard II's favorites and was executed by Henry in 1399, as is reported in *Richard II* (3.2.142). In 1.3.265 of *1 Henry IV*, where Wiltshire is incorrectly identified as the Archbishop's brother, this execution is said to have sparked the prelate's rebellion against Henry. Although Shakespeare took his information from HOLINSHED, it is not true. The archbishop supported the new king until 1405, when he and a number of northern barons—among them his brother-in-law Northumberland—joined to oppose the heavy taxes Henry had levied in order to finance his wars against earlier rebels. Once in revolt, the archbishop was not betrayed by Northumberland; instead, he impetuously began his campaign against the king before his allies were prepared to fight, and he accordingly found himself outnumbered—and then outsmarted—at GAULTREE FOREST.

Bardolph Character in *1* and *2 Henry IV*, *The Merry Wives of Windsor*, and *Henry V*, a follower of Falstaff. In *1 Henry IV* Bardolph participates in the highway robbery of 2.2, and in *2 Henry IV* he assists the fat knight in his illicit recruiting efforts in 3.2, collecting bribes from men who wish to avoid service. When Falstaff is rejected by Prince Hal in 5.5, Bardolph goes to prison with him. In *The Merry Wives* Bardolph is only a minor figure who occasionally delivers messages to Falstaff. In *Henry V* he is a soldier in the army of King Henry V. In 2.1 he defuses the feud between Pistol and Nym. In 3.2.28–57 the Boy convincingly describes him as a coward and thief. In 3.6 we learn that Bardolph is to be executed for having stolen a sacramental vessel from a French church, and in 4.4 the Boy reports that Bardolph has indeed been hung.

Despite his swaggering, Bardolph has little distinctive personality. His peacemaking role in *Henry V* ironically counters King Henry V's bellicosity in an antiwar reading of the play, but if one interprets Henry as a epic hero, then Bardolph remains a comic soldier, a petty villain whose end helps to demonstrate the King's dedication to justice. Bardolph's most prominent characteristic is his diseased facial complexion, florid and fiery, "all bubukles, and whelks, and knobs, and flames o'fire" (*Henry V*, 3.6.105–106). He is teased mercilessly about his skin disorder by Falstaff and other characters, finding himself compared to lamps, torches, blushing maids, red wine, red petticoats, hellfire, and even "Lucifer's privy kitchen" (*2 Henry IV*, 2.4.330).

Bardolph was originally called Rossill, but after *2 Henry IV* was written the name was changed, probably to avoid offending a prominent aristocrat, William Russill, Earl of Bedford. The fact that the name Bardolph had already been assigned to another character in *2 Henry IV*, Lord Bardolph, is only one instance of Shakespeare's tolerance for minor confusions and inconsistencies in his plays.

Blunt, Sir Walter (d. 1403) Historical figure and character in *1 Henry IV*, a follower of King Henry IV. Blunt is a respected adviser and emissary, and his calm personality contrasts with that of the tormented Henry and the temperamental Hotspur. In 1.3 Blunt attempts to mediate the quarrel between the king and Hotspur. In 3.2.163–179 he brings the dramatic news that the rebel forces are gathering at SHREWSBURY, a report that propels Prince Hal into action. In 4.3 Blunt acts as the king's ambassador, and he is properly short with the bellicose Hotspur. In 5.3 he is dressed as the king, in a standard medieval battlefield tactic, and is killed by Douglas. The sight of his corpse causes Falstaff to remark ironically, "There's honour for you!" (5.3.32).

The historical Blunt was a longtime follower of King Henry's father, John of Gaunt. He was Gaunt's executor, and he naturally became one of Henry's chief advisers. He was indeed killed at Shrewsbury, but he was not among those disguised as the king. He bore the king's standard, a position of honor that suggests a sound reputation as a military man. He was the father of Sir John Blunt, who appears in *2 Henry IV*, and great-grandfather of Sir James Blunt of *Richard III*.

Carrier Either of two minor characters in *1 Henry IV*, freight haulers who prepare to take a cargo to LONDON from ROCHESTER in 2.1. The Carriers comically complain about conditions at the inn. They tellingly distrust the highwayman Gadshill when he asks to borrow a lantern, but they unwittingly supply him with information, commenting that they expect gentlemen carrying valuables to accompany them on the road. At least one of the Carriers is apparently among the Travellers who are ambushed in 2.2, for he appears in London with the Sheriff in 2.4, having recognized Falstaff during the robbery.

Chamberlain Minor character in *1 Henry IV*, an inn employee who scouts for the highwayman Gadshill. In 2.1 the Chamberlain tells Gadshill of two likely victims who are staying at his inn and who will soon be leaving for LONDON. He is promised a share in the highwayman's take. In 2.2 Gadshill, Falstaff, and others rob the unfortunate Travellers. In Shakespeare's day the employees of inns were generally mistrusted, and contemporary writings describe many instances of this particular arrangement among thieves.

Douglas, Archibald, Earl of (1369–1424) Historical figure and character in *1 Henry IV*, the leader of the Scottish army that joins the rebels against King Henry IV. Douglas's appearance is preceded by word of his reputation for courage and military prowess. In 3.2 the King speaks of his renown by way of praising Hotspur, who has captured him at the battle of HOLMEDON, and Falstaff describes him as "that sprightly Scot of Scots, Douglas, that runs a-horseback up a hill perpendicular . . ." (2.4.338–340). In accordance with Worcester's plan, Hotspur frees Douglas and recruits him for the rebellion against Henry. A bold talker (". . . there is not such a word spoke of in Scotland as this term of fear" [4.1.84–85]) and fighter, Douglas's fiery temperament resembles Hotspur's, and both men urge the rebels into the battle of SHREWSBURY without waiting for reinforcements. During the battle, in 5.3–4, Douglas seeks out Henry, first slaying Sir Walter Blunt. He nearly kills the king, but Prince Hal drives him away. He then attacks Falstaff, who feigns death. In 5.5 Douglas's capture is reported, but Prince Hal declares that he shall be freed without the payment of ransom, as a tribute to his valor.

Black Douglas, as the historical figure was known, was indeed a famous warrior, although he may have been a bad commander, for he was never on the winning side in a major battle. He was not in fact released at Shrewsbury; he was only freed five years later, after the payment of a very large ransom. Shakespeare followed his source, HOLINSHED, in this error. Douglas later fought against the English for King Charles VII of France in the HUNDRED YEARS' WAR, and he died in FRANCE.

Falstaff, Sir John   Character in *1* and *2 Henry IV* and *The Merry Wives of Windsor*. Falstaff—physically huge, stunningly amoral, and outrageously funny—is generally regarded as one of the greatest characters in English literature. Lecherous, gluttonous, obese, cowardly, and a thief, he lies to the world but is honest with himself. His monumental presence, both literal and metaphoric, dominates the plays in which he appears, and he has become one of the most familiar of Shakespeare's creations, having inspired work ranging from pub signs and ceramic mugs to operas and symphonic works.

In the *Henry IV* plays, Falstaff, although an entirely credible human being, also functions as a symbol of an extreme lifestyle. In *1 Henry IV* young Prince Hal begins to come to grips with his role as the future king of England, and he is presented with strong figures who suggest modes of adulthood. Unlike Hal's father, the calculating and politically shrewd King Henry IV, and unlike the intensely single-minded warrior Hotspur, Falstaff, in the free and dissolute ambience of the BOAR'S HEAD TAVERN, indulges in food, drink, and adventure, whether sexual or criminal, and rejects life's demands for courage or honor. From the beginning the Prince states his intention to reject Falstaff's world, in the famous "reformation" speech (1.2.190–212). Still, throughout the play he is clearly delighted with his friend's bold effronteries and witty lies; at its close he promises to support Falstaff's claim to have killed Hotspur. In *Part 1* Falstaff is a decided rascal, cowardly and deceitful, but his common sense and tolerance counter the values of Hotspur and King Henry.

In *2 Henry IV* the Prince is closer to his assumption of power, and he is accordingly more remote from Falstaff. Falstaff dominates this play entirely. He is still very funny—as he puts it, "I am not only witty in myself, but the cause that wit is in other men" (1.2.8–9)—but he is presented in a significantly darker light, contributing to the play's atmosphere of disease and death. He is ill; his first words deal with a diagnosis (1.2.1), and he describes himself as sick on several occasions. He refers to his age several times, as when he doubts his attractiveness to Doll Tearsheet, saying, "I am old, I am old" (2.4.268). In *Part 1* he says he is in his 50s (2.4.418–419), while in *Part 2* his acquaintance with Shallow is said to date from "fifty-five year ago" (3.2.205), making him at least 70.

Most important, his misdeeds are distinctly more serious in *2 Henry IV*. In *Part 1* his extortion of bribes from draft evaders is merely reported (4.2.11–48), while we actually see it happen in *Part 2*, 3.2. Moreover, his impressed soldiers, anonymous victims in *Part 1*, take human shape in *Part 2* as such sympathetic, if minor, figures as Shadow and Feeble. The recruiting scene is hilarious, but it remains on the record as evidence of Falstaff's criminality. In fact, the episode was clearly intended as a satirical condemnation of a real practice that plagued the English poor in Shakespeare's time. Perhaps Falstaff's most serious offense is his selfish exploitation of his friends. He promises love but instead bleeds money from his loyal admirer the Hostess, as she herself describes in 2.1.84–101. The preposterous Shallow is a natural victim, but Falstaff's cynical rationale for fleecing him—"If the young dace be a bait for the old pike, I see no reason in the law of nature but I may snap at him" (3.2.325–326)—is, however wittily put, morally repugnant.

Hal is distant and hostile to Falstaff when they meet in 2.4, and when the knight seeks to profit from Hal's succession to the crown, the new king forbids his presence. Hal is cold and forceful—although he mercifully provides his former friend with a generous pension—and Falstaff's fall seems abrupt, although it has been prepared for throughout both plays. The needs of the greater political and military world of Prince Hal triumph in the end.

Still, however fully one may endorse Prince Hal's rejection of Falstaff (and many people do not accept it at all), the fat knight remains a generally sympathetic figure. If his misdeeds would be offensive in real life, they are frequently delightful on stage. He deflates pretension with the needle of his satire, and he counters excessive rigor with his entertainingly flexible morals. His combination of grandiose rhetoric, penetrating wit, and common sense shines in such virtuoso passages of comic monologue as his battlefield rejection of courage (*1 Henry IV*, 5.4.110–120)—leading to a particularly outrageous gesture, the stabbing of Hotspur's corpse—and his tribute to wine (*2 Henry IV*, 4.3.85–123), long acclaimed as one of the most delectable discourses in English literature. In the plays' tavern scenes (2.4 in each) he is uproarious and hearty. His ceaseless flow of parody and imitation evokes a wide and enjoyable range of personages from aristocrats to highwaymen.

Falstaff is a figure of immense psychological resonance; through him we can enjoy our own fantasies of life without responsibilities. When it seems he can offer no excuse for some misdeed and must surely be brought down, like the rest of us, he devises some extravagant lie or joke and escapes. His vitality seems limitless; as he puts it himself, "banish plump Jack, and banish all the world"

Sir John Falstaff (seated on tabletop) in a scene from a modern production of *1 Henry IV*. Shakespeare's corrupt but outrageously funny knight teaches Prince Hal things he cannot learn from more conventional role models. *(American Shakespeare Festival, Stratford, Connecticut. Photo courtesy of Billy Rose Theater Collection: New York Public Library at Lincoln Center; Astor, Lenox and Tilden Foundations)*

(*1 Henry IV*, 2.4.473–474). However, Falstaff *is* banished, for he also represents amoral disloyalty, criminal exploitation, and weak social values. Less sternly, he is often compared to springlike weather in autumn (e.g., in *1 Henry IV* 1.2.154–155), a common metaphor for youthful energy in old age. The fat knight clearly reflects Shakespeare's fond appreciation of tavern life and its pleasurable delinquencies, but one of the values most important to the playwright—as is especially plain in the HISTORY PLAYS—was the maintenance of social order. Thus Falstaff is repudiated in no uncertain terms, both in the *Henry IV* plays and in *The Merry Wives*.

Part of Falstaff's humor lies in his burlesque of the chivalric values of the aristocracy, and part of his vital force in his energetic individuality. These traits lead many modern readers to think of the *Henry IV* plays as ironical satires of war and government and of Falstaff's rejection as proof that human authenticity is tragically at odds with the practice of politics. However, this ascribes to Shakespeare the views of our own age, when the worth of the individual is placed above that of traditional societal values. But in earlier times Falstaff was held to be flatly villainous. The first great Shakespearean editor, Nicholas ROWE, called him "a Thief, Lying, Cowardly, Vainglorious, and in short every way vicious" in his 1709 edition of the plays. A little later, Samuel JOHNSON wrote that Falstaff "has nothing in him that can be esteemed." Although Shakespeare himself was surely less critical of his creation, he certainly would have understood their point of view. In the RENAISSANCE the potential of the individual was beginning to be recognized, as Shakespeare's interest in and respect for human psychology exemplify, but the ancient, biblically sanctioned, hierarchical society of medieval Europe is persistently championed in the plays, as well as in other works of Elizabethan literature. Therefore, necessity—that national order be restored after a civil war—demands the rejection of the thoughtless pleasures and the irresponsibility that Falstaff displays.

Falstaff's popularity on the Elizabethan stage prompted Shakespeare to announce, in the EPILOGUE to *2 Henry IV*, that the fat knight would appear in another play. However, he does not appear in *Henry V*, although he may have been a character in a lost, probably unacted version of that play. A number of textual peculiarities make it clear that *Henry V* was altered after it was first written; most strikingly, Pistol takes on Falstaffian characteristics in several passages. Following his humiliation in 5.1, he speaks of growing old and of losing Doll Tearsheet, lines that are plainly more appropriate to Falstaff. Also, Pistol's capture of the French Soldier parallels Falstaff's comic achievements in *1* and *2 Henry IV*. Scholars speculate that, in an original draft of the play, Falstaff was the chief comic character, that he was deleted by the playwright—for it appears that the present version of the play derives from Shakespeare's manuscript— and that much of his part was transferred to Pistol. This theory cannot be proven, but it does explain the textual evidence.

Why would Shakespeare have eliminated Falstaff? Two answers present themselves. The first supposes that the controversy surrounding Falstaff's original name, Oldcastle, was still current and that pressure from the son of Lord COBHAM necessitated another change, finally ending the enmity of a powerful aristocrat toward the CHAMBERLAIN'S MEN, Shakespeare's company. However, Shakespeare may simply have thought better of resurrecting his mammoth exemplar of immorality in a play that is dedicated to the English triumph at AGINCOURT. Falstaff had already been rejected on well-established grounds, and his powerful presence may have seemed too distracting from the patriotic themes of *Henry V*.

However, the fat knight's death is described in *Henry V*, 2.3, by Pistol, the Hostess, Bardolph, and Nym, and their affection for him reflects the playwright's. When Bardolph wishes he were with Falstaff "wheresome'er he is, either in heaven or in Hell!" (2.3.7–8), the Hostess asserts that he is surely in heaven; she goes on to describe his deathbed touchingly: ". . . after I saw him fumble with the sheets and play with flowers and smile upon his fingers' end, I knew there was but one way; for his nose was as sharp as a pen, and a' babbled of green fields . . . a' cried out 'God, God, God!' three of four times . . ." (2.3.14–20). Thus Falstaff's humanly believable end summons our sympathy one last time for the knight who had "more flesh than another man, and therefore more frailty" (*1 Henry IV*, 3.3.167–168).

The Merry Wives of Windsor was written before *Henry V*, probably during the creation of *2 Henry IV*, and here Falstaff is a less complex figure than the giant of the *Henry IV* plays. His function is more purely comic and stands at the center of the play rather than in contrast to the realities of history. He is more nearly a traditional character type, the comic villain whose downfall is obvious from the outset. He is also associated with another type, the foolish and boastful would-be lady's man, although in attempting to seduce the wives to get at their husbands' money, Falstaff is not erotically inclined. However, he is thereby linked with the familiar theme of the jealous husband, and the sexual side of his story links him with the SUBPLOTS centered on the courting of Anne Page.

The complications caused by Falstaff's greedy impulses lead him to receive a humorous retribution and then forgiveness. His personality has not changed—he is still brassy, shrewd, and amorally selfish—but the resourceful prankster and brazen reprobate of the *Henry IV* plays no longer has the initiative. He is easily tricked by the wives, not once but three times. This is sometimes regarded as an unfortunate trivialization of a great character, but it may also be argued that Falstaff's lesser magnitude in *The Merry Wives* suits his simpler function as a comic butt. In the world of Prince Hal, Falstaff was a shrewd courtier in addition to his other roles, and he never forgot his status—indeed, several of his fantastic excuses for his misbehavior refer to the exalted position of the Prince. In Windsor he assumes regal attitudes: he tyrannically bullies Pistol and Nym, and he attempts to lord it over the townspeople. His changed behavior—in addition to demonstrating Shakespeare's acute perception of social relations—makes Falstaff an entirely appropriate target for a comic comeuppance.

This aspect of the character is particularly evident in Falstaff's apologetic confession following his final humiliation (5.5.122–129)—often seen, in its "un-Falstaffian" quality as evidence of a lost source play. However, in the MASQUE-like finale, where none of the characters present their ordinary characteristics, symbolic expression is given to the play's implicit moral—the triumph of domesticity. Here, then, Falstaff makes the formal surrender that his status as a traditional comic butt requires.

In this respect, Falstaff has been seen as a representation of an ancient fertility spirit in a tradition that in the playwright's time was still alive in remote regions of Britain and was still generally understood. As such, his figurative role was that of the sacrificial victim punished for the sins of society in ancient religious practices. This image need not be taken literally to see that the Falstaff of *The Merry Wives* is identified with common human foibles.

Indeed, Falstaff has the same function in the *Henry IV* plays as well. He moves us in a way that Hal or Hotspur or Anne Page cannot, because, like him, we all often feel irresponsible, dishonest, selfish inclinations. We know that Falstaff is part of us, like it or not. In the *Henry IV* plays he represents a childish, self-centered universe of pleasure that adults are doomed to leave and that is defeated by a harsh and demanding political ideal, insistent on duty and order. In *The Merry Wives* Falstaff is again opposed by a triumphant principle, in this case the world of domestic security. In both cases, he embodies the need of each of us to rebel against the constraints of society and thus find our individual potential, and his defeat symbolizes the need to sublimate that rebellion in light of our innate dependence on each other.

In his first appearance, Hal excuses Falstaff from even an awareness of time, "unless hours were cups of sack, and minutes capons, and clocks the tongues of bawds, and dials the signs of leaping-houses, and the blessed sun himself a fair hot wench in flame-coloured taffeta" (*1 Henry IV*, 1.2.7–10). The essential nature of Falstaff's personality is revealed in this passage, for the thrust of his wit, and of his life, is to elaborate this fantasy and to defend it against the demands of reality. We delight in the brilliant energy of his efforts, and we mourn the impossibility of their success.

Francis Minor character in *1* and *2 Henry IV*, an indentured servant at the BOAR'S HEAD TAVERN. In 2.4 of *1 Henry IV* Prince Hal teases Francis, engaging him in conversation while Poins, by prearrangement, summons him. The endearingly simple-minded

Francis can only reply with the well-known protest of the harried waiter, "Anon, anon," as Hal has predicted. Hal suggests that Francis might run away from the tavern, and then he extravagantly promises Francis £1,000 for a packet of sugar. He next asks if Francis will rob the innkeeper and goes on to speak of Francis's likely future. "Why then your brown bastard is your only drink," he says, "for look you, Francis, your white canvas doublet will sully. In Barbary, sir, it cannot come to so much" (2.4.72–74). Francis is now hopelessly confused, and he exits hurriedly as Poins, Hal, and his boss, the Vintner, all call him at once.

This puzzling exchange has elicited a number of explanations, the simplest of which is that Hal is merely playing a practical joke on Francis, an example of the idle tavern life that he will later reject. However, while a joke is clearly intended, the Prince is deliberately placing himself on familiar terms with an "underskinker" (2.4.24), continuing his exploration of the lives of the common people whom he will later rule. Thus the episode helps to demonstrate that Hal's participation in Falstaff's world is part of his preparation for his greater role, and not simply dissipation. He suggests as much when, asked by Poins what the point of the joke was, he replies that he is now "of all humours" (2.4.90) and compares his good mood with Hotspur's mania for war. In Francis's humble life, he has seen a contentment that the warrior can never discover. Further, Hal observes that, if Francis will not be tempted by theft or flight, he must accept the low life of a servant. This may reflect, albeit in a resigned manner, Hal's attitude toward his own destiny to become a leader, rather than a participant in the easier, irresponsible world of the tavern.

In *2 Henry IV* Francis appears to have been promoted, as he organizes the service for Falstaff's dinner in 2.4.

Gadshill   Character in *1 Henry IV*, a highway robber and friend of Falstaff and Prince Hal. In 2.1 of *1 Henry IV* Gadshill uses a well-known highwayman's tactic: an accomplice, the Chamberlain of an inn, tips him off about the travel plans of rich guests. Then he and Falstaff and others rob these Travellers in 2.2, only to be robbed in their turn by the Prince and Poins. Gadshill—a professional thief,

unlike Falstaff and the Prince—serves to demonstrate the depths of delinquency from which the Prince must emerge.

Gadshill is a nickname taken from Shakespeare's anonymous source, THE FAMOUS VICTORIES, where it is applied to a highwayman whose favorite working locale was GAD'S HILL.

Glendower, Owen (ca. 1359–ca. 1416)   Historical figure and character in *1 Henry IV*, military leader from WALES who joins rebellious English noblemen against King Henry IV. In 3.1, at a rebel council of war, Glendower boasts of supernatural powers, displaying the superstitiousness traditionally associated with the Welsh, to the disgust of Hotspur. The clash of these two personalities almost upsets the alliance, though Glendower, admiring his hotheaded ally, makes peace several times during the scene. In a lighter vein, Glendower interprets for his daughter, Lady Mortimer, who is in love with her husband, Lord Mortimer, but does not speak English. Father and daughter together reveal their lyrical sentimental streak and a love of music, also traits stereotypically associated with the Welsh.

Later, in 4.4.16–18, Glendower is reported to have absented himself from the crucial battle of SHREWSBURY, "o'er-rul'd by prophecies." This episode adds Glendower's superstitiousness to the general weakness and incapacity that plague the rebel cause. Also, the account lends Hotspur's defeat an ominous, fated quality that is in keeping with the play's condemnation of rebellion.

Although Shakespeare's sources mention Glendower's training in law and his youthful service at the English court, he is chiefly portrayed as a barbaric and ruthless Welsh outlaw, as is reflected in the report on him by the Earl of Westmoreland in 1.1.40–46. However, Shakespeare amplifies and softens this figure, and his Glendower is a composer and scholar whom Mortimer can describe as "a worthy gentleman, . . . valiant as a lion, and wondrous affable, and as bountiful as mines of India" (3.1.159–163). Traditional English bias against the Welsh may account for the brute of the chronicles; the music-loving sage of the play may reflect Shakespeare's acquaintance with Welsh residents of London. Glendower's superstitiousness may also derive from the playwright's personal knowledge, for the English stereotype of the superstitious Welshman was grounded in the survival of a strong Celtic religious sensibility in Wales. Although Hotspur finds this trait ridiculous (3.1.142–158), Shakespeare himself apparently regarded it more sympathetically, as a humorous failing. Glendower is on the whole a positive figure, if a weak one. Even Hotspur's raillery against him is enjoyable rhetoric.

The historical Glendower led the last and most nearly successful Welsh rebellion against the English. In 1400, shortly after Henry IV's deposition of Richard II, Glendower led an uprising that grew from a quarrel with his English neighbor into a full-scale revolt. In 1403 the Welsh rebels joined with those from northern England led by Hotspur, and only Henry's decisive advance on Shrewsbury prevented their forces from combining. That Glendower's superstition led him to abandon the rebels at Shrewsbury is not reported in Shakespeare's sources; Raphael HOLINSHED, in fact, mistakenly says that Glendower was at the battle, and Samuel DANIEL, like modern historians, attributes his absence only to King Henry's superior generalship. In 1404, with most of Wales under his control, Glendower established a national government at Harlech, where a parliament elected him Prince of Wales, and he entered into an alliance with England's enemy, FRANCE. In 1405, with French troops reinforcing his own, he invaded England but was defeated by Henry. This was the high-water mark of his rebellion, and by 1409 Glendower had lost even Harlech and had retreated deep into the mountains. After 1410 he disappeared from history, though he is thought to have lived somewhat longer. Although only briefly successful, Glendower united Wales—a land of petty principalities before the English invaded in the 12th century—and led it to an independence it never again attained. He remains a great hero of Welsh culture.

A minor character in *Richard II*, the Captain, is sometimes thought to have been intended as Glendower, and the famous leader is specifically referred to in that play as Glendor (3.1.43). He is also inaccurately said to have imprisoned his son-in-law Mortimer in *2 Henry VI* (2.2.40–41). His death is reported (several years too early, due to an error in Holinshed) in *2 Henry IV* (3.1.103).

Hal, Prince   See Prince of Wales, Henry.

Harvey   Original name of Peto in *1* and *2 Henry IV*. When the name Peto was substituted for Harvey, shortly after the plays were written, in 1596–97, one instance of the original designation inadvertently remained in the early texts of *1 Henry IV*, in 1.2.158, revealing that the change had occurred. Since the 18th century, this reference has also been altered in most editions. The change of name was made at the same time that Oldcastle became Falstaff—at the insistence of William Brooke, Lord COBHAM, a descendant of the historical Oldcastle—presumably in the hope of avoiding a similar problem with another prominent aristocrat, Sir William HERVEY (also known as Harvey).

Henry IV, King of England (1366–1413)   Historical figure and title character in *1* and *2 Henry IV*. (The same figure appears in *Richard II* as Henry Bolingbroke.) King Henry is not the most prominent character in the plays that take his name, but he is nonetheless an important figure. The major concern of the plays is the growth of his son and successor, Prince Hal. The question of what constitutes a good ruler is thus paramount, and as king, Henry personifies the issue. He is viewed from three distinct points of view in *Part 1:* He sees himself as a weary but effective monarch; Hotspur regards him as a dishonorable politician who first deposed a king (as is enacted in *Richard II*) and then betrayed those who helped him do so; and Falstaff considers him a cold, rigid opponent of comfort and license. By *Part 2* Henry is almost a tragic figure. The cost of power shows itself in his illness and fatigue, while he himself suggests that his decline and death are the deserved fate of a usurper.

Henry is presented as a strong ruler: for instance, his dismissal of Hotspur and Northumberland in 1.3.116–122 of *Part 1* makes it clear that he does not tolerate insubordination, and in 3.1 of *Part 2* he overcomes his illness and melancholy to face the rebellion squarely, saying, "Are these things then necessities? then let us meet them like necessities"

(3.1.92–93). He is also politically astute to the point of cynicism. In *Part 1* (3.2.39–59) he describes the appearance of regal splendor that he assumed during his rebellion against Richard II in order to win the hearts of the populace (Richard also describes this in *Richard II*, 1.4.23–36), and his distinctly Machiavellian deathbed advice to Hal—divert potential rebels by engaging in wars abroad—is chilling.

But despite his strength, Henry's principal characteristic is weariness. From the first line of *Part 1* Henry presents himself as a sick and tired man who wants to embark on a crusade to the Holy Land to atone for his role in the murder of Richard II. Moreover, his disappointment over Prince Hal's dissolute life embitters him. In 3.1 of *Part 2* he comments that the terrible burden of power prevents him from sleeping; he broods, "uneasy lies the head that wears a crown" (3.1.31). He goes on to wish, "Oh God, that one might read the book of fate . . ." (3.1.45), in tones that foreshadow the darkly brilliant meditations of Shakespeare's tragic heroes.

Hotspur sees Henry as a treacherous usurper who has turned against his allies. Henry himself is very much aware that he has been a rebel. In his deathbed conversation with Hal, he plainly suffers guilt for the "by-paths and indirect crook'd ways" (*2 Henry IV*, 4.5.184) by which he gained power, a reference to the deposition and murder of Richard II. He observes that many of his allies against Richard later resented his assumption of power. He anticipates that Hal will have an easier time when he ascends the throne, being legitimately descended from a sitting king. This indeed proves to be so, as the end of *2 Henry IV* and all of *Henry V* demonstrate. However, as Shakespeare and his contemporaries were well aware, the disputes over the royal succession that Henry's actions had triggered were settled only by the disastrous WARS OF THE ROSES, and Henry's sense of guilt is a reflection of the curse that his sinful usurpation has brought upon himself, his family (see LANCASTER FAMILY), and his country. Nevertheless, Henry is the established power in these plays, and Hotspur and his allies sin in rebelling against him and are repeatedly condemned as a result.

Henry's ultimate significance in the drama is as the holder of the position for which Prince Hal must equip himself. While Henry's cold, Machi-

avellian world of political manipulation is too rigid and inhumane for the young man to grow up in, he does in the end enter it. In 4.5, in a reprise of the king's lament over the stresses of kingship (*2 Henry IV*, 3.1.4–31), Hal rhetorically addresses Henry's crown and speaks of the burden that kingship demands. He accepts that burden for himself, emphasizing his decision by placing the crown on his own head. One consequence of this decision is that he must become like Henry to some degree; he must enact in the real world the disciplinarian's role he had taken in the tavern burlesque of *Part 1*. Hal is often criticized for his icily brutal dismissal of Falstaff in 5.5; readers have thought that, in rejecting Falstaff, Hal also rejects part of his own humanity, but it may equally well be argued that he is simply adopting a different type of humanity, that of his weary, careworn father.

The history of Henry's reign is strenuously compressed in the plays, producing an impression of greater civil disorder than in fact occurred. While the various rebellions of the play did take place, they were widely spaced and relatively easily suppressed. Henry was a strong king, although he was not a competent administrator and his regime had persistent financial troubles. Two significant variations from history in the plays concern Henry personally. First, in *Part 1* Henry is committed from the very beginning (indeed, from *Richard II*, 5.6.49–50) to a crusade to ease his conscience, thus stressing sin and retribution as the ultimate causes of the unrest of Henry's reign. In fact, and in Shakespeare's sources. Henry did not propose a crusade until late in his reign, when it seems to have been intended to expand his influence in European diplomacy. Second, Henry's illness, which he actually developed only a year before his death, plagues him for most of his reign in the plays, dominating all his appearances in *2 Henry IV*. Shakespeare may have been influenced in this direction by Samuel DANIEL, whose *Civil Wars* stresses Henry's deathbed struggles with his bad conscience. The effect that is produced, a melancholy sense of impending death, makes more fateful and solemn Hal's acceptance of his kingly burden.

Hostess (Mistress Quickly, Nell Quickly)   Character in *1* and *2 Henry IV* and *Henry V*, the proprietress of the BOAR'S HEAD TAVERN in EASTCHEAP. The Hostess, a good-hearted woman whose affection for Falstaff withstands his exploitation of her purse, is comically loquacious. Aspiring to conversational brilliance, she displays a considerable vocabulary, but she unfortunately misplaces one word for another in an ancient comedy routine, going so far, in a state of great excitement, as to confuse "honeyseed" and "honeysuckle" for "homicide" and "homicidal" (*2 Henry IV*, 2.1.49–51). She is a denizen of the quasi-criminal underworld of London—(she associates with highwaymen and harlots and is arrested when a murder is said to have occurred in her tavern)—but no crimes are explicitly attributed to her. Indeed, her amiable and forgiving nature contains no hint of villainy.

The Hostess's role in *1 Henry IV* is very minor. In 2.4 she is an amused spectator of the mock drama played by Prince Hal and Falstaff, and in 3.3 she disputes with Falstaff over his debt to her. He mocks her, and his insults spark her honest indignation.

In *2 Henry IV* the Hostess is a somewhat more substantial character. She escalates her dispute with Falstaff by summoning two officers, Fang and Snare, to arrest the fat knight for debt. She elaborates on her complaint, remembering at length (2.1.83–101) that he had promised to marry her in order to borrow money. However, Falstaff not only talks her into calling off her legal action but also into lending him more money. She weeps, but she agrees, showing the gullibility and kindness that mark her relationship with him. In 2.4, when Falstaff is called to join the armies assembling to oppose the rebels against Henry IV, the Hostess displays her sentimental attachment to him, weeping and saying, "Well, fare thee well. I have known thee these twenty-nine years, come peascodtime, but an honester and truer-hearted man—Well, fare thee well" (2.4.379–382). Even the Hostess's credulousness does not extend to a belief in Falstaff's honesty; she is merely expressing her love with conventional sayings that come first to her mind. The Hostess's tolerance and affection for Falstaff are important in Shakespeare's presentation of the fat rogue as a humane, though flawed, person. It comes as a shock when the Hostess and her friend Doll Tearsheet are arrested in 5.4, in a demonstra-tion of the rigorous law enforcement of the new regime, anticipating Prince Hal's rejection of Falstaff in 5.5.

In *Henry V* the Hostess (now married to Pistol) has a small but striking role, as she describes her attendance at Falstaff's deathbed, in a speech (2.3.9–27) that is one of the masterpieces of English comic literature, being simultaneously extremely funny, even bawdy, and touchingly tender. Her efforts to comfort a dying and conscience-stricken sinner reflect Shakespeare's own forgiving humanity.

The Hostess is given the name Mistress Quickly in all three plays (e.g., in *1 Henry IV*, 3.3.90; *2 Henry IV*, 2.1.44; *Henry V*, 2.1.19 [where she is "Nell Quickly"]), but she is plainly a different person from the Mistress Quickly of *The Merry Wives of Windsor*; Shakespeare simply reused the name and comical verbal habit of the Hostess with his customary disregard for questions of consistency. Some scholars hold that the correct pronunciation of Quickly should be "quick-lie," a legitimate Elizabethan variant that carries an obvious implication that she is a prostitute. Falstaff hints that she is (e.g., in *1 Henry IV*, 3.3.110–127), but although she consorts with Doll, who is a courtesan, there is no other evidence to support this. It is more probable that her name, pronounced ordinarily (as it commonly was in the 16th century), is simply intended to suggest the hustle and bustle of an inn-keeper's life.

Hotspur (Henry Percy) (1364–1403) Historical figure and character in *1 Henry IV*, a rebel against King Henry IV; the same figure appears as Henry Percy in *Richard II*. Hotspur, a fiery warrior, is repeatedly contrasted with Henry's son, Prince Hal. The Prince's dissipation in the company of Falstaff is compared unfavorably with Hotspur's military prowess and chivalric honor. The play's major theme is Prince Hal's decision to abandon the tavern for the field and to compete with Hotspur, whose example inspires the Prince to adopt his proper role as a military hero. At the play's climax, the two young men meet in hand-to-hand combat at SHREWSBURY, where the Prince kills his rival. The play makes clear that Hotspur's volatile temper has led to his defeat and to the failure of his rebellion: he has carried his ideal of chivalric honor to excess.

In this sense, he is contrasted with Falstaff, whose self-indulgent cowardice represents an opposite extreme. Hotspur thus resembles a figure from the MORALITY PLAYS, a symbol of a value or attitude.

Even before he appears, Hotspur is associated with military honor and prowess, as well as with excessive pride, in King Henry's account (1.1.66–94) of his capture—and arrogant possession—of Douglas. Hotspur begins the play in the service of the king, but the Percy family harbors a simmering resentment over Henry's apparent ingratitude for the help they gave him when he usurped the throne (as enacted in *Richard II*). When a dispute erupts over Hotspur's failure to relinquish custody of Douglas, and the king refuses to ransom a Percy relative, Lord Mortimer, the Percys decide to rebel. Hotspur's reputation for courage and his proven success in combat make him the natural leader of the rebellion, but his older relatives—his father, Henry Percy, Earl of Northumberland, and his uncle, the Earl of Worcester—must struggle to curb the young man's temper. Ultimately they are unable to do so, and Hotspur's rash insistence on fighting against the odds at Shrewsbury dooms the rebellion to defeat.

Hotspur's virtues are manifest; he is a fine military leader in a world that values this trait highly. King Henry's regret that his own son is not more like Hotspur is genuine, and the Prince himself, after killing his rival, acknowledges his worth in a warm eulogy (5.4.86–100). However, Hotspur represents, like Falstaff, an unbalanced attitude toward life. He lives only for battle and identifies himself entirely with his reputation for military valor. His rhetoric grows windy on the subject, as in 1.3.199–206 and 4.1.112–123. As his wife, Lady Percy, tells us in 2.3.48–63, he even fights battles in his sleep. Utterly single-minded, he rejects even sex, declaring that "this is no world to play with mammets, and to tilt with lips" (2.3.92–93).

Hotspur's impetuosity makes him as much a liability as an asset to his allies. He has no control over his emotions, letting his enthusiasm for honor dominate all other considerations; his own father calls him "a wasp-stung and impatient fool" (1.3.233). At Shrewsbury, messengers present a steady procession of reasons for caution, as the rebel fortunes grow increasingly uncertain, but Hotspur's response is almost ludicrously inappropriate: "Come, let us take a muster speedily— / Doomsday is near; die all, die merrily" (4.1.133–134). His foolish refusal to wait for reinforcements condemns his cause to defeat; he is so overwrought at the approach of battle that he cannot even read his despatches, saying that life is too short to waste on such petty activity. Hotspur's impulsiveness is evident even in minor details of his speech—e.g., in his habit of interrupting himself, as in 1.3.155–184. Characteristically, he dies in mid-sentence. However, he is not merely a stock emblem of fiery and foolish chivalry; he displays intelligence, humor, and high spirits, and he has a loving wife whose affection emphasizes his humanity.

The historical Hotspur was as celebrated—and evidently as vain and foolish—as Shakespeare's character, and the play presents his role at Shrewsbury accurately, except in two important respects. First, his death in the battle cannot definitely be attributed to Hal, or to anyone else. Second, and more significant, he was not Hal's contemporary, being in fact older than King Henry. The alteration in his age serves to make him a more satisfying foil to Prince Hal, but at the time of Shrewsbury, when Hal was 16, Hotspur was a veteran soldier of 39, having been a famous warrior on the Scottish border—where he won the nickname Hotspur—for more than 20 years. The alteration in Hotspur's age is established in *Richard II*, in which young Percy, who becomes Hotspur, is introduced as a boy.

A theatrical tradition of playing Hotspur as a stutterer—an effective indication of his excitability—seems to have arisen in 19th-century Germany, where the respected translator SCHLEGEL interpreted Lady Percy's recollection of her husband's "speaking thick" (*2 Henry IV*, 2.3.24) as stammering. Shakespeare may have been referring to his Northumbrian dialect or, more likely, to his habit of speaking rapidly. In any case, there is no record concerning the historical Hotspur's speech.

Hotspur's son, another Henry Percy, was still a boy when first his father and then his grandfather were killed fighting against King Henry. Prince Hal, upon his accession as King Henry V, pardoned young Percy and permitted him to resume the family title. As a result, he fought for Hal's son, Henry VI; he was the Earl of Northumberland whose death in the first battle of ST. ALBANS is reported in 1.1.4–9 of *3 Henry VI*. His son and successor, Hotspur's grandson, appears as Henry Percy, Earl of Northumberland, later in that play.

Lady Mortimer, Catherine (active 1403–1409) Historical figure and character in *1 Henry IV*, daughter of Owen Glendower and wife of Lord Mortimer. Lady Mortimer speaks only Welsh (with the consequence that her lines are dropped from many productions of the play) and must converse with her husband through the interpretation of her father. Glendower reports that she is upset that her husband is leaving for battle and that she is likely to cry. Through him, she asks her husband to lie in her lap while she sings to him. She sings in Welsh, to the amusement of the fiery Hotspur, in an episode that lends humanity to the rebel cause. It is thought that the scene may have been prompted by the presence of actors from WALES in the CHAMBER-LAIN'S MEN, one of whom played Lady Mortimer.

Practically nothing is known of the historical Lady Mortimer. She is thought to have died in London after being taken prisoner when her father was defeated and her husband killed at Harlech in 1409.

Lady Percy, Elizabeth (1371–ca. 1444) Historical figure and character in *1* and *2 Henry IV*, wife and then widow of Hotspur. In 2.3 of *1 Henry IV* Lady Percy is distressed that her husband apparently intends to return to war. She playfully attempts to extract his plans from him, but he teasingly refuses to tell her. In 3.1, just before Hotspur departs for SHREWSBURY, she joins him. He affectionately teases her about her refusal to sing while Lady Mortimer serenades her husband. He finds another target in her mild oath "in good sooth" (3.1.240), and he fondly scorns her temperance. These episodes reveal that the fiery Hotspur, whose rivalry with Prince Hal is the play's major theme, is also a loving husband who has plainly inspired affection in his wife. Hotspur's warm relationship with his wife complements the fierce fixation with battle that otherwise dominates our picture of him. Without these scenes, Hotspur might seem so one-dimensional that we could not accept the favorable opinion of him held by King Henry IV and Hal.

Lady Percy also displays a personality of her own, that of a modest, possibly somewhat stiff, but spirited and pleasant young matron.

In 2.3 of *2 Henry IV* Lady Percy makes a single appearance, joining her mother-in-law, Lady Northumberland, in persuading Lord Northumberland not to rejoin the revolt. Lady Percy bitterly observes that the elderly lord had failed to assist the rebels when Hotspur was still alive, and she goes on to eulogize her late husband glowingly.

Lady Percy's name in Shakespeare's source, HOLINSHED's *Chronicle*, is given inaccurately as Elianor, but Hotspur calls his wife Kate. Shakespeare was decidedly fond of this name—he frequently used it, perhaps most notably for Katherina in *The Taming of the Shrew*—and he may have regarded it as an affectionate nickname for a woman, regardless of her real name.

Lancaster, Prince John of (1389–1435) Historical figure and character in *1* and *2 Henry IV*, son of King Henry IV and brother of Prince Hal. (The same figure appears in *Henry V* and *1 Henry VI* as the Duke of Bedford.) In *1 Henry IV* Lancaster first appears in Act 5 at the battle of SHREWSBURY, where his energy and valor are praised by the king and Prince Hal. He speaks only five lines, but his presence heralds his greater role in *2 Henry IV*. In that play he negotiates a truce with the rebels led by the Archbishop, only to seize the unsuspecting leaders once they have disbanded their troops. This treachery is followed by Lancaster's self-righteous utterance, "God, and not we, hath safely fought today" (4.2.121). Then, in 5.5.97–101, he sanctimoniously praises Hal's rejection, as King Henry V, of Falstaff.

Lancaster is portrayed as an uncompromisingly cold, calculating, humorless man. Falstaff says of him, ". . . . this same young sober-blooded boy doth not love me, nor a man cannot make him laugh; but that's no marvel, he drinks no wine" (*2 Henry IV*, 4.3.85–88). He presents an extreme alternative to Falstaff's irresponsibility. But although Falstaff is a far more attractive character, Shakespeare clearly felt that Hal's course as king must lie closer to Lancaster. Prince John's ruse at GAULTREE FOREST is not disparaged in the play. Such ploys were common in late medieval warfare, and neither Shakespeare's sources nor the playwright himself treat it as particularly heinous when compared to the much greater crime of rebellion against an anointed ruler.

Shakespeare inaccurately depicts the historical Prince John. His presence in *1 Henry IV* is fictional; he was only 13 years old at the time of Shrewsbury, and he does not appear in Shakespeare's sources until several years later. However, in addition to preparing for *2 Henry IV*, Shakespeare wished to bring the LANCASTER FAMILY together at a point of crisis. Also, the 16-year-old Lancaster was not responsible for the negotiations at Gaultree; as Shakespeare knew, they were conducted by Ralph Neville, Earl of Westmoreland. The playwright wished to attach this maneuver to King Henry's family, thus focusing on the web of treachery and conflict that followed Henry's usurpation of the throne (enacted in *Richard II*). John was not Duke of Lancaster—Hal bore that title, in fact—but Shakespeare's sources were confused on this point, and the playwright doubtless thought he was correct. The historical Prince John was a successful military leader who achieved distinction against the Scots and who later, as Bedford, helped govern the kingdom when Henry VI was a minor.

Messenger   Any of several minor characters in *1 Henry IV* who bring messages to Hotspur. A Messenger informs Hotspur of his father's illness on the eve of the battle of SHREWSBURY in 4.1. Two more Messengers appear in 5.2, just before the battle, in an episode that heightens the excitement of the occasion. One brings letters that Hotspur, in his agitation, refuses to read, and the second brings word that King Henry IV's army is approaching.

Michael, Sir   Minor character in *1 Henry IV*, friend of the Archbishop of York. In 4.4 the Archbishop and Sir Michael discuss the rebels' likely defeat against King Henry IV at SHREWSBURY. The episode introduces the Archbishop's subsequent further rebellion against the King, to be enacted in *2 Henry IV*.

No historical Michael is known among the Archbishop's associates. Sir Michael's presence in the play may reflect a lost source that the playwright consulted, or he may be Shakespeare's invention.

Mistress Quickly   See Hostess.

Monmouth, Harry (Henry Monmouth)   Another name for Prince Hal, later King Henry V (see Prince of Wales, Henry). Both as prince and king, this character is occasionally called Harry or Henry Monmouth, after his birthplace on the Welsh border (e.g., *1 Henry IV*, 5.4.58; *2 Henry IV*, 2.3.45; *1 Henry VI*, 2.5.23).

Mortimer, Edmund (1376–1409)   Historical figure and character in *1 Henry IV*, a rebel against King Henry IV. Originally an army commander for the King, Mortimer's capture by Owen Glendower is reported in 1.1. However, the king learns that Mortimer has married Glendower's daughter, and he refuses to ransom him. This becomes a bone of contention between the king and Hotspur—whose wife, Lady Percy, is Mortimer's sister—as the revolt begins. Mortimer appears at the rebels' council of war in 3.1, where he proves to be a moderate negotiator among more difficult personalities. He attempts to maintain amity between Hotspur and Glendower. He tries to control Hotspur's temper, and he forthrightly defends his father-in-law against the firebrand's slurs. Mortimer can only speak to his bride, now Lady Mortimer, through the translations of her father, for he speaks no Welsh and she no English. Nevertheless, he sentimentally asserts his love for her in an episode that lends humanity to the rebel cause.

Following errors in his sources, Shakespeare confused Mortimer with his nephew, another Edmund Mortimer, who was Earl of March and thus an heir to the English throne. The rebels speak of his claim several times (e.g., in 1.3.142–157 and 4.3.93–95) in making the case for their fight against Henry. Although an explicit intention to place him on the throne if their rebellion succeeds is not mentioned, Mortimer is to receive England in the division of the kingdom contemplated at the war council.

The historical Mortimer had supported Henry's usurpation of the crown several years earlier, which Shakespeare depicted in *Richard II*, although Mortimer does not appear in that play. The rebels of 1403, depicted in *1 Henry IV*, intended to place the younger Mortimer on the throne, and this Mortimer acted in support of his nephew, as well as for Glendower. After SHREWSBURY, Mortimer and Glendower were pursued by the king, as Henry stipulates he will do in 5.5.40, and Mortimer died in the unsuccessful defense of Glendower's capital at Harlech in 1409.

Northumberland, Earl of See Northumberland, Henry Percy, Earl of, in *Richard II*.

Oldcastle Original name of Falstaff in *1* and *2 Henry IV*. Shakespeare called one of Prince Hal's companions Sir John Oldcastle, following his source, *The Famous Victories of Henry the Fifth*. In THE FAMOUS VICTORIES Oldcastle speaks very little and does not resemble his successor in any important way. Shakespeare simply took over the name and applied it to his own creation, the extraordinary figure we know as Falstaff. Soon after writing the plays (1596–97), the playwright changed the name of the character, evidently in response to protests from William Brooke, Lord COBHAM, a descendant of the historical John Oldcastle. The name was changed before *1 Henry IV* was registered for publication, in early 1598, for Falstaff is referred to in its subtitle at that time. (The names Harvey and Rossill were also changed in this text for similar reasons.)

Several traces of the name Oldcastle survive in the plays. For example, the alteration from three syllables to two produces anomalies in the METER at several points (e.g., in *1 Henry IV*, 2.2.103). There are more overt clues as well: In *1 Henry IV*, 1.2.41, Falstaff is called "old lad of the castle"; in the QUARTO edition of *2 Henry IV* (1600), a single speech prefix (1.2.119), inadvertently uncorrected, retains the name Oldcastle; in *2 Henry IV*, 3.2.25, Falstaff is said to have been a page to Thomas Mowbray, which is thought to have been true of the historical Oldcastle. Moreover, the EPILOGUE to *2 Henry IV* specifically dissociates Falstaff from the historical Oldcastle. Also, another play, SIR JOHN OLDCASTLE was produced by the ADMIRAL'S MEN in 1599, clearly in response to the popularity of Falstaff. It presented the life of Oldcastle in a glowing light, and it opened with a prologue drawing an express distinction between its hero and Shakespeare's character. (Oddly, this play was published as Shakespeare's work by William JAGGARD in the FALSE FOLIO of 1619, and it later appeared in the third and fourth FOLIO editions of Shakespeare's work.)

The historical Oldcastle (ca. 1375–1417) had been a friend of Prince Hal. His surname referred to a family estate on which there was a ruin, probably of a Roman fort. The extent to which Oldcastle was involved in the prince's youthful excesses is unknown. He converted to Lollardy, a proto-Protestant religious movement, was convicted of heresy in 1413, and imprisoned. He escaped and led an unsuccessful religious rebellion against Hal, now King Henry V, and was captured and executed in 1417. After the Reformation, Oldcastle came to be regarded as a Protestant martyr and was held in great respect by the strict English Protestants, becoming known, in Shakespeare's time, as Puritans. That Shakespeare applied the name of a Lollard hero to a criminally debauched character seems to reflect his satirical disapproval of the growing Puritanism in English life.

Despite the name change, the association of Oldcastle with Shakespeare's celebrated reprobate lingered. The name Oldcastle was sometimes used in 17th-century performances of *1* and *2 Henry IV* despite Shakespeare's alteration, and in several other writings of the period the name appears as a humorous reference to the vices we associate with Falstaff.

Ostler Minor character in *1 Henry IV*, groom at an inn. The Ostler shouts his one brief line from offstage, lending an impression of hectic activity to the inn yard depicted in 2.1.

Peto Minor character in *1* and *2 Henry IV*, a follower of Falstaff. Peto participates in the highway robbery in 2.2 of *1 Henry IV*, and he later tells Prince Hal how Falstaff attempted to disguise his cowardice. In 2.4 of *2 Henry IV* Peto brings the Prince news of King Henry's preparations against the rebellion, stirring Hal to action.

Peto was originally given the name Harvey, but the name was changed after early performances, probably to avoid offending a prominent aristocrat, William HARVEY. (See also Oldcastle; Rossill, Sir John.)

Poins, Ned Character in *1* and *2 Henry IV*, friend of Prince Hal. Poins suggests the two jokes that he and Hal play on Falstaff. In *1 Henry IV*, 1.2.156–185, he devises the plan to rob Falstaff of his takings in the highway robbery of 2.2, and in *2 Henry IV*, 2.2.164–165, he proposes that he and the Prince disguise themselves as Drawers and spy on Falstaff. He also participates in the Prince's joke on Francis in 2.4 of *1 Henry IV*. In 2.4 of *2 Henry IV*, Falstaff, unaware of Poins's presence, describes him, insulting but with considerable accuracy, in a hilarious presentation of a rowdy, empty-headed party boy (2.4.241–250). In 2.2.42 Poins demonstrates his blindness to Prince Hal's true character, expecting him to be pleased at the imminent death of his father, King Henry IV. But in 2.2.61–65 he is conscious of his position as part of the world of delinquency that the Prince must reject, and he accepts his own limitations.

Poins is Shakespeare's version of a character named Ned in THE FAMOUS VICTORIES, his chief source for the material on Hal's riotous early life. His last name may refer to the lace ribbons, known as points, that were a prominent feature of a 16th-century courtier's elaborate garb.

Prince of Wales, Henry (Prince Hal, later King Henry V) (1387–1422) Historical figure and character in *1* and *2 Henry IV*, the oldest son of King Henry IV. The central concern of the *Henry IV* plays is Prince Hal's preparation for assuming the throne. (He appears as the king in Act 5 of *2 Henry IV* and as Henry V in *Henry V*.) The Prince must find his way between two undesirable extremes—anarchy and obsessiveness—represented, respectively, by the irresponsible debauchery of Falstaff and the exaggerated sense of honor of the war-loving Hotspur. In neither play is the Prince the most prominent character, but Hotspur in *Part 1* and Falstaff in both plays derive their importance from their relationship to the Prince. In *Part 1* the Prince becomes a chivalric hero by conquering Hotspur, though he remains friendly with Falstaff. In *Part 2* he integrates himself more fully into the world of statecraft, assumes the throne upon his father's death, and makes the final, irrevocable break with Falstaff in his famous "rejection" speech in 5.5.

The comparison of Hal and Hotspur is foreshadowed in *Richard II*, when Hotspur, then known as Percy, tells of Hal's disreputable life among harlots in London (5.3.13–19). In *1 Henry IV* the dissolute Prince is contrasted with the valorous Hotspur. However, Hal assures his father that "the time will come" (3.2.144) when he will conquer Hotspur. Significantly, the Prince does not have to change his character to arrive at this resolution, for he is conscious of his destiny from the outset. As he makes clear in his famous "reformation" speech (1.2.190–212), he intends to fulfill his inherited duties. He simply chooses to remain in EASTCHEAP until "being wanted he may be more wonder'd at" (1.2.196). Once Hal has asserted his readiness to assume his proper position as Prince when the time comes—and of course, Shakespeare and his original audiences were very much aware of Hal's future success as Henry V—the ground is laid for the climactic hand-to-hand combat in which the Prince kills Hotspur.

Shakespeare took care to have Hal spurn some of the temptations offered by Falstaff, as when he rejects the old man's lascivious suggestions about a barmaid in 1.2.46. The playwright thus establishes that the Prince is not the reckless and vicious playboy of the well-known farce *The Famous Victories of Henry the Fifth* (see FAMOUS VICTORIES, THE), but rather a good king in the making.

The essential question of the *Henry IV* plays is Can a ruler successfully combine cold-blooded political skills with the spiritual values that derive from social contacts and appreciation of one's fellows? Hal's development take place in the irresponsible world of Eastcheap because the Machiavellian world of King Henry cannot nurture humane values. At the BOAR'S HEAD TAVERN, however, Prince Hal learns about the lives of ordinary people, and he knows that this education has a purpose. "When I am King of England, I shall command all the good lads in Eastcheap," he says in 2.4.13–14. At the same time, the Prince is learning about himself as well. He places himself in different contexts: highway robbery in 2.2 of *Part 1* and menial service in 2.4 of both plays. In the mock drama he enacts with Falstaff in 2.4 of *Part I*, he even samples the role of king. In Eastcheap the Prince is free to make mistakes, to take positions he will later reject—in short, to learn.

In *Part 1*, although Hal plans to forsake Eastcheap life at some point, he still participates fully in it. He rejects duty in favor of pleasure, sending Falstaff to dispose of the king's messenger, and when the rebellion against his father is introduced, he boldly suggests, in the callous manner of a soldier, that a campaign brings the opportunity to "buy maidenheads . . . by the hundreds" (2.4.358–359). His merriment in the same scene includes a disrespectful charade of his father. While he does go to SHREWSBURY and defeats Hotspur, the battle seems to be only an interval in his life with Falstaff. At the end of the fighting, he is ready to corroborate Falstaff's lie about his courage "with the happiest terms I have" (5.4.156).

However, as his kingship draws closer, the Prince avoids Falstaff. In *Part 2* Hal returns to Eastcheap only once. The Prince arrives in LONDON from the battlefield in 2.2, and the uproarious tavern scene (2.4) closes with his being called back to action. Falstaff's world is now an interlude for the Prince, rather than a primary focus. Moreover, his exchange with Falstaff is more hostile than friendly; he does not accept Falstaff's bantering excuses, as he has in the past, and Hal departs with only a cool "Good night, Falstaff." Therefore, when, as Henry V, Hal coldly spurns Falstaff in 5.5, we have no reason to be surprised.

Prince Hal's rejection of Falstaff is often considered callous and unfair, but in its historical context it may be seen as both necessary and relatively mild. Falstaff's behavior is downright criminal in both plays—in fact, the scenes dealing with his corrupt recruitment of troops (*1 Henry IV*, 4.2; *2 Henry IV*, 3.2) were designed as incriminating satires of contemporary practices—yet Hal merely dismisses him with a pension. (The imprisonment imposed by the Chief Justice—to an institution reserved for aristocrats—was understood by the playwright and his audience to be lenient and temporary.) While Hal can be thought to be rejecting part of his humanity in order to make himself fit for power, he is in fact simply adopting a different humanity, that of his weary father. In *Henry V* the new king will apply the capacity for fellowship he has learned in Eastcheap; first, in *2 Henry IV*, he becomes a king.

The crucial moment of Hal's development, and the climax of *2 Henry IV*, is Hal's encounter with his dying father in 4.5. Addressing the crown as it lies beside the king, Hal recognizes the burden that kingship demands and he accepts that burden, emphasizing his decision by placing the crown on his own head. Henry, thinking that Hal has selfishly desired his death in order to wear the crown, delivers an impassioned speech on the dangers England will face once his son is king, crying, "The wild dog shall flesh his tooth on every innocent" (4.5.131–132) and regretting the collapse of the order he has striven to preserve. This speech asserts powerfully, if negatively, the value of social discipline. After Hal has sworn loyalty to his father— and, implicitly, to the values just expressed—the king advises that Hal keep would-be opponents busy with overseas wars. This militarist solution— honorable in Shakespeare's world, though reprehensible in our own—is related to Henry's view of a ruler's basic duty, the maintenance of order and the avoidance of civil war. The Prince accepts this lesson and receives his father's wishes for a peaceful reign and a final blessing (4.5.219).

Shakespeare altered Hal's biography to suit his dramatic ends. Hal is introduced as an adult at a time when he was only 12 years old, as part of the playwright's strategy of presenting him and Hotspur as contemporaries, though Hotspur was in fact a generation older. Also, Hal did not fight Hotspur at Shrewsbury; the rebel died at the hands of an anonymous warrior. Shakespeare may have believed that the two heroes had met—his sources are ambiguous—but he would surely have had them do so in his play, even if they had not historically done so, to enhance the play's impact.

Prince Hal's wild life was evidently real, for contemporaries recorded his conversion to good behavior upon being crowned. It was reported that the Prince was given to drunken brawling—and even gang warfare—in Eastcheap. Shakespeare and his contemporaries believed in the truth of a tradition that Hal had hit the Chief Justice and been imprisoned for it, but since this story cannot be traced earlier than 1531 (to an account that omits physical assault), its authenticity is dubious. A more reliable early account stated that Hal had robbed his own agents on the highway; a later version changed the victims to bearers of the king's money. Shakespeare omitted a striking anecdote, well known to the Elizabethans, that is probably true: Hal, perhaps in a spirit of atonement, approached his father wearing a dog collar and a strange garment with many needles sewn to it. This mystifying story has never been explained, and Shakespeare may have simply found it too distracting to use. Hal's unwise wearing of his dying father's crown came from Shakespeare's sources, but it is quite plainly apocryphal.

In any event, reports of "wild Prince Hal" probably reflect only isolated incidents, and not a committed way of life, in the youth of a privileged and high-spirited soldier. Certainly, much of the Prince's energy was devoted to serious military training, for he fought in WALES beginning in 1400, and he was considered competent at the age of 16 to command a wing of Henry's army at Shrewsbury. He governed part of Northumberland shortly thereafter, and he served in increasingly important offices over the next eight years. In 1411 Hal was dismissed from the king's council, an event that is alluded to in *1 Henry IV,* 3.2.32, where it is associated with the supposed assault on the Chief Justice. In fact, it appears that King Henry suspected his son of treasonous disloyalty; a reconciliation was effected a year later, not long before Henry's death, and this appears to be the germ of the reconciliation scenes in the plays.

Rossill, Sir John (Sir John Russell) Original name of Bardolph in *1* and *2 Henry IV.* When the name Bardolph was substituted for Rossill, shortly after the plays were written in 1596–97, several occurrences of the original name inadvertently remained in the early texts of the plays, revealing that the change had taken place. Since the 18th century these references have also been altered in most editions. The change of name was made at the same time that Oldcastle became Falstaff—at the insistence of Lord Cobham, a descendant of the historical Oldcastle—presumably in the hope of avoiding a similar problem with another prominent aristocrat, William Russell, Earl of Bedford (ca. 1558–1613). (See also Peto.)

Servant Minor character in *1 Henry IV,* a member of Hotspur's household. In 2.3 Hotspur summons the Servant to question him about the availability of a new horse. This brief episode helps quicken the pace of a scene—otherwise involving only the nobleman and his wife—that points to the forthcoming military crisis of Hotspur's rebellion.

Sheriff Minor character in *1 Henry IV,* a policeman who investigates the highway robbery committed by Falstaff. The Sheriff, who has a witness who knows Falstaff, accepts Prince Hal's word that Falstaff is not present at the inn and that the Prince will guarantee the return of any stolen money; he then leaves.

Traveller Either of two minor characters in *1 Henry IV,* victims of highway robbery at the hands of Falstaff and others in 2.2. The Travellers are presumably the Kentish franklin and the auditor described to Gadshill by the Chamberlain of the inn in ROCHESTER in 2.1.52–59.

Vernon, Richard (d. 1403) Historical figure and character in *1 Henry IV,* a supporter of Hotspur. Vernon arrives at the rebel camp before the battle of SHREWSBURY with news that the King's armies are approaching. He describes Prince Hal's forces in a speech (4.1.97–110) famous for its vivid imagery. In 4.3 he advises vigorously against Hotspur's insistence on entering battle before his reinforcements arrive, and in 5.1 he participates, with Worcester, in the negotiations that precede the battle. Captured in the battle, he is sentenced to death by King Henry IV in 5.5.

The historical Vernon, a powerful magnate of Cheshire, in western England, was in fact captured and beheaded at Shrewsbury, although he was not a participant in the negotiations between the two sides.

Vintner Minor character in *1 Henry IV,* an employee of the BOAR'S HEAD TAVERN. The Vintner appears only briefly, in 2.4, to chasten Francis and announce the arrival of Falstaff. He contributes to the atmosphere of a busy tavern.

Westmoreland, Ralph Neville, Earl of (1364–1425) Historical figure and character in *1* and *2*

Henry IV and *Henry V*. In *1* and *2 Henry IV* Westmoreland is a loyal adviser to King Henry IV, though he is rather faceless. In 1.1 of *1 Henry IV* he brings grave news of military setbacks, introducing the unrest that besets Henry's reign. He later appears briefly at the battle of SHREWSBURY. In *2 Henry IV* Westmoreland is again a solid supporter of the king, defending Henry against the rebellious noblemen's claims of mistreatment. In 4.2 he seconds Prince John of Lancaster in his fraudulent offer of a truce to the rebels at GAULTREE FOREST, and he arrests the leaders after they have unsuspectingly sent their troops home. In 4.4 he brings news of the final defeat of the rebels, closing the history of revolts against Henry.

In *Henry V* Westmoreland has a minor role and is notable only for expressing a wish for reinforcements just before the battle of AGINCOURT, provoking King Henry V's famed "St. Crispin's Day" speech (4.3.18–67). The historical Westmoreland was not present at Agincourt, having been placed in command of the Scottish border. His more prominent role in the *Henry IV* plays reflects his historical position more accurately, though here, too, Shakespeare altered reality. Westmoreland backed Henry Bolingbroke, later Henry IV, in his deposition of Richard II, although Richard had granted him his earldom. He served the new king loyally, as the plays show. It was he who actually tricked the rebel leaders at Gaultree, not Prince John, who was a youth at the time. Shakespeare de-emphasized Westmoreland in order to keep the focus on Henry's family.

Westmoreland married twice and fathered 16 children, and several of his descendants appear in Shakespeare's plays. By his first wife he was the grandfather of the Earl of Westmoreland who appears in *3 Henry VI*; by the second he was the father of the Earl of Salisbury of *2 Henry VI* and grandfather of the Earl of Warwick, known as the "kingmaker," of *2* and *3 Henry VI*.

Worcester, Thomas Percy, Earl of (1343–1403) Historical figure and character in *1 Henry IV*, Hotspur's uncle and a leader of the rebels against King Henry IV. Worcester is presented as a malevolent figure who introduces the idea of rebellion against

Henry, beginning in 1.3.185, and formulates its strategy later in the same scene. In 5.2, in an illustration of the evil that attends rebellion, Worcester destroys the rebels' last chance for peace on the eve of the battle of SHREWSBURY by concealing Henry's offer of amnesty, fearing that in a state of peace, the king would single him out for punishment. Although his efforts to control Hotspur's impetuosity in 4.1 and 4.3 show that Worcester well understands the likelihood of catastrophe in the coming battle, he calculatingly permits his cause to court defeat because his personal interest may be at stake. After the battle, in which he is captured, Henry sentences him to death, and he justifies himself, saying, "What I have done my safety urg'd me to" (5.5.11).

Shakespeare followed his primary historical source, Raphael HOLINSHED, in presenting a perfidious Worcester. Modern scholarship finds the truth unclear, but, while Worcester was certainly a leader of the revolt, he was probably not its instigator. He was in fact executed after Shrewsbury, but the tale of the negotiations is probably untrue. On the day of the battle it was apparently Henry who broke off the talks and began fighting. Before the time of the play, Worcester had served ably in the government of King Richard II, who had made him an earl in 1397. Two years later he allied himself with Henry Bolingbroke when he usurped the crown and became Henry IV (as is enacted in *Richard II*; although Worcester does not appear in that play, his actions are described in 2.2.58–61 and 2.3.26–30).

Henry IV, Part 2
SYNOPSIS

Induction

A personification of Rumour announces that he has put forth a false report, following the victory of King Henry IV at the battle of SHREWSBURY— where Prince Hal has killed the rebellious Hotspur—that the king and Prince were killed and the rebels were victorious. This report, Rumour says, is now reaching WARKWORTH CASTLE, home of Hotspur's father, the Earl of Northumberland.

Act 1, Scene 1

Lord Bardolph brings Northumberland the false news of Hotspur's victory; however, Travers appears with two reports, one corroborating Lord Bardolph's account and the other telling of Hotspur's death and the rebels' defeat. Morton, an eyewitness, arrives to confirm the truth of the second story. In addition, he says that the victorious king has sent troops, under the Earl of Westmoreland and Prince John of Lancaster, to capture Northumberland. The earl rages madly, but his followers counsel calm; the revolt may still be alive. Morton says that the Archbishop of York has raised a rebel army to avenge the death of King Richard II, whom Henry deposed and murdered. Northumberland begins to make plans for the renewal of the war.

Act 1, Scene 2

Falstaff jests about the comical disparity between his own huge bulk and that of his diminutive Page (1). He encounters the Chief Justice, who upbraids him for having refused to answer a summons, observing that, although Falstaff's service at Shrewsbury has allowed earlier offenses to be overlooked, he must behave better in the future. Falstaff wittily dismisses this warning. The justice attempts to shame the old man for his foolishness, but to no avail. The knight asks to borrow money from the justice, who leaves. Falstaff then sends the Page with letters to the Prince, Lancaster, Westmoreland, and a woman whom he says he has promised to marry. Complaining of his gout, he declares that a limp will prove useful: he will seem to have been wounded in the war and will get a bigger pension.

Act 1, Scene 3

The rebels, led by the Archbishop, lay their plans. Lord Bardolph advises that they postpone action until they can be sure of Northumberland's support. Lord Hastings, however, argues that the King's forces are divided, facing threats from the French and the Welsh as well as from themselves, and suggests that the rebels launch their campaign at once. The Archbishop agrees, citing the turn of public opinion against Henry, and they leave to assemble their forces.

Act 2, Scene 1

The Hostess of the BOAR'S HEAD TAVERN enlists the officers Fang and Snare to arrest Falstaff for debt, but when they try to do so, he and his friend Bardolph draw their swords and prepare to fight. The furor brings the Chief Justice and his men. He asks the Hostess to explain her claim, and she states that Falstaff has proposed to her, in addition to owing her a great deal of money. Falstaff says that the Hostess is insane, but the Chief Justice insists that he recompense her. Falstaff speaks to the Hostess in private, and he wheedles another loan from her, along with a promise of dinner. The Chief Justice receives word that immediate preparations for battle against the rebels are being made.

Act 2, Scene 2

Prince Hal jests with Poins, but when Poins twits him for not displaying sadness at his father's illness, the Prince observes bitterly that his dissipated life has left him with such a bad reputation that a show of melancholy could only be taken for hypocrisy. Bardolph and Falstaff's Page arrive with a saucy letter from the knight to Hal. The Page (1) reports that Falstaff is dining with the Hostess and a harlot, Doll Tearsheet; the Prince and Poins concoct a plot to surprise him at his meal by disguising themselves as Drawers.

Act 2, Scene 3

Lady Percy and Lady Northumberland try to dissuade Northumberland from joining the rebel armies. He pleads his duty, but Lady Percy reminds him that he failed to assist his own son, her late husband, Hotspur, whom she eulogizes. Humiliated, the Earl agrees to flee to Scotland.

Act 2, Scene 4

At the Boar's Head, the Hostess, Doll Tearsheet, and Falstaff banter drunkenly. Pistol arrives and makes so much noise that Falstaff drives him away. The Prince and Poins, disguised, overhear Falstaff's assertions that they are inconsequential louts. When Hal confronts Falstaff, the fat knight says that he had disparaged the noblemen only in order to protect them from the ignominy of finding themselves admired by such wicked sorts as Doll and the Hostess, Peto appears with news that the king's army is urgently assembling. The Prince, conscience-stricken that he was indulging himself, hurries away. A further summons arrives for Falstaff, and he departs as well.

Act 3, Scene 1

King Henry sends a Page (2) with letters to the Earls of Surrey and Warwick. He reflects on his heavy responsibilities, which keep him awake at night while his subjects sleep. Warwick and Surrey arrive and attempt to calm him, but he morosely speaks of the inevitable ravages of time and recalls the prophecy of Richard II (in *Richard II*, 5.1) that Northumberland would rebel. Warwick remarks that Northumberland's essentially false nature made such an outcome inevitable, and the observation restores Henry to a sense of the necessity for action. Warwick assures the king that the rebellion seems under control, for the Welsh leader Glendower's death has been reported.

Act 3, Scene 2

The country justices Shallow and Silence leisurely await the arrival of the king's army recruiter, Falstaff, for whom they have assembled a group of villagers. Shallow reminisces windily on his student days in LONDON, where he knew Falstaff. Falstaff appears with Bardolph and comically interviews the potential soldiers, selecting several for enlistment before adjourning for a drink with the justices. Bardolph collects bribes from two of the recruits, and upon Falstaff's return tells him which ones are to be released from duty, Falstaff justifies his choice of the least likely recruits in a humorous parody of military standards. After promising another visit, Falstaff leaves. In a soliloquy he asserts that on his return he shall fleece the gullible Shallow.

Act 4, Scene 1

In GAULTREE FOREST the Archbishop tells his fellow rebels that Northumberland has deserted. Westmoreland appears and demands an explanation for the rebellion. The Archbishop asserts that the illness of the realm requires that they take up the role of surgeons. Westmoreland states that Lancaster, the commander of the king's army, is prepared to hear their grievances during a period of truce. Mowbray is opposed to this offer, but the Arch-

bishop states their complaints against the king, and Westmoreland leaves. Mowbray asserts that the king will always distrust them and that they should continue to pursue victory, for only then can they be safe. The Archbishop and Hastings, however, argue that Henry genuinely desires peace.

Act 4, Scene 2

Lancaster meets the rebels and promises to redress all their grievances if they will disband their forces. The Archbishop and Hastings agree, but Westmoreland arrests them once their forces have dispersed. Lancaster says that he had promised only that their grievances would be redressed, not that they themselves would be pardoned, and he sentences them to death.

Act 4, Scene 3

Falstaff encounters a rebel officer, John Colevile, who recognizes him and surrenders. Falstaff transfers his prisoner to Lancaster, who sends Colevile to be executed. Lancaster announces that he must go to London, where his father, King Henry, is very sick. Lancaster grants Falstaff permission to return through Gloucestershire, and he leaves. Alone, Falstaff reflects that he cannot make the unconvivial Lancaster laugh because the prince does not drink. In a long, humorous soliloquy he praises strong drink, saying that it both improves the wit and warms the spirit. He asserts that Prince Hal is courageous only because the cold blood he inherited from King Henry has been heated by his drinking.

Act 4, Scene 4

The dying King Henry is attended by his younger sons, the Dukes of Gloucester and Clarence, and by Warwick. Learning that Prince Hal is at his old haunts in London, the King rails against his dissipated son. Warwick defends Hal, asserting that he is merely studying the ways of evil men, the better to judge them as king. News arrives of the final defeat of the rebels, but the king suddenly feels much weaker and is taken into a bedroom.

Act 4, Scene 5

Prince Hal arrives and watches alone at his sleeping father's bedside. He addresses the royal crown, declaring that the cares and stress it represents have killed the king. Believing that his father has died, the Prince meditatively puts on the crown and absently wanders from the room. The king awakes and assumes that Hal has demonstrated an impatience to see him dead. When the Prince is found, weeping in another room, the king predicts dire disorder for England when he succeeds to the throne. The Prince explains why he took the crown and prays for the return of the king's health. The king, convinced, expresses his pleasure with the Prince and offers him advice. Having become king only through usurpation, Henry says he had made enemies. While the Prince, inheriting the crown, will be more widely accepted, he will still have some of the same enemies. The king recommends overseas wars to divert the would-be rebels and to provide an arena in which Hal can prove his valor and undo his sullied reputation. The others return, and the king asks to be taken back to the JERUSALEM CHAMBER, where he wishes to die.

Act 5, Scene 1

Shallow, with the help of his steward Davy, prepares to entertain Falstaff with a dinner. Before accompanying his host indoors, Falstaff belittles his intended victim.

Act 5, Scene 2

Warwick and the Chief Justice regret the death of the king and the accession of the delinquent Prince. The Chief Justice expects trouble, for he once jailed the Prince. The Prince, now called Henry V, arrives, and he suggests that the Chief Justice may regret that incident. The jurist defends his action, however, asserting the rule of law. Hal agrees and reappoints him to his post, vowing to mend his ways and become a proper king.

Act 5, Scene 3

After dinner Shallow, Silence, and Falstaff drink together in Shallow's orchard. Shallow is drunkenly hospitable, and Silence sings snatches of various songs. Pistol arrives from London with word that the king has died. Falstaff, assuming that Hal, now king, will provide richly for his old friends, makes haste to go to London and claim his fortune. He

promises Shallow and Pistol all they desire, and he vows vengeance on the Chief Justice.

Act 5, Scene 4

The Hostess and Doll Tearsheet are under arrest, having apparently been involved in a murderous tavern brawl. They revile the Beadle who arrested them, but to no avail.

Act 5, Scene 5

Falstaff and his entourage, including Shallow, attend the coronation parade. Falstaff boasts that the new king will welcome him, but when Hal appears, he rejects the old man, promising him a pension but requiring him to live at least 10 miles from court. Falstaff assures Shallow that the king has only put on a public front and will send for him later that night. Shallow is dubious. The Chief Justice, accompanied by Lancaster, arrives and sends the entire group to prison, pending their expulsion from London. Lancaster expresses satisfaction with Hal's kingly behavior and predicts that the new king will lead a military expedition to France.

Epilogue

A speaker, identifying himself as the author, apologizes for a recent unpopular play and hopes that this one has been more satisfactory. He then speaks of himself as a dancer whose performance may make up for the play's defects. He promises that another play featuring Falstaff will continue the story. In closing he observes that Falstaff does not represent the martyr Oldcastle.

COMMENTARY

Henry IV, Part 2 is concerned with the demands of kingship, although Falstaff plays a much greater role than he did in *Part 1*. From the INDUCTION and 1.1, with their emphasis on the disruptions of rebellion, to the close, when Prince Hal assumes the heavy mantle of kingship as Henry V, the lessons of *2 Henry IV* are political. Hal rejects Falstaff in 5.5, the final scene, and this incident symbolizes the ethic of a ruler: strict justice, though tempered by mercy.

To an even greater degree than in *Part 1*, Shakespeare here presents a picture of all England—the common people who underlie history as well as the aristocrats who make it. Palace chambers and battlefields are set against dissolute EASTCHEAP and bucolic GLOUCESTERSHIRE. In addition to several familiar Eastcheap denizens from *Part 1*, Shakespeare here presents two other extraordinary figures: the Ancient Pistol and Doll Tearsheet. In Gloucestershire, rural England is represented by Justice Shallow and a number of splendid countrymen, including Davy and Silence. In assembling these citizens, *2 Henry IV* continues the unprecedented achievement of *Part 1*, the creation of a comprehensive sense of the diverse life of England in the context of key historical events.

As in *Part 1*, Prince Hal's development is central to the history being presented, though here he becomes a statesman rather than a warrior. However, he is an unimportant character until 4.5, when he meditates on and accepts the burden of kingship. Then, having become king in Act 5, he accepts the Chief Justice, a symbol of honesty and duty, and rejects Falstaff, an emblem of irresponsibility. Hal is committed to becoming a good king, and this is the end to which the rest of the play leads as well, but the focus of the dramatic action is elsewhere, on values opposed to good government, represented by Falstaff on one hand and the rebels on the other.

Falstaff makes quite a different impression than he did in *1 Henry IV.* He is older and in bad health, as he remarks in 1.2.229–233; the prospect of his death looms, as Doll reminds him in 2.4.229–232. He is more distinctly and unpleasantly a swindler, preying on Shallow and the Hostess and sending Feeble and his fellows to their probable deaths; in *Part 1* his robbery victims were the anonymous— and supposedly rich and powerful—Travellers, and his soldiers remained unseen. Further, he justifies his selfishness in *Part 2* with a flagrantly cynical appropriation of "the law of nature" (3.2.326). He thus seems singularly ripe for a downfall.

The groundwork for Hal's rejection of Falstaff in 5.5 was laid in *Part 1*, and it is anticipated throughout *Part 2*. Falstaff's awkward encounters with the Chief Justice in 1.2 and 2.1 foreshadow this end. In addition, Hal is conspicuously absent from Falstaff's early scenes; their only encounter prior to 5.5 is Hal's somewhat hostile appearance at Falstaff's tavern party in 2.4, which ends with

the Prince's cursory farewell to his old friend as he leaves to help suppress the rebellion. Hal shows no interest in Falstaff's world after that point. But after the new king so coldly and firmly dismisses him, Falstaff persists in supposing that Hal is only putting up a public front, although by this time, even the gullible and unsophisticated Shallow sees the truth. Falstaff's rejection comes as no surprise to anyone but himself. His folly in leaping boldly into Hal's coronation scene only seals his fate. His lack of judgment is, of course, the fundamental reason why he is not acceptable company for a king.

It has often been contended that one's response to Hal's rejection of Falstaff reflects one's attitude toward Shakespeare's political sensibility, perhaps toward all political philosophy. According to this theory, the extent to which one sympathizes with Falstaff, who represents comic license and freedom, limits the value that one can simultaneously place on social order. This view, however, not only denies Shakespeare's breadth of vision, which encompassed both freedom and order, but, more important, it also depends on a more sentimental outlook than that of the 16th century. The playwright's plain purpose was to bring Falstaff to a reckoning and to complete the elevation of Prince Hal to his intended destiny as the just King Henry V.

Shakespeare is clearly more sympathetic to the fat scoundrel than the Prince is, for Falstaff is still intended as an essentially delightful character. His inventive humor is still appealing; as he says himself, "I am not only witty in myself, but the cause that wit is in other men" (1.2.8–9). In his famous praise of wine (4.3.84–123), Falstaff compares himself favorably to the cold and calculating Lancaster, and we are irresistibly inclined to agree with him. At the end of 2.4 the Hostess and Doll Tearsheet touchingly show their affection for him, although they are fully aware of his nature. His ways may bar him from being close to a responsible ruler, but they do not prevent others from appreciating his high spirits. Shakespeare's fondness for Falstaff is further demonstrated by the remarkable leniency with which the new king treats him, however frostily Hal may address him. He is allowed to live as he pleases, with a comfortable pension; clearly, the playwright did not wish to deprive his remarkable creation of sack and capons. Moreover, as the EPILOGUE indicates, Shakespeare intended to bring him back in another play. Falstaff is very much a part of Shakespeare's England and thus of the historical context within which the play's political questions are set.

The rebellion of the nobles is at the political core of *2 Henry IV*. The threat of social disorder runs through all the HISTORY PLAYS, and in *2 Henry IV* it manifests itself both in the petty crimes of Falstaff and in the more grievous offense of the rebels. Rebellion is cast in a highly negative light. Northumberland's apocalyptic rage in 1.1.153–160 demonstrates the anarchic morals of the rebel leaders, who are willing to permit society to collapse. And to stress his worthlessness, Northumberland is presented as treacherous to his own treacherous cause in the Induction (lines 36–37) and in 2.3. Morton describes, in 1.1.200–209, the Archbishop's sacrilegious use of religion to stimulate armed revolt; Westmoreland elaborates on the Archbishop's particular guilt in 4.1.30–52. However, Shakespeare rarely settled for a single viewpoint on any subject, and the Archbishop makes a plainly sincere response to Westmoreland, in which he states the dilemma of the royalist who nevertheless is provoked into rebellion by misgovernment. Here and in 4.2.30–42, he offers to disband the rebel forces if his complaints are heard by the king, and it is precisely this that is promised when Lancaster deceives and traps the rebel leaders.

Nonetheless, the playwright thoroughly disparages the rebels, and it is striking that he does not similarly deplore Lancaster's treachery against them. Such a scheme, common enough in the histories Shakespeare read, seems acceptable in the play's terms, because it works against the greater evil of the uprising. It may also serve as an example of the woeful state of public life amid the dynastic struggles that dominate most of the history plays. The rebellion itself is a continuing reminder of King Henry's situation: He is a usurper, under whom the nation cannot be calm. He himself observes this several times (e.g., 3.1.57–79, 4.5.183–186), and in dying he takes comfort that Hal, a legitimate heir, will not encounter the same difficulty.

The play's focus on political turmoil is sharpened by several secondary themes, the most impor-

tant of which is the unreliability of human knowledge. This motif is repeatedly stressed. At the play's outset, Rumour summons a baffling array of "surmises, jealousies, conjectures" (Ind. 16) that humanity must face. Among the false impressions that pervade the play are the king's fear that Hal will prove a disastrous heir, Falstaff's contrary assumption that he will prove a delightful one, the rebels' expectation of aid from Northumberland, and their betrayed hopes at Gaultree. The Archbishop seems entirely justified in his plaint "What trust is in these times?" (1.3.100). Only Prince Hal is aware—from the beginning of *1 Henry IV*—that his own position will be regal. He alone is free of misunderstanding, as befits his ultimate heroic stature as Henry V.

Recurrent references to disease and death add to the atmosphere of urgent uncertainty. Both the king and his rival, Northumberland, are physically ill, and the king's fatal sickness is particularly prominent. Falstaff, as we have seen, encounters his mortality as well: Hal notices his white hairs and says that his "grave doth gape" (5.5.53). Henry says of his kingdom, "How foul it is, what rank diseases grow" (3.1.39), and the Archbishop constructs an elaborate metaphor on the diseased nation, asserting the need to "purge th' obstruction which begin to stop / Our very veins of life" (4.1.65–66).

Animal imagery, a favorite device of Shakespeare's, serves to represent the brutal energy of civil disruption: the Archbishop likens the fickle public to a dog eating its own vomit in 1.3.95–100; Northumberland speaks of the civil conflict as "a horse [that] madly hath broke loose, and bears down all before him" (1.1.9–11). And, when the king paints a hysterical picture of England under the rule of a profligate Hal, he says, "the wild dog / Shall flesh his tooth on every innocent" (4.5.131–132).

Political realities prohibit any festive, comic resolution of *2 Henry IV*. Even Hal's succession to the throne, while an optimistic conclusion to the conflicts that have married his father's reign, is not a consummation; rather, it points onward to the wars of Henry V. The several worlds that are juxtaposed in *2 Henry IV*—fictional versus historical, aristocratic versus plebeian, urban versus rural—are each disturbed by political events. Their rich interactions yield a convincing portrait of difficult times, pertinent in the nervous Elizabethan era when fears of rebellion pervaded political thought, and no less relevant in our own troubled time.

SOURCES OF THE PLAY

Shakespeare's chief source for the historical material in *2 Henry IV* was Raphael HOLINSHED's *Chronicles of England, Scotland, and Ireland* (2nd ed., 1587), modified by the account of Henry's reign in Samuel DANIEL's epic poem *The Civil Wars between the two Houses of York and Lancaster* (1595). In particular the playwright was influenced by Daniel's elaborate treatment of Henry's deathbed and of his guilt as a usurper. In addition, in developing the Chief Justice, who is merely mentioned in his other sources, Shakespeare drew either on John STOW's *Annales of England* (1592), where he found an account of Hal's encounters with the jurist, or on Stow's source, Thomas ELYOT's *The Boke called the Governour* (1531). Additional details seem to have come from the anonymous farce known as THE FAMOUS VICTORIES (before 1588) and from the life of Owen Glendower in the popular anthology of biographies A MIRROR FOR MAGISTRATES (1559). It has been suggested that both *Henry IV* plays may have been derived from an earlier play by Shakespeare on the same subject, but this speculation is unprovable.

TEXT OF THE PLAY

The composition of *2 Henry IV* can be dated only approximately. The play was probably begun early in 1597 and completed before the end of 1598. The revised Epilogue refers to *Henry V*, while the version used in the earliest productions does not. We may assume, therefore, that *2 Henry IV* was in performance before *Henry V* was begun, in the spring of 1599. The survival of the name Oldcastle in the QUARTO edition of the play indicates that Shakespeare had at least begun the play before this name was changed to Falstaff. This alteration followed the first production of *1 Henry IV* in the winter season of 1596–97.

A Quarto edition of *2 Henry IV* was published in 1600 by Andrew WISE and William ASPLEY. Printed by Valentine SIMS, this edition, known as Qa, omitted 3.1. Later, the same individuals published Qb, a reprint of Qa that included the missing scene; although the large number of surviving copies of Qa suggests that it was in circulation for some time before Qb was printed, that interval is unknown. The 1600 Quarto (Q) is considered to consist of Qa plus 3.1 from Qb. Q evidently derives from Shakespeare's FOUL PAPERS; in addition to the usual imperfections of detail associated with foul papers, Q includes the strange spelling Scilens, for the character Silence, an idiosyncrasy that helps to identify the "Hand D" pages of *Sir Thomas More* as Shakespearean. No other edition of the play was published prior to the FIRST FOLIO of 1623 known as F.

Because it was derived from Shakespeare's manuscript, Q has been the basic text for modern editions, but it is supplemented by material available only from F. Eight Folio passages, ranging in length from 3 to 36 lines, are not found in Q. Some of these apparent cuts in Q may have been intended to shorten the performing time of the play; others may imply CENSORSHIP. The Folio editors took this material from an unknown source, possibly a PROMPTBOOK, that itself probably derived from Q plus a now-lost manuscript, perhaps the same one that Q was originally printed from. F varies from Q in other ways: many words and phrases are different, its punctuation is greatly reworked, and its stage directions are almost entirely altered and improved.

In addition to the published texts, there exists a 17th-century handwritten copy of a play that combines *1* and *2 Henry IV*, the DERING MANUSCRIPT. With respect to *2 Henry IV*, it derives from Qb. Because it includes minor details from the Folio versions of both plays, it is dated 1623–24. Its variations from the published texts are not thought to reflect either alterations by Shakespeare or the practices of early productions, and modern editions do not follow it.

THEATRICAL HISTORY OF THE PLAY

The Quarto of *2 Henry IV* (1600) states that it had been "sundrie times publikely acted" by the CHAMBERLAIN'S MEN, and several references to its characters in various writings of the early 17th century testify that it continued to be staged. The earliest known record of a specific performance is of Thomas BETTERTON's adaptation of 1700 (revived 1720), *The*

Sequel of Henry the Fourth. As this title suggests, *2 Henry IV* has generally been less popular than *1 Henry IV*, which has been produced much more frequently. In the 1720 revival Colley CIBBER was a great success as Shallow, a part he took in another adaptation that was staged in 1731 and 1736.

The play was relatively popular throughout the 18th century, and numerous adaptations appeared, frequently in conjunction with *Part 1*. James QUIN played Falstaff several times, and David GARRICK played Henry IV. King George II (incognito) played Henry in a public performance of 1753, to the scandal and delight of London. Theophilus CIBBER played Pistol in his own adaptation, *The Humourists* (1754). The play was produced as part of George III's coronation ceremonies in 1761 (and W. C. MACREADY revived this production for the coronation of William IV in 1821). In 1804 J. P. KEMBLE played Henry IV opposite his brother Charles KEMBLE as Hal; Charles took the same role in Macready's coronation production. In 1853 Samuel PHELPS revived Betterton's version of the play, appearing as both the king and Shallow, a widely acclaimed virtuoso accomplishment. Phelps revived this version again in both 1864 and 1874; in the latter production the young Johnston FORBES-ROBERTSON played Hal. Another revival of 1874, by Charles CALVERT, was scrupulously Shakespearean.

In the 20th century *2 Henry IV* was often produced as part of the numerous cycles of the history plays that have been popular, notably those at STRATFORD in 1906, 1951, and 1964. Ralph RICHARDSON's performances as Falstaff in a 1945–46 production of both *Henry IV* plays were particularly admired. Several history cycles on TELEVISION since the 1950s have included *2 Henry IV*. A 1987 London production demonstrated the continuing popularity of the *Henry IV* plays; both parts, along with *Henry V*, were staged on different nights of the week, and, most strikingly, theatergoers responded with enthusiasm to marathon Saturday performances featuring all three works in succession. In 2000 the ROYAL SHAKESPEARE COMPANY again staged both *Henry IV* plays.

CHARACTERS

Archbishop of York, Richard Scroop See Archbishop of York, Richard Scroop, in *Henry IV, Part 1*.

Bardolph, Lord Thomas (1368–1408) Historical figure and character in *2 Henry IV*, a follower of the Earl of Northumberland and a rebel against King Henry IV. He is invariably referred to as Lord Bardolph to distinguish him from Bardolph, who appears in the same play. Lord Bardolph brings Northumberland a mistaken report of a rebel victory in 1.1, and he helps to encourage the crestfallen Earl after the real news arrives. In 1.3 he urges caution on his fellow rebels, Lord Hastings and the Archbishop of York, who insist on challenging the king. Although he then disappears from the play, the defeat of Lord Bardolph and Northumberland is reported in 4.4; he thus seems associated with Northumberland's betrayal of the rebel cause.

The historical Lord Bardolph, like the historical Northumberland, did not desert the rebellion. He fought with distinction and died in battle several years after GAULTREE FOREST.

A speech prefix in the QUARTO edition of the play (1600) indicates that Lord Bardolph's part in 1.1 was originally written for Sir John Umfrevile, another follower of Northumberland's, whose part was assigned to Lord Bardolph in order to reduce the number of actors required.

Beadle Any of several minor characters in *2 Henry IV*, petty London officials assigned to whip the Hostess and Doll Tearsheet. In 5.4 the Beadles drag the two women across the stage. One of them speaks, remarking that the punishment has been decreed because the women have been involved in a murder. Both women insult the chief Beadle, referring to his skeletal appearance. In the QUARTO edition of the play, a stage direction identified this Beadle as John SINCKLO, a very thin actor, and it is presumed that Shakespeare wrote this scene with him in mind.

Blunt, Sir John (d. 1418) Historical figure and minor character in *2 Henry IV*, an aide to Prince John of Lancaster. Blunt appears only once and says nothing; he is assigned to guard the captive Colevile (4.3.73). Blunt was also mentioned in two stage directions in the QUARTO edition of the play (1600), but these references are absent in the FIRST FOLIO (1623) and have generally been omitted since. It is speculated that this alteration may reflect minor cuts made for an early production, perhaps by Shakespeare himself. The historical John Blunt was a minor courtier, the son of Walter Blunt, who appears in *1 Henry IV*.

Bullcalf, Peter Minor character in *2 Henry IV*, one of the men whom Falstaff recruits for the army in 3.2. Bullcalf claims to be ill, despite the robust appearance his name suggests, but he is recruited anyway. However, his friend Ralph Mouldy secures release for them both by bribing Corporal Bardolph. The episode satirizes the notoriously corrupt practices of 16th-century recruiters.

Chief Justice, Lord Character in *2 Henry IV*, the highest-ranking judicial officer of England. The Chief Justice chastises Falstaff twice. In 1.2 he observes that only Falstaff's success at the battle of SHREWSBURY has kept him from being prosecuted for the highway robbery at GAD'S HILL in *1 Henry IV*, and he warns the knight against continuing his dissolute life. In 2.1 he orders Falstaff to repay a debt to the Hostess. In both cases the Chief Justice has enough intelligence and humor to appreciate Falstaff's wit and to recognize that the fat knight cannot be cajoled into an honest life, but his own sense of public morality urges him to make the attempt.

In 1.2.55–56 Falstaff's Page calls the Chief Justice "the nobleman that committed the Prince for striking him about Bardolph," referring to an earlier imprisonment of Prince Hal. In 5.2, after the death of Henry IV, the Chief Justice expects to find the new king vengeful, but when he defends his action, noting that he was right to follow the law irrespective of the offender's rank, the former prince approves entirely and confirms him in his office. The young king asserts that he will be guided by the justice, and when he rejects Falstaff in 5.5, his formal diction seems to reflect the judge's influence. The Chief Justice later implements Hal's decision to banish Falstaff.

The story of Hal's assault on the Chief Justice was part of the popular legend of "wild Prince Hal": He is said to have been reprimanded by the justice for seeking a favorable ruling on behalf of a delinquent acquaintance, whereupon he struck the

judge and was jailed for it; as in the play, he maintained the justice in office upon becoming Henry V. However, this tale is almost surely fictitious; the earliest written reference to any such event did not appear until 1531, more than a century later, in Thomas ELYOT's *The Boke named the Gouernour*. Moreover, Elyot reports no assault, merely the Justice's reprimand, which the Prince accepted meekly. The assault and incarceration occur only in THE FAMOUS VICTORIES, a 16th-century farce that has no historical validity whatsoever. Shakespeare doubtless knew this, but the tale was too dramatic to waste. The Chief Justice of Hal's day, unnamed in the play or in any of Shakespeare's sources, was Sir William Gascoigne (ca. 1350–1419), a distinguished jurist who had long served King Henry IV, having been his attorney when he was in exile as Henry Bolingbroke (as enacted in *Richard II*). As King Henry's chief legal officer, Gascoigne had presided over the sentencing and execution of the rebels captured at GAULTREE, although Shakespeare does not associate him with this event in the play.

Clarence, Thomas, Duke of (1388–1421) Historical figure and minor character in *2 Henry IV* and *Henry V*, son of King Henry IV and younger brother of Prince Hal. In *2 Henry IV* Clarence receives advice from his dying father on dealing with Hal after he succeeds to the throne. In *Henry V*, although he receives a command from the king in 5.2.84, he does not reply, nor is he named in the stage directions or the dramatis personae in most editions of the play.

The historical Clarence was an important figure in the regimes of his father and brother. A young governor of Ireland in the first years of Henry IV's reign, Clarence replaced Hal on the king's council when the latter was dismissed in 1411, and he led a successful military expedition in GASCONY in 1412. Late in the reign of Henry V, Clarence was killed in battle in FRANCE.

Colevile of the Dale, Sir John (Sir John Coleville of the Dale) (d. 1405) Historical figure and minor character in *2 Henry IV*, a rebel knight captured by Falstaff. After the rebels have been tricked into dispersing without a battle,

Colevile peaceably surrenders to Falstaff, who makes much of his own valor as he turns his prisoner over to Prince John of Lancaster. Lancaster sends Colevile to be executed. The episode provides a comical glimpse of Falstaff in the long and otherwise entirely political Act 4.

Shakespeare took Colevile's name from HOLINSHED, who lists him among the executed rebels, but it is possible that Colevile was pardoned and lived to be recorded as Sir John Colvyl, who fought in FRANCE with Henry V.

Davy   Character in *2 Henry IV*, steward to Justice Shallow. In 5.1 Davy makes the necessary arrangements when Falstaff visits Shallow and conducts ordinary business—seeing to minor repairs, planting, paying the blacksmith, and so on—at the same time. As a typical resident of GLOUCESTERSHIRE, he is part of the play's delightful presentation of English country life. On behalf of his friend William Visor, Davy asks his master for a favorable ruling in a lawsuit, offering a humorous look at small-time legal chicanery. At Shallow's drinking party in 5.3, Davy manages to function as host, guest, and servant.

Doll Tearsheet   Character in *2 Henry IV*, referred to in *Henry V*, lover of Falstaff. Doll joins Falstaff at his uproarious dinner at the BOAR'S HEAD TAVERN in 2.4. She is clearly a prostitute, but her affection for Falstaff is more than commercial. Although they fight with gusto, Doll's sentimental fondness for the fat knight is evident. She invokes their long-standing friendship in a hard world: "Come, I'll be friends with thee, Jack, thou art going to the wars, and whether I shall ever see thee again or no there is nobody cares" (2.4.64–66). He feels comfortable enough with her to admit, "I am old, I am old," and she assures him, "I love thee better than I love e'er a scurvy young boy of them all" (2.4.268–270). When Falstaff departs to join the troops, Doll is genuinely upset, unable to speak for tears.

In 5.4 Doll and the Hostess are arrested for their involvement in a murder, and Doll's capacity for invective and deceit comes to the fore as she berates the Beadle while claiming a fictitious pregnancy, potentially useful in court. This episode emphasizes the criminality of Falstaff's world and indicates a change in the lax moral climate that has existed in LONDON, foreshadowing the crucial scene in which Prince Hal rejects Falstaff.

Doll was a name conventionally applied to prostitutes. Moreover, as other allusions in 16th- and 17th-century literature make clear, Doll's last name is also related to her profession, implying vigor in its practice. In *Henry V* Pistol says that Doll is in the hospital with a venereal disease (2.1.74–77), and her death is reported in 5.1.85.

Drawer   Any of several minor characters in *2 Henry IV*, servants at the BOAR'S HEAD TAVERN. In 2.4 the Drawers, who "draw" wine from casks for their customers, prepare for Falstaff's dinner party. They enjoy an anecdote in which Prince Hal taunts Falstaff about his age, and they plan for entertainment with a musician named Sneak. Among their number is Francis, who also appears in *1 Henry IV*. The Drawers present one of the many glimpses of working-class life in the *Henry IV* plays.

Falstaff, Sir John   See Falstaff, Sir John, in *Henry IV, Part 1*.

Fang   Minor character in *2 Henry IV*, a constable who attempts to arrest Falstaff for debt. In 2.1 the Hostess employs Fang and his assistant, Snare, to arrest the fat knight, but when Falstaff and his companion, Bardolph, draw their swords, the officers are helpless. The Chief Justice appears and resolves the situation without their assistance. Fang's name, which in Elizabethan English meant "snare" or "trap," is appropriate to his function, if not to his abilities.

Feeble, Francis   Minor character in *2 Henry IV*, one of the men whom Falstaff recruits for the army in 3.2. Feeble is selected over hardier men who bribe their way out of service, and Falstaff justifies the choice by saying that Feeble will be useful in retreat, being already inclined to run. However, Feeble is willing to fight if he has to, saying, "I will do my good will, sir, you can have no more" (3.2.155), and ". . . he that dies this year is quit for the next" (3.2.233). Feeble gives his occupation as a "woman's tailor," which gives rise to ribaldry: "tailor" was Elizabethan slang for the genitals, male or female.

Francis   See Francis, in *Henry IV, Part 1*.

Gloucester, Humphrey, Duke of   See Gloucester, Humphrey, Duke of, in *Henry VI, Part 1*.

Gower   Minor character in *2 Henry IV*, a messenger. In 2.1 Gower brings the Chief Justice a report that King Henry IV and Prince Hal have returned to London from fighting rebels in WALES, and he answers the judge's questions about military news. His knowledge suggests that he is in the army, but there is no other evidence to link him with Captain Gower in *Henry V* and he is generally regarded as a different character.

Groom   Any of two or three minor characters in *2 Henry IV*, servants who strew the London streets with rushes in preparation for the crowds attending Prince Hal's coronation as Henry V. Their presence at the opening of 5.5 sets the scene. They are identified as two Grooms in the FOLIO edition of the play, and as three Strewers in the QUARTO edition; modern editions vary.

Hal, Prince   See Prince of Wales, Henry, in *Henry IV, Part 1*.

Harcourt   Minor character in *2 Henry IV*, a messenger. In 4.4 Harcourt brings King Henry IV news that Lord Bardolph and the Earl of Northumberland have been defeated, thus ending the rebellion that began in *1 Henry IV*.

Hastings, Lord Ralph (d. 1405)   Historical figure and character in *2 Henry IV*, a rebel against King Henry IV. An ally of the Archbishop of York, Hastings makes several errors of judgment, first advocating that the rebels proceed against the King despite the desertion of Northumberland and then, when they find themselves outnumbered at GAULTREE FOREST, recommending that they accept the peace offered by Prince John of Lancaster. Lancaster's offer proves treacherous, and Hastings and the other rebels are arrested and sentenced to death. The historical Hastings was a minor nobleman of northern Yorkshire.

Henry IV   See Henry IV, King of England, in *Henry IV, Part 1*.

Henry V   See Prince of Wales, Henry, in *Henry IV, Part 1*.

Hostess   See Hostess, in *Henry IV, Part 1*.

Lady Northumberland (Margaret Neville) (d. ca. 1400)   Historical figure and character in *2 Henry IV*, the wife of the Earl of Northumberland. In 2.3 Lady Northumberland and her daughter-in-law Lady Percy plead with the earl not to join the rebels against King Henry IV. He bows to their pressure and flees to Scotland. The incident demonstrates the weakness of Northumberland's allegiance. The historical Lady Northumberland died some time before the period of the play, but Shakespeare revived her in order to create a situation in which family loyalties oppose political ones. She was a sister of the Archbishop of York, a relationship that Shakespeare ignored.

Lady Percy   See Lady Percy, Elizabeth, in *Henry IV, Part 1*.

Lancaster, Prince John of   See Lancaster, Prince John of, in *Henry IV, Part 1*.

Messenger   Minor character in *2 Henry IV*, a soldier. In 4.1 the Messenger brings the rebel leaders a report that the army of Prince John of Lancaster is approaching.

Mistress Quickly   See Hostess, in *Henry IV, Part 1*.

Monmouth, Harry   See Monmouth, Harry, in *Henry IV, Part 1*.

Morton   Minor character in *2 Henry IV*, follower of the Earl of Northumberland and rebel against King Henry IV. In 1.1 Morton arrives at WARKWORTH CASTLE with an eyewitness report—settling a distressing uncertainty—that the rebels have lost the battle of SHREWSBURY and that the Earl's son, Hotspur, has been killed by Prince Hal. He then joins with Lord Bardolph in rousing Northumberland from the despair this news causes him. In doing so, Morton announces (1.1.187–209) the plans of the Archbishop of York, whose continuation of the rebellion will provide the central action of the rest of the play. Morton's account presents rebellion in terms of subverted religion that help to establish the play's disapproving attitude toward revolt (although Morton himself, as a rebel, finds it acceptable).

Mouldy, Ralph   Minor character in *2 Henry IV*, a countryman enlisted by Falstaff in his capacity as an army recruiter in 3.2. After joking about his name, Falstaff drafts Mouldy over the man's objections. However, once recruited, Mouldy bribes Corporal Bardolph to secure his own release from service, along with that of his friend Peter Bullcalf.

Mowbray, Thomas, Lord   (1386–1405)   Historical figure and character in *2 Henry IV*, a rebel against King Henry IV. An ally of the Archbishop of York and Lord Hastings, Mowbray argues against accepting the peace offered by Prince John of Lancaster at GAULTREE FOREST in 4.1, but he is ignored. When Lancaster's offer proves treacherous, in 4.2, Mowbray is arrested with the others and sentenced to death. The historical Mowbray, not yet 20 years old when he was executed, was the son of Thomas Mowbray, whose quarrel with Henry Bolingbroke, later to become Henry IV, was enacted in *Richard II*.

Musicians   Minor characters in *2 Henry IV*. In 2.4 the Musicians, led by Sneak, perform for Falstaff at his drunken dinner with the Hostess and Doll Tearsheet at the BOAR'S HEAD TAVERN.

Northumberland, Earl of   See Northumberland, Henry Percy, Earl of, in *Richard II*.

Page (1)   Character in *2 Henry IV*, Falstaff's attendant. For the most part, the Page simply performs routine tasks and says little. However, in 2.2, where he bests Bardolph in a battle of wits and is rewarded with money by Prince Hal and Poins, the Page saucily comes into his own, in the manner of the pert young pages in the plays of John LYLY, whose works were well known to Shakespeare.

The Page's diminutive stature is frequently referred to in humorous terms by the other characters; e.g., in 1.2.1, he is a "giant"; in 2.2.82, an "upright rabbit"; in 5.1.55–56, "my tall fellow." It is thought that these references, with others in other plays, reflect the presence of a particularly small boy

actor (see ELIZABETHAN THEATER) in the CHAMBERLAIN'S MEN, for whom Shakespeare wrote the play. The same character appears in *The Merry Wives of Windsor* as Robin and in *Henry V* as the Boy.

Page (2)   Minor character in *2 Henry IV*, a servant of King Henry IV. The Page, who does not speak, carries messages for the King in 3.1.

Perkes, Clement   GLOUCESTERSHIRE countryman named in *2 Henry IV*, a legal adversary of Davy's friend William Visor of Woncot. Davy, the steward of Justice Shallow, asks his master to rule in Visor's favor in his lawsuit against "Clement Perkes a'th'Hill" (5.1.35), in a glimpse of rural corruption that is part of the play's depiction of English manners and mores. Perkes is thought to represent someone Shakespeare knew, a member of a family named Purchase or Perkis that lived near Woodmancote, the play's "Woncot," in an area traditionally called "the Hill."

Peto   See Peto, in *Henry IV, Part 1*.

Pistol   Character in *2 Henry IV*, *The Merry Wives of Windsor*, and *Henry V*, a braggart soldier and follower of Falstaff. The comical Pistol serves as Falstaff's aide in King Henry IV's campaign against the rebels in *2 Henry IV*. He first appears at Falstaff's dinner party at the BOAR'S HEAD TAVERN in 2.4, and he offends everyone present with grandiose insults while asserting his chivalric honor with distorted snatches of rhetoric from Elizabethan drama and literature. This vigorous mode of address is Pistol's principal attribute in all of his appearances. To some extent, Pistol satirizes military pretensions, but his rhetoric is more pointedly a literary parody; Shakespeare exaggerates the florid language of Marlowe and his followers. Pistol is called an ancient; ancient, or ensign (standard-bearer), is a military rank, the equivalent of lieutenant, which Bardolph calls Pistol in *Henry V*, 2.1.38. Pistol may actually be an ancient, or he may have simply appropriated the title, for part of his absurdity is his singular unsuitability for command.

Like the 16th-century sidearm for which he is named, Pistol is violently loud but incapable of serious damage. Also, the pistol was commonly associated, in Elizabethan humor, with the penis; much is made of this in *2 Henry IV*, 2.4.109–135. When the QUARTO edition of *2 Henry IV* was published in 1600, its subtitle made particular reference to Pistol, whose appeal was already recognized, and he has been among Shakespeare's most popular characters ever since. His extravagant rhetoric makes him hilarious even to audiences for whom the original parodies are meaningless.

In *The Merry Wives* Pistol is again in Falstaff's entourage (apparently as a civilian), but he refuses to deliver his master's love letters, rejecting the task as unsoldierly, and Falstaff fires him. He and Nym seek revenge, and they inform Ford and Page that Falstaff has designs on their wives, thereby triggering the principal SUBPLOT of Ford's jealousy. Pistol is insignificant thereafter, although he does appear in the final MASQUE-like scene, disguised as a fairy. This may simply reflect the employment of the actor who played Pistol in another role, but Pistol's appearance in character might have been taken by 16th-century audiences as a clue to the ceremonial nature of the scene, in which personality is wiped out.

In *Henry V*, Pistol mourns the passing of Falstaff with his new wife, the Hostess, whom he has presumably dazzled with his extravagant braggadoccio. Once on campaign in France, he proves himself a coward in 3.2; following this episode, the Boy remarks on the villainy of Pistol, Nym, and Bardolph. In 3.6 Pistol pleads unsuccessfully for Fluellen's intercession on behalf of Bardolph, who has been sentenced to death for looting; in 4.1 he is one of the soldiers whom the incognito King Henry V encounters the night before the battle of AGINCOURT, though he has little to say, merely making a nasty remark about Fluellen.

In 4.4 Pistol captures a French Soldier and demands ransom of him, threatening to kill him otherwise. Since he speaks no French and the soldier no English, the scene is comical, but Pistol is unquestionably an unpleasant character, vicious and overbearing. The Boy acts as interpreter, saving the soldier's life, and he remarks afterward of Pistol, "I did never know so full a voice issue from so empty a heart" (4.4.69–70). Pistol is last seen in 5.1, where Fluellen forces him to eat a leek. The last survivor of Falstaff's followers, Pistol in *Henry V* serves to show that the anarchic element represented by Falstaff is finally rendered both harmless and completely disreputable. On the other hand, Pistol may also be seen as a symbolic parallel to King Henry's militarism: He satirizes notions of military honor, while most of the combat actually presented involves Pistol at his most degenerate. Most strikingly, his threat to kill his prisoner in 4.4 foreshadows Henry's own order that "every soldier kill his prisoners" (4.6.37).

It is thought that Falstaff appeared in an early, unacted version of *Henry V* and was then excised by Shakespeare, with remnants of his part going to Pistol, who displays Falstaffian characteristics in several scenes, particularly 5.1. This theory cannot be proven, but it is supported by textual evidence.

Porter Minor character in *2 Henry IV*, gatekeeper at WARKWORTH CASTLE, home of the Earl of Northumberland. The Porter admits Lord Bardolph in 1.1. At the outset of the play, he embodies ordinary lives amid the doings of the aristocracy, an important aspect of the play.

Prince of Wales, Henry See Prince of Wales, Henry, in *Henry IV, Part 1*.

Rumour Allegorical figure in *2 Henry IV*, the speaker of the INDUCTION (Ind.). Rumour serves as a CHORUS and introduces the play. Rumour wears a costume "painted full of tongues" (Ind. 1, stage direction) and represents a medieval tradition ultimately derived from a passage in VIRGIL's *Aeneid*, written in the first century B.C. An unpleasant figure full of scorn for human credulity, he describes his own potential to cause disruption and states that he is now going to give the Earl of Northumberland the false news that the rebels against King Henry IV, led by the Earl's son, Hotspur, have won the battle of SHREWSBURY. Act 1 then commences with Northumberland's receipt of this news.

Rumour serves three functions. First, he recounts that Henry has won the battle and that there remain other rebels, under Northumberland, who are still active. Then, in asserting that Northumberland has missed the battle by being "crafty-sick" (Ind. 37), he introduces the idea that treachery infects the rebel cause, part of the play's unfavorable presentation of revolt. Most significantly, Rumour, introduces the idea that uncertainty cannot be avoided, saying, "which of you will stop the vent of hearing when loud Rumour speaks?" (Ind. 1–2). This pessimistic proposition reflects the play's dark mood and is an underlying element of the play's message that order must be maintained in society.

Shadow, Simon   Minor character in *2 Henry IV*, one of the men whom Falstaff recruits for the army in 3.2. Simon Shadow is extremely thin, and much is made of the appropriateness of his name. While hardier men bribe their way out of service, Falstaff justifies his choice of Shadow by observing that he will be as hard for a marksman to hit as "the edge of a penknife" (3.2.262). It is thought that Shadow was originally played by John SINCKLO, an exceptionally thin actor who was among the CHAMBERLAIN'S MEN, the company for whom Shakespeare wrote the play.

Shallow, Robert   Character in *2 Henry IV* and *The Merry Wives of Windsor*, a GLOUCESTERSHIRE Justice of the Peace. A garrulous old man who thinks himself sophisticated but is in fact very gullible, the Shallow of *2 Henry IV* is a perfect victim for Falstaff's exploitation. Given to lying about his youthful adventures with Falstaff and pluming himself on his status as a justice, he is somewhat ridiculous. As Falstaff remarks in a soliloquy at 3.2.296–322, he remembers the youthful Shallow as a laughingstock, and he is certainly a comical figure in old age. However, he is never simply laughable, despite Falstaff's elaborate and comically uncomplimentary description. Upon their initial appearance, Shallow and his cousin Silence seem amusingly empty-headed as their conversation shifts from the deaths of old acquaintances to the price of livestock in 3.2.1–52, but while the exchange is a tour de force of subtle comedy, the characters are also movingly human: two old men whose minds wander as they confront mortality. Shallow's age and something more of his earlier life are mentioned in 3.2.205, where Silence remarks that it

was "fifty-five year ago" that Shallow entered Clement's Inn, a law school. Supposing him to be about 20 years old at that time, we see that he is about 75 at the time of the play. Clement's Inn, as Shakespeare's audience will have known, was an institution similar to the INNS OF COURT but less socially and intellectually elite. As his capacities in old age suggest, he was not accepted by the top law schools in youth. Such a circumstantial biography helps make Shallow a real person and not simply a comic butt.

Throughout the play, Shallow is a sympathetic character. He presents the pleasant world of the small landowner in *2 Henry IV*'s remarkable panoply of English scenes, hosting Falstaff and his men with a bountiful dinner of home-grown food. His incautious friendship is repaid when he is jailed along with Falstaff in 5.5, when Falstaff is banished by Prince Hal.

In *The Merry Wives*, although Shallow is more prominent and appears in far more scenes than in *2 Henry IV*, he is less strikingly drawn. He is the avuncular promoter of a marriage between his dim-witted young relative Slender and the desirable Anne Page. Also, seconding the Host in 2.1, 2.3, and 3.1, he helps avert the duel between Evans and Caius, in a SUBPLOT that contributes to the play's conciliatory quality.

As *The Merry Wives* opens, Shallow—making pompous claims of aristocratic ancestry—threatens a lawsuit against Falstaff; this suit is immediately forgotten in the play, and it is sometimes thought that its purpose was solely to link the laughable country justice with some real person whom Shakespeare had disputed with and was now making fun of (see GARDINER, WILLIAM; LUCY, THOMAS). However, this is highly questionable, and the episode's peculiarly truncated quality probably reflects the haste with which the play was apparently written, or perhaps it survives from a lost play sometimes hypothesized as a source for *The Merry Wives*.

Silence   Character in *2 Henry IV*, a rural justice of the peace, cousin of Justice Shallow. Silence, as his name suggests, says very little. In 3.2 he clearly admires his cousin's youthful career as "lusty Shallow" (3.2.15), and he politely responds to Shallow's remarks. In 5.3, at Shallow's delightful garden party, Silence comes to life under the influence of wine: Six times he breaks into SONG—two of these excerpts are from known 16th-century ballads, and the others are presumed to derive from lost works—and he has to be carried to bed at the end of the evening. Although we hear of his daughter Ellen and his son William (3.2.6, 8), Silence's own first name is never mentioned.

In the QUARTO edition of *2 Henry IV,* Silence's name is spelled Scilens on 18 occasions. This edition derives from Shakespeare's manuscript, and therefore the spelling is presumed to have been used by the playwright. Its only other known occurrence is in the "Hand D" pages of the manuscript of *Sir Thomas More* (where it is a common noun); this piece of evidence, along with others, leads scholars to conclude that Shakespeare wrote these pages.

Snare Minor character in *2 Henry IV,* subordinate to the constable Fang. In 2.1 Fang and Snare are hired by the Hostess to arrest Falstaff for debt. Snare is nervous about the likelihood of armed resistance, and indeed, when Falstaff and his companion, Bardolph, draw their swords, Fang and Snare are helpless. Snare's name, like Fang's, indicates his function, if not his capabilities.

Sneak Musician referred to in *2 Henry IV,* the leader of the Musicians who play for Falstaff at dinner at the BOAR'S HEAD TAVERN. In 2.4.11 "Sneak's noise" is stipulated as the desired music, and in line 21 a Drawer goes in search of him. Another reference to Sneak, in a play of 1613, suggests that there was an historical Sneak who enjoyed some renown in LONDON, but nothing more is known of him.

Strewers See Groom.

Surrey, Thomas Fitz-Alan, Earl of (1381–1415) Historical figure and minor character in *2 Henry IV,* a follower of King Henry IV. In 3.1 Henry sends for Surrey and Warwick and tells them of his troubles. Surrey does not speak.

The historical Surrey was much more important than this slight role suggests. His father had been executed in 1397, along with Thomas of Glouces-

ter, by King Richard II in the conflict that was to trigger the events enacted in *Richard II.* Surrey, who fled to Flanders after his father's arrest, joined Henry IV, when, as Henry Bolingbroke, he deposed Richard, and he remained a strong supporter of the king against the rebellions enacted in *1* and *2 Henry IV.* He was a friend of Prince Hal, who later, as King Henry V, entrusted him with the command of major military expeditions.

Travers Minor character in *2 Henry IV,* follower of the Earl of Northumberland and a rebel against King Henry IV. In 1.1 Travers brings Northumberland the mistaken news that the rebel forces have won the battle of SHREWSBURY, an account shortly belied by the eyewitness account of Morton. The episode helps to develop a secondary theme of the play, the uncertainty of knowledge.

Umfrevile, Sir John (active 1403) Historical figure mentioned in *2 Henry IV* as an ally of the rebel Earl of Northumberland, perhaps the original speaker of some lines assigned to Lord Bardolph. In 1.1, as Travers approaches WARKWORTH CASTLE with news of the battle of SHREWSBURY, Lord Bardolph tells of having encountered Travers and given him such news as he had. When he arrives, Travers reports that he met Umfrevile en route and that Umfrevile had gone ahead of him with his news, which he accordingly omits, proceeding to tell of a later encounter. The QUARTO edition of the play (1600) gives a speech prefix to Umfrevile at 1.1.161—later editors give the line to either Lord Bardolph or Travers—and in 1.3.81 Lord Bardolph reveals his ignorance of information provided in this scene. Scholars conclude that Lord Bardolph's part in 1.1 may originally have been written as Umfrevile's, and that Umfrevile's lines were later assigned to someone else in order to eliminate one character as an economy measure for an acting company.

Visor, William GLOUCESTERSHIRE countryman named in *2 Henry IV,* a friend of Davy. Davy, steward of Justice Shallow, wishes his master to rule in favor of his friend "William Visor of Woncot" (5.1.34) in a lawsuit against one "Clement Perkes a'th'Hill" (5.1.35). Shallow observes that "Visor is an arrant knave" (5.1.37), but Davy disingenuously asserts the greater right of a knave to favor since, being a knave, he is likely to be denied it. He goes on to claim the privilege of a loyal servant to "once or twice a quarter bear out a knave against an honest man" (5.1.44), and Shallow promises that Visor "shall have no wrong" (5.1.49). We are given a humorous glimpse of small-time country corruption, one of the many vignettes of common life that the play features.

Visor is thought to represent a real person, a member of a family named Visor or Vizard, known to have lived for centuries in the village of Woodmancote, the "Woncot" of the play. Why Shakespeare chose to present William Visor as "an arrant knave" is not known.

Wart, Thomas   Minor character in *2 Henry IV*, one of the men whom Falstaff recruits for the army in 3.2. Wart, who is dressed in rags, is initially rejected as being too poor a specimen of soldier. However, after two draftees offer bribes to Falstaff's assistant, Bardolph, they are released from service and Wart is taken. He is put through an incongruous marching exercise in 3.2.267–272. The episode satirizes the notorious greed of 16th-century recruiters.

Warwick, Earl of   See Warwick, Richard Beauchamp, Earl of, in *Henry VI, Part 1*.

Westmoreland, Earl of   See Westmoreland, Ralph Neville, Earl of, in *Henry IV, Part 1*.

Henry V
SYNOPSIS

Prologue
The Prologue laments that the players cannot adequately represent such great events as King Henry V's war against FRANCE. But he begs the audience's indulgence and says that he will serve as Chorus.

Act 1, Scene 1
The Archbishop of Canterbury and the Bishop of Ely discuss a movement in Parliament to appropriate huge amounts of the church's wealth. Canterbury says that the king, despite his decadent youth (as enacted in *1* and *2 Henry IV*), is likely to support the church; he marvels at length that the king has proved himself a wise statesman. He adds that he has just offered the king an immense sum of church money to support a war in France and assure his support against Parliament, but before Henry could accept it, the arrival of an Ambassador from France postponed their conversation. Canterbury and Ely leave to witness the king's reception of the Ambassadors.

Act 1, Scene 2
The king summons Canterbury for a conference before receiving the Ambassadors. The archbishop delivers a long and learned justification of Henry's claim to the throne of France. Ely, the Duke of Exeter, and the Earl of Westmoreland second him in recommending a war to support that claim, and Henry decides to invade. He receives the Ambassadors, who bring an insulting message from the Dauphin: Henry has gone too far in claiming certain French dukedoms; he should stay home and play games, as suits his dissolute character. A barrel of tennis balls accompanies this insolence. Henry sends the Ambassadors home with a declaration of war.

Act 2, Chorus
The Chorus tells of English preparations for war in highly rhetorical terms. He also states that three men intend to kill the king in SOUTHAMPTON before he can sail for France. The Chorus assures the audience that the play will transport them to France—without seasickness—after first taking them to Southampton.

Act 2, Scene 1
Lieutenant Bardolph encourages Corporal Nym to forgive Pistol, who has married the Hostess to whom Nym had been betrothed. Bardolph wishes them reconciled before they all go to fight in France, but Nym talks of violence against Pistol. Pistol and the Hostess appear, and he and Nym exchange insults and draw swords. Bardolph's threat to kill the first to use his weapon prevents immediate bloodshed. The Boy arrives, summoning the Hostess to help Falstaff, who is very ill, and she leaves with him. Pistol and Nym quarrel further,

but Bardolph effects a truce. The Hostess returns to report that Falstaff's sickness has worsened, and they all leave to visit him.

Act 2, Scene 2
Exeter, Westmoreland, and the Duke of Bedford discuss King Henry's cool pretense that he does not know of the treason intended by the Earl of Cambridge, Henry Scroop, and Thomas Grey. Henry arrives with the three traitors, and he mentions to them his intention to pardon a drunken soldier who has been arrested for speaking disloyalty of him. They all recommend severity against any challenge to the king's authority. He then shows them the formal charges against themselves. They plead for mercy, but he cites their own arguments and sentences them to death. They acknowledge his justice before being taken away to be executed.

Act 2, Scene 3
Falstaff's friends mourn him before departing for France. The Hostess touchingly describes his death.

Act 2, Scene 4
The French King lays defensive plans against the English. The Dauphin belittles Henry's military potential, but the Constable and the king remember earlier English triumphs led by Henry's ancestors. Exeter arrives as Henry's ambassador, and he delivers a demand that the French King relinquish his crown or be conquered.

Act 3, Chorus
The Chorus asks the audience to imagine the glorious English fleet sailing to France and, further, to imagine a French ambassador offering Henry a marriage to Princess Katharine, with a dowry of dukedoms, and being turned away as English cannons begin the fighting.

Act 3, Scene 1
At the siege of HARFLEUR, Henry encourages his troops with a speech extolling the traditional courage of English soldiers, ending with a battle cry.

Act 3, Scene 2
Bardolph enthusiastically shouts a battle cry, but Pistol Nym, and the Boy seek safety. Fluellen appears and harasses the reluctant soldiers up to the front, though the Boy stays behind long enough

to soliloquize on the cowardice and dishonesty of his masters, reflecting that he hopes to leave their service soon. Gower, an English officer, talks with Fluellen, Macmorris, and Jamy, who are Welsh, Irish, and Scottish, respectively. They discuss the tactics of siege warfare in a conversation made comical by their various dialects and stereotypical temperaments.

Act 3, Scene 3
Henry addresses the citizens of Harfleur, vividly describing the horrors of an army sacking a town. The Governor of Harfleur appears and surrenders.

Act 3, Scene 4
In French, Princess Katharine receives a comical lesson in English from her waiting-woman, Alice, enlivened by gross mispronunciations and inadvertent sexual references.

Act 3, Scene 5
The French leaders marvel at the fighting abilities of the English, and the French King orders a massive assault. The Constable remarks that this show of force will surely make the English offer ransom rather than fight, for their forces are sick, hungry, and greatly outnumbered.

Act 3, Scene 6
Gower and Fluellen discuss the English success in taking a bridge. Fluellen praises Pistol's accomplishments there but is disappointed when Pistol appears and seeks his intervention to save Bardolph, who has been sentenced to death for stealing from a church. Fluellen refuses, favoring stern discipline, and Pistol curses him and leaves. Fluellen recollects that Pistol's supposed bravery at the bridge had consisted only of bold words, and Gower elaborately describes the sort of cowardly rogue who avoids fighting and then brags of his heroics in London taverns. Henry arrives, and Fluellen tells him of Bardolph's sentence; the king approves. A French herald, Montjoy, arrives with a proposed truce if Henry will offer a large ransom. While admitting that he is at a disadvantage, Henry refuses to pay and prepares for battle.

Act 3, Scene 7
The night before the battle, a group of the French leaders converse idly, anticipating an easy victory.

Act 4, Chorus

The Chorus asks the audience to imagine the two opposing camps, busy in the night preparing for battle. The overconfident French play games, gambling prospective English prisoners with each other. The rueful English contemplate defeat and death. However, he says, Henry moves among his troops, raising their spirits. He adds that the actors will depict the ensuing battle of AGINCOURT, although their petty presentation will disgrace the battle's fame.

Act 4, Scene 1

King Henry's cheerful approach to the coming battle is mirrored by an aged knight, Sir Thomas Erpingham. Henry dismisses his attendants and, incognito, encounters several soldiers in his army. The disguised king is roundly cursed by Pistol when he defends Fluellen. Henry then overhears a conversation between Fluellen and Gower and reflects that Fluellen is a good and careful officer. He next meets three English soldiers, one of whom. Michael Williams, asserts that, while common soldiers will be killed, the king risks only capture, after which he will be ransomed. Henry, speaking as another commoner, insists that this is not so; the king has vowed to die rather than be taken prisoner. Williams doubts that this will happen. After a brief argument, Williams agrees to fight his opponent after the battle, if they both live, and they exchange tokens of identity, so that they can recognize each other in the daytime: Each will wear the other's glove on his hat. The soldiers depart, and Henry, in a long soliloquy, meditates on the cares of kingship. Erpingham appears and delivers a request that the king confer with his nobles, and Henry sends him to convene a meeting at his tent. Alone again, the king prays that God will not permit his soldiers to fail as punishment for his father's deposition and murder of Richard II (enacted in *Richard II*), since he has reburied Richard and made other formal atonements for the crime.

Act 4, Scene 2

The French nobles, about to begin the battle, remark on the feeble opposition.

Act 4, Scene 3

The English nobles, though ready to fight, comment on the degree to which they are outnumbered. Westmoreland wishes they had reinforcements from England, but Henry observes that their triumph will be the greater because they are fewer. He would prefer that the fainthearted depart so that the honor of the battle need be shared only by those who are worthy. He predicts that the day will be long remembered as a great one for England and that all those present will value the experience for the rest of their lives. Montjoy reappears with another offer of peace for ransom, but Henry sends him back with a proud refusal.

Act 4, Scene 4

Pistol captures a French Soldier and threatens bloody death if he is not paid a ransom, but the soldier doesn't understand English. Pistol comically but viciously rants at his helpless prisoner, until the Boy interprets into English the Frenchman's offer of money, and Pistol marches off with him. Alone, the Boy reflects that Pistol has avoided the fate of Bardolph and Nym—both hanged for theft—only through cowardice, having been afraid to steal. He observes that only he and other boys are with the army's baggage train, which makes it a good target for the French.

Act 4, Scene 5

The French nobles hysterically try to organize a counterattack against the English, who are winning the battle.

Act 4, Scene 6

Exeter gives Henry a touching account of the death of the Duke of York. When it appears that French reinforcements have entered the battle, Henry orders all prisoners killed.

Act 4, Scene 7

Fluellen and Gower discuss the cowardly French massacre of the unarmed boys tending the baggage train. Praising Henry's response to this outrage—ordering the death of all prisoners—Fluellen presents a long and comical comparison between the king and Alexander the Great. Henry arrives and sends a messenger to tell the remaining French knights that they should prepare to fight or flee, for all French prisoners are to be killed. Montjoy reappears to ask that the fighting stop so that the French can bury their dead, and he concedes that the English have won the battle. Fluellen praises the king, noting his Welsh blood. Williams appears and tells the king of the oath that the glove on his hat represents. Henry sends him with a message to Gower. The king then gives Fluellen a glove to wear on his hat, saying that he had captured it in the battle and that anyone who challenges it is a friend of the French and should be arrested. Fluellen, proud of his assignment, is also sent to Gower. Henry then instructs Warwick and Gloucester to follow Fluellen and prevent a fight between him and Williams.

Act 4, Scene 8

Williams encounters Fluellen and strikes him; Fluellen prepares to fight, as Warwick and Gloucester prevent him. The king arrives, explains the circumstances, and gives Williams a glove full of coins. Fluellen attempts to increase the reward with his own shilling, but William rejects it. Henry reads a long list of French noblemen killed in the battle, along with only four English knights, and he orders that religious rites of thanksgiving be observed.

Act 5, Chorus

The Chorus tells of Henry's triumphal return to London, of the peace negotiation between England and France, and of Henry's subsequent return to France.

Act 5, Scene 1

Fluellen tells Gower that Pistol has insulted the leek, symbol of WALES, that he wears in his hat. Pistol appears, and Fluellen cudgels him and forces him to eat the leek. The humiliated Pistol decides that he will return to England and take up a life of petty crime. He will pretend the scars from Fluellen's beating were obtained in battle.

Act 5, Scene 2

King Henry, the French King, and their respective entourages meet to sign a peace treaty. The Duke of Burgundy makes an eloquent plea for peace, and Henry replies that peace must be bought, as the treaty provides. The French King requests a final consultation on certain points, and Henry sends his noblemen to negotiate with the French. Henry is left with Princess Katharine and Alice. The king courts the princess, and their language difficulties

are humorous. She is uncertain what to think, but she concedes that, if her father agrees to the marriage, she will also consent. The negotiators return, and all parties accept the marriage. Henry orders that wedding preparations begin.

Epilogue

The Chorus states in a SONNET that this ends the presentation of Henry's glory. Conquered France was left to the infant Henry VI, during whose reign it was lost through English discord and mismanagement, as the actors have often depicted on stage.

COMMENTARY

Henry V completes the second TETRALOGY of Shakespeare's HISTORY PLAYS, and this work restates a problem first dealt with in *Richard II*: Can sensitivity and warmth—the spiritual values that elevate human life—coexist with the ruthless strength and shrewdness that a ruler needs to govern? In *Henry V* this question can be plausibly answered in two ways that seem to be mutually exclusive. Some readers find the play a patriotic tribute to Henry, who is seen as an ideally heroic leader who takes England to new heights of power and defeats a traditional enemy; he is a hero suited to the threatening times England endured in the late 16th century, when the play was written, and the play has been popular in times of national crisis ever since. Alternatively, though, the play is a mordant commentary on politics and war, in which Henry is a Machiavellian militarist, a cold-blooded, power-hungry hypocrite who uses religion to justify the horrors of an unnecessary war. This antiheroic view has found its audience primarily in recent decades, but the observations that war is hellish and that it is often conducted for selfish ends are not new, and Shakespeare could easily have found them suitable material for a play.

Both readings are equally valid, and they may reflect Shakespeare's own ambivalence toward the subject of power. In either interpretation, *Henry V* is a powerful dramatic work whose epic quality is plainly intended to invoke the grandeur of the ancient world, whether seriously or sardonically. For instance, the use of the Chorus, itself a direct reference to ancient Roman drama, places the action in a timeless, semimythical context. Such lines as the Prologue's desire for "a Muse of fire" (Prologue.1) and the description of the night as filling "the wide vessel of the universe" (4.Chorus.3) are unquestionably grand, and they lend a monumental air—ironic or otherwise—to the work. A sense of great moments passing into legend is often called forth in this play, as when Henry declares, "Then call we this the field of Agincourt, fought on the day of Crispin Crispianus" (4.7.92–93).

However, Shakespeare remains committed to the great portrait of the common people of England that he began so successfully in the *Henry IV* plays. A group of new characters, led by Fluellen, provides a glimpse of Henry's army. Part of their function is to exemplify the stalwart bearing of the common soldier, lending dignity to Henry, but they also offer a frequently humorous cross-section of the British public. In 3.2, known as the "international" scene, Gower, Macmorris, Jamy, and Fluellen represent England, Ireland, Scotland, and Wales, respectively, in a tribute to British unity under Henry. Jamy and Macmorris are simple stereotypes, but Fluellen and Gower have more depth. Likewise, Henry's conversation with Bates and Williams in 4.1 is humanly complex and real and stirs our feelings in preparation for his important soliloquy on the difficulties of kingship (4.1.236–290). These vignettes reveal that Henry's strength derives from his subjects, who in turn respond to him and are proud to be British.

However, the world of the BOAR'S HEAD TAVERN, familiar from *1* or *2 Henry IV*, is treated less sympathetically. Falstaff dies offstage almost immediately, and the Hostess's role is brief, if poignant. Then Bardolph and Nym die ignominiously, and the Boy is killed in an atrocity of war. Finally, Pistol is humiliated by Fluellen in 5.1. These incidents serve both interpretations of the play, for while they may represent a defeat for anarchy by the new order of the epic hero, at the same time they present Henry as an unforgiving, unfeeling politician who can cite principles of discipline while permitting an old friend to die.

Earlier, the account of Falstaff's death makes this point more explicitly. We hear of his illness and death in two sentimental scenes, 2.1 and 2.3, that give emotional resonance to his EASTCHEAP cronies; Pistol and Nym, in particular, are otherwise little better than mindlessly vicious. Their grief lends them a pathos that helps sustain the epic quality of the play, but on the other hand, Falstaff's final agony is expressly attributed to Henry's cold and Machiavellian nature—"The king hath killed his heart" (2.1.88), the Hostess says, referring to Falstaff's rejection in *2 Henry IV*—and this contributes to the play's sardonic and cynical viewpoint.

Various sorts of evidence reflect the likelihood that Falstaff was originally the chief comic character of the play, and Shakespeare's deletion of the fat knight is indicative of his purposes. Henry's central role could be compromised only by the presence of so massive a personality; in either interpretation Falstaff's cheerful immorality would only distract from its primary focus, be it an epic vision of England's greatness or a biting assessment of Henry's calculating militarism.

Henry's invasion of France and the victory at Agincourt were already legendary peaks of English glory in Shakespeare's day, and national pride is patently evident at many points in the play; several passages—especially 3.1.1–34 and 4.3.20–67—have been standard items of patriotic rhetoric since they first appeared. However, the play is not merely rousing pageantry; the morality of Henry's war is questioned throughout. The major justification for the war is presented by the Archbishop of Canterbury in 1.2.33–95, and while this speech may be read with great solemnity, it also has a more ironic side—for example, in Canterbury's assertion that his complicated and legalistic argument makes Henry's claim to the French crown "as clear as is the summer's sun" (1.2.86). That the archbishop and not Henry makes the argument demonstrates Henry's manipulative nature: He places the onus on the archbishop, cautioning him, in 1.2.13–28, that the justification of war is a mighty responsibility, but he refuses to accept that responsibility when Williams makes a similar point in 4.1.

More boldly, the play commingles with its sense of heroic chivalry several passages that are explicit condemnations of war, including Henry's "conjuration" to the archbishop just mentioned. Best known is Burgundy's plea for peace in 5.2.24–67, in which the plight of a war-torn land is movingly evoked. Significantly, Henry's response is the cool insistence that France must "buy that peace" (5.2.70).

Most important, the savagery of war is repeatedly described in vivid speeches that compellingly counter the heroic idea of warfare that they ostensibly promote, beginning subtly with the archbishop's strangely inappropriate equation of war booty with the peaceful activity of bees gathering honey and quickly escalating to Henry's inflamed response to the Dauphin's mockery in 1.2.261–296. At Harfleur the king describes in grisly detail the fate the town will undergo if his soldiers loot it (3.3.1–41). While Henry is in fact merciful to the citizens—because they do in fact surrender, sparing him the trouble of a battle—his graphic threat is a stark reminder of the horrors of war. Williams's description of a battle also illustrates the terrifying reality of warfare, in terms that are far from conventionally heroic rhetoric: ". . . all those legs and arms and heads, chopped off in a battle" (4.1.137–138).

Moreover, the only actual combat we see involves Pistol, who is systematically deplored throughout the play. He is decried at length for cowardice, vanity, and downright criminality by Gower in 3.6 and the Boy in 3.2 and 4.4. Further, Pistol makes us aware of a frequent consequence of war: the social havoc that can be wreaked by hardened and embittered soldiers returning to a civilian population. Having failed in war, he declares that he will become a professional thief on his return to London (5.1.89–95).

Thus the evils of war are abundantly demonstrated, even as the triumph of English arms is glorified. Both messages are strongly reinforced by the seemingly anticlimactic courtship scene, 5.2. First, Henry's development as an epic hero is brought to its proper climax by his marriage; he woos his bride briskly, with joyous predictions of a happy marriage and fine offspring. He is now a complete hero whose fine traits and accomplishments can be carried forward into the future. Moreover, the supremacy of England over France is again emphasized. However, Henry's aggressive wooing of Katharine may also be seen as an extension of his brutal conquest. In addition, the final bankruptcy of Henry's cause is frankly, if subtly, asserted: Henry predicts great heroism for his son, but we know that this son will become the ineffectual Henry VI, under whom England's French conquests will be lost; this is expressly mentioned in the Epilogue. These references remind

us, as they reminded Shakespeare's original audience—to whom all of these matters were much more familiar—that *Henry V* actually presents a mere interlude in the bloody and tragic tale of England's disruption by the selfish ambitions of feuding aristocrats. This heavy irony chillingly closes the play on a note of failure and resignation that does much to offset the epic nature of the story.

Some critics view the play's ambiguities as unintentional, claiming that Shakespeare intended a portrayal of heroic idealism but failed to present it convincingly, perhaps due to an unconscious revulsion against authority. Others assert that the play's emphasis on Henry's Machiavellian nature conflicts with his status as a national hero, resulting in a confused political statement. Perhaps a compromise position permits the fullest response: Shakespeare may have accepted Henry's status as a hero while also being aware of the sordidness of political life. In the tetralogy that closes with *Henry V*, Shakespeare developed his ideal of a king whose human sensitivity matches his capacity for ruthlessness, but in doing so he perhaps discovered the limitations imposed on this ideal by the nature of power.

Shakespeare's instinctive response to the irreducible complexity of life was to be further reflected in the great plays of the next several years. *Julius Caesar,* another play about power and idealism, followed almost immediately; the great tragedies pose questions about the reliability of human motives, whether political or otherwise—questions that are implicit in the ambiguities of *Henry V.* The need for social order is an important issue throughout Shakespeare's work; however, so is an evident distrust of those who hold authority. We can only conclude that the playwright recognized the paradox that underlies much political thought from the late Middle Ages to the present: The only forms of power that seem fully moral—such as those outlined in Thomas MORE's *Utopia* and its successors—are impossible to achieve. Thus the ambivalence of *Henry V* reflects our most profound political ideals as well as our most disturbing fears of political power.

SOURCES OF THE PLAY

Shakespeare's chief source for the historical material in *Henry V* was Raphael HOLINSHED's *Chronicles of*

England, Scotland, and Ireland (2nd ed., 1587), supplemented by *The Union of the Two Noble and Illustre Families of Lancaster and York* (1548) by Edward HALL. Other historical details may have come from the chronicles of Robert FABYAN (1516) and John STOW (1592). Shakespeare may also have read several Latin biographies of King Henry, written during the monarch's lifetime or shortly thereafter: the *Henrici Quinti Angliae Regis Gesta*, written by an army chaplain who was present at Agincourt; the *Vita et Gesta Henrici Quinti*, whose anonymous author is known as Pseudo-Elmham; and the *Vita Henrici Quinti*, by Tito Livio, which was translated as *The First English Life of King Henry the Fifth* (1513).

Several fictional episodes may have been inspired by other works. The Dauphin's insulting gift of tennis balls in 1.2, Pistol's capture of the French Soldier in 4.4, and Henry's courtship of Katharine in 5.2 probably derive from similar scenes in an earlier play about Henry V, THE FAMOUS VICTORIES (before 1588). Also, Katharine's language lesson in 3.4 closely resembles several scenes in 16th-century French farces, suggesting that Shakespeare had read some of these plays, although they were published only in France and never translated into English. Henry's clemency to the drunken soldier, described in 2.2.39–43, may derive from a similar episode in PLUTARCH's *Lives of the Noble Grecians and Romans*, translated by Thomas NORTH (1579). And the Archbishop's comparison of human society to a hive of bees (1.2.187–204) was probably inspired by a passage in the *Georgics* of VIRGIL.

TEXT OF THE PLAY

We know that *Henry V* was written in the spring or summer of 1599, for it contains a plain allusion to a contemporary event. In 5.Chorus.30–32, the Chorus refers to the military expedition of Robert Devereux, Earl of ESSEX, to Ireland, hoping that he would return triumphantly. Essex left London in March 1599 and returned ignominiously in September. The reference was probably made in the spring, for it quickly became known that the expedition was destined for failure.

The play first appeared in print in a QUARTO edition of 1600, printed by Thomas CREEDE for publishers Thomas MILLINGTON and John BUSBY. This edition, known as Q1, is a BAD QUARTO—that is, it was recorded from memory by actors who had appeared in it, and its text is seriously flawed. Moreover, Q1 lacks the Prologue, Epilogue, all of the speeches of the Chorus, three other whole scenes, and long portions of six others. Q2 (1602) and Q3 (1619), both published by Thomas PAVIER, are reprinted from Q1; they differ from it only accidentally and omit the same material. Q3 was part of the notorious FALSE FOLIO and is spuriously dated 1608.

The FIRST FOLIO version of the play (1623) is the first to present the missing material, and it has been the basis of all subsequent editions. Descriptive stage directions, the presence of a GHOST CHARACTER, and idiosyncratic spellings known to have been used by Shakespeare suggest that the Folio text was printed from the playwright's FOUL PAPERS. Minor details derived from Q3 indicate that the printers also used a copy of that edition.

THEATRICAL HISTORY OF THE PLAY

The title page of the 1600 edition of *Henry V* asserts that the play had already been "sundry times played," but the earliest known performance was held at the court of King JAMES I on January 7, 1605. No other 17th-century production is known, and the play has been popular only intermittently since then. A 1723 adaptation eliminated the comic characters from Eastcheap. David GARRICK produced Shakespeare's text in the 1750s, playing the Chorus. John Philip KEMBLE played Henry V in his own quite successful version of the play between 1788 and 1811. W. C. MACREADY also played Henry several times, culminating in a memorably spectacular production of 1839. Nineteenth-century producers were inclined to extraordinary effects; in 1859 Charles KEAN staged a triumphal march after Agincourt that employed 550 actors. Charles CALVERT presented *Henry V* in both London (1872) and New York (1875).

At about the turn of the 20th century, F. R. BENSON played Henry, but the play was not often staged thereafter until its patriotic aspect made it successful during both world wars. *Henry V* has been performed frequently as an antiwar play in Britain and America since the 1950s, as the nuclear age and its series of small but vicious conflicts have generated strong pacifist sentiments in Western society. Among the most notable productions was that of Peter HALL at STRATFORD in 1960. The play was also produced as part of a number of cycles of the HISTORY PLAYS, notably those at Stratford in 1901, 1906, 1951, and 1977 and on British TELEVISION in 1960, one of six television versions of the play. *Henry V* has twice been made a FILM: Laurence OLIVIER's patriotic wartime version (1944; music by William WALTON) contrasts with the bleaker 1989 movie by Kenneth BRANAGH. A 1987 London stage production demonstrated the continuing public interest in the play: both *Henry IV* plays and *Henry V* were staged on different nights of the week, and, most strikingly, theatergoers responded with enthusiasm to marathon Saturday performances featuring all three works in succession.

CHARACTERS

Alice Minor character in *Henry V*, lady-in-waiting to Princess Katharine of France. In 3.4 Alice, said to have been in England, gives her mistress a brief lesson in English, telling her the names for such body parts as the hand, the fingers, and so on, in an exchange marked by comical mispronunciation and unintentional sexual references. This oddly charming episode, conducted entirely in French, appears immediately after King Henry V's dire threats to sack HARFLEUR and thus subtly contributes to the play's sardonic presentation of Henry's career of conquest, parallel to its glorification of him. The scene also foreshadows Henry's aggressive bilingual courtship of Katharine in 5.2, where Alice is also present.

Ambassador Any of several minor characters in *Henry V*, diplomats representing FRANCE at the court of King Henry V. In 1.2 one of the Ambassadors conveys the arrogant message of the Dauphin, including a mocking delivery of tennis balls, implying the king's fitness only for childish games. The insult offers Henry an occasion to declare war.

Bardolph See Bardolph, in *Henry IV, Part 1.*

Bates, John Minor character in *Henry V*, one of the soldiers who encounter the incognito King Henry V on the eve of the battle of AGINCOURT.

Bates is a grumbler who wishes he were elsewhere, even if the King were left alone in FRANCE, but he also says, "yet I determine to fight lustily for him" (4.1.196). He tries to allay the quarrel between Williams and the stranger (the King), saying, "Be friends, you English fools, be friends: we have French quarrels enow . . ." (4.1.228–229). Bates is a typical English soldier, part of the scene's varied presentation of the army's morale before the battle.

Beaumont Minor character in *Henry V*, a French nobleman. Beaumont is a GHOST CHARACTER; i.e., he appears but does not speak. He is named in 3.5.44 and in a stage direction in 4.2.1. His death in the battle of AGINCOURT is reported in 4.8.102. Shakespeare apparently took the name from the list of casualties in HOLINSHED's *Chronicles*, perhaps intending to develop the character further.

Bedford, John Plantagenet, Duke of See Bedford, John Plantagenet, Duke of, in *Henry VI, Part 1.*

Berri, Jean of France, Duke of (1340–1416) Historical figure and minor character in *Henry V*, a follower of the French King. Berri does not speak, but he is referred to in 2.4.4 and 3.5.41. The historical Berri was the uncle of Charles VI, the French King of the play, and sometimes served as regent during Charles's bouts of insanity. He was thus an important figure in the French political conflict that resulted from the King's incapacity, although Shakespeare ignored this aspect of Henry V's conquest. Berri is now famed for his great collection of medieval books of hours, whose beautiful illuminations inspired the costumes and sets for Laurence OLIVIER's well-known FILM of *Henry V*.

Bourbon, Jean, Duke of (1380–1434) Historical figure and minor character in *Henry V*, a French nobleman. In 4.5, in the confusion of the French defeat at AGINCOURT, Bourbon determines to launch a counterattack. However, in 4.8 he is a prisoner of King Henry V. Following the QUARTO edition of the play, some editions assign to Bourbon the lines of Bretagne in 3.5; this reflects the elimination of Bretagne's part in an early production. The quarto also gives the lines of the Dauphin in

3.7 to Bourbon, suggesting that the actor who played the Duke in the same early production was held in high regard.

The historical Bourbon, after being taken prisoner at Agincourt, spent the rest of his life in captivity in England. The Bourbon who appears in *3 Henry VI* was his illegitimate son.

Boy   Character in *Henry V*, servant of Bardolph, Pistol, and Nym. Having been employed by Falstaff as a page—the same figure appears in *2 Henry IV* as the Page and in *The Merry Wives of Windsor* as Robin—he accompanies his late master's cronies to France as part of King Henry V's army. In 3.2.28–57 he elicits our sympathy by regretting his association with such cowardly thieves. At the battle of AGINCOURT he acts as an interpreter between Pistol and the captive French Soldier in 4.4, and after this sorry episode he again bemoans his continued connection with Pistol; he also reveals that Bardolph and Nym have been hung. In this speech (4.4.69–80) he remarks that only he and other boys guard the English baggage train, which would thus make a good target for the French, if only they knew the situation. With this observation the Boy grimly heralds his own death, for in 4.7.5 Gower reports the French massacre of all these youngsters.

Bretagne, Jean, Duke of (Jean, Duke of Britaine; Duke of Brittany) (1389–1442)   Historical figure and minor character in *Henry V*, a follower of the French King. In 3.5 Bretagne and other French noblemen marvel at the fighting abilities of the English. Brittany was still an independent state in the 14th century, and the historical Duke of Bretagne (Brittany) was an important ally of FRANCE. He was the son-in-law of Charles VI, the French King of the play.

Burgundy, Philip, Duke of   See Burgundy, Philip, Duke of, in *Henry VI, Part 1*.

Cambridge, Richard, Earl of (1376–1415)   Historical figure and character in *Henry V*, a traitor who plans to assassinate King Henry V but is foiled and condemned to death. In 2.2 Henry, who knows of the intended treason, asks Cambridge and his co-conspirators, Lord Scroop and Sir Thomas Grey, how to deal with a drunken soldier who has spoken against him. They all insist that Henry be firm against any hint of disloyalty. Then Henry reveals his knowledge of their treason and applies their own advice, denying them clemency and sentencing them to death. Cambridge, who has no distinctive personality, welcomes death with conventional remorse, as do the others, in a passage intended to emphasize Henry's godlike majesty.

The historical Cambridge benefited from Henry's benevolence, for the king had restored his older brother to the dukedom of York, despite his history of rebellion against HENRY IV, and had elevated Cambridge to his earldom. However, the Earl firmly opposed Henry IV's usurpation of the throne from Richard II, and he continued to rebel. In *Henry V* French gold alone motivates the traitors, although in 2.2.155–157 Cambridge observes that he wants the cash for a purpose that Shakespeare did not specify because he wished his audience to focus on Henry's enemies in France. The historical traitors, however, planned to replace Henry on the throne with Edmund Mortimer, Cambridge's brother-in-law, whose father was held to have been the rightful heir to Richard II. Mortimer himself was loyal and turned in the conspirators, which Shakespeare does not mention, but his claim to the throne was revived by Cambridge's son, the Duke of York of the *Henry VI* plays, and the WARS OF THE ROSES ensued as a result. Thus this minor scene in *Henry V* carries the germ of future English disasters, as many people in Shakespeare's original audiences will have recognized.

Canterbury, Henry Chichele, Archbishop of (1362–1443)   Historical figure and character in *Henry V* who gives King Henry V a rationale for going to war with FRANCE. In 1.1 Canterbury, speaking with the Bishop of Ely, expresses his hope that a state of war—especially when supported by the large donation he has offered the king—will divert the introduction of legislation requiring a vast state seizure of church property. In 1.2 he presents the king with a long, legalistic argument in support of his hereditary claim to the French crown, and he joins others in encouraging a conquest of France.

Shakespeare's portrayal of Canterbury is flawed, though only because his sources were. The historical Henry Chichele did not become archbishop until some time after the war began; until then he was Henry's ambassador to France. Shakespeare followed Edward HALL in this error. More significant, the church was not particularly instrumental in promoting the war, and the archbishop's motives, although Shakespeare took them from HOLINSHED, are unhistorical. In fact, although the legislation to seize church property had been proposed under King Henry IV (as Canterbury observes in 1.1.2–3), it was not reintroduced under Henry V. Thus the church had no reason to promote the war, and, although it contributed to the King's war fund, as was customary, its donation was not exceptionally great, as it is in the play.

Charles VI, King of France See French King.

Chichele, Henry, Archbishop of Canterbury See Canterbury, Henry Chichele, Archbishop of.

Chorus Allegorical figure in *Henry V,* speaker of the PROLOGUE (where he is identified in a stage direction as the Prologue), an introduction to each act, and the EPILOGUE. The Chorus apologizes for the inadequacy of the theater to present historical events in a sufficiently grand manner, and he therefore offers a supplementary account of the events dramatized. He uses a stylized and artificial diction that is in marked contrast with the realism of the dramatic scenes, and the Chorus's grand rhetoric contributes to the epic quality so important to the play. However, if *Henry V* is considered as an acid satire on politics, then the Chorus's epic voice has an ironic quality, sardonically at odds with the cynical waging of an unnecessary war by a hypocritically religious king. In the Epilogue—a formally correct SONNET—the Chorus again remarks on the inadequacy of historical drama, and he praises the accomplishments of Henry V anew. Then he goes on to observe that all of Henry's gains in FRANCE were almost immediately lost under Henry VI, closing with a reference to Shakespeare's well-known *Henry VI* plays, which depict this loss.

The Chorus repeatedly invokes imaginary scenes: In the Prologue he asks the audience to "piece out our imperfections with your thoughts" (Prologue.23) and thereby to "carry [characters] here and there, jumping o'er times" (line 29). In 3.Chorus.18 he requests, "Grapple your minds," and later, "Work, work your thoughts, and therein see . . ." (line 25), and lastly, "eke out our performance with your mind" (line 35). Thus the Chorus, by insisting on the audience's part in shaping the narrative, supplying with their imaginations what cannot be provided in a theater, helps to provide an almost cinematic sweep of time and events.

Clarence, Thomas, Duke of See Clarence, Thomas, Duke of, in *Henry IV, Part 2.*

Constable of France, Charles d'Albret (Charles Delabreth) (d. 1415) Historical figure and character in *Henry V,* a high-ranking officer in the French army. Although the Constable recognizes that King Henry V is not the dissolute figure the Dauphin believes him to be, he nonetheless falls prey to the overconfidence of the French prior to the battle of AGINCOURT. His death in the battle and his name are reported in 4.8.94.

Court, Alexander Minor character in *Henry V,* soldier who meets the incognito King Henry V on the eve of the battle of AGINCOURT. His companions, Bates and Williams, converse with the king, but Court speaks only one line.

Dauphin Lewis (1396–1415) Historical figure and character in *Henry V,* son of the French King. The Dauphin—who bore the traditional title of the eldest son of a king of FRANCE—leads the French nobles in their cocky overconfidence before the battle of AGINCOURT. In 1.2 the French Ambassador delivers a sneering message to Henry from the Dauphin, accompanied by a shipment of tennis balls, said to be appropriate weapons for so foolish a monarch; the insult gives Henry an occasion to declare war on France. When the English invade, the Dauphin and his friends are preposterously boastful and arrogant caricatures, presented only to be put down by events. In 4.5 a hysterically suicidal Dauphin is shown in defeat.

Shakespeare's Dauphin, besides being a stock figure, misrepresents the historical Dauphin in several small matters of fact as well. He mocks Henry for his youth, as in 2.4.28, but he was in fact nine years younger than his foe. Nor was he present at Agincourt; too sick to fight, he died two months after the battle.

Ely, John Fordham, Bishop of (d. 1435) Historical figure and character in *Henry V* who supports the Archbishop of Canterbury in urging King Henry V to war. In 1.1 Ely and Canterbury express their hope that a state of war—especially when supported by a large donation from the church—will forestall the introduction of legislation requiring a vast state seizure of church property. In 1.2 Ely, Canterbury, and others encourage Henry to invade FRANCE.

Erpingham, Sir Thomas (1357–1428) Historical figure and minor character in *Henry V*, officer in the army of King Henry V. In 4.1, on the eve of the battle of AGINCOURT, Erpingham rejects Henry's suggestion that he is too old to sleep on the hard ground, asserting that he enjoys being able to say, "Now lie I like a king" (4.1.17). Henry congratulates him on his spirit, thus contributing to the episode's emphasis on the high morale of the English army.

The historical Erpingham supported the King's father, Henry Bolingbroke, later King Henry IV, when he deposed King Richard II (enacted in *Richard II*) and later served as his chancellor. He was one of the highest-ranking officers at Agincourt.

Exeter, Thomas Beaufort, Duke of See Exeter, Thomas Beaufort, Duke of, in *Henry VI, Part 1*.

Fluellen Character in *Henry V*, a Welsh officer in the army of King Henry V. Fluellen, although hot-tempered, rather humorless, and pedantic, is open, honest, and courageous as well. He is further distinguished by a comically extravagant Welsh accent. His prickly insistence on military traditions leads him to speak sharply to Captain Macmorris in 3.2, Pistol in 3.6, Williams in 4.8, and Gower at several points. Irked by Pistol's anti-Welsh mockery, Fluellen forces him to eat a leek, the Welsh national emblem, in 5.1. The king remarks that Fluellen is "touch'd with choler, hot as gunpowder" (4.7.185).

Fluellen's bravery and sense of military honor mark him as a fine soldier, and his enthusiasm for Henry—especially in his comical comparison of the king and Alexander the Great (4.7.12–55)—supports the play's presentation of the king as an epic hero. On the other hand, his fiery irrationality and suffocating self-confidence are also to be associated with the king and thus color the alternative view that Henry is a vicious militarist and the play a satirical picture of war and political power. Shakespeare intended both aspects of the play to be felt, and Fluellen, in his small way, contributes to this effect.

Fluellen's name is a variant of the more common Welsh name Llewelyn; Shakespeare may have borrowed the surname of one William Fluellen, an associate of his father, John SHAKESPEARE. Fluellen's Welshness helps to demonstrate the unity of the peoples of Britain under Henry V, especially in the "international scene" (3.2), where WALES, England, Ireland, and Scotland are represented by Fluellen, Gower, Macmorris, and Jamy, respectively. Also, the emphasis on Fluellen's accent probably reflects the presence of a Welshman in Shakespeare's acting company.

French King (Charles VI of France) (1368–1422) Historical figure and character in *Henry V*, the opponent of King Henry V. The French King plays an inconsequential role. He presents a brief history of earlier English conquests in FRANCE in 2.4.48–64; he encourages his noblemen before the battle of AGINCOURT in 3.5; and in 5.2 he accepts the terms of the treaty of TROYES, surrendering to Henry the inheritance of his crown, as well as the hand of his daughter, Princess Katharine. The ineffectual French King complements another model of French inadequacy, the caricature of foolish bravado that is his son the Dauphin.

This perfunctory portrait omits the most important fact about the historical Charles VI: He was intermittently insane. His illness—later to surface in his grandson King Henry VI of England—was known to Shakespeare, but the playwright, who had not touched on madness in the *Henry VI* plays either, may have disliked pointing out defects in the ancestral line of his own ruler, Queen Elizabeth (see Elizabeth I in *Henry VIII*). Also, focusing on Henry V's greatness, he probably did not wish to elaborate on France's weakness. For in failing to mention Charles's lunacy, Shakespeare also omitted its most important consequence—a state of virtual civil war in France that made the English conquest much easier.

Two factions vied with each other for the regency of France when the King was sick. When Henry invaded, the party in power at first refused to fight him, fearing that their rivals would seize Paris in their absence. This led to the Dauphin's failure to relieve HARFLEUR, of which its Governor complains in 3.3. The French pulled themselves together—note the French King's roll call, including noblemen of both factions, in 3.5.40–45—but the victory at Agincourt saved the English. When Henry again entered France, in 1417, the same situation prevailed; as a result, the English were able to conquer Normandy and claim the French crown. (See also HUNDRED YEARS' WAR.)

French Soldier Minor character in *Henry V*, a gentleman taken prisoner by Pistol at AGINCOURT. In a grimly comic scene Pistol, who speaks no French, attempts to extract ransom from the Soldier, who tries to offer it but does not speak English. Finally the Boy interprets, and Pistol agrees not to kill his captive.

Gloucester, Humphrey, Duke of See Gloucester, Humphrey, Duke of, in *Henry VI, Part 1*.

Governor of Harfleur Minor character in *Henry V*, a French official. The Governor surrenders the town of HARFLEUR to Henry V, confessing in 3.3.44–50 that, without the support of the Dauphin, the town is indefensible.

Gower Minor character in *Henry V*, an officer in the army of King Henry V. Gower functions chiefly as a foil to Fluellen, a calm and restraining friend of—and audience for—the irascible Welshman. Gower, a stolid military man, reveals his own per-

sonality only when he voices his heartfelt disapproval of Pistol, whom he sees as a petty thief and braggart impersonating a soldier, in 3.6.67–82, his sole substantial speech.

Grandpré Minor character in *Henry V*, a French nobleman. Grandpré appears only once, to describe, in 4.2.38–55, the listless and dispirited English army just before the battle of AGINCOURT. The speech contributes to the presentation of French overconfidence. Grandpré's death is reported in 4.8.101. Shakespeare apparently took the name from the list of casualties in HOLINSHED's account of the battle.

Grey, Thomas (d. 1415) Historical figure and minor character in *Henry V*, a traitor who plans to assassinate King Henry V but is captured and sentenced to death. In 2.2 Henry, who knows of their plot, asks Grey and his fellow conspirators, Lord Scroop and the Earl of Cambridge, for advice about a drunken soldier who has criticized him. They all recommend severity, insisting that Henry be firm against any hint of disloyalty. Then Henry reveals his awareness of their treason and applies their own rule against them, sentencing them to death. Grey, like the others, offers a conventionally remorseful speech, thanking God for the defeat of the conspiracy and welcoming death. Grey has no personality; the episode merely serves to emphasize Henry's godlike majesty.

The historical Grey was a landowner in Northumberland and is thought to have been allied to the Percy family, persistent rebels against King Henry IV. The revolt led by Cambridge may have been a final spasm of the civil conflict enacted in *1* and *2 Henry IV*.

Henry V, King of England (1387–1422) Historical figure and title character in *Henry V*, victorious leader of an English invasion of FRANCE during the HUNDRED YEARS' WAR. (The same individual appears as Prince Hal in *1* and *2 Henry IV*.) Henry may be seen in two very different ways, in accordance with the play's essential ambivalence. The play may be taken either as an epic patriotic drama or as a satirical exposure of vicious hypocrisy, depending on one's interpretation of its protagonist; many episodes support both points of view. Henry has two dramatic functions: He is a hero whose exuberant leadership carries England to triumph over a traditional foe, yet he is also a coldly Machiavellian politician who is indifferent to the human costs of war.

Henry's stature as a model of kingship is evident from the outset. In 1.1 the Archbishop of Canterbury extols Henry as a thoughtful and devout ruler, praising his understanding of religious, military, and political matters. The king's statesmanship is demonstrated in 2.1, when he solemnly warns of the grave consequences of war. Once agreed that honor requires him to invade France, his inflammatory response to the French Ambassador displays an invincible martial spirit. Henry's rule is secure within his realm, and he easily foils the assassination plot of Cambridge, Scroop, and Grey in 2.2 and sentences the conspirators to death. The skill with which he manipulates them demonstrates his ability to handle men, while his clemency to the drunken soldier, described in 2.2.39–43, mitigates his severity. On the eve of the invasion of France, we are told, "all the youth of England are on fire . . . following the mirror of all Christian kings" (2.Chorus.1–6). Henry inspires his forces with one of the most famous patriotic speeches in English literature (3.1.1–34). His chivalric behavior stands out especially by comparison with his boastful opponents, the vain and foolish French. His anger at the mocking delivery of tennis balls from the Dauphin in 1.2 is proportionate to the foolishness of the gift. On the battlefield, Henry's dignified refusal to avoid conflict in 3.6 is followed immediately by the prattle of the cocky French nobility.

At AGINCOURT, in Act 4, we see the King at his most heroic. Henry shares the anxieties of the common soldiers in 4.1, and his triumphant courage and high spirits are reflected in his officers, particularly after another famous morale-raiser, the "St. Crispin's Day" speech (4.3.18–67). His weeping response to the deaths of York and Suffolk in 4.6 belongs to an ancient tradition of vignettes in which great heroes grieve for their slain companions. Displaying the decisiveness of a great general, he reacts harshly in a moment of danger, ordering death for the French prisoners in 4.6.37, but this

action is associated in the next two scenes with revenge for a French atrocity. In 4.7 Henry's righteous anger and the approval of Gower and Fluellen reflect the opinion of both Shakespeare's sources and 16th-century military theory that Henry's act was praiseworthy.

Following the battle, Henry is betrothed to Princess Katharine of France. This completes the portrait of an epic hero, who, especially if he is a king, must produce offspring to carry on his line. Henry predicts that their son shall be a great Christian hero, rescuing Constantinople from the Turks. Further, by a dramatic convention of the day, the marriage signifies a happy ending: The war has been resolved, and a bright future is promised.

Most important to Henry's stature as an epic hero, God is on his side. His battle cry asserts, "God for Harry . . ." (3.1.34), and the traitors acknowledge God's hand in their downfall (2.2.151, 158). Henry utters frequent prayers and assertions that earthly affairs are controlled by God. He is particularly concerned about his relations with heaven in view of his father's sins of usurpation and murder, as he reveals in his prayer for victory on the eve of Agincourt (4.1.295–311). He refuses credit for the subsequent victory, saying, "Praised be God, and not our strength, for it!" (4.7.89) and orders that psalms of thanksgiving be sung.

Henry seems a proper epic hero, but a contrary view is also suggested from the first. The sincerity of Canterbury's praise in 1.1 is dubious, for the archbishop frankly wants to win the king's support against Parliament. The sentimental 2.1 and 2.3, in which Falstaff's followers regret his illness and then mourn his passing, place the king in a moral shadow, for the knight's death is expressly attributed to Henry—"The king hath killed his heart" (2.1.88), the Hostess says, referring to Falstaff's rejection in *2 Henry IV*. For many, this act is a coldly ungrateful example of personal betrayal, however appropriate in terms of public policy; a germ of disapproval toward Henry is thus planted before he even appears.

Henry often seems sanctimonious rather than genuinely religious. He chiefly calls on God to justify his own intentions, and he turns ostensibly religious sentiment into a casual anti-French slur in

3.6.155–157. More significantly, Henry's prayer for victory in 4.1.295–311 may be seen as a crass material bargain with God, an invoice, as it were, for the charitable works he has paid for since becoming king. Henry's prayer follows a long passage on the difficulties of kingship, during which it did not occur to him to seek divine assistance. Had Shakespeare intended his hero as a seriously religious person, that would have been a telling and touching moment to have him turn to God. This omission is not in itself very important, but it contributes to a sense that Henry does not truly possess the Christian spirit that he projects.

These suspicions of hypocrisy are supported by the impression that Henry is that most un-Christian figure, the ruthless militarist. The morality of Henry's war is sharply questioned. In 1.1 the play's only formal representatives of Christianity plot to foment a war to protect church property, and we must doubt the propriety of Henry's cause. In Henry's angry speech to the French ambassadors he justifies himself as an instrument of God's will, but he brandishes ugly threats that are far from Christian in spirit. His God seems to offer an all too convenient excuse to do what he already wants to do—that is, conquer France. At this point we may recall the advice that Henry received from his dying father in *2 Henry IV*—namely, to fight a foreign war to distract potential rivals at home.

The apparent dishonesty of the archbishop's justification for war, noted above, is striking; that it is the archbishop and not Henry who makes the argument is equally telling. Henry has placed the onus on the prelate, having cautioned him, in 1.2.13–28, that the making of war is a mighty responsibility that he refuses to accept himself. This evasion recurs when the soldier Williams makes a similar point in 4.1. Henry responds with a lecture on the sinfulness of all the soldiers (4.1.150–192), cleverly deflecting moral responsibility away from himself.

Henry's military heroism has a negative side as well, for he repeatedly reveals a nasty viciousness. His spirited reply to the French ambassadors is also brutally violent, threatening death to "many a thousand" and grief for those "yet ungotten and unborn" (1.2.284, 287) as vengeance for a petty insult. His handling of the traitors in 2.2 is effec-

Shakespeare's Henry V (here played by Laurence Harvey) can be seen either as a model of English heroism or as a hypocritical adventurer indifferent to the cost of war. *(Courtesy of Culver Pictures, Inc.)*

tive, but it also suggests a catlike delight in cruelty as Henry toys with his prey. The king's threats to HARFLEUR, though not carried out—the town surrenders and spares him the trouble—are extreme, promising a list of horrors including "naked infants spitted upon pikes" (3.3.38). The references to his killing of prisoners (4.6.37, 4.7.9–10, 4.7.65), while justifying the act, are all seemingly insistent on the image of the king as executioner. And lastly his cool response to Burgundy's plea for peace in 5.2—". . . you must buy that peace" (5.2.70)—is quite chilling when viewed in light of Henry's demonstrated brutality on the battlefield.

In less-political contexts, Henry also seems unfeeling. As we have seen, the death of Falstaff raises this point in Act 2, and the fat knight's rejection is referred to again in 4.7.47–53, where it is associated with Alexander the Great's murder of a friend. Moreover, in 3.6.110 Henry lets Bardolph die for a petty offense in the name of discipline. The king's cold, Machiavellian nature is thus illustrated several times, contributing to the portrait, alongside that of the epic hero, of a cynical politician.

Henry's aggressive courtship of Princess Katharine, while possessing a certain bluff charm, may also seem repellent. Not only is the king falsely humble, claiming to be a "plain soldier" (5.2.153), but he is clearly aware that she is already properly his as a trophy of war. This scene harbors the crowning irony of the play: as Henry crows over the prospective greatness of his and Katharine's future child, we know that this son is to be the hopelessly ineffective Henry VI, who will lose the conquests Henry is presently celebrating. This is bluntly stated in the EPILOGUE, ending the play on a note of resignation and loss that flatly oppose the idea of Henry as an epic hero.

Nonetheless, Henry V was undeniably a monumental figure in the eyes of Elizabethan England, universally accepted as a great king, and Shakespeare took this status as a given. The king is the major figure in the play in either interpretation, and the playwright took pains to emphasize his importance. It appears that Falstaff was removed from the play after it was written, presumably in order to avoid impinging on Henry's significance. Further, Shakespeare altered the historical reality of Henry's reign to the same purpose. The battle of Agincourt, fought in 1415, is the central event of the play and appears to lead directly to the surrender of France. But the decisive campaign in Normandy in 1417–19, and the importance of naval warfare in its success, is not mentioned; nor is the English alliance with Burgundy, which made Henry's final victory possible five years after Agincourt. In the battle itself the king's role is overstated by the striking omission of a crucial and well-known element, the devastation wrought by the English longbowmen. This aspect of the English victory was already legendary in Shakespeare's time, but it was not suited to the playwright's focus on Henry.

Henry V must dominate the play, for the play's essential ambivalence toward power depends entirely on the extraordinary dual nature of the protagonist, who must function as two quite differ-

ent figures at the same time. Henry V is in this way unparalleled in Shakespearean drama, though many characters are greater than he in other respects. Thus he brings us to a renewed awareness of the range of his creator's genius.

Herald   Minor character in *Henry V*, a messenger who brings King Henry V a written account of the French fatalities at AGINCOURT. The Herald speaks only one line.

Hostess   See Hostess, in *Henry IV, Part 1*.

Isabel, Queen of France (1370–1435)   Historical figure and character in *Henry V*, the wife of the French King. Queen Isabel appears only in 5.2, where she blesses the marriage of King Henry V and her daughter, Princess Katharine.

The historical Queen Isabel was a princess of Bavaria who married Charles VI, the French King of the play, at the age of 14. She was a notoriously self-indulgent, licentious, and extravagant woman. When it became evident that her husband was insane, Isabel became a leader of the factional strife that was probably most responsible for the victories of Henry V. She went so far as to declare that her second son, the successor to the Dauphin as the heir to the throne, was illegitimate, her love life being too rich to permit identification of the father. He nevertheless managed to claim the crown upon the death of the king, and he appears as Charles VII in *1 Henry VI*.

Jamy   Character in *Henry V*, a Scottish officer in the army of King Henry V. Jamy appears only in the "international" scene, 3.2, with the Welsh Fluellen, the English Gower, and the Irish Macmorris. The episode emphasizes the diversity of British subjects serving together under Henry. Although Fluellen speaks of him as a fine soldier, Jamy merely lends color, uttering commonplaces in an almost impenetrable brogue.

Katharine (Princess Catherine, Princess Katherine) (1401–1438)   Historical figure and character in *Henry V*, the daughter of the French King, later betrothed to King Henry V. Princess Katharine is an innocent girl. She is comically instructed in English by her waiting-woman, Alice, in 3.4, and she is the upright but somewhat baffled subject of King Henry's aggressive courtship in 5.2. Most of her lines are in French or broken English. She has little personality; she is simply the object of King Henry's affections and part of his reward for victory over FRANCE.

The historical Katherine of Valois was the youngest child of Charles VI, the French King of the play, and Queen Isabel. She was married to Henry as part of the treaty of TROYES. After Henry's death, she married an obscure Welsh nobleman, Owen Tudor; their grandchild was to become King Henry VII of England, and he appears as the Earl of Richmond in *3 Henry VI* and *Richard III*.

Macmorris Character in *Henry V*, an Irish officer in the army of King Henry V. Macmorris appears only in the "international" scene, 3.2, with the Welsh Fluellen, the Scottish Jamy, and the English Gower. Hot-tempered, Macmorris takes offense at Fluellen's reference to the Irish, assuming he means an insult, and they nearly come to blows, though both respond professionally to the call of duty and postpone their quarrel. The episode exploits ethnic stereotypes to demonstrate the diversity of British subjects working to a common end under King Henry.

Messenger Any of several minor characters in *Henry V*, servants in the court of the French King. In 2.4 a Messenger announces the arrival of an English ambassador. In 3.7 and 4.2 Messengers, perhaps soldiers, bring word of English troop dispositions prior to the battle of AGINCOURT.

Montjoy Minor character in *Henry V*, a French herald. Montjoy arrogantly delivers the French King's challenge in 3.6.122–141 and patronizingly offers mercy on behalf of the Constable in 4.3.79–88, but he must humbly concede French defeat at AGINCOURT in 4.7.72–85. He is a dramatic pawn without personality, adding to the chivalric tableau of medieval warfare while formally presenting French attitudes to England, a more civil version of the overconfident French nobility represented by the Dauphin and the Duke of Orléans. Montjoy was actually the title of the chief herald of France, not his name, though 3.6.142–143 suggests that Shakespeare did not know this.

Nell Quickly See Hostess, in *Henry IV, Part 1*.

Nym Character in *The Merry Wives of Windsor* and *Henry V*, a follower of Falstaff. In *The Merry Wives* Nym is a minor figure, being dismissed by his master early in the play for refusing to deliver love letters. But in three brief scenes he is memorably established as an eccentric character, using the word *humour* in almost every speech, applying it in every imaginable way, to the point where it ceases to have meaning. This word was a fashionable and widely parodied term in late-16th-century London (see COMEDY OF HUMOURS); in fact, a character in a play of 1596, George CHAPMAN's *The Blinding Beggar of Alexandria*, had the same verbal habit and clearly seems to have influenced Shakespeare's creation of Nym.

In *Henry V* Nym feuds with Pistol, who has married the Hostess, to whom Nym was engaged. Bardolph reconciles the two. Nym is one of the companions of Falstaff who mourn his death in 2.3, but he says little. In 3.2, as part of King Henry V's army in France, Nym is cowardly and is upbraided by Fluellen. The Boy comments on the villainous characters of Nym, Pistol, and Bardolph in 3.2.28–56, describing them as braggarts, petty thieves, and cowards. In 4.4.75 the Boy reports that Nym has been hung, apparently for theft.

In *The Merry Wives*, Nym's function is comical, although he remains an undeveloped character. In *Henry V* his more unsavory aspects are stressed; he is part of the underworld that is put down by King Henry. His very name suggests petty villainy; it meant "steal" or "filch" in Elizabethan English.

Orléans, Charles, Duke of (1391–1465) Historical figure and character in *Henry V*, one of the fatuously overconfident French nobles before the battle of AGINCOURT. Like his fellows, Orléans has no distinctive personality; he joins them in feeble humor and idle insults to the English. They are simply caricatures, braggarts set up to take a fall.

The historical Orléans, nephew of Charles VI, the French King of the play, was an important figure in the complicated French politics of the time. He was married to the former English queen Isabel, the widow of Richard II. He was seriously wounded and captured at Agincourt (as is reported in 4.8.78), and he was imprisoned in England for 26 years. During his captivity, he began to write poetry, continuing to do so after his release, and he is regarded as one of the greatest French medieval poets.

Pistol   See Pistol in *Henry IV, Part 2.*

Prologue   Allegorical figure in *Henry V,* the speaker of the PROLOGUE that opens the play. Although he is designated in the opening stage direction as the Prologue, he identifies himself as the Chorus in line 32, and his rhetorical invocation of the Muses is taken up again, in remarks delivered under that designation, before each subsequent act (2–5) and in the EPILOGUE.

Rambures, Lord   Minor character in *Henry V,* a French nobleman. Rambures, who speaks only a few lines, shares in the French overconfidence prior to the battle of AGINCOURT in 3.7 and 4.2. His death is reported in 4.8.96, where he is said to have been the "master of the cross-bows." Shakespeare took this information—and the character's name—from the account of the battle in the *Chronicles* of Raphael HOLINSHED. In speech headings and stage directions of the BAD QUARTO edition of the play (1600), Rambures is designated "Gebon," presumably indicating the actor who played the part. Scholars suppose he was either Thomas GIBBORNE or Samuel GILBURNE.

Salisbury, Duke of   See Salisbury, Thomas Montague, Earl of, in *Henry VI, Part 1.*

Scroop, Henry (Henry de Scroop, Henry Scroope, Henry Scrope) (ca. 1376–1415)   Historical figure and minor character in *Henry V,* a traitor who plans to assassinate King Henry V but fails and is sentenced to death. Scroop and his fellow conspirators, the Earl of Cambridge and Sir Thomas Grey, are asked by Henry to advise him on punishing a drunken soldier who has defamed him. They all

recommend severity. Then the king reveals his knowledge of their plot and applies their own rule to them, refusing them mercy. They each thank God for preventing their success, in conventional speeches intended to emphasize Henry's own majesty.

Henry judges Cambridge and Grey in a few words, but he chastises Scroop at great length (2.2.93–142). Scroop's treason is deemed particularly heinous, for he has been Henry's close friend and confidant for many years. Henry goes so far as to call Scroop's offense "another fall of man" (2.2.142). The combination of Henry's grief at his friend's betrayal and his unswerving sternness demonstrates both the humanity and the maturity of the king.

The historical Scroop was indeed close to Henry, but he was also associated with a history of rebellion against the LANCASTER dynasty. Although Shakespeare does not mention it in *Henry V,* Scroop's father, Stephen Scroop, had been a supporter of Richard II, who was deposed by Henry's father, Lord Bolingbroke, later King Henry IV, as is enacted in *Richard II.* Further, Scroop's uncle, the Archbishop of the *Henry IV* plays, led two revolts against Henry IV. Scroop and his father disassociated themselves from the Archbishop, and Scroop was given high office under Henry V. Accordingly, his involvement in Cambridge's plot was punished with particular rigor: Grey and Cambridge were each beheaded, while Scroop was drawn and quartered.

Suffolk, Michael de la Pole, Earl of (1394–1415)   Historical figure mentioned in *Henry V.* This Earl of Suffolk was one of the few English noblemen killed at the battle of AGINCOURT; his death is described grandly in 4.6.10–32. He is not to be confused with his younger brother, William de la Pole, Earl of Suffolk, who succeeded to the title and appears in *1* and *2 Henry VI.*

Warwick, Earl of   See Warwick, Richard Beauchamp, Earl of, in *Henry VI, Part 1.*

Westmoreland, Earl of   See Westmoreland, Ralph Neville, Earl of, in *Henry IV, Part 1.*

Williams, Michael   Character in *Henry V,* a soldier who unknowingly argues with King Henry V, who is disguised as a common soldier, in 4.1. Henry finds that Williams doubts the virtue of the English invasion of France and asserts that, if Henry's cause is not righteous, the king must accept responsibility before God for the sin of unjustifiable killing committed by his men. Henry argues irrelevantly that the king cannot be held accountable for the soldiers' sins committed before the battle, and Williams concedes the point but doubts the king's reputed promise to fight to the death rather than be ransomed. The two men exchange gloves, to be worn on their hats as identification, and each agrees to challenge the other to a fight if he sees him after the forthcoming battle of AGINCOURT. However, when Henry, undisguised, sees Williams in 4.7, he does not acknowledge their prior meeting but sends the soldier on an errand. He then gives the glove that he holds to Fluellen and sends him to the same place as Williams, ensuring an encounter. When the two meet in 4.8, they prepare to fight; Henry appears and explains matters but demands a defense from Williams for having dared to abuse the monarch. Williams makes the obvious explanation—that he could not have known the king—and Henry returns him his glove, filled with money. Williams sharply rejects Fluellen's offer of a further gratuity.

This episode may be viewed in either of two lights, depending on one's interpretation of the play, which Shakespeare deliberately made ambiguous. If King Henry is seen as an epic hero, his encounter with Williams may be seen as evidence of the king's commendable ability to relate to the common soldiers of his army. The dispute in 4.1, from this point of view, offers the king a lesson in humility by displaying the virtues of forthright courage that may be found in all men, and it leads to the king's great soliloquy (4.1.236–290) in which he regrets his royalty. When the king generously rewards Williams in 4.8, he recalls the magnanimity of his youth as Prince Hal, enacted in *1* and *2 Henry IV*. On the other hand, if the play is taken as a satire on war and politics, and Henry as a hypocritical militarist, then emphasis shifts to Williams's scepticism about the morality of Henry's war. The soldier's honest doubt is shuffled off by a sophistic evasion. The business of the gloves displays Williams as a courageous commoner who is patronized by a superior who first makes a riskless challenge and then diverts it to Fluellen, seemingly for mere entertainment. Shakespeare set up a number of such ambivalent situations in this play, and Williams, a convincing British soldier—his name suggests that he may be Welsh—contributes much to the realism of this one.

York, Edward, Duke of (ca. 1373–1415) Historical figure and minor character in *Henry V*. (The same figure appears as the Duke of Aumerle in *Richard II*.) In 4.3 York asks King Henry V for permission to lead the vanguard at the battle of AGINCOURT, offering an instance of English valor. His brave death in combat is touchingly reported by the Duke of Exeter in 4.6.7–32, a passage that helps to maintain the epic tone of the play's presentation of the battle.

The historical York inherited the title from his father, the York of *Richard II*, several years after the time of that play. He was pardoned by Henry V for his rebellions against Henry IV (one of which is enacted in *Richard II*). As he demonstrated at Agincourt, he remained loyal to the new king, but his younger brother, the Earl of Cambridge, was executed for treason, as is enacted in *Henry V*, 2.2. When York died childless, the title passed to Cambridge's son, the Duke of York of the *Henry VI* plays. The York of *Henry V* died at Agincourt, but not in the courageous manner described in the play. Quite fat, York suffered a heart attack or some other sort of fatal seizure after falling from his horse. His heroic death is Shakespeare's invention; he may have had in mind the great popularity of his earlier description of John Talbot's death in battle in *1 Henry VI*, 4.7.

Henry VI, Part 1
SYNOPSIS

Act 1, Scene 1
The play opens on the funeral of King Henry V; the Duke of Bedford notes astrological portents of disaster. The Duke of Gloucester and the Bishop of Winchester argue, disrupting the ceremony. A Messenger arrives with news of disastrous military

defeats in FRANCE. A second Messenger arrives, bringing news of a general rebellion of France against England, featuring the crowning of the Dauphin as King Charles VII, in violation of the treaty enforced by Henry V, and the rallying to his cause of several important noblemen, including the Bastard of Orléans, Reignier, and the Duke of Alençon. Another Messenger arrives to tell of the defeat of England's leading knight, Talbot, wounded and captured due to the cowardice of another English commander, Sir John Fastolfe. Bedford vows to lead reinforcements to France, and the Messenger relates that the army under the Earl of Salisbury is pinned down outside ORLÉANS.

Act 1, Scene 2

At the siege of Orléans, Charles VII, Alençon, and Reignier exult in their recent good fortune and mock the English. An assault occurs, and the French are driven offstage. The three French leaders reenter, cursing the English, and decide that they will abandon the town. The Bastard of Orléans arrives. He describes a young woman, Joan La Pucelle, who has been sent by a vision from heaven to aid the French forces. Joan enters and offers to demonstrate her God-given military capacities in single combat with Charles. Charles accepts the challenge and is overwhelmed. He accepts her offer of assistance. Alençon and Reignier ask about plans for Orléans, and the newly inspired Charles declares that they will fight it out.

Act 1, Scene 3

The Duke of Gloucester and the Bishop of Winchester argue about the right to command the TOWER OF LONDON. They and their men come to blows. The Mayor of LONDON enters, with the king's order commanding public peace. The disputants separate with insults and challenges.

Act 1, Scene 4

The Master-gunner of Orléans instructs a Boy to keep watch on a tower where English soldiers come to observe the besieged city. Several Englishmen, including Salisbury and Talbot, appear on the tower. Talbot explains that he has been exchanged for a captured Frenchman. They begin to plan an attack on the city, but they are struck by a cannon-ball. Salisbury falls badly wounded, and another man is killed. Talbot cries out against the loss of Salisbury's heroism and leadership. A Messenger arrives with the news that Charles and Joan have arrived with an army to raise the siege.

Act 1, Scene 5

Skirmishing, Joan pursues a group of Englishmen across the stage. Talbot and Joan fight to a draw. Joan says that Talbot's time has not yet come, and she enters the city with the successful French troops, leaving Talbot to bemoan the poor state of English morale. In another skirmish, the English are driven back into their trenches, and Talbot concedes defeat.

Act 1, Scene 6

Joan, Charles, Reignier, and Alençon assemble on the walls of Orléans to celebrate their victory over the English.

Act 2, Scene 1

With a group of soldiers, Talbot, Bedford, and the Duke of Burgundy, an ally of the English, assault Orléans. The French leaders are driven over the walls. The Frenchmen exchange recriminations, but Joan encourages them to think of counterattack. However, an English Soldier (1) enters, shouting Talbot's name as a war cry, and the French party flees in panic.

Act 2, Scene 2

Bedford, Burgundy, and Talbot mourn the dead Salisbury. A Messenger arrives with an invitation for Talbot from a French noblewoman, the Countess of Auvergne, who wishes to entertain the valorous conqueror. Talbot leaves with the Messenger, but he first whispers something to a Captain.

Act 2, Scene 3

The Countess of Auvergne gloats over her plan to capture Talbot. He arrives, and she mocks his physique. Offended, he begins to leave, and she announces his capture. But he springs his counterplot, blowing his horn to summon a waiting troop of soldiers, who immediately free him.

Act 2, Scene 4

Richard Plantagenet argues hotly with the Duke of Somerset in the company of several other men.

Plantagenet plucks a white rose from a garden tree and calls on those who support him to do likewise. Somerset immediately takes a red rose as his own emblem. The Earl of Warwick joins Plantagenet; Suffolk sides with Somerset. Both Plantagenet and Somerset agree that the dispute should be settled by a majority vote among the group. However, when most support Plantagenet, Somerset hints at a duel. He goes on to cast aspersions on Plantagenet, referring to the execution of his father, the Earl of Cambridge, for treason. Plantagenet counters that the execution had not been carried out legally. He threatens action against Somerset, who replies in kind and departs. Warwick assures Plantagenet that he will be reinstated as Duke of York.

Act 2, Scene 5

In the Tower of London, Plantagenet visits a dying relative, Mortimer, who is a prisoner. Plantagenet wants to know the story of his father's death. Mortimer tells of the deposition of King Richard II by Henry IV, head of the Lancastrian branch of the royal family. Mortimer, of the YORK branch, had been the legitimate heir to the throne, but an attempt to install him as king has resulted in his imprisonment for life while still a young man. In the reign of Henry V, Mortimer's brother-in-law, who had been Richard Plantagenet's father, had repeated the attempt to crown Mortimer and was executed for it. Mortimer names Plantagenet his successor, and he dies, after cautioning the younger man not to act against the house of LANCASTER, which is too strong to be removed. Plantagenet vows that he will begin to seek vengeance for his family by becoming reinstated as Duke of York at the forthcoming Parliament.

Act 3, Scene 1

In the Parliament House, Winchester and Gloucester and their respective supporters argue violently. King Henry VI, still a child, pleads for peace between the factions. The Mayor enters, reporting that the followers of Gloucester and Winchester are battling in the streets. Two Serving-men burst in, fighting. The king continues to plead for peace; Gloucester says he is willing. Winchester, reluctant, finally agrees, and the Serving-men are dismissed. The king agrees to restore Plantagenet as Duke of

York. Gloucester announces that all the preparations have been made for Henry to be crowned King of France in Paris. As the others depart, the Duke of Exeter remains and, in a soliloquy, predicts disaster for the English forces.

Act 3, Scene 2

Outside the gates of ROUEN, Joan and four Soldiers (2) gain entrance to the city disguised as tradesmen. She signals to the French troops, who take the city. The French leaders taunt the English, who are now outside the walls. Talbot and Burgundy exchange vows to recapture the town immediately. The dying Bedford, confined to an invalid's chair, refuses to leave the scene of battle. The skirmishing begins, and Fastolfe appears, fleeing in panic. The French are defeated, and Bedford, pronouncing himself satisfied, dies in his chair. Talbot and Burgundy exult in their victory and eulogize Bedford.

Act 3, Scene 3

The French leaders call the Duke of Burgundy to a parley to convince him to desert the English. Joan speaks to him of the misery of his homeland and asserts that the English are not his true friends. While suggesting that he may have been bewitched by Joan, Burgundy does change sides, declaring himself an ally of France.

Act 3, Scene 4

Talbot is knighted by Henry in Paris, where the king has come to be crowned. Vernon and Basset engage in another round of the York-Somerset rivalry, exchanging insults and threats.

Act 4, Scene 1

Winchester crowns the king, and the Governor of Paris kneels and accepts the oath administered by Gloucester. Fastolfe arrives with a message from Burgundy. Talbot tears off the Order of the Garter that Fastolfe wears, declaring him a coward, and the king banishes Fastolfe. Gloucester reads Burgundy's letter, in which he declares his changed allegiance. Talbot is ordered to march against Burgundy and departs spiritedly. Vernon and Basset appear, demanding a trial by combat. Their dispute spreads, and York challenges Somerset to a duel. Gloucester intervenes, and the king attempts to restore order.

To demonstrate his even-handedness, he foolishly divides the command of the English forces, assigning the infantry to York and the cavalry to Somerset.

Act 4, Scene 2
Talbot appears before the walls of BORDEAUX and demands the surrender of the city. A General on the walls refuses, confident in the strength of the approaching French army. Talbot recognizes danger, and he urges his troops to fight fiercely.

Act 4, Scene 3
York receives a Messenger, who tells of the force that is marching to attack Talbot, and he curses Somerset for not providing cavalry support. Sir William Lucy arrives from Bordeaux with an urgent plea for reinforcements. He is resisted by York, who continues to accuse Somerset.

Act 4, Scene 4
Lucy approaches Somerset with the same plea, and Somerset refuses, criticizing York for a bad plan. He refuses to send cavalry without an explicit request from York. Lucy cries out that Talbot will be defeated and killed, and he blames Somerset for feuding.

Act 4, Scene 5
Talbot tells his young son, John, that he should flee the certain death to be expected in the upcoming battle. John refuses, citing the honor of the family. They debate the matter, but the boy insists that he will stay.

Act 4, Scene 6
In the midst of the battle, Talbot rescues his son, fighting off surrounding attackers. The father describes the fierce fighting that has occurred, and he renews his insistence that his son should flee, but John again refuses.

Act 4, Scene 7
Talbot, mortally wounded, mourns the death of his son, killed in the battle, and then dies also. The victorious French leaders talk of John Talbot's valor and express thanks for York and Somerset's absence. Lucy appears, under a flag of truce, to retrieve the bodies of the two Talbots.

Act 5, Scene 1
Gloucester tells King Henry that a peace treaty has been arranged and that a marriage, intended to secure the peace, has been proposed between the king and the daughter of a French nobleman, the Earl of Armagnac. The king agrees to the treaty and marriage, and the visiting ambassadors are summoned to receive his formal acceptance.

Act 5, Scene 2
The French leaders rejoice at the news that Paris has risen against the English, but they are then disturbed by further news that the English army, reunited, is approaching.

Act 5, Scene 3
Joan uses witchcraft to summon a group of Fiends, but these spirits silently refuse to aid her, and she realizes that all is indeed lost. After a skirmish, York defeats Burgundy and takes Joan prisoner. He leads her away as Suffolk enters with Margaret of Anjou as his prisoner. He has already fallen in love with her, and he devises a plot to make her his lover, although he is already married. He offers to marry her to King Henry and make her Queen of England if she will be his lover. She accepts, on the condition that her father, Reignier, agree. Reignier is summoned, and he does agree, provided that he be awarded his home territories, Anjou and Maine. Suffolk promises to arrange this, and he leaves Margaret with her father.

Act 5, Scene 4
Joan, condemned to be burned, encounters her father, a Shepherd, but she refuses to acknowledge him, claiming descent from royalty. She declares that her death will bring damnation to her executioners. She is nevertheless ordered to the stake. Next she claims she is pregnant, but she is sent to her death, cursing England. The French leaders arrive to settle the details of the peace. Charles at first refuses to declare himself a subject of the English king, but Reignier and Alençon convince him to sign, for he can always break his word later.

Act 5, Scene 5
Suffolk's description of Margaret's virtues has caused the King to desire her. Gloucester objects, citing the earlier marriage agreement. However, the king orders Suffolk to return to France to arrange a marriage to Margaret. The play closes with a solilo-

quy by Suffolk, in which he proposes to rule the kingdom himself, through Margaret.

COMMENTARY

Henry VI, Part 1 was probably the first of Shakespeare's HISTORY PLAYS to be written, though scholars generally believe that it (like *Edward III*, another very early history play) was a collaborative effort by Shakespeare and at least one other playwright, possibly some combination of Thomas NASHE (particularly associated with Act 1), Robert GREENE, and Christopher MARLOWE, with only certain elements (especially 2.4, 2.5, and 4.2–4.7) credited to Shakespeare. This early play shares with the later works a particular emphasis on the disastrous consequences for England of rivalry among the high aristocrats who constituted the government. The development of individual characters is not very important, for the theme is English history. This play commences the TETRALOGY of dramas dealing with the WARS OF THE ROSES, the great crisis that formed the English nation as it was known to Shakespeare and his contemporaries. Here the playwright deals with the earliest of the disruptions, beginning during the last phase of the HUNDRED YEARS' WAR, a series of conflicts in which the French resisted English attempts to conquer them.

The action starts after the death of King Henry V, who had led his forces to great victories, establishing English control over large stretches of France (as Shakespeare was later to recount in *Henry V*); in the course of this play, these territories are almost all lost. However, narrative history is unimportant, here, as the play amplifies the theme that England's misfortunes were the result of selfish ambitions unchecked by a weak monarch's incompetence. King Henry VI is an infant when the play begins and only a young man when it ends. Ambitious noblemen felt they had plenty of opportunity to increase their personal power, and to indulge in feuds that a more assertive monarch would have curtailed.

These themes are immediately set out in 1.1. The outbreak of verbal sparring between the Duke of Gloucester and the Bishop of Winchester introduces the disorder among the nobles. Moreover, the effects of this dissension are already beginning to be felt, as the Messengers arrive to tell of military losses in France, including the catastrophic capture of a great English leader, Talbot.

French successes in the war are juxtaposed with brawling disorders in England. For example, the disagreement between Gloucester and Winchester at the Tower of London in 1.3 follows the arrival of Joan La Pucelle (Joan of Arc) to boost the morale of the French forces. Similarly, the rock fight that spreads even into the king's deliberations in 3.1 immediately precedes Joan's successful ruse at Rouen in 3.2. The feuding of Vernon and Basset begins in 3.4, just after the defection of the Duke of Burgundy, and it continues in 4.1, providing a sorry prelude to the death of Talbot.

This disorder in the realm is reflected in the repeated instances of hypocrisy and dishonesty on the part of various characters. Mortimer advises Plantagenet to conceal his opposition to the Lancasters (2.5). The Bishop of Winchester plots to kidnap the infant king, although this strand of the plot goes undeveloped, and he pretends to be reconciled with Gloucester after the fight in Parliament (1.1, 3.1). In the Temple garden dispute (2.4), Somerset refuses to abide by the majority vote he had agreed to honor. Suffolk plots to deceive the king in Act 5, and in the final scene even the saintly Henry is prevailed upon to go back on his agreement to marry the daughter of Armagnac. Another recurrent motif, representing the English dissension, is the interrupted ceremony. Three times, in 1.1, 3.1, and 4.1, ceremonial occasions are disrupted, each time more than once.

Shakespeare's chief contribution to *1 Henry VI* is thought to have been the development of the English hero, Talbot, who counterbalances these ominous developments. Talbot, a model knight who symbolizes the lost English supremacy under Henry V, stands out from the array of rhetorical quarrelers. He is knightly courtesy itself at the beginning of the coronation scene, and he personifies righteous indignation when he refuses to tolerate the wearing of the Garter, symbol of valor, by the coward Fastolfe. Talbot's praises are sung repeatedly by English and French alike. But his virtues cannot survive in the prevailing climate of deceit and disorder, and his courageous death in 4.7 is presented as the direct result of the York-Somerset struggle.

Historically, the episode of York and Somerset's divided command took place in Normandy during the 1440s, while Talbot's death occurred in southern France some years later. However, to increase the contrast between the brave and honorable Talbot on the one hand and the selfish, scheming factions on the other, the play provides a direct connection between the rise of the nobles and the loss of England's hero. Neither the playwrights nor their audiences were concerned with historical accuracy, but *1 Henry VI* is nevertheless strikingly at odds with the record as Shakespeare and his contemporaries knew it. For instance, although the Duke of Burgundy did indeed change sides during the Hundred Years' War, he did so some years after Joan's death. Moreover, this defection resulted from two decades of minor disputes and disagreements between the English and the Burgundians. For dramatic reasons, Shakespeare compressed all this into one highly charged, if entirely fictitious, scene; this enabled him to emphasize the duplicity of the French and Joan's associations with sorcery.

Similarly, the play describes, in close succession, Talbot's death, Joan's execution, and Henry's marriage: The fall of the great English hero prepares for that of the French heroine, who in turn is succeeded in the play by another Frenchwoman, the focus of a plot against Henry's power. To achieve these emotionally resonant juxtapositions, Shakespeare willfully ignored the chronicles, which correctly record a rather different arrangement. Joan was burned in 1431, Henry was married in 1444, and Talbot died in 1453. Smaller distortions of the historical record occur throughout the play.

The playwright and his collaborators also invented a number of scenes for dramatic impact. Talbot's encounter with the Countess of Auvergne (2.3), for instance, points up aspects of the hero's soldierly nature and contrasts his honesty with the Countess's deceit. A more important invention is the confrontation between the future Duke of York and his rival Somerset in the Temple garden (2.4), in which they select as emblems a white and a red rose. This scene objectifies the rivalry that was to develop into civil war in the sequels to this play. Although historically it did not happen, it is so dramatically appropriate that we might wish it had.

Such inventions and obvious errors are much more evident to a reader than to an audience. The Hundred Years' War and the English political scene are made real through a highly theatrical counterpoint of formal spectacle and unpredictable violence. The disrupted ceremonies noted above are obvious manifestations of this dramatic tension; the cool equanimity of the dying Bedford amid the hurly-burly of battle in 3.2 is a subtler instance. And Joan's brief dismissal of Sir William Lucy's elegiac recital of Talbot's noble titles brings us with a jolt from the formal dignity of medieval pomp to a renewed awareness of the carnage of battle (4.7.75–76).

King Henry himself is a humanly interesting character, unlike the caricatures of ambitious courtiers around him, although his personality is more developed in *2* and *3 Henry VI*. The conflict between his nature and the requirements of his situation fuels some of the development in this play and becomes highly significant in its sequels. Henry is gentle and thoughtful. He is distressed by the dissensions around him but is unable to contain them, not only on account of his youth but also because of his innate dislike of involvement in worldly matters.

In general, however, character development is not a strength of this play, which partly explains its general unpopularity with modern audiences. The play's style is rhetorical and formal, its content is largely expository, and the poetry tends to be somewhat stilted. Another problem arises from the playwrights' need to consider the play as one of a series; a certain amount of dramatically undirected material must be used in order to establish concerns that will be dealt with only in the sequels. Most glaring of these incidents is the relationship between the Earl of Suffolk and Margaret of Anjou, which seems unrelated to anything else in the play. It is certainly used to establish a major theme of the next play. However, it also provides a natural climax to this one, completing the devastation of England's position in France with the loss of Anjou and Maine. Also, Margaret becomes the strong adversarial figure that Joan had been. That Margaret first appears just as Joan is rendered powerless is typical of Shakespeare's later dramatic strategies, whether or not he devised the scheme in *1 Henry VI*.

Among the conventional stances that the play adopts are a vicious anti-French bias and a contemptuous attitude toward Joan that now seems excessive. These traits have been regarded as evidence that the play could not have been written by Shakespeare, such attitudes being thought beneath a great writer, but such virulent Francophobia was quite in tune with Elizabethan attitudes. The picture of Joan as a whorish sorceress comes from Shakespeare's sources and he may well have regarded it as historically sound, but the literary crudity of these passages suggests to modern scholarship the work of other hands.

On the whole, *1 Henry VI* cannot be regarded as a successful play. It lacks cohesion, being composed of scenes whose connections are more often contrasting than developmental. It is rhetorical to an extent that inhibits an audience's responses, and it does not reflect the insights into human nature that we associate with the mature Shakespeare. On the other hand, the play does present an extensive tract of complicated history, and it does so in a manner that enables us to apprehend it intellectually and also taste something of the nerve-racking reality of confused warfare. To whatever extent the young Shakespeare was involved in its creation, *1 Henry VI* was an early effort at a new form, the drama of historical narrative, and the maturing playwright was to improve upon it in each of its sequels, before going on to the glories of the major tetralogy.

SOURCES OF THE PLAY

Shakespeare's chief sources for *1 Henry VI*, and its sequels were the best-known English histories of his day, Raphael HOLINSHED's *The Chronicles of England, Ireland, and Scotland* (second edition, 1587) and *The Union of the Two Noble and Illustre Families of Lancastre and York*, by Edward HALL (third edition, 1550). An older text, *The New Chronicle of England and of France*, by Robert FABYAN (1516), provided some supplementary material, such as an account of the stone-throwing skirmish in 3.1.

TEXT OF THE PLAY

It is impossible to date the composition of Shakespeare's early history plays with absolute certainty;

the evidence is sparse, complex, and contradictory. However, *1 Henry VI* contains several minor resemblances to Edmund SPENSER's *Faerie Queene*, dated December 1589, and the play was referred to by Thomas Nashe, in the summer of 1592, as already very popular. Since the theaters were closed by plague after June of that year, the play must have been performed that spring. Therefore we do know that it was written between 1589 and 1592.

Although it is sometimes contended that *Part 1* was written *after* the other *Henry VI* plays, modern opinion tends to support common sense in supposing that the plays of the minor tetralogy, including *Richard III*, were written in the order in which they are read. *Richard III* seems to have been known to Marlowe by early 1592; therefore, it seems likely that the four plays were composed between early 1590 and late 1591, with *1 Henry VI* being written near the beginning of this period.

The only early publication of the play was in the FIRST FOLIO edition of 1623, and this text has necessarily been the basis for all subsequent editions. The Folio version's many errors and inconsistencies have provided grist for much scholarly dispute over minor points, but the text is not seriously flawed. Some characteristics—the casual stage directions and the retention of flagrant contradictions that would probably have been corrected in a performance script—seem to indicate that the Folio was printed from the author's manuscript.

THEATRICAL HISTORY OF THE PLAY

Nashe's reference to the play as an established hit just before the theaters closed in 1592 proves that it had been performed that spring. However, no other early productions are known. After Shakespeare's time, *1 Henry VI* was all but ignored for almost three centuries, being revived only in 1738 and 1899. However, elements from it were occasionally used in abridgments of the complete set of Henry VI plays. In the 20th century it was somewhat more frequently produced, especially in cycles presenting the history plays in clusters. It has also continued to provide material for abridged combinations, on both stage and TELEVISION. It has never been a FILM, but it was made for television in 1983 and was incorporated in two BBC series: *AN AGE OF*

KINGS (1960) and *The Wars of the Roses* (1964), which combines the *Henry VI* plays and *Richard III*.

CHARACTERS

Alençon, John, Duke of (1409–1476) Historical figure and character in *1 Henry VI*, one of the French noblemen who lead the forces of Charles VII against the English. Like his fellows, the Bastard of Orléans, Reignier, and Charles himself. Alençon is depicted as a type, a bragging but inept, treacherous, and cowardly warrior. Alençon's father was the French knight whose glove Henry V of England is said to have taken during the battle of AGINCOURT (*Henry V*, 4.7.159).

Basset Minor character in *1 Henry VI*, a supporter of the Duke of Somerset. Basset disputes with Vernon, a partisan of the Duke of York, in 3.4 and 4.1. By demonstrating the involvement of lesser figures, these incidents magnify the damage to English morale caused by the dissensions among the noblemen.

Bastard of Orléans (Jean Dunois) (1403–1468) Historical figure and character in *1 Henry VI*, one of the leaders of the French forces. Though the historical Bastard, who was well known by that appellation, was one of the leading soldiers of the 15th century, he is presented in the play as a boastful but cowardly and inept warrior. His personality resembles that of the other French noblemen, whose collective role was simply to demonstrate that France could not have been victorious but for dissensions among the English.

Bedford, John Plantagenet, Duke of (1389–1435) Historical figure and character in *1 Henry VI* and *Henry V*, the younger brother of King Henry V and uncle of Henry VI. (The same individual appears as Prince John of Lancaster, in *1* and *2 Henry IV*.) In *1 Henry VI* Bedford is a regent, ruling FRANCE for the infant King Henry. Bedford opens the play memorably, mourning the deceased Henry V in portentous terms: "Hung be the heavens with black, yield day to night!" (1.1.1). In Act 2 Bedford proves himself a capable warrior when Orléans is captured, but in Act 3 he is an aged invalid, confined to a chair,

whom Joan La Pucelle taunts as "good grey-beard" (3.2.50). He dies happily after witnessing the English victory at ROUEN.

The historical Bedford did die in Rouen, though at the age of 45 or 46, while the city was under English rule; the battle scene in the play is fictitious. He outlived Joan of Arc by several years. In fact he played a major role in Joan's capture and trial, but Shakespeare transferred this important aspect of his career to York in order to lend importance to the character who was to be a leading figure in the civil wars to come.

In *Henry V* a younger Bedford is an inconsequential member of the king's entourage. The historical Bedford, however, played an important role in the English conquest of France. Although he is present at the battle of AGINCOURT in the play, he was actually in England at the time, ruling in Henry's absence. Then he won a crucial naval battle in the second of Henry's campaigns in France. This campaign is ignored by Shakespeare, although it was actually more important than Agincourt in precipitating the final French surrender depicted in 5.2.

Boy Minor character in *1 Henry VI*, the son of the Master-Gunner of ORLÉANS. In 1.4 the Boy is instructed by his father that their cannon is trained on a tower where the English leaders are known to stand watch, and he subsequently fires the shot that kills the Duke of Salisbury.

Burgundy, Philip, Duke of (1396–1467) Historical figure and character in *1 Henry VI* and *Henry V*, an ally of the English in the HUNDRED YEARS' WAR who defects to the side of FRANCE. Early in *1 Henry VI* Burgundy assists the English at ORLÉANS and ROUEN; then in 3.3 Joan La Pucelle persuades him to align himself with France. In *Henry V*, set some years earlier, a younger Burgundy encourages Henry V and the French King to make peace in 5.2.23–67. He speaks at length on the horrors of war, in a passage that contributes much to the play's modern reception as an antiwar work. Burgundy then attends the French King in the final negotiations of the treaty of TROYES, which occur offstage while Henry courts Katharine. Upon returning, Burgundy jests lewdly with Henry about his forthcoming marriage.

The historical Burgundy was not an ally of France at Troyes, and he was a much more important figure than his role suggests. He was a cousin of Charles VI, the French King of the play, and he ruled the most powerful of the independent French duchies. His grandfather, the first Duke of Burgundy, appears as Philip in *Edward III*, and his father, Duke John (1371–1419), was the Duke of Burgundy mentioned in *Henry V* 3.5.42 and 4.8.99. Duke John fought against Henry at AGINCOURT. He was murdered in the factional disputes over the rule of France during Charles's frequent bouts of insanity, and Philip of Burgundy, upon inheriting the duchy, sought support from outside the circle of French rivalries. He sided with England and thus assured Henry V's victory, a phenomenon that Shakespeare, focusing on the accomplishments of the English king, ignored in *Henry V*. Burgundy's subsequent alliance with England under Henry VI was marred by many disputes over policy and by his feud with the Duke of Gloucester; he eventually restored his family's traditional amity with France, helping to drive the English from the country in the 1450s, as is depicted in *1 Henry VI*. However, both historically and in Shakespeare's sources, Joan of Arc had nothing to do with Burgundy's defection, which took place four years after her death. This alteration serves to amplify the importance of Joan, who is Shakespeare's chief representative of the deceitful and villainous French.

Captain Minor character in *1 Henry VI*, an English officer. When Talbot is invited to visit the Countess of Auvergne, in 2.2, he rightly suspects a trap and confers with the Captain. Though he is not seen in 2.3, the Captain is presumably responsible for the troop of soldiers who immediately free Talbot when the trap is sprung.

The same character (or perhaps a different captain) challenges the cowardly Fastolfe, who is fleeing from the battle in 3.2. And, in 4.4, a captain precedes Sir William Lucy in seeking reinforcements from the Duke of Somerset.

Charles VII, King of France (1403–1461) Historical figure and character in *1 Henry VI*. The historical Charles VII became king of FRANCE upon the death of his father Charles VI (the French King of *Henry V*), as is recorded in 1.1. However, he is throughout the play referred to as the Dauphin (sometimes rendered as Dolphin), a title traditionally applied to the eldest son of a French monarch and not to a king. This reflects the historical English position that the treaties following the conquests of Henry V gave the French crown to the English king. Charles's enthronement was therefore an act of rebellion, and the French subsequently drove the English from their lands.

In the play, Charles is not readily distinguishable from the other French noblemen, who are all depicted as boastful but inept, treacherous, and cowardly warriors. Charles moons lovingly over Joan La Pucelle at first—for instance, in 1.2.107–117—but he is quick to turn on her at the first misadventure of their campaign (2.1.50–53). In his final scene (5.4), he takes the advice of his nobles and agrees to a peace treaty with the intention of violating it later. (Historically, the treaty referred to was a mere truce, followed by the fighting—already undergone in the play—that drove the English out of France.)

Countess of Auvergne Minor character in *1 Henry VI* a French noblewoman who attempts to capture Talbot by means of a ruse. She invites him to visit her castle, pretending an innocent desire to meet so valiant a hero in person. He receives the invitation in 2.2, but, suspicious, he plans a counterploy. In 2.3 she springs her trap, but following his plan, a troop of soldiers immediately frees him. Talbot gracefully accepts the Countess's apology.

This episode is entirely fictitious, probably derived by the playwright from similar events in the "Robin Hood" cycle of tales. It serves to emphasize the virtues of Talbot, whose eventual death in battle is one of the climaxes of the play. In attributing such deceit to the French, implicitly denying their military strength, the episode contributes to the play's chief point—that the successes of the French could not have occurred without dissensions among the English.

Exeter, Thomas Beaufort, Duke of (1337–1427) Historical figure and character in *1 Henry VI* and *Henry V*, illegitimate son of John of Gaunt and younger brother of Henry Beaufort, the Bishop of Winchester. In *1 Henry VI* Exeter speaks of his position as the "special governor" (1.1.171) of the infant King Henry VI, which reflects his historical appointment, under the will of Henry V, as the new King's tutor. Although the historical Exeter died a few years thereafter, before most of the events of the play, Shakespeare kept him alive to function as a periodic commentator on the action, like a Greek CHORUS, predicting disaster for the feuding English. For instance, he closes 3.1 with a grim forecast of the WARS OF THE ROSES, hoping that his own "days may finish ere that hapless time" (3.1.189–201).

In *Henry V,* set a decade earlier, Exeter is a valued follower of his nephew the king, but he has no distinctive personality. He bears a boldly defiant message from Henry to the French King and the Dauphin in 2.4, and in 4.6 he recounts the death of the Duke of York at AGINCOURT, in tones reminiscent of courtly epic poetry. Thus Exeter's formulaic speeches help to maintain a distinctive tone in both plays.

The historical Exeter, though born a bastard, was granted princely titles and incomes even before being legitimized by his father at the age of 40. He was an important military commander under both Henry IV and Henry V, and he was named an executor of the latter's will. As in *Henry V,* 3.3.51–54, Exeter was made governor of HARFLEUR after its capture by Henry, though it is unclear whether or not he fought at Agincourt. He was not named Duke of Exeter until after most of the events of *Henry V;* Shakespeare took this minor inaccuracy from HOLINSHED's *Chronicles.*

Falstaffe, Sir John (Sir John Falstaff) Name given to Sir John Fastolfe in some editions of *1 Henry VI.*

Fastolfe, Sir John (ca. 1378–1459) Historical figure and character in *1 Henry VI,* an English officer in the HUNDRED YEARS' WAR. In the play Fastolfe is depicted as a cowardly soldier whose hasty retreats cause great losses to the English. His retreat at Patay, near ORLÉANS, was recorded in the chronicles that were Shakespeare's sources, but the playwright magnified this single event in order to

create a striking contrast to the heroism of the play's most important figure, Talbot. The defeat at Patay is reported in 1.1 by a Messenger, who says that Fastolfe has "play'd the coward" (1.1.131). In 1.4 Talbot describes his resultant captivity, and he rails against the "treacherous Fastolfe" (1.4.34). Fastolfe first appears on stage in 3.2; he is fleeing ignominiously during the assault on ROUEN, an entirely fictitious episode. Asked whether he is abandoning Talbot, Fastolfe replies, "Ay, all the Talbots in the world, to save my life" (3.2.108). Finally, in 4.1, Talbot angrily tears the Order of the Garter from Fastolfe's leg, describing again the action at Patay. The king promptly banishes the coward, who departs in silence.

The historical Fastolfe had a very different career. The incident at Patay, which did not result in Talbot's captivity, is viewed by modern historians as having been chiefly due to bad generalship by Shakespeare's hero, necessitating a sensible withdrawal by Fastolfe, his fellow commander. The Duke of Bedford seems to have been most upset by the episode; it is he, not Talbot, who stripped Fastolfe of his Garter (temporarily and probably without authority) while an investigation was conducted at Talbot's request. The investigators exonerated Fastolfe completely, and he went on to complete a distinguished career as a general and diplomat.

The only early text of *1 Henry VI,* that in the FIRST FOLIO of 1623, names this character Falstaffe. Subsequent editors, however, generally have used the historical figure's correct name, thereby avoiding confusion with Shakespeare's great comedic figure Falstaff.

Fiend Any of several minor characters in *1 Henry VI,* the supernatural beings that Joan La Pucelle summons by means of sorcery in 5.3. Joan asks the assistance of these creatures "cull'd / out of the powerful regions under earth" (5.3.10–11) in fighting England. However, they silently refuse, leading her to realize that all is lost. Her capture follows immediately.

Gargrave, Thomas (d. 1429) Historical figure and minor character in *1 Henry VI,* an officer who is killed by the same cannon shot that kills the Earl of Salisbury at the siege of ORLÉANS in 1.4. The historical Gargrave is a minor figure in Shakespeare's sources, a nobleman who is recorded as having been killed at the siege.

General Minor character in *1 Henry VI*, a French officer on the walls of BORDEAUX. He rejects Talbot's demand for the surrender of the city in 4.2.

Glansdale, Sir William (fl. 1429) Historical figure and minor character in *1 Henry VI*, an officer present when the Earl of Salisbury is killed at the siege of ORLÉANS in 1.4. The historical Glansdale is a minor figure in Shakespeare's sources as well; he was an officer who is recorded as having been present at the siege.

Gloucester, Humphrey, Duke of (1390–1447) Historical figure and character in *1* and *2 Henry VI*, *2 Henry IV*, and *Henry V*, the youngest son of King Henry IV and the brother of King Henry V and the dukes of Clarence and Lancaster. Gloucester is an important figure in the aristocratic disputes of the *Henry VI* plays, presented as the chief cause of the English loss to FRANCE in the HUNDRED YEARS' WAR. In the later works, where he is a younger man, he is a minor character.

In the *Henry VI* plays, Gloucester engages in a running dispute with his uncle the Bishop of Winchester. He is depicted as a valorous defender of England's honor, whereas Winchester is an opportunistic politician. Their feud rages through 3.1 of *Part 1*, after which it is replaced in importance by that between York and Somerset. In *Part 2* Gloucester's wife, the Duchess of Gloucester, is convicted on charges of witchcraft and banished. Then, in 3.1, Gloucester himself is arrested at BURY ST. EDMUNDS, falsely charged with treason, and killed. Hired murderers flee the scene of the crime at the beginning of 3.2; the Second Murderer regrets the deed because the duke's death had been marked by religious penitence.

After Gloucester's death the country slides into civil war, and we are meant to see him as having been the guardian against such an event. In order to magnify the duke's virtues, two otherwise irrelevant anecdotes are inserted into the story. In 2.1

Gloucester demonstrates his perceptiveness by exposing the imposter Simpcox, and in 3.1 he wisely postpones a potentially explosive issue, York's appointment as regent in France, until a marginally related dispute can be resolved. These incidents demonstrate the qualities of prudence and judgment that are shortly to be denied the country by the duke's murder.

The historical Gloucester was very different from the "good Duke Humphrey" (*2 Henry VI*, 3.2.122) of these plays. Shakespeare, following his sources and the established opinion of his own time, was opposed to the political position of Gloucester's enemies and he thus depicted Humphrey as a patriot. Winchester headed a "peace party" that advocated a withdrawal from a war virtually lost. Gloucester and the "hawks" of the day, however, insisted that the war go on. In the HISTORY PLAYS Shakespeare presents the view that the French were able to drive the English from France only because of English disunity, and Gloucester's insistence on continuing the war was taken to demonstrate a patriotic faith in English arms that the "peace party" lacked.

Gloucester was in fact selfishly ambitious, quite willing to pursue his own interests at the expense of the country's, once the restraining influence of Henry V was gone. After Henry's death Gloucester's power was restricted by a council of nobles who recognized his headstrong selfishness. He rebelled; the dispute with Winchester at the TOWER OF LONDON (*1 Henry VI*, 1.3) reflects Gloucester's actual coup attempt of 1425. A year later he eloped with the wife of a close friend of the Duke of Burgundy, England's most important ally, and then recruited an army to support his new wife's claims. A duel with Burgundy was avoided only by the annulment of the marriage. This affair was among the grievances that Burgundy cited when he eventually defected from the English alliance against France. Later Gloucester scandalously married his mistress, Eleanor Cobham, who, as Duchess of Gloucester, was found guilty of treason and witchcraft.

No evidence has ever been offered to support the belief that Gloucester was murdered. Although he died while in Suffolk's custody, historians generally believe that his death was natural. No question of murder arose at the time, and Suffolk's banishment only occurred some years later, for different reasons.

In *2 Henry IV* and *Henry V*, set years earlier, Gloucester's role is minor. He is present at his father's deathbed in 4.4 and 4.5 of the first play, and in 5.2 he commiserates with the Chief Justice on the treatment the jurist expects to receive from the new king, whom he believes is an enemy. In *Henry V* Gloucester is an almost anonymous member of the king's entourage.

Governor of Paris Minor character in *1 Henry VI*, an official commanding the capital of English-occupied FRANCE. The Governor wordlessly takes an oath of allegiance to Henry VI when the king is crowned monarch of France in 4.1.

Henry VI, King of England (1421–1471) Historical figure and title character of *1, 2,* and *3 Henry VI*. Despite their titles, King Henry is not the leading figure in any of the *Henry VI* plays. In *Part 1* he is a child, and even the story of the nobles who presume upon his weakness is overshadowed by the account of the military loss of FRANCE and the bravery of Talbot. In *Part 2* Henry is merely a witness to the political developments that occupy the play: the fall of Gloucester and the rise of York. In *Part 3* he is more articulate but no less helpless. Pious and plaintive, he is crushed between the contending forces that his weakness has allowed to rise. He is finally killed, and his corpse appears early in *Richard III*.

Henry is a virtuous man; he is gentle, thoughtful, and governed by a sense of moral values. However, fate has placed him on a throne and he lacks the ruthless vigor required of a medieval ruler. In fact, he is a paragon of weakness—a vacuum into which disorder rushes—and the HISTORY PLAYS are about order and disorder.

In *1 Henry VI* the king is an infant at the outset and only a young man at the end. He is distressed by the rivalries he sees around him but is unable to resolve them, being entirely incompetent in worldly matters. In his most important action in the play (4.1.134–173), Henry makes a grave error in his haste to defuse the hostility between York and Somerset, dividing the English military command

between the two disputants. At the close of the play, he succumbs to the unscrupulous arguments of the Earl of Suffolk and agrees to marry Margaret, a decision that the subsequent plays demonstrate to have been disastrous for England and for Henry himself.

In *2 Henry VI* the king, although an adult, is no more in control of his kingdom than he was in his youth. His chief interest is religion, and in the face of dangerous dissensions, his only response is to preach the virtues of unity and peace. He is thoroughly manipulated by others, first by Suffolk and then, after that lord's death, by Queen Margaret. He permits the ruin of Gloucester, although he knows it to be unjust. Even when faced with the bloody rebellion led by Jack Cade, the king cannot take decisive action, but again thinks first of his religion. When York rebels, opening the WARS OF THE ROSES, Henry is again quite helpless. He realizes his own unsuitability for command and regrets his position in life.

In *3 Henry VI* the king attempts to bring about an end to the growing civil war, but the leaders of the two factions, York and his son Richard (Richard III) on one side and Margaret on the other, will not be appeased. Henry protests the barbarities that ensue. He is the only important character in the play who does not espouse the principle of revenge, but he cannot influence the action. His position as king is well exemplified during the dispute among the nobles in 2.2, where he twice demands to speak (at 117 and 119–120) and has no chance to say another word in the scene. In 2.5, a scene central to the play, Henry withdraws from a raging battle to meditate lyrically on the virtues of a pastoral existence that is as far removed from his reality as it imaginably could be. In stark contrast, he immediately witnesses the grief of the Son That Hath Killed His Father and the Father That Hath Killed His Son. He is completely dispirited after these incidents; this gentle man is finally crushed by his world. Only as he is killed does Henry again come alive on the stage, prophesying the future crimes of his murderer, in anticipation of the next play in the cycle, *Richard III*.

The character and career of the historical Henry VI are less clearly delineated. While he was certainly not the strong, activist monarch that his father, Henry V, had been, it is uncertain how much his courtiers manipulated him. He possessed the powers of a medieval king and could not be defied if he were to insist on something. Even in Shakespeare, when he decrees the banishment of Suffolk, the earl leaves. However, it is uncertain when and on what points he stood firm, so we cannot know how much he is to blame for the wartime policies of the 1440s (in *Part 1*), for the unrest of the following decade (in *Part 2*), or for the policies of the civil war period. It is known that, in the early 1450s, Henry was literally incompetent for a time, being beset with a mental illness that rendered him speechless and almost immobile. The playwright chose to ignore this episode (during which York ruled and the country remained stable and at peace)—perhaps because it would have aggrandized York, perhaps because he wished to avoid offending the dignity of a ruler.

In any case, Shakespeare was more concerned with drama than with history, and as Henry's character develops through the plays, we can observe the young playwright learning how to devise a suitable tragic figure whose very virtues are his undoing. The germ of some of Shakespeare's great characters is here: A man who is good finds himself in a situation where his limitations generate an evil that crushes him. In *Richard II*, and later in *Hamlet* and *King Lear*, the drama can rest upon this predicament. However, in the *Henry VI* plays the playwright had not yet honed his skills so finely, and Henry VI can merely speak of his woeful ineffectuality while the world sweeps him away.

Joan La Pucelle (Joan of Arc) Historical figure and character in *1 Henry VI*, a leader of the French forces in the HUNDRED YEARS' WAR. The historical Joan of Arc was known as La Pucelle, "the virgin," in her own lifetime, and Shakespeare takes the name from the chronicles. In Acts 1–4 Shakespeare's Joan is in some respects difficult to distinguish from the other French leaders, Charles VII, Alençon, and Reignier; like them, she is intended to show, by her trickery and lack of military valor, that a French victory would have been impossible without the English dissension that is the play's chief theme. Unlike her fellows, though, Joan can be a charismatic leader. In 1.2 she revives the morale of the French after a lost skirmish, and in 1.5 she leads them in breaking the English siege of ORLÉANS, as the historical Joan had done.

This is as much of the real John of Arc's life as the play reflects, however. The English capture of Orléans in 2.1 is entirely unhistorical, as is, of course, the French leaders' flight from a single English soldier. Similarly, Joan's devious tactic while taking ROUEN in 3.2, is fictitious; in fact, the actual anecdote that Shakespeare drew upon tells of an *English* strategy in a different battle. In 3.3 Joan convinces the Duke of Burgundy to abandon the English cause; in actuality, Burgundy did not withdraw from his alliance with England until well after Joan's death.

In Act 5 the playwright recasts Joan as a villainess in an altogether more absolute manner. Joan's sorcery in 5.3, where she calls up Fiends, is simply intended to blacken her image. (Similarly, the other characters insult Joan freely throughout the play, casting aspersions on her courage and her virginity and frequently accusing her of witchcraft.) Lastly, in Shakespeare's most glaring misrepresentation of Joan, she makes a cowardly attempt, in 5.4, to avoid execution, first by claiming royal birth and refusing to acknowledge her father, the Shepherd, and then by disavowing her virginity and claiming to be pregnant. She goes to her death cursing England and the English.

The play's uncharitable attitude toward Joan of Arc has stimulated much hostile criticism. In fact, this feature was once taken as evidence of non-Shakespearean authorship, on the grounds that no great writer would stoop to such propagandistic viciousness. However, such keen anti-French sentiments were common in Elizabethan times, as well as in the play's source material, such as the chronicles of HALL and HOLINSHED, and modern authorities, whatever their opinions as to the authorship of *1 Henry VI*, do not find it odd that a playwright should have portrayed Englishmen insulting Joan in this manner.

The historical Joan, born Jeanne d'Arc, began, at the age of 12, to hear voices that she understood to be those of angels and of God, advising her to lead a holy life. Later the voices instructed her to help Charles VII drive the English from FRANCE. In

1428 she persuaded a local military commander to take her to Charles's court, where she convinced Charles to permit her to lead a small army to relieve besieged Orléans. Remarkably, her troops were victorious, and she is still known as "the maid of Orléans." Her continued participation in the war infused the French with the courage and confidence that turned the tide of the conflict. She was captured by Burgundian forces in 1430. Her captors sold her to the English under Warwick, who arranged for a "show trial" for heresy before a French ecclesiastical tribunal. She was convicted and burned at the stake on May 30, 1431. Her conduct at the trial was, by all accounts, dignified and honorable, entirely unlike that of the Joan of the play. In 1456 her admirers obtained a retrial, at which her innocence was pronounced. She was declared a saint by the Catholic Church in 1920.

John Talbot (Young Talbot) (1425–1453)   Historical figure and character in *1 Henry VI*, the son of Lord John Talbot, England's heroic general. Also known as Young Talbot, John appears in 4.5, fighting courageously beside his father. When Talbot realizes that the coming battle is a doomed one, he attempts to persuade John to flee and save his life. The young man, citing the family honor, refuses in 4.6.42–53. John does die, and, in 4.7, Talbot, dying himself, addresses his son's corpse, praising John's exploits in the battle.

Shakespeare intended the melodramatic deaths of Talbot and John to contrast with the selfishness of York and Somerset, whose disputes denied the heroes reinforcements. To increase the poignancy of the comparison, Young Talbot is said to be his father's only son, but in fact several others carried on the Talbot line. Further, John appears quite young, although the historical figure was in his late 20s and had a number of children.

Keeper   Minor character in *1 Henry VI*, one of the guards who attends the imprisoned Mortimer in the Tower of London in 2.5.

Lawyer   Minor character in *1 Henry VI*, an observer of the quarrel between the Duke of Somerset and Richard Plantagenet. Called upon by Somerset for an opinion, the Lawyer answers with comical exactitude, "Unless my study and my books be false, / The argument you held was wrong in law . . ." (2.4.57–58).

Legate   Minor character in *1 Henry VI*, the papal ambassador who is to receive the money the Bishop of Winchester owes the pope for his promotion to cardinal. He acknowledges his errand in his single line, 5.1.55. The episode typifies anti-Catholic sentiment in England in Shakespeare's time.

Lucy, Sir William   Character in *1 Henry VI*, an officer who seeks reinforcements for Talbot during that general's fatal battle in Act 4. Lucy approaches both York and Somerset, but these noblemen are feuding; each blames the other for Talbot's position, and each refuses to send assistance. Lucy grieves for the loss of England's conquests in FRANCE, emphasizing Shakespeare's point that only dissensions among the English made a French victory possible.

Margaret of Anjou (1430–1482)   Historical figure and character in *1, 2,* and *3 Henry VI* and *Richard III*, the French-born queen, and later widow, of King Henry VI. Taken as a single role, running through four plays, Margaret is surely the greatest female part in Shakespeare. She develops from an ingenuous young woman thrust into prominence, through a career as a scheming plotter and a courageous and persistent military leader, to a final appearance as a raging, Furylike crier of curses against her triumphant enemies.

In *1 Henry VI* Margaret plays only a brief role as a French prisoner of war intended as a bride for King Henry by the devious Suffolk, who loves her himself. Her importance is chiefly to prepare the groundwork for the action of *2 Henry VI*. She replaces Joan La Pucelle (Joan of Arc) as the symbolic Frenchwoman who plagues an England that is divided by the selfish ambitions of the aristocracy. Her appearance marks the completion of one disaster, the loss of FRANCE, and begins another, a civil war.

In *2 Henry VI* Margaret's flawed personality is demonstrated early on. She conspires with Suffolk to bring about the fall of Duke Humphrey of Gloucester because she resents Gloucester's influence over the king and her own resulting insignificance. She displays an evil temper when she abuses the Petitioners in 1.3.37–40; later in this scene she mocks her husband's piety. When Gloucester is forced by his wife's disgrace to leave his position as Lord Protector, Margaret exults, comparing Gloucester's relinquished sceptre of office to an amputated limb (2.3.42). We are not surprised when this bloodthirsty woman proposes killing her enemy to ensure against his possible return to power. When the king mourns Gloucester's subsequent murder, Margaret dares to complain that Henry is paying too little attention to her. Henry banishes Suffolk from England for his part in the crime, and as the queen and the duke bid each other farewell, they reveal their passionate love. Shakespeare, aware as always of the complexities of human nature, offsets his portrait of this villainess by evoking a glimmer of sympathy for a woman losing her lover.

In *3 Henry VI* the queen assumes a major role in the civil war, replacing the ineffectual king at the head of his armies. Her bold and cruel nature reveals itself most fully at the battle of WAKEFIELD, when York has been captured. Margaret insists on postponing his death so that she may torment him with barbs and, most chillingly, with evidence of the murder of his child, Rutland. Before he dies, York rages at her, calling her a "she-wolf of France" (1.4.111), an epithet that has been applied to her by writers ever since, and as a "tiger's heart wrapp'd in a woman's hide" (1.4.137), a line that was parodied in the earliest reference to Shakespeare that has survived (see GREENE, ROBERT).

At the crucial battle of TOWTON, Margaret is plainly the leader of the king's forces; in fact, she orders Henry to stay away from the fighting. Although the battle is lost and York's son Edward (Edward IV) is enthroned in Henry's place, Margaret refuses to give up, and she goes to France in search of military aid. When she is once again prepared to fight, she sends word to Edward, "Tell him my mourning weeds are laid aside, / And I am ready to put armour on" (3.3.229–230). Despite her viciousness, this dauntless warrior does command some admiration.

The subsequent battle of TEWKESBURY results in Margaret's final defeat. Forced to witness the killing of her son, the Prince of Wales, Margaret is reduced to lamentations and curses ironically similar to those delivered by York just three acts earlier. Richard, later Richard III, wishes to kill Margaret, saying, "Why should she live to fill the world with words?" (5.5.43). He aptly predicts her role in *Richard III*.

Margaret's role in that work is limited to only two scenes, but it is a very powerful element of the play, for she represents Nemesis, the personification of retribution through fate, a theme that underlies the entire minor TETRALOGY, which *Richard III* closes. In 1.3 she heaps elaborate curses upon her victorious foes, reserving for Richard her choicest and subtlest imprecations, hoping that his punishment not come to pass until his "sins be ripe" (1.3.219). In the formal and theatrical manner of a Greek CHORUS, Margaret restates past grievances and suggests future developments. She departs with the prediction that her enemies will come to regard her as "a prophetess" (1.3.301). Before her return, in 4.4, many of her curses will have been substantially fulfilled through Richard's murderous malignity, and Richard's own downfall is in progress. Several of Richard's victims reflect on Margaret's curses as they go to their deaths, thereby making more evident her role as Nemesis.

In 4.4 Margaret gloats over the misfortunes of Queen Elizabeth and leaves for France, content that she has stayed in England long enough to witness the fall of those who brought about her decline. As she departs, the climax of the play is about to unfold, and she has fulfilled her function. As an almost supernatural embodiment of Vengeance, she has represented an amoral world that is now to be overcome by the Christian reconciliation of Richmond.

Although Margaret of Anjou was a central figure in the WARS OF THE ROSES, Shakespeare took considerable liberties with her story. He magnified the importance, and the evil, of a queen who only naturally used her strengths to shore up the fortunes of her incompetent husband. Her foreignness and her gender made her useful as a witchlike figure at the center of the web of treachery and violence that characterize the plays of the minor tetralogy.

For instance, Margaret's love affair with Suffolk, from its beginnings in *1 Henry VI*, is entirely fictitious. In *Part 2* Shakespeare ascribes to her an important role in English politics almost from the moment she sets foot in England in 1444. In fact, Margaret was a 14-year-old bride with no political experience, placed in an unfamiliar court and country, and she had little or no impact on English affairs for a decade. The fall of the Duchess of Gloucester, which she helps bring about in the play, occurred historically before her arrival. The Duke of Gloucester was probably not murdered, and Margaret had little to do with his political defeat in any case. In 1453 she attempted to assume the Regency of the realm during the period of her husband's insanity (ignored by Shakespeare). However, government by a Frenchwoman was unacceptable to the English aristocracy, and York was appointed Protector. His replacement by the queen's protégé, Somerset, eventually led to the opening of the wars, with the first battle of ST. ALBANS.

Queen Margaret was not present at that conflict, as she is in Shakespeare, but in the period immediately following it, she became an important leader of Henry's forces. However, the central incidents in the playwright's version of Margaret's role as a leader are fictitious. The queen was not present to seize control on the occasion of Henry's concessions to York, enacted in 1.1 of *3 Henry VI*; nor was she a party to the killing of York, depicted with such extravagance in 1.4. Although she was indeed a force behind the later renewal of Lancastrian hopes (see LANCASTER FAMILY), Warwick was far more important. She was in any case neither captured at Tewkesbury nor forced to witness her son's death; he was actually killed in the fighting, and she escaped to be captured a week later. She was imprisoned for several years and then ransomed by the King of France, to whose court she retired for the last six years of her life.

In *Richard III*, Margaret's mere presence constitutes a final distortion of history, for she first appears on an occasion that actually took place only after her death in France. Shakespeare ignored this reality in order to use once more, in a highly symbolic manner, the strong but malign character he had developed in the course of the *Henry VI* plays.

Master-Gunner Minor character in *1 Henry VI*, a French soldier in the besieged city of ORLÉANS.

The Master-Gunner instructs his Boy in 1.4 that their cannon is trained on a certin tower where the English leaders are known to stand watch. The Boy subsequently fires the shot that kills Salisbury.

Mayor of London Minor character in *1 Henry VI*. In 1.3 the Mayor breaks up a brawl between the men of the Duke of Gloucester and those of the Bishop of Winchester. In 3.1 he tells the king's conference of further disorders. The incidents serve to illustrate the spreading social chaos that aristocratic dissensions have engendered.

Messenger Any of several minor characters in *1 Henry VI*, mostly soldiers who deliver accounts of battle situations. In the opening scenes, the repeated interruptions of Henry V's funeral by Messengers bearing tidings of English defeats establish the theme of loss and disruption. In 4.3 a Messenger announces to the Duke of York the commencement of the battle that will prove fatal to Talbot. In 2.2 a French Messenger brings Talbot the deceitful invitation from the Countess of Auvergne.

Mortimer, Sir Edmund, Earl of March (1391–1425) Historical figure and character in *1 Henry VI*, uncle of Richard Plantagenet, to whom he bequeaths his claim to the throne. In 2.5 Plantagenet visits his aged and dying uncle in the TOWER OF LONDON, where he is a prisoner. Mortimer tells of the deposition of King Richard II by Henry IV, head of the Lancastrian branch of the royal family. Mortimer, of the York branch (see YORK FAMILY), had been the rightful heir to the throne (see LANCASTER FAMILY). An attempt to install him as king had resulted in his imprisonment for life while still a young man. Mortimer names Plantagenet his successor, and he dies. Mortimer's appearance in the play establishes York's claim to the throne, anticipating developments in *2* and *3 Henry VI*.

Mortimer's claim to royal descent was rather more controversial than the play suggests, for it depended on succession through a woman, a principle of inheritance often not accepted in the medieval world. In any case, the play mistakes this Mortimer for other historical personages, for Shakespeare's sources were likewise confused. By his reference to his mother (2.5.74), this Mortimer seems to be Edmund Mortimer, actually his uncle and neither an earl nor in the royal line of descent. (However, Edmund Mortimer appears in *1 Henry IV*, where the confusion continues and he is given this Mortimer's ancestors.) In his lifelong captivity, the character in *1 Henry VI* resembles both a historical cousin of his and a Lord Gray of Ruthven (a brother-in-law of the other Edmund Mortimer), both of whom died in prison late in life. The actual Edmund Mortimer, Earl of March, died a free man at the age of 36. His loyalty to the crown had been demonstrated. In 1415, his brother-in-law (and York's father), the Earl of Cambridge, plotted to kill King Henry V and place Mortimer on the throne. This was the attempt that is inaccurately described in *1 Henry VI*. In fact, Mortimer himself revealed the conspiracy when he learned of it, and Cambridge, with two others, was executed for treason. His sentencing is enacted in *Henry V*, 2.2, though Mortimer is not mentioned.

Plantagenet, Richard   See York, Richard Plantagenet, Duke of.

Porter   Minor character in *1 Henry VI*, a servant of the Countess of Auvergne who assists in her attempt to capture Talbot in 2.3.

Reignier, Duke of Anjou and King of Naples (1409–1480)   Historical figure and character in *1 Henry VI*, one of the French leaders and father of Margaret of Anjou. Like the other French leaders, Reignier is depicted as a boastful but ineffectual warrior who demonstrates that the French could not have defeated England but for dissensions among the English. He is not himself of any importance in the play, but his presence paves the way for the appearance of his daughter in Act 5. She will marry Henry VI and become a principal character in *2* and *3 Henry VI*.

The historical figure on whom Reignier is based is better known as René the Good, a proverbially popular ruler of Anjou and parts of Provence, who governed his territories wisely and displayed a penchant for literature and the arts. He wrote the text and may have painted the illustrations of one of the

most beautiful of late medieval manuscripts, known as *King René's Book of Love*. René inherited the kingdom of Naples, including most of southern Italy, from a distant relative, but he ruled there for only four years; he was driven out in 1442 by Alfonso of Aragon, who ruled in Sicily. However, while René retained no kingly income or power (from Naples or from more remote claims to the kingdom of Hungary and the former crusader kingdom of Jerusalem), his royal status made him an important figure in European international relations. His daughter was thus a fitting bride for a king of England.

Salisbury, Thomas Montague, Earl of (Thomas Montacute) (1388–1428)   Historical figure and minor character in *1 Henry VI* and *Henry V*, an English general. In *1 Henry VI* Salisbury appears only in 1.4, to be killed by a cannonball fired from the walls of ORLÉANS, dying in the arms of Talbot. The incident emphasizes the increasing revival of French fortunes in the HUNDRED YEARS' WAR. In his even briefer appearance in *Henry V*, set 13 years earlier, Salisbury adds a note of epic valor to the victory of the badly outnumbered English at AGINCOURT, saying, just before the battle, "If we no more meet till we meet in heaven, then, joyfully, . . . adieu!" (4.3.7–10).

The historical Salisbury chiefly served King Henry V as a diplomat and administrator, and under Henry VI he was one of England's most successful generals. Salisbury was indeed killed by a cannonball at Orléans, but he did not die immediately, lingering in pain for a week. Talbot was not present, and Salisbury's funeral in 2.2 is also fictitious, for his body was in fact brought back to England for burial.

Scout   Minor character in *1 Henry VI*, the French soldier who brings news of the English army's approach in 5.2.

Sentry   Any of several minor characters in *1 Henry VI*, French soldiers. Posted on the walls of ORLÉANS at the beginning of 2.1, the Sentries fail to warn their superiors of the English assault, which retakes the town. This episode, along with others, serves to ridicule the French, thus furthering the central point that only dissensions among the English could have resulted in the loss of FRANCE.

Sergeant   Minor character in *1 Henry VI*, a French soldier. In 2.1, just before the English retake the town of ORLÉANS, the Sergeant posts lookouts who then fail to warn the others of the English attack. This, with numerous other incidents, points up the military inadequacies of the French, thus helping to emphasize the importance of dissensions among the English in promoting France's victories.

Servant   Minor characters in *1 Henry VI*. In 4.7 the Servant aids the mortally wounded Talbot on the battlefield and mournfully announces the arrival of the corpse of the hero's son, John, killed in the fighting, with an agonized cry (4.7.17) that vividly expresses the grief of the English at their losses.

Serving-man   Any of several minor characters in *1 Henry VI*, feuding servants of the Bishop of Winchester and the Duke of Gloucester. In 3.1 the king and his noblemen, assembled in the PARLIAMENT HOUSE to settle the feud between the bishop and the duke, learn that the large household staffs of these two are fighting in the streets. These Serving-men have been forbidden to carry arms because of earlier conflicts, but they are now pelting each other with rocks. Several Serving-men burst into the meeting, still fighting, and refuse to stop. One asserts, ". . . if we be forbidden stones, we'll fall to it with our teeth" (3.1.89–90). The episode serves to point up the increasing disorder that has arisen in England because of rivalries among the aristocracy.

Shepherd   Minor character in *1 Henry VI*, the father of Joan La Pucelle, or Joan of Arc. This humble figure encounters his daughter after she has been captured and condemned to death, but she refuses to acknowledge him, claiming to be descended from a long line of kings. He responds by cursing her. This incident, entirely fictitious, is simply part of the play's strong anti-French bias.

Soldier (1)   Minor character in *1 Henry VI*, an English infantryman. In 2.1, during the retaking of

the town of ORLÉANS by the English, the Soldier, crying the name of the great English warrior Talbot, drives the French leaders, including Charles VII and Joan La Pucelle, from the stage. He gleefully claims the clothing they have left behind in their panic. This episode, entirely fictitious, emphasizes the importance to the English cause of the noble Talbot. It also serves to ridicule the French, thus furthering the play's point that only dissensions among the English could have resulted in French victories.

Soldier (2)   Any of several minor characters in *1 Henry VI*. Four French Soldiers, disguised as peasants, accompany Joan La Pucelle and gain entrance to the English-held city of ROUEN in 3.2. They spy out the weakest gate and signal the other French troops, who enter and capture the city. This episode emphasizes the treacherous nature of the French by contrasting Joan's deceitful ruse with the unalloyed valor of the English hero, Talbot.

Somerset, John Beaufort, Duke of   (1403–1444) Historical figure and character in *1 Henry VI*, the rival of Richard Plantagenet, Duke of York. Somerset selects a red rose as his emblem in response to Plantagenet's adopting a white one in the Temple garden scene (2.4). Thus, fictitiously, do the WARS OF THE ROSES begin. Somerset is depicted as dishonorable. He is unwilling to fulfill his agreement to accept the opinion of a majority in his dispute with Plantagenet, declaring that his argument was "here in my scabbard" (2.4.60), and he goes on to taunt his rival about his father's execution some years earlier. When their quarrel erupts again at Henry VI's coronation in PARIS (4.1), the king unwisely attempts to settle it by dividing the command of the troops in FRANCE between them. Then the death of Talbot is attributed to York's and Somerset's refusal to provide him with reinforcements.

The historical Somerset quarreled with York over the divided command in Normandy in the early 1440s, and Shakespeare uses this material in the sequence culminating in Talbot's death, which actually took place nine years after Somerset's own. Moreover, Somerset was a prisoner in France in 1421–38 and thus could not have had taken part in the quarrel with York at the king's coronation or in the Temple garden scene. Thus, John Beaufort's younger brother Edmund, his successor as Duke of Somerset and a character in *2 Henry VI*, is sometimes considered to have been a co-model for the Somerset of *1 Henry VI*. However, Edmund did not succeed to the title until 1448—later than all the events in *1 Henry VI* except the death of Talbot, which Shakespeare linked to an episode that unquestionably involved John Beaufort, the divided command. Therefore it seems best to regard John Beaufort as the Somerset of this play.

Suffolk, William de la Pole, Earl of (later Duke of Suffolk) (1396–1450) Historical figure and character in *1* and *2 Henry VI*, an ambitious nobleman. Suffolk attempts to control King Henry VI through his influence on Queen Margaret, whose marriage to Henry he engineers in *1 Henry VI*. With Cardinal Beaufort, Suffolk leads the plot against Duke Humphrey of Gloucester and personally engineers his murder. The downfall and death of "good Duke Humphrey," presented as a man whose judgment and honesty might have saved the country from the WARS OF THE ROSES, dominates the first half of *2 Henry VI*. Suffolk is thus largely responsible for a national catastrophe, and he is accordingly treated as an arch-villain, calculatingly treacherous and unscrupulous, who will stop at nothing.

In *1 Henry VI* Suffolk emerges as a figure of importance for the first time in 5.3. He has captured Margaret of Anjou in battle and has fallen in love with her on sight. Plotting to make her his paramour, although he is already married, he decides to marry her to King Henry. He offers her a bargain; he will make her Queen of England if she will be his lover. She defers to her father, Reignier, who demands the cession of two territories, Anjou and Maine (parts of English-controlled FRANCE), before he will give his consent. Suffolk agrees to arrange it. In 5.5 Suffolk overcomes the scruples of Gloucester and convinces the king to break a previous marriage agreement and wed Margaret. Suffolk closes the play with a soliloquy in which he proposes to rule the kingdom through Margaret when she is queen. Thus Suffolk's ambition lays the groundwork for the disasters of the civil strife to come.

At the outset of *2 Henry VI*, Suffolk presents Margaret to Henry, who is delighted with his bride, although the terms of the marriage contract include the cession of Anjou and Maine, to the anger and disgust of the assembled nobility. Suffolk's capacity for intrigue is immediately made evident in 1.2, when the renegade priest Hume, having agreed to recruit sorcerers for the Duchess of Gloucester, reveals that he is being paid by Suffolk to set the Duchess up for arrest and prosecution. (The Duchess's séance produces a prediction that Suffolk will die by water.) In 1.3 Suffolk takes advantage of the minor episode of the armorer Horner to embarrass the Duke of York, a potential rival. When Margaret complains to Suffolk of the arrogance of various nobles, he replies that his plots will conquer all her enemies. One of them, the Duchess, is banished in the next scene. In 3.1, after Gloucester has been arrested for treason, Suffolk urges that he be murdered by any means necessary, lest he be acquitted of the charge.

Suffolk hires the Murderers, and we see him arranging to pay them in 3.2. However, he has gone too far; King Henry, stimulated by a furious reaction from the Commons and his own grief at Gloucester's death, banishes Suffolk from England for life. Suffolk proceeds to vent his anger with a bloodcurdling series of imprecations on his foes (3.2.308–327).

The farewells of Suffolk and Margaret at the end of 3.2 reveal their passionate love. Shakespeare often, as here, made a point to emphasize the complexities of human character by evoking some sympathy for a villain. We can, astonishingly, forget Suffolk's viciousness for a moment as he laments the prospect of dying without Margaret.

Suffolk comes to an appropriate end. We see him for the last time on a beach in Kent, as the prisoner of pirates who have captured the ship carrying him into exile. The Lieutenant of the pirates assigns each captive to a different crewman, who can collect a ransom for each life. However, the pirate who receives Suffolk has lost an eye in the battle for the ship; he wants vengeance and proposes to kill his prisoner. He identifies himself as Walter Whitmore, and as Walter was pronounced "water" by the Elizabethan, Suffolk sees that his death could fulfill the prophecy made to the Duchess of Gloucester in 1.4. The Lieutenant proves to be an English patriot who detests Suffolk for the damage his ambitions have done the English cause in France, and he recites Suffolk's political offenses in virulent terms before turning him over to Whitmore for execution. Suffolk dies with an arrogant courage that can be admired.

The historical Suffolk was a grasping, ambitious, and extortionate aristocrat, but he probably did not earn the place he occupies in Shakespeare and in the chronicles that were the playwright's sources. He was an inept general and unsuccessful minister who bore some of the responsibility for the loss of France at the end of the HUNDRED YEARS' WAR, and he did receive a dukedom, which he abused monstrously, for his role in arranging the marriage of Henry and Margaret. But his love affair with the queen is entirely fictitious, based on a passing remark in the chronicle of Edward HALL. The cession of Anjou and Maine occurred some time after the marriage, on the king's initiative; while Henry was doubtless influenced by Margaret, who was possibly supported by Suffolk, the duke did not arrange the matter himself. Suffolk was Gloucester's enemy, and he instituted his arrest at BURY ST. EDMUNDS, having called Parliament to that remote location, within his own territories, in order to do so. But Gloucester was probably not murdered, although rumor immediately and ever after laid his death to Suffolk. In any case, Suffolk was neither charged nor punished; in fact, his position grew stronger than ever after the deaths of Gloucester and Cardinal Beaufort. Not until three years later, when Normandy was finally and irrevocably lost, did Suffolk's enemies find their opportunity to undo him, and even then he was banished for only five years, not life. However, as in the play, his ship was captured by another one, whose crew took it upon themselves to execute the man they believed had slain "good Duke Humphrey." This murder proved to be the opening event in the revolt of Kentishmen led by Jack Cade (presented in Act 4 of *2 Henry VI*).

Talbot, Lord John (before 1388–1453) Historical figure and character in *1 Henry VI*, the principal English military hero in the HUNDRED YEARS' WAR. In 1.1 Talbot's reported capture seems to magnify

English woes. The Messenger who brings this news describes how Talbot's actions in battle had raised English morale. Talbot's account of his captivity, related in 1.4, after he has been ransomed, further demonstrates his capacity to daunt the French enemy. The king acknowledges Talbot's virtues when he repeats his father, Henry V's, remark, "A stouter champion never handled sword" (3.4.19).

Talbot's fate is closely linked with that of Joan La Pucelle in an alternating sequence of victories and defeats that closes with Joan's ignoble capture and death in Act 5, presented in contrast to Talbot's own glorious fall in the immediately preceding battle. The war reaches its theatrical climax in these scenes (4.2–7), in which the brave Talbot fights and dies, along with his young son, John. He is doomed by the dispute between the Dukes of York and Somerset, which prevents reinforcements from reaching him. Sir William Lucy, who comes to collect his corpse, delivers a formal, elegiac recital of Talbot's feudal titles, reminding us how little removed Shakespeare was from the Middle Ages.

Throughout the play, Talbot carries the burden of destiny for the English in their struggle with the French. He is also contrasted with the selfish noblemen whose ambitions cause dissensions within the English leadership that lead to the losses to FRANCE. While the noblemen engage in squabbles and arguments, Talbot is consistently virtuous. Heightening the contrast, Shakespeare rearranged history so that the jealous rivalry of York and Somerset becomes a direct cause of Talbot's death.

In his *Pierce Penniless*, a book of social commentary published in 1592, Thomas NASHE remarked on the contemporary theater's capacity to thrill its public with works depicting patriotic stories "long buried in rusty brass and worm-eaten books." He chose a single example as sufficient to prove his point: "How would it have joyed brave Talbot, the terror of the French, to think that after he had lien two hundred years in his tomb he should triumph again on the stage, and have his bones new-embalmed with the tears of ten thousand spectators at least, at several times, who in the tragedian that represents his person imagine they behold him fresh bleeding." This passage, the earliest known literary reference to *1 Henry VI*, suggests to us how successful the young Shakespeare had been when he created Talbot, a clean-cut hero for his times similar to those played by John Wayne in ours.

Vernon Minor character in *1 Henry VI*, a follower of Richard Plantagenet, later Duke of York. Vernon backs Plantagenet against the Duke of Somerset, in the scene (2.4) that establishes the rivalry that will eventually lead to civil war. Later, in 3.4 and 4.1, he disputes with Basset, a backer of Somerset. By demonstrating the involvement of lesser figures, these incidents illustrate the damage to English morale caused by the dissensions among the noblemen.

Warders Minor characters in *1 Henry VI*, soldiers manning the TOWER OF LONDON who refuse admittance to the Duke of Gloucester in 1.3, citing orders from the Bishop of Winchester. The term *warder* referred to a soldier whose duty was to act as a guard, especially at the entrance to a building or fortification.

Warwick, Richard Beauchamp, Earl of (1382–1439)   Historical figure and character in *1 Henry VI, 2 Henry IV,* and *Henry V.* In *1 Henry VI* Warwick declares for Plantagenet (see WARS OF THE ROSES) in 2.4, and in 3.1 he presents King Henry VI with a petition in favor of Richard Plantagenet's restoration as Duke of York. He is present but unimportant in later scenes. In *2 Henry IV* and *Henry V* we see Warwick as a younger man. In *2 Henry IV* he is an adviser to King Henry IV. He soothes the king's melancholy and rouses him to action in 3.1, and he defends Prince Hal in 4.5, asserting that his debauchery is instructing the young man in the ways of evil, from which he will reform himself. This passage is intended to confirm the essential nobility of the future King Henry V. In *Henry V* Warwick speaks only one line as a member of the King's court.

The historical Warwick was much more important in the affairs of his time than the character is in the plays. As a young man, under Henry IV, he distinguished himself in the army, serving against Owen Glendower's Welsh rebellion and at the battle of SHREWSBURY. He was a highly successful general under Henry V and governed the occupied towns of CALAIS and ROUEN at various times. Upon the king's death, the infant Henry VI was placed in Warwick's care. In *1 Henry VI* Warwick is overshadowed by York, whom Shakespeare wished to emphasize, although the earl was actually a more successful and prominent figure. When he died, Warwick was governing occupied FRANCE as regent for Henry VI.

Shakespeare confused Richard Beauchamp with Richard Neville, a later holder of the same title: in *2 Henry IV,* 3.1.66, Beauchamp is misnamed Neville, and in *2 Henry VI,* 1.1.118–120, episodes from his military career are claimed by Neville. It is sometimes thought that Neville was expressly intended as the Warwick of *1 Henry VI,* but, although the chronology of that play is hopelessly skewed, certain key features point to Beauchamp. While Shakespeare was seemingly unaware of the distinction, it seems likely that Richard Beauchamp is the Warwick depicted.

Winchester, Henry Beaufort, Bishop of (1374–1447)   Historical figure and character in *1 Henry VI,* illegitimate son of John of Gaunt, older brother of the Duke of Exeter, and uncle of the Dukes of Somerset. The same historical figure appears in *2 Henry VI,* where he is known as Cardinal Beaufort. In *1 Henry VI,* 1.1, Winchester's feud with the Duke of Gloucester interrupts the funeral of Henry V, introducing dissension as a major theme of the play. Winchester reveals depths of criminality by plotting to kidnap the infant king, Henry VI, although this plan is not followed up; it seems to be presented solely as an indication of the bishop's character, although it may constitute a remnant inadvertently left in place after a revision. The bishop and Gloucester wrangle further, until their followers are battling in the streets. The king pleads for peace, and while Gloucester is willing, Winchester only reluctantly and hypocritically agrees to a truce.

The quarrel between York and Somerset takes precedence in the rest of the play, and the bishop's role diminishes. In 5.1 he turns over to the papal Legate a bribe owed to the pope for his promotion to cardinal. This does not affect the course of the play, but it confirms Winchester's image as an unscrupulous villain.

Shakespeare depicts Winchester as a MACHI-AVEL, unscrupulously ambitious and persistently at odds with "good Duke Humphrey" of Gloucester. The historical Winchester led a "peace party" that opposed Gloucester in the 1440s. To some extent, Winchester's stance was dictated by his rivalry with Gloucester; each aspired to power in the vacuum created by the king's extreme youth. On the other hand, Gloucester, as brother of Henry V and a veteran of the battle of AGINCOURT, was committed to total victory in France and adamantly opposed any compromise. Winchester favored an accommodation with the enemy to end the long and costly conflict. Shakespeare's position, which his sources and most of his contemporaries shared, was that England lost France as a result of internal dissension that counteracted English valor, which would otherwise have won out. Thus both the sources and the playwright favored the "hawk" Gloucester—in reality something of a monomaniac whose actions significantly hurt the English cause—over the "dove" Winchester, probably the sounder statesman.

Woodville, Lieutenant Richard (Lieutenant Richard Woodvile) (d. ca. 1440)   Historical figure and minor character in *1 Henry VI*, the commander of the WARDERS at the TOWER OF LONDON. Woodville refuses to admit the men of the Duke of Gloucester in 1.3, citing orders from the Bishop of Winchester. The historical Woodville became the father of Elizabeth Woodville, Lady Grey, later queen of England, and of Lord Rivers, both of whom appear in *3 Henry VI* and *Richard III*.

York, Richard Plantagenet, Duke of (1411–1460) Historical figure and character in the three *Henry VI* plays, claimant to the throne of England against the Lancastrian branch of the PLANTAGENET FAMILY (see LANCASTER FAMILY; YORK FAMILY). York attempts to seize the throne at the end of *2 Henry VI*, launching the WARS OF THE ROSES. He fails, dying early in *3 Henry VI*, but his son becomes King Edward IV. The Yorkist cause thus succeeds, only to be brought to ruin (in *Richard III*) by the greedy machinations of

York's younger son, Richard III, who inherits his father's ruthless ambition.

In *1 Henry VI* York's claim to the throne is established. His father, the Earl of Cambridge, has been executed for treason (as is depicted in Shakespeare's *Henry V*) for supporting the royal claims of Edmund Mortimer. The dying Mortimer bequeaths his claim to York, his nephew, in 2.5 of *1 Henry VI*, thus laying the groundwork for the conflict to come. York feuds with the Duke of Somerset, even at the expense of military disaster in the HUNDRED YEARS' WAR.

In *2 Henry VI* York's story is at first overshadowed by that of Humphrey, Duke of Gloucester, whose murder is seen as making the civil war inevitable. Early in the play, York reveals his ambition to seize the throne, but this crafty planner keeps a low profile, even when his appointment as Regent in FRANCE is given to another Somerset, the brother and successor to his old rival. York participates in the plot against Gloucester, but the chief conspirators are the Duke of Suffolk and Cardinal Beaufort.

York is placed in command of an army and sent to crush a revolution in Ireland. He sees that these troops will permit him an opportunity to seize the crown. Despite the grand boldness of his scheme and his demands on himself for extraordinary courage, York's morality is sorely limited; he is prepared to expend any number of lives in the pursuit of his own ambition. He arranges for Jack Cade to foment a revolt in England, providing an excuse for him to bring in his army.

After Cade's rebellion, staged in Act 4, York returns with his army, demanding the imprisonment of Somerset. When this is not done, he announces his claim to the throne and proceeds to battle the king's troops at ST. ALBANS. York's forces are victorious, but the king escapes to London. Thus the civil war has begun as the play ends.

In *3 Henry VI* York compromises: King Henry will be permitted to rule in his own lifetime but will pass the crown to York or his heirs. Richard persuades his father to seize the throne anyway, just as Queen Margaret, who has herself rejected Henry's deal, arrives with an army. In the ensuing battle, York is captured; after a dramatic scene (1.4) in which Margaret mocks him viciously, the Queen and Lord Clifford stab him to death. In his last moments, York heaps insults on Margaret and weeps over the death of his young son Rutland, with whose fate the Queen had taunted him.

York generally functions more as a foil for other characters or incidents than as a well-developed figure himself. In *1 Henry VI* his ambitious rivalry with Somerset functions as a dark backdrop to the upright and patriotic career of Lord Talbot; in *Part 2* his machinations are similarly contrasted with the fate of "good Duke Humphrey" of Gloucester. In the latter half of *Part 2* and in *Part 3,* York simply exemplifies aristocratic ambition in a mechanical manner dependent largely on mere assertion, backed by the tableaux of the battlefield. Even his death scene serves chiefly to present Margaret in the vicious, warlike personality she assumes in that play. Only in his darkly malevolent speeches of *Part 2* is he a stimulating villain, and even then he is overshadowed by Suffolk. In any case, as an agent of evil York pales before the grand MACHI-AVEL that his son Richard is to embody.

York's function as an archetype of selfish ambition is achieved at the expense of historical accuracy. The historical York actually had little role in the action of *1 Henry VI*; his presence is magnified in order to prepare for his role in *Parts 2* and *3.* The character's rise begins with the return of his dukedom to him in 3.1 of *Part 1,* but in fact York had never been kept from that title and so could not be restored to it. York and the Duke of Somerset launch their quarrel in *Part 1,* though in reality the contest between York and Lancaster was not consequential until many years later. Further, the quarrel is made the cause of Talbot's defeat and death, but the divided command depicted by Shakespeare had occurred elsewhere and 10 years earlier. Also, York is assigned elements of the career of the Duke of Bedford. All of these fictions serve to foreshadow the conflict to come, establishing as a longstanding feud a rivalry that actually only developed some years later.

The greatest difference between the historical York and Shakespeare's character is a basic one: York's ambition is presented as a long-meditated plot to usurp the king's power. In fact, although he

was undeniably a powerful figure who attempted to dominate the political world of England in the 1450s, York has nonetheless been considerably misrepresented by Shakespeare. He showed no intention to seize power until very shortly before he actually attempted to do so in 1455, the action that sparked the fighting at St. Albans. He had competed fiercely with Somerset for power, but only for power as a minister under King Henry. He seems to have acted to usurp royal authority only when it became evident that his career and very possibly his life would be in great danger from Somerset and Margaret if he did not. Shakespeare has simply eliminated a great deal of intricate and fascinating politics, most notably any reference to York's capable rule in 1453–54, when King Henry was insane and unable to speak.

It was not the playwright's concern in composing the *Henry VI* plays to render history accurately. He depicted unscrupulous aristocratic rivalry leading to civil war, thus demonstrating the importance of political stability. One of the ways in which he achieved his end was to make the Duke of York a simple paragon of selfish ambition, and his success is demonstrated in the effectiveness of this fairly one-dimensional character in providing the impetus for a great deal of complicated action in the three *Henry VI* plays.

Henry VI, Part 2
SYNOPSIS

Act 1, Scene 1

The court of Henry VI is assembled to welcome the King's new bride, Margaret of Anjou, whom the Earl of Suffolk has brought to England. The Duke of Gloucester reads aloud the terms of the marriage contract, by which Anjou and Maine, French territories that England had conquered, are ceded to Margaret's father. This so upsets him that he cannot read on. Cardinal Beaufort continues, reading that Margaret shall pay no dowry. The king accepts the terms. He then promotes Suffolk to a dukedom and temporarily suspends the appointment of the Duke of York as regent of FRANCE. The royal newlyweds and Suffolk depart. Gloucester, backed by York, the Earl of Salisbury, and the Earl of Warwick, rails against the marriage contract. He leaves, prophesying the loss of France. The Cardinal suggests that Gloucester, the heir apparent to the throne, is quarreling only because he seeks to replace the king. He observes that Gloucester is popular and thus doubly dangerous. The Duke of Buckingham agrees and proposes a plot to unseat Gloucester from his position as Lord Protector. The Cardinal leaves to recruit Suffolk for the plot, and in his absence, the Duke of Somerset contends that the Cardinal is himself ambitious to fill the Protector's office. Salisbury and Warwick speak of the good of the country and decide to back Gloucester, an honest and competent Protector. They recruit York to their cause, but when they leave, York, in a soliloquy, confides that he thinks of himself as the rightful king and of Henry as a usurper. He determines that he will ally himself with the backers of Gloucester and await a good time to seize the throne by force.

Act 1, Scene 2

The Duchess of Gloucester encourages Gloucester to aspire to the throne, but he rejects the idea and rebukes her for it. A Messenger summons the duke, who leaves. Alone, the Duchess speaks of her intention to pursue the crown for her husband. She summons Hume and arranges for a séance with a witch and a sorcerer whom he has contacted on her behalf. She pays Hume and leaves, and he reveals in a soliloquy that he is also in the pay of Suffolk and the Cardinal, arranging a scandalous exposure of the Duchess that will bring down Gloucester as well.

Act 1, Scene 3

Peter, an armorer's apprentice, reports that his master, Horner, has heard the Duke of York express a claim to the throne. Suffolk has Peter taken into custody and Horner sent for. The new queen complains to Suffolk that the king seems merely the equal of his noblemen. Suffolk assures her that his plots will undo the noblemen, but that she must be patient. The king arrives with the nobles of the court. They discuss the regency of France; Gloucester backs York for the position. The queen attacks Gloucester, as do Suffolk, the Cardinal, Somerset, and Buckingham. Gloucester storms off, and the

queen provokes a quarrel with his wife, striking her, and the Duchess leaves also. Buckingham follows her. Gloucester returns, his anger cooled, and again proposes York for the regency, but Suffolk accuses York of treason, and Horner is brought in. Horner denies having said anything about York and asserts that his apprentice is lying. Gloucester calls for a trial by combat. Peter despairs, saying he cannot fight, but the combat is scheduled.

Act 1, Scene 4

Hume assembles the witch Margery Jourdain and the sorcerers Roger Bolingbroke and John Southwell to call a spirit for the Duchess of Gloucester. The spirit Asnath appears and is asked about the future of the king. He replies ambiguously. He predicts a death by water for Suffolk, and he advises that Somerset should avoid castles. The spirit is dismissed, and York and Buckingham appear, placing everyone present under arrest.

Act 2, Scene 1

The members of the court are hunting with falcons. Gloucester and the Cardinal quarrel to the point of arranging a duel. The king opposes the dispute but cannot stop it. A citizen of nearby ST. ALBANS approaches, proclaiming a miracle: a man blind since birth can suddenly see. Gloucester interviews the man, one Simpcox, suspecting a fraud, and his clever questioning confirms his guess. Buckingham appears with news of the arrest of the Duchess of Gloucester as a user of witchcraft and leader of a conspiracy against the king. When his enemies gloat, Gloucester announces that if his wife has indeed done these things, he will reject her and leave her to the process of the law.

Act 2, Scene 2

York outlines his claim to the throne to Salisbury and Warwick. Convinced, they swear allegiance to him, but he cautions them that he is not king yet. They should conceal their plot, he says, and wait for Suffolk, the Cardinal, and their allies to bring down Gloucester, who is the most important Lancastrian.

Act 2, Scene 3

King Henry sentences the conspirators who were arrested in 1.4. The commoners are sentenced to death. The Duchess of Gloucester will be paraded ignominiously through the streets of London and then exiled. The king orders Gloucester to surrender his staff of office. He does so and leaves. Horner and Peter appear for their trial by combat. Horner, expected to win the contest, is too drunk to fight and is killed by Peter. Dying, he confesses having lied and exonerates his apprentice.

Act 2, Scene 4
The Duke of Gloucester witnesses his wife's humiliation in the streets. She forecasts that he will soon be threatened with death by Suffolk and his allies. Gloucester asserts that his unblemished loyalty and honesty will be his protection.

Act 3, Scene 1
The queen's clique insists to the king that Gloucester is planning a coup. The king denies it. The Duke of Somerset appears to announce the loss of all the English territories in France. The king accepts this defeat as the work of God, but York is bitter. Gloucester arrives, and Suffolk accuses him of treason. Gloucester leaves under arrest, and the king, saying that he is grief-stricken, relinquishes his authority to the queen's clique and leaves. The conspirators decide that Gloucester is still too dangerous and agree to have him murdered. A Messenger arrives from Ireland with news that a revolt is in progress there. Suffolk assigns York an army and sends him to suppress the rebels. All but York depart, and the duke reveals his plans in a long soliloquy. He exults that he has an army at his disposal, and he plans a rebellion to be staged by his hired agent, Jack Cade. Then he will take advantage of the unrest and seize the throne.

Act 3, Scene 2
Several murderers flee from Gloucester's chambers and are met by Suffolk, who promises them their pay for the deed. The king and his court arrive, and Suffolk is sent to summon Gloucester. He returns to announce Gloucester's death. The king faints, awakening to mourn. Margaret responds with an extravagant plaint, lamenting that she will be slandered with implications of guilt and that Henry now wishes her dead. She is interrupted by Warwick and Salisbury, who arrive with a crowd of commoners. Warwick reports that the people are distressed by rumors that Gloucester has been mur-

dered. Warwick examines the corpse and points out signs that the duke was indeed slain. He accuses Suffolk. The two agree to a duel and depart, but they return immediately, just ahead of a mob. Salisbury reports that the people demand death or banishment for Suffolk. The king formally banishes Suffolk from England and leaves with his loyal noblemen. The queen and Suffolk are left to make their farewells, revealing that they love each other. Vaux enters with news that the Cardinal is dying.

Act 3, Scene 3
The king, Warwick, and Salisbury witness the Cardinal's death. The delirious Cardinal reveals his guilt.

Act 4, Scene 1
On a beach, members of the crew of a pirate ship assemble their three captives, recently seized from another ship. A Lieutenant of the pirates awards the prisoners to his men, who will collect ransom from them. Suffolk is awarded to the pirate Walter (pronounced "water" in Elizabethan English) Whitmore. Whitmore, having lost an eye in the battle, insists on vengeance and declares that Suffolk must die. Suffolk recalls his predicted death by water. He identifies himself, and the Lieutenant speaks against him, reciting his political crimes. Whitmore takes Suffolk off to be beheaded. The Lieutenant releases one captive, a Gentleman, to carry ransom messages to London. Whitmore returns to deposit Suffolk's head and body at the feet of the Gentleman, who vows to carry them to the king and queen.

Act 4, Scene 2
Bevis and Holland discuss the rebellion of Jack Cade and join the uprising when the rebels arrive. Cade claims to be a PLANTAGENET and the proper heir to the crown. Comically, he promises his followers preposterous rewards. One rebel proposes killing all lawyers, and Cade agrees, ranting against the use of documents. The Clerk of Chatham is brought in as a prisoner, and he is sentenced to death for being literate. A Messenger arrives to warn of the approach of troops led by Sir Humphrey Stafford. Stafford insultingly demands that the rebels surrender, but they refuse.

Act 4, Scene 3

In a skirmish, Stafford and his Brother are slain. Cade proposes to march on London.

Act 4, Scene 4

In the king's palace in London, Margaret, carrying Suffolk's head, mourns her lover's death, while Henry and Buckingham plan how to deal with the rebellion. A Messenger reports the approach of the rebels, and Buckingham recommends that the king retreat until the revolt is suppressed. Another Messenger reports that the rebels have reached London and that some of the citizens are rising in sympathy with them. The king and queen depart with Buckingham.

Act 4, Scene 5

A Citizen reports to Lord Scales, the commander of the TOWER OF LONDON, that the rebels are successfully assaulting London Bridge and that the Lord Mayor has requested Scales's assistance. Scales promises to send aid and issues orders.

Act 4, Scene 6

Cade declares himself Lord of London and commands that the water fountain be made to flow wine for a year. He further declares that it shall be treason to address him as anything but Lord Mortimer. A Soldier enters, calling out for Cade, unaware of the new regulation. Cade orders him set upon, and he is killed. Cade orders that London Bridge and the Tower of London be burned down.

Act 4, Scene 7

Lord Say is brought to Cade's camp. Cade derisively accuses him of various deeds that are usually considered praiseworthy, such as building a grammar school. Say pleads for his life, but after several exchanges Cade sends him off to be beheaded with his son-in-law. Some soldiers return with the two heads on poles. Cade orders these trophies paraded through the streets.

Act 4, Scene 8

Buckingham and Lord Clifford offer the king's pardon to all rebels who will declare allegiance to the throne. A great roar of "God save the king" goes up. Cade counters with a speech that evokes a similar cry in his favor. Clifford, however, seduces the fickle mob back to the king's side. Cade flees.

Act 4, Scene 9

The king laments his fate. Buckingham and Clifford enter and announce Cade's flight. They are accompanied by many former rebels seeking the king's forgiveness, which he grants. News arrives that York has returned from Ireland with a strong army, demanding the removal of the Duke of Somerset. The king, distressed, sends Buckingham to negotiate with York and temporarily orders Somerset to the Tower.

Act 4, Scene 10

Cade hides in the walled garden of an estate and is discovered by its owner, Alexander Iden. After a brief quarrel, the two fight and Cade is killed.

Act 5, Scene 1

York, at the head of an army, announces that he has returned from Ireland to claim the throne, but he observes that he must still pretend loyalty to Henry. Buckingham delivers a message from the king and informs York that Somerset is a prisoner; York accordingly dismisses his soldiers. The king arrives, and York expresses his allegiance. Iden appears with the head of Cade, which he offers to the king. The king knights him. The queen arrives with Somerset. When he sees that Somerset is not in prison, York angrily declares that he shall no longer regard Henry as king and claims the throne for himself. Somerset and Margaret challenge him. York's sons, Edward (Edward IV) and Richard (Richard III), enter to support him, opposing Clifford and his son, Young Clifford, whom the Queen has summoned. Warwick and Salisbury arrive and side with York. Warwick and Clifford vow to fight each other in the battle that is now necessary, and Young Clifford exchanges insults with York.

Act 5, Scene 2

York kills Clifford on the battlefield. The younger Clifford discovers his father's body and, in a lament, compares death to the Last Judgment. He asserts his intention to kill the children of the Yorkists as they have killed his aged father. York and Somerset enter fighting, and Somerset is slain. York notes that the prediction that Somerset should avoid castles has come true; he has been killed beneath a tavern sign depicting a castle. York exits, and the king and queen arrive in retreat. Henry hesitates, but Margaret insists that they must flee in order to fight again.

Act 5, Scene 3

Near the battlefield, Salisbury proposes to York that they should pursue their fleeing enemies. York agrees, as does Warwick, who comments that the battle is likely to become famous.

COMMENTARY

Henry VI, Part 2 is a political play rather than a drama of human interaction or development. It tells of England's collapse into the anarchy and civil strife of the WARS OF THE ROSES due to selfish ambitions unleashed by the weakness of a young and indecisive ruler. As part of the minor TETRAL-OGY of HISTORY PLAYS, this work also furthers the underlying themes of inexorable tragedy caused by the usurpation of the crown by the LANCASTER FAMILY and of the eventual retribution delivered to that dynasty. In *2 Henry VI* these concerns are developed in two episodes. The first, occupying Acts 1–3, involves the political downfall and eventual murder of Duke Humphrey of Gloucester, who is presented as a just and prudent statesman whose leadership might have preserved the kingdom. The second is an account of the final steps the Duke of York takes toward his own seizure of the crown. This episode begins with a popular rebellion led by York's agent, Jack Cade, a comical affair providing relief after the relentless unfolding of Gloucester's fate. It turns vicious, however, illustrating the evil of anarchy unloosed by the murder of "good Duke Humphrey." York capitalizes on the uprising to advance his own claim and brings the nation to civil war at the first battle of St. Albans, with which the play closes.

Shakespeare was dramatizing history in the *Henry VI* plays, but he was not at all averse to alter-ing actual events for dramatic purposes, although *Part 2* uses less such distortion than *Part 1*. The greatest misrepresentation is the depiction of York's ambition, presented as a carefully deliberated plot by a determined usurper. Historically, York, who had nothing to do with the outbreak of Cade's rebellion, made no attempt to seize the crown until very

shortly before the war broke out. Prior to that time he does not seem to have contemplated doing so; he had fiercely competed with the Duke of Somerset for power as a minister under King Henry, but he attempted to rule himself only when it became clear that Margaret's influence on Somerset's behalf was too great to be finally overcome and that Somerset planned to destroy his own power altogether. In order to emphasize the rivalry of the Lancaster family and YORK FAMILY and to stress the evils of aristocratic ambition, Shakespeare humanized the confused political process that had in fact uncoiled in the 1440s and 1450s by making a convincing schemer of York. Much exciting history has simply been eliminated—most notably, York's capable assumption of the regency in 1453–54, when the king fell helplessly insane and was unable to speak.

The story of Gloucester's fate is tightened and given a melodramatic sense of inevitability by com-pressing many events, widely separated historically, into a swiftly flowing narrative. The tale of the Duchess of Gloucester's sorcery and exile is histori-cal, but it occurred four years before the arrival of Queen Margaret. The two women are made con-temporary, thereby involving Margaret in Glouces-ter's fall, and the episode is made to contribute directly to that fall, which it did not actually do. Similarly, the exile and death of Suffolk are moved back by several years and are thereby associated directly with Gloucester's death. Thus six years of aristocratic maneuverings are collapsed into a mat-ter of months in order to heighten the drama of Gloucester's fall and clearly establish it as the spark for the events that follow.

Though the play's point is made by its sequence of events, Shakespeare created a number of believ-able, humanly distinct characters to execute them, marking a great improvement on the masses of quarreling nobles in *1 Henry VI*. King Henry him-self—enthralled by religion, well-meaning but inef-fectual—is moving toward the pathetic, almost tragic figure he becomes in *3 Henry VI*. Also strik-ing are Queen Margaret and the Duke of Suffolk, who are convincing as scheming villains and at the same time inspire sympathy as lovers in their farewell scene (3.2). One sees that Shakespeare is developing the capacity to produce such great later characters as the villains Iago (in *Othello*) and Richard III and the lovers Romeo and Juliet.

Richard III, in fact, makes his first appearance late in this play. His role is unimportant, and he is present simply as a harbinger of the next two dramas in the tetralogy, but he is a cleanly drawn figure, sardonically epigrammatic. Another minor figure, Buckingham, sounds an aristocratic note of peremptory command, and two men who will figure prominently in the next play, Warwick and Clifford, are strongly delineated minor characters in this one.

Given this range of characters and events, the poetic style in *2 Henry VI* is necessarily varied. The speeches of Cade and his rebels are comically gross, while Margaret and Suffolk's farewells draw on the tradition of courtly love. The vicious repartee of the feuding nobles differs from the high poetry of the pirate Lieutenant. In contrast with *1 Henry VI*, Shakespeare here shows his increasing mastery of the difficult task of writing credible speech in verse.

Shakespeare's willful manipulation of his historical sources is successful on the whole but does misfire in some instances. Most notable in this respect are two episodes taken from widely separated accounts in the sources and used to illustrate the good judgment of the Duke of Gloucester. The incident involving Horner's reported remarks about York's ambition provides an occasion for the Duke to exercise prudence. He withholds office from York pending resolution of the matter. However, the resolution never comes. The dying Horner admits that he had made the incriminating comment, but no note is made of the obvious implications concerning York's loyalty and the matter is never again referred to; the playwright has left his audience dangling. In the other incident, Gloucester cleverly exposes the impostor Simpcox. Here, the scene is dramatically complete and quite amusing, but it is too trivial to stand up to the more important events with which it is juxtaposed.

Henry VI, Part 2, although it marks a considerable advance on *Part 1*, is still plainly the work of a young, less than masterly, playwright. Moreover, it suffers from its position in a sequence of plays. Much of the early exposition is intended to provide a link to the action of *1 Henry VI*, and several dramatically unnecessary characters, such as Richard

and Young Clifford, appear in Act 5, where they foreshadow *3 Henry VI*. Nevertheless, it is an exciting play, composed of varied and interesting scenes that generate two plausible climaxes, and it is full of the promise of greater things to come.

SOURCES OF THE PLAY

As in the other history plays, Shakespeare adapted material from the available chronicles. For *2 Henry VI*, his chief source was *The Union of the Two Noble and Illustre Families of Lancastre and York*, by Edward HALL (third edition, 1550), supplemented by Raphael HOLINSHED's *The Chronicles of England, Ireland, and Scotland* (second edition, 1587). He also used John FOXE's *Book of Martyrs* (fourth edition, 1583), from which he took the story of Simpcox's false miracle, along with other details. Various minor suggestions seem to have come from other chronicles, including those of Robert FABYAN and Richard GRAFTON, along with a popular anthology of biographies, A MIRROR FOR MAGISTRATES.

TEXT OF THE PLAY

It is impossible to date the early history plays with certainty, but since *1* and *2 Henry VI* both contain minor resemblances to Edmund SPENSER's *Faerie Queene*, dated December 1589, these plays cannot have been written earlier than 1590. It is thought by many that the four plays of the tetralogy were written in the order in which they are read, and the last of them, *Richard III*, was apparently known to MARLOWE by early 1592. Therefore, it seems likely that the four plays were composed between early 1590 and late 1591. If the second of them is assigned the second quarter of this span of time, we may date *2 Henry VI* to the latter half of 1590.

The play was first published in the form in which we know it in the FIRST FOLIO, in 1623, and that text has been the basis for all subsequent editions. However, a BAD QUARTO edition, known as *The Contention*, was published by Thomas MILLINGTON in 1594 and again in 1600; these editions are known as Q1 and Q2, respectively. Thomas PAVIER published another QUARTO edition (Q3) that included a bad quarto of *3 Henry VI* (see *The Whole Contention*), as part of the FALSE FOLIO (1619). While Q3 may have provided some details for the

Folio text (notably in the genealogy recited in 2.2, adapted by Pavier from John STOW's chronicles), the quarto editions are chiefly of historical interest.

THEATRICAL HISTORY OF THE PLAY

No specific performances of *2 Henry VI* during Shakespeare's lifetime are recorded, but it is clear that all of the *Henry VI* plays were popular, and they were doubtless performed often. In about 1612 Ben JONSON referred to them as well-known works. The architect and designer Inigo Jones drew a costume for Jack Cade at around the same time or a little later, probably reflecting an unrecorded production. However, the earliest known performances are much later, in 1681 and 1723, and both of these were heavily reworked adaptations.

The first performance of the whole play since at least the early 17th century was given in 1864. The play was more successful in the 20th century. F. R. BENSON produced it several times, beginning in 1899. It appeared in a number of history-play cycles, notably in two BBC TELEVISION productions: *AN AGE OF KINGS* (1960) and *The Wars of the Roses* (1964), which incorporates the *Henry VI* plays and *Richard III*.

CHARACTERS

Asnath Minor figure in *2 Henry VI*, a supernatural spirit or devil summoned in 1.4 by the witch Margery Jourdain, with help of spells cast by the sorcerers Southwell and Bolingbroke. The spirit is questioned by Bolingbroke; the queries are provided by the Duchess of Gloucester, who wishes to examine the prospects for a coup. Asnath displays the traditional reluctance of such spirits to answer, but the laws of magic compel him to obey. He is ambiguous about the future of the King; he forecasts a death by water for the Duke of Suffolk, and he cautions that the Duke of Somerset should avoid castles. Bolingbroke then dismisses him. It is thought that Shakespeare intended his name as an anagram of "Sathan," a common 16th-century spelling of "Satan."

Beadle Minor character in *2 Henry VI*, a constable of the village of ST. ALBANS who is assigned to whip the imposter Simpcox in 2.1.

Bevis, George Minor character in *2 Henry VI*, a follower of Jack Cade. Bevis discusses Cade's rebellion with his friend John Holland in 4.2, and the two men join the revolt. In 4.7 Bevis, here called George, serves as the guard over the captured Lord Say. Since John Holland is known to have been a minor actor of the early 1590s, George Bevis probably was also, and his name was likely given to this character, by either Shakespeare or the keeper of a PROMPTBOOK, as a convenience.

Bolingbroke, Roger (d. 1441) Historical figure and minor character in *2 Henry VI*, a sorcerer who, along with John Southwell and Margery Jourdain, is hired by Hume to summon and question a spirit for the Duchess of Gloucester, who wishes to know the prospects for a coup. Bolingbroke addresses the spirit, Asnath. He asks it questions, provided by the duchess, about the futures of the king and nobles. They are all arrested by the Dukes of York and Buckingham. In 2.3 the king sentences Bolingbroke to be strangled.

The historical Bolingbroke was a priest. His execution was of a sort reserved for particularly heinous criminals: he was hanged and then publicly disembowelled and quartered.

Brother Minor character in *2 Henry VI*, brother of Sir Humphrey Stafford. Accompanying Sir Humphrey on a mission to put down the revolt led by Jack Cade, the Brother supports Stafford in his undiplomatic approach to the rebels in 4.2; they are both killed in the skirmish in 4.3. It is known from historical sources that the brother's name was Sir William Stafford (d. 1450).

Buckingham, Sir Humphrey Stafford, Duke of (d. 1455) Historical figure and character in *2 Henry VI*, an ally of the Duke of Suffolk against Gloucester and later of King Henry VI against the Duke of York. Buckingham enters Suffolk's conspiracy cheerfully, nominating himself as a possible replacement for Gloucester as Lord Protector (1.1.177–178). When the Duchess of Gloucester is driven from the assembled court by Queen Margaret, Buckingham volunteers to follow her, remarking that the woman's anger will make her "gallop far enough to her destruction" (1.3.151), and in the next scene, indeed, Buckingham is able to arrest the Duchess for witchcraft. When Gloucester himself is arrested, Buckingham impatiently urges on the action (3.1.186–187). In 4.4 Buckingham counsels the king during the rebellion led by Jack Cade, and, with Clifford, he later (4.8) defuses that uprising by presenting the rebels with the king's offer of pardon. In 5.1 he acts as the king's representative to the Duke of York. Shakespeare's peremptory, sharp-spoken Buckingham rings one of the notes of individual personality among the group of fractious nobles that mark this play as an improvement over *1 Henry VI*.

The historical Buckingham died in the battle of Northampton, and his death is noted in *3 Henry VI* (1.1), though it is placed at the battle of ST. ALBANS, fought at the close of *2 Henry VI*. His son, Henry, Duke of Buckingham, figures in *Richard III*.

Cade, Jack (d. 1450)   Historical figure and character in *2 Henry VI*, the leader of a rebellion and pretender to the throne of England. Cade, whose revolt occupies most of Act 4, is presented as a buffoonish but brutal figure. He makes preposterous promises to his followers and proposes to legislate on such matters as the length of Lent. He also whimsically executes people for being literate or for being ignorant of an arbitrary change in his title. He enthusiastically seconds Dick the Butcher's proposal, "The first thing we do, let's kill all the lawyers" (4.2.73). In the case of Lord Say, the victim's actual virtues, such as having been a benefactor of education, are used by Cade as grounds for his death. Cade orders the destruction of London Bridge, the TOWER OF LONDON, and the INNS OF COURT as well. All this viciousness is explained as having been commissioned by the Duke of York in order to give him a reason to bring an army into England and suppress the rebels.

In presenting this episode, Shakespeare took remarkable liberties with history, for not only did the historical York have nothing to do with Cade's rebellion, but the uprising itself is based in part on accounts of a different event, the Peasants' Rebellion of 1381, when there were attempts to destroy London Bridge and the Inns of Court. The proposal

to kill the lawyers also dates from the earlier revolt, which was a much more anarchic and bloody affair than the one actually led by Cade.

The historical Cade was probably Irish; he had married into a minor landholding family in KENT, and the rebels he led were lesser gentry, artisans, and tradesmen—that is, members of the nascent middle class. Their revolt was intended to achieve well-defined ends that were expressed in a document, the "Complaint of the Commons of Kent," which demonstrates an informed awareness of real political problems. It refers to the loss of France and subsequent Kentish business losses, and to excessive taxation and the extravagance of the royal household. It complains of the dominance of the Duke of Suffolk among the king's councillors, for Suffolk was hated in Kent as an unreasonable and extortionate magnate.

As Cade and his men approached London in June 1450, they ambushed a party of royal troops and killed the commander, Sir Humphrey Stafford, and his Brother, as in the play. At this point the royal government placed Lord Say in the Tower of London as a sop to popular sentiment, and fled to the countryside. (Say was a widely detested Kentish landowner and not the model aristocrat Shakespeare presents.) On July 4 the people of London welcomed the rebels into the city, and Say was taken from the Tower and executed. After several days, the Kentishmen had seemingly worn out their welcome, for the citizens, aided by the Tower guards under Lord Scales, who appears in the play, drove them south across the Thames into SOUTHWARK. There the King's pardon was offered to all who would disperse, and most did. Cade himself did not, and he was pursued and killed by Alexander Iden, who was the Sheriff of Kent and not the simple, patriotic landowner of the play.

Shakespeare thus took a real episode from the period of his play and altered its character in order to make certain points. From the prevalent Elizabethan point of view, which Shakespeare shared, Cade and others like him were traitors pure and simple, propagators of vicious and immoral doctrines that could only undermine society. Thus the playwright felt perfectly justified in depicting Cade's undertaking as a more brutal and violent event than it in fact was, for an important point addressed by the history plays is the value of political stability. The distinction between Cade's revolt and the 1381 uprising was unimportant to Shakespeare; each constituted an unacceptable subversion of a properly ordered society.

The episode of Cade, as it is presented, serves three purposes. First, it provides comic relief after the sustained political battle, ending in the murder of Gloucester, of Acts 1–3. The buffoonery of Cade and his followers is in an old tradition of comical rusticity that Shakespeare always favored. However, the humor quickly turns vicious, and the evil of anarchy is abundantly demonstrated, which is the second function of the action. The uncontrolled common people mirror the dissensions of the nobles and demonstrate, conversely, Shakespeare's most important political point—that all social good derives from a stable monarchy. Third, the episode is associated with the rise of York and thus serves to introduce the final sequence of the drama, the ambitious advance to open rebellion by that lord. Thus, aristocratic ambition is demonstrated to have directly produced tragic disorder among the common people.

Cardinal Beaufort, Henry (1374–1447)   Historical figure and character in *2 Henry VI*, a leader of the plot against the Duke of Gloucester that dominates the first half of the play. The Cardinal, the illegitimate son of John of Gaunt, is a great-uncle of the king and a powerful secular lord in his own right. (The same historical person appeared in *1 Henry VI* as the Bishop of Winchester, where his rivalry with Gloucester is developed; he is sometimes referred to in *2 Henry VI* as Winchester, as in 1.1.56.) In 1.1 the Cardinal smoothly recruits other noblemen to his cause, accusing Gloucester, the heir apparent to the throne, of self-interest, turning against him what should be to his credit—his patriotic anger at the king's foolish cession of lands in his marriage contract. The Cardinal and Gloucester agree to fight a duel in 2.1, but they are interrupted. At the end of that scene, word is brought that Gloucester's wife has been arrested for witchcraft, and the Cardinal gloats that his rival, abruptly humiliated, will not have the heart to fight.

When Gloucester himself is arrested for treason, in 3.1, the Cardinal and his confederates agree that the Duke should be murdered, and the Cardinal volunteers to hire the murderer, although Suffolk actually performs that deed. After Gloucester's murder, word is brought to the king that the Cardinal is dying of a sudden illness. When the king and Warwick visit him in 3.3, he appears to have a bad conscience. The Cardinal's ravings are not quite specific, but they nonetheless convict him.

Historically, Cardinal Beaufort, although he was a rival of Gloucester, was not his murderer; in fact, Gloucester was probably not murdered at all. The cardinal may not even have had anything to do with Gloucester's arrest by Suffolk, which led to the duke's death, for Beaufort by this time had largely abandoned his political role and retired from public life. Shakespeare's version of the cardinal's death is pure fiction; he actually died at home in a normal manner at the age of 73, some months after Gloucester's death. However, the playwright held the opinion, along with his sources, that "good Duke Humphrey" had been victimized by his rivals (see Winchester, Henry Beaufort, Bishop of, in *Henry VI, Part 1*), and he accordingly made an unscrupulous villain, or MACHIAVEL, of the cardinal, who was actually a far more prudent and statesmanlike figure than Gloucester.

Citizen   One of several minor characters in *2 Henry VI*. In 4.5 one of a group of citizens reports to Lord Scales, the commander of the TOWER OF LONDON, that the rebels led by Jack Cade are successfully assaulting London Bridge and that the Lord Mayor has requested Scales's assistance.

Clerk   Minor character in *2 Henry VI*, a victim executed by the rebels led by Jack Cade. Cade and his men are suspicious of the clerk's literacy, which they construe as a sign of hostility toward the peasantry. They are particularly infuriated by the fact that his given name is Emmanuel, a word often used to head legal documents in Shakespeare's time as a token of piety. Cade orders him hung "with his pen and ink-horn about his neck" (4.2.103–104). The incident is one of several that Shakespeare uses to depict Cade's rebellion as an anarchic uprising by ignorant peasants concerned only with killing their betters, although historically this was not the case.

Clifford, Lord Thomas (1414–1455) Historical figure and character in *2 Henry VI*, a backer of King Henry VI against the claims of the Duke of York. Clifford first appears as a representative of the king, offering a pardon to the rebel followers of Jack Cade in 4.8. Following York's declaration of rebellion in 5.1, Clifford supports the king and exchanges insults and challenges with the Earl of Warwick, but in the ensuing first battle of ST. ALBANS, he is killed by York. His son, Young Clifford, on seeing his father's corpse, vows revenge on the followers of York, anticipating events in *3 Henry VI*. In a famous instance of Shakespeare's carelessness, Clifford's death is reported in different ways in *3 Henry VI*. In 1.1.7–10, it is stated that Clifford was killed by common soldiers, which almost surely is historically accurate. However, in 1.3.5 and 1.3.46, his son declares that he was killed by York. The playwright was following separate accounts in his sources, making good dramatic use of the son's reported remark—probably a rhetorical one—and forgetting to omit the altogether more plausible version.

Clifford, Young See Clifford, Lord John, in *Henry VI, Part 3*.

Commons Group of extras in *2 Henry VI*, members of the parliament assembled at BURY ST. EDMUNDS. These representatives of the common people gather in an unruly crowd in 3.2 to protest the murder of the Duke of Gloucester and demand punishment for the Duke of Suffolk. As is usual in Shakespeare, the common people en masse, as distinguished from individual characters, are presented as a thoughtless rabble, controlable only by aristocrats, here the Earls of Warwick and Salisbury. Warwick refers to them as "an angry hive of bees / That want their leader" (3.2.124–125), and Salisbury speaks for them in their address to the king. They prepare the audience for the later appearance of the rebels led by Jack Cade, as the disorder in the state intensifies.

Cromer, Sir James (d. 1450) Historical figure mentioned in *2 Henry VI*, the son-in-law of Lord Say. Cromer himself does not appear in the play, but the rebel Jack Cade orders him executed, along with his father-in-law, in 4.7, and the revolutionaries carry his head on a pole at the end of that scene.

Dick the Butcher Minor character in *2 Henry VI*, a follower of the revolutionary Jack Cade. After making several small jokes at his leader's expense when the rebels are introduced in 4.2, Dick also delivers the famous line "The first thing we do, let's kill all the lawyers" (4.2.73). Elsewhere in the depiction of Cade's uprising, Dick further displays the anarchic brutality that Shakespeare attributed to the episode.

Duchess of Gloucester, Eleanor Cobham (d. 1454) Historical figure and character in *2 Henry VI*, the wife of Duke Humphrey of Gloucester. The Duchess is ambitious for her husband, the heir apparent to King Henry VI, but the Duke repudiates her desire that he be king. She therefore proceeds behind his back. In 1.2 she meets with a renegade priest, John Hume, who has hired conjurers for her so that she may see the future in order to plan a coup. Hume, however, is in the pay of Gloucester's enemy, the Duke of Suffolk, and the Duchess is arrested in 1.4, along with the sorcerers Southwell and Bolingbroke and a witch, Margery Jourdain. These commoners are sentenced to death in 2.3, but the Duchess's punishment is limited to the humiliation of public exposure in a parade through the streets of London, followed by lifelong banishment to a castle on the Isle of Man, in the Irish Sea. Her unscrupulous attempt to harness the supernatural as an aid to treason marks the first stage in the downfall of "good Duke Humphrey," the chief business of Acts 1–3.

The historical Eleanor Cobham was a young woman of relatively low standing, compared to the PLANTAGENET lineage of her husband, and her position seemed to some degree scandalous, both to her own contemporaries and to Shakespeare's. Duke Humphrey had married her after an earlier marriage, to a Burgundian noblewoman stolen from her husband, had been annulled. The new duchess dabbled in witchcraft, and she apparently attempted to divine the date of King Henry's death through the assistance of Hume and the others. However, there seems to be no evidence that she plotted against the king's life. Nor is there evidence that Gloucester's enemies plotted against her; they did not need to, for the duchess initiated her indiscretions herself. She was tried and convicted of using sorcery, and, as in the play, she was sentenced to public humiliation—a punishment usually reserved for common prostitutes—and banishment. She died on the Isle of Man some years later, after enforced residence in several other, less remote locations.

Shakespeare's only important departure from the historical record of this incident is chronological. The duchess's disgrace actually occurred four years prior to the arrival of Queen Margaret in England, with which the play begins, and while the incident was troublesome for her husband, it did not contribute directly to his own ultimate collapse in fortunes. However, the playwright wished to compress all the Duke's embarrassments into a brief sequence of bad luck, and to associate them with Margaret and Suffolk. In this way the play emphasizes the degree to which selfish ambition undercut the one man whose judgment and honesty, in the light of history as Shakespeare and his contemporaries understood it, might have prevented civil war.

Edward (later King Edward IV) See Edward IV, King of England, in *Henry VI, Part 3*.

First Murderer One of "two or three" characters in *2 Henry VI*, the killers of the Duke of Gloucester. Several men, two of whom speak, flee the scene of the crime at the beginning of 3.2. The First Murderer calmly accepts payment for the crime from the Duke of Suffolk, thus distinguishing himself from the Second Murderer, who is conscience-stricken.

Gentleman Either of two minor characters in *2 Henry VI*, captives of pirates in 4.1, along with the Duke of Suffolk. After the gentlemen agree to pay a ransom for their lives, Suffolk is executed by the pirates. One of the gentlemen is released to carry ransom messages to London, and he also receives Suffolk's severed head to deliver to Queen Margaret.

Gloucester, Humphrey, Duke of See Gloucester, Humphrey, Duke of, in *Henry VI, Part 1*.

Henry VI, King of England See Henry VI, King of England, in *Henry VI, Part 1*.

Herald Minor character in *2 Henry VI*, a messenger from the king summoning the Duke of Gloucester to a meeting of Parliament in 2.4.70.

Holland, John Minor character in *2 Henry VI*, a follower of Jack Cade. Holland discusses Cade's rebellion with his friend George Bevis in 4.2, and they join the rebels when they appear. Holland also makes several joking asides in 4.7. A John Holland is known to have been an actor with STRANGE'S MEN in the early 1590s, and it is believed that he played this part. His name was given to the character as a convenience by either Shakespeare or the keeper of a PROMPTBOOK.

Horner, Thomas Minor character in *2 Henry VI*, an armorer who is reported to have remarked that his client the Duke of York was "rightful heir to the crown" (1.3.26). Horner's apprentice, Peter, informs the Duke of Suffolk of Horner's assertion, and Suffolk brings them both before the court in an effort to embarrass York. Horner denies Peter's assertion, and a trial by combat is ordered by the Duke of Gloucester, the Lord Protector. Thus a potentially explosive issue is postponed and diverted into what will prove a minor spectacle for the court. Also, at Gloucester's recommendation, the reappointment of York as regent of FRANCE is withheld until this question should cool off. Thus the episode serves to illustrate Gloucester's qualities of prudence and discretion—ironically not long before his downfall.

Horner, though expected to win the combat against the cowardly Peter, arrives at the contest drunk in 2.3 and is slain by his apprentice. Dying, he confesses that Peter's account had been true, and the apprentice is exonerated. Although the combat is not treated seriously by the court, it prefigures

York's rebellion in the WARS OF THE ROSES, which begins later in the play.

Hume, John (active 1441)   Historical figure and character in *2 Henry VI*, a dishonest priest who arranges to hire a witch, Margery Jourdain, and two sorcerers, John Southwell and Roger Bolingbroke, for the Duchess of Gloucester. The Duchess wishes to read the future so that she can prepare for a possible coup against King Henry VI. In 1.2.87–107 Hume reveals in a soliloquy that he is also in the pay of the Duke of Suffolk, who seeks the Duchess's downfall as part of his campaign against her husband, the Duke of Gloucester. Consequently, Hume's information leads to the arrest of the Duchess, along with that of Hume and the magicians, at a séance in 1.4. Hume's confederacy with Suffolk does him little good, for the king sentences him to death in 2.3 for his part in the plot.

Historically, Hume, whose first name was actually Thomas, was pardoned, for reasons that the chronicles do not specify; there is, however, no other evidence that he was an agent of Gloucester's enemies. Shakespeare's reason for omitting Hume's pardon, seemingly appropriate to his presentation, is not apparent. Perhaps the playwright intended a subtle intimation of treachery on Suffolk's part. Or this may simply be an instance of the petty inconsistencies to which the playwright was persistently susceptible.

Iden, Alexander (active 1450)   Historical figure and minor character in *2 Henry VI*, a landowner who kills the rebel Jack Cade, who has hidden in his garden, in 4.10. Iden represents an ideal of the English country gentleman and small landowner. He is the very opposite of the subversive and destructive Cade and also of the scheming noblemen whose ambitions are the chief business of the play. We see Iden before he knows of Cade's presence, enjoying his garden and rejoicing in his lot. Challenged by the desperate and angry Cade, Iden refuses to send for help. They fight, and Iden kills Cade, cursing the rebel as he does so. In 5.1 he presents King Henry VI with Cade's head and is knighted.

Shakespeare created this paragon of the minor gentry from a bare mention of Cade's killer in the chronicles. The historical Iden was a sheriff of Kent who presumably killed Cade for the sizable bounty that was offered for the rebel's head, which he in fact collected.

Lieutenant   Minor character in *2 Henry VI*, an officer, sometimes called a Captain, of a pirate ship. In 4.1 the Lieutenant distributes among his crew the prisoners his ship has taken; each crewman is entitled to extract a ransom from his prisoner. When Walter Whitmore asserts a desire to kill his instead, the Lieutenant counsels mercy. However, upon learning that the prisoner is the Duke of Suffolk, the Lieutenant patriotically vows to see him slain, knowing that the Duke's ambitious conspiracies have harmed England. He delivers a virulent recital of Suffolk's political offenses and sends him off to be executed by Whitmore.

Some editions of *2 Henry VI*, following the play's BAD QUARTO (see *The Contention*), designate the Lieutenant as a Captain. This small difference seems to have resulted from an assumption that the leader of the pirates would be called their captain. However, the Quarto probably presents a reconstruction of the play from memory, by an actor or viewer, while the Lieutenant's rank in the FIRST FOLIO edition and its successors is believed to come from Shakespeare's original FOUL PAPERS and thus to be what the playwright intended.

Margaret of Anjou   See Margaret of Anjou, in *Henry VI, Part 1*.

Margery Jourdain (d. 1441)   Historical figure and minor character in *2 Henry VI*, a witch hired by Hume to summon a spirit for the Duchess of Gloucester. In 1.4, at a séance, Margery summons the spirit Asnath, and, after it has been questioned by the sorcerer Roger Bolingbroke, she is arrested, with her fellows and the Duchess, by the Dukes of York and Buckingham. In 2.3 the king sentences her to be burned at the stake. The historical Jourdain claimed to have magical powers and was convicted of using them in the employ of the Duchess, and she was indeed burned at the stake.

Master   Minor character in *2 Henry VI*, a petty officer on a pirate ship. In 4.1 the Lieutenant of the ship awards to the Master the ransom of a Gentleman, one of several captured by the pirates.

Mate Minor character in *2 Henry VI*, a sailor on a pirate ship. In 4.1 the Lieutenant of the ship awards the Mate the ransom of a Gentleman, one of several captured by the pirates.

Mayor of St. Albans Minor character in *2 Henry VI*. The Mayor accompanies Simpcox, a confidence man who is presented to the king's hawking party in 2.1.

Messenger Any of several minor characters in *2 Henry VI*, whose announcements spark action by greater figures or provide news of events offstage. In 1.2 a Messenger summons the Duke of Gloucester to a royal hawking party, leaving his wife the Duchess alone to pursue the plot that will eventually bring them both down. In 4.4 a Messenger informs the king of the progress of Jack Cade's rebellion, and in 4.7 another man announces to Cade the capture of an important nobleman, Lord Say. Lastly, in 4.9, a Messenger brings the king the momentous news that the Duke of York has returned from his duty in Ireland at the head of an army, an event that heralds the coming civil war.

Michael Minor character in *2 Henry VI*, a follower of the rebel Jack Cade. In 4.2 Michael brings word that Sir Humphrey Stafford is approaching with troops to put down the rebellion.

Neighbor Any of three minor characters in *2 Henry VI*, supporters of Thomas Horner when he appears, in 2.3, to defend himself in a trial by combat with his apprentice, Peter. Unfortunately for Horner, his friends ply him with liquor by way of cheerful support, and, drunk, he is slain.

Old Clifford See Clifford, Lord Thomas.

One Minor character in *2 Henry VI*, a citizen who approaches the royal hawking party in 2.1, proclaiming that a miracle has occurred: A blind man, who proves to be the imposter Simpcox, has recovered his sight.

Peter Minor character in *2 Henry VI*, an apprentice to an armorer, Thomas Horner. In 1.3 Peter reports that his master has said that the Duke of York is "rightful heir to the crown" (1.3.26). This bit of hearsay is seized upon by the Duke of Suffolk, who accuses York of treason and has Peter repeat his account later in the scene. Horner denies having said such a thing, and the question is referred to a trial by combat. This procedure, a judicious postponement of a potentially explosive issue, is ordered by the Lord Protector, the Duke of Gloucester. In the meantime, at Gloucester's suggestion, York's reappointment as regent of FRANCE is postponed until the matter is resolved. Thus, as his downfall approaches, "good Duke Humphrey" is given an opportunity to display the qualities of prudence and judgment that are shortly to be denied the country through the selfish ambitions of Suffolk and others.

Although Peter is desperately afraid to fight, Horner arrives for the contest drunk in 2.3, and Peter slays him. The dying armorer confesses the truth of Peter's report, and the apprentice is exonerated. Although the nobles do not take this clownish incident seriously, the episode prefigures York's actual treason, which sparks the WARS OF THE ROSES, later in the play.

Petitioners Any of several minor characters in *2 Henry VI* who arrive at court in 1.3 with pleas for justice. The Petitioners, two of whom have spoken lines, join with Peter in planning to address their grievances to the Duke of Gloucester. Queen Margaret and the Duke of Suffolk appear instead and demand to see their petitions; one is personal and the other requests protection from Suffolk himself, who has incorporated common lands into his estates. Peter's business proves useful to Suffolk, but Margaret scornfully rejects the other Petitioners, tearing up their written pleas and abusively ordering them to leave.

Post Minor character in *2 Henry VI*, a messenger who brings word of an Irish rebellion in 3.1.

Prentice Either of two minor characters in *2 Henry VI*, apprentices and friends of the armorer's apprentice Peter, who must fight his master,

Thomas Horner, in a trial by combat. The Prentices encourage Peter before the event, in 2.3.

Queen Margaret of England See Margaret of Anjou in *Henry VI, Part 1*.

Richard Plantagenet (later Duke of Gloucester) See Gloucester, Richard Plantagenet, Duke of, in *Henry VI, Part 3*; Richard III, King of England, in *Richard III*.

Salisbury, Richard Neville, Earl of (1400–1460) Historical figure and character in *2 Henry VI*, a patriotic nobleman, distinguished from the selfishly ambitious aristocrats around him. In 1.1 Salisbury and his son, the Earl of Warwick, determine to support the Duke of Gloucester, an honest and capable minister, against his enemies. In general, Salisbury is overshadowed by Warwick, who is to be a major figure in *3 Henry VI*. For example, in 3.2 Salisbury, speaking for the enraged Commons, demands that Suffolk be punished for Gloucester's murder. However, it was Warwick, a hundred lines earlier, who had established Suffolk's guilt.

Salisbury's finest moment comes in 5.1, when he announces his support of York's claim to the throne. Reminded by King Henry VI of his oath of allegiance, Salisbury replies, "It is great sin to swear unto a sin, / But greater sin to keep a sinful oath . . ." (5.1.182–183).

The historical Salisbury was the son of the Earl of Westmoreland, who appears in *1* and *2 Henry IV*. He was also the son-in-law, and thus successor to the title, of the Salisbury who dies at the siege of ORLÉANS in *1 Henry VI*. Shakespeare distorted Salisbury's political career considerably. Although he was not an enemy of Gloucester, he was not a notable ally of that lord either. As a great magnate of northern England, Salisbury was rather more limited in his concerns than the patriot depicted in *2 Henry VI*. His chief rivals were the Percy family, of neighboring Northumberland, and he did not become close to York until, well after most of the events in the play, York's rival, Somerset, fell into a dispute over land with Warwick. As Somerset's enemy, York became the Nevilles' friend, and the family allied itself with York in time for the beginning of the WARS OF THE ROSES. Salisbury was later captured at the battle of WAKEFIELD and executed at POMFRET CASTLE, although this is not mentioned when the battle occurs in *3 Henry VI*.

The early backing of York's cause by Warwick and Salisbury in *2 Henry VI* seems intended to show how even the apparently upright patriots among the aristocracy became caught in the web of hypocrisy and falsehood that pervades all of these plays. It also serves to foreshadow Warwick's importance as the chief Yorkist in *3 Henry VI*. It is sometimes argued on textual grounds that Salisbury originally had a small role in 1.2 of *3 Henry VI*, but that the character was eliminated, perhaps before any performance was given, as a measure of economy for the acting company, and Salisbury's lines were given to Montague.

Say, James Finnes, Lord (d. 1450) Historical figure and character in *2 Henry VI*, treasurer of England who is captured and killed by Jack Cade's rebels. Lord Say is presented as a noble and courageous man who volunteers to stay in London when the rebels approach in 4.4, although he knows that they particularly hate him, for unspecified reasons. He refuses to retreat with the king, lest his presence endanger the monarch. Seized by the rebels and taken before their leader in 4.7, Say is roundly insulted by Cade and accused of deeds ordinarily considered good, such as founding a school. He pleads his own virtues but is beheaded by the rebels.

Shakespeare incorporated this merciless execution of a patently good man into his version of Cade's rebellion in order to paint it as thoroughly evil. Just as the reality of the revolt was different, so was Say a different sort of nobleman than the one depicted here. He was a widely despised landowner in Kent—greedy, oppressive, and a close associate of the equally detested Duke of Suffolk. Moreover, as Treasurer he was generally held responsible for the high taxes necessitated by the same misrule that had sparked the rebellion. When the rebels neared London, Henry VI's government did not hesitate to imprison Say in the TOWER OF LONDON as a sop to public sentiment before fleeing itself. When the rebels were welcomed into the city, one of their first acts was to execute Say, who made no defense that was recorded.

Scales, Lord Thomas de (d. 1460) Historical figure and minor character in *2 Henry VI*, the commander of the TOWER OF LONDON during the rebellion led by Jack Cade in 4.5. Scales, whose historical role is accurately presented, helps drive the rebels from London. Scales is also mentioned in passing in *1 Henry VI* as having been captured by the French (1.1.146), as indeed he had been historically.

Second Murderer One of "two or three" characters in *2 Henry VI*, the killers of the Duke of Gloucester. Several men, two of whom speak, flee the scene of the crime at the beginning of 3.2. The Second Murderer regrets the deed because their victim had died religiously. (See also First Murderer.)

Servant Minor character in *2 Henry VI* who accompanies the Duke of Gloucester in 2.4 when he watches his wife, the Duchess paraded ignominiously through the streets of London as part of her punishment for conspiring against the king. The Servant suggests that he and his fellows could rescue the Duchess, but the duke rejects the idea. The episode emphasizes the Duke's magnanimous concern for civil order.

Sheriff Minor character in *2 Henry VI*, an officer who is assigned the task of parading the Duchess of Gloucester through the streets of London in 2.4 as part of her sentence for dabbling in witchcraft and conspiring against King Henry VI.

Simpcox, Saunder Minor character in *2 Henry VI*, an imposter who claims to have been blind and had his sight miraculously restored. In 2.1 the gullible villagers of ST. ALBANS present him to the king's hawking party, and the equally credulous Henry VI begins to congratulate him, but the Duke of Gloucester exposes the fraud through clever interrogation. Simpcox, who has also said he is lame, is whipped on Gloucester's orders, and he naturally runs away from the whipper, further revealing his imposture. Gloucester orders Simpcox and his Wife to be whipped through every

town until they arrive at the remote village they have claimed to come from. The incident, besides providing a bit of low comedy, was intended by Shakespeare to demonstrate the sound judgment of Gloucester.

Smith (Smith the Weaver) Minor character in *2 Henry VI*, a follower of the revolutionary Jack Cade. As the rebels are introduced in 4.2, Smith indulges in several joking asides at the expense of his leader, exhibiting the buffoonery that was one aspect of Shakespeare's characterization of Cade's uprising. As "Weaver" he gets one more such line in 4.7.

Soldier Minor character in *2 Henry VI*, a messenger who enters the camp of the rebel leader Jack Cade in 4.6, unaware that Cade has just declared it an act of treason to address him as anything but "Lord Mortimer." The Soldier, knowing no better, calls out for "Cade"; the leader orders him set upon, and he is killed. This incident serves to present a vicious side of the uprising, which has earlier been treated as a focus of broad humor. Now Cade, in addition to being a buffoon, is shown to be a bloodthirsty tyrant in the making.

Somerset, Edmund Beaufort, Duke of (1406–1455) Historical figure and character in *2 Henry VI*, a Lancastrian rival of the Duke of York. (See LANCASTER FAMILY; YORK FAMILY.) Edmund, the younger brother of John Beaufort, the Duke of Somerset in *1 Henry VI*, inherited both the rivalry and the title after John's death in 1444. The Somerset-York feud is a central feature in *1 Henry VI*; however, *2 Henry VI* focuses first on the fall of the Duke of Gloucester and later on the sudden rebelliousness of York, and this Somerset is a relatively minor figure.

He is sufficiently consequential, however, that the Duchess of Gloucester, seeking political advice from the supernatural world, questions a spirit (Asnath) about his future in 1.4. It is prophesied that Somerset should fear castles, a warning that at the time seems incomprehensible. In 1.3 Somerset is appointed King Henry VI's regent in FRANCE, and he reappears in 3.1 to announce the loss of France, evidencing the harm that infighting among ambitious noblemen has done to England. When York returns from Ireland with an army, he demands Somerset's imprisonment. Somerset volunteers to go to the TOWER OF LONDON if the king wishes, and York is placated. However, York encounters Somerset, still free, in 5.1 and takes the fact as cause for an armed rebellion. In the ensuing battle, the first of the WARS OF THE ROSES, Somerset is killed by York's son (later Richard III) beneath a tavern sign depicting a castle, thus fulfilling the prophecy. (In 1.1 of *3 Henry VI*, Richard displays Somerset's head as a demonstration of his prowess in battle.)

One theme of *2 Henry VI* is the death of "good Duke Humphrey" at the hands of scheming nobles, who thereby deprived England of its only chance of avoiding the civil war that erupted during Henry's weak reign. Shakespeare desired to compress the events that led to that war, and he eclipsed Somerset's political importance in the process. Somerset was the favorite of Queen Margaret after the fall of Suffolk in 1450. However, Somerset had been the commander under whom Normandy was lost in the late 1440s, and he was Henry's chief minister in 1453, when England was irrevocably defeated in southern France. He was therefore in extreme disfavor at the time. So even though Margaret would have preferred Somerset to act as regent in the summer of 1453, when King Henry succumbed to a disabling form of insanity, his unpopularity with both the aristocracy and the public inhibited her, and York was given the post. He governed well and faithfully until late in 1454, when the king recovered. At this point, Somerset was restored to office, and it was this action, probably taken at Margaret's insistence, that led York to gather an army and eventually declare himself king. Shakespeare thus omits several years of intricate political maneuvering in order to clarify York's drive for the throne.

Southwell, John (d. 1441) Historical figure and minor character in *2 Henry VI*, a sorcerer whom Hume employs, along with Roger Bolingbroke and Margery Jourdain, to summon a spirit for the Duchess of Gloucester, who wishes to see the future to prepare for a possible coup. In a séance in 1.4, Southwell helps Bolingbroke to cast a magic spell that summons the spirit Asnath, who answers questions about the king and certain noblemen. South-

well is arrested, along with his fellows and their client, by the Dukes of York and Buckingham. In 2.3 the king sentences him to be strangled. The historical Southwell was a priest who died in prison the night before his scheduled execution.

Stafford, Sir Humphrey (d. 1450) Historical figure and minor character in *2 Henry VI*, a nobleman sent, in 4.2, to deal with the rebellion led by Jack Cade. An arrogant aristocrat, Stafford takes the position *least* likely to defuse an uprising, addressing the mob as "Rebellious hinds, the filth and scum of Kent . . ." (4.2.116). He and his Brother are killed in the skirmish that follows in 4.3. Stafford was not related to the Duke of Buckingham, another figure in the play, although he bore the same name.

Stanley, Sir John (actually Sir Thomas Stanley) (ca. 1406–1459) Historical figure and minor character in *2 Henry VI*, a nobleman to whose castle on the Isle of Man the Duchess of Gloucester is banished in 2.3.–13. In 2.4 Sir John escorts the Duchess from London after she has been humiliated by being paraded through the streets. He is sympathetic to her for her husband's sake, and promises to treat her "Like to a duchess, and Duke Humphrey's lady" (2.4.98). The Isle of Man, in the middle of the Irish Sea, is remote and isolated even now; in the 15th century it was an ideal place of exile. Sir Thomas Stanley inherited the island from his father, Sir John, with whom Shakespeare confused him. John had received it in 1406 from Henry IV as a reward for supporting the deposition of Richard II.

Suffolk, Duke of See Suffolk, William de la Pole, Earl of, in *Henry VI, Part 1*.

Vaux, Sir William (d. 1471) Minor character in *2 Henry VI*, a messenger who announces the terminal illness of Cardinal Beaufort in 3.2. Vaux gives a vivid account of the Cardinal's guilty raving about the murder of the Duke of Gloucester. The historical Sir William Vaux was a minor member of the entourage of the Cardinal. He later died fighting for Henry VI at the battle of TEWKES-

BURY. His son was the Sir Nicholas Vaux who appears in *Henry VIII*, and his grandson was the poet Sir Thomas VAUX.

Warwick, Richard Neville, Earl of (1428–1471) Historical figure and character in *2* and *3 Henry VI*, the chief backer of the Duke of York and then the leader of an effort to dethrone York's son Edward IV after he has become king. The Earl of Warwick in *1 Henry VI* was his father-in-law, Richard Beauchamp, and Shakespeare confused the two. Early in *2 Henry VI*, Shakespeare has Neville laying claim to certain of Beauchamp's military accomplishments (1.1.118–120).

The young nobleman of *2 Henry VI* is a bold, hot-tempered soldier, unswerving in his devotion to serving the cause of right. A proud and spirited youth, Warwick is unafraid to contradict such high-ranking lords as Cardinal Beaufort. Like his father, the Earl of Salisbury, he seeks the good of England rather than personal advancement, in contrast to the other aristocrats. York confides in the Nevilles his intention to seize the throne, claiming descent from Richard II, whose crown had been usurped by Henry VI's grandfather (see LANCASTER FAMILY; YORK FAMILY). Warwick and his father agree to support York, accepting the validity of his right to rule. In Act 5 Warwick distinguishes himself as a warrior, fighting with York's forces at the opening battle of the WARS OF THE ROSES. He closes the play exulting in their success and hoping for more to come, thus anticipating the action of *3 Henry VI*.

It is in the later play that Warwick becomes a major figure in the wars. After York is murdered by Queen Margaret, Warwick becomes the leading lieutenant for the Duke's sons. He boosts their spirits, encouraging Edward to claim the throne himself, and he leads them to war against Margaret. When the battle of TOWTON is all but lost, Warwick's rousing vow to revenge the death of his brother restores Yorkist morale, and the day is saved.

In consequence, Edward is crowned and Warwick seems to have accomplished his goal. He goes to FRANCE and negotiates a political marriage for Edward, thus securing the Yorkist position by acquiring a strong ally. However, his arrangements are peremptorily canceled when word arrives that Edward has married an English commoner, who becomes Queen Elizabeth. Warwick, furious that his plans have been dismissed and that his promises to the French king have been dishonored, immediately allies himself with Margaret and the displaced Henry VI. He succeeds in capturing Edward and restoring Henry to the throne, but Edward escapes and himself captures Henry. In 5.2 Warwick is mortally wounded at the battle of BARNET. He dies musing on the insignificance of his former power and influence.

The historical Warwick, known as the "kingmaker," was indeed the chief architect of Yorkist success, and Shakespeare's account of his drive and ambition ring true. However, in his need to compress the sequence of historical events, the playwright distorted the developments behind Warwick's defection to Margaret, which in the play seems so sudden as to be almost frivolous. Shakespeare preserved the essential features of the story, but Warwick's motives were rather more complicated and humanly interested than those of the fickle figure in the play.

Relations between the kingmaker and his former protégé became strained once Edward was in power. Although Warwick disapproved of Edward's marriage, it did not occur while he was in Paris arranging another one; nor was it the principal cause of their split, which did not occur until years later. The two fought over foreign policy, and Warwick's opinions were increasingly ignored. Moreover, when Warwick tried to arrange a marriage between his daughter and Edward's brother George, the king angrily rejected the idea. In 1469, eight years after Edward's coronation, George and Warwick staged a coup. Warwick ruled for nine months in Edward's name, but the king gathered loyalist supporters and drove the usurpers from the kingdom. It was at this point that Warwick, desperate, accepted the proposition of King Lewis, Louis XI of France, that he ally himself with Margaret and restore Henry to the throne. Accordingly, his other daughter, Anne, was betrothed to the onetime Prince of Wales, Margaret and Henry's son. As in the play, this alliance briefly placed Henry back on the throne before losing the battle of Barnet, where Warwick did indeed die.

Whitmore, Walter   Minor character in *2 Henry VI*, a sailor on a pirate ship and the executioner of the Duke of Suffolk in 4.1. The Lieutenant of the vessel gives Whitmore the authority to collect a ransom from Suffolk, whom the pirates have captured from another ship. Whitmore, having lost an eye in the battle for the ship, wants revenge, not ransom, and he insists, over the Lieutenant's protests, that he will kill Suffolk. When he identifies himself by name, it is as "Water" Whitmore, the Elizabethan pronunciation of his name, and Suffolk is reminded of the prediction made by Asnath in 1.4 that he would die by water. When the Lieutenant learns who Suffolk is, he denounces the Duke's political crimes and sends him with Whitmore to be beheaded. Whitmore returns with Suffolk's head and body and gives them to a released prisoner, a Gentleman, who is to take them to London.

Wife   Minor character in *2 Henry VI*, the wife of the imposter Simpcox. In 2.1 the pair appear before the king's hawking party near ST. ALBANS. She supports her husband's false story of miraculously repaired blindness, and, when the Duke of Gloucester unmasks their fraud, she is condemned with her husband to be whipped through every town between St. Albans and the distant village they had claimed as their home.

York, Duke of   See York, Richard Plantagenet, Duke of, in *Henry VI, Part 1*.

Young Clifford   See Clifford, Lord John, in *Henry VI, Part 3*.

Henry VI, Part 3
SYNOPSIS

Act 1, Scene 1
The Duke of York, his sons Edward (Edward IV) and Richard (Richard III), and their followers discuss the first battle of ST. ALBANS, with which *2 Henry VI* closed. Richard displays the head of the Duke of Somerset, whom he killed in the previous

play. York seats himself on the throne, which is present for an anticipated meeting of the king's council. King Henry VI arrives with a retinue. He restrains his followers from seeking immediate vengeance on the Yorkists, and the two sides parley. York states his claim to rule, based on the proposition that Henry had inherited a usurped crown, taken by his grandfather, Henry IV, from Richard II, whose true heir York claims to be. The king counters weakly that Richard II had voluntarily given the kingdom to Henry IV. Lords Clifford and Warwick escalate the argument, and Warwick summons his hidden soldiers. The king, hoping to avert further violence, agrees to name York as his heir if he be permitted to retain the throne in his own lifetime. York accepts the offer and vows to refrain from rebellion. York and his men depart, satisfied. The king's supporters leave dissatisfied, expressing their disdain for the king's act. Queen Margaret and the Prince of Wales arrive. Margaret reviles Henry for disinheriting their son the Prince, and declares herself divorced. She and the Prince depart to continue the battle against York.

Act 1, Scene 2
York's sons contend that he may properly seize the crown without violating his oath. Richard makes the case that the oath is invalid because it was not made to a proper monarch but rather to a usurper. York accepts this idea with delight and begins to plan a campaign. News arrives that Margaret's army of 20,000 men is approaching. York decides to engage the queen's army immediately, although he is outnumbered four to one.

Act 1, Scene 3
At the battle of WAKEFIELD, York's young son Rutland is taken by Clifford, who declares that he will kill the child in revenge for his own father's death at York's hands. Rutland's pleas for mercy are ignored, and Clifford kills the boy.

Act 1, Scene 4
York appears on the battlefield and describes the courage of his sons in a losing cause. As his pursuers approach, he realizes that he is doomed. Margaret and the Prince appear, accompanied by Northumberland and Clifford. The queen mocks York for his

failure. She further taunts him by giving him a hand-kerchief that has been dipped in Rutland's blood. As her mood grows increasingly vicious, she orders him beheaded. York responds with a long condemnation of the queen, and he weeps for the death of Rutland. Northumberland is moved to pity the captive, but the queen and Clifford stab York to death.

Act 2, Scene 1

Richard and Edward, wondering about their father's fate, see three suns in the sky, which they interpret as an omen of success. News arrives of York's capture and death, and Warwick arrives with more bad news: The duke's forces have been defeated by the queen's. However, he assures the brothers that they can still achieve victory and install Edward as king.

Act 2, Scene 2

Outside the walls of YORK, Margaret points out the Duke of York's head, which has been placed on the city gate; King Henry is dismayed by the sight. Clifford chastises him for being too soft, encouraging him to fight, if only for the inheritance of his son. Henry is unimpressed, arguing that evil cannot produce success. The Yorkist leaders arrive, headed by Warwick and Edward. Edward claims to be king and demands that Henry kneel to him. Margaret and Clifford respond sharply; Richard and the other lords enter the bitter argument. Henry is ignored by all. Amid a barrage of insults, the parley breaks up.

Act 2, Scene 3

At the battle of TOWTON, Warwick, wounded and exhausted, seeks rest. Edward and his brother George enter and fear that the battle is lost. Richard arrives to report that Warwick's brother, slain by Clifford, had cried out with his last breath for Warwick to avenge his death. Warwick, reinvigorated, vows to return to the conflict and not rest again before winning or dying. Their morale restored, the brothers go back to the battle with him.

Act 2, Scene 4

Richard and Clifford prepare to fight hand to hand, with declarations of intended vengeance, when Warwick arrives and Clifford flees.

Act 2, Scene 5

King Henry, having withdrawn from the fighting, musingly wishes that he had been born a shepherd whose time passes uneventfully in the company of his flock. He watches a soldier carry a body from the field in order to loot it, only to discover that his victim had been his own father. Henry, unseen shares the devastating grief of the Son That Hath Killed His Father. Another soldier, with another body and the same intent, discovers that he carries the corpse of his own son. Henry is likewise stricken with the horror that fills the Father That Hath Killed His Son. Margaret and the Prince enter in full retreat from the victorious Yorkists, and they take the king with them.

Act 2, Scene 6

Clifford, wounded in the neck, regrets his own imminent death because he knows it spells disaster for the king's cause. He wishes that the king had been a stronger man, for the war would not have been necessary in that case. He faints just before Edward and his followers arrive, discussing their victory and wondering where Clifford is. They discover his body just as he dies; not realizing that he is dead, they revile and taunt him. Once his death is apparent, Warwick orders that his head replace York's on the city gate. Next, Warwick says, Edward shall be crowned. Then he, Warwick, will go to FRANCE and arrange Edward's marriage to the French king's sister-in-law, Lady Bona. Edward agrees, conferring on Warwick the authority to act as though he were king himself.

Act 3, Scene 1

At a game park, two Keepers come across King Henry. He is a refugee, having fled after the battle. The Keepers accost him, and, although Henry chastises them mildly for their inconstant loyalty, he goes with them to be taken into captivity.

Act 3, Scene 2

In LONDON, King Edward hears the plea of Lady Elizabeth Grey that her late husband's sequestered lands be returned to her. He agrees, but only on condition that she become his mistress. She refuses, and he, infatuated, declares that he will marry her. Richard, in a long soliloquy, makes a frank declaration of his intention to become king. He cynically analyzes his own capacity for villainy, acknowledging that he will have to murder those who precede him in the order of succession.

Act 3, Scene 3

In France, Queen Margaret explains her and her deposed husband's plight to a sympathetic King Lewis. Warwick arrives with Edward's proposal of marriage to Lady Bona, and Lewis, accepting Edward as king, consents. Then Edward's marriage to Elizabeth is announced. Warwick, furious at the dishonorable position this places him in, volunteers to abandon Edward's cause and ally himself with Margaret and the Earl of Oxford in an effort to restore Henry to the throne. Lewis, seeking to avenge the insult to Bona, agrees to assist them, and an invasion is planned.

Act 4, Scene 1

George and Richard oppose the ill-considered marriage, but Edward insists that his royal prerogative negates all criticism. News of the impending invasion arrives. George's dissatisfaction comes to a boil, and he declares that he will join the rebels; he leaves, along with the Duke of Somerset. Richard declares his loyalty to Edward after an aside confirming his true interest—the pursuit of the crown.

Act 4, Scene 2

Warwick and Oxford have landed with the invasion force. They encounter George and Somerset and accept their alliance.

Act 4, Scene 3

Warwick's forces rout the Watchmen in Edward's camp and capture the king, although Richard escapes. Warwick plans to march to London and reinstate Henry as king.

Act 4, Scene 4

Queen Elizabeth, as Edward's wife is now known, knows of her husband's capture. Pregnant, she proposes to flee to the legal sanctuary of a church to protect the unborn Yorkist heir to the crown.

Act 4, Scene 5

Richard and others help Edward escape from captivity.

Act 4, Scene 6

Henry, released from the TOWER OF LONDON by Warwick and George, assigns his power of command to them. The young Earl of Richmond is present, and Henry acclaims him as a future king. Word arrives of Edward's escape, and plans are made against him. Somerset and Oxford take Richmond into exile abroad to protect him against the possibility of Edward's victory.

Act 4, Scene 7

Edward has arrived at York to find the city gates closed by the Mayor, who cites the town's allegiance to Henry. Edward contends that he claims only his position as Duke of York, and he is admitted. Montgomery arrives with troops to support Edward, but only if he resumes his claim to the throne. Edward agrees and makes a formal assertion of kingship.

Act 4, Scene 8

Warwick deploys various of Henry's supporters to raise troops and meet him in COVENTRY. They all depart, leaving Henry to be captured by Edward and Richard, who suddenly appear on their way to meet Warwick in battle.

Act 5, Scene 1

Warwick, within the walls of Coventry, is besieged by Edward and Richard; he receives reinforcements from several noblemen. George also arrives with troops, but Richard persuades him to abandon Warwick and rejoin Edward.

Act 5, Scene 2

At the battle of BARNET, Warwick lies wounded, meditating on the insignificance of his former power now that he is near death. Oxford and Somerset, retreating, tell him that the battle is lost and that they are going to join Margaret, who has an army in the field. As they speak, Warwick dies.

Act 5, Scene 3

Edward, Richard, and George, triumphant, plan to march to TEWKESBURY and fight the queen's army.

Act 5, Scene 4

At Tewkesbury, Queen Margaret makes a stirring speech, and her courage inspires her followers. The Yorkist leaders arrive, and Edward and Margaret each make brief statements signaling the start of battle.

Act 5, Scene 5

The queen and her followers are prisoners of Edward. The Prince defies his captors, insulting Edward and his brothers, and they stab him. Richard departs for London, stating that he has important business there. Helpless, Margaret rails against the killers of her son.

Act 5, Scene 6

Richard accosts Henry in his cell in the Tower of London. Henry reviles Richard for his villainy, predicting the future tragedy he will cause many people and referring to the evil omens that accompanied his birth. Richard kills him and accepts, in a soliloquy, his own evil nature, proposing to use his capacity for crime to achieve the throne.

Act 5, Scene 7

King Edward rejoices in his resumption of power and delights in his son, the new Prince of Wales, and in the support of his brothers. Richard's dark asides demonstrate the king's naiveté.

COMMENTARY

Like Shakespeare's other HISTORY PLAYS, *Henry VI, Part 3* is essentially concerned with civil disorder. As the young playwright's skills matured, his handling of the theme improved, and this third play of the minor TETRALOGY marks a notable advance. Shakespeare's ability to organize a confused mass of material is superior to that in *1* and *2 Henry VI*. Also, and more important in light of his later development, his presentation of chaos includes disorder in the individual as well as in the state; malfunctions of personality underlie those of politics. The painter of tableaux and pageantry is becoming a tragedian.

The dissolution of the government is the major concern of the play, which describes the overthrow of King Henry VI, but this major theme is also reflected in minor keys. Just as the organizational principle of society, the state, is disrupted, so, too, the basic social bond of the family is disturbed. Henry disinherits his own son to purchase relief from York's threats of war, and the action sparks Margaret's unilateral declaration of divorce. The opposing clan, the Yorks, are no better off. George abandons his brother's cause after Edward turns his attentions to the relatives of his new bride. Richard plots the deaths of both his brothers. The theme of familial collapse is given spectacular exposure in 2.5, the scene involving the Son That Hath Killed His Father and the Father That Hath Killed His Son. Further, an abandonment of individual honesty characterizes the world of the play. As Edward quite coolly asserts in 1.2.16–17, ". . . for a kingdom any oath may be broken: I would break a thousand oaths to reign one year."

These themes, so suggestive of chaos, are developed within a regularly alternating cycle of changes of fortune, beginning and ending with the ascendancy of the house of York. Yorkist success at the outset is countered by the Lancastrian victory at Wakefield and York's ignominious death. However, Warwick rallies the Yorkists, who are victorious at Towton in Act 2. In Act 3 Edward's perfidy triggers the defection of Warwick and the consequent reinstatement of Henry as king. But the last swing of the pendulum produces the defeat and death of Warwick and Richard's murders of Henry and his heir. This easily perceived sequence imposes order on the turbulent events.

Dramatic unity is furthered by the persistence of images that reflect the violence of nature. Throughout the play, the characters refer to their conflicts in terms of the killing of animals by men, as in 1.4.61–62 and 2.4.13, or the taking of prey by animals, as in 2.1.14–17 and 5.6.7. Even more evocative are references to the power of tempests, such as Henry's striking description of the battle of Wakefield in 2.5.5–9 and Margaret's more elaborate nautical analogy at the beginning of 5.4. Our awareness of the brutality and viciousness of the play's action is constantly reinforced by this recurrent imagery.

Moreover, Shakespeare frequently has his characters refer to the past and predict the future—devices that serve to bring all the parts of the play to the repeated attention of the audience. For instance, in 1.1.130–133 Henry foretells the coming battles and his own death; the dying York, in 1.4.165–166, wishes upon Margaret a fate that comes to pass in 5.5. Clifford, in 2.6, summarizes King Henry's hapless reign. Henry, before his murder in 5.6, predicts Richard's future crimes. Many such allusions, both plain and subtle, reverberate throughout the play.

More important than this clever technique, however, is Shakespeare's increasing ability to make his characters much more convincing. Henry VI in particular has grown greatly as the playwright's skill has advanced. The king's gentleness is touchingly rendered in his revulsion at the sight of York's head in 2.2, in his wish to be a simple shepherd (2.5.1–54), and in his forgiving his prison guard in 4.6. However, Henry's virtue has a negative side, causing him to become more and more dissociated from his surroundings. The consequences are both subtly recorded, as when the king demands to speak but is ignored and remains speechless in 2.2, and obvious, as upon his virtual abdication in 4.6. Henry's position involves a tragic paradox: his goodness ought to be given scope by his power, but it is precisely his power that places him in the way of historical forces that goodness cannot resist. That Henry is believably both weak and good makes this situation humanly tragic as well as politically disturbing.

Queen Margaret also displays greater dimensions than in the earlier plays. The strength that enables her to organize the resistance to York is fueled by intemperate rage. When she has York at her mercy in 1.4, her viciousness comes to the fore, and we are faced with a fearsome shrew in one of the most powerful scenes Shakespeare had yet written. Though Margaret is undeniably savage—as in 2.2, where she encourages Henry to gloat over York's severed head—she also possesses a capacity for military leadership and strength that is not without a noble appeal. Her persistence in the face of setbacks and her readiness to resume battle when the tide turns, in 3.3, make credible her leadership in the face of final defeat at Tewkesbury. Her inspiring speech in 5.4 rings true, for we have seen that she is a real warrior.

Edward, too, is a well-developed figure. His stature as York's heir to the throne proves illusory once he is crowned, for he shows no regard for the responsibilities of kingship. He is willful in pursuing his lust, and his behavior brings on further civil war. In the conflict, he indulges in pointless bravado and permits himself to be captured. In 5.5.84, after the final victory, Edward casually permits Richard to murder Henry, evincing a lack of concern for civil order that will eventually result in his own victimization in *Richard III*.

But Shakespeare's greatest accomplishment in the play is the creation of his first great villain—Richard. Richard's extraordinary personality bursts forth in 1.1, when he abruptly throws down the head of Somerset, saying, "Speak thou for me, and tell them what I did" (1.1.16). Richard's violence is mixed with sardonic wit throughout the play. He gloats over Clifford's corpse in 2.6, his speech darkening from morbid humor to vicious rhetoric. Later, after killing Henry, Richard raises his bloody sword and sarcastically crows, "See how my sword weeps for the poor King's death" (5.6.63). Richard is conscious of his own character, and he shares his self-awareness with the audience, enlarging our appreciation of his villainy. In his famous soliloquy at the end of 3.2, he observes that he "can smile, and murder whiles I smile"; he associates himself with a paragon of atheism and amorality in claiming he will "set the murderous Machiavel to school" (see MACHIAVEL). His appreciation of his own viciousness seems very modern, as does his psychological motivation: his personality is formed in part by his physical deformity, a hunched back. In 3.2.153–171, he attributes his own malevolence to this defect. Richard, established in *3 Henry VI* as misshapen and monstrously evil, will achieve heights of villainy in the following play in the sequence, which bears his name.

Shakespeare ties together his various strands in a spectacularly ironic final scene. The victorious Edward congratulates himself on his success, in pointed contrast to Richard's Judas kiss, which prepares us for the horrors of *Richard III*. In the final line, Edward carelessly rejoices in a future happiness that the audience knows very well to be doomed. The author has combined the consummation of his play's action with a foreshadowing of its sequel.

SOURCES OF THE PLAY

Shakespeare's main source for *3 Henry VI*, as for the other *Henry VI* plays, was *The Union of the Two Noble and Illustre Families of Lancastre and York*, by Edward HALL (3rd ed., 1550). The playwright supplemented Hall's basic information with ideas from other sources, as was his habit. Most notably, the poem *Romeus and Juliet* (1562), by Arthur BROOKE, provided the germ of Queen Margaret's rousing speech at the beginning of 5.4, and Edmund SPENSER's *Faerie Queene* influenced the descriptions of the sun in 2.1. Minor elements can also be traced to A MIRROR FOR MAGISTRATES, a popular anthology of biographies, and to *The Spanish Tragedy* (1588–89) and *Soliman and Perseda* (1590), plays by Thomas KYD.

TEXT OF THE PLAY

It is impossible to date the early history plays with certainty, but since all three *Henry VI* plays contain minor reflections of Edmund Spenser's *Faerie Queene*, published December 1589, they cannot have been written earlier than 1590. It is thought that the four plays of the minor tetralogy were written in the order in which they are read, and the last of them, *Richard III*, was apparently known to Christopher MARLOWE by early 1592 (see *Richard III*, "Text of the Play"); therefore, it seems likely that the four plays were composed between early 1590 and late 1591. If we assume the third of them to have been written in the third quarter of this span of time, we may date *3 Henry VI* to the first half of 1591.

The play was first published in the form in which we know it in the FIRST FOLIO of 1623, and that text has been the basis for all subsequent editions. However, a BAD QUARTO edition, known as *The True Tragedy*, was published by Thomas MILLINGTON in 1595 and again in 1600: these editions are known as Q1 and Q2, respectively. In 1619 a third quarto edition, Q3, was published by Thomas PAVIER in the same volume with a bad quarto of *2 Henry VI*. This edition is known as *The Whole Contention*. Its text for *Part 3* is very close to that of Q1. While some minor details of the Folio text of the play may have come from the quartos, these editions are chiefly of historical interest.

Scholars believe that the Folio edition was derived largely from Shakespeare's FAIR COPY, as is indicated by the presence of elaborate stage directions, along with other minor clues. The editors of the Folio probably used a copy made by a scribe, for their text includes various small adjustments of a sort known to have been common in the work of Elizabethan scribes.

THEATRICAL HISTORY OF THE PLAY

Henry VI, Part 3 seems to have been popular in Shakespeare's day, although we have no documentary evidence of any particular performances. However, the title page of *The True Tragedy* informs us that the play had been performed by PEMBROKE'S MEN before they disbanded in 1593. The play's several quarto editions indicate a continuing public interest, as does the remark made by the CHORUS at the end of *Henry V* that "oft our stage hath shown" (Epilogue, 13) the events of the *Henry VI* plays. Further, Ben JONSON, writing in about 1612, referred to these works as particularly popular.

Subsequently, however, the play has not been notably well received. Favorable critical attention in the second half of the 17th century suggests that it was still read and regarded as a successful work, but the only performances known from the period were greatly altered, containing very little of Shakespeare's text (see, e.g., CROWNE). Two such productions are also known from the 18th century. A German production of *3 Henry VI* to celebrate the tercentenary of Shakespeare's birth in 1864 seems to have provided the only performances of the 19th century. The play was produced a number of times in the 20th century, generally in cycles with the other plays of the minor tetralogy. It has been made for TELEVISION (1983) and also incorporated in two BBC series that abridge and combine the history plays: AN AGE OF KINGS (1960) and *The Wars of the Roses* (1964), which presents the *Henry VI* plays and *Richard III*.

CHARACTERS

Bona, Lady (after 1447–1485) Historical figure and character in *3 Henry VI*, the proposed French bride of Edward IV, whose rejection of her sparks the defection of the Earl of Warwick. In 3.3 Bona, the sister-in-law of King Lewis, is agreeable to the marriage, having heard good things of Edward, but Edward has instead married an English commoner. Bona adds her voice to a chorus of demands for revenge for this slight, and thus approves of the alliance among Lewis, Warwick, and Margaret, aimed at deposing Edward and reinstating Henry VI. This episode is one of many in the *Henry VI* plays in which broken oaths result in catastrophe for England—in this case, another phase of the WARS OF THE ROSES. It is analogous to the similar abandonment of a marriage agreement by King Henry in order to marry Margaret at the close of *1 Henry VI*.

The historical Lady Bona of Savoy, Louis XI's sister-in-law, was indeed proposed as a bride for Edward, but the matter never progressed very far. She subsequently married a Duke of Milan, and after his death she briefly ruled that duchy as regent for her son.

Bourbon, Lewis, Lord (Louis, Lord Bourbon) (active 1460s)   Historical figure and minor character in *3 Henry VI*, an admiral in the service of King Lewis of FRANCE. In 3.3, when Lewis decides to provide soldiers for Margaret and Warwick, he orders Bourbon to arrange their passage to England. Bourbon does not speak. The historical admiral was the illegitimate son of the Duke of Bourbon, who appears in *Henry V*.

Clifford, Lord John (ca. 1435–1461)   Character in *2* and *3 Henry VI*, the obsessed avenger of his father's death, who kills both the Duke of York and his young son Rutland. As Young Clifford, this character appears briefly in Act 5 of *2 Henry VI* as a supporter of King Henry VI against the Duke of York and as a participant in the battle of ST. ALBANS. On the battlefield, he sees the dead body of his father, Thomas Clifford, whom York has killed, and he delivers a famous speech (5.2.40–65), a rhetorical comparison of his death with the last judgment, closing with a vow of revenge that prefigures some of the most dramatic action in *3 Henry VI*.

In the later play Clifford's bloodthirsty quest for revenge reflects the bestiality that England's aristocracy has descended to as the civil war progresses. "Patience is for poltroons," he cries (1.1.62) when King Henry tries to placate an angry earl. In 1.3, when he encounters Rutland, a child attempting to flee the battle of WAKEFIELD, he kills the boy despite his pleas for mercy, citing his own father's death as justification. When York is captured in 1.4, Queen Margaret can only with difficulty restrain Clifford long enough to enjoy herself tormenting her enemy with an account of Rutland's murder. Finally, unable

to wait any longer, Clifford kills York also. In 2.2, before the battle of TOWTON, Clifford chastises King Henry for his "harmful pity" in a speech filled with the animal imagery that contributes to the impression of savagery that runs so strongly throughout the play. Ironically, it is another bloody deed by Clifford that costs his side the battle: When Warwick hears that Clifford has killed his brother, that seemingly defeated leader is aroused and inspires the Yorkists to rally and win the day. In 2.6 Clifford appears, wounded in this battle, to deliver a deathbed speech in which he regrets the weakness of the monarch who has brought the country to this bloody pass. He recognizes that his enemies are upon him, and he dies daring them to wreak their vengeance on him. When they recognize him, before they realize he is dead, they taunt and mock him.

Shakespeare took his account of Clifford's revenge on Rutland from HALL, but it is entirely unhistorical. Rutland was not a child; he was an officer in the Yorkist army. While he did die at Wakefield, it was never known who killed him. Moreover, it is not known who killed Clifford's father at St Albans either; he died in the thick of the battle, as the playwright also reports in *3 Henry VI* (in 1.1.7–10), in a famous instance of Shakespearean carelessness. Lastly, Clifford did not die at Towton but in a skirmish several days earlier. He was struck in the neck by an arrow, as in the play, but was reported at the time to have died instantly.

Edward IV, King of England (1442–1483)   Historical figure and character in *2* and *3 Henry VI* and *Richard III*. Known simply as Edward until Act 3 in *3 Henry VI*, King Edward IV receives his crown as a result of the machinations of his ambitious father, the Duke of York, and his heirs are murdered later by his brother, who succeeds him as Richard III.

In *2 Henry VI* Edward appears in 5.1 to support his father in his claim to the throne. Edward has only one line, which Richard immediately tops. In *3 Henry VI*, although Edward comes into his own, he continues to be overshadowed by his brother. He becomes king, but the leadership of the Yorkist cause is clearly provided by Warwick, prior to that lord's defection, and by Richard. Edward displays the unscrupulous ambition that characterizes the aristocrats in all the *Henry VI* plays. He baldly displays his own dishonesty, claiming that "... for a kingdom any oath may be broken: / I would break a thousand oaths to reign one year" (1.2.16–17). However, Edward is outclassed in criminality by his brother Richard.

Edward demonstrates a selfish disregard for the responsibilities of kingship, and his behavior necessitates a renewal of the WARS OF THE ROSES. He ignores the benefits of an alliance with FRANCE and abandons a marriage to Lady Bona in order to satisfy his lust for Elizabeth Woodville. In the resulting war, he indulges in pointless bravado and permits himself to be captured in 4.3. After the final Yorkist victory, Edward casually allows Richard to murder the finally displaced King Henry, demonstrating a lack of concern for civil order that typifies England's corrupt public life. In *Richard III* Edward appears only in 2.1, on his deathbed. He learns of the death of George York, Duke of Clarence, and his dismay, it is implied, leads to his own rapid demise. His death is reported in 2.2.

Shakespeare's treatment of the reign of Edward IV is extremely unhistorical, for the playwright wished to emphasize the disruption of English public life that the coming of the TUDOR DYNASTY repaired. Edward's 22-year tenure is presented as a rapid succession of quarrels and battles. In fact, though, Edward was a very competent ruler. He was judiciously merciful to most of the Lancastrians; he introduced badly needed financial reforms; he withdrew from France—at the cost of considerable personal popularity, but to the immense benefit of the country. His marriage to Elizabeth was not the chief, or even an important, cause of Warwick's rebellion. Although his lusty appetites, given much emphasis in the play, were well known to his contemporaries, they do not seem to have interfered with his public duty, although it has been suggested that overindulgence in wine and women may have resulted in his early death.

Elizabeth Woodville (Elizabeth Woodvile, Lady Grey, Queen Elizabeth) (1437–1492) Historical figure and character in *3 Henry VI* and *Richard III*, the wife of King Edward IV. Her brother is Lord

Rivers in the same plays, and her father is Richard Woodville in *1 Henry VI*. Known as Lady Grey until Act 4 of *3 Henry VI*, Elizabeth becomes queen when Edward marries her after she refuses to become his mistress. Edward was already promised to Lady Bona of FRANCE, so the marriage becomes a stimulus for warfare. Elizabeth is a pawn in the troubled politics of the time. However, she displays dignity in an awkward position, as in her speech at 4.1.66–73, and her instinct to protect her unborn child in 4.4 is also noteworthy. She quite properly distrusts the treacherous and violent noblemen of the disturbed nation, but she is powerless.

In *Richard III* Queen Elizabeth is cursed in 1.3 by the former queen, Margaret, and sees her enemy's wishes come true as Edward dies and Richard murders her two sons by Edward. He also has her brother Rivers and a son, Grey, executed, while another son, Dorset, is forced into exile. However, Richard fails to exploit her family further. Elizabeth resists him in 4.4, when he attempts to win her approval of his plan to marry her daughter. She rejects his efforts to swear an oath, stifling him until he is reduced to wishing ill on himself, fatefully (4.4.397–409). Elizabeth suspends the conversation at 4.4.428–429), leaving the resolution of the matter in doubt. (Her daughter is betrothed to the victorious invader Richmond at the play's end.)

Historically, Warwick's alienation from Edward was provoked by disagreements over policy and not simply by the king's marriage, as Shakespeare would have it, but among the minor causes was the behavior of the greedy Woodvilles. Elizabeth Woodville was the first commoner to become Queen of England, and her many male relatives exploited her new position by marrying the cream of eligible heiresses. However, Elizabeth attracted supporters when, after the death of King Edward, her son inherited the crown. Edward had appointed Richard the boy's protector, with ruling power, before he died; Elizabeth's allies attempted to circumvent this arrangement with a coup. They were defeated by Richard, as in the play, though he treated Elizabeth herself with great generosity and provided her with a distinguished place at his court.

Richard repeatedly denied rumors that he planned to marry Elizabeth's daughter. In fact, since he had in part based his claim to the throne on the charge that Edward himself was illegitimate, an attempt to marry his daughter would seem self-defeating. However, Shakespeare's sources reported the rumors, and the playwright expanded them into a powerful scene. Elizabeth herself had other plans; it appears that she secretly allied herself with Richmond (later King Henry VII) before his invasion, with the agreement that, should he succeed, he would marry the daughter, which he did. Elizabeth lived out her life as an honored dowager at the court of her son-in-law.

Exeter, Henry Holland, Duke of (1430–1473) Historical figure and minor character in *3 Henry VI*, a supporter of King Henry VI and Queen Margaret. Exeter acknowledges the claim to rule of the Duke of York in 1.1, but he remains loyal to Henry. This may represent a slip by the playwright, or it may be a subtle reminder of the difficulty of the issue for the participants.

Falconbridge, William Neville, Lord (Lord Fauconberg, Lord Faulconbridge) (d. 1463) Historical figure mentioned in *3 Henry VI*, sometimes assigned the lines of the Marquess of Montague in Act 1. Montague's assertions of kinship with Edward would make more sense if spoken by Falconbridge, who was Edward's brother-in-law. His connection with the sea, at 1.1.216, also applies better to Falconbridge, who was at the time a military commander responsible for the English Channel defenses, as is mentioned 30 lines later. It is supposed that Falconbridge was deleted and his lines reassigned, possibly before any performances were given, as an economy measure for the production.

Father That Hath Killed His Son Minor but significant character in *3 Henry VI*, a participant in the battle of TOWTON in 2.5. The Father, a soldier, prepares to loot the corpse of an enemy he has killed, when he discovers that the body is that of his own son. He mourns for himself and for the times: "O, pity, God, this miserable age! / What stratagems, how fell, how butcherly, / Erroneous, mutinous, and unnatural, / This deadly quarrel daily doth beget!" (2.5.88–91).

The Father's discovery and grief are witnessed by King Henry VI, who has withdrawn from the battle to wish despairingly that he were a rustic shepherd, rather than a combatant. This incident, along with that of the Son That Hath Killed His Father, is juxtaposed ironically with Henry's pastoral musings to highlight the horrors of civil war.

George York, Duke of Clarence (1449–1478) Historical figure and character in *3 Henry VI*, the untrustworthy younger brother of Edward IV. George returns from exile following the death of his father, the Duke of York. He supports Edward in his pursuit of the crown, becoming Duke of Clarence upon his brother's accession. However, resenting the advancement of his brother's in-laws, he joins Warwick in his rebellion, leaving Edward's court in 4.1. After helping Warwick reinstate Henry VI, George is persuaded to defect again by his younger brother Richard (Richard III) in 5.1, and he returns to Edward's cause. After fighting for Edward at BARNET and TEWKESBURY and participating in the murder of the Prince of Wales, George is present in the final scene to pledge his rather doubtful loyalty to his elder brother. In *Richard III* the same figure appears as Clarence, and he is often so called, by himself and other characters, in *3 Henry VI*.

The historical George remained abroad in exile until Edward was crowned, at which time he was still only 12 years old. Shakespeare brings him into the action before that time, and as an adult, in order to establish him as a member of Edward's court well before he deserts it. Also, George's prominence in the play does much to emphasize the disloyalty and lack of honor that prevailed at the time of the WARS OF THE ROSES.

Gloucester, Richard Plantagenet, Duke of (1452–1485) Title held by the future Richard III after 2.6 of *3 Henry VI* until he is crowned king in 4.2 of *Richard III*. (For his career, see Richard III in *Richard III*.) Some modern editions of these plays follow 16th- and 17th-century practice and designate the character as Gloucester (Gloster) in stage directions and speech headings in Acts 3–5 of *3 Henry VI* and Acts 1–3 of *Richard III*. Other editions name him Richard throughout.

The prior holder of Richard's dukedom had been the ill-fated Humphrey, Duke of Gloucester, whose murder occurs offstage in 3.2 of *2 Henry VI*. Therefore, as Shakespeare's audience will have recognized, the title bodes evil for its holder. Richard himself points this out in 2.6.107 of *3 Henry VI*. His words ironically prefigure his own fall, in a technique Shakespeare frequently used in the HISTORY PLAYS: references in the dialogue to past or future events serve to heighten dramatic tension, which is threatened by the long period of time over which the action takes place.

Hastings, Lord William See Hastings, Lord William, in *Richard III*.

Henry VI, King of England See Henry VI, King of England, in *Henry VI, Part 1*.

Huntsman Minor character in *3 Henry VI*, a servant assigned to escort the captive Edward IV. Surprised by Edward's rescuers in 4.5, the Huntsman elects to travel with the escapee's party, saying, "Better do so than tarry and be hang'd" (4.5.26). This one-liner provides a hint of comic relief amid a grim series of political and military maneuverings.

Keeper Either of two minor characters in *3 Henry VI*, gameskeepers who capture the refugee King Henry VI in 3.1. Henry chastises the Keepers for their inconstant allegiance, which they once gave to him but now proclaim to be owed to Edward IV. They respond with rationalizations before arresting him. This incident is another instance of changeable loyalties in the disrupted world depicted in the play.

In the FIRST FOLIO text of the play, the Keepers are designated in a stage direction as "Sinklo" and "Humfrey." These are presumably the actors who played the parts in an early production, probably John SINCKLO and Humphrey JEFFES.

Lady Grey See Elizabeth Woodville.

Lewis, King of France (1423–1483) Historical figure and minor character in *3 Henry VI*, King Louis XI of FRANCE. In 3.3 Lewis is insulted when King Edward IV of England voids his agreement to marry the French king's sister-in-law, Lady Bona. Lewis agrees to back an effort by Margaret and Warwick to invade England and reinstate the deposed Henry VI as king, thereby beginning another phase of the WARS OF THE ROSES.

In a gross oversimplification of years of foreign-policy maneuverings, Shakespeare presents a cardboard French king who simply wavers from sympathy with Margaret to alliance with Edward and back again. In reality, Louis XI, known as "the Spider" for his ruthless diplomacy, had long enjoyed good relations with Warwick. Upon Edward's accession, Warwick had backed an English alliance with France and had proposed the marriage to Bona, though nothing came of the idea. Edward, on the other hand, had opted for a connection with Louis's enemy, Burgundy. When Warwick initiated his coup in 1469, Louis discreetly provided him funds. Then, when Warwick was forced to flee England, it was Louis who initiated the alliance with Margaret in June 1470, six years after Edward's marriage to Lady Elizabeth. He financed Warwick's invasion and surely regarded the money as well spent, despite Warwick's ultimate failure, because the incident disrupted English politics significantly.

Lieutenant Minor character in *3 Henry VI*, a guard in the TOWER OF LONDON. When Henry VI is released from the Tower upon his reinstatement as king in 4.6, the Lieutenant asks and receives the monarch's pardon for having been his jailer. Henry assures him that he appreciates the Lieutenant's civil behavior as a guard. When Richard, the Duke of Gloucester, comes to murder the reimprisoned Henry in 5.6, he dismisses the Lieutenant from his guard post.

Margaret of Anjou See Margaret of Anjou, in *Henry VI, Part 1*.

Mayor of Coventry Minor character in *3 Henry VI*, a supporter of Warwick in his attempt to reinstate Henry VI as king. The Mayor, who does not speak, appears on the walls of Coventry with Warwick in 5.1, lending local authority to the effort.

Mayor of York Minor character in *3 Henry VI*, the chief officer of the city of York. In 4.7 the

Mayor cites his loyalty to King Henry VI as the reason for refusing to open the gates of the city to Edward IV. Lying, Edward asserts that he will make no claim on the crown but wishes only to be Duke of York. Believing him, the Mayor admits him. The incident illustrates the lack of honor among the feuding royalty during the WARS OF THE ROSES.

Messenger Any of several minor characters in *3 Henry VI*, soldiers bringing military reports. The Messengers simply report troop movements, except for the first of two in 2.1, who brings a detailed account of the death of the Duke of York.

In the FIRST FOLIO text of the play, believed to have been printed from Shakespeare's manuscript, the Messenger is referred to in the stage direction at 1.2.47 as "Gabriel." This apparently refers to the actor Gabriel SPENCER, who presumably played the part in the original production.

Montague, John Neville, Lord (ca. 1428–1471) Historical figure and minor character in *3 Henry VI*, a supporter of the Duke of York and his sons who deserts their cause to join his brother, the Earl of Warwick, in his revolt. Montague is a Yorkist through 4.1.141, when he declares his loyalty to King Edward IV, although Warwick's rebellion has begun. However, when he next appears, in 4.6, he is with Warwick. His death in the battle of BARNET is reported in 5.2.

The motives of the historical Montague, omitted by Shakespeare, are interesting for the light they cast on the politics of the WARS OF THE ROSES. Upon his accession, Edward had confiscated the estates of the Earl of Northumberland and given them to Montague. After Warwick's defection, seeking allies in the north, Edward gave them back to Northumberland's heir. Edward thought he had appeased Montague with new titles, but he was wrong. When Warwick landed in England with his invasion forces, Montague joined him and a large body of troops was placed under his command. This event is depicted in 5.1.

Montgomery John (actually Thomas Montgomery) (ca. 1430–1495) Historical figure and minor character in *3 Henry VI*, a supporter of King Edward IV. In 4.7 Montgomery arrives at YORK with troops with which he proposes to aid Edward, but only if Edward will attempt to regain the throne. Edward promptly declares himself king, renouncing his oath that he would not claim the crown, sworn earlier in the scene in order to gain admission to the city. The incident provides one of the many instances of broken promises in these plays.

Although Montgomery is referred to and addressed as "Sir John" (4.7.40, 43, 51) in both the FIRST FOLIO and the quarto (or Q1) texts of the play, Shakespeare's source, Raphael HOLINSHED's history, accurately names him Thomas. The playwright seems to have confused Thomas Montgomery with his father, John (d. 1449).

The historical Montgomery was a loyal Yorkist, having been knighted on the field at TOWTON. He subsequently served Edward as a diplomat on many occasions. He gained great notoriety in 1475 as one of the ministers who negotiated a treaty with FRANCE that aborted an English invasion attempt under terms that were widely viewed as dishonorable to England and that included an annual payment from Louis XI to each of the ministers and to King Edward.

Mortimer, Sir Hugh (d. 1460) Historical figure and minor character in *3 Henry VI*, an uncle and supporter of the Duke of York. In 1.2 Sir Hugh arrives with his brother, John Mortimer, to offer aid to York before the battle of WAKEFIELD. Sir Hugh does not speak; the deaths of the brothers in the battle are reported in 1.4.2.

Mortimer, Sir John (d. 1460) Historical figure and minor character in *3 Henry VI*, an uncle and supporter of the Duke of York. In 1.2 Sir John arrives with his brother, Hugh Mortimer, to offer aid to York before the battle of WAKEFIELD. Sir John speaks one line; the deaths of the brothers in the battle are reported in 1.4.2. The historical figures appear only as names in the death list of the battle, where they are mentioned as "bastard uncles" of York.

Nobleman Minor character in *3 Henry VI*, a messenger. In 3.2.118–119 the nameless Nobleman brings word to King Edward IV of the capture of Henry VI. He is merely a messenger, but like many of Shakespeare's messengers he has the significant function of spurring a sudden change in the play's emotional tone. Here, in signaling the complete success of the rebels against Henry, he provides the occasion for the future Richard III to soliloquize on his own malevolence, in a famous speech.

Norfolk, John Mowbray, Duke of (1415–1461) Historical figure and minor character in *3 Henry VI*, a supporter of the Yorkist cause in the WARS OF THE ROSES. Norfolk's paternal grandfather was the Thomas Mowbray of *Richard II*. His uncle was the Lord Mowbray of *2 Henry IV*.

Northumberland, Henry Percy, Earl of (1421–1461) Historical figure and minor character in *3 Henry VI*, a supporter of King Henry VI. Northumberland is among the nobles who depart from Henry in anger, when the king agrees to bequeath the throne to York in 1.1. He appears with Queen Margaret and Lord Clifford in 1.4, when the captive York is murdered; his sympathy for York, who is tormented with evidence of his young son's murder before his own, is chastised by the queen. He later dies at the battle of TOWTON.

This Northumberland was the grandson of Henry Percy, known as Hotspur, who figures in *Richard II* and *1 Henry IV*. His father, Hotspur's son, died at the first battle of ST. ALBANS, as is described in the opening lines of *3 Henry VI*.

Nurse Minor character in *3 Henry VI*. A non-speaking character, the Nurse tends to the infant Prince of Wales in the final scene.

Oxford, John de Vere, Earl of (1443–1513) Historical figure and minor character in *3 Henry VI* and *Richard III*, a follower of Queen Margaret and King Henry VI in the former play and of Richmond in the latter. In *3 Henry VI* Oxford supports Margaret against Warwick at the French court in 3.3. When Warwick changes sides and joins Margaret, Oxford participates in the campaign to reinstate Henry. He is captured at the battle of TEWKESBURY and sentenced to imprisonment. The historical

Oxford was not present at Tewkesbury, having fled the country after the earlier battle of BARNET. Several years later he attempted another invasion but was defeated and captured, beginning the imprisonment mentioned in the play. After 10 years he escaped and joined the Earl of Richmond in Paris. In *Richard III* Oxford, though historically an important general in Richmond's campaign, speaks only two lines.

Pembroke, William Herbert, Earl of (d. 1469) Historical figure and minor character in *3 Henry VI*, a supporter of Edward IV. Pembroke, who does not speak, is present when the Yorkist leaders learn that Warwick has deserted their cause in 4.1. He is ordered, with Lord Stafford, to raise an army.

In 1469 the historical Pembroke, who received his title from Edward for his services in the civil war, was commissioned, with Stafford, to put down a local rebellion that Warwick had sponsored; because of a personal dispute, Stafford withheld his forces from a battle, and the rebels captured and beheaded Pembroke. The historical Pembroke was the father of Sir Walter Herbert, who appears in *Richard III*. Through an illegitimate son, he was also the great-grandfather of Henry Herbert, Earl of PEMBROKE, the sponsor of PEMBROKE'S MEN, the actor's company with which Shakespeare was probably associated when he wrote this play.

Post Either of two minor characters in *3 Henry VI*, express messengers. One Post carries messages between King Edward IV and the French court in 3.3, and returns with answers in 4.1. The replies are quite venomous, and the Post asks assurance that he will not be punished for the contents of his report. In 4.6 another Post carries word to Warwick of Edward's escape from captivity.

Prince of Wales, Edward (1453–1471) Historical figure and character in *3 Henry VI*, the heir apparent to King Henry VI. The young Prince Edward, son of Henry and Queen Margaret, has inherited his mother's bold and courageous spirit, and unlike his father, he strongly opposes the efforts of York and his sons to seize the throne. He reproaches his father for his weakness on several occasions, and he presents a consistently fiery front to the rebels; in consequence, he is stabbed to death by the usurper, King Edward IV, and the other York sons after being taken prisoner in the battle of TEWKESBURY in 5.5. The young Prince is a model of chivalry and thus rather dull, but he is intended as a symbolic figure rather than a developed personality. He serves as a foil for his father's more complex and human weakness, and, further, as a suggestion of what might have been—an instance of the rigor and pride kingship demands. Shakespeare saw its absence in Henry VI as having been tragic for England. The Ghost of the young Prince appears in *Richard III.*

The murder of the captive prince was part of the Tudor version of the WARS OF THE ROSES, but it is apparently fictitious. Shakespeare took it from his chief source, Edward HALL, but according to earlier accounts, the prince was killed in the battle, a much more likely end.

Queen Margaret of England   See Margaret of Anjou, in *Henry VI, Part 1.*

Richard Plantagenet   See Gloucester, Richard Plantagenet, Duke of.

Richmond, Earl of (Henry Tudor)   See Richmond, Earl of, in *Richard III.*

Rivers, Earl of   See Rivers, Anthony Woodville, Earl of, in *Richard III.*

Rutland, Edmund York, Earl of (1443–1460) Historical figure and character in *3 Henry VI,* the murdered son of the Duke of York. Rutland, though only a child, is killed by the vengeful Lord Clifford as he attempts to flee from the battle of WAKEFIELD in 1.3, accompanied by his Tutor. His blood, preserved on a handkerchief, is used in 1.4 to torment his father, whom Clifford kills as well. These highly dramatic encounters exemplify the barbarity of the WARS OF THE ROSES. Shakespeare took the incident from his source, Edward HALL, but it is entirely fictitious. Rutland was not a child but, at 17 years old, an adult by the standards of the time. He fought in the battle of Wakefield and was slain there, but, as is normal for 15th-century warfare, no particular combatant can be positively identified as his killer.

Soldier   Minor character in *3 Henry VI.* When Edward IV decides to declare his renewed claim to

the crown, in 4.7, he calls on the Soldier to read his proclamation.

Somerset, Duke of   Character in *3 Henry VI*—a combination of two historical figures—who betrays King Edward IV to support Warwick in his rebellion. Shakespeare confused two dukes of Somerset who participated in the WARS OF THE ROSES, Henry (1436–64) and his younger brother Edmund (ca. 1438–71), both of them sons of the Duke of Somerset of *2 Henry VI.* In 4.1 of *3 Henry VI* Somerset leaves Edward's court with George to join Warwick and fight for the reinstatement of the deposed King Henry VI. This Somerset must be Henry, who deserted the Lancastrians and then rejoined them, at which point he is depicted here. Henry was finally captured and beheaded by the Yorkists. All of the subsequent appearances of Somerset in the play occur well after the date of Henry's execution and thus must portray Edmund, who succeeded to his brother's title. Edmund was always a firm Lancastrian, and it is he who is shown aiding the young Richmond in 4.6, supporting Warwick and Margaret in Act 5 and, in 5.5, being sentenced to death after the battle of TEWKESBURY, as Edmund in fact was.

Somerville, Sir John (d. 1492) Historical figure and minor character in *3 Henry VI,* a supporter of Warwick in his rebellion against King Edward IV. Somerville reports to Warwick on troop movements in 5.1.

Son That Hath Killed His Father   Minor but significant character in *3 Henry VI,* a participant in the battle of TOWTON in 2.5. The Son, a soldier, begins to loot the corpse of an enemy he has killed, only to discover that the fallen foe is his own father. He bewails his fate and prays, with an allusion to the Crucifixion, "Pardon me, God, I knew not what I did: / And pardon, Father, for I knew not thee" (2.5.69–70). He is witnessed by King Henry VI, who has withdrawn from the battle to wish despairingly that he were a rustic shepherd rather than a combatant. This incident, along with that of the Father That Hath Killed His Son, is juxtaposed ironically with King Henry's pastoral musings to highlight the horror of civil war.

Stafford, Lord Humphrey (1439–1469) Historical figure and minor character in *3 Henry VI*, a supporter of King Edward IV. Stafford, who does not speak, is present in 4.1 when the Yorkist leaders learn that Warwick has deserted their cause, and he is ordered, with Lord Pembroke, to raise an army. The historical Stafford, who was knighted by Edward during the battle of TOWTON, was sent with Pembroke in 1469 to subdue a local uprising that Warwick had incited. Because of a personal dispute between the two commanders, Stafford withheld his forces from a battle, with the result that Pembroke was captured and beheaded by the rebels. Stafford was declared a traitor and was hunted down and executed by the local authorities.

Stanley, Sir William (ca. 1436–1495) Historical figure and minor character in *3 Henry VI*, a supporter of King Edward IV. In 4.5 Stanley helps Edward to escape from captivity. He is mentioned in *Richard III*, in 4.5.13, as one of the supporters of the Earl of Richmond.

The historical Stanley was the son of Sir Thomas Stanley, misnamed by Shakespeare as John Stanley in *2 Henry VI*, and he was the younger brother of Sir Thomas Stanley, a prominent figure in *Richard III*. William Stanley had been a consistent Yorkist prior to Richmond's invasion, when he joined his brother in supporting the usurper. His nephew George, Richard's hostage, betrayed him, and Richard declared him a traitor prior to the battle of BOSWORTH FIELD. Nevertheless, following a family tradition of ambivalent loyalty, he held his troops back during that fight until he saw that he could join the winning side. Then his appearance with 3,000 troops turned the tide for Richmond, who amply rewarded him after acceding to the throne as Henry VII. Ten years later, however, Stanley became associated with another attempted coup and was beheaded.

Tutor Minor character in *3 Henry VI*, adult companion of the child Rutland, the son of the Duke of York. In 1.3 the Tutor unsuccessfully attempts to spirit the boy away from the battle of WAKEFIELD, but Lord Clifford captures them and, in his pursuit of vengeance against York, declares he will murder Rutland. The Tutor tries to dissuade the killer, but he is unceremoniously taken away by Clifford's soldiers, and the avenger does indeed slay the child.

Watchmen Three minor characters in *3 Henry VI*, soldiers who guard the tent of King Edward IV. On guard in 4.3, the Watchmen remark on Edward's insistence on courting danger when he could be housed in greater safety, but they claim pridefully that they will protect their king. Warwick and his soldiers appear and capture Edward, routing the guard instantly. The episode offers an instance of Edward's immaturity, as his bravado makes difficulties for his cause. It also provides a touch of rustic humor when the Watchmen comically fly just as they proclaim their own virtues as guards.

Westmoreland, Ralph Neville, Earl of (ca. 1404–1484) Historical figure and minor character in *3 Henry VI*, a Lancastrian nobleman (see LANCASTER FAMILY). Westmoreland is one of the supporters of King Henry VI who angrily leave the monarch's presence when he agrees to bequeath the throne to York in 1.1.140. Following his sources, Shakespeare erred in assigning this Westmoreland a role in the WARS OF THE ROSES. He took no part in the conflict and is thought to have been an invalid. He was the grandson of the Earl of Westmoreland who appears in *1* and *2 Henry IV* and *Henry V*.

York, Duke of See York, Richard Plantagenet, Duke of, in *Henry VI, Part 1*.

Henry VIII

SYNOPSIS

Prologue

The Prologue disclaims any attempt at humor. The play, he says, will be serious, full of important issues and unhappiness. Its noble scenes will inspire pity and also present the truth. For those who simply like a splendid show, it will prove satisfying. But it will not be a frivolous play, with foolery and fighting. The audience should prepare to be sad, for they will see great and noble people fall upon misery.

Act 1, Scene 1
The Duke of Norfolk tells the Duke of Buckingham about the recent meeting in FRANCE between King Henry VIII and the French ruler. The two courts competed in displaying their wealth, and elaborate jousts were held. Norfolk notes that Cardinal Wolsey arranged the meeting. Lord Abergavenny joins the conversation, and the three men criticize Wolsey, especially for having seized too much power over England's affairs. They declare that the peace he negotiated with France is no good, for France is still seizing English trade goods. Norfolk, who has heard that Buckingham is feuding with Wolsey, warns him that his foe is dangerous. Wolsey himself arrives and exchanges glares with Buckingham. He speaks with his Secretary about a pending interview with Buckingham's Surveyor, or overseer, and declares that its results will cut the duke down to size. When he leaves, Buckingham rages against him, accusing him of treason. He asserts that the cardinal deliberately negotiated a weak treaty with France after being bribed by the Holy Roman Emperor, who feared a genuine peace between France and England. Brandon appears and arrests Buckingham and Abergavenny for treason; Buckingham says that his Surveyor has doubtless been bribed.

Act 1, Scene 2
At a meeting of his council, the king thanks Wolsey for having suppressed Buckingham's conspiracy. The queen, Katherine of Aragon, arrives and speaks on behalf of the people against the unjust taxes introduced by Wolsey. Norfolk adds that uprisings are occurring as a result. The king, who knows nothing of these taxes, orders Wolsey to invalidate them and pardon the rebels. In an aside the cardinal instructs his Secretary to issue these orders but to make it seem as though the relief came from him. Queen Katherine regrets the arrest of Buckingham, and King Henry suggests she hear the evidence. Buckingham's Surveyor is brought in and testifies that Buckingham had planned to become king if Henry died. Katherine doubts his testimony, but he goes on, reporting that the duke spoke of killing Wolsey and the king. Convinced, Henry rages against Buckingham.

Act 1, Scene 3
The Lord Chamberlain, Lord Sands, and Sir Thomas Lovell jest about the recent, deplorable rise of the French influence in manners and clothes. They then leave for a dinner being given by Wolsey, praising the cardinal's bountiful table.

Act 1, Scene 4
The guests gather at Wolsey's banquet and jest bawdily with the young women there. On his arrival Wolsey encourages his guests to drink and enjoy one another. The Lord Chamberlain introduces a group of masquers (see MASQUE) who, dressed as shepherds, dance with the women. One of them is King Henry, who is clearly attracted to his partner. After the dance, the Lord Chamberlain introduces her to him as Anne Bullen, one of the queen's ladies-in-waiting.

Act 2, Scene 1
On a street in LONDON, a Gentleman (1) meets a friend, who tells him of Buckingham's trial and conviction. Presuming that Wolsey was behind the duke's fall, the Gentlemen discuss the cardinal's political maneuverings. They remark that Wolsey is as hated by the common people as Buckingham is beloved. Buckingham then appears, under guard, and makes a speech, forgiving his enemies and asking for his friends' prayers. He compares himself to his father, who was also betrayed by a servant and unjustly killed as a traitor. After he leaves for his execution, the Gentlemen rue his fate. They go on to talk of a rumor that Wolsey's next victim will be Queen Katherine. The king, they say, has been incited to divorce her by Wolsey, who seeks to embarrass the Holy Roman Emperor—Katherine's nephew—who refused Wolsey an archbishopric he wanted. Another cardinal, Campeius, has come from ROME, allegedly to oversee the divorce.

Act 2, Scene 2
The Lord Chamberlain discusses the king's possible divorce with Norfolk and the Duke of Suffolk. They, too, see the influence of Wolsey. They hope the king will come to his senses, remember the virtues of his 20-year marriage, and recognize the cardinal for the schemer he is. After the Lord Chamberlain leaves, the dukes approach the king,

who is reading. He is angry at their interruption but welcomes the arrival of Wolsey and Campeius. Norfolk and Suffolk leave, muttering curses at Wolsey. Henry then confers briefly with his secretary, Gardiner, and Wolsey informs Campeius that Gardiner will do whatever he, Wolsey, tells him to. Henry sends Gardiner with a message to the queen and announces that a hearing will be convened on the divorce question.

Act 2, Scene 3

Anne Bullen, talking with an Old Lady, pities the queen and says it would be better to be born poor than to be queen and subject to injustice and rejection. The Old Lady accuses her of hypocrisy and asserts, with bawdy quibbles, that she herself would gladly give up virginity for a crown. Anne declares that she would not. The Lord Chamberlain appears and announces the king's gift to Anne of a rich estate and title; she receives the news with great modesty, and the Chamberlain praises her in an aside. After he leaves, the Old Lady chortles over the gift, predicting that Anne will soon be a duchess. Anne, however, is offended and thinks again of the unfortunate queen.

Act 2, Scene 4

After a grand procession and formal proclamations by a Crier, the divorce proceedings begin. Addressing Henry, Katherine argues that she has always been a good and faithful wife. When Wolsey and Campeius object to her personal remarks, she replies that she refuses to be judged by an enemy. She demands a hearing from the pope and leaves. Henry, while praising her, also declares Wolsey innocent of any enmity toward her or any influence on himself. He asserts that he fears that his marriage is sinful because Katherine was once married to his elder brother. Though the church approved his marriage to Katherine at the time, he wants another ruling, to clear his conscience. Campeius declares an adjournment until the queen can be made to attend. In an aside Henry deplores these formalities and wishes his adviser Cranmer were present to expedite matters.

Act 3, Scene 1

Wolsey and Campeius visit Katherine and suggest that she abandon her defense and accept the king's decision to avoid the scandal of a divorce trial. Raging at them, she decries her helplessness but finally subsides into acceptance.

Act 3, Scene 2

Norfolk, Suffolk, Lord Surrey, and the Lord Chamberlain discuss Wolsey's downfall: Henry has learned that the cardinal secretly opposed the divorce (now completed) and did not wish the king to marry the virtuous Anne Bullen. But Henry has secretly done so and plans to make her queen; moreover, Wolsey's enemy, Cranmer, has been appointed Archbishop of Canterbury. Wolsey appears, seeming troubled, and muses in an aside that he intends to see the king marry a French duchess and not Anne Bullen. The king arrives and tells the noblemen that Wolsey has mistakenly included personal financial records among state papers sent to the king. Henry is shocked at the cardinal's wealth. He approaches Wolsey and sardonically praises him for putting his duty above personal gain. After giving him a folder of papers, Henry leaves angrily with the noblemen. When Wolsey sees that the papers include his records and his letters opposing the divorce, he realizes that all is lost. The noblemen return and recite a long series of formal charges against him, adding that the king has ordered all his possessions confiscated. They leave and the cardinal soliloquizes on his loss of greatness, comparing it to humanity's common end in death. He now recognizes the futility of his pride and riches. When his follower Cromwell approaches him, Wolsey declares that his downfall had led him to a fresh, healthier view of life. His conscience is finally free, and he has the fortitude to withstand whatever earthly miseries may be in store. Cromwell grieves for his master's downfall, but Wolsey encourages him to serve as an adviser to the king. For himself, he regrets not having given as much energy to religion as to the state.

Act 4, Scene 1

The two Gentlemen (1) meet again, at the coronation parade of Queen Anne. A grand procession passes by, including Suffolk, Norfolk, and Surrey—all now high officers of the realm—as well as the new queen. A Third Gentleman (1), who has seen the actual coronation, describes the ceremony in great detail. The discussion turns to political gossip: Gardiner, who is now Bishop of Winchester, is an enemy of Archbishop Cranmer, but the latter has a new and powerful ally in Cromwell, who is a close adviser of the king.

Act 4, Scene 2

At KIMBOLTON, Katherine learns of Wolsey's death from her attendant, Griffith. According to Griffith, the cardinal repented before his death and died at peace with God. When Katherine speaks bitterly of Wolsey, Griffith offers a charitable view of him, describing him as an excellent public servant who, though greedy for wealth, was also generous with his ill-gotten gains—founding two colleges, for instance. Katherine, who is near death, thanks Griffith for pointing to the Christian viewpoint. She falls asleep and sees a vision, which appears onstage: six dancing figures ceremoniously present her with garlands of bay leaves. When she awakes, her waiting-woman Patience observes that she is near death. She then receives a visitor, Lord Capuchius, the ambassador to England from her nephew the emperor. She asks him to take King Henry a letter, in which she asks to be remembered to their daughter and requests that he treat her followers and servants well. She then retires to bed, prepared to die.

Act 5, Scene 1

Bishop Gardiner meets Lovell in the middle of the night and learns that Queen Anne is in labor and may die. Gardiner hopes she does and insists, over Lovell's objection, that for them and their allies, it would be best if Anne, Cranmer, and Cromwell were all dead. He adds that he believes he has brought the king's council to move against Archbishop Cranmer's Protestant opinions. The council will interrogate the archbishop in the morning. After Gardiner leaves, the king arrives and meets Cranmer, whom he has sent for. Though Lovell tries to eavesdrop, the king orders him away. Henry tells Cranmer that he will have enemies at the council meeting in the morning. Cranmer declares that he has nothing to fear, but Henry warns him against false witnesses. Observing that the council may try to jail him, he gives him a ring to signify the king's protection. Cranmer leaves, and Anne's companion the Old Lady arrives to inform the king

that he has a daughter. She first comically identifies the infant as a boy and then complains about the size of the tip the king gives her.

Act 5, Scene 2

Cranmer arrives for the council meeting but, insultingly, is kept waiting outside. Doctor Butts brings the king to an upper room, where he can watch the proceedings. After Cranmer is admitted, the Chancellor accuses him of spreading heresies; Gardiner adds that severe treatment is called for, lest civil disorders arise from the heresy, like the religious wars then raging in Germany. Although Cranmer asserts his opposition to civil disorder, Gardiner insists that he must be imprisoned. Cromwell says Gardiner is too harsh, and Gardiner accuses him of involvement in heresy himself. The Chancellor then orders Cranmer to prison, but the archbishop produces the king's ring. His enemies are dumbfounded, realizing that the king has stymied them. The king then emerges from his vantage point and castigates them mercilessly. He confirms his support for Cranmer by asking him to baptize his daughter.

Act 5, Scene 3

On the day of the christening, the Porter and his Man are unable to prevent a crowd of celebrating commoners from invading the palace courtyard. They make comical remarks about the riotous celebrants.

Act 5, Scene 4

A grand procession escorts the infant Elizabeth. It is led by the Garter, who recites a prayer for her. Cranmer addresses the assembled court, predicting a great future for the child and happiness for the country. The king thanks him and declares the day a holiday for all.

Epilogue

An actor asserts that people may criticize the play for various reasons, but that all must concede that it has glorified good women, and so he supposes it will get applause, for no men will withhold it when their ladies prompt them.

COMMENTARY

Henry VIII, though classed with the HISTORY PLAYS, treats English history in a very different way. The play does not realistically enact a political conflict, as the other history plays do. Rather, it is a symbolic tribute to the TUDOR DYNASTY, presented in the manner of Shakespeare's other late plays, the ROMANCES. Like these plays, it uses an episodic plot line, studded with spectacles and tableaux, and closes with the promise of a new generation. Moreover, *Henry VIII* makes the same moral point as the romances—that humanity depends on divine providence, which requires that we exercise our capacity for good through a steadfast spirit, mercy, and forgiveness. The play celebrates King Henry VIII's attainment of wisdom and the country's simultaneous rejection of the authority of Catholic Rome, but Henry does not guide the play's development so much as he is simply its leading figure. A national myth is embodied in *Henry VIII*—that England is chosen by providence for Protestant freedom—and it is Henry who leads the country there. The final tableau confirms Henry's virtues in those predicted for his daughter Elizabeth, the last and greatest of Tudor monarchs. In the earlier history plays, the qualities of the characters, good and bad, generated events; here, history is driven by destiny.

As in the romantic literature on which Shakespeare's last plays were based, the rise or fall of great personages is displayed in a series of brief, almost actionless scenes that enact a pattern of loss and regeneration. Buckingham is executed, and Queen Katherine humiliated because of Cardinal Wolsey's enmity; then Wolsey is exposed and discredited. Anne Bullen (better known today as Anne Boleyn) is crowned, and Cromwell and Cranmer assume high office. Finally, Cranmer's enemies—led by Wolsey's onetime underling, Bishop Gardiner—are confounded. All these events are given significance in relation to the growth of Henry. The king is easily deceived by Wolsey about Buckingham, and his moral qualms about his first marriage help Wolsey bring about the fall of Katherine. Although the intervention of chance is necessary to expose the cardinal, the king then masterfully subdues him. The king recognizes good in the virtuous—and Protestant—Anne, despite Wolsey's attempts to keep her from him, and the king's maturing wisdom contributes to the rise of Cromwell and Cranmer, two fine men, the latter an important Protestant religious hero. Finally, the king saves Cranmer from

Gardiner's machinations. When the monarch has thus arrived at a summit of wisdom and maturity, he brings forth a glorious successor in Elizabeth, who is rhapsodically praised by Cranmer in 5.4. Cranmer's eulogy even extends to the monarch ruling at the time the play was written, Elizabeth's successor, King JAMES I.

Henry VIII also resembles the romances in its use of pageantry. The play opens with a description of elaborate ceremonies and closes with the enactment of one. Between the opening and the close there are several spectacular tableaux, often with heavily descriptive stage directions that indicate their importance to the play. These episodes are more than mere entertainment, however. In the first half of the play, they demonstrate the effects of evil on the play's world; in the second, they evidence the exaltation of its recovery from evil.

In 1.1 the meeting of monarchs in France is described in terms that convey greed and corruption. One side's display resembles "heathen gods" (1.1.19); the other then makes "a fool and beggar" (1.1.28) of its competitor. The women "almost sweat to bear" (1.1.24) their jewelry. Most significant, "these fierce vanities" (1.1.54) are associated with the villainies of Wolsey; moreover, the treaty being celebrated is shown to be worthless. In 1.4 the cardinal's banquet offers an aura of decadence, especially in the risqué conversation before the king's masque, which is important to our sense of Wolsey's evil effect on the court. (On the other hand, the masque, during which Henry falls in love with Anne—a development that counters Wolsey's evil—is a lovely, ordered dance.) In 2.1 Buckingham is solemnly led to execution with "tipstaves before him, the axe with the edge towards him, halberds on each side" (2.1.53, stage direction); the grandeur of the play's world becomes increasingly ominous. An extremely elaborate stage direction at the opening of 2.4 describes in detail the panoply of Katherine's divorce trial. Particularly gaudy is the ecclesiastical pomp of the two cardinals, clad in their scarlet robes and escorted by "two Gentlemen bearing two great silver pillars." However, their rich display cannot help the king, who is attempting to rectify a sin that has deprived the nation of an heir to the throne. As the scene ends, Henry rejects the "dilatory sloth and tricks of Rome" (2.4.235) in favor of the "well-beloved" (2.4.236) Cranmer. Here, the play's luxuriant splendor is associated with Catholicism, but the path of recovery is evident.

After Wolsey's downfall and the revelation that Anne is to become queen in Act 3, we again find spectacle in Act 4, but now the association is entirely positive. At 4.1.37 a complex, 10-part stage direction presents the coronation procession. The Gentlemen remark on the participants, including Anne: ". . . the sweetest face I ever look'd on . . . an angel" (4.1.43–44). The Third Gentleman then provides a description of another ritual ceremony, the actual coronation, in entirely positive terms. The splendid and spectacular are now associated with the good of England and the triumph of virtue. Although Katherine's vision in 4.2 is in a very different key, it, too, is presented in great detail; it is also entertaining on stage and distinctly linked with virtue, in this case more personal and religious. Lastly, there is another procession preceding Cranmer's speech at Elizabeth's christening. This sumptuous parade provides a fitting culmination to the play's use of ceremony and ritual as expressions of moral tone. Here, the triumph of virtue is confirmed in another formal display of religion, but this time it is a Protestant religion—a distinction immediately evident to Shakespeare's audience, through costume as well as Cranmer's presence.

Divine intervention underlies the play's developments. In the first half this is clear in the way chance brings Anne to the king's attention and exposes Wolsey. It is also evident in the forgiving attitude and acceptance of God's will of Wolsey's victims. In the second half of the play, the religious theme becomes prominent, limiting the importance of personality among the play's chief characters. Henry demonstrates the significance of personal growth—the wisdom and maturity he attains in the course of the play are necessary to its happy conclusion—but he simply displays differing outlooks, without going through a process of internal development.

More striking as personalities are the "tragic" characters, who embody the importance of patiently accepting fate. However, they are restricted in emotional range, precisely to emphasize their thematic significance. Buckingham, Katherine, and Cardinal

Wolsey appear only briefly before meeting their fates; they achieve importance only at their downfalls, when they respond to adversity with dignity and wisdom.

Upon his arrest, Buckingham's anger against Wolsey—his only trait so far—disappears, and he simply says, "The will of heav'n / Be done . . . I obey" (1.1.209–210). In this he is supported by his fellow victim, Abergavenny. On his way to be executed in 2.1, Buckingham forgives his enemies and accepts his downfall as a blessing. Though he reveals some bitterness in recollecting his father's similar fate, he controls it and departs with a prayer: "I have done, and God forgive me" (2.1.136).

Queen Katherine's conduct at her trial—her dignity as she presents her case, her fire as she turns against Wolsey, and her resolute departure—is truly impressive. Even when she recognizes defeat, she finds powerful poetry to express it: "like the lily / That once was mistress of the field and flourish'd, / I'll hang my head and perish" (3.1.151–153). (This episode is introduced with the SONG "Orpheus with his lute" [3.1.3–14], which in its union of mysticism and music is a typical ploy of Shakespearean romances.) Perhaps most important is Katherine's joint demonstration, with Griffith, of forgiveness toward Wolsey. In her mild way, the deposed and dying queen is bitter toward her enemy, but after Griffith's recital of the cardinal's hidden virtues, she confirms that "religious truth and modesty" require her declaration, "peace be with him" (4.2.74, 75). She approaches her death "meditating / On that celestial harmony I go to" (4.2.79–80). Her vision adds supernatural sanction to our impression of her virtues, as well as reinforcing the importance of divine intervention in the play's world.

Most significant, the play's only important villain, Wolsey, makes a similar demonstration of acceptance. Once his downfall is certain, in 3.2, the cardinal recognizes the futility of his struggle for wealth and power and rejects the "Vain pomp and glory of this world" (3.2.365). Free from the temptations of intrigue and ambition, he finds "A peace above all earthly dignities, / A still and quiet conscience" (3.2.379–380), and he thanks the king, who has overthrown him, for his newly found "fortitude of soul" (3.2.388). He considerately advises Cromwell on both worldly advancement and spiritual health, before departing from the court with the wish that he had "but serv'd my God with half the zeal / I serv'd my king" (3.2.455–456). In 4.2 Griffith repeats the lesson in describing the cardinal's death: "His overthrow heap'd happiness upon him, / For then, . . . [he] found the blessedness of being little / And . . . died fearing God" (4.2.64–68). Thus, Wolsey's end, like those of Buckingham and Katherine, points to the ultimate superiority of the divine over the mundane. The eulogies Shakespeare provides for the cardinal are all the more important when we consider what a departure they were from the standard English view of his day. For most English Protestants of the 16th and 17th centuries, Wolsey was a chief villain of pre-Reformation English Catholicism; to present him as a recipient of God's mercy was to make mercy a prominent theme indeed.

Like the romances, *Henry VIII* stresses the triumph of good and the importance of patience in adversity, elevating these propositions by placing them in a schematic plot in which it is clear that God controls all. However, unlike the romances, the plan is set in the historical world, one still very well known to the play's original audience. It is not only a moral tale of suffering borne with dignity, it is a national myth. Here the regenerative pattern of the romances is employed to display the redemption of a particular country at a particular time: England as it acquired the state church—and the anti-Catholic stance—with which its people largely identified in Shakespeare's time. In the spirit of the romances, this process yields great optimism: Old errors are expiated in an atmosphere of reconciliation, and the future offers the promise of a new generation. The providence that lends strength to the allegorical characters of *Pericles*, *Cymbeline*, *The Winter's Tale*, and *The Tempest* is here devoted to an entire people. *Henry VIII* is history in a romantic mode.

SOURCES OF THE PLAY

Shakespeare's principal source for most of *Henry VIII* was Raphael HOLINSHED's *Chronicles of England, Scotland, and Ireland* (Second edition, 1587), supplemented by the account of Henry's reign in *The Union of the Two Noble and Illustre Families of Lancaster and York* (1548) by Edward HALL. However, for the trial of Cranmer in 5.1–2, the playwright relied on John FOXE's *Book of Martyrs* (1563).

TEXT OF THE PLAY

Since 1850, Shakespeare's authorship of *Henry VIII* has been disputed. Some scholars have thought the play was too badly organized to be the work of a single author and have attributed much of the play to John FLETCHER. Some go so far as to hold that Shakespeare did not write any of it, ascribing it to Fletcher and Philip MASSINGER. The question is still argued, but increasingly scholarly opinion tends to find the play wholly, perhaps largely, Shakespearean for a variety of reasons. For one, the FIRST FOLIO editors accepted *Henry VIII* while rejecting the plays known to be Fletcher-Shakespeare collaborations (*The Two Noble Kinsmen* and *Cardenio*). Moreover, the use of sources seems consistent throughout the play, and it is different from Fletcher's practice elsewhere. Finally, the "disorganization" of *Henry VIII* seems less significant if one compares the play with Shakespeare's contemporary romances, which are intentionally episodic, rather than with his histories, which are more narrative in structure.

Henry VIII was written between late 1612 and June 1613, when the GLOBE THEATRE burned down during a performance of it. (A report of this event calls the play *All Is True*, apparently a subtitle.) By its style *Henry VIII* can be identified as a very late work, so it was probably written not long before this performance. It may have been composed specifically for the celebration of the marriage of the princess ELIZABETH STUART in February 1613, as is suggested by its patriotism and its particular attention to the princess's namesake. In any case, its suitability for Elizabeth's marriage also made it an appropriate offering to the public that spring. In sum, most commentators agree that it was first performed in early 1613 and written not long before.

Henry VIII was first published in the First Folio (1623). The text derives from the author's FOUL PAPERS (or possibly from the FAIR COPY made by a professional scribe), for it has elaborate and literary stage directions (some taken directly from source material), which would have been abbreviated in a PROMPTBOOK. The Folio offers the only early text and has therefore been the basis for all subsequent editions.

THEATRICAL HISTORY OF THE PLAY

As already noted, *Henry VIII* may have been first performed as part of the festivities celebrating the marriage of Princess Elizabeth in the winter of 1612–13. However, it is not in the list of 14 Shakespeare plays staged by the KING'S MEN during the winter's wedding festivities (though it may have been the play canceled due to scheduling conflicts on February 16). The earliest recorded performance (but clearly not the first) was on June 29, 1613, when cannon fire—called for in the stage direction at 1.4.49—set fire to the thatched roof of the Globe and burned the theater to the ground. A tradition first reported in 1708 held that John LOWIN was the original Henry and "had his instructions" from Shakespeare himself, which suggests that the playwright may have directed the production. One other early staging is known: a private performance in July 1628, commissioned by King Charles I's favorite, George Villiers, Duke of Buckingham. Though no relation to the play's Buckingham, Villiers reportedly left the performance after the duke is led away to be executed in 2.1. (He was himself assassinated a few weeks later.)

After the reopening of the London theaters following 18 years of revolutionary government, *Henry VIII* was staged by William DAVENANT in 1664, with Thomas BETTERTON as King Henry and Henry HARRIS as Wolsey; Samuel PEPYS saw it, but his account of a play about Henry "with all his wives" suggests that it may have been considerably altered by Davenant. It was recorded as a "stock play" for Davenant's company over the next few decades, though no specific performance was noted. It then disappeared for a generation.

In 1716 *Henry VIII* was revived by Colley CIBBER, who produced it frequently during the next decade and added increasingly spectacular scenic effects, especially for the coronation procession in 4.1. Appropriately, Cibber presented the play at the coronation of King George II in 1727. Barton BOOTH played the title role in Cibber's presentations.

The coronation procession from *Henry VIII* was often performed separately in the middle of the 18th century, as part of a program of pantomimes or even along with other plays. David GARRICK continued the trend to spectacle; his production, revived many times between 1742 and 1768, required 140 actors in 4.1. Other elements were cut to make time for this one, most notably the vision of Queen Katherine in 4.2. Garrick played Henry opposite the Queen Katherine of Hannah PRITCHARD.

After a 20-year hiatus, J. P. KEMBLE revived *Henry VIII* in 1788, with his sister Sarah SIDDONS as Queen Katherine, a role for which she was particularly acclaimed throughout her career. Kemble himself played Cromwell (to whom he assigned Griffith's part, as well). After 1803, as manager of the Covent Garden Theatre, Kemble revived the play numerous times, often playing Wolsey, and after his retirement in 1817, his younger brother Charles KEMBLE continued the tradition. In 1830 Charles's daughter Fanny KEMBLE, though only 20 years old, was successful as Queen Katherine.

Henry VIII naturally appealed to the 19th-century taste for spectacle, and the next notable production, that of Charles KEAN in 1855, was probably the most elaborate. His 5.4 opened with (in his words) "the Lord Mayor and City Council proceeding to the royal ceremonial in their state barges, to give a panoramic view [on a moving backdrop] of London, as it then appeared." He managed nonetheless to restore material often dropped from earlier productions, such as the role of Griffith and Katherine's vision (in which Ellen TERRY, as a small child, played an angel in a revival of 1858). Henry IRVING staged *Henry VIII* in 1892, with Terry as Katherine, Irving himself as Wolsey, and Johnston FORBES-ROBERTSON as Buckingham. Irving's production was no less sumptuous than its predecessors, and it was wildly popular.

In the 20th century, the popularity of *Henry VIII* waned somewhat, but a number of notable productions were staged. Beerbohm TREE presented the play in a characteristically extravagant adaptation that cut Act 5 entirely. This spectacular, starring Tree as Wolsey, was a hit in London (1910) and New York (1916). Sir Lewis CASSON produced the play with Sybil THORNDIKE as Katherine in 1925. Margaret WEBSTER presented it in New York in 1946, as the inaugural production of the American

Repertory Company, with Eva Le Gallienne (b. 1899) as Katherine. Tyrone GUTHRIE has staged it three times: in 1933 at SADLER'S WELLS THEATRE, with Charles LAUGHTON in the title role; in 1949 at STRATFORD, with Anthony QUAYLE as Henry; and at the OLD VIC THEATRE in 1953, in honor of the coronation of Queen Elizabeth II. Michael BENTHALL's OLD VIC (1958) production starred John GIELGUD as Wolsey and Edith EVANS as Katherine. In the last quarter of the century, Joseph PAPP and the ROYAL SHAKESPEARE COMPANY each presented the play, the latter twice.

Tree's 1910 production of *Henry VIII* was the basis for a brief silent FILM made in 1911, but since only five scenes were filmed over a period of only two hours including rehearsals, it is fair to say that *Henry VIII* has not yet been produced as a movie. It was made for TELEVISION in 1979, with Claire Bloom (b. 1931) as Queen Katherine.

CHARACTERS

Abergavenny, George Neville, Lord (d. 1535) Historical figure and minor character in *Henry VIII*, son-in-law of the Duke of Buckingham. As the play opens, Abergavenny joins Buckingham and the Duke of Norfolk in their complaints about Cardinal Wolsey's abuse of power. At the end of 1.1, Abergavenny and Buckingham are arrested for treason, the victims of a plot by Wolsey. Like his father-in-law, Abergavenny calmly accepts his fate. "The will of Heaven be done, and the king's pleasure / By me obey'd" (1.1.215–216), offering a strong contrast with Wolsey's villainy. Shakespeare took Abergavenny's involvement from HOLINSHED's *Chronicles*, and the lord is merely an echo of Buckingham. At 1.1.211 of the FIRST FOLIO edition of the play, Abergavenny's name is spelled "Aburgany," indicating its ordinary pronunciation.

Anne Bullen (Anne Boleyn) (ca. 1507–1536) Historical figure and character in *Henry VIII*, the lover and later the wife of King Henry VIII, and the mother of Queen Elizabeth. At Cardinal Wolsey's banquet in 1.4, Anne chats pleasantly with Lord Sands before meeting Henry. The king is charmed by Anne when he dances with her, though she does not speak. In 2.3 Anne tolerantly accepts the Old

Lady's bawdy jesting about her potential relationship with the king, but her own mind is on the suffering of the rejected Queen Katherine. Thus, Shakespeare disassociates Anne's rise from Katherine's fall, which is blamed on Cardinal Wolsey. Anne appears but does not speak at her own coronation in 4.1, and she is not present at the christening of her daughter Elizabeth in 5.4. She is depicted as a saintly woman whose Protestantism is said to be a healthy influence on the king and the country. Her role in the play's events, however, is very understated, probably in order to avoid reminding the audience of her well-known fate: Only three years later, after failing to produce sons, she was divorced and executed on trumped-up charges of adultery and treason. Any allusion to this would undermine the play's emphasis on King Henry's growth to wisdom and on the general virtues of the TUDOR DYNASTY, of which Elizabeth was so prominent a member.

The historical Anne Boleyn was very different from Shakespeare's Anne, and the course of her affair with the king is only sketchily presented in the play. We are not informed that the king had already had an affair with Anne's older sister Mary, nor that Anne was pregnant with Elizabeth when the king married her. Anne's personality is hard to discern today, after centuries of accusation and defense, but she was certainly not the high-minded virgin of the play. She appears to have had other affairs before Henry—with the poet Thomas WYATT, at least—and her upbringing was notoriously scandalous. Anne's father, Thomas Boleyn (1477–1539), an ambitious merchant who had married a daughter of the Duke of Norfolk, was a determined participant in the power politics of the king's court. His power and influence increased greatly as a result of his daughters' sexual relationships, and it seems likely that both girls were brought up with such possibilities in mind. Boleyn served Henry as ambassador to FRANCE, and from the age of about 12, Anne was a lady-in-waiting at the licentious court of King Francis I, where sexual intrigue was a way of life. King Francis later described Mary Boleyn as "a great prostitute, infamous above all"—and though Anne is not implicated in such accounts, she was certainly close to the participants. Henry knew Anne slightly at this time; he considered having her marry an Irish nobleman as part of a diplomatic settlement, apparently at her father's suggestion.

Anne returned to England around 1522, when her older sister became Henry's mistress. Anne was soon banished from court for a romantic entanglement that interfered with a proposed political marriage, and it was only after her return in 1526 that Henry fell in love with her. She seems to have resisted his desire for sex for several years, probably in the hope of becoming a wife rather than a mistress, but once sure of her eventual legitimacy, she surrendered. In the meantime she and the king scandalized the court and humiliated Queen Katherine with such behavior as public caresses and mocking remarks. In marked contrast to Shakespeare's portrait, Anne seems to have taken pains to show her disrespect for the older woman. Such behavior made Anne widely unpopular with both courtiers and commoners, and her ultimate destiny was welcomed by many.

Bishop   Any of three minor characters in *Henry VIII*, attendants to the Cardinals Wolsey and Campeius as they enter the formal hearing on King Henry VIII's prospective divorce. The three—the Bishops of Ely, Rochester, and St. Asaph—are mentioned only in the elaborate stage direction at the opening of 2.4, and they do not speak, serving merely to swell the scene. Shakespeare knew of their presence from the account given by his main historical source for the play, Raphael HOLINSHED's *Chronicles*.

Boleyn, Anne   See Anne Bullen.

Boy   Minor character in *Henry VIII*, an attendant of Bishop Gardiner. Identified in the stage directions opening 5.1 as the bishop's page, the Boy carries a torch for his master and in his three words confirms that it is one o'clock. He thus establishes the time of night while also indicating by his presence the high rank of Gardiner, once the king's secretary.

Brandon   Minor character in *Henry VIII*, an officer who arrests the Duke of Buckingham and Lord

Abergavenny. Brandon appears in 1.1 and instructs a Sergeant at arms to arrest the two noblemen. Brandon is sorry to have this duty and civilly explains that they are alleged to be part of a conspiracy against the king. His apologetic attitude helps convey the play's point of view, that Buckingham's enemy Cardinal Wolsey is in the wrong.

Brandon may be the same person as the Duke of Suffolk, who appears later in the play and whose name was Charles Brandon. The designation of one character by two names might indicate joint authorship of the play, or it might simply be an instance of Shakespeare's carelessness in such matters, evident throughout his plays.

Buckingham, Edward Stafford, Duke of   (1478–1521)   Historical figure and minor character in *Henry VIII*, a nobleman falsely convicted of treason and sentenced to death, a victim of Cardinal Wolsey's intrigues. In 1.1 Buckingham's anger at Wolsey's duplicitous misuse of power establishes the cardinal as a villain. His own contrasting goodness is demonstrated as he calmly accepts his arrest for treason, even though it becomes apparent that Wolsey has bribed the duke's former Surveyor to commit perjury. In 2.1, on his way to be executed, Buckingham furthers the contrast by forgiving his enemies, wishing King Henry VIII well, and humbly preparing for death. Buckingham's victimization marks one end of the play's most important development—the growth of King Henry—for the ease with which the king is deceived by Wolsey and the Surveyor is soon replaced by increasing maturity and wisdom.

In 2.1.107–123 Buckingham compares himself to his father, also executed for treason. That Duke of Buckingham appears in *Richard III*, and *his* father, this duke's grandfather, is the Buckingham of *2 Henry VI*.

Butts, Doctor (William Butts)   (d. 1545)   Historical figure and minor character in *Henry VIII*, King Henry VIII's physician. In 5.2 Doctor Butts leads Henry to an upper room where he can secretly view his council's meeting below, in order to thwart the councillors' attempt to imprison Thomas Cranmer, Archbishop of Canterbury. Butts informs the king that the archbishop has been humiliated by having to wait with the servants outside the meeting room, and this adds to the king's anger. Shakespeare took Butts's role in this incident from his source, FOXE's *Actes and Monumentes.* Butts was King Henry's personal physician for many years, and his death is said to have distressed the king greatly. His personal appearance has been preserved in a fine portrait by Hans Holbein the Younger (ca. 1497–1543).

Campeius, Cardinal Laurence (Lorenzo Campeggio) (1472–1539) Historical figure and minor character in *Henry VIII,* the pope's ambassador to the court of King Henry VIII. Campeius comes to England to consider the legality of Henry's proposed divorce of Queen Katherine. Cardinal Wolsey has assured the king that Campeius will rule in his favor, but in 2.4 the Roman cardinal merely postpones a decision. Irritated, Henry complains, "These cardinals trifle with me: I abhor / This dilatory sloth and tricks of Rome" (2.4.234–235). Here—as throughout—Campeius embodies the untrustworthiness of Catholicism from the play's point of view. The episode also demonstrates Henry's growing mistrust of Wolsey, as he moves from gullibility to wisdom, a principal theme of the play. In 3.2 Campeius is said to have "stolen away to Rome . . . / [having] left the cause o'th'king unhandled" (3.2.57–58).

The historical Campeggio—Shakespeare uses the Latin form of his name—was responsible for English affairs at the Vatican and had visited England before he arrived to adjudicate Henry's divorce in 1528. In fact, Henry had appointed him absentee Bishop of Salisbury in 1524. Unknown to Wolsey, he was under instructions to delay Henry's divorce as long as possible, for the pope did not want to offend the Holy Roman Emperor, Queen Katherine's nephew. He succeeded in postponing the trial for nine months and then, when it seemed likely that Henry would win his case, he declared an adjournment and left for Rome. Henry eventually declared himself divorced when he assumed papal powers in England as part of the Reformation, and at that time Campeggio lost his English bishopric.

Capuchius, Lord (Lord Capucius, Eustace Chapuys) (active 1530s) Historical figure and minor character in *Henry VIII,* ambassador to England from the Holy Roman Empire, a visitor to Queen Katherine. In 4.2 Capuchius bears a message from King Henry VIII wishing good health to the dying Katherine. She observes mildly that the gesture comes too late. She asks Capuchius to take the king a letter, in which she requests that he look after their daughter—and remember her to the child—and treat her followers and servants well. She then retires to die. The episode, which Shakespeare knew from his source, HOLINSHED's *Chronicles,* offers a final demonstration of Katherine's virtue.

Following Holinshed, Shakespeare used the Latin form of the ambassador's name. Chapuys's surviving official correspondence casts light on the intrigues of the period. One letter declares that Cardinal WOLSEY had written to him recommending that the pope excommunicate King Henry and use arms to enforce Catholicism in England. In an unrelated treason trial of 1533, it was alleged that Chapuys had planned an invasion of England in support of Katherine, but that the emperor had vetoed the idea. This may not have been taken seriously, because Chapuys continued in his post and, as we have seen, was permitted to visit Katherine.

Chamberlain, Lord Character in *Henry VIII,* an official of King Henry VIII's household, overseer of the king's travel, entertainment, and wardrobe. In 1.4 he assists Sir Henry Guilford with Cardinal Wolsey's banquet, where he introduces the king to Anne Bullen. In 2.2 and 3.2 he appears briefly as a plotter against Wolsey with the Dukes of Norfolk and Suffolk, and in 5.2 he is a member of the royal council, though he speaks only a few lines. In 5.3 he helps prepare for the christening of Princess Elizabeth. Throughout he is representative of the elaborate world of courtly entertainment. Historically, the Chamberlain was Sir William Sands, but Shakespeare mistakenly gave that nobleman another part in the play.

Chancellor Minor character in *Henry VIII,* the highest-ranking official of King Henry VIII's government and keeper of the Great Seal of England, used to signify royal approval of any document. In

5.2 the Chancellor chairs the meeting of the royal council at which Bishop Gardiner attacks Archbishop Cranmer. He sides with Gardiner, but when the king intervenes for Cranmer, the Chancellor declares that their intention was simply to provide the archbishop with a chance to clear his name. He typifies the malevolence that the king overcomes in the final political episode of the play.

We hear in 3.2.393–394 that Sir Thomas MORE has succeeded Cardinal Wolsey as Chancellor, but Shakespeare's Chancellor is nameless. In fact, More held the office for only three years, and the Chancellor at the time of 4.1 and 5.2 was Sir Thomas Audley (1488–1544). However, the specific identification is immaterial; the Chancellor is present simply as a representative of the highest levels of government.

Cranmer, Thomas (1489–1556)   Historical figure and character in *Henry VIII*, an adviser to King Henry VIII and later Archbishop of Canterbury. Cranmer is the central figure in 5.1–2, as Bishop Gardiner and the Lord Chancellor attempt to charge him with heresy at a meeting of the royal council, only to be thwarted by the king's intervention. The episode demonstrates the king's mastery of the situation—Henry's increasing wisdom is an important theme of the play. It also illustrates the triumph of the Protestant leaders—Cranmer and the king—over the pro-Catholic conspirators.

Cranmer is sometimes confused with another Archbishop of Canterbury in the play, whom the king addresses in 2.4.215–217. However, this figure—who remains mute—is Cranmer's predecessor, Archbishop William Warham (d. 1532), for Cranmer is abroad at this point. Henry wishes Cranmer were present in 2.4.236–237; his return and his appointment as Archbishop are reported in 3.2.74.

At the close of the play, Cranmer's prediction of glory for the infant Elizabeth even includes praise of her successor, JAMES I, and thus extends *Henry VIII* into Shakespeare's own time. In this the play differs from all the other HISTORY PLAYS. Cranmer, well known to 17th-century audiences as a martyred religious hero, is a suitable vehicle for such a spiritual evocation of "the happiness of England" (5.4.56).

The historical Cranmer was a professor at Cambridge University in the 1520s who was influenced by continental Protestant doctrines, especially on papal authority. He proposed that King Henry did not need the pope's permission to divorce Queen Katherine if he had the approval of other authoritative clerics. Henry sent Cranmer and others to solicit opinions, some of them approving, from religious thinkers throughout England and Europe. When Cranmer was appointed archbishop in 1533, he declared the king's marriage invalid. Cranmer's greatest historical importance, however, lies in his work as the chief creator of a liturgy for the new Protestant Church of England. He supervised the production of the first two editions (1549, 1552) of a prayer book and promulgated a formal statement of doctrine in 42 articles (1552), later reduced to 39. An oath of adherence to the 39 Articles, as they were known, was required of all Anglican clergymen and became a bone of contention in English politics for generations. Cranmer also edited and wrote parts of the first book of *Homilies* (1547), intended to be used for sermons in Anglican churches. For these works and his leadership as archbishop, Cranmer is regarded as the principal founder of the Church of England. Under the Catholic queen Mary (ruled 1553–58), he was ousted from his archbishopric and charged with heresy. He formally recanted but was condemned anyway and burned at the stake.

Crier   Minor character in *Henry VIII*, petty official at the divorce trial of Queen Katherine. In 2.4.7 and 10, upon the orders of the Scribe, the Crier formally demands the presence of King Henry VIII and the queen. In this he emphasizes the pomp and ceremony with which the king is proceeding against Katherine, thereby increasing our sense of her vulnerability.

Cromwell, Thomas (ca. 1485–1540)   Historical figure and character in *Henry VIII*, secretary to Cardinal Wolsey and later to King Henry VIII's council. In 3.2, as Wolsey's downfall becomes clear, Cromwell's demonstration of loyalty improves our image of Wolsey. He seems genuinely grieved, crying out, "O my lord, / Must I then leave you? must I needs forgo / So good, so noble and so true a master?" (3.2.421–423). The episode also offers an opportunity for the fallen cardinal to display magnanimity—concerning himself with Cromwell's welfare amid the debacle of his own affairs and thereby demonstrating his capacity for moral regeneration in adversity, an important theme of the play. Cromwell's subsequent political rise is mentioned by the Third Gentleman, who calls him "A man in much esteem with th'king" (4.1.109). In 5.2 Cromwell defends Archbishop Cranmer against heresy charges and is himself accused of Protestant leanings by the orthodox Bishop Gardiner. The episode points up the political importance of religious rivalries in the play's world. Also, that the onetime aide to Wolsey should become the king's ally demonstrates the progress from evil to good so central to *Henry VIII*.

The historical Cromwell served as Wolsey's secretary, but Shakespeare invented his sympathetic response to the cardinal's plight. Cromwell eventually succeeded Wolsey as the king's chief minister. A vigorous administrator, he devised and oversaw the dissolution of English monasteries to enrich the Crown and set up an intensive domestic intelligence service, sometimes called the first prototype of a secret police force. Eventually, however, Cromwell shared Wolsey's fate. He tried to ally England with the Protestant powers of northern Europe, and to that end arranged Henry's fourth marriage, in 1540, to the German princess, Anne of Cleves (1515–57). The rapid failure of the marriage was the minister's downfall. He was convicted of treason and executed. (His fate is obscurely alluded to in 3.2.448–449.) His career was the subject of the play THOMAS LORD CROMWELL, at one time attributed to Shakespeare.

Denny, Sir Anthony (1501–1549) Historical figure and minor character in *Henry VIII*, a member of King Henry VIII's court. In 5.1.80–81 Denny reports that he has brought Archbishop Cranmer to a midnight meeting with the king, as Henry has instructed. After escorting Cranmer to the king, he disappears from the play. Shakespeare took Denny's tiny role from a source, FOXE's *Actes and Monumentes*, and used it to intensify the air of intrigue surrounding the meeting, which begins the

major episode of Act 5. The historical Denny was a close friend of the king.

Elizabeth I, Queen of England (1533–1603) Ruler of England for much of Shakespeare's life and a very minor character in *Henry VIII*, written 10 years after her death. Elizabeth appears as an infant—that is, as a prop held by an actor—in 5.4 of the play, where she is the subject of a long eulogy by Archbishop Cranmer. Queen Elizabeth was the most important patron of ELIZABETHAN THEATER: Her influence was essential in protecting the theatrical profession from Puritan-inspired prohibitions, and her court provided an important source of income and prestige for the leading LONDON acting companies. She especially favored Shakespeare's company, the CHAMBERLAIN'S MEN, and he often performed for her.

Elizabeth I ruled while England became a world power. The works of Shakespeare are only the most prominent of many great artistic and intellectual achievements that occurred in England during her reign. *(Courtesy of Colonial Williamsburg)*

The queen is said to have been so pleased with Falstaff in the *Henry IV* plays that she commanded the playwright to produce a play in which the fat knight falls in love; the result was *The Merry Wives of Windsor*—written, according to legend, in two weeks. There may be a germ of truth to the tale, for *The Merry Wives* was probably written for a royal occasion. In any case, Elizabeth's fondness for Shakespeare's plays is testified to in Ben JONSON's accolade, printed in the FIRST FOLIO, in which he refers to the playwright's "flights . . . That so did take Eliza . . ."

Shakespeare rendered appropriate tribute. In *Henry V* the Chorus, analogizing the English victory at AGINCOURT with a hoped-for English victory in Ireland in 1599 (when the play was written), refers to "our gracious empress" in 5.Chorus.30. This was Shakespeare's only overt reference to Queen Elizabeth in her lifetime, though twice in *A Midsummer Night's Dream*, passages subtly allude to her, probably because she was expected to be present at the wedding celebration for which the play is believed to have been written. In 2.1.155–164 she is complimented by a lyrical description that evokes the conventional allegorical representations of the queen in popular prints of the day. In 5.1.89–105 Duke Theseus praises a monarch's benevolent reception of tongue-tied subjects, behavior that Elizabeth is known to have prided herself on.

Cranmer's eulogy to Elizabeth in *Henry VIII*, delivered by an important English national hero, doubtless reflects the nostalgia for her reign felt by England a decade after her death. Elizabeth was the only child of King Henry VIII and Anne Boleyn, the Anne Bullen of *Henry VIII*. After succeeding her Catholic half sister Mary (ruled 1553–58), she had a long and successful reign. Under Elizabeth, Protestantism was firmly established in England, and the nation showed its strength against its Catholic enemies with the defeat of the Spanish Armada in 1588. Elizabeth's reign also encompassed magnificent achievements in English literature. Although drama itself was not appreciated as art, the great value of the prose and poetry of Philip SIDNEY, Edmund SPENSER, Thomas NORTH, and others—including the Shakespeare of *Venus and Ado-*

nis and *The Rape of Lucrece*—was recognized and appreciated. In the early 17th century, Elizabeth's reign was already considered—as it has been ever since—England's golden age.

Gardiner, Stephen (d. 1555)   Historical figure and character in *Henry VIII*, a follower of Cardinal Wolsey and later his successor as the play's principal villain. In 2.2 Gardiner appears as King Henry VIII's new secretary; in an aside he assures Wolsey of his personal loyalty, and the cardinal tells Campeius that Gardiner will do as he tells him. When we next see Gardiner, in the coronation parade in 4.1, he has become a bishop, and a Gentleman remarks that he is the powerful enemy of the Archbishop of Canterbury, Thomas Cranmer. In 5.1 and 5.2 Gardiner leads an effort to convict Cranmer of heresy, but the king intervenes and he is stymied. In Act 5 Gardiner is the unscrupulous, pro-Catholic schemer that Wolsey was before his fall, but here the king is more than a match for the villain. This indicates Henry's growth from gullibility to wisdom, an important theme of the play.

The historical Gardiner, a bright young priest, was employed by Wolsey to represent him in ROME before becoming the cardinal's secretary. Wolsey promoted his protégé into the king's service, presumably for the reasons given in the play, and Gardiner prospered. He became the king's secretary in 1529 and Bishop of Winchester in 1531. A conservative cleric, his opposition to Cranmer centered on the archbishop's prominent role in the Reformation in England. Henry balanced one against the other, but after the king's death, Cranmer gained power and Gardiner was imprisoned. However, under the Catholic queen Mary (ruled 1553–58), Gardiner was restored to power and Cranmer was executed, though Gardiner died before his enemy went to the stake.

Garter (Garter King-at-Arms)   Minor character in *Henry VIII*, an official of the court of Henry VIII. The Garter, whose duties include making formal proclamations at official ceremonies, is present, though mute, at the coronation of Anne Bullen, and he recites a brief prayer after the christening of the future queen Elizabeth in

5.4.1–3. His small role adds pomp and circumstance to the picture of the court.

Gentleman (1) Any of three minor characters in *Henry VIII*, members of the court of King Henry VIII. In 2.1 two of the Gentlemen discuss the trial and conviction of the Duke of Buckingham. They attribute the duke's fall to Cardinal Wolsey, who they say is hated by the common people as much as Buckingham is loved. After witnessing Buckingham's moving farewell, they discuss Wolsey's effort to bring down Queen Katherine and mention the arrival of Cardinal Campeius as part of that story. Thus they convey much important information about the plot, while stirring the audience's responses to the villain and his victims.

In 4.1 the Gentlemen reappear, this time at the coronation of Queen Anne. They speak of the deposed Katherine's exile to KIMBOLTON, and as the royal procession passes by, they identify and remark on its participants. They are then joined by a Third Gentleman, who describes the actual coronation ceremony in exalted terms that foster the play's depiction of Anne as a saintly queen, rejoiced in by the country. They go on to discuss the advancement of Thomas Cranmer and Thomas Cromwell in the wake of Wolsey's fall, and they mention the rivalry between Cranmer, now Archbishop of Canterbury, and Bishop Gardiner. This foreshadows the political developments of Act 5. Once again, the Gentlemen convey information while also suggesting the play's point of view.

Gentleman (2) Minor character in *Henry VIII*, an attendant to Queen Katherine. In 3.1 the Gentleman announces the arrival of "two great cardinals" (3.1.16), Wolsey and Campeius, thus introducing the main business of the scene.

Griffith (Gentleman Usher) Minor character in *Henry VIII*, an attendant to Queen Katherine. Griffith is the Gentleman Usher to the queen in 2.4, but in 4.2 he has a more intimate function, as a faithful servant who continues to attend the now-deposed queen in exile at KIMBOLTON. Griffith tells Katherine that Cardinal Wolsey repented of his evil deeds before dying. As Wolsey's victim, Katherine speaks harshly of him, but Griffith suggests a more charitable view of the cardinal, emphasizing his good works. Katherine thanks Griffith for reminding her of the proper Christian attitude toward her enemy, since she is near death herself. Griffith is tender with the dying queen; along with the waiting-woman Patience, he helps surround the queen's death with an atmosphere of virtuous mildness. Griffith is named in Shakespeare's sources, but only in connection with his duties as the queen's gentleman usher; the playwright invented his role in 4.2, as part of his association of Katherine with the themes of forgiveness and patience in adversity.

Guilford, Sir Henry (Sir Henry Guildford) (1489–1532) Historical figure and minor character in *Henry VIII*, a steward to Cardinal Wolsey. In 1.4 Guilford, welcoming the guests to the cardinal's banquet, cheerfully delights in the "good company, good wine, good welcome" (1.4.6). He speaks briefly as the scene opens and then disappears from the play, having served to establish the mood of this occasion, when King Henry VIII meets his future bride Anne Bullen. The historical Guilford later became a steward to King Henry and functioned as his MASTER OF REVELS, before that office was formally created.

Henry VIII, King of England (1491–1547) Historical figure and title character of *Henry VIII*. King Henry is nominally the protagonist of the play, but he does not create the action; rather, he is placed in a series of situations and the change in the nature of his responses—as he grows from an easily influenced tool of evil men to a wise and mature ruler—illuminates the play's themes. The play's dominant moral point concerns the importance of humanity's capacity for good, which is represented in Henry's development. On another level, the play is about the establishment of England as a Protestant country, and as such it is a celebration of the TUDOR DYNASTY. Unlike Shakespeare's other English kings (see HISTORY PLAYS), Henry is not a realistic participant in political or military events, but rather a symbol for the greatness of England.

King Henry is dramatically subordinate to other figures in each of the play's episodes, though he alone appears throughout. In Acts 1 and 2 he is manipulated by Cardinal Wolsey. First, the cardinal deceives him about the Duke of Buckingham, so that he sends an innocent man to death. However, Shakespeare makes certain that we do not blame Henry. Wolsey's evident villainy and Buckingham's saintly forgiveness indicate that the king's only offense is ignorance. In 1.4 the king meets and falls in love with the virtuous Anne Bullen, who will become the mother of Elizabeth and who, as a Protestant, anticipates the English Reformation. Henry's connection to this righteous woman prepares us to sympathize with his moral qualms about his marriage to Queen Katherine of Aragon. He fears his sin in marrying his brother's widow has prevented him from fathering an heir to the throne of England, and this worry makes him susceptible to Wolsey's machinations. The king is again manipulated, but this time only through his own scrupulous morality. Moreover, because Katherine's fall leads to the ascendancy of Protestantism and the birth of Elizabeth, Shakespeare's audience could be expected to find the result satisfactory. When Henry rejects the "dilatory sloth and tricks of Rome" (2.4.235) in favor of the "well-beloved servant Cranmer" (2.4.236)—the famous Protestant leader Thomas Cranmer—we see that from the play's point of view, Henry is progressing toward wisdom.

In 3.2 Wolsey is accidentally exposed as a profiteer and an opponent of Henry's marriage to Anne, and Henry responds forcefully, though he mercifully spares the cardinal's life. Wolsey then finds atonement with God, for which he thanks the king. Henry's actions are now unmistakably a force for good, even if it has taken a providential accident to spur him.

Act 4 offers a celebration of Anne—and indirectly of the Tudors generally—along with a restatement of the mercy and forgiveness that characterize the stories of Katherine and Wolsey. These themes further free Henry from blame, in a general atmosphere of blessedness. In Act 5 Henry's actions in support of good are taken on his own initiative, as he preserves Cranmer from the wiles of Bishop Gardiner, Wolsey's successor as villain. Here we see the culmination of Henry's development. He is now a wise and masterful ruler, capable of foiling the evil intentions of Catholic sympathizers and preserving the Reformation's most important leader. It is at this pinnacle of maturity that Henry, in the play's finale, can pass on to the infant Elizabeth a virtuous realm and the prospect of prosperity for England.

The historical Henry VIII was far from the wise, benevolent, and virtuous ruler Shakespeare depicts. Shakespeare de-emphasized Henry's ruthlessness and altered history in order to refocus the play on the themes of forgiveness and mercy. Only a small segment of Henry's reign is dealt with. His expensive, inconclusive wars and his court's wasteful extravagance are not mentioned, and the vicious despotism of his later years is ignored. The future execution of Anne Boleyn (as Anne is known to history) is not so much as hinted at, nor is the existence of Henry's four other ill-fated wives.

At the time of his accession in 1509, Henry was an intelligent and well-educated young man who was determined to be a good king. However, his egocentric desire to be a chivalric hero led him to wars and extravagance. He wasted the considerable treasury amassed by his father, the highly competent Henry VII, and left his successors with a serious debt problem. Moreover, he was a brutally tyrannical ruler, inclined to suspect treason without cause and to punish without mercy, especially as he got older. In contrast to the play, Henry probably ordered the trumped-up execution of Buckingham, for he feared that the duke, a distant relative, might try to seize the throne. Similarly, he beheaded the last PLANTAGENET, 68-year-old Margaret (the Girl of *Richard III*), simply because she was a theoretical rival.

The divorce of Katherine of Aragon was also Henry's idea, and he was much less kind to his longtime wife than in the play. Katherine, however, was permitted to live out her life in peace; the king was less considerate of his later wives. Anne soon fell victim to Henry's need for a male heir. Henry was already involved with his next wife-to-be when Anne's second pregnancy ended in stillbirth. The king arranged false charges of adultery, incest (with a brother), and treason, and within weeks—less than three years after her coronation—Anne was beheaded. Henry was to marry four other wives, one of whom was also executed. His viciousness extended to others as well: he often chose execution as a punishment for failure or opposition. Thomas Cromwell and Sir Thomas MORE were among his victims.

The king's behavior in his later years has often been diagnosed as psychotic. Although this diagnosis is hypothetical, Henry VIII was undeniably a violent and arbitrary ruler. Shakespeare and his contemporaries, however, had a very positive image of Elizabeth's father: he was a national hero who had led England to Protestantism and freed the country from the corrupt influence of the Vatican. This view was widely disseminated by the historians of the Tudor dynasty, including Shakespeare's chief source for the play, HOLINSHED's *Chronicles*.

Katherine of Aragon, Queen of England (Katharine of Aragon) (1485–1536) Historical figure and character in *Henry VIII*, the rejected wife of King Henry VIII. The focus of most of Acts 2 and 3 is on Henry's finally successful effort to divorce Katherine and marry Anne Bullen. Katherine appears first in 1.2, where she opposes the unjust taxes introduced by Cardinal Wolsey. The episode establishes the queen as a good person and Wolsey, already designated a villain, as her enemy—and it is Wolsey's influence that leads the king to divorce her. In 2.4, at her divorce trial, Katherine spiritedly defies Wolsey, refusing to submit to his judgment and demanding an appeal to the pope. In 3.1, when she is visited by Wolsey and Cardinal Campeius, she concedes her helplessness but refuses to cooperate in her own downfall. Finally, in 4.2 she is seen dying in exile at KIMBOLTON, after the king has married Anne and crowned her as queen. She hears of Wolsey's death, and though bitter, she accepts Griffith's advice and forgives the cardinal. Throughout she is a spirited woman, insisting on the respect due a queen. Her virtues are stressed in the enactment of her dream, in which supernatural beings crown her with garlands.

Katherine's role in the play is largely symbolic. As a paragon of goodness, she makes a suitable victim for Wolsey, whose villainy dominates the first half of the play. Henry is susceptible to Wolsey's

influence, but his evident affection for Katherine makes it clear that he is not himself a villain, despite the divorce. The loss of Katherine is seen as a misfortune that is compensated for by the king's later wisdom and maturity, and by the birth of Elizabeth at the play's close.

For dramatic purposes, Shakespeare places Katherine's death immediately after Wolsey's death and Anne's coronation, though she in fact lived for six years after the first event and three after the second, almost long enough to see Anne's downfall. Aside from chronology. Shakespeare's presentation of Katherine's story is fairly accurate. The daughter of King Ferdinand and Queen Isabella of Spain (ruled 1479–1516), Katherine (usually spelled Catherine) was married to Henry's elder brother, Prince Arthur (1486–1502), the heir apparent to King Henry VII, in 1501. Prince Arthur died shortly after marrying Katherine, and she declared, then and later, that the marriage had not been sexually consummated. Henry disputed this later, when he sought an annulment and cited Katherine's marriage to his brother as having disqualified her for marriage to him. (Though traditionally called a divorce, what Henry actually obtained was a declaration that he had never been married in theological terms.) Yet when Henry had acceded to the throne in 1509, he had actually received papal approval to marry Katherine.

In marrying Katherine, Henry had wished to maintain the Spanish alliance that she represented, but he apparently loved her as well. However, when she did not produce a suitable heir to the throne—their only child was a daughter, not considered acceptable at the time, although she did eventually rule as "Bloody Mary" (1553–58)—Henry considered a new marriage. Thus, on falling in love with Anne, he proceeded to dispose of his wife of 20 years. Though Katherine was badly humiliated by Henry before and after the divorce, he allowed her to live out her life in some comfort, and it was thought by contemporaries—and most modern historians agree—that his affection and respect for her never completely disappeared.

Keeper Minor character in *Henry VIII*, the doorman at a meeting of the king's council. In 5.2 the

Keeper, following his orders, prevents Cranmer, the Archbishop of Canterbury, from entering the meeting to which he has been summoned. This is plainly an insult to a person of his rank, as King Henry VIII realizes angrily when he is informed of it by Doctor Butts. The incident demonstrates the enmity of Bishop Gardiner and the councillors toward Cranmer, whose support by the king is the theme of 5.1–2.

Lincoln, Bishop of (John Longland) (1473–1547) Historical figure and minor character in *Henry VIII*, confessor to King Henry VIII. In 2.4.209–214 Lincoln confirms the king's statement that as his confessor, he, Lincoln, advised Henry to pursue a divorce of Queen Katherine. His small part helps justify the king's action.

Longland, Bishop of Lincoln and Henry's longtime confessor, was later to record that the king hounded him at length about the divorce, insisting on his consent. Although Longland did consent—and was on one occasion stoned by a disapproving public—he later declared a change of mind. After the establishment of the Church of England, Longland became known for his religious intolerance and his support of the king's supremacy in matters of religious doctrine.

Lovell, Sir Thomas (d. 1524) Historical figure and minor character in *Henry VIII*, a follower of Cardinal Wolsey and later Bishop Gardiner. Lovell appears as a member of Cardinal Wolsey's entourage in Acts 1 and 3. In 1.3.16–57 his bawdy banter helps establish the decadent flavor of King Henry VIII's court while it is under the influence of Wolsey. In 2.1 he appears briefly to escort Buckingham to his execution, a fate arranged by Wolsey. Here, however, he expresses sympathy for the Duke, in an incident that provides evidence of Buckingham's virtues in contrast to Wolsey's vices. In 5.1 Bishop Gardiner has become Wolsey's successor as villain, and Lovell's support signifies as much; a pawn of the plot, he also provides the audience with information on the new political situation. The historical Lovell was a distant cousin of Sir Francis Lovell, who appears in *Richard III*.

Man Minor character in *Henry VIII*, assistant to the Porter. In 5.3, on the day of the christening of Princess Elizabeth, the Man defends his inability to prevent a crowd of celebrating commoners from entering the courtyard of the royal palace. He comically exaggerates, in military terms, the combats he has undergone.

Messenger Minor character in *Henry VIII*, a servant of Queen Katherine. In 4.2 the Messenger, announcing the arrival of Lord Capuchius, addresses the now-deposed queen as if she were a mere duchess. She instantly rebukes him and orders Griffith to see that he is never sent to her again. The episode, which derives from an historical incident, offers a last demonstration of strength in the victimized and dying Katherine.

Norfolk, Thomas Howard, Duke of (1443–1524) Historical figure and character in *Henry VIII*, a nobleman at the court of King Henry VIII. Through the first three acts, Norfolk is an enemy of Cardinal Wolsey. In 1.1 he warns the Duke of Buckingham against Wolsey's power, and in 1.2 he supports Queen Katherine's complaint against Wolsey's illicit taxes. In 2.2 he leads a group of noblemen in railing against the cardinal, and in 3.2 he delightedly levels formal treason charges against Wolsey, whose downfall has finally come to pass. Finally, in 5.2, he takes a small part in resisting the attack on Archbishop Cranmer by Bishop Gardiner. Though he is no longer prominent, he remains on the side of right in the play's scheme of the things.

The historical Norfolk—one of the great English military heroes of his day—died in 1524, before most of the events in the play took place. He was succeeded as Duke of Norfolk by his son, the play's Earl of Surrey. Shakespeare ignores Norfolk's death, perhaps through error or perhaps to keep this dignified hero as a fitting opponent of Wolsey and Gardiner.

Norfolk gained heroic stature by leading the English army to a decisive victory over SCOTLAND at the battle of Flodden Field in 1513. Earlier, however, he was an enemy of the TUDOR DYNASTY, for he fought for Richard III in 1485 at BOSWORTH FIELD, where Henry VII established the Tudors as English monarchs. Norfolk appears in *Richard III* as the Earl of Surrey; his father, *Richard III*'s Norfolk, was killed at Bosworth Field. Henry VII deprived the family of its ducal rank, but at the age of 70 this Norfolk won it back at Flodden.

Old Lady Minor character in *Henry VIII*, a waiting-woman to Anne Bullen. In 2.3 the Old Lady jests bawdily with Anne, who insists that she would not trade her virginity for a throne. The Old Lady contradicts her, declaring that for "England / You'd venture an emballing: I myself / Would for Carnarvonshire" (2.3.46–48). The episode exploits the spicy aspects of a courtly romance while not sullying the play's presentation of Anne as a saintly woman. Anne's tolerance of the Old Lady's sharp tongue also keeps her saintliness from seeming stiff-necked and inhumane.

In 5.1, where Anne is the wife of King Henry VIII, the Old Lady informs the king of the birth of his and Anne's daughter. Confronted with the king's demand for news of a son, she fudges her announcement: ". . . a lovely boy: the God of heaven / Both now and ever bless her: 'tis a girl / Promises boys hereafter" (5.1.164–166). As she had anticipated, the traditional tip for the bearer of news is a small one, and she complains vigorously, "I will have more, or scold it out of him" (5.1.173). The Old Lady gives a light and comic touch to the introduction of the play's final motif, the auspicious birth of the future queen Elizabeth.

One Within Minor character in *Henry VIII*, a LONDON commoner. The One Within is part of a crowd of enthusiastic celebrants of the christening of Princess Elizabeth who invade the royal court-yard, despite the efforts of the Porter. He speaks from offstage, claiming to be a worker in the court of King Henry VIII in 5.3.4 and baiting the Porter in 5.3.27. His voice contributes to the riotousness of the occasion. The speech prefixes in the FIRST FOLIO edition of the play designate this character as "Within"; however, most subsequent editors have prefaced this with "One."

Patience Minor character in *Henry VIII*, an attendant to Queen Katherine. In 4.2 Patience faithfully attends the deposed and dying queen in her exile at KIMBOLTON. Patience speaks very little, remarking on Katherine's ghastly appearance as she approaches death and saying, "Heaven comfort her" (4.2.99); her mere presence—with that of Griffith—tells us of the loyalty the good Katherine inspires. Her name is so striking that it is often thought Shakespeare created her for its sake. Griffith addresses her, "Softly, gentle Patience" (4.2.82), as they watch their mistress sleep, and Katherine, approaching death, says, "Patience, / You must not leave me yet" (4.2.165–166). The quality her name evokes is Katherine's signal trait and an important theme in the play: the virtue of patience in adversity. In gentle Patience, Shakespeare created an embodiment of the virtue itself, an allegorical figure like those of the medieval MORALITY PLAY. This technique is characteristic of *Henry VIII*, which is filled with tableaux, MASQUEs, and other emblematic episodes.

Porter Minor character in *Henry VIII*, a doorman at a royal palace in LONDON. In 5.3, on the day when Princess Elizabeth is to be christened, the Porter and his Man are unable to prevent a crowd of celebrating commoners from invading the palace courtyard. They make comical remarks about the riotous celebrants, until the Lord Chamberlain announces the arrival of the royal party, and they return to their efforts to control the crowd. The incident demonstrates the enthusiasm of the common people for Elizabeth and the TUDOR DYNASTY, an important theme of the play, and it offers comic relief that separates the intrigue of 5.1–2 from the grand ceremony of 5.4, with which the play closes.

Prologue Allegorical figure in *Henry VIII*, the speaker of the PROLOGUE that opens the play. The Prologue tells the audience that the play will be serious and sad, containing "Such noble scenes as draw the eye to flow" (Prologue 4), and that it purports to tell the historical truth. It will include pleasing spectacles, but it will not be "a merry bawdy play" (Prologue 14). (Scholars believe this last remark refers to an earlier, decidedly nonserious play about King Henry VIII by Samuel ROWLEY.) The Prologue prepares the audience for the solemnity of the play to come, which was a different sort of history play than Shakespeare's audiences were accustomed to. Scholars who believe that *Henry VIII* was written by

more than one author usually ascribe the play's prologue to Shakespeare's collaborator.

Sands, Lord (William Sands, William Sandys)
(d. 1540) Historical figure and minor character in
Henry VIII, a nobleman at the court of King Henry
VIII. Sands jests with the Lord Chamberlain in 1.3
and attends Cardinal Wolsey's banquet in 1.4,
where he flirts with Anne Bullen. He helps establish the cheerfully decadent tone that characterizes
the king's court while still under the influence of
Wolsey in the early part of the play.

Shakespeare was confused about the status of
the historical Sands. At the time of the play's
events, Sands was the Lord Chamberlain, though
Shakespeare adds an anonymous holder of that
office. Although he is designated as "Sir Walter
Sands" in the stage direction at 2.1.53, this nobleman's name was William, as Shakespeare knew
from his source, HOLINSHED's *Chronicles*; the error
probably resulted from a printer's misreading of an
abbreviation for the name.

Scribe Minor character in *Henry VIII*, petty official at the divorce trial of Queen Katherine. In
2.4.6 and 8–9, the Scribe orders the Crier to formally demand the presence of King Henry VIII and
the queen, thus opening the proceedings. His tiny
role stresses the pomp and ceremony of the occasion, thereby pointing up Katherine's vulnerability
to the king's power.

Secretary Minor character in *Henry VIII*, an
aide to Cardinal Wolsey. In 1.1 the Secretary
speaks two half-lines, to inform the cardinal that
the Surveyor who is to testify against the Duke of
Buckingham is ready to be interrogated. As part
of Wolsey's businesslike retinue, the Secretary
contributes to our sense of the cardinal's energy
and power.

Sergeant Minor character in *Henry VIII*, a soldier who formally arrests the Duke of Buckingham.
In 1.1.198–202 the Sergeant follows the orders of
Brandon and reads a formal charge of treason
against Buckingham. He then disappears from the
play. His small role adds a note of pomp and cere-

mony that stresses the great power underlying
Buckingham's downfall.

Servant Minor character in *Henry VIII*, a worker in
the household of Cardinal Wolsey. At the cardinal's
banquet, the Servant announces the arrival of "A
noble troop of strangers" (1.4.53), who prove to be
the Masquers (see MASQUE) led by King Henry VIII.
The Servant lends an air of opulence to the occasion.

Suffolk, Charles Brandon, Duke of (ca. 1485–
1545) Historical figure and character in *Henry
VIII*, a nobleman at the court of King Henry VIII.
Suffolk is among the enemies of Cardinal Wolsey.
In 2.2 he joins the Duke of Norfolk and the Lord
Chamberlain in hoping for the cardinal's downfall,
and in 3.2 he takes part in the formal recitation of
Wolsey's crimes and punishments. Suffolk is also
present but unimportant in Act 5.

The historical Suffolk was the son of Henry VII's
devoted follower, Sir William Brandon, who dies at
BOSWORTH FIELD in *Richard III*. From childhood on,
Suffolk was a close friend of Henry VIII, as their
friendly card game in 5.2 suggests. He married
Henry's younger sister Mary, widow of the King of
France, in 1515; their granddaughter was the unfortunate Lady Jane Grey, executed in 1554 after the
failure of a conspiracy to place her on the throne.

Surrey, Thomas Howard, Earl of (1473–1554)
Historical figure and character in *Henry VIII*, a
nobleman at the court of King Henry VIII. In 3.2
Surrey joins his father, the Duke of Norfolk, in
bringing down Cardinal Wolsey; he thus avenges
the death of his father-in-law, the Duke of Buckingham, who was earlier framed and sent to execution
by Wolsey. In 2.1 the First Gentleman asserts that
Wolsey has had Surrey assigned to a post in Ireland
"lest he should help his father[-in-law]" (2.1.44);
this circumstance makes him a doubly appropriate
addition to the play's roster of Wolsey's enemies.
Surrey is present but inconspicuous in 5.2.

The historical Surrey was indeed sent to Ireland
by Wolsey, almost certainly because the cardinal
wanted an enemy out of England, but this occurred
some time before Buckingham's treason trial and
may not have been directly related to it. Shake-

speare took Wolsey's motive from Raphael HOLIN-SHED's *Chronicles* and certainly believed it was true. However, the playwright gave Surrey a wrong name and rank, for by the time he appears in the play, his father had died and he had become the Duke of Norfolk. Yet since Norfolk remains alive in the play, Surrey must remain an earl. Surrey was an uncle of Anne Boleyn (Anne Bullen), whose mother was his sister. He was the father of the famed poet Henry Howard, Earl of SURREY.

Surveyor Minor character in *Henry VIII*, a treacherous steward to the Duke of Buckingham. The Surveyor, bribed by Cardinal Wolsey, gives false testimony that convicts Buckingham of treason and leads to his execution. After performing his task in 1.2, the Surveyor disappears from the play. The episode emphasizes the atmosphere of duplicity that surrounds Wolsey in the first half of the play. Historically, the Surveyor was one William Knyvet or Knevet, otherwise unknown, who had been fired by Buckingham in response to his tenants' complaints that he mistreated them.

Vaux, Sir Nicholas (d. 1523) Historical figure and minor character in *Henry VIII*, member of the court of King Henry VIII. In 2.1 Vaux, with Sir Thomas Lovell, escorts the Duke of Buckingham to the TOWER OF LONDON. He speaks only three lines, suggesting that the prisoner should be treated in accordance with his rank, but Buckingham contradicts him, humbly accepting the loss of his duchy as his fate. Vaux's tiny part helps point up the virtues of Buckingham, which contrast with the evil of his enemy, Cardinal Wolsey.

Vaux's father, Sir William Vaux, who appears in *2 Henry VI*, had lost his estates for having supported King Henry VI in the WARS OF THE ROSES, but they had been returned to Sir Nicholas by Henry VII. Nicholas Vaux's son was the courtier-poet Sir Thomas VAUX.

Within See One Within.

Wolsey, Thomas Cardinal (ca. 1475–1530) Historical figure and character in *Henry VIII*, the overpowerful chief adviser to King Henry VIII. Wolsey is the villain of the first half of the play. He sends his enemy Buckingham to execution by buying the perjured testimony of the Surveyor, and then, to further his foreign policy aims, he encourages the king to divorce Queen Katherine. Moreover, he opposes the king's marriage to the saintly Anne Bullen. His arrogance and pride are vividly presented in such vignettes as his vicious rebuff of Buckingham in 1.1 and his later disdain for a good man he is said to have driven mad: "He was a fool,/ For he would needs be virtuous" (2.2.131–132). However, when his evils are uncovered and he is brought low, Wolsey comes to realize that his life has been wasted in the pursuit of wealth and power. He reflects that now, removed from politics and its temptations, he can rejoice in a "still and quiet conscience" (3.2.380). Further, we learn from Griffith's touching description that on his deathbed the cardinal has "found the blessedness of being little" (4.2.66) and made his peace with God. Good has arisen from evil, with right balancing wrong in a spiritual sense—an important theme of the play.

Wolsey's evils contribute strongly to several of the play's other themes. His victims are good people and offer important images of forgiveness and forbearance. In the play's opposition of justice and injustice, Wolsey exemplifies the latter. He also represents Catholicism, as understood by the Protestant England of Shakespeare's day. Greedy, proud, and corrupt, he is allied with ROME, in the person of Cardinal Campeius, against the virtuous—and Protestant—Anne Bullen. Perhaps most significant, early in the play the role of King Henry is defined in terms of his response to Wolsey. About Buckingham, the king is completely duped; with respect to Katherine, he finds his own approach—a blameless one, from the play's point of view—and when he finally realizes Wolsey's faults, especially his opposition to Anne, he angrily drives him from office. Thus, the king's growth from immaturity to wisdom begins with his increasing awareness of the cardinal's evil influence.

Wolsey was one of the great villains for the historians inspired by the TUDOR DYNASTY, including Shakespeare's chief source for the play, Raphael HOLINSHED's *Chronicles*, and the playwright's treatment of the cardinal is particularly noteworthy in this light. The dignity the cardinal is permitted in his fall and the virtue the audience is clearly expected to find in his repentance had a great impact in the 17th century because of the contrast with the expected picture of a wholly evil figure. As in his other late plays, the ROMANCES, Shakespeare's emphasis was on the restoration of good, rather than on the evil that had prevailed earlier. His humanly forgivable Wolsey helps him present this theme in *Henry VIII*.

The historical Wolsey was the son of a prosperous, middle-class livestock dealer and wool merchant. (Wolsey's enemies habitually labeled his father a butcher—Buckingham calls the cardinal a "butcher's cut" [1.1.120]—and this became an historical commonplace, but it was not true.) As a bright young priest, he was a tutor to the sons of the Marquess of Dorset (who appears in *Richard III*). His intelligence and drive impressed the aristocrats he met, and he was repeatedly advanced until he became Henry VII's chaplain. When Henry VIII became king in 1509, Wolsey was one of his most important advisers. He promoted Henry's invasion of FRANCE in 1512, supplied the army, and negotiated the highly advantageous peace of 1514. He was rewarded with the archbishopric of York; then in 1515 the pope made him a cardinal and he became Lord Chancellor of England. At this point he virtually governed England for the king. He became very wealthy by accepting bribes and keeping for himself the feudal incomes from various church properties. This was perfectly normal in the 16th century, but as a nonaristocrat, Wolsey aroused great enmity by displaying his power and wealth with extravagant houses, clothes, and entertainment. He was thought, perhaps rightly, to aspire to the papal throne and to have cultivated foreign alliances to that end.

Among Wolsey's principal enemies was Buckingham, who was a leader of the aristocratic clique that had been displaced as the king's main source of advice. However, Buckingham's fate was probably ordered by Henry, who feared him as a relative of the Plantagenets and a potential claimant to the throne. Wolsey doubtless manipulated the surveyor, and he may have been pleased with the outcome, but the motivating force was the king's. Shakespeare, however, followed Holinshed in attributing the deed entirely to Wolsey.

It was the power of the emperor, which Wolsey vainly sought to harness, that finally brought about his fall. Henry ordered Wolsey to see to his divorce from Katherine. Wolsey almost certainly did not instigate this scheme; the play's intimations to that effect come from Holinshed. However, the opposition of Katherine's nephew, the Holy Roman Emperor Charles V (ruled 1519–55), proved insuperable. Charles controlled the papacy—his troops sacked Rome in 1527, just as Henry's divorce effort began—so approval from that quarter was never possible. Wolsey probably realized this, but Henry persisted, and the cardinal's failure to achieve the impossible meant his ruin. Henry—who knew of and accepted the cardinal's other activities—could not accept frustration, and once the failure was evident, he disposed of his minister quickly in 1529. The cardinal's accidentally revealed inventory in 3.2 is an anecdote from Holinshed, but it happened to a different person, 20 years earlier; it is an excellent demonstration of Shakespeare's inventive use of his sources. In actuality, Henry simply invoked the laws defining papal interference in English affairs as treason. He dismissed Wolsey from office and confiscated most of his possessions but spared his life. The cardinal continued to communicate with Rome and the emperor, in the hope of retrieving his situation; within a year this was discovered, and he was again charged with treason. He died while traveling to London for his trial.

Wolsey's contribution to history was great, though it is generally overshadowed by his role in the story of Henry's divorce. He reformed the English judiciary to establish more control for the central government, thereby contributing to England's growth into a modern nation-state, free from the dominance of feudal lords. In foreign policy he was less successful in the short term, but we see in his strategies the first experiment in balance-of-power politics in Europe, with England providing a potential counterweight to any expansion of either French or Hapsburg power. This arrangement was to characterize European international relations for centuries.

Woman Any of several minor characters in *Henry VIII*, attendants to Queen Katherine. In 3.1.3–14 one of the women sings a SONG, "Orpheus with his lute," in an effort to cheer the despairing Katherine. The incident helps establish a melancholy atmosphere around the defeated queen.

Julius Caesar

SYNOPSIS

Act 1, Scene 1

Two tribunes, Flavius and Marullus, disperse a crowd that is celebrating the return of Julius Caesar to ROME, though not before a Cobbler makes some flippant jokes. The tribunes rebuke the Commoners for disloyalty in welcoming the conqueror of another Roman, Pompey, whom they had also celebrated in the streets. The two officers remove the decorations that have been placed on public statues.

Act 1, Scene 2

At the feast of Lupercalia, Caesar arranges for Mark Antony, who is to participate in a fertility rite, to ritually touch Calphurnia, Caesar's wife. A Soothsayer warns Caesar to beware the ides (the 15th day) of March; Caesar ignores him and leads his entourage to the festival. Cassius and Brutus remain behind and speak of Caesar's ambition to rule alone, a violation of the Roman political tradition that all aristocrats share power equally. Cassius says that Rome looks to Brutus for leadership in this crisis, and they hear cheering from the festival, which, they fear, means that Caesar is being acclaimed king by the Commoners. Cassius observes resentfully that he does not wish to be ruled by a man no better than himself, as another cheer erupts. Cassius continues to speak against Caesar's rule and refers to an ancient revolt against a king that Brutus's ancestor had led. Brutus hints that he has contemplated a similar action. Caesar's group returns; Caesar confides to Antony that he distrusts Cassius and then exits. Brutus and Cassius detain Casca and hear an account of the festival from him. Caesar was offered the crown three times, Casca reports, and he refused it each time, though only with regret. Casca and Brutus leave, and Cassius soliloquizes that Brutus, though a very important fig-

ure, is easy to manipulate, and he plans to further influence him with letters purporting to be from angry citizens who seek action against Caesar.

Act 1, Scene 3

Amid thunder and lightning, Casca meets Cicero and tells of omens that have accompanied the storm, foretelling extraordinary events. Cicero dismisses this superstitiousness and departs. Cassius appears and recruits Casca for a plot against Caesar, naming a meeting place for later that night. Another conspirator, Lucius Cornelius Cinna, arrives, and Cassius directs him to leave messages, which he provides, in places where Brutus will receive them.

Act 2, Scene 1

Brutus, having been awake all night, decides at dawn that Caesar's ambition makes it necessary to kill him. He receives one of Cassius's anonymous letters urging him to protect Rome, and he resolves to lead the conspirators in assassinating Caesar. Cassius and other plotters arrive, and they lay their plans. Brutus insists that Antony not be killed, arguing that they must not seem bloodthirsty and that Antony will be helpless without Caesar. Decius volunteers to ensure that Caesar will attend the day's Senate session, where the assassination is to take place. The conspirators depart. Brutus, seeing his sleeping servant, Lucius, muses on his own sleepless life. His wife Portia appears and asks why he is disturbed. He promises to tell her later, as a last conspirator, Ligarius, arrives, and she leaves. Ligarius agrees to follow Brutus in any exploit, and they leave together for the Senate.

Act 2, Scene 2

Calphurnia tells Caesar of the many appalling omens that have been seen and insists that he stay home rather than go to the Senate. He refuses, insisting that one must face death if it comes, but then he decides to humor Calphurnia and stay at home, pleading illness. However, Decius arrives and claims that the omens are favorable and that the Senate proposes to offer Caesar a crown. Caesar changes his mind again.

Act 2, Scene 3

Artemidorus reads aloud a message naming the conspirators and warning Caesar against them. He vows to present it to Caesar at the Senate.

Act 2, Scene 4

Portia worries hysterically about Brutus. The Soothsayer appears, saying that he hopes to warn Caesar of impending harm, and he goes on to the Senate. Portia sends Lucius on a pointless errand to Brutus, with orders to return and tell her how he seems.

Act 3, Scene 1

At the Senate, Caesar encounters the Soothsayer, who warns that the ides of March is not yet over. Artemidorus attempts to deliver his message, but Caesar rejects him and proceeds with Senate business. One conspirator draws Antony away from the meeting, while another presents Caesar with a petition that he has already rejected. Caesar's continued refusal is the signal: the conspirators stab him. Caesar, dismayed that his friend Brutus should be among the attackers, dies. The assassins, led by Brutus, ritually bathe their hands in Caesar's blood, declaring their devotion to political liberty. A message arrives from Antony: He is prepared to ally himself with the conspirators if they can provide a rationale for their deed. Though Cassius has reservations, Brutus approves. Antony arrives and volunteers to die with Caesar if the conspirators wish to kill him, but Brutus insists on their alliance, and he grants Antony's request to speak at Caesar's funeral. The conspirators depart, and Antony soliloquizes about his intention to avenge Caesar's death by launching a civil war. News comes of Octavius's approach to Rome.

Act 3, Scene 2

Brutus addresses the Plebeians, assuring them that the assassination was necessary in order to preserve the Republic. They applaud him, proposing that he be crowned himself. Antony arrives with Caesar's body, and Brutus tells the crowd to listen to Antony's funeral oration. Brutus leaves, and Antony addresses the Plebeians, praising Caesar while seeming to acknowledge the honor of the assassins. Gradually, Antony generates a mood of hostility toward the conspirators while denying his intention to do so. Introducing Caesar's will, which designates a generous bequest to be distributed among the people, he sparks a riotous response to the assassination. The Plebeians rage into the

streets, intending to burn the houses of Brutus and the others. Antony exults. Learning of Octavius's presence in Rome, he goes to join him; as he leaves he hears that Brutus and Cassius have fled the city.

Act 3, Scene 3

A mob of Plebeians encounters the poet Gaius Helvetius Cinna and kills him, mistaking him for the conspirator with the same name.

Act 4, Scene 1

Antony, Octavius, and Lepidus decide who must be executed to protect their new power in Rome. Antony sends Lepidus on an errand and then belittles him as an insignificant man who is not fit to rule but who will be useful for a while. Antony and Octavius begin to plan a campaign against Brutus and Cassius, who have raised an army.

Act 4, Scene 2

At Brutus's camp, Lucilius returns from a visit to Cassius's troops and reports that Cassius has not displayed the warmth of earlier meetings. Brutus interprets this as a sign of waning friendship between Cassius and himself. Cassius arrives and immediately asserts that Brutus has wronged him; Brutus suggests that they enter his tent to talk privately.

Act 4, Scene 3

Cassius charges that Brutus has ignored his arguments and punished an officer for taking bribes. He insists that they cannot be overstrict in a time of crisis, and Brutus remarks that Cassius himself is reputed to be corrupt and accuses him of withholding funds. The infuriated Cassius, declaring that he never expected such insults from his comrade, offers his dagger and suggests that Brutus kill him. Brutus gently mocks Cassius's excess but apologizes for being overheated himself, and the two shake hands in reconciliation. A Poet arrives and chastises the two generals for their disharmony. Cassius is amused, but Brutus dismisses him abruptly. Brutus then tells Cassius that he has been short-tempered in part because he has just learned of Portia's suicide due to her fear of the immense army that Octavius and Antony are sending against her husband. Messala arrives with news from Rome: Octavius and Antony have executed many political enemies and are on the march. He also reports

Portia's death. Brutus hides his prior knowledge and pretends to receive the news stoically, arousing Messala's admiration. Brutus then proposes marching on PHILIPPI, where their enemies have camped. Cassius argues that they should stay where they are and let Antony and Octavius use up their energy marching, but Brutus insists that his plan is superior and Cassius gives in. Brutus then retires for the night, and the others leave. The Ghost of Caesar appears to Brutus, announces that they shall meet again at Philippi, and disappears.

Act 5, Scene 1

Octavius and Antony reflect on their good fortune that Brutus and Cassius have taken disadvantageous positions. Octavius insists on commanding the more important right wing, despite Antony's seniority. Brutus, Cassius, and their army appear, and the opposing commanders parley. They quickly begin to exchange insults, and Octavius and Antony leave. Cassius confides to Messala that he is uneasy about the forthcoming battle. Brutus and Cassius tell each other that they will commit suicide rather than be captured.

Act 5, Scene 2

Brutus orders an attack on Octavius's forces, which he can see weakening.

Act 5, Scene 3

Titinius and Cassius, pressed hard by the enemy, see that Brutus has launched his attack too soon and left them at a disadvantage. Pindarus arrives with news that troops are approaching their headquarters; Cassius sends Titinius to investigate and tells Pindarus to watch from a nearby hill. Pindarus reports that Titinius is captured, and Cassius, believing that his own capture is imminent, impales himself on his sword, assisted by Pindarus. Pindarus flees, as Titinius returns safely with Messala to announce that Brutus has defeated Octavius. They find Cassius's body and realize what has happened. Messala leaves to tell Brutus, who appears and mourns his comrade. He announces that they shall launch another attack before nightfall.

Act 5, Scene 4

Brutus is forced to retreat. Lucilius pretends to be Brutus and is captured. Antony arrives, realizes that the captive is not Brutus, and praises Lucilius for courageously diverting attention from his commander.

Act 5, Scene 5

Brutus, defeated, asks several companions to help him commit suicide, but they refuse. As enemy troops approach, he prevails upon Strato to help him, and he dies on his sword. Antony and Octavius appear, triumphant, and find Brutus's body. They praise him and order his honorable burial.

COMMENTARY

Julius Caesar is a play about moral ambiguity in a political setting and the personal tragedy that results. It resembles both the HISTORY PLAYS, written somewhat earlier, and the great TRAGEDIES, soon to come. Like the tragedies, it presents a protagonist who aspires to heroism and fails because of his own moral shortcomings. At the same time, *Julius Caesar* also reflects the political philosophy

"This was the noblest Roman of them all" (*Julius Caesar* 5.5.68). Antony (Marlon Brando) eulogizes Brutus (James Mason) in the 1953 film version. *(Courtesy of Movie Star News)*

that had informed the playwright's picture of English civil war in the history plays. Because civil disorder and violence are tragic for the entire society, their avoidance is a higher moral obligation than the pursuit or control of power, even for apparently just or moral purposes. Therefore, for Shakespeare the preservation of the political status quo is a primary good.

Brutus, the protagonist of *Julius Caesar,* is an ambivalent figure who may be seen as both good and evil—an honorable man dedicated to the good of his country, but also a destroyer of its peace. The play's central action—the murder of Caesar—may seem an act of disinterested idealism or one of inflated self-love. Twentieth-century views of the play reflect these possibilities: With the rise of fascism in the 1920s and 1930s, Brutus was aggrandized as a model of republican virtues, and Caesar was identified with Mussolini and Hitler. More recently, however, Caesar has been defended as a hero who is destroyed by a neurotically envious Brutus, who pursues glory without regard for the disaster he provokes.

These positions are not as mutually exclusive as they may seem; *Julius Caesar* is sometimes grouped with the PROBLEM PLAYS as a work about the uncertain outcome of human endeavors. In this light, the heart of *Julius Caesar* is the tension between Brutus's idealistic rejection of a dominating leader and the reality that human society requires the discipline that Caesar imposes. From another angle, the conflict occurs between the protagonist's obsessive demand for a perfect world and the catastrophe that follows in the real, imperfect world. Thus Brutus's actions are both virtuous and disastrous. Precisely because this ambiguity is possible, Brutus is a tragic hero who attempts the humanly impossible and fails.

At first glance, it seems odd that the play's title character is killed less than halfway through the work, but Caesar, though his part is small, dominates the whole drama. First, his assumption of power in Rome stimulates the conspiracy; later, the inescapable memory of him inspires Antony and haunts Brutus.

The telling comparisons between Brutus and Caesar demonstrate the play's most essential ambivalence: The tyrant and his opponent are not easily distinguishable. In this fashion, the morality of the assassination is questioned, and the importance of Caesar's leadership—first resented and then absent—remains evident. Both Brutus and Caesar have great leadership qualities, and, being certain of his virtues, each is susceptible to flattery and manipulation by lesser men. In murdering Caesar, Brutus follows the Caesar-like course of attempting to change society in accordance with his views. Similarly, in the war that follows the assassination, Brutus behaves as imperiously as Caesar did, enacting precisely the failings of autocratic leadership—the isolation from his followers, the presumption of sound decision making, the potential for tyranny—that he had acted to prevent in killing Caesar. Significantly, Caesar's Ghost identifies itself as Brutus's "evil spirit" (4.3.281).

Nevertheless, Caesar is superior to Brutus in his analysis of Cassius and in his recognition that a single leader is needed to control Rome. Moreover, Brutus persistently makes bad judgments, and he suffers the consequences, going from error to error. He refuses to share leadership of the conspiracy with Cassius or Cicero. His arrogant overconfidence is plainly demonstrated when he dismisses Antony as an inconsequential underling in 2.1.181–183. Later, he twice rejects the advice of the more experienced Cassius, resulting in the failure of his cause at Philippi. He is persistently blind to reality, following his own superficial rectitude to disaster. The patriotism he invokes is certainly a living ideal for Brutus, but it is also a cover for his vanity and his unacknowledged need to be like Caesar himself.

As Brutus deteriorates morally in the second half of the play, becoming ever more Caesar-like, so Caesar himself seems to grow in worth as Rome collapses in the leadership vacuum created by his death. This important point is made especially clear by the behavior of the Plebeians after the murder. Ironically, they hail Brutus as an autocrat—"Let him be Caesar" (3.2.52)—just after he has murdered Caesar to prevent him from becoming one. However, the fickle mob is immediately turned against Brutus by Antony's oration, and their brutality in killing the wrong Cinna in 3.3 heralds the disorder that later prevails on a larger scale in the civil war. Brutus has unleashed a whirlwind.

Brutus's attempts to dignify the assassination by invoking the gods through ritual are pointedly undercut. Brutus wishes to make a ceremony of the killing, saying, "Let's be sacrificers, but not butchers" (2.1.166), but he immediately goes on to reveal an unconscious awareness of public opinion: ". . . so appearing to the common eyes, / We shall be call'd purgers, not murderers" (2.1.179–180). Another attempt to ritualize the murder occurs when Brutus leads the assassins in washing their hands in Caesar's blood, an act that only accentuates the violence of the deed.

In the second half of the play, Antony, heretofore an unimportant figure, suddenly comes into his own. He dominates the conspirators, taking control of Rome by the end of 3.2. In 4.1, where he bargains the lives of his relatives with Octavius and Lepidus, and then disdains the latter as an impotent tool, we see Antony as both a cynical political operative and a strong leader, a complex figure whose ambivalent nature deepens the moral ambiguity of the play's world.

Later developments confirm that Brutus's decision to kill Caesar was wrong both politically and morally. Antony's dire prediction of the bloody course revenge will take, in 3.1.258–275, strongly invokes the conventions of the REVENGE PLAY, a popular genre of ELIZABETHAN and JACOBEAN DRAMA that Shakespeare had exploited earlier in *Titus Andronicus* and would again in *Hamlet* and *Macbeth*. In a revenge play an inexorable rule operates: a murder must be punished with another one, usually under the eye of the victim's ghost; the first murderer is doomed, regardless of politics or personality. Thus such factors as the possible benefit to Rome of Caesar's death are swept aside. Brutus's moralizing has been useless; Antony will inevitably triumph. The would-be savior of Rome has produced only a morally chaotic situation in which final victory goes not to the high-minded assassin, nor to the hot-blooded avenger, but to the cool opportunist Octavius. This icily commanding figure takes control from Antony in 5.1.20 and disposes of matters at the play's close. Roman history was much more familiar in Shakespeare's time than in ours, and the playwright knew that his audience would immediately recognize the irony that Brutus's attempt to prevent one tyranny merely paved the way for the greater autocracy of Octavius, known to history as the first Roman emperor, Augustus Caesar. (Shakespeare was to dramatize the final consolidation of Octavius's power in *Antony and Cleopatra*.)

As he did in the history plays, Shakespeare altered the historical record considerably in writing *Julius Caesar*. Following PLUTARCH, the playwright accurately presented the broad outlines of Roman history but altered many details for dramatic purposes. Notably, he compressed the chronology of events from months to a few days or hours in order to achieve a more dramatic sequence of events. For instance, Caesar's triumphant return to Rome occurred in October of 45 B.C., while the feast of Lupercalia fell in the following February. Only some weeks after this event were the tribunes Flavus (the play's Flavius) and Marullus ousted after removing public decorations that honored Caesar. Shakespeare combined all these events into a single day, enacted in 1.1–1.2.

Similarly, the aftermath of the assassination covers only several hours in the play. In Plutarch the same events took months. Antony's speech followed Brutus's by several days, rather than immediately, and Brutus, whose flight is reported after the speech, did not in fact leave Rome until mid-April. Similarly, Octavius's arrival coincides with the orations in the play, but he did not actually appear in Rome until six weeks afterward. And though Antony welcomes Octavius in the play, the two actually quarreled to the point of warfare, and their alliance was not arranged for almost 20 months, though in the play it follows immediately.

The battle of Philippi is a dramatic example of Shakespeare's compression of events. In the play, the battle directly follows the meeting of Cassius and Brutus in 4.2–3, whereas it actually occurred more than six months later. In fact there were two battles at Philippi, as Plutarch reports: The first was a draw, in which Cassius killed himself; in the second, 20 days later, Brutus was defeated and also committed suicide. Shakespeare compresses the two conflicts into a single afternoon.

Other changes involve the historical figures themselves. In 1.2 Cassius refers to an estrangement between himself and Brutus, and Brutus replies that his private worries have made him distant to his friends. In fact, according to Plutarch, the hostility between the two stemmed from their rivalry for a political position. Shakespeare's version draws attention to Brutus's worries about Caesar's aspirations and also makes him seem thoughtful and conscientious, rather than politically ambitious.

Further, Shakespeare substantially elaborated Plutarch's accounts of the speeches of Brutus and Antony in 3.2 and of the riot of the Plebeians in 3.3. Plutarch merely alludes to the two orations, attaching no great importance to their styles, while Shakespeare creates antithetical deliveries—rational versus emotional—that reflect on the characters who speak them and on the very nature of politics. Similarly, while Plutarch mentions the actions of the mob, the playwright gives the crowd life and thus transforms their volatility and fickleness, even their grim sense of humor, into a significant political phenomenon.

Shakespeare had to emphasize politics in *Julius Caesar*, for otherwise Brutus's fate would be meaningless. Brutus himself never sees his mistake in murdering his best friend and the leader of his country. His fate is dramatically satisfactory only in light of the impact of his action on Roman society as a whole, that is, in its political consequences. His error stems from an unconscious desire for a political world in which evil is impossible. Thus his political blindness has a psychological element, reflecting Shakespeare's progress toward the psychological portraiture of the great tragedies.

SOURCES OF THE PLAY

The primary source for *Julius Caesar* was Sir Thomas NORTH's translation of the ancient Roman biographical collection Plutarch's *Lives* in either its first or second edition (1579, 1595). Isolated passages suggest other materials that the playwright knew, including a biography of Caesar by John HIGGINS in *A MIRROR FOR MAGISTRATES*; the philosophical poem *Nosce Teipsum* ("Know Thyself") by John DAVIES, published in 1599; and several works by CICERO. Nevertheless, three of the lives in Plutarch—those of Caesar, Brutus, and Antony—supply all of the incidents in the play. In addition, English plays about Caesar had been popular since

at least the early 1580s, and this tradition must have helped stimulate the writing of *Julius Caesar*. While there is no evidence that any of these plays influenced Shakespeare directly, the famous phrase "Et tu, Brute" (3.1.77) may have come from such a work, for it does not appear in any Latin source yet was a well-known tagline in Shakespeare's day.

TEXT OF THE PLAY

Julius Caesar was probably written in early 1599. The diary of Thomas PLATTER records a performance of the play on September 21, 1599, and it is not on the list of Shakespeare's plays published by Francis MERES in September 1598. While Meres's list does not pretend to be complete, *Caesar* was a strikingly popular work, as contemporary references indicate, and it is not likely to have been omitted if it had been staged. While it might have been written during the latter part of 1598, it is fairly certain that *Much Ado About Nothing* and *Henry V* were written then, so *Julius Caesar* is thought to have followed them.

Caesar was not printed during Shakespeare's lifetime; the first edition is that of the FIRST FOLIO (1623). This text, known as F1, is relatively error-free—it is generally held to be the least corrupt text in the Folio—indicating that it was probably printed from a copy of Shakespeare's own manuscript, or FOUL PAPERS. This copy had probably been used as or taken from a PROMPTBOOK, in which the playwright's characteristic misspellings and unnecessarily elaborate stage directions had been corrected. The later folios—and a series of late-17th-century QUARTOS—vary slightly from F1, but all are clearly based on it, as are all modern editions.

THEATRICAL HISTORY OF THE PLAY

The earliest known performance of *Julius Caesar* was held on September 21, 1599, as recorded in Thomas Platter's diary, and many references from 1599 and the early 17th century indicate that the play was very popular with its original audience, as does the existence of a competing play about Caesar produced by Philip HENSLOWE in 1602. Leonard DIGGES wrote about *Caesar*'s enthusiastic audiences as late as the 1620s, and it was performed at the royal court at least twice, in 1613 and 1638. In the

1660s the play was included in the repertoire of Thomas KILLIGREW's company and was one of the few Shakespearean plays to be popular in the late 17th century; Charles HART played Brutus for Killigrew, and later Thomas BETTERTON was successful in the part. The play was published six times between 1684 and 1691.

In the 18th century Spranger BARRY was a notable Antony, while Barton BOOTH and James QUIN played Brutus in several productions. The celebrated Peg WOFFINGTON appeared as Portia in the 1750s, though that small part has not generally attracted leading actresses. In the 19th century most major English actors portrayed one or more of the play's important roles, and the play was also very popular in America, where Lawrence BARRETT, Edwin FORREST, and Edwin BOOTH were particularly associated with it. In 1864 Booth and his brothers Junius Brutus BOOTH and John Wilkes BOOTH played Brutus, Cassius, and Antony, respectively, performing on the same stage for the first and only time. In London, a very popular 1895 production, presented by Beerbohm TREE, featured sets and costumes by perhaps the most famous English painter of the day, Sir Lawrence Alma-Tadema (1836–1912).

Perhaps because the rise of totalitarianism in Germany and Russia between the world wars generated a concern with political tyranny, *Julius Caesar* was often produced in the 20th century. In 1934 the Italian composer Gian Francesco MALIPIERO, having offended the Fascist dictator Benito Mussolini (ruled 1922–43), attempted to ingratiate himself by dedicating his next opera to the ruler. Mussolini was unappeased, perhaps because the work, *Giulio Cesare*, derived from *Julius Caesar*, a play about a tyrannicide. More memorable was Orson WELLES's modern-dress rendering of 1938, in which Caesar was attired as Mussolini. More recently, *Julius Caesar* has continued to be frequently presented. The ROYAL SHAKESPEARE COMPANY produced it several times in the last quarter of the 20th century, including noted productions by Terry HANDS in 1987 and Peter HALL in 1995.

Julius Caesar has also yielded a number of FILMS, notably MGM's 1953 version starring Marlon Brando as Antony. The play has likewise been produced several times on TELEVISION, beginning as long ago as 1938; in 1963 the British Broadcasting Corporation presented THE SPREAD OF THE EAGLE, based on all three ROMAN PLAYS.

CHARACTERS

Antony, Mark (Marcus Antonius) See Antony, Mark, in *Antony and Cleopatra*.

Artemidorus (active 44 B.C.) Historical figure and minor character in *Julius Caesar*, an ally of Caesar. In 2.3 Artemidorus writes a memorandum detailing the plot against Caesar's life, of which he has learned. However, in 3.1 he is unable to prevail upon the busy general to read it, and moments later Caesar is murdered. According to Shakespeare's source, PLUTARCH's *Lives*, Artemidorus, a professor of rhetoric, knew of the plot through his acquaintance with some of the conspirators, but the playwright ignored this information and simply used the futile warning as an illustration of Caesar's overconfidence.

Brutus, Marcus (ca. 85–42 B.C.) Historical figure and character in *Julius Caesar*, leader of the assassins of Caesar and of the forces opposing Mark Antony in the subsequent civil war. Brutus, the protagonist of *Julius Caesar*, is representative of the moral ambiguity that is the play's central theme. He seems both good and evil: a patriotic and honorable man who nonetheless brings about Rome's downfall and his own.

When Caesar's apparent ambition to rule alone begins to disturb Roman aristocrats, Brutus is drawn by Cassius to lead a plot against him. "With himself at war" (1.2.45), Brutus debates the murder of his friend and mentor: Shall his patriotism be stronger than his love and respect? He concludes that Caesar must be killed, despite his personal virtues, to save Rome from tyranny. Brutus then approaches the assassination as a moral imperative, but Shakespeare offers much evidence that Brutus is not the wholly selfless figure he believes himself to be. Not only does his decision prove to be politically catastrophic, but it also appears to be morally flawed, for Brutus is unconsciously in pursuit of power himself.

Brutus's self-appraisal has often been mistaken for Shakespeare's portrait of him, but the playwright, while acknowledging his protagonist's patriotism and honorable intentions, presents a host of opposing indications that paint another picture. Brutus is willful and arrogant, resembling the tyrant he kills and growing more like him as the play unfolds. As leader of the conspiracy, he peremptorily opposes anyone else's initiative, refusing to share leadership with either Cassius or Cicero. His disdainful overconfidence is disastrous when he dismisses Antony as a man of little importance in 2.1.181–183. He overrules Cassius, insisting that Antony be spared and then that Antony be permitted to speak at Caesar's funeral. Both decisions prove fateful. As the battle of PHILIPPI approaches, Brutus once again demands his own way—and leads his cause to defeat. In insisting on his own way at all times, Brutus displays the dictatorial behavior he had feared in Caesar. But unlike Caesar, he is not a competent leader. Lacking insight into other men's motives, as he abundantly demonstrates with respect to Cassius and Antony, he is an inadequate politician. He is also an inexperienced and impatient general.

Brutus's self-delusion is startlingly apparent on several occasions. On one level he considers the assassination a high moral duty; yet, subconsciously guilty, he also needs to justify it, saying, "Let's be sacrificers, but not butchers" (2.1.166). Further, when Caesar has been stabbed to death, Brutus improvises a cleansing ritual—the assassins bathe their hands in their victim's blood—but this act accentuates, not alleviates, the violence of the deed. Brutus does not see the gore through his own vision of rectitude.

Particularly striking is Brutus's unconscious hypocrisy in praising himself for refusing to acquire funds through graft or by accepting bribery, saying, "I can raise no money by vile means" (4.3.71), while at the same time castigating Cassius for refusing to share with him his own ill-gotten gains. In another instance, in 4.3.180–194, he pretends to accept with great stoicism the news of the death of Portia, when he has in fact known of it for some time. (It has been contended that Shakespeare had excised this passage from the play, and it survived only because of a printer's error; however, the ploy suits Brutus's imperiousness quite well, and the rejection of the passage seems unnecessary.) This deception may be defended as good for the morale of his underlings, but it is nevertheless quite as patronizing as Caesar's feigned reluctance to accept a crown, as reported in 1.2.231–272.

A possible source of Brutus's self-deception is his repeated denial of his emotions and thus his inability to recognize his own drives. He rejects his love for Caesar, for Cassius, even for Portia, lest they contaminate the higher faculty of his reason. His errors in trusting Antony and relying on the support of the Plebeians stem from his assumption that they, like he, will act rationally. Not only does he undervalue the significance and power of passion in others, he does not see its operation in himself. Thus blinded, Brutus never sees the error of

Brutus, a protagonist of *Julius Caesar*. While trying to save Rome from Caesar's dictatorship, he becomes, ironically, like a dictator himself. *(Courtesy of Culver Pictures, Inc.)*

his attack on Caesar. The unnecessary disaster of the civil war has resulted from his own obsession with controlling the Roman political world, but he honestly sees only his own idealistic point of view. Thus his actions are virtuous in their intent but evil in their consequences. Precisely because of this contradiction, Brutus resembles a tragic hero, attempting great things and failing through his own psychological flaws.

Julius Caesar is not simply the story of a man who injures his society by an illicit rebellion or of a man who murders a friend for bad reasons. Rather, the tragic grandeur of Brutus's moral imperfection lies in his effort to transcend human limitations and create a political world without the potential for evil and exploitation. Like Othello or Hamlet, Brutus possesses an integrity that impels him toward a wrong course. Attempting the impossible, he can produce only chaos, and he brings about the downfall of both his world and himself. Antony's final eulogy not only acknowledges the nobility of Brutus's conscious intentions in killing Caesar but also reminds us of his weakness, observing that he was an honorable man who did not recognize the dishonor of his actions.

The historical Brutus was a rather different person than Shakespeare's patriotic but deluded idealist, and much of his career is neither enacted nor alluded to in *Julius Caesar*. Renowned in his own day as an admirable Roman nobleman—upright in his dealings and grave in demeanor—Brutus was descended from an illustrious patrician family. His mother was Caesar's mistress for many years, giving rise to the rumor that Brutus was Caesar's son (alluded to in *2 Henry VI,* 4.1.136), though the relationship probably began only after Brutus's birth. Brutus had a highly successful political career; he received profitable appointments as an administrator of Roman territories abroad. He was also a prominent player in the factional politics of the period. Prior to the time of the play, Brutus was a follower of Pompey the Great (106–48 B.C.) in his civil war against Caesar, but after Caesar's decisive victory at the battle of Pharsala (48 B.C.) he switched sides. Caesar rewarded him with appointments to high offices. However, Brutus seems to have regretted his betrayal of Pompey; he published a defense of Cato,

a prominent Pompeian, and he married Portia, Cato's daughter, which his contemporaries recognized as a gesture of opposition to Caesar.

Brutus and the conspirators compared themselves to Brutus's ancestor, Junius Brutus, a legendary Roman patriot (who figures in Shakespeare's *The Rape of Lucrece* and *Coriolanus)*, as Shakespeare indicates in 1.2.157 and 2.1.53–54, but in fact their ends were more selfish than patriotic. They stood for the privileges and vested interests of the Roman aristocracy, threatened by Caesar's long-standing dictatorship—normally a temporary office held during a crisis. Caesar seemed to be establishing a new order, in which the nobles would be subordinated to him and to his government.

Brutus's ritual bloodbath, described above, is Shakespeare's invention, intended to emphasize both the violence of the deed and its political nature. PLUTARCH, Shakespeare's source, reports the murder in brutal imagery drawn from hunting, presenting just the sort of picture Brutus attempts, in the play, to avoid. Thus the playwright distorted his source material in order to create a telling effect.

Shakespeare greatly compressed the complicated events following Caesar's death for dramatic reasons, and Brutus's struggles to maintain a political position in Rome are ignored. After the assassination, Brutus and the conspirators negotiated with Antony and other Caesarians, and for several weeks the two groups governed Rome jointly, although the citizenry frequently rioted against the assassins. Numerous intrigues, now obscure, dominated Roman politics; Brutus and Cassius attempted to recruit followers among the rural aristocrats with only modest success. In mid-April they left Rome for good. They remained in Italy throughout the summer, during which a possible alliance between Antony and Octavius Caesar began to seem threatening. Brutus then left for Macedonia, where he held a government appointment. Negotiations between the assassins and Antony continued throughout the winter, but the civil war began in the spring of 43 B.C., with Antony defeating Decius in northern Italy. In November, Antony and Octavius formed the Triumvirate with Lepidus, and the following summer they launched the campaign that led to Philippi.

Except for collapsing two battles into one, Shakespeare's account of Brutus's defeat and death at Philippi is accurately retold from Plutarch, although other sources indicate that Cassius did not oppose the decision to march to Philippi; the conspirators' forces were supported by the local population, while Antony and Octavius were short of supplies. One other mild distortion of Brutus's nature follows from Shakespeare's compression of events: In the 20 days between battles, Brutus most fully revealed his serious incompetence as a general, for he had only to wait for time and hunger to defeat his enemies, and he could not do it.

Caesar, Julius (102–44 B.C.) Historical figure and title character of *Julius Caesar*, ancient Roman political leader assassinated by conspirators led by Marcus Brutus. Caesar's role is not a large one, but the character dominates the play even after his murder early in Act 3. He is an enigmatic figure, representative of the central theme of the play, the moral ambiguity surrounding his murder. The assassination victim is both a valuable leader of ROME and an arrogant tyrant; thus the conspiracy against him seems alternately malevolent and noble.

Caesar is undeniably imperious. When he first appears, in 1.2, surrounded by admiring followers, he is clearly accustomed to command. Irritated by the warning of the Soothsayer to beware the ides of March, he coolly dismisses him. Knowing the outcome, as Shakespeare assumed his audience would, we see immediately that Caesar's self-confidence is misplaced. Caesar's smug sense of power is strikingly evident in his language; he frequently refers to himself with the royal "we," as in 3.1.8, and sometimes even in the third person, as when he declares his intention to defy bad omens and go the Senate, saying, "Caesar should be a beast without a heart / If he should stay at home to-day for fear. / No, Caesar shall not. Danger knows full well / That Caesar is more dangerous than he" (2.2.42–45). His wife, Calphurnia, warns that his "wisdom is consum'd in confidence" (2.2.49), and we clearly see that he is ripe for a fall. In the last moments of his life, Caesar's arrogance extends almost to blasphemy, as he dismisses all argument with the order, "Hence! Wilt thou lift up Olympus?" (3.1.74). The assassination, which follows immediately, seems entirely justified.

On the other hand, Caesar is also presented as "the foremost man of all this world" (4.3.22), as Brutus calls him. He is certainly a strong leader; the only weaknesses attributed to him are physical: some deafness and mild epilepsy (1.2.210, 251) and the poor swimming and susceptibility to illness that Cassius complains of in 1.2.99–114, matters so patently unimportant that they tell us more about Cassius's petty envy than they do about Caesar. In 2.1.20–21 Brutus observes that Caesar has never let his emotions alter his judgment, and we learn the value of that judgment when we hear his acute portrayal of Cassius in 1.2.189–207. The funeral orations of Brutus and Antony in 3.2 offer evidence of his virtues, and indeed Caesar's greatness is evident in the respect that almost all the other characters show him.

It may seem odd that a figure killed before the halfway point should be the title character of a play, but it is appropriate here, for Caesar's spirit continues to dominate the action after his death. Not only does Antony's revenge for Caesar's murder provide the plot of the play's second half, but the thought of Caesar recurs repeatedly to Brutus and Cassius as well. Notably, each speaks of Caesar at his death. Moreover, Caesar's arrogance is taken up by Brutus in a subtle demonstration of the psychology of power. The survival of Caesar's spirit is made tangible by the appearance of Caesar's Ghost in 4.3 and at the battle of PHILIPPI (reported by Brutus in 5.5.17–20).

Caesar's greatest importance lies in the action he stimulates, his assassination. The murder of the seemingly tyrannical Caesar triggers a civil war and—as Shakespeare and his audiences were aware—would soon lead to much greater despotism under the Roman Empire of Octavius, later known as Augustus Caesar (see *Antony and Cleopatra*). Thus Caesar symbolizes a social good that is flawed by the potential evil of tyranny, as opposed to the social disruption created by Brutus's ideal of a political world in which no such evil exists.

Shakespeare added salient details to the Caesar he found in his source, PLUTARCH's *Lives*, humanizing the leader by inventing physical defects that the historical figure did not have: deafness and poor swimming. He also ascribed to Caesar a concern with superstition in his last days, stressing an intellectual corruption produced by power, in preparation for the audience's sympathetic response to the assassins when the murder is committed. On the other hand, he did omit a number of anecdotes from Plutarch that would have portrayed Caesar too negatively, leaving less room for doubt about the killing. For instance, Caesar is said to have looted a famous temple and to have unjustly dishonored an earlier wife in order to divorce her.

More significantly, Shakespeare followed Plutarch in exaggerating Caesar's real threat to the privileges of the Roman aristocracy that spurred the assassins historically. In fact, modern scholars find, Caesar's policies were surely not directed toward creating a monarchy, as the conspirators—and Plutarch— believed. They were to some extent not directed at all, being largely driven by events.

After his well-known conquests in Gaul and Britain, Caesar had, at the time of the play, recently won a civil war against another Roman political and military leader, Pompey the Great (106–48 B.C.). As the head of a faction intent on admitting new members to Rome's small ruling class, Caesar had fought a group of conservatives and had more nearly represented the republican ideals later associated with Brutus—in part because of Shakespeare's presentation—than Brutus himself did. He was in no sense a revolutionary, however. In the course of his conflict with Pompey, Caesar had assumed the dictatorship, a legitimate office of the Roman government that carried extensive powers and was temporarily awarded to leading military commanders in times of crisis. Caesar had been dictator briefly in 49 B.C., but this time he had held the dictatorship for several years, using its powers to protect his gains in the civil war. In early 44 B.C. the Senate—which Caesar had greatly enlarged and filled with his followers— declared him dictator for life. This event sealed the conspirators' determination.

It was rumored that Caesar intended to be crowned and to move the capital to Ilium, a Roman possession in the Near East. However, this was never likely—the ceremony in which he rejected the crown, as reported by Casca in 1.2, was planned

by Caesar expressly to defuse these rumors—and it seems probable that Caesar was more conservative than the nobility feared. He assumed his extraordinary powers because the forces of Pompey's son (the Pompey of *Antony and Cleopatra*) still threatened him and because he was aware of the threat of assassination. To preserve the government, newly established after years of disorder, Caesar needed dictatorial power to suppress his enemies. He did, however, protect ancient privileges to a considerable degree, resisting pressures from his more radical followers for drastic reforms.

Moreover, Caesar understood the need for a strong ruler to maintain order in a nation that had been disrupted by years of internal strife. He is said (though not by Plutarch) to have anticipated his end, observing that his assassination would produce terrible consequences for Rome; the actual result was the effective elimination of the old Roman Republic—and of its aristocracy—under the Empire. As Shakespeare felt, although he did not clearly see the underlying historical reality, Caesar's assassination unnecessarily disrupted the Roman state, already weakened by civil wars, and it only led to a much greater tyranny.

Calphurnia (Calpurnia) (active 59–44 B.C.) Historical figure and character in *Julius Caesar*, the wife of Caesar. In 2.2 Calphurnia, alarmed by accounts of dire omens, begs Caesar not to attend the Senate session on the ides of March. She asserts that his "wisdom is consum'd in confidence" (2.2.49) and prevails on him to stay home. However, her work is immediately undone by Decius, and Caesar goes to his death. The episode demonstrates Calphurnia's devotion to her mighty husband and casts a softer light on him than we would otherwise have. Further, it reminds us that his assassination was a domestic tragedy as well as a political event, thus humanizing the play's account of murderous intrigue and civil war.

Caesar married the historical Calpurnia—as her name was spelled in Latin—in 59 B.C. to cement a political alliance with her father. Although Caesar was blatantly unfaithful and came close to divorcing her a few years later in order to make another political marriage, Calpurnia was thought by contemporaries to have been a genuinely devoted wife; the tale of her entreaty, as reported in Shakespeare's source, PLUTARCH's *Lives*, is probably true. After the assassination, Calpurnia assisted Mark Antony's campaign against the conspirators by turning over to him Caesar's papers and a large amount of cash. Little else is known of her life.

The spelling Calphurnia, though less familiar than Calpurnia and incorrect in Latin, is increasingly used by modern editors, restoring the style of the FIRST FOLIO (1623), which was also followed by most of Shakespeare's contemporaries in other writings about Caesar. (In Shakespeare's source, Sir Thomas NORTH's English translation of Plutarch, both forms are used.) In the 18th century, editors of Shakespeare chose to revert to the Latin form, establishing a different tradition.

Carpenter (First Commoner) Minor character in *Julius Caesar*, a Commoner. In 1.1 the Carpenter, who speaks one line (1.1.6), is part of a crowd being dispersed by the tribunes Flavius and Marullus. He identifies himself by profession, establishing the social class of the group. In some editions the Carpenter is identified as the First Commoner.

Casca, Publius Servius (d. 42 B.C.) Historical figure and character in *Julius Caesar*, one of the assassins of Caesar. In 1.2 Casca officiously orders the festival crowds to be silent in Caesar's presence, but later he speaks contemptuously to Brutus and Cassius about Caesar's rejection of the crown and his fit of epilepsy. In addition, he pokes fun at the pedantry of Cicero and his companions, who had remarked on Caesar in Greek; Casca delivers one of Shakespeare's most-quoted lines, "It was Greek to me" (1.2.281), implying that he scorned to know a foreign language. Brutus calls him a "blunt fellow" (1.2.292), but Cassius defends him as a bold man, useful in any difficult enterprise. Casca, who is vain, holds the same opinion, saying, "I will set this foot of mine as far as who goes furthest" (1.3.119–120). However, earlier in the same scene he has shown himself to be cowardly, trembling at reports of dire omens, in telling contrast to Cicero's coolness. Casca is also a hypocrite; in 2.1.143 and 153, as the con-

spirators hatch their plot, he swiftly reverses his opinion of Cicero to agree with Brutus's. In 3.1 Casca is the first of the conspirators to stab the defenseless Caesar, although he disappears from the play thereafter. (It has been speculated that Shakespeare discontinued the role at this point in order to free an actor to take the part of Octavius, who appears somewhat later).

Little is known about the historical Casca, aside from his participation in Caesar's murder. Shakespeare's source, PLUTARCH, states that he was the first to stab Caesar and that Caesar called him "vile" or "vicious" (in different accounts of the assassination), and these two brief mentions are the basis of Shakespeare's fairly elaborate portrait. The playwright omitted two other episodes concerning Casca—that he almost revealed the conspiracy inadvertently and that he was responsible for the brutal killing of prisoners at PHILIPPI—but these inglorious moments doubtless contributed to the playwright's vision of Casca's unpleasant personality. Plutarch does not record Casca's suicide after the battle of Philippi, an honorable end by Roman standards and an episode that might have altered Shakespeare's characterization.

Cassius (Caius Cassius Longinus) (d. 42 B.C.) Historical figure and character in *Julius Caesar*, one of the assassins of Caesar, and, with Brutus, a leader of the forces opposing Mark Antony in the subsequent civil war. Cassius presents two quite different aspects in the course of the play. He first appears as a cynical, unscrupulous conspirator whose scheming stresses the evil side of political ambition. However, he later proves to be a courageous fighter, a sensible general, and a friend to Brutus. Cassius can thus be seen as a foil for Brutus and *his* two sides, first as a noble conspirator and then as an increasingly imperious leader; further, Cassius's two faces reinforce the play's insistence that the qualities that make up a political leader result from the continuous interaction of good and evil.

Prior to Caesar's murder, Cassius is bitterly envious of his power, and his diatribes against his leader in 1.2 and 1.3 are hysterically petty. Although it is typical of Brutus that he does not recognize Cassius for what he is, Caesar analyzes him with great perceptiveness in his famous remarks on his enemy's "lean and hungry look. . . . Such men as he be never at heart's ease / Whiles they behold a greater than themselves, / And therefore are they very dangerous" (1.2.191, 205–207).

Cassius knows that Brutus's sense of honor makes him susceptible to manipulation, and his soliloquy at the close of 1.2 reveals his intention to seduce Brutus into leading the conspiracy against Caesar. This speech presents Cassius as a MACHIAVEL, the typical political villain of ELIZABETHAN DRAMA. It also pointedly contrasts Cassius's cynical scheming with Brutus's honorable motives (though these are seriously questioned elsewhere), and it thus establishes two possible points of view toward the assassination of Caesar.

Cassius has an unstable personality. He rages over trifles like Caesar's poor swimming and susceptibility to illness (1.2.99–130). During the assassination he loses his nerve, and Brutus has to reassure him that Popilius does not know of their plot. In 5.1.71–89 he wavers in the face of unfavorable omens before PHILIPPI. His weakness has great consequences, for it causes him to give in to Brutus's insistence that Antony should be spared and then permitted to speak at Caesar's funeral. Later, he similarly accedes to Brutus's strategy at Philippi with equally catastrophic results. Cassius's death at Philippi, when he too hastily believes a report of defeat, reflects this character flaw; a stronger man would have resisted longer.

However, in Acts 4 and 5 Cassius is generally a finer figure than he is before the assassination. He is an experienced and sensible general, although he permits himself to be overruled, and he attracts the loyalty and admiration of his officers. He displays a touching affection for Brutus, especially when he learns of his friend's grief over the death of Portia, and he generously forgives Brutus his fatal errors. When they exchange farewells before the battle, in 5.1.116–122, their mutual affection rings true, reflecting Shakespeare's constant inclination to believe that people are not wholly bad.

The historical Cassius was noted in his own day for his violent temper and sarcastic speech, as is reflected in Shakespeare's source, PLUTARCH's *Lives*, and other ancient documents. Before the time of the play, Cassius had fought against Caesar in an earlier civil war, and Caesar had forgiven him. He apparently originated the plot against Caesar; his motives are unclear, though Shakespeare followed Plutarch's contention that his private dislike for Caesar stimulated his public hatred of tyranny. Shakespeare's account of Cassius's death at Philippi is also accurately retold from Plutarch. However, other sources indicate that Brutus and Cassius did not disagree on the decision to march to Philippi; their forces were supported by the local population, while Antony and Octavius were short of supplies. The loss of Cassius was decisive. Shakespeare compressed two battles of Philippi, which actually occurred 20 days apart, into one; it is thought that Cassius, a more experienced general than Brutus, would not have fought the second one, in which the forces of Caesar's assassins were finally defeated.

Cato Minor character in *Julius Caesar*, soldier in the army of Brutus. In 5.4.4–6, at the battle of PHILIPPI, Cato's bold battle cry declares that his father was Marcus Cato, a famous opponent of Caesar. He is killed shortly afterward. Shakespeare took this gallant but fatal exploit—a motif popular with Elizabethan audiences—from PLUTARCH's *Lives*. Cato's sister was Brutus's wife, Portia.

Cicero, M. Tullius (106–43 B.C.) Historical figure and minor character in *Julius Caesar*, a senator of ROME. Cicero appears only to dismiss Casca's concern about omens in 1.3. Earlier Casca had described in comical terms Cicero's pedantic use of Greek ("It was Greek to me" [1.2.281]), and later Brutus rejects the suggestion that Cicero be included in the conspiracy against Caesar as an elder statesman. Brutus says that Cicero is too independent and will "never follow any thing that other men begin" (2.1.151–152). Cicero's execution by Antony and Octavius is reported in 4.3.176–177.

Although he is an interesting background presence, Cicero is of no real importance to the play. Probably his inclusion simply reflects his immense stature as a writer. Cicero was perhaps the most influential of all classical authors. His works were highly respected in his own lifetime and throughout the period of the Roman Empire; during the Middle

Ages he was revered as a master of rhetoric. In the RENAISSANCE his works were well known to all educated people, and they influenced humanistic writers on a broad range of subjects. In Shakespeare's time Cicero was certainly one of the best-known ancient Romans, and it was therefore natural for the playwright to present him on stage. Cicero was often known in the 16th century as "Tully," from his middle name, and he is so referred to in *2 Henry VI*, 4.1.136, and *Titus Andronicus*, 4.1.14.

Cicero was also a highly successful lawyer and politician. He was among the most important men in the Roman world at the time of the play. He was a leader of the opposition to Caesar's party, although he had no part in Brutus's plot, and after the assassination he denounced Antony in a series of speeches. As is reported in the play, he was executed as a result.

Cinna, Gaius Helvetius (Gaius/Helvius Cinna) (d. 44 B.C.)   Historical figure and minor character in *Julius Caesar*, victim of a mob of Plebeians. In 3.3 Cinna, a poet, is mistaken for Lucius Cornelius Cinna, one of the assassins of Caesar, and he is killed by the ferocious Roman mob incited by Mark Antony's funeral oration for Caesar. The historical Cinna—called Helvetius Cinna for his birth in what is now Switzerland—was a noted poet of his day. His epic poem *Zmyrna* was famous for generations as a difficult "modernist" masterpiece, but it is now lost. Not mentioned in Shakespeare's source, PLUTARCH's *Lives*, is Cinna's political role; he was Caesar's ally, and he became a tribune when Caesar deposed Flavius and Marullus. His murder by the pro-Caesar mob was therefore all the more ironic, but the playwright did not know this.

Cinna, Lucius Cornelius, the Younger (active 44 B.C.)   Historical figure and minor character in *Julius Caesar*, one of the assassins of Caesar. In 1.3 CASSIUS assigns Cinna to distribute anonymous letters encouraging Brutus to join the conspiracy against Caesar. When Caesar is stabbed, Cinna cries, "Liberty! Freedom! Tyranny is dead!" (3.1.78).

The historical Cinna—whose father (d. 84 B.C.) had been a famous radical leader under whom Caesar had served in the earlier Roman civil wars—had

been appointed to high office under Caesar. Shakespeare's source, PLUTARCH, mentioned Cinna as one of the conspirators and reported that, after the assassination, he made a speech against Caesar that infuriated the crowd. It is not historically certain, however, that Cinna was actually one of Caesar's murderers; he may merely have been among those who supported the assassins after the fact. In either case, he was identified with the killing in contemporary minds; as is enacted in 3.3, a pro-Caesar mob encountered Helvetius Cinna and, believing him to be Lucius Cornelius Cinna, beat him to death.

Claudius (Claudio)   Minor character in *Julius Caesar*, a soldier in the army of Brutus. Claudius and Varro, serving as messengers, sleep through the appearance of the Ghost of Caesar in Brutus's tent and are awakened by Brutus to confirm that they have seen nothing.

In the first edition of *Julius Caesar*, that is in the FOLIO (1623), Claudius's name is rendered as Claudio, and some modern editors follow this practice. Others, however, use Claudius, which is correct in Latin and appears in Shakespeare's source, NORTH's translation of PLUTARCH's *Lives*.

Clitus (active 42 B.C.)   Historical figure and minor character in *Julius Caesar*, a soldier in the army of Brutus. In 5.5 Clitus—like Dardanius and Volumnius—refuses to help Brutus to commit suicide after the battle of PHILIPPI, saying "I'll rather kill myself" (5.5.7). The episode shows the fondness with which Brutus's subordinates regard him, fostering an aura of sentiment around his death. Little is known of the historical Clitus, whose role Shakespeare took from PLUTARCH's *Lives*.

Cobbler (Second Commoner)   Minor character in *Julius Caesar*, a Commoner. In 1.1, as the tribunes Flavius and Marullus disperse a crowd of artisans gathered to cheer Caesar, the Cobbler jests impertinently when they ask about his profession. He calls himself "a mender of bad soles" (1.1.13) and asserts that he has joined the crowd to encourage the others to wear out their shoes and thus gain extra business. This brief bit of comedy immediately brings the audience into the reality of ancient ROME and prepares them for the contrasting spectacle of the rioting Plebeians in Act 3. In some editions the Cobbler is identified as the Second Commoner.

Commoner   Any of several minor characters in *Julius Caesar*, working people of ROME. In 1.1 the tribunes Flavius and Marullus disperse a crowd of Commoners who have gathered to cheer Caesar. Two of the Commoners speak, the Carpenter only to identify himself, the Cobbler to bandy crude witticisms with the officers. (In some editions the speakers are identified as the First and Second Commoners.) This pleasingly vital episode comically introduces the urban mob that, as the Plebeians, flares into riot in Act 3.

Dardanius (Dardanus)   (active 42 B.C.)   Historical figure and minor character in *Julius Caesar*, a soldier in the army of Brutus. At PHILIPPI, Dardanius, along with Clitus and Volumnius, refuses to help Brutus to commit suicide, saying, "Shall I do such a deed?" (5.5.8). The episode demonstrates that Brutus was regarded with affection by his subordinates, adding sentiment to the presentation of his death. Shakespeare misspelled the name of the historical figure Dardanus. Little is known of this individual, whose role Shakespeare took from PLUTARCH's *Lives*.

Decius Brutus (Decimus Brutus)   (d. 43 B.C.)   Historical figure and minor character in *Julius Caesar*, one of the assassins of Caesar. In 2.2 Decius persuades Caesar to proceed with his fateful plans after Calphurnia has convinced him to stay at home. Caesar thus goes to the Senate and is assassinated.

The historical figure was named Decimus Brutus, not Decius; the error originated with Jacques AMYOT, who translated PLUTARCH into French. His work was retranslated into English by Sir Thomas NORTH, who transmitted the incorrect name to Shakespeare. Decimus Brutus (a cousin of Marcus Brutus) had distinguished himself as a commander under Caesar in Gaul. Although awarded high office under Caesar, he joined the conspiracy against his leader and played the part enacted in the play. He was killed in the ensuing civil war.

Flavius (L. Caesetius Flavus)   (active 44 B.C.)   Historical figure and minor character in *Julius Caesar*, a tribune of ROME and an ally of Brutus. In 1.1 Flavius, with his fellow tribune Marullus, disperses a crowd that has assembled to cheer Caesar upon his triumph over Pompey in a civil war. The tribunes criticize the Commoners for their disloyalty to Pompey, whom they had earlier supported. After the crowd has dispersed, Flavius and Marullus decide to strip the city's statues, which are decorated in Caesar's honor, because they fear the triumphant general will become a tyrant. In 1.2.282–283 Casca reports that Flavius and Marullus have been "put to silence" for this deed. The episode establishes a widespread mistrust of Caesar. Flavius also appears briefly in 5.4 as a member of the army of Brutus at the battle of PHILIPPI.

Shakespeare followed an error of his source, PLUTARCH's *Lives*—transmitted through the translations of AMYOT and NORTH—in misspelling the name of the historical tribune, Flavus. Little is known of Flavus beyond the incident enacted; he and Marullus were dismissed from their positions by Caesar. Flavus's appearance at Philippi is Shakespeare's invention.

Ghost   Character in *Julius Caesar*, the spirit of the assassinated Caesar. In 4.3, as Brutus rests in his tent near SARDIS, the Ghost appears to him, identifies itself as Brutus's "evil spirit," and warns, "thou shalt see me at Philippi" (4.3.281, 283)—that is, at the subsequent battle of PHILIPPI. In 5.5, defeated and preparing for suicide, Brutus recounts that the Ghost of Caesar has appeared to him a second time and concludes, "I know my hour is come" (5.5.20). Shakespeare's presentation of the Ghost closely follows the account in PLUTARCH's *Lives*.

Lepidus, Marcus Aemilius   See Lepidus, Marcus Aemilius, in *Antony and Cleopatra*.

Ligarius, Caius (Quintus)   (d. 44 B.C.)   Historical figure and minor character in *Julius Caesar*, one of the assassins of Caesar. In 2.1 Ligarius (designated Caius in the FIRST FOLIO text and some modern editions), although ill, accepts the invitation of Brutus to engage in an honorable exploit, saying,

"By all the Gods that Romans bow before, I here discard my sickness" (2.1.320–321). Though Brutus does not specify the nature of the deed, he refers to the planned assassination of Caesar, and Ligarius is among the conspirators who accompany Caesar to the Senate in 2.2, although he does not appear in the murder scene (3.1). Ligarius represents the stoical Roman virtues in disregarding poor health to follow duty; more important, his immediate, unquestioning acceptance of Brutus's leadership also demonstrates the authority that Brutus holds among the conspirators.

In 2.1.215–216 Ligarius is said to "bear Caesar hard, who rated him for speaking well of Pompey." In fact, the historical Ligarius had fought long and hard for Pompey the Great (106–48 B.C.) against Caesar in an earlier civil war and had been pardoned. In Shakespeare's source, PLUTARCH's *Lives*, he is said to have joined the conspirators out of hatred for Caesar's tyranny. He died shortly after the assassination, probably of natural causes. His name was actually Quintus; the error was Plutarch's.

Lucilius (active 42 B.C.) Historical figure and minor character in *Julius Caesar*, an officer in the army of Brutus. Brutus confides in Lucilius, clearly a trusted subordinate, at SARDIS in 4.2 and 4.3 and at PHILIPPI in Act 5. In 5.4, as Brutus's army is overrun by the soldiers of Mark Antony, Lucilius pretends to be Brutus—daring his opponents to kill him and be acclaimed—in an effort to divert attention from his commander. He is taken prisoner, and Antony, who realizes his captive is not Brutus, praises Lucilius's bravery and orders that he be treated kindly.

Lucilius's diversionary tactic was admired in ancient and medieval literature (and, presumably, in warfare) and was popular on the Elizabethan stage. Shakespeare had used it in *1 Henry IV*, where Sir Walter Blunt is killed while impersonating King Henry IV. The playwright took Lucilius's exploit from PLUTARCH's *Lives*, where the officer is reported to have been a friend of Brutus and to have remained loyal to Antony after Philippi.

Lucius Minor character in *Julius Caesar*, a young servant of Brutus. In 2.1 Lucius falls asleep while the conspirators plot the death of Caesar, and Bru-

tus expresses envy of the boy's carefree state. In 2.4 Lucius appears as an innocent foil to the near-hysterical worry of Portia. In 4.3, at Brutus's camp near SARDIS, Lucius plays a lute at his master's command, and Brutus shows consideration and affection for the boy in a scene that shows the zealous conspirator in an unusually soft light.

The episodes in which Lucius appears have a distinctive emotional tone. His role offers an important touch of domestic tenderness and loyalty in a work that is dominated by the darker themes of murderous politics and civil war.

Marullus, C. Epidius (C. Epidius Murellus) (active 44 B.C.) Historical figure and minor character in *Julius Caesar*, a tribune of ROME and an ally of Brutus. In 1.1 Marullus and his fellow tribune Flavius disperse a crowd that has assembled to greet the triumphant Caesar. The tribunes criticize their disloyalty to Pompey, whom they had supported earlier and whom Caesar has defeated in civil war. After the crowd has gone, Flavius and Marullus destroy the public decorations that have been put up in Caesar's honor because they fear the triumphant general will become a tyrant. In 1.2.282–283 Casca reports that Flavius and Marullus have been "put to silence" for this deed. The episode establishes a widespread mistrust of Caesar from the outset of the play.

Little is known of the historical Marullus, but Shakespeare's source, PLUTARCH's *Lives*, reports that Caesar dismissed the two tribunes from their positions because they had made the gesture dramatized in the play. However, in Plutarch's account this occurred months after Caesar's triumph. Shakespeare compressed these events for dramatic purposes.

In the FIRST FOLIO, where the play was first published, Marullus is identified throughout as "Marellus," and some modern editions preserve this spelling, though others follow the historically correct rendering of the name.

Messala, Marcus Valerius (Messale Corvinus Valerius) (64 B.C.–A.D. 8) Historical figure and minor character in *Julius Caesar*, a general under Brutus and Cassius. In 4.3 Messala brings Brutus news of the death of Portia and witnesses Brutus's feigned stoicism, to which he responds with misplaced admiration, saying "Even so great men great losses should endure" (4.3.192). Messala appears frequently at the battle of PHILIPPI in Act 5, but his only important moment comes when he discovers the corpse of Cassius in 5.3. In 5.5 he has been captured by Octavius and Antony.

The historical Messala, better known as Messala Corvinus Valerius, was offered the command of Brutus's army as it crumbled at Philippi, but he joined Octavius and Antony instead. Ten years later he fought for Octavius against Antony at ACTIUM (though he does not appear in *Antony and Cleopatra,* where that battle is enacted). Under Augustus Caesar, as Octavius became known, Messala held various offices, was a patron of a group of pastoral poets, and wrote books on history and literature; his work—famous in its day—was a source for Shakespeare's source, PLUTARCH, though none of it has survived.

Messenger   Minor character in *Julius Caesar,* a soldier in the army of Octavius and Antony. In 5.1 the Messenger announces the approach of the army of Brutus and Cassius just before the battle of PHILIPPI.

Metellus Cimber (L. Tillius Cimber)   (d. ca. 44 B.C.)   Historical figure and character in *Julius Caesar,* one of the assassins of Caesar. In 3.1.49–51, as part of the assassination plot, Metellus requests that Caesar pardon his brother, who has been banished; since Caesar has refused this plea once, the conspirators are confident that he will do so again, and this refusal is to be the signal—and ostensible stimulus—for their attack. Metellus has no distinctive personality; he simply performs his role and then stabs Caesar along with the others.

The historical figure was actually named Lucius Tillius Cimber; the error comes from Shakespeare's source, PLUTARCH's *Lives,* where Cimber is given two different names, both of them wrong. Cimber had been an associate of Caesar's but abandoned him and joined Brutus's conspiracy. He probably died in combat at PHILIPPI; he fought with Brutus's forces, but no further record of him has survived.

Murellus   See Marullus, C. Epidius.

Octavius (Gaius Octavius Caesar, Octavian) (63 B.C.–A.D. 14)   Historical figure and character in *Julius Caesar,* Antony's ally against Brutus and Cassius. (The same figure appears as Caesar in *Antony and Cleopatra.*) Octavius is a cool, self-possessed, and efficient leader, whether hearing out Antony's criticisms of Lepidus in 4.1, claiming command of the right wing—properly Antony's—before the battle of PHILIPPI in 5.1, or ordering the honorable burial of Brutus in 5.5. Though his part is small, it is boldly drawn and clearly anticipates the briskly calculating victor of the later play.

Shakespeare captures something of the personality of the historical Octavius but ignores the events of his life for the most part. In his will, Julius Caesar formally adopted Caius Octavius—the grandson of his sister—and made him the heir to his name and three-quarters of his immense fortune. (In legally accepting this inheritance after Caesar's murder, Octavius changed his name to Caius Julius Caesar Octavianus, and to English-speaking historians he is generally known as Octavian from this time until his assumption of the title Augustus in 27 B.C. However, Shakespeare was probably unaware of this distinction, and the character is called Octavius throughout *Julius Caesar.*) Octavius, who had been a physically frail child, was a 19-year-old student in Athens when Caesar died. When he returned to Italy to claim his inheritance, he immediately asserted himself politically but was not taken seriously at first. However, the name of Caesar was a powerful one, and he was soon at the head of an army of the pro-Caesar forces assembling to combat the assassins.

Unlike in *Julius Caesar,* Octavius was a rival of Antony's from the outset, and their alliance—joining with Lepidus in the Triumvirate—was sealed only after 18 months of antagonism that approached full-scale war. While his political acumen was considerable, Octavius was still inclined to illness and was not a competent military man; at Philippi he was notably unsuccessful, and the defeat of Brutus and Cassius was largely the work of Antony. However, Octavius was soon to assume the leadership of much of the Roman world—the situation with which *Antony and Cleopatra* opens—and his cool efficiency in the closing lines of *Julius Caesar* effectively foreshadows this achievement.

Pindarus (active 42 B.C.)   Historical figure and minor character in *Julius Caesar*, a captured Parthian slave belonging to Cassius. In 5.3, at PHILIPPI, Pindarus helps Cassius to commit suicide. Pindarus mistakenly reports the capture of Titinius, and Cassius, in despair, decides that, rather than be captured himself, he will die. He gives Pindarus his freedom in exchange for holding the sword upon which he falls. Pindarus, now free, "yet would not so have been" (5.3.47), elects to run far away and disappears from the play. Shakespeare took the episode, which fittingly ends the career of the emotional Cassius, from PLUTARCH's *Lives*, where Pindarus is reported to have beheaded Cassius before disappearing and to have been suspected by some of having murdered his master.

Plebeians   Minor but significant characters in *Julius Caesar*, the citizens of ROME who react to the assassination of Caesar. In 3.2 the Plebeians are addressed at Caesar's funeral, first by Brutus and then by Antony, and they respond enthusiastically to the orations of each. First, when Brutus explains the rationale behind the assassination (3.2.13–48), the crowd excitedly approves his assertions. Ironically, however, the Plebeians shout, "Let him be Caesar" (3.2.52), and speak of crowning Brutus, who has just killed Caesar in order to prevent a crowning and preserve the Republic. Conversely, they can now say of Caesar, whom earlier they had hailed, "This Caesar was a tyrant" (3.2.71). Moreover, their change in attitude merely foreshadows another one.

Antony's famous oration (3.2.75–254) plays on the emotions of the Plebeians, whereas Brutus had appealed to their reason, and Antony's impact is much greater. Before he is halfway through, the Plebeians are calling Brutus and the conspirators " . . . traitors . . . villains, murderers!" (3.2.155–158), and they go on to raise a confused cry of "Revenge! . . . Burn!—Fire!—Kill!—Slay!" (3.2.206–207). Finally, the Plebeians run amok, hurrying to burn the houses of the conspirators, and Antony exults, "Mischief, thou art afoot" (3.2.262). Almost immediately he receives news that Brutus and Cassius have had to flee the city.

In 3.3 the mob encounters Gaius Helvetius Cinna, and simply because he has the same name

as one of the assassins—Lucius Cornelius Cinna—they beat him to death. In this brief and grimly humorous scene, the Plebeians are almost incoherent, asking questions of their victim without listening to his answers and finally, realizing that he is not their proper prey, declaring, "It is no matter, his name's Cinna; pluck but his name out of his heart" (3.3.33–34). Having demonstrated their irrational power, they disappear from the play. The civil war that Antony had hoped to foment (in 3.1.254–275) has begun with their riot.

The term *plebeian* was an ancient designation for the ordinary citizens of the Roman Republic, as distinguished from the patricians, or aristocrats. Its use suggests the intense political context of the play at this point, in contrast to the use of Commoner in 1.1. Shakespeare valued individual humans regardless of social standing—as is evidenced by many of his characters, including, in this play, the Cobbler—but he distrusted the common people as a class. Two of the most important political points he made in *Julius Caesar* are that the masses are unreliable and that their ascendancy is a key symptom of social disorder. The Plebeians of the play, in their fickleness, brutality, and manipulability, demonstrate the dangers of a political world that includes them. In this respect they resemble the rebels led by Jack Cade in *2 Henry VI* and the rabble of *Coriolanus*.

Poet   Minor character in *Julius Caesar*, a wandering bard who accosts Brutus and Cassius and advises them against discord. He is plainly a fool, and in any event he arrives (in 4.3.122) after the two generals have reconciled. While Cassius tolerates the Poet, Brutus arrogantly dismisses him, demonstrating in a small way the deterioration in his character that is a major theme of the play. Also, the brief episode provides a moment of needed comic relief between the dispute between the two leaders' and the revelation of the death of Portia.

Shakespeare took this episode from PLUTARCH's *Lives*, where the figure was not a poet but a self-declared philosopher, a seemingly lunatic imitator of the wandering ascetics known as Cynics. (Cynicism, founded by Hellenistic philosophers in the fourth century B.C., held that independence and self-control constituted the only human good, and they preached a "natural" lifestyle, ostentatiously rejecting wealth, prestige, and even the comforts of ordinary life.) Cassius calls the Poet a "cynic" in 4.3.132. In Plutarch, the would-be Cynic quotes a line from the *Iliad* of HOMER, which, after being transmuted through AMYOT and NORTH, appears comically in 4.3.130–131, where Shakespeare— perhaps mistakenly—attributes it to the speaker himself, who is therefore called a poet.

Popilius Lena (active 44 B.C.) Historical figure and minor character in *Julius Caesar*, a senator of ROME. Popilius Lena, present as the assassins prepare to kill Caesar at the Senate, alarms Cassius by conversationally hoping his "enterprise to-day may thrive" (3.1.13) and then speaking to Caesar; Cassius fears the plot is known. However, it proves a false alarm. The episode, which Shakespeare took from PLUTARCH's *Lives*, heightens the tensions of the moment. Little is known of the historical Popilius Lena.

Portia Historical figure and character in *Julius Caesar*, the wife of Brutus. In 2.1, observing her husband's great emotional distress, Portia insists on sharing his trouble. He has in fact been agonizing over the assassination of Caesar, and he is reluctant to reveal this grave plan. She insists that her stature as the wife of a great Roman and the daughter of another warrants her inclusion in matters of importance. She shows Brutus a wound in her thigh that she has given herself to demonstrate that she has the Roman virtue of self-control. He is impressed, saying, "O ye gods, render me worthy of this noble wife!" (2.1.302–303), and he agrees to take her into his confidence, but then they are interrupted.

Although we do not see him tell her of the conspiracy against Caesar, he evidently has done so by the time she reappears in 2.4, where she is almost hysterical with concern. In both scenes Portia's concern for her husband's welfare is strong, giving the audience another positive viewpoint of Brutus, and her distress also raises the emotional pitch of the play as the first great climax, Caesar's murder, approaches.

In 4.3 we learn that Portia, in Rome as her husband campaigns against Caesar's successors, Antony

and Octavius, has committed suicide, convinced that he cannot survive against the tremendous power that she knows has been sent against him. Portia is intended to exemplify the Roman virtues of courage and self-sacrifice. Her virtues were legendary by Shakespeare's time; he also used the name for the splendid heroine of *The Merchant of Venice*, Portia, in which her suitor alludes to her namesake, asserting that his love is "nothing undervalu'd to Cato's daughter, Brutus' Portia" (1.1.165–166).

The historical Portia was the daughter of Marcus Porcius Cato (95–46 B.C.), a tribune famous for his honesty and dedication; the Cato of the play is Portia's brother. Their father had opposed Caesar in an earlier civil war, committing suicide rather than be captured, only two years before the time of the play. Her own suicide was regarded as similarly honorable. In the play she is said to have "swallow'd fire" (4.3.155). This reference follows Shakespeare's source, PLUTARCH's life of Brutus, where Portia is said to have put hot coals in her mouth and kept her mouth closed until she choked to death. This seems improbable, and scholars have speculated that this report may reflect her actual death by carbon monoxide poisoning, produced by a smoky charcoal fire in a closed room.

Publius Minor character in *Julius Caesar*, a witness to the assassination of Caesar. In 3.1 Publius accompanies Caesar to the Senate, and when the killing takes place, he watches, horrified; he is the only figure onstage not in violent action. Brutus reassures him that no harm is intended to him or any other citizen, and he is sent to pass along this message to others. He remains silent throughout the episode.

Publius is usually designated as a senator in the list of characters, but the text offers no indication of his status; the first such list only dates from ROWE's 1709 edition of the plays. The same Publius may be referred to when Antony consents to the condemnation of his nephew, Publius, in 4.1.4–6. Although no such relationship has been mentioned before, the name recalls the earlier figure and intensifies the picture of Antony as a ruthless politician. Not only does he condemn his own relative to solidify his political position, but he also undoes Brutus's explicit mercy of 3.1.

Publius, unlike the other named characters in *Julius Caesar*, does not appear in Shakespeare's source, PLUTARCH's *Lives*. Antony had no nephew named Publius, and no one of that name appears in Plutarch's account of the assassination. Having decided to present an innocent bystander in 3.1, Shakespeare simply invented an extra character and gave him a handy Latin name (one that he also used in 3.1.53 to identify the brother of Metellus, who is also unnamed in Plutarch). His various uses of the name may simply be an instance of the minor carelessness that recurs throughout his plays.

Servant (1) Minor character in *Julius Caesar*, messenger for Caesar. In 2.2.5–6 Caesar sends the Servant to request an augury—a forecast of the future through the ritual examination of an animal's entrails—from the priests. He returns to report a disastrous outcome in 2.2.37–40: An animal was sacrificed and discovered to have had no heart. The episode reinforces the sense of mounting tension as Caesar's death approaches. However, Shakespeare's source, PLUTARCH's *Lives*, states that Caesar performed the augury himself; rather than attempt a spectacle—probably impractical to stage—that would distract the audience by providing a false climax before the assassination scene, the playwright moved the event offstage and added this character to convey its essence.

Servant (2) Minor character in *Julius Caesar*, a messenger employed by Mark Antony. The Servant delivers a speech in his master's name to Caesar's assassins, offering them an alliance. In an eloquent passage (3.1.123–137) that anticipates Antony's funeral oration, the Servant establishes a sense of Antony's cunning and strong personal style before he makes an important appearance himself.

Servant (3) Minor character in *Julius Caesar*, a messenger for Octavius. In 3.1 the Servant tells Mark Antony of Octavius's approach to ROME. Arriving just after the assassination of Caesar, his shock reminds us of the enormity of the deed. The Servant reappears in 3.2, after Antony's oration at

Caesar's funeral, to report that Octavius has arrived. His brief appearances indicate the onset of Rome's future in the person of the emperor-to-be, and remind us of the inexorability of the events that unfold in the wake of Caesar's murder.

Soldier Any of several minor characters in *Julius Caesar*, members of the armies of Antony and Octavius on the one hand, and Brutus and Cassius on the other, in the civil war that follows the assassination of Caesar.

Soothsayer Minor but notable character in *Julius Caesar*. The Soothsayer bids Julius Caesar, "Beware the ides of March" (1.2.18, 23). Later, when the overconfident Caesar remarks that the ides of March have arrived without bringing harm, the Soothsayer replies ominously, "Ay, Caesar, but not gone" (3.1.2). Seventy-five lines later, Caesar is killed.

In Shakespeare's source, PLUTARCH's *Lives*, the Soothsayer is reported to have delivered his warning long before; the playwright compressed this account in order to achieve greater dramatic impact. The Soothsayer was probably not a real person; predictions such as his were commonly devised after the fact in ancient accounts of great events.

Strato (active 42 B.C.) Historical figure and minor character in *Julius Caesar*, a soldier in the army of Brutus. At the battle of PHILIPPI, Strato helps Brutus to commit suicide. When Octavius's troops arrive, Strato defiantly proclaims that they are too late to capture his master. The victorious Octavius, admiring his spirit and Brutus's, takes Strato into his service. Strato represents an ideal of Roman martial virtue, confirming the sense of grim rectitude that surrounds the defeat and death of the conspirators who killed Caesar. Little is known of the historical Strato, whose role Shakespeare took from PLUTARCH's *Lives*.

Titinius (d. 42 B.C.) Historical figure and minor character in *Julius Caesar*, friend of Cassius. In 5.3, during the battle of PHILIPPI, Cassius sends Titinius to determine the status of a group of approaching horsemen, and Pindarus's mistaken report of Titinius's capture shocks Cassius. Grieving that he has sent his "best friend" (5.3.35) to be captured, and believing that he himself is liable to be taken, Cassius kills himself. Titinius returns to find his friend and commander dead, and he kills himself also. Shakespeare took this illustration of stoic Roman military virtue from PLUTARCH's *Lives*, where Titinius is said to be one of Cassius's closest friends.

Trebonius, Gaius (d. 43 B.C.) Historical figure and minor character in *Julius Caesar*, one of the plotters against Caesar. In 3.1 Trebonius plays an important, if silent, role in the assassination, drawing Mark Antony away from the scene at the critical moment.

The historical Trebonius was a Roman aristocrat who had been an ally of Caesar in his earlier conflicts and had served as a general in Caesar's conquest of Gaul. Turning against him, he performed the part in the assassination that is enacted in the play. He died in the ensuing civil war.

Varro (Varrus) Minor character in *Julius Caesar*, a soldier in the army of Brutus. In 4.3 Varro and Claudius are ordered to sleep in the same tent with Brutus to be available as messengers. They sleep through the visitation of the Ghost of Caesar, and Brutus wakes them to confirm that they have seen nothing.

In the first edition of *Julius Caesar*, that in the FIRST FOLIO, Varro's name is rendered as Varrus, and some modern editors follow the Folio in this respect. Others, however, use Varro, which is correct in Latin and appears in Shakespeare's source, NORTH's translation of PLUTARCH's *Lives*.

Volumnius (active 42 B.C.) Historical figure and minor character in *Julius Caesar*, a soldier in the army of Brutus. In 5.5 Volumnius—like Clitus and Dardanius—shrinks from helping the defeated Brutus to commit suicide, saying "That's not an office for a friend, my lord" (5.5.29). The episode illustrates the fondness with which Brutus is regarded by his subordinates, thereby contributing to the aura of sentiment surrounding his death. Little is known of the historical Volumnius, though Shakespeare's source, PLUTARCH, asserts that he had been a schoolmate of Brutus.

King John
SYNOPSIS

Note: Act and scene numbers in *King John* vary significantly from edition to edition. Traditionally editions since THEOBALD's (1726) have altered the FIRST FOLIO's scene divisions in Acts 2 and 3; some modern editions revert to the Folio's arrangement, while others do not. In this volume citations to *King John* follow the New Arden edition, which uses the Folio designations. Where there is a difference from the traditional citation, the latter is given in parentheses or brackets.

Act 1, Scene 1
King John and his mother, Queen Eleanor, receive a French ambassador, Chatillon, who delivers a demand from Philip Augustus, King of France: John must relinquish the crown of England to his young nephew Arthur. John replies defiantly that he will invade FRANCE, and Chatillon departs. Eleanor supports John's decision, implying that, since his rule is illegal, it must be maintained through force. Robert Faulconbridge and his older brother, the Bastard, enter and ask the king to judge a dispute: Robert claims their father's estate, asserting that his brother is illegitimate, having been sired by the late King Richard I. Eleanor and John recognize the strong resemblance of the Bastard to the late king, and they like his bold and saucy manner. They offer him a knighthood if he will leave the Faulconbridge estate to his brother and go to war in France with them. He accepts, and after the others have left to prepare for the campaign, he soliloquizes humorously on the manners of the courtly world he is about to enter. His mother, Lady Faulconbridge, arrives, having followed her sons to court to defend her honor. However, when the Bastard tells her he has renounced his inheritance in favor of greater glories, she admits that King Richard was indeed his father. He revels in his newly discovered patrimony.

Act 2, Scene 1
Outside ANGIERS, an English-occupied city in France, King Philip, his son Lewis, and Arthur greet the Archduke of Austria, who has agreed to fight in support of Arthur's claim to the English

crown. Austria is thanked effusively by Arthur and his mother, Constance. Chatillon appears with news that an English army, led by John, is approaching. John and his entourage enter, and Philip questions John's legitimacy, noting that Arthur is the son of John's older brother and thus the proper heir. John simply denies Philip's right to judge the matter, and the two parties trade insults. A Citizen of Angiers appears on the city walls and states that the city will admit neither ruler until it can be ascertained which one represents the true King of England. The two armies skirmish, but Hubert, speaking for Angiers, reiterates the city's refusal to open its gates. The Bastard suggests that the two parties ally temporarily and conquer the recalcitrant town. As they prepare to do so, Hubert proposes a peaceful settlement: Lewis can marry John's niece Blanche of Spain, uniting the two parties. Lewis and Blanche are agreeable, and a treaty is concluded. John grants many of the English territories in France to Philip, and Philip implicitly recognizes John's legitimacy in return. Arthur is to be given high rank and the rule of Angiers. Everyone enters the town to prepare for the wedding except the Bastard, who muses in a soliloquy on the dishonor that the kings have incurred—John for giving away much of his kingdom to secure the rest, Philip for having abandoned an allegedly sacred cause. He rails against "commodity," or self-interest, but then confesses that he does so only because he has not yet had the opportunity to pursue it himself.

Act 2, Scene 2 (Act 3, Scene 1)

The Earl of Salisbury brings word to Constance and Arthur of the settlement between France and England. Constance rants wildly against Salisbury for bringing the news, against Philip for abandoning Arthur's cause, and against fortune for favoring King John.

Act 3, Scene 1 (Act 3, Scene 1 continued)

The wedding party appears, and Constance resumes her cursing. A papal legate, Cardinal Pandulph, arrives with a demand from Rome that King John surrender to the pope's authority in a dispute over the archbishopric of Canterbury. John flatly refuses. Pandulph excommunicates him and insists

that Philip abandon his new alliance with England and make war on John—or face excommunication himself. When Philip hesitates, Pandulph delivers an equivocal argument justifying the breaking of an oath. Philip rejects the alliance with John, and the two parties prepare for war.

Act 3, Scene 2

The armies skirmish. Resting from the battle, the Bastard displays the severed head of Austria. John arrives with the captive Arthur, whom the king turns over to Hubert, now allied with the English.

Act 3, Scene 2 continued (Act 3, Scene 3)

After further skirmishing, John and the Bastard enter, accompanied by Arthur, Hubert, and Eleanor. John sends the Bastard back to England with orders to loot the monasteries there. Eleanor takes Arthur aside to comfort him, while John speaks with Hubert. After flattering him and speaking of future rewards, the king hints that he has a secret desire. Hubert offers to fulfill it, whatever it may be. John observes that Arthur is a potential problem to him, and he speaks the single word "death." Hubert responds that Arthur shall die, and John expresses his satisfaction.

Act 3, Scene 3 (Act 3, Scene 4)

Philip and Lewis discuss the English victory with Pandulph. Constance appears, mad with grief at her son's capture. When she leaves, Philip follows her, fearing that she may harm herself. Pandulph tells Lewis not to lose heart and suggests a plan: John will surely kill Arthur and thus alienate his own followers, and Lewis, as Blanche's husband—she being Arthur's cousin—may claim the throne. Moreover, Pandulph urges the Bastard's ransacking of the monasteries will also antagonize the English so that a French invasion will be welcomed by rebels in England. Pandulph and Lewis go to present this plan to King Philip.

Act 4, Scene 1

Hubert prepares hot irons to put out Arthur's eyes. Hubert summons Arthur, who says that the only comfort he has had in his imprisonment has been the affection of Hubert. The older man, in asides, reveals his torment, but he nevertheless tells Arthur that he must put out his eyes. Arthur pleads for mercy. Hubert relents, but he insists that Arthur's death must be feigned to protect himself, Hubert, from the king's anger.

Act 4, Scene 2

Pembroke and Salisbury tell John that many nobles are dismayed that Arthur is kept imprisoned, and they urge him to free his nephew. He agrees, as Hubert arrives to confer with the king. The two noblemen remark that they know Hubert was assigned to kill Arthur. When John announces that Hubert has brought word of Arthur's death, they are not surprised, and they leave angrily. News arrives that the French have invaded and that Queen Eleanor has died. The Bastard appears and reports that the country is inflamed over Arthur's reported murder. John sends him to summon the disaffected nobles; in view of the invasion, he must attempt to win back their allegiance. Hubert returns and tells of superstitious fears among the populace. John blames Hubert for killing Arthur, claiming that he had not ordered him to do so. Hubert confesses that Arthur is not in fact dead, and John, relieved, tells him to carry this news to the rebellious lords.

Act 4, Scene 3

Arthur attempts to escape by leaping off the castle wall, but he dies from the fall. Pembroke, Salisbury, and Lord Bigot pass by, discussing their plan to join the French invaders, who have offered them an alliance. The Bastard accosts the noblemen with the king's request that they join him. They refuse. Discovering Arthur's body, they rage with increased venom, vowing revenge on John. Hubert enters, claiming that Arthur lives; when shown the body, he is shocked, but the lords do not believe him. They depart, intent on joining Lewis's army.

Act 5, Scene 1

King John yields his crown to Pandulph and receives it back again, thus acknowledging the pope as the source of his authority. In return, Pandulph promises to persuade the French to leave England. The Bastard arrives with news of French successes and of Arthur's death. He rebukes the king for inaction. John explains that he has Pandulph's promise to rely on, and the Bastard is mortified, first that a papal alliance has been formed and

second that no military response to France has been prepared. John tells him to make such arrangements himself.

Act 5, Scene 2

In the French camp, the dissident nobles seal their alliance with Lewis. Salisbury weeps, lamenting the necessity to fight against his own countrymen. Pandulph appears and reports John's reconciliation with the pope, but Lewis refuses to halt his onslaught. The Bastard arrives under a flag of truce and is informed of Lewis's intransigence; he responds with a challenge to continued war. The two sides prepare for battle.

Act 5, Scene 3

During the battle, Hubert reports to King John that his armies are losing. John admits that he is sick, with fever and at heart. A message from the Bastard requests that the king leave the battlefield. John replies that he shall go to SWINSTEAD ABBEY. The Messenger (1) adds that French reinforcements have been lost at sea and that their army has retired to defensive positions. John is too ill to respond to this good news, and he departs for Swinstead.

Act 5, Scene 4

A French nobleman, Lord Melun, mortally wounded and conscience-stricken, tells the rebellious English lords of Lewis's plan to have them executed once John is defeated. Salisbury replies for the group that they will rejoin King John.

Act 5, Scene 5

Lewis receives news of Melun's death, the disaffection of the English lords, and the wreck of his supply ships. He prepares for hard fighting the next day.

Act 5, Scene 6

In the middle of the night Hubert encounters the Bastard and informs him that King John has been poisoned and is dying. The Bastard, whose own forces have been badly damaged by the storm, hastens to rejoin the king.

Act 5, Scene 7

John, burning with fever and aware that he is near death, is brought to his son Prince Henry. The

Bastard arrives with news of the war, but the king dies as he speaks. Salisbury tells the Bastard that Lewis has made offers of peace and has already begun to return his forces to France. The nobles acknowledge Henry as the new king, and the Bastard delivers a patriotic speech, observing that, now that its internal disputes are over, England will once again be invulnerable to invasion.

COMMENTARY

Aside from the very early and collaborative play *Edward III* and the very late and uncharacteristic play *Henry VIII, King John* is the only one of Shakespeare's HISTORY PLAYS that is not part of a TETRALOGY. Further, its narrative is not linked to the others, which together cover an unbroken 87-year period in English history, but rather deals with a much earlier and more obscure era. Thus *King John* has been somewhat neglected, being viewed as a minor and transitional work between the two tetralogies. However, its subject matter is basically the same—the disruption of English public life by dynastic disputes—and its moral weight is as great as that of most of the other histories. Moreover, it is especially closely linked to the contemporary concerns of the playwright's own time.

One of the issues that Shakespeare's history plays most persistently raise is the nature of good government. In *King John* the playwright impresses us with the need for a sound political ethic by presenting a near-catastrophe that stems from ethical weakness. In *Richard III* a melodramatic villain had generated the problem, and his supernaturally aided defeat at BOSWORTH FIELD had solved it. In this more intellectual work Shakespeare examines political realities and problems that require compromises, not heaven-sent intervention.

The chief political concern in the frequently disrupted monarchy of medieval and early modern England was that of the legitimacy of the ruler, and this is the play's primary focus. Shakespeare felt no compunctions about taking liberties with historical reality, and *King John* is one of his least accurate history plays. Besides using such minor anachronisms as John's threat to use cannon in 1.1.26 (gunpowder did not come into use in Europe until the HUNDRED YEARS' WAR, about 150 years later),

he simply rewrote the main lines of John's reign. Compressing the events of 17 years into a single brief sequence, the playwright juxtaposes conflicts that were in fact widely separated in time. John's defense of his right to rule against the partisans of Arthur occupied the first few years of his reign and was completed by 1203, when Arthur was killed. Arthur's death is the central event of the play, but it simply closed the earliest epoch of John's actual reign. In the play the death stimulates the rebellious barons to oppose John and join the invading French. But historically the barons' revolt occurred 10 years after Arthur's death and had nothing to do with it; murder was, after all, an ordinary political event in medieval times. Further, the French invasion came only after the barons' revolt had been settled by the signing of the Magna Carta in 1215 and then resumed in the following year.

The most important issue of John's reign, at the time and to Shakespeare's contemporaries, was John's dispute with Pope Innocent III. However, the playwright lessened its importance and interwove it with the other two conflicts, Arthur's claim and the barons' revolt. In fact, John's dispute with Innocent III began several years after Arthur's death, and it ended before the barons rebelled. The king surrendered to the pope—permitting Pandulph to recrown him, as in the play—precisely because he was concerned about the barons, and Pandulph was in fact John's ally against them. As depicted by Shakespeare, Pandulph's opposition to John revives Arthur's claims, which had been rejected by the marriage treaty of 2.1; the papal legate then stirs up a French invasion in anticipation of Arthur's death, and he finally proves incapable of ending the war in return for John's surrender to papal authority. All of this is flagrantly unhistorical; as always, Shakespeare was less concerned with history than with dramatic effect, and he made John's usurpation of the crown from Arthur the dominant issue in the play in support of his all-important theme: political legitimacy.

Shakespeare's John, then, is an illegitimate ruler, and illegitimacy is a recurring motif in the play. Most prominently, the Bastard raises the issue of illegitimate birth, in speech and in person; significantly, he proves nobler in his steadfast loyalty than all of the other characters, whose treachery and dishonor exemplify illegitimacy in a broader sense: illegitimate actions in terms of the courtly code that all of the aristocrats profess. The Bastard is seen as England's saving grace: He maintains the English resistance, and English honor, when John has succumbed to his moral crisis. Most important, the Bastard gives expression to the value of legitimate succession when he leads the nobles in patriotic support of Henry III in 5.7. It is clear that positive results have come from loyalty to John— that is, that this usurper has his own legitimacy.

The issue of legitimacy was not only a historical one: Queen Elizabeth I (see Elizabeth I in *Henry VIII*) faced similar political problems to a lesser degree. She was conceived outside marriage, as was well known, and Rome did not recognize her legitimacy, either in birth or as a ruler. Similarly, Innocent III had declared John an illegitimate king against whom revolt was lawful, as Pandulph affirms in 3.1.100–101 (3.1.174–175). Further, on several occasions conspiracies against Elizabeth's life were discovered, and Robert Devereux, Earl of ESSEX, actually attempted rebellion toward the end of her reign. Advocates of Mary, Queen of Scots, compared her claim against Elizabeth with Arthur's claim against John; their voices were not silenced until Mary was executed. Monarchs of the TUDOR DYNASTY were aware of their own dynastic roots in rebellion (as is enacted in *Richard III*), and they incorporated a new doctrine in their laws, declaring that the holder of the crown is not only in fact the wielder of power, he or she is also the proper ruler in law, despite the legitimacy of any other claim. This is the implicit principle on which the Bastard bases his loyalty to John. John makes the same claim for himself—"Doth not the crown of England prove the king?" (2.1.273)—and the play reinforces it through remarks such as Eleanor's acknowledgment that "strong possession much more than . . . right" (1.1.40) must secure his throne, as well as through the analogy that the Bastard's possession of the Faulconbridge estates is sufficient evidence of right, even in the face of a legal bequest (1.1.126–133). Further, Arthur is presented as not only a tool of France, but—inaccurately—as a mere child, clearly unsuited to be king. John's legitimacy, like Elizabeth's, must be continuously reaffirmed.

Parallels between John and Elizabeth abound in the play, and Shakespeare's original audience will have recognized them immediately. Pandulph's excommunication of John (3.1.99) [3.1.173] is plainly a reference to the excommunication of Elizabeth in 1570. His promise, four lines later, of canonization to an assassin of John was an inflammatory glance at fairly current events: In 1589 Henri III of France had been murdered by a monk who contended that the King was soft on Protestantism; the assassin's canonization was publicly sought by Catholic groups in France, to the shock and revulsion of Protestants (and some Catholics) throughout Europe. It was widely believed in England that a similar bounty was offered in the case of Elizabeth, and Pandulph's words must have evoked patriotic horror. The conflict between Reformation and Counter-Reformation in the 16th century inspired Protestants to think of John as a predecessor who attempted to rebel against the power of Rome, and they made much of his notorious—but fictitious—poisoning at the hands of a monk. Shakespeare's Pandulph is a stereotype of the malevolent Catholic of fearful Protestant imaginations; John's insulting address to him (3.1.73–86) [3.1.147–160] is an example of 16th-century rhetoric, reflecting the attitudes of Shakespeare's England, not of John's.

Shakespeare is often regarded as a sympathetic to Catholicism (see e.g., SPIRITUAL TESTAMENT OF JOHN SHAKESPEARE), and although *King John* would seem to douse that speculation thoroughly at first glance, the religious issue is nevertheless far less prominent in the play than it was in the actual historical period or in the playwright's sources. Although public interest would certainly have justified a strong presentation of the struggle between Rome and England, Shakespeare refrained. *King John* is primarily a play about a usurpation that did not in fact occur, rather than about the religious conflict that did. To Shakespeare, the religious question is less important than the issue of political legitimacy.

Readers today are often puzzled to find that *King John* makes no mention of what today seems the most salient feature of John's reign, the signing of the Magna Carta in 1215. However, in Shakespeare's day, when the aristocracy was definitely subordinate to the crown, John's concessions to his fractious noblemen seemed unimportant. Our own conception of the Magna Carta as the wellspring of democratic freedom from royal control was not formulated until shortly after Shakespeare's death. Opponents of King Charles I, seeking legal precedents to cite in their struggle, discovered that King John had made concessions, 400 years earlier, that could be said to establish the principle that a ruler was obliged to consult his subjects. This interpretation helped fuel a dispute that led to civil war in 1642. However, the charter signed by John was rather reactionary, restoring to the barons certain feudal rights that the central government was absorbing and would absorb again, especially under the Tudors. The political establishment of Shakespeare's day, intent on preserving its own relatively unrestricted power, certainly had no use for the Magna Carta, and Shakespeare, a supporter of a strong central government, shared this attitude.

King John is sometimes thought of as a failure, with an episodic, undirected plot and confused characterizations, but these seeming defects are actually purposeful techniques. The play's ambiguities and contradictions illustrate the dangers of an unreliable political world, and this is the principal point of the play. The course of the action continually varies, with the vagaries of fortune constantly before us. The characters change their natures repeatedly: John is variously a patriotic hero, resisting France and Rome; a villain, murdering Arthur; a traitor, surrendering his authority to the pope; and a simple failure, collapsing into pathetic uselessness in the face of a crisis. The Bastard first appears as a satirical baiter of aristocratic society, but he becomes the noblest of the Englishmen at the end. Hubert is first a cagey Angevin diplomat caught between big powers, then a sycophantic courtier prepared to murder a child to gain favor with the king, and finally a sorrowing penitent. Our point of view changes repeatedly, our sympathies are continually shifting, and we are drawn into the play as if into an intrigue. Such ambiguity is appropriate for a study of political confusion and uncertainty.

SOURCES OF THE PLAY

It has traditionally been assumed that Shakespeare adapted another play, THE TROUBLESOME RAIGNE OF KING JOHN, in writing *King John*, but the proposition that the former play was derived from Shakespeare's work has gained ground in recent years. In any case, the principal source for whichever play came first was Raphael HOLINSHED's *Chronicles of England, Scotland, and Ireland* (2nd ed., 1587). Shakespeare also referred to John FOXE's *Book of Martyrs* (probably in the 4th ed., 1583), and he took various details from other sources as well. For instance, from the *Chronica Majora*, a Latin history by Matthew Paris (d. 1259), Shakespeare reworked the Bastard's account of his losses in a storm (5.6.39–42, 5.7.61–64) and elements of Salisbury's lament in 5.2. Also, Shakespeare probably knew the popular romances concerning Richard Coeur-de-Lion, from which he may have taken the erroneous identification of Austria with Limoges. His attitudes toward John and his reign may have been influenced by further reading, perhaps including the *Annals* of John STOW, in which John is taken to task as a usurper.

TEXT OF THE PLAY

The date of *King John*'s composition is difficult to determine, if *The Troublesome Raigne of King John* was Shakespeare's source for the play. *The Troublesome Raigne* was published in 1591, and *King John* had been performed by 1598, for it appears in the list of Shakespeare's works that Francis MERES compiled then. Every year between those dates has been proposed for the writing of the play. Stylistically, it is generally thought to fall between the two major tetralogies—that is, in the first half of the 1590s.

If *The Troublesome Raigne* was derived from Shakespeare's play, however, then the date of *King John* must be 1590 or 1591: *King John* contains a reference (1.1.244) to a character in a popular play of 1590, *Soliman and Perseda* (probably by Thomas KYD). A dating of 1590 for *King John* is also supported by the play's frequent allusions to the Spanish Armada (1588)—more than in any other work by Shakespeare—suggesting that it was written soon after the attempted invasion.

King John was first published in the FIRST FOLIO edition of the plays (1623), and that text has been the basis of all subsequent editions. It is thought that the Folio was printed either from Shakespeare's FOUL PAPERS, probably slightly emended by the Folio editors, or from a PROMPTBOOK, perhaps one that Shakespeare himself had revised.

THEATRICAL HISTORY OF THE PLAY

Numerous early-17th-century references to *King John* testify to the play's popularity at that time, but no production of it is known before a revival in 1737. In 1745 Colley CIBBER staged an adaptation emphasizing the French invasion, attempting to capitalize on the patriotism stimulated by the defeat of the Jacobite Rebellion in that year. However, Shakespeare's play, starring David GARRICK as John, was produced at the same time, and the Cibber play folded immediately. *King John* was staged several times in colonial America, beginning with a Philadelphia production in 1768. In London in 1803, during the Napoleonic Wars, another adaptation stressing French iniquities appeared. It was wildly popular and played for years throughout Great Britain. The 1823 production by Charles KEMBLE, designed by J. R. PLANCHE, inaugurated the 19th-century Shakespearean tradition of striving for historical accuracy in costumes and stagings. Kemble's example was followed in William Charles MACREADY's successful production of 1842, and elaborate versions were staged in New York (1846) and London (1852) by Charles KEAN.

A great favorite in times of British national crisis, when the Bastard's patriotic speeches have proved inspiring, *King John* was staged a number of times in the 20th century. In 1945 Peter BROOK directed a striking production featuring Paul SCOFIELD as the Bastard. The play was produced for television twice, in 1951 (with Donald Wolfit as King John) and in 1984 as part of the BBC's inclusive Shakespearean cycles. Although *King John* has not been made as a movie, excerpts from Beerbohm TREE's 1899 stage production of the play were recorded, when cinema was still experimental, in the earliest appearance of Shakespeare on film.

CHARACTERS

Arthur, Prince of England (1187–1203) Historical figure and character in *King John,* nephew and victim of King John. John has usurped Arthur's crown as the play opens. A defenseless boy, Arthur is supported by King Philip of FRANCE and the

Archduke of Austria, who go to war with England. Arthur is captured and is taken to England in the custody of Hubert, who is instructed to kill him. However, Hubert grows fond of his prisoner and cannot bring himself to carry out his orders. First, he decides to blind the boy; then, in 4.1, in response to Arthur's heart-rending pleas for mercy, he spares him altogether. To protect himself, Hubert reports that Arthur has died. Arthur, in the meantime, attempts to escape and perishes jumping from a castle wall. His death provokes a rebellion by John's nobles, whose reservations about the royal succession are now reinforced by revulsion at Arthur's murder, as they believe it to be.

Historically, Arthur had little claim to the English crown, although he was the son of John's older brother, for the rule of primogeniture—succession passing to eldest sons of eldest sons—was not yet accepted in England. John was named heir to the throne in Richard I's will, and he succeeded his brother peacefully, as Shakespeare's sources make clear. Philip's sponsorship of Arthur was intended purely to justify a war and had no legitimacy for the English, but the playwright wished to develop the theme of usurpation.

Further ignoring his sources, Shakespeare made Arthur a young boy, said to be about three feet tall (4.2.100), so as to stress the pathos of his treatment. The historical Arthur was an adult by medieval standards. He was a soldier, the nominal leader, at 15 years old, of the force that besieged Queen Eleanor at Mirabeau, Shakespeare's ANGIERS. Captured in battle there, Arthur was at first in the custody of Hubert but was transferred to an English-held castle at Rouen. He was never taken to England, as in the play.

It is unclear how Arthur died. One contemporary account held that John had proposed blinding and castrating his prisoner to make him unfit for kingship; Hubert dissuaded the King from this course and then falsely announced Arthur's death, intending to discourage his followers. Another source reported that Arthur drowned attempting to escape. Shakespeare combined these two anecdotes. According to a third version of the story, John killed Arthur himself in a fit of drunken rage. The detailed truth cannot be known, but guilt for Arthur's death must ultimately lie with John. The murder did not trigger the barons' revolt, as it does in the play—that event occurred many years later—but it may have contributed to the spate of desertions by various nobles that affected the final year of the war against France, which John lost decisively.

Austria, Limoges, Archduke of (Lymoges, Archduke of Austria)   Character in *King John*, ally of Arthur and King Philip of FRANCE. Austria undertakes to fight King John and place Arthur on the throne of England. He claims to have killed the former English king, the famed Richard Coeur-de-Lion, and he wears a lion's skin as a trophy of this act. Austria is boastful, but when he is baited by the Bastard, as in 3.1.56–59 (3.1.130–133), he reveals his cowardice. In 3.2 (3.3) the Bastard displays Austria's head.

Shakespeare confused two historical figures in creating the Archduke. In the 16th century Austria was a major European power, and the playwright treats it as such, but in King John's day it was a minor German state. Leopold of Babenberg, a duke of Austria who died in 1194, five years before the earliest events of the play, had feuded with Richard Coeur-de-Lion when they were both crusaders in Palestine; he then captured and held Richard for two years, until he received a great ransom. Later, in an unrelated battle, Richard died while besieging the castle of Waldemar, Viscount of Limoges (d. 1199), who may have been killed in revenge by Richard's illegitimate son (who did not otherwise resemble the fictitious Bastard of the play). Thus Shakespeare makes the territory of one of Richard's foes the first name of another. The playwright apparently took this error from 16th-century popular romances, which recounted Richard's life with little or no regard for accuracy.

Bastard, the (Philip Faulconbridge)   Character in *King John*, illegitimate nephew of King John. The Bastard, the most prominent character in the play, is a complicated figure. Early in the play he satirizes courtly manners while revealing the self-serving behavior he mocks. He impulsively insults others and makes humorous asides to himself, yet he is at the same time a calculating social climber. His illegitimacy parallels the king's status as a usurper, and just as John defies the French challenge to his rule, so the Bastard relies on his strength of character to maintain himself in aristocratic society. Yet while John falls, the Bastard prospers; his rise is concurrent with John's fall, and the contrast lends piquancy to the king's collapse. He begins as a comical figure, but by the end of the play he is clearly the mainstay of the English forces. He has remained true to the king, unlike the other noblemen, and it is he who first acknowledges Prince Henry as the new king, emphasizing the restoration of social order.

The Bastard also functions as a CHORUS, commenting on the foibles of society, sometimes contradicting his role in the plot. For instance, he deplores "commodity," or self-interest, in a famous soliloquy (2.1.561–598), yet he is guilty of commodity himself, as he admits in the last dozen lines of the speech. Shakespeare uses the fictitious Bastard somewhat in the manner of the allegorical figures of a MORALITY PLAY, while at the same time making his spirited courage and loyalty humanly admirable. Most strikingly, while the Bastard bears some resemblance to the ancient dramatic figure of the VICE—in his repeated identification with the devil (e.g., in 2.1.134–135), and in his presentation of satirical monologues directly to the audience—he is also in some sense the hero of the play, an exemplar of patriotic virtue. He closes the play with a speech (5.7.112–118) that has been a staple of British patriotic literature since it first appeared.

The Bastard is not based on any single historical figure, although elements of his situation are drawn from the lives of several historical bastards. King Richard I did have an illegitimate son named Philip, and although very little is known of him, he is reputed to have killed the Viscount of Limoges in revenge for his father's death; the Bastard has his first name and kills Austria, who is identified with Limoges in the play. The name Faulconbridge was borne by another noteworthy bastard, William Neville, Lord Falconbridge, who is mentioned in *3 Henry VI*. An illegitimate Norman nobleman, Faukes de Bréauté (d. ca. 1227), led John's armies against the rebellious barons, as the Bastard does in the play, but Shakespeare's character bears no resemblance to this man, a notoriously cruel and oppressive mercenary soldier who finally had to be driven from England by force in 1224. Another famous figure, Jean Dunois, the Bastard of Orléans, apparently contributed to Shakespeare's character as well. Dunois appears in *1 Henry VI*, but that play does not present this famed general with historical accuracy. However, his proclamation, reported in HOLINSHED's *Chronicles*, that he would rather be the bastard of a great man than the legitimate heir of a humble one, is clearly echoed by the Bastard of *King John* (1.1.164, 259–276).

Bigot, Roger (Roger Bigod) (d. 1220) Historical figure and minor character in *King John*, a rebel against King John. Bigot is one of the noblemen who oppose the king, responding to the death of Arthur, and who treacherously ally themselves with the invading French. Bigot speaks in only one of the four scenes in which he appears.

The historical Bigot was one of the barons who opposed John in 1214 and forced him to sign the Magna Carta. He was a great landowner in eastern England.

Blanche of Spain (Blanch of Spain) (1188–1252) Historical figure and minor character in *King John*, the niece of King John, who marries Lewis, the French Dauphin, after 2.1. Blanche finds herself with mixed loyalties when hostilities break out between her uncle and her new husband. In 3.1 she unsuccessfully attempts to persuade her husband and his father, King Philip, to refrain from fighting England. She is reduced to a bewildered lament that plaintively expresses the helplessness of the noncombatant.

The historical Blanche of Castile, as she is better known, was raised in Spain. Her mother was John's sister Eleanor, and her father was the king of Castile. A treaty between John and Philip provided for the marriage of Lewis to a princess of Castile, and Queen Eleanor traveled to Spain and selected Blanche from among several eligible sisters. Thus, at 12, Blanche was taken by her grandmother, whom she had not met before, to another country to marry a man whom she had never met. Although her initial depression in her new home

was noted in a contemporary chronicle, she went on to become one of the great women in French history. After the brief reign of Lewis (Louis VIII), Blanche acted as regent for her son, Louis IX, known to history as St. Louis. She put down several rebellions and completed the subjection of southern France to royal rule. St. Louis spent much of his reign crusading in the Holy Land, and Blanche governed effectively in his absence.

Chatillon (Chatillion) Minor character in *King John*, the ambassador of King Philip Augustus of France to King John. A haughty lord, Chatillon opens the play by delivering an ultimatum to John in terms that are obviously meant to be insulting. He reappears only briefly, bearing the news of John's invasion of France in 2.1; while belittling the English, he must speak of their military success. Chatillon's role helps to develop a strong sense of the arrogance of power, heightening the impact of treachery in high places, one of the play's major themes.

Citizen Minor character in *King John*, a citizen of ANGIERS who appears on the walls of the city in 2.1 to explain to the kings, Philip Augustus of France and John of England, why the gates are closed. He declares the town's allegiance to the king of England but adds that, until it is established whether John or Arthur is properly the holder of that office, the citizens have "ramm'd up our gates against the world" (2.1.272). The Citizen's suspicion of his leaders illuminates the treacherous nature of royal politics, a major theme of the play.

In the FIRST FOLIO, where *King John* was first published, the Citizen departs at 2.1.282 and Hubert acts as representative of Angiers to the forces outside after entering at line 325. However, in some modern editions, Hubert's lines in 2.1 are given to the Citizen. Conversely, in other editions, the Citizen's part in its entirety is given to Hubert.

Constance, Duchess of Brittany (d. 1201) Historical figure and character in *King John*, mother of Arthur. Before the play begins, Constance has gained the support of King Philip Augustus of France in her attempt to place Arthur on the throne of England, from which King John, his uncle, has displaced him. In 3.1 she rages furiously at the betrayal of her cause by Philip and the Archduke of Austria, emphasizing the theme of treachery that runs throughout the play. However, she then helps persuade Philip to another betrayal as he turns on his new ally, King John. In 3.3 (3.4), Constance grieves hysterically over Arthur's capture by King John. She raves about making love to death (3.3.25–36), and Philip fears that she will harm herself. Her death "in a frenzy" is reported in 4.2.122. Her agonizing madness helps to stress the evil of John's usurpation.

The historical Constance was the daughter of a rebellious duke of Brittany whom King John's father, Henry II, defeated. In an effort to assure Brittany's loyalty, Henry insisted that Constance marry his son Geoffrey. After Geoffrey's death, Constance ruled Brittany for Arthur, whose name may suggest her ambition to see her son rule England. Her ambition is reflected in Shakespeare's sources, but the playwright altered the details of her life freely. For instance, Constance bemoans her "husbandless" state in 2.2.14 (3.1.14), but in fact she married twice after Geoffrey's death. Also, in order to continue a deliberate pairing of Constance with Eleanor, he has the two women die at the same time, although in fact Constance had died three years earlier.

Eleanor of Aquitaine, Queen of England (Elinor of Aquitaine) (1122–1204)   Historical figure and character in *King John*, mother of King John. Queen Eleanor is a bold and forthright character, quick to respond to possible insult to her son, whether from Chatillon (1.1.5) or from Philip Augustus, King of France (2.1.120). She is fully prepared to fight (1.1.40), but she is also a wise diplomat, equally ready to make peace when it seems profitable (2.1.468–479). It is clear that she is a very important figure in John's life, and his distraction following her death just as the French invade (4.2) is completely understandable.

The historical Eleanor of Aquitaine was one of the most remarkable women of the Middle Ages. The daughter of the Duke of Aquitaine, she inherited her father's duchy, a powerful independent territory in what is now the south of FRANCE, at the age of 15. Three months later she married the Dauphin of France; one month after that, her new father-in-law died, and she became queen of France. However, she bore no heirs to Louis VII. This fact, the great personality differences between herself and the king, and her marital infidelities, referred to in 2.1.125, resulted in their divorce in 1152. Eleanor was publicly humiliated in the process, but as Duchess of Aquitaine, the greatest heiress in Europe, she was able to avenge herself immediately by marrying Louis's greatest rival, Henry II of England. By Henry she bore four sons, among them both Richard I and John. However, her relations with her second husband were no better than with her first, and she incited her sons to rebel against him. When the revolt failed, she was imprisoned for 15 years, being released only upon Henry's death. She devoted the rest of her life to supporting her sons, and her death in 1204, at 83, must indeed have seemed a monumental loss to John, although it occurred many years before the crisis with which it is associated in the play.

Essex, Geoffrey FitzPeter (d. 1213)   Historical figure and minor character in *King John*, follower of King John. Essex appears only in 1.1 and has only one short speech. Textual scholars speculate that Essex's lines were assigned to Lord Bigot—perhaps in 1601, after the failed rebellion of the later Earl of ESSEX, Robert Devereux—and that this alteration was overlooked in the one speech in the FIRST FOLIO text. The historical Essex, no relation to Shakespeare's contemporary, had been named an earl by John and remained a loyal follower of the king.

Executioner   Any of two or more minor characters in *King John*, Hubert's assistants in the preparations to blind Arthur. Before Hubert dismisses the Executioners, one of them, the First Executioner, voices the distaste with which these hardened men view the prospect of practicing their profession on a boy. His qualms heighten the pathos of the scene.

Falconbridge (Faulconbridge)   Any of several characters in *King John*, including the Bastard, Lady Faulconbridge, and Robert Faulconbridge.

Gurney, James Minor character in *King John,* a friend or servant of Lady Faulconbridge. Gurney speaks only half of one line (1.1.231), a friendly response to his dismissal from the scene (and the play) by the Bastard, Lady Faulconbridge's son. This moment illuminates the world of rural informality that the Bastard has come from.

Henry, Prince (later King Henry III of England) (1207–1272) Historical figure and minor character in *King John,* the son of King John. Henry appears only in the final scene, 5.7, in which he witnesses the death of his father and accepts the submission of the noblemen to him as the next King. He is thus a symbol of the restoration of social order after the dislocations of John's reign.

Shakespeare's Henry is a young man but definitely an adult, capable of musing on the nature of disease and death. The historical Prince was only nine years old upon his succession. He ruled England well for 56 years. His great-great-grandson was Edward III (see PLANTAGENET FAMILY).

Herald Either of two minor characters in *King John,* the respective representatives of King John of England and King Philip Augustus of France, to the city of ANGIERS in 2.1. Each Herald formally proclaims the victory of his king in the preceding skirmish and demands that the city declare its loyalty to that ruler and open its gates to his soldiers. The symmetrical opposition of the Heralds emphasizes the difficulty in resolving competing claims to power, an important theme of the play.

Hubert Character in *King John,* a follower of King John and custodian of Arthur. Hubert first appears as a representative of the city of ANGIERS, proposing a compromise between John and King Philip Augustus of France. His opening remarks (2.1.325–333) emphasize the balance between opposing forces that recurs throughout the play. By 3.2 (3.3), Hubert has joined King John's entourage. When Arthur is captured in battle, Hubert accepts John's implicit order to kill him. In 4.1, one of Shakespeare's most terrifying and moving scenes, Hubert, touched by the boy's innocence, hides Arthur and tells the king that he has died. Arthur's

supposed death proves politically catastrophic to the king; yet, when Hubert reveals that Arthur is alive, it turns out that the young prince has in the meantime died attempting to escape. Thus Hubert's career mirrors the changes in fortune and the ambiguities of good and evil that are a principal theme of the play.

Shakespeare's character bears almost no resemblance to the historical figure who provided the name. Hubert de Burgh (d. 1243), although he briefly had custody of Arthur, seems not to have been involved in his death; he may have actually tried to prevent it. In any case, he certainly was not the bourgeois opportunist depicted in the play. On the contrary, he was one of the highest-ranking aristocrats in England, being descended directly from Charlemagne, and he was an important administrator both before and during the period of the play and under John's successor, Henry III (Prince Henry in the play). Furthermore, he won a great naval victory over a French fleet that was attempting to reinforce the forces of Lewis in England. Shakespeare translates this battle—the first in Britain's long tradition of naval supremacy—into a storm, reported in 5.3.9–11, rather than give credit to Hubert. The playwright may have felt that depicting Hubert as a commoner made the unscrupulous ambition that leads him to agree to kill a boy more believable, while the character's lack of commitment to the high politics of the realm could make his subsequent mercy credible.

John, King of England (1167–1216) Historical figure and title character in *King John.* John is a complicated protagonist of a complicated play. Not quite hero or villain, he espouses values of English patriotism while his selfish ambition leads the country to catastrophe. John passes from unscrupulous strength to dispirited weakness, and his own moral failings are at the heart of his collapse. He is ultimately an inadequate leader, controlled by events rather than controlling them. As the play opens, John has usurped the English throne from his nephew Arthur. Nevertheless, he initially appears to be a strong king: In 1.1 he boldly defies the challenge to his rule from Arthur's supporter Philip Augustus, King of France. However, he soon displays his weakness when, in the treaty concluded in 2.1, he surrenders a great deal of English territory in order to protect his claim to the rest. He exhibits strength again, in a context particularly significant to 16th-century Protestant England, when he refuses to obey the dictates of the pope, conveyed by Pandulph in 3.1, and renewed war with FRANCE results. John's forces capture Arthur, and the king dishonorably orders him killed by Hubert in 3.2 (3.3). He also commands the Bastard to loot England's religious houses to pay for the war.

Shakespeare's handling of Arthur's death, the central event of the play, illuminates John's ambiguous nature. Before learning that Hubert has not killed the boy, John expresses regret for the crime and dishonestly tries to excuse himself in 4.2.103–105 and 205–248; he rejoices when he discovers that Arthur is alive. Yet Arthur does die when he tries to escape his captors. John is thus blamed for the death anyway and suffers the political consequences.

John's fortunes deteriorate from this point on. His barons desert him; his mother, Queen Eleanor, dies; a wandering seer, Peter, predicts that he will give up his crown. The Dauphin Lewis of France invades England, and several barons join his forces. In 5.1 John formally acknowledges the supremacy of the pope over England, in return for Pandulph's promise to make the French withdraw. Lewis will not abandon his successful invasion, however, and only the efforts of the Bastard keep England's defenses functioning. Demoralized and sick, John withdraws to SWINSTEAD ABBEY, where a monk, enraged by the king's pillaging of the churches, poisons him. John dies in torment, just as an urgent message of fresh disaster is being delivered. His death returns peace and stability to England, as the French finally withdraw and the Bastard leads the nobles in pledging allegiance to John's successor, Henry.

According to modern scholarship, the sources Shakespeare used in creating his John were not very accurate, and the playwright altered many details in any case. The historical John was not a usurper; he did not lose the support of his barons by killing an innocent boy; he was not murdered. He was indeed an unsuccessful king, though probably due more to the assets of his enemies than to his own defects. Philip Augustus of France was a powerful soldier and statesman, and Innocent III was one of the greatest of medieval popes. John did not, however, lack leadership skills himself. Many of his nobles remained loyal to him, and he never withdrew from the fight against the rebels and their French allies; he died of a sickness contracted on the battlefield. His personality is not well recorded, but he appears to have been highly temperamental, perhaps deranged; according to one account, he beat Arthur to death in a drunken rage. However, Shakespeare did not attempt to delineate John's true nature; the character is a fiction designed to illustrate the nature of misused power. The king's moral weakness is central to an intellectual drama of politics, and his personality is not relevant.

Lady Faulconbridge (Falconbridge) Minor character in *King John*, mother of the Bastard and Robert Faulconbridge. Lady Faulconbridge follows her two sons to court, where Robert has claimed that his older brother is the illegitimate son of the late King Richard I. She hopes to preserve her reputation, but when the Bastard tells her that he has renounced his status as a Faulconbridge in favor of royal illegitimacy, she confesses that Richard was indeed his father. Her role serves merely to allow her son's spirit to manifest itself.

Lewis, the Dauphin (later King Louis VIII of France) (1187–1226) Historical figure and character in *King John*, son of Philip Augustus, King of France. Lewis joins his father in supporting Arthur, whose rightful inheritance of the English crown has been prevented by King John. The French abandon Arthur's cause for a favorable peace, under whose terms Lewis marries John's niece Blanche. In 3.1, despite his bride's pleas, Lewis urges his father to support the pope and turn on John, and he later leads an invasion of England. He refuses to cease fighting when John makes his peace with Rome, insisting that FRANCE would be dishonored by retreat. He withdraws only when deserted by the disaffected English lords who had been aiding him. Lewis is a superficially civil but treacherous Frenchman of a type that Shakespeare often depicted; here the stereotype not only heightens the patriotic sentiments of *King John* but also stresses the motif of faithlessness that runs through the play.

The historical Lewis did invade England and was successful at first. However, the invasion was not prompted by the pope's quarrel with John, which had been settled earlier. In fact, it was undertaken in defiance of a papal prohibition; it was intended to place Lewis on the English throne, at the invitation of rebellious English barons. A reunited England under John's successor, Henry, drove Lewis back to France. Lewis is frequently referred to as the Dauphin, or Dolphin, a title traditionally given to the eldest son of a King of France, as Prince of Wales is given to his English equivalent. However, this practice began only in 1350, so its application to Lewis is inaccurate.

Melun (Melune), Giles de, Lord (d. 1216) Historical figure and minor character in *King John*. The fatally wounded Melun, a French lord, relieves his conscience before dying by warning the rebellious English nobles who have aided the French invasion that Lewis, the French leader, intends to kill them after he has defeated King John. This information spurs the rebels, led by the Earl of Salisbury, to return to the English forces.

Shakespeare took this incident from Raphael HOLINSHED's history, but it is probably not accurate. In any case, little more is known of Melun. In the play he speaks of his English grandfather, who may have been Robert de Melun, Bishop of Hereford (d. 1164); this cannot be confirmed by known records, however.

Messenger (1) Minor character in *King John*. In 4.2 the Messenger brings King John news of both the French invasion and the death of John's mother, Queen Eleanor, and in 5.3 he reappears with a message from the Bastard, urging the king to remove himself from battle. Thus this underling marks the beginning and end of John's collapse.

Messenger (2) Minor character in *King John*. In 5.5 the Messenger brings Lewis three pieces of bad news: the death of Lord Melun, the desertion from the French forces of the English barons who had been in revolt against King John, and the loss of French ships at sea. These tidings collectively spell doom for the French invasion of England.

Pandulph (d. 1226) Historical figure and character in *King John*, papal legate and enemy of King John. Pandulph appears in 3.1 to demand John's submission to the pope in the appointment of an archbishop. When John refuses, Pandulph threatens King Philip Augustus of France with excommunication if he does not break his new alliance with England and declare war on John. Pandulph offers an elaborate and specious argument (3.1.189–223 [3.1.263—297]) justifying the breaking of an oath. In 3.3 he offers the Dauphin Lewis a plan whereby he may conquer England and claim the throne. Having thus launched an invasion of England, Pandulph promises John that he will call it off in exchange for his oath of submission to the pope. John agrees, and he relinquishes his crown to Pandulph, who recrowns him, thus symbolically asserting papal supremacy over the government of England. However, in 5.2 Lewis refuses to withdraw and is defeated only when his traitorous English allies return to King John's side. Pandulph's unscrupulous warmongering and his inability to fulfill a promise fit the stereotype he represents: that of the steely, hypocritical Jesuit, capable of arguing any side of a question to suit the ends of the Catholic Church.

The historical Pandulph, a native of Rome, was sent to England in 1211—long after the marriage of Lewis and Blanche in 1200, with which his arrival is associated in the play—to insist that the papal candidate be installed as Archbishop of Canterbury, as in the play. But Shakespeare's condensation of history has skewed Pandulph's subsequent role, for by the time of the barons' revolt he was John's ally. After receiving John's submission to the pope in 1213, Pandulph supported him against his rebellious nobles, excommunicating those of them who extracted the Magna Carta from the king. John rewarded him with the bishopric of Norwich. Pandulph attempted unsuccessfully to prevent Lewis's invasion in 1216. He remained an influential bishop in England after John's death, serving as one of the regents for the young King Henry until 1221, when Henry exiled him, apparently on personal grounds. Pandulph died in Rome, but he was buried in Norwich, at his own request.

Pandulph was never a cardinal, the rank he holds in the play. Shakespeare may have taken this error from an early-16th-century play on King John, but there is no other evidence that he knew the work. It is more likely that Pandulph was elevated in rank for a simple and sensible theatrical reason: to dress him in the boldly dramatic scarlet robes of a cardinal, an ordinary item in the wardrobes of acting companies.

Pembroke, William Marshall, Earl of (ca. 1146–1219)   Historical figure and minor character in *King John*, a rebel against King John. Pembroke, like Lord Bigot, is merely a representative rebellious baron with no distinctive personality.

The historical William Marshall was a famous soldier who in fact remained loyal to John throughout his reign. Shakespeare confused him with his son, who did join the French invasion forces.

Peter of Pomfret (d. 1213)   Historical figure and minor character in *King John*, a wandering "prophet" whose public forecasts of the fall of King John are recounted by the Bastard in 4.2. Peter himself, who has been brought to the king, speaks only one line (4.2.154), affirming his belief that John will have surrendered his crown by the following Ascension Day. John orders him imprisoned, to be hung on Ascension Day, and he does not reappear. On Ascension Day, when John does indeed give up his crown—only to receive it again from the papal legate Pandulph—he recalls the prophecy and observes that it has been fulfilled, in an unanticipated way. We are not informed of Peter's fate, however. The incident illustrates popular dissatisfaction with John's reign and also suggests that his fall was inevitable.

Shakespeare read of this prophecy in HOLINSHED's *Chronicles*, where Peter, a hermit "in great reputation with the common people" for his powers of prophecy, offered himself to be executed if he proved wrong. On Ascension Day, John still being in power, he was hung, along with his son. Holinshed thought that the prophet was a fraud, but he records that Peter's death was popularly held to be

an injustice in light of John's temporary surrender of his crown to Pandulph, which had occurred the day before and seemed to fulfill the prediction.

Philip Augustus, King of France (1165–1223)   Historical figure and character in *King John*, enemy of King John and supporter of Arthur. Philip is presented as an opportunist intent on political and military advantage over England by any means available, while mouthing graceful sentiments about honor. In 2.1 he backs Arthur's claim to the English throne, which John has usurped, but he willingly enters into a treaty by which his son Lewis marries John's niece Blanche, receiving in her dowry a large grant of English-held territory. Philip then breaks this alliance—under Pandulph's threat of excommunication—and launches a war that results in Lewis's invasion of England in Acts 4–5. Philip himself disappears from the play in 3.3 (3.4), after Arthur's mother, Constance, delivers a fierce tirade against his treacherous abandonment of the boy.

The historical Philip is regarded as one of the great kings of FRANCE. He was a successful general who regained much of English-held France, to the north and west of Paris, seized territories from Flanders, and began the Albigensian Crusade, which was to result, under Blanche, in the accession of what is now southern France. Philip also successfully opposed the independence of the great barons of France, doing much to establish the powerful monarchy that was to bring France into early modern times. For these achievements he was known as Augustus, after the founder of the Roman Empire.

Plantagenet, Richard   In *King John*, the name granted to the Bastard in acknowledgment that he is the illegitimate son of the late king Richard I. The Bastard is fictitious; King Richard did have an illegitimate son, but his name was Philip.

Robert Faulconbridge (Robert Falconbridge)   Minor character in *King John*, younger brother of the Bastard. Robert comes to King John in 1.1, seeking to claim his father's estate. He asserts that his brother is illegitimate, having been fathered by the late King Richard I. When the Bastard accepts this lineage and joins the royal court, Robert is awarded the estate and disappears from the play. Content with comfortable nonentity, he is depicted as inferior to the Bastard, who seeks glory.

Much is made of Robert's extraordinarily thin face, as in 1.1.138–147. This is thought to indicate that the actor who originally played Robert was John SINCKLO, whose appearance is similarly noted in several other roles.

Salisbury, William Longsword, Earl of (d. 1226) Historical figure and character in *King John*, the leader of the English noblemen who rebel against John. Salisbury is the spokesman for the other rebels, the Earl of Pembroke and Lord Bigot. They desert John and join a French invasion force, believing that the king has foully murdered young Prince Arthur. They return to John's side when they learn from Melun that the French leader, Lewis, plans treachery against them. The rebellious barons represent an evil consequence of John's evil behavior, and Salisbury effectively expresses their motives, both in disrupting the realm and in returning to loyalty.

The historical Salisbury was King John's half brother, an illegitimate son of King Henry II. He was not a leader of the rebellious barons but remained loyal to the king through the settlement that produced the Magna Carta in 1215. However, upon the resumption of civil war, Salisbury joined the alliance of the barons and the invading French, leaving it only after John's death. He was no relation to the other earls of Salisbury who appear in Shakespeare's plays.

Sheriff Minor character in *King John*, a petty official who escorts Robert Faulconbridge and the Bastard into the king's presence in 1.1.44. The Sheriff, who does not speak, represents the world of country gentry from which the brothers come.

King Lear
SYNOPSIS

Act 1, Scene 1
The Earl of Gloucester introduces his illegitimate son Edmund to the Earl of Kent and observes that he has a legitimate son as well. King Lear arrives with his daughters, Goneril, Regan, and Cordelia, and explains his intention to abdicate and distribute Britain among his sons-in-law, the Dukes of Albany and Cornwall—married to Goneril and Regan, respectively—and either the Duke of Burgundy or the King of France, suitors of Cordelia. He will give the largest share of the kingdom to whichever daughter can convince him she loves him the most. Goneril and Regan declare their love effusively, but Cordelia simply states that her love is that of a daughter to a father, and that she will also love her husband when she has one. Infuriated, Lear disinherits her; Kent attempts to dissuade him, and Lear banishes him. Burgundy rejects the disinherited Cordelia, but France decides to marry her and take her back to France. Regan and Goneril confer on the need to control their obviously senile father lest he turn against them.

Act 1, Scene 2
Edmund bewails his illegitimacy and decides to steal his brother Edgar's inheritance with the help of the letter he holds. Gloucester enters, and Edmund pretends to hide the letter, but his father insists on reading it. It is supposedly from Edgar, proposing to Edmund that they murder Gloucester. Edmund pretends to believe the letter is merely a test of his morals, and he offers to arrange for Gloucester to overhear a conversation between the half brothers. Gloucester agrees and leaves; Edmund remarks on his naiveté. Edgar appears, and Edmund tells him that their father is viciously angry with him, warning him to go armed lest he be attacked.

Act 1, Scene 3
Goneril desires to humble her father and instructs her steward Oswald to treat Lear and his followers disdainfully when they arrive.

Act 1, Scene 4
Kent, disguised, plans to rejoin the king's court at Goneril's castle. Lear arrives with his followers, and Kent is accepted among them. Oswald is surly to the king, and to Lear's delight, Kent rails against him, knocks him down, and drives him away. Lear's Fool mocks the king for having surrendered his

A scene from an early-20th-century *King Lear*. Lear (Robert Bruce Mantell) disinherits Cordelia, saying, "Nothing will come of nothing" (1.1.89). *(Courtesy of Culver Pictures, Inc.)*

authority. Goneril appears and scolds Lear for the conduct of his men. She demands that he halve their number, and he declares that he will leave and go to Regan. He departs. Albany protests over Goneril's behavior, but she silences him and sends Oswald with a letter to Regan that details her tactics with their father.

Act 1, Scene 5
Lear sends Kent with a letter to Regan. The Fool again taunts the king for being at the mercy of his daughters.

Act 2, Scene 1
Edmund encounters Edgar and advises him to flee for his life. As Gloucester approaches, Edmund tricks Edgar by saying that he must pretend to prevent Edgar's flight but that he will actually help him escape. He draws his sword and fakes a fight, hustling Edgar away. He then tells Gloucester that Edgar had assaulted him when he opposed the murder plot. Gloucester declares he will have Edgar captured and executed, and he vows to legitimate Edmund. Cornwall and Regan arrive on a visit to Gloucester; they praise Edmund and take him into their service.

Act 2, Scene 2
Outside Gloucester's castle, Kent insults and pummels Oswald as Edmund, Cornwall, Regan, and Gloucester appear. Asked to explain his behavior,

Kent declares that Oswald is a hypocrite. Cornwall places Kent in the stocks despite his status as messenger of the king. Gloucester protests but is ignored. When the others leave, Kent muses on a letter he has received from Cordelia, who has learned of Lear's humiliation.

Act 2, Scene 3
Edgar has escaped from a search party and overheard a proclamation that he is outlawed. He decides to disguise himself as a wandering lunatic, taking the name Tom O'Bedlam.

Act 2, Scene 4
Lear, seeking Regan, arrives at Gloucester's castle and finds Kent in the stocks. The Fool calls Kent a fool for attaching himself to a powerless master. Gloucester reports that Regan and Cornwall will not receive Lear, who begins to rage but restrains himself. Regan and Cornwall appear, and Kent is freed. Regan defends Goneril against Lear's complaints as Goneril arrives. The two unite in demanding that Lear dismiss his retinue. The distressed Lear wavers between tears and anger and rages out into a storm that has arisen, followed by Gloucester and the Fool.

Act 3, Scene 1
Kent meets a Gentleman (1) who reports that Lear is raging madly in the storm, accompanied only by the Fool. Kent asks him to report Lear's situation to Cordelia, who has arrived in DOVER with a French army.

Act 3, Scene 2
Lear raves in the storm, cursing his daughters. Kent appears and urges the king to take shelter in a nearby hovel. The Fool bitterly predicts disruption for England, whatever lies in store.

Act 3, Scene 3
Gloucester tells Edmund that Cornwall, his feudal lord, has forbidden him to take Lear in. He confides, however, that he has received a letter assuring that Lear's revenge is at hand in the form of the French invasion. Edmund decides to inform on his father so he can get his inheritance sooner.

Act 3, Scene 4
Lear, Kent, and the Fool approach the hovel. Lear declares that he prefers the storm to the thoughts

he would have if he were sheltered, but he sends the Fool inside. He reflects on the woes of the poor and homeless, whom he had never considered when he ruled. The Fool reappears, terrified of a madman in the hovel. He is followed by Edgar, disguised as Tom O'Bedlam, who raves about being pursued by devils. Lear sympathizes with him, assuming that he too has been betrayed by his daughters. Edgar asserts that his demons are punishment for certain offenses: He had been a decadent and immoral servant who slept with his mistress, among other sins. Gloucester appears and offers them shelter. He confides to Kent that Lear's daughters seek the king's death.

Act 3, Scene 5
Edmund has revealed Gloucester's correspondence with the French army, and Cornwall orders him to have his father arrested.

Act 3, Scene 6
Gloucester leaves Kent, Lear, the Fool, and Edgar in a warm room. Lear acts out a criminal trial of Goneril and Regan and finally falls asleep just as Gloucester returns and warns them to flee immediately. Kent and the Fool leave, carrying the sleeping Lear. Edgar, left behind, reflects that his own fate does not seem so bad compared with that of the mad king.

Act 3, Scene 7
Gloucester, under arrest, is brought before Cornwall and Regan. When he says that he will see them punished by fate, Cornwall puts out his eyes. The duke is attacked by a Servant, who cannot abide such evil. Cornwall kills the Servant, but not before being badly wounded. Regan takes him away, and the remaining Servants agree to take the blinded Gloucester to the wandering madman, who can help him safely escape.

Act 4, Scene 1
An Old Man leads the blind Gloucester to Edgar, who grieves to see his father in such condition. However, still an outcast, he resumes his madman's disguise. He agrees to lead Gloucester to the cliffs of Dover.

Act 4, Scene 2

Oswald meets Goneril and Edmund and tells them that Albany has learned of Cordelia's invasion, which pleases him, and of Edmund's informing on Gloucester, which does not. Goneril sends Edmund with a message to Cornwall to hastily muster an army; they exchange loving farewells, accompanied by hints of a murder plot against Albany. Albany appears and berates Goneril for her evil; she replies that he is merely a coward. A Messenger (1) arrives with news of Cornwall's death and Gloucester's blinding. In an aside, Goneril worries that Regan has possible designs on Edmund, now that she is a widow. Albany vows privately to revenge Gloucester.

Act 4, Scene 3

In Dover the Gentleman tells Kent of Cordelia's tearful response to news of Lear. Kent replies that Lear is in Dover but refuses to see Cordelia, out of shame.

Act 4, Scene 4

Cordelia hears that Lear has been seen wandering wearing a crown of weeds and flowers, and she orders a search party. The Doctor assures her that Lear's madness may be eased by rest, and that sedatives are available. News arrives that the armies of Albany and Cornwall are approaching.

Act 4, Scene 5

Oswald reports to Regan that Goneril has convinced Albany to fight against Cordelia's invasion. He also has a letter from Goneril to Edmund, which sparks Regan's jealousy; she gives Oswald a token from herself to give Edmund with Goneril's letter. She adds that if Oswald finds and kills Gloucester, he will be rewarded.

Act 4, Scene 6

Edgar convinces Gloucester that they have reached the top of the cliffs at Dover and then pretends to leave him. In an aside to himself he says that he must humor his father's despair in order to cure it. Gloucester leaps forward and falls to the ground. Edgar then pretends to be a passerby at the bottom of the cliff and says that he had seen Gloucester at the top with a hideous demon. Gloucester accepts the idea that the gods have miraculously preserved him from an evil impulse, and he vows to accept his

affliction in the future. Lear appears, covered with wildflowers and raving madly. The Gentleman arrives with a search party and takes Lear to Cordelia. Edgar learns from him the location of the British army. Oswald appears and attacks Gloucester, but Edgar kills him. As he dies, Oswald asks his killer to deliver his letters to Edmund. Edgar reads a letter from Goneril proposing that Edmund murder Albany and marry her.

Act 4, Scene 7

Cordelia greets her father, but Lear mistakes her for a spirit and only gradually realizes that he is still alive. The Doctor says that he needs more rest, and he is taken indoors, leaving Kent and the Gentleman to discuss the coming battle. Kent declares that his life will end that day.

Act 5, Scene 1

Jealously, Regan interrogates Edmund about Goneril, and Goneril says to herself that she would rather lose the battle than see Regan get Edmund. Edgar appears in disguise and takes Albany aside. He gives him the letter he got from Oswald. He proposes that after the battle Albany call for a challenger to prove in trial by combat that its contents are true. In a soliloquy Edmund reflects that Albany's leadership will be needed during the battle, but he hopes Goneril will then see to killing him. He observes that Albany has proposed mercy for Lear and Cordelia, but he, Edmund, will not permit it.

Act 5, Scene 2

Edgar leaves Gloucester and goes to fight. Fleeing soldiers pass by, and Edgar returns, saying that Cordelia's forces have been routed and she and Lear captured. Gloucester fatalistically elects to stay, but he recovers when reminded of his resolution to endure, and the two flee together.

Act 5, Scene 3

Edmund sends the captured Lear and Cordelia to prison. Lear rejoices at being with Cordelia, despite the circumstances. Edmund sends an Officer (1) after them, telling him to carry out his written instructions mercilessly. Albany arrives with Regan and Goneril. He arrests Edmund and Goneril for treason, asserting that a challenger will appear to back the charge in trial by combat. Regan departs, suddenly sick. Edgar appears, unrecognizable in full armor, and he and Edmund fight until he wounds Edmund badly. Albany displays the letter, and Goneril departs hastily. The dying Edmund confesses his crimes. Edgar identifies himself and tells of escorting Gloucester, adding that when he finally told his father who he was, the emotional shock killed the old man. A hysterical Gentleman (2) reports that Goneril has confessed to poisoning Regan and then committed suicide. Edmund reveals that he has ordered someone to kill the king and hang Cordelia in her cell, an apparent suicide. Edmund is carried away and a soldier is sent to halt the killer, but Lear appears, carrying the dead Cordelia in his arms. He mourns her death, but at intervals believes she may be still alive. He sees Kent but cannot recognize or understand him; the others realize that he is mad again. Edmund's death is reported, and Albany declares that he will return Lear's kingdom to him. Lear suddenly announces that he sees Cordelia breathing, and as he does so, he dies. Albany orders funeral preparations and appoints Kent and Edgar to be his associates in rule, though Kent says that he will soon die. Edgar closes the play with the assertion that such woes as Lear's shall not be seen again.

COMMENTARY

As was his habit, Shakespeare altered his sources considerably when he wrote *King Lear*, and his most important alteration changed the nature of the story entirely. In the many versions of the tale that preceded Shakespeare's, Lear does not go mad but recovers his throne and leaves it to Cordelia. The old story is essentially reassuring: One may make a catastrophic mistake and still survive to live a peaceful and happy life. Shakespeare plainly felt that life makes more strenuous demands than a happy ending can illustrate, and at the core of his story is human failing. Gloucester's blindness is foreshadowed in his lack of judgment about Edgar, and Lear's madness by his egotistical demand for total love. These failings are seen in conjunction with the unscrupulous ambition for power represented by Edmund, Cornwall, Goneril, and Regan, and we are repelled by crimes within families, violations of the most basic human solidarity. Our hor-

ror is compounded by the vivid depiction of villainy triumphant, which is only slightly lessened by the villains' deaths, as these are more than matched by those of Gloucester, Lear, and Cordelia. Edmund's remorse at the play's close does little to compensate for his evil, and Regan and Goneril display no final repentance at all. Our pity for Lear and Gloucester is increased by the knowledge that they brought their sufferings on themselves.

The enormity of the tragedy is unmistakable, and the play leaves us with a troubling question: How can we reconcile human dignity with human failure in the face of life's demands? This is finally unresolvable; however, several possible ways of addressing the question emerge through Shakespeare's rich presentation of human tragedy.

Perhaps most striking is the play's obvious religious interpretation, emphasized by numerous allusions to religious matters. These range from the trivial—as in the many mentions of pagan gods—to serious remarks such as Edgar's "The Gods are just, and of our pleasant vices / Make instruments to plague us" (5.3.169–170). Also, numerous references to the end of the world are made, most strikingly in the cries of Kent, Edgar, and Albany at the horror of Cordelia's death, in 5.3.262–263. Most significantly, Cordelia, who suffers through no fault of her own and accepts her fate with uncomplaining fortitude and undiminished love, is often seen as a personification of the Christian virtues of self-sacrifice and acceptance of God's will. In fact, many commentators have found her to be a Christlike figure whose death symbolizes Christ's crucifixion. This offers a positive interpretation of the play's fatal close: the tragedy is a manifestation of God's will, a reminder of the coming redemption of humanity through Christianity. On the other hand, a non-Christian interpretation of Cordelia's sacrifice is also compelling. She lacks the Christian's reward in the afterlife because she is a pagan, thus her virtue is its own reward. Her conduct is therefore all the more stirring, and our admiration of her heroic courage is increased.

The sufferings of Lear and Gloucester, which they have brought upon themselves, may be compared to punishment for sins by God. They recognize that they are at fault and are then reconciled with their children, and this development suggests God's forgiveness for those who are penitent. Their forgiveness is accompanied by death, and this points up the doctrinal importance of the Christian afterlife and its eternal mercy. However, this promise is lacking in Lear's pagan world, and, as with Cordelia, a nonreligious interpretation could be that Lear's endurance is heroic in itself, and his triumph lies in his recognition and acceptance of his failings before he dies. Most commentators agree, in any case, that the suffering of the characters in *Lear* is finally redemptive, for it is heroic, it leads to heightened consciousness in Lear and Gloucester, and it provides the example of Edgar's and Cordelia's undiminished loyalty and love. Also, many commentators hold that Shakespeare intended Lear to die believing that Cordelia is alive, as his last words indicate, which implies a happy resolution in death akin to that of Gloucester, whose heart "burst smilingly" (5.3.198).

Another positive conclusion can be drawn from the tragedy. Politics are as important in *King Lear* as religion. In fact, in Shakespeare's time, the references to the end of the world carried a political implication, for people commonly believed that the world's end was more or less imminent, and that one of the symptoms of approaching apocalypse would be a collapse of social structures, including political bonds. Much reassurance was found in the peaceful accession of King JAMES I—civil war was feared at the time—with its promise for the unification of England and Scotland. The threat of civil war, several times alluded to in *Lear,* raises a point that was important to Shakespeare and which dominates the HISTORY PLAYS: the belief that personal immorality in the ruling class is a disease that spreads evil throughout society, in extreme cases causing it to fall apart. Though Lear, Gloucester, and Cordelia do not live to appreciate it, Britain at large is rescued from the evil that has overrun the highest reaches of its society; civil war in Britain is avoided, and the French invasion caused by Lear's lack of judgment is defeated by Albany. The play is thus supportive of civil authority; the catastrophe of Lear's reign might be compared, by the 17th-century playgoer, with the strength and harmony expected from that of James. It is worth noting that in 1606 *Lear* was performed at James's court on a very festive occasion, the day following Christmas.

Another point addressed in *King Lear* is that a sovereign is responsible for his subjects. Raving madly in the storm, Lear realizes that he had been unaware of hunger and homelessness when he was king, and he sees that his present experience could have been valuable to him as a ruler. He says to himself: "Take physic, Pomp; / Expose thyself to feel what wretches feel, / That thou mayst shake the superflux to them, / And show the Heavens more just" (3.4.33–36). Lear recognizes that his errors are more important than other people's because he is a king.

A more particular social question is also addressed in *King Lear.* In Shakespeare's day, the newly prosperous gentry and the commercially active bourgeoisie were rising in prosperity and power, largely at the expense of the old aristocracy. This conflict is plainly the cause of the extraordinary venom displayed by Kent toward Oswald in 2.2.13–81. Oswald is a caricature of a 17th-century social climber, as Kent's accusation, phrased largely in terms of social status, makes clear. Edmund also represents the new classes, with his lack of chivalric scruples and his concern for his own advancement. In his first soliloquy Edmund identifies himself with a typical modern rejection of tradition by declaring, "Thou, Nature, art my goddess" (1.2.1), a reference to the RENAISSANCE rediscovery of classical paganism and the sophisticated agnosticism that was thought to accompany it. In placing these sentiments in the mouth of a self-declared villain, Shakespeare stresses his alliance with the old world of the aristocracy, just as he does in ridiculing Oswald through Kent.

However, though *King Lear* may lend itself to numerous interpretations, Christian or humanistic, political or moral, our response to the play is largely governed by its conclusion. Act 5 brings no relief for our anguish, despite the expectations raised by the reunion of Lear and Cordelia. The finality of death may suggest that the play reflects a morbidly depressed response to life on Shakespeare's part (without denying that other plays express other responses). Such a viewpoint has led some to compare *Lear* to the Book of Job and see the play as an explication of the power of fate, or God. However, both Edgar and Albany survive to carry on, conscious of the fragility of happiness and on guard against the errors of Lear and Gloucester, for as Edgar (Albany, in some editions) says, "The weight of this sad time we must obey" (5.3.322).

The extraordinary woe that is at the heart of *King Lear* can make it a harrowing experience for audiences. Shakespeare maintains this atmosphere of wretched despair through a variety of subtle effects. Most striking perhaps is the repeated depiction of pain and disease, capped by Lear's madness and Gloucester's blinding but also represented by Edmund's self-mutilation in 2.1, Edgar's feigned lunacy, and Lear's convulsion of the throat known as *Hysterica passio* (2.4.55), among other instances. Further, painful metaphors of torment and sickness are extensively used. For instance, the Fool compares the rejected Lear to a bird that "had it[s] head bit off" (1.4.214); Edgar speaks vividly of self-mutilation, in 2.3.14–16; and Lear speaks of his daughters' rejection as a "mouth . . . tear[ing a] hand" (3.4.15). In a famous image, Gloucester compares humanity's relationship to the gods with that of "flies to wanton boys . . . They kill us for their sport" (4.1.36–37).

Another aspect of the theme of disease is the play's morbid attitude toward sex. In *King Lear* sexual love is seen as evil and is only presented in the monstrous rivalry of Regan and Goneril for Edmund. It is also seen as the source of other evils. The misdeeds of Lear's daughters are firmly connected by Lear to the sexual acts from which they were conceived, and Edgar points out that Edmund was the product of illicit sex. Also, in his disguise as Tom O'Bedlam, Edgar declares that intercourse, "the act of darkness" (3.4.85), is responsible for his painful madness. Lear goes so far as to condemn human procreation, demanding that the gods "Crack Nature's moulds, all germens spill at once / That makes ingrateful man!" (3.2.8–9). In the extreme, the raving Lear links female sexual anatomy with evil, saying, "there's hell, there's darkness, / There is the sulphurous pit—burning, scalding, / Stench, consumption; fie, fie, fie!" (4.6.126–128). This incrimination of a natural

drive is an indication of the troubled world in *King Lear* and of the disturbed minds of its inhabitants. Happiness is offered only in the isolated and asexual world of the reunited but imprisoned Lear and Cordelia, where all other human contact is willingly forsworn; the exhausted king declares that "Upon such sacrifices . . . / The Gods themselves throw incense" (5.3.20–21).

The play's treatment of psychological distortion is well served by its disjointed and varying tone. This is largely provided by its complex SUBPLOT, whose differing elements include Gloucester's blinding, Edgar's exile as mad Tom, and Regan and Goneril's sexual rivalry. The intercutting of these developments with Lear's story was once much criticized; early-19th-century commentators such as Charles LAMB declared that *Lear* was a bad play in theatrical terms, while acknowledging its power as poetry. This was long a traditionally accepted idea, influencing 20th-century critics to elaborately consider the plot's "failings," despite the play's unquestionable success with modern audiences.

The subplot actually anchors the play's dramatic structure. The wanderings of Edgar and Gloucester are presented in sequential incidents, as are the machinations of Edmund and the cruel sisters. Together they provide a well-defined structure that the main plot—Lear's foolish choice and subsequent isolation—does not offer. Indeed, the principal action can hardly be called a plot at all; it is simply a progression, taking the central character from vanity and folly through deepening madness to a recovered consciousness and ultimate collapse. As we watch this progression, we do not think about the next step in the plot so much as we simply observe Lear's personal qualities and contemplate their evolution. The events of Lear's progress are less important and are not presented in a structured way, unlike the plotting in, for example, *Julius Caesar*, but are indicated by discrete and almost unconnected subsidiary developments.

The play also offers disconcerting suggestions of comedy that complicate our response and thus increase its emotional power. In *King Lear* Shakespeare employed a number of elements traditionally associated with comedy: a double plot, the use of a jester to comment on the action, the use of disguise, the progression of the action from royal court to country and back to court, and the counterpoint of youth and age. Moreover, Kent's ridicule of Oswald, a number of Edgar's remarks as Tom O'Bedlam, and the Fool's routines are all quite funny. These elements suggest the potential for a different sort of story altogether, not a simple tale of evil triumphant.

King Lear is complex also in its repeated emotional polarities. We are presented with oppositions of weeping and laughing, silence and speech, honesty and guile, madness and intelligence, delusion and clearsightedness, love and hate. Cordelia's frankness and spirituality is contrasted with the deceit and lasciviousness of her sisters; Kent's moral firmness with Oswald's self-serving oiliness and his strength with Lear's weakness; the merciful Albany with the cruel Cornwall. Individual characters present contrasts within themselves as well, though the playwright is careful to motivate each change so as not to dilute a character's strength as a representative figure. Kent, for instance, announces that he will "other accents borrow / That can my speech defuse" (1.4.1–2), and he adopts a plainspoken prose and only reverts to verse when he cannot be heard by Lear or when he expresses his love and concern for his demented master, as in 3.2.42–49, 60–67. Edgar similarly effects prose as Tom O'Bedlam but speaks poetry as himself, and the hypocritical sisters use verse to flatter their father and prose to plot against him. *Lear*'s great range of characters stimulates our strong awareness of the play as a philosophical statement about the human condition.

SOURCES OF THE PLAY

The main plot of *King Lear* was well known in Shakespeare's day—at least 40 versions have been uncovered by scholars—but it is clear that the playwright relied chiefly on an earlier, anonymous play, KING LEIR (ca. 1590). This work contains the general story of Lear's relations with his daughters, though at the play's close King Leir is restored to his throne and Cordelia lives. Some scholars think Shakespeare may have acted in *King Leir* in the 1590s, playing a character corresponding to Kent, for a number of passages that are especially closely echoed in *Lear* are spoken when that figure is onstage.

Shakespeare also knew the story from an account in Raphael HOLINSHED's *Chronicles of England, Scotland, and Ireland* (2nd ed., 1587), which inspired several passages. Holinshed's account of Lear is based on the work of a medieval historian, GEOFFREY OF MONMOUTH. Details of Gloucester's attempted suicide were probably inspired by another story in Holinshed, that of a giant who was thrown to his death from the cliffs of Dover. John HIGGINS's version of the tale in A MIRROR FOR MAGISTRATES (1587) provided Shakespeare with a number of significant details, including France's praise of Cordelia's virtues. Other details can be ascribed to a variety of sources, most notably Edmund SPENSER's *The Faerie Queene* (1589), Ben JONSON's *Sejanus* (1605), Gerard LEGH's *Accedens of Armory* (1562), and, possibly, William CAMDEN's *Remaines* (1605).

Shakespeare found the subplot involving Gloucester, Edmund, and Edgar in a tale from Sir Philip SIDNEY's *Arcadia* (1590), about a king who is betrayed by one son and saved by another. It may also have influenced the main plot, for Sidney's tragic hero is not restored to his former glory, like King Leir, but dies of mingled joy and exhaustion, like Shakespeare's Gloucester. Also, Sidney's king is driven out into a storm, like Lear, and lives as a beggar, like Edgar. Another anecdote in *Arcadia* may have influenced Edmund's plot to disgrace Edgar, and a poem in *Arcadia* is a meditation on suicide that is echoed in several passages of the play.

Two other works contributed to the play's themes, though not to the actual plot: Samuel HARSNETT's *A Declaration of Egregious Popish Impostures* (1603), which provided the lore of demons for Edgar's assumed lunacy, and John FLORIO's English translation of the *Essays* of Michael de MONTAIGNE (1603), whose scepticism influenced Edmund's disdain for the conventional attitude toward illegitimacy, as well as his unscrupulous attitude toward morals. It is also possible that a contemporary case of insanity resembling Lear's (see ANNESLEY, BRIAN) may have sparked Shakespeare's imagination, for in no earlier version of the tale is the king mad.

TEXT OF THE PLAY

King Lear was written between the spring of 1603 and early 1606, for one of the play's sources—

Samuel Harsnett's book—was published in March 1603, and a play that was influenced by *Lear*—*The Fleir*, by Edward SHARPHAM—was registered for publication in May 1606. A more precise date is difficult to determine; some passages in the play seem to offer clues, but no agreement can be reached. Similarly, relationships between *Lear* and other works published between 1603 and 1606 are generally problematic, as it is impossible to tell which is in debt to which.

The play was first published in 1608 by Nathaniel BUTTER in a QUARTO edition known as Q1. Twelve copies of Q1 exist, but they encompass 10 slightly different texts, since proofreading and correction were carried on simultaneously with printing. Q1 is sometimes called the "Pied Bull Quarto" because its title page refers to Butter's shop "at the signe of the Pide Bull." Q1 is a BAD QUARTO, assembled from the recollections of spectators or of actors who had performed in the play, but scholars differ in their conclusions about who these reporters were and whether or not they had access to a manuscript. It is a poor text with many errors, little punctuation, missing or inadequate stage directions, and many passages of verse set as prose and vice versa. A second quarto (Q2), printed from a copy of Q1, was dated 1608 and attributed to Butter, but it was actually produced in 1619 as part of the pirated FALSE FOLIO.

King Lear appears in the FIRST FOLIO (1623), and this version (F) is a far better text than Q1, incorporating many corrections, including amplified stage directions. Most significantly, it is a radically altered script. More than 300 lines of dialogue from Q1 are omitted in F—including a number of significant passages—and about 100 lines are added, including Lear's final lines (5.3.309–310).

It is generally believed that the omissions from Q1 reflect shortening made for performances sometime between 1608 and 1623, and that the additions are Shakespeare's, made before he retired around 1613. Scholars are divided on the form in which the printers of the Folio received the alterations, but the most widely accepted theory is that F was printed from a copy of Q1 that had been heavily annotated with amendments and references from the PROMPTBOOK used by the KING'S MEN. However, a recently popular theory holds that the Folio text represents a rewriting of the play by Shakespeare, from which it follows that there exist two different *King Lears*, each distinctive in tone and emphasis. One edition of Shakespeare's works, that of Oxford University Press (1986), prints them as such, though most editors have combined the two in a single text that omits nothing of consequence while relying on F, the superior text, where the two conflict.

THEATRICAL HISTORY

The earliest known performance of *King Lear* is recorded in the publisher's registration of the play, which asserts that it was performed at the court of King James on December 26, 1606. Scholars believe that the play was not well received in Shakespeare's day, for there are few surviving references to it in contemporary documents. However, it is known that Richard BURBAGE was the original Lear.

After the 1660 reopening of the English theaters—they had been closed during the Puritan Revolution—*Lear* was staged only twice, in 1660 (by William DAVENANT) and 1675. It was replaced in 1681 by an adaptation, Nahum TATE's *History of King Lear*. Tate's *Lear* retained much Shakespearean dialogue, but amid vast changes in plot, including a happy ending in which Lear is restored to his throne. Thomas BETTERTON played Lear for Tate. Though modern commentators condemn this version as a travesty, it was one of the most successful plays in the history of the English theater, continuing to be staged—with Shakespeare's text sometimes restored in varying degrees—until as late as 1843 (and occasionally in modern times as an historical curiosity). Published, Tate's *Lear* went through 22 editions before the end of the 18th century.

The restoration of Shakespeare's text began with David GARRICK's production of 1742, and the process was furthered by George COLMAN (though he also added his own alterations) in 1768. In the late 18th and early 19th centuries the play was suppressed by the government, which disliked its focus on a mad monarch at a time when King George III was insane. It reappeared in 1809 in a version by John Philip KEMBLE that restored most of Tate's text. Edmund KEAN, under the influence of the critics

Charles LAMB and William HAZLITT, restored Lear's death in his production of 1823, though the text was still largely Tate's. Not until 1838 were Tate's words completely removed in Charles William MACREADY's production, though Gloucester's travails were still omitted. It remained for Samuel PHELPS to produce a genuinely Shakespearean version in 1845. Edwin BOOTH played Lear with Tate's text early in his career, but by 1876 he was presenting Shakespeare's play. No subsequent production reverted to Tate, but considerable editing of the original text remained common; Henry IRVING, for instance, cut more than half the play in his presentation of 1892 that starred himself and Ellen TERRY.

In the 20th century *King Lear* was extremely popular. Most leading actors played Lear; among the most notable were Robert Bruce MANTELL early in the century; John GIELGUD and Donald WOLFIT in the 1940s; Michael REDGRAVE, Orson WELLES, and Charles LAUGHTON in the 1950s; Paul SCOFIELD, especially in a famed 1962 staging by Peter BROOK; and James Earl JONES in Joseph PAPP's production of 1973. The role of Cordelia attracted leading actresses, among them Peggy ASHCROFT and Zoë CALDWELL. Recent productions include the OLD VIC THEATRE staging directed by Peter HALL in 1997 and the 2002 presentation at Stratford, Ontario, directed by Jonathan MILLER and starring Christopher PLUMMER.

Lear has been presented on FILM eight times; the two most famous, by Brook and the Russian Grigori KOZINTSEV, were made simultaneously as the two directors, shooting in Denmark and Russia, respectively, corresponded, comparing notes on their projects (1969). The play has been made for TELEVISION five times. Also, Akira KUROSAWA's *Ran* (1985) is based on *Lear*. The play has also inspired six OPERAS—though only one, by Aribert REIMANN (1978), has entered the general operatic repertoire—and at least one well-known orchestral work, the *King Lear Overture* by Hector BERLIOZ (1831).

CHARACTERS

Albany, Duke of   Character in *King Lear*, the virtuous but weak husband of Lear's villainous daughter, Goneril. Albany, who does not discover his wife's wickedness until too late, eventually aids the banished Lear and formally restores him to power just before his death. In this way he represents an instance of moral growth in a degraded world. At the play's close he is the ruler of Britain, sharing power with Edgar and Kent and intent on repairing the damage to the state that Lear's crisis has produced. In the final lines, Albany offers a possible lesson to be drawn from the tragedy, saying, "The weight of this sad time we must obey" (5.3.322); he recognizes the need to be aware of human susceptibility to catastrophic error, as Lear did not. (Albany's lines here are often given to Edgar, as in the FIRST FOLIO text.)

In his early appearances Albany is ineffectual. He is governed entirely by his wife, who dismisses his question about her rift with Lear by curtly ordering, "Never afflict yourself to know more of it" (1.4.289). After Act 1 he does not reappear until 4.2, when, having learned of the treacherous blinding of Gloucester, he denounces Goneril as an evildoer. "You are not worth the dust which the rude wind / Blows in your face," he declares (4.2.30–31). Nevertheless, he goes along with her alliance with Edmund against Cordelia's French army, though he privately asserts his intention to revenge Gloucester. Informed by Edgar of Edmund and Goneril's plot against his own life, Albany exposes the villains in 5.3. By this time Albany is clearly intent on rectifying the misdeeds of his wife and her allies, but his earlier weakness has already helped them. His poor judgment in patriotically fighting the French has an unintended and fatal result when Edmund gains control of Lear and Cordelia. Thus, though well-intentioned and finally benevolent, Albany reinforces the play's theme of human fallibility.

Burgundy, Duke of   Minor character in *King Lear*, a suitor who rejects Cordelia when she is disinherited by King Lear. Burgundy appears only in 1.1; he and the King of France have been summoned to determine which of them will marry Lear's youngest daughter and thus govern one-third of Britain. Burgundy's concern is with a politically and materially advantageous match, and when Cordelia is disinherited he simply loses interest in her. She dismisses his frank but polite apology coolly, saying, "Peace be with Burgundy! / Since that respect and fortunes are his love, / I shall not be his wife" (1.1.246–248). Burgundy's conventionally greedy behavior contrasts tellingly with the response of France, who recognizes Cordelia's virtues and marries her.

The Duke's equal footing with the King of France reflects a reality of medieval Europe: The Duchy of Burgundy, though formally a client state of FRANCE, was an independent and wealthy country (as evident in *1 Henry VI* and the character of Philip, Duke of Burgundy). However, this medieval context is an anachronism, for in the early period in which *King Lear* is set, the Duchy of Burgundy did not yet exist.

Caius In *King Lear*, the name adopted by the Earl of Kent as part of his disguise as a yeoman. This Roman name is inappropriate to the pre-Roman Britain in which the play is ostensibly set, but such anachronisms abound in *King Lear* and the playwright doubtless felt that "Caius" was appropriately antique for the ancient world in which the work is set. However, Kent uses his alias only at the very close of the play, in 5.3.282, where it attracts little notice. Shakespeare may have thought he had used it earlier; the slip would be typical of the many small errors and inconsistencies to which he was inclined.

Cordelia Character in *King Lear*, the virtuous daughter whom King Lear mistakenly rejects. Knowing she will marry, Cordelia refuses to assert that all of her love will forever go to her father, unlike Regan and Goneril, her hypocritical sisters. Lear mistakes Cordelia's honesty for a lack of affection and disinherits her, though the King of France recognizes her innate worth and marries her anyway. She leaves Britain with him at the end of 1.1 and does not reappear until Act 4, when she arrives with an army. She intends to restore her father to his throne, for he has been humiliated and banished to the wilderness by Regan and Goneril. Lear and Cordelia are reunited, but they are nonetheless defeated in battle, and the villainous Edmund imprisons them and orders their murder, in 5.3. Although Edmund is defeated by Edgar, it is too late; the assassin has killed Cordelia, though Lear kills him. In the play's final episode, Lear grieves over his daughter's corpse and dies of a broken heart.

During her long absence from the play we are not permitted to forget Cordelia, for her goodness and self-sacrifice are central to the tragedy: The Fool is said to have "much pined away" for her, in 1.4.72; in 2.2, the loyal Kent reveals that she knows of Lear's situation; Lear himself refers to her in 2.4.211; and her invasion force is mentioned several times, beginning in 3.1.30.

Many commentators believe that Shakespeare specifically intended Cordelia as an example of the Christian virtues of self-sacrifice and acceptance of God's will. Cordelia accepts her undeserved fate while she displays undiminished love for her erring father. In this view she is a Christlike figure in a pagan world who offers a suggestion of Christianity's coming redemption of humanity. Her death thus symbolizes Christ's crucifixion, and the tragedy's lesson is the mysterious nature of God's will.

A nonreligious interpretation of Cordelia's sacrifice is also proposed by many critics, who see her virtue as its own reward, for as a pagan she lacks the Christian's promise of recompense in the afterlife. In this humanistic view her goodness inspires our admiration all the more for being unrewarded, and the pure light of her courage offers the most compelling sense that the play's tragedy is not utterly futile. Also, many critics hold that Shakespeare intended Lear to die believing that Cordelia is still alive, in which case his own fate is greatly eased, and we can feel more strongly the redemptive effect of her virtues. A final variation on her importance does not diminish it: Some writers hold that *King Lear* reflects a despairing and pessimistic view of life that denies aid for human folly in a tragic universe. In this interpretation Cordelia's virtues, combined with the injustice of both her rejection by her father and her ultimate death, offer striking confirmation of the dire point of view attributed to the playwright.

In almost any view, Cordelia's manifest virtue is a dominating element of the play, giving her an importance seemingly unjustified by her relatively few appearances on stage. In her pure honesty and unqualified love she seems almost devoid of ordinary human personality traits, and her saintly qualities are especially stressed by the Gentleman (1) who reports on her in 4.3, preparing the audience for her return to the drama. In a passage rich in imagery and rhetoric, he describes her mingled joy and sorrow at news of Lear, saying, for instance, ". . . she shook / The holy water from her heavenly eyes" (4.3.29–30). Later she is described as one "Who redeems nature from the general curse" (4.6.203). Evoked in these terms, Cordelia resembles an angel more than she does a worldly character. Her vague personality contributes to our sense of dislocation in *King Lear*. She is remote from the more active figures, even the fighters against evil, Edgar, Kent, and Albany, and this draws attention to the failure of human interaction in the play's tragic universe.

Cordelia may also be seen in a more human light. In fact, some writers declare that she exhibits a prideful stubbornness in Act 1, only adopting an attitude of loving generosity when she sees the damage that has been done. In this light her moral progress may be said to parallel that of her father. This is a minority view, however, for most commentators feel that Shakespeare intended her initial insistence on honesty to be an obvious virtue.

Cornwall, Duke of Character in *King Lear*, the villainous husband of King Lear's usurping daughter Regan. Cornwall takes a prominent part in the evil deeds that spark much of the play's action. In 2.1 he declares that Edgar, who has been falsely accused of a murder plot against his father, Gloucester, shall be executed, and he adopts as a follower Edgar's persecutor, Edmund. He places Lear's loyal follower Kent in the stocks, and he supports his wife and his sister-in-law Goneril in their expulsion of Lear. At his most cruel, in 3.7 he puts out Gloucester's eyes when the earl remains loyal to the outcast former king. For this offense he is killed by an appalled Servant. His death is proof that the triumph of villainy will not be total, but at the same time the enormity of his final deed contributes greatly to the general atmosphere of horror that so distinguishes the play.

Curan Minor character in *King Lear*, a follower of the Earl of Gloucester. In 2.1 Curan tells Edmund of

a rumor that the Dukes of Cornwall and Albany—the husbands of Regan and Goneril, to whom King Lear has foolishly given power—are soon to fall into civil war. This is the first hint that Lear's error, already disastrous for him personally, is also a potential catastrophe for the kingdom as a whole.

Doctor Character in *King Lear*, a physician who reports to Cordelia on the condition of her father, King Lear. In 4.4 he tells Cordelia that Lear's sanity can be restored through rest, saying, "Our foster-nurse of nature is repose" (4.4.12). He assures her that he can provide drugs to sedate the mad king. Later he oversees the touching reunion of the rested Lear with his daughter. He ends the meeting for the good of his patient, but again reassures Cordelia that "the great rage . . . is kill'd in him" (4.7.78–79). His kindly ministrations contrast with the evil that has permeated Lear's world to this point.

Edgar Character in *King Lear*, the banished son of the Earl of Gloucester. Misled by his illegitimate son Edmund, Gloucester formally exiles Edgar to the wilderness; this action parallels King Lear's rejection of his daughter Cordelia. In 2.3, under threat of execution, Edgar disguises himself as a wandering lunatic. When Lear is banished by his villainous daughters, the disguised Edgar accompanies him, in 3.4 and 3.6. When Gloucester is blinded and expelled because he has remained loyal to Lear, Edgar, still disguised, becomes his father's guide in 4.1 and saves him from suicide and a murder attempt by Oswald in 4.6. In Act 5 Edgar finally takes control of the play, exposing Edmund and Goneril's plot to murder the Duke of Albany and defeating Edmund in a trial by combat. At the play's close Edgar is invited by Albany to share in the rule of Britain; with his final lines, he offers a possible lesson to be drawn from the play—that we must be aware of our human susceptibility to folly, as Lear was not—saying, "The weight of this sad time we must obey" (5.3.322). (In some editions these lines are given to Albany, following the common practice in ELIZABETHAN DRAMA of assigning the closing lines of a play to the character of the highest social rank among those on stage at the time—in this case Albany, who is a duke.)

As the insane Tom O'Bedlam, Edgar embodies the play's theme of disease and misery as products and emblems of human folly. Tom blames his insanity on his sexual promiscuity, thus illustrating the morbid attitude toward sex that permeates the world of the play. Similarly, when he is again himself, Edgar attributes Gloucester's tragedy to "The dark and vicious place" (5.3.171) where Edmund was conceived, that is, to sex outside of marriage.

On the other hand, Edgar's loving loyalty to his father parallels Cordelia's to Lear. Both present a Christlike willingness to sacrifice themselves that is often cited as a lesson in accepting the will of God. Even from a nonreligious viewpoint, Edgar is an agent of redemption, preserving order and goodness where chaos and evil have threatened by acting as a guide and savior first for Lear, then for his father, and finally for Britain as a whole. When he saves his father from suicide in 4.6, he offers a way to renew acceptance of life. Deceiving Gloucester into believing he has jumped from a cliff and lived, Edgar declares his father's survival to be "a miracle" (4.6.55); the blind man concludes that he should not give in to despair, but endure. Thus, Edgar illuminates a basic principle that is at the core of the tragedy; we must struggle to make the best of our lives, accepting death only when its time comes. As he says to his father, "Men must endure / Their going hence, even as their coming hither: / Ripeness is all" (5.2.9–11).

Edmund   Character in *King Lear*, the unscrupulous and ambitious illegitimate son of the Earl of Gloucester. Edmund conspires against his legitimate brother Edgar, who is banished into the wilderness in 2.1; he betrays his father to King Lear's evil daughter Regan and her husband, the Duke of Cornwall, who puts out the old man's eyes in 3.7; and he pursues a love affair with Lear's other daughter Goneril, with whom, in 4.2, he plots to murder her husband, the Duke of Albany. When Cornwall is killed, the widowed Regan schemes to take Edmund from Goneril, and this unsavory love triangle is an important part of the play's atmosphere of moral collapse.

In Act 5 Edmund leads Cornwall's army against the supporters of Lear's faithful daughter Cordelia; victorious, he thwarts Albany's plans for mercy and imprisons Lear and Cordelia, ordering their execution. Edgar learns of the plot against Albany, charges Edmund with treason, and challenges him to a trial by combat, wounding him fatally. The dying Edmund confesses his intention toward Lear, but it is too late to prevent Cordelia's death, and Lear dies of a broken heart soon thereafter.

Edmund's villainy is a central element in *King Lear*; his schemes are crisply executed and do much to provide a dramatic structure in the SUBPLOT that the more idea-oriented main story lacks. However, Edmund is a stereotypical villain with little human complexity—his deeds are more interesting than he is himself—and his schemes are effective due to the moral weakness of others, not his compelling personality. His declaration of repentance—"some good I mean to do / Despite of mine own nature" (5.3.242–243)—is perfunctory and unconvincing. It serves to spark the final episode—Lear's fatal grief—after which Edmund is carried away to die. Albany's brusque dismissal of the news of his death demonstrates the extent of the villain's defeat; compared to the lessons to be absorbed from Lear's end, Edmund's demise is "but a trifle here" (5.3.294).

Shakespeare identified Edmund's unscrupulous ambition with a troubling social phenomenon of his own day: the rise of the new commercially active classes—the bourgeoisie of the cities and the lesser landowners, or gentry, of the countryside. The success of these groups depended on their willingness to engage in trade and banking, as opposed to the traditional dependence on the land, and in this they were at odds with the great territorial nobles of the old aristocracy. A worldly emphasis on practical finance characterized the commercial classes, and this was regarded as unscrupulous by hostile eyes. From this point of view, Edmund represents the new man in his lack of chivalric scruples and his concern for his own advancement.

Traditionalists conventionally associated such an attitude with a new, "modern" strain of thought, and Edmund quite plainly identifies himself with this new mode. In his first soliloquy he declares, "Thou, Nature, art my goddess" (1.2.1), boldly stating his independence of "the plague of custom" (1.2.3) and its man-made moral standards. Such sophisticated agnosticism arose in part from the RENAISSANCE rediscovery of classical paganism, and it was reflected in such works as the *Essays* of MONTAIGNE, which Shakespeare had read and which he admired in some respects. However, in placing these sentiments in the mouth of a self-proclaimed villain, Shakespeare declares his alliance with the old world of the aristocracy that is quite clearly represented by Lear, Gloucester, and Edgar, Edmund's enemies.

Fool Character in *King Lear,* the court jester or FOOL to King Lear. The Fool sees that Lear should not have rejected Cordelia and placed himself in the power of Regan and Goneril, and he repeatedly reminds his master of this. He employs barbed quips, for instance, having caused Lear to observe that "nothing can be made out of nothing," the Fool remarks, ". . . so much the rent of his land comes to" (1.4.130–132). He also utters simple

Nicholas Pennell as the Fool in the 1985 Stratford (Ontario) festival production of *King Lear. (Photograph by David Cooper)*

truths, such as "Thou should'st not have been old till thou hadst been wise" (1.5.41–42). He strives to use his wit to ease Lear's mind as the king goes insane, and he accompanies him into the stormy wilderness in Act 3. The Fool is last seen leaving with Lear and Kent after Gloucester has warned them of a murder plot against the king. His last line, "And I'll go to bed at noon" (3.6.83), suggests an early death, but his fate is not reported.

The Fool is deeply moved by Lear's plight, but he is capable of detachment from it. Lear's Fool shares with other Shakespearean jesters, such as Feste and Touchstone, an irony that permits him to comment on the action of the play, as does a CHORUS. With jokes, riddles, and scraps of SONG, he clarifies the central situation by commenting on it more intelligently than the other characters. Especially pertinent is his observation, ". . . the Fool will stay, / And let the wise man fly" (2.4.79–80); with it he makes a declaration of loyalty that helps contrast a moral world with the tragic one that dominates the play. Similarly, his sanity is a foil for Lear's increasing disintegration.

The Fool is closely associated with Cordelia at two significant points. Before his first entrance, he is said in 1.4.72 to have "much pined away" for her, the first mention of Lear's daughter since her departure in 1.1. At the play's close, Lear, grieving over Cordelia's corpse, says, "And my poor fool is hang'd" (5.3.304). "Fool" was a common term of endearment in Shakespeare's day, and Lear seems to be referring to his lost daughter (who has in fact been hanged), but the line provides an occasion to compare the two characters. The Fool resembles Cordelia in both his devotion to Lear and his commitment to a truthful assessment of life. He replaces her as the exponent of these virtues during her long absence from the play. In fact, some scholars suggest that the two roles may have been taken by the same actor in the original productions by the KING'S MEN. Others, however, hold that the part of the Fool was probably played by the famed comedian Robert ARMIN, whose notoriety would have made him an unlikely Cordelia.

France, King of Character in *King Lear,* the suitor and later the husband of Cordelia, King

Lear's rejected daughter. France, as the king is called, appears only in 1.1. He recognizes the honesty and virtue in Cordelia and thus emphasizes Lear's moral blindness. He agrees to marry her, saying "She is herself a dowry" (1.1.240), and takes her back to FRANCE. Cordelia is thus absent for most of the action as her sisters humiliate and banish their father. The Earl of Kent soon knows that "from France there comes a power" (3.1.30) to aid Lear, but France himself does not reappear; he has returned home to deal with "something he left imperfect in the state" (4.3.3), while a French general unsuccessfully attempts to reestablish Lear on the throne. The subject of foreign invasion was a touchy one in Shakespeare's day because Protestant England felt threatened by Catholic enemies, including France, and scholars believe that the playwright found it expedient, in view of government CENSORSHIP, to de-emphasize the role of France, both man and country, in *King Lear*.

Gentleman (1)   Minor character in *King Lear*, a follower of Lear. The Gentleman assists the loyal Kent in his efforts to aid the wandering and insane king. Primarily a useful attendant, the Gentleman delivers two important descriptions that help form the audience's responses to the play in significant ways. In 3.1 he reports vividly to Kent on Lear's raging in the storm and prepares the audience for the wild scene to follow. In 4.3 he movingly describes Cordelia's haunting response to the news of her wretched father. Rich in religious imagery, this passage provides a strong sense of Cordelia's saintly nature, a central image of the play. In 4.6 the Gentleman leads a search party, sent by Cordelia, that finds Lear.

Gentleman (2)   Minor character in *King Lear*, a follower of the Duke of Albany. In 5.3 the horrified Gentleman announces the deaths of Goneril and Regan. Goneril has stabbed herself after confessing that she poisoned Regan. The character adds to the increasing hysteria of the final scene.

Gloucester, Earl of   Character in *King Lear*, father of Edgar and Edmund. Gloucester is the central figure of the play's SUBPLOT, in which his illegitimate

son Edmund's villainy and his own error lead him to disaster and suffering from which he recovers only to die. This progression parallels the story of King Lear in the main plot. Deceived by Edmund, who wants to inherit the earldom, Gloucester disinherits and banishes his legitimate son Edgar. Because Gloucester is faithful to the outcast and insane Lear, Edmund turns him over to Lear's enemy, the Duke of Cornwall, who puts out Gloucester's eyes and banishes him into the wilderness. Edgar, disguised as a wandering lunatic, tends to his father. He saves him from suicide, in 4.6, and renews in him the strength to endure. Finally, however, when Gloucester learns Edgar's identity, the old man dies; "his flaw'd heart, . . . 'Twixt two extremes of passion, joy and grief, / Burst smilingly" (5.3.195—198).

Gloucester's tale offers a significant parallel to that of Lear; like the king's, Gloucester's tragedy is self-induced, for his actual blinding is preceded by figurative blindness when he fails to see either Edgar's virtue or Edmund's villainy. Like Lear, Gloucester recognizes his error—"I stumbled when I saw" (4.1.19), he confesses—when it is too late. His helpless wanderings, dependent on the aid of a seeming lunatic, suggest powerfully the similar straits of the mad king. The similarity between the two reaches a horrific climax, in 4.6, when they encounter each other on the beach at DOVER; it is one of the most touching passages in Shakespeare. The mad and the blind old men recognize each other and acknowledge their joint status as victims; their consciousness, though it is flawed by their handicaps, is clearly more acute than it was before.

Their parallel tales, and the close sympathy of Lear and Gloucester when they meet, is highly significant for our interpretation of the play's final moments. Gloucester's death immediately precedes Lear's at the close of the play, and because their parallel development has been stressed, we may read in the king's death the same "extremes of passion" and presume that his heart, too, "burst smilingly." Thus, Gloucester's tragedy helps confirm the nobility of human suffering, a central message of the play.

Goneril   Character in *King Lear*, one of the villainous daughters of King Lear. Goneril and her sister Regan declare their great love for Lear in 1.1, when in fact they merely want the portion of his kingdom that he has foolishly promised to whichever daughter can assure him she loves him most. They share the prize when their honest younger sister Cordelia enrages the king with a frank admission that her love will be given in part to her future husband. Goneril takes the lead in the two sisters' villainy. She introduces the idea of humiliating Lear in 1.1, and she orders her steward, Oswald, to commence the practice in 1.3. In 1.4 she starts the dispute over Lear's followers that sends the ex-king fleeing into the storm, where he descends into madness. In 4.2 Goneril's wickedness becomes more pronounced as she enters into a love affair with the ambitious Edmund and hints at the existence of a murder plot against her husband, the virtuous but weak Duke of Albany. She and Regan both desire Edmund, and Goneril declares that she would rather lose the battle against the avenging forces led by Cordelia than lose Edmund to her sister. This rivalry depicts the vicious sexuality that is part of the play's general atmosphere of moral and physical unhealthiness. When Goneril and Edmund's plot against Albany is exposed, she poisons Regan and then commits suicide as the Gentleman (2) reports in 5.3.225–226.

Goneril's extravagantly evil nature is so boldly and unsubtly drawn that only her greater aggression distinguishes her from her sister. Her manipulation of her husband foreshadows Shakespeare's Lady Macbeth, but Goneril, a less-sophisticated creation, is simply an imitation of a standard male villain, cruel and ambitious. Unlike Lady Macbeth, she cannot compare herself with conventional femininity, nor does she succumb to illness through a bad conscience, for she is a much less complex character and serves chiefly as an emblem of evil.

Herald Minor character in *King Lear*, an official at the duel in which Edgar kills Edmund. In 5.3.110–116 the Herald announces to the troops of Albany, Goneril, and Regan that Edmund will defend himself against any challenger who dares to assert that "he is a manifould traitor" (5.3.112), as Albany has said someone intends to do. When Edgar, disguised, appears, the Herald formally asks him to identify himself, though once Edgar replies

his answer is taken up by Albany and Edmund, and the Herald is not heard from again. His small part helps create a sense of chivalrous order to the final retribution upon Edmund.

Kent, Earl of Character in *King Lear*, nobleman faithful to King Lear. Kent attempts to dissuade the king from his catastrophic decision to banish Cordelia when she honestly admits that her love will go to her husband as well as her father, but Lear banishes him as well for interfering. Kent then disguises himself and attempts to assist Lear when he is rejected by his other daughters, Regan and Goneril. He succeeds in keeping Lear safe from possible murder, and he reunites the king and Cordelia at DOVER. His conflict with Goneril's steward Oswald stresses an important value in the play, the association of virtue with gentlemanly behavior. Kent's steadfast honesty and loyalty is contrasted with the courtier's self-serving ambition. However, when Cordelia's invasion fails and she and Lear are captured by Edmund, Kent is helpless. As he witnesses Lear's death at the play's close, he exclaims, "Break, heart; I prithee, break!" (5.3.311). Whether he refers to his own heart or Lear's, this forsaken cry is emblematic of the sorrowful view of humanity's plight that is an important theme of the play. Yet Kent's final declaration of his own imminent death, "I have a journey, sir, shortly to go; / My master calls me, I must not say no" (5.3.320–321) also contributes to the play's sense of the nobility of human suffering.

Kent corresponds to a character named Perillus in Shakespeare's chief source for *Lear*, the play KING LEIR (ca. 1588). Some scholars think Shakespeare may have played Perillus for the CHAMBERLAIN'S MEN in the 1590s, for a number of passages in the older play are especially closely echoed in *Lear* when Kent is onstage.

Knight Minor character in *King Lear*, a follower of King Lear. In 1.4 the Knight is sent by Lear to summon Oswald, steward to the king's ungrateful daughter Goneril. He returns to report that Oswald insolently refuses to come, and he goes on to remark that "your Highness is not entertain'd with that ceremonious affection as you were wont"

(1.4.56–57). This summarizes the main plot so far: Goneril and her sister Regan are purposefully humiliating the king. The Knight also mentions Cordelia, the virtuous daughter whom Lear had rejected in 1.1, and reminds us that the king's plight lies in his own foolishness. Thus the Knight serves to mark the plot's development just before it intensifies with Lear's expulsion into the wilderness in the next scene.

Lear Title character of *King Lear*, an ancient king of Britain. Lear rejects Cordelia, his only honest daughter, when he mistakes her frankness for a lack of affection. He is then rejected by his other two daughters, Regan and Goneril, to whom he has granted his kingdom, and finds himself wandering in the wilderness, outcast and insane. His prideful wrath has blinded him to the difference between good and evil, but before the play's end he recovers his sanity in part, although too late to prevent the tragedy of Cordelia's death. However, in the course of his trials he does come to recognize his failings, which constitutes the play's most important lesson.

Lear's descent into madness, the central event of the play, illustrates the extent to which humanity can be degraded by its errors. Lear is both victim and perpetrator, for his own egocentricity has sparked the events that lead to his collapse; his ensuing suffering is a result of his inadequacy as a human being. Thus his story presents to us a powerful demonstration of humanity's frailty and the consequent potential for tragedy in life.

Our horror at Lear's tale is alleviated somewhat by his partial recognition and acceptance of his failings. Lear's trials have been variously interpreted. They may be seen as comparable to God's punishment for sins; his recognition of his fault is followed by reconciliation with Cordelia, which is suggestive of God's forgiveness following a sinner's repentance. That the relief is accompanied by death suggests the importance of the Christian afterlife and its eternal mercy, but this promise is lacking in Lear's pagan world. In a nonreligious interpretation, Lear's endurance is heroic in itself, and his triumph lies in his acceptance of his errors before he dies. These two interpretations are not, of course, mutually exclusive: Lear is heroic in both senses.

Also, most commentators agree that Lear's suffering is finally redemptive, in that it leads to heightened consciousness on his part. Further, Lear's last words seem to indicate (though the question is disputed) that he dies believing that Cordelia is alive, which implies a happy resolution in death akin to that of Gloucester, whose heart "Burst smilingly" (5.3.198), and whose sufferings conspicuously parallel Lear's.

In the course of his wanderings, both physical and mental, the distracted Lear is able to understand his folly. He first recognizes a general lack in his conduct as a ruler. Raving madly in the storm, Lear suddenly realizes that he had been previously unaware of hunger and homelessness, and he sees that the knowledge would have been valuable to him as king. He tells himself, "Expose thyself to feel what wretches feel, / That thou mayst shake the superflux to them, / And show the Heavens more just" (3.4.34–36).

Lear comes to a more personal acknowledgment of fault, though his progress is fitful. At first, his guilt takes an unhealthy, morbid form, as he castigates himself for having fathered his daughters, seeing the fault in the sexual process rather than in his egotistical demands. While still on the stormy moor, he declares his torment to be "Judicious punishment! 'twas this flesh begot / Those pelican daughters" (3.4.73–74). He elaborates on these sentiments when he equates female sexuality with the torments of hell, in 4.6.117–128. Lear's attitude toward sex—also displayed by Edgar—is evidence of the unhealthy mental and moral state of the play's world.

However, before his lowest point, Lear learns of Cordelia's faithfulness and realizes the wrong he has done her. As Kent reports, "burning shame" (4.3.46) drives him from her camp. While wandering in the fields nearby, he encounters the blinded Gloucester and, stirred by the sight of another sufferer, acknowledges his own weakness—"they told me I was every thing," he says of his former courtly flatterers, adding sardonically, "'tis a lie, I am not ague-proof" (4.6.104–105). Later, as part of his remarks on patience, he declares the weakness of all humanity, firmly including himself. He is raving, but the tone of his lament is clear enough; the arrogance that informed his earlier vow of revenge is entirely gone. Finally, in Cordelia's presence, he declares himself "a very foolish fond old man" (4.7.60) and admits that he has wronged her. He asks her to "forget and forgive" (4.7.84), and later, as father and daughter are taken to prison, he is pleased at the prospect of perpetual atonement: "I'll kneel down, / And ask of thee forgiveness: so we'll live . . ." (5.3.10–11).

Still, his insight is at best flawed. That a catastrophe and such a great degree of unhappiness has been necessary to elicit in Lear the acknowledgment of his faults and the existence of human ingratitude has been held against him by many readers. Shakespeare accepted no simple views on the complexities of life, and Lear is distinctly not a perfectly reformed man. Strikingly, no trace of guilt is found in his grief over Cordelia's death, and his enthusiasm for imprisonment with her is disturbingly egocentric in his lack of any sense of her life, as was his original demand for love, in 1.1. This point has been central to much recent feminist criticism of the play. However, Cordelia acquiesces, and so do most audiences; the play's emphasis on forgiveness and redemption seems clear, and in this light, Lear's residual defects are perhaps best viewed as evidence of Shakespeare's honesty about human frailty. Finally, *King Lear* is a play that raises more questions than it answers, and the extent to which Lear's tragedy is illuminating to him—as opposed to us, for its potential for illumination is unquestionably clear—remains for us to contemplate.

Shakespeare doubtless believed that there was a historical king of Britain named Lear, as is recorded in his sources, but he is in fact a mythical figure. The name derives from a Celtic god of the sea, Llyr. The legendary king is reported to have founded the town of Leicester, whose name is related to his own (Lear + *castrum*, Latin for "camp").

Messenger (1) Minor character in *King Lear*, a servant of Regan. In 4.2 the Messenger interrupts a dispute between Goneril and Albany with the news that Gloucester has been blinded and Cornwall is dead. Goneril immediately withdraws to plan her selfish response to the latter event, in contrast to her husband's shocked dismay over the former. The Messenger then adds that Gloucester had been betrayed by his son Edmund. The episode stresses the evil that Albany realizes he must oppose as the play approaches its climax.

Messenger (2) Minor character in *King Lear*, a follower of Cordelia. In 4.4 the Messenger brings his mistress the news that the armies of Goneril and Regan are approaching. His brief announcement immediately throws the newly arrived Cordelia into the fury of battle, thereby increasing the play's pace as it reaches its climax.

Officer (1) Minor character in *King Lear*, the murderer of King Lear's daughter Cordelia. In 5.3 Edmund orders the Officer, a captain (designated as "Captain" in some editions), to kill the captured king and his daughter, hanging Cordelia to make her death seem a suicide. The officer is a petty representative of the evil that permeates the play. He responds to Edmund's promise of reward in a cynically mercenary spirit, saying, "I cannot draw a cart nor eat dried oats; / If it be man's work I'll do 't" (5.3.39–40). He succeeds in disposing of Cordelia, but he is killed by her father when he does so, as we learn from Lear himself in 5.3.273.

Officer (2) Any of several minor characters in *King Lear*, followers of the Duke of Albany. In 5.3.109 an Officer relays Albany's order for a trumpet blast. A little later, an Officer (perhaps the same one) is sent after the fleeing Goneril, but he does not speak. When it is learned that an assassin has been ordered to kill Cordelia and Lear, a different Officer (the pursuer of Goneril does not return) is sent to prevent him. He returns and confirms, in half a line (5.3.274), Lear's account of how he killed Cordelia's murderer. The Officers, whether two or three in number, function merely to swell the ranks of the victorious Albany's entourage in the busy climactic moments of the play.

Old Man Minor character in *King Lear*, a vassal of the Earl of Gloucester. In 4.1 the Old Man escorts the blind Gloucester who has had his eyes put out by the evil Duke of Cornwall. The demoralized and fatalistic Gloucester orders him away, but the Old Man observes that he has been tenant to the Earl and his father for "fourscore years" (4.1.14) and does not obey until he has turned his master over to an escort, the wandering lunatic Tom O'Bedlam (who is actually Gloucester's son, Edgar, in disguise). The frailty of the Old Man emphasizes Gloucester's weakness, while at the same time his devotion offers evidence that some good remains in the increasingly violent and evil world of the play.

Oswald Character in *King Lear*, the steward of King Lear's villainous daughter Goneril. In 1.3 Oswald coolly accepts Goneril's instructions to treat her father insolently, for she wishes to humiliate him thoroughly. In 1.4 Oswald acts upon these orders. Thus, the steward is identified with his mistress as a villain, and when Lord Kent beats him and drives him away, we approve. In 2.2 Kent encounters Oswald again and berates him in a long, comical series of insults that focus on the steward's pretensions to gentlemanly status. Kent's speech is a scathing critique of the vain, self-serving "lily-livered, action-taking, whoreson, glass-gazing, super-serviceable, finical rogue . . . nothing but the composition of a knave, beggar, coward, pandar, and the son and heir of a mongrel bitch" of a courtier that Oswald seems to be (2.2.15–21). Less prominent after these encounters, Oswald principally serves Goneril as a messenger, until, in 4.5, he delivers a letter to Regan and accepts her implied commission to kill the outcast and blinded Earl of Gloucester. When he encounters Gloucester in the next scene he attempts to do so, only to be killed himself by the blind man's son, Edgar. With his dying breath he begs his killer to make amends by delivering his letters. He thus demonstrates loyalty to his mistress—he is indeed "super-serviceable"— while at the same time he reveals her secrets and provides for her ultimate downfall in the final scene.

Oswald represents a familiar character type found in the satirical comedy of JACOBEAN DRAMA, a caricature of an ambitious commoner attempting to climb into aristocratic social circles. The rise of the gentry and the birth of the bourgeoisie during the reigns of Queen Elizabeth I (see Elizabeth I in *Henry VIII*) and King JAMES I resulted in a crisis of confidence among the aristocracy, who attempted to distinguish themselves from the newly rich by insisting on proper manners and values. This social conflict is the subject of humor in many plays of the period (e.g., Malvolio, of *Twelfth Night*). In the clash between Kent and Oswald, the advantage is given clearly to the old nobility at the expense of the rising class, reflecting Shakespeare's conservative social instincts. Some scholars have speculated that Oswald is further intended as a satire on an actual person, perhaps William FFARINGTON, the obnoxious steward of the ELIZABETHAN THEATER patron Lord STRANGE, but this cannot be proven.

Regan Character in *King Lear*, one of the villainous daughters of King Lear. In 1.1 Regan and her sister Goneril hypocritically claim to love their father in order to share the portion of the kingdom lost by the honest Cordelia, their younger sister, who frankly admits that her husband as well as her father will receive a share of her love. Regan follows Goneril's lead, and they humiliate Lear once he has surrendered power to them and their husbands. She is led on also by her husband, the Duke of Cornwall, and supports him when he performs the play's most appalling act of cruelty and puts out the eyes of the Earl of Gloucester, in 3.7. Cornwall is killed while performing this deed, and Regan sets her sights on Goneril's lover, the ambitious Edmund, but her stronger sister poisons her. Regan is last seen as she withdraws, overcome by sickness. Only later is word of her death, and of Goneril's confession as to its cause, brought to the other characters. Regan is the least distinguished of the play's villains, being chiefly a follower of her sister and her husband, though her somewhat cool and aloof quality presents a contrast with the more energetic Goneril.

Servant Any of several minor characters in *King Lear*, members of the household of the Duke of Cornwall. In 3.7, one of the Servants, designated the First Servant, attacks Cornwall in an effort to prevent him from barbarously putting out the eyes of the Earl of Gloucester. The First Servant is killed, but he wounds the duke, who dies later. The Second and Third Servants assist the wounded Gloucester, and they comment on the evil natures of the duke and his wife Regan. The episode stresses the horror that has been loosed by King Lear's folly in granting power to Regan and her sister Goneril. At the same time, the Servants demonstrate that good still resides in some people, and thereby offer some relief from the increasing violence and terror of the plot.

Lover's Complaint, A

Poem accompanying the *Sonnets* in their first edition (1609). A 329-line poem in RHYME ROYAL, *A Lover's Complaint* has often been declared non-Shakespearean, chiefly due to its inferior poetry, but current scholarly opinion finds it likely to be an early work of Shakespeare's. The poem consists largely of a monologue delivered to an aged shepherd (who never speaks and goes unmentioned after his introduction) by a distraught young woman who has been betrayed by her lover. Her complaint is overheard by an unnamed narrator who also disappears from the poem once he has set the scene.

The woman tells of having encountered a man whom everyone loved, a paragon of male beauty and wit. She realized, however, that he had repeatedly broken his vows of love and fathered many illegitimate children, and she vowed not to succumb to him. However, when he approached her, he acknowledged his reputation but insisted that only in knowing her had he experienced true love. He wept because she could not love him, and she gave in and slept with him. Now, in disgrace and apparently abandoned, she regrets having fallen prey to his wiles, while admitting that he was so attractive that she might do the same thing again.

The COMPLAINT, the genre to which the poem belongs, was very popular in the 1590s, and *A Lover's Complaint* may be, like *Venus and Adonis* and *The Rape of Lucrece*, a product of the young playwright's enforced idleness during the period when the London theaters were closed by a plague epidemic (June 1592–May 1594). If Shakespeare wrote it, it is unquestionably an immature and undeveloped work, particularly in its presentation of personality—as a result of which some have felt

it may date from even earlier in Shakespeare's career—but it does contain pleasing passages, and it is in fact a quite respectable example of Elizabethan verse. On the other hand, it is an essentially trivial work—unlike the two narrative poems, most of the *Sonnets*, and "The Phoenix and Turtle," the acknowledged Shakespearean poems—and it contains a high percentage of words not found elsewhere in Shakespeare's works; these considerations argue against its inclusion in the Shakespearean CANON. The matter cannot be satisfactorily settled unless new evidence appears, which is unlikely, so *A Lover's Complaint* is best appreciated as a piece of good Elizabethan poetry that can suggest something of the poet's relation to the literary world of his day. If it is by Shakespeare, it is certainly among the least of his works.

Love's Labour's Lost
SYNOPSIS

Act 1, Scene 1
The King of Navarre proposes to dedicate himself and his courtiers to the pursuit of scholarship. He requires his three gentlemen-in-waiting to sign an oath, swearing off revelry, banqueting, and the company of women for three years. Longaville and Dumaine sign readily, but Berowne argues against such rigor. He points out a problem with forbidding the company of women: The Princess of France is scheduled to arrive shortly. The King agrees that she will have to be an exception. Dull, a constable, appears with Costard, a CLOWN, and delivers a comically rhetorical letter from Armado, a visiting Spaniard whose ludicrous pedantry is well known. The letter accuses Costard of speaking with Jaquenetta, contrary to the King's proclamation against consorting with women. The King sentences Costard to a week's diet of bran and water, to be overseen by Armado.

Act 1, Scene 2
Armado and his page, Moth, exchange pedantries; the saucy page mocks his master, who is too slow-witted to notice. Armado confesses his love for Jacquenetta, but he feels ashamed of it because she

is a common country girl. Costard, Dull, and Jaquenetta appear. Dull announces Costard's scheduled fast. Before Jaquenetta departs with Dull, Armado speaks to her of his love; she is cool. Armado angrily sends Costard away to be imprisoned, in the custody of Moth, and soliloquizes ruefully on the power of love.

Act 2, Scene 1

The Princess of France and her entourage arrive. In light of rumors concerning the King's vow to exclude women from his court, the Princess sends her adviser Boyet ahead to announce her approach. She talks with her waiting-women about the King of Navarre's courtiers, whom they have met before. Maria praises Longaville, Katharine admires Dumaine, and Rosaline is taken with Berowne. Boyet returns and announces that the King, who is arriving with his courtiers, plans to house the visiting women in tents outside the court, in accordance with his vows. The King and his courtiers arrive. The Princess upbraids the King for his poor hospitality, and she delivers a written message from her father. The courtiers converse with the ladies. Berowne and Rosaline exchange witty remarks: she sharply parries his advances. The King apologizes for the accommodations he must provide because of his oath, and he and his retinue depart. Dumaine, Longaville, and Berowne each reenter in turn to inquire of Boyet the name of the gentlewoman he has been conversing with.

Act 3, Scene 1

Armado orders Moth to free Costard, who is to deliver a love letter to Jaquenetta. Moth goes, after teasing his master about his infatuation, and returns with Costard, who is given the letter. Berowne enters and commissions Costard to deliver a letter to Rosaline. Costard departs, and Berowne, in a soliloquy, despairs that he has been captured by love.

Act 4, Scene 1

Costard interrupts the Princess's deer-hunting party to deliver Berowne's letter to Rosaline. The Princess gleefully asks Boyet to open it and read it aloud. However, Costard has delivered the wrong letter; it is Armado's letter to Jaquenetta, and its preposterous style causes great glee.

Act 4, Scene 2

Holofernes, a comically pedantic schoolmaster, and his follower Nathaniel discuss the deer hunt in absurdly scholastical terms, to the consternation of Dull. Jaquenetta appears with Costard, seeking a literate person to read her the letter she has received. Nathaniel reads it; it is a SONNET by Berowne, intended for Rosaline. Holofernes realizes that it has been misdelivered, and he instructs Jaquenetta to take it to the King, for it may be important.

Act 4, Scene 3

Berowne, alone, again bemoans the fact that he is in love. He hides himself as the King approaches. The King reads a poem he has written and reveals that he, too, is in love. The King also hides when Longaville appears, and Longaville does the same thing, hiding in his turn when Dumaine appears and also reads a love poem. As Dumaine finishes, Longaville comes forth to tease him, but the King in turn chastises them both for breaking their ascetic vows. Berowne comes forth to rebuke the King for hypocrisy, and he takes a superior attitude to them all until Jaquenetta arrives with his letter to Rosaline. Admitting his love, Berowne then provides a rationale for romantic behavior. He says that their vows are unnatural for young men, and, further, that love, superior to all else, should be their proper subject of study. The King and the other courtiers rejoice in his solution and lay plans for festive entertainments to help woo their intended lovers.

Act 5, Scene 1

Armado, while bragging grandiloquently of his close relations with the King, announces that he has been asked to arrange a pageant to entertain the Princess. He consults with Holofernes, who proposes a presentation of "The Nine Worthies," a traditional tableau.

Act 5, Scene 2

The Princess and her gentlewomen mock their suitors, comparing the gifts of jewelry and poems they have received. Boyet arrives to report that he has overheard the courtiers planning to approach the ladies disguised as a delegation of Russians. The Princess devises a counterplot: The ladies shall be masked, and shall each wear the jewelry given to another of them, so each suitor will address the wrong woman. The gentlemen enter, and the ladies teasingly refuse to dance with them. Each suitor then proceeds to take aside the wrong lady and profess his love. The women continue their ridicule, and soon the gentlemen beat a retreat. The ladies exult in their triumph. Shortly, the gentlemen return undisguised. The women tease the men further by jesting about the fools garbed as Russians that had been present earlier. The embarrassed gentlemen realize that the women had known them all along, and Berowne makes a confessional speech disavowing "perjury." The King, reaffirming his earlier vows of love, is perplexed when Rosaline claims to have received them, rather than the Princess. Berowne realizes what has happened and rails against Boyet as a spy and teller of tales.

Costard arrives, announcing that the pageant of The Nine Worthies is about to begin. The noblemen heckle the commoners; they drive Nathaniel and then Holofernes from the stage. Costard, misunderstanding part of Armado's performance, breaks in and reveals that Jaquenetta is pregnant by the Spaniard. Armado and Costard are egged on toward a duel by the gentlemen, but Marcade appears with news of the death of the King of France, the Princess's father.

The emotional tone of the play changes instantly. The "Worthies" are dismissed; the Princess prepares to depart and, in a new mood of sadness, apologizes to the King for the ridicule that she and her maids have used. The King, aided by Berowne, persists in courtship; the Princess responds by promising him her love only if he will adopt a severely monastic life for a year. Katharine and Maria also require a year's wait for Dumaine and Longaville. Rosaline, observing that Berowne has an excessively mocking wit, requires that he spend the same year visiting dying patients in hospitals to learn a more proper seriousness. Armado returns and requests that the nobles hear the song intended to close the pageant. The assembled commoners then conclude the play with a song "in praise of the owl and the cuckoo" (5.2.878–879).

COMMENTARY

Love's Labour's Lost is a difficult play for modern readers, but it can prove to be a rewarding one. Its basic story line, in which pretensions are deflated and love conquers all, has a universal appeal. It is well plotted and constructed, and it contains a number of attractive lyrical passages and many comical sketches. Its cheerfully unrealistic atmosphere of games and festive play yields, at the last, to a sterner but nevertheless attractive vision of achieved maturity in the real world and the promise of future happiness.

Nevertheless, the play can seem unapproachable. It is full of in-jokes for Shakespeare's contemporaries, and much of its more accessible humor concerns the use of overelaborate language, which is of course even further from our own English than most Elizabethan dialogue. Its characters are often types drawn from older traditions and based on social roles that no longer exist. And its four sets of lovers who barely know each other seem implausible, to say the least. However, the playwright's organizational and linguistic genius carries the audience through the development of the play's comic situation to the satisfactions of its resolution.

The reader can dispose of many of the play's difficulties by dealing with them in a fashion that makes its virtues more evident. The witticisms in *Love's Labour's Lost* are frequently baffling to the most committed scholars and may simply be ignored. It is enough to know that they refer to lost controversies that were possibly obscure even to much of the original audience. Similarly, the inflated rhetorical posturings of Armado and Holofernes are amusingly pretentious, although we may not recognize the once-fashionable manners being parodied. Indeed, the greater part of the humor of a scene such as 4.2, which introduces Holofernes and Nathaniel, lies in its incomprehensibility—to the audience no less than to Dull. Shakespeare's point—that pomposity and pretension in language are laughable—is easy to enjoy in itself, and it also is linked to the main plot, where pretensions are also deflated.

The romance of the gentlemen and ladies provides the main interest. The play begins with the King's unnatural demand for a dry and rigorous asceticism in the name of learning. This strange proposition, counter to common sense and human instinct, is established in order that it may be refuted. Berowne begins, even in 1.1, to oppose it; his sense of reality never completely deserts him, and he is the first to shake off the fakery that the gentlemen have entangled themselves in. We see the extent to which the false ideal of ascetic scholarship has been manifested in language, and the SUBPLOT's connection to the main plot emerges. Just as the gentlemen violate their own natures in attempting to emphasize dry learning over real living, so do the lesser characters err in reducing learning itself to foolish verbiage. In a sense, these figures may be said to be parodies of the King's gentlemen as well as of contemporary manners and mores.

The dramatic conflict between the high-flown pretensions of the King and the sensible humor of the Princess of France and her ladies is established early, and the comedy of the main plot lies in two chief manifestations of that tension: the embarrassed attempts by the gentlemen to resist and then deny love; and the practical joke played on them by the disguised ladies. The story alternates with the subplot, scene by scene, with very little overlap. A third component, the element of pageantry, integrates the two plots to some degree, although Shakespeare had not yet mastered the complex interwoven plots of his later, richer works.

If the characters in *Love's Labour's Lost* tend to be rather one-dimensional, this is not inappropriate to the somewhat abstract nature of the play. It is a comedy of notions, in which a blatantly false ideal is overcome by common sense and love is permitted to prevail. The humorous characters of the subplot derive mostly from the comical archetypes of the Italian COMMEDIA DELL'ARTE; the lords and ladies are simply courtly representatives of the warring ideals. The exception is Berowne, whose humanity provides a foil for the cold, ascetic withdrawal proposed by the King. His humorous self-mocking soliloquy in which he admits to having fallen in love (3.1.168–200) propels the play toward its lively series of climaxes, and his energy drives the comic tour de force in 4.3, when the King and his three courtiers discover that they have all succumbed to love.

Although Berowne is the most fully developed character in the play, several other figures briefly exhibit flashes of Shakespearean life. The Princess, for instance, is also humanly believable; from her first speech (2.1.13–34), she is intelligent and sensible. Rosaline's sharp wit and balanced sensibility also inspire affection. Katharine has one touching moment of reality, when she is reminded of the death of her sister (5.2.14–18). Costard, primarily a character type, a combination of clown and FOOL, also engages our sympathy in a more personal way when he shamefacedly apologizes for misreading a line in the pageant of the Worthies (5.2.554–555) and when, shortly thereafter, he speaks up for Nathaniel, who is stricken with stage fright (5.2.575–579).

On the whole, however, the play does not exploit or depend on the delineation of character. It is a formal exercise, balancing the fantastic and the actual, and is as near to dance as it is to psychological realism. As such it must be crisply organized. The alternations of verse and prose, of main plot and subplot, merge in the pageantry of the final scene. Acts 1–2 constitute the exposition, Acts 3–4 develop both story lines, and Act 5 creates a transcendent world of romance and festivity, enabling the audience to forget the mundane world. The unreal atmosphere of the play is finally shattered by the appearance of Marcade, a messenger from the real world.

This bold and unexpected stroke, a coup de théâtre, changes the tone of the play instantly. "The scene begins to cloud," Berowne observes (5.2.714), and the final few minutes take place in a more sober atmosphere. But although the interval of festive mirth is ended, it is not repudiated. It must be found in a larger universe, the real world that includes grief and business, but it is allowed its place. A maturation that has taken place permits this, for the gentlemen have advanced from a self-absorbed withdrawal in the name of abstract ideas to a more humane involvement with others. The ladies require of the gentlemen a testing period before their loves can be consummated, but beyond this chastening trial, the prospect of a happy conclusion is unmistakable. The reappearance of the entire company to sing the opposing songs of Winter and Spring expresses the reality of ongoing life.

SOURCES OF THE PLAY

No written source for the plot of *Love's Labour's Lost* has ever been found, although it has been speculated that an earlier play may have been revised, as is true of other Shakespearean dramas. However, there is no actual evidence that such a predecessor existed, and most authorities conclude that the playwright invented his own stories in this play.

Nevertheless, many details may be traced to the general public knowledge of the day concerning the French Wars of Religion, then drawing to a close. English interest in that conflict was very great, largely because English troops participated in it, in 1591–93, on the side of the Protestant rebel Henri, King of Navarre, later Henri IV of France. Thus Shakespeare and his audience were familiar with the events in France that *Love's Labour's Lost* alludes to. The central figure in the play is also the King of Navarre, and the names of his courtiers correspond to well-known political figures in Henri's world. Also, Henri did receive a delegation from France headed by a princess; although he was married to her at the time, they were on opposite sides in the war and were engaged in renegotiating her dowry, an important component of which was Aquitaine, the focus of the Princess's embassy in the play. Moreover, Henri of Navarre was one of many 16th-century rulers to found an academy based on Italian Renaissance models. All of these facts were common knowledge in England, thanks to the presence there of many Protestant refugees from the wars and through many printed accounts.

However, a prominent literary work may also have figured in the genesis of the play: it has been theorized that *Love's Labour's Lost* was written as a rejoinder to "Shadow of Night," a long poem by George CHAPMAN that extols a life of contemplation and study, as opposed to the concerns of mundane existence. According to this theory, the playwright was involved in a literary dispute among politically hostile aristocratic cliques; references to some of the participants in this feud (see, e.g., Thomas NASHE) are certainly hidden in the now-obscure passages of by-play that baffle most modern readers, such as 3.1.81–95. An attack on Chapman, and on esoteric knowledge, was an attack on Sir Walter RALEIGH and his friends, made on behalf of a rival group led by Robert Devereux, Earl of ESSEX, whose close friend, Henry Wriothesley, Earl of SOUTHAMPTON, was Shakespeare's patron.

The Russian masquerade in 5.2 is thought to have been inserted in a revision of the play made no earlier than 1595, for it, too, can be associated with historical evidence. In 1594 the annual Christmas revels at Gray's Inn (see INNS OF COURT) included a comical pageant of Russians (probably stimulated by the publication in 1591 of a popular and influential book on Russia by Giles FLETCHER, an early English traveler to Moscow). We may suppose that Shakespeare knew of this event, for *The Comedy of Errors* was performed at the same festival, a production in which the playwright probably acted. Moreover, certain details in *Love's Labour's Lost* correspond with accounts of the Gray's Inn pageant of Russians.

TEXT OF THE PLAY

Scholars agree, for a number of reasons, that the text of *Love's Labour's Lost* reflects two renderings of the play. Most prominently, there are several passages that are printed in two versions. Also, there is variation in the names provided for several characters in stage directions and dialogue headings, and there is an evident change in the casting of the pageant of the Nine Worthies between its planning in 5.1 and its presentation in 5.2. Further, it has been speculated that the play may originally have ended at 5.2.870, before the anticlimactic songs of Winter and Spring, and that a scene involving Armado and Moth was cut, leaving Costard's puzzling lines at 4.1.145–150. Internal evidence suggests dates for both an original version and a revision (see "Sources of the Play"). The original composition of *Love's Labour's Lost* probably dates from around 1593, at the height of the literary dispute with which it is associated and while England was still involved in the French wars; the play was apparently revised after 1594.

The earliest surviving text of the play is the QUARTO edition of 1598, by William WHITE for publisher Cuthbert BURBY; this is, incidentally, the earliest play text to carry Shakespeare's name on the title page. The phrase *newly corrected and augmented* also appears on the title page, suggesting that an earlier edition, of which no copy has survived, had been printed. (However, the phrase may simply refer to the revision of the play.) The 1598 edition was very clumsily printed, with many typographical errors, but it has nevertheless served as the basis for all subsequent editions, including that in the FIRST FOLIO of 1623.

THEATRICAL HISTORY OF THE PLAY

The title page of the Quarto edition of 1598 records that *Love's Labour's Lost* was performed at the court of Queen Elizabeth I during the Christmas festivities of 1597, and it had probably been staged previously as well. The only other specifically recorded early production was also held at court, in 1604, although the Quarto of 1631 asserts that the play had been performed at the BLACKFRIARS THEATRE, where Shakespeare's works were not produced before 1608. The very existence of the second Quarto edition suggests that the play remained popular through the first decades of the 17th century. It then completely disappeared from the stage for two centuries, although its songs were occasionally adapted in other works.

First revived in 1839, *Love's Labour's Lost* was both staged and published a number of times in the 19th century. In the 20th it received a great deal of scholarly and critical attention, and it is now regarded as one of Shakespeare's most important early works. As such, it has been presented in several major productions and has proven to be quite popular with theatergoers. The composer Nicolas NABOKOV based an OPERA (1973) on the play, with a libretto by W. H. AUDEN and Chester Kallman (1921–75). *Love's Labour's Lost* was made as a FILM by Kenneth BRANAGH in 2000, as a musical (with much of the play's text cut), set in 1939, featuring songs by Irving Berlin, Cole Porter, and George and Ira Gershwin, and starring Branagh as Berowne. The play has been presented twice on TELEVISION.

CHARACTERS

Armado, Don Adriano de Character in *Love's Labour's Lost*, a comically pedantic and pompous Spaniard who participates in the humorous subplot. Armado's language is ludicrous whether he is ingratiating himself with royalty or wooing his rustic sweetheart, Jaquenetta. Armado is mocked by his own page, the saucy Moth, and his preposterously rhetorical letters are read aloud as entertainment by the other characters. His pompously inflated language, like that of the similar characters Holofernes and Nathaniel, is a satirical target of the play.

Armado participates in the pageant put on by the comic characters in 5.2. In its course, it is revealed that Jaquenetta is pregnant by the Spaniard, and at the end of the play he announces that he has taken a vow to his beloved similar to the promises made by the aristocratic lovers, thus providing a link between the two plots.

Armado boasts of his acquaintance with the King of Navarre in a richly comical passage (5.1.87–108) and clearly demonstrates his descent from the comic character type known in ancient Roman drama as the MILES GLORIOSUS, a foolish, bragging soldier. In the Italian COMMEDIA DELL'ARTE, this figure was a Spaniard, an enemy of Italy and also of Shakespeare's England. Armado's very name, attached to so ludicrous a character, is a derisive reference to the Spanish Armada's grand failure to invade England in 1588.

Berowne (Biron) Character in *Love's Labour's Lost*, one of the gentlemen in the court of the King of Navarre. Berowne is the witty exponent of the play's two main points: that love is superior to the pursuit of knowledge; and that pretensions, especially verbal ones, cannot be successful. When the King demands that his courtiers follow a three-year ascetic regimen dedicated to scholarship, Berowne argues that this is unhealthy and doomed to failure, because young men will naturally succumb to love. Berowne's common sense is opposed to the affection of scholarly devotion, and his awareness of real emotion counters the fakery of academic rhetoric.

Unlike the other lovers in *Love's Labour's Lost*, who function simply as vehicles for the conventional proposition that the emotions should take precedence over the intellect, Berowne is a humanly believable character, as well as a funny one. The gentleman mocks himself in a humorous soliloquy at the end of 3.1, confessing that he has fallen under the sway of "this signor junior, giant-dwarf, dan Cupid" (3.1.175). He is delighted to find that the King and the other courtiers, Dumaine and Longaville, are similarly smitten, in the comic high point of the play, a stock eavesdropping scene repeated three times to a height of absurdity (4.3). Berowne proclaims a manifesto in favor of love, using his wit and warmth in a speech that contains perhaps the best verse in the play (4.3.285–361).

The gentlemen attempt to court the ladies with a masquerade and high-flown sentiments, and they are mocked by the women they would woo. Berowne realizes that their pretensions have failed them, and he eloquently advances the play's campaign against foolish rhetoric, rejecting "Taffeta phrases, silken terms precise, / Three-pil'd hyperboles, spruce affection, / Figures pedantical . . . / Henceforth my wooing mind shall be express'd / In russet yeas and honest kersey noes . . ." (5.2.406–413).

During the pageant in the same scene, Berowne is merciless in his heckling, perhaps evidencing the essential immaturity of the gentlemen. As a result of his wounding wit, Rosaline, at the play's denouement, requires that Berowne must spend a year visiting the sick in hospitals before she will accept him. Berowne, no cardboard character as are his fellows and the King, has human faults that must be corrected, even though he is also the chief exponent of the honest emotional life promoted by the play.

Berowne's name, pronounced "B'roon," is taken from that of a contemporary French Protestant general, the Duc de Biron, who was a principal adviser to the historical King of Navarre (see "Sources of the Play").

Boyet   Minor character in *Love's Labour's Lost*, a gentleman in the entourage of the Princess of France. Boyet is a smooth courtier, a familiar type in the Elizabethan court. We first see him flattering his mistress and being put in his place. He often serves as a messenger. He happens to overhear the plans of the King and his gentlemen to masquerade as Russians, and he warns the Princess and her ladies. Berowne expresses his dislike for Boyet in 5.2.315–334.

Costard   Character in *Love's Labour's Lost*, a quick-witted CLOWN who is at the center of the rustic SUBPLOT. In 3.1 Costard is employed by Armado to send a love letter to Jaquenetta and by Berowne to send another one to Rosaline. He delivers each

to the wrong woman, resulting in two comical outcomes: Armado's pompous rhetoric is read aloud to the amusement of the Princess of France and her retinue; and Berowne's love poem exposes to his fellow courtiers his own susceptibility to romance, just as he is chastising them for the same failing.

To a great degree, Costard is simply a character type derived from the Italian COMMEDIA DELL'ARTE tradition—that of the servant or rustic yokel descended from the comic slave figures of ancient ROMAN DRAMA. He engages in several bits of standard by-play—for instance, when he comes to believe that "remuneration" means a three-farthing coin and "guerdon" a shilling. However, he displays realistic touches of humanity that rank among the play's literary gems. A participant in the comical pageant of the Nine Worthies, Costard muffs his lines and shamefacedly apologizes, in 5.2.554–555. Some 20 lines later, Costard demonstrates an appreciation for his fellows that exceeds the restricted humanity of a stock figure when he speaks up for Nathaniel the Curate, who has been driven away by stage fright.

Costard's name is an old word meaning "apple" or "head," which stimulates a cluster of jokes in 3.1.

Dull, Anthony   Minor character in *Love's Labour's Lost*, the slow-witted rustic constable. Dull is a character type whose name summarizes his nature. Dull acts as a foil to the comical pedants Armado, Holofernes, and Nathaniel, offsetting their elaborate contortions of language by being himself. At one point, Holofernes observes, "*Via*, goodman Dull! Thou hast spoken no word all this while." Dull replies, "Nor understand none neither, sir" (5.1.141).

Dumaine (Dumain)   Character in *Love's Labour's Lost*, one of the gentlemen who fall in love and thus disrupt the ascetic academic program of the King of Navarre. Although committed to the King's idea at the outset of the play, Dumaine falls in love with Katharine, a lady-in-waiting of the Princess of France. Along with the King and the other courtiers, he breaks his vows and abandons scholarship for love.

The Duc de Mayenne, well known in Shakespeare's London for his role in the French Wars of

Religion, is usually thought to have provided the name Dumaine. Unlike the originals of Longaville and Berowne, he was not an aide to the historical King of Navarre; rather, he was a principal enemy of the insurgent monarch, but this inconsistency would probably not have bothered either the playwright or his audience. An alternative, the less notable General D'Aumont, who was an aide to the King of Navarre at the time, has been proposed.

Forester Minor character in *Love's Labour's Lost*, the guide for a royal hunt. The Forester's naive honesty provides a foil for the wit of the Princess of France in 4.1.

Holofernes Character in *Love's Labour's Lost*, a comical pedant. Named for Dr. Tubal Holofernes, a tutor in Rabelais's *Gargantua*, Shakespeare's scholar is so Latinate in his speech that he can hardly be understood. Holofernes, never without his obsequious follower, Nathaniel the Curate, is the subject of much mirth on the part of the other characters. Moth says of Holofernes and his fellow grotesque, Armado, that "they have been at a great feast of languages, and stolen the scraps" (5.1.35–36). Although Holofernes is consistently wrongheaded, conceited, and intolerant of those he considers his intellectual inferiors, we nevertheless feel sorry for him when he attempts to perform in the pageant of the Nine Worthies and is mercilessly heckled by the gentlemen. Driven from the stage, he cries, justly, "This is not generous, not gentle, not humble" (5.2.623).

While Shakespeare's audiences will have made more of Holofernes's ranting than we can, it is nonetheless good comedy, for much of the fun lies in its near-incomprehensibility. Some of his references are clearly to topical jokes that are now hopelessly obscure. It has been speculated that Holofernes was intended as a parody of some contemporary literary figure—John FLORIO and Gabriel HARVEY have been suggested—but this theory cannot be proven.

Jaquenetta Minor character in *Love's Labour's Lost*, the young dairymaid wooed by both Armado and Costard. Jaquenetta receives a love letter that Berowne intended for Rosaline and turns it over to King Ferdinand, on the advice of Holofernes. This embarrasses Berowne, who must acknowledge his susceptibility to love. In 5.2 Costard reveals that Jaquenetta is pregnant by Armado, and the Spaniard vows fidelity to her at the end of the play.

Katharine (Catherine, Katherine) Character in *Love's Labour's Lost*, the beloved of Dumaine and a lady-in-waiting to the Princess of France. Although primarily a stock figure in the play's courtly tableau of lovers, she is given a flash of true human feeling. In 5.2 Rosaline teases her about a sister who was said to have died of love, and Katharine is overtaken by her memory of the occasion. "He made her melancholy, sad, and heavy; / And so she died: had she been light, like you, / Of such a merry, nimble, stirring spirit, / She might ha' been a grandam ere she died. . . ." (5.2.14–17) This brief remark not only gives us a glimpse of a young woman's recollected grief, but we receive an impression of Rosaline's character as well.

It is thought that Shakespeare derived the story of Katharine's sister's death from a current account of a similar demise among the attendants of the historical Princess of France of the day, Marguerite of Valois, who was in fact married to the King of Navarre. The same tale may also have influenced Ophelia's death in *Hamlet*.

King Ferdinand of Navarre Character in *Love's Labour's Lost*, the ruler whose decision to make "a little academe" (1.1.13) of his court leads to the action of the play. Although opposed by the sardonic humor of Berowne, the King bans all mirth, banqueting, and even the company of women in order to promote disinterested study. The King's humorless desire to make of his courtiers "brave conquerors . . . / That war against your own affections / And the huge army of the world's desires" (1.1.8–10) is focused on an abstract idea, not a love of scholarship, and is therefore vain. This self-centered seriousness is overcome by love as the play develops. The King himself succumbs to the charms of the Princess of France, and when, at the close of the play, she requires that he prove his love with a year of monastic life, he willingly assumes the task, asserting, "My heart is in thy breast" (5.2.808).

Longaville (Longueville) Character in *Love's Labour's Lost*, one of the gentlemen who falls in love and thus disrupt the ascetic academic program of the King of Navarre. In 1.1 Longaville is enthusiastic about the King's idea, but he falls in love with Maria, one of the ladies-in-waiting to the Princess of France, and, along with the King and the other courtiers, he breaks his vow and abandons scholarship for love.

Longaville's name was taken from that of a French contemporary of Shakespeare, the Duc de Longueville, a well-known figure in the Wars of Religion. Longueville was an aide to Henri de Bourbon, who was the historical King of Navarre and later ruled France as Henri IV.

Marcade (Mercadé) Minor character in *Love's Labour's Lost*, the messenger who brings the Princess of France news of her father's death in 5.2, thus changing the tenor of the play in its closing minutes.

Maria Character in *Love's Labour's Lost*, the beloved of Longaville and one of the ladies-in-waiting to the Princess of France. Maria, like her lover, functions simply as a figure in the courtly pageant of love that constitutes the play's main plot. She has no distinctive personality traits, although she may be said to anticipate more fully developed secondary female characters, such as Nerissa, in *The Merchant of Venice*.

Mercadé See Marcade.

Moth (Mote) Character in *Love's Labour's Lost*, a page employed by the Spanish braggart Armado. Moth's quick wit is employed to ridicule his master, subtly to his face and blatantly behind his back. Moth appears only in scenes that function as set pieces, humorous sketches intended simply as entertainment. Moth is apparently an energetic teenager or child, small and slight of build. He is described as "not so long by the head as *honorifica-bilitudinitatibus*" (5.1.39–40) (the longest word in Latin, and in Shakespeare). His name, pronounced "mote" in Elizabethan English, suggests both the erratic flight of an insect and the elusiveness of a

particle of dust. In the pageant of the Nine Worthies (5.2), he plays the infant Hercules. He is the vehicle for a number of the obscure topical jokes that make *Love's Labour's Lost* the most cryptic of Shakespeare's plays. He is believed to have been intended as a parody of the peppery Elizabethan pamphleteer and satirist Thomas NASHE.

Nathaniel Character in *Love's Labour's Lost*, the obsequious companion of the comical pedant Holofernes. Nathaniel emulates his friend, seconding his opinions with less Latinity but no less pretension. Although Nathaniel is no more than an object of derision for the most part, Costard presents him in a more human light, standing up for him in 5.2 when he has fled the pageant, stricken with stage fright.

Princess of France Character in *Love's Labour's Lost*, the head of an embassy from France to the court of the King of Navarre, who falls in love with her. When we first encounter the Princess, in 2.1, she reprimands her courtier, Boyet, for his flattery in sharp but sensible terms that immediately establish her as a straightforward woman. But, although we do have a sense of the Princess as a real person, her chief role in the play is as a participant in the courtly tableau of lovers that draws the King and his gentlemen to an awareness that their narrow world of asceticism is insufficient compared to the power of love.

In 5.2, when she learns of her father's death, the Princess prepares to leave Navarre immediately. She responds to the King's suit by requiring him to live as a hermit for a year to test the strength of his love. She recognizes that the process of maturation that the gentlemen have undergone in the course of the play is not complete—a recognition that makes her the character who perhaps most clearly represents the play's point of view.

Rosaline Character in *Love's Labour's Lost*, the beloved of Berowne and one of the ladies-in-waiting to the Princess of France. Rosaline is largely a stock figure—a witty, charming lady who takes part in the courtly pageant of love that is the main business of the play. However, at times we are made to sense her humanity. For instance, we hear a real person, a mischievous young woman, as she contemplates tormenting the lovestruck Berowne: "How I would make him fawn, and beg, and seek, / And wait the season, and observe the times, / And spend his prodigal wits in bootless rimes, / And shape his service wholly to my hests / And make him proud to make me proud that jests! / So Pair-Taunt like would I o'ersway his state / That he should be my fool, and I his fate. . . ." (5.2.62–68).

Described as having a strikingly dark complexion, and demonstrating a provoking wit, Rosaline is presumed to have been linked, in Shakespeare's mind, to the Dark Lady of the *Sonnets*, although this cannot be proved. She does seem to anticipate later Shakespearean heroines who are plainly among his favorite types—attractive and assertive young women such as Beatrice, Portia, and her near-namesake Rosalind (in *Much Ado About Nothing, The Merchant of Venice,* and *As You Like It,* respectively).

Love's Labour's Won

Possible lost play by Shakespeare. In 1598 Francis MERES listed *Love's Labour's Won* among Shakespeare's comedies. This title was for many years identified with *The Taming of the Shrew,* the only pre-1598 Shakespearean COMEDY that Meres omitted. However, the question was raised anew in 1953 with the discovery of a 1603 bookseller's catalogue listing both *Shrew* and *Love's Labour's Won. Won* could still be *Shrew,* published under another title sometime before 1603 in an edition that has not survived. It could also be such an edition of one of the other comedies appearing after 1598—and so not in Meres's list—but before 1603. The most likely nominees are *All's Well That Ends Well* and *Much Ado About Nothing,* though *As You Like It* and *Troilus and Cressida* have also been suggested.

Macbeth

SYNOPSIS

Act 1, Scene 1

Three Witches meet during a storm and declare their intention to encounter Macbeth.

Act 1, Scene 2

The wounded Captain tells King Duncan of Scotland and his son Malcolm of the bravery of Macbeth and Banquo in battle against rebels led by the Thane of Cawdor. Angus and Rosse arrive and report that the battle has been won and that Cawdor has surrendered. The King orders them to see that Cawdor is executed and to convey the rebel's title and estates to Macbeth.

Act 1, Scene 3

The Witches gather and boast of their evil deeds. Macbeth and Banquo encounter them, and they address Macbeth as Thane of Cawdor and as the future king. They also declare that though Banquo will not be king, his descendants will rule. The Witches disappear despite Macbeth's pleas for more information. Rosse and Angus arrive and inform Macbeth that he is now the Thane of Cawdor. Banquo and Macbeth are stunned by this confirmation of part of the Witches' prophecy. Macbeth muses to himself on his ambition to be king, which has been strengthened by these events.

Act 1, Scene 4

King Duncan praises Macbeth greatly and tells him that he wishes to visit his castle at INVERNESS. Duncan also announces that when he dies, Malcolm shall inherit the throne. Macbeth volunteers to travel ahead and prepare to receive the king; he reflects to himself that his ambition to be king is hindered by Malcolm's new status.

Act 1, Scene 5

Lady Macbeth reads a letter from her husband that tells of the Witches' prophecy and its partial fulfillment. She is delighted, but fears that Macbeth's emotional weakness will prevent him from becoming king. Word arrives of Duncan's approach, and Lady Macbeth exults in this unexpected opportunity to kill Duncan. Macbeth arrives, and he is less enthusiastic, but she declares spiritedly that she will take charge of the murder.

Act 1, Scene 6

Lady Macbeth greets King Duncan courteously on his arrival at Inverness.

Act 1, Scene 7

Macbeth worries about his fate in the afterlife if he becomes a murderer. Lady Macbeth mocks him and fiercely stirs his ambition with the fury of her own. He declares that he will go ahead with the murder.

Act 2, Scene 1
Banquo and Macbeth speak briefly of the Witches. Macbeth discounts their importance as Banquo warns of the temptations that might arise from their prophecies. Left alone, Macbeth sees a hallucination of a bloody dagger. He acknowledges that he is horrified at the prospect of murdering the king, but he forces himself to proceed.

Act 2, Scene 2
Lady Macbeth has drugged the king's guards, and she awaits Macbeth's return. He comes to report that he has killed Duncan, but he is fearful of divine punishment because when he heard Duncan's sons Malcolm and Donalbain praying, he could not say "Amen" to himself. He also says he heard a voice that predicted he would never again be able to sleep. Lady Macbeth upbraids him because he has brought the bloody daggers with him instead of leaving them in the hands of the guards, as they had planned. She goes to complete the deed, and as she returns they hear a knock at the castle entry. She insists that they must go to bed and pretend they have been asleep.

Act 2, Scene 3
The knocking continues as a drunken Porter amuses himself with the pretense that he is the doorkeeper of hell. He finally admits Macduff and Lenox, and Macbeth arrives to greet them. He pretends to have been awakened by their arrival. Macduff goes to greet the king, while Lenox tells Macbeth of the night's violent and ominous storm. Macduff reappears and cries that the king has been murdered; he raises the alarm as Macbeth runs to the king's chamber. Lady Macbeth, Banquo, Malcolm, and Donalbain arrive in great confusion. Macbeth returns and reports that in his fury at the murder, he has killed the guards, who he says are the murderers. As the group departs to dress and meet again, Malcolm and Donalbain confer. They fear that they will be suspected of the murder. They also fear for their lives, and they decide to flee SCOTLAND.

Act 2, Scene 4
An Old Man tells Rosse of the strange omens that had preceded the king's death. Macduff reports that the flight of Malcolm and Donalbain has convinced everyone of their guilt and that Macbeth is to be crowned as Duncan's successor.

Act 3, Scene 1
Banquo, alone, voices his suspicion that Macbeth killed Duncan, and he reflects on the Witches' prophecy that his own heirs will rule. Macbeth, now the king, arrives. He learns that Banquo proposes to go horseback riding with his son Fleance, and he insists that they return in time for the evening meal. Banquo leaves and Macbeth plans his murder, lest the Witches' prophecy come true. He sends for the First Murderer and his companion and arranges for them to kill Banquo and Fleance as the victims return from riding.

Act 3, Scene 2
Macbeth and Lady Macbeth discuss the danger Banquo presents, and Macbeth hints darkly at the plot he has set in motion.

Act 3, Scene 3
The two Murderers, joined by a Third Murderer—sent by Macbeth—attack Banquo and Fleance. Banquo is killed, but Fleance escapes.

Act 3, Scene 4
The First Murderer reports to Macbeth during a banquet. When the king returns to his guests, the Ghost of Banquo appears and sits in his chair. No one sees it but Macbeth, who reacts with horror. Lady Macbeth tells the guests that he is suffering from an old illness, and when the Ghost disappears, Macbeth recovers. But it soon reappears and evokes a strong response from Macbeth; the banquet is disrupted, and the nobles leave. Macbeth tells Lady Macbeth that he will consult the Witches, to learn of all possible threats.

Act 3, Scene 5
Hecate chastises the Witches because they have not included her in their dealings with Macbeth. She tells them that they must prepare especially potent spells to delude Macbeth when he consults them.

Act 3, Scene 6
Lenox and another Lord discuss the suspicious deaths of Duncan and Banquo, the exiled Malcolm's support from the King of England, and Mac-

duff's defection to his cause. They hope for aid from England against Macbeth.

Act 4, Scene 1

The Witches and Hecate cast spells, and Hecate departs as Macbeth arrives. The Witches summon three Apparitions to answer Macbeth's questions. The first, an armed head, warns Macbeth against Macduff; the second, a bloody child, declares that no man born of a woman can harm him; the third, a crowned child, assures him that he will not be conquered until the forest at Birnam marches to DUNSINANE. Macbeth concludes that he is certain of continued success. Macbeth asks if Banquo's descendants shall ever rule Scotland. A parade of eight Kings appears, escorted by Banquo's Ghost, which smilingly indicates that these are his offspring. The apparitions and Witches disappear. Lenox brings news of Macduff's desertion, and Macbeth decides he will kill all of Macduff's family and followers as punishment.

Act 4, Scene 2

Lady Macduff bemoans her husband's departure. She tells her Son that his father is dead, but the clever boy realizes this isn't true, and he engages his mother in a humorous exchange. A Messenger appears, quickly delivers a warning of their imminent danger, and flees. The Murderers appear, kill the boy, and chase his mother as she attempts to escape.

Act 4, Scene 3

In England, Malcolm tests Macduff's loyalty to Scotland. He pretends to confess to extreme depravity, and when Macduff mourns for his country, Malcolm knows he is a true patriot. Rosse brings the news that Macbeth has slaughtered Macduff's family. Macduff vows revenge, and he and Malcolm prepare to launch an army against Macbeth.

Act 5, Scene 1

Observed by a Gentlewoman and a Doctor (2), Lady Macbeth walks in her sleep and raves about the blood on her hands. She mentions the murders of Duncan, Lady Macduff, and Banquo.

Act 5, Scene 2

A group of Scottish rebels against Macbeth speak of the approaching English army led by Malcolm,

Macduff, and Siward, They prepare to rendezvous at Birnam Wood, near the castle at Dunsinane where Macbeth has established his defense.

Act 5, Scene 3

Macbeth boasts that he does not fear the invaders because of the assurances of the Apparitions. The Doctor (2) reports that Lady Macbeth is troubled by hallucinations, which he cannot cure. Macbeth rejects him angrily.

Act 5, Scene 4

Malcolm orders that each of his soldiers, assembled at Birnam Wood, shall carry a branch cut from a tree to provide camouflage and confuse the enemy as to their numbers.

Act 5, Scene 5

On the castle walls, Seyton reports to Macbeth that Lady Macbeth is dead. Macbeth laments the nature of life. His Messenger arrives and reports that, unbelievably, Birnam Wood appears to be moving toward the castle. Macbeth recognizes the danger predicted in the Apparition's prophecy, but he declares himself ready to die.

Act 5, Scene 6

Malcolm, Siward, and Macduff approach the castle.

Act 5, Scene 7

Macbeth fights Young Siward, kills him, and leaves to fight elsewhere. Macduff appears and follows him.

Act 5, Scene 8

Macduff finds Macbeth, and they fight. Macbeth boasts that he cannot be killed by any man born of a woman, but his opponent counters with the information that he, Macduff, was taken surgically from his mother's womb before birth, and in this sense was not born of a woman. They fight, and Macduff kills Macbeth.

Act 5, Scene 9

Macduff appears with Macbeth's head and hails Malcolm as king of Scotland. Malcolm declares that when he is crowned, his supporters shall be made earls, in celebration of the defeat of Macbeth.

COMMENTARY

Macbeth is a study of the human potential for evil; it illustrates—though not in a religious context—

the Judeo-Christian concept of the Fall, humanity's loss of God's grace. We see the triumph of evil in a man with many good qualities. We are made aware that the potential for evil is frighteningly present in all of us and needs only the wrong circumstances and a relaxation of our desire for good. The good in Macbeth cries out poignantly through his feverish imagination, but his worldly ambition, the influence of Lady Macbeth (though she too has an inarticulate angel struggling against her own evil), and the instigation of a supernatural power all combine to crush his better nature. By the end of the play Macbeth has collapsed beneath the weight of his evil, and the desperate tyrant has so isolated himself from society—and from his own moral sensibility—that for him life seems "a tale / Told by an idiot, full of sound and fury, / Signifying nothing" (5.5.26–28).

Macbeth's despair strikes a responsive chord in modern audiences and readers partly because it resembles an existentialist response to the uncertainties of modern life. Though Shakespeare was not a philosopher, and in the 17th century existentialism had not been formulated, he nevertheless understood the potential for social and emotional collapse in the absence of morality. Macbeth and his lady chill us with their monstrous perversion of principles so obviously pertinent to people in all periods.

Shakespeare's depiction of evil in *Macbeth* has two aspects, natural and supernatural. The former is the portrait of the man, Macbeth; the latter is the representation of the supernatural world. Evil exists outside the protagonist in the world of black magic, represented most strikingly by the Witches. The appearance of these embodiments of the devil in 1.1 establishes the play's tone of mysterious evil. The Witches cause Macbeth to respond in ways that are "Against the use of nature" (1.3.137), and his mind "is smother'd in surmise, / And nothing is, but what is not" (1.3.141–142). When Macbeth finally recognizes that their predictions were not what they seemed, he denounces "th'equivocation of the fiend, / That lies like truth" (5.5.43–44). He thus touches on their most important quality: The Witches deform the lives they interfere with because they disturb a necessary element of human society: its dependence on mutual trust.

Other emblems of the supernatural in *Macbeth* are the omens associated with the murder of Duncan. As he approaches the deed, Macbeth remarks on the ominous night: "Nature seems dead, . . . Witchcraft celebrates . . ." (2.1.50–51). Moments later, Lady Macbeth hears an owl's hoot and the sound of crickets, both traditional omens of death. Lenox's account of the night's terrifying storm is full of ancient superstition told in explicit detail, with "strange screams of death" (2.3.55), earthquakes, and dire prophesies by owls. In 2.4 the Old Man and Rosse intensify the motif when they discuss the day's strange darkness, the killing of a hawk by an owl, and the deadly combat among Duncan's horses. These are gross disruptions of nature that signify the presence of active evil.

The supernatural world is the most extreme example of power that is beyond human control, and it is therefore an apt symbol for the unpredictable forces of human motivation. This larger aspect of evil influences our impression of its more particular manifestation in the man Macbeth. Thus, the pervasive magic in the world of *Macbeth* supports our awareness that the behavior of the protagonist is, in human terms, unnatural. The portrayal of the evildoer, while convincing, is not psychological in intent; instead, it emphasizes the mystery of human behavior. The play presents possibilities and influences—Macbeth's political ambition, Lady Macbeth's urging, the Witches' bald temptation—but we still wonder why Macbeth does what he does. Macbeth is revolted by himself, and his self-awareness makes his descent even more appalling; it also maintains our consciousness of the power of evil. He succumbs to temptation in an almost ritualistic way. He acknowledges each evil and then proceeds, prepared to accept "deep damnation" (1.7.20) from the time he first recognizes temptation until he is left with no alternative but death.

Macbeth's relation to evil is symbolic. Lady Macbeth, too, though she rejects her husband's scruples, is entirely aware that the proposed murder is evil. She avoids mentioning it too explicitly, and she cannot bring herself to do the deed herself. Finally, her anguished madness—presented in 5.1 and confirmed by her suicide—demonstrates her inability to absorb what she has helped to unleash. Thus, she too presents the weakness of humanity in the face of evil. We recognize that they are susceptible to the mental ravages of guilt, and this keeps us from seeing either Macbeth or Lady Macbeth as simply a monstrous sociopath. In fact, much of the play's tension is created because neither of them can simply accept their evil callously. Thus, Macbeth is as much a victim of evil as its instrument, and he is doubly symbolic as a negator of the good in humanity.

Macbeth clearly sees that his evil is a perversion of human values, and the fact that he persists in the face of this awareness demonstrates a profound moral disorder. Indeed, disorder permeates his world. Disrupted sleep—commonly considered a symptom of guilt in Shakespeare's day and in our own—plagues both Macbeth and his wife. He hears a voice predict, "Macbeth shall sleep no more!" (2.2.42) as he commits the murder, and later he speaks of "these terrible dreams that shake us nightly" (3.2.18–19). Lady Macbeth demonstrates the disorder physically in the sleepwalking scene (5.1). Macbeth even envies the murdered Duncan, for "After life's fitful fever he sleeps well" (3.2.23).

Emotional disorder is particularly strongly presented in a repeated emphasis on sexual dysfunction. Lady Macbeth makes sex a weapon in her efforts to spur Macbeth's ambition. She casts aspersions on his sexuality when she equates it with his fear. "Such I account thy love" (1.7.39), she says, and adds, "When you durst do it, then you were a man" (1.7.49). In 3.4 she uses the same technique when she urges him to conquer his fear of Banquo's Ghost. She calls the bloody-handed Macbeth "My husband!" (2.2.13) when he has just killed the king. This—the only time she calls him "husband"—suggests that she finds him sexually impressive in his gore. She also distorts her own gender in a startling fashion when she prays, "Spirits . . . unsex me here" (1.5.40–41), and she perversely elevates and then denies her maternal instincts in a vivid description of infanticide in 1.7.54–59. In 2.3.28–35 the Porter delivers a short description of sexual dysfunction from drink just at the moment when Duncan's murder, accomplished but not yet discovered, hangs over the play's world, emphasizing the motif. Macbeth's later withdrawal from his wife—he excludes her from his plans for Banquo and she takes no part

in his story thereafter—suggests that their marriage has been destroyed, not strengthened, by their immersion in evil.

This motif, combined with the obvious pleasure that Macbeth and Lady Macbeth take in each other upon their first meeting in the play (1.5.54 ff.), has led most modern actors and directors to present their relationship as highly charged sexually, sometimes including sadomasochistic bouts of slapping and grappling. However, the text could also support the suggestion of an icy incapacity to express themselves sexually. In either light, sex is an issue between Macbeth and Lady Macbeth, and the normal marital relationship is pathologically distorted—one way or another—by the force of the evil to which they commit themselves.

The theme of unnatural disorder is reinforced throughout the play. When Macbeth first considers murdering the king, he acknowledges the evil of the deed with a vivid image of the disorder of the elements, "Stars, hide your fires!" (1.4.50). His doubts are stimulated by his subconscious recognition that there is no possible way to integrate his desires with the proper order of things. Once Macbeth is fully committed to his evil course, this lack of integration is manifested in 3.4. He is horribly isolated at the banquet when only he sees Banquo's Ghost. His response, the decision to return to the Witches, illustrates nicely the widening difference between himself and other men.

The contrast is stressed in the comparison of Macbeth and Macduff, which becomes an important theme at this point in the play. In 3.6 Lenox and another Lord discuss Macduff's opposition to Macbeth in terms of holiness versus evil. Perhaps most forceful are the parallel impressions of Macduff and Macbeth in grief. Macduff's response to news of the massacre of his family is a powerful demonstration of true humanity—he must "feel it as a man" (4.3.221). Macbeth's reaction to Lady Macbeth's death—"To-morrow, and to-morrow, and to-morrow, / Creeps in this petty pace . . ." (5.5.19–20)—is the wretched cry of a man so used to evil that he has lost his emotional reflexes. Macbeth's advanced disorder also manifests itself more violently when he alternates between despair and rage in Act 5. He now lacks the capacity for normal emotions.

The force that affects the man also affects the whole society in which he lives. The evil created by the Witches inspires mistrust throughout the world of the play. Significantly, after the Witches' "overture" in 1.1 the play opens with the suppression of a treasonous rebellion. Duncan's "absolute trust" (1.4.14) in the Thane of Cawdor was misplaced, and with broad irony, Shakespeare permits the king to award the defeated rebel's title to another man he should not trust. Though trust is still available to the characters, it is already misplaced. Once Duncan has been killed, doubt and confusion grow. This development is signaled by the Porter's allusions to treachery and to the doctrine of "equivocation," a justification for lying (see GARNET, HENRY). Duncan's sons feel the world is faithless. They fear that they shall themselves be murdered, and they suspect everyone, particularly one who would be most reliable in a morally sound world, their own relative, Macbeth: ". . . the near in blood / The nearer bloody" (2.3.138–139).

Rosse describes vividly the overwhelming lack of trust that afflicts the land ruled by Macbeth: ". . . cruel are the times, when we are traitors, / And do not know ourselves . . . [and] know not what we fear, / But float upon a wild and violent sea" (4.2.18–21). The subsequent quasi-comical dialogue on treachery between Lady Macduff and her Son offers another slant on the same phenomenon, as does the deliberately false nature assumed by Malcolm to test Macduff, in 4.3. At the play's climax, Macbeth discovers that he has been the victim of the "equivocation of the fiend / That lies like truth" (5.5.43–44), and thus reprises the Porter's motif. Only with Macbeth's defeat and death can honesty return. Siward is proud that his son died having "paid his score" (5.9.18). When he hails Malcolm as the new king, Macduff wants to express what is in his mind; and Malcolm, in response, declares his wish to be "even with" his supporters (5.9.28). The malaise generated by Macbeth's evil is dissolved, and "the grace of Grace" (5.9.38) has returned to the world of the play.

As Malcolm begins to conduct the business of the state, we see that the motif of mistrust has been significant for the play's secondary theme, a political one. Throughout his career, Shakespeare was concerned with the influence on society of the moral quality of its leaders—this issue dominates the HISTORY PLAYS, for instance—and in *Macbeth* he applies his ideas to a tale of ancient Scotland. Like many of the histories, *Macbeth* begins and ends with a battle (one reported, one enacted), and the fate of the country is never ignored. The travails of Scotland while governed by the evil usurper are clearly presented, especially in the conversation among Malcolm, Macduff, and Rosse in 4.3. The fate of Scotland is a parallel development to Macbeth's descent into evil. This strengthens our awareness of his decline, but it also stresses the important lesson that the immoral behavior of a society's leader is a dangerous disease, capable of producing widespread catastrophe.

The political aspect of the play also had a contemporary significance for Shakespeare's original audiences. The alliance of English and Scottish forces against Macbeth predicts the joining of the two countries under King JAMES I in 1603, a recent event still prominent in the public eye, and James's rule is pointed to more directly in the apparition of future rulers presented in 4.1. Moreover, the enormity of regicide, combined with the Porter's allusions to the trial of Henry Garnet, will have brought forcibly to mind the recently exposed Gunpowder Plot, giving the play a thrilling relevance to the biggest political story in many years.

When he devised his drama of personal evil and public affairs, Shakespeare drew on the history of Scotland as presented in his source, Raphael HOLINSHED's *Chronicles*, but much of his version varies from Holinshed for he was interested in drama, not history. These inaccuracies are of no consequence, for the play's bold art generates more power than could a dispassionate presentation of real facts. *Macbeth*, which contains some of Shakespeare's greatest poetry, offers one of literature's most striking accounts of an individual soul's descent into the darkness of evil, and its resulting isolation from society. Macbeth's rejection of morality, and its consequences—the loss of his soul and the disruption of the society that he influences—horrifies us. This is a drama that is as terrifying as the plots and wars of real usurpers and kings.

SOURCES OF THE PLAY

The chief source for *Macbeth* was Raphael Holinshed's *Chronicles of England, Scotland, and Ireland* (2nd ed., 1587), whose account of Scotland was derived from the Latin *Scotorum Historiae* (1527) of Hector BOECE. Shakespeare used Holinshed's report of Macbeth's encounter with witches and subsequent usurpation of the throne, though the playwright altered the story considerably. He also used an account in Holinshed of another Scottish regicide that provided the details of Macbeth's crime and included his wife's involvement. Other details may have come from other Scottish tales in Holinshed. Another history of Scotland, George BUCHANAN's Latin *Rerum Scotiarum Historia* (1582), may also have influenced the playwright in the development of Macbeth's character and in several political details.

Various other sources contributed to *Macbeth* in minor ways. Reginald SCOT's *Discovery of Witchcraft* (1584) contributed to the depiction of the Witches, as did a work by King James I, *Daemonologie* (1599). Another tract by James, his *Counterblaste to Tobacco* (1604) provided additional details. The Latin memoirs of Erasmus, *Colloquia* (1500)—which the playwright may have read in school—provided the original version of Macbeth's remarks on dogs and men in 3.1.91–100. Lines from two contemporary plays are echoed in *Macbeth*: Samuel DANIEL's *The Queen's Arcadia* (1605) and John MARSTON's *Sophonisba* (1606). Another play, Matthew GWINNE's Latin work, *Tres Sibyllae* (1605), may have suggested the subject matter in the first place. Some scholars believe, however, that the idea may have come from a lost play on Macbeth thought to have been performed in the 1590s. Also, Shakespeare exploited the plays of SENECA in *Macbeth*, particularly in the depiction of Lady Macbeth. He also used details from three of his own earlier works, *2 Henry VI*, *Richard III*, and, especially, *The Rape of Lucrece*.

TEXT OF THE PLAY

Macbeth was probably written between 1603 and 1606. It is dated after King James's accession to the throne in the former year and before the publication in 1607 of THE PURITAN, a play whose author—probably Thomas MIDDLETON—had clearly seen *Macbeth*. Some critics feel that the references to James were added later and that the play was written before he came to power, perhaps as early as 1599. However, most scholars believe that the style suggests the later dates. Also, several pieces of evidence—the probable influence of Matthew Gwinne and John Marston, the reference in 1.3.7 to the ship TIGER, and certain allusions to the treason of Henry Garnet—suggest the summer of 1606 as a more precise date. However, these items could also have been added, and the date of composition remains uncertain.

The scenes involving Hecate in *Macbeth*—3.5 and 4.1.39–43—were obviously added. They include material that came from Middleton's play *The Witch* (ca. 1610–20), and it is traditionally assumed that Middleton wrote them. However, some scholars point out differences in style and conclude that some other writer, now unknown, was responsible. The scenes were presumably written for a KING'S MEN production sometime after Shakespeare's retirement, but before the publication of the play.

Macbeth was first published in the FIRST FOLIO (1623). At 2,500 lines, it is the shortest of the tragedies, and scholars generally believe that the play was cut considerably before publication and that the surviving text is the acting version of a longer original work. Other alterations are suspected—by Shakespeare or another writer—and the relationship of the published text to the playwright's original manuscript is unknown. The FOLIO text was probably printed from a PROMPTBOOK, or a transcript of a promptbook made for the purpose. As the only old text, the Folio has been the basis for all subsequent editions.

THEATRICAL HISTORY OF THE PLAY

Simon FORMAN recorded the earliest known performance of *Macbeth* in April 1611, but since the play influenced a work published in early 1607, we know it must have been performed at least as early as 1606. Richard BURBAGE is thought to have created the title role. No other early stagings are recorded, but alterations evident in the Folio text (1623) imply that several productions had been mounted by that time.

The English theaters were closed for 18 years while the Puritan government was in power, and when they reopened, William DAVENANT produced an adaptation of *Macbeth* (1663) that altered the play greatly. Much of Shakespeare's text was omitted or "refined" (e.g., "The devil damn thee black, thou cream-faced loon!" [5.3.11] became "Now Friend, what means this change of Countenance?"), and musical numbers featuring singers and dancers were added to the Witches' scenes. These scenes were satirized in Thomas DUFFET's *The Empress of Morocco* (ca. 1673). Among the actors who were noted for their portrayals of Macbeth in the adaptation were Thomas BETTERTON and James QUIN.

Davenant's version was quite popular, and it was not until David GARRICK's 1744 production that Shakespeare's *Macbeth* was partially restored. Though Garrick consulted Samuel JOHNSON about the text, he still cut some 300 lines, retained many of Davenant's operatic embellishments, and added some lines of his own. Macbeth was one of Garrick's great roles, and he played it for many years. He ceased only upon the death of his longtime Lady Macbeth, Hannah PRITCHARD, in 1768. Another popular 18th-century Macbeth was Charles MACKLIN, who introduced the use of Scottish kilts and plaids in 1773. In the late 18th and early 19th centuries, Sarah SIDDONS was a very popular Lady Macbeth, and she frequently played opposite her brother, John Philip KEMBLE.

Samuel PHELPS's production of 1847 omitted Davenant's operatic elements for the first time. Edwin BOOTH was an especially acclaimed Macbeth in the 19th century, and he often played opposite Helena MODJESKA. Charlotte CUSHMAN played Lady Macbeth opposite both William MACREADY and Edwin FORREST. Cushman and Siddons, in particular, were noted for the ferociousness of their interpretations, but styles changed later in the century when Ellen TERRY played the character as a less assertive partner to Henry IRVING's dominating Macbeth. In the 1890s, Sarah BERNHARDT introduced an explicit sexuality to the role that was also stressed in the 20th century.

Macbeth remains extremely popular with modern audiences, and most leading actors and actresses aspire to the roles of Macbeth and his Lady. There were many remarkable productions in the 20th century, beginning with the 1928 modern-dress presentation by Barry JACKSON. Another was Orson WELLES's notorious "voodoo" *Macbeth* of 1936, which was set in 18th-century Haiti and featured a gigantic mask as Banquo's Ghost, a Hecate with a 12-foot bullwhip, and a band of onstage drummers. The 1941 New York production directed by Margaret WEBSTER, which starred Judith ANDERSON and Maurice EVANS, and Trevor NUNN's 1976 staging at STRATFORD, with Ian MCKELLEN and Judi DENCH, were both memorable. Other notable Macbeths have included Robert Bruce MANTELL, Laurence OLIVIER, and John GIELGUD. Zoë CALDWELL and Sybil THORNDIKE have been acclaimed as Lady Macbeth. In 1981 a company from the University of Illinois adapted *Macbeth* to kabuki, the traditional, stylized Japanese drama, and performed in several American cities.

Macbeth has been made into a FILM 17 times. The earliest of these was in 1908, when the first of seven silent versions was made; the last of them, by D. W. Griffith, starred Beerbohm TREE. Orson Welles directed and starred in a movie of 1948, and Maurice Evans and Judith Anderson re-created their stage success on the screen in 1960. Probably the best-known (and by virtually unanimous critical acclaim the best) film of *Macbeth* is an adaptation, Akira KUROSAWA's *Throne of Blood* (1957). Five TELEVISION productions of the play have been broadcast, the first in 1949, though one of these simply recorded a performance of Nunn's 1976 stage production.

CHARACTERS

Angus, Thane of Gilchrist (active 1056) Historical figure and minor character in *Macbeth*, a Scottish nobleman. A minor follower of King Duncan in Act 1, with Rosse he brings Macbeth the news that he has been named Thane of Cawdor, in 1.3.89–116. Angus reappears in 5.2 and 5.4 as one of the Scottish rebels against Macbeth who join the army of Prince Malcolm. Angus speaks very little, though he does deliver a telling description of the depraved Macbeth, who feels ". . . his title / Hang loose about him, like a giant's robe / Upon a dwarfish thief" (5.2.20–22). His mere presence in Malcolm's army is significant, for the rebellion of the nobles demonstrates the extreme disorder in SCOTLAND caused by Macbeth's evil.

The historical Thane of Angus, whose surname was Gilchrist, ruled a small territory in eastern Scotland. In 1056, as a reward for his services to Malcolm, he was named Earl of Angus, as is anticipated in 5.9.28–30, but little more is known of him. Shakespeare took his name from a list of Malcolm's allies in his source, Raphael HOLINSHED's history.

Apparitions Minor characters in *Macbeth*, supernatural phenomena shown to Macbeth by the Witches, in 4.1. These specters are designated as the First, Second, and Third Apparition; each has a distinctive appearance and message. The First Apparition is described in the stage direction at 4.1.69 as "an armed head," and it warns Macbeth to beware of Macduff. The Second, "a bloody child" (4.1.76), declares that ". . . none of woman born / Shall harm Macbeth" (4.1.80–81). The Third Apparition is "a child crowned, with a tree in his hand" (4.1.86), and it adds that "Macbeth shall never vanquish'd be, until / Great Birnam wood to high Dunsinane hill / Shall come against him" (4.1.92–94). Macbeth naturally receives these prophecies as "Sweet bodements!" (4.1.96) and assurances that he will not be killed by his enemies. The tensions of the play tighten with this episode, the first intimation of its climax. Macduff is brought into sharp focus for the first time, yet Macbeth's defeat is made to seem all but impossible. These portents come from the same supernatural agency whose prediction of Macbeth's rise—in the Witches' prophecy of 1.3—was gravely accurate.

In Act 5 the prophecies of the Apparitions are borne out, though not as Macbeth anticipates. With hindsight we can see that the Apparitions bear clues as to Macbeth's true fate, for their appearances are symbolically significant. The armored head that is the First Apparition forecasts the severing of Macbeth's own head after 5.8. The Second Apparition, a bloody child, suggests Macduff "from his mother's womb / Untimely ripp'd" (5.8.15–16). The Third Apparition, the child crowned, foretells the reign of the young Prince Malcolm with which the play

closes, and the tree it bears refers to his decision to have his soldiers bear boughs cut from Birnam wood as they march on DUNSINANE.

Banquo Character in *Macbeth*, friend and later victim of Macbeth. In 1.3 Banquo and Macbeth encounter the Witches, who predict that Macbeth will become Thane of Cawdor and King of SCOTLAND. They add that Banquo, whom they describe as "Lesser than Macbeth, and greater" (1.3.65), shall father a line of rulers, though he shall not be one himself. Macbeth, inspired by this encounter to fulfill his ambition, kills King Duncan and seizes the throne. He then worries about the possibility that his kingdom will fall to Banquo's heirs, and he orders Banquo and his son Fleance murdered. In 3.3 the First Murderer and his companions kill ·Banquo, though Fleance escapes. Banquo's Ghost later appears to Macbeth, aggravating his bad conscience. In 4.1 the Ghost confirms the Witches' prediction that his descendants will be Kings. King JAMES I, England's ruler in Shakespeare's day, was believed to be descended from an historical Lord Banquo.

Banquo is a decent and honorable nobleman who senses that the Witches are evil and thus not to be relied on. He warns Macbeth that "oftentimes, to win us to our harm, / The instruments of Darkness tell us truths" (1.3.123–124), and his concern contrasts strikingly with Macbeth's susceptibility to the Witches. Banquo's resistance points up Macbeth's failure to resist and stresses his tendency toward evil, the flaw that makes the tragedy possible. When he decides to murder Banquo, Macbeth acknowledges his "royalty of nature" (3.1.49). He fears that Banquo's righteousness may turn him into an enemy. Thus, we see that Banquo's fate is dictated by his virtue, just as Macbeth's is determined by his villainy.

In Shakespeare's source for *Macbeth*, HOLINSHED's *Chronicles*, Banquo collaborates with Macbeth in the murder of Duncan and is killed because he knows too much. The playwright may have altered Banquo simply to avoid depicting the king's ancestor as a murderer, though Banquo could merely have been omitted to achieve this end. However, Shakespeare probably realized that the play is stronger with only a single villain, and Banquo's supposed ancestry to the king made him an apt choice to stand in opposition to that villain as a pointedly virtuous comrade. That this was Banquo's more important function for Shakespeare is suggested by the playwright's disregard for Fleance's fate or for the question of Banquo's descendants, once Fleance's survival ensures that he could have had some.

Though Holinshed, Shakespeare, and King James himself had no reason to doubt the belief that Banquo was a predecessor of the STUART DYNASTY, modern scholarship has established that this was not true. Banquo may reflect some ancient chieftain of Scotland, but outside Holinshed's source, the semilegendary history of Hector BOECE, he has no historical standing.

Captain (Sergeant) Minor character in *Macbeth*, a wounded soldier who describes the brave Macbeth's achievements in battle against the rebels who oppose King Duncan. In 1.2 the Captain offers an image of Macbeth as a hero, and the shock of Macbeth's later treason is the greater because this initial image is shattered. The effect is furthered by the Captain's considerable dignity; he speaks in measured rhetorical cadences and his own suffering is bravely suppressed until he closes touchingly with, "But I am faint, my gashes cry for help" (1.2.43). He is not seen further, however, being important only as a commentator on the opening situation.

Some modern editors note that the Captain is referred to by Malcolm as "the Sergeant" in 1.2.3 and designate him with that rank in the stage directions and speech headings. However, he is called "Captain" in those places in the first edition of the play and in the FIRST FOLIO (1623), and other editors retain this designation. It is supposed that "Sergeant" refers to the character's function as a valued but not high-ranking subordinate.

Cathness, Thorfin Sigurdsson, Earl of (Earl of Caithness) (active 1014–1065) Historical figure and minor character in *Macbeth*, a Scottish nobleman. In 5.2 Cathness, with Menteth, Angus, and Lenox, marches to join the army led by Malcolm and Macduff against Macbeth. In 5.4 they prepare to march on DUNSINANE, though Cathness does not

speak. This Scottish soldier helps to suggest the play's national scope, for the rebellion of which he is a part results in the restoration of good government and social stability in SCOTLAND.

The historical Earl of Caithness was in fact a Viking lord, the powerful independent ruler of the Orkney and Hebrides Islands and parts of mainland Scotland, including Caithness on the northernmost coast. Known as Thorfin the Mighty, he is also a minor figure in *King Harald's Saga*, a classic of medieval Norse literature. His daughter (or possibly his sister) later married Malcolm.

Cawdor, Thane of In *Macbeth*, a noble title forfeited by a defeated rebel against King Duncan of SCOTLAND and granted, with its lands and income, to Macbeth, as a reward for valor in 1.2.67. Thereafter, the title refers to Macbeth, though he does not know of this development when the Witches predict, in 1.3, that he will become Thane of Cawdor and then king. When he receives Cawdor's title the reinforcement of the prophecy stimulates his ambition to be king. The title thus comes to carry a reference to the aura of evil that attends Macbeth's rise to power. The original Cawdor's repentant acceptance of his execution is reported to Duncan with the famous remark, "Nothing in his life / Became him like the leaving it" (1.4.7–8). In this the first Cawdor contrasts with his successor, Macbeth, who struggles to preserve his life even after it has become a burden and he is "aweary of the sun" (5.5.49). On the other hand, there is also irony in the resemblance between the two, as the rebel yields his title to a man who thereupon becomes a usurper himself.

Doctor (1) Minor character in *Macbeth*, an English physician serving King Edward the Confessor of England (ruled 1042–66). In 4.3 the Doctor tells Malcolm and Macduff of King Edward's power to miraculously cure disease by merely touching the victims. This is a reference to a well-known superstition that any English sovereign could cure scrofula, a tuberculosis of the lymph nodes that could leave its victims "All swoln and ulcerous, pitiful to the eye" (4.3.151), as Malcolm puts it. The positive magic of the saintly king is contrasted with the evil machinations of the Witches who support Macbeth. The episode may also have been intended as a compliment to the new King of England, JAMES I; it suggests the sacred status of his office. Some scholars believe that the entire passage, 4.3.139–159—probably written by Shakespeare—may have been interpolated into the original text of the play on the occasion of a performance before the king.

Doctor (2)   Minor character in *Macbeth*, a physician who attends Lady Macbeth. The Doctor witnesses Lady Macbeth's hallucinations in the sleepwalking scene (5.1) and understands the allusions to the murders she has on her conscience. He observes, "Unnatural deeds / Do breed unnatural troubles . . . More needs she the divine than the physician" (5.1.68–71). This emphasizes the play's connection of evil with psychological disorders. Further, the Doctor points up the atmosphere of fear and distrust that surrounds the rule of Macbeth when he departs, saying, "I think, but dare not speak" (5.1.76). In 5.3 at besieged DUNSINANE, the Doctor reports to Macbeth that Lady Macbeth continues to suffer from mental disturbances; he confesses that he cannot cure them and incurs the king's disdain. Again, he has a pertinent exit line: "Were I from Dunsinane away and clear, / Profit again should hardly draw me here" (5.3.61–62), a salty reminder of Macbeth's evil influence as it was felt by ordinary citizens of SCOTLAND.

Donalbain (ca. 1033–1099)   Historical figure and character in *Macbeth*, the younger son of the murdered king Duncan of Scotland. Donalbain plays a very minor part in the play; after he attends his father in three scenes of Act 1, he speaks for the first time in 2.3, after Duncan's murder. He suggests to his brother Malcolm that they flee, lest suspicion fall upon them. He declares that he will go to Ireland while Malcolm goes to England. Malcolm returns to reclaim the kingdom from Macbeth, but Donalbain does not reappear in the play though he is mentioned several times, lastly in 5.2.7–8, where it is observed that he is not with Malcolm's army of invasion. However, in the play's final speech, Malcolm says that he intends "calling home our exil'd friends abroad" (5.9.32), a remark that may remind us of Donalbain.

The historical Donalbain was a child when Macbeth seized the throne from Duncan in 1039. His name is a corruption of Donald Ban, or Donald the White, which suggests that he was flaxenhaired. For dramatic purposes, Shakespeare altered the story and increased the ages of the brothers, but they did in fact leave Scotland—taken by adults, however—for separate exiles, Donalbain going to the Hebrides Islands off Scotland's northwest coast. He may have spent some time in Ireland, but it is from the Hebrides that he reentered history years later. Donald became the leader of the conservative Celtic nobility of northwestern Scotland who opposed the European orientation that Malcolm, as king, gave the country. When Malcolm died fighting the Norman rulers of England in 1093, Donald invaded Scotland and deposed Malcolm's heir, Duncan II, with the help of one of Duncan's brothers. They ruled jointly for three years. However, another brother reconquered Scotland with the assistance of England—gained by accepting feudal subordination to the English king—and in 1099 Donald was captured, blinded, and imprisoned for the last few months of his life.

Duncan, King of Scotland (ca. 1001–1039)   Historical figure and character in *Macbeth*, ruler of SCOTLAND whom Macbeth murders for his throne. Shakespeare's Duncan is an elderly man, a respected and noble figure; as Macbeth reflects, he "Hath borne his faculties so meek, hath been / So clear in his great office, that his virtues / Will plead like angels, trumpet-tongu'd" against / The deep damnation of his taking-off (1.7.17–20). Duncan's generous and trusting nature contrasts strikingly with the evil that surrounds Macbeth. Though he appears only in Act 1, he is an important symbol of the values that are to be defeated and restored in the course of the play. His generosity and fatherly affection for Macbeth make his murder even more appalling. The unconscious irony is sharp when he greets Macbeth, who is already plotting against him, with a declaration of his *own* ingratitude, in 1.4.14–16. Duncan's faith, misplaced first in the rebellious Cawdor and then in Macbeth, provides the audience with an introduction to the atmosphere of betrayal that exists throughout the world of the play.

The historical Duncan was a much younger man than Shakespeare's character, only a few years older than Macbeth. The playwright altered Duncan's age to stress the evil of Macbeth's crime, but in fact Macbeth did not murder Duncan; he usurped the crown through a civil war, and Duncan died in battle. The two were first cousins, both grandsons of Duncan's predecessor on the throne of Scotland, King Malcolm II (ruled 1005–34). Duncan's claim to the throne was somewhat stronger than Macbeth's as it appears that Malcolm II had named Duncan as his heir, although the facts are obscure. However, Macbeth's action was an ordinary political maneuver in 11th-century Scotland; King Malcolm II took the throne previously by murdering his cousin, Kenneth III (997–1005). Shakespeare devised his version of Duncan's death from an account of an earlier royal assassination, that of Malcolm II's uncle, King Duff (d. 967), in his source, Raphael HOLINSHED's history.

First Murderer Minor character in *Macbeth*, an assassin recruited by Macbeth. In 3.1 the First Murderer and his accomplice, the Second Murderer, accept Macbeth's assignment to kill Banquo and Fleance. They are virtually indistinguishable from each other. Neither speaks much, although each makes a brief complaint (3.1.107–113) about the desperation of his unfortunate life and his determination to perform any deed that may improve his lot. In 3.3 the Murderers, assisted by the Third Murderer, undertake their commission. They cooly assault their targets and kill Banquo, though Fleance escapes. In 3.4 the First Murderer reports the deed succinctly to Macbeth. He takes pride in their fierceness and describes Banquo's wounds as "twenty trenched gashes on his head; / The least a death . . ." (3.4.26–27).

In 4.2 an unspecified number of Murderers, probably the First and Second, kill the Son of Lady Macduff and chase her off stage where they kill her, as we learn in 4.3. Their cold-bloodedness is here particularly horrifying as one of them notes his victim's youth, calling the Son an "egg" (4.2.82) as he kills him.

The Murderers are not distinct from each other as individuals. The First Murderer offers a pleasing

description of a sunset in 3.3.5–7, but we do not imagine that he is a man of esthetic sensibility. He is merely a vessel for Shakespeare's poetic lyricism, which here helps to establish the eerie atmosphere of dusk for a scene that, in the playwright's theater, was performed without modern stage lighting to set the mood.

Fleance Minor character in *Macbeth*, the son of Banquo and the intended murder victim of Macbeth. The Witches predict to Macbeth that he will be king but that Banquo's descendants will rule, rather than his own, so once Macbeth has seized the throne of SCOTLAND, he decides that he must kill Banquo and Fleance to prevent the prediction coming true. Fleance appears briefly in 2.1, simply to establish his existence, and when Banquo is killed in 3.3, Fleance escapes after an even briefer appearance. Thus, the possibility is preserved that Banquo's line will eventually replace Macbeth's, and this is Fleance's sole function in *Macbeth*. Once his survival is noted, he is not mentioned in the remainder of the play.

Banquo and Fleance are named as forefathers of the STUART DYNASTY in Shakespeare's source for the play, HOLINSHED's *Chronicles*. A Stuart ruled England at the time *Macbeth* was written in the person of King JAMES I, and the playwright dutifully included the information (the connection to the Stuarts is made by Banquo's Ghost). However, this was simply a legend recorded as fact in Holinshed's source, the semilegendary history by Hector BOECE. Fleance in fact never existed, although the name may well have been used by some ancient Scottish lord.

Gentlewoman Minor character in *Macbeth*, an attendant to Lady Macbeth. The Gentlewoman confers with the Doctor (2) on her mistress's somnambulism, and together they witness Lady Macbeth's hallucinatory manifestations of guilt in the famous sleepwalking scene (5.1). Before Lady Macbeth appears, the Gentlewoman refuses to tell the Doctor what she has heard—her mistress's obsession with Macbeth's murders—without a witness to back her up. This demonstrates the distrust that permeates the play's world, one of *Macbeth*'s important themes.

Ghost Character in *Macbeth,* the spirit of the murdered Banquo. The Ghost appears at the banquet hosted by Macbeth and Lady Macbeth in 3.4. It can be seen only by Macbeth, who had ordered Banquo's murder and is the only one present who knows he is dead. It appears again in 4.1 in the company of the ghostly procession of future KINGS shown to Macbeth by the Witches. In both cases the Ghost is silent. In 4.1 Macbeth observes that it "points at them [the Kings] for his" (4.1.124); this confirms the Witches' prediction that Banquo's descendants will be kings. On both occasions the Ghost appears when Macbeth names Banquo: first, when he hypocritically praises him at the banquet, in 3.4, and then when he demands to know about the prediction, in 4.1. This highlights the connection between the Ghost and Macbeth's internal state. Moreover, in 3.4 the Ghost is seen only by Macbeth, which further points up his disturbed state of mind in the aftermath of his crimes.

That no one else can see the Ghost in 3.4 is sometimes taken as evidence that the specter does not in fact exist and is merely Macbeth's hallucination. However, it was believed by many in Shakespeare's day that ghosts and other supernatural beings could limit their visibility at will to particular individuals at particular times. (For instance, the Ghost in *Hamlet* is seen by Hamlet and several other characters in Act 1, but is invisible to Gertrude when Hamlet sees it again in 3.4.) Banquo's Ghost thus serves as both a supernatural and a natural—that is, psychological—phenomenon, and no conclusions can be drawn as to Shakespeare's belief in ghosts. In any case, whether it is real or not, Banquo's Ghost adds to the eerie supernatural atmosphere that permeates the play and stresses the unnaturalness of Macbeth's evil.

The Ghost is usually played by the actor who has played Banquo, though some productions employ film or slide projections or some other image, like the huge mask in Orson WELLES's controversial "voodoo" *Macbeth.* In other productions Macbeth is presented as hallucinating, and the Ghost does not actually appear.

Hecate (Hecat, Heccat) Minor character in *Macbeth,* a supernatural being allied with the Witches. In 3.5 Hecate appears to the Witches and chides them because they did not include her in their entrapment of Macbeth. She goes on to plan for another encounter with him and promises to devise extremely powerful spells for the occasion. Then ghostly music begins, and Hecate is called away by invisible singers. In 4.1 she appears briefly to the Witches as they prepare for their second meeting with Macbeth. She praises their witchcraft and leaves to the accompaniment of another spectral song.

Hecate's appearance in *Macbeth* was obviously added to the play after it was originally written (ca. 1606) but before it was published (1623). This can be determined because the songs were written by Thomas MIDDLETON for a play, *The Witch,* probably written sometime between 1610 and 1620, and because 3.6 has been moved from its proper chronological position (it should follow 4.1), in order to separate the two Witch scenes, 3.5 and 4.1, which would otherwise be in direct sequence. Because Middleton was associated with the KING'S MEN, the theatrical company that performed *Macbeth* in the early 17th century, and because the Hecate episodes are clearly designed to introduce Middleton's songs, it has been traditionally assumed that he wrote them. However, the Hecate passages of *Macbeth* are quite different in style from Middleton's work, and most modern scholars believe that someone else wrote these lines, possibly—though it is a minority opinion—Shakespeare himself.

Hecate was a familiar figure in classical literature and was frequently invoked, for instance, in SENECA, whose plays were well known to Shakespeare. She was a fearsome goddess of the underworld, associated with witchcraft and other ghostly and uncanny things. The ancients commonly worshipped three-faced statues of her at lonely country crossroads, where she glared down a side lane and both directions of the main trail. She remained well known throughout the Middle Ages, especially in connection with black magic, and Shakespeare was clearly familiar with her. Whether or not he employed her as a character in *Macbeth,* he had his protagonist mention her twice, in 2.1.52 and 3.2.41 (in passages that were definitely written by Shakespeare). Further, she is also invoked in *Hamlet* (3.2.252), *A*

Midsummer Night's Dream (5.1.370), and *King Lear* (1.1.109). Her name is a synonym for witch in *1 Henry VI* (3.2.64), though here the name has three syllables—pronounced *heckity* rather than *heckit*—and, partly for this reason, some scholars think this passage may have been written by someone else.

Kings Minor characters in *Macbeth*, eight ghostly figures who appear to Macbeth, representing future rulers. In 4.1 Macbeth seeks to learn from the Witches whether their earlier prediction, that Banquo would father a line of rulers, is still true. In response, the eight spectral Kings appear in a procession led by Banquo's Ghost, who indicates, with a smile and a gesture, that they are indeed his descendants. Macbeth observes that some of the Kings carry "twofold balls and treble sceptres" (4.1.121). This is a topical reference to the coronation regalia of the newly crowned ruler of England and SCOTLAND in Shakespeare's day, King JAMES I. James was of the STUART DYNASTY and was believed (though inaccurately) to be descended from Banquo. Moreover, the eight Kings correspond to the eight Stuart kings, the first of whom was crowned in 1371. (Shakespeare omits the one queen in the line—Mary, Queen of Scots, James's mother—presumably because she had been the enemy of England's Queen Elizabeth I and had been executed by her in 1587.) These allusions were much more obvious to Shakespeare's original audiences than they are today.

Through this episode Macbeth sees that the Witches' earlier prediction is confirmed. He realizes that his ambition must remain incompletely satisfied. Thus, figuratively, Macbeth's downfall has begun. The significant message that Macduff has abandoned him—the first step in his actual defeat—follows immediately.

Lady Macbeth (ca. 1005–ca. 1054) Historical figure and character in *Macbeth*, the wife of Macbeth. Lady Macbeth shares her husband's lust for power, and her fierce goading in Act 1 leads him to murder King Duncan in 2.2 and seize the throne of SCOTLAND. He is reluctant and fears detection. He recognizes that the deed is evil, but Lady Macbeth's ferocious will inspires him with the perverse inten-

sity necessary to overcome his scruples. However, the evils unleashed by the murder prove too much for the new queen, and she goes insane. Reduced to sleepwalking and hallucinations in 5.1, she eventually dies, as is reported at 5.5.16. Her death is declared a suicide in 5.9.35–37.

Lady Macbeth's principal importance lies in her ability to influence her husband early in the play when she urges him to murder the king. When she learns of Duncan's approach to INVERNESS—which offers the opportunity for murder—she fervently prays, "Come, you Spirits . . . unsex me here, / And fill me, from the crown to the toe, top-full / Of direst cruelty!" (1.5.40–43), and she asks that the milk of her breasts be changed to gall. This speech introduces an important motif: the distortion of sexuality, which is a symbol of moral disorder. She goes on to summon "the dunnest smoke of Hell" (1.5.51) to obscure her deeds from Heaven's sight. This invocation of supernatural horrors is chilling, and reminds us of the Witches, already established as a source of evil.

With hypocritical charm, Lady Macbeth welcomes King Duncan to Inverness in 1.6, after which she must deal with her husband's qualms. She insinuates that he is not an adequate man if he gives in to his fears. "When you durst do it, then you were a man" (1.7.49), she taunts. This tactic is another instance of dysfunctional sexuality as a manifestation of evil. She goes on to exploit her own sexuality when she describes the experience of nursing a loving infant. She insists that she would have ruthlessly "plucked my nipple from his boneless gums, / And dash'd the brains out" (1.7.57–58), if it had been necessary to achieve their goal. Shamed by her vigor, Macbeth agrees to proceed, but in 2.2 it is left to her to break the horror-struck trance into which he falls after he murders Duncan and to bring their plan to completion. Her ruthless intensity has brought the throne within reach, and Macbeth is crowned soon thereafter.

Lady Macbeth's viciousness has horrified generations of readers and audiences. However, her grim fervor not only makes her fascinating—the role has consistently attracted major actresses of all periods—but it also illuminates the most important element of the play: Macbeth's relationship to evil.

He clearly would not have carried out the regicide, although he had already considered it, without the impetus from her. She, on the other hand, willingly commits herself to evil. The contrast makes clear the potential goodness in Macbeth that he abandons when he kills his king. Lady Macbeth thus functions as a symbol of evil until she falls victim to it herself.

However, Shakespeare's major characters are never one-dimensional, and Lady Macbeth is not a simple cartoon of villainy. She, too, is repelled by the evil inherent in murder, though only subconsciously. She can refer to the regicide only euphemistically—Duncan must be "provided for" (1.5.67); the killing is "this enterprise" (1.7.48) or merely "it" (5.1.34), and she is unable to bring herself to do the deed because Duncan too closely resembles her father. When Macbeth speaks of evil just after he has killed Duncan, she prophetically declares, "These deeds must not be thought / After these ways: so, it will make us mad" (2.2.32–33). Finally, her anguish in the sleepwalking scene demonstrates convincingly that she simply cannot tolerate her too-hastily accepted immersion in evil. Lady Macbeth's madness, along with her husband's profound emotional malaise, is essential to one of the play's strongest effects. Because we see their dreadful breakdown so vividly, we must acknowledge that they are victims of evil as well as its instruments.

There may also be another cause for her madness. She and Macbeth are obviously fond of each other, as we see when they first meet in 1.5. Macbeth's letter to her—read in her first speech—makes clear that they have long confided in each other, and that their ambitions are closely shared. Yet when they accomplish their long-sought goal, it has an unforeseen consequence for her. Once Duncan has been killed, Lady Macbeth becomes increasingly unimportant to her husband as he begins to undergo the emotional collapse that is the play's principal development. She does not become Macbeth's "dearest partner of greatness" (1.5.11), as both had anticipated, but is instead excluded from his confidence. He does not inform her of his plan to kill Banquo, and after her ineffectual attempts to control him when he sees Banquo's Ghost, in 3.4, she disappears from the plot. The

evil she was so willing to accept betrays her—as it betrays Macbeth—and produces only anguish in place of the rewards she had envisioned. Not only does she lose her husband to his increasingly dead emotional life, she also loses the access to power that had motivated her in the first place. Nothing

Lady Macbeth, one of Shakespeare's grandest creations, is played here by Ellen Terry, one of the most acclaimed of Shakespearean actresses. *(Courtesy of Billy Rose Theatre Collection; New York Public Library at Lincoln Center; Astor, Lenox and Tilden Foundations)*

remains to her, and she goes insane. When she stimulates action, in Act 1, Lady Macbeth overflows with vitality; in 5.1 she is reduced to fear of the dark. Though she seemed much stronger than her husband, in the end she lacks the animal strength he uses to bear the aftermath of their deed to its fatal conclusion.

The intimacy between Macbeth and Lady Macbeth combined with the use of perverse sexuality as a symbol of moral disorder has led to a theatrical tradition (dating to the interpretation of Sarah BERNHARDT, in the late 19th century) that presents their relationship as highly charged sexually, and she as a bold flaunter of her sexual charms. However, the play could also suggest sublimated passions whose energies have been displaced onto political ambition. In any case, it is clear that their relationship—however construed—withers in the atmosphere of mistrust and emotional disturbance that is unleashed with Duncan's murder.

The historical Lady Macbeth, whose first name was Gruoch, was the granddaughter of a Scottish king who was murdered in A.D. 1003, 36 years before the time at which the play begins. Macbeth was Gruoch's second husband. By her first, a nobleman from northern Scotland, she bore a son, Lulach, whom Shakespeare presumably had in mind when Lady Macbeth remembers nursing a child, in 1.7.54–58. When Macbeth seized the throne, his wife's royal descent doubtless supported his pretensions, though it was not necessary to his claim. There is no evidence at all that she attempted to persuade her husband to make such a claim, nor that she needed to. In fact, Gruoch is very little in evidence at any point in the history of Macbeth's reign, though after his fall her influence may be supposed. Lulach ruled briefly after Macbeth's defeat and death in 1057 before being killed by the triumphant Malcolm. Since Lulach was known as "the Simple," some historians think that his mother engineered his assumption of power. Perhaps her spirit passed down to Lulach's grandson Angus, Lady Macbeth's last known descendant, who attempted unsuccessfully to seize the throne in 1120.

Lady Macduff Character in *Macbeth*, wife of Lord Macduff and a victim of Macbeth's hired Murderers.

In 4.2 Lady Macduff is afraid that her husband's departure for England to join the rebellion against Macbeth has placed her and her children in danger. ROSSE attempts to reassure her, but he can only say "I dare not speak much further: / But cruel are the times . . ." (4.2.17–18). This exchange makes plain the extent to which evil has triumphed in Macbeth's SCOTLAND. Rosse leaves, and the Lady, in her distress, blurts out to her Son that Macduff is dead. He is an intelligent lad who realizes that stress has made her say it, and her loving appreciation of his childish wit shines through her distracted grief. This touching moment is interrupted by the Messenger who warns them to flee, and the immediate appearance of the Murderers, who kill the Son and chase Lady Macduff out of the room and off the stage. Her death is reported in 4.3.

Though a minor figure, this pathetic character—created only to be unjustly killed—is a striking example of the well-crafted small role of which Shakespeare was a master. In her brief appearance she is vivid enough to contrast powerfully with Lady Macbeth. As a loving mother, domestic life is more important to her than politics, and she is everything in a woman that Lady Macbeth is not. As she is the only other female character (except the Witches), the contrast is firmly impressed on us. She also affects us in another way, for her helpless bewilderment is another of the many instances of the nation's disorder. The terror she experiences in her last moments alive constitutes the depths of the play's horror. Her death is an important turning point, for it motivates Macduff, in 4.3, to undertake the fight against Macbeth with a stronger will than politics alone could prompt.

Lenox, Thane of (Thane of Lennox) Character in *Macbeth*, a Scottish nobleman. Lenox functions as an attendant for most of the play. He is a silent companion of King Duncan in Act 1, and he speaks only a little when he arrives to join the king in 2.3, at the time of Duncan's murder. After Macbeth is crowned, Lenox transfers his services to the new king and attends him silently in 3.1 and with a few words in 3.4 and 4.1. Only in 3.6—a misplaced scene (in the FIRST FOLIO text) that should follow 4.1—does Lenox assume any importance. In this scene he speaks against Macbeth and makes clear the extent to which his evil is loathed in SCOTLAND. Like his fellow thanes Rosse and Angus, Lenox's chief significance lies in his rebellion, which demonstrates the extremity of the nation's disorder once evil has been permitted to flourish. In Act 5 Lenox serves the cause of Prince Malcolm. Shakespeare's use of the name Lenox may have been intended as a compliment to the new English king, JAMES I, who was descended from an earl of Lenox.

Lord Any of several minor characters in *Macbeth*, members of Macbeth's royal court. In 3.4 several Lords are present at a banquet and witness Macbeth's distress at the appearance of the Ghost of Banquo. They accept Lady Macbeth's explanation—that the king is suffering the effects of an old illness—and depart. In 3.6 a single, unidentified Lord meets with Lenox, and they observe that Prince Malcolm has arrived in England, and that Macduff has defected to his cause. In both scenes, the anonymous noblemen bear witness to the unraveling of Macbeth's power.

Some scholars agree with the suggestion of Samuel JOHNSON that the FIRST FOLIO stage direction calling for "Lenox and another lord" at the opening of 3.6 was an error that resulted from the misinterpretation of a manuscript abbreviation— "An."—for Angus, who was actually intended as Lenox's companion. This idea cannot be proven, and in any case, as Angus is a minor character like the Lords, the effect would be identical.

Macbeth (ca. 1005–1057) Historical figure and title character of *Macbeth*, a Scottish nobleman who kills King Duncan of Scotland and rules the country until he is killed in combat by Lord Macduff. The evil of Macbeth's deed, and its effects on him and on SCOTLAND, are the central elements of the play. He is conscious of the evil his ambition gives rise to, but he cannot overcome temptation. His weakness is compounded by the urging of the equally ambitious Lady Macbeth and the encouragement given him by the Witches, whose supernatural powers seem certain to help him though in fact they bring him to his doom. As a man who abandons his own potential for good, Macbeth may

be seen as an illustration of the fall of man, the prime Judeo-Christian example of sinful humanity's loss of God's grace. Eventually, Macbeth is destroyed by two virtuous men—Macduff, and Duncan's son Malcolm—who are his opposites in the play's balance of good and evil.

One of the play's manifestations of the power of evil is the collapse of Macbeth's personality. Macbeth commits, or causes to be committed, more than four murders: first, that of the king, which he performs himself in 2.2, and then those of Banquo in 3.3 and of Lady Macduff and her children in 4.2. His behavior during and after each of these events is different, and in this progression is the heart of the drama.

We hear of Macbeth before we see him. In 1.1 the Witches reveal that he is their target, and in 1.2 King Duncan hears of his prowess on the battlefield. He appears to be a brave and loyal follower of the king, but when the Witches suggest, in 1.3, that Macbeth is to become king himself, we see that he has already entertained the possibility of usurping Duncan's crown. However, in 1.7, as he contemplates the prospect of killing King Duncan, he wavers. He still remembers his society's crude discipline, the "even-handed Justice" (1.7.10), which dictates that if he kills the king, someone else may kill him. He further acknowledges that in simple decency he should not kill the man who is his kinsman and his guest, and who has, moreover, been notably kind to him. On another ethical level, he recognizes that it is evil to deprive society of a virtuous man and a fine ruler.

Macbeth still retains the moral sensibility to declare, "I dare do all that may become a man. / Who dares do more is none" (1.7.46–47), but Lady Macbeth encourages him to overcome his scruples, and in 2.2 he kills the king. He is immediately plagued by his conscience; he tells of how he "could not say 'Amen'" (2.2.28) and of the voices that foretold sleeplessness. His absorption with his bloody hands foreshadows his wife's descent into madness in 5.1. Nevertheless, he carries his plot through and is crowned between 2.4 and 3.1.

Though the influence of the Witches and of Lady Macbeth is very prominent and reflects different aspects of the ways one can fall into evil, Macbeth is basically not controlled by them. His story is one of a moral choice and the consequences of that choice. It is clear that Lady Macbeth's influence helps him on his way, but once he has killed Duncan he withdraws from her, and she has no role in his subsequent plots; he plainly *can* get along without her. At the same time, his response to the supernatural is carefully contrasted with Banquo's suspicion of the Witches. Macbeth has every opportunity to avoid his fate: he could have ignored Lady Macbeth, or followed the lead of Banquo. However, he made a different choice, for he is a driven, self-destructive man.

Once installed as king, he considers murdering Banquo. He hopes to dispose of the Witches' prediction that Banquo's descendants will rule. He is troubled and cannot rest; he sees life as a "fitful fever" (3.2.23), and he cries out, "O! full of scorpions is my mind" (3.2.36). But he hires murderers to dispose of Banquo and his son Fleance. Again he is tormented by his conscience, especially by the sight of Banquo's Ghost. He returns to the Witches a second time and is warned by the Apparitions against Macduff. He determines to eliminate this threat also, with the result that the murderers kill Macduff's wife and children, although Macduff has already escaped to England.

By now, however, Macbeth's qualms have disappeared, replaced by a more fundamental disorder. We next see him in 5.3 as he prepares to defend himself against the army of Malcolm and Macduff, and he has become a different person. He veers wildly between rage and despair and has lost any emotional connection to his fellow humans. He declares that he is "sick at heart" and has "lived long enough" (5.3.19, 22), and he realizes that all that he might once have expected in his old age, "honour, love, obedience, troops of friends" (5.3.25), is irrevocably lost. Informed of Lady Macbeth's death, he can only reflect on the meaninglessness of life. He has lost his ordinary human repertoire of responses to life and death.

Even his courage, the only virtue he has retained, has an inhuman quality: "bear-like, I must fight the course" (5.7.2), he growls. Only when he finally understands the deceptive prophecies of the Apparitions does he succumb once again, too late,

to a genuine human emotion. He feels sheer terror—"it hath cow'd my better part of man," he cries (5.8.18) when he realizes that Macduff is not "of woman born" (5.8.13). He recovers courage enough to die fighting, and thus in death he is not wholly lost.

His basic strength is also demonstrated in his capacity to face and withstand the ugly truth about himself. He sees the evil to which he has subjected himself and his world. He recognizes his own immorality, and he is not satisfied with the position he attains, but he nevertheless defends this position with continued murder. He is aware of this irrational phenomenon; one of his most fascinating features is that he is conscious of the goodness he abandons. When he first contemplates the murder of Duncan, he says its "horrid image doth unfix my hair" (1.3.135). He recognizes the "deep damnation" (1.7.20) to be expected, and his hallucination of the dagger confirms the force of this knowledge. After he commits the murder, his immediate concern is not with being discovered but with his conscience. "To know my deed, 'twere best not know myself" (2.2.72), he says. And at the end of the play he is tormented by the awareness that his life could have been altogether different. It is the contrast with what might have been that makes Macbeth a tragic figure. Though Malcolm understandably refers to "this dead butcher, and his fiend-like Queen" (5.9.35), the real point of the play resides in the extent to which Macbeth is not simply a monster. He cannot accept his evil callously; he suffers for it.

The historical Macbeth did indeed seize the throne from his cousin Duncan, but Shakespeare's depiction of the man and his reign is otherwise entirely fictional. Shakespeare took some of his errors from his source, HOLINSHED's *Chronicles*, which itself depended on the unreliable, quasi-legendary history of Hector BOECE. However, much of the playwright's version varies from Holinshed, anyway, for he was interested in drama, not history.

Though in the play the stigma against Macbeth's action is immense, his usurpation was fairly ordinary in 11th-century Scotland. Duncan's predecessor, King Malcolm II, had taken the throne when he murdered his cousin, Kenneth III. By the standards of the day, Macbeth's claim to the throne was fairly legitimate, as Holinshed makes clear. Macbeth, like Duncan, was a grandson of Malcolm II and thus a plausible heir. He might also have asserted a claim as the husband of Gruoch (the real Lady Macbeth), who was a granddaughter of Kenneth III. However, there is no evidence that he received—or needed—any prodding from his wife to usurp power. Tradition dictated that any male member of the royal family who could establish that he had regal qualities—usually interpreted as control of an armed force—was qualified to succeed to the crown. In principle, an election within the family settled conflicting claims, though a resort to force was ordinary.

Macbeth, however, did not murder Duncan; he launched a civil war, and Duncan died in battle. Shakespeare took from Holinshed an account of an earlier royal assassination and ascribed it to his protagonist. Further, the play shows Scotland convulsed by the usurper's crime and tormented by his tyranny, but in fact Macbeth was a benign and successful king who ruled in peace for 15 years. Holinshed reported Macbeth's virtues as a king, but Shakespeare ignored them in the interests of drama. As in the play, Macbeth's reign ended when the exiled Prince Malcolm invaded the country with English forces. Malcolm's first attempt at conquest was only partially successful. Siward won a victory at DUNSINANE Castle in 1054, but it was not until 1057 that Macbeth was finally defeated in a battle nowhere near Dunsinane.

Macduff, Thane of Fife (active ca. 1054) Quasi-historical figure and character in *Macbeth*, the rival and vanquisher of Macbeth. After Macbeth murders King Duncan of Scotland and succeeds him on the throne, Macduff joins Duncan's son Malcolm in exile in England. There he learns that Macbeth has massacred his family, and when he and Malcolm lead an army against Macbeth, Macduff seeks out the usurper at DUNSINANE to exact personal vengeance. Macbeth relies on the supernatural assurance that no man "of woman born" (4.1.80, 5.8.13) can harm him, but it turns out that Macduff was "from his mother's womb / Untimely ripp'd" (5.8.15–16)—that is, delivered by Caesarean section and thus not "born" in the ordinary construc-

tion of the word. In the subsequent fight, Macduff kills Macbeth; he presents the usurper's severed head to Malcolm in 5.9.

Shakespeare painstakingly establishes Macduff as the play's agent of retribution. We first notice Macduff in 2.4, when he returns to FIFE rather than attend Macbeth's coronation. In 3.4 Macbeth suspects Macduff is hostile, and in 3.6 we hear that he has fled to join Malcolm. Thus, even before he takes a prominent role, Macduff distinguishes himself because he refuses to accept Macbeth's succession to the crown. In 4.1 Macbeth is told by the Apparitions to "Beware Macduff" (4.1.71), and it is evident that the Thane of Fife will be the usurper's rival, though Macbeth is calmed by the Apparitions' other predictions. In 4.3 Macduff proves that he is a disinterested patriot. Malcolm fears that Macduff may be Macbeth's agent and tests him. The prince pretends to be a degenerate who would make a terrible king. Macduff despairs for Scotland, and Malcolm accordingly accepts him. Thus, the playwright places Macduff's virtue in clear opposition to the villainy of Macbeth.

As a symbol of triumphant good, Macduff is a somewhat stylized character. He rejects Macbeth, he proves himself dedicated to Scotland, he is able to overcome the magic that Macbeth relies on, and in the end he kills the villain. A multifaceted persona is not required for such a character, and generally we do not see one. However, he has one majestic moment that powerfully evokes our sympathy for him as a man. In one of Shakespeare's most moving episodes, Macduff grieves for the death of his wife, Lady Macduff, and their family at the hands of Macbeth's hired killers. At first he can hardly believe it: "All my pretty ones? / Did you say all?—O Hell-kite!—All?" (4.3.216–217), he cries. When Malcolm encourages him to revenge and says, "Dispute it like a man" (4.3.220), Macduff replies with great dignity, "I shall do so; / But I must also feel it as a man: / I cannot but remember such things were / That were most precious to me" (4.3.220–223). We are deeply moved, aware that the grieving thane is profoundly engaged with his love and sorrow. The source of Macduff's virtue is exposed: He is a complete human being who cannot sever the bonds of kinship and love. We see

In Orson Welles's 1948 film version of *Macbeth*, Malcolm (Roddy McDowell) prepares to lead his army against Macbeth's fortress, Dunsinane, to avenge the murder of his father, Duncan. Malcolm's trick of camouflaging his men with tree branches is instrumental in Macbeth's downfall. *(Courtesy of Culver Pictures, Inc.)*

that Macduff's strong acceptance of his grief is the opposite of the cold inhumanity of Macbeth and Lady Macbeth.

It is uncertain whether Macduff existed in history. Shakespeare found him in HOLINSHED's *Chronicles,* which was based on the quasi-legendary history of Hector BOECE, but he cannot be certainly identified with anyone recorded in 11th-century documents. Nevertheless, the name probably represents a historical ruler of Fife who was an ally of Malcolm against Macbeth. His birth by cesarean section is even more speculative. The procedure, though known to have existed since ancient times, was certainly extremely rare in medieval Scotland, if practiced at all. In pre-modern societies the strangeness of this mode of birth led to its being associated with the extraordinary figures of history and legend—such as Julius Caesar, for whom it is named—and this doubtless accounts for the belief that Macbeth's killer entered the world in this fashion.

Malcolm (Prince Malcolm Canmore) (d. 1093) Historical figure and character in *Macbeth,* son of the murdered King Duncan of Scotland. In 1.4 Malcolm is named his father's successor to the dismay of Macbeth, who plots to take the crown himself. However, when Duncan is murdered, Malcolm and his brother Donalbain fear for their lives and worry that suspicion will fall on them. They flee the country in 2.3 and leave Macbeth to occupy the throne. Malcolm seeks refuge at the court of the English king, where we find him in 4.3 Macduff joins him there, and they lead an army to Scotland in Act 5, defeating and killing Macbeth. At the play's close, Malcolm makes a stately speech that thanks his supporters and announces his forthcoming coronation as king of SCOTLAND.

Like Macduff, the young prince is a figure of goodness placed in opposition to Macbeth's evil, and as such he is somewhat two-dimensional. He is clever when he devises a form of camouflage—each soldier carries a branch of a tree as the army marches on DUNSINANE—that proves significant in Macbeth's downfall. However, Malcolm is most distinctive when he tests Macduff's patriotism, in 4.3.1–139. The prospective king describes himself as an intemperate and dishonest degenerate, certain to be bad for the country. When Macduff despairs for Scotland, Malcolm reveals himself as a virtuous prince and accepts Macduff as a leader of his invasion army. This episode has two functions. Most important, it stresses the atmosphere of distrust that Macbeth's evil has loosed on Scotland. It also presents Malcolm as a sensible, cautious young man who seems likely to be a successful ruler. This impression, along with our recollection of the clever camouflage, helps establish the sense of healing that comes with his triumph at the play's close. Cathness refers to him, appropriately, as "the med'cine of the sickly weal" (5.2.27).

The historical Malcolm did return from exile to defeat Macbeth, but Shakespeare's treatment of his career is otherwise almost entirely altered. Malcolm was a young child when Macbeth seized the throne in 1039. Duncan was not murdered, so Malcolm did not flee to avoid suspicion. He was in fact sent to his uncle, Earl Siward, and he later lived at the court of King Edward the Confessor of England, as in the play. Only 15 years later, once he was a man, did Malcolm attempt an invasion of Scotland in 1054. The attack was repulsed, though some territory was taken. Three years later a second attempt succeeded; Macbeth was defeated and killed, and Malcolm took the throne.

Malcolm's reign began a highly important period in Scottish history, the first European orientation for the country. Malcolm's second wife, later known as St. Margaret, was an English princess who had been raised at the cosmopolitan medieval court of the kings of Hungary. Under her influence, Scotland accepted the Roman rather than the Celtic church and the arts and culture of Europe as opposed to those of ancient Britain. Margaret had been a refugee from the Norman conquest of England in 1066, and Malcolm engaged in periodic warfare against William the Conqueror. He died in battle in 1093, during his fifth invasion of England. His successor was Duncan II, his oldest son by his first wife (the sister or daughter of Cathness). Duncan was overthrown by his uncle, Donalbain, but eventually another of Malcolm's sons (by Margaret) ruled Scotland as King David I (1124–53). Through him, Malcolm was an ancestor of JAMES I, the ruler of England in Shakespeare's time.

Menteth, Walter Dalyell, Thane of (Thane of Menteith) (active 1056) Historical figure and minor character in *Macbeth*, a Scottish nobleman. In 5.2 Menteth, with Cathness, Angus, and Lenox, joins the army led by Malcolm and Macduff against Macbeth. They are presumably among the "many worthy fellows" (4.3.183) reported earlier to have risen in arms against Macbeth's tyranny. In 5.4 they prepare to march on DUNSINANE. Though his character is not developed, Menteth's presence helps strengthen the political aspect of the play. The rebellion of the nobles indicates the extent of political and social disruption in SCOTLAND due to Macbeth's evil.

The historical Walter Dalyell ruled Menteith, a territory in central Scotland. Little more is known

of him; Shakespeare took his name from a list of Malcolm's allies in his source, HOLINSHED's history.

Messenger Minor character in *Macbeth*, a servant of Macbeth. In 1.5 the Messenger brings Lady Macbeth the news that King Duncan, whose murder she has just been contemplating, approaches. Her startled response to this sudden opportunity for the crime serves to escalate the plot's tension. In 4.2 the Messenger (or, possibly, another one) betrays his master when he warns Lady Macduff that Macbeth's hired killers approach. He is bravely willing to stand up against Macbeth's villainy, and his action provides a moment of relief from the growing evil of the plot. In 5.5 the Messenger, still employed by Macbeth (unless, again, he is a different person), brings his master word that the forest appears to be moving. This message signals Macbeth's downfall, and his wrathful response emphasizes his desperate position. Though they seem unimportant, all three of the Messenger's appearances mark a change in the play's emotional tone, a striking Shakespearean technique.

Old Man Minor character in *Macbeth*. The Old Man converses with Rosse in 2.4 and comments on the evil omens that have accompanied the murder of King Duncan. This conversation, like a Greek CHORUS, offers a commentary on the action so far. The description of the omens—especially that of Duncan's horses eating each other—stresses an important theme of the play: Duncan's murder and its perpetrator are horribly unnatural. The Old Man states the theme explicitly when he describes the eerie darkness of the day. "'Tis unnatural, / Even like the deed that's done" (2.4.10–11), he says.

The Old Man presents himself as venerable but unsophisticated—"Threescore and ten I can remember well" (2.4.1), he says when he introduces himself. This, along with his distinctively rustic image of the "mousing owl" (2.4.13) that killed the falcon, helps establish that the play's catastrophe is universal. SCOTLAND's collapse due to Macbeth's evil is a major motif of the play, and the country as a whole is represented by this aging peasant.

The episode is a good instance of a technique that Shakespeare was fond of: The plot is interrupted by the introduction of an anonymous figure who comments on it and then disappears from the play. In *Macbeth* the Porter serves a similar function in a more elaborate manner; the Grave-digger of *Hamlet* is another particularly well-known example.

Porter Minor character in *Macbeth*, a doorkeeper at the castle of Macbeth. In 2.3, immediately following Macbeth's murder of King Duncan, the Porter appears in response to a knocking at the gate. His humorous drunkenness contrasts strikingly with the grim murder scene, and thus he reinforces the suspenseful horror that we have just been exposed to. Also, in his drunkenness the Porter pretends to be the gatekeeper of hell, and this motif emphasizes the fact that Macbeth has just lost his soul.

Shakespeare's original audiences will have recognized immediately that the Porter was imitating a familiar figure of the medieval MORALITY PLAY; the gatekeeper of hell who admits Christ to Limbo in the ancient legend of the "Harrowing of Hell." This gatekeeper guarded the literal mouth of hell—a familiar image from the painted backdrops of a gigantic, flaming lion's mouth (derived from Rev. 13:2) used in the morality plays. The Porter makes it clear that we are to see Macbeth's castle as hell, and leaves no doubt whatever that the enormity of Macbeth's evil is of the greatest importance in the play. When the Porter finally opens the door and admits Macduff, a subtle analogy between Macduff and Christ is suggested. This foreshadows Macduff's role as the final conqueror of the evil Macbeth.

The Porter also provides comic relief. His humor is both topical, with references to a contemporary treason trial (see GARNET, HENRY)—a resonant theme in a play on regicide—and simply vulgar, as in his remarks on the effects of drink, in 2.3.27–35. This vulgarity inspired high-minded commentators such as Alexander POPE and Samuel Taylor COLERIDGE to declare the Porter a non-Shakespearean addition, on the grounds that a genius of literature would not stoop to such low comedy. However, modern critics recognize that the Porter is a typically humorous Shakespearean representation of unsophisticated humanity. With his comedy and his simple mind that nevertheless

offers important commentary on the situation, the Porter is the nearest thing to a FOOL in *Macbeth*. Also, like the Old Man of 2.4, he serves the function of a CHORUS and offers a point of view entirely outside that of all the other characters.

Rosse, Thane of (Thane of Ross) Character in *Macbeth*, a Scottish nobleman. Rosse is a pawn of the plot; he often is the bearer of news. In 1.2 Rosse tells King Duncan of Macbeth's success in battle, and in 1.3 he conveys to Macbeth the king's thanks. In 2.4 he discusses evil omens with the Old Man and speaks with Macduff of Macbeth's coronation. In 4.2 he attempts to encourage the bereft Lady Macduff. In this scene he delivers a speech that stresses the play's motif of fear and mistrust. "Cruel are the times, when we are traitors, / And do not know ourselves" (4.2.18–19), he says. In 4.3 he reports her murder to her husband, whom he joins in revolt against Macbeth. In 5.9 he tells SIWARD of the death of his son, Young Siward. Rosse's greatest significance is seen in his gradual revolt against Macbeth. He represents SCOTLAND as a whole, which suffers from Macbeth's evil and then rejects him.

Historically, the Thane of Ross (the correct spelling, which has been adopted by many editors instead of the FIRST FOLIO's "Rosse") was Macbeth himself, who had received the title years before the time of the play. Shakespeare took his error from his source, Raphael HOLINSHED's history, where the name appears in a list of Scottish noblemen who revolted against Macbeth.

Second Murderer See First Murderer.

Servant Any of several minor characters in *Macbeth*, workers in Macbeth's household. In 3.1 a Servant is sent to bring the Murderers to Macbeth; in 3.2 Lady Macbeth sends a Servant (possibly the same one) to summon her husband; and in 5.3, a Servant (again, perhaps the same one) reports to Macbeth that the woods appear to be advancing on DUNSINANE. In all three instances, the Servant's function is to effect a transition or provide information and, in the final scene, Macbeth's fury at the innocent Servant demonstrates his desperate and baleful state of mind.

Seyton Minor character in *Macbeth*, an attendant to Macbeth. Seyton appears briefly in 5.3, where he endures Macbeth's impatient abuse, and even more briefly in 5.5, where he informs Macbeth of the death of Lady Macbeth. This triggers Macbeth's famous soliloquy on the meaninglessness of "to-morrow, and to-morrow, and to-morrow" (5.5.19). He is a patient servant who functions as a sounding board for Macbeth's increasing dementia.

The men of a Scottish family named Seyton (Seton, Seaton) were hereditary armorers to the kings of Scotland, and Shakespeare may have intended Seyton as one of them. However, the Seytons' position did not exist until the rule of King Edgar (ruled 1097–1107), who was a son of Macbeth's foe and successor Malcolm. Some scholars think Shakespeare may also have intended the name to be a pun on "Satan," a reference to Macbeth's last loyal servant who stresses the king's depravity as he approaches his end.

Siward, Earl of Northumberland (Sigurd the Dane) (d. 1055) Historical figure and minor character in *Macbeth*, English ally of Malcolm and Macduff against Macbeth. Siward, a famous soldier who commands an army of 10,000 men, is provided by England's king to the exiled Prince Malcolm of SCOTLAND. As a noble and knightly figure, Siward stands for the virtues lost to the world of the play through Macbeth's evil, and as a foreigner who must be brought in to restore the country's health, he points up the extremity of Scotland's need. He appears briefly several times in Act 5 and is a direct and simple soldier. His most notable moment comes when he is informed that his son, Young Siward, has died in combat. With noble fortitude he observes, "Why then, God's soldier be he! / Had I as many sons as I have hairs, / I would not wish them to a fairer death: / And so, his knell is knolled" (5.9.13–16).

The historical Siward, or Sigurd, was of Danish royal descent. His family had seized Northumberland during the Danish conquest of England a few generations earlier; in Northumberland it was traditionally said that his grandfather was a bear. Siward was a famous warrior who had fought for the English kings Hardicanute (ruled 1040–42) and Edward the Confessor (1042–66), and he was thus a fitting choice to command Malcolm's army of invasion, quite aside from his kinship to the prince. He was either Malcolm's brother-in-law or uncle—11th-century references differ. Shakespeare's source, Raphael HOLINSHED's history, mistakenly called him Malcolm's grandfather, for he was considerably older than Malcolm's father, King Duncan. The playwright made him Malcolm's uncle—perhaps thereby unknowingly correcting an error—to place him in the same generation as Duncan.

Much more than the legendary Banquo, Siward deserved to be called "the root and father / Of many kings" (3.1.5–6). His oldest son, Osberne, died fighting against Macbeth, as in the play. His younger son, Waltheof (d. 1075), led the last British resistance to William the Conqueror and was later canonized for it as Saint Waldeve. He had a daughter, Matilda, who married Malcolm's son, later King David I of Scotland (ruled 1124–53). Two of their sons were kings of the Dunkeld dynasty, as were a grandson and great-grandson. A third son of Matilda and David was an ancestor of King Robert II (ruled 1371–90) who was the founder of the Stewart (later STUART) dynasty. Thus Siward is an ancestor of Shakespeare's sovereign, King JAMES I, whose supposed descent from Banquo is celebrated in the play. All this was certainly unknown to Shakespeare, who simply followed Holinshed, and presumably to King James as well, for he seems to have enjoyed his supposed connection to Banquo.

Son Minor character in *Macbeth*, Lady Macduff's child, who is killed by Macbeth's hired Murderers, in 4.2. The Son sees that his mother is distressed by Macduff's departure to England to join the rebellion against Macbeth, and he attempt to understand the situation with pertly humorous questions and remarks. His wit and intelligence make his slaughter all the more vicious and contribute greatly to the power of the episode, which stresses the depths of evil to which Macbeth has descended. The boy's courage in death—he calls one of the Murderers a "shag-hair'd villain" (4.2.82), and with his last breath he futilely attempts to warn his mother—contrasts tellingly with the villainy of his killers.

Third Murderer Minor character in *Macbeth*, one of the assassins hired by Macbeth to kill Banquo and Fleance. The Third Murderer joins his colleagues as they approach their targets. He was not with them when they were recruited in 3.1, and they initially distrust him, but his exact instructions convince them that he has been sent by Macbeth. His presence suggests that with the distrust typical of despots, Macbeth has felt the need to plant an agent among his hired assassins. The Third Murderer is indistinguishable from his fellows and speaks only a few brief lines.

Witches Group of characters in *Macbeth*, supernatural beings who encourage Macbeth in his evil inclinations. In 1.1 three Witches appear in the thunder and lightning of a storm; they say that they will meet again to encounter Macbeth. In 1.3 the boast of their evil deeds before they accost Macbeth and Banquo. They greet the former with titles he does not possess: Thane of Cawdor and "King hereafter" (1.3.50)—though we already know that Macbeth has been named Thane of Cawdor (in 1.2.67–69)—and they assure Banquo that he shall not be a king but that his descendants shall. After they make these puzzling remarks, they disappear. When Macbeth and Lady Macbeth learn that he is in fact Thane of Cawdor and the Witches' prophecy is corroborated, their ambition is sparked to murder King Duncan so that Macbeth can rule SCOTLAND. Then, once he is king, Macbeth worries over the Witches' pronouncement that Banquo's heirs will replace his own, and he murders him as well. Thus, the Witches inspire the central action of the play.

In 3.5 we see the three Witches with a more powerful spirit, Hecate, who is accompanied by several more witches. (However, most scholars believe that this scene was not written by Shakespeare, and that *Macbeth*'s Witches were originally only three in number.) In 4.1 the Witches concoct a magical brew in a cauldron. They are preparing for another visit from Macbeth, who wishes to learn what he must do to assure his safety now that he is king. They summon the Apparitions, whose predictions seem to promise safety but actually foretell his destruction. Finally, in a passage that may be a non-Shakespearean interpolation, the Witches perform a ritual dance, after which they vanish.

Though their appearance are brief, the Witches have an important function in *Macbeth*. The play opens with their grim and stormy meeting, and this contributes greatly to its pervasive tone of mysterious evil. Moreover, they offer another important theme of the play: the psychology of evil. The Witches are an enactment of the irrational. The supernatural world is terrifying because it is beyond human control, and in the play it is therefore symbolic of the unpredictable force of human motivation. At their first appearance, the Witches state an ambiguity that rules the play until its close: "Fair is foul, and foul is fair" (1.1.11). Their deceptive pictures of the future—both in their initial predictions of Macbeth's rise and in the prophecies of the Apparitions—encourage in Macbeth and Lady Macbeth a false sense of what is desirable or even possible. The magic of the Witches is thus an image of human moral disruption. Through their own uncertain nature, they demonstrate—and promote—the disruption in the world of the play. When Macbeth meets them a second time, he describes their capacity for disorder: they "untie the winds, and let them fight / Against the Churches . . . palaces and pyramids, do slope / Their heads to their foundations . . . Even till destruction sicken" (4.1.52–60). They declare that their activity comprises "A deed without a name" (4.1.49). Their world is without definition; similarly, Macbeth's disordered sense of the world comes to encompass the assumption that "Life's . . . a tale / Told by an idiot, full of sound and fury, / Signifying nothing" (5.5.24–28).

Many people in Shakespeare's day believed in the reality of the supernatural world, but at the same time a recognition that many folk beliefs were merely superstitions had arisen as well. Shakespeare's opinion on the subject cannot be determined, for his handling of the Witches is ambiguous. Banquo asks them, "Are ye fantastical, or that indeed which outwardly ye show?" (1.3.53–54). After they leave, he wonders if he and Macbeth have "eaten on the insane root" (1.3.84) and have simply imagined them. Their nature is never clearly stated. Moreover, the extent to which they have powers other than those of persuasion is also uncertain, which perhaps reflects—or exploits—the generally uncertain sense of such things in the playwright's original audiences. Shakespeare may have shared his audiences' ambivalence as to the supernatural, or he may simply have played on it to devise a dramatic grouping of characters. Despite a modern disbelief in the supernatural, we can respond to its dramatic use in *Macbeth* and find in it a symbol of obscure regions of the human psyche. In this light the Witches can be thought of as manifestations of Macbeth's ambition and guilt. That Banquo also sees them and Lady Macbeth accepts their reality does not argue against such an interpretation of Shakespeare's intentions; it merely points up the ambivalence of 17th-century attitudes toward the supernatural.

It is interesting to note that Shakespeare altered the nature of the Witches considerably when he took them from his source, Raphael HOLINSHED's *Chronicles*. There the beings who appear to Macbeth are described as "nymphs or fairies" who could read the future through magic. A number of references connect them with the three Fates, ancient goddesses who are figures of dignity and grandeur, quite unlike the hags of British folklore. Nymphs and female fairies were traditionally beautiful, but the Witches of *Macbeth* are "So wither'd and so wild in their attire, / That [they] look not like th'inhabitants o'th'earth" (1.3.40–41). Scholars have surmised that Shakespeare replaced Holinshed's classical spirits with his own, earthier creatures in light of King JAMES I's well-known interest in contemporary witchcraft. However, the traditionally horrifying creatures of folklore are entirely appropriate to the association in *Macbeth* of these beings with the potential evil in humankind.

Young Siward (Osberne of Northumberland)
(d. 1054) Historical figure and minor character in *Macbeth*, an English soldier killed by Macbeth. Son of Siward, the English ally of Malcolm and Macduff, Young Siward appears with the leaders in 5.4 but does not speak. In the ensuing battle he bravely challenges Macbeth to personal combat, in 5.7, and dies in the encounter. The youth has no personality and serves only as a foil to Macbeth, whose evil is emphasized by the contrast with Young Siward's noble bravery, and whose malign nature is demonstrated in the otherwise unnecessary death of so fine a young man. The actual son of Siward was named Osberne. He did indeed die in combat at an early age during Malcolm's invasion of Scotland, but nothing more is known of him.

Measure for Measure
SYNOPSIS
Act 1, Scene 1
As he prepares to leave the city, Duke Vincentio of Vienna appoints Escalus second in command to Angelo, the deputy who will exercise power in the Duke's absence. Angelo receives his orders, and the Duke praises him for his life of devotion to duty.

Act 1, Scene 2
Mistress Overdone, a bordello keeper, interrupts the lewd banter of Lucio and two Gentlemen to tell them that Claudio has been sentenced to death for having made Juliet pregnant. Pompey tells Mistress Overdone of a new law that orders the destruction of bordellos; he assures her that she will survive and that he will continue to work for her. The Provost appears and exhibits Claudio in the streets as part of his punishment. Claudio tells Lucio that he had slept with Juliet in the belief that they would soon be married, but that her relatives had held up her dowry. Then, after Juliet became pregnant, Angelo began to enforce a long-neglected law making sexual immorality a capital crime. Claudio tells Lucio of his sister who is about to enter a convent, and asks Lucio to ask her to seek mercy from Angelo.

Act 1, Scene 3
The Duke visits the Friar and tells him that he has placed Angelo in charge during a revival of disused morality laws. He fears that to revive these laws under his own authority might give them too great a force; this way he can see how they are received and act accordingly. He intends to secretly return to Vienna and oversee the process, disguised as a friar.

Act 1, Scene 4

Lucio visits Claudio's sister, Isabella, at the convent. He tells her of Claudio's predicament, and she agrees to plead for mercy from Angelo.

Act 2, Scene 1

Escalus proposes mercy for Claudio, but Angelo refuses. Constable Elbow brings Pompey and Froth before the officials; in comically confused speech he charges his prisoners with running a bordello for Mistress Overdone and adds that they attempted to recruit his wife. Pompey's wittily long-winded reply drives Angelo away; he leaves the case to Escalus. After further comical exchanges, Escalus releases Froth and Pompey with a warning that law enforcement is becoming stricter; Pompey leaves sassily.

Act 2, Scene 2

Despite the Provost's pleas, Angelo orders Claudio's execution for the next day. Isabella arrives and pleads at length for mercy. Angelo promises only to reconsider and tell her of his decision the next day. Angelo, alone, reflects distractedly that he has fallen in love with Isabella and is tempted to sin by offering a pardon for Claudio in exchange for her love.

Act 2, Scene 3

The Duke, disguised as "Friar Lodowick," ministers to the inmates of the prison. He encounters Juliet, urges her repentance, and promises that he will visit her condemned lover.

Act 2, Scene 4

Angelo soliloquizes that he cannot pray for strength against temptation because his thoughts are filled by Isabella. Isabella arrives and renews her plea. Angelo tells her he will have mercy on Claudio only if she will become his lover. She refuses, and he swears that he will have Claudio tortured. He gives her a day to change her mind and leaves. Alone, she declares her confidence in Claudio. As a man of honor, he will agree that her avoidance of sin is more important than his rescue.

Act 3, Scene 1

The Duke, as a friar, counsels Claudio to prepare for death by considering the ills of life. Isabella arrives, and the "friar" eavesdrops as she tells Claudio of Angelo's evil ultimatum. Though Claudio at first supports her refusal, he is overcome by fear of death

and pleads with her to save him. Furious, she berates him hysterically and leaves. The "friar" intercepts her and tells her he knows of Angelo's intentions. He proposes a plot to her. Angelo had once abandoned a woman he was supposed to marry named Mariana, and she still loves him. If Isabella arranges to have sex with Angelo on condition that the transaction be silent and in the dark, Mariana could actually keep the appointment. Isabella agrees.

Act 3, Scene 2

Elbow brings Pompey to the prison; Lucio appears, and Pompey asks him for bail but is refused. Lucio speaks with the Duke, thinking he is actually a friar. He claims to be an intimate of the Duke, gossips about him slanderously and leaves. Mistress Overdone is imprisoned despite her claim that Lucio has informed on her because she keeps his illegitimate child. Before he leaves to visit Claudio, Escalus observes to the "friar" that the absent Duke would not have been so merciless as Angelo. Alone, the Duke reflects on the virtues needed in a ruler and rails against Angelo's violation of these standards.

Act 4, Scene 1

The Duke, as the "friar" visits Mariana. Isabella arrives and reports that she has agreed to meet Angelo that night in his garden. Mariana accepts her part in the plot.

Act 4, Scene 2

The Provost offers Pompey parole if he will serve as assistant to the executioner, Abhorson, in the beheadings of Claudio and another man, Barnardine; he agrees. The disguised Duke arrives and predicts that Claudio will be pardoned. However, a Messenger brings the order that Claudio is to be killed immediately and his head sent to Angelo. "Friar Lodowick" suggests that Barnardine's head be substituted for Claudio's. The Provost says he cannot do this because of his duty. The "friar" confides that he knows the Duke's intentions and produces letters from him as proof.

Act 4, Scene 3

Pompey and Abhorson summon Barnardine to be executed, but he refuses because he has a terrible hangover. The Provost appears, and the "friar" observes that Barnardine is so unrepentant that if he died he would surely go to hell, placing a moral burden on his executioners; the Provost remarks that another prisoner has by chance died that morning, and they agree that his head can be used as the substitute for Claudio"s. Isabella arrives, and the disguised Duke decides to postpone telling her of the plot to spare Claudio. He tells her instead that Angelo has demanded and received Claudio's head. He promises her revenge; she is to take a letter to a friar who will bring her to the Duke, and Angelo's guilt will be exposed. As she leaves, Lucio arrives; he brags that he has abandoned a pregnant woman and claims to know the Duke has done the same.

Act 4, Scene 4

Angelo and Escalus discuss the Duke's peculiar instructions: They are to proclaim that any complaints of injustice should be made publicly and then meet him outside the city. Escalus leaves to send out this decree; alone, Angelo bemoans his guilty conscience. Not only did he deflower Isabella, he had Claudio killed for fear he would someday seek revenge. He regrets his decision and cries that one sin leads to more.

Act 4, Scene 5

The Duke visits the Friar again and plans his return to Vienna.

Act 4, Scene 6

Isabella and Mariana ready themselves to encounter Angelo and the Duke; "Friar Lodowick" has warned Isabella that she must expect to be mistreated before she triumphs. The real Friar, Friar Peter, arrives to escort them to the Duke's ceremonial return.

Act 5, Scene 1

The Duke returns, and Isabella demands justice. The Duke refuses to believe her tale and has her arrested; she claims that Friar Lodowick can support her. Friar Peter says that he will present the evidence of Friar Lodowick, who is sick. He calls Mariana, who reveals her role as Angelo's sexual partner. Angelo denies having seen her for years and accuses Friar Lodowick of plotting against him. The Duke sends the Provost for Friar Lodowick and orders Angelo and Escalus to handle the investigation while he leaves briefly. The Provost returns with Friar Lodowick—the Duke in his disguise—who loudly declares Angelo's guilt. The Provost and Lucio attempt to arrest the disguised Duke for slander, and in the struggle his identity is revealed. Angelo realizes his guilt is known and confesses. The Duke orders him to marry Mariana immediately, and Friar Peter takes the two away to be wed. When Angelo returns with his new wife, the Duke sentences him to death for having killed Claudio. Mariana, joined by Isabella, pleads for his life, but the Duke refuses. The Provost declares that in repentance for having executed Claudio, he has left another prisoner alive. The Duke sends for that man. Barnardine appears, accompanied by Claudio, and the Duke pardons them both. He proposes marriage to Isabella and then pardons Angelo. He declares that Lucio must marry the woman he had abandoned; afterward, he will be whipped and hung, but in the spirit of forgiveness he withdraws the punishments. He insists on the marriage of Claudio and Juliet, thanks the Provost and Escalus for their good services, and closes the play with an elaboration of his proposal to Isabella.

COMMENTARY

Measure for Measure is a dark play in its focus on evil and its seemingly cynical attitude toward two basic human concerns: sex and the ordering of society. These elements place it among the PROBLEM PLAYS, and like its fellows, *Troilus and Cressida* and *All's Well That Ends Well*, it has generally been among the least popular of Shakespeare's plays during almost four centuries, though they have all increased in popularity during our troubled age. Nevertheless, although its subject matter may have more appeal in the 20th century, the play continues to dissatisfy many readers and viewers. As in the other problem plays, the realistic characters do not readily mesh with the artificial plot or with the happy ending and marriages traditional in COMEDY.

As a TRAGICOMEDY, *Measure for Measure* purposefully combines tragic development with a comic resolution, utilizing irony to distance the story line; this technique emphasizes the play's symbolic significance. The play addresses its issues—questions of good government and personal morality—through teachings from the Bible, though in a highly secular context. When this is taken into consideration, *Measure for Measure* may seem the least problematic of the problem plays, for its elements then cohere in a convincing manner to justify the traditional happy ending in marriage.

The play's title refers to Christ's Sermon on the Mount, "measure for measure" being a well-established proverbial abridgment of one of its lessons. In Matthew. 7:2 and Luke 6:38 (and in Mark 4:24, in the context of a different sermon) we are taught to use a full, unstinting measure in distributing grain to others, for we shall receive measures in the same way that we distribute them. This lesson was commonly used by preachers and religious books of Shakespeare's day. On a particular Sunday, the version in Luke was by rule the subject of the sermon in all English churches. Thus, we can be sure that Shakespeare was familiar with the text that the proverbial expression referred to, and he could presume that his audience was, too. (He had, in fact, used "measure for measure" before, in *3 Henry VI*, 2.6.55 and *King John*, 2.1.556–557.)

In Luke and Matthew the "measure for measure" passages are closely linked to Christ's important pronouncements on the doctrine of Christian forgiveness. The proverb insists on such forgiveness, for only by practicing mercy can one expect to receive it. In the play, Angelo's lack of mercy is strikingly compared with Isabella's pleas for it, especially when she seeks mercy for Angelo himself, in 5.1. The biblical passages also contain the familiar instruction not to judge others lest you incur judgment, another lesson in reciprocation. Both ideas were specifically linked with the exercise of power, as well as with personal ethics, by 16th- and 17th-century English Bible commentators. *Measure for Measure* is particularly concerned with the proper exercise of power, at least with respect to the administration of justice; a good ruler, the Duke, uncovers and punishes a bad one, Angelo.

The subject was appropriate in 1604 when Shakespeare wrote *Measure for Measure*. The duties of a Christian ruler were being widely discussed in London, for England had a new king, JAMES I, who was interested in theological matters and had raised the issue himself. In the 17th century it was

believed that a ruler's authority came from God, and a good ruler was expected to attempt to be like God in justice and mercy alike. Because of this relationship, it was almost universally held, a ruler was exempted from the prohibition against vengeance and the exaction of punishment. The ruler was specifically required to use his power to punish wrongdoers, not only to preserve social order but to act as God's weapon in the fight against evil. As such, the ruler could use extraordinary methods that might in others be immoral. Thus, the Duke's disguise and other deceptions, including the bed trick, were entirely acceptable to Shakespeare's audiences. Similarly, the Duke's position justifies his attempts to circumvent the rulings of Angelo, who as a ruler's deputy is also God's appointee. This point is clearly made in the play when the Provost refuses to act against Angelo until the disguised Duke produces a letter indicating that the "friar" acts for the supposedly absent Duke.

Christian interpretations of the play can be highly literal—some critics have found in it an allegory of divine atonement, in which Angelo is an Everyman figure and the Duke represents Christ, Lucio the Devil, and Isabella the soul. In a more general sense, many commentators have seen Isabella as a particularly Christian figure in her desire to be a nun, her adamant chastity, and her ultimate mercy. However, one need not view the play as purposeful religious doctrine, though it plainly reflects Christian sentiments. Shakespeare's other plays are distinctly *not* allegorical or sermonizing and *Measure for Measure* does not resemble traditional allegory, for most of its characters are believable human beings set in a socially realistic world. The play is easily understood as a traditional secular comedy whose themes have been drawn from a prominent Christian text.

The specifically Christian nature of the play's issues did not have to be raised; the playwright expected his audience to take these ideas for granted and go on to consider their application to the rather grim sex scandal being enacted. As a tale of official misconduct, the play evoked one aspect of the Christian lesson; through its presentation of human psychology a more personal application could be considered. *Measure for Measure* vividly offers both, and in both contexts the final lesson is the same: The power of good (in the form of Christian charity, as stressed by the title) can effect a reconciliation that untangles all plots, rights all wrongs, and leads to marital happiness, just as surely as does secular love in the traditional comedic mode.

As a play on the misuse of authority, *Measure for Measure* opposes two different sorts of bad government, an arrangement appropriate to its title. The Duke's administration of justice prior to the play has been too lax, as he himself admits, saying, " . . . Liberty plucks Justice by the nose, / The baby beats the nurse, and quite athwart / Goes all decorum. / . . . 'twas my fault to give the people scope . . ." (1.3.29–35). It is to rectify this situation that the Duke has transferred his authority to Angelo, but the deputy proves to be the opposite sort of bad governor. He is uncompromisingly strict and cannot apply mercy where it is appropriate, as in Claudio's case. The Duke's lax government is also represented in the comic SUBPLOT by Escalus's release of Pompey. Thus the long comic "trial" scene featuring Constable Elbow results in freedom for a career pimp, while Claudio, an honorable young man who wishes only to become a husband and father, is still condemned to death. The consequences of the dramatic situation are more extreme than in Shakespeare's other comedies. Angelo's intention toward Isabella is quite simply rape (and he believes he carries it out); then he further blackens himself by going back on his word, and Claudio is very nearly killed.

The remedy begins with the Duke's idea to monitor Angelo, which he actually adopts before the play opens. Significantly, the ruler takes on a religious role. He disguises himself as a friar, thus stressing the divinity of authority. The result, in addition to the preservation of Isabella's honor and Claudio's life, is the emphasis on the Duke's mercy and forgiveness at the play's close. This denouement might seem exaggerated to modern sensibilities but is utterly fitting to a proper ruler in the world of the play.

In terms of human psychology, the play places Angelo and Isabella in opposition. Angelo's inexcusable refusal of mercy stems from an excess of zeal for the rule of law. This position is related to his notion of himself as a virtuous public servant, one who is beyond examination because he is dutiful. In this Angelo is contrasted with the Duke, who acknowledges his failings and investigates his own government. Because Angelo has not questioned himself, he cannot see the humanity in Claudio, as Isabella points out. His stiff assumption of virtue deprives him of the capacity for honest judgment. Moreover, so confident is he in his own rightness that he is entirely incapable of resisting lust—though he wishes to—when it arises.

The heroine, like the villain, is strictly virtuous. Not only is she prepared to enter a nunnery, she regrets that its rules are not strict enough. Like Angelo, she insists that her own ideas about life be applied to others, "wishing a more strict restraint / Upon the sisters stood" (1.4.4–5) and demanding that Claudio "Take my defiance, [and] Die, perish!" (3.1.142–143). Her assertiveness, while attractive in its bold spirit, is uncharitable, also proving Isabella an unlikely nun. Thus, we need not be surprised when she accepts the Duke's proposal of marriage at the close; once her enthusiasm has been allied with a forgiving tolerance, she can adopt a more natural destiny than seclusion from the world.

The stiff, unyielding attitudes of the two chief characters establish the play's major conflict. This quality is fittingly expressed in the play's general atmosphere, for all of Acts 2 and 3 and much of Act 4 take place within a prison or courthouse, and of the nine remaining scenes, three take place in the Friar's cell or the nunnery and one in Mariana's "moated grange" (3.1.265), a doubly isolated place, both rustic and fortified. Four more scenes (1.1,2; 4.4,6) are in nondescript locales, but they are all distinctly anxious in tone; only the final scene of reconciliation (5.1) takes place in a setting of openness and freedom—"at the gates" (4.4.4), the site of the Duke's ceremonious reentry of Vienna.

The play's comic subplot both reinforces the claustrophobic atmosphere and relieves it. The shady world of Pompey, Lucio, and Mistress Overdone deals with similar themes as the main plot—sex and criminal justice—but contrasts with it greatly in tone, being bawdy about sex and jocularly dismissive of the courts. The tension of Claudio's fate is thus relaxed, but at the same time the sub-plot offers a dark view of VIENNA's civic life that supports a sense of imminent doom. The jesting on venereal disease by Lucio and his friends in 1.2, Mistress Overdone's assertion that Lucio has betrayed her, and the association of Pompey with the executioner Abhorson all contribute to our growing recognition that these humorous figures do not represent an idyllic world of irresponsibility but rather an unpleasant one of commercialized sex and a collapse of values.

In the main story the conflict between Angelo and Isabella becomes unbearably tense. Claudio pleads with Isabella to sin and save him, and she denounces him hysterically; by 3.1 it seems painfully clear that either Isabella must break or Claudio must die. The nature of the play changes at this point. No longer an enactment of psychological tension and moral extremism, it becomes a symbolic representation of the power of reconciliation to produce harmony and love where strife had been. The presence of the disguised Duke suggests such an outcome from the beginning. With a balance that is reflected in the title, the second half of the play counters the first. The Duke takes control of the plot, and Angelo, Isabella, and Claudio become much less important. The highly expressive poetry of the first half is replaced by a more mundane mixture of poetry and prose, and the aura of impending tragedy becomes ironic comedy. Through his somewhat absurd plotting, the Duke replaces punishment and death with pardons and marriages. While this development often strikes modern readers as silly, it was for Shakespeare's original audiences a recognizable variant on traditional comedy as well as on medieval MORALITY PLAYs, which generally centered on an undeniable sinner who is forgiven. In Shakespeare's world the fact that Angelo's crime is exceptionally dreadful suggests strongly that he will be forgiven, particularly in light of the play's title.

However, the power of Shakespeare's realistic portrayals of Angelo and Isabella in the first half of the play made a significant change in his source material necessary. In all the variants of the tale the playwright saw, the Angelo figure had his way with the Isabella figure, and then, in the final resolution,

was forced to marry her in order that her honor could be restored. However, given the psychological strength with which the two characters have earlier been invested, they simply cannot be made to accept each other without losing their power to move an audience, and much of the play's power also. Mariana therefore replaces Isabella through the use of the bed trick, an ancient comedic device that Shakespeare also used in *All's Well*. Here, the Duke's unquestioned authority makes it seem a less squalid device, though like a deus ex machina, this coup de théâtre disposes of the impending tragedy with an ease and convenience that is troubling to modern sensibilities. However, in Shakespeare's day this conclusion was perfectly acceptable, the triumph of good had been made explicit in a manner that was satisfying to the sentimental feelings of his audiences.

Mariana also triggers the sequence of pardons in 5.1 by pleading for Angelo's life. More important, she persuades Isabella to join her. Mariana's plea is essentially selfish—she wishes to preserve the husband she has so long sought. Isabella's intercession is, however, more objective; indeed, it goes against her natural enmity toward the man who is her intended rapist and the apparent killer of her brother. The Duke points this out when he says, "Her brother's ghost . . . would . . . take her hence in horror" (5.1.433–434). But Isabella not only kneels in support of Mariana's plea—which is as much as Mariana asked—but goes on to make a reasoned case for mercy toward her tormentor. Her act flies in the face of common sense, just as does Christ's command in the Sermon on the Mount to love one's enemies. Whether under the influence of Mariana's example of love, or because she remembers her claim to Angelo that she would be merciful if she had his power, or, perhaps, to make up for her willingness to sacrifice Claudio for a principle, Isabella has arrived at the giving of a full measure in the spirit of the text that inspired the play's title.

Thus the play yields a satisfactory outcome on its own terms, those of Christian moral doctrine presented in the form of traditional comedy. The drama is one of ideas, rather than real life. However, Shakespeare's strengths as a dramatist actually diminish this effort, for the psychological and social realism of the play combine to smother the spiritual aura that might otherwise make the play's message more dramatically effective. In the later ROMANCES, Shakespeare more successfully combines the symbolic and the real. Like *All's Well That Ends Well*—which it resembles in many ways—*Measure for Measure* charts the playwright's evolution from a master of personal and societal portraiture toward a more ethereal, intellectual drama. While it is not a successful example of the genre, it marks a significant experiment in its development.

SOURCES OF THE PLAY

Measure for Measure derives from a striking range of sources. The main plot stems originally from a real incident which took place in Italy in 1547: the extortion of sex from the wife of a condemned murderer by a judge who promised mercy and then executed the criminal anyway. The aggrieved widow went to the authorities, and the judge was forced to marry his victim and was then executed. These events were recounted in many works in several languages, and Shakespeare drew on at least one of them, Thomas LUPTON's account in *Too Good to Be True* (1581), which is echoed in the encounters of Angelo and Isabella in Act 2.

More important as a source, however, was a fictional work stimulated by the event, a novella by the Italian author CINTHIO, published in his collection *Hecatommithi* (1565). Here the criminal's offense is less serious—the seduction of a virgin—and the abused pleader for mercy is his sister, rather than his wife. At the close she pleads for the life of her violator, now her husband, and a virtuous ruler grants it; a happy ending replaces revenge. Cinthio reworked his novella as a drama, *Epitia* (1583), which also influenced Shakespeare. In *Epitia* the young criminal is spared because a merciful official substitutes a dead man's head for his, as in *Measure for Measure*, and a secondary heroine is featured, a sister of the judge who joins his victim/wife in pleading for his life; she is the original of Mariana.

Miscellaneous details suggest that Shakespeare knew Cinthio's work directly, rather than through the English version of the tale by George WHETSTONE. He could have read Cinthio in the original Italian, in a French translation, or in some now-lost

English translation; he certainly did one of these, for another, untranslated Cinthio tale inspired *Othello*. However, Shakespeare was definitely influenced by Whetstone's play on the same subject, *Promos and Cassandra* (1578), which has a comic subplot involving harlots and panders who contrast with the virtuous major characters. Also, Whetstone first presents the object of the young criminal's seduction, the model for *Measure for Measure*'s Juliet. Whetstone also elevates the seduction to a respectable act of love that merely precedes formal marriage, as in Shakespeare.

Tales of disguised princes who investigate the workings of their governments were common in 16th-century England, and derived originally from legends concerning the Roman emperor Alexander Severus (reigned A.D. 222–235). Shakespeare was doubtless influenced by numerous accounts, including one in Whetstone's *A Mirrour for Magistrates of Cityes* (1584), an account of the vices of Londoners. A popular romance dealing with similar material, *The Adventures of Brusanus Prince of Hungary* (1592), by Barnabe RICH, was probably the source for Lucio's interactions with the disguised Duke.

The political attitudes of the play, such as those expressed by the Duke in 1.1, may reflect a very popular book on kingship, *Basilicon Doron* (1603), by King James, and the Duke may have been modeled on James himself. At any rate, Shakespeare's remarks on crowd behavior, in 1.1.67–70 and 2.4.24–30, clearly echo a tract of 1604, *The Time Triumphant*, probably by Shakespeare's fellow actor, Robert ARMIN, describing King James's arrival in London. One further source may have contributed to the political sensibility of the play, the most famous contemporary guide for statesmen, *De Optimo Senatore* (1568), by Laurentius GOSLICIUS (anonymously translated as *The Counsellor* [1598]), which develops criteria to distinguish good and bad public officials that seem reflected in the Duke's opinions on the subject.

TEXT OF THE PLAY

Measure for Measure was written during the spring or summer of 1604. Angelo's remarks on the nuisance of adoring crowds echo a source published in the spring of that year, and Lucio's references to peace talks in 1.2.1–3 are thought to refer to English negotiations with Spain, resulting in a treaty signed in August. Also, Mistress Overdone mentions "the war, . . . the sweat, . . . the gallows" (1.2.75–76), probably referring to England's continuing war with Spain, an outbreak of plague in London, and the execution of a number of the alleged co-conspirators of Sir Walter RALEIGH, all noteworthy events of early 1604.

The play was first published in the FIRST FOLIO (1623). This text was printed from a copy of the play that had been transcribed by Ralph CRANE, as distinctive punctuation and spelling reveal. Scholars dispute whether Crane's transcription was of Shakespeare's FOUL PAPERS or a later revision of the play—by Shakespeare or someone else—which may have been responsible for irregularities in several scenes, such as the divided soliloquy whose halves appear in 3.2.179–182 and 4.1.60–65. As the only early text, the Folio version has served as the basis for all subsequent editions.

THEATRICAL HISTORY OF THE PLAY

Measure for Measure was performed at court on December 26, 1604, though some topical references in it suggest that it had been performed in public somewhat earlier, perhaps during the previous summer. It was apparently not very popular; the next recorded production was over a century later. It was exploited in two notorious adaptations: one, THE LAW AGAINST LOVERS (1662) by William DAVENENT, which incorporated some material from *Much Ado About Nothing*; and a second, based on the first, Charles GILDON's *Measure for Measure, or Beauty the Best Advocate* (1699), which featured a full-scale operatic MASQUE (taken from Henry PURCELL) that comprised the subplot. Thomas BETTERTON and Anne BRACEGIRDLE starred in the latter work.

Measure for Measure was popular in the 18th century. In 1720 John RICH staged a version that was close to Shakespeare's play, and after more than a decade's popularity it was replaced by a version by Colley CIBBER. Like the adaptations, both of these versions and most of their 18th-century successors eliminated all or most of the subplot, which was viewed as grossly undignified. Isabella was a particularly esteemed role, and many of the leading 18th-century actresses played her, including Mary Ann YATES, Ann BARRY, and Sarah SIDDONS.

In the early 19th century John Philip KEMBLE restored the subplot in a staging that was much more purely Shakespearean, but the play was not greatly liked nor often produced during the century. Adelaide NEILSON was a noted Isabella in the 1870s. The play was more popular in the 20th century: Among the memorable productions were those of Oscar ASCHE (1906), Peter BROOK (1950, starring John GIELGUD as Angelo), and John BARTON (1970). In 1998 the ROYAL SHAKESPEARE COMPANY produced a controversial staging, in which Angelo and the Duke are presented as modern-day military tyrants engaged in coup and countercoup, their armed followers coming to blows in the final scene. This production, directed by Michael BOYD, was attacked by some critics as egregiously un-Shakespearean and praised by others as a pertinent and welcome breath of relevance for new audiences. *Measure for Measure* has twice been done on FILM, once each in Italian (1942) and German (1963), and has once been broadcast on TELEVISION, in a 1979 BBC production starring Kate Nelligan. The great German composer Richard WAGNER's third OPERA (and his first produced), *Das Liebesverbot* (1836), was based on the play.

CHARACTERS

Abhorson Character in *Measure for Measure*, an executioner. Abhorson appears in 4.2, where he undertakes to train the pimp Pompey as his assistant, and in 4.3, where he and Pompey summon the condemned criminal Barnardine to be executed, only to be comically frustrated by the victim's refusal to cooperate. Abhorson is part of the comic SUBPLOT, but he serves chiefly to help create the ominous atmosphere of the prison. Abhorson's name, which suggests both the verb *abhor* and the insulting noun *whoreson*, serves the same two purposes. It conveys clearly the repellent aspects of the man's profession, thereby reinforcing the atmosphere of impending doom that has been established earlier in the play, even as its absurdity helps defuse that tension.

Angelo Character in *Measure for Measure*, deputy to Duke Vincentio of Vienna and lustful pursuer of Isabella. Angelo abuses his office by refusing mercy to Claudio when it is obviously due. Then he attempts to extort sex from Isabella with a promise of a pardon for Claudio. Once he has slept with her (or so he thinks), he goes back on the deal and orders Claudio's execution. Angelo is saved, however, from actually committing these unforgivable deeds by the Duke's machinations—Mariana, whom Angelo had deserted years earlier, replaces Isabella in his bed and, instead of Claudio's head, he is shown that of a criminal who has died naturally. Angelo is himself pardoned at the play's close, as part of its emphasis on forgiveness.

Angelo's criminality is a facet of the play's theme of good government. His downfall results from an excess of zeal. The Duke is too lax, but Angelo errs in the other extreme. At first a righteous public servant—the Duke calls him "A man of stricture and firm abstinence" (1.3.12)—he proves to be unreasonably stern. A grievous injustice, Claudio's death sentence, is the result. Angelo's rigid personality is seen to be a cause of evil. He ignores pleas for mercy; he is so confident in his own rightness that he never examines his own humanity—a point made by Isabella in 2.2. As W. H. AUDEN observed in his *Lectures on Shakespeare*, Angelo "demonstrates the difference between the superego and the conscience." Blind to human nature, he is not only a bad ruler, he is also incapable of resisting his sudden lust for Isabella. His initial misdeeds lead him further into evil. He sees this himself and cries, "Alack, when once our grace we have forgot, / Nothing goes right . . ." (4.4.31–32). It is the Duke who saves him from his own intentions and, after he marries Mariana, forgives him.

Once Isabella's refusal to meet Angelo's demand has left Claudio facing death in 3.1, the Duke takes over the play, and Angelo is not seen very much until his conviction and reprieve in 5.1. Because Shakespeare wished to employ the happy ending of traditional COMEDY, he was compelled to abandon the psychological portrait of Angelo, though the fallen deputy remains stern at the close, seeking death rather than marriage and forgiveness. Whether the villain's reduced importance is seen as a flaw in the play or simply as a strategy in the service of a nonrealistic end depends on one's view of *Measure for Measure*, but in any case Angelo remains a powerful creation.

Barnardine Minor character in *Measure for Measure*, a condemned criminal whose undeserved pardon epitomizes the play's theme of unqualified mercy. Barnardine is a comical brute who is "drunk many times a day, if not many days entirely drunk" (4.2.147–148). He declares he will not come forward to be executed on the day appointed—when he is to substitute for Claudio—because he has "been drinking hard all night, and [needs] more time to prepare . . ." (4.3.52–53). Duke Vincentio postpones the execution, saying that under the circumstances it could only send the victim to instant damnation, a responsibility the Duke will not take. In 5.1 the ruler pardons Barnardine and remands him into the custody of Friar Peter as part of the mercy and forgiveness of the play's denouement.

Barnardine is funny in his stubborn refusal to be killed and helps provide relief from the oppressiveness of the prison, where much of the middle of the play is set. Yet he is a callous murderer "unfit to live or die" (4.3.63). Although Barnardine is specifically designated as a proper subject for execution, he is pardoned as part of the play's final conciliation; his evilness then highlights the magnanimity of the Duke's mercy.

Boy Minor character in *Measure for Measure*, servant of Mariana. At the opening of 4.1 the Boy sings a stanza of the SONG "Take, O take those lips away" and is dismissed. The Boy provides the relief of a song as the plot tightens and helps, by his presence, to indicate the social status of Mariana.

Claudio Character in *Measure for Measure*, a condemned prisoner and brother of Isabella. Claudio has impregnated Juliet out of wedlock, and has been condemned to death, under an antiquated law, by Angelo, the deputy of Duke Vincentio of Vienna. This is the basic situation from which the play's central conflict arises—Angelo's demand of sex from Isabella in exchange for Claudio's life. Claudio's intentions are clearly honorable, however; he wants only to marry Juliet. Their sexual relations would have been perfectly legal but for a delay in marriage arrangements, and his condemnation is an evil excess on Angelo's part, as all the other characters agree.

Claudio's situation is a result of the Duke's lax regime in VIENNA. Despite his aristocratic upbringing, the young man is familiar with the bordello world of Lucio, Pompey, and Mistress Overdone, from whom we first learn of his plight, in 1.2. We recognize the stereotype of an immature young man in bad company, and we are not surprised that his ascetic sister is disappointed in him when his fear of death overcomes his sense of nobility. The moving passage in which he begs her to accommodate Angelo begins, "to die, and go we know not where" (3.1.117). His reaction is touchingly human and we do not share Isabella's hysterical condemnation; the episode helps us realize that she is, in her way, as extreme as Angelo. Claudio's moral character is favorably compared with Angelo's in the contrast between his loving relationship with Juliet and Angelo's desertion of Mariana.

Duke Vincentio of Vienna Character in *Measure for Measure,* the ruler of VIENNA. The Duke, who appoints the stern Angelo as his deputy and then spies on his performance, personifies a major theme of the play: the relationship of government to Christian doctrines of forgiveness and mercy. The Duke's government has been lax, as he admits to the Friar in 1.3, but in designating Angelo to restore a strict public morality he errs to the opposite extreme. His deputy is incapable of applying the law flexibly, and the result is a harsh injustice, the death sentence for the honorable Claudio. However, the Duke is intent on personal improvement—Escalus says of him that he "above all other strifes, contended especially to know himself" (3.2.226–227)—and his effort teaches him to acknowledge the need for mercy to counteract human weakness.

Significantly, the Duke's disguise as he investigates Angelo's governance is that of a friar; in adopting a religious role he manifests the God-given authority that Shakespeare and his original audiences ascribed to all rulers. Angelo's lust for Isabella, Claudio's intercessor, produces a seemingly unresolvable conflict. However, the Duke, in his friar's guise, takes over the play and effects two improbable schemes: the substitution of another head for that of the supposedly executed Claudio, and of another woman, Mariana, for Isabella. Having thus negated Angelo's evil intent, the Duke reemerges, in 5.1, to bring the play to a close in a flurry of pardons and marriages.

Many commentators have found this denouement lacking in credibility, but Shakespeare's purpose was symbolic, and realism should not be expected. The Duke controls the outcome and thus fulfills the ruler's proper role in the play's scheme of things. He offers the mercy of God to the deserving and undeserving alike. It is he who recognizes in Barnardine, the vicious murderer, a mere "creature unprepar'd" (4.3.66), and he forgives Lucio his slanders, despite the insult to both his personal pride and his authority. Most important, he proves susceptible to the pleas of Mariana and Isabella for mercy toward the villainous Angelo. Finally, though he has earlier claimed immunity from "the dribbling dart of love" (1.3.2), he proposes marriage to Isabella. In striking contrast to the negative attitudes of both Angelo and Isabella, early in the play, the Duke underscores Shakespeare's belief in the happy marriages that traditionally close a COMEDY.

Elbow Minor character in *Measure for Measure,* a comic constable of VIENNA. In 2.1 Elbow brings Pompey to court and attempts to prosecute Froth for an unspecified insult to his, Elbow's, wife. However, with his comical mispronunciations and unconscious double meanings he is a stereotypical CLOWN, and he cannot make a sensible accusation. He is foiled by Pompey's humorous evasions, which result in the dismissal of the case. The episode serves as comic relief from the increasingly tense main plot. It also illustrates vividly the SUBPLOT's world of petty vice and crime, standing in striking contrast with the more rigid world of the Duke, Angelo, and Isabella. In 3.2 Elbow has the satisfaction of bringing Pompey to prison, though his triumph is not so humorous as his defeat. Compared to his better-known predecessor Dogberry (in *Much Ado About Nothing*), Elbow is a less successful version of an ancient character type—the bumbling, foolish constable. His is a familiar figure in traditional English drama: In 2.1.169 Escalus compares Elbow and Pompey to Justice and Iniquity, characters in a MORALITY PLAY.

Escalus Character in *Measure for Measure*, a subordinate to Duke Vincentio of Vienna. Escalus is a respected elder—the Duke praises the "art and practice" of "Old Escalus" (1.1.12, 45). He is appointed second-in-command to Angelo in the Duke's absence, and serves as his foil in the play. He consistently advocates mercy for Claudio, in opposition to Angelo's determination to execute the young man for fornication. Though his pleas are dismissed, he continues to defend the ideal of justice tempered with mercy. On the other hand, in the comical trial scene of 2.1 Escalus represents the opposite failing of government in being too lax when he releases the pander Pompey with a warning—one for which the pimp has no respect. This produces the anomaly that a hardened promoter of prostitution goes unpunished while the honorable Claudio remains under sentence of death. Escalus contrasts with Angelo in another respect: He is true to his duty while the Duke's deputy is corrupted by his lust for Isabella. Though he disagrees with Angelo's severity toward Claudio, he limits his resistance to argument and makes no effort to forestall the decision of his superior officer. The Duke recognizes his devotion to duty at the play's close. Escalus's chief function is to serve as a symbol of both dutiful submission and kindness.

Friar Peter (Friar Thomas) Character in *Measure for Measure*, helper of the Duke Vincentio of Vienna. In 1.3 the Duke asks the Friar to disguise him as another friar so that he can return to Vienna incognito and observe the administration of his deputy, Angelo. In 4.5 the Duke revisits the Friar, who assists in his plans to expose the misconduct of Angelo, and in 4.6 the Friar escorts Isabella and Mariana as part of those plans. Finally, in 5.1 he introduces the two women as witnesses to Angelo's evil doings. Though the Duke speaks of him in 1.3 as an intimate friend, the relationship is not developed; the Friar serves merely to further the plot.

The Friar is named Thomas in the stage direction at the beginning of 1.3, but the name is never used elsewhere, and in a later appearance he is named Peter. Shakespeare—who made such minor slips throughout the plays—apparently gave the Friar a name when he first created him, but then forgot about it before writing Act 4, where he gave him another one. The earliest text of the play, that of the FIRST FOLIO, was printed from a transcription of Shakespeare's manuscript, and his original note was erroneously included.

Froth Minor character in *Measure for Measure*, a customer of Mistress Overdone's bordello and bar who is arrested by the comical constable Elbow. In an episode of comic relief, Froth is brought to court along with Mistress Overdone's accomplice, Pompey, in 2.1. Froth says very little and serves only as the subject of the humorous dispute between Elbow and Pompey. Dismissed by the judge Escalus, Froth makes his only substantial remark, a joke that seems to account for his name. He jests that he never enters a taproom willingly, but is drawn in—a reference to the foam, or froth, "drawn" by a tapster in the course of serving ale.

Gentlemen Two minor characters in *Measure for Measure*, friends of Lucio. The Gentlemen appear briefly in 1.2, where they help establish the ambience of the play's SUBPLOT, the atmosphere of vice and degradation amid good spirits that characterizes the underworld of VIENNA. They are soldiers who callously regret the prospects of peace and go on to jest about venereal disease, especially when Mistress Overdone appears. The Gentlemen have no distinct personalities and are not distinguishable from each other. After this brief scene they disappear from the play.

Isabella Character in *Measure for Measure*, a would-be nun and the object of the illicit lust of Angelo. Isabella pleads with Angelo to pardon her brother Claudio, who has been sentenced to death for sexual immorality; in doing so, she arouses the official's desire, and he demands sex of her in exchange for the pardon. She refuses and asserts that to avoid such a sin is worth a life; she objects hysterically when Claudio begs her to give in. She is, in her strict insistence on morality, as extreme as Angelo was when he sentenced Claudio. She realizes her error by the end of the play and requests mercy for Angelo when he is condemned to death by Duke Vincentio. Finally, she abandons her earlier intention to become a nun and agrees to marry the Duke, thus bringing about the play's happy ending in marriage, the traditional closing of a COMEDY.

Isabella undergoes a great change of heart in the course of the play, for neither acceptance nor leniency seem part of her nature at first. Like Angelo, before he succumbs to her beauty, she is strictly insistent on virtue. Not only is she about to enter a nunnery, she regrets that its rules are not strict enough. Like Angelo, she wants to see her own ideals applied to others, "wishing a more strict restraint / Upon the sisters stood" (1.4.4–5) and demanding that Claudio "Take my defiance, / [and] Die, perish!" (3.1.142–143). When she seeks mercy for Claudio, she holds fast to her morals, pleading that the fault be condemned rather than the doer of it. When this fails to work, she goes on to demand that Angelo behave as God would. Her strict attitudes appeal to Angelo's obsessiveness, sparking his lust as no simple offer of a sexual bribe could. Her extremism matches his.

As with other Shakespearean heroines, Isabella's assertiveness is an attractive feature to audiences, but here it is counterproductive and brings nearer the potential tragedy of Claudio's death. This serves, of course, to further the plot, but it also emphasizes an important point: mercy may not be brought about through evil means. If Claudio is to be saved it must be through the action of good, and Isabella, concerned wholly with a rigid sense of morality, cannot provide that action.

Isabella's obsession with her virginity covers her own strong sexuality, which is startlingly apparent in her response to Angelo's proposition. She declares that she'd rather die under torture, saying, "Th' impression of keen whips I'd wear as rubies, / And strip myself to death as to a bed / That longing have been sick for . . ." (2.4.101–103). The strength of her subconscious passion suggests—as does her assertiveness—that she is not a good candidate for the convent, and at the end of the play when her judgmental attitude has softened, her assent to the Duke's marriage proposal seems appropriate, a step toward fulfillment.

Resolution is only made possible by the substitution of Mariana in the "bed trick," permitting the entrapment of the villain without compromising the heroine. Shakespeare's introduction of this device, which is not present in his sources, suggests his attitude toward Isabella. In the original story, the Angelo figure sleeps with the Isabella figure and then is forced to marry her and restore her honor. However, Angelo and Isabella have been shown in the first half of the play to be enemies, and their obsessiveness has been presented with powerful realism. Even within the play's aura of forgiveness, these two characters simply cannot be made to accept each other without losing their dramatic power. Mariana therefore replaces Isabella, and a resolution becomes possible. What is more, Isabella participates in the resolution. She makes the arrangements for the assignation with Angelo, though a message would have sufficed, and then tells Mariana of the plot, a task that could have been performed by the Duke. Shakespeare kept Isabella in the action at this point, thus making her an active force.

Most important, Isabella pleads for Angelo. As the Duke points out, "Her brother's ghost . . . would . . . take her hence in horror" (5.1.433–434). Isabella's intercession opposes her natural feelings toward Angelo, her intended rapist and the apparent killer of her brother, but she supports Mariana's plea. She argues in rational terms for mercy, in a fashion suited to the case, rather than in the absolute terms in which she had pleaded for Claudio. Isabella is no longer a moral extremist. Perhaps she is under the influence of Mariana's example of love, or perhaps she remembers her claim, in 2.2.67–70 that she would be merciful if she had power, or possibly she wishes to atone for her willingness to sacrifice Claudio for a principle. Her act flies in the face of common morality with its demand for justice, just as does Christ's command in the Sermon on the Mount to love one's enemies. Isabella has arrived at the giving of a full measure in the spirit of the biblical text that inspired the play's title.

While the play's ending often seems arbitrary to modern readers, its convenient resolution of the impending tragedy was not only perfectly acceptable in Shakespeare's day, it was highly satisfying: the triumph of good, in a clear and traditional manner, gratified the sentimental feelings of audiences. While

Isabella is somewhat diminished as a character by her symbolic quality in the play's denouement, she is nonetheless sufficiently well developed to rank among Shakespeare's most interesting heroines.

Juliet Minor character in *Measure for Measure*, the pregnant fiancée of Claudio. Claudio's death sentence for having illicit sex with Juliet is the central element of the play's plot, but the young woman is nevertheless a shadowy and undeveloped character. She speaks in only one of the three scenes in which she appears (2.3), and though she is touching in her combination of repentance and love, she remains a minor figure. The role of Juliet is small, and this has suggested to some scholars that the play was at some point extensively revised—by Shakespeare or someone else—and her role was awkwardly cut. However, other commentators feel that her function as a pathetic victim is fully realized by her mere presence, and any enlargement of her role would be distracting.

Justice Minor character in *Measure for Measure*, a magistrate of VIENNA. The Justice appears only in 2.1, speaking three lines to his superior, Escalus. This brief exchange serves to remind the audience of the condemned Claudio after the diversion of the long comic trial of Pompey. The Justice and Escalus depart together at the close of the scene.

Some scholars believe that the Justice's absence elsewhere in the play is evidence that it was considerably revised. Another theory supports only a tiny revision, holding that the Justice's lines had originally been written for the Provost, but that in production they had been reassigned. Normal stage practice in Shakespeare's day frowned on an immediate reentrance after an exit, and since the Provost opens the next scene, he could not close this one by leaving with Escalus. So possibly a new character was invented by Shakespeare or someone else. As a matter of economy, the Justice is often cut from modern productions and his lines eliminated or given to the Provost.

Lodowick In *Measure for Measure*, the name taken by the disguised Duke Vincentio of Vienna.

Lucio Character in *Measure for Measure*, a dissolute gentleman who befriends the condemned Claudio and slanders Duke Vincentio of Vienna. Although, as Claudio's friend, Lucio supports Isabella in her encounters with the obsessively strict official, Angelo, he is nonetheless an unsavory character. He maliciously defames the Duke and callously admits to having abandoned a pregnant woman; that he is forgiven his crimes in the end is an important part of the play's emphasis on the value of forgiveness.

We first see Lucio in 1.2, jesting lewdly about venereal disease with his friends. A customer of the bordello run by Mistress Overdone and Pompey, Lucio represents the degenerate life that has flourished in VIENNA because of the Duke's lax regime. He is not without good qualities, however. In standing by Isabella, in 2.2 and 2.4, he seems a positive figure, but beginning in 3.2 he takes on another aspect. He flippantly refuses to help Pompey avoid imprisonment, and Mistress Overdone declares that he has informed on her; these episodes make us realize that Lucio's Vienna is an ugly one. In 3.2 and 4.3 Lucio amuses himself by making up the libelous stories about the Duke for which he is punished in 5.1. He does not realize that the "friar" with whom he converses is the disguised ruler himself.

While Lucio's slanderous lies are plainly malicious, he seems funny, not evil, to modern sensibilities. But abuse of a ruler—believed to have been appointed by God to maintain order in society— was a much more serious matter in Shakespeare's day than in our own, and Lucio's offense, although comical, is decidedly criminal. Seventeenth-century audiences would not have been surprised by the severity of the Duke's proposed punishment: "Let him be whipp'd and hang'd" (5.1.511). Nevertheless, Lucio remains wittily uncompromising at the end. This testifies to Shakespeare's sympathy with the rebellious individual, even in a play that stresses the importance of authority and the values of society at large.

Mariana Character in *Measure for Measure*, the abandoned fiancée and eventual wife of Angelo. By means of the "bed trick" instituted by Duke

Vincentio, Mariana replaces Isabella—from whom Angelo has attempted to extort sex—in Angelo's bed. When Angelo's evil is exposed, the Duke orders Angelo to marry Mariana—thereby legitimizing her action—following which he will be executed. Mariana pleads for mercy, convincing Isabella to join her, and the Duke finally relents in the atmosphere of reconciliation and forgiveness that closes the play. Aside from her rather formal melancholy as she pines for Angelo in seclusion when we first meet her in 4.1, Mariana is not a developed character, though her plea in 5.1 is touchingly expressive of the play's charitable point of view. She insists that "best men are moulded out of faults, / And . . . become much more the better / For being a little bad" (5.1.437–439).

Her plea gives Mariana special significance, for with it she triggers the sequence of pardons and forgiveness that close the play. Perhaps most important, she persuades Isabella to join her. Though Isabella's intercession goes against her natural enmity toward Angelo, she nevertheless proceeds to offer a sensible case for mercy. It is her conversion to this forgiving point of view—one quite removed from her earlier insistence on morality even if it meant the death of her brother—that is the play's climax. Mariana's plea is essentially selfish; she wishes to preserve the husband she has so long sought. But Isabella is totally objective, and it is this that makes her action impressive. Only the existence of Mariana as a proper mate for Angelo makes this possible.

No hint of Mariana is to be found in Shakespeare's sources for *Measure for Measure,* and the character has particular importance as she is an invention of the playwright that changes the nature of his story in a significant manner. In all of the sources for the play, the Angelo figure successfully extorts sex from the Isabella figure, and then, when exposed, he is forced to marry her. However, in Shakespeare's rendering of the tale, Isabella and Angelo have effectively been presented as intense figures whose opposing psychological strengths make such a union impossible to contemplate. Mariana therefore replaces Isabella. The bed trick, an ancient comedic device that Shakespeare also used in *All's Well,* accomplishes this end. Isabella is preserved as the virtuous counterpart to Angelo's corruption, and Mariana can influence her toward forgiveness as her rigidity relaxes. The device may seem arbitrary to modern readers—like a deus ex machina, it disposes of the impending tragedy with ease and convenience—but in Shakespeare's day this conclusion was not only perfectly acceptable, it was highly gratifying to the audience's sentimental feelings.

Messenger Minor character in *Measure for Measure,* servant of Angelo. In 4.2 the Messenger delivers to the Provost Angelo's command for the execution of Claudio, though a pardon has been expected. Angelo's employment of the Messenger makes his deed seem even more monstrous as he distances himself from it.

Mistress Overdone Character in *Measure for Measure,* the keeper of a bordello in VIENNA. Mistress Overdone's principal role is as a stereotypical member of Vienna's underworld, which stands in contrast to the world of the major characters. Her servant Pompey is the most important figure of this comic SUBPLOT. Mistress Overdone is a familiar figure to Lucio and his friends; her entrance inspires the Gentlemen to jest about venereal disease, establishing the bawdy, depraved tone of the subplot. She also introduces a major element of the main plot when she first appears in 1.2 and tells of the prosecution of Claudio. She is comically presented as a typical innkeeper, worried about business, though this also includes worrying about the government's attempts to fight prostitution. When she is imprisoned in 3.2, she complains that she has been informed against by Lucio. This reminds us that her world of petty vice is not truly a comic one.

A comic subplot featuring a bordello madam and her servant was found by Shakespeare in one of the sources for *Measure for Measure,* George WHETSTONE's *Promos and Cassandra* (1578). However, Shakespeare invented the preposterous names they bear in his play; Mistress Overdone's name reflects her status as a veteran of her profession.

Nun (Francisca, Francesca) Minor character in *Measure for Measure,* a member of the convent that Isabella intends to join. The Nun appears only briefly, in 1.4, when she listens to Isabella's complaint that the restrictions imposed on the nuns seem insufficient. When she hears Lucio's voice, she asks Isabella to receive him, for she may not speak to a man except in the presence of the prioress and then only while hiding her face; if showing her face, she must be quiet. Having established these regulations for the audience, the Nun disappears from the play; except for a momentary disturbance at the approach of Lucio, she displays only the quiet of the stereotypical nun. The episode illustrates Isabella's extremism, as we see that she is determined to adopt a sterner rule of withdrawal than that required of the Nun.

The Nun is named Francisca (or Francesca) in the stage direction at the beginning of 1.4, but the name is not used thereafter. Scholars believe that Shakespeare named his character when he created her but then never used the name. Its survival in the earliest published text, the FIRST FOLIO (1623), is viewed as evidence that the printed text came from Shakespeare's manuscript.

Pompey Bum Character in *Measure for Measure*, a pimp and servant of Mistress Overdone. Pompey is a humorous petty criminal, a representative of the underworld of VIENNA, and the major figure in the comic SUBPLOT, which contrasts with the main story and offers relief from its tensions. Tried as a procurer by Escalus, in 2.1, he outwits Constable Elbow, who testifies for the prosecution, with long-winded evasions and subtle double entendres. He sassily asks the judge if he intends, through laws against prostitution, "to geld and splay all the youth of the city" (2.1.227–228). His bawdy wit makes a mockery of the court, helping to establish that the authority of the Duke has degenerated due to his lax regime. Pompey is eventually jailed in the same prison as Claudio, whose condemnation for illicit sex is at the center of the main plot's conflict. As assistant to Abhorson, the executioner—a position taken in return for a promise of parole—Pompey continues to jest, and his comedy lightens the oppressive atmosphere as Claudio's execution approaches.

As Escalus observes in 2.1.169, Pompey resembles Iniquity, a character from the medieval MORALITY PLAY. He represents a type that was well known,

the clownish criminal (he is designated as a CLOWN throughout the FOLIO text of the play). A comic subplot featuring a madam and her servant was found by Shakespeare in a principal source for *Measure for Measure*, George WHETSTONE's *Promos and Cassandra* (1578), and its appeal was surely immediate for the creator of Falstaff. Pompey's preposterous name was Shakespeare's invention: An ancient Roman hero, Pompey the Great, is provided with a surname that is slang for buttocks.

Provost Character in *Measure for Measure*, the warden of the prison in which Claudio is jailed. From his first appearance—when he exposes Claudio to public humiliation at the orders of Angelo but declares, "I do it not in evil disposition" (1.2.110)—we see the Provost to be a kind and honorable man. He pleads with Angelo to be merciful toward Claudio and clearly presents a sensible view of the young man's offense, thereby emphasizing Angelo's extremism. Nevertheless, the Provost is prepared to do the duty of his office and oversee the young man's execution. In this way he offers a contrast to the moral laxity that created the problem in the first place.

In a telling episode, the Provost demonstrates Shakespeare's position that social order has a high value. This clearly sympathetic character who obviously favors mercy for Claudio nevertheless resists the attempts of the disguised Duke to find a way to save the young man until the Duke produces letters that reveal his authority. Then, supported by the knowledge that he will not be opposing the ruler—Shakespeare and his original audiences believed that rulers were appointed by God—he can enthusiastically help.

Servant Minor character in *Measure for Measure*, an attendant to Angelo. The Servant receives the Provost in 2.2 and announces Isabella's arrival in 2.4. His presence reminds us of Angelo's importance and power.

Varrius Minor character in *Measure for Measure*, a follower of the Duke of Vienna. Varrius is addressed by the Duke in 4.5 and is mentioned in the stage direction opening 5.1, the Duke's formal entry to Vienna, but he does not speak, nor does he appear in the list of characters in the first published text of the play, in the FIRST FOLIO. Some scholars believe that this is evidence that the play had been cut before it was published. On the other hand, Varrius may be seen as a representative of the Duke's entourage whose tiny part in 4.5 prepares the audience to perceive the Duke's return in 5.1 as a ceremonious occasion.

Merchant of Venice, The

SYNOPSIS

Act 1, Scene 1

Salerio and Solanio attempt to cheer up their friend Antonio; they are assisted by Bassanio, Lorenzo, and Gratiano. Antonio denies that he is worried about his investments in far-flung trading voyages, for he is confident of their success. The friends, except Bassanio, depart. Antonio inquires about the love affair Bassanio has promised to speak of. Bassanio replies that his extravagant lifestyle, which he has supported with loans from friends, especially Antonio, may pay off if he can successfully woo and marry Portia, a rich heiress. However, he wishes to borrow more money in order to present himself as an impressive enough suitor to compete with his wealthy rivals. Antonio assures his friend that he will loan him as much as he needs. Because Antonio's funds are all invested in ships at the moment, he promises to borrow the money to support Bassanio's courtship.

Act 1, Scene 2

Portia discusses her late father's will with her maid, Nerissa. Under its terms, she must marry the man who selects from among three chests or caskets— one each of gold, silver, and lead—the one that contains the consent placed in it by her father. Portia worries about the sort of husband she may win in this lottery. She and Nerissa discuss and humorously dismiss a number of potential suitors, and Nerissa reveals, to the relief of her mistress, that all of them have decided not to choose among the caskets because of a penalty that Portia's father has decreed for those who pick either of the wrong ones. Nerissa reminds Portia of Bassanio, who had visited some time before, and they agree that he

would make an acceptable suitor. Word comes that a new suitor, the Prince of Morocco, has arrived.

Act 1, Scene 3

Bassanio and Antonio ask the Jewish moneylender Shylock for a loan. Antonio remarks that he is opposed to usury, the lending of money at interest, and Shylock defends the practice. Further, Shylock observes that Antonio has often spat on him and insulted him for being a Jew, and he asks why he should be expected to assist his tormentor. Antonio frankly acknowledges that Shylock must regard the loan as one made to an enemy. Shylock, however, insists that he wishes to be friendly and offers to lend him the money interest-free for three months, requiring only a humorous collateral: If Antonio cannot repay the loan when it comes due, he will permit Shylock to cut from his body one pound of flesh. Although Bassanio is uneasy about this arrangement, Antonio signs a legal contract for the loan, confident that his business ventures will soon bring him nine times the amount required.

Act 2, Scene 1

Morocco declares his love for Portia and agrees to be bound by her father's will: If he selects the right casket, he will marry her, but he must solemnly swear that, if he chooses one of the others, he will never marry anyone.

Act 2, Scene 2

Shylock's clownish servant, Launcelot Gobbo, soliloquizes humorously on his desire to run away from his master. His blind father, Old Gobbo, appears. Launcelot teases his father, pretending to be a stranger, but finally speaks seriously of his plan to desert Shylock and work for Bassanio, a more liberal and generous master. Bassanio happens by, and Gobbo, with much comical prompting from his son, speaks to him about employing Launcelot. Bassanio, finding the youth amusing, agrees, and Launcelot departs to give notice to Shylock. Gratiano enters and asks to accompany Bassanio when he travels to Portia's estate. Bassanio agrees but insists that Gratiano curb his usual wild humor.

Act 2, Scene 3

Shylock's daughter Jessica bids Launcelot farewell and gives him a letter to deliver to Lorenzo. Alone, she regrets that she is Shylock's daughter but takes heart in the prospect of marrying Lorenzo and converting to Christianity.

Act 2, Scene 4
Lorenzo, with Gratiano, Salerio, and Solanio, are preparing for a MASQUE, when Launcelot arrives with the letter from Jessica. Lorenzo gives him a message for Jessica: he, Lorenzo, shall not fail her. Salerio and Solanio leave, and Lorenzo tells Gratiano that he and Jessica plan to elope that evening.

Act 2, Scene 5
Launcelot delivers an invitation to dinner from Bassanio to Shylock and hints to Jessica that Lorenzo is about to arrive.

Act 2, Scene 6
Lorenzo, accompanied by Gratiano and Salerio, takes Jessica from Shylock's house. Antonio enters and gives Gratiano the message that Bassanio is preparing to leave for BELMONT, Portia's estate.

Act 2, Scene 7
With Portia, Morocco reads the inscriptions on the caskets. The gold one promises "what many men desire"; the silver offers as much as the chooser deserves; the lead warns that the chooser "must give and hazard all he hath." Morocco rejects the lead as a plainly foolish choice and the silver as inadequate. He selects the gold casket but finds inside it a rhyme informing him that he has lost. He departs, to Portia's relief.

Act 2, Scene 8
Salerio and Solanio gossip about Shylock's hysterical discovery that Jessica has fled and taken much of his money. They reflect that Shylock's anger will affect Antonio if he fails to repay his debt, and they worry that a rich Venetian ship, reported lost, may be one of his.

Act 2, Scene 9
The Prince of Arragon ventures to choose one of the caskets and win Portia's hand. He rejects the gold's offer of "what many men desire" as the choice of the foolish multitudes who value outward appearance. Feeling that he is quite worthy, he elects the silver casket's promise of as much as he

deserves. However, a rhyme inside the casket announces his failure, and he leaves. A Messenger brings word that a young Venetian intends to enter the lottery of the caskets. Portia and Nerissa hope that he will prove to be Bassanio.

Act 3, Scene 1
Solanio and Salerio discuss the rumored loss of Antonio's ship. Shylock appears and curses Jessica; he also rails against Antonio, vowing that he will collect his pound of flesh as revenge for Antonio's anti-Semitism. Shylock observes that Jews are like Christians in bodily respects, and he will prove that their desire for revenge is also the same. A message from Antonio causes the gentlemen to depart, and Shylock's friend Tubal arrives. Tubal reports that he has been unable to find Jessica, but he has heard of her extravagance with her father's money. Shylock is frantic about his lost wealth, but Tubal also tells his friend that Antonio has suffered further losses and is said to be bankrupt. Shylock becomes exultant.

Act 3, Scene 2
Portia asks Bassanio to postpone choosing among the caskets, for he must leave if he fails and she has fallen in love with him. Bassanio, however, cannot tolerate the suspense, and he proceeds to his selection. He rejects the gold and silver as representing false glamor and expensive show, and he opens the lead casket. Inside he finds Portia's picture and a text confirming that he has won her hand. She gives him a ring, which he swears to wear until he dies. Gratiano and Nerissa reveal that they have also fallen in love, and a double wedding is proposed. Salerio arrives from Venice with Lorenzo and Jessica. He tells Bassanio that Antonio has lost all his vessels and that Shylock has said that he will demand the pound of flesh. Portia offers to pay Shylock many times over.

Act 3, Scene 3
Antonio, in the custody of a Gaoler, approaches Shylock, but the Jew will not speak to him; he angrily repeats his demand for the pound of flesh and departs. Antonio prepares to die; he hopes only to see Bassanio again.

Act 3, Scene 4
Portia announces her intention to enter a religious retreat while Bassanio tries to help Antonio in Venice. She instructs her servant Balthasar to

deliver a letter to her cousin in PADUA. He is then to meet her with the documents and clothing the cousin will give him. She tells Nerissa of her plan: They shall go to Venice disguised as men.

Act 3, Scene 5

Launcelot, in his capacity as a professional FOOL, impudently jests with Jessica and Lorenzo, who then banter affectionately.

Act 4, Scene 1

The Duke of Venice convenes a court to try Shylock's claim. Shylock is asked to be merciful, but he refuses. The Duke announces that he has sent to a Paduan scholar for a legal opinion. Portia and Nerissa arrive, disguised as a lawyer and his clerk sent by the scholar. Portia interviews Shylock and Antonio. After Shylock repeatedly demands strict justice, she awards him his pound of flesh but prohibits him from drawing any blood—for blood is not mentioned in the contract—on pain of death. Realizing that he is beaten, Shylock says he will accept the money, but Portia rules that he shall have only the exact justice he has demanded: He may attempt to extract his bloodless flesh, or he may withdraw his suit, but he cannot claim the money. Shylock concedes defeat and is about to leave when Portia further rules that, as a non-Venetian who has attempted to take the life of a citizen, he is subject to the death penalty—unless the Duke pardons him—and to the confiscation of all his possessions. The Duke permits him to live, and Antonio suggests that he be allowed to keep half of his earthly goods in exchange for converting to Christianity and deeding the other half to Lorenzo and Jessica. Shylock agrees to these terms. The Paduan lawyer (Portia) refuses a fee but asks Bassanio for his ring as a token of thanks. He refuses, saying that it was a sacred gift from his wife, but he repents after she leaves, accusing himself of ingratitude. He sends Gratiano to give the ring to the lawyer.

Act 4, Scene 2

Gratiano gives the ring to Portia, who asks him to direct her clerk (Nerissa) to Shylock's house to deliver the deed that the moneylender must sign. Nerissa tells Portia that she will contrive to get Gratiano to give her his ring as well.

Act 5, Scene 1

Lorenzo and Jessica enjoy the moonlight and music at Belmont, joyfully comparing themselves to various famous lovers. Word arrives that Portia and Nerissa are returning from the monastery, and Launcelot, comically imitating a hunting horn, heralds the approach of Bassanio. The lovers resume their contemplation, and Lorenzo reflects on the harmony of the spheres. Portia and Nerissa enter, just ahead of Bassanio, Gratiano, and Antonio. The women "discover" that their husbands no longer have their rings, and they chastise them severely, evoking pained excuses. Finally Portia reveals the truth, and the party moves indoors to celebrate their reunion.

COMMENTARY

The Merchant of Venice is a richly complicated work in which several themes are presented in the framework of a traditional COMEDY, which calls for the triumph of young lovers over their unromantic elders. Before this end is achieved, three distinct plots are resolved: the winning of Portia by the lottery of the caskets, the settlement of Shylock's claim, and the final complication of the betrothal rings. All of these developments further the traditional romantic purpose of the play.

But before looking at Shakespeare's intentions and devices, let us consider the evidently anti-Semitic nature of the play, which is particularly repellent in light of the Holocaust (1933–45), in which 6 million European Jews were executed in Nazi concentration camps. Great historical events unavoidably affect the thoughts and sensibilities of later generations, and this terrifying 20th-century manifestation of anti-Semitism must color our response to *The Merchant of Venice*. Its villain is a stereotypical Jew, and his Jewishness is persistently derided by the Christians in the play. Even though Shylock has his moments of sympathetic humanity, they are rather qualified, and he is finally found deserving of treatment that is unquestionably shabby by modern Western ethical and legal standards. He is deprived of his life's earnings and coerced into renouncing his religion by avowed anti-Semites who preach justice and mercy all the while. Many have asked how Shakespeare could have depicted such behavior in characters clearly intended to be taken as good people—Portia, Antonio, and their friends—when in the rest of his work his characterizations are so strikingly humane. One must conclude that, to at least some extent, Shakespeare shared in the anti-Semetic biases of his age.

Of course, the anti-Semitism of Shakespeare's England was rather theoretical: practicing Jews had been few in number there since their expulsion from the country in 1290, and active anti-Jewish bigotry was accordingly unusual. But while 16th-century Londoners may have found Jews more exotic than malevolent, they also had a generally negative image of Judaism that was the legacy of centuries of bias. Christian tradition, from the New Testament on, stimulated anti-Semitism, and if the 16th-century English version was milder than others, it was nonetheless real. Shakespeare, very much a man of his time and place, probably harbored it to some degree; he was at least willing to accommodate his public, which had responded with great delight to *The Jew of Malta,* by Christopher MARLOWE, whose spectacularly villainous title character probably influenced the creation of Shylock. Also, the trial and execution of Roderigo LOPEZ in 1594, not long before Shakespeare wrote this play, generated a spate of more overt expressions of bigotry. (Elizabethan prejudices are similarly addressed in the play's negative presentations of a black man, Morocco, and a Spaniard, Arragon.) In any case, English anti-Semitism was only one expression of a widespread European phenomenon, and there is unquestionably a historical connection across the centuries between the attitudes of Shakespeare's characters and the atrocities of the Holocaust.

Anti-Semitism contributed to the development of Shylock's character simply by providing the only well-known image of a Jew. Sixteenth-century Englishmen tended to attribute to Jews only two important characteristics, both negative: first, that Jews detested Christians and gave much energy to devising evils for gentiles to undergo; and second, that Jews practiced usury. The latter assumption was grounded in an old, though disappearing, reluctance on the part of Christians to lend money, due to biblical injunctions against the practice within one's own religious community. Despite the growth of modern banking in the 16th century, it remained true in much of Europe—including Italy, the source of Shakespeare's story—that lending money at interest was confined by law to non-Christians. In England, however, Christians could and did practice usury, at a legally sanctioned rate of 10 percent. Usury's increasing importance in everyday life was a prominent and widely disliked aspect of economic development in Shakespeare's day, a phenomenon that doubtless led the playwright to adapt a tale that condemned it. That it also condemned a Jew was as much a result of actual Continental practices at the time as of Shakespeare's prejudices. His source featured a Jewish usurer as a villain, and he borrowed this character. He gave the role more life than he found in the source, as he typically did, but he did not alter its anti-Semitic overtones.

Although Shakespeare was influenced by the anti-Semitism of his day in writing *The Merchant of Venice,* the play was not itself motivated by anti-Semitism, nor was it intended to spread anti-Semitic doctrines. Instead, *The Merchant of Venice* illustrates a theme that occupied Shakespeare in most of his comedies: the triumph of love over false and inhumane attitudes toward life.

The central plot of the play deals with Bassanio's courtship of Portia. Antonio goes to Shylock for a loan only because his friend wishes to woo Portia, and the usurer's undoing comes about through Portia's desire to help the friend of her beloved. The seemingly strange ending of the play is the culmination of Portia and Bassanio's betrothal.

The courtship is based on an ancient folk motif, that of a choice among caskets, the suitor's correct choice being rewarded with marriage to the maiden in question. Bassanio expresses his distrust of rich appearances in 3.2.73–107, as he selects the casket of lead. Such sentiments, attached to similar stories, were common in Elizabethan literature and reflected the ideal of true love. Only a true lover would value the maid for herself and choose the plainest casket, which requires him to "give and hazard all he hath" (2.7.9). This ideal is not sullied by Bassanio's frank assessment of Portia's wealth in 1.1.161–176, for such considerations were normal when contemplating marriage in the 16th century;

Bassanio could not reasonably bring up the subject with Antonio and fail to mention Portia's wealth, particularly since he was asking to borrow money to accomplish his courtship.

The tale of the caskets also casts light on another theme of the play, that of the misuse of wealth. The title character of any work may be supposed to represent its essential spirit, and the title character here is Antonio, who risks his wealth—and his life, as it turns out—to aid his friend Bassanio. His enemy, Shylock, is a grotesque miser who loves his ducats more than his daughter. Though his stereotypical Jewishness is essential to his personality, Shylock is more significantly related to another tradition, that of the miser whose mean-spiritedness is contrasted with, and overcome by, the power of love felt by the romantic young. However, the conflict is not simply between money and love, but rather between two different attitudes toward money. Both Antonio and Shylock engage in commerce, but only Antonio is willing to use his wealth in the service of others, resembling Bassanio in his willingness to "hazard all" for his friends. Shylock has the same blind pride as Arragon, assuming that he deserves as much as he is capable of getting.

In Shakespeare's time, money was a particularly troubling subject. Commercial banking was a relatively new phenomenon in England, where land-based wealth had been the norm for centuries, and it inspired much distrust and resentment. Shakespeare's own position seems somewhat ambiguous: His sympathies with old England and his conservative social and political orientation are evident throughout his work, but he himself was a competent businessman, on good terms with the leading usurer of STRATFORD, John COMBE. It has been speculated that his ambivalence may have inspired him to create so three-dimensional a figure as Shylock where a conventional stage villain might have served his traditional comic aims just as well. However, Shylock's humanity gives him great weight; he forcefully represents money's great power to foster hatred and strife, and the open generosity of Antonio and Portia are more convincingly triumphant over Shylock's lust for vengeance when we can clearly see the psychology of his evil need.

As greed is set against love in *The Merchant of Venice*, so is justice placed in opposition to mercy, especially in the trial scene (4.1). The Duke, asking Shylock to excuse Antonio's penalty, asks him, "How shalt thou hope for mercy rend'ring none?" (4.1.88); he is referring to the usurer's expectations in the afterlife. So is Shylock when he answers, "What judgement shall I dread doing no wrong?" (4.1.89). This exchange refers implicitly to a conventional comparison of the Old Testament and the New, in which the former is seen to emphasize strict obedience as humanity's obligation to God while the latter stresses God's mercy. Shylock stands for the strict interpretation of law, for justice in its most rigorous and unbending form. Portia argues for divine clemency, observing, "The quality of mercy is not strained" (4.1.180), at the opening of her most famous speech.

But Shylock is not wholly evil. His position is defensible, and his demand for vengeance is made humanly understandable. He has earlier traced his own evil to a plausible source in remarking to his tormentors Salerio and Solanio that "the villainy you teach me I will execute" (3.1.65). Further, Portia, once her battle is won, is not particularly given to mercy, depriving Shylock of any repayment of his loan and then sentencing him to death as well. Shakespeare invented Portia's invocation of a capital punishment statute; it is not in his sources. Thus he emphasized the paradoxical conclusion that Shylock's downfall results from his own insistence on strict justice.

Antonio mercifully rescinds the death penalty, but Shylock is deprived of all his support in life—as Shakespeare permits him to observe in 4.1.370–373. The main thrust of the trial scene is clear: Shylock has been given enough rope to hang himself, and then harsh justice has been tempered by the mercy of the title figure. Antonio, whose affairs have both promoted Bassanio's romantic success and produced his own woes, remains the source of the play's action.

The two primary plots demonstrate and reconcile opposing principles. We see how wealth can aid romance as well as hinder it, and that justice can be merciful as well as vengeful. These themes are tied together in the seemingly gratuitous anecdote of the betrothal rings. Portia's ploy is not simply a practical joke; the rings are carefully presented as tokens first of love, then of gratitude, and finally of forgiveness. Bassanio understands the dilemma he faces when he gives his ring to the lawyer "Balthasar"; he is not disloyal to Portia, but he recognizes that he owes a debt of gratitude to the young lawyer who has saved his friend. Portia knows this, and while she effectively adopts Shylock's position, insisting on the letter of the oath with which the ring was received originally, she clearly intends to forgive Bassanio after teasing him a bit. The story of the rings—a well-known tale in Shakespeare's day—was introduced by the playwright in order to recapitulate in a lightly comic manner the lessons won from the stressful trial. The other elements of 5.1—the rhapsodic musings of Lorenzo and Jessica and the meditations on music—serve a similar purpose. Although often seen as an ill-considered aberration, this scene alleviates the mood of the preceding one. It provides an anticlimax that returns us to the lovers and their world. Without it, *The Merchant of Venice* would resemble the later PROBLEM PLAYS, which tend to deal with unpleasant social phenomena in an ambiguous way. Here, even such a grossly sentimental—and wholly implausible—event as Portia's announcement that Antonio's ships have miraculously survived (5.1.274–279) can be accepted wholeheartedly. The audience is permitted to share in the triumph of love and playfulness—the spirit of comedy—over the selfish and inhumane stinginess that Shylock represents.

Modern readers, aware of the extremes to which anti-Semitism can lead, tend to give Shylock more sympathy than his place in the play's tight structure can bear. Shakespeare and his audiences were comfortable with a formal, allegorical presentation of human truth that often seems obscure to modern sensibilities, which are far more attuned to realism. Shylock's symbolic role, that of an obvious villain opposed to characters representing generosity and love, is more important to the play's themes than is his Jewishness or his personality. Eighteenth- and 19th-century theatrical tradition humanized the character, presenting to our own century a very different figure from the one whom Shakespeare originally conceived.

The Merchant of Venice presents great opportunity for such varying approaches; indeed, it demands them. For example, Shylock can be sympathized with, but he may also be seen as an overdeveloped figure who interferes with a romantic comedy. On the other hand, sometimes 5.1 is seen as a defective scene that draws attention away from Shylock. Portia's strategem of leading Shylock on in his claims to justice can be seen as high-handed and the trial scene regarded as a satire on law and its cruel strictures. Some critics see the focus of the play as the relationship between Antonio and Bassanio; the theme of friendship among men was prominent in medieval literature and was more plainly employed by Shakespeare in *The Two Gentlemen of Verona*. Some go so far as to hold that Shakespeare intended Antonio's affection to be taken as homosexual. These varied interpretations demonstrate the richness of *The Merchant of Venice*: Many different views of the play can be plausibly presented. Its diverse complications are not stiffly theatrical, despite their roots in dramatic conventions and old tales. Instead, they derive from the problems and ambiguities of human experience.

SOURCES OF THE PLAY

The primary source for *The Merchant of Venice* was a story in an Italian collection, *Il Pecorone (The Simpleton)*, by Giovanni FIORENTINO, published in Milan (1558). This tale presents all the components of Shakespeare's play in considerable detail, except for the lottery of the caskets and Shylock's practice of usury (his equivalent loans money at no interest). A possible intervening source has often been proposed: A lost English play, *The Jew*, mentioned in a publication of 1579, may have been reworked by Shakespeare. However, the only known reference to *The Jew* is brief and ambiguous, and such complicated plots as that of *The Merchant of Venice* were virtually unknown in the 1570s. This hypothesis is thus generally unpopular.

The introduction of the usury theme could have been suggested by several contemporary sources, including Anthony MUNDAY's novel *Zelauto* (1580) and a well-known ballad, "Gernutus," both of which tell of a similarly forfeited loan, in each case to a usurer. The lottery of three caskets is an ancient motif that the playwright also may have known from a number of sources. The *Confessio Amantis,* by John GOWER, which Shakespeare unquestionably knew, contains a variation taken from BOCCACCIO, but the most closely corresponding version is in a translation by Richard ROBINSON of the *Gesta Romanorum,* a famed medieval collection of tales, published in 1577 and 1595. The elopement and conversion of Jessica may have been suggested by similar characters in either *Zelauto* or Marlowe's *The Jew of Malta* (ca. 1592). The latter's immense popularity is often thought to have sparked Shakespeare's adaptation of Fiorentino's tale (or *The Jew*) in the first place, and its title character probably influenced the creation of Shylock.

TEXT OF THE PLAY

The Merchant of Venice was written between the summer of 1596 and the summer of 1598. The later date is certain because the play was registered for publication in July of that year, and it is mentioned as a produced play in Francis MERES's book, published in September 1598. The earlier date, though less certain, seems probable in view of Salerio's reference in 1.1.27 to the ship ANDREW—that is, the *St. Andrew,* a Spanish vessel captured by the English in 1596. (Although such a reference could have been added some time after the play was written, earlier dates seem unlikely in view of the play's stylistic similarities to such later works as *1* and *2 Henry IV* and *Much Ado About Nothing.*)

The Merchant of Venice was first published in 1600 in a QUARTO edition known as Q1. It was printed by James ROBERTS for the publisher Thomas HEYES. Its stage directions, which contain many superfluous remarks, suggest that Q1 was printed from Shakespeare's manuscript, though whether from his FOUL PAPERS or from the FAIR COPY, is uncertain. A second edition, Q2, was a reprint of Q1, produced in 1619 by William JAGGARD for Thomas PAVIER as part of the FALSE FOLIO. The publisher, who was reprinting the play without authorization, asserted on the title page that the edition had been printed by Roberts in 1600—that is, that it was in fact Q1. Until the early 20th century, scholars believed it to be the first edition of the

play. But although taken from Q1, Q2 contains several minor alterations of the original text, as well as many new errors. Q3 (1637) and the FIRST FOLIO text of 1623 were based on Q1, and Q1 has also served as the basic text for most subsequent editions. However, the Folio edition contains improved stage directions (probably derived from a text used in early productions), and these have frequently been followed by modern editors.

THEATRICAL HISTORY OF THE PLAY

According to the title page of the first edition of the play in 1600, *The Merchant of Venice* had been performed "divers times" by that date, but the first performance of which a record has survived was held at the court of King JAMES I in the spring of 1605. It was so well received that the king ordered a second performance several days later, but no other 17th-century performance is known. In 1701 George GRANVILLE produced an adaptation, *The Jew of Venice,* in which Shylock was played for laughs by a popular comic. This version was still quite popular in 1741, when Charles MACKLIN restored Shakespeare's play, portraying Shylock as a melodramatic villain. The play was performed in various versions throughout the rest of the 18th century, with most of the important actors of the day playing the Jew. Shylock was apparently treated as the major figure in the play, and, following Macklin's example, he was depicted as thoroughly malignant.

The first Shylock intended to arouse sympathy was that of Edmund KEAN, whose Jew was scornful of his enemies and raged against their pretensions to mercy. William HAZLITT, in a famous review, said of Kean's Shylock, "He is honest in his vices; they are hypocrites in their virtues." Other notable 19th-century Shylocks included William Charles MACREADY, Charles KEAN, and Edwin BOOTH. Beginning in 1879, Henry IRVING was particularly successful playing the villain in a grandly tragic manner. A somewhat later production went so far as to have Shylock commit suicide onstage following his last lines.

In the 20th century the emphasis on Shylock was modified, and various interpretations were offered. In a famous 1921 production, the German producer Max REINHARDT presented the villain as a buffoon and the play as a farce with a notorious blue and white Cubist-style set, but most attempts have been soberer. In general it was found that, with Shylock somewhat de-emphasized, productions were able to assert the essential unity of the play.

The Merchant of Venice has remained among the most popular of Shakespeare's plays, and many leading players have performed in it, including John GIELGUD and Sybil THORNDIKE. An award-winning 1999 production directed by Trevor NUNN was adapted for TELEVISION in 2001. The *Merchant* has been televised a number of other times, perhaps most memorably in 1970, directed by Jonathan MILLER and starring Laurence OLIVIER and Joan PLOWRIGHT. It had been produced as a silent FILM six times by 1923 but has only once been filmed since, in Italian in 1952. Mario CASTELNUOVO-TEDESCO, who composed numerous works using Shakespearean texts, wrote a popular OPERA based on *The Merchant of Venice* in 1956.

CHARACTERS

Antonio Title character in *The Merchant of Venice*. Antonio borrows money from Shylock and agrees to let the usurer cut away a pound of his flesh if he defaults on the repayment. Antonio represents the ideal of selfless generosity that the play advocates. He borrows only in order to help his spendthrift friend Bassanio, who wishes to appear wealthy as he woos Portia. Antonio's extravagant willingness to risk his money—and his life—stands in opposition to Shylock's calculating greed. Also, his often-expressed fondness for Bassanio represents another literary ideal of Shakespeare's day— that of close friendship between males—which the playwright dealt with more extensively in *The Two Gentlemen of Verona*. Although this motif was a common one, some scholars contend that the intensity of Antonio's affection for Bassanio may demonstrate homosexual tendencies in Shakespeare. Whether or not this is the case, Antonio is a passive, melancholy, somewhat colorless man, stoical in the face of death and lonely amid the lovers' happiness at the play's end.

Arragon (Aragon) Character in *The Merchant of Venice*, Spanish prince and unsuccessful suitor of Portia. In selecting among the caskets of silver, gold, and lead to win Portia's hand, Arragon reveals the arrogance that his name suggests. He rejects the lead casket as unworthy and the gold because its inscription promises "what many men desire" (2.9.24), and he feels himself superior to the "common spirits" (2.9.32). Although Arragon is a somewhat comic figure—he is a caricature Spaniard of a sort familiar to 16th-century English theatergoers—his failure to select the correct casket illuminates the thematic values of the play. He is presented as a foil to Bassanio, who chooses the humble lead casket and wins the lottery and whose victory reflects on the Spaniard's vanity. Further, the villainous Shylock resembles Arragon in his pride, refusing to relinquish an iota of what he feels he deserves. An unselfish sense of community with others is necessary for romantic success, in the play's scheme of things, and Arragon demonstrates its opposite.

Balthasar Minor character in *The Merchant of Venice*, servant of Portia. In 3.4 Balthasar is sent with a letter to Portia's cousin, setting in motion her plan to impersonate a lawyer at the hearing of Shylock's suit against Antonio. Portia later takes Balthasar's name as part of her disguise.

Bassanio Character in *The Merchant of Venice*, friend of Antonio and suitor of Portia. In requesting money from Antonio in order to court Portia in style, Bassanio is indirectly responsible for the peril in which the merchant finds himself when he borrows from Shylock and risks his flesh. But Bassanio is also an important figure in his own right. He wins Portia by choosing the correct casket in the lottery required by her father, and in so doing he demonstrates a 16th-century ideal of romantic love. He distrusts the rich appearance of the gold and silver caskets (3.2.73–107) and instead selects the casket of lead. Such a choice was a conventional indication of selfless love. Only a true lover would value the maid for herself rather than her "outward shows" (3.2.73). Bassanio is a leisured gentleman, presumably able to find a wife elsewhere, but he is willing to risk his chances of matrimony in order to win Portia. Like Antonio, he finds value in reaching for the greatest happiness, and he is thus placed in opposition to Shylock's stinginess. Similarly, like Antonio and Portia and unlike Shylock, Bassanio gives what he has. He is a good-hearted spendthrift who cannot refuse a request, as when Gratiano announces that he has a favor to ask and is immediately told, "You have obtain'd it" (2.2.169).

Bassanio is sometimes seen in a rather different light. Some critics regard him as an heiress-hunting playboy whose irresponsibility endangers Antonio. However, Bassanio objects to Antonio's acceptance of Shylock's bond (1.3.150–151) and is persuaded only by his friend's assurances that he will certainly be able to repay the loan. And although Bassanio refers to Portia's wealth when he first mentions the idea of marrying her (1.1.161–176), this does not necessarily make him a gold digger. Such considerations were normal in the 16th century; one would not discuss courtship without bringing up the subject of wealth. For Shakespeare's audience, and for the playwright himself, such behavior was ordinary, and Bassanio was surely intended as a romantic hero, a personification of good fortune in love.

Bassanio's name—not found in Shakespeare's sources for the play—may have been taken from one of several Bassanios, natives of Venice, who were musicians in the household of Queen Elizabeth I (see LANIER, EMILIA).

Duke of Venice Minor character in *The Merchant of Venice*, the ruler of VENICE. The Duke presides over the trial of Shylock's suit against Antonio. He is helpless to influence matters, being bound by the laws of the state, a position in which Shakespeare often places his rulers (e.g., the Duke of Ephesus in *A Comedy of Errors*). In this way the Duke emphasizes a principle to which the playwright was strongly committed: the importance of the law in a well-ordered society. Although the Duke is prepared to see Antonio die, as the full rigor of the law dictates, he is merciful to Shylock after the case is resolved in Antonio's favor, thus highlighting another virtue Shakespeare saw in an ideal ruler.

Gaoler Minor character in *The Merchant of Venice*, the custodian of Antonio, who is arrested for debt, in 3.3. The Gaoler, who does not speak, repre-sents the authority of the state, mutely showing that Antonio may not be exempted from the law. Shakespeare believed such rigor to be necessary, however undesirable the personal consequences.

Gobbo, Old Minor character in *The Merchant of Venice*, father of Launcelot Gobbo. Old Gobbo, nearly blind, is teased by Launcelot, who pretends to be a stranger and informs the old man that his son has died. Rewarded by his father's distress, Launcelot tells him the truth and enlists him to help approach Bassanio about a job. After providing these few moments of incidental mirth, Gobbo disappears from the play.

Gratiano Character in *The Merchant of Venice*, friend of Bassanio and lover of Nerissa. Gratiano is a crude and frivolous companion. As Bassanio himself puts it, "Gratiano speaks an infinite deal of nothing" (1.1.114). He can be tactless, as in 1.1, where he is the only one of Antonio's friends who fails to see the propriety of leaving Antonio and Bassanio to confer privately. Bassanio, fearful that his friend will embarrass him before Portia, feels constrained to chastise him, "Thou art too wild, too rude, and bold of voice . . ." (2.2.172). Gratiano's bluff heartiness turns ugly in the trial scene (4.1), when he baits the desperate Shylock, and his lewd remarks, as in 3.2.216, mark him as a lesser person than the gentlemanly Bassanio. His courtship of Nerissa is simply an echo of Bassanio's wooing of Portia and seems to have no point but symmetry; such doubling was very popular among Elizabethan audiences. Gratiano's name comes from the Italian COMMEDIA DELL'ARTE tradition, where it was used for a stock character, the comical doctor.

Jessica Character in *The Merchant of Venice*, daughter of Shylock and lover of Lorenzo. Jessica is an apparently demure young woman who nevertheless abandons her father and her religion willingly in eloping with Lorenzo, and she also steals Shylock's money. Tubal reports her extravagance with these funds in 3.1. In 5.1 the romantic rhapsodies of Lorenzo and Jessica provide the play's finest lyric poetry and establish the triumph of love, a major theme of the work.

Jessica's behavior to her father has often been criticized, and if Shylock is viewed as a sympathetic or tragic character, his daughter can only seem immoral. Moreover, her desertion and theft seem to be related to the anti-Semitism that infects this play. Referring to Jessica's enthusiastic readiness to steal from her father, Gratiano avers that she is "a gentle [i.e., gentile], and no Jew" (2.6.51). That is, she qualifies as a Christian by her actions against a Jew. However, the play is clearly a traditional romantic COMEDY, and Jessica's role in that context is a simple one. She flees to romantic love from the prison of her father's miserly household, which she describes as "hell" (2.3.2). In doing so, she illustrates a bold example of the opposition between love and greed that lies at the heart of the play. Further, her theft of her father's funds reflects Shylock's traditional function as a comic villain (although Shakespeare enlarged the character considerably) and was probably received by the play's original audiences as a comeuppance to the miser, a traditional subject of comical raillery. Jessica is humorous as she steals, archly asserting that the weight of a purloined casket is "worth the pains" and saying she will "gild myself / with some moe ducats" as she leaves (2.6.33, 49–50). She is essentially a secondary character, graceful but uncomplicated. Only her relationship to Shylock inspires comment.

Launcelot Gobbo (Lancelot Gobbo) Character in *The Merchant of Venice*, comical servant, first of Shylock and then of Bassanio, for whom he is also a professional jester. Launcelot carries messages and announces impending arrivals, but his role in the action is otherwise unimportant. His humor is clever and resourceful, but often broad and laced with standard devices. In 2.2.1–30, when he first appears, he wittily imitates legal precision in describing the overcoming of his conscience; in the same scene he draws on the ancient comic routine of mistaken identity, teasing his blind father, Old Gobbo. He frequently misuses words—a regular feature of Shakespearean clowning—as when he mistakes "reproach" for "approach" (2.5.20) and "impertinent" for "pertinent" (2.2.130). He engages Lorenzo in a battle of puns and deliberate misunderstandings in 3.5.35–58, and in 5.1.39 he raucously

imitates the blare of hunting horns. He has no particular personality aside from his buffoonish wit.

Launcelot is called "clown" in the stage directions of old editions, but he does not have the rustic qualities sometimes associated with that stock theatrical figure (although the terms *clown* and *fool* were somewhat interchangeable; see CLOWN and FOOL), and here the term may merely indicate that the part was played by the clown of the company, who specialized in broadly comic roles.

Launcelot provides evidence of Elizabethan anti-Semitism. In 2.2 he delivers a comic monologue in which he recounts a dispute between his conscience and a fiend as to whether or not he should leave Shylock's service. This passage and Launcelot's subsequent conversation with his father help to establish Shylock's reputation as a miser in virulently anti-Semitic terms. Similarly, in 3.5.1–24 he jests with Jessica on the likelihood of her damnation as a Jew, reflecting centuries of Christian prejudice. Although plainly intended as comical, Launcelot's attitude surely indicates something of the spirit in which Shakespeare's audience received Shylock—as an obvious villain, at least in part simply because he is Jewish.

Leonardo Minor character in *The Merchant of Venice*, servant of Bassanio. In 2.2 Leonardo speaks one line when he is instructed to arrange Bassanio's trip to BELMONT.

Lorenzo Character in *The Merchant of Venice*, suitor and then husband of Jessica. A friend of Antonio and Bassanio, Lorenzo is a stock theatrical figure, a stylish young aristocrat with little distinctive personality. However, the rhapsodies of Lorenzo and Jessica on moonlight and music in 5.1 provide the play's finest lyric poetry. Lorenzo's musing on the music of the spheres (5.1.55–65) presents an idea of universal harmony that is appropriate to the play's conclusion, in which the oppositions that have been its principal substance—love versus greed, justice versus mercy—are resolved.

Messenger Minor character in *The Merchant of Venice*, servant of Portia. In 2.9 the Messenger tells Portia that Bassanio is approaching.

Morocco (Morochus) Character in *The Merchant of Venice*, an African prince and unsuccessful suitor of Portia. Faced with the choice among three caskets ordained by Portia's father, Morocco rationalizes his choice in a long speech (2.7.13–60) that presents a viewpoint that the play as a whole invalidates. Morocco is attracted by the richness of the gold casket, which promises "what many men desire" (2.7.5), but he finds within it an image of a death's head and a scroll whose message begins with the now-familiar line "All that glisters is not gold" (2.7.65). Morocco fails because he equates appearance with inner worth and because he cannot imagine hazarding all in pursuit of happiness, unlike Bassanio, who wins Portia by selecting the lead casket, and Antonio, who risks everything for his friend in accepting Shylock's perilous loan.

Portia dislikes the prospect of marrying Morocco because he is black. She makes the conventional Elizabethan association of black skin and evil when she first learns of his approach (1.2.123–125). In 2.1 she politely assures him that she recognizes his virtues as a man and a prince, but after his defeat, she is relieved. *The Merchant of Venice* is a play that acknowledges and makes use of Elizabethan prejudices; not only is it distinctly anti-Semitic, but the two unsuccessful suitors—both presented as examples of flawed values—are a black man and a political enemy of England, the Spaniard Arragon.

In both the QUARTO and FIRST FOLIO editions of the play, the name Morocco is rendered in Latin, Morochus, and some modern editions follow this practice.

Musicians Minor characters in *The Merchant of Venice*, servants of Portia. The Musicians appear in two important episodes. In 3.2 their song "Tell me where is Fancy bred" provides an interlude that heightens the suspense as Bassanio contemplates his fateful choice among the three caskets, and it also makes a point about the nature of beauty. Further, it may offer Bassanio a clue as to which casket to select. In 5.1 the Musicians add to the romantic charm of BELMONT, dissipating the disturbing and anxious atmosphere of the preceding courtroom scene. Musicians were a normal feature of a wealthy household in Shakespeare's day.

Nerissa Character in *The Merchant of Venice*, lady-in-waiting to Portia. Nerissa is a pert and lively companion to her mistress. In the early scenes involving the lottery of the three caskets, she assures the uneasy heiress that all will be well, and she seconds Portia in the practical joke of the betrothal rings in 5.1. Her courtship by Gratiano echoes that of Portia by Bassanio; such symmetical couples were quite popular in ELIZABETHAN THEATER.

Old Gobbo See Gobbo, Old.

Portia Character in *The Merchant of Venice*, lover of Bassanio and defender of his friend Antonio. Portia, disguised as a lawyer, saves Antonio from the revenge of Shylock. Initially a passive young woman at the mercy of her father's odd matchmaking device, the lottery of caskets, she emerges as a touching lover with Bassanio in 3.2 and achieves a grand maturity when she defends Antonio in 4.1. Her address to Shylock on the virtues of mercy (4.1.180–198) is renowned as one of the finest passages Shakespeare wrote; it is certainly his most effective presentation of Christian ideals. Her tactics in the trial—leading Shylock to believe he can win his case and thus eliciting from him his demands for the strictest interpretation of the law—have been deplored as high-handed, and they are certainly unethical by modern standards. But Shakespeare was composing an allegory, not a legal precedent, and Portia's strategy emphasizes the instructive paradox that Shylock's rigid insistence on the letter of the law proves to be his own undoing. Portia, defending Antonio because he is the friend of her beloved, evidences the power of love itself, conquering Shylock, whose calculating usury is opposed to the generosity of the young lovers and Antonio.

Portia's final act—accepting, in the person of the young lawyer "Balthasar," her own ring from Bassanio and then twitting him with disloyalty—has been seen as arbitrary and graceless, but the episode fittingly closes the play. It recapitulates the lesson that love and forgiveness are superior to self-centered greed. By invoking Shylock's attitude, insisting on the letter of Bassanio's oath, Portia reasserts a negative value that she immediately repudiates when she forgives her new husband, and the play closes on a note of loving reconciliation.

Before she appears, Portia is described by Bassanio in extravagantly poetic terms (1.1.161–172), and we envision her as an almost supernatural ideal of womanhood. However, with her opening line, " . . . my little body is aweary of this great world" (1.2.1–2), she instantly becomes human. Her simultaneously grand and companionable nature charms us throughout the play. She is an open young woman who can describe herself as "an unlessoned girl, unschooled, unpractised" (3.2.159) and who can giggle with Nerissa over the disguises they will wear (3.4) and over the trick they will play on their husbands-to-be (4.2). At the same time she inspires Bassanio's rhapsody, and most important, she is a resourceful and commanding figure who takes Antonio's fate in hand and delivers him. Shakespeare thus enshrines in virginal youth a gallant, courageous, and worldly woman.

However, Portia has an unattractive feature, to modern sensibilities: She clearly partakes of the 16th-century English racial prejudice and anti-Semitism that are reflected in this play. Addressing Shylock in court, in 4.1, she repeatedly calls him "Jew," and she is frank about her distaste for Morocco's black complexion in 1.2.123–125 and 2.7.79. On the other hand, she is willing to marry the African prince if he wins the lottery of caskets, as she declares in 2.1.13–22, and her attitude toward Shylock's Jewishness—manifested only in the trial scene—is extremely mild, compared to that of other characters. *The Merchant of Venice* accommodates the prejudices of its original audiences, but Portia is not a significant bearer of this theme, and we are in no doubt that Shakespeare intended her as a delightful heroine.

Portia is a fine example of the frank and fearless young women who appear in many of the plays; like Rosaline, Beatrice, and Rosalind (in *Love's Labour's Lost*, *Much Ado About Nothing*, and *As You Like It*, respectively), she seems to embody an ideal of femininity that the playwright held and put forth often. Spirited and capable, she is willing to enter a man's world—in this case, that of the law—in pursuit of her aims, yet she ultimately accepts the conventional Elizabethan woman's status, that of a wife, at least theoretically subservient to her husband.

Salerio (Salarino)   Character in *The Merchant of Venice*, a friend of Antonio. Salerio, whose conversation in elegant verse reflects his position as a cultured gentleman of VENICE, is difficult to distinguish from his companion Solanio. They present certain facts to the audience, as when, consoling the melancholy Antonio in 1.1, they refer to his status as a wealthy and successful merchant. In 2.8 the same figures discuss Shylock's despair and rage at Jessica's elopement (which Salerio has assisted) and speculate that the Jew will vent his anger on Antonio if he can. In 3.1 they tease Shylock, eliciting from him his famous speech claiming equality with Christians. Salerio is simply a conventional figure whose role is to further the development of more significant characters.

In some editions Salerio's part, except in 3.2, is assigned to Salarino, who is thought of as a separate character. However, most modern scholarship holds that the latter name is simply a 16th-century typographical error.

Serving-man (1)   Minor character in *The Merchant of Venice*, servant of Portia. The Serving-man brings his mistress word that four unwanted suitors are leaving and that another suitor, the Prince of Morocco, is arriving.

Serving-man (2)   Minor character in *The Merchant of Venice*, servant of Antonio. In 3.1 the Serving-man tells Salerio and Solanio that his master wishes to see them.

Shylock   Character in *The Merchant of Venice*, Jewish moneylender who seeks to kill the title figure, Antonio, by claiming a pound of his flesh, as provided for in their loan agreement. Shylock is a stereotypical Jew, shaped by anti-Semitic notions that were prevalent in Shakespeare's England. He accordingly possesses the two standard features ascribed to Jews at the time: a vicious hatred of Christians and the practise of usury, the latter entailing an obsessive miserliness. However, Shakespeare's portrayal of Shylock does not demonstrate

With Shylock, Shakespeare transforms a stock character from earlier literature, the miser, into a richer, more complex character. More than just a comic villain, Shylock is also a sympathetic victim. *(Courtesy of Culver Pictures, Inc.)*

enters in the same scene, Shylock reveals in an aside (1.3.36–47) his deep-seated hostility toward the merchant, "for he is a Christian." Yet his first words to Antonio are fawning compliments, and we immediately recognize the cruel usurer as a hypocrite as well. Throughout the play he is repeatedly associated with the devil (e.g., in 3.1.19–20). The famous speech in which he seemingly asserts his basic humanity—"Hath not a Jew eyes? . . ." (3.1.47–66)—is actually a baleful and chilling assertion of his intention to murder Antonio. Shylock grows more and more malevolent until, in the trial scene (4.1), he melodramatically hones on his shoe the knife with which he hopes to kill the merchant while obstinately refusing to grant mercy, even for huge sums of money.

As is true of all comic villains, there is never any doubt that Shylock will be defeated in the end, and he is therefore never truly threatening. Further, Shylock is broadly comical at times; in this respect he somewhat resembles the VICE of the medieval MORALITY PLAY. His stinginess has a humorous quality of caricature to it, and he is depicted as a subject for ridicule in all but one of his scenes, even in the trial scene. In his first meeting with Antonio, he justifies his usury by citing instances from the Bible, but he comically selects stories of crafty dealing (1.3.66–83) that actually cast him in a bad light. In 2.5 his dream is mocked by Launcelot, and his obsessive insistence on locking his house is humorously crotchety. In 3.1, following the renowned speech in which he asserts his thirst for revenge, a change of tone—preparing the audience for a return to BELMONT in 3.2—presents him as a farcical villain who becomes ludicrous as he oscillates hysterically between rage and delight when Tubal tells him of Jessica's extravagance and Antonio's misfortune. Even at the trial, Shylock repeatedly makes himself clownish, chortling over the absence of a surgeon, naïvely exulting in the pretense of Portia that he will win his case and hastily trying to recover his money when he finds he has lost. Only in 3.3 is Shylock purely evil, making more imperative the development of Portia's counterplot in 3.4.

As villain, Shylock embodies the negative element in several sets of opposing values whose conflicts provide the major themes of the play. First, he

his intent to promote or display anti-Semitism; he simply took the figure from his anti-Semitic source and used it for traditional comic purposes. But his genius also transformed the character into something far grander. Shylock has so fascinated generations of readers and theatergoers that, although his name has become a byword for the warped personality of the unscrupulous miser, few can avoid feeling sympathy for him.

The miser was a frequent comic villain in the drama and literature of the Middle Ages and early RENAISSANCE, and Shylock belongs to this lineage. He represents the killjoy against whom pleasure-loving characters unite. He is a schemer whose icy shrewdness daunts Bassanio in 1.3. When Antonio is the crabbed old man who opposes the expansive young lovers. His daughter flees him, saying that his "house is hell" (2.3.2), and his contrast to Bassanio is carried forward to Portia's victory over him in the courtroom. The final scene (5.1) rings with Shylock's absence, as young love triumphs. Further, he represents justice as opposed to mercy, insisting on the letter of the law and refusing to accept any reduction of the terms of his contract with Antonio. Most significantly, he personifies greed, in contrast to the generosity of Antonio and Portia. In comically crying, "My daughter! O my ducats! O my daughter!" (2.8.15), Shylock reveals that he loves money as much as, if not more than, Jessica. Among the reasons he gives for hating Antonio is a commercial one: the merchant, in making interest-free loans, has depressed the going rate. Thus Shylock's love of money generates acrimony and strife.

It is evidence of Shakespeare's creative empathy that even an evil stereotype is developed to the extent that Shylock is. Not content with a conventional stage villain, the playwright gives Shylock's personality an extraordinary duality. Many of his speeches, even the most humorous and/or malicious, can be construed as cries of anguish: the villain is also a victim, we sense. It is easy to deride the two-faced miser who comically equates his daughter and his ducats, but it is also easy to perceive an old man, enraged by betrayal, who has begun to lose his mind. The usurer is given an opportunity to justify his practice in 1.3, and his solemn citations from the Bible have dignity and are not to be taken as only self-incriminating. He is finally subjected to a total and humiliating defeat: His oaths on his religion are nullified, and he is forced to convert. Yet our response to him remains complex. When the crushed moneylender last exits at the close of 4.1, he may be seen as an unrepentant malingerer ("I am not well . . ." [4.1.392]), as a hopeful Christian convert ("I am content" [4.1.389]), or simply as a properly beaten cur and an appropriate target for the cruel jests of Gratiano. The scene may also be effectively played so as to give Shylock his pride, broken but not vanquished; this image diminishes the righteous triumph of Antonio's defenders. Most strikingly, perhaps, Shylock so vividly evokes Venetian anti-Semitism in

3.1.47–66 that this speech is generally taken as a plea for fair and humane treatment, when it is in fact a justification for an extremely inhumane demand. Repeatedly, the playwright offers the possibility of contradictory responses (as he did, at about the same time, in creating Falstaff). However, it is basic to the nature of the character that, although Shylock has come to his extreme behavior through suffering, his behavior is nonetheless unacceptable: He is fundamentally a ruthless villain who plans to kill Antonio. Shakespeare does not ignore the process whereby Shylock has become what he is, but he is nonetheless appallingly vicious. Shylock himself says, ". . . since I am a dog, beware my fangs" (3.3.7).

This complex and powerful character dominates the play, despite his relatively small part: He appears in only five scenes and speaks fewer than 400 lines. His multifaceted nature complicates the work substantially, and it has sometimes inspired criticism on the grounds that it upsets the graceful development proper to a romantic comedy. Shakespeare may have been aware of this problem when he disposed of his villain in Act 4; the final act affirms the triumph of the lovers without his disturbing presence.

Like many of Shakespeare's characters, Shylock lends himself to many interpretations, and he remains as compelling as ever, anticipating the power and pathos of such later protagonists as Othello and Lear. But although we may recognize the deformed grandeur and nobility of Shylock, we must not lose our awareness of the ideal of loving community that is at the heart of the play, an ideal to which Shylock at bottom runs counter. Nevertheless, the playwright's complex and humane sensibility brought forth a villain whose downfall cannot be wholeheartedly enjoyed. We are forced to recognize the moral cost involved in his defeat, and to acknowledge that hatred is not easily overcome.

Shylock's name has puzzled scholars. Shakespeare may have derived it from *shallach*, the Hebrew word meaning "cormorant," a term often used abusively to describe usurers, who were equated with that greedy fish-eating bird. The name has also been associated with Shiloh, a name used in Genesis 49:10 for the coming Messiah, and with Salah or Shelah, the father of Eber, from whom the Hebrews took their name (Genesis 10:24, e.g.). Also, Shakespeare may have adapted a 16th-century English word for a contemptible idler, *shullock* or *shallock*.

Solanio   Character in *The Merchant of Venice*, friend of Antonio. Solanio is a cultured gentleman of VENICE whose conversation in elegant verse reflects the advanced civilization of his city. He is difficult to distinguish from his companion Salerio. In commenting on the action, these two gentlemen present facts and ideas. For instance, consoling the melancholy Antonio in 1.1, they speak of his status as a wealthy and successful merchant, and in 2.8 they offer a picture of Shylock's despair and rage at Jessica's elopement and speculate that the Jew will vent his anger on Antonio if he can. In 3.1 they tease Shylock, eliciting from him his famous speech claiming equality with Christians. Solanio is simply a conventional figure whose main purpose is to further the development of more significant characters.

Stephano   Minor character in *The Merchant of Venice*, a servant of Portia. In 5.1 Stephano tells Lorenzo and Jessica that his mistress will be returning to BELMONT shortly.

Tubal   Minor character in *The Merchant of Venice*, friend of Shylock. In 3.1 Tubal tells Shylock that he has been unable to find his friend's daughter, Jessica, who has eloped, but that he has heard reports of her extravagance with the money she has stolen from her father. Tubal also discloses that Antonio has suffered grave commercial losses, thus putting him at the mercy of Shylock, who has loaned him money. Shylock's responses, alternating from delirious anger to exultant delight, are grimly humorous. Tubal's name occurs among the list of descendants of Noah in Genesis 10:2. Biblical scholars of Shakespeare's day thought it meant "confusion" or "slander," though modern scholars believe it refers to an ancient tribe.

Merry Wives of Windsor, The
SYNOPSIS

Act 1, Scene 1
Shallow, in Windsor to sue Falstaff, confers with his young relative Slender and the local parson, the Welshman Evans. Shallow boasts that his noble ancestry is equal to Falstaff's, and Evans offers to arbitrate the quarrel. Slender mentions his inclination to marry, and Evans suggests Anne Page, an attractive young woman who has just inherited some money. Shallow suggests that they call on her father, George Page, whom, Evans says, Falstaff is also visiting. They knock on Page's door and speak with him briefly; Falstaff emerges with Bardolph, Nym, and Pistol. Shallow accuses Falstaff of assaulting his men, poaching deer, and breaking into his hunting lodge. Falstaff grandly admits to these deeds and asserts that if Shallow takes the case to the king's council, he will be laughed at. Slender adds that Falstaff's companions have robbed him. They deny it. Evans insists that he, Page, and the Host of the local tavern shall form a committee to settle these disputes. Mistress Page, Anne, and Mistress Ford appear with refreshments, and everyone goes indoors except the nervous Slender. Shallow and Evans emerge to say that his marriage to Anne has been proposed. Anne enters to summon the men to dinner, and Shallow and Evans leave her with Slender. Slender is too embarrassed to go in with her, and he makes awkward conversation until Page comes out and insists.

Act 1, Scene 2
Evans sends Slender's servant, Simple, to the house of Dr. Caius with a letter for his housekeeper, Mistress Quickly, asking her to encourage Anne Page to marry Slender.

Act 1, Scene 3
Falstaff persuades the tavern's Host to hire Bardolph as a tapster. He tells Pistol and Nym of his plan to get money: He will seduce both Mistress Ford and Mistress Page. He believes that each woman has found him attractive, and he knows that each controls her family's funds. He has written letters to them, and he asks his followers to deliver them. However, they spurn such a task as unworthy of soldiers, and he dismisses them, giving the letters to his page, Robin, and then leaving. Pistol and Nym decide to avenge their dismissal by telling Ford and Page of Falstaff's intentions.

Act 1, Scene 4
Mistress Quickly tells Simple that she will assist Slender's courtship. At Dr. Caius's approach,

Quickly puts Simple in the closet. Caius finds him, and when he tells of his errand, the doctor rages against Evans for sending him, for he—Caius—intends to marry Anne Page himself. Caius writes a letter challenging Evans to a duel and sends Simple back with it. Caius leaves, and Fenton appears. Quickly assures him that his courtship of Anne is going well. Pleased, he gives her money and asks for her continuing assistance.

Act 2, Scene 1

Mistress Page reads Falstaff's love letter. She feels insulted, as does Mistress Ford, who appears with a similar letter. The two women plot revenge: They will tempt Falstaff to spend his money courting them—to no avail—until he is bankrupt. Mistress Ford is particularly irritated with Falstaff because of her husband's quick jealousy. The two women withdraw to discuss their plot, and their husbands appear, accompanied by Pistol and Nym. Pistol and Nym tell the husbands that Falstaff is pursuing their wives, and they leave. The wives reappear as Mistress Quickly arrives, and they decide to employ her as their messenger to Falstaff; the three women leave together. Page and Ford talk; Page doesn't believe the stories of Pistol and Nym, but Ford is worried. The Host and Shallow enter on their way to oversee the duel between Caius and Evans. Shallow tells Page of a plan to interfere with the duel. Ford bribes the Host to introduce him to Falstaff as "Brook." He says to himself that he will see what he can find out about Falstaff and his wife.

Act 2, Scene 2

Quickly delivers messages from the wives to Falstaff. Mistress Page writes of her desire for a meeting, but Mistress Ford makes an appointment for that morning. Quickly leaves, and Ford, disguised as "Brook," arrives. "Brook" gives Falstaff a gift of money and confesses that he has fallen in love with Ford's wife but that her marital fidelity puts him off. He therefore asks Falstaff to seduce her so that he—"Brook"—may catch her in adultery and thus justify his own advances. Falstaff accepts the bargain; he tells "Brook" of his appointment with Mistress Ford for that very morning, and he leaves. Ford soliloquizes jealously and vows revenge.

In 2.1 of *The Merry Wives of Windsor*, Mistress Ford and Mistress Page discover that Falstaff is courting them both with love letters. They plot their revenge. In this 19th-century production Ada Rehan (left) stars as Mistress Ford. *(Courtesy of Culver Pictures, Inc.)*

Act 2, Scene 3

Dr. Caius awaits the arrival of Evans to start the duel. Instead, the Host, Shallow, Slender, and Page appear. All but Slender (who can only moon over Anne Page) talk with the doctor, complimenting him on his valor while pointing out the good fortune that has kept him from having to kill Evans. The Host tells Shallow and Page to find Evans, who has been sent elsewhere to duel, and they will meet later. He then tells Caius that he will take him to visit Anne Page.

Act 3, Scene 1

Evans awaits the arrival of Dr. Caius to start the duel. Page, Shallow, and Slender arrive, and Evans heaps insults on Dr. Caius. The Host appears with Caius. The two would-be duelists argue over where they were to meet, and the Host reveals that he has misled them; he proposes that they be friends again. Evans suggests to Caius that they unite in seeking vengeance on the Host, who has made fools of them both. Caius agrees, and they become allies.

Act 3, Scene 2

Ford encounters Mistress Page, accompanied by Robin, who is on loan from Falstaff. He believes that the situation confirms the infidelity of both women. He proposes to himself to unmask Falstaff, disillusion Page, and punish his wife all at once. The group returning from the averted duel appears, and Ford invites them to his house, although Shallow and Slender go to call on Anne Page. Page remarks that he favors Slender as a son-in-law, while his wife prefers Caius. He rejects Fenton as a suitor, observing that the young aristocrat—too high-ranking to marry Anne—is probably a fortune hunter, being poor despite his rank, and is notably dissolute, having been friends with Prince Hal and Poins (of *1* and *2 Henry IV*).

Act 3, Scene 3

The wives lay their plan: they instruct two Servants to be ready to carry away a big basket of laundry and dump it in the river. Falstaff arrives and woos Mistress Ford; Mistress Page appears, and Falstaff hides behind the curtains. Mistress Page announces that an angry Ford is approaching, seeking his wife's lover. Falstaff leaps from his hiding place into the laundry basket, which the two Servants carry out as Ford enters. Ford searches the house, watched by Page, Evans, and Caius, who assert that he is foolish. Left together, the two wives exult over Falstaff's discomfiture and decide to try it again the next morning. Unable to find any lover in the house, Ford admits his error. Page invites the men to go hawking the next morning. Evans and Caius confer about their revenge on the Host.

Act 3, Scene 4

Anne asks Fenton to continue to try to befriend her father before they think of elopement. Quickly

arrives with Shallow and Slender. Slender is bashful, but Shallow leaves him to talk with Anne. Anne asks him frankly what his intentions are, and he replies that he himself has none but that others say he should marry her. Anne's parents arrive and announce their approval of Slender's suit and disparage Fenton's presence. Page and Slender leave. Fenton appeals to Mistress Page to support his loving courtship, and Anne states her dislike of both Slender and Caius. Mistress Page relents to the point of promising to consult with Anne, and the two women leave. Quickly takes credit for softening Mistress Page, and Fenton gives her some money. She soliloquizes that, having promised to help all three suitors, she will do so, but she favors Fenton.

Act 3, Scene 5

Falstaff laments having been dumped in the river. Quickly brings him an apologetic message from Mistress Ford, who extends another invitation for that morning, while her husband is hawking. Ford arrives, again disguised as "Brook." Falstaff tells of his escape in the laundry and of his new opportunity. He leaves, and Ford rages angrily that this time he will catch Falstaff in his house.

Act 4, Scene 1

Evans drills young William Page in his Latin grammar, and Quickly listens with comical misunderstanding.

Act 4, Scene 2

Falstaff calls on Mistress Ford, and once again Mistress Page arrives, sending him into hiding. Again, she tells of Ford's angry approach. The wives disguise Falstaff as the old woman of Brainford, a reputed witch whom Ford particularly despises. Ford arrives with a group of witnesses and ransacks the laundry in search of Falstaff; then, in his fury he drives the "old woman" from the house, beating "her" mercilessly. He begins to search the house once more, and in his absence the wives decide to tell their husbands of their campaign against Falstaff so that all four may participate in another round of imposture.

Act 4, Scene 3

Bardolph informs the Host that the agents of a German count, soon to arrive at the king's court, wish to hire horses. The Host agrees to let them use his, proposing to overcharge them.

Act 4, Scene 4

The Pages and Fords, with Evans, concoct a plot against Falstaff. They will arrange to have the fat knight meet the women at an ancient sacred oak in the woods at midnight, disguised as a mythological creature, Herne the Hunter, who wears stag's antlers. When he arrives at the rendezvous, he will be accosted by a group of Children disguised as fairies and elves, led by Anne. They will pinch him and ridicule him until he admits his shabby dealings. Then all the hidden adults will emerge to mock him. As they lay their plans, Ford muses to himself that he may take advantage of the occasion to spirit Anne away with Slender and have them married. Mistress Ford plots similarly with Dr. Caius in mind.

Act 4, Scene 5

Simple has followed the old woman of Brainford to Falstaff's rooms to ask her questions of behalf of his master. Falstaff says that he has spoken with the witch, and he gives Simple trick answers when he asks about Slender's chances of winning Anne Page. Bardolph reports to the Host that the Germans have made off with the horses; Evans and then Caius arrive with warnings that the Germans are not to be trusted. Realizing that he has been robbed, the Host rages and rushes off. Quickly appears with a message to Falstaff from the two wives, and he takes her to his chamber to hear their proposition in detail.

Act 4, Scene 6

Fenton bribes the Host to help him. Anne has learned of her parents' respective schemes, and the two lovers have hatched a counterplot. The Host agrees to arrange for a minister to marry the couple that night.

Act 5, Scene 1

Falstaff sends Quickly to prepare for his masquerade that night, just as Ford arrives, disguised as "Brook." Falstaff assures him that tonight all they had planned will be accomplished.

Act 5, Scene 2

Page, Shallow, and Slender lie in wait, planning for Slender's elopement with Anne.

Act 5, Scene 3

The wives, with Caius, lie in wait, planning for the doctor's elopement with Anne.

Act 5, Scene 4

Evans and the Children lie in wait, planning to accost Falstaff.

Act 5, Scene 5

Falstaff, disguised as Herne, arrives at the rendezvous and compares himself with Jupiter, who took the forms of animals for sexual purposes. The wives appear; Falstaff is jubilant, thinking that his liaison is finally to occur, but the women hear a noise and flee. Evans and the Children, with Pistol and Quickly, all disguised as fairies and elves, come out and conduct a ceremony. They then torment Falstaff, burning him with their candles and pinching him. Slender and Caius arrive, and each steals away with a different fairy; Fenton takes Anne, Page, Ford, and the wives come forward and reveal their hoax to Falstaff, who is mortified. Slender returns to complain that his intended bride has proved to be a boy; Caius appears with the same story. Fenton and Anne return and explain that they have married. The Pages make the best of it and accept Fenton as their son-in-law. In a conciliatory spirit of fellowship, Falstaff is invited to join the others in a festive celebration at the Ford household.

COMMENTARY

The Merry Wives of Windsor was probably written for a ceremonial occasion (see "Text of the Play"), and it is clearly intended primarily as an entertainment. Unlike such earlier comedies as *The Comedy of Errors* and *The Two Gentlemen of Verona*, *The Merry Wives* is not colored by any possibility of serious unhappiness that must be forestalled. In this respect it is the shallowest COMEDY of Shakespeare's plays, and it is therefore sometimes thought of as an unimportant diversion in Shakespeare's development, an essentially trivial work that does not warrant attention. However, the play's success on the stage—historical and current—has affirmed its value, and modern commentators have increasingly found it to be a particularly interesting work.

The Merry Wives is a variation on a medieval moral tale, and thus it draws on the theatrical traditions of Shakespeare's day. But Shakespeare added contemporary elements; it is the only one of his works to focus exclusively on English life in his own time. Moreover, in *The Merry Wives* the playwright gave the initiative in the play's plot to the wives rather than to male characters, as was normal in earlier comedies, including his own. This points intriguingly to the prominence of heroines in his later comedies.

As a moral tale *The Merry Wives* recounts the triumph of domestic values over the threat of corruption brought in by an outsider, Falstaff, whose amoral selfishness is contrasted with the communal solidarity of the townspeople and whose status as a courtier makes him a social alien. In an ancient tradition, known in Shakespeare's day through both Roman drama and the medieval MORALITY PLAY, satirical comedy exposed human foibles by making fun of them. The happy resolution that defines the genre usually consisted in precisely the sort of humiliation and forgiveness that befall Falstaff in the play. Thus Shakespeare applied a familiar formula, immediately understood by his audience and so self-evident in its intentions that subsequent readers and theatergoers have responded just as instinctively.

The play also offers another sort of tale, a standard plot in Elizabethan comedy: the triumph of young lovers—Anne Page and Fenton—over the machinations of the girl's parents and her mercenary suitors. The final comic resolution of this story buttresses that of the Falstaff plot. Moreover, the double denouement is both forecast and supported by the SUBPLOT of the enmity and reconciliation of Caius and Evans, whose proposed duel is defused by the collective efforts of various townspeople. Thus the play's theme—the power of good over evil—is developed in several mutually reinforcing ways.

The contemporaneity of *The Merry Wives* is one of its strikingly novel features. In this work, as in the *Henry IV* plays, written at almost exactly the same time, Shakespeare dramatizes his own world with unprecedented theatrical realism. He doubtless created the BOAR'S HEAD TAVERN in *1 Henry IV* to strengthen that play's historical themes by associating them with a more mundane aspect of English society. In *The Merry Wives*, which is concerned solely with entertainment, historical markers are

almost nonexistent (although a few references are made—e.g., in 3.2.66–67—to the world of Henry IV), and the entire play is a detailed slice of Elizabethan rural life. The characters enjoy such country entertainments as greyhound racing (1.1.81–89) and hunting with small hawks (3.3.214–215); they are familiar with stiles (3.1.32), goose-pens (3.4.40), bilberries (5.5.46), and the ways of the cuckoo (2.1.121). The specific geographical references—FROGMORE (2.3.81), Eton (4.5.63), Datchet Mead (3.3.12), Herne's oak in Windsor Forest (4.4.40)—lend great realism to the play's setting.

More sophisticated tastes are also provided for in the literary humor of William's Latin lesson (4.1) and in the inside jokes about the Count of MÖMPELGARD in 4.3 and 4.5, accessible only to the highest ranks of courtly society. Also, several minor jests involve quotations from the works of SIDNEY and MARLOWE, requiring an educated familiarity with contemporary literature, although Shakespeare's audience will have recognized these references much more readily than modern readers can.

The play was also conspicuously part of the contemporary vogue for the COMEDY OF HUMOURS, in which social types are represented by boldly identifiable characters, each sporting a notable eccentricity of speech or behavior. Most of the secondary figures in *The Merry Wives* exhibit such traits: Evans and Caius each speak with a comic foreign dialect, Welsh and French respectively. Pistol is an archetypal swaggerer, Slender a foolish bumpkin, the Host a jovial gladhander. Ford, though more humanly complex, belongs to a very ancient tradition, that of the unreasonably jealous husband. Even Falstaff takes on the role of a character type, the unsuccessful lecher, although his motive in approaching the wives is actually mercenary.

The play's many comic characters are ranged around Falstaff, who, although he is a less masterful figure than in the *Henry IV* plays, is nonetheless as brassy, zestful, and humorously rhetorical as ever, brandishing language like a torch to baffle and confuse his intended victims. The difference is that in *The Merry Wives* he does not succeed, even temporarily. He is a comic butt, destined from the outset to be defeated by the forthright and faithful wives. That the resourceful rogue of *1 Henry IV* should be so easily bested, not just once but three times, has been regretted by some, who see in Falstaff's downfall the trivialization of a great comic figure. However, in *The Merry Wives* Falstaff's function is different. He is not placed in contrast with a historical plot involving politics and war, a circumstance that gives his wit extraordinary resonance in the *Henry IV* plays; here he has an almost abstract, allegorical role as the spirit of malevolence that, while comic and releasing, must be roundly crushed. The Falstaff of *The Merry Wives* has been seen as similar to the scapegoat, a sacrificial animal of pre-Christian religious traditions, who is figuratively laden with the misdeeds of the people and then released into the wilderness or killed, taking with it the sins of the community. Certainly 5.5 is suggestive of such rites, which were still remembered and understood in Shakespeare's day, having disappeared only recently—they may, in fact, have still been alive in the remotest parts of Britain. In any case, at the close of the play, Falstaff's humiliation is mitigated by the fact that Page and his wife have also been foiled in their plans for Anne, and the fat villain is included in the final forgiveness and good cheer that embody the spirit of Shakespearean comedy.

The Merry Wives anticipates Shakespeare's later work in its emphasis on women. While the wives, comfortably settled in middle-aged domesticity, are not much like the bold and venturesome heroines that the playwright was soon to create—Beatrice (*Much Ado About Nothing*), Rosalind (*As You Like It*), Viola (*Twelfth Night*), and Helena (*All's Well That Ends Well*)—they nonetheless prefigure them. They are clearly the most sensible and competent people in Shakespeare's Windsor. They know who they are, and they firmly assert themselves; we are left in no doubt that they are "merry, and yet honest too," as Mistress Page says (4.2.96). Falstaff's greed is the first stimulus to the plot, but the wives are his target precisely because they are the important figures in their households, and the initiative in the plot's development lies squarely with them. They repeatedly lead Falstaff on—and thus, indirectly, Ford—although the men think they are imposing their wills on the world. The wives' vigor is evident not only in the execution of their plans but in their language; for instance, Mistress Page passes boldly from technological to classical to sexual imagery in condemning Falstaff's use of identical love letters (2.1.71–78), closing with the ornithological: "I will find you twenty lascivious turtles [turtledoves] ere one chaste man" (2.1.78). The merry wives are the defenders of domesticity against promiscuity—of order against misrule, that is—and their symbolic importance clearly indicates, for the first time in the plays, the high value Shakespeare placed on female influence in human affairs, a position that he would reassert, perhaps more strikingly, in later works.

The Merry Wives of Windsor is not one of Shakespeare's greatest plays; it lacks stirring poetry and monumental characters, and its concerns are not so sophisticated as the political philosophy and psychological exploration of some of the more important works. However, it is a bold reminder of the popular morality theater of medieval England, and it also presents a delightfully picturesque view of 16th-century rural life. An expertly plotted farce that ranges from gentle charm to high hilarity, it deploys a dozen splendid comic characters in a world of solid virtue that is exemplified by its commendable though understated heroines. As such, the play has been appreciated by generations of theatergoers, and increasing attention from scholars and critics will reinforce its continuing popularity.

SOURCES OF THE PLAY

A number of loose ends in *The Merry Wives of Windsor*—especially Shallow's threatened and then forgotten lawsuit—have suggested to some scholars that the play is based on another one, now lost. This would have been a logical tactic for Shakespeare to use, if it is true that the play was written in two weeks at Queen Elizabeth's command (see "Text of the Play"). However, no evidence exists to link *The Merry Wives* to any earlier play, and the inconsistencies within the play may simply be evidence of hasty composition, whether in response to a royal command or not. In any case, nothing in *The Merry Wives* seems beyond the invention of a well-read and creative mind. Its incidents and characters resemble material that had long been current in European literature and folklore. Jealous husbands and lovers who triumph over adversarial parents are staples of Western storytelling, and Shakespeare could simply have thought of stories he had heard or read without referring to particular works. Also, the contemporary vogue for the comedy of humours must have influenced *The Merry Wives,* which, while transcending the genre, certainly incorporates features from it.

Nevertheless, several likely literary sources may be mentioned. A number of details of Falstaff's escapes from the jealous Ford may have been appropriated from a story from Giovanni FLORENTINO's collection *Il Pecorone (The Simpleton),* published in Milan (1558) and a source for *The Merchant of Venice.* A comical English prose work, Robert Copland's *Gyl of Braintfords Testament* (1560) may have suggested Falstaff's disguise as the old woman of Brainford, and his departure in the laundry basket may derive from a story by Barnabe RICH in his *Farewell to Militarie Profession* (1581). The personality of the Host was probably influenced by Geoffrey CHAUCER's famous innkeeper in *The Canterbury Tales,* and George CHAPMAN's *The Blind Beggar of Alexandria* (1596), a highly successful comedy of humours, contained a character whose comical overuse of the word *humour* clearly contributed to the creation of Shakespeare's Nym. The famous "Latin" scene, 4.1, is representative of a set piece in several contemporary French farces, which Shakespeare would have known of and may have read. Lastly, Falstaff's torment at the hands of fairy impersonators was perhaps based on a scene in John LYLY's play *Endimion* (1588), in which a lecher is punished for his lust by fairies.

TEXT OF THE PLAY

Although absolute proof is lacking, scholars, led by Dr. Leslie HOTSON, have convincingly established that *The Merry Wives* was commissioned for a particular occasion, a feast hosted by Queen Elizabeth I on April 23, 1597, in honor of newly elected members of the knightly Order of the Garter. In 5.5.56–75 Quickly, in the guise of the Queen of Fairies, issues instructions to prepare Windsor Castle for the Knights of the Garter. Apparent references to the German count of Mömpelgard also reflect this occasion, as does the setting of the play

in Windsor, rather than in Shakespeare's native WARWICKSHIRE or some other rural location. Among the noblemen joining the Order of the Garter on this occasion was George Carey, Lord HUNSDON—patron of Shakespeare's company, HUNSDON'S MEN—who had just become Elizabeth's Lord Chamberlain (the company was called the CHAMBERLAIN'S MEN from then on), and he probably commissioned the play. These circumstances appear to confirm a longstanding tradition that *The Merry Wives* was written in 14 days to fulfill a desire expressed by Queen Elizabeth to see Falstaff in love. This notion does not appear in print until 1702, but it fits well with the evident purpose of the play's composition: If a play were offered to the queen, it is quite possible that she would specify a choice of subject. It is known that Hunsdon's Men had performed at court several times in the winter of 1596–97, and it is likely that they presented their most recent popular success, *1 Henry IV,* in which Elizabeth would have become acquainted with Falstaff.

The play is therefore dated to early 1597. A change in the apparent home of Justice Shallow in *2 Henry IV* (see GLOUCESTERSHIRE) suggests that the composition of that play was interrupted by the writing of *The Merry Wives,* in which Shallow explicitly comes from Gloucestershire (1.1.5). *Henry IV, Part 2,* was probably begun in early 1597, thus pushing the creation of *The Merry Wives* a little closer to the beginning of rehearsals for its April presentation; this allows very little time for the job, perhaps only 14 days, although this cannot be known precisely, of course.

The play was first published in 1602 in a BAD QUARTO edition by Arthur JOHNSON, who bought the rights to it from John BUSBY. This edition, known as Q1, was printed by Thomas CREEDE. It was reprinted with minor alterations in 1619 by William JAGGARD for the FALSE FOLIO of publisher Thomas PAVIER. This edition is known as Q2. The 1623 FIRST FOLIO version of *The Merry Wives* is a greatly superior text. It includes five scenes omitted in the Quartos, and it provides more comprehensible, smoother readings throughout. Scholars believe that the Folio was printed from a transcript of Shakespeare's manuscript, perhaps in a version reflecting a court performance of 1604 (see under Brook); certain idiosyncrasies in the text point to the hand of Ralph CRANE, a professional scribe whose work is well known. Q1 represents an already abridged version of the play, one intended for the public theater rather than for the play's original aristocratic audience at the queen's banquet. It omits the scenes dealing with the Order of the Garter, along with the "Latin" scene, presumably thought inappropriate for the relatively uneducated public. The Folio was immediately recognized as the superior text, and subsequent editions have been largely based on it, with occasional alterations deriving from Q1.

THEATRICAL HISTORY OF THE PLAY

The Merry Wives was enthusiastically received by its original audience. The subtitle of the 1602 edition of the play asserts that it had been performed "divers times" both before the queen and elsewhere, and it specifically mentions Falstaff, Evans, Shallow, Slender, Pistol, and Nym, attesting to the fame of these figures. The earliest specific performance of which a record survives was held at the court of King JAMES I in 1604. An ambiguous record of 1613 may or may not refer to *The Merry Wives*, but the play was certainly played at the court of Charles I in 1638, testifying to its ongoing popularity. After the theaters were reopened following their 20-year closure by the Puritan revolution, *The Merry Wives* was one of the first plays to be staged. Samuel PEPYS saw it in 1660, 1661, and 1667. The program of an unsuccessful adaptation of 1702, *The Comical Gallant* by John DENNIS, implies that *The Merry Wives* had been produced several times in the intervening years, though no late-17th-century performances are recorded. In 1704 Shakespeare's text was staged by Thomas BETTERTON, who played Falstaff, and James QUIN duplicated the project a year later. Since the 1720s the play has been extremely popular in both Britain and America, and many major Shakespearean actors of the 18th and 19th centuries played Falstaff, Ford, or both.

The Merry Wives remained a favorite in the 20th century; the many productions of the play included those of Oscar ASCHE and Theodore KOMISARJEVSKY. More recently, Terry HANDS directed a London production (1995) starring Geraldine Fitzgerald as Mistress Ford. *The Merry Wives* was twice a silent FILM

(1910, 1917), but it has not been a movie since. It has been made for TELEVISION four times, including the 1955 production of Glen Byam SHAW, starring Anthony QUAYLE. A number of OPERAs have been based on the play, beginning in 1824, when Fredric REYNOLDS produced an opera with music by Henry BISHOP. Among others have been such well-known works as Karl Otto NICOLAI's *Die lustigen Weiber von Windsor* (1849); Ralph VAUGHAN WILLIAMS's *Sir John in Love* (1929); and, by general consent the greatest of them, Giuseppe VERDI's *Falstaff* (1893). Another musical work inspired in part by *The Merry Wives* is the English composer Edward Elgar's symphonic study *Falstaff* (1913).

CHARACTERS

Anne Page Character in *The Merry Wives of Windsor*, a marriageable young woman pursued by Slender, Dr. Caius, and Fenton. Anne's father, George Page, favors Slender because he is rich, although completely vacuous. Her mother, Mistress Page, prefers Dr. Caius, who is an obnoxious but prestigious physician at Windsor Castle. Anne herself is in love with Fenton. A demure daughter, she urges Fenton to do his utmost to win over her father before they consider elopement. However, she has the good sense to see that the other two suitors are totally unacceptable. After Slender has proposed by observing that it is not his idea to marry her but that of his uncle and her father, Anne forthrightly pleads, "Good mother, do not marry me to yond fool" (3.4.81), and when Mistress Page assures her that Dr. Caius is more likely, she cries, "Alas, I had rather be set quick i' th' earth, and bowl'd to death with turnips!" (3.4.84–85). When her parents each arrange her abduction by their chosen son-in-law, she rebels and urges Fenton to arrange their secret marriage, which her parents accept in the spirit of conciliation that closes the play.

Bardolph See Bardolph, in *Henry IV, Part 1*.

Brook Name used by the disguised Ford in *The Merry Wives of Windsor*. Ford, unreasonably jealous, believes that his wife, Mistress Ford, intends to commit adultery with Falstaff. He visits Falstaff posing as Brook, a would-be lover of Mistress Ford, and he encourages Falstaff to seduce his wife, pretending to hope to follow in his footsteps as Brook. He actually wants to catch his wife in her adultery with the fat knight. His assumed name figures in several jokes, as in 2.2.145–146 and 5.5.241–242.

It is thought that this alias was Shakespeare's subtle, jesting reference to an alteration in his work that had recently been forced upon him. A Puritan leader, William Brooke, Lord COBHAM—or perhaps his son Henry Brook—had been offended by a fat, lecherous, ne'er-do-well character in *1 Henry IV* whose name, Oldcastle, was the same as that of one of his revered ancestors. Cobham was a powerful aristocrat, and his complaint was honored: Oldcastle became Falstaff. However, in the first play in which the new name was used from the outset, *The Merry Wives*, Shakespeare permitted himself a mild revenge, associating the Cobham family name with a character whose foolishness might be said to resemble their own pridefulness. Since the Oldcastle furor was well known in London, the joke, if it was one, would certainly have been widely understood.

However, Shakespeare's jest was itself subject to revision. In the FIRST FOLIO edition of the play (1623), Ford uses the name Broome throughout. Since the 1602 QUARTO uses Brooke, this change must have been made between 1602 and 1623. It may be that Henry Brooke demanded the change, although its apparent late date seems to distance the alteration from the original controversy. Several other theories have been proposed; the most convincing asserts that the name was changed for a performance at the court of King JAMES I in November 1604, 18 months after his accession. In the previous year both Henry Brooke and his brother George had attempted coups against the new King and had been convicted of treason. George was executed, and Henry was imprisoned for life. Their surname may have been removed from the play to avoid an unnecessary reminder of James's difficulties.

Caius, Doctor Character in *The Merry Wives of Windsor*, a French physician and suitor of Anne Page. Caius is descended from a traditional stock figure of COMEDY, the blustering, arrogant, and ineffective doctor, although his profession is not important in the play; his bad temper and aggressive nature are exemplified by his explosive reiterations of the expletive "By gar"—e.g., in 5.5.203–207. Caius is also a stereotypical foreigner, mangling the English language and behaving with notable wrong-headedness. He challenges Evans to a duel for having attempted to assist Slender, a rival for Anne's hand. The duel is averted by a group of townsmen, led by the Host. Caius and Evans then conspire against the Host, arranging to steal his horses. Although Caius's combativeness is generally amusing, this petty vengeance, combined with his vanity, isolates him from the generally mild temper of the play, and it is probably significant that he and Evans, a Welshman, are WINDSOR's only foreigners. Caius is also the only character to withdraw willfully from the reconciliations in 5.5.

Children Minor characters in *The Merry Wives of Windsor* who imitate fairies and elves to torment Falstaff. In 5.5 Anne and William Page, and other Children, disguised as diminutive supernatural beings, help to carry out Mistress Page's plot for the final humiliation of Falstaff, devised in 4.4.28–64. When the lecherous Falstaff meets Mistress Page and Mistress Ford in the forest, seeking double adultery, the Children appear, led by Mistress Quickly, Pistol, and Evans. They dance in a circle (while ceremonial references to the Order of the Garter are made—see "Text of the Play"), and they hold candles to Falstaff and pinch him, while singing a song condemning "lust and luxury" (5.5.95).

Evans, Sir Hugh Character in *The Merry Wives of Windsor*, a Welsh clergyman and schoolmaster. A peaceable busybody, Evans is distinguished by his heavy Welsh accent—Falstaff says he "makes fritters of English" (5.5.144). In 1.1 he volunteers to form a committee to settle a dispute between Falstaff and Shallow, and he repeatedly tries to allay the irrational jealousy of Master Ford. When he attempts to promote Slender's marriage to Anne, he is challenged to a duel by Dr. Caius. The clergyman is daunted by this prospect, describing himself as "full of . . . trempling of mind" (3.1.11–12). To calm himself, he sings a popular Elizabethan love SONG (with words by Christopher MARLOWE), comically borrowing a line from the Bible. The Host defuses the duel by sending the two men to different rendezvous. To preserve his honor, Evans proposes an alliance with Caius against the Host, claiming that they have been made fools of. They later are apparently responsible for the theft of the Host's horses.

Evans also figures in the famous "Latin scene" (4.1), in which he quizzes young William Page on his Latin lessons. In lines that parody the standard Latin textbook of Shakespeare's day, Lily's *Latin Grammar*, Evans's accent, and Mistress Quickly's capacity for misunderstanding join to make fritters of Latin. The scene is full of double entendres and bilingual puns, presumably intended especially for the educated audience for whom the play was originally written. The episode may also reflect Shakespeare's own memories of childhood: He learned Latin from Lily's *Grammar* at school in STRATFORD, where he probably had a teacher of Welsh ancestry, Thomas JENKINS.

Evans was popular with London theatergoers of the late 16th century. When *The Merry Wives* was first published, in 1600, he figured in the subtitle— as "Syr Hugh the Welch Knight"—for it was thought that his name would attract buyers. Shakespeare was plainly aware of the popular English stereotype of the Welsh as stubbornly foreign and naturally given to music and theft. Also, along with the interest in WALES demonstrated in several other works, especially *1 Henry IV* and *Henry V*, the character of Evans probably indicates that Shakespeare's acting company included one or more Welshmen in the late 1590s.

Falstaff, Sir John   See Falstaff, Sir John, in *Henry IV, Part 1*.

Fenton   Character in *The Merry Wives of Windsor*, suitor of Anne Page. Fenton, a conventional young romantic lead, has little personality, although we are told that he "kept company with the wild Prince and Poins" (3.2.66–67). Anne's father, George Page, objects to Fenton on this ground and on the related one that he is too socially high-

ranking to be an appropriate husband for the bourgeois maid. Moreover, Page suspects Fenton is a treasure hunter. Fenton himself admits to Anne in 3.4.12–18 that, although he has fallen in love with her since, Page's money was his original motive for courting her. Nevertheless, he compares favorably with Anne's other suitors, Slender and Caius, and when Anne's parents each plot to have her abducted and married by one of these misfits, her elopement with Fenton comes as a natural course of action. When Fenton announces their marriage in 5.5.217–227, her parents gracefully accept the situation in the spirit of reconciliation that closes the play.

Ford, Frank   Character in *The Merry Wives of Windsor*, jealous husband of Mistress Alice Ford. Ford is to some extent a character type, representing a traditional figure in European folklore and literature, the jealous husband, but he is also humanly credible. His emotional excess is not only a source of simple comedy; it also adds to our rich sense of domestic life in Windsor. Ford's jealous tendencies are established before he appears, when his wife remarks on them to her friend Mistress Page in 2.1.97–103. Then, in a psychologically masterful manner, Shakespeare demonstrates the growth of an episode of jealousy. At first Ford disbelieves Pistol's assertion that Falstaff is courting his wife, though only for a rather uncomplimentary reason— "Why, sir, my wife is not young" (2.1.109)—but then he tersely directs himself to look into this possibility, in lines scattered within Nym's insinuations of a similar adultery to George Page and he refuses to follow Page in his dismissal of the accusations. When his wife observes that Ford appears reoccupied, he snaps at her. She remarks that he has "some crotchets in thy head now" (2.1.148), and we are aware that mistrust and anxiety have taken control of him. When Mistress Quickly says that his wife "leads an ill life with him: he's a very jealousy man" (2.2.85), we easily believe her.

Ford's strategy—taking the name Brook and encouraging Falstaff to approach his wife so that he can catch him at it—is a simple-minded device suitable to the jealous husband in a farce, and the wily wives make Ford foolish at the same time that they dupe Falstaff. Although we do not sympathize with Ford, his heart-felt relief when the situation is revealed to him is touching. Moved to impromptu rhetoric, he asserts to his wife, "I rather will suspect the sun with cold than thee with wantonness" (4.4.7–8), inspiring Page to remark tellingly, "Be not as extreme in submission as in offence" (4.4.11–12).

Host Character in *The Merry Wives of Windsor*, the keeper of the Garter Tavern. The bluff and ebullient Host is a peacekeeper whom Evans nominates to the committee intended to arbitrate between Shallow and Falstaff and who later leads the effort to prevent the duel between Evans and Dr. Caius. The would-be combatants, the only two foreigners in Shakespeare's WINDSOR, reward the Host's good intentions by having his horses stolen. The Host's heartiness is evident in his extravagant rhetoric. For instance, when directing a visitor to Falstaff's rooms at the inn, he says, "There's his chamber, his house, his castle, his standing-bed, and truckle-bed; 'tis painted about with the story of the Prodigal, fresh and new. Go, knock and call; he'll speak like an Anthropophaginian unto thee; knock, I say" (4.5.5–9). His bold language encompasses an extraordinary range of epithets, from "bully rook" (1.3.2, et al.) , "Cavaliero" (2.1.186; 2.3.70), and "bully Hercules" (1.3.6), to such fanciful constructs as "Bohemian-Tartar" (4.5.18) and "Castalian-king-Urinal" (2.3.31).

Mistress Alice Ford One of the title characters in *The Merry Wives of Windsor*, wife of Frank Ford. When Mistress Ford and her friend Mistress Page receive identical love letters from Falstaff, they feel their honor has been insulted by a gross lecher, and they plot revenge. In their plan Mistress Ford serves as bait for Falstaff, who comes to her house, where the appearance of her jealous husband causes the lecher's humiliating flight, first in a hamper of dirty laundry and then in disguise as an old woman, pummeled by Ford. Mistress Ford suffers from her husband's neurotic jealousy, but she bears with him, and we sympathize when she quietly observes that Mistress Page's more reasonable man makes her "the happier woman" (2.1.103). By the same token we share her delight when Ford's jealousy leads him to be made as foolish as Falstaff; "I know not which

pleases me better," she exults, "that my husband is deceived, or Sir John" (3.3.164–165).

Mistress Margaret Page One of the title characters in *The Merry Wives of Windsor*, wife of George Page and mother of Anne and William Page. In 2.1 Mistress Page's response to Falstaff's love letter establishes the position of the honest and forthright wives as enemies of Falstaff's amorality. After reviewing the insult to her wifely honor, she concludes, "How shall I be revenged on him? For revenged I will be, as sure as his guts are made of puddings" (2.1.29–31). When Mistress Ford receives an identical letter, the two friends join forces. Mistress Page's role is to break in on Falstaff's visits to Mistress Ford, sparking his humiliating exits, first hidden in a hamper of dirty laundry and then beaten into the streets while dressed in an old woman's clothes. In 4.4 Mistress Page devises Falstaff's final punishment, his torment by children disguised as fairies. If she seems insensitive in seeking to marry Anne to the obnoxious Dr. Caius, she accepts the outcome graciously when Anne elopes with Fenton, saying, "Master Fenton, Heaven give you many, many merry days!" (5.5.236–237), and she proposes the pleasant resolution of the play, that all the chief characters "laugh this sport o'er by a country fire, Sir John [Falstaff] and all" (5.5.239–240).

Mistress Page's ebullient strength is well matched with her husband's milder cheerfulness. With him, she contributes a large share of the play's charm, in both her vigorous good humor and her confident assertion of traditional values.

Nym See Nym, in *Henry V*.

Page, George Character in *The Merry Wives of Windsor*, the husband of Mistress Margaret Page. Unlike his jealous friend Ford, Page believes in his wife's fidelity. He is consistently mild and cheerful, pleasant evidence of the solid virtues of the bourgeois life of Windsor. He is part of the group, led by the Host, who mediate the quarrel between Evans and Caius, and he repeatedly tries to cajole Ford out of his irrational jealousy. If Page seems unpleasantly mercenary in attempting to marry his daughter Anne Page to the ridiculous Slender, we should remember that such motives were ordinary, indeed expected, in Elizabethan fathers, and we note that Page accepts Anne's elopement with Fenton with good grace. Page's solid common sense is exemplified in his dry reply to Ford's exaggerated protestations of trust in his wife once he has been proven wrong. Page suggests, "Tis well, 'tis well; no more. Be not as extreme in submission as in offence" (4.4.10–13). Once Falstaff is properly humiliated for his deeds, in 5.5, it is Page who ends the punishment, saying, "Yet be cheerful, knight: thou shalt eat a posset to-night at my house . . ." (5.5.171–172).

In 1.1.42 Evans gives Page the name Thomas, though he is called George by his wife in three places (2.1.143, 2.1.151, 5.5.199). While this may represent an error by Evans, it is more probably just a typical instance of Shakespeare's tolerance for minor inconsistencies.

Pistol   See Pistol in *Henry IV, Part 2*.

Quickly, Mistress   Character in *The Merry Wives of Windsor*, housekeeper for Dr. Caius. Mistress Quickly is a shrewd yet comically foolish servant who meddles in other people's affairs. She serves as a messenger between the merry wives and Falstaff, and she impartially supports three different suitors in their pursuit of Anne Page. Mistress Quickly is a traditional, humorously loquacious comic character, given to the misuse of fancy words and the misinterpretation of other people's speeches. For instance, in the famous "Latin scene," 4.1, she finds bawdy puns in Latin grammatical exercises.

In 5.5 Mistress Quickly takes the part of the fairy queen in the ceremonial taunting of Falstaff that is his final humiliation at the hands of the wives. She is entirely out of character in this scene, and her presence in the texts of the play may merely reflect the playhouse practice of having the actor who played her also play the anonymous fairy imitator. Alternatively, her distinctively uncharacteristic presence may have been intended by Shakespeare to suggest the MASQUE-like unreality of the scene, emphasizing its ritualistic quality.

Mistress Quickly bears the same name as the Hostess of *1* and *2 Henry IV* and *Henry V*, and she shares the Hostess's comical way with words, but she is nonetheless best considered as a different person, living in a different world. She is unacquainted with Falstaff when she encounters him in *The Merry Wives*, and she has certainly never had anything to do with the BOAR'S HEAD TAVERN in London. It seems likely that, in the haste with which *The Merry Wives* was written, Shakespeare simply made use of an earlier creation in a new way. Neither he nor his audience was distressed by the inconsistencies this involves.

Robin   Character in *The Merry Wives of Windsor*, Falstaff's page. Robin is briefly loaned by Falstaff to Mistress Page and is let in on their plot against his master, which he enters with apparent enthusiasm. His role is minor, limited to announcing entrances, with the exception of a remark in which he both displays his own spirit and casts a mocking aspersion on Falstaff's size and, possibly, arrogance. Speaking to Mistress Page, he says, "I had rather, forsooth, go before you like a man than follow him like a dwarf" (3.2.5–6).

The same character appears in *2 Henry IV* as the Page, and in *Henry V* as the Boy. Robin's small size is alluded to several times in *The Merry Wives*— e.g., in 3.3.19, where he is called an "eyas-musket," or baby sparrow hawk. Along with similar references in the other plays, these are thought to reflect the presence of a particularly small boy actor in the CHAMBERLAIN'S MEN.

Rugby, John   Minor character in *The Merry Wives of Windsor*, servant of Dr. Caius. Rugby, who says little, is merely an emblem of his bullying master's status, thus filling out the social world of WINDSOR.

Servant   Either of two minor characters in *The Merry Wives of Windsor*, workers in the Ford household. In 3.3 Mistress Ford has the Servants, whom she addresses as John and Robert, carry Falstaff out of the house in a laundry basket and dump him in the river. In 4.2 they again carry out the basket, and they remark humorously on the great weight it contained before. The Servants contribute to the sense of bourgeois prosperity that pervades Shakespeare's WINDSOR.

Shallow, Robert See Shallow, Robert, in *Henry IV, Part 2*.

Simple, Peter Minor character in *The Merry Wives of Windsor*, the servant of Slender. Simple reveals himself to be no smarter than his name suggests, as he carries messages and announces arrivals. In his most developed moment 4.5.24–53, he is fooled by Falstaff's elementary verbal tricks.

Slender, Abraham Character in *The Merry Wives of Windsor*, dull-witted suitor of Anne Page. For financial reasons, a marriage between Anne and Slender is supported by Anne's parents and by Slender's elderly relative Justice Shallow, but Slender himself, although attracted to the idea, can only sigh vacantly at the prospect—". . . sweet Anne Page!" (3.1.38, 66, 105)—and make awkwardly embarrassed conversation. When he finally proposes, he can only blurt that it isn't his idea, "Truly, for mine own part, I would little or nothing with you. Your father and my uncle hath made motions. . . . You may ask your father . . ." (3.4.61–64). Anne beseeches, "Good mother, do not marry me to yond fool" (3.4.81), and the audience can only sympathize. However, Mistress Page arranges for Slender to elope with Anne during the mock fairy ceremonies in 5.5. Fortunately, Anne and her true love, Fenton, foil the plan, and Slender has a boy foisted off on him, as he only discovers during the marriage ceremony.

Slender's name suggests both his appearance and his lack of self-reliance. Such feeble characters were stock figures in Elizabethan comedy. It has been speculated that Slender was also intended by Shakespeare as a satirical portrait of the stepson of his enemy William GARDINER, but this cannot be proven.

William Page Character in *The Merry Wives of Windsor*, son of George Page and Mistress Page. William appears only in the famous "Latin" scene (4.1), where he is quizzed by his schoolmaster, Evans. Evans's Welsh accent and the confusion of an observer, Mistress Quickly, combine to produce a parody of the standard Latin textbook of Shakespeare's day, William LILY's *Latin Grammar*. William stumbles through the interview, none too well prepared, until he is finally forced to admit, "Forsooth, I have forgot" (4.1.67). He is then excused from the impromptu lesson. The scene, with its bevy of double entendres and bilingual puns, was presumably intended especially for the educated audience for whom the play was written, but the episode may also reflect Shakespeare's childhood memories. He had himself learned Latin from Lily's *Grammar* at school in STRATFORD; perhaps William's name was not without sentimental significance for the playwright.

Midsummer Night's Dream, A
SYNOPSIS

Act 1, Scene 1

Theseus, Duke of Athens, discusses with Hippolyta their forthcoming marriage, only days away. Egeus arrives with his daughter Hermia and her two suitors, Demetrius and Lysander. Since Hermia will not marry Demetrius, whom her father prefers, but insists that she loves Lysander, Egeus wants her subjected to a law that will condemn her to death or a life as a nun for refusing to marry the groom her father has chosen. Theseus reluctantly rules that he must enforce the law, but he gives Hermia until the day of his own wedding to decide what she will do. Lysander, declaring himself the better marital prospect, reveals that Demetrius had earlier courted Hermia's friend Helena and made her fall in love with him. Theseus leaves, taking with him all but Lysander and Hermia, who decide to elope, agreeing to meet in the woods the next night. Helena appears, pining for Demetrius; Lysander and Hermia encourage her by telling of their plan and asserting that, with Hermia gone, Demetrius will be free again. The lovers leave, and the lovesick Helena, in a soliloquy, devises a plot to curry favor with Demetrius: She will tell him of the planned elopement and accompany him to the woods to intercept the pair.

Act 1, Scene 2

Quince, with his fellow artisans Snug, Flute, Snout, Starveling, and Bottom, gather to rehearse the

A fairy procession from the 1935 film of *A Midsummer Night's Dream* by Max Reinhardt. The Austrian-born director was famous for his lavish sets and costumes. *(Courtesy of Culver Pictures, Inc.)*

INTERLUDE they are to perform at Theseus and Hippolyta's wedding. Quince, the director, announces the subject of their playlet—the tale of PYRAMUS AND THISBE—and distributes the parts among the players. Bottom, who is to play Pyramus, is so confident of his acting abilities that he wants most of the other parts as well. Quince declares that, in order to keep their spectacle a surprise, they will rehearse in secret, meeting the next night in the woods.

Act 2, Scene 1

Puck and a Fairy discuss the conflict between the King of the Fairies, Oberon, whom Puck serves, and the Fairy Queen, Titania, the Fairy's mistress. Titania and Oberon arrive and begin arguing. She refuses to give up a changeling boy whom Oberon covets. She leaves, and Oberon vows vengeance. He instructs Puck to gather for him a certain flower that he will apply to Titania's eyes while she sleeps and that will cause her to fall in love with the first living being she sees when she wakes. While awaiting Puck's return, Oberon overhears Demetrius and Helena, who are now in the woods, and when Demetrius persistently repulses his admirer, the Fairy King decides that he will dose him with the flower also. Puck returns with the magical herb, and Oberon takes some of it to give to Titania. He tells Puck to find the Athenian couple who are roaming in the woods and to apply the rest of the potion to Demetrius.

Act 2, Scene 2

Titania's retinue sings her to sleep. Oberon appears and puts juice from the plant on her eyes. He leaves, and Lysander and Hermia enter, exhausted from wandering. They sleep, though only after Hermia has insisted that they maintain a proper distance from each other. Puck arrives, sees that they are Athenians, and, assuming that their physical separation implies a lack of love, supposes that he has found his target. He administers the juice to Lysander's eyes and leaves. Demetrius appears, pursued by Helena. He shakes her off and goes on alone. Lysander awakes and, seeing Helena, falls in love with her. Offended by his seeming fickleness, she leaves, and he follows her. Hermia wakes to find herself alone; Titania remains asleep.

Act 3, Scene 1

Quince, Bottom, and their colleagues rehearse in the woods. Puck happens on them and decides to make mischief; he gives Bottom an ass's head, which all but he can see. The other artisans are frightened by this transformation and flee. Bottom, unaware of it, concludes that they are attempting to scare him. To demonstrate his courage, he sings a song, thus waking Titania, who falls in love with him as a result of Oberon's magic. Claiming him, she assigns him an entourage of four fairies, Peaseblossom, Cobweb, Moth, and Mustardseed.

Act 3, Scene 2

Puck reports on Titania's ludicrous infatuation, to Oberon's delight. Demetrius and Hermia appear, arguing. She leaves angrily, and Demetrius, worn out, falls asleep. Oberon realizes that the wrong man has been treated with the magical juice. He commands Puck to lure Helena, while he himself charms Demetrius with the herb. When Helena arrives, Lysander follows, pleading his love. Demetrius wakes; he falls in love with Helena and begins to praise her beauty. She concludes that the two men are mocking her, and she chastises them. Hermia enters in search of Lysander. She expresses bewilderment at her lover's new preference for Helena. Helena takes this as a deliberate insult and concludes that Hermia has joined the men in belittling her. After a series of exchanges, during which first the men and then the women almost come to blows, Lysander and Demetrius stalk off to fight a duel, Helena flees Hermia's wrath, and Hermia leaves, baffled. Oberon directs Puck to summon a dense fog and then to impersonate each man to the

other and lead them away from any conflict. Then he is to apply an antidote to Lysander's eyes. Puck leads the men on separate chases until each falls exhausted on an opposite side of the stage. Helena and Hermia, both lost in the woods, find spots to sleep. Puck squeezes the juice on Lysander's eyes, singing a song of reconciliation.

Act 4, Scene 1

Watched by Oberon, Titania leads Bottom into the clearing where the lovers sleep. Bottom is pampered by his fairy attendants, and he requests hay to eat. Titania speaks adoringly to Bottom and curls up to sleep with him. Puck appears, and Oberon confides that Titania has surrendered her changeling to him; he decides to release her from his spell. He wakes her and tells Puck to remove the ass's head from Bottom. After casting a spell of deep sleep on the mortals, the fairies leave. Theseus, Hippolyta, and Egeus enter; they are hunting with hounds. They discover the lovers and wake them. Lysander tells of his and Hermia's intended elopement, and Egeus angrily demands his execution for having attempted to prevent Hermia's marriage to Demetrius. However, Demetrius announces his intention to marry Helena. Theseus is delighted and commands that the two reunited couples shall be married that day, along with himself and Hippolyta. They all return to Athens, leaving Bottom, who awakes amazedly and muses on the strange dream that he can't quite remember.

Act 4, Scene 2

Quince, Flute, Snout, and Starveling wonder at Bottom's absence, and Snug arrives to tell them that the Duke's festivities are about to begin. Their distress is relieved when Bottom arrives, not quite able to recount what he has seen but prepared to lead them onstage.

Act 5, Scene 1

Theseus discounts the lovers' experiences in the woods, attributing to them a madness that also affects lunatics and poets. The newlyweds arrive, and Theseus calls for entertainment. Quince's production of *Pyramus and Thisbe* is performed, provoking amusement. Following the performance, everyone departs, and the fairies, led by Puck, arrive to bless the marriages. They leave, and Puck delivers an EPI-

LOGUE suggesting that, if the audience is offended by being asked to believe in fairies, they should simply pretend that they have slept and dreamed.

COMMENTARY

Scholars generally agree that *A Midsummer Night's Dream* was written to be performed at an aristocratic wedding. Everything in the play is related to the theme of marriage. Theseus and Hippolyta's nuptials are the goal toward which all the action is directed—the fairies have come to Athens to bless the occasion; the artisans' performance is intended for it; Hermia's judgment, and thus the climax of the lovers' story, is scheduled to coincide with it, and finally the young lovers are married along with the ducal couple. The very first line emphasizes the importance of the forthcoming "nuptial hour" (1.1.1), and the denouement is a blessing of the three weddings in terms that suggest a performance within a dwelling, as Oberon orders the fairies to distribute blessings "through this house" (5.1.388). (See "Theatrical History of the Play.")

The play suits such an occasion well, for it has the formality of a MASQUE, an entertainment often performed at noble weddings. Like many masques, this comedy presents a world of magic and metamorphosis in brilliant spectacles involving picturesque supernatural beings. It also makes much use of music and dance, and its finale is itself masquelike. It is given over to celebration, with further dancing and a comical performance (*Pyramus and Thisbe*) similar to an anti-masque—the realistic farce that was commonly part of a masque itself. Like a masque again, Acts 1–4 are very symmetrically plotted, moving from the court of Theseus to the woods and back again. In part, this reflects an archetypal plot pattern of withdrawal and return, common in the romance literature preceding Shakespeare and in his own work, but the arrangement here is particularly formal. (Compare, for example, *The Two Gentlemen of Verona* or *Cymbeline*.) There are internal symmetries also. For example, two songs are used—one to put Titania to sleep in 2.2, and the other to wake her in 3.1—and Quince and his cast appear four times, twice on either side of Bottom's adventure.

As is natural in such a formal context, the characters are stylized and unrealistic: they do not inter-

act as people normally do. Theseus and Hippolyta are remote ideals of classical calm; Puck is a typical goblin; and Titania and Oberon are distant in their regal immortality, elemental forces of nature with the power to influence the climate and to bless marriages. Only Bottom and his fellow artisans represent ordinary people, and they are plainly character types with little personality beyond their buffoonery.

The lovers, too, are static; although Lysander and Demetrius are transformed by Oberon's magical herb, they are altered only in their stance toward another character, and in Lysander's case the change is only temporary. Demetrius is left in a position he had held before the opening of the play and thus is ultimately unchanged also. Change occurs only in the pattern of the lovers' relationships, which has often been compared to a dance: first, the two men address one of the women while the other woman is alone; then one man's affection is changed, and a circular chase unfolds. Lysander woos Helena, who is still pursuing Demetrius, who continues to court Hermia, who still wants Lysander. Next, when Demetrius is put under Oberon's spell, the two men face the other woman, and the first woman is alone. Finally the only stable arrangement is achieved, with Lysander and Demetrius each returned to his original love interest.

Such intricate masquelike plotting is appropriate not only to a festive occasion but also to the world of dreamy confusion that is central to the story. Much of the action, from 2.1 into 4.1, takes place at night; the lovers assert several times that they are looking at the stars (e.g., 3.2.61, 3.2.188), thus drawing attention to the nighttime setting (which was usually enacted in afternoon sunlight in an Elizabethan public theater). The nocturnal universe of shadowy strangeness is further evoked in the play's imagery. The moon is referred to prominently, beginning in the very first few lines (1.1.3,4,9); moonlight is mentioned three times more often in *A Midsummer Night's Dream* than in all of Shakespeare's other plays combined. In many different contexts the moon is used in figures of speech: to indicate time of day (1.1.209–210) and of month (1.1.83); with reference to catastrophic flooding (2.1.103) and to the speed of fairies (2.1.7, 4.1.97); cuckoldry (5.1.232); and in connection with chastity (1.1.73, 2.1.162) and opposition to chastity (3.1.191–193). "Moonshine" is even a character in the artisans' play. The eerie quality of moonlight is reinforced by frequent evocations of the beauty of the woods at night.

Flowers are frequently mentioned as well, as in 1.1.185 and 2.1.110, and of course the magical aphrodisiac is a flower (2.1.166). Even the doggerel of *Pyramus and Thisbe* provides a floral motif (3.1.88–89). Birds, too, are alluded to throughout the play. Afoot (5.1.380) and in flight (3.2.20–24), as emblems of sight (2.2.113, 3.2.142) and of sound (1.1.184, 1.2.78, 5.1.362), they sing (5.1.384) and soar (3.2.23) in the play's highly lyrical language. Even Bottom, when he sings, brings forth a country ditty about birds (3.1.120–128).

Animals also inhabit the enchanted woods, though they lurk ominously for the most part. Even a bee poses a threat (4.1.15–16), however slight. The image of preying carnivores is invoked by Helena to describe her desperate pursuit of Demetrius in 2.1.232–233. Dead sheep are part of Titania's vision of disordered nature (2.1.97). Theseus evokes a nighttime fear that a bush may be a bear (5.1.22). Potential tragedy is presented in a humorous context only in the artisans' interlude, but in that episode tragedy is wrought by a ravening lion. Puck, introducing the fairies' blessings with a reminder of the cruel world that they may also be associated with, remarks that "the hungry lion roars, / And the wolf behowls the moon" (5.1.357–358).

Indeed, the dreamworld of the play involves several hints of nightmare, providing a contrast to its harmonies of love. Hermia awakes from a nightmare at the end of 2.2, and the "drooping fog, as black as Acheron" (3.2.357) summoned by Puck to deceive Lysander and Demetrius carries a hint of terror, though its purpose is benign. Shakespeare never lets the fairy world seem altogether sweet and light; Puck has a touch of malice to his personality, and he reminds the audience of the fairies' alliance to dark powers in the speech, cited above, that introduces the final ritual, the blessing of the house.

One of the functions of that blessing, indeed, is to exorcise all potential evil at last. The interlude has just performed a similar task in rendering a lovers' tragedy as farce. In fact, Quince, Bottom,

and the boys act as an earthy counterweight to the uncanny airiness of the fairies. This is like an exorcism, because the unreal world of Puck and Oberon, Titania and Peaseblossom is supremely alien and potentially dangerous. The mortals can be manipulated and never know it: The lovers, returning to Athens, believe themselves to have awakened from dreams (4.1.197–198), as does Bottom (4.1.204).

But generations of viewers and readers and critics have felt compelled to ask whether Shakespeare intends us to take the enchanted woods as dream or as reality. The title of the play—related to "midsummer madness," proverbially a lovers' sickness—suggests that the mortals' experience in the woods is but a figment of the imagination, perhaps that the whole play is. Theseus sees only fiction or lunacy when the "imagination bodies forth / The forms of things unknown [and] the poet's pen / Turns them to shapes, and gives to airy nothing / A local habitation and a name" (5.1.14–17), but we the audience, having witnessed it ourselves, may agree with Hippolyta that "all the story of the night told over, . . . grows to something of great constancy . . . strange and admirable" (5.1.23–27). And we can realize even more: that the play, the poet's embodiment of imaginary things, has made the unreal real.

We must return to our starting point, the occasion for which the play was evidently written. Shakespeare's original audience, guests at a wedding, were removed from the world of reality, just as modern audiences are, and then returned to it by the ritual at its close. The exact definition of reality is not addressed by the play; indeed, the play's ambiguity on the point is deliberate. The experience is all that matters, and the experience, as Bottom knew, is a profound one. When he wakes from his experience in the woods and observes, "The eye of man hath not heard, the ear of man hath not seen, man's hand is not able to taste, his tongue to conceive, nor his heart to report, what my dream was" (4.1.209–212). Bottom has experienced, though he is unable to express it, the depths of mystery that underlie all things, real and unreal alike. By evoking such awareness, the play fulfills its original and primary function as a celebratory hymn to the beauties of married love.

SOURCES OF THE PLAY

A Midsummer Night's Dream is one of the few Shakespearean plays that seem to have been generated principally from the playwright's own imagination; no known literary work is a source for it. However, it draws on a number of diverse traditions—the courtly spectacle or pageant, the folklore of fairies, and a delight in the antics of the rustic CLOWN—that were common in Shakespeare's day. The playwright did make use of a number of ideas and images that came from literature, and *A Midsummer Night's Dream*—more, perhaps, than a work that is based firmly on another work, such as *Romeo and Juliet* or *Hamlet*—suggests the range of the author's reading.

At least a dozen works provided general ideas for or bits and pieces of this play. Prominent among them is one of the most famous of ancient books, well known to Shakespeare and his audience, *The Golden Ass,* by APULEIUS, written in the second century and translated into English by William ADLINGTON in 1566; this tale tells of a man transformed into an ass. Shakespeare also took ingredients from several works by his greatest English predecessor, Geoffrey CHAUCER, notably "The Knight's Tale," which provided the characters Theseus and Hippolyta as Duke of Athens and Queen of the Amazons, as well as several situations in the play; the marriage of Chaucer's ducal couple is postponed by the arbitration of a dispute, for example, and Theseus uses his authority to uphold a supernatural resolution of complicated lovers' quarrels. He also interrupts a duel between rivals, as Oberon does in the play. Further, Chaucer's "The Merchant's Tale" presents a fairy king and queen who are at odds over a human being and who intervene in mortal affairs. Also, his "Sir Tophas," a satire of knightly romance, features a comical knight-errant who dreams of marrying an "elf-queene."

One of Shakespeare's favorite books, OVID's *Metamorphoses* (in the 1567 translation by Arthur GOLDING) was the source of the legend of Pyramus and Thisbe as presented in the interlude in 5.1. That the playwright also knew Ovid in the original Latin is demonstrated by his use of the name Tita-nia, which is not in Golding but which the Roman poet used several times in contexts relevant to the play's motifs—as another name for Diana, the moon goddess, and for Circe, who transformed men into animals.

The Fairy King, Oberon, was a well-known figure both in folklore and in medieval literature. In *Huon of Bordeaux,* a 13th-century French adventure tale translated by Lord BERNERS (1534), he resembles Shakespeare's character in presiding over a magical forest where mortals become lost and in explicitly distinguishing himself from evil spirits; in both stories he intervenes to bring about a happy ending.

The play incorporates many minor echoes of a work of Shakespeare's own time, *The Discoverie of Witchcraft* (1584) by Reginald SCOT, a tract opposing the prosecution of witches. Shakespeare used Scot's accounts of fairy lore, especially about Robin Goodfellow, or Puck, although Scot derides belief in such things as groundless superstition. Scot also tells of a magical procedure reputed to give a man the head of an ass.

Shakespeare's knowledge of other works is also reflected in the play. These works include Edmund SPENSER's *Shepheardes Calender* (1579), Bartholomew YONG's translation of *Diana Enamorada,* by the Portuguese author Jorge de MONTEMAYOR (a chief source of *The Two Gentlemen of Verona*), several plays by SENECA and several by John LYLY, plus novels *Euphues* (1578) and *Euphues and His England* (1580). In addition, Thomas NORTH's translation of PLUTARCH's "Life of Theseus" (1579) provided a number of proper names; this was Shakespeare's first use of a source that would become very important to him.

TEXT OF THE PLAY

Dating the composition of *A Midsummer Night's Dream* precisely is not possible with the existing evidence, but we can assume it was written in 1595 or early 1596. The comical worry about the possible ferocity of a theatrical lion (1.2.70–75, 3.1.26–44, 5.1.214–221) was almost certainly inspired by an account, published in London in late 1594, of a planned appearance by a lion at a christening, canceled as possibly dangerous and certainly alarming. Further, Titania's description of the cataclysmic weather caused by her dispute with Oberon (2.1.88–114) apparently refers to a series of three extraordinarily cold, wet summers in 1594–96. This allows us to assume that the play was written between 1595 and 1598, when it was recorded in the list of Shakespeare's works assembled by Francis MERES. However, we know that from 1596 onward Shakespeare was working on plays—*The Merchant of Venice, 1* and *2 Henry IV,* and *The Merry Wives of Windsor*—very unlike the lyrical *Dream.* The latter work, moreover, is linked stylistically to several plays—*Love's Labour's Lost, Romeo and Juliet,* and *Richard II*—that can be dated to 1593–95.

The first edition of the *Dream* was published as a QUARTO by Thomas FISHER in 1600. It appears to have been printed from Shakespeare's FOUL PAPERS, with irregular stage directions and other mistakes that would have been corrected in any later manuscript. This edition is known as Q1. The next edition, Q2, was printed by Thomas PAVIER and William JAGGARD in 1619, as part of the notorious FALSE FOLIO; it was dated 1600 in order not to seem a new, unauthorized publication. Q2 was simply an inaccurate reprint of Q1, with many minor errors. It nonetheless served as the basis for the FIRST FOLIO edition of 1623, though its editors also referred to a PROMPTBOOK of the play, resulting in superior stage directions in their version. Q1, derived from Shakespeare's own manuscript, is regarded as the most authoritative text, and it has been the basis for all modern editions, except with respect to stage directions, for which the Folio text is favored.

THEATRICAL HISTORY OF THE PLAY

The first performance of *A Midsummer Night's Dream* was almost certainly at an aristocratic wedding of the 1590s, although no record of the event exists. The occasion may have been the marriage in February 1596 of Elizabeth Carey, granddaughter of Henry Carey, Lord HUNSDON the patron of the CHAMBERLAIN'S MEN, with whom Shakespeare was associated at the time. Another possible wedding was that of William Stanley, Earl of DERBY, a year earlier, for Derby's older brother, Fernando Stanley, Lord STRANGE, had been the same company's patron before his death in 1594.

In 1600 the title page of the first Quarto edition of the play asserted that it had "been sundry times publickely acted" by the Chamberlain's Men, but the earliest recorded performance, perhaps of an adaptation, was held at the court of King James I in 1604 under the title *A Play of Robin Goodfellow.* No other productions during the playwright's lifetime are known.

A scandal was aroused in 1631 by a Sunday performance of the *Dream* in the house of a bishop, and an excerpt from the play was performed surreptitiously between 1642 and 1660, when the theaters were closed by the revolutionary government. This abridged version was published as a DROLL—*The Merry Conceits of Bottom the Weaver*—in 1661 by Henry MARSH and Francis KIRKMAN. The diarist Samuel PEPYS attended a performance of the *Dream* in 1662 and called it "the most insipid ridiculous play that ever I saw in my life."

This was the last recorded performance for more than a century and a half, though many adaptations were popular throughout the period. The first and most successful of these was Henry PURCELL's OPERA *The Fairy Queen,* produced in 1692 by Thomas BETTERTON, who provided the libretto (which preserved not a single line of Shakespeare's play). Musical versions continued to be produced in the 18th century, most notably Richard LEVERIDGE's operetta *A Comic Masque of Pyramus and Thisbe* (1716, revived 1745), which satirized the current London enthusiasm for Italian opera. As its title suggests, this work included only the SUBPLOT of *A Midsummer Night's Dream.* This material was also tapped by Charles JOHNSON, who incorporated the comical interlude into LOVE IN A FOREST (1723), his version of *As You Like It.* David GARRICK used the main plot of Shakespeare's play, eliminating Bottom and his friends, in *The Fairies* (1755), an opera incorporating 27 songs by various authors. Frederic REYNOLDS continued the musical tradition in 1816, with an operatic medley based on the *Dream.*

The earliest restoration of Shakespeare's text occurred in 1827, in Ludwig TIECK's Berlin production of SCHLEGEL's German translation featuring the famous overture and incidental music by Felix MENDELSSOHN, composed in the previous year. Mendelssohn's music also accompanied the first

English revival, in 1840. Subsequent 19th-century productions included a grandly scenic staging by Charles KEAN and a more restrained version by Samuel PHELPS. The 19th-century tendency to spectacular presentations of the *Dream* reached its height in Beerbohm TREE's 1900 production, which featured live rabbits and birds amid dense foliage.

A *Midsummer Night's Dream* was among the most frequently performed of Shakespeare's plays in the 20th century. Harley GRANVILLE-BARKER's avant-garde rendering of 1914 (New York, 1915) employed a rigorously Shakespearean text, but it also featured stylized botanical motifs in place of realistic scenery and fairies who were painted gold and used mechanical gestures to emphasize their exotic nature. This highly controversial production was influenced by the *Ballets Russes* of Diaghilev. Max REINHARDT presented highly altered versions of Shakespeare's text on the London stage in the 1920s and in a FILM of 1935, starring James Cagney as Bottom and Mickey Rooney as Puck. More conventional productions included those of Tyrone GUTHRIE and Peter HALL. In 1970 Peter BROOK aroused as much controversy as Granville-Barker had a half-century earlier, with a *Dream* incorporating circus acts and costumes in a bare white set. Michael BOYD's ROYAL SHAKESPEARE COMPANY production of 1999–2000 drew raves as well as protests against its eroticism. Operas have continued to be based on the *Dream*, perhaps most notably those by Benjamin BRITTEN (1960) and Carl ORFF (1962). Purcell's *The Fairy Queen* was revived in 1946. *Swinging the Dream* (1939) was a jazz version featuring the Benny Goodman Sextet, with Louis Armstrong as Bottom. The play has been made as a film eight times (five of them silent movies). Most recently, Michael Hoffman produced and directed *William Shakespeare's A Midsummer Night's Dream* (1999), featuring Michelle Pfeiffer as Titania and Kevin Kline as Bottom. The play has also been seen on TELEVISION eight times.

CHARACTERS

Bottom, Nick Character in *A Midsummer Night's Dream*, a weaver of ATHENS. His comical ignorance and his tendency to mangle language make Bottom a typical Shakespearean CLOWN. He is repeatedly placed in ludicrous situations, but his supremely good opinion of himself is unshakeable. As the leading player in the amateur production of PYRAMUS AND THISBE, Bottom cuts a silly figure as a know-it-all who is unaware of his true ignorance. Given the head of an ass by the fairy Puck, Bottom temporarily becomes the beloved of the magically charmed Titania, and his decorum in this extraordinary situation is ridiculous.

However, Bottom is a sympathetic figure as well. He is not pompous, and he is unfailingly civil to everyone. He is not patronizing to his fellow artisans when he lectures them (preposterously) on stagecraft, and he is courteous to his fairy attendants, Peaseblossom, Cobweb, Moth, and Mustardseed. His self-confidence, though humorous in its fog-like density, is not entirely misplaced: he is a leader among his fellows, as they are quite aware, and we can believe he is surely an excellent craftsman. His comedy lies in the contrast between his circumstances and his lack of awareness, but he is not a victim. His courage makes him admirable as well as amusing.

It is ironic that Bottom, who remains absurdly unperturbed, is the only mortal who actually meets any of the fairies. Yet in the end, he is plainly moved by his experience. Awakening from what he calls "a most rare vision" (4.1.203), he discovers that he cannot quite recollect it. He expresses his bafflement in comically garbled terms that reflect, among other things, St. Paul's description (1 Cor. 2:7–9) of the "hidden wisdom which God ordained before the world." We do not need to know the source to sense the power of these words. Bottom aptly observes of his vision, "It shall be called 'Bottom's Dream,' because it hath no bottom" (4.1.214–215); he has sensed that something profound has happened to him.

Bottom's name had no anatomical connotations in Elizabethan English. It refers to a tool of his trade, the core on which a skein of yarn is wound, or, figuratively, the skein itself; its suggestions of the fundamental or basic element of something are equally appropriate to this representative of the common man. To "get to the bottom" of a subject is to find its essential quality, and Bottom displays the combination of practicality, courage, and blind confidence that underlies much human achievement.

Cobweb Character in _A Midsummer Night's Dream_, a fairy, an attendant to the Fairy Queen Titania. In 3.1 Titania assigns Cobweb to the retinue of the comical rustic Bottom because the Queen has been magically induced to love him. Cobweb serves Bottom by hunting for honey in 4.1. Bottom refers to the ancient use of cobwebs to stop small cuts from bleeding (3.1.176); perhaps, the name suggests that Cobweb possesses medicinal lore.

Demetrius Character in _A Midsummer Night's Dream_, the lover of Hermia whose affections are magically diverted to Helena. Chosen by Egeus to be Hermia's husband, Demetrius had wooed Helena earlier, before the opening of the play, but had abandoned her. In addition to fickleness, Demetrius shows an unpleasant shortness with Helena, who pursues him, but on the whole he is—like Hermia's beloved, Lysander—a colorless young man who exists merely to be manipulated by Oberon's spells.

Egeus Character in _A Midsummer Night's Dream_, the father of Hermia. Egeus's angry demand for severe punishment of his daughter for refusing to marry Demetrius interrupts the blissful anticipation of marriage with which the play opens. Duke Theseus hopes to persuade Egeus to abandon his inten-

James Cagney as Bottom in Max Reinhardt's 1935 film of _A Midsummer Night's Dream_. Given the head of an ass by the mischievous Puck, Bottom temporarily becomes the beloved of the magically charmed Titania. _(Courtesy of Movie Star News)_

tions, but we see in 4.1, when Egeus and the Duke discover the sleeping lovers in the enchanted woods, that his attempts have not succeeded. Egeus insists that Lysander be executed for having tried to elope with Hermia. His harshness makes him no more sympathetic to the Duke than to the audience, and Theseus takes evident pleasure in announcing, "Egeus, I will overbear your will" (4.1.178). Shakespeare apparently took the name Egeus from CHAUCER's "The Knight's Tale," in which Egeus is Theseus's father.

Fairy Any of several minor characters in *A Midsummer Night's Dream*, attendants of Titania and Oberon. In 2.1 a nameless Fairy encounters Puck (a Fairy himself), and their conversation establishes the nature of the quarrel between Titania and Oberon. In 2.2 Titania is accompanied by several Fairies, who sing her to sleep. Other Fairies in the play are Cobweb, Moth, Mustardseed, and Peaseblossom.

Flute Character in *A Midsummer Night's Dream*, a bellows-mender of ATHENS and a performer in the comical amateur production of PYRAMUS AND THISBE staged at the wedding celebration of Duke Theseus and Queen Hippolyta. Flute plays Thisbe in this INTERLUDE, which is directed by Peter Quince. In 1.2 Flute resents being cast as a woman, asserting that he has "a beard coming" (1.2.43–44). His objection makes clear that in fact he is still a beardless youth. Flute's name, like those of his fellow artisans, refers to his trade; the flute is the nozzle through which a bellows expels air. The name also suggests the high-pitched quality of the character's voice, and Shakespeare may well have selected the name, and then the occupation, to suit the player of Thisbe.

Helena Character in *A Midsummer Night's Dream*, the lover of Demetrius. Helena is obsessed with Demetrius, who has betrayed her, and while she realizes she is shaming herself, she cannot stop pursuing him, even to the extent of betraying her friend Hermia. That she has lost her self-respect is evident in her first words, "Call you me fair? That fair again unsay!" (1.1.181). When, through Oberon's magic, both men woo her, she can construe their praise

only as ridicule. Her frustration leads her to insult Hermia viciously in the four-way quarrel in 3.2. Her flawed personality has nothing to do with her finally winning Demetrius, as she knows: she treats the outcome as a miracle, saying, "I have found Demetrius like a jewel, / Mine own, and not mine own" (4.1.190–191).

Hermia Character in *A Midsummer Night's Dream*, one of the four lovers whose adventures in the enchanted wood are the centerpiece of the play. In 1.1, when Hermia's father, Egeus, demands that she be punished for refusing to marry Demetrius, her civil but firm response reveals a determined nature. Her first words, a straightforward assertion of her beloved Lysander's virtues, indicate that she will not easily be deterred. When Lysander's love is magically diverted to Helena, Hermia is prepared to fight for her man, and she drives her friend away. Several remarks indicate that Hermia is a brunette with a dark complexion, and she has often been associated with the "Dark Lady" of Shakespeare's *Sonnets*, which he was writing at about the same time.

Hippolyta Character in *A Midsummer Night's Dream*, Queen of the Amazons and the bride of Duke Theseus of ATHENS. Hippolyta's role is small, but she is a sympathetic figure who contributes to the play's theme of domestic love. In 1.1 her distress at the prospect of Hermia's punishment highlights the young lovers' plight. In 5.1 she disagrees with Theseus about the lovers' accounts of their experiences in the enchanted wood. He has doubted their story, but she observes that "all the story of the night told over / . . . grows to something of great constancy / . . . strange and admirable" (5.1.23–27). Her mythical origins as leader of the Amazons are hinted at only fleetingly, in her recollected acquaintance with Hercules and Cadmus, in 4.1. Shakespeare took her name and gentle nature from a character in CHAUCER's "The Knight's Tale."

Lysander Character in *A Midsummer Night's Dream*, the lover of Hermia. When mistakenly anointed with a magical love potion, however, his affections are transferred to Helena. Lysander is the least distinctive of the lovers in the play. His love interest changed from one young woman to another and back again by the magic of Oberon's herbs, Lysander is merely a pawn in Shakespeare's game of rotating lovers.

Moth Character in *A Midsummer Night's Dream*, a fairy attendant to the Fairy Queen Titania. In 3.1 Titania assigns Moth to the retinue of the comical rustic Bottom, whom the Fairy Queen has been magically induced to love. As the smallest and least important fairy in the group attending Bottom, Moth is never addressed by his temporary master and is given no particular task. His name means— and in Elizabethan English was pronounced— "mote" and suggests the tiny size of a speck of dust.

Mustardseed Character in *A Midsummer Night's Dream*, a fairy attendant to the Fairy Queen, Titania. Titania assigns Mustardseed to the retinue of the comical rustic Bottom, whom the Queen has been magically induced to love. Bottom has been endowed by Puck with the head of an ass, but he does not know of his new adornment, and Mustardseed, with Peaseblossom, serves him by helping to scratch his strangely itching face. The fairy's name suggests the several references to the tiny mustard seed in the Gospels (e.g., Luke 17:6).

Oberon Character in *A Midsummer Night's Dream*, the Fairy King who works the magic that ensures the triumph of love that is the focus of the play. Oberon gives an unpleasant first impression in 2.1, quarreling with his queen, Titania, and resolving to "torment" her (2.1.147) because she will not surrender to him a changeling he desires to raise. However, it is clear that he intends his revenge, a dose of a magic aphrodisiac, to be only temporary. Once he knows he will have his way, he is a gentle king, overseeing the confusions of the lovers' plot with good-natured amusement. When Titania, magically made to fall in love with the ass-headed Bottom, has surrendered the changeling, he feels sorry for her and lifts his spell, as he had said he would. For the remainder of the play, he is a benign figure, blessing the marriages and the palace of Duke Theseus. Oberon was the traditional King of Fairies, and Shakespeare must

have known of him from several sources, though the one most prominent in the play is a 13th-century French adventure tale, *Huon of Bordeaux*.

Peaseblossom Character in *A Midsummer Night's Dream*, a fairy attendant to the fairy Queen Titania. In 3.1 Titania assigns Peaseblossom to the retinue of the comical rustic Bottom, whom the queen has been magically induced to love. Bottom has been endowed by Puck with the head of an ass, but he does not know it, and Peaseblossom, assisted by Mustardseed, serves him in 4.1 by scratching his strangely itchy face.

Philostrate Minor character in *A Midsummer Night's Dream*, the MASTER OF REVELS under Duke Theseus. Philostrate arranges the entertainment for the wedding of Theseus and Hippolyta and presents the duke with a list of prospective acts. A pompous courtier, Philostrate argues against Theseus's selec-

The fairy Peaseblossom in Max Reinhardt's 1935 film of *A Midsummer Night's Dream* is made an attendant to Bottom by Titania. *(Courtesy of Culver Pictures, Inc.)*

tion of the artisans' production of PYRAMUS AND THISBE on the grounds that it is blatantly undignified. Shakespeare apparently took the name Philostrate from CHAUCER's "The Knight's Tale," in which one character uses it as an alias.

Puck (Robin Goodfellow) Character in *A Midsummer Night's Dream*, a fairy and aide to Oberon, the Fairy King. Puck is a powerful supernatural creature, capable of circling the earth in 40 minutes (2.1.176) and of manipulating the elements—for example, he summons a fog in 3.2—but he is more mischievous than awe-inspiring. He reminds us of a small boy when he boasts of his talents as a trickster in 2.1.42–57 and when he calls out, "I go, I go, look how I go!" (3.2.100). Like Bottom, he is a humorous character, but where Bottom is a CLOWN, intended to be laughed at, Puck more closely resembles a FOOL, like Shakespeare's jesters Touchstone and Feste. He is removed from the practical world and expresses himself through an idiosyncratic sense of humor. He prefers "things that befall prepost'rously" (3.2.121).

There is some malice in Puck's taste for pranks, and Puck reminds us that the fairy world is not all sweetness and light; this contributes to an undertone of potential evil that makes the comedy, while still benign, a more richly textured tale. He speaks in horrifying terms of the cruel and awesome world that is also the domain of the fairies (5.1.357–373), only to assure us that "we fairies . . . / Now are frolic." However, when his error in anointing Lysander causes trouble, Puck is immune to Oberon's regret that this has happened, replying only, "Then fate o'er-rules" (3.2.92). He is coolly indifferent to human suffering.

While Puck explicitly calls himself a fairy in 5.1.369, quoted above, and elsewhere, there is some ambiguity in his relationship to the FAIRY in 2.1, and in 3.2.399 he identifies himself as a "goblin." Shakespeare did not care about such minor inconsistencies, and they do not interfere with Puck's effectiveness in the drama. They do, however, reflect the fairy lore known to Shakespeare, who combined in Puck two supernatural creatures that had earlier been thought of as separate beings. Robin Goodfellow, a name interchangeable with

In *A Midsummer Night's Dream*, Puck (played here by Mickey Rooney in the 1935 film) is a mischievous trickster who creates trouble by anointing Lysander with a love potion. *(Courtesy of Culver Pictures, Inc.)*

Puck in the 16th century, was a household spirit also associated with travelers. A "puck" was not a fairy, but a small elf or goblin fond of playing practical jokes on mortals, especially at night. The puck was originally a Norse demon, identified in England with the devil.

Quince, Peter Character in *A Midsummer Night's Dream*, a carpenter and the director of the comical production of PYRAMUS AND THISBE, performed by several artisans of ATHENS. Quince organizes an INTERLUDE to be performed at the wedding of Duke Theseus and Queen Hippolyta. Though overshadowed by his leading man, Bottom, he directs the performances of Snug, Flute, Snout, and Starveling, and he reads the PROLOGUE himself. Despite the supposedly Athenian setting of *A Midsummer Night's Dream*, Quince and his fellows are typical English artisans, excellent representatives of the humorous workers Shakespeare was fond of creating.

Quince comically performs several of the tasks of a real Elizabethan acting company. Not only the director, he has also written the script and is responsible for the properties and staging. He is something of a pedant, given to such high-flown locutions as "I am to entreat you, request you, and desire you . . ." (1.2.92–93), but he is a tactful director, flattering Bottom into accepting his role in 1.2.79–82, and a resourceful reviser, prepared to create additional dialogue in 3.1. Less talented as an actor, he misreads his initial speech (5.1.108–117). (Quince's comical mispunctuation of the passage was a standard Elizabethan routine dating from the first English COMEDY, Nicholas UDALL's *Ralph Roister Doister* [ca. 1553].)

The name Quince refers to certain tools of the carpentry trade, wooden wedges called "quoins" or "quines." Quince is thought to have been originally played by Richard COWLEY.

Robin Goodfellow   See Puck.

Snout, Tom   Character in *A Midsummer Night's Dream*, a tinker of ATHENS and a performer in the comical amateur production of PYRAMUS AND THISBE staged at the wedding of Duke Theseus and Queen Hippolyta. Snout plays the Wall in this INTERLUDE, which is directed by his fellow artisan Peter Quince. Snout's name, like that of the other artisans, refers to his trade; a tinker's most common task was repairing the spouts, often called snouts, of kettles and teapots.

Snug   Character in *A Midsummer Night's Dream*, a joiner of ATHENS and a performer in the comical amateur production of PYRAMUS AND THISBE, directed by Peter Quince and staged at the wedding of Duke Theseus and Queen Hippolyta. Snug plays the Lion in this INTERLUDE. He presents himself as "slow of study" (1.2.63), and he is mute during the rehearsal scene (3.1), but he carries off his role commendably at the performance in 5.1. In the woodworking trades, Snug's name means "tightly fitting," an appropriate name for a joiner.

Starveling, Robin   Character in *A Midsummer Night's Dream*, a tailor of ATHENS and a performer in the comical amateur production of PYRAMUS AND THISBE staged at the wedding of Duke Theseus and Queen Hippolyta. Starveling, the least competent of the actors, plays the Moonshine and can utter only two of his lines before reverting to prose to inform the audience what the rest of his verses would have said.

Starveling's name refers to the proverbially skinny nature of tailors, and Shakespeare's choice of name and occupation probably reflects the presence in the acting company of John SINCKLO, a strikingly thin actor who is presumed to have played the part.

Theseus   Character in *A Midsummer Night's Dream*, the Duke of ATHENS. Theseus's wedding to Queen Hippolyta is the climax toward which the play moves. He is a sympathetic lover, though as a middle-aged man he is not given to the passions of youth. He is responsive to Hippolyta's moods, noting, for example, her distress at the plight of Hermia in 1.1.122. Hermia's situation disturbs Theseus, too; it raises an issue that was important to Shakespeare—the relationship between authority and the law. Theseus is a model ruler who respects the laws of his domain, but he regrets the harsh consequences that they may entail for Hermia. He will attempt to help her by persuading Egeus and Demetrius with "private schooling" (1.1.116); but if that effort fails, he is committed to carrying out the law.

Theseus is a constitutional monarch, as the rulers of the TUDOR DYNASTY of England declared themselves to be. Thus he is associated with Queen Elizabeth I (see Elizabeth I in *Henry VIII*). A closer identification of the two is implied in 5.1.89–105, in which Theseus proclaims that he responds favorably to his citizens' speeches of welcome, even when, hopelessly tongue-tied, they fail to speak at all. Elizabeth was known to take great pride in doing the same thing, and this passage is thought to embody a compliment to the sovereign and thus to suggest that she was present to receive it at the first performance of the play.

Titania   Character in *A Midsummer Night's Dream*, the Fairy Queen, wife of Oberon and, temporarily, the magically charmed lover of Bottom. Titania's infatuation with Bottom is Oberon's revenge on her for having persisted in keeping a changeling whom he wants. She asserts that she will keep the body in memory of his mother, who died in childbirth. She is icily haughty and insists on having her way, although, since she and Oberon are elemental forces of nature, their dispute is causing bad weather, as she vividly describes in 2.1.88–117. During Titania's enchantment she is a vapid lover, and afterward she merely serves a decorative role. Her chief qualities are regal pride and grand diction. She is a highly stylized character, generally magnificently costumed, who symbolizes the supernatural at its most glamorous.

Much Ado About Nothing

SYNOPSIS

Act 1, Scene 1

A Messenger tells Leonato, governor of MESSINA, that Don Pedro, Prince of Aragon, is approaching. He reports the prince's victories in war and tells of the knightly accomplishments of Claudio, a young gentleman in Don Pedro's court. Leonato's niece, Beatrice, asks about another gentleman, Benedick; she responds to the Messenger's good report with sharp raillery, which Leonato explains as part of an ongoing rivalry of wits between his niece and the young nobleman. Don Pedro arrives, accompanied by the two young men and his brother, Don John. Benedick and Beatrice exchange humorous insults, each of them asserting an extreme aversion to love, particularly for the other. Leonato offers a special welcome to Don John, who has lately been reconciled with his brother. Most of the group departs, leaving Claudio and Benedick alone; Claudio confesses that he has fallen in love with Leonato's daughter, Hero, and wishes to marry her; Benedick derides marriage. Don Pedro returns, and Benedick reveals Claudio's desire. Don Pedro teases Benedick, predicting that he will fall in love one day. Then he helpfully offers to court Hero himself, disguised as Claudio at the MASQUE scheduled for that evening; once assured of Hero's response, he will approach her father on Claudio's behalf.

Act 1, Scene 2

Leonato's brother, Antonio, reports that a servant has overheard Don Pedro telling Claudio of his intention to marry Hero.

Act 1, Scene 3

Don John complains to his attendant Conrade of his bitter melancholy. Conrade replies that he should disguise his attitude to preserve his newly restored place in Don Pedro's court. Don John asserts that he can only be himself and that he wishes to be a villain, spreading discontent. Another follower, Borachio, brings news of Don Pedro's plan to woo Hero on Claudio's behalf. Don John proposes to make mischief with this information, hurting Claudio, whose advancement he envies.

Act 2, Scene 1

Beatrice acidly compares the ferociously silent Don John to the overly talkative Benedick. Leonato asserts that her attitude toward men will prevent her from getting a husband. He then reminds Hero to respond to the prince's expected wooing, though Beatrice wittily preaches against marriage. Don Pedro and his courtiers arrive for the festivities, and all the participants put on masks. Don Pedro takes Hero aside as other couples flirt. Benedick and Beatrice, in disguise, trade insults, supposedly stating other people's opinions. Don John tells Claudio that he has heard the prince courting Hero. Claudio is shocked, believing that Don Pedro is stealing his prospective bride. He leaves embittered. When Don Pedro appears, Benedick berates him for betraying Claudio, but the prince assures him that he means well by their friend. The talk turns to Beatrice, and Benedick reveals that he is angered and hurt by her sharply expressed disdain for him. Claudio and Beatrice appear, and Benedick leaves. Don Pedro tells Claudio that he has arranged his marriage to Hero, and Claudio rejoices. Beatrice leaves, and the prince reveals a plan to Leonato and Claudio: He will trick Benedick and Beatrice into falling in love with each other.

Act 2, Scene 2

Borachio proposes to Don John a scheme to thwart Claudio's marriage: he, Borachio, will recruit Hero's waiting-woman, Margaret, to disguise herself as Hero and admit him into Hero's window that night. If Don John, pretending concern for Claudio's honor, can get him and Don Pedro to witness this charade, they will believe that Hero has a lover and Claudio will repudiate her.

Act 2, Scene 3

In the garden Benedick reflects on the seductiveness of love. When Don Pedro, Claudio, and Leonato appear, he hides himself in an arbor. They see him, and, following Don Pedro's plan, they speak loudly about Beatrice's passionate love for him. They profess to be reluctant to tell him of her ardor, knowing his hostility toward her. They leave, and Benedick observes that he has misjudged matters and that he will marry Beatrice. Beatrice appears to summon him to dinner. She says that she dislikes her errand and leaves, but Benedick comically imagines that he sees double meanings in her words that prove her love.

Act 3, Scene 1

Ursula, a waiting-woman, is sent to tell Beatrice that Hero and Margaret are talking about her in the garden. As expected, Beatrice eavesdrops on the two, and they speak loudly of Benedick's passion for her, praising him highly as they do so. They profess reluctance to tell her this news, fearing her mockery. They leave, and Beatrice decides that she will return Benedick's love, and she looks forward to happiness with him.

Act 3, Scene 2

Don Pedro and Claudio tease Benedick about his changed appearance, saying that he must be in love. He claims toothache, but he takes Leonato aside to speak privately, presumably about marrying Beatrice. Don John appears and tells Claudio and Don Pedro of Hero's infidelity, offering to prove the truth of his accusation that night.

Act 3, Scene 3

The rustic Constable Dogberry, assisted by Verges, assembles the Watchmen for their nightly patrol. In a comically confused passage, they assert that all sorts of disorder and dereliction are proper procedures. Then Conrade and Borachio appear. Borachio describes the success of his plan to deceive Claudio and tells of Claudio's determination to disgrace Hero at the wedding. The Watchmen, though perplexed, realize that some villainy has been committed, and they arrest the two men.

Act 3, Scene 4

Margaret and Hero tease Beatrice about her seeming love sickness.

Act 3, Scene 5

Leonato, late for Hero's wedding, interrupts Dogberry's comically long-winded account of Conrade and Borachio. He tells Dogberry to interrogate the prisoners and submit a written report.

Act 4, Scene 1

During the marriage ceremony, Claudio rejects Hero, asserting that he has witnessed her rendezvous with a lover. This report is confirmed by Don Pedro, and even Leonato believes it. Hero faints, and Claudio and Don Pedro leave. Leonato rages at her, wishing she were dead, but Friar Francis, who had been officiating at the wedding, calms Leonato and states his belief in Hero's innocence. Beatrice and Benedick also support her, and Leonato recovers his faith in his daughter. The Friar suggests they pretend that Hero has died, thus silencing gossip and possibly stirring Claudio to grief and reviving his love. Then, if Hero is not exonerated, she can at least be secretly transferred to a nunnery. Leonato and the Friar leave, taking Hero into seclusion. Beatrice and Benedick reveal their feelings for each other, but Beatrice demands that Benedick prove his love by challenging Claudio to a duel in support of Hero. He agrees to do so.

Act 4, Scene 2

Dogberry tries to interrogate Conrade and Borachio, but his comical ineptitude spurs the Sexton to take over. He questions the Watchmen, who tell of Don John's plot. The Sexton, knowing about the abortive wedding and aware that Don John has fled from Messina, realizes that this story is true. He orders the prisoners bound and taken to Leonato, and he goes to report what he has learned. Conrade insults Dogberry, who responds with humorously pompous self-praise.

Act 5, Scene 1

Leonato and Antonio berate Claudio and Don Pedro, exiting just as Benedick arrives. Benedick challenges Claudio to a duel and leaves, declaring that they will fight later. Dogberry arrives with his prisoners, and Borachio confesses all. Leonato returns, having been told the truth by the Sexton, and Claudio begs his forgiveness, promising to perform any penance. Leonato states that he must

In *Much Ado About Nothing*, 4.2, the comically inept constable Dogberry attempts an interrogation of Borachio and Conrade. *(Courtesy of Culver Pictures, Inc.)*

publicly mourn Hero and then marry Hero's cousin. Claudio assents.

Act 5, Scene 2

Benedick tells Beatrice of his challenge to Claudio, and they tease each other on the subject of love. Ursula tells them that Don John's plot has been exposed.

Act 5, Scene 3

Claudio reads an epitaph for Hero at Leonato's family crypt, believing that she is buried in it. Balthasar completes the rite with a mournful song. Don Pedro comes to escort Claudio to his wedding to Hero's cousin.

Act 5, Scene 4

Benedick receives Leonato's permission to marry Beatrice. Claudio prepares to marry the veiled cousin, who reveals herself to be Hero. Benedick and Beatrice cannot bring themselves to admit their love for each other, returning to their barbed wit, but Claudio produces a love poem that Benedick has written about Beatrice, and Hero presents a similar lyric by Beatrice about Benedick. Exposed, Beatrice and Benedick agree to be married. As plans are made for a double wedding, word comes that Don John has been apprehended. Benedick promises to devise some suitable punishment, but he turns to celebration in the meantime. The assembled people dance.

COMMENTARY

Much Ado About Nothing shares a theme common to Shakespearean COMEDY: A romance is disrupted, but love triumphs. However, unlike such earlier works as

The Two Gentlemen of Verona and *A Midsummer Night's Dream*, this play is a comedy of character, rather than of situation; its major development—the defeat of the threat to romantic happiness—comes about through a psychological change on the part of the major characters, rather than through changes in their circumstances. While elaborate and melodramatic coincidences bring the play to its climax, that climax—Beatrice and Benedick's commitment to each other—is one of personal crisis and response.

The conflict between Beatrice and Benedick is the central element of the play, although it is sometimes seen as a SUBPLOT, being humorous and lacking the villainous interference that adds suspense to the story of Hero and Claudio. The two scorners of love are unquestionably the brightest and most vital characters in the play, and their lively battle of wits engages much of our attention. It is introduced before Claudio and Hero even meet, and Claudio's feebly motivated love at first sight has none of its appeal. The comic trap that brings the former foes together holds our interest in the second half of the play; the tale of the foolish Claudio and his passively victimized lover seems most important as the stimulus for the growing trust between Beatrice and Benedick, who are much more fully developed characters.

The gulf that at first separates Beatrice and Benedick is not created by any outside interference; rather, the lovers themselves have established it. We are immediately aware that they love each other, despite their protestations to the contrary: in 1.1 Beatrice cannot refrain from asking after Benedick's fate in battle, though she affects scorn in doing so, and Benedick thinks first of Beatrice as a model with which to compare Hero (unfavorably) when he mocks Claudio's intention to marry. Beatrice and Benedick have apparently quarreled in the past; she speaks of "our last conflict" (1.1.59) and implies an earlier unhappy romance, in 2.1.261–264. He is overly sensitive to her criticism, declaring himself unable to abide her company in 2.1.257–258. These hints lead us to believe that both parties are trying to protect themselves against a repetition of their previous unhappiness.

Thus their relationship develops in a way that makes it stirringly real. When Don Pedro's plot makes them fall in love with each other, it seems entirely appropriate and their responses are convincing. Each, once convinced of the other's love, accepts affection and reciprocates it. Their reactions are both comical and humanly touching, as they halfheartedly attempt to disguise their new feelings with transparent complaints of toothache (3.2.20) and head cold (3.4.40). When their friends tease them, we feel a pleasurable sense of escape, seeing on stage, at a safe distance, a kind of foolishness to which we ourselves might be susceptible.

The reaction of these vital and good-humored figures to the denunciation of Hero lies at the moral heart of the play. The scene of Hero's rejection in church (4.1), which alludes to such religious concepts as "grace" and "damnation" (4.1.171, 172), presents a crisis of spiritual values. Beatrice acts on her faith in her cousin, and Benedick acts on his faith in Beatrice. This involvement in a serious issue brings them together utterly, completing the work of their friends' earlier ploys. This process permits them to return to the world of normal relations, where earlier they had isolated themselves from it.

Although Beatrice and Benedick dominate the play—significantly, it was long known by the title "Beatrice and Benedick"—Claudio and Hero reinforce their lesson of love and faith. While these lovers are undeniably shallower than Benedick and Beatrice, this very fact makes them effective in their own way. Hero and Claudio are conformists who believe in the romantic norms that their more spirited friends reject. Their conventionality supports the comic tone of the play by preventing our emotional or sentimental involvement in their situation.

Hero is a typically pliant and acquiescent young Elizabethan woman. She shows no interest in Claudio until Don Pedro tells her that she is betrothed to him. She is mildly charming, and she is spirited enough to help trick Beatrice into loving Benedick, but she is mostly a docile participant in an arranged marriage. Claudio plays a more prominent role; if Benedick and Beatrice must learn that their opposition to love is a false sentiment, Claudio must also be freed from the naive pseudo-love that he at first declares for Hero, an emotion not grounded in experience. Claudio has often been condemned as a cad, a mere cardboard figure, or both. However, he should be taken at his word when he professes love for Hero; even as he rejects her, he does so in sorrow, regretting that his love has been disappointed. His vicious attempt to humiliate Hero reflects the extent of his hurt. Moreover, as a conventional young man, Claudio is concerned about the offense to his honor—and to that of his prince, Don Pedro—caused by what he believes to be a plot to foist a promiscuous bride on him. While this consideration is almost meaningless today, it will have been appreciated by Elizabethan audiences, and thus we should recognize that, while Claudio is plainly foolish and gullible, he may reasonably plead in his own defense that he has sinned "but in mistaking" (5.1.269).

Claudio's repentance at Hero's supposed tomb is often criticized as cynical, too slight and superficial to be taken seriously, but the text of the scene (5.3) offers no justification for this view; it presents a solemn, if brief, ritual of grief and atonement, followed by a formal quatrain, spoken by Don Pedro (5.3.24–27), that invokes hope for the future. However, even though Claudio is properly repentant, he remains uninteresting, and it is fitting that he and Hero are simply ignored at the end of the play, when attention turns to Benedick and Beatrice.

Don John is also a conventional figure, a "plain-dealing villain" (1.3.30), for whom "any bar, any cross, any impediment will be medicinable to me" (2.2.4–5). His true nature is hidden even from his brother, Don Pedro, even though he has recently rebelled against him. (In 16th-century melodrama, the evil of a villain often remains unknown to his victims until he is overtly exposed.) He is a plot device more than a truly complex character—a sort of anticomic symbol who opposes the happy ending. Such a mechanical villain is necessary, because a true villain, like Richard III or Iago, would destroy the comic assurance that all will be well for the crossed lovers. Significantly, Don John is not present at the final reconciliation, for his nature is utterly at odds with it.

Much Ado's central plot device is the readiness of the characters to accept error and misinformation: Don John's false presentation of Hero is merely the most important incident in a series of erroneous reports and misunderstandings. While Don John maliciously misleads his intended victims, Don Pedro benevolently tricks Benedick and Beatrice. Dogberry is fully capable of confusing himself and everyone else.

Disguise, another source of error, is also a prominent motif. At the masque in 2.1, Beatrice and Benedick converse in masks, and their dialogue, more vitriolic than usual, marks the extreme extent of their hostility. In the same scene, Claudio is pretending to be Benedick when Don John tells him that Don Pedro loves Hero. More important, the play turns on Margaret's use of a disguise, Hero's clothes, as part of Don John's plot to slander Hero. This episode is lent further mystery by being only reported (twice—by Borachio in 3.3.139–158 and, slightly differently, by Don Pedro in 4.1.89–94) and not actually shown on stage.

The theme of error and confusion is also enhanced by various other dramatic devices. Prominent is the repeated importance of overhearing, an act that lends itself to misinterpretation and error. Don Pedro's plan to help Claudio woo Hero is overheard and misunderstood by Antonio's servant, as is retold by Antonio in 1.2, and it is also overheard—correctly but with malice—by Borachio, leading to Don John's first piece of villainy. Don John's scheme involves the invention of another overheard conversation, with which he deceives Claudio. Don Pedro uses overhearing benevolently to convince Beatrice and Benedick that each is loved by the other, and the Watchmen overhear Borachio's account of Don John's second villainy, leading to the eventual exposure of his plot. The frequent recurrence of this motif lends strength to the role of luck and timing in the comedy's gratifying resolution.

The very title of the play may contain a pun on this subject, for "nothing" was probably pronounced like "noting," which in Elizabethan English could mean "overhearing" or "eavesdropping." This possibility seems to be supported by the wordplay in 1.1.150–152 and 2.3.57. The casual title serves a thematic purpose in any case, affirming the play's comic nature by implying that the lovers' trials will prove in the end to have been of no consequence.

The various plots of *Much Ado* are intricately interwoven in a fabric that both suggests and reinforces the complex confusions that are central to the play. From the beginning our attention is repeatedly transferred from one set of lovers to the other. One plot is conventionally melodramatic, while the other is a series of clever rejections of conventional romance; each of these qualities contradicts the other, preventing a single tone from dominating. The Claudio-Hero plot is written entirely in verse, whereas Beatrice and Benedick spar in particularly loose and lively prose. (An exception, Beatrice's lyrical outburst when she hears that Benedick loves her [3.1.107–116], is sometimes seen as evidence that Shakespeare adapted *Much Ado* from a lost play in verse [see "Sources of the Play"], though it is just as likely to have been intended as a sign of her sudden receptivity to romance.)

While the two stories are thus antithetical in some ways, they are similar in others. Both plots feature heroes who err in renouncing their lovers out of pride in both cases—Benedick's pride of overvalued independence, Claudio's pride required by a conventional sense of honor. Both men, however, are plainly going to end up married. Similarly, Beatrice and Hero are alike in destiny and opposed in personality. The two stories combine when they both come to their dissimilar climaxes in 4.1. In fact, Claudio's rejection of Hero sparks the cooperation and trust between Beatrice and Benedick.

Other features of plotting emphasize the play's confusions. Strikingly, Don John's villainy is first spent on a scheme that goes nowhere, the attempt to make Claudio believe that Don Pedro is taking Hero for himself. This ruse makes us aware of important aspects of both the villain and his victim. Similarly, the third plot element, that of Dogberry and his Watchmen, is also full of confusion. But it is handled with a precision that makes *Much Ado* respected as among the most deftly plotted of Shakespeare's works. Dogberry's Watchmen appear exactly at the crucial moment when Don John's second, more potent villainy has been unfolded to us, though not to its victims. When the Watchmen overhear Borachio and Conrade, we are assured that Hero will be exonerated. Yet Dogberry's comical ineptitude ensures that she won't be cleared immediately, and the lovers' stories are allowed to continue to their resolutions.

Thus hints of tragedy alternate with comical reassurances. We learn the truth while the characters operate in ignorance of it; thus we laugh, preserving the comic nature of the play. Our emotions are insulated from the distress that the deluded characters would evoke in a tragedy or in real life. Nevertheless, the melodrama of Hero's unjust disgrace, shockingly brutal because it is set at her wedding, forbids escapism. Like the later PROBLEM PLAYS, *Much Ado* has the capacity to disturb, and we are morally engaged. The happiness that is finally attained is made more valuable by the difficulty with which it is achieved. At the end, though, as in *The Merchant of Venice*, these hardships are forgotten, and love and happiness prevail. The final reconciliation stems from the essential goodness of the world of Leonato's court; its denizens are cheerfully at home with each other, too witty to be sentimental and too kind to be unfeeling. While Claudio and Don Pedro prove vulnerable to Don John's manipulations, their error is rectified. Evil is undone through the redeeming power of love and faith and through the timely grace of chance. We can agree with Benedick when he says, "man is a giddy thing, and this is my conclusion" (5.4.107), but perhaps it is Dogberry who most truly, if unwittingly, states the play's nature when he chastises Borachio, asserting, "Thou wilt be condemned into everlasting redemption" (4.2.53–54).

SOURCES OF THE PLAY

The main plot of *Much Ado About Nothing* is an example of an old European tradition—dating at least to late classical times—of stories in which a lover is deceived into believing that his beloved is unfaithful. Shakespeare drew on a version that first appeared in Ludovico ARIOSTO's massive poem *Orlando Furioso*, which he may have known in both an Italian edition (probably that of 1532) and the English translation by Sir John HARINGTON (1591). He also used another Italian rendering, itself an adaptation of Ariosto, a story by Matteo BANDELLO that was published in a 1554 collection. Between the two Italian texts, most of the details of Claudio's courtship of Hero, its villainous thwarting, and the final happy reunion of the protagonists are foreshadowed. An English version of Ariosto's story, in George WHETSTONE's collection of tales *The Rocke of Regard* (1576), may have suggested Claudio's rejection of Hero at her own wedding.

Some scholars have argued that Shakespeare modified an earlier play to create *Much Ado*, but this viewpoint is highly speculative and largely unpopular, particularly since no existing text is offered as the missing source, although the mysterious *Love's Labour's Won* is sometimes suggested.

Ariosto and derivative texts account only for the Hero-Claudio plot, while it is the other plots in *Much Ado*—the romance of Benedick and Beatrice and the crucial intervention of the comical constabulary—which make the play a comedy; the older works are straight melodramas. Dogberry is certainly a Shakespearean original, in that no particular literary source provides a forerunner. However, humorous constables—characterized by confused speech and ludicrous logic—were a very old theatrical staple. Indeed, Shakespeare had already used the type in a more minor character, Constable Dull, of *Love's Labour's Lost*. Just as important as any model for Dogberry, in all probability, was Shakespeare's awareness of the onstage personality of Will KEMPE, the actor for whom the role was written.

As witty scorners of romance, Beatrice and Benedick are also part of a tradition that was well established in the 16th century, but an important stimulus probably came from the Italian Baldassare CASTIGLIONE's *The Book of the Courtier* (1528), one of the most important and widely read works of the time. Shakespeare almost certainly read it, either in Italian or in the popular English translation by Thomas HOBY (1561, three eds. by 1588). Castiglione presents an ideal of courtly life that included the revolutionary idea that women had much to contribute to it. To illustrate this point, he composed a series of sprightly debates between a man and a woman that may well have inspired the verbal sparring between Beatrice and Benedick.

TEXT OF THE PLAY

Much Ado About Nothing is thought to have been written in mid- or late 1598, although this date cannot be proven. Francis MERES omits *Much Ado* from his list of Shakespearean comedies, published in the summer of 1598 (though it is sometimes maintained that the title *Love's Labour's Won* refers to *Much Ado*). Meres's omission suggests that the play did not exist when he wrote, although he may simply have omitted it. However, a late date is supported by the fact that the play was registered with the STATIONERS' COMPANY in 1600 as "to be stayed"—that is, *not* to be published. This ploy was generally associated with new work, being an attempt to protect a currently popular play from piracy by unlicensed publishers. Still, even if *Much Ado* was a recent success in 1600, it was certainly written somewhat earlier, for Will Kempe, for whom the role of Dogberry was written, left Shakespeare's company, the CHAMBERLAIN'S MEN, in January or February 1599.

The company apparently sold the rights to Andrew WISE and William ASPLEY, for they published a QUARTO edition of the play (known as Q) late in 1600. This text was probably printed (by Valentine SIMMES) from Shakespeare's own manuscript, or FOUL PAPERS, as is evidenced by casual stage directions, some of which name the actors who played Dogberry and Verges, and some of which name Innogen, a GHOST CHARACTER.

The next publication of the play was in the FIRST FOLIO of 1623, where it was printed from a copy of Q that had been partially amended, particularly with respect to stage directions. The Folio also made two brief cuts in the play, probably to avoid offending the court or violating the 1606 statute against profanity (see CENSORSHIP). The two texts remain very similar, and modern editions are based on both.

THEATRICAL HISTORY OF THE PLAY

The 1600 edition of *Much Ado About Nothing* asserts that the play had been "sundrie times publikely acted." Although it was not reprinted between 1600 and 1623, it is evident that *Much Ado About Nothing* was immediately popular, for many references to it have survived from the early 17th century. When Leonard DIGGES compared the popularity of the plays of Shakespeare and JONSON in 1640, he observed, "let but Beatrice and Benedick be seen, lo, in a trice the Cockpit, Galleries, Boxes, all are full." Several performances at the court of King JAMES I are recorded, among them a presentation at the wedding festivities of the princess ELIZABETH STUART in 1613. Later, King Charles I was sufficiently familiar with the play to amend the table of contents of his copy of the Second Folio (1632) by changing its name to "Benedik and Betrice" (sic).

In the Restoration period William DAVENANT owned the rights to produce the play, but he merged it with *Measure for Measure* in THE LAW AGAINST LOVERS (1662). Another production of *Much Ado* itself is not recorded until 1721, when John RICH revived it, restaging it several times over the next quarter-century. The play was again cannibalized in two popular adaptations of this period: LOVE IN A FOREST (1723) by Charles JOHNSON, a rendering of *As You Like It,* contained bits of *Much Ado;* and James MILLER combined Shakespeare's play with one by Molière in 1737.

Much Ado was very popular throughout the rest of the 18th century and has remained so ever since. David GARRICK played Benedick many times between 1748 and 1776, and it was often said to be his best role. Among the notable Benedicks of the 19th century were Charles KEMBLE and Henry IRVING; Beatrice was principally associated with two actresses, first Helen FAUCIT and then Ellen TERRY. Hector BERLIOZ wrote an OPERA—*Béatrice et Bénédict* (1862)—based on *Much Ado;* it omitted the Claudio-Hero plot.

Among the most notable of many 20th-century productions of *Much Ado* were John GIELGUD's highly successful London presentation of 1949, revived in 1950, 1952, and 1955; Franco ZEFFIRELLI's production of 1965; Joseph PAPP's 1972 New York version, set in the turn-of-the-century United States; a more conventional Papp presentation in 1988; and the 1976 STRATFORD staging by John BARTON, set in British India. The play has been produced as a FILM several times, most recently by Kenneth BRANAGH in 1993. Several productions have been adapted for TELEVISION, including Zeffirelli's (1967) and Papp's (1973).

CHARACTERS

Antonio Character in *Much Ado About Nothing,* brother of Leonato. Antonio is a charming old gentleman, especially when he flirts with Ursula at the MASQUE in 2.1, undismayed when his identity is betrayed by his palsy. He is an unimportant member of Leonato's entourage until 5.1, when, sharing his brother's anger at Don Pedro and Claudio over their humiliation of Hero, he challenges the two younger men to a duel. His extravagant and blustery rage is somewhat comic, particularly since the audience is aware of the imminent resolution of Hero's dilemma, but it is also touching evidence of Antonio's loyalty to his brother and niece.

Balthasar Minor character in *Much Ado About Nothing,* a musician and singer employed by Don Pedro. In 2.3 Don Pedro instructs Balthasar to sing the SONG "Sigh no more, ladies," though Balthasar insists he is not a good singer. In 5.3 he sings the solemn "Pardon, goddess of the night," as Claudio mourns the supposed death of Hero. Balthasar makes feeble attempts to be witty, especially when he fishes for compliments in 2.3, but he has no real personality. He is part of the play's atmosphere of aristocratic decorum and hospitality, here expressed through courtly music, a standard feature of the great noble households of both RENAISSANCE Italy and Elizabethan England.

In a stage direction in the FIRST FOLIO edition of the play (1623), Balthasar is identified as "Iacke Wilson," a reference to the actor who played the part. It cannot be known for certain who this was, but scholars frequently propose either Jack WILSON or John WILSON.

Beatrice Character in *Much Ado About Nothing,* sharp-tongued rival in wits—and later the lover—of Benedick. Beatrice, who initially disparages love and Benedick, later rejects these attitudes and becomes his betrothed. She in fact loves him all along, as the audience knows; her own awareness comes only with the assurance that he loves her. Their relationship matures when they act together to defend her defamed cousin Hero at the crisis point of the play.

Beatrice bluntly disdains love, sneering, "I had rather hear my dog bark at a crow than a man swear he loves me" (1.1.120–122), but her first words (1.1.28–29) have already betrayed her interest in Benedick, although she covers it with a veneer of witty insults and teasing. She has suffered through an earlier unhappy romance with Benedick, as she suggests in 1.1.59 and 2.1.261–264, and her barbed wit is plainly defensive, disguising her true feelings even from herself. Her brashness is nicely contrasted with Hero's reticence in 2.1: Hero is twice prompted about her response to the expected courtship of Don Pedro, and on both occasions Beatrice's comments about marriage prevent her reply.

Tricked into believing that Benedick loves her, Beatrice immediately discards her cynicism, saying, "contempt, farewell, and maiden pride, adieu!" (3.1.109–110), in a lyrical 10-line outburst—almost her only verse lines in the play—that emphasizes her elation. Swallowing her pride, she must accept her friends' teasing in 3.4.

When Hero is cruelly rejected on false evidence of promiscuity, Beatrice proves her essential goodness, believing in her cousin's innocence in the face of the evidence and demanding support from Benedick. The two witty lovers become involved in a serious conflict, bolstered by each other's trust. In asking for Benedick's aid, Beatrice confirms her love and acknowledges his.

Nevertheless, once Hero's problem is solved, Beatrice and Benedick briefly retreat from love in 5.4. Their strength is almost not great enough to overcome their old habits, but when their friends produce their love poems, they are forced to reaffirm their true feelings. Beatrice's quick wit cannot resist an attempt at having the last word (5.4.94–96), so Benedick silences her with a kiss.

This rather abrupt close to Beatrice's part suggests an important aspect of the playwright's attitude toward women: Beatrice, like other Shakespearean heroines, such as Katherina in *The Taming of the Shrew,* displays a spirited individuality, but in the end she willingly accepts a position subordinate to a man, as was conventionally expected of Elizabethan women. At first, denying that she wants or needs a husband, Beatrice asserts her independence, demonstrating the freedom of will that enlivens Shakespeare's most attractive female characters. However, when she seeks to defend Hero's innocence, she concedes that a male presence is required, saying of the vengeance she desires on

her cousin's behalf, "It is a man's office" (4.1.265). She asks Benedick to fulfill the role that she cannot, reminding us of the ultimately dependent position of women in Shakespeare's world.

Intriguingly, Beatrice shares two further characteristics with Shakespeare's other bold young women, including the "Dark Lady" of the *Sonnets*: a sharp wit and a dark complexion. It seems plausible, though altogether unprovable, that these were the traits of a woman (entirely unidentifiable) who was romantically important to Shakespeare.

Beatrice is sometimes seen as shrewish, but this is a misconception; Shakespeare plainly intended to present a delightful young woman—defensive about love but charming and candid. While her repartee can be made to seem malicious or mean-spirited in performance, it is more fittingly delivered with great mirth and gaiety; Don Pedro remarks that she is "a pleasant-spirited lady" (2.1.320). Shakespeare took Beatrice's name from the Latin name *Beatrix,* meaning "she who blesses." She is thus appropriately matched with Benedick (from the Latin *Benedictus,* meaning "blessed").

Benedick Character in *Much Ado About Nothing,* rival of Beatrice in contests of wit and later her lover. Benedick initially ridicules love, insisting that cuckoldry is the inevitable fate of married men, but he becomes a joyous bridegroom at the play's end. His playful dislike of Beatrice, which predates the beginning of the play, extends to all women, including Hero, whom his friend Claudio loves, but Benedick subtly reveals an underlying readiness to abandon his misogyny when he contrasts his "custom, as being a professed tyrant to their sex" with his "simple true judgement" (1.1.154–157). Tricked by Claudio and Don Pedro into believing that Beatrice loves him, Benedick permits his own suppressed affection to emerge. At the play's climax, when Beatrice asks him to support the maligned Hero, he agrees, though this means turning from the comfortable companionship of Claudio and Don Pedro. Trusting in his certainty of Beatrice's essential decency, Benedick has grown from shallow misogyny to implicit faith in his lover. His maturation, along with Beatrice's corresponding development, is the chief psychological theme of the play.

Benedick is essentially a comic figure. His friends value him for his sense of humor; Don Pedro says of him, "from the crown of his head to the sole of his foot he is all mirth" (3.2.8–9). He is also sometimes a figure of fun. He crosses verbal swords with Beatrice, but she is too quick-witted for him, and he can respond only in her absence, as in the humorous speech that he delivers to Don Pedro in 2.1.223–245. Tricked into believing that Beatrice loves him, he comically imagines romantic double meanings in her derisive words. Even filled with passion, he can be funny: "I will live in thy heart, die in thy lap, and be buried in thy eyes; and moreover, I will go with thee to thy uncle's" (5.2.94–96).

However, Benedick is no buffoon; his essential honor is often displayed. In 2.1, although hurt and humiliated himself, he accosts Don Pedro on Claudio's behalf when it appears that the older man is stealing Hero. When he defends the falsely accused and dishonored Hero in 5.1, Benedick manfully resigns from Don Pedro's service and challenges Claudio to a duel. At the end of the play, fully committed to marrying Beatrice, he recants his earlier misogyny with no loss of dignity whatever. He admits freely that he had been wrong and is prepared to accept any ridicule that may be attempted against him, saying, ". . . since I do purpose to marry, I will think nothing to any purpose that the world can say against it" (5.4.103–105). In acknowledging his earlier foolishness, he offers a motto that might well sum up Shakespeare's comedies: "man is a giddy thing, and this is my conclusion" (5.4.107).

Benedick, a common name in medieval England, comes from the Latin *Benedictus,* meaning "blessed;" he is thus appropriately matched with Beatrice (from *Beatrix,* or "she who blesses"). Shakespeare's character has become so firmly entrenched in the imagination of generations of readers and theatergoers that his name, sometimes spelled "Benedict," has become a common noun meaning a newly married man who has long been a bachelor.

Borachio Character in *Much Ado About Nothing,* follower of Don John. Borachio, Don John's chief lieutenant, receives 1,000 ducats from his master for devising a scheme to prevent the marriage of Claudio, whom Don John resents and despises, to the desirable Hero. Borachio masquerades with Hero's waiting-woman, Margaret, as Hero and a clandestine lover. This charade convinces Claudio and Don Pedro that Hero is promiscuous, and she finds herself publicly humiliated as an unfaithful fiancée. However, when Borachio brags of his success to his friend Conrade, the Watchmen overhear him, and the plot is eventually exposed. In the general reconciliation that closes the play, Borachio repents, confessing his guilt freely and adding that he duped Margaret.

Some modern editors give the lines of Balthasar in 2.1.92–102, where he flirts with Margaret, to Borachio. Errors in some of these speech prefixes suggest that the printers of the early editions were confused, and, since Borachio is elsewhere associated with the waiting-woman, he is sometimes given that connection here as well. Borachio's name comes from the Spanish *borracho,* meaning "drunkard." This rather undignified appellation reflects the petty villainy of the character while also implying a relative innocence that makes his acknowledgment of guilt at the end of the play more believable.

Boy Minor character in *Much Ado About Nothing,* servant of Benedick. In 2.3 Benedick sends the Boy on an errand whose sole purpose seems to be to permit the mention that the scene is set in an orchard or garden. The Boy flippantly asserts that his speed will be such that "I am here already, sir" (2.3.5), an effervescent pleasantry suited to the early action of the play.

Claudio Character in *Much Ado About Nothing,* lover of Hero. Claudio falls in love with Hero on sight, but he rejects her when the deceitful Don John presents him with false evidence of her infidelity. Once aware of his error, and believing that Hero has died of shame, Claudio repents and agrees to marry Hero's supposed cousin, who turns out to be Hero herself, and the couple is at last united. Claudio's apparent lack of awareness and his haste to mistrust his beloved make him seem shallow and insensitive, and modern audiences tend to find him one of the least likeable or interesting of Shakespeare's young noblemen.

However, Claudio may be considered from another point of view that more likely reflects Shakespeare's intentions. Claudio, like Hero, is a model young Elizabethan. Even before he appears, he is extolled by the Messenger as a paragon of knightly virtues, "doing, in the figure of a lamb, the feats of a lion" (1.1.13–14). His youth and inexperience make him a plausible target for Don John's lies; his passive wooing of Hero, dependent on Don Pedro's assistance, emphasizes his vulnerability. He is often faulted for a seemingly mercenary interest in Hero (1.1.274), but his inquiry about her inheritance is merely conventional: any young man of Shakespeare's day would ask such a question of a prospective bride, and the query simply demonstrates his interest in marriage. Gullible, he believes Hero has been unfaithful, but Shakespeare takes care to make his credulousness less ridiculous by having Don Pedro seem duped as well. The viciousness of Claudio's response indicates the extent to which he has been hurt by his seeming rejection. Both Claudio and Don Pedro regret the understandable anger of Leonato and Antonio in 5.1, and they refrain from a violent response. Their awkward jesting confirms their embarrassment over the situation. Claudio's repentance and atonement are sometimes regarded as cursory and hypocritical, but Shakespeare treats them seriously. Although the scene at Hero's supposed tomb is brief, it is solemn. In 5.4 Claudio's return to happiness is complete, and he is unquestionably accepted in Leonato's generous and cheerful court.

This more charitable interpretation of Claudio better suits the play, which is after all a COMEDY. Don John, the villain, is plainly saddled with all the blame. In any case, the play revolves around Beatrice and Benedick; as Claudio's conventionality suggests, he is a relatively unimportant figure whose personality need not be well developed. Significantly, after the disguised Hero is revealed, the reunited lovers do not speak, as the focus of the play immediately shifts to Beatrice and Benedick. As Claudio's usefulness as a character is spent, he recedes into the background.

Conrade (Conrad) Character in *Much Ado About Nothing,* follower of Don John. In 3.3 Conrade listens as his friend Borachio tells of the scheme to implicate the innocent Hero as a promiscuous woman. This conversation is overheard by the Watchmen, which leads ultimately to the exposure of Don John's villainy. Conrade is a simple pawn, needing no personality, but he does display a vehement temper when, irritated by Constable Dogberry's interrogation, he blurts out, "You are an ass, you are an ass" (4.2.70). This triggers one of Dogberry's best comic bits, his indignant repetition of the insult.

Dogberry Character in *Much Ado About Nothing,* comical rustic constable in charge of the Watchmen. Dogberry, his second-in-command Verges, and the Watchmen are humorously inept, but their apprehension of Borachio and Conrade nonetheless exposes the nefarious plot of Don John against Claudio and Hero. However, Dogberry's officious bumbling postpones this result long enough that Claudio is deceived and Hero humiliated. The tensest moment of the play occurs when Dogberry's tediousness prevents Hero's father, Leonato, from learning the truth before the wedding, where Hero is to be accused of promiscuity. We are exasperated by the constable's foolishness and infuriated by his preening when he is appointed to interrogate the suspects, but he is nonetheless endearingly amusing.

Although the ridiculous policeman who garbles language was an ancient theatrical character type—Shakespeare had used the figure before in Constable Dull of *Love's Labour's Lost*—Dogberry is one of Shakespeare's most impressive comic creations. A typical Shakespearean CLOWN, he affects a more pretentious vocabulary than he can master, misusing the language spectacularly. He is very much a distinctive personality, however. Preposterously long-winded, smugly self-assured, touchingly (though absurdly) incredulous that Conrade could call him "an ass" (4.2.70), Dogberry has a naive dignity that has charmed audiences and readers for centuries.

In part, this response reflects our gratitude for the relief from melodrama that his comedy produces. Dogberry is an important element in Shakespeare's strategy to lighten Hero's plight and maintain a comic tone throughout the play. His foolish locutions and ideas provide comic relief at several points. In 3.3, just after Don John's scheme has begun to bear fruit, we first encounter Dogberry and the Watchmen; our knowledge that the villain's plot will eventually be exposed makes Hero's humiliation less painful. Dogberry's laughable confusion during the interrogation of Conrade and Borachio takes the edge off the revelation of their evil, and in 5.1 his arrival as a comical deus ex machina resolves the plot on a note of hilarity.

In the early texts of the play, a number of Dogberry's speech prefixes in 4.2 refer to "Kempe" or "Kemp"; it is accordingly believed that the actor William KEMPE first played the role. Dogberry's odd name refers to the fruit of the wild dogwood, a common English shrub. "Berry" may also designate fish roe, a common Elizabethan usage. The anomalous reference thus produced—dog roe—seems appropriate to the constable's absurdity.

Friar Francis Minor character in *Much Ado About Nothing*, clergyman who supports the slandered Hero, restoring her father Leonato's faith in her. The Friar officiates at the wedding of Hero and Claudio, only to see the ceremony disrupted. Claudio, misled by Don John, rejects his bride, accusing her publicly of promiscuity. Hero faints in response, and Leonato, humiliated, curses her. However, the Friar believes Hero is innocent, and his spiritual authority persuades Leonato. The Friar then proposes a plan intended to rouse Claudio's guilt and sympathy and renew his love for Hero: Hero should be said to be dead. While this plan has no effect on Claudio, it provides an interesting detour in the plot, during which Don John's scheme is exposed by other means. The Friar marries Hero to Claudio and Beatrice to Benedick as the play closes.

Hero Character in *Much Ado About Nothing*, daughter of Leonato and beloved of Claudio. Hero is a demure and pliant maid, a conventional representative of the Elizabethan ideal of docile womanhood. She accepts an arranged marriage, first to Don Pedro and then to Claudio. She is pleasant and has enough sparkle to engage in the ploy whereby her cousin Beatrice is tricked into accepting Benedick's love, but she largely lacks personal-

ity or spirit. A pawn, first proffered in marriage to Claudio and then rejected by him, she can only faint when unjustly accused of promiscuity. Beatrice, Benedick, and Friar Francis stand up for her, and Constable Dogberry's timely exposure of the villainous Don John finally clears her, but she is herself inactive. Significantly, once she and Claudio are finally reunited, they barely speak, as the play's focus immediately shifts to Beatrice and Benedick.

Hero's name—which bears no relation to the common noun *hero*, though it is pronounced the same—comes from an ancient Greek tale of two lovers that was very well known in Shakespeare's day as the subject of the immensely popular poem "Hero and Leander," by Christopher MARLOWE. In naming his tractable heroine after a famous romantic lover, Shakespeare may have intended a mild irony.

Innogen GHOST CHARACTER who is mentioned in the stage directions in some editions of *Much Ado About Nothing* (at the opening of 1.1 and 2.1) but does not appear, the wife of Leonato. The existence of a ghost character, apparently reflecting an unrealized intention of the playwright, is evidence that the original published text, the QUARTO of 1600, was printed from Shakespeare's FOUL PAPERS—his unpolished manuscript—and is therefore highly authoritative.

John, Don Character in *Much Ado About Nothing*, the villainous brother of the prince, Don Pedro. With the help of his follower Borachio, Don John schemes to mortify Claudio by slandering his betrothed, Hero. After Borachio arranges for an incriminating impersonation of Hero, the would-be bride is humiliatingly rejected by the deluded Claudio, but by a fortuitous accident the plot is uncovered and Don John flees from MESSINA, only to be captured and brought back. However, his flight and final comeuppance occur offstage and are only reported (in 4.2.58 and 5.4.123–124); Don John himself is absent at the close of the play, for his vicious nature would be out of place amid the general spirit of reconciliation.

Don John resents Claudio because "that young startup hath all the glory of my overthrow. If I can cross him any way, I bless myself . . ." (1.3.62–64). Claudio's advancement in Don Pedro's court has come at Don John's expense, for Claudio has shone in the war that suppressed Don John's rebellion against his brother. However, this motive is relatively unimportant; Don John plots to cause as much trouble to those around him as he can, apparently out of a simply evil nature. He declares that he would "rather be a canker in a hedge than a rose" and describes himself as "a plain-dealing villain" (1.3.25, 30). His is a generalized, undirected discontent; he envies other people's happiness and is therefore misanthropic.

Although Borachio compares him to the devil in 3.3.150, Don John is a slight figure, a study for a portrait of a villain. He is neither as grandiose as Richard III nor as direct as Macbeth. Nor is he as threateningly mysterious as Iago, whom he anticipates in both his ill-defined motivation and his manipulation of the conventional sexual attitudes of his victims. Most important, he lacks the human complexity of any of these larger, more fully developed characters. Don John is a simple stereotype, intended chiefly to advance the plot of a COMEDY, offering just enough evil to necessitate a triumph for happiness but not enough to evoke terror, as in a TRAGEDY.

Leonato   Character in *Much Ado About Nothing*, father of Hero and uncle of Beatrice. The governor of MESSINA, Leonato displays the formality that his position demands, but he is clearly a warm person, fond of his daughter and pleasant to all, offering avuncular advice to Beatrice and friendship even to the villainous Don John. He enjoys a joke and is quite willing to participate in Don Pedro's ruse to trick Benedick and Beatrice into falling in love. But Leonato displays little real personality until the crisis of the play. The deluded Claudio rejects Hero at the altar, asserting—with the backing of the prince, Leonato's superior, Don Pedro—that he has seen her with a lover. Leonato is so sensitive about his honor that his immediate reaction is abysmal shame for himself and furious rage at his daughter. In a hysterical passage (4.1.120–154) that foreshadows the laments of King Lear, Leonato wishes Hero dead. Friar Francis quickly restores his belief in her innocence, however, and he sternly pro-

claims that he shall have vengeance; in 5.1.59–76 he challenges Claudio to a duel. However, in 5.4, Leonato presides over the general air of reconciliation that closes the play, forgiving the errant Margaret and accepting the repentant Claudio with a practical joke, disguising Hero as a mysterious cousin whom the sinner must marry in atonement.

Lord   Minor character in *Much Ado About Nothing*, follower of Claudio. The Lord walks with Claudio in Hero's supposed funeral procession in 5.3; he speaks only one line.

Margaret   Character in *Much Ado About Nothing*, attendant to Hero. Drawn into Don John and Borachio's plan to slander Hero, Margaret dresses in her mistress's clothes and meets Borachio at night, although this occurs offstage. Hero's betrothed, Claudio, is lured to the scene by Don John, and, believing that Hero is seeing a lover, he refuses to marry her. When the villainy is finally exposed, however, Margaret is judged to have been an unwitting accomplice.

An impersonator of Hero is necessary to the plot, but Shakespeare wished to minimize the villainy in *Much Ado*, stressing comedy over melodrama, and he provided a number of proofs of Margaret's innocence. She is clearly a valued member of the genial circle of friends surrounding Hero; we see her only in scenes of mirthful fun, and she has a playful sense of humor; Benedick says her "wit is as quick as the greyhound's mouth" (5.2.11). Moreover, Borachio's recruitment of Margaret, like the charade itself, is kept offstage, and when Borachio confesses in 5.1, he insists that Margaret "knew not what she did . . . but always hath been just and virtuous" (5.1.295–296). Once Hero is finally cleared, Leonato remarks, "Margaret was in some fault for this, although against her will, as it appears" (5.4.4–5). Her participation resembles, in fact, a well-known masquerading game, recorded in accounts of 16th-century courtly pastimes, in which a woman would dress herself as a bride and thereby demand more elaborate endearments from her sweetheart. In a small but telling touch, Margaret's fondness for clothes is presented in her delighted description of an elaborate gown in 3.4.17–20.

Messenger   Minor character in *Much Ado About Nothing,* a servant of Don Pedro. In 1.1 the Messenger tells Leonato of Don Pedro's successes in war, citing the noble deeds of Claudio and Benedick and thus providing expository material on the play's romantic leads. The mention of Benedick subjects the Messenger to Beatrice's sharp verbal sallies; the passage (1.1.28–83) presents one of the play's major motifs, the witty—though prickly—independence of its heroine. In 3.5.50–51 and 5.4.123–124 the Messenger presents brief reports of offstage action.

Musicians   Minor characters in *Much Ado About Nothing,* entertainers hired by Leonato. In 5.3 the Musicians accompany Balthasar when he sings the mournful SONG "Pardon, Goddess of the night" as Claudio grieves at Hero's tomb, believing her dead. They may also accompany "Sigh no more, ladies" in 2.3, though the stage direction is ambiguous. Musicians were a normal feature of a grand household in Elizabethan times, and their presence here helps to maintain the splendidly festive atmosphere of Leonato's court.

Oatcake, Hugh   Minor character in *Much Ado About Nothing,* one of the Watchmen. Oatcake, with Seacoal, is nominated in 3.3.11 for the post of constable, for both are literate, but Dogberry appoints Seacoal. Oatcake is presumably one of the Watchmen who reappear in 4.2 and 5.1, but he is not again mentioned specifically. His comical name—which helps heighten the Watchmen's comical foolishness—is typical of a Shakespearean CLOWN.

Pedro, Don   Character in *Much Ado About Nothing,* the Prince of Aragon, who attempts to promote romances on behalf of two of his followers, Claudio and Benedick. Visiting the court of Leonato, governor of MESSINA, Don Pedro volunteers to help Claudio marry Leonato's daughter, Hero, whom he courts on the younger man's behalf. He also decides on the scheme that tricks Benedick and Beatrice into falling in love. However, his success as a cupid is qualified at best.

The prince has just defeated an uprising led by his brother, Don John, whom he has forgiven and who accompanies him. However, Don John

remains a villain, and his plot to trick Claudio into believing that Hero is promiscuous fools Don Pedro as well. The prince is offended, as is Claudio, at the dishonor involved in having courted such a woman; he encourages Claudio's humiliating rejection of his bride and coolly accepts her apparent death from shame.

Benedick, like Beatrice, remains loyal to Hero and severs his relations with Don Pedro. The prince and Claudio seem decidedly at fault for the audience knows that Hero is innocent. When Don John's trickery is exposed, Don Pedro is genuinely remorseful, and he leads Claudio to his penitential marriage to Hero's cousin, who proves to be Hero herself. The two couples are reunited, and the play ends in a spirit of reconciliation, in which Don Pedro joins.

The original of Don Pedro in the playwright's source, Matteo Bandello's novella, is completely insignificant; Shakespeare elaborated the character to create an elderly, dignified figure who presides over the action, thus enhancing the courtly air that suffuses the play. Although vulnerable to Don John's machinations, being too concerned with personal honor to respond humanely when presented with apparently convincing evidence of Hero's guilt, Don Pedro is otherwise a gentle and likable figure. His initial forgiveness of Don John after subduing his revolt testifies to his good will, and he participates prominently in the celebration of renewed harmony that closes the play. Like Claudio, he may be defended as having sinned "not / But in mistaking" (5.1.268–269). With the two young couples united, Don Pedro, somewhat poignantly, is left single himself. His awareness of this misfortune is evident a few lines from the end of the play, when the exultant Benedick teasingly enjoins "Prince, thou art sad; get thee a wife, get thee a wife!" (5.4.120–121).

Shakespeare took Don Pedro's name from Bandello's tale, in which the King of Aragon, who has just conquered Sicily, is named Piero. The playwright used the Spanish form of the name, but there is no reason to believe that he was aware of the historical figure whose name he was borrowing. Aragon, one of several medieval kingdoms located in what is now Spain, ruled Sicily beginning in

1282, when a great rebellion arose there against the French. King Pedro III (1236–85)—generally known in English as Peter the Great of Aragon—was invited by the rebels to assume the crown. He invaded and quickly drove out the French, beginning a period of Aragonese—and later Spanish—rule that was to last until 1713.

Seacoal, George Minor character in *Much Ado About Nothing*, one of the Watchmen of MESSINA. In 3.3.11 Seacoal is recommended to Dogberry, the chief constable, as a likely leader of the watch because he is literate, and he is appointed to the position. He has no particular personality and cannot readily be distinguished from the other Watchmen. However, Seacoal may be assumed to be the speaker of commands—such as "We charge you in the Prince's name, stand!" (3.3.159, where the speech heading reads "Second Watchman")—by virtue of his office.

A Francis Seacoal is mentioned by Dogberry at 3.5.54; he is apparently the Sexton, who appears in 4.2. The unnecessary and unlikely coincidence of surnames is best explained as one of the many minor errors in the plays. Here the playwright hastily gave an inconsequential character a name that happened to be handy, forgetting that he had just used it for another such figure.

Sexton Minor character in *Much Ado About Nothing*, a scribe who records Constable Dogberry's comically inept interrogation of Conrade and Borachio in 4.2. Exasperated, the Sexton assumes control of the investigation and deduces that the Watchmen have uncovered the plot by which the villainous Don John has slandered Hero. His common sense thus allows the exposure of wrongdoing that Dogberry's antics cannot.

The Sexton seems to be referred to in 3.5.53–55, where Dogberry calls him Francis Seacoal, giving him the same distinctive surname as George Seacoal, one of the Watchmen. The minor confusion brought about by this unlikely coincidence is hardly noticeable onstage; it is probably simply one of the many minor slips that Shakespeare made throughout his career.

Ursula Minor character in *Much Ado About Nothing*, attendant to Hero. A cheerful member of Leonato's court, Ursula has no important function and little personality. She flirts with the aged Antonio at the MASQUE in 2.1, and she helps her mistress fool Beatrice into believing that Benedick loves her in 3.1.

Verges Character in *Much Ado About Nothing*, Constable Dogberry's second-in-command. Verges is chiefly a straight man for Dogberry to play against; his eager assistance is rejected by his superior, who prefers to do things himself. Though praised as "an old man, . . . honest as the skin between his brows" (3.5.10–12), Verges has little personality, being rather like the other Watchmen—and Dogberry—in his confusion and comical misuse of language.

Speech prefixes in 4.2 give Verges's lines to "Cowley." It is therefore assumed that the actor Richard COWLEY first played the part. Verges's name is traditionally said to be a rustic pronunciation of the word *verjuice*, meaning "the acid juice of green or unripe fruit," but the character is not notably acid. Verges's name is more probably associated with his office, a *verge* being a rod or staff symbolizing authority, usually carried by an underling or assistant to the holder of power.

Watchmen Minor characters in *Much Ado About Nothing*, the police patrol of MESSINA. In 3.3 the Watchmen prepare for their night's patrol in a comical sequence in which all of the obvious duties of watchmen are denied. For instance, when their commander, Dogberry, orders, "You shall also make no noise in the streets," a Watchman replies, "We will rather sleep than talk" (3.3.34–37), and Dogberry responds to a query about "laying hands" on a thief with the observation, ". . . by your office you may, but I think they that touch pitch will be defiled" (3.3.55–56). It has been suggested that this passage parodies a London statute of 1595 that attempted to control nighttime activity in the city.

However, for all their foolishness, these absurd lawmen play a significant role in the drama: They overhear Borachio speaking of the deception he has staged as part of the plot of Don John against Hero and Claudio. Although still confused, they recognize villainy, and they arrest Borachio and his companion, Conrade, and testify against them in 4.2 and 5.1, acts that lead to the exposure of the scheme and the happy resolution of the play.

Most of the Watchmen's speeches were not specifically assigned by Shakespeare to one or another of them, and they are largely indistinguishable, though Hugh Oatcake and George Seacoal are said to be literate, and the latter is appointed the leader of the night's patrol. Scholars speculate that Shakespeare may have been inspired to create the Watchmen by a similar group in John LYLY's play *Endimion* (ca. 1588, published 1591).

Othello

SYNOPSIS

Act 1, Scene 1
Roderigo, who has been courting Desdemona, is distressed at Iago's news that she has eloped with Othello, a Moorish general in the service of VENICE. Iago, who is Othello's aide, assures Roderigo that he also hates the Moor because Othello has denied him a promotion that went instead to Cassio. He says that he only continues to serve the general in the hope of revenge. Iago and Roderigo awaken Desdemona's father, Brabantio, to inform him of the elopement.

Act 1, Scene 2
Iago tells Othello of Brabantio's anger, as Cassio arrives with word that the general has been summoned by the Duke to a council of war. Brabantio and Roderigo arrive. The angry father, informed of the Duke's council, plans to accuse Othello there.

Act 1, Scene 3
The Duke and several Senators receive news of an immanent Turkish attack on the Venetian island of CYPRUS. Othello and Brabantio arrive, and Brabantio makes his accusation. Othello replies that Desdemona loves him and has married him of her own free will. When she is summoned she supports his account. Brabantio concedes, and the meeting

turns to business: Othello is ordered to leave for Cyprus. Desdemona is to live there with him, and Iago is to escort her in a later ship. Privately, Iago assures Roderigo that Desdemona will soon repent marriage to a Moor, and that if Roderigo will come to Cyprus he will continue to help him with his suit by delivering presents to Desdemona. Roderigo agrees and leaves; Iago reflects on how easy it is to get money from this fool. Saying that Othello is rumored to have cuckolded him, he goes on to plot revenge upon both Othello and Cassio; he will make the general believe that Cassio is the lover of his new wife.

Act 2, Scene 1
In Cyprus the Venetian governor, Montano, and two friends discuss the great storm that may have destroyed the Turkish fleet. A third Gentleman brings news that Cassio has arrived with word that this has indeed happened, but that the ship carrying the new governor, Othello, has also disappeared. Iago arrives with Desdemona, his wife Emilia, and Roderigo. Iago engages the two women in a courtly exchange of witticisms while they await word about Othello. The general arrives safely and greets Desdemona with affection. The group moves indoors, except for Iago and Roderigo. Iago proposes a plot: He says that Desdemona is in love with Cassio and proposes that Roderigo pick a fight with the lieutenant while he commands the guard that night, in the hope that fighting on duty will disgrace Cassio and remove him as potential competition for Desdemona. Roderigo agrees. Alone, Iago meditates on the course of his plans: He will abuse Cassio to Othello and get credit from the general, while at the same time making him sick with jealousy.

Act 2, Scene 2
A Gentleman reads Othello's proclamation of a public holiday. All the soldiers are at liberty until 11:00 at night, when they must return to duty.

Act 2, Scene 3
Despite Cassio's insistence that a little wine will make him very drunk, Iago convinces him to drink for the sake of the holiday. They join some others, including Montano, and when Cassio goes to take his guard post he is drunk. Iago sends Roderigo

after Cassio; he shortly reappears, pursued by the drunken lieutenant, who gets into a fight with Montano. Iago sends Roderigo to sound the alarm, and Othello appears and angrily dismisses Cassio from his post. Left alone with a dismayed Cassio, Iago convinces him that his only hope of recovering his position is to get Desdemona to present his case to Othello. Cassio agrees and leaves, and Iago exults in the success of his scheme: Now Othello will witness—and jealously misconstrue—Desdemona's interest in Cassio.

Act 3, Scene 1

Cassio has hired Musicians to play before the general's quarters in the hope of influencing his mood. Iago sends Emilia to Cassio; she assures him that Desdemona favors his cause and agrees to take him where he may meet with the general's wife.

Act 3, Scene 2

Othello prepares to conduct an inspection of the fortifications.

Act 3, Scene 3

Desdemona assures Cassio she will plead his case to Othello. Cassio withdraws as Othello and Iago approach; Iago pretends to regard this suspiciously. Desdemona asks Othello to take Cassio back, and he agrees, saying that he loves her and can deny her nothing. She leaves, and Iago begins to ask seemingly innocent questions about Cassio. He pretends to be reluctant to express his suspicion, but goes on to inflame Othello with the idea of a sexual affair between Cassio and Desdemona. He suggests that if Othello delays Cassio's reappointment, he can see if Desdemona supports the lieutenant to an excessive degree. Othello fears that Desdemona has been unfaithful because he is black or because he is old, but he tries to resist the thought. Desdemona and Emilia arrive to accompany him to a state banquet, and Othello disguises his distress. As they leave, Desdemona drops a handkerchief that was Othello's first gift to her. Emilia picks it up, and Iago takes it from her as she leaves. He states his intention to plant it on Cassio. Othello returns and angrily demands proof of Desdemona's infidelity. Iago asserts that Cassio has Desdemona's handkerchief. Enraged, Othello goes

on his knees to formally swear ve[...] affirms his loyalty and joins him in [...] ising to kill Cassio himself and to [...] Desdemona.

Act 3, Scene 4

Desdemona speaks of Cassio, but Othello demands his handkerchief. He says it was charmed by an Egyptian sorceress so that the woman who lost it would be damned in the eyes of her lover. Desdemona denies that it is lost. She tries to change the subject back to Cassio, and Othello leaves in a rage. Iago and Cassio appear; Desdemona remarks on Othello's strange anger, and Iago volunteers to go see the general. Emilia observes that Othello may be jealous of his wife, even though he has no reason, and Desdemona decides she must approach him again. The women leave Cassio as Bianca appears. She humorously chastises Cassio for not seeing her more often. He asks her to make him a copy of the embroidered handkerchief he has found.

Act 4, Scene 1

Iago says that Cassio has admitted to sleeping with Desdemona. Beside himself with rage, Othello babbles incoherently and then faints. Cassio appears, and Iago tells him he has important news that he will give him once Othello has recovered and they can speak alone. Cassio leaves, and when Othello awakens Iago tells him that if he eavesdrops on the meeting he has arranged with Cassio, the general will hear Cassio speak of his affair with Desdemona. Cassio returns, and Iago speaks to him of Bianca, his lover. With amused disrespect, Cassio laughs about how she presumes to think she'll marry him, and Othello, crying out in asides, believes he is speaking of Desdemona. Bianca arrives, angry about the handkerchief, which she believes was given to Cassio by another woman. Othello now thinks that Cassio has given Desdemona's love token to a harlot. Bianca and Cassio leave, and Othello says he will kill Desdemona; Iago promises to kill Cassio that night. Desdemona appears with Lodovico, who brings a message from Venice calling Othello back and placing Cassio in command of Cyprus. When Desdemona is pleased, Othello hits her; enraged, he can barely speak. He orders her away and then leaves. Lodovico is surprised at this

...avior, but Iago confides that it is sometimes much worse.

Act 4, Scene 2

Othello quizzes Emilia, who says there is no reason to suspect Desdemona and Cassio. He does not believe her and sends her to summon his wife. When Desdemona appears he accuses her and ignores her denials. He leaves in a rage as Emilia reappears. When Desdemona tells Emilia of Othello's state, she fetches Iago, and the two try to reassure her. Desdemona and Emilia leave as Roderigo arrives. He complains that Iago has taken his money and jewels and done nothing for him. Iago tells him that because Cassio is to replace Othello as governor, the general is leaving and will take Desdemona with him. Iago promises to help Roderigo kill Cassio so that Othello will have to stay, and Desdemona will remain within reach.

Act 4, Scene 3

On his way out, Othello tells Desdemona that she is to prepare for bed and dismiss Emilia. Desdemona says that she loves Othello despite his unreasonable anger, though she also has a presentiment of tragedy; she sings a song that was sung by an abandoned woman while she died. Though Desdemona is revolted by the idea of sexual infidelity, Emilia declares that men deserve it.

Act 5, Scene 1

Iago sets Roderigo up to ambush Cassio; he hopes that Roderigo and Cassio will kill each other, for Roderigo may claim repayment from him and Cassio may disprove his story. Cassio appears and Roderigo attacks him, but is wounded by Cassio. Iago then wounds Cassio from behind and flees. Othello sees the wounded Cassio crying for help and exults in the sight. He leaves as Lodovico and Gratiano arrive. Iago returns, pretends to be enraged at the assault on Cassio, and kills Roderigo. Bianca arrives. Iago declares that she is probably involved in the attempted murder and places her under arrest.

Act 5, Scene 2

Othello, at the bed of the sleeping Desdemona, is overcome with love for her and declares that he will not harm her beauty but will kill her bloodlessly. She wakes, and he tells her to prepare for

A scene from the 1965 film of *Othello* with Laurence Olivier as the Moor and Maggie Smith as Desdemona. The same great passion with which Othello loves his wife leads him to murder her when his faith turns into jealousy. *(Courtesy of Culver Pictures, Inc.)*

death. He says the handkerchief is proof of her adultery. She says that Cassio will clear her, but Othello triumphantly reports his death. She pleads for mercy, but Othello smothers her. Emilia appears, and Desdemona recovers enough to declare that she is dying in innocence. She dies, and Othello proclaims that he has murdered her because she was unfaithful. Emilia denies it, and Othello declares that Iago has proved it. She calls for help, and Montano, Gratiano, and Iago appear. Othello speaks of Desdemona's handkerchief, and Emilia reveals the truth. Iago kills her and flees. Montano chases him, leaving Othello to his mounting grief. When Iago is brought back, Othello attacks him and wounds him before being disarmed. Othello declares himself a fool but not a dishonorable one, stabs himself with a hidden weapon, and dies.

COMMENTARY

The most striking difference between *Othello* and Shakespeare's other tragedies is its more intimate scale. The terror of the supernatural is not invoked, as it is in *Hamlet* and *Macbeth;* extremes of psychological derangement, as in *King Lear,* are not present. Kingdoms are not at stake, and the political consequences of the action are not emphasized as they are in varying degrees in all of the other tragedies. Here Shakespeare focuses on personal rather than public life; Othello's plunge into obsession occurs mostly in private—only he and Iago know it is happening—and he murders Desdemona in the seclusion of their bedroom. The play has been described as a domestic comedy gone wrong. Its tragedy lies in the destruction of the happy personal lives of the general and his bride by the perverse malice of a single unsatisfied man. Yet *Othello* is profoundly social, for the human quality that Iago lacks and that he destroys in Othello is trust, the cement that holds people together. Jealousy, the play's central motif, is simply a particularly virulent form of interpersonal distrust. The tragedy of *Othello* is that a noble man loses faith and is reduced to a bestial frenzy. As a result, a love and a life are destroyed, and this loss inspires horror in the audience, which, combined with our pity for Desdemona, gives the play tremendous power. Significantly, *Othello* stands out as one of Shakespeare's plays that has been altered very little over the centuries by its producers, for its capacity to overwhelm audiences has always been recognized.

The central dynamic in *Othello* is the hero's change in attitude toward Desdemona. At first the couple are happily matched; when they defend their elopement, in 1.3, they establish themselves as mature lovers whose passion is both spiritual and sexual, mutually satisfying and based on self-knowledge. But Othello's weakness destroys his happiness as his trust in his wife turns to jealousy and then murderous hatred under the influence of Iago. On the other hand, his trust in his aide never flags until he is finally exposed. Othello comes to see love through Iago's eyes rather than Desdemona's. In a sense, Iago and Desdemona represent internalized features of the hero: He rejects his loving and generous self—that aspect of humanity that makes society possible—in favor of the dark passions of his self-centered ego. In the end, the forces of trust and love regain their strength as Othello finally recognizes the goodness of Desdemona, and Iago is formally condemned, but in the meantime the action of the play has demonstrated the power of evil.

The motif of trust destroyed dominates the interactions of Iago and Othello on the one hand and Othello and Desdemona on the other. Othello is placed between Iago—who cannot trust or love—and Desdemona—who offers an ideal, unconditional love. This situation closely resembles the traditional MORALITY PLAY, whose central character, usually symbolic of the human soul, is placed between an angel and a devil who each demand his loyalty. This dramatic form was still familiar to Shakespeare and his audience, and *Othello* reflects it in its distinctly allegorical quality. Iago is associated with the devil several times, and Desdemona—in her martyrlike acceptance of her entirely undeserved end—may be seen as a symbol of Christian love and resignation to the will of God.

In its structure, *Othello* continually focuses our attention on its main theme, jealous mistrust. The relationships of Othello to Iago and Desdemona are paralleled in those between several minor characters in the play. For instance, Othello's credulousness is foreshadowed in that of Roderigo, whose victimization by Iago is established in the opening scene. Similarly, later in the play, Cassio's disastrous reversion from distrust to trust of the villain echoes the development of the main plot. Also, Cassio's admiring recognition of Desdemona's virtues offers the opposite image to Othello's loss of perception, while her appreciation of Cassio reflects ironically on Othello's mistaken opinion of Iago.

Perhaps most striking are the two "marriages" paralleling that of Othello and Desdemona. Cassio is linked with Bianca, and while they are not formally married, a comparison is irresistible because Iago substitutes Bianca for Desdemona when he deceives Othello about the handkerchief, in 4.1. More pointedly, Bianca's jealousy of Cassio—expressed in her complaint that he has avoided her, in 3.4, and her anger when she thinks that he has been given Desdemona's handkerchief by another woman—echoes Othello's emotion but in a context where jealousy seems justified. Iago and Emilia's marriage, while plainly lacking affection, let alone love, is not immune from sexual jealousy. Iago remarks several times that he is suspicious of his wife's adultery with either Othello (1.3.385–386) or Cassio (2.1.302). His assumption that his wife's lover was Othello sounds intended only to justify his campaign against the general, but he seems to have some cause for suspicion: Emilia clearly states that she would indeed commit adultery, in 4.3.70–76, 84–103, as she believes that unfaithfulness is a woman's only weapon against a bad husband. The mutual distrust in which these two live offers another instance of the play's major motif: jealousy. All three marriages, with their stress on this emotion, demonstrate abundantly the fragility of trust between humans.

Iago's jealousy is particularly significant, as it suggests that when he misleads Othello he is simply transferring his own psychic ailment. In fact, Iago's jealousy extends beyond a purely sexual context; he is motivated in large part by envy, the jealous sense that others have advantages over him. He fears that the free and virtuous natures of the other characters, especially Desdemona, may demonstrate his own worthlessness. It is precisely Othello's "constant, noble, loving nature" (2.1.284) that he cannot endure, and he recognizes that Cassio "has a daily beauty in his life, / That makes me ugly" (5.1.19–20). He accordingly proposes to "out of [Desdemona's] goodness make the net / That shall enmesh 'em all" (2.3.352–353).

The parallels that reinforce the theme of jealousy illustrate the craftsmanship of the playwright, and indeed, *Othello* is a particularly well-constructed play. Most strikingly, Shakespeare introduces—and then contrives to disguise—what seems to be a serious defect of the plot, namely, that Desdemona's infidelity should be utterly implausible to Othello for the simple reason that she has had absolutely no opportunity for it. Iago presents this fictional "love affair" as though it had been going on for some time, while in fact Othello and Desdemona have only been married a few hours when they depart for Cyprus—on different ships, with Cassio on a third—and once there, Othello passes the first night with Desdemona and kills her on the second. The haste with which the plot unfolds contributes tremendously to its almost unbearable tension, and for this reason Shakespeare chose an unrealistic time span rather than a weeks-long scenario in

which an adulterous affair could evolve realistically. He carries it off by means of a clever device that critics refer to as "double time." While the two days' development is nonsensical, it is effectively disguised by a number of strategic references suggestive of a different time frame. For instance, Iago speaks of ". . . how oft, how long ago, and when" (4.1.85) Cassio and Desdemona have made love, and Othello later justifies her murder with the claim that this lovemaking had occurred "a thousand times" (5.2.213); Emilia says that Iago has asked her "a hundred times" (3.3.296) to steal Desdemona's handkerchief, and she suggests that Desdemona has had "a year or two" (3.4.100) to become acquainted with Othello; Cassio is said to have been absent from Bianca for a week, with the implication of an established relationship before that; orders recalling Othello to Venice arrive, reflecting time enough for news of the situation on Cyprus to have reached Venice and the orders returned. These hints, among numerous others, serve to keep before us a convincing sense that more has transpired than could actually be the case.

However, "double time" is unworkable for exposition, and Act 1 differs from the rest of the play in being performed in real time. Here, in Venice, we are introduced to the characters and their world under more realistic circumstances. Events are not compressed into a short time for before the main action is underway the playwright does not need to deceive us about the pace of events, and he can properly establish the nature of his characters, especially Iago. In the long interchanges between him and Roderigo in 1.1 and 1.3, in his lie that opens 1.2, and especially in his soliloquy that closes the act, Iago's villainous nature and his enmity toward Othello are made clear, and we are primed for the developments to follow.

Act 1 also differs from the rest of the play in its setting. This is very telling, for Othello's place in the society of Venice plays an important, if subtle, role in his downfall. As Brabantio's response to Desdemona's marriage makes abundantly clear, Venice is a closed society, racist in its distrust of Othello. Also, Venice is seen to be influenced by inhumane commercial values. Iago exploits the degraded values of Roderigo, who thinks love is a commodity, and many commentators have seen a satire on mercantile society—Venetian and English, both—in Iago's repeated advice to Roderigo to "put money in thy purse" (beginning at 1.3.342). This is a world that cannot appreciate Othello's virtues. The general is thus isolated from the world he has married into; Iago can convince him that Desdemona might "repent" the "foul disproportion" (3.3.242, 237) of a mixed marriage, and Othello lacks the assurance of a respectable social position that might temper the fear of rejection that his jealousy feeds on.

The racial bias of Shakespeare's Venice is important and quite prominent, especially in Act 1. Brabantio's sneer at Othello that Desdemona could not love "the sooty bosom / Of such a thing as thou" (1.2.70–71) is based on the racist assumption that such love would be "against all rules of nature" (1.3.101). Iago and Roderigo have stimulated Brabantio's rage with labels, such as "old black ram" (1.1.88), "Barbary horse" (1.1.111), and "lascivious Moor" (1.1.126), associating race with animals, sex, and the devil, characteristically racist ploys, even today. No one disputes Brabantio's statement that Desdemona has subjected herself to "general mock" (1.2.69) by marrying a black man; prejudice is plainly widespread in Venice.

Othello is the earliest sympathetic black character in English literature, and the play's emphasis on prejudice must have had particular impact in Shakespeare's LONDON, which was a distinctly biased society. Though Africans were present in London in some numbers beginning around 1550—especially once the English slave trade got underway in the 1560s—little distinction was drawn between North African and sub-Saharan blacks. Africa and Africans had figured in English drama from an even earlier date; dozens of 16th-century plays made use of African settings or characters, though virtually all of them were wildly inaccurate and blatantly racist, depicting Africans in simple stereotypes as idle, lustful, and likely to be treacherous. Not surprisingly, the biases of English society as a whole was equally blatant. In 1599 and 1601 the government made an effort to deport all of the "Negars and Blackamoores which [have] crept into this realm."

The Venice of *Othello*, like London in its greed and racism, has another aspect, however. As represented by the Duke and the Senators, the society offers a model of trust and cooperation. In 1.3 we see these figures arriving through consensus at a collective response to the Turkish threat, and in the same workmanlike spirit they insist that Othello be permitted a defense against Brabantio's charges. They recognize his innocence and accept him as their general, and Brabantio agrees entirely, accepting his society's collective judgment. On the whole, Venice is not a promising milieu for Iago's purposes; significantly, Shakespeare removes the action from Venice when the main plot is to get under way. On Cyprus the action is isolated; no social or political distractions remove Othello from Iago's influence, and Desdemona can have no recourse to advice or intervention. It is only when Venetian envoys come to Cyprus that the truth can be unfolded, though too late.

In another manipulation of time, Shakespeare tightens the tension rapidly as we approach the play's climax by subtly increasing the pace with which things seem to occur. As Iago puts it, "Dull not device by coldness and delay" (2.3.378). For instance, when Iago first makes Othello desire revenge against Desdemona and Cassio, the general demands Cassio's death "within these three days" (3.3.479) and Desdemona's death is not scheduled. But when the matter is next discussed, Othello insists on killing Desdemona "this night . . . this night" (4.1.200–202) and Iago promises to kill Cassio "by midnight" (4.1.207). This sudden acceleration creates an effect of heightened tension that reflects Othello's mental state. It also diverts attention from the illogicality of time's so-swift passage while increasing the pace.

Only once, and in a very telling maneuver, does Shakespeare slacken the pace of events—in the famed "willow" scene (4.3), in which Desdemona prepares for bed and, unknowingly, for death. This lull prepares us for the final storm of Act 5's violence. Desdemona's melancholy at Othello's changed and angry manner yields a morbid fantasy that is, in effect, a slow, grand elegy of her innocence and virtue. She imagines herself dead, shrouded in her wedding sheets, and she remembers her mother's maid, who died of love, singing "a song of 'willow', / An old thing [that] express'd her fortune, / and she died singing it" (4.3.28–30). Ominously, Desdemona sings it herself, and its plaintive sadness soothes her even as it chills us with its portent of her death. Her calm and beautiful acceptance of fate is contrasted at the scene's close with Emilia's cynical speech on adultery. Our appreciation of Desdemona in this scene makes the approaching climax all the more horrible. Despite its languid tone, this brilliantly conceived interlude actually succeeds in heightening our anxiety.

Through a simple plot with minimal comic relief, Shakespeare avoids distractions that would permit the audience to recuperate temporarily from the increasing tension into which they are drawn. The few diversions from the main plot are mostly anxiety-producing disturbances. The midnight brawl of 2.3 that results from Cassio's drunkenness; Othello's cruel rudeness as he pretends to take his wife's bedroom for a bordello, in 4.2; another fight scene, in which Roderigo wounds Cassio and Iago kills Roderigo—all of these events offer the reverse of comic relief, tightening our emotional screws for the next stage of Iago's plot against Othello. Even at the play's close, the tension is similarly maintained as the eerie privacy in which the murder of Desdemona takes place is followed by the raucous tumult in which Iago kills Emilia and Othello wounds Iago and kills himself. Only in the very last lines of the play is there relief when Lodovico disposes of practical matters in the wake of the death of the Venetian commander on Cyprus.

Not only is the rule of society reestablished at the close, but Iago's triumph over Othello is undercut by the hero's recognition of his error. The trust that had been violated is at least acknowledged in the end. In the world of tragedy, death and defeat are inescapable, thus mirroring the tragic aspects of human existence. Othello is not a hero through triumph but because he is an incarnation of basic human energies, both good and bad. When he joins Desdemona in death, he offers recompense for his grievous self-centeredness earlier, and while this compensation is obviously useless to her, it offers *us* a cathartic sense of reconciliation with tragedy. The lives—and deaths—of Othello and Desde-

mona are in the end transcended by their involvement with each other. She sacrifices herself to her love and he himself to his grief that he was inadequate to it. Without the support of his love for Desdemona, Othello could only say, "Chaos is come again" (3.3.93); with his recognition of his error, order is implicitly restored as the ethical meaning of the story is revealed.

SOURCES OF THE PLAY

The source for *Othello* was a novella by the Italian author, CINTHIO, published in his collection *Hecatommithi* (1565). No surviving English translation of the tale was made until much later, and scholars dispute whether the playwright read Cinthio in Italian, in a French or Spanish translation, or in some now lost English translation. In any case, Shakespeare made a number of significant changes in Cinthio's tale. He accelerated the course of events to produce a tauter drama, and he altered the personalities of the major characters, making Othello and Desdemona nobler and Iago more coldly malevolent. He also added such minor characters as Roderigo, Brabantio, and the Venetian officials.

An actual murder may also have been a source for the play. In 1565 an Italian serving the French government was diverted from a diplomatic mission by false reports of his wife's infidelity, circulated by his enemies. Returning home, he accepted her denials, but after earnestly seeking her forgiveness, he strangled her anyway in the name of honor. Scholars speculate that knowledge of this historical event may have influenced Shakespeare in his choice of Cinthio's tale, though no known English source can be cited.

Other minor literary sources include LEO AFRICANUS's *A Geographical History of Africa* (translated by John PORY; publ. 1600) and the *Natural History* of PLINY the Elder (translated by Philemon HOLLAND). Also, Shakespeare's odd mention of two otherwise unknown characters—"Signior Angelo" and "Marcus Luccicos" (1.3.16, 44)—suggests the existence of some minor source material that is now lost.

TEXT OF THE PLAY

Othello was probably written in 1603 or 1604, just before its earliest recorded performance. Some scholars believe that the BAD QUARTO of *Hamlet* (Q1, 1603) is contaminated by recollections of lines from *Othello*, favoring an earlier date (possibly 1602) for *Othello*, though others find the evidence uncertain. On grounds of style and content, *Othello* cannot be dated earlier than 1602.

The play was first published in 1622 by Thomas WALKLEY, in a QUARTO edition, known as Q1, printed by Nicholas OKES. It was printed from a manuscript whose nature has been the subject of considerable scholarly debate. It may have been a FAIR COPY of Shakespeare's manuscript, or it may have been a transcript of either his FOUL PAPERS or of the PROMPTBOOK kept by the KING'S MEN. The transcription may originally have been made for Walkley's publication or for use by the King's Men, or, possibly, for an individual, a theater enthusiast. Given the surviving evidence, none of these theories can be positively proven or disproven.

In 1623 *Othello* appeared in the FOLIO edition of plays, and this text (known as F) was probably printed from Q1 but amended according to another manuscript whose nature is also perplexing. It may have been Shakespeare's fair copy; it may have been a promptbook; it may have reflected alterations resulting from years of productions; it may have included errors made by someone relying on their memory of performances; it may have incorporated Shakespeare's own alterations. Again, no hypothesis can be established firmly.

Whatever this manuscript was, it differed significantly from Q1. There are over a thousand variants, most of them minor, but F contains about 160 lines not present in Q1, including a few substantial passages. The longest fragment (4.3.31–52, 54–56) contains much of the "willow" song, for instance. On the other hand, Q1 contains 10 brief passages (the longest being four lines) not in F. Whether these variations represent additions to one text or cuts from the other is debated by scholars; in practice, modern editors have generally found F to be the superior text and have used it as the basis for their versions, while also using variants from Q1 in many particular instances. However, some editors reverse the priority.

THEATRICAL HISTORY OF THE PLAY

The earliest known performance of *Othello* took place at the court of King JAMES I on November 1, 1604. Numerous other performances in various theaters and at court are recorded prior to the closure of the theaters by the civil war in 1642; and it appears to have been among the most popular of Shakespeare's plays in his own lifetime, as it has been ever since. Richard BURBAGE was the first Othello, and though the original Iago was not recorded, it is known that after 1619 Joseph TAYLOR was famous in the role.

After the Restoration, *Othello* was among the first plays to be staged in the reopened theaters. On December 8, 1660, Thomas KILLIGREW's version, in which Margaret HUGHES played Desdemona, featured the first woman to perform on an English stage. William DAVENANT's company performed the play as well, attesting to its continuing popularity. A number of anecdotes from this period tell of enthralled spectators leaping onto the stage to prevent the murder of Desdemona. Charles HART played Othello, but Thomas BETTERTON was acknowledged the greatest Moor of the day. Michael MOHUN was a notable Iago.

In the 18th century, *Othello* continued to be among the most-often performed of Shakespeare's plays. Most leading actors undertook the title role, with Barton BOOTH, James QUIN, and Spranger BARRY prominent among them, while John HENDERSON and Charles MACKLIN were successful Iagos. In the early 19th century, Edmund KEAN was acclaimed as the greatest Othello of all time, a status that some critics believe may still apply, though his legend has doubtless been enhanced by the fact that he collapsed onstage while playing the part (into the arms of Iago, played by his son Charles KEAN) and never recovered, dying a few weeks later. Othello was a natural vehicle for Ira ALDRIDGE, the first black Shakespearean actor. William MACREADY played both Othello and Iago at various times, as did Edwin FORREST and Edwin BOOTH. Forrest's performances as Othello in New York in 1826 are said to have inaugurated the popularity of Shakespearean tragedy in America. Charlotte CUSHMAN was acclaimed as Desdemona, opposite Forrest, in London in 1846. Booth alternated playing Othello and Iago with Henry IRVING in a famous London run of 1881, with Ellen TERRY as Desdemona and the soon-to-be-famous playwright Arthur Wing Pinero (1855–1934) as Cassio. Tommaso SALVINI played Othello in Italian, often with an English-speaking company, in productions that were immensely popular in both England and America throughout the 1870s and 1880s.

Among many noteworthy 20th-century stagings of *Othello*, perhaps the most renowned were two American productions featuring extraordinary performances: that of Paul ROBESON as Othello—directed by Margaret WEBSTER (1943)—and Christopher PLUMMER as Iago opposite the Othello of James Earl JONES in Nicol WILLIAMSON's presentation (1982). Other 20th-century Othellos included Oscar ASCHE, Earle HYMAN, Ralph RICHARDSON, and Donald WOLFIT. In 1981 an American company under a Japanese director adapted *Othello* to Kabuki, the traditional, stylized Japanese drama, and performed in several American cities.

Eleven FILMS have been made of *Othello*—seven of them silent movies. An Italian movie shot in Venice in 1909 was the first attempt to film Shakespeare on location. The best-known films are those starring Orson WELLES (who also directed; 1952) and Laurence OLIVIER (1965). Also, the Italian avant-garde director Pier Paolo Pasolini (1922–75) presented a puppet play of *Othello* in the 1967 film *Capriccio all'Italiana*. More recently, Kenneth BRANAGH was acclaimed as Iago in a 1995 film that starred Laurence Fishburne as the title character. *Othello* has also been made for TELEVISION several times, perhaps most notably by Trevor NUNN in 1990. In addition, *Othello* has inspired several OPERAS. The 1816 work by Gioachimo ROSSINI is considered the first great Shakespearean opera, but it was surpassed by Guiseppe VERDI's *Otello* (1887), with libretto by Arrigo BOITO, which is considered among the greatest of all operas. In 1997 composer Elliot Goldenthal (b. 1954) and choreographer Lar Lubovitch (b. 1943) created a modern ballet rendering of *Othello* (recorded for television in 2001).

CHARACTERS

Bianca Character in *Othello*, a courtesan of Cyprus and the lover of Cassio. Iago calls Bianca "A housewife that by selling her desires / Buys herself bread and clothes" (4.1.94–95), where "housewife" is intended with the common Elizabethan meaning of "courtesan." However, she is not a lowly prostitute; she has her own house (and is thus a literal housewife) and has the pride to be offended by the insults of Emilia in 5.1. Moreover, her obviously genuine concern for the wounded Cassio in the same scene touchingly demonstrates that she is a fundamentally decent person. This degree of dignity makes it possible for her relationship with Cassio to function as a foil for that of Othello and Desdemona. The comparison is emphasized when Iago makes Cassio a part of his campaign to arouse Othello's jealousy of his wife. More pointedly, Bianca is jealous of Cassio—she complains, in 3.4, that he has avoided her, and in 4.1 she rages at him when she suspects that he has another lover. Her emotion echoes Othello's with the pointed difference that it is justified: Bianca's love for Cassio cannot be based on trust for she knows that, in the nature of relations between soldiers and courtesans, he will eventually leave her. In this context her jealousy seems both entirely rational and entirely futile, thus pointing up Othello's grievous error in two different ways.

Brabantio (Brabanzio) Minor character in *Othello*, Desdemona's father. Brabantio, a senator of VENICE, learns from Iago of Desdemona's secret marriage to the Moorish general Othello and is outraged at the thought of his daughter on "the sooty bosom / Of such a thing as [Othello]" (1.2.70–71). He accuses Othello of having "enchanted her . . . with foul charms . . . with drugs or minerals" (1.2.63–74) and seeks his imprisonment as a sorcerer, but he is foiled when Desdemona testifies to her love for the general. Defeated, he departs, but his final speech carries heavy irony as he warns Othello, "Look to her, Moor, have a quick eye to see: / She has deceiv'd her father, [and] may do thee" (1.3.292–293). Brabantio disappears from the play at this point, though we are told in 5.2 that he has died of grief at Desdemona's marriage. He serves chiefly to establish, through his racial prejudice and enmity toward Othello, the extent to which the Moor is isolated in Venetian society.

Cassio Character in *Othello*, a Florentine officer serving under Othello. Iago is the enemy of both Othello and Cassio because Cassio has been appointed Othello's lieutenant, a post Iago had coveted for himself. Iago gets Cassio drunk and incites Roderigo to fight him; the lieutenant disgraces himself by brawling drunkenly while on guard duty and is demoted. More important, Iago convinces Othello that his wife, Desdemona, is Cassio's lover, going so far as to plant on Cassio a handkerchief that Othello has given Desdemona. The enraged general commissions Iago to kill Cassio, and Iago again employs Roderigo. However, Cassio survives the attack and testifies against Iago in the play's closing moments.

The change in Othello's attitude toward Cassio is paralleled by Cassio's change toward Iago. Before his disgrace, Cassio is distant and refuses to be friendly with Iago, as we see at the beginning of 2.3. However, when Iago befriends him after he is discharged by Othello, he accepts him entirely. He calls him "honest Iago" (2.3.326) and says, "I never knew / A Florentine more kind and honest" (3.1.40–41). He is grateful for what seems like excellent advice from Iago to ally himself with Desdemona. Though this is to have disastrous consequences, Cassio does not see through Iago until much too late, after the villain is exposed in the wake of Desdemona's murder.

Cassio's relationship with Bianca, a courtesan of CYPRUS is another echo of the main plot. Though they are not married we compare them with Othello and Desdemona, partially because Iago employs the unwitting Bianca in deceiving Othello about the handkerchief, in 4.1. More pointedly, though Bianca is jealous on Cassio's account—just as Othello is on Desdemona's—Cassio disdains her, in striking contrast to Desdemona's intense love for Othello. Cassio's tawdry affair casts light on the nature of Othello's blessed but rejected marriage.

Cassio's relationship with Bianca and his account of it to Iago, in 4.1, reflect the worldliness of a professional soldier accustomed to finding women wherever he is stationed. As a competent soldier, he is respected and valued by Othello before Iago's poison begins its work. We see this in his appointment as lieutenant and in the general's

easy conversational tone as Cassio assumes guard duty, in 2.3. The lieutenant is apparently a gentleman, and he has enough learning to be mocked by Iago for his "bookish theoric" (1.1.24). In 2.1.61–87 he expresses his reverence for Desdemona in courtly formal rhetoric that reflects his respect for Othello as well, establishing clearly an aura of gentlemanly honor and stately virtue.

On the other hand, while Cassio's soldierly dignity helps stress the vulgarity of Iago, he is often without that dignity, being drunk in 2.3 and awkwardly humiliated most of the time after that. Though his remorse at his irresponsibility is genuine and honorable—he regrets having "deceive[d] so good a commander, with so light, so drunken, and indiscreet an officer" (2.3.269–271)—he is nevertheless somewhat ridiculous: he foolishly drinks wine he doesn't want and then quickly falls into Iago's next trap. His speech is often ludicrously high-flown; he declares, "O thou invisible spirit of wine, if thou hast no name to be known by, let us call thee devil!" (2.3.273–275).

Yet Cassio "has a daily beauty in his life" (5.1.19) that stirs Iago's envy, and his reputation and dignity are restored by the end of the play. He is given the command of Cyprus, and he shows a quiet assurance in insisting to Othello, "Dear general, I did never give you cause" (5.2.300). At the close it is fitting that Cassio is the only person to recognize the grandeur of the suicidal general, declaring "This did I fear, . . . For he was great of heart" (5.2.361–362).

Clown Minor character in *Othello*, a jester, or FOOL, in the retinue of Othello. The Clown jokes lewdly with the Musicians in 3.1, before dismissing them with Othello's payment. In 3.4 he briefly jests with Desdemona before carrying a message for her. As comic relief, the Clown does not do much to interrupt the play's increasing tension; he may well have been merely a conventional figure, expected by Shakespeare's audiences and therefore supplied by the playwright.

Desdemona Character in *Othello*, the wife of Othello. Desdemona is unjustly suspected of adultery and murdered by her jealous husband, who has believed the lies of his villainous aide, Iago. She is a strong, outspoken woman, unafraid to challenge the racial bias of VENICE or the opinions of her imposing husband, and she is also touching in her sorrow as Othello's love turns to hostility. Desdemona's function, however, is largely symbolic; she represents the spirit of self-sacrifice traditionally associated with the most intense and spiritual love. Indeed, in her martyrlike resignation to an entirely undeserved death, many commentators see her as symbolizing Christian love and acceptance of God's will. In Desdemona, Shakespeare created an emblematic figure that was familiar to his original audiences from the medieval MORALITY PLAY, still a well-known theatrical form in the early 17th century. She resembles the angel that opposes the devil in such a play, struggling for control of the central character, who is a symbol of humanity. Like the angel, Desdemona evokes the forgiveness of God, and, as in the medieval play, the good she represents is acknowledged at the close and thus is seen to be the play's central theme.

Desdemona's role is a passive one; her only significant action—marrying Othello—has been taken before the play opens. She is the chief repository of the play's values. Othello knows this when he says, "I do love thee, and when I love thee not, / Chaos is come again" (3.3.92–93). She alone has recognized his inner worth. She says she "saw Othello's visage in his mind" (1.3.252), and even when his virtue is obscured she retains her vision. As she puts it, ". . . his unkindness may defeat my life, / But never taint my love" (4.2.162–163), and even as she dies, she declares her love of the inner, obscured Othello, saying, "Commend me to my kind lord" (5.2.126).

At first, Desdemona's nobility of spirit is matched by that of her new husband. When the couple justify their elopement before the Duke, in 1.3, they display a mature love that is both spiritual, in their mutual appreciation of each other's virtues, and sensual, in their excited anticipation of the physical side of married life. Desdemona's strength of character is evident in her calm resistance to her father, Brabantio, who holds that loving a black man is "Against all rules of nature" (1.3.101). She firmly and courageously stands up to the prejudices of the only society she has ever

known. Once committed to Othello she is steadfast; the central fact of the play is her unswerving loyalty. The suspicion that Iago induces in Othello is always seen to be completely unjustified. In 4.3 Emilia defends adultery, but Desdemona spurns this temptation in an episode that parallels Othello's failure to resist Iago. Desdemona recognizes that Othello's jealousy is ignoble, but she continues to give him her love to its fullest extent, saying, ". . . my love doth so approve him, / That even his stubbornness, his checks and frowns, /. . . have grace and favour in them" (4.3.19–21). Her love is literally unconditional, standing in stark contrast to the malevolence of Iago.

Duke of Venice Character in *Othello,* the ruler of VENICE. In 1.3 the Duke meets with his advisers to decide on a response to the Turkish assault on CYPRUS. Summoning Othello, their chief general, they are faced with Brabantio's accusation that Othello has used witchcraft to marry his daughter, Desdemona. When Desdemona confirms that theirs is a love match, Brabantio is bitter, but the Duke offers wise proverbs on emotional moderation, such as, "To mourn a mischief that is past and gone, / Is the next way to draw more mischief on" (1.3.204–205). He represents a social wisdom that is markedly lacking in the main plot.

Emilia Character in *Othello,* lady-in-waiting to Desdemona and wife of Iago. Despite Emilia's loyalty to and fondness for Desdemona, she is manipulated by Iago as he convinces Othello that Desdemona is having a love affair with Cassio. Unwittingly, Emilia aids Iago in this deception when she provides him with Desdemona's handkerchief, a love token from Othello that Iago plants on Cassio. In 5.2 after the jealous Othello has been driven to murder, Emilia fearlessly denounces him, and when Iago's involvement becomes apparent, she exposes his schemes just as boldly. In reprisal Iago stabs her. Dying, she asks to be placed next to Desdemona and makes a final oath that her mistress was faithful to Othello.

Except in this final scene, Emilia serves principally as a foil to her mistress. A sharp-tongued woman whose worldly cynicism makes plausible her marriage to the ambitious and unscrupulous Iago, her nature contrasts tellingly with Desdemona's loving innocence. Though Emilia does not suspect Iago's motives, their marriage is obviously unhappy. She stoically receives his insults, but when alone with Desdemona she rails against men and marriage, declaring, in 4.3, that she would commit adultery, given the chance. Despite her unhappiness, Desdemona rejects this idea firmly, in contrast with Othello's failure to repudiate Iago's sentiments.

Gentleman Any of three minor characters in *Othello*, Venetian noblemen and members of the occupation force on CYPRUS. In 2.1 two Gentlemen talk with Montano about the dispersal of the Turkish fleet by storm, then a third appears with news of Othello's arrival to take command of the island. In 2.2 one of the Gentlemen (designated as Othello's Herald in the FIRST FOLIO and some other editions) reads the general's formal proclamation declaring a holiday, and in 3.2 another accompanies Othello on an inspection of the fort, uttering a single line. These figures are representative of the Venetian military presence, serving to further the plot.

Gratiano (Graziano) Minor character in *Othello*, a Venetian nobleman, Desdemona's uncle. Gratiano is a member of the delegation from VENICE that comes to CYPRUS at the close of the play and witnesses the climax of Othello's madness. He ineffectually responds to the cries of Cassio and Emilia for assistance in 5.1 and 5.2, respectively. In both cases he fails to prevent Iago's wicked schemes. In this respect he is representative of the society at large, whose racial prejudice has helped make Othello vulnerable to Iago. In his most important remark, Gratiano declares that Desdemona's father, Brabantio, has died of grief at her marriage to Othello.

Iago Character in *Othello*, Othello's villainous aide. The play centers on Iago's effort to destroy Othello's happiness by convincing him that his wife, Desdemona, has been having a love affair with Cassio, his lieutenant. One of Shakespeare's most thoroughly villainous characters, Iago has intrigued audiences for generations through his combination of realistic malice and seemingly unjustified lust for revenge, his "motiveless malignity," in Samuel Taylor COLERIDGE's famous words. However, Shakespeare does provide his villain with stimuli that provoke his evil. In fact, if Iago's motives seem unclear, it is because he is motivated in several ways, rather than not at all.

Shakespeare provides us with much evidence of Iago's motives in his soliloquies. He has been passed over for promotion in favor of Cassio, and in his first soliloquy he schemes to reverse this development and considers entangling Desdemona and the lieutenant as a step in this direction. Much later, Iago's wife, Emilia, unknowingly comes close to guessing the cause of Othello's jealousy when she remarks, "Some busy and insinuating rogue, / . . . to get some office, / [Has] devis'd this slander" (4.2.133–135).

Military ambition is commonplace, and this is an entirely credible motive, but it does not preclude the simultaneous operation of others. A second motive is sexual jealousy, the emotion which Iago transmits to Othello. Iago suspects Emilia's adultery with Othello in 1.3.385–386, and in his second soliloquy jealousy is his only stated motive. His suspicions are sometimes thought to be only a justification in his campaign against the general, but he expresses them in soliloquy, when he need not lie, and he is also jealous of Cassio (2.1.302). Emilia speaks of his suspicions, in 4.2.149, and Iago seems to have some general grounds for his jealousy, as Emilia states explicitly that she would commit adultery, given the opportunity (4.3.70). It is telling that the weapon Iago fashions to destroy Othello is precisely the one that hurts himself. The power of sexuality as a goad is further revealed in Iago's obsessive references to bestial sex (as in 1.1.88–89) and in his vivid description of Cassio in bed with him (3.3.425–432). It is obvious that Iago's suspicions stem from his morbid imagination, but from Iago's point of view they are no less effective as inducements to action.

Both of these motives reflect an even deeper level of feeling. Iago's professional and sexual jealousies cause him to "hate the Moor" (1.3.384), but they also stem from a greater, generalized jealous sense, an envy of those who have advantages over him that extend beyond promotions or access to his wife. He senses that the open and virtuous qualities in others may point up his own worthlessness. He cannot "endure . . . [Othello's] constant, noble, loving nature" (2.1.283–284), and he sees in Cassio "a daily beauty in his life, / That makes me ugly" (5.1.19–20). Like Satan—and not coincidentally, as we shall see—Iago is envious of those who are spiritually greater than he.

Iago's multiple motives make him a humanly credible character, but these are joined by an inhuman ferocity that adds a dose of terror to our perception of him. His envy and anger are so strong that they compel him to risk his life in his passionate effort to damage Othello. Though he has motives, his response outweighs the stimulus, and thus a less easily understood motive merges with the others: Iago loves evil for its own sake. He clearly delights in what he is doing. He speaks of fooling Roderigo as "my sport" (1.3.384); his delighted irony all but bubbles over when he exults, "And what's he then, that says I play the villain . . ." (2.3.327); and his enjoyment is obvious when he says, "Pleasure, and action, make the hours seem short" (2.3.369). After his triumph in the temptation scene (3.3), he cannot refrain from returning to manipulate his enemy some more. When accident brings him Desdemona's handkerchief, he comfortably contemplates the damage he may do with it, like an artist savoring a new and exciting idea— "this may do something" (3.3.329), he slyly understates. After reducing Othello to hysteria, he gloats, "Work on, / My medicine, work" (4.1.44–45), and even in utter defeat his final refusal to talk smacks of self-satisfaction.

With his pleasure in evil, Iago resembles the VICE of medieval drama. The Vice was an allegorical figure whose delight in horseplay and mischievous humor made him a popular character. Iago, however, is a realistic, rather than an abstract, embodiment of evil. Although Iago is not a comic character, he is occasionally funny. In 1.1.118, for example, he returns Brabantio's "Thou art a villain" with "You are a senator," and in his many ironic remarks on his own honesty, as in 2.3.258 and 318, the humor is unrecognized by anyone but himself and the audience. He also adopts a jocular attitude for his own purposes, as in the conventional battle

of wits in 2.1.109–166 and the drinking bout of 2.3. Many commentators and theatrical directors agree with the advice of Edwin BOOTH, who insisted that actors playing Iago should "not sneer or glower" and suggested that "the 'light comedian' . . . not the 'heavy man'" should play the part.

Many people have a problem with the plot of *Othello*: The hero is unrealistically gullible, murdering his wife on the strength of a suggestion that has no serious credibility. However, Shakespeare relied on an established dramatic convention: Iago has a double role as villain to the audience but trustworthy friend to the characters in the play. He is seen as good by everyone but the audience, which fosters a high degree of suspense. For this reason, Shakespeare made Iago's villainy evident immediately in his first exchange with Roderigo in Act 1, and his evilness is repeatedly confirmed in his soliloquies. Iago is frank about his double role, saying "I am not what I am" (1.1.65). Even his name—that of the patron saint of England's great enemy, Spain—indicated his evil nature to a 17th-century audience. Shakespeare's audiences presumed that Iago's victims would be taken in—and most modern audiences believe this as well.

Iago deceives Othello by also manipulating other people to achieve his ends. At Iago's instigation, Cassio urges Desdemona to intervene for him, thus unwittingly inflaming Othello's jealousy, and Roderigo attacks Cassio, who might expose Iago. Iago gets Desdemona's incriminating handkerchief from Emilia, and he exploits the affair of Bianca and Cassio to mislead Othello further. He describes his schemes aptly as spiderwebs, in 2.1.168. At the close of the play he fails when his network of villainy begins to unravel. When Cassio fails to kill Roderigo, Iago does it himself—or thinks he does, though actually Roderigo lives to testify against him, as is revealed in 5.2.325–330. Only as he recognizes these possibilities does Iago's cool self-confidence leave him, and he hastily mutters to himself, "This is the night / That either makes me, or fordoes me quite" (5.1.127–128).

In the end the power of Iago's envy expires, and the forces of trust and love recover, though it is a bleak victory. Othello finally recognizes the goodness of Desdemona, and Iago is condemned, but in the meantime Iago has demonstrated the power of evil. His power depends, however, on the weakness in Othello. In his motives, his judgments, and his single-minded savagery, Iago embodies his victim's psychological flaws. Iago can triumph only because Othello rejects his own potential for love and trust in favor of the self-centered desperation of jealousy and envy, the passions that dominate Iago.

Iago is the evil influence on Othello, in opposition to Desdemona's good. This situation closely resembles that of the medieval MORALITY PLAY, still familiar in Shakespeare's day, in which a central character must choose between an angel and a devil. Iago is associated with satanic evil at several points in the play. For example, when Othello, fainting with rage at the image of Desdemona's infidelity cries out, "O devil!" (4.1.43), Iago, on cue, exults, "Work on, / My medicine, work" (4.1.44–45). Iago hints at the hellish nature of his undertaking early on when he openly (to Roderigo) claims as his allies "all the tribe of hell" (1.3.358), and in his soliloquy declares, "Hell and night / Must bring this monstrous birth to the world's light" (1.3.401–402). Later, when he says that his "Dangerous conceits . . . Burn like the mines of sulpher" (3.3.331–334), he reminds us of the conventional metaphor for hellfire.

Finally, at the play's close, Iago overtly identifies himself with the devil. Othello makes the connection first, after Iago's malevolence has been exposed. He looks at the villain's feet to see if they are cloven and says, "If that thou be'st a devil, I cannot kill thee" (5.2.288), as he attempts to stab him with his sword. Iago, wounded, gloats defiantly, "I bleed, sir, but not kill'd" (5.2.289), fully accepting the implication. It is the last thing he says before refusing to speak any further. In this final refusal Iago brazenly displays his malice, for all along his power has been in his words, talking his evil ends into existence. In making Iago's nature so strikingly evident at the play's close, Shakespeare helps assuage our horror, for we see that the villain's uncanny malevolence is even more immense than we had thought. It is as vast as hell itself, the abode of infinite evil, and we are therefore doubly glad that his career is finished, not only in relief from the play's agonizing developments, but also in satisfaction at the suppression of a truly satanic menace.

Lodovico   Character in *Othello,* an emissary from VENICE to CYPRUS. Lodovico appears only toward the end of the play, arriving on Cyprus just as Othello's madness approaches its climax. He serves a symbolic function, representing the life of normal society from which the main characters have been isolated since Act 1. On Cyprus, Iago's influence can work its poison free of social or political affairs that might engage Othello's attention, and Desdemona cannot seek advice or intervention from other Venetian aristocrats. Lodovico is unable to prevent the catastrophe of Desdemona's murder, but in the final scene after Iago's duplicity has been exposed and Othello has committed suicide, Lodovico assumed the mantle of leadership and disposes of practical matters in the wake of the tragedy.

Messenger   Minor character in *Othello,* bearer of a dispatch from Montano to the Duke of Venice. In 1.3 the Messenger delivers news of the Turkish attack on CYPRUS that Othello will be sent to oppose. His brief part increases the urgency of the scene.

Montano   Minor character in *Othello,* the governor of CYPRUS who is replaced by Othello. Montano is acknowledged by the Duke of Venice to be a competent governor, "of most allowed sufficiency" (1.3.224), though Othello, as a tried battle leader, is to replace him. Montano agrees with this judgment and declares his approval of the appointment as soon as he hears of it, in 2.1. He is wounded by the drunken Cassio in 2.3, and his rank makes Cassio's offense even greater. In 5.2 he witnesses the furor following Othello's murder of Desdemona, and he displays soldierly alertness in chasing and capturing Iago when he flees, but then Lodovico arrives and takes charge, and it is clear that Montano is an inconsequential figure.

Musicians   Minor characters in *Othello* strolling players hired by Cassio to serenade Othello, with whom he is out of favor. Cassio's gesture is rejected, however, when Othello's Clown pays them to leave, saying "If you have any music that may not be heard, to 't again, but . . . to hear music, the general does not greatly care" (3.1.15–17). The Clown jests lewdly on the sexual symbolism of their instruments and associates them with venereal disease, suggesting a criticism of the courtly flattery their performance represents.

Officer   Either of two minor characters in *Othello*, soldiers of VENICE. In 1.2 an Officer tells Brabantio of the council meeting called by the Duke of Venice, and in 1.3 another Officer announces the arrival of news from the Venetian fleet. They serve merely to increase the frantic activity surrounding the prospect of war.

Othello   Title character in *Othello*, the husband of Desdemona, whom he murders because he has been misled by the villainous Iago. A Moorish general in the service of VENICE, Othello has just married the much-younger Desdemona as the play opens. The central dynamic of the drama is his alteration from a noble lover to a raving killer under the malevolent influence of his aide, Iago, who convinces him that his wife is having a love affair with another officer, Cassio. Unable to trust Desdemona—he lacks this basic element of love—Othello disintegrates morally. His destructiveness extends to his own suicide when his error is exposed. He suffers emotional agonies throughout this process, and we suffer with him, grieving for the destruction of his inherent nobility and the beauty that his marriage exemplifies at its outset.

Through 3.2 Othello is a grandly positive character—a leading figure in the Venetian establishment, a respected military man, and a loving husband. He carries himself with impressive dignity while frankly delighting in his young wife, whose love he values above "the sea's worth" (1.2.28). When the couple defend their elopement, in 1.3, we see that their love is both spiritually satisfying and imbued with a healthy sexuality. However, in the second half of the play he abandons this transcendent love for a blind jealousy too strong to see reason. He loses faith not only in Desdemona but also in himself. When he rejects her love and trust, Othello also rejects his own capacity for love, in favor of a demanding but unsatisfiable self-centeredness.

When he collapses in 4.1, Othello can only babble as he falls at Iago's feet in a trance. He recovers his wits, but from this point he has only one goal:

the deaths of Desdemona and Cassio. In his single-minded malice, Othello now shares Iago's malevolent spirit. Indeed, as the play progresses he even comes to resemble the villain in his speech, using staccato repetitions, broken sentences, and Iago's violent, sexual animal imagery. In 4.1 he cruelly insults his wife publicly, and in 4.2, the so-called brothel scene, he indulges in a savage exaggeration of his jealousy when he says he believes Desdemona a harlot and Emilia her bawd. In the end, though he can still contemplate his love for his wife when he sees her asleep, he kills her with a coolness that stresses the power of his fixation. His reaction once Desdemona's innocence has been established is just as potent. He recognizes that he is no longer noble—he calls himself "he that was Othello" (5.2.285)—and equating himself with the heathen enemies he used to conquer, he kills himself.

Iago can effect this extraordinary response only because Othello is lacking in trust. This lack is implicit in the Moor's situation from the outset, for he cannot partake of the social solidarity that encourages and reinforces trust between humans. He is an outsider in Venice because of his profession—a mercenary soldier, unacquainted with civilian society "even from [his] boyish days" (1.3.132)—and his race. Though Othello's military skills are valued and he is not denied the protection of a hearing on Brabantio's charge of witchcraft, he is nonetheless an alien in a prejudiced society. He is isolated from the world he has married into. Iago can convince him that Desdemona might have come to detest him because he is black; he lacks the support of a solid position in Desdemona's world that might temper the fear of rejection that his jealousy feeds on.

Though the evidence in the play is clear, some commentators have declared that Othello is not actually black—usually on the racist grounds that so noble a figure could not be a "veritable negro," as Samuel Taylor COLERIDGE put it. Most frequently, a Moor is held to be of an Arab-related racial type, rather than a Negro. However, Shakespeare (like his contemporaries) drew no such distinction, and Othello is clearly a black African; decisively, Roderigo calls Othello "the thicklips" (1.1.66). (Significantly, Shakespeare's other notable Moor,

Aaron of *Titus Andronicus,* calls his child "thick-lipp'd" and himself "coal-black," and he refers to his "fleece of woolly hair" [*Titus* 4.2.176, 99; 2.3.34].)

Shakespeare plainly intended Othello's race to have a great impact on his original audiences, many of whom, he knew, were as prejudiced as Brabantio. Othello is the earliest black character in English literature with a credible personality, let alone a sympathetic one. Shakespeare deliberately emphasized this, for in CINTHIO's tale, his source, Othello's race has little importance, while in the play it is frequently mentioned, especially in Act 1, where the nature of Venetian society is stressed. The obvious racist caricature offered before Othello appears is entirely in line with the standard English stereotypes of the day, but his actual bearing is strikingly noble. This is emphasized numerous times—Othello even claims royal birth in 1.2.21–22, a point that had much greater importance in Shakespeare's day than in ours—and the playwright must have been aware of the impact of this bold departure. For one thing, Desdemona's strength is greatly magnified by her willingness to courageously defy society's biases. Further, Shakespeare's sympathetic portrait of an alien figure, combined with the compassionate presentation of his repentance and suicide at the play's close, emphasizes that the potential for tragic failure is universal.

Othello's race helps determine his status as an alienated outsider in Venice, and this makes him susceptible to Iago's persuasions, for he is grievously naive about Desdemona's world. Iago assures him, "I know our country disposition well" (3.3.205), and Othello, reminded of his own ignorance, accepts at face value the preposterous claim that adultery is the moral norm among Venetian women. Iago is absolutely correct when he says to Emilia, "I told him . . . no more / Than what he found himself was apt and true" (5.2.177–178). Most significantly, once distracted, Othello is not capable of appreciating Desdemona; he knows enough of Venice to see its prejudice, but he does not recognize her steadfast courage in opposing it. Like Coriolanus and Macbeth, Othello has succeeded as a soldier and is accordingly endowed with dignity and pride, but he can only misunderstand the world outside the military camp.

With his suicide, Othello acknowledges his fault, but his final recognition of Desdemona's goodness offers us—if not him—the consoling sense that in dying he recovers something of his former nobility. He honestly admits that he "lov'd not wisely, but too well" and was "perplex'd in the extreme" (5.2.345, 347). We see a vestige of pride when he refers to his former service to the state, and when he identifies his errant self with the "malignant . . . Turk" (5.2.354) he once slew, we see that in dying he is as triumphant, in a way, as he was "in Aleppo once" (5.2.353).

Othello has returned to sanity too late, but that he returns at all provides us with some sense of reconciliation. Othello's fate shows us that a noble person may fall to the depths of savagery, but that an essential humanity remains within the troubled soul. The tradition of the medieval MORALITY PLAY was still familiar in Shakespeare's day and certainly influenced him. Othello's striking placement between Iago and Desdemona resembles the situation of the central character in a morality play: Symbolic of the human soul, he was placed between an angel and a devil who each demanded his loyalty. Though the devil succeeded for a time, and the character sinned (entertainingly), the mercy of God nevertheless prevailed, and the character was reclaimed by the angel and forgiven in the end. Similarly, *Othello* offers redemption at its close. Othello is emblematic of one aspect of human life; he incarnates the inexorable guilt and ultimate death that we recognize as the tragic element in humanity's fate, but his eventual awareness offers a redeeming catharsis.

Roderigo Character in *Othello,* a Venetian gentleman who is duped by Iago. Roderigo believes Iago is serving him as a go-between in his attempted seduction of Othello's wife, Desdemona, though Iago has simply pocketed the expensive presents intended for the young woman. Iago's exploitation of Roderigo figures prominently early in the play, helping to establish him as a villain. Though he eventually serves as a pawn in Iago's scheme against Othello—he is persuaded to attempt the murder of Cassio—Roderigo's story is subsidiary to the main plot, and he functions chiefly as a foil. His gullibility foreshadows Othello's credulous acceptance of Iago, and his crass attempt to buy Desdemona's affections contrasts with both the mature love of Othello before he is corrupted and the gentlemanly adoration of Cassio.

Sailor Minor character in *Othello*, a messenger. In 1.3 the Sailor brings news of the Turkish attack on CYPRUS and disappears from the play; he has no personality and serves only to increase the frantic activity of the scene.

Senators Several minor characters in *Othello*, lawmakers of VENICE. The Senators meet with the Duke, in 1.3, to discuss the threat presented by a Turkish attack on CYPRUS. When they summon their chief general, Othello, they hear Brabantio's complaint that Othello has stolen his daughter Desdemona. With the Duke, they find Othello innocent of any crime, appoint him commander of Venetian forces in Cyprus, and order him abroad. The Senators are spoken for by the First Senator (except for one brief passage by a Second Senator), who asks appropriate questions. The Senators and the Duke illustrate the pomp and power of the Venetian state; they also demonstrate a collective capacity for social cooperation and judgment by consensus, aspects of society that are notably absent when the main plot unfolds on Cyprus.

Pericles, Prince of Tyre
SYNOPSIS

Act 1, Chorus
The ghost of John Gower identifies himself and introduces the play as the enactment of an ancient tale. It opens in ANTIOCH, where King Antiochus practices incest with his beautiful Daughter. He has stipulated that she may marry only the suitor who can solve a certain riddle, and that any suitor who attempts to do so and fails will be executed.

Act 1, Scene 1
Pericles, Prince of TYRE, hears the riddle, and realizes that its solution reveals Antiochus's incest. He declines to give his answer, but he makes it clear that

he knows the secret. The king decides to humor him and grants him a 40-day respite before he must answer. Pericles realizes that Antiochus will attempt to silence him, and he decides to flee. Antiochus orders Thaliard to kill Pericles, but word comes that Pericles has left Antioch. Thaliard is sent in pursuit.

Act 1, Scene 2
In Tyre, Pericles fears that Antiochus, who is a much more powerful ruler, will attack and devastate his country. A group of fawning courtiers appears, but among them is Helicanus, who strongly disapproves of flattering a monarch. Pericles admires his spirit and confides his fears to him. Helicanus advises him that he should travel for a time, until Antiochus's rage has cooled. Pericles agrees and decides to go to THARSUS. He appoints Helicanus to rule in his absence.

Act 1, Scene 3
Thaliard has come to Tyre. He learns of Pericles' departure and leaves to inform Antiochus.

Act 1, Scene 4
Cleon, the Governor of Tharsus, and Dionyza, his wife, are worried because a famine has overtaken their once-rich country. Pericles has heard of their plight and arrives with shipments of food.

Act 2, Chorus
Gower tells the audience that Pericles is adored in Tharsus. In a DUMB SHOW, Pericles receives a message, which Gower tells us is from Helicanus, who warns the prince of Thaliard's evil intent and suggests further flight. Gower tells us that Pericles fled by sea and was shipwrecked.

Act 2, Scene 1
Shipwrecked, Pericles encounters three Fishermen, who inform him he is in PENTAPOLIS. They tell him that their king, Simonides, is holding a tournament the next day at which knights will joust for the hand in marriage of his daughter. Pericles' armor is brought up in the Fishermen's net, and he decides to use it in the king's tournament.

Act 2, Scene 2
At the tournament, the king's daughter, Thaisa, receives greetings from each Knight who will compete for her hand. Pericles' rusty armor is

ridiculed by some courtiers, but cheers celebrate his victory offstage.

Act 2, Scene 3
At a celebratory banquet, Pericles is welcomed by Thaisa as the victor and therefore her fiancé.

Act 2, Scene 4
In Tyre, Helicanus tells Escanes that the gods have punished Antiochus and his daughter by killing them with a heavenly fire. A group of noblemen declare that they cannot be without a king any longer and ask Helicanus to declare himself king. He refuses but agrees to do so if Pericles has not returned after another year.

Act 2, Scene 5
To test Pericles, Simonides pretends to be angry that the young man has falsely gained the affection of Thaisa, and he calls him a traitor. Pericles rejects the insult manfully, to Simonides' secret delight. Thaisa appears and says it would please her if Pericles loved her. Simonides reveals his pleasure and declares that she and Pericles shall marry.

Act 3, Chorus
Gower reveals that Thaisa, now married to Pericles, is pregnant. In a dumb show, Pericles receives another letter, which he shows to Thaisa and Simonides. Gower tells us that the letter is from Helicanus, summoning Pericles to Tyre. He goes on to report that Pericles and Thaisa leave by ship, only to be caught in a great storm.

Act 3, Scene 1
Aboard ship during the tempest, the nurse Lychorida tells Pericles that Thaisa has died in childbirth. She shows him the infant, a daughter. A Sailor insists that Thaisa must be buried at sea or the ship is cursed, and the distracted Pericles agrees. Pericles orders the ship to stop at Tharsus, where he will leave the infant. He is afraid she may not survive a longer voyage.

Act 3, Scene 2
At EPHESUS a chest washed up by the great storm is brought to the nobleman and physician Cerimon. He opens it and finds the apparently dead Thaisa, but he recognizes that she is merely unconscious and revives her with medicines.

Act 3, Scene 3
At Tharsus, Pericles leaves his daughter Marina in the care of Cleon and Dionyza.

Act 3, Scene 4
In Ephesus, Thaisa decides to enter a convent devoted to the goddess Diana since she will never find her husband again.

Act 4, Chorus
Gower tells us that Marina has grown into a gracious and beautiful young woman. So fine a person is she, he says, that she overshadows Cleon and Dionyza's daughter. Dionyza has become so jealous that she decides to have Marina killed.

Act 4, Scene 1
Dionyza reminds Leonine of his oath to murder Marina, for he is reluctant. Marina appears and is persuaded to take a walk on the beach with Leonine. As he prepares to kill her, a boatload of Pirates come ashore and kidnap her. Leonine escapes and is relieved not to have to kill Marina. He plans to tell Dionyza that he has done so anyway.

Act 4, Scene 2
In a brothel in MYTILENE, the Pandar, the Bawd, and their servant Boult discuss the sorry state of business. They regret that they don't have more attractive young women to offer. A Pirate appears and offers to sell them Marina, and they accept. Despite Marina's pleas and objections, they make plans to offer her to their customers.

Act 4, Scene 3
In Tharsus Cleon is distressed to learn that Dionyza has had Marina murdered. She has also poisoned Leonine to keep him quiet. She is cynically pleased with the success of her plan and tells Cleon that they will inform Pericles that Marina died naturally.

Act 4, Scene 4
Gower appears by Marina's gravestone in Tharsus with the information that Pericles has come to get his daughter. A dumb show presents his grief when he is shown the tomb by Cleon. Gower reads the flowery epitaph on the monument and contrasts its flattery with Marina's unhappiness in Mytilene.

Act 4, Scene 5

Two Gentlemen (2) of Mytilene discuss the wondrous virtue of a harlot they have encountered, and they vow to reform their lives.

Act 4, Scene 6

The Bawd, the Pandar, and Boult despair at the damage Marina is doing to their business. Lysimachus, the governor of Mytilene, appears and is offered Marina. She implores him as an honorable man not to use her as a harlot, and he declares that his intention has merely been to test her virtue, of which he has heard. He leaves, but he refuses to give money to Boult. Boult angrily threatens to deflower Marina himself so that her virtue will not further upset the brothel's business. However, she shames him into agreeing instead to help her establish herself as a teacher of music, dance, and handicrafts to young women.

Act 5, Chorus

Gower tells of Marina's success in Mytilenian society. He adds that the grief-stricken Pericles, who has been wandering at sea, has arrived in Mytilene.

Act 5, Scene 1

Lysimachus boards Pericles' ship to greet the visitor, but he is informed by Helicanus that the prince has been made speechless by his grief. A Mytilenian courtier suggests that the charms of Marina could cure Pericles, and she is sent for. When she arrives she is left alone with Pericles, and he speaks because he is startled by her resemblance to Thaisa. In the course of their conversation their relationship becomes apparent, and they are happily reunited. Exhausted by the excitement, Pericles is left alone to sleep, and the goddess Diana appears to him in a vision. She directs him to go to her temple in Ephesus and proclaim the history of Marina's birth and their separation and reunion.

Act 5, Scene 2

At the Temple of Diana in Ephesus, Thaisa, the High Priestess, stands by the altar. Gower appears and tells us that Lysimachus and Marina are engaged but will not marry until Pericles fulfills Diana's instructions, so the couple have accompanied Pericles to Ephesus.

Act 5, Scene 3

At the Temple altar, Pericles identifies himself and tells of Marina's birth and adventures. Thaisa recognizes him and faints. Cerimon is present, and he reveals her identity to Pericles. When Thaisa recovers, she and Pericles are reunited, and Thaisa and Marina meet for the first time since Marina's birth. When he learns of Simonides' death, Pericles declares that he and Thaisa shall reign in Pentapolis and Lysimachus and Marina will rule in Tyre.

Epilogue

Gower compares the heavenly destruction of Antiochus and his daughter with the ultimate happiness of Pericles, Thaisa, and Marina. He goes on to praise Helicanus and Cerimon, and adds that the people of Tharsus were enraged when they heard of Marina's murder and massacred Cleon and Dionyza. He then announces that the play is over.

COMMENTARY

Pericles, Prince of Tyre is the first of Shakespeare's ROMANCES. Even though the opening acts are probably not his work (see "Text of the Play"), Shakespeare took this opportunity to develop several ideas and techniques. These techniques—such as the melding of COMEDY and TRAGEDY and the use of strange, elaborate plots and boldly symbolic characters—are the ones that he began to use in the PROBLEM PLAYS and continued to experiment with in works such as *Timon of Athens*. Most important is the growth of a theme that runs through all of the late plays: that humankind cannot alter its destiny in an inexplicable but finally benevolent universe. *Pericles* is flawed, in part due to both collaboration and a very faulty text, but also due to the nature of its imperfectly combined elements. However, it constitutes a significant step toward the magnificent achievements of *The Winter's Tale* and *The Tempest*.

Though *Pericles* was extremely popular in the early 17th century, it has since been considered one of the least satisfying of Shakespeare's plays. Despite the flawed surviving text, it contains much good poetry, especially in the reunion of Pericles and Marina in 5.1, but the play's virtues are largely outweighed by its defects. Its major figures seem lifeless; it is episodic; its events are often described rather than enacted; and all this is presented in a nearly shapeless plot that is full of extreme improbabilities and absurd situations. For instance, why would Antiochus describe his sin in the riddle he invites the world to solve? Why does Thaisa enter a convent instead of going on to Tyre to rejoin her husband? Why does Pericles leave Marina in Tharsus for 14 years? Each question can be answered by reference to the conventions of folklore and narrative romance, but taken together, the whole story lacks plausibility and dramatic interest.

Nevertheless, *Pericles* has increased in popularity in the 20th century. The bold extremes of characterization and theme found in folklore and narrative romance may be more acceptable to a century familiar with abstraction and montage. The play is more rewarding on the stage than in print, in any case, for it depends in good part in MASQUE-like spectacle. It also entertains us with a wide range of human behavior—however baldly represented—and of good and bad fortune. Its very conventionality is reassuring: We can suspend our sense that life cannot be both randomly threatening and neatly resolved and simply enjoy its bizarre episodes and its happy ending.

Pericles centers on the title character—and, late in the play, on Marina—but it features a number of boldly drawn minor figures. These are not, for the most part, endowed with real human personalities, but they demonstrate the nature of humanity. Antiochus is a regal villain, full of power and sin, while Dionyza represents the archetypal evil stepmother. On the other hand, Helicanus is a paragon of loyalty and strength, while Cerimon is a benevolent nobleman and a master of the far reaches of human knowledge. These figures are not realistic, but this is part of their point. They are symbols of the human potential for good and evil that is so much more complex and obscure in reality, or even in realistic drama. The Fishermen of 2.1 and the staff of the Mytilenian brothel in Act 4 not only provide comic relief, they also remind us of our own parallel universe, mirrored allegorically in the play.

The play is unified by a repeated pattern of loss and recovery. On the largest scale, Pericles loses his confident idealism and is tainted by sexual evil; he suffers as a result, and he recovers goodness and love at the end of his life. This pattern is repeated within the overall development, as Pericles encounters love and loses happiness three times, only to recover each time. The cycle is strikingly punctuated with storms. When he flees the horror represented by Antiochus's daughter, Pericles becomes a shipwrecked exile, but he finds love anew in Thaisa. Beset by another tempest, Pericles loses Thaisa but takes comfort in the birth of Marina. Finally, though he is driven to despair by the apparent loss of Marina as well, fate changes its course, and he recovers both daughter and wife. Significantly, the storm that Pericles endures at this point is merely mentioned briefly, in 5.Chorus.14, and is not given the emphasis of the first two. Like ancient festival rituals, *Pericles* offers an analogy to the eternal cycles of winter and spring, death and rebirth. This pattern is the play's "plot."

Our sense of this plot is reinforced by the play's most prominent motif, resurrection. First Thaisa and then Marina seem to die, only to be revived, literally in Thaisa's case and figuratively with Marina's release from the brothel (after which "she sings like one immortal" [5.Chorus.3]). When Pericles discovers that his daughter is dead, he withdraws into himself and may be said to have suffered a mock death, from which he is revived by Marina. Once restored, he cries that Marina "beget'st" him (5.1.195), which suggests his reborn state, and demands "fresh garments" (5.1.213). The symbolic value of this gesture is difficult to ignore. He has been returned from death as surely as Marina and Thaisa seem to have been. Finally, at the play's close, the ritual cycle of death and birth is brought full circle, and Pericles' mourning for his daughter is forgotten in plans for her marriage. The recurring theme is touched on one last time when Simonides' death is reported. This allows Marina and Lysimachus to take their destined place—once that of the play's protagonist—as rulers of Tyre.

Another major motif of the play, incest, appears only once, but the issue is raised again at sensitive moments. In the play, incest suggests the deepest evil to which humanity is susceptible. Pericles, drawn to Antiochus's daughter, is tainted by her sin although he is innocent, for the "gods . . . inflame'd desire in [his] breast / To taste the fruit" (1.1.20–22). The episode's place at the opening of the play gives it great weight, and its point is further made by contrast when the hero encounters Thaisa and Simonides. Their healthy love is apparent when Simonides delightedly surrenders his daughter to Pericles in marriage. The theme is subtly and dramatically reworked in Pericles' cry to Marina: "Thou . . . beget'st him that did thee beget" (5.1.195). The horrifying potential of incest—inbred offspring—is inverted. Finally Pericles, like Simonides and unlike Antiochus, can willingly separate himself from Marina as she joins her husband in a new life.

At the play's close, then, the influence of evil has been destroyed and the misfortunes of the hero have been ended, but neither he nor Marina have been responsible for the happy ending. Dramatic coincidence, good luck, and the intervention of the gods have propelled events. Marina, in resisting the brothel world, influences her fate to some degree, but only sheer accident reunites her with her father. The other characters, especially Pericles—who is extraordinarily passive throughout—simply suffer or succeed as fate decrees. The play emphasizes that the characters cannot control their destiny, and that the patience to accept the misfortunes of life is the best way to survive them. The most important of the external forces that drive the action is the sea. Its impersonal violence is both the occasion and the symbol of Pericles' recurring losses. Further, help comes to famine-beset Tharsus by sea in 1.4; in 2.1 the shipwrecked Pericles' only remaining emblem of princely dignity, his inherited armor, is brought up in the Fishermen's net; and in 4.2 Marina's unlikely rescuers appear from the sea. Not for nothing does the reunion of Pericles and Marina take place on a feast day dedicated to Neptune. This fact is emphasized by pointed repetition (5.Chorus.17; 5.1.17) and by reiteration of the word *sea* and references to the sea throughout the scene. The spectacular appearance of Diana makes the divine influence on the play's events completely clear. It is only sensible that Gower should summarize the tale of Pericles' family by saying that they have been "Led on by heaven" (Epilogue.6).

Another aspect of the characters' dependence on fate is the element of surprise that recurs throughout the play. In 1.1 Pericles is shockingly disillusioned about Antiochus's daughter; in 1.3 Thaliard finds his prey escaped; in 1.4 Cleon is astonished by the arrival of succor from famine, and so on. In almost every scene but Gower's narrations, which serve to anchor us amid seas of uncertainty, are instances of such startled amazement. Indeed, Marina feels that "This world to me is as a lasting storm, / Whirring me from my friends" (4.1.19–20). The sublimely spiritual quality of the last act owes much to the appearance of a cause for the play's random surprises. As mistrust yields to confidence that the promised joy is real, we, like the characters, can believe that the irrational brutality of the world is a survivable danger; such a solace is to be valued as much as any human achievement.

SOURCES OF THE PLAY

The original source for *Pericles, Prince of Tyre* was an ancient tale known as "Apollonius of Tyre." Though the earliest surviving version is a Latin text of the fifth–sixth centuries, scholars recognize from its style that it is a translation of a Greek work of 300 years earlier. This tale was extremely popular throughout the Middle Ages and the RENAISSANCE, and Shakespeare (and his collaborators, if any) surely knew it in several different versions that were current in 17th-century England. However, only two of these possible sources are specifically represented in the play: the 14th-century *Confessio Amantis* of John Gower in a 1554 edition and Laurence TWINE's *The Patterne of Painefull Adventures* (ca. 1576).

Gower's version of the tale, which was derived from a history of the world in Latin verse by the medieval chronicler Godfrey of Viterbo (ca. 1120–ca. 1196), was most important to the play. It provided the general outline of events, the locations, and most of the characters. Moreover, a number of passages—including Antiochus's riddle (1.1.65–72) and Pericles' note in Thaisa's coffin (3.2.70–77)—follow Gower fairly closely.

Twine's rendering of Apollonius's adventures, which he translated from a French version of the famous *Gesta Romanorum*, a medieval collection of Latin tales, was less important. It was only used extensively in Marina's story, especially in 4.3, where Dionyza cynically defends the supposed murder of Marina (though similar arguments made by Lady Macbeth and Goneril also foreshadow this episode). Minor echoes of Twine's words occur elsewhere in the play as well.

Though Shakespeare's Gower resembles and must have been influenced by the allegorical Chorus of the playwright's own *Henry V*, the idea of using the author of a well-known source as a ghostly CHORUS was probably stimulated by a contemporary play, *The Devil's Charter* (1607), by Barnabe BARNES. This play was derived from a work by the Italian historian Francesco Guicciardini (1483–1540) and featured Guicciardini as a choric narrator. Several of Gower's speeches contain echoes of the words of Barnes's Guicciardini.

Lastly, the hero's name—and thus that of the play—was probably inspired by Pyrocles, a major character in Sir Philip SIDNEY's pastoral romance *Arcadia* (1590). Two passages in the play—Pericles' appearance in rusty armor in 2.2 and Marina's description of a storm in 4.1—reflect episodes in *Arcadia*.

TEXT OF THE PLAY

Many scholars believe that *Pericles* was the product of a collaboration between Shakespeare and George WILKINS, Wilkins writing Acts 1 and 2, and perhaps, 5.2, while Shakespeare wrote the remainder and probably revised the whole. However, some commentators hold that the many faults of Q1 (see below) are sufficient to account for the discrepancies between parts of the play, while others consider John DAY or Thomas HEYWOOD to have been the coauthor. The matter has been a subject of controversy since the 18th century, and it will surely continue to be.

Pericles was probably written in 1607. The likely influence of Barnes's *The Devil's Charter* on the play suggests that *Pericles* was probably not completed before Barnes's play was staged early in 1607. It apparently had been completed, and probably performed, by May 1608, when the text was registered with the STATIONERS' COMPANY as "A booke called *The booke of Pericles prynce of Tyre.*" This wording almost certainly refers to a theatrical PROMPTBOOK. Also, there are no surviving references to this extremely popular play that date from before 1608, which implies that it appeared in or just before that year.

Edward BLOUNT registered the play, but he did not publish it, a maneuver that scholars believe was a "stopping action," intended to prevent publishing piracy. The effort was unsuccessful, however, for *Pericles* was published the next year by Henry GOSSON in a QUARTO edition printed by William WHITE known as Q1 (1609). Q1 is a BAD QUARTO, an inaccurate text put together from the recollections of actors or viewers. Some scholars believe that two different recollections were used, which produced the difference between Acts 1–2 and Acts 3–5. Based on this hypothesis, the text may be wholly Shakespeare's. Q1 was so popular that Gosson produced another edition (Q2) in the same year. (*Richard II* was the only other Shakespeare play to appear in two quartos in one year.) An unknown publisher brought out Q3 (1611), and Q4 (1619) was part of Thomas PAVIER's FALSE FOLIO. Q5 And Q6 appeared in 1630 and 1635. *Pericles* was not published in the FIRST FOLIO (1623), for reasons that are unknown. Perhaps the editors knew that much of the play was not written by Shakespeare, or they may have found the bad quarto too poor a text to reproduce. *Pericles* does appear, along with several definitely non-Shakespearean works (see APOCRYPHA), in the Third FOLIO (F3; 1664). F3 was printed from Q6, and Q2–Q6 are all derived from Q1. The original quarto, therefore, despite its faults, has been the basis of all subsequent editions.

THEATRICAL HISTORY OF THE PLAY

Undated diplomatic papers record that a performance of *Pericles* was attended by the Venetian and French ambassadors to England sometime between May 1606 (when the French delegate arrived in London) and the closure of London's theaters by a plague epidemic in July 1608. Scholars generally date the play to 1607, so the initial production probably opened during that year or early in 1608. The KING'S MEN made an unsuccessful effort to prevent the pirated publication of *Pericles* in 1608 because the play was already extremely popular. George WILKINS's 1609 novel based on the play capitalized on this popularity, which is further stressed by contemporary references. These include a 1609 remark that great crowds attended the play and the 1619 record of an elaborate production and intermission banquet with which the government entertained visiting dignitaries. As late as 1631, Ben JONSON complained in print that *Pericles* was outdrawing his own works.   .

However, though *Pericles* was among the first Shakespearean plays revived when the theaters were reopened following the English civil war— Thomas BETTERTON was acclaimed in the title role in 1660 and 1661—the play was not popular thereafter. In fact, it was not produced again—except in a very un-Shakespearean adaptation by George LILLO (1738)—until Samuel PHELPS revived it in 1854. Phelps's version was greatly abridged; Gower was eliminated entirely, for instance. It was also sanitized; Victorian tastes could not tolerate the brothel scenes in particular, so Phelps condensed Act 4 and "disinfected it of its impurities," as a contemporary reviewer put it.

Only three other productions—two of them German—are known from before World War I, but since then the play has grown somewhat in popularity. Among the most notable 20th-century productions were the first modern staging of the unaltered play by Robert ATKINS at the OLD VIC THEATRE (1921) and two productions starring Paul SCOFIELD (1947, 1950). *Pericles* has never been made into a FILM, though it has been produced once for TELEVISION, in 1983.

CHARACTERS

Antiochus, King of Syria (ca. 238–187 B.C.) Historical figure and character in *Pericles*, the incestuous father of the Daughter courted by Pericles. In 1.1 Antiochus proposes a riddle. He who solves it will win the hand of his daughter in marriage, but any who fail will be executed. A row of severed heads attests to many failures. Pericles solves the riddle, but it reveals the king's incest, and, horrified, he withdraws his suit. Antiochus realizes that his secret has been uncovered and he decides to kill Pericles, though he attempts to delude his victim by giving him an extra 40 days to answer the riddle. When Pericles flees, Antiochus sends Thaliard in pursuit with orders to murder

him. Antiochus appears only in the opening scene and is a conventionally false and vicious villain. In Act 2 the good King Simonides is contrasted with him, and Antiochus's death by "a fire from heaven" is reported in 2.4.9.

As the play's only historical figure, Antiochus provides us with a date for its action. However, this was unimportant to Shakespeare, who took the name from his sources, which included Antiochus because he was one of the most famous rulers of the Greek lands of the eastern Mediterranean. Known as Antiochus the Great, he was a king of the Seleucid dynasty, heirs to a portion of the empire founded by Alexander the Great. Antiochus waged a number of largely unsuccessful wars and is known as "the Great" because he carried a campaign to "India" (actually Afghanistan) rather than for any lasting accomplishments. However, he did develop his capital city and made it one of the great metropolises of its day, after which, as ANTIOCH, it bore his name. No evidence exists that Antiochus was incestuous, though he did have daughters, one of whom, Cleopatra, was married to a ruler of Ptolemaic Egypt and was thus the ancestor of Shakespeare's Egyptian queen. However, the playwright probably did not know of this connection.

Bawd Minor character in *Pericles*, the keeper of a brothel in MYTILENE, who, with her husband the Pandar, buys the kidnapped Marina. The Bawd is a hard-boiled madam. She coolly assesses her wenches as "creatures . . . [who] with continual action are even as good as rotten" (4.2.6–9). She rejects her husband's scruples: "Other sorts offend as well as we" (4.2.34), she says grumpily. She is prepared to be friendly with the newly bought Marina and assures her that she "shall live in pleasure [and] taste gentlemen of all fashions" (4.2.72–76). When Marina grieves at her plight, however, the Bawd turns nasty and declares, "you're a young foolish sapling, and must be bow'd as I would have you" (4.2.83–85). The Bawd jokes cynically with her employee Boult about the venereal diseases of their clients. This was a traditional subject of humor in Shakespeare's day, but placed in contrast with the virginal Marina, it seems shocking. When Marina's virtues begin to encourage moral reform among her customers, the

Bawd complains comically, "Fie, fie upon her! She's able to freeze the god Priapus, and undo a whole generation" (4.6.3–4). In her energetic sinfulness, the Bawd resembles such other Shakespearean ladies of the demimonde as the Hostess and Mistress Overdone (in *1 Henry IV* and *Measure for Measure*, respectively), though the underworld of Mytilene is not so developed as those of LONDON and VIENNA. The Bawd contributes to the comic—and realistic— relief from the elevated and melodramatic romance of the main plot.

Boult Minor character in *Pericles*, brothel employee responsible for training and advertising the kidnapped Marina. The energetic Boult ("Performance shall follow" [4.2.59], he says proudly) pretends to be cruel and cynical. When he speaks of Marina's modesty, he declares that "these blushes of hers must be quench'd with some present practice" (4.2.122–124). However, though he threatens to destroy her innocence through rape, in 4.6, she recognizes that she can appeal to his inner revulsion at his profession, and tells him his job would shame "the pained'st fiend / Of hell" (4.6.162–163). He can only plead, "What would you have me do? go to the wars, would you? Where a man may serve seven years for the loss of a leg, and have not money enough in the end to buy him a wooden one?" (4.6.169–172). This brief, compelling outburst demonstrates the breadth of Shakespeare's humanity: he transforms a minor character's crisis into a striking commentary on a pervasive scandal of Elizabethan times; the distressing status of military veterans. Boult agrees to help Marina escape the brothel, which we later learn she does. In addition to helping Marina, Boult also contributes to the comic relief from melodrama provided by the brothel scenes.

Cerimon, Lord Character in *Pericles*, a nobleman and physician of EPHESUS who revives the seemingly dead Thaisa. Cerimon's benevolence as well as his expertise as a scientist is conveyed in his conversation with two neighbors, in 3.2. He assists a Servant who has suffered the great storm of the night before—the storm during which the unconscious Thaisa was mistakenly buried at sea, in 3.1—and he speaks of his long study of "physic, [the] secret art

[of] the blest infusions / That dwells in vegetives, in metals, stones" (3.2.32–36). Today we might call him an alchemist. He revives Thaisa by invoking the spirit of Aesculapius, the Greek god of healing, which suggests ancient medical wisdom. Cerimon guides Thaisa to the famous Temple of Diana—one of the most important ancient pagan temples— when the revived queen, certain she will never see her husband again, desires "a vestal livery" (3.4.9). In 5.3, when Thaisa, by then a high priestess at the Temple, is reunited with Pericles, Cerimon is there and, as the only calm person present, is able to confirm Thaisa's story. This kind and intelligent scholar foreshadows Shakespeare's last great protagonist, the magician Prospero of *The Tempest*.

Cleon Character in *Pericles*, governor of THARSUS and husband of Dionyza. In 1.4 Cleon bemoans the catastrophic famine that has beset Tharsus, and when Pericles brings relief, he is very grateful. He curses anyone who may ever harm his benefactor, including "our wives, our children, or ourselves" (1.4.103). This remark proves very ironic when Dionyza attempts to murder Pericles' daughter, Marina, who has been left in their care. Cleon disapproves of his wife's deed, but he gives in to her harangue against his cowardice, and as the head of the family, he eventually receives much of the blame for it. The play's spokesman, Gower, tells us in the EPILOGUE that Cleon and his entire family have been massacred by the citizens of Tharsus, who were incensed when they learned of the murder. When his bravery is questioned by Dionyza, Cleon resembles Macbeth (in *Macbeth* 1.7, 2.2, and 3.4) and the Duke of Albany (in *King Lear* 4.2), but he is a very minor figure whose function is to depict man's weakness in the face of evil.

Daughter Minor character in *Pericles*, incestuous lover of her father, King Antiochus of Syria. Pericles attempts to win the Daughter in marriage by solving Antiochus's riddle, but when the solution reveals the incest, he withdraws in horror, repelled by the sin and fearful of Antiochus's wrath. When she appears in 1.1, the Daughter is presented as a personification of fertility, "apparell'd like the spring" (1.1.13). However, a warning is immediately voiced by her father, who calls her "this fair Hesperides, / With golden fruit, but dangerous to be touch'd" (1.1.28–29). She speaks only two lines and approves of her suitor, but when Pericles learns the truth, he rejects her and says "Good sooth, I care not for you" (1.1.87). He later speaks of her and her father as "both like serpents . . . who though they feed / On sweetest flowers, yet they poison breed" (1.1.133–134). In Act 2 Thaisa and her father, Simonides, are implicitly contrasted with the Daughter and Antiochus, whose deaths by divine vengeance are reported in 2.4.: "A fire from heaven came and shrivell'd up / Their bodies . . ." (2.4.9–10). The Daughter has no personality and is a convenient agent of evil in the play's melodramatic plot.

Diana Pagan goddess and minor character in *Pericles, Prince of Tyre*. After Pericles has been reunited with his daughter Marina, Diana appears to him in a vision, in 5.1.238–247. She instructs him to go to her temple at EPHESUS and publicly tell of his continued separation from his wife, Thaisa. In 5.3 he does so and is thereby reunited with Thaisa, for she is a priestess at the temple. The play's protagonist thus finds final relief from his suffering through supernatural intervention, and this stresses the play's most important theme: the helplessness of humanity in the face of destiny.

Diana, the ancient goddess of the moon and the hunt, was a familiar theatrical personage in Shakespeare's day. She appears in a number of 16th- and 17th-century dramatic productions, generally clad in a costume decorated in silver with emblems of the moon, and carrying a silver bow (which she mentions here, in 5.1.246). Her appearance in *Pericles*, the first of Shakespeare's ROMANCES, heralds the supernatural atmosphere and dreamlike quality that characterizes these late plays.

Dionyza Character in *Pericles*, would-be murderer of Marina. In 3.3 Pericles leaves his daughter Marina in the care of Dionyza and her husband Cleon. However, Dionyza grows jealous of the girl as she overshadows their own daughter, and in 4.1 she forces her servant Leonine to agree to kill Marina. Though he does not do so, he tells his mistress he

has, and in 4.3 Dionyza faces Cleon's horror at her deeds—she has also poisoned Leonine to ensure secrecy. In response to his dread, she says, "I think you'll turn child again" (4.3.4) and compares his qualms to complaining that "winter kills the flies" (4.3.50). She clearly resembles her forerunner Lady Macbeth but is a much less developed character. In 1.4 we see her as she echoes her husband's distress over a famine, and her transition to evil seems unmotivated. She is merely a stereotype of the wicked stepmother, evil because the plot requires it.

Escanes Minor character in *Pericles*, a lord of TYRE. Escanes appears with Pericles' deputy, Helicanus, in 1.3 and 2.4—mute in the former scene and speaking two short lines in the latter. In 4.4.13–16 he is said to be governing Tyre while Pericles and Helicanus are abroad. His presence adds dignity to Helicanus, for whom he serves as a retinue.

Fishermen Three minor characters in *Pericles*, poor men of PENTAPOLIS. In 2.1 the Fishermen assist the shipwrecked Pericles and inform him that the ruler of Pentapolis is King Simonides, whose daughter, Thaisa, is to marry the winner of a jousting tournament. When Pericles' armor is brought up in the Fishermen's net, he decides to use it in the king's tourney, and the Fishermen agree to guide him to Simonides's court.

This episode introduces the next scene in the play, but the Fishermen also have a greater significance, as they reflect the play's major theme. Before they encounter Pericles they speak of the shipwreck and regret their inability to help the victims "when, well-a-day, we could scarce help ourselves" (2.1.22). They also philosophize on the ways of the world in a humorous vein. They observe, for instance, that fish live "as men do a-land: the great ones eat up the little ones" (2.1.28–29). Thus, the Fishermen present the idea that people are at the mercy of forces outside themselves, whether natural or social. This helplessness is the central element of the play's world.

The First Fisherman is the leader of the group; he refers to the Second and Third Fishermen by their names—Pilch and Patch-breech—both humorous terms for raggedy clothes. These labels suggest the general appearance of the Fishermen, which is that of a traditional comic character, the rustic CLOWN.

Gentlemen (1) Two minor characters in *Pericles*, neighbors of the physician Lord Cerimon. In 3.2, after a great storm, the Gentlemen encounter Cerimon and he remarks on his medical practice and knowledge of arcane herbal treatments. This establishes the physician's credentials to the audience, in readiness for the next episode—his revival of Thaisa—which the Gentlemen observe and comment on briefly. The Gentlemen serve to carry the plot forward.

Gentlemen (2) Two minor characters in *Pericles*, visitors to a bordello who are converted to virtue through their encounter with Marina. In 4.5 the two Gentlemen discuss the young woman whose virtuous nature has shamed them. They marvel that "divinity [has been] preach'd there" (4.5.4), and one of them declares, "I'll do anything now that's virtuous" (4.5.8). With this very brief (nine-line) scene, Shakespeare establishes Marina's superiority to her circumstances. We have just seen her sold to the bordello by Pirates who had kidnapped her earlier, and this scene makes it clear that good is in the process of triumphing over evil.

Gentlemen (3) Any of several minor characters in *Pericles*, attendants of Pericles. In 5.1 the Gentlemen are summoned to receive Lysimachus, the governor of MYTILENE, who is visiting Pericles' ship. One Gentleman acknowledges the call in four words, but otherwise these courtiers do not speak. They are extras, intended to increase the atmosphere of ceremonious formality that surrounds Pericles.

Gower, John (ca. 1330–1408) English poet, a historical figure and a character in *Pericles*. Gower's major work, the *Confessio Amantis* (1390), was Shakespeare's chief source for *Pericles* and a possible influence on *The Comedy of Errors* and *The Merchant of Venice*. In *Pericles* Gower acts as a CHORUS who summarizes offstage action and moralizes on the course of developments. He appears in brief PROLOGUE-like passages before each act and also in

4.4 and 5.2. At the play's close he delivers a brief EPILOGUE. His manner of speaking is quaintly old-fashioned by the standards of the 17th century, which indicates his historical position as well as clarifying the remote and romantic nature of the story being enacted. Occasionally, Shakespeare's character clearly imitates the real Gower's poetic style, as in 3.Chorus. Also, two passages not spoken by the character—1.1.65–72 and 3.2.70–77—follow the real poet's verse quite closely.

Gower's *Confessio Amantis* contained 141 ancient tales from various sources, rendered in English verse. One of its stories, the Greek "Apollonius of Tyre," dates to at least the third century A.D., though Gower took it from the work of a later chronicler, Godfrey of Viterbo (ca. 1120–ca. 1196). A 1554 edition of Gower's *Confessio* provided Shakespeare with the general outline of events, the locations, and most of the characters of *Pericles*. The same tale may also have inspired the SUBPLOT concerning Egeon in *The Comedy of Errors* and the episode of the three caskets in *The Merchant of Venice*.

Gower was a minor nobleman who pursued his literary career in London, supported by rents from two small country estates. He wrote major works in Latin, French, and English, though the *Confessio* (which may have been commissioned by King Richard II) is by far the most important. Its 33,000 lines of eight-syllable couplets constitutes one of the greatest achievements of 14th-century English poetry. Gower was a contemporary and friend of Geoffrey CHAUCER, who dedicated his *Troilus and Criseyde* to him. However, the two poets may have become estranged, for a tribute to Chaucer in the first manuscript edition of the *Confessio* is omitted from later ones produced in Gower's lifetime.

Helicanus Minor character in *Pericles*, adviser to and surrogate ruler for Prince Pericles of TYRE. In 1.2 Helicanus stands out among a group of flattering courtiers when he makes a speech that stresses the value of honest criticism to a ruler. Impressed, Pericles leaves Helicanus in charge of Tyre when he must flee from the powerful King Antiochus of Syria. In 2.4 the Tyrian nobles desire a ruler who is in residence and suggest that Helicanus declare himself Pericles' successor, but the faithful adviser summons

Pericles home instead. In Act 5 Helicanus serves Pericles again. He acts as Pericles' spokesman when the grief-stricken prince—he has been separated from his wife and daughter—refuses to speak. He witnesses Pericles' reunions with Marina, in 5.1, and Thaisa, in 5.3. Helicanus demonstrates that loyalty and goodness do continue to exist among humans, despite the misfortunes that plague Pericles. Pericles praises Helicanus's virtues several times, and calls him "fit counsellor and servant for a prince, / Who by thy wisdom makes a prince thy servant" (1.2.63–64), and "a grave and noble counsellor" (5.1.182). This wise elder's presence seems appropriate to the play's conclusion in divinely wrought happiness and good fortune.

Knights   Several minor characters in *Pericles*, jousters who compete with Pericles for the hand of Thaisa. In 2.2 five Knights—along with Pericles—are presented to Thaisa and her father, King Simonides, and Thaisa describes their elaborate coats of arms. None of them speak. In 2.3, at the banquet that follows, one of the Knights—designated as the First Knight—offers brief courtly remarks to Pericles and the king. In 2.5 each of three Knights—First, Second, and Third—speaks a single line as they leave Simonides's court, having been told that Thaisa refuses to marry. The Knights are required for the jousting, and they add to the ceremony of Simonides's court, but they do not have individual character attributes.

Leonine   Minor character in *Pericles*, the murderer hired by Dionyza to kill Marina. In 4.1 Dionyza urges Leonine to ignore his conscience, for he is reluctant to murder so fine a young woman; however, he agrees to uphold his sworn oath to do so. A civil murderer, he offers Marina time to say her prayers, and while she is doing so, he is interrupted by the coincidental arrival of marauding Pirates, who kidnap his intended victim. Relieved to be freed from his obligation, Leonine nevertheless proposes to tell Dionyza he has in fact done the deed. As we learn in 4.3.10, Dionyza believed him, but she has also poisoned him to ensure secrecy. Leonine's brief appearance is thus filled with surprises, as first his conscience, then his viciousness,

and finally his deceit all prove insufficient. Such ironic changes are found throughout the play, and demonstrate that humanity is helpless before fate, an important theme for *Pericles* and Shakespeare's late plays in general.

In the *Confessio Amantis* of John GOWER, Shakespeare's chief source for the play, Leonine, which means "lionlike," is the name of the Pandar. The playwright presumably transferred the name to the murderer to make better use of its reference to a ferocious beast.

Lord (1)   Any of several minor characters in *Pericles*, gentlemen of Pericles' court. The Lords appear briefly in 1.2, flattering Pericles. Helicanes denounces them and thereby gains the confidence of Pericles, who puts him in charge when he leaves TYRE. In 2.4 a group of Lords insist that Tyre needs a resident ruler and that if Pericles does not return, Helicanes should take his place. Helicanes puts them off for a year while he sends for Pericles, who returns to Tyre and is thus separated from his wife and child. Thus, the Lords further the inexorable workings of fate.

Lord (2)   Minor character in *Pericles*, a gentleman of THARSUS. In 1.4 the Lord brings Cleon word that a convoy of ships approaches. Though Cleon fears invasion, the Lord observes that the ships bear flags of truce. Sent to escort the arrivals to Cleon, the Lord returns with Pericles. The Lord is not a developed character, though his common sense presents a mild opposition to Cleon's pessimism.

Lord (3)   Any of several minor characters in *Pericles*, attendants of Simonides, king of PENTAPOLIS. At the king's jousting tournament in 2.2, three of the Lords mock Pericles, who is wearing rusty armor. This elicits Simonides's observation that "Opinion's but a fool, that makes us scan / The outward habit by the inward man" (2.2.55–56). The Lords speak only eight lines between them and serve to introduce this single point.

Lord (4)   Minor character in *Pericles*, an attendant of Lysimachus. In 5.1 Lysimachus confers with Helicanus about the speechless despair of Pericles, and a member of his retinue, the First Lord, reminds his master of the extraordinary qualities of Marina, who may be able to "win some words of him" (5.1.43). This timely suggestion brings about the climactic reunion of Pericles and Marina. The fact that the suggestion is made by a minor figure maintains the dignity of Lysimachus—who should not seem preoccupied with Marina—and adds to the atmosphere of courtly formality with which the play abounds.

Lychorida   Minor character in *Pericles,* the nurse of Marina and the servant of Pericles and Thaisa. Lychorida accompanies the pregnant Thaisa and Pericles as they embark on a sea journey, shown in the DUMB SHOW in 3.Chorus. In 3.1, aboard ship, she presents the newborn Marina to Pericles and reports that Thaisa has died in childbirth. In 3.3 she carries Marina but does not speak when Pericles leaves infant and nurse in THARSUS. Marina's grief at Lychorida's death 14 years later is probably mentioned in 4.1.11, though the text is unclear. In Shakespeare's world the company of a nurse was a regular attribute of a well-born young woman. Through her service to Thaisa and then her daughter, Lychorida embodies dedicated domestic service and contributes to the play's atmosphere of ceremonious and courtly life.

Lysimachus   Character in *Pericles,* the governor of MYTILENE who becomes betrothed to Marina. In 4.6 Lysimachus visits the brothel to which the kidnapped Marina has been sold. His familiar banter with the Bawd and Boult suggests that he is a regular customer. Once alone with Marina, he seems baffled by her refusal to acknowledge the situation, and he insists "Come, bring me to some private place; come, come" (4.6.89–90). She counters, "If you were born to honour, show it now" (4.6.91) and goes on to express her revulsion for the brothel. Lysimachus is impressed and shamed. He claims to have come "with no ill intent" (4.6.109), and says that he wished only to observe Marina's already famous virtue. However, his flight is hasty, and without being funny he suggests the comic potential of the exposed hypocrite. In any case, he serves admirably as a foil for Marina's virtue, courage, and wit. The Lysimachus of Shakespeare's

sources is much more plainly a lecher, and when the playwright provided him with an excuse, he certainly intended us to take it as an indication of the governor's essential decency.

In 5.1 Lysimachus witnesses the reunion of Marina and her father Pericles. When he learns that she is a suitable bride for a ruler, he asks Pericles for her hand. In the final reconciliations and reunions of 5.3 his engagement to Marina is formally declared, and the couple is assigned the rule of TYRE, though Lysimachus does not speak. He is merely a conventional high-born figure, a suitable husband for the heroine.

Marina   Character in *Pericles,* daughter of Pericles and Thaisa. Marina appears only in Acts 4–5 (except as a newborn infant—i.e., as a stage prop—in 3.1), but she is nevertheless a major character. Along with her father, she bears the weight of the play's central lesson: the value of patience in the face of fate. Marina, like Pericles, is helpless before her destiny, which subjects her to the loss of her family and great dangers as well. Her name, which implies her birth at sea, suggests her destiny-driven life. Her spirit does not flag, however; she resists despair, as her father does not, and becomes his savior. Finally, her moral virtues are rewarded by reunion with her parents and a prospective marriage with Lysimachus.

Like Pericles, Marina suffers great misfortune— separation from her parents in infancy, a murder attempt by her foster mother, a kidnapping and sale to a brothel—through no fault of her own and despite her extraordinary virtue. Also like her father, she is an idealized character, more important as an emblem than as a personality. She represents absolute innocence and purity; she says, "I never spake bad word . . . never kill'd a mouse, nor hurt a fly . . . But I wept for't" (4.1.75–79). However, though she resembles "Patience gazing on kings' graves, and smiling / Extremity out of act" (5.1.138–139), she is not without spirit. She demonstrates patience by never giving up on the world, but she is not passive like her father. Her stubborn refusal to surrender her virginity saves her, as she first talks her way out of the brothel and then becomes such a model of grace and kindness that she is called upon to cure the depression of the man who proves to be her father. Marina is typical of Shakespeare's plucky, spirited heroines, even though she does not seek out her adventures but is cast into them by fate.

Marina's ideal virtue and the simplicity and inflexibility of her motives places her in a disturbing contrast with the social reality of the Bawd, the Pandar, and Boult. This contrast is often seen as a defect, but the objection ignores the playwright's allegorical purposes, which are emphasized by the contrast. Like Shakespeare's other late heroines, Perdita and Miranda (in *The Winter's Tale* and *The Tempest,* respectively), Marina represents a sort of redemption, a renewal of life. Her spirit revives that of Pericles, who calls her "Thou that beget'st him that did thee beget" (5.1.195). Through her, he can transcend the buffetings of fate and be reconciled with a life whose disillusionments have been too much to bear. Her healing nature also affects the customers of the brothel and even the hard-boiled Boult. Moreover, Marina has been symbolically dead: She was believed dead by Pericles and has undergone a journey through the underworld of the brothel. She thus is representative of resurrection, the play's most important motif. She is an appropriate symbol of the spirit of hope and renewal with which the play ends.

Marshall   Minor character in *Pericles,* an official of the court of King Simonides. In 2.3 the Marshall designates a seat for Pericles at the royal banquet; he speaks only four lines and serves merely to indicate the grandeur of the occasion.

Messenger   Minor character in *Pericles,* a servant of King Antiochus of Syria. In 1.1 the Messenger informs Antiochus that Pericles—whom the king intends to kill—has fled the country. The Messenger, who speaks only a single line, helps heighten the melodramatic tension of the scene.

Mytilenian Sailor   See Tyrian Sailor.

Pandar   Minor character in *Pericles,* the keeper of a brothel who, with his wife, the Bawd, buys the kidnapped Marina. The Pandar is somewhat less

hard than his wife. He contemplates retirement from a trade whose practice puts them on "sore terms . . . with the gods" (4.2.33). However, he does have a business to run, and when Marina's glorious innocence begins to produce moral reform among the clientele, he despairs. He moans, "I had rather than twice the worth of her she had ne'er come here" (4.6.1–2). He then curses her with a contradictory pair of sexual problems: "the pox upon her green-sickness" (4.6.13). Thus the Pandar offers comic relief from the melodramatic romance of the main story.

Patch-breech   See Fishermen.

Pericles   Title character of *Pericles,* the ruler of TYRE. Through no fault of his own, Pericles undergoes tremendous misfortunes. He is driven into exile and becomes separated from both his wife and daughter, only to be finally reunited with them at the play's close. He accepts his fate passively, and thus he embodies a major theme of the play: that we cannot control our destiny, and the acceptance of suffering is humanity's only choice.

Pericles encounters love three times, but each time he loses it. In 1.1 he loves the Daughter of Antiochus, but when he learns of her incestuous relationship with her father, he withdraws his suit in horror. He is sullied by her sin although he is innocent, for the "gods . . . inflame'd desire in [his] breast / To taste the fruit" (1.1.20–22). Disillusioned, he loses his youthful assurance and flees into exile, a tribulation that ends when he is shipwrecked on the coast of PENTAPOLIS, in 2.1. He finds love again when he meets and marries Thaisa, but suffers a great loss when he wrongly believes that she has died in childbirth during a storm at sea. This is eased by the compensation of Marina's birth, but he leaves Marina with Cleon and Dionyza because he fears for her survival at sea. When he returns for her in 4.4, he learns—again wrongly—of her death. Significantly, he endures another storm at this point, but it happens offstage and is merely mentioned, in 5.Chorus.14, for his fortunes have now begun to turn. Distraught and without hope, he succumbs to despair. He only recovers when he accidently encounters Marina. The goddess Diana then guides him to a reunion with Thaisa. Thus, in the course of his life Pericles manifests youthful illusions, the misery of incomprehensible suffering, and the ultimate happiness that follows from his patient acceptance of the will of the gods.

His passiveness makes Pericles a strange hero to modern tastes. However, this trait should not be seen as an aspect of his personality, but rather as an emblematic feature that offers an allegory of a possible human relationship to the universe. Like most of the play's characters, Pericles is more emblematic than real and does not have a complex, fully developed personality. He is wholly good and without flaws. Unlike Antiochus, he *is* "a man on whom perfections wait" (1.1.80). He does not cause his misfortunes, nor does he resist them. He expresses his resignation clearly after the shipwreck. He addresses the tempest and says, "earthly man / Is but a substance that must yield to you; / And I, as fits my nature, do obey you" (2.1.2–4). His marriage is not his own doing, either. Thaisa courts him more than he does her, and though he loves her, he declares that he has "never aim'd so high to love" her (2.5.47). He is not without spunk—he responds with fiery indignation when Simonides pretends to believe him a "traitor" (2.5.54)—but in the world of the play he must suffer or prosper as fate decrees. Finally, his passiveness leads to his complete withdrawal when he believes Marina is dead. He retreats into speechlessness, a deathlike trance of despair from which only Marina can revive him. The play's theme of regeneration is embodied in part by this, Pericles' resurrection.

The play's strongest treatment of evil is its presentation of incest. Here Pericles is pointedly contrasted with Antiochus and proves himself a vessel of goodness. The episode is confined to 1.1, but it is mentioned at several points throughout the play, and it makes the point that humanity is capable of gross unnaturalness. It is countered by the example of Simonides and Thaisa, but more dramatically we see the father-daughter relationship reformulated in the union of Pericles and Marina. Pericles recognizes her impact on his despair and calls Marina "Thou that beget'st him that did thee beget" (5.1.195); thus, incest's horror is reversed. At the play's close, Pericles, unlike Antiochus, willingly surrenders Marina

to a husband. He demonstrates the healthy paternal love that promotes the natural cycles of regeneration that are an important theme of the play.

In his summary of *Pericles*, John Gower speaks of the hero and his family in words that could refer to Pericles alone. He calls them "Led on by heaven, and crown'd with joy at last" (Epilogue.6). Pericles is an extremely simple character, and Shakespeare, like many readers, may have found him a little too simple, for the subsequent ROMANCES were to contain a pattern of sin and remorse from which Pericles' story is exempt. Nevertheless, in this first of these late comedies the title character is a fine example of an allegorical protagonist, and he is a dramatic success when viewed in the terms set by the play.

The play stems from the ancient Greek tale "Apollonius of Tyre," and the protagonist's name remained Apollonius in Shakespeare's main sources for the play. The new name was probably suggested by Pyrocles, a hero of Sir Philip SYDNEY's *Arcadia*, one of the play's minor sources. Shakespeare's hero bears no resemblance at all to the Athenian statesman named Pericles (ca. 495–429 B.C.), though the playwright undoubtedly read the Athenian's biography in PLUTARCH's *Lives*. The great stature of the historical Pericles may have made his name seem appropriately grand for a fictional ruler of Tyre.

Philemon Minor character in *Pericles*, a servant of Lord Cerimon. Philemon, summoned by Cerimon, leaves immediately to carry out his master's orders to "Get fire and meat" (3.2.3) for the victims of a storm. He speaks only four words and helps illustrate Cerimon's concerned care for others.

Pilch See Fishermen.

Pirates Three minor characters in *Pericles*, buccaneers who kidnap Marina. In 4.1 the Pirates interrupt Leonine, who is about to murder Marina, and take her from her would-be killer. In 4.2 they sell her to a brothel in MYTILENE and disappear from the play. When they effect this melodramatic change in heroine's fortunes, the Pirates bring about one of the play's many surprises, which helps demonstrate the human dependence upon fate, an important theme. The Pirates, who speak four short lines between them, display an abrupt vigour ("A prize! A prize!" cries the Second Pirate [4.1.93], in his only speech) but their function is mainly to further the plot.

Sailor Either of two minor characters in *Pericles*, seamen aboard whose ship Marina is born and Thaisa apparently dies. In 3.1, during a raging storm, the Sailors believe that Pericles' wife Thaisa has died, though in fact she is merely unconscious. They demand that she be buried at sea, for they believe that a corpse aboard ship will bring disaster. The distracted Pericles agrees, and Thaisa is cast overboard in a watertight coffin. Thus begins the long separation of husband and wife, a central development in the play's sequence of exiles and disconnections. The Sailors are hearty seamen, conspicuously unafraid of the storm. The First Sailor addresses it contemptuously, "Blow, and split thyself" (3.1.44), to which the Second Sailor responds, "But sea-room, and the brine and cloudy billow kiss the moon, I care not" (3.1.45–46). Shakespeare makes it clear that they are not evil; they are merely unknowing implements of fate.

Servant (1) Minor character in *Pericles*, the victim of a storm who is aided by the physician Cerimon. In 3.2 Cerimon informs the Servant that his master will soon die, apparently making the diagnosis based on information the Servant has given him before the scene opened. The Servant then leaves, having spoken only briefly. He serves to help illustrate Cerimon's talents as a physician.

Servant (2) Any of several minor characters in *Pericles*, employees of Lord Cerimon. The Servants deliver a large chest that has been washed ashore by a storm. It proves to be a coffin that contains the body of the supposedly dead Thaisa. A Servant is sent to fetch the medical supplies with which Cerimon revives her. One Servant speaks briefly, but they serve mainly to bring stage properties into the scene.

Simonides Character in *Pericles*, king of PEN-TAPOLIS and father of Thaisa. In 2.2 Simonides hosts a tournament, the winner of which is to have his daughter's hand in marriage. He welcomes the anonymous Pericles to the contest despite his poor appearance in rusty armor. "Opinion's but a fool, that makes us scan / The outward habit by the inward man" (2.2.55–56), he says. Pericles wins the tournament, and Simonides is delighted. Pericles admires Simonides and compares him to his own royal father. In 2.5 Simonides tests the couple's readiness for marriage and pretends to distrust Pericles' motives. This elicits a manly denial from Pericles and a declaration of affection from Thaisa, following which Simonides announces his approval.

Simonides appears only in Act 2, but his symbolic importance is great. We are reminded of this when his death is reported in 5.3 after the perils and separation of Thaisa and Pericles are finally ended. His virtues are made clear before he appears, in the remarks of the Fishermen in 2.1. Most important, Simonides' healthy love permits him to be pleased with his daughter's marriage. This presents a powerful contrast to the relationship of Antiochus and his Daughter, the incestuous love with which the play opens and which causes Pericles' exile. The hero's encounter with Simonides and Thaisa signals the beginning of the recovery of his fortunes, and this connection is confirmed at the play's end when Pericles cries, "Heavens make a star of him!" (5.3.79).

In Shakespeare's sources for the play, the character corresponding to Simonides has another name. Why Shakespeare adopted the name Simonides is not known, but he presumably knew that the name belonged to two ancient poets, Simonides of Amorgos (active ca. 660 B.C.) and Simonides of Ceos (ca. 556–468 B.C.).

Thaisa Character in *Pericles*, wife of Pericles and mother of Marina. The daughter of King Simonides of PENTAPOLIS, Thaisa is the prize of a knightly tournament won by Pericles in 2.2. She marries him and sails with him to TYRE. En route, Marina is born, and Thaisa, mistakenly declared dead in childbirth, is buried at sea, in 3.1. She is revived by Cerimon in 3.2, but in 3.4, convinced she will never find Pericles again, she enters a convent dedicated to the goddess Diana. She does not appear again until 5.3, when Diana sends Pericles to the temple where Thaisa serves, and the two are reunited.

Thaisa's resurrection in 3.2 is one of the play's semi-supernatural marvels. What seems to be an ill-motivated retreat into a nunnery is merely a convention of romantic literature, as is her final reunion with her husband. However, she is not simply a cardboard figure. In Act 2 we see that she is a delightful, strong-minded young woman, like many of Shakespeare's other, more developed, heroines. She is delighted by Pericles' victory in the tournament, for though the exiled prince hides his identity, he seems to her "like diamond to glass" (2.3.36). He is reluctant to press his right to marry her, so she pursues the matter and insists to her father that she'll marry Pericles "or never more to view nor day nor light" (2.5.17). When Simonides pretends to be angry that Pericles has allegedly proposed to her, she declares, "who takes offence / At that would make me glad?" (2.5.70–71). In the final scene, this strength of personality lends resonance to her speech as she recognizes Pericles: "Did you not name a tempest, / A birth and death?" (5.3.33–34).

In the *Confessio Amantis* of John GOWER, Shakespeare's chief source for the play, Thaise is the name of Pericles' daughter, and his wife is nameless. Having selected the name Marina for his heroine, the playwright adapted the daughter's name for the mother. The name is traditionally associated with the legendary beauty of Thais, the mistress of Alexander the Great.

Thaliard Minor character in *Pericles*, assassin sent by King Antiochus of Syria to kill Pericles. In 1.1 Thaliard accepts his assignment with cool professionalism, but in 1.3, once he has followed Pericles to TYRE, he expresses reluctance. He declares that he only contemplates committing the deed out of fear of punishment if he refuses and a sense of obligation to his oath of loyalty to Antiochus. He is relieved to learn that his quarry has fled. Thaliard, as a potential assassin, represents an unjust fate, but he is also a victim, trapped by his place in the world. He is thus a part of a major theme of the play: that humanity is helpless in the face of destiny.

Tyrian Sailor Minor character in *Pericles*, a seaman on Pericles' ship. As 5.1 opens the Tyrian Sailor tells Pericles' aide, Helicanus, of the visit of Lysimachus, the governor of MYTILENE. He then relays Helicanus's request for courtiers to greet the governor, and he finally introduces the visitor to Helicanus. This busy episode points up the formality with which Pericles is surrounded, and adds to the ceremonious atmosphere of the play.

The designation of this character as Tyrian is the consequence, first, of the QUARTO edition of the play, which provided two sailors. Later, scholars assumed that one of them was in Lysimachus's service and was thus Mytilenian; the other, Pericles' sailor, was therefore distinguished in like fashion. Editors have varied in their distribution of the episode's lines: Sometimes 5.1.11–13 are given to the Mytilenian Sailor, but he is often dropped, and the Tyrian (or First) Sailor speaks all the lines. Sometimes a First and Second Sailor are provided who are both assumed to be Tyrian.

"Phoenix and Turtle, The"

Shakespeare's allegorical poem on the mystical nature of love. "The Phoenix and Turtle" (sometimes known by its first line, "Let the bird of loudest lay") was published with Robert Chester's LOVE'S MARTYR, a long allegorical poem celebrating the marriage of Sir John SALUSBURY and his wife. "The Phoenix and the Turtle" tells of the funeral of two lovers: the phoenix, a mythological bird associated with immortality, and the turtledove (usually called "turtle" in Elizabethan English), a symbol of fidelity. The two birds have burned to death and are forever joined in love. The allegory celebrates an ideal of love in which an absolute spiritual union of the lovers, defying rationality and common sense, is chastely achieved through death, the ultimate rejection of the world.

The poem consists of 13 quatrains (four-line stanzas) rhyming *abba*, followed by five triplets (stanzas of three rhyming lines) all in iambic tetrameter (see METER). The first five quatrains summon various birds to the funeral. The owl and other birds of prey—considered omens of evil—are refused admittance, while the crow and the swan, whose color and song, respectively, are traditionally associated with death, are welcomed. The next eight stanzas comprise a funerary "anthem" (line 21). The lovers are praised for having successfully achieved a total union, defying reason in the process. This defeat of worldly wisdom is celebrated in lyrical paradoxes, such as "Two distincts, division none; Number there in love was slain" (lines 27–28) and "Either was the other's mine" (line 36). Reason itself is constrained to cry out, "Love hath reason, reason none" (line 47). Reason composes a funeral song, the "threnos," which is presented in the last five stanzas, the solemn triple rhymes. The phoenix and the turtle are said to have embodied truth and beauty and, through their deaths, to have conveyed these qualities to all who "are either true or fair" (line 66).

This allegory reflects a notion that was widespread in the RENAISSANCE: Ideal love was felt to transcend reason and thus to represent a truer state of being than that of the material world. This idea, whose roots lay in the writings of Plato, is also related to the Christian concept of the state of grace that God offers to believers, and "The Phoenix and Turtle" has been interpreted as a specifically Christian allegory. More generally, it may be seen as illustrating the possibility of transcendence through love, an ideal that informs much of Shakespeare's work, particularly the COMEDIES.

"The Phoenix and Turtle" does not have a particular literary source, although the idea of an assembly of birds was a common one; for example, it appears in CHAUCER's *The Parliament of Fowls* and a famous mock funeral in OVID's *Amores*, to name only two great authors whom Shakespeare is known to have read and admired. The more specific motif of love between phoenix and turtledove was determined by its use in *Love's Martyr*. Shakespeare's poem was apparently written to be published with that work in 1601. The idea of love between these two symbolic birds was novel, originating with either Chester or his patron.

Salusbury and his wife are the likeliest subjects of any specific symbolism the phoenix and the turtledove may carry, in addition to their joint role as an emblem of ideal love. Also, scholars have long speculated on possible hidden meanings in *Love's Martyr* and/or "The Phoenix and Turtle," and various obscure references have been proposed. Some commentators who accept the idea of Shakespeare as a "crypto-Catholic" (see SPIRITUAL TESTAMENT OF JOHN SHAKESPEARE) believe the poem may be an esoteric celebration of that faith—which was that of *Love's Martyr*'s dedicatees, Salusbury and his bride—or of identify-shrouded Catholic martyrs, known to Salusbury's circle of friends, the prospective readers. But the two birds also have been seen as Queen Elizabeth I (see Elizabeth I in *Henry VIII*) and Robert Devereux, Earl of ESSEX, and as Essex and Henry Wriothesley, Earl of SOUTHAMPTON, among other pairings. However, such hypotheses are not provable, and in any case the poem transcends whatever particular purposes it may have had, surviving as a mystical and powerful invocation of love.

Rape of Lucrece, The

Narrative poem by Shakespeare that retells the ancient Latin story of the sexual assault on Lucretia—anglicized as Lucrece—a high-ranking Roman woman, by Sextus Tarquinius, or Tarquin, the son of the Roman king. Tarquin, tormented by an awareness of his own evil, proceeds to rape his victim nonetheless. Lucrece's distress is described at length, and her subsequent suicide is presented as a high-minded response to the dishonor of having slept with a man other than her husband. Before dying, Lucrece tells her husband and others of Tarquin's crime and elicits an oath of vengeance from them. The last stanza reports that they subsequently drove Tarquin and his father from Rome. An introductory ARGUMENT makes clear that, in expelling the royal family, the avengers, led by Junius Brutus, replaced the kingdom with the Roman Republic.

Lucrece complements the slightly earlier *Venus and Adonis*, and it is clearly the "graver labour" promised in *Venus*'s dedication to Henry Wriothesley, Earl of SOUTHAMPTON. Both works deal with sexual desire, but the reluctant male of *Venus* is a comic subject, while the ravished female of *Lucrece* is tragic. In contrast to the essential frivolity of the earlier poem, *Lucrece* is an expressly moral work, offering the lesson that disaster will result from a serious moral offense. Scholars speculate that the notoriety achieved by the somewhat salacious *Venus*—a notoriety that is evident in many surviving references—encouraged Shakespeare to appease those possibly offended—including patrons of literature or the theater—with a second effort of greater propriety. If this was indeed his intent, he succeeded: The critic Gabriel HARVEY noted, "The younger sort takes much delight in Shakespeare's *Venus and Adonis,* but his *Lucrece* and his tragedy of *Hamlet* . . . have it in them to please the wiser sort."

The association with *Hamlet* is no accident, for *Lucrece* is an example of a genre that 16th-century theorists classed with tragedy, the COMPLAINT, a poem intended to reflect on the hardships of life or of a particular event. Samuel DANIEL's *The Complaint of Rosalind* (1592), an extremely popular poem, is thought to have influenced Shakespeare's choice of genre. RHYME ROYAL, the verse pattern in which both *Lucrece* and Daniel's work were composed, was regarded as the most appropriate vehicle for such elevated expressions of dismay.

The bold rhyme scheme, with each stanza ending in two couplets, is also appropriate to formal rhetoric, and *Lucrece* is extremely rhetorical, filled with antitheses, virtuoso digressions, and elaborate comparisons. Often a reader can feel overwhelmed by these forced effects and tire of Lucrece's seemingly endless laments. Such baroque passages as the 26-line description of Lucrece's complexion (lines 52–77) seem excessive to modern taste, for example. In general, however, the poet's techniques enhance his points, often in ingenious ways.

But the poem is clearly more than simply a clever technical exercise. Shakespeare was fascinated by the story, and references to it recur in his plays. The character of Junius Brutus is compared to that of the king in *Henry V* (2.4.37); Macbeth, contemplating his intended murder in *Macbeth* 2.1.52–56, thinks of Tarquin approaching his victim in terms quite similar to those used in lines 162–168. In a

more casual way, Lucrece is cited as a model of chastity in *The Taming of the Shrew* (2.1.289).

Although *Lucrece* is tragic, it is not like the great plays that followed it. Instead, it resembles the early tragedy *Titus Andronicus*—a drama whose central event is a rape and which contains several references to the story of Lucrece. Both works are crude and unsubtle, contrasting absolute good and absolute evil in a context of horrible violence. Nevertheless, in *Lucrece* several of the most important themes and motifs of Shakespeare's later work appear. In writing *Macbeth* Shakespeare expanded on an interest in the psychology of evil that is presented forcefully in Tarquin's tortured self-awareness. Tarquin's inability to resist an impulse he detests also foreshadows Othello's similar plight. Moreover, the same episode of the poem, in which Tarquin's emotions and motives and indecisions are intensely explored, seems likely to have established a precedent that the playwright followed in creating Hamlet. (Perhaps significantly, both Hamlet and Lucrece refer to the same symbol of despair, Hecuba—he in 2.2.496, 552–553, she in lines 1447–56.) As late as the writing of *Cymbeline* (1609), Shakespeare was still intrigued with Tarquin. As the subtle villain Iachimo enters the heroine's bedchamber, he compares himself to Tarquin (2.2.12). Clearly, Shakespeare was fascinated with individuals who are willing to cut themselves off from basic morality, and his portrayal of Tarquin merits attention as an instance of that interest.

Lucrece also illustrates a type of which Shakespeare was fond, for although at first glance she may seem simply a passive victim, she is actually an interesting variation on the bold young women who star in the COMEDIES, such charmingly independent characters as Beatrice in *Much Ado About Nothing* and Portia in *The Merchant of Venice.* Lucrece, though she is indeed victimized, dictates the ultimate outcome of the catastrophe with a resolute will that demonstrates the same strength of character as Shakespeare's other Roman suicides, such as Marcus Brutus, "the noblest Roman of them all" (*Julius Caesar,* 5.5.68). Her decision may disgust or perplex modern readers, but in terms of ancient Roman psychology and ethics, at least as understood by Shakespeare, she is a true heroine; her sense of honor guides her to the only response she could find correct. Realizing that her despair is vain, she determines to take action (lines 1016–1029) and she lays a plan as efficiently as Portia devised hers against Shylock; ignoring the opinions of the men around her (lines 1708–1710), she displays the confidence in her own sensibility that Beatrice shows when she defends her slandered cousin Hero. Like several of Shakespeare's best-loved plays, *The Rape of Lucrece* has a female lead.

Numerous touches in *Lucrece* reveal the poet's experience as a playwright. The poem begins at a point well along in the narrative provided by the argument, reflecting a theatrical instinct to grab the reader with immediate excitement. The long digression to describe the painting of the siege of Troy (lines 1366–1561) allows time for Lucrece's messenger to perform his errand, a feature that will naturally have occurred to a playwright. Tarquin and Lucrece both question themselves in sharp exchanges that resemble the stichomythia that Shakespeare and other Elizabethan dramatists took from the plays of SENECA. And Shakespeare builds sympathy for one of his characters at the expense of the other. Lucrece's extensive pleading with Tarquin serves to further deepen his villainy when he remains untouched. The more reasonably she pleads, the more monstrous is his refusal to heed her. In a like fashion, Jack Cade is blackened by refusing mercy to Lord Say in *2 Henry VI* (4.7); Clifford behaves similarly to Rutland in *3 Henry VI* (1.3).

Also, *Lucrece* contains many passages of considerable power. The detailing of the Trojan painting, mentioned above, is extraordinary; Tarquin's torchlit approach to Lucrece's chamber (lines 302–371) is a vivid vignette of evil on the prowl, and Lucrece is touchingly vulnerable in the four stanzas of lines 386–413. Another four-stanza passage (lines 1121–1148), in which Lucrece rhetorically addresses the mythological Philomel—another rape victim—is a fine Elizabethan poem in its own right. Thus, although the poem's antique rhetoric and great length can be frustrating, *The Rape of Lucrece* deserves closer examination than it usually gets, for in it the young Shakespeare demonstrated that much greater work was to come.

Lucrece was written between April 1593, when *Venus and Adonis* was registered for publication with the STATIONERS' COMPANY, and May 1594, when it was registered itself. During the period from June 1592 to May 1594, when the London theaters were closed because of a plague epidemic and the young Shakespeare's playwriting career was interrupted, the young dramatist turned to a more prestigious mode of literature. Poetry was then regarded as the only serious form of literature—the stage was still somewhat disreputable (see ELIZABETHAN THEATER)—and poetry was potentially much more profitable under the patronage system that prevailed at the time. As was customary, Shakespeare offered his poems to a patron by formally dedicating them to him. Shakespeare chose to address both *Venus* and *Lucrece* to the Earl of Southampton, and the earl apparently accepted them, as the dedication to *Lucrece* implies, for its air of intimacy between writer and patron is unlike any other such passage in the literature of the time. Shakespeare's friendship with Southampton is accordingly regarded as a certain feature of the playwright's life, at least in the 1590s; this is one of the few biographical facts not supported by documentary evidence that almost all scholars accept without reservation.

The tale of Lucrece and Tarquin was well known to readers in Shakespeare's day, and the poet drew on a number of familiar sources. He used two Latin texts: OVID's *Fasti* and LIVY's *Ab urbe condita*, the two earliest surviving versions of the story. Shakespeare also used an English translation of Livy from *Palace of Pleasure* (1566), by William PAINTER, and he was also indebted to CHAUCER's *The Legend of Good Women* (ca. 1386), which was itself based on both Ovid and Livy. At least one detail in the description of the siege of Troy was taken from the *Aeneid* of VIRGIL.

The Rape of Lucrece was first published in 1594 by John HARRISON in a QUARTO edition (known today as Q1) printed by Richard FIELD. All subsequent early editions of *Lucrece* were published in octavo format, though they are conventionally known as Q2 and so on. Q6 (1616) was the last edition to appear in Shakespeare's lifetime. Each of these editions was simply a reprint of one of its predecessors, incorporating such minor changes as the printers saw fit to make, and, while they all contain variant readings, none is thought to reflect any changes that Shakespeare made. Q1 is therefore regarded as the only authoritative text, and it is the basis for modern editions.

Remarkably, *The Rape of Lucrece* has inspired not one OPERA but two. Composer Ottorino RESPHIGI died while finishing his *Lucrezia;* completed by his widow, it was produced posthumously in 1937. It is now rarely performed, but it was the inspiration for a 1946 chamber opera, a smaller-scale production, *The Rape of Lucretia*, by Benjamin BRITTEN, still popular.

CHARACTERS

Brutus, Junius (active 509 B.C.)   Quasi-historical founder of the Roman Republic and minor figure in *The Rape of Lucrece*. He avenges Tarquin's assault on Lucrece and expels the last king of Rome, Tarquin's father. (The same figure appears in *Coriolanus*, though as a very different character—Marcus Brutus.) Brutus appears only in the closing stanzas of *Lucrece*, beginning in line 1807. He rallies the grief-stricken husband and father of Lucrece, Collatine and Lucretius, to pursue the villain, with the consequence, stated briefly in the last line of the poem, that Tarquin is banished. Shakespeare described this conclusion slightly more elaborately in the final sentence of the ARGUMENT: ". . . the Tarquins were all exiled, and the state government changed from kings to consuls."

Brutus is said to have been a foolish young man, best known "for sportive words and utt'ring foolish things" (line 1813), before finding maturity in undertaking this act of revenge and revolution. Shakespeare took this characterization from his Latin sources, OVID and LIVY. However, these writers lived five centuries after Brutus; very little is actually known of the historical figure, if he actually existed. His name, meaning "brutish" (like that of Hamlet), was probably an insult, originally, perhaps, referring to his careless early life. However, Roman tradition revered Brutus as the leader of the revolt that established the republic in 509 B.C., though all that was recorded of him, and only recorded somewhat later, was that he was one of the first two consuls, the officers who replaced the kings and ruled jointly for a year at a time. (The

association of the revolution with a rape is entirely legendary.) Marcus Brutus, the assassin of Julius Caesar, claimed descent from him, as is mentioned several times in *Julius Caesar* (e.g., in 2.1.53–54). Brutus is also mentioned in *Henry V,* 2.4.37, where his legendary misspent youth is compared with Prince Hal's.

Collatine (Tarquinius Collatinus)   Semilegendary husband of the Roman matron Lucretia and minor figure in *The Rape of Lucrece*, the husband of Lucrece. After being sexually assaulted by the king's son, Tarquin, Lucrece sends for her father and Collatine, or Collatinus, as he is occasionally called (e.g., in line 218). Collatine does not appear until line 1584, and he is mostly tongue-tied by grief for the rest of the poem, for Lucrece informs the men what has happened and kills herself after demanding vengeance. Collatine is roused to revenge only by another witness of Lucrece's account, Junius Brutus.

The last words of the poem's introductory ARGUMENT observe that the vengeance that Brutus exacted upon Tarquin resulted in the fall of his father's kingdom and the establishment of the Roman Republic. Shakespeare took this conclusion from his sources, OVID and LIVY, but the association of the birth of the republic with a rape has no historical truth. All that is known of the historical Tarquinius Collatinus is that in 509 B.C. he was (with Brutus) one of the first two consuls, the executives who jointly ruled the republican government of Rome. His name suggests that he was Etruscan, like the departing royal family.

Lucrece (Lucretia)   Legendary Roman matron and central figure in *The Rape of Lucrece*, the victim of a rape by Tarquin. Lucrece kills herself rather than accept the disgrace of having slept with someone other than her husband. The bulk of the 1,855-line poem—from her first awareness of Tarquin's menace in line 442 until her death in line 1724—is dedicated to Lucrece's responses, fearful, horrified, ashamed, and determinedly suicidal. Her great wordiness is often considered a weakness of the poem, but her meditations are nonetheless studded with brilliant passages and also reflect an aspect of Shakespeare's attitude toward women.

Sometimes seen as a victim who is further victimized, Lucrece is actually rather like the boldly assertive young women of Shakespeare's work who have charmed COMEDY audiences for generations. She is admittedly less well realized, however, and her situation is less rewarding, both for herself and for modern readers. Lucrece's values, impossibly remote from modern ones, lead her to adopt a course of great bravery against the advice of the men around her (see lines 1709–1710). She realizes that only her death can repair the damage done to her self-esteem, and through her suicide she achieves heroic stature. In an aristocratic value system that gives great weight to marital loyalty—especially in women, who bear children and thus transmit the family line—Lucrece has been forcibly removed from the ranks of the pure, a status in which she has plainly taken great pride. She poignantly expresses her sense of her predicament by comparing herself to a damaged tree: ". . . the bark pill'd from the lofty pine, / His leaves will wither and his sap decay; / So must my soul, her bark being pill'd away" (lines 1167–1169).

In ancient heroic traditions, these situations are no more subject to rationalization than are natural catastrophes. Lucrece's response preserves her honor, all that remains within her control. Although Lucrece's action is criticized by Brutus (lines 1822–1827), she is nevertheless presented as a heroic figure, and her actions stimulate a heroic act, the revolution against the Tarquinian kings and the establishment of the Roman Republic. Moreover, Lucrece's tale was so perfectly in accord with notions of honor and heroism that it survived through almost 2,000 years and several upheavals in European civilization to find continued acceptance among the Elizabethans.

Shakespeare took the story of Lucrece's rape and its political consequences from his Latin sources, LIVY and OVID, but it is not historical, deriving in fact from pre-Latin traditions. Someone involved with the establishment of the republic may have had a wife named Lucretia (the Latin spelling of Lucrece), but nothing at all is known of her.

Lucretius Legendary Roman and minor figure in *The Rape of Lucrece*, the father of Lucrece. Lucretius appears only late in the poem. He is implicitly present from line 1583 but is not mentioned until line 1732, after Lucrece has told of Tarquin's crime against her and killed herself. He delivers a touching, three-stanza outburst of grief (lines 1751–1771), but it is one of the other witnesses, Brutus, who rallies the mourners to exact vengeance against Tarquin, finally resulting in the fall of the monarchy. Shakespeare took Lucretius from his Latin sources, OVID and LIVY, who lived several centuries after these events supposedly took place; modern historians have found no record of Lucretius from his own time.

Tarquin (Sextus Tarquinius) Semilegendary Roman prince and figure in *The Rape of Lucrece*, the rapist who assaults Lucrece. In the first quarter of the poem, Tarquin, though aware that his act will dishonor him forever, is gripped by sexual desire and continues, "pawning his honour to obtain his lust" (line 156). He condemns himself at some length (lines 190–245, 260–280), but he finally commits himself to satisfying his lust. He is held between "frozen conscience and hot burning will" (line 247), in the grip of an evil impulse "strong past reason's weak removing" (line 243). In this respect Tarquin's story anticipates a major theme of *Macbeth*, and he is specifically referred to in that play (2.1.55).

Once Tarquin assaults Lucrece in her bedroom, the poet's attention turns to the victim (line 442), and after committing his crime, Tarquin flees (line 740). He does not reappear, though in the last line of the poem it is reported that Lucrece's avengers, led by Junius Brutus, have expelled him from Rome. Earlier, in the last sentence of the ARGUMENT to the poem, Shakespeare also mentions this development, saying, ". . . the Tarquins were all exiled, and the state government changed from kings to consuls." Thus Tarquin's crime is said to have led to the establishment of the Roman Republic.

In Shakespeare's sources, OVID and LIVY, Sextus Tarquinius is the son of the last king of the Romans, Tarquinius Superbas, and the king, deposed in favor of the Republic in 509 B.C., may have had a son who bore this name. However, the tale of Lucrece's rape has its roots in pre-Roman traditions, and Tarquin may well be totally legendary. In any case the name Tarquinius suggests that these rulers of Rome were Etruscans, whose principal city was Tarquinia.

Richard II

SYNOPSIS

Act 1, Scene 1

Henry Bolingbroke appears before his cousin King Richard II and accuses Thomas Mowbray of treason for having embezzled funds, hatched unspecified plots, and murdered Thomas, Duke of Gloucester, uncle of Bolingbroke and the king. Mowbray claims innocence and demands a trial by combat. Despite Richard's appeals, seconded by Bolingbroke's father, John of Gaunt, the two noblemen insist on fighting; Richard gives in and designates a time and place for the encounter.

Act 1, Scene 2

The Duchess of Gloucester, widow of Thomas, demands that Gaunt avenge her husband's murder, but he replies that, since the murder was ordered by the king, God's deputy, vengeance can be exacted only by God. The Duchess then prays that Mowbray shall be killed in the trial by combat.

Act 1, Scene 3

Mowbray and Bolingbroke prepare for the trial by combat, but at the last moment the king rules that the two disputants shall be banished from England—Bolingbroke for 10 years, Mowbray for life. Before departing, Mowbray asserts that Bolingbroke's disloyalty will eventually surface, to Richard's regret. Richard, seeing Gaunt's despair at his son's banishment, reduces the sentence to six years, but Gaunt replies that he shall die before that time is up. The king, unmoved, departs. Gaunt attempts to cheer up his disheartened son, but to no avail.

Act 1, Scene 4

The Duke of Aumerle, who has pretended friendship with Bolingbroke, reports to the king that that nobleman has left England. Richard reveals his enmity toward Bolingbroke, on account of the latter's widespread popularity. Sir Henry Greene remarks that a rebellion in Ireland requires the king's attention, and Richard says that he will lead an army there. This expedition will be financed by selling to entrepreneurs the right to collect taxes and by forcing loans from wealthy noblemen. Sir John Bushy brings news that John of Gaunt is very sick and has asked to see the king. Richard hopes for his immediate death so that he may confiscate his wealth for the Irish campaign.

Act 2, Scene 1

The dying Gaunt confides to his brother the Duke of York his desire to give good counsel to Richard before he dies, and he goes on to rage against the king's shady financial practices. The king arrives with a group of nobles. Gaunt reprimands him, and the angry Richard reminds his uncle of his power to have him killed; Gaunt dares him to do so, accusing him of the murder of Gloucester and asserting that the shame the king has brought on the family will kill him in any case. Gaunt retires to bed, asserting that he will soon die. The Earl of Northumberland brings word that Gaunt has in fact died, and Richard immediately declares that he will confiscate his late uncle's wealth. York, horrified, chastises the king for this illegal seizure, comparing it ominously with the usurpation of a crown. He then exits. The king, ignoring this outburst, plans his departure for Ireland and appoints York to be governor of England in his absence. He leaves with his entourage. The remaining nobles—Northumberland, Lord Ross, and Lord Willoughby—discuss the king's abuses. They fear that the seizure of Gaunt's estate will set a precedent that threatens all aristocrats. Northumberland reveals that Bolingbroke is returning to England with an army, and the noblemen decide to join him.

Act 2, Scene 2

Queen Isabel speaks to Bushy and Bagot of her strange grief and depression, stimulated by Richard's departure for Ireland. Greene arrives with news that Bolingbroke has invaded England and been joined by several noblemen. York arrives, bewailing the difficulty of defending the realm when Richard has taken all available armed forces with him. A Servant (1) brings word of the death of the Duchess of Gloucester, from whom York had hoped to borrow money. York, undone by this news, wishes Richard had cut off his head so that he would not have to deal with his present dilemma: Both king and invader are his kinsmen, and he feels he owes loyalty to each of them. Uncertain what to do, York leaves with the Queen. Bushy, Bagot, and Greene decide to flee, realizing that trouble lies ahead for the king's favorites.

Act 2, Scene 3

Bolingbroke and Northumberland, on the march, meet Northumberland's son Harry Percy, who brings news that York and a small force are stationed nearby at Berkeley Castle. Ross and Willoughby also join the invading army. Lord Berkeley enters. He bears York's demand that Bolingbroke explain his presence in England. York himself follows, and he castigates his nephew for disloyalty to the king. Bolingbroke insists that he has returned only to claim what is rightfully his—the estate of his father, Gaunt. Bolingbroke's supporters back him up. York continues to insist on the treasonous nature of their opposition to the king, but he declares that he will remain neutral, lacking power enough to oppose them, and he offers them the hospitality of the castle. Bolingbroke says that he must first go to BRISTOL to capture Bushy and Bagot.

Act 2, Scene 4

A Welsh Captain tells the Earl of Salisbury that his troops cannot be prevented from deserting Richard's cause, after 10 days with no word from the king. He tells of rumors that Richard is dead and cites dire omens that seem to support them. Salisbury foresees Richard's fall.

Act 3, Scene 1

Bushy and Greene are prisoners of Bolingbroke, who condemns them to death, asserting that they have misled the king and caused bad relations between the king and his queen. Further, Bolingbroke alleges that they caused the king to banish him and that they then took his property in his absence.

Act 3, Scene 2

Richard, having returned from Ireland, responds to news of Bolingbroke's successes with wild emotional swings, veering between confidence in divine support and dark despair. Finally, informed that York has joined Bolingbroke, he subsides into resignation and concedes defeat.

Act 3, Scene 3

Bolingbroke, outside FLINT CASTLE, learns that the king has sequestered himself within, and he sends Northumberland to negotiate with him, offering to submit completely to Richard provided that Gaunt's estates are restored to him and that his banishment is repealed. Richard appears with kingly pomp and arrogance, but he immediately agrees to Bolingbroke's terms. Awaiting Bolingbroke himself, Richard falls into despair, ranting about his own deposition and death. When Bolingbroke appears, Richard accepts the successful rebel's pretended submission but remarks that he has merely yielded to strength.

Act 3, Scene 4

The disconsolate Queen hides herself in a garden, hoping to overhear political news in the conversation of the Gardener and his assistants. The Gardener tells of the executions of Bushy and Greene and speculates that the king, having been seized by Bolingbroke, will soon be deposed. The Queen erupts in anger, demanding to know why the Gardener thinks this; he asserts that Richard's situation is common knowledge in London. The Queen, enraged and in despair, leaves for the city.

Act 4, Scene 1

Bolingbroke holds court in WESTMINSTER HALL. Bagot, who has turned informer, accuses Aumerle of having plotted to murder the Duke of Gloucester. After much argument, the debate is postponed, to be settled at a future trial by combat. York brings word of Richard's willingness to abdicate. The Bishop of Carlisle speaks against the deposition of God's appointed ruler, predicting civil war as a consequence. He is arrested by Northumberland and placed in the custody of the Abbot of Westminster. Richard is summoned, and he reluctantly surrenders his crown and scepter to Bolingbroke. Looking in a mirror, he reflects on the fragility of kingly glory, and he smashes the glass to prove his point. Richard is taken away, and Bolingbroke, departing with his entourage, sets the date for his own coronation. Aumerle, the Abbot, and Carlisle are left behind, and they agree to plot against Bolingbroke's usurpation.

Act 5, Scene 1

The Queen intercepts Richard as he is escorted to the TOWER OF LONDON and tries to raise his spirits.

He recommends patient resignation. Northumberland appears with a change of plans: Richard is to be taken to POMFRET CASTLE, and the Queen is to be banished to FRANCE. Northumberland resists their pleas that they be permitted to remain together, and the royal couple bid each other an emotional farewell.

Act 5, Scene 2
The Duke of York, after describing Bolingbroke's triumphant entry into London to his Duchess, asserts his adherence, however dismayed, to the new king. He discovers that his son, Aumerle, is part of a plot against Bolingbroke, and he sets off to warn the king and, to alleviate the stain on his honor, turn in his son. The Duchess fails to persuade him against this course; she then tells Aumerle to ride at top speed and reach the King before his father can and plead for mercy.

Act 5, Scene 3
Bolingbroke laments that his delinquent son, the Prince, spends his time with criminals and harlots, but he hopes for better behavior in the future. Aumerle enters and extracts a promise of a pardon for an offense that he wishes to confess. York arrives and warns the king of the plot against him, recommending severity. The Duchess enters and pleads for mercy for Aumerle, and Bolingbroke grants it.

Act 5, Scene 4
Sir Piers Exton, reflecting on remarks made by Bolingbroke, believes that the new king wants Richard killed, and he resolves to do the deed himself.

Act 5, Scene 5
Richard, in his prison cell, meditates on his lonely, defeated state. A former Groom of Richard's appears, offering sympathy and raising the prisoner's spirits. However, he is ousted by the Keeper, who brings Richard's meal. The Keeper refuses to taste the food for poison, as is his usual practice, citing orders from Exton. Aggravated, Richard strikes him, and the Keeper's cries summon a group of murderers, led by Exton, who assault Richard. He fights back but is killed. Exton, conscience-stricken, regrets the deed.

Act 5, Scene 6
Bolingbroke receives word of the final defeat of resistance to his rule, including that of the Bishop of Carlisle, who is brought in as a prisoner. Bolingbroke forgives him magnanimously. Exton arrives with a coffin bearing Richard. He expects thanks, but Bolingbroke repudiates him, deploring the deed and regretting that his words had sparked it. He declares that he will lead a crusade to the Holy Land to atone for his part in Richard's death.

COMMENTARY
Shakespeare wrote *Richard II* entirely in verse. The measured cadences of iambic pentameter lend a musical grandeur to the play's most didactic and explanatory passages, and the medium of verse is natural to its highly charged language. In this play emotions are expressed by means of heightened rhetoric. For instance, the parting of Richard and Queen Isabel in 5.1 sparks an exchange of mechanical couplets that may seem emotionally sterile. But taken over the entire work, such language impels respect, for it is boldly apparent that the characters are in the grip of something higher and more important than their own personalities. The total dominance of poetry lends the play a pointedly aesthetic tone, in striking contrast to its ostensible subject matter, a military coup. The play depicts no battles; in fact, there is little action of any kind. A trial by combat is scheduled but does not take place; an army is assembled but does not fight. York vows to resist Bolingbroke but lacks the strength to do so, and Richard crumbles immediately. Action is systematically thwarted until Richard's murder in Act 5. Language, in the form of poetry, is paramount. The disparity between political history and poetic tone points to the existence of a second level of meaning: This play is about more than the deeds of historical figures. *Richard II* basically deals with the disturbing nature of historical change rather than the events themselves.

In addition, *Richard II* is a moving human document. Richard's personality is the most prominent feature of the play, and in one of his most brilliant portraits, Shakespeare shows us a gallant but failing human effort to come to terms with change. Richard marks a significant stage in the development of the playwright's art, for he is the first of Shakespeare's tragic heroes whose personal flaws help to bring about his own downfall. His own inadequacies as king lead inexorably to his deposition. However, Richard's greater significance lies in his response to his fate. He does not resist his destiny but accepts it. In 5.5, stirred by the beauty of music and by the love of the Groom who visits him, the imprisoned Richard comes to terms with his humanity and the suffering that goes with it. With this acceptance, Richard—and we who respond to him—transcend the universal fate and thus triumph over death.

Furthermore, Richard is persistently contrasted with the world around him. At its most superficial level, the play depicts the fall of one king and the rise of another, and this automatically invites comparison between the two rulers. Richard's poetic diction and his assertion of transcendent values stand in marked contrast with the prosaic speech and practical concerns of Bolingbroke and York, and even of the Queen, who exhorts him to fight. The play presents a bold juxtaposition of utilitarian and artistic temperaments.

Yet the play also involves a comparison of worlds. Richard's sensibility, his poetic utterances, and his self-conscious awareness of his royal status are grounded in a world of ceremonious spectacle. The gorgeous tournament of 1.1 and Richard's brilliant rhetoric on the divine right of kings, as in 3.2.36–62, have a heavy grandeur that is reinforced by such formal speeches as the conventionally high-flown grief of the Queen in 3.4 and the elaborate metaphor constructed by the Gardener in the same scene. Richard is a medieval king, fully conscious of his divine appointment to rule; his personal weaknesses emphasize the pathos of being the last such ruler in history. Bolingbroke represents a new world, that of the Renaissance. He is a Machiavellian, ready to assume any posture required by the needs of the moment. This brings him political success, but it also makes him an unknowable personality, a symbol of faceless ambition. By contrast, Richard's emotional self-exposure is much more humanly sympathetic. The rising and falling monarchs are most strikingly opposed in 4.1, in which the mere presence of the nearly silent Bolingbroke has as powerful an effect as Richard's polemics. Each regal figure attempts to impose his own reality on the scene: Richard plays the tragically overthrown representative of God, while Bolingbroke maintains the importance of legal rights and social order.

It is profoundly ironic that the anointed ruler has subverted public order, while the blasphemous rebel upholds legality. Richard, though legitimate, has failed to lead his nation and moreover has exploited the kingdom shamelessly, while the usurper Bolingbroke acts in the name of legal redress and proves to be a strong leader who brings England into a new era. Underlying this paradox is a question that was posed by Shakespeare's portrayal of King Henry VI and that was to be answered by that of Henry V. Can the spiritual qualities that seem to offer the greatest human rewards coexist with the practical, manipulative skills needed to govern a society? In *Richard II* a potentially successful government has been created, but only at the cost of eroding the spiritual underpinnings of society. The civil disorders to come are the direct result, as Carlisle's predictions in 4.1.136–147 and 322–323 remind us.

Both principal figures of *Richard II* achieve their potential yet remain ungratified: Richard's spiritual depths open upon an abyss, while Bolingbroke's political success is dampened by the need for suppression, beginning with Richard's murder. This situation reflects a contradiction at the heart of the Elizabethan conception of power: a monarch was still considered to be ordained by God, as had been true in medieval times, but a newer notion dictated that he or she was expressly sent to serve the people. This concept, which was part of early modern Europe's emergence from feudalism, was related to political developments—in England, it was part of the TUDOR DYNASTY's justification of Henry VII's conquest (enacted in *Richard III*): the deposed king had failed to serve the people, and the new king had been sent by God to do so. Thus a ruler should not be deposed, but if he were, the usurper should not be replaced either. In this conundrum rested the legitimacy of the reign of Queen Elizabeth I (see Elizabeth I in *Henry VIII*) and the established politics of Shakespeare's own day. In *Richard II* it is demonstrated in the ultimate inadequacy of both the usurped king and the successful rebel.

Possible solutions to this puzzling irony are offered by Shakespeare, but only as hints concerning the play's sequels. *Richard II* was consciously written as the first in a series of plays, and it is not intended to come to a conclusion. Bolingbroke, soon to be King Henry IV, becomes more magnanimous as the play closes, pardoning Carlisle and Aumerle and spurning Exton. He turns to religion as well. Thus an improvement in the character of the usurper is at least tentatively proposed. However, Bolingbroke's essential cynicism in this play makes such a solution difficult to believe. More promising is the introduction of a character who does not actually appear: Bolingbroke's son, Prince Hal. His bold ridicule of his father's success, as reported by Percy in 5.3.16–19, may seem immature and unproductive, but it is undeniably fresh and youthful; Hal, at least, is entirely outside the coils of politics. His time will come (as the audience knows)—as Henry V, he will be a successful king. Thus history generates its own solution to history's dilemma: Whatever may befall a king or a world, youth is always preparing new history.

Finally, too, the invocation of the future suggests the larger framework of *Richard II* and of all the HIS-TORY PLAYS. *Richard II* introduces the grand theme of the entire cycle: the passage of England from prosperity lost through lack of respect for a divinely ordained order, to civil disruption and war, to a resumption of prosperity under the Tudors.

As was his custom, Shakespeare took some liberties with the history his play chronicles, tightening the pace where it is dramatically desirable—particularly in 2.1 and 4.1, where in each case the happenings of months are compressed into a single day—but the treatment of historical events is much more straightforward than is the case in the earlier histories. Bolingbroke is probably a more deliberate rebel than the playwright's sources demand, and Richard is certainly a more ineffective king, but these distortions serve an aesthetic purpose, illuminating greater issues. Shakespeare always subordinates historical details to a playwright's values, and *Richard II* is, above all, a dramatic presentation of human responses to inexorable change.

SOURCES OF THE PLAY

Shakespeare's primary source for the historical material in *Richard II* was Raphael HOLINSHED's *Chronicles of England, Scotland, and Ireland* (2nd ed., 1587). In addition, Act 5 was particularly influenced by an epic

poem, *The Civil Wars between the two Houses of York and Lancaster,* by Samuel DANIEL, which was published in early 1595, just as Shakespeare was working on this play. Another important source was a popular anthology of biographies in verse, A MIRROR FOR MAG-ISTRATES (1559), which contains lives of Richard, Northumberland, Mowbray, and the Duke of Gloucester. Shakespeare's John of Gaunt, very different from Holinshed's, was probably derived from the characterization of the Duke of Gloucester in the anonymous play WOODSTOCK (ca. 1592–95), which provided many other small hints to Shakespeare. Another influence may have been the Gaunt presented in Jean FROISSART's *Chroniques,* a French history that Shakespeare could have known in the English translation (1523–25) by Lord BERNERS. Two French works written in defense of Richard in his own time, an anonymous chronicle known as the TRAÏSON and a poem by Jean CRÉTON, *Histoire du Roy d'Angleterre Richard,* may have been available to Shakespeare and have been suggested by scholars as possible sources for minor elements. *Edward II* (ca. 1592) by Christopher MARLOWE may have influenced Shakespeare's general conception of a flawed king whose downfall is triggered by immoral behavior.

TEXT OF THE PLAY

Shakespeare completed the text of *Richard II* sometime before its publication in mid-1597 and after the publication of Daniel's *Civil War* in early 1595. The similarity of its lyrical tone to that of *Love's Labour's Lost, Romeo and Juliet,* and *A Midsummer Night's Dream,* all written in 1594 and 1595, suggest that *Richard II* was probably written in 1595.

The play was published by Andrew WISE in a QUARTO edition, known as Q1, in 1597. The play must have been popular, because Wise brought out two more quartos (Q2, Q3) in 1598. (*Pericles* is the only other Shakespeare play to have appeared in two quartos in the same year.) These editions were reprinted from Q1 and are inferior to it, having many more errors, although some corrections were also made. Wise sold his right to print the play to Mathew LAW in 1603, and Law produced Q4 (1608) and Q5 (1615), each drawn from its immediate predecessor. Q4 contains the first printing of the deposition scene (4.1.154–318), which had earlier been withheld, presumably due to government CEN-SORSHIP. It seems to have been printed from a "memorial" version, dictated or written from memory by an actor. In 1623 the FIRST FOLIO contained a version of the play (F1) that appears to have been printed from Q3, except for its last few columns, taken from Q5. (This peculiarity is thought to reflect a damaged copy of Q3, repaired with two pages from Q5.) However, F1 contains a version of the deposition scene that is greatly superior to that in Q4 and Q5, where it is clearly corrupt. This is assumed to have come from a PROMPTBOOK that was also used to correct the Quarto copy.

Q1 is thought to have been printed from a transcript of Shakespeare's own manuscript, for it contains irregular stage directions and other signs of the author's informal version, along with errors that seem likely to have been made by someone who already knew the play, probably a member of the cast in an early production. Thus Q1 is the basis for most modern editions, supplemented by F1, from which is taken, in particular, 4.1.154–318.

THEATRICAL HISTORY OF THE PLAY

Its repeated publication in the 1590s and early 17th century suggests that *Richard II* was quite popular with early audiences. The earliest surviving record of a particular performance is a startling one. On February 7, 1601, the CHAMBERLAIN'S MEN were commissioned by backers of Robert Devereux, Earl of ESSEX, to perform the play at the GLOBE THEATRE. The earl's abortive rebellion against Queen Elizabeth took place on the following day, and it was apparently thought that the enactment of Richard's deposition would encourage the population of LONDON to support a latter-day usurpation. It had no such effect, and although inquiries were made by the government, no action was taken against the acting company or Shakespeare.

The second known performance of the play is also surprising: in 1607 it was performed aboard an English ship off the coast of Africa. No other particular performances during Shakespeare's lifetime are known, although the play was staged at the Globe again in 1631.

In 1681 Nahum TATE produced an adaptation of *Richard II, The Sicilian Usurper,* that was suppressed

by a nervous government, despite its changed setting. Other adaptations were produced over the next century, often with material borrowed from other plays, including *King Lear* and *Titus Andronicus.* Shakespeare's play was produced several times in the late 1730s, but the play was not generally popular again until the 19th century. In a highly successful production of 1857, Charles KEAN used more than 500 extras in a spectacular rendition of Bolingbroke's triumph. Beerbohm TREE and William POEL also directed versions of the play. *Richard II* was extremely popular in the 20th century. John GIELGUD and Maurice EVANS were particularly successful Richards. The play was produced many times, both by itself and in cycles with other history plays, on stage and on TELEVISION. Most recently, in 2003 the BBC televised a live performance of *Richard II* from the new Shakespeare's Globe Theatre in London. (See also WANAMAKER, SAM.)

CHARACTERS

Abbot of Westminster (William Colchester) (ca. 1345–1420) Historical figure and character in *Richard II,* a conspirator against Henry Bolingbroke. After Richard II is formally deposed in 4.1, the Abbot conspires with the Bishop of Carlisle and the Duke of Aumerle to kill the usurper. The plot is discovered, and the Abbot's death, apparently of a bad conscience, is reported in 5.6.19–21. The historical abbot (born William Colchester) was pardoned by Bolingbroke, by then King Henry IV, after one month in prison, and was permitted to retain his office, which he held until his death. Shakespeare may have confused the abbot's fate with Carlisle's, as reported (inaccurately) by HOLINSHED. The Bishop is said to have died upon capture, "more through feare than force of sicknesse."

Another Lord Minor character in *Richard II,* an accuser of the Duke of Aumerle in 4.1. The Lord asserts that Aumerle falsely denied his complicity in an earlier murder plot, and he challenges Aumerle to a trial by combat. His accusation and challenge follow several others and lend a vivid sense of excess and confusion to the scene, thereby suggesting the potential for chaos produced by the victory of Henry Bolingbroke over King Richard II.

Aumerle, Edward York, Duke of (ca. 1373–1415) Historical figure and character in *Richard II*, a supporter of Richard II. Aumerle is a flattering courtier whose loyalty to King Richard is later undercut by his willingness to betray his fellow conspirators, who attempted to restore the deposed king, in order to save his own life. Aumerle displays his hypocrisy with seeming pride in 1.4, when he boasts of having feigned affection for Henry Bolingbroke. He offers advice to Richard at several points; in 3.2 he suggests firmness in resisting Bolingbroke but then shifts to less honorable stalling tactics (3.3.131–132). After Bolingbroke has triumphed, Bagot accuses Aumerle of complicity in Richard's murder of the Duke of Gloucester; Bolingbroke postpones the question, but we hear in 5.2 that Aumerle has been stripped of his dukedom (though he continues to be designated Aumerle throughout the play). In this scene Aumerle's father, the Duke of York, discovers his son's involvement in the Abbot's plot against Bolingbroke and angrily declares that he will inform the new king. Aumerle's mother, the Duchess of York, sends him to court to beg for mercy before York can expose him. She follows and successfully pleads for his life. This episode contrasts Aumerle's devious character with his father's forthright patriotism, his mother's maternal passion, and Bolingbroke's generosity.

The historical Aumerle was a favorite of King Richard; when the Duke of Gloucester was killed, before the play opens, Aumerle was awarded much of the dead man's property and was created Duke of Albemarle (corrupted to Aumerle in Elizabethan English), Aumerle accompanied Richard to Ireland, and it was apparently his bad advice that led the king to delay his return to England upon Bolingbroke's arrival and then to dismiss his army when he got there. Further, in an episode probably unknown to Shakespeare, Aumerle abandoned Richard for Bolingbroke at that point; therefore, when he joined the Abbot of Westminster's conspiracy against Bolingbroke, he was being doubly treacherous, and he was shortly to betray his fellow conspirators as well. His father's part in this action is probably not historical, although it is reported in Shakespeare's chief source, HOLINSHED's *Chronicles*. In any case, Aumerle was pardoned by Bolingbroke, by then HENRY IV, but his mother's involvement is entirely Shakespeare's invention; the duchess had actually been dead for six years. Moreover, to increase the pathos of her plea, Shakespeare presented Aumerle as an only child; the duke actually had a younger brother, the Earl of Cambridge, who is a character in *Henry V*. Aumerle himself reappears as the Duke of York in that play.

Bagot, Sir John (d. ca. 1400) Historical figure and character in *Richard II*, a supporter of Richard II. Bagot, with his colleagues John Bushy and Henry Greene, is one of the "caterpillars" (2.3.165) whose influence on the king is said by Bolingbroke to have been disastrous for England. They recognize that their position as favorites of the king is likely to prove dangerous if Bolingbroke defeats him, and in 2.2 they decide to seek safety when Bolingbroke appears. Bushy and Greene are captured and executed, but Bagot joins the king in Ireland and thus lives to appear before the triumphant Bolingbroke at the beginning of 4.1. He brings an accusation against the Duke of Aumerle, presumably in exchange for clemency, and then disappears from the play.

The historical Bagot was a lesser aristocrat of WARWICKSHIRE and had originally been a supporter of the murdered Duke of Gloucester. He was later recruited to Richard's cause and became close to the king; it was at Bagot's residence in COVENTRY that Richard stayed at the time of the trial by combat between Bolingbroke and Mowbray that is depicted in 1.3. After the fall of the king, Bagot was imprisoned by Bolingbroke in the TOWER OF LONDON, where he is last known to have been alive.

Barbary Horse named in *Richard II*. The Groom who visits Richard II in prison in 5.5 tells the deposed king that his successor, Bolingbroke, has ridden Barbary at his coronation and that the horse carried its new rider "So proudly as if he disdain'd the ground" (5.5.83). Richard is initially angry with his former steed, but he then berates himself for railing at the animal.

Shakespeare apparently invented this episode, which appears in none of his sources. Barbary is also the name of a highly valued breed of horse exported from North Africa, itself known as Barbary.

Berkeley, Lord Thomas (d. 1417) Historical figure and minor character in *Richard II*, an ally of the Duke of York. A GLOUCESTERSHIRE nobleman whose castle has assumed strategic importance in the rebellion of Henry Bolingbroke against King Richard II, Berkeley greets Bolingbroke on York's behalf.

The historical Berkeley apparently allied himself with Bollingbroke when York did, for he served on the commission of noblemen that issued the formal declaration of Richard's deposition, and he opposed the rebellion against the new king, capturing the Duke of Surrey and the Earl of Salisbury. He turned his prisoners over to a mob, who killed them; their deaths are reported in 5.6.8. In later years Berkeley fought for Henry IV, as Bolingbroke became known, against Owen Glendower.

Bolingbroke, Henry (Henry Bullingbrook, later King Henry IV) (1366–1413) Historical figure and character in *Richard II*, the usurper of the throne from King Richard II. (The same individual appears as King Henry IV in *1* and *2 Henry IV*.) Bolingbroke's rise to the throne balances Richard's fall, and Bolingbroke, like Richard, undergoes personal change. In 1.1 he uses elaborate rhetoric to accuse Mowbray of murdering the Duke of Gloucester, triggering a trial by combat. This duel is averted in 1.3 when King Richard banishes both combatants from England. We learn in 1.2 that Gloucester's murder was Richard's doing, as Bolingbroke must have known. It is clear that Bolingbroke is hostile to Richard from the very beginning and that the King has no effective response. Bolingbroke's triumph can already be foreseen. (Shakespeare will have assumed that his audience knew that Bolingbroke was to become King in any case.) Although Bolingbroke accepts his banishment, we know that he will shortly reappear as Richard's enemy. Thus Bolingbroke seems an unscrupulous schemer from the beginning.

When he returns from exile to claim his inheritance—the estates of his father, John of Gaunt—his first actions reinforce this impression. In 2.3 he welcomes Percy, Ross, and Willoughby as his allies with apparently frank gratitude, but having seen his ambition, we doubt his sincerity. Moreover, the playwright will probably have counted on his audience's familiarity with the fate of Percy, who later died in rebellion against Bolingbroke (as is enacted in *1 Henry IV*). Later in this scene, Bolingbroke offers an elaborate rationale for his rebellion against the crown when he is criticized by the Duke of York; it is clear that he thinks it important to maintain an appearance of justified innocence, masking his ambition with assertions of political rectitude. Further, he proclaims that he has come only to claim his inheritance, but he also proceeds to execute the alleged villains Bushy and Greene for "crimes" that are actually offenses against Bolingbroke personally rather than against the state.

Significantly, Bolingbroke's diction changes at this point. As Richard's strikingly poetic manner of speaking becomes prominent in his emotional collapse, Bolingbroke adopts a plainer mode of speech intended to reveal his motives. His practical realism is emblematic of the new era in politics that he represents. Bolingbroke is a Machiavellian leader, prepared to take whatever measures are necessary to acquire and preserve power, whereas Richard, relying on long-standing tradition, believes in the ancient theory of divine right. The passing of the romantic medieval world represented by that tradition is a major theme of the play. Bolingbroke's easy reliance on his own strength is a new attribute of kingship, reflected in his speech and manner as soon as he begins to assert his power.

A third Bolingbroke, the generous victor, begins to assume importance in 3.1. Although he undertakes a ruthless act of state in condemning Bushy and Greene, he anticipates his later development in demonstrating his sympathy for Richard's Queen, instructing that she be treated well. Bolingbroke's magnanimity is further stressed in Act 5, when he pardons Carlisle and Aumerle and when he repudiates Richard's murder. The playwright is clearly paving the way for Bolingbroke's appearance as Henry IV.

The historical Bolingbroke was Richard's close contemporary, although the playwright makes the usurper younger than the deposed King (e.g., in 3.3.204–205) to emphasize his greater vitality. Henry Bolingbroke was so called because he was born at Bolingbroke, a castle in Lincolnshire. (The alternative version of his name, Bullingbrook, first used in the Q1 edition of the play, suggests its probable pronunciation in Elizabethan English.) As a young man, Bolingbroke belonged to a political faction, led by Gloucester, that nearly dethroned Richard in 1387. However, he remained aloof from the politics of the court throughout the 1390s, spending much of his time as a crusader in Lithuania, and he seems to have had nothing to do with the conflict of 1397 that resulted in Gloucester's death. His motivation in challenging Mowbray two years later is unclear, although the play makes it appear to be ambition for the throne. Actually, even after his invasion, Bolingbroke may have intended only to claim his inheritance; it is unclear when he decided to seize power.

Shakespeare invented several aspects of Bolingbroke's assumption of the crown. The deposition scene, in which Bolingbroke formally displaces Richard, is entirely fictitious; the triumphant usurper had no interest in providing his defeated opponent with a public platform. Similarly, his instigation of the murder of Richard by Piers EXTON is unhistorical. The episode, in which Bolingbroke vows to go on crusade to atone for Exton's crime, is intended to introduce the religious tendencies of Henry IV. Although the playwright took this incident from his chief source and certainly believed it, Bolingbroke's repudiation of Exton after the murder is Shakespeare's fiction. A similar story concerning Thomas à Becket and Henry II was one of several apocryphal anecdotes that the playwright might have used as a model; an account in PLUTARCH was another.

Bushy, Sir John (Sir John Bussy) (d. 1399) Historical figure and character in *Richard II,* a supporter of Richard II. Bushy, John Bagot, and Henry Greene are the "caterpillars" (2.3.165) whose influence on the king is alleged by Henry Bolingbroke to have been disastrous for England. Bushy attempts to comfort the distraught Queen Isabel in 2.2; his elaborate courtier's language seems merely grotesque to modern ears, unaware that it parodies 16th-century religious meditations. Later in 2.2 Bushy, Bagot, and Greene recognize that their position as favorites of the king is likely to prove dangerous if their master is defeated by Bolingbroke. The three decide to flee when Bolingbroke approaches; Bushy and Greene seek safety in BRISTOL Castle, but Bolingbroke captures them and sentences them to death.

The historical Bushy was a minor politician; he was frequently Speaker of the House of Commons—not an important post in his day—and was also three times Sheriff of London. Originally a supporter of the Duke of Gloucester, he was recruited to Richard's party in the 1390s, before the murder of the duke.

Captain Minor character in *Richard II,* the Welsh commander of troops who desert the cause of Richard II in 2.4, after the king has not appeared for many days. The Captain tells of rumors that Richard has died and cites menacing omens that seem to substantiate them. Shakespeare may have associated the Captain with Owen Glendower, who is mentioned in 3.1.43.

Carlisle, Thomas Merke, Bishop of (d. 1409) Historical figure and character in *Richard II,* a supporter of King Richard II. Carlisle accompanies Richard on his return from Ireland to face Henry Bolingbroke, and he warns the king against inaction, but his speech is equivocal. His ambivalence is immediately emphasized by the Duke of Aumerle's much more pointed statement of the same warning. Nonetheless, Carlisle is the only defender of Richard in the deposition scene (4.1). In a formal speech he appeals to the assembled aristocrats not to violate the sanctity of a king divinely placed on the throne—"What subject can give sentence on his king?" (4.1.121), he asks rhetorically—and he predicts disaster for England if the deposition is carried out. Northumberland promptly arrests him for treason, and he is placed in the custody of the Abbot of Westminster. At the close of the scene Carlisle joins the Abbot and Aumerle in a plot against Bolingbroke. At the end of the play he is brought before Bolingbroke, now King Henry IV, who pardons him, referring to his honorable character.

The historical Carlisle was a Benedictine monk who served Richard ably as an administrator and was rewarded with his bishopric as a result. He did not protest Henry's accession; his speech is drawn from accounts of his opposition to a later proposal to try Richard on criminal charges. These accounts may have been invented, however, for they derive from an unreliable, propagandistic tract, probably written by a member of Queen Isabel's French household, that was the source for Shakespeare's source, HOLINSHED's *Chronicles*. However, regardless of its historical reality, Carlisle's speech presents an important aspect of Tudor political dogma: the citizenry may not judge its monarch in any way. This idea is emphasized in Holinshed, and it is present throughout the HISTORY PLAYS.

Carlisle did participate in the abbot's conspiracy, but he was not willingly pardoned by Henry. Tried and convicted, he was dismissed from his see, and his life was spared only by papal intervention.

Duchess of Gloucester, Eleanor de Bohun (1367–1399)   Historical figure and minor character in *Richard II*, sister-in-law of John of Gaunt and widow of Duke Thomas of Gloucester. In 1.2 the Duchess visits Gaunt to discuss her husband's murder. She blames King Richard II for his death and passionately entreats Gaunt to avenge it. He insists that vengeance against a king may be taken only by God, and the Duchess wrathfully expresses the hope that Henry Bolingbroke will kill Mowbray, whom she says murdered Gloucester at the king's order. Then she resignedly asserts that she will soon die of grief and departs for her home. Her death is reported in 2.2.97. The episode casts light on the conflicts of 1.1 and 1.3, making clear to the audience that Richard is implicated in Gloucester's murder and that Bolingbroke's accusation of Mowbray is embarrassing to the king.

Although the Duchess appears to be Gaunt's contemporary, she was actually a generation younger, being only 32 when she died, reportedly of grief at the death of her only son. Shakespeare's rendering of her as an older woman helps to heighten the pathos of the vanishing medieval world that colors his story of the king's fall.

Duchess of York, Isabel of Castile (1355–1393) Historical figure and minor character in *Richard II*, mother of the Duke of Aumerle. When her husband, the Duke of York, discovers Aumerle's part in a plot against the new king (Henry Bolingbroke), he insists on protecting the monarch by revealing the conspiracy, exposing his son to charges of treason. The Duchess's objections go unheeded, and in 5.3,

after sending Aumerle ahead, she goes to the king herself and argues against her husband, opposing her motherly anguish to his concern for the state. She receives Bolingbroke's pardon of Aumerle with great gratitude. A powerful dramatic presentation of maternal passion, the episode also serves to stress the magnanimity of Bolingbroke in preparation for his role as King Henry IV in *1* and *2 Henry IV*.

The incident is entirely fictitious; the real Duchess Isabel had been dead for years before the events depicted in the play took place. The Duke of York had remarried, but the second duchess, besides not being Aumerle's mother, had nothing to do with his being pardoned by King Henry.

Exton, Sir Piers (Pierce)   Character in *Richard II*, the murderer of Richard II. Exton, an ambitious nobleman who wishes to curry favor with Henry Bolingbroke, the new king, decides in 5.4 that he will murder the old one, believing that Bolingbroke has expressed a desire that this deed be done. In 5.5 Exton leads a gang of hired murderers against Richard in his cell at POMFRET CASTLE, and they kill the ex-king, although Exton suffers pangs of conscience. He presents the corpse to Bolingbroke, now Henry IV, hoping for a reward, but the king rejects him.

Shakespeare took the account of Exton's deed from his chief source, HOLINSHED, but the anonymous French author of Holinshed's source, probably a member of Queen Isabel's household, apparently invented the story. No other early source mentions Exton or supposes that Richard died violently; the only other contemporary chronicler asserts that Richard was starved to death, either by his gaolers or by his own will. This source, also French, has its own propagandistic bias, and Richard may well have died of natural causes. His skeleton was exhumed and examined in the 1870s, and no evidence of violence was found.

We cannot say conclusively how the ex-king died, but, in any case, Henry IV's rejection of the murderer appears to be Shakespeare's own addition to the tale, possibly in anticipation of the opening of *1 Henry IV*. A similar story concerning Thomas à Becket and Henry II was only one of several apocryphal anecdotes that might have served the playwright as a model; an account in PLUTARCH was another.

Fitzwater, Lord Walter (Lord Walter Fitzwalter) (ca. 1368–1407) Historical figure and minor character in *Richard II*, a supporter of Henry Bolingbroke. In 4.1 Fitzwater seconds Bagot's assertion that Aumerle had boasted of killing the Duke of Gloucester, and he challenges Aumerle to a trial by combat. He is in turn challenged by the Duke of Surrey, as the scene erupts in charges and counter-charges. The episode reflects England's political chaos, for Bolingbroke has just displaced King Richard II. In 5.6 Fitzwater reports the defeat of a rebellion against Bolingbroke, and he is promised rewards by the new king.

Gardener Minor character in *Richard II*, a worker in the household of the Duke of York. In 3.4 the Gardener and his assistants discuss the news of the capture and likely deposition of King Richard II by Henry Bolingbroke. In their conversation the garden is an extended metaphor for the state: Just as a garden must be constantly tended if it is to bear flowers and fruits, so must the state be kept in order by its rulers if it is to function healthily. Thus the Gardener summarizes one of the play's important moral points.

The episode also has another function. Queen Isabel overhears the Gardener's remarks and reacts with hysterical anger. Although she curses him, the Gardener is sympathetic to her grief, and his response neatly emphasizes the human side of Richard's story. Up to this point we have been encouraged to judge the King harshly as a self-centered and unreliable ruler; here, the Gardener's pity stirs an awareness that Richard's fall, however deserved it may be, has a personal dimension. Our sympathies begin to shift, preparing us for the tragic and philosophical Richard of the second half of the play.

Gaunt, John of (Duke of Lancaster) (1340–1399) Historical figure and character in *Richard II*, King Richard II's uncle and father of Henry Bolingbroke. Gaunt, though he dies in 2.1, is an important figure. He represents a grand tradition of statesmanlike

patriotism and honor, encouraging Bolingbroke, in 1.1 and 1.3, toward the ideal of obedience to the King, whom he believes rules by divine right. On the same grounds, he resists the Duchess of Gloucester's demands in 1.2 for vengeance against the King for the murder of her husband, Gaunt's brother. Yet he is aware of Richard's failings, and before dying he chastises the King severely for ruining the country through overtaxation and self-indulgence. Preparing himself for this final encounter with Richard, he meditates on England in a patriotic passage that has been famous since it was first performed: "This royal throne of kings, this scept'red isle, . . . This blessed plot, this earth, this realm, this England, . . ." (2.1.40–50).

The historical Gaunt was a very different sort of man from the paragon of virtue presented in the play. Shakespeare altered the much more accurate portrait found in his principal source, HOLINSHED's *Chronicles*, in part because Queen Elizabeth I traced her ancestry to Gaunt, but also in order to hold up an ideal representative of the chivalric age, whose passing is a major theme of the play. Gaunt, named for his birth in English-occupied Ghent, in Flanders, was a greedy and aggressive aristocrat, devoted to his own interests, not to the common welfare. Before the time of the play, he spent several years—and vast amounts of English wealth—fighting in Spain in an unsuccessful attempt to seize the crown of Castile for himself. He was widely detested in England, and during the great revolt of 1381 his palace in London was thoroughly sacked by gleeful crowds.

Gloucester, Thomas of Woodstock, Duke of (1355–1397) Historical figure mentioned prominently in *Richard II*, brother of John of Gaunt, uncle of King Richard II, and husband of the Duchess of Gloucester. Although he does not appear in the play, the Duke of Gloucester, often called Woodstock, is an important figure in Acts 1–2. His murder, which occurred six months prior to the play's opening, sparks the crises that lead to Richard's deposition.

In 1.1 Henry Bolingbroke accuses Mowbray of complicity in the death of Gloucester, who died in Mowbray's custody in the prison of the English fortress at Calais. In 1.2 Gaunt and the Duchess discuss Gloucester's death: they know that Mowbray did indeed kill the duke, and that he did so under the king's orders. In 4.1, just before Richard's deposition, the murder is again mentioned—Richard's favorite, the Duke of Aumerle, is now implicated—to reinforce our sense of Richard's guilt. Gloucester's murder is given importance as a symptom of illness in the body politic, evidence that Richard's fall has been made inevitable by his own misdeeds.

Gloucester is presented as a splendid figure of humanity. Gaunt, in his dying speech to Richard, refers to Gloucester as a "plain, well-meaning soul" (2.1.128), alluding both to his sturdy, unfashionable dress and his frank and open mode of speech. He is several times referred to as "noble." The duchess loved him as a husband, and she calls him "the model of [his father, the late King Edward III's] life" (1.2.28), thus equating him with England's greatest contemporary hero. Furthermore, the duchess points out that his royal blood should have made him sacrosanct; with his death, an important tradition has been defiled. Gloucester is thus a focus of nostalgia: He symbolizes the chivalric ethic of Edward III's day, a glorious age whose passing is one of the major themes of the play.

Shakespeare's Gloucester presents an image of the man that was widely held in the 16th century and that is reflected in a number of the playwright's sources, particularly the anonymous play WOODSTOCK. However, Shakespeare's principal source for *Richard II*, HOLINSHED's *Chronicles*, depicts Gloucester as a willfully violent man of little judgment. Modern scholarship finds Holinshed much nearer the mark. The historical Gloucester was a scheming, power-hungry aristocrat who clearly attempted to subvert the rule of his nephew.

When Edward III died in 1377, Gloucester, though young, was markedly abler than his older brothers, and he became the power behind the throne of the preadolescent King Richard. As Richard matured, he attempted to assume power himself. The resulting conflict with his uncle escalated into a brief civil war in 1387. Gloucester's faction was victorious, forcing the exile or execution of several of Richard's favorites and effectively ruling the country for a time. In 1389 Richard, now 22

years old, declared that he would rule, and the coalition of nobles accepted his sovereignty. Richard was a successful king, and he cultivated his own group of supporters, including former followers of Gloucester such as Mowbray and Bolingbroke. Another rupture between the king and his uncle came in 1397. This time Richard quickly prevailed, imprisoning his opponents with little difficulty. Gloucester was placed in Mowbray's custody and died in the prison at Calais, as the play states. Whether or not he was murdered under Richard's orders cannot be confirmed, but modern scholarship seconds the contemporary popular opinion that he was.

Greene (Green), Henry (d. 1399) Historical figure and character in *Richard II*, a supporter of King Richard II. Greene, John Bagot, and John Bushy are the "caterpillars" (2.3.165) whose influence on the King is alleged by Henry Bolingbroke to have been disastrous for England. In 1.4 Greene, the least prominent of the three, advises the king that he must address the pressing problem of a rebellion in Ireland. The three favorites recognize that their closeness to the king is likely to prove dangerous if their master is defeated by Bolingbroke. In 2.2 they decide to flee when Bolingbroke appears; Bush and Greene seek safety in BRISTOL Castle, but Bolingbroke captures them and sentences them to death.

Little is known about the historical Greene, a member of the gentry who was recruited for Richard's faction from among the supporters of the Duke of Gloucester some time before the Duke's murder.

Groom Minor character in *Richard II*, a supporter of Richard II. The Groom visits the imprisoned Richard in 5.5, in a demonstration of allegiance that raises the ex-King's spirits. He tells Richard of the use of the horse Barbary by Henry Bolingbroke. This major incident illustrates that Richard could inspire loyalty in a simple servant and thus heightens the pathos of the deposed ruler's murder, which follows immediately.

Herald Either of two minor characters in *Richard II*, petty officials at the trial by combat between

Henry Bolingbroke and Thomas Mowbray in 1.3. Each Herald cries out a formal statement of purpose for one contestant.

Keeper Minor character in *Richard II*, the jailer of the deposed King Richard II. The Keeper brings Richard a meal in 5.5, but he refuses to taste it for poison, as had been routine, asserting that Sir Piers Exton has forbidden him to do so. Richard strikes him in anger, and the Keeper's cries summon Exton and his murderers, who kill the prisoner.

Lady Either of two minor characters in *Richard II*, attendants of Queen Isabel. In 3.4 the Ladies try without success to alleviate the Queen's grief at the fall of King Richard II.

Man Minor character in *Richard II*, the Gardener's assistant. The Man asks the Gardener why they should bother to tend their plans when the larger "garden," the country as a whole, is falling into ruin due to neglect. In other words, he maintains that the state must be kept in order by its rulers, just as a garden must by its humbler caretakers.

Marshal (Lord Marshal) Minor character in *Richard II*, the nobleman who presides over the trial by combat between Bolingbroke and Mowbray in 1.3. Historically the Marshal on this occasion was the Duke of Surrey, a supporter of Richard II and thus an enemy of Bolingbroke. Shakespeare apparently forgot this fact, which appears in his chief source, HOLINSHED's history, when he presented the Marshal as a friend of Bolingbroke in 1.3.251–252. This is one of the many minor errors and inconsistencies that appear throughout the plays.

Mowbray, Thomas, Duke of Norfolk (ca. 1365–1400) Historical figure and character in *Richard II*, an enemy of Henry Bolingbroke. The play opens with Bolingbroke's accusation to King Richard II that Mowbray has committed treason by embezzling military payrolls, engaging in unspecified plots, and, most important, having murdered the king's uncle, Thomas, Duke of Gloucester. Mowbray hotly denies these charges, and a trial by combat is scheduled. In their vehement, fiery rhetoric,

both contestants evoke the stylized pageantry of a medieval world that was remote even in Shakespeare's day and whose passing is a basic theme of the play. Before the trial by combat begins, in 1.3, two decidedly sympathetic characters, John of Gaunt and the Duchess of Gloucester, the widow of the murdered duke, make it clear that Mowbray had in fact killed Gloucester and that he had done so on Richard's orders. The king, presumably hoping to avoid potential embarrassment, cancels the combat and banishes both disputants from England. Mowbray's response is again highly oratorical, but it contains one particularly distinctive passage (1.3.159–173), in which he regrets his departure to non-English-speaking lands, asserting a psychological dependence on the ability to express himself through language. This attitude surely reflects Shakespeare's own. Later Carlisle declares (4.1.91–102) that Mowbray has died in Venice after fighting bravely against the Saracens in a Crusade.

The historical Mowbray, like Bolingbroke, belonged to a faction, headed by Gloucester, that had rebelled against Richard in the late 1380s, and, with Bolingbroke, he subsequently joined the king's party. When Richard was again opposed by Gloucester, in 1397, the king arrested his uncle and placed him in the custody of Mowbray, who commanded the English fortress at Calais. Gloucester died in prison, and while it cannot be confirmed, 14th-century rumor and modern scholarship alike agree with Shakespeare that Mowbray most likely had the duke killed at the king's command. When he was expelled from England, Mowbray went on a pilgrimage to the Holy Land, but he did not fight there; the Crusades had ended a full century earlier.

Mowbray's son, Thomas Mowbray, later rebelled against his father's foe, when Bolingbroke had become Henry IV. He was captured and executed in 1405, as is enacted in *2 Henry IV.*

Northumberland, Henry Percy, Earl of (1342–1408) Historical figure and character in *Richard II* and *1* and *2 Henry IV*, a supporter of Henry Bolingbroke against Richard II in the first play, and a rebel against him—after he has begun to rule as Henry IV—in the two later works. In *Richard II*

Northumberland is Bolingbroke's chief lieutenant; in 2.1 he leads others into rebellion against Richard by providing a rationale for revolt: "The king is not himself, but basely led by flatterers . . ." (2.1.241–242). In 2.3 Northumberland himself resorts to flattering his leader unctuously, and in 3.3 he hypocritically conveys Bolingbroke's false declaration of loyalty to Richard. In 4.1 Northumberland takes on the most boldly disrespectful functions in the process of removing the king from his position, and in 5.1 he is the hard-hearted deputy who separates Richard and the grieving Queen Isabel. On that occasion he tersely states a cruel principle that aptly represents the new world of Machiavellian politics that Bolingbroke has inaugurated: replying to a request for mercy, he observes, "That were some love, but little policy" (5.1.84).

In the *Henry IV* plays Northumberland is a less prominent but no more likable figure. He and his son, the fiery Hotspur, join in rebellion against King Henry, whom they perceive as ungrateful to the Percy family. However, the earl fails to appear with his forces at the crucial battle of SHREWSBURY, sending word that he is ill; the rebel forces are defeated there, and Hotspur killed. At the outset of *2 Henry IV* the personification of Rumour claims that Northumberland was "crafty-sick" (Ind. 37), and in 2.3 Lady Percy, Hotspur's widow, chastises her father-in-law for having dishonorably abandoned his son; no other evidence is presented that Northumberland's illness was feigned, however. The earl then deserts the rebels again, fleeing to Scotland rather than supporting the renewed efforts of the Archbishop of York. His final defeat is reported in 4.4.97–101.

The historical Northumberland (like all the Percy men in Shakespeare, a descendant of Henry Percy, who figures in *Edward III*) did first rebel with Bolingbroke and then against him, but Shakespeare exaggerates his treachery and alters the facts of his life considerably. A man of King Henry's age in the *Henry IV* plays, Northumberland was actually a generation older; this change is part of Shakespeare's development of the rivalry between Hal and Hotspur by making them contemporaries. Northumberland, a major landowner in northern England and a distinguished warrior in the Scottish border conflicts, was a close friend and supporter of King Henry's father, John of Gaunt. Like Gaunt, he had supported Richard II against Thomas of Gloucester, but he was alienated by Richard's seizure of Gaunt's estate, and when Bolingbroke returned from exile, the earl became one of his chief allies, as in *Richard II*. His despicable personality as Bolingbroke's lieutenant may derive from the playwright's knowledge of a famous incident that, surprisingly, he did not use. Sent by Bolingbroke to negotiate with Richard, Northumberland swore a sacred oath that Bolingbroke intended to allow Richard to remain in power if he were restored to Gaunt's title and estates. Richard was thus induced to forgo escape by sea and leave the castle in which he had taken shelter. He was promptly ambushed by Northumberland and taken to LONDON, where he was deposed. It is not known whether or not Northumberland used this ploy under orders, but it was reported in Shakespeare's source, HOLINSHED's *Chronicles*, as a heinous betrayal.

Once Henry was in power, disputes arose between him and the Percys, eventually leading to their revolt. However, Northumberland's role in it in the *Henry IV* plays is almost wholly fictitious. According to Shakespeare, his unforeseen illness shocks the rebels, disturbs their plans, and contributes to their defeat at Shrewsbury, but in reality he had been sick for some time and his absence had been anticipated. The playwright's version is dramatically more interesting, and it allows the rashness of Hotspur and Douglas to be emphasized. The earl's pretending to be ill is also unsupported by Shakespeare's sources; it is simply an appropriately nasty rumor to associate with his Machiavellian character. Further, his betrayal of the Archbishop is untrue; Northumberland was the elected leader of the renewed rebellion, and the Archbishop commenced the uprising prematurely, before Northumberland could join him. Only after the disaster at GAULTREE FOREST, when Henry marched on his headquarters at WARKWORTH CASTLE, did Northumberland flee to Scotland. Several years later, after recruiting arms and money in Flanders and FRANCE, he again revived the rebellion and invaded England, dying in unsuccessful but valorous combat, according to Holinshed. This account of tenacious courage did not at all suit Shakespeare's model of a contemptible rebel, and he simply ignored it.

Percy, Henry (1364–1403) Historical figure and character in *Richard II*, a supporter of Henry Bolingbroke and a son of the Earl of Northumberland. The same historical figure appears as Hotspur in *1 Henry IV*. In *Richard II* Percy is a minor figure who primarily delivers information. He is plainly introduced solely in anticipation of his far greater importance in *1 Henry IV*. Presented as younger by a generation than he really was, Percy is thus made the contemporary of Bolingbroke's son, Prince Hal, who is to be his great rival. Significantly, it is Percy who tells Bolingbroke the disreputable news of his son in 5.3.13–19. Percy's role is clear evidence that Shakespeare had already formulated the general outline of *1 Henry IV* while writing *Richard II*.

Queen Isabel of England (1389–1409) Historical figure and character in *Richard II*, the wife of Richard II. The Queen is so completely different from her historical counterpart that she is virtually fictitious. Shakespeare introduces her to help provide a human context for the political events of the play. In 2.3 she glumly regrets the temporary absence of her husband—"so sweet a guest as . . . sweet Richard" (2.2.8–9)—casting the vain and headstrong king in a very different light than he has yet been seen. Later, after she overhears the Gardener's remarks on Richard's capture and likely deposition by Henry Bolingbroke, she responds with hysterical grief. She last appears in the famous farewell scene with Richard (5.1), which restates, on a personal level, the breach in the political fabric that Bolingbroke's usurpation has effected. (Richard refers to this in his speech beginning with the expostulation "Doubly divorc'd!" [5.1.71].) The Queen's pleas that she be permitted to accompany her husband are rejected by the stony Earl of Northumberland, and the sorrowing couple are forcibly separated, just as Richard has been parted from his crown. The historical is presented on a human level, with a degree of poignancy far greater than any dismay we may feel for Richard's fall from worldly greatness or for the collapse of England's feudal traditions.

The historical Isabel was no happier than Shakespeare's Queen, but she was a child of 10 when these events occurred. The daughter of Charles VI, the French King of *Henry V*, she was married to Richard when she was 7. While this couple seems to have been genuinely fond of each other, they had no opportunity to develop the mature relationship that Shakespeare depicts. Although she is banished to France in the play, she was actually detained in England for two years following Richard's deposition, virtually a prisoner, because the new government was reluctant to return her dowry. When she finally returned home, Isabel was still an eminently eligible princess, and she was married in 1404 to Prince Charles of Orléans (who appears in *Henry V*). She died in childbirth five years later, at the age of 20.

Richard II, King of England (1367–1400) Title character of *Richard II*, king deposed by Henry Bolingbroke. Richard is a self-centered man and an inept ruler; his fall seems both deserved and inevitable. Nevertheless, Shakespeare elicits strong sympathy for the fallen king as he suffers painful psychological trauma before coming to accept his fate.

It is quickly established that Richard is an incompetent king. In 1.2 we learn that before the play begins, Richard had arranged the murder of his uncle the Duke of Gloucester, an admired member of the royal family. Furthermore, his ordinary conduct as king is persistently disastrous. When his "coffers, with too great a court / And liberal largess, are grown somewhat light" (1.4.43–44), he turns to extortionate abuses of the public. He also seizes the estate of John of Gaunt, rightly the inheritance of the exiled Bolingbroke. This not only stimulates Bolingbroke's rebellion, but it alarms many other nobles, who fear that their own holdings may similarly be in jeopardy. Richard's wrong-headedness is exemplified by his obstinate refusal to heed the good advice of his uncles, Gaunt and the Duke of York. He delights in ceremony and the trappings of power, and his rhetoric is windy. Narcissistic and arrogant, he does not rule; he enjoys himself in the role of ruler. Despite all his boasting, Richard cannot use the power of his position, and Bolingbroke's triumph, when it comes, is almost effortless.

However, in political decline Richard becomes a more sympathetic character. His speech is no less extravagant, but now his mannered style is plainly a manifestation of inner distress. He is a more complex person than he had seemed earlier; in his isolation he is intensely introspective and racked with anxiety, alternating between unjustified hope and exaggerated despair. Finally, imprisoned and due to be killed, he acknowledges that his own failings have played some part in his fall: "I wasted time, and now doth time waste me" (5.5.49). Richard, with his penchant for strong imagery and elaborate metaphor, is the first of Shakespeare's protagonists to demonstrate an extraordinary imagination and artistic sense. A complex and ambiguous personality, Richard foreshadows the great heroes of Shakespeare's later TRAGEDIES.

Richard's poetic language and love of ceremony place him in striking opposition to the prosaic and practical Bolingbroke. This powerful contrast reflects a basic human conflict between the doer and the dreamer. It also enhances Richard's strong symbolic role as the last representative of the medieval England of King Edward III, in which the ethos of chivalry was still dominant. The passing of this nostalgically romantic period is a major theme of the play.

The historical Richard is for the most part ignored by Shakespeare, who focuses entirely on the last year of a 22-year reign. When Edward III died, his grandson and heir, Richard (see PLANTAGENET FAMILY), was only 10 years old. The young king seems to have been fond of pomp and splendor, and he had a reputation as a dilettante, but he was also courageous. At 14 he faced a murderous crowd during the great peasants' rebellion of 1381 and convinced them to disperse. However, England was governed during Richard's minority by his uncles, especially the Duke of Gloucester. When Richard attempted to assert himself 10 years later, an armed conflict ensued, and Richard was nearly forced from the throne. A coalition of nobles ruled for two years, but Richard gathered supporters and successfully began to rule at the age of 22. He seems to have governed well. His reign was noted for its emphasis on peace; he concluded truces in Ireland in 1394 and, more important, in the HUN-DRED YEARS' WAR against FRANCE in 1396. (By the latter treaty, he agreed to marry the young Princess Isabel, who was a child, not the adult Queen of the play.) In 1397 another rupture between the king and Gloucester resulted in the duke's imprisonment and death. Modern scholarship tends to confirm the contemporary opinion that Richard was responsible for his uncle's murder, but the truth cannot be ascertained.

The political events of the play are roughly accurate—Shakespeare followed his sources, for the most part—but the emphasis on Richard's incompetence is distinctly overdrawn. His departure for Ireland, shortly after seizing Gaunt's estate and alienating the nobility, was a grave error, but even worse was his delay in returning once Bolingbroke's invasion had begun. This procrastination, as well as the dismissal of much of his force upon arrival in England, appears to have been advised by Richard's second-in-command, Aumerle, who promptly deserted his master, an event that Shakespeare omits. Richard was given sworn oaths by Northumberland, who was speaking for Bolingbroke, that the latter did not intend usurpation and would disarm if Gaunt's titles and estates were restored to him. Richard accepted these terms and unknowingly allowed himself to be taken prisoner. Thus his final fall was due as much to treachery as to wrongdoing on his part. The deposition scene (4.1) is entirely fictitious; Bolingbroke certainly could not afford to give his enemy a platform, and he did not. Sir Piers Exton's murder of Richard is also a fiction, although Shakespeare took it from his source and doubtless believed it. A contemporary report states that Richard died of starvation, either deprived of food by his jailers or because he refused to eat. The actual circumstances of Richard's death are not known, although his bones were exhumed in 1871 and no signs of violence were found.

Ross, William de (William de Ros) (d. 1414) Historical figure and minor character in *Richard II*, a supporter of Henry Bolingbroke. In 2.1 Ross, Lord Willoughby, and the Earl of Northumberland agree to join Bolingbroke's rebellion against King Richard II. They fear that their own estates are endangered by such acts as Richard's illegal seizure of Bolingbroke's inheritance. In 2.3 they accompany Bolingbroke as he marches against the king. The historical Ross, a prominent landowner in northern England, went on to serve for a time as Lord Treasurer of England during Bolingbroke's reign as King Henry IV.

Salisbury, John Montague, Earl of (John Montacute) (ca. 1350–1400) Historical figure and minor character in *Richard II*, a supporter of King Richard II. In 2.4 Salisbury receives notice from the Welsh Captain that his troops will no longer remain in Richard's army, and he mourns the likely downfall of the king. He himself stays loyal and is eventually killed fighting against Bolingbroke; his death is reported by the Earl of Northumberland in 5.6.8.

The historical Salisbury was a trusted adviser to Richard for many years; in 1396 he negotiated the king's marriage to Queen Isabel. A year after Richard's deposition, Salisbury was captured in battle, along with the Duke of Surrey, by Lord Berkeley, who turned his prisoners over to a mob, which beheaded them. Salisbury's son was the Earl of Salisbury in *Henry V* and *1 Henry VI*.

Scroop, Stephen (Stephen de Scroop, Stephen Scroope, Stephen Scrope) (ca. 1350–1406) Historical figure and minor character in *Richard II*, a supporter of Richard II. In 3.2 Scroop tells Richard of the popular acceptance of Henry Bolingbroke, the execution of Bushy and Greene, and the defection of the Duke of York. These tidings undo the king, plunging him into near-hysterical despair, and Scroop remarks pointedly on the king's state: "Sweet love, I see, changing his property, / Turns to the sourest and most deadly hate" (3.2.135–136).

The family of the historical Scroop did not accept Bolingbroke's rule. Stephen's brother Richard, the Archbishop of York, appears as a rebel in *1* and *2 Henry IV*. Stephen dissociated himself from that rebellion, but his son, Henry Scroop, betrayed Bolingbroke's son, Henry V, and was executed for treason, as depicted in *Henry V*.

Servant (1) Minor character in *Richard II*, a messenger serving the Duke of York. In 2.2 the Servant

brings new of the death of the Duchess of Gloucester. This poignant moment emphasizes the duke's helplessness in the face of onrushing events.

Servant (2) Minor character in *Richard II*, the attendant of Sir Piers Exton. The Servant supports Exton in his assumption that Henry Bolingbroke wants to have the deposed Richard II murdered.

Surrey, Thomas Holland, Duke of (Earl of Kent) (1374–1400) Historical figure and minor character in *Richard II*, a supporter of King Richard II. In 4.1 Surrey disputes Lord Fitzwater's account of the Duke of Aumerle's role in the murder of the Duke of Gloucester. Fitzwater challenges him to a trial by combat, one of many similar conflicts that erupt in this scene. The episode serves to demonstrate the widespread disorder that the illicit assumption of power by Henry Bolingbroke has engendered.

Although he is not seen again in the play, Surrey subsequently joins the revolt against Bolingbroke, for his execution is announced by Northumberland in 5.6.8, where he is called Kent. Thomas Holland had been named Duke of Surrey by Richard in 1397, but Bolingbroke revoked that status at the time of the rebellion, so Northumberland refers to him by his lesser title, the Earl of Kent. Kent and the Earl of Salisbury were captured in battle by Lord Berkeley, who turned them over to a mob, who beheaded them.

Willoughby, William de (d. 1409) Historical figure and minor character in *Richard II*, a supporter of Henry Bolingbroke. In 2.1 Willoughby and Lord Ross join the Earl of Northumberland in rebellion against King Richard II, agreeing that their status as aristocrats is imperiled by Richard's seizure of Bolingbroke's inheritance. In 2.3 they accompany Bolingbroke as he marches against the king.

The historical Willoughby, a prominent landowner in Lincolnshire, was descended from a knight in the army of William the Conqueror and thus had great prestige among the aristocracy. He later married the widow of the Duke of York, Joan of Kent—the successor to the Duchess of the play—who went on to marry a third Shakespearean character, Henry le Scroop (in *Henry V*).

York, Edmund of Langley, Duke of (1341–1402) Historical figure and character in *Richard II*, uncle of King Richard II. Like his brother John of Gaunt, York deplores the misguided rule of their nephew but believes strongly in the divine appointment of kings and is doggedly loyal to Richard. Richard, even as he is censured by York, appoints him Governor of England to rule in the king's absence, observing that "he is just" (2.1.221). However, he is helpless to prevent the usurpation of the Crown by Henry Bolingbroke, and, once this is accomplished, he transfers his loyalty to the new king, despite his own grief at Richard's fall. He even denounces his son, the Duke of Aumerle, as a traitor.

York is a representative of a vanishing medieval world of inviolable political and social hierarchies. In 2.3.96–104 he consciously identifies himself with that system, nostalgically recalling his comradeship with the Black Prince in the days of King Edward III. Ironically he speaks just as Bolingbroke is preparing the triumph of a more modern world of opportunistic, Machiavellian politics. York's sympathetic character is intended to heighten the pathos that colors the passing of that older world, one of the principal themes of the play.

The historical York apparently resembled Shakespeare's character. He was noted for his gentle, peace-loving nature, combined with a marked incapacity in political and military matters. He was the founder and namesake of the YORK FAMILY, a branch of the PLANTAGENET FAMILY: through a son younger than Aumerle, the Earl of Cambridge, who appears in *Henry V*, York's great-grandson would eventually claim the crown and rule as King Edward IV.

Richard III

SYNOPSIS

Act 1, Scene 1

Richard III observes in a soliloquy that the victory of the York faction has ended England's civil strife. He says that he himself is unsuited for times of peace, being deformed and thus not able to engage in the games of love that occupy the court. Therefore he proposes to be a villain, and he reveals that he has convinced his eldest brother, King Edward IV, that his other brother, the Duke of Clarence, intends treason. Clarence appears, under arrest; Richard hypocritically sympathizes with him and promises to secure his release. As Clarence is taken away, Richard reveals in another soliloquy that he intends to have him killed. He discusses with Lord Hastings the news that the king is near death from illness. In a third soliloquy, Richard details his plans to kill Clarence and to marry Lady Anne, whose late husband Richard helped to murder in *3 Henry VI*.

Act 1, Scene 2

Lady Anne, attending the funeral procession of her father-in-law, the late King Henry VI, who was murdered by Richard in *3 Henry VI*, curses the murderer. Richard appears and accepts her scorn, asserting that his proper place in the world is in her bed and claiming that it was the thought of her beauty that caused him to kill her husband. She spits in his face as he asserts his love. He offers her his sword with which to kill him, but she cannot do it. He continues to talk, gradually hypnotizing her with words, and she finally accepts a ring from him and agrees to meet him again. She leaves, and in a soliloquy Richard derides her susceptibility.

Act 1, Scene 3

Queen Elizabeth tells her brother Rivers and her sons Dorset and Grey of her fear that, when the king dies, Richard will rule in the name of her son the Prince of Wales. Other noblemen appear, including Richard, who argues with Elizabeth. Queen Margaret, the widow of Henry VI, enters and heaps curses on her old enemies. She desires an early death for the king and the Prince of Wales, as well as for Dorset, Rivers, and Hastings. She wishes on Elizabeth her own fate—to continue living after seeing her husband and sons killed and herself deposed. She curses Richard most elaborately and, before departing, goes on to warn Buckingham against him. The others are called away, and Richard instructs two murderers whom he has hired to kill Clarence.

Act 1, Scene 4

Clarence, in the TOWER OF LONDON, tells of a nightmare in which he was drowned and went to hell, where he encountered the spirits of men whom he had betrayed and murdered. The murderers arrive. The Second Murderer feels pangs of conscience; in a comic exchange, the First Murderer reminds him of the money that Richard has promised them, and he recovers. Clarence pleads for mercy, and the Second Murderer begins to relent. But the First stabs Clarence and carries him offstage to drown him in a large barrel of wine.

Act 2, Scene 1
The ailing King Edward orders reconciliation among the peers, and vows of friendship are exchanged. Richard arrives and announces the death of Clarence, to the consternation of the king, who had canceled the death warrant. Edward is stricken by remorse.

Act 2, Scene 2
The son of Clarence, a Boy, reveals that Richard has told him that the king is responsible for his father's death. The Duchess of York curses Richard, her son, but the Boy refuses to believe that his uncle has lied. The queen arrives with news of the king's death, and mourning becomes general. Richard arrives with other nobles, and plans are made to bring the young Prince of Wales to London to be crowned. When the others depart, Richard and Buckingham conspire to join the Prince's escort and keep him from his protecting relatives.

Act 2, Scene 3
Three Citizens discuss the rivalry between Richard and the queen's relatives. They conclude that there is trouble ahead for England.

Act 2, Scene 4
The queen, the Duchess of York, and the Prince's younger brother, the Duke of York, await the arrival of the Prince. They are told that Richard has imprisoned several of the queen's allies. The queen decides that she and her son York must enter a church and claim sanctuary.

Act 3, Scene 1
The Prince is formally welcomed. Cardinal Bourchier goes to remove his brother from his sanctuary. Richard informs the Prince that he and York will be housed in the Tower of London, a prospect that dis-

turbs the boy. The younger prince arrives, and the two are escorted to the Tower. Richard makes plans with Buckingham and Catesby: If Hastings resists Richard's proposed seizure of the throne, he is to be executed. Richard promises that when he is king, he will reward Buckingham with an earldom.

Act 3, Scene 2
Hastings receives a message from Stanley telling of an ominous dream of danger from Richard, but he dismisses it. Catesby enters and suggests Richard's enthronement; Hastings disapproves. Stanley arrives, still full of misgivings. The naive Hastings engages in small talk before leaving for a scheduled council meeting.

Act 3, Scene 3
Richard Ratcliffe leads Rivers, Grey, and Vaughan to execution. The victims recollect Margaret's seemingly clairvoyant curses.

Act 3, Scene 4
The council is in session. Richard withdraws to confer with Buckingham about Hastings. He reenters, raging about plots against himself, and when Hastings speaks reassuringly, Richard accuses him of protecting the supposed plotters and sentences him to death.

Act 3, Scene 5
Richard explains to the Mayor that the danger presented by Hastings's plot had made it necessary to execute him immediately, without a trial. The Mayor assures Richard of his approval and leaves. Richard instructs Buckingham to spread the rumor that the imprisoned princes are illegitimate sons of the late king's illicit liaisons.

Act 3, Scene 6
A Scrivener shows a document approving the execution of Hastings. He knows that this justification was prepared long beforehand. He grieves that such deceitfulness should prevail.

Act 3, Scene 7
Buckingham reports that the Mayor has been induced to discuss the possibility of Richard's becoming king. He recommends that Richard feign reluctance to rule. When the Mayor arrives, he is told that Richard is engaged in religious devotions and cannot be disturbed. Buckingham leads the

Mayor to insist, and finally Richard appears, accompanied by clergymen. Buckingham, purporting to speak for the Mayor and people, asks Richard to take the throne. Richard refuses, and Buckingham leads the delegation away, but Richard has them called back and accepts their acclaim as king.

Act 4, Scene 1

Queen Elizabeth and the Duchess of York, with Dorset, meet Lady Anne, now Richard's wife. They are not permitted to enter the Tower to visit the princes, by Richard's order. Stanley arrives to say that Richard has been declared king. He helps the women make plans: Dorset is sent abroad to join the Earl of Richmond; Anne goes to be crowned, having no choice; Elizabeth will return to sanctuary.

Act 4, Scene 2

Buckingham shows reluctance as Richard, now king, insinuates that the princes should be murdered. Richard, angry, summons Tyrell. Richard orders a rumor started that Anne is deathly ill; he reveals his intention to marry the daughter of Queen Elizabeth. Tyrell agrees to murder the princes. Buckingham returns and wishes to claim the earldom promised him in 3.1; Richard refuses him and departs. Left alone, Buckingham plans his desertion of Richard.

Act 4, Scene 3

Tyrell reports that he has killed the princes; Richard reflects that he has imprisoned Clarence's son and married his daughter to a commoner who cannot claim the crown, and that the princes and Anne are all dead. Knowing that Richmond thinks of marrying Queen Elizabeth's daughter, he proposes again to do so himself. News arrives that the Bishop of Ely has fled to join Richmond, and that Buckingham has raised an army against Richard.

Act 4, Scene 4

Margaret joins Elizabeth and the Duchess of York, who are bewailing Richard's murder of the princes. Margaret thanks God for this development but goes on to call for vengeance on Richard. She gloats over Elizabeth's misfortunes and departs, just before Richard arrives with a military entourage. Elizabeth and the Duchess confront him with his misdeeds; he orders his drummers and trumpeters

to drown them out with noise. The Duchess delivers a tirade against her son before departing. Richard now proposes to Elizabeth that he marry her daughter. After an extended argument, she pretends to agree and leaves. News arrives of Richmond's invasion fleet, and Richard panics, blurting out confused orders and curses. Fearing treachery from Stanley, Richard orders him to leave his son as a hostage. More news arrives of Buckingham's growing rebellion, but then comes a message that his forces and Richmond's fleet have been dispersed by a great storm, followed by word that Buckingham has been captured. His spirits restored, Richard takes command and orders his troops to march.

Act 4, Scene 5

Stanley meets with Sir Christopher, a representative of Richmond, and says that he will have to postpone his intended defection to the invading Earl because Richard has seized his son.

Act 5, Scene 1

Buckingham is escorted to his execution. He remembers Margaret's warning to him in 1.3.

Act 5, Scene 2

Richmond, in England, speaks cheerfully of the coming battle with Richard's forces.

Act 5, Scene 3

Richard arrives at BOSWORTH FIELD and has his tent pitched at one side of the stage. Richmond arrives and has his tent pitched at the other side. He sends a messenger to Stanley. Richard sends his own message to Stanley, a threat that his son will be killed if he deserts. Richard retires to his tent. Stanley comes to Richmond, promising at least to delay his troops. Richmond prays and goes to bed. Between the tents, a succession of spirits appears, each one the Ghost of a character murdered by Richard. Each delivers a similar set of messages: They remind Richard of his misdeeds and bid him "despair and die"; turning to Richmond, they assure him of supernatural aid. Richard wakes and despairingly acknowledges his guilt. Richmond awakens, refreshed by the visions, and addresses his troops, asserting that Richard's soldiers will willingly lose, to escape being governed by such a villain. Richard curses his pangs of conscience and speaks to his army, heaping insults on his foes. A messenger reports that Stanley refuses to march; Richard orders the hostage killed but postpones the action, for the combat has begun.

Act 5, Scene 4

During the battle, Richard enters, crying out for a horse, rhetorically offering his kingdom in exchange for one.

Act 5, Scene 5

Richmond kills Richard in hand-to-hand combat and declares victory. Stanley offers him Richard's crown. Richmond proclaims an end to England's civil wars. He announces his intention to marry Elizabeth's daughter, thus uniting the feuding factions, and prays for continued peace.

COMMENTARY

Richard III seems at first glance to be a fairly simple work in its general outlines: a drama with a striking central character whose rise and fall provide a straightforward entertainment, set within a context that lends moral weight to the tale. This description is adequate up to a point, and it suggests the playwright's interest in individual human capacities for good and evil, a characteristic concern of the RENAISSANCE. But because our experience of the play is dominated by its protagonist, we may lose an appreciation of its primary theme, which is a social one: the redemption of English public life through the coming of the TUDOR DYNASTY. Only secondarily, in the magnificence of its dazzling villain-hero, does it concern individuality.

Richard's immense capacity for crime is a final, climactic instance of the disruptive aristocratic ambitions that have spurred the action in all the plays of the minor TETRALOGY. Thus Richard exemplifies something larger than his own fascinating personality. Further, even more important than his negative relationship to peace and public order is the role of fate, which inexorably brings Richard's dominance to an end. Divine providence punishes the fractious Plantagenets through the crimes of their own last representative and grants England a restoration of grace with the advent of the Tudors. The workings of fate are revealed in the developments of the plot, of course, but they are also reflected in the organization of the drama. The play is powered by subtle tensions, generated by contrasting its bold protagonist with its equally bold structural symmetry.

In *Richard III* Shakespeare twice used the potent device—a favorite of his—of two matching scenes, one early in the play and the other late. The second scene echoes the first but differs in revealing ways. In one instance, Richard's attempt in 4.4 to gain Queen Elizabeth's approval of his plan to marry her daughter recalls his courtship of Lady Anne in 1.2. This time, however, Richard is in decline; not only have we seen his downfall begin in earlier scenes, but here he is not the same wooer. He apologizes for his deeds in 4.4.291–298, whereas with Anne he had boldly attributed them to his love (1.2.125ff.). Elizabeth baffles him with rejections of his oaths, stifling his assertions until he is reduced to wishing ill on himself (4.4.397–409). Elizabeth suspends the conversation in 4.4.428–429, leaving its resolution in doubt, where Anne was told where to await Richard's later visit (1.2.214–220). We feel the difference and know that Richard will not have his way this time; in fact, as soon as Elizabeth departs, his downfall resumes with quickened speed. The repetition of motifs increases the strength with which we respond to the differences in situation; we feel that there lurks something fateful in the coincidences linking success and failure.

Similarly, the appearance of the Ghosts to the sleeping Richard in 5.3 reminds us of Clarence's dream in 1.4. Again, a situation where Richard's downfall is imminent is compared with an earlier one in which his villainy is triumphant. In using this device, Shakespeare took each later incident from his sources and invented the earlier ones, which makes his intention very clear. These links unite the different stages of the narrative.

This quality in the play is heightened by the repeated presentation of fulfilled predictions. For instance, the dreams of Clarence and Richard both deal with the dreamer's later death. Moreover, much is made of specific forecasts. Queen Margaret in particular is used by Shakespeare as "a prophetess," as she calls herself in 1.3.301. In 1.3 she predicts a rash of deaths. As Richard's victims fall, they allude to Margaret's prophecy, and when she

reappears in 4.4, we recollect the truth of her predictions (which she refers to, in case we do not)
with some degree of awe. When she asserts that
Richard nears "his piteous and unpitied end"
(4.4.74), we believe her. Similarly, characters predict the future even when they are unaware of it, as
when Richard names his own fate to Elizabeth, even
as he thinks he is warding it off, in 4.4.397–409.

Omens are equally evocative of a world governed by fate, and *Richard III* is rife with them.
Hastings's tendency to ignore them is almost comical. A Citizen of London couches his uneasiness
about the political future in terms of augury
(2.3.32–35); the young Duke of York's request for
Richard's dagger has a foreboding quality, as
Richard's reply (3.1.111) makes clear. The strawberries so pointedly introduced in 3.4 had an emblematic association with serpents and the devil that was
quite familiar to Shakespeare's audiences. Most
ominous of all are the omens that had attended
Richard's birth, which are mentioned several times.

All of these devices create an air of myth that is
supported by the uniform tone that persists
throughout the play. There is no SUBPLOT, nor
faintest evidence of romantic interest. Aside from
Richard's sardonic enthusiasm for his own villainy,
there is very little humor. Even the violence takes
place offstage, for the most part. The plot and
themes unfold largely through talk—however
absorbing and varied—rather than action. The
only exceptions are the stabbing of Clarence
(though not his drowning) and Richard's death in
single combat, each of which constitutes a climactic moment in the play's development. Each is
fairly stylized. Such a restrained rendering, despite
the many opportunities for bloody tableaux—
which were as popular in Shakespeare's day as they
are now—produces a pronounced solemnity. Combined with the flavor of sorcery discussed above,
the play's pervasive calm contributes to a sense of
ritual, of magical demonstration. This surreal aura
supports the mythic denouement: Richard and
Richmond—opposing paragons of Evil and Good—
face each other in a grand trial by combat.

In lesser hands these ideas might have yielded a
set of sermons illustrating the inevitability of divine
providence. However, *Richard III* is animated by the
presence of Shakespeare's first great protagonist,
Richard himself. Not only does this astonishing villain speak nearly one-third of the play's lines, but he
delivers all of the major soliloquies as well. Significantly, many of his prominent speeches appear early
in the play so that we become accustomed to his
point of view. Thus he seems to be in control of the
action, until fate intervenes. His wit, his acute political acumen, and his energy enthrall us at the same
time that we are appalled by his diabolical sadism.
The final defeat of this extraordinary figure makes
the power of fate seem all the more awesome.

Richard was a product of a newly established
16th-century tradition of magnificent villain-heroes
that stemmed from MARLOWE's Tamburlaine. Marlowe's works were wildly popular when *Richard III*
was written, and Shakespeare was not the only playwright to exploit the example they set. Shakespeare's
superior talent produced a greater character, a figure
whose language is not only more credibly idiomatic
but also has greater lyrical power. However, Richard's
dominance of the play reminds us of the somewhat
derivative character of the young playwright's work.
He was later to develop the capacity to create believable characters of greatly varying types in a single
play, thereby surpassing Marlowe utterly.

In fact, a number of the lesser characters in
Richard III testify to that developing talent. Buckingham's woolly rhetoric marks him as a politician
who prefers evasiveness to clarity; if he were not
malevolent, he would be funny. Clarence is a moving psychological portrait of a tormented sinner
whose fear of hellfire makes him writhe in agony.
The unfortunate but fatuous Hastings inspires both
disdain and pity. None of these figures is fully
developed, but each animates effective episodes.

Richard III is a very unreliable guide to the history of the period it purports to describe. As he did
in all of the HISTORY PLAYS, Shakespeare took liberties with his sources, and these were themselves
biased and unreliable. The last 12 years of Edward's
reign are compressed into 1.1–2.1 as a cluster of
related incidents. Richard's career has been notably
distorted, first by Tudor historians, especially
Thomas MORE, whose account was the basis for
much of the tale as Shakespeare received it; and
then by the playwright himself, who was concerned

not with historical accuracy but rather with the aggrandizement of his villain. At the end of the play, Richard's two-year reign is collapsed into a few frantic weeks, as the success of the usurper is immediately superseded by his fall. Thus the sequence of plays that began with *1 Henry VI* comes to its close. Where King Henry V had just been lost to England at the beginning of the cycle, Richmond arrives to play the part of a new hero at its end. The death of Talbot, accompanying the loss of English hopes in the first play, is balanced by Richard's death and their renewal in the last one. Patriotic history is combined in *Richard III* with grand entertainment, creating a drama that has always been popular.

SOURCES OF THE PLAY

Shakespeare's chief source for *Richard III* was *The Union of the Two Noble and Illustre Families of Lancaster and York* by Edward HALL (1548), supplemented by Raphael HOLINSHED's *Chronicles of England, Scotland, and Ireland* (1587 edition). Hall's account is itself an adaptation of Thomas MORE's *History of King Richard III* (1543). More's chief source, in turn, was Polydore VERGIL's Latin *Historia Anglia*. Shakespeare also adapted various details from a number of other works, including several of the plays of SENECA, OVID's *Metamorphoses,* Thomas KYD's *The Spanish Tragedy* (1588–89), Edmund SPENSER's *Faerie Queene* (1590), and a popular anthology of biographies, A MIRROR FOR MAGISTRATES. In addition, the influence of the plays of Christopher MARLOWE was plainly felt by the young Shakespeare. An anonymous play of the 1590s, *The True Tragedie of Richard the Third,* has sometimes been thought to be a source for *Richard III.* However, most current scholarly opinion holds that the slight similarity between the two plays, if it reflects any relationship, shows an influence of Shakespeare on the other playwright.

TEXT OF THE PLAY

It is impossible to date the early history plays exactly, but several echoes of *Richard III* in Marlowe's *Edward II* indicate that Shakespeare's play was the earlier of the two. The title page of *Edward II* reports that it was performed by PEMBROKE'S MEN,

presumably before the closing of the theaters by plague in June 1592. It cannot have been written, therefore, after early 1592, nor can *Richard III* have been written after late 1591. All three *Henry VI* plays contain minor reflections of Spenser's *Faerie Queene,* published in December 1589. Thus the composition of Shakespeare's cycle seems to span the years 1590–91, and it is thought that the four plays were written in the order in which their events occur. *Richard III,* the last of them, would therefore have been written in late 1591.

The play was not published until 1597, when Andrew WISE published the first QUARTO edition (known as Q1). It was followed by seven subsequent quarto editions (known as Q2–Q8) over the next four decades. Each of these later editions was derived from its predecessor, adding progressively greater numbers of errors; they all derive ultimately from Q1. Q1 differs considerably from the version of the play that appeared in the FIRST FOLIO in 1623. The Folio text (F1) is much superior. Not only does it contain some 200 lines missing from Q1, but its lines are more metrical, its grammar better, and its poetry more impressive. Thus, F1 is the basis for most modern editions. But Q1 remains important, for it contains some material, both dialogue and stage directions, that F1 omits.

Close study of the texts has revealed that Q1 is a "memorial" version of the play—that is, it consists of the lines as recollected by actors who had performed them—and thus it is sometimes classed as a BAD QUARTO. However, unlike most such editions, this is a solid, actable version of the play. It even includes elaborate and accurate stage directions that are generally superior to those of F1. It has been concluded that this version was prepared by an entire acting company, rather than by only a few players, as in the more corrupt quartos. This was probably done because the company had lost its copy of the play. (Only a single copy of a play was ordinarily kept, to discourage pirate publishers.) The company that performed *Richard III* in the years just prior to 1597 was Shakespeare's own group, the CHAMBERLAIN'S MEN, and the playwright may have had a hand in reconstructing the play.

Textual study further suggests that the printers of F1 worked from a manuscript, probably

Shakespeare's FOUL PAPERS, that was collated with one or more quarto copies of the play, certainly a copy of Q3 (of 1602) and possibly a copy of the then-newest edition, Q6 (1622).

THEATRICAL HISTORY OF THE PLAY

Richard III has always been among the most popular of Shakespeare's plays. The very large number of editions published in the late 16th and early 17th centuries suggests immediate enthusiasm for the work, and this is confirmed by many allusions to it in surviving documents of the period. Richard BURBAGE is known to have played the title role in the 1590s (see MANNINGHAM, JOHN), but a 1633 performance at the court of King Charles I is the earliest performance to be mentioned explicitly. The play is presumed to have been staged until the closing of the theaters by the Puritan Revolution in 1642, and several productions are mentioned in records of the Restoration period, later in the 17th century.

In 1700 Colley CIBBER introduced a radically altered version of the play, which was the basis for subsequent productions for more than 150 years. It was much shorter than Shakespeare's, and more than half its lines were written by Cibber himself. This version of *Richard III*, presented in New York in 1751, was the first Shakespeare play staged in America, in any form. In the 19th century, elaborate productions using scores of extras were in vogue. Shakespeare's text resumed on the stage in the 1870s, though it has often been considerably cut. Significant 20th-century productions included those of Terence Gray (active 1926–33) in Cambridge, England (1928), and Tyrone GUTHRIE (1953; Stratford, Ontario).

Richard III has been made a FILM five times, four of them silent films, including Max REINHARDT's 1919 version. Laurence OLIVIER's notable movie of 1956 introduced many people to the play, but it is a significantly altered version—most strikingly in its elimination of Queen Margaret's furious raging. In the 1990s two films of *Richard III* attracted much acclaim. Ian MCKELLEN starred in Richard Loncraine's 1995 version, set in the 1930s. It presents Richard's reign as a 20th-century fascist dictatorship and dramatically displays such 20th-century phenomena as tanks, antiaircraft guns, and drug addiction. A year later the actor and director Al Pacino (b. 1940) produced *Looking for Richard*, a documentary about Shakespeare and, in particular, about a film production of *Richard III*, starring Pacino himself. Featuring pithy interviews with the likes of Kenneth BRANAGH and Peter BROOK, it presents ten fully dramatized scenes from the play, building to its proper climax at Bosworth Field.

Richard III has been made for TELEVISION once by itself, in 1983, and twice as part of a BBC series incorporating groups of the history plays: AN AGE OF KINGS (1960) and *The Wars of the Roses* (1964), which combines the *Henry VI* plays and *Richard III*.

CHARACTERS

Anne, Lady (Anne Neville) (1456–1485)   Historical figure and character in *Richard III*, the wife of King Richard III. Courted by Richard—the murderer of her late husband, the Prince of Wales, and his father, King Henry VI—Anne is half-hypnotized by his words and accepts a ring from him in 1.2. When she appears again, in 4.1, she is Richard's wife, and she is called to be crowned following his coup d'état. She predicts that he will murder her, and the play implies that he does so.

The historical Anne is alluded to, although in error, in 3.3.242 of *3 Henry VI*, when the Duke of Warwick agrees that his eldest daughter shall marry the Prince. Actually, Anne was Warwick's younger daughter, and, although she and the Prince were betrothed, they apparently did not actually marry. In any case, she married Richard in 1474. Historically, she did not attend the funeral of Henry VI, and her dialogue with Richard is entirely fictitious; Shakespeare invented it in order to create a scene that contrasts with Richard's later effort to negotiate a marriage with the daughter of Queen Elizabeth. Also, there has never been any evidence that Anne was murdered; she seems to have died a natural death.

Archbishop of York, Thomas Rotherham (1423–1500)   Historical figure and minor character in *Richard III*, friend of Queen Elizabeth. In 2.4, when news arrives of the imprisonment of the queen's allies, the Archbishop urges her to seek sanctuary, and he offers her his assistance, even to the illegal extent of giving her the Great Seal of England, with which he has been entrusted. This incident, which Shakespeare took from HALL, emphasizes the villainy of Richard III by presenting opposition to it from a venerable figure.

The historical Rotherham was a powerful clergyman who held a number of secular posts, including that of Chancellor of England, bearer of the Great Seal. He was imprisoned for opposing Richard's accession, but he was soon released. He withdrew from court politics for the remainder of his life, although he remained a prominent churchman.

In some modern editions of the play, the Archbishop of York is eliminated and his lines are given to Cardinal Bourchier, following the 16th-century QUARTO editions. This change was presumably made as an economy for the acting company.

Berkeley   Minor character in *Richard III*, one of two named gentlemen among the group that accompanies Lady Anne and the corpse of Henry VI in 1.2.

Bishop   Either of two minor characters in *Richard III*, clergymen who accompany Richard III as he receives the Mayor in 3.7. They convey the impression that Richard has been busy with devotional concerns. In fact, this is a contrived deception, and the "Bishops" are actually unscrupulous lower-ranking clergymen, John Shaa and Friar Penker, whom Richard has summoned for the purpose.

Blunt, Sir James (d. 1493)   Historical figure and minor character in *Richard III*, a follower of Richmond. Richmond uses Blunt as a messenger before the battle of BOSWORTH FIELD. Blunt is the great-grandson of Sir Walter Blunt, who appears in *1 Henry IV*. He may have been selected for his tiny role, from all the possible officers in Richmond's army, as a gesture toward the Blunt family, who were STRATFORD landowners of Shakespeare's day and were related to the playwright's friends in the COMBE family.

Boy (Edward Plantagenet, Earl of Warwick) (1475–1499)   Historical figure and minor character in *Richard III*, the son of Clarence. The Boy appears in 2.2, in which he refuses to believe that his uncle, Richard III, has killed his father. He is

not seen again, but we hear of his imprisonment by Richard in 4.3.36. Crimes against children are a recurring motif in the *Henry VI* plays and *Richard III*, and this instance is clearly intended to add to the enormity of Richard's crimes. The villain has felt it unnecessary to kill the Boy, despite his position as a possible claimant to the throne, only because the Boy is "foolish" (4.2.55), meaning mentally retarded. It is unclear whether or not this was so, but it is known that the historical Boy, Edward of Warwick, was in fact imprisoned not by Richard but by his successor, Henry VII, the Richmond of the play. In fact, although the record is obscure, it is thought that Richard may have named Warwick his successor after the death of his own son (who does not appear in the play) in 1484. Later, after a number of people attempted to impersonate the imprisoned Warwick and seize power, Henry finally had him executed.

Brakenbury, Robert (Robert Brackenbury) (d. 1485)   Historical figure and character in *Richard III*, the commander of the TOWER OF LONDON and thus the chief jailer of, first, Clarence and, later, the young Prince Edward and his brother York. Some editions of the play follow the first QUARTO and assign Brakenbury the lines of the Keeper in 1.4.

The historical Brakenbury was a Constable of the Tower, but not at the time of Clarence's death. The inconsistency doubtless resulted from Shakespeare's marked compression of historical time in the early part of the play. Brakenbury was killed at the battle of BOSWORTH FIELD, as is reported in 5.5.14.

Brandon, Sir William (d. 1485)   Historical figure and minor character in *Richard III*, a follower of the Earl of Richmond. In 5.3 Brandon is among Richmond's officers and is designated as the Earl's standard bearer in the forthcoming battle of BOSWORTH FIELD. In 5.5 his death in the battle is reported. Historically, Brandon was the father of the Duke of Suffolk, who appears in *Henry VIII*.

Buckingham, Henry Stafford, Duke of (1455–1483)   Historical figure and character in *Richard III*, the most important supporter of Richard III before he deserts the king in response to his ingratitude.

Buckingham acts as a spokesman for Richard's positions, especially to the Mayor and the people of London. His style of speaking, bombastic and obscure, is typical of devious politicians, and his wily, conspiratorial nature makes him an important adviser to Richard at several junctures, notably in hatching the plot against Hastings. He prides himself on his capacity for deceit in the remarkable conversation that opens 3.5.

However, in 4.2, when Richard, now enthroned, proposes to go further and kill the young Prince of Wales and his brother, Buckingham is somewhat reluctant, perhaps sensing that a king should be more cautious. Richard, angered, then refuses Buckingham the earldom he had promised him. Buckingham perceives that he is in danger of suffering Hastings's fate, and he decides to abandon the king. He raises an army in rebellion but is quickly captured. In 5.1 Buckingham, about to be executed, formally reflects on his circumstances, recollecting past oaths and prophecies almost in the manner of a Greek CHORUS. Thus, in a prelude to the approaching doom of Richard, Buckingham invokes the sense of ordained fate that is central to the play.

Shakespeare's sources offered several possible motives for Buckingham's revolt, but Shakespeare chose one that was definitely untrue, for Richard had given Buckingham his earldom prior to his defection. The question cannot be answered with the surviving evidence; he may simply have anticipated Richard's overthrow by Richmond. It has been suggested that Buckingham was ambitious to rule, for he had a distant claim to the throne himself, being descended from Thomas, Duke of Gloucester, the youngest brother of Richard II. Buckingham's father was the Duke of Buckingham of *2 Henry VI*, and his son appears as Buckingham in *Henry VIII*.

Cardinal, Lord (Thomas Bourchier) (ca. 1404–1486) Historical figure and minor character in *Richard III*, the Archbishop of Canterbury. In 3.1 the Cardinal is persuaded by Buckingham to remove the young Duke of YORK from sanctuary in a church. The historical Bourchier was a politically accommodating prelate who crowned Edward IV, Richard III, and Henry VII, the Richmond of the play.

In some modern editions of the play, the Archbishop of York is eliminated and his lines are given to the Cardinal, following the 16th-century QUARTO editions. This change was presumably made as an economy for the acting company.

Catesby, Sir William (d. 1485) Historical figure and character in *Richard III*, a follower of King Richard III. Catesby is a useful underling who appears in many scenes, mostly as a messenger, and he lacks a distinct personality. The historical Catesby was a lawyer who served as estate manager for Lord Hastings. He was captured and executed after the battle of BOSWORTH FIELD.

Christopher (Sir Christopher Urswick) (1448–1522) Historical figure and minor character in *Richard III*, a follower of Richmond. Prior to Richmond's invasion of England, Sir Christopher Urswick makes contact with Lord Thomas Stanley, Richmond's stepfather, who confirms his intention to defect from Richard III. The historical Urswick was a priest in the employ of Margaret Beaufort, Richmond's mother and Stanley's wife.

Citizens Several minor characters in *Richard III*, common people of LONDON who respond to the sinister affairs surrounding the crown. In 2.3, three Citizens discuss the death of King Edward IV and the ambitions of Richard III in tones of anxious foreboding. One of them summarizes their viewpoint: "All may be well; but if God sort it so / 'Tis more than we deserve, or I expect" (2.3.36–37). In 3.7 a number of Citizens accompany the Mayor to witness Richard's charade of unwillingness to accept the crown, and their silence speaks volumes about the usurper's impropriety.

Clarence, George York, Duke of (1449–1478) Historical figure and character in *Richard III*, the victimized brother of Richard III. Richard reveals in his opening soliloquy (1.1) that he has turned King Edward IV, his oldest brother, against Clarence, his next oldest. When Clarence is arrested in the same scene, Richard sympathizes with him and promises him assistance, but in fact he proceeds to hire two murderers to kill him. Thus Clarence is to be removed from the succession to the crown, leaving Richard in his place.

In 1.4 we see Clarence in his cell in the TOWER OF LONDON. He has just awakened from a terrible nightmare, in which he was drowned and went to hell. There he encountered the spirits of both the Earl of Warwick, whom he had betrayed, and the one-time Prince of Wales, whom he had helped to murder. (Both events are enacted, with Clarence appearing as George in *3 Henry VI.*) Awake but still afraid, he admits that his conscience is heavy.

The murderers arrive, and Clarence learns that Richard, whom he had thought he might rely on in his distress, has hired them. He piteously bewails his fate. The Second Murderer, who had displayed pangs of conscience earlier, is prepared to relent, but the First Murderer proceeds to stab Clarence and, for good measure, seals him in a cask of wine to ensure that he won't survive.

Clarence's death scene is an emotional highlight of the play. It has tremendous impact, shocking the audience, for Richard's villainy, which has been seductively entertaining up to this point, is now seen to have serious consequences. Clarence's account of his dream reveals a soul in torment; he speaks in passionate verse, the most lyrical in the play. His spiritual suffering—his heavyhearted loss of hope and fear of death—is intense. The scene anchors much of the action that follows: Although Richard's coldhearted machinations result only in offstage violence, they nevertheless cannot be witnessed without recalling this chilling evidence of their real weight.

Shakespeare's account of Clarence's death has little relation to history, though the playwright certainly believed it to be true; he took it from his chief source for the HISTORY PLAYS, the account of the WARS OF THE ROSES written by Edward HALL. Historically, Richard actually protested against Clarence's imprisonment and execution. However, Clarence's position was irreparable, for he had persisted in involving himself in plots against King Edward. After forgiving his brother several times (one of these occasions is dramatized in *3 Henry VI*), Edward finally ordered Clarence's trial for treason, appearing in person as the prosecutor.

Clarence was sentenced to death, and a few days later his death was announced, although there was no public execution, as would have been ordinary. This last detail may account for the persistence of the rumor that Richard had Clarence murdered, which was, by Shakespeare's time, accepted as fact.

Dorset, Thomas Grey, Marquis of (1451–1501) Historical figure and character in *Richard III*, the son of Elizabeth Woodville by her first marriage. Dorset appears with his mother, the Queen of England, several times in the early scenes of the play. In 2.2 he offers her the rather cold comfort, on the occasion of the death of King Edward IV, that God is simply taking back the gift of royalty that He had given. In 4.1, when the Queen receives word that Richard III has seized the crown, Dorset is sent abroad to join Richmond. Following the FIRST FOLIO stage directions, many modern editions include Dorset among Richmond's followers at BOSWORTH FIELD in 5.3, although he does not speak. In actuality, the invading Earl had left Dorset in France as a hostage to ensure the cooperation of his mother's party.

Duchess of York, Cicely Neville (1415–1495) Historical figure and character in *Richard III*, the mother of Richard III and his brothers, Edward IV and Clarence. The widow of Richard, Duke of York, a major figure in the *Henry VI* plays, she was also the mother of Rutland, who figures briefly in *3 Henry VI*. The Duchess is a symbolic figure whose role is to lament Richard's evil nature in a stylized manner reminiscent of a Greek CHORUS. Shakespeare's sources hardly mention her; it is thought that the playwright was influenced by similar characters in the plays of SENECA. The historical Cicely Neville was a daughter of Ralph, Earl of Westmoreland, who appears in *1* and *2 Henry IV* and *Henry V*.

Edward IV, King of England See Edward IV, King of England, in *Henry VI, Part 3*.

Ely, John Morton, Bishop of (ca. 1420–1500) Historical figure and minor character in *Richard III*, a pawn in the scenario arranged by Richard III as he strikes at Lord Hastings in 3.4. At a council meeting, Richard requests that the genial Ely send for some strawberries from his garden, thereby establishing a mood of cordiality that he shortly shatters with his accusations of treason. Both Hastings and the audience have been lulled into a false sense of security that is rudely smashed, in a manner symbolic of Richard's effect on the entire realm. As ineffectual as Ely seems here, he is later, at 4.3.46, said to have joined the forces of the Earl of Richmond, thus contributing to Richard's downfall.

The historical John Morton had been a rising young ecclesiastical lawyer when the WARS OF THE ROSES broke out. He became a firm Lancastrian, to the extent of joining Queen Margaret in exile. However, after the Yorkist victory, he submitted to the victors and resumed his clerical and legal career with great success. He was appointed Bishop of Ely in 1479, and he was the executor of the will of King Edward IV. But under Richard he fared less well. After the incident described above, Ely, as an adherent of the young Prince, was among those arrested. He was placed in the TOWER OF LONDON, but the Duke of Buckingham took over his custody after several years and recruited him to his rebellious conspiracy. Ely joined Richmond abroad, and when that earl was crowned as Henry VII, the bishop became a prominent member of his government. Morton was also to become the patron of the young Thomas MORE, whose history was Shakespeare's source for the strawberry anecdote. Thus its historical accuracy seems certain.

First Murderer   Character in *Richard III*, one of two hired assassins employed by Richard III to kill his brother the Duke of Clarence. The First Murderer coolly accepts his role as a killer, whereas the Second Murderer has an attack of conscience as they approach their victim in 1.4. Later in this scene, when Clarence pleads for mercy and the Second Murderer seems inclined to yield, the First stabs the Duke, carries him off stage, and drowns him in a large barrel of wine.

Gentleman   Minor character in *Richard III*. The Gentleman vainly attempts to prevent Richard III from interrupting the funeral procession of Henry VI, early in 1.2, and then restarts the procession, at Richard's command, later in this scene. He speaks one line on each occasion. His first line is sometimes assigned to a Halberdier, for the abuse the character takes from Richard is thought inappropriate for a gentleman. Villainous though he is, it is supposed that Richard would observe the formal distinctions between aristocrats and commoners.

Ghost   Any of 11 minor but significant characters in *Richard III*, the ghosts of the victims of Richard III, who appear to King Richard and his enemy Richmond in 5.3, on the eve of the battle of BOSWORTH FIELD. The ghosts each deliver brief messages, insisting that Richard shall "despair and die" and assuring Richmond of victory. The ghosts appear in the order in which they died: the ghosts of the Prince of Wales and his father, Henry VI, hark back to murders Richard committed in *3 Henry VI*, the preceding play in Shakespeare's TETRALOGY. Next appears the ghost of Richard's brother Clarence, followed by those of Lords Rivers, Grey, and Vaughan. The ghost of Lord William Hastings comes forth next, succeeded by those of the two children Richard had ordered killed—Edward, Prince of Wales, and his brother, Richard, Duke of York. Richard is then faced by the ghost of his wife Anne, only recently eliminated so that the King could make a politically convenient second marriage. The ghost of Richard's closest ally in his bloody rise to power, the Duke of Buckingham, executed only two scenes earlier, appears last. Shakespeare's source, the history by Edward HALL, mentions rumors that Richard had complained of nightmares before the battle, but the content of the dreams appears to be the playwright's invention.

Girl (Margaret Plantagenet)   (1473–1541)   Historical figure and minor character in *Richard III*, the daughter of Clarence. The Girl mourns her father's murder in 2.2 and is present but silent in 4.1. Richard is fearful that a husband of the Girl might claim the throne, her father having been the heir apparent. He remarks in 4.3.37 that he has therefore married her to a low-ranking husband, who cannot claim the crown. Historically, this maneuver was performed by Richard's conqueror and successor, Henry VII, the Richmond of the play. At the age of

68, being the last surviving PLANTAGENET, Margaret was beheaded by a paranoid Henry VIII.

Gloucester, Duke of   See Richard III, King of England.

Grey, Sir Richard (d. 1483)   Historical figure and character in *Richard III*, a kinsman of Queen Elizabeth and a victim of Richard III. Grey simply functions as a pawn in Richard's game of power politics. He is executed in 3.3 solely because he is the Queen's relative. As he goes to his death, along with Rivers and Vaughan, he recollects the curses of Queen Margaret, who had anticipated this event in 1.3.

Shakespeare was apparently confused about Grey's relationship to Elizabeth, although his habitual carelessness about minor matters suggests that he probably did not concern himself about it. Historically, Grey was Elizabeth's son by her first marriage, but in the play he is implied to be her brother. However, in recalling Margaret's curse, he speaks as though he were Dorset, unquestionably a son of Elizabeth.

Halberdier   Minor character in *Richard III*, one of the soldiers guarding the coffin of King Henry VI in 1.2. The Halberdier vainly attempts to prevent Richard III from interrupting the King's funeral procession. (A halberd, the weapon assigned this character in the stage directions, was a combination of lance and battle-ax, mounted on a long pole.)

The Halberdier's single speech is attributed to him by modern editors who feel that older editions err in giving it to the Gentleman. A gentleman, it is argued, would neither receive nor accept the abuse that Richard heaps on the unfortunate soldier. Villainous though he is, it is supposed that Richard would observe the formal distinctions between aristocrats and commoners.

Hastings, Pursuivant   Minor character in *Richard III*, a petty official. In 3.2 Lord William Hastings, converses briefly with his like-named acquaintance, conveying the information that his enemies, the allies of Queen Elizabeth, have been imprisoned.

The Lord remarks that they had last met when he himself had been under arrest and in danger of execution; the audience is aware that, ironically, he is about to be imperiled again. This curious incident, although it depicts a historical event recorded in Shakespeare's sources, seems to have little point in the drama, unless it is intended to help to emphasize the intricate workings of fate, by virtue of the coincidences of names and circumstances. However, many editions of the play have followed the FIRST FOLIO version in ignoring this character's name, referring to him only by his title, Pursuivant, which signifies a minor subordinate of a herald.

Hastings, Lord William (ca. 1430–1483)   Historical figure and character in *3 Henry VI* and *Richard III*, a Yorkist supporter who becomes a victim of political murder. In *3 Henry VI* Hastings is only a minor nobleman attached to Edward IV, but in *Richard III* he is more prominent. He exemplifies the pettiness of English public life during the WARS OF THE ROSES. He profits from Richard's rise, as his old enemies are imprisoned and sentenced to death, but he is unwilling to aid his leader's attempt to seize the crown; he is reluctant to oppose the legal heirs. Richard accordingly turns on him, but Hastings, ignoring warnings, has too little imagination to conceive that his situation has changed. In 3.4 Richard fabricates a tale of treason, accuses Hastings, and condemns him to death in one sentence, as his victim sits speechless. In 3.7 Richard justifies Hastings's immediate execution, citing the dangers of the supposed plot.

The historical Hastings played an obscure role in the events surrounding Richard's accession. Shakespeare followed his source in having Richard fabricate Hastings's treason, but it was probably real. In June 1483 he apparently joined in an attempt to unseat Richard from his position as Protector of Edward's young heir. The plot failed, and Richard arrested Hastings and had him executed without a trial, as in the play.

Herbert, Sir Walter (ca. 1462–after 1485)   Historical figure and minor character in *Richard III*, an officer under Richmond. Herbert, whose father, William of Pembroke, has a nonspeaking role in

3 Henry VI, speaks one line in 5.2 and is present but silent in 5.3.

Keeper   Minor character in *Richard III*, the jailer of Clarence in the TOWER OF LONDON. The Keeper listens sympathetically to Clarence's report of a nightmare in 1.4. Some editions follow the first QUARTO and assign the Keeper's part to Brakenbury. The dropping of the character doubtless reflects an economy measure by a 16th-century acting company.

Lovell, Sir Francis (Sir Francis Lovel) (1454–1487)   Historical figure and character in *Richard III*, a supporter of Richard III. Lovell is willing to undertake Richard's dirty work; he assists Ratcliffe in the execution of Lord Hastings, bringing that lord's severed head to Richard in 3.5.

The historical Lovell was Richard's Lord Chamberlain. He escaped capture after the battle of BOSWORTH FIELD and died two years later, fighting in an uprising against Richmond, by then King Henry VII. He was a distant cousin of Sir Thomas Lovell, who appears in *Henry VIII*.

Mayor of London   Minor character in *Richard III*, a subservient figure who is cowed by Richard III. The Mayor appears in several scenes in Act 3. He provides a cover of legality for Richard's actions, approving an execution and acclaiming Richard as king when he moves to seize the throne.

Messenger   Any of several minor characters in *Richard III*, bearers of news. In 2.4 a Messenger brings word to Queen Elizabeth that her son and brother have been imprisoned, and in 3.2 a Messenger delivers to Hastings an account of an ominous dream from Stanley. In a highly dramatic use of messengers, Shakespeare brings four on stage successively in 4.4, within a few lines, to demonstrate Richard's lack of control as news floods in of rebellion against him. In 5.3 one last Messenger brings Richard word of Stanley's desertion at BOSWORTH FIELD.

Norfolk, John Howard, Duke of (ca. 1430–1485)   Historical figure and minor character in *Richard III*, commander of the forces of Richard III at the battle of BOSWORTH FIELD. A quiet follower of orders, Nor-

folk brings Richard a note warning of treachery in the forthcoming battle, in 5.3. His death in the fighting is noted at 5.5.13. His son, his second in command, is the Earl of Surrey (who appears in *Henry VIII* as Norfolk). Norfolk was a grandson of Thomas Mowbray, who appears in *Richard II*.

In 1483 the historical Norfolk received his dukedom for his services in securing for Richard the office of Protector. This may account for his silent presence in the stage directions to 3.4.

Northumberland, Henry Percy, Earl of (1446–1489)   Historical figure mentioned in *Richard III*, an apparent follower of Richard III. On the eve of the battle of BOSWORTH FIELD, Richard refers to "the melancholy Lord Northumberland" (5.3.69) as one of his officers. This is the son of the Northumberland of *3 Henry VI*, who had died in the battle against the Yorkist king Edward IV (and against Richard) at TOWTON and whose lands and title had been seized by the victors. After the defection of Warwick, King Edward sought new allies, and he returned the Northumberland fiefdom to this Northumberland, who was accordingly with Richard at Bosworth. However, Shakespeare did not mention the denouement of the relationship: Northumberland refused to bring his many troops into the fighting, and after the battle he immediately found favor with Richmond.

Oxford, Earl of   See Oxford, John de Vere, Earl of, in *Henry VI, Part 3*.

Page   Minor character in *Richard III*, an attendant to Richard III. In 4.2 Richard asks the Page to recommend an ambitious nobleman to do a desperate deed. The youth names James Tyrell, whom Richard commissions to murder his nephews.

Penker, Friar (Friar Pynkie) (active 1483)   Historical figure and minor character in *Richard III*, one of two clergymen who, disguised as Bishops, accompany Richard III as he receives the Mayor in 3.7. This imposture is intended to lend an air of religiosity to the would-be usurper. Penker and Doctor Shaa were summoned by Richard in 3.5.

In Thomas MORE's history, one of Shakespeare's sources for this anecdote, Penker's name is Pynkie, and he is described as a Provincial of the Augustine friars, a fairly high-ranking administrator.

Priest   Minor character in *Richard III*, a friend of Lord Hastings. Hastings engages in small talk with the Priest in 3.2, demonstrating his naive lack of concern about the danger from Richard that he has been warned about.

Prince of Wales, Edward (Edward V, King of England)   (1470–ca. 1483)   Historical figure and character in *Richard III*, the son and heir of King Edward IV whom Richard III murders. The Prince appears only once, when he arrives in London after his father's death. Although technically king, he is never crowned and is known as the Prince throughout the play. Being taken to the TOWER OF LONDON and his eventual death, the Prince, 12 years old, impresses us with his serious concern for history. He also provides an ironic commentary on the way the story of his own death has been transmitted, officially unrecorded but nonetheless known: "But say, my lord, it were not register'd / Methinks the truth should live from age to age . . ." (3.1.75–76). The murder—at Richard's instigation—of the Prince and his younger brother, the Duke of York, is reported in 4.3 and mourned thereafter. It is clearly intended to be taken as the most heinous of Richard's crimes.

Shakespeare had no doubt as to Richard's guilt, and posterity, greatly influenced by Shakespeare, has agreed. Modern scholarship, however, has thrown doubt on the whole question of the fate of the princes. It is known that they entered the Tower in June 1483 and never emerged, but how they died and who was responsible are not clear (see TYRELL, SIR JAMES) and may never be, except in the unlikely event that new evidence is uncovered.

In *3 Henry VI* the Prince appears in the final scene as an infant, virtually a stage property, to be displayed by his father. The baby is kissed by his uncles, as a token of loyalty to King Edward. This incident is noteworthy for the behavior of Richard, who characterizes himself in an aside as comparable to Judas, in kissing one to whom he intends harm.

Pursuivant   See Hastings, Pursuivant.

Queen Elizabeth   See Elizabeth Woodville, in *Henry VI, Part 3*.

Queen Margaret   See Margaret of Anjou, in *Henry VI, Part 1*.

Ratcliffe, Sir Richard   (d. 1485)   Historical figure and character in *Richard III*, a follower of Richard III. Ratcliffe is a minor underling, distinctive chiefly for his efficient executions of Rivers, Grey, and Vaughan in 3.3 and Hastings in 3.4. The historical Ratcliffe was a longtime and trusted adviser of Richard who had fought with him at TEWKESBURY. He died at the battle of BOSWORTH FIELD.

Richard III, King of England (Richard Plantagenet, Duke of Gloucester)   (1452–1485)   Character in *2* and *3 Henry VI* and title character of *Richard III*. Known simply as Richard or Gloucester until he is crowned in 4.2 of *Richard III*, his ambition never ceases to drive him toward that moment. Richard is more than simply a villain; his dazzlingly evil nature, combining viciousness and wit, makes him as important and valuable to the drama, especially in *Richard III*, as any hero. He was Shakespeare's first great creation, marking a tremendous advance over earlier, more ordinary characters.

Richard makes his first appearance late in *2 Henry VI*, when he is called to support his father, the Duke of York. His role is minor; he is present chiefly as a foreshadowing of the sequels to the play. He is nevertheless a cleanly drawn figure, sardonically epigrammatic. For instance, he encourages himself in battle with the cry, "Priests pray for enemies, but princes kill" (5.2.71). His bold and willfully, even pridefully, cruel nature is already evident, after only a few lines.

In 1.1 of *3 Henry VI* Richard's extraordinary personality bursts forth. As the nobles recount their exploits at the battle of ST. ALBANS, Richard abruptly throws down the head of Somerset, saying, "Speak thou for me, and tell them what I did" (1.1.16). Richard's bloodthirstiness, not unmixed with dry humor, is evident throughout the play, pointing toward the horrors he is to commit in *Richard III*. In his famous soliloquy at the end of 3.2, he describes himself as able to ". . . smile, and murder whiles I smile"; he will "set the murderous Machiavel to school" (3.2.182, 193). Killing the imprisoned King Henry VI, Richard raises his bloody sword and sarcastically crows, "See how my sword weeps for the poor king's death" (5.6.63). This bloody villain is fully conscious of his own viciousness and savors it with a cocky irony that seems very modern. At the close of the play, he even delightedly identifies himself with the arch-traitor of Christian tradition, Judas Iscariot. Richard's monstrously evil nature is thoroughly established in *3 Henry VI*, in order that it may attain fullest fruition in *Richard III*.

In *Richard III* the title character has the second-longest part in all of Shakespeare's work (only Hamlet speaks more lines). He murders his way to the throne, killing his brother, his young nephews, his wife, and a number of political opponents. He is still a spectacular villain, with a fondness for com-menting humorously on his atrocities before com-mitting them. Once he becomes king, however, his wit and resourcefulness desert him; he clumsily alienates his allies and quite simply panics when he first learns of the approach of Richmond. In Act 5 he dies in battle, defeated at BOSWORTH FIELD. Richmond's triumph releases England from the vio-lence and treachery of the WARS OF THE ROSES.

The personality of Shakespeare's Richard is formed in part by his physical deformity—a hunched back—referred to many times in the plays, often by Richard himself. At the end of *3 Henry VI*, for instance, he says, ". . . since the heav-ens have shap'd my body so, / Let hell make crook'd my mind to answer it" (5.6.78–79). He rationalizes his rejection of human loyalties by theorizing that his physical nature has placed him beyond ordinary relationships. Thus he can claim, "I am myself alone" (5.6.83). Others agree with him: A number of characters associate Richard's deformity with his evil nature. Queen Margaret, for example, asserts, "Sin, death, and hell have set their marks on him . . ." (*Richard III*, 1.3.293), and various of his enemies identify him with a range of carnivorous animals and with such repulsive creatures as spi-ders, toads, and reptiles.

However, our fascination with Richard derives largely from the disturbing reality that he has undeniably attractive qualities as well. He has charisma and self-confidence, and he is plainly quite intelligent. He has great energy combined with immense self-control, and, probably most tellingly, he is extremely witty. He cracks a joke even as he plots the murder of his brother in 1.1.118–120 of *Richard III*.

Richard wins admiration even as he repels because he plays to the audience directly. Through his monologues and asides, he brings us into an almost conspiratorial intimacy with him. He some-times tells us what is shortly going to occur, and then he comments on it afterward. In practicing deceit, he also takes on different roles, much as an actor does: He plays a loyal follower of his brother King Edward IV, a lover opposite Lady Anne, a friend to his brother Clarence, and a pious devotee of religion before the Mayor and his entourage.

With the collapse of his fortunes, Richard's per-sonality changes. He loses his resilience and sub-tlety; he panics and is disorganized in the face of crisis. We learn that his sleep is troubled; such insomnia was a traditional consequence for royal usurpers, and Shakespeare's sources impute it to Richard conventionally, but the playwright makes more of it, letting both Anne and Richard himself remark on it, before presenting us with an actual nightmare vision in 5.3 of *Richard III*. At this low ebb, Richard seems almost deranged. He recognizes his terrible isolation from humanity and despairs, crying out in anguish that his death will neither receive nor deserve pity from anyone. However, Richard recovers his spirit later in the scene and leads his men into battle with renewed flippancy.

Richard represents a well-known type who was a popular figure on the Elizabethan stage, the grandiose villain, first embodied in *Tamburlaine*, by Christopher MARLOWE, still popular when *Richard III* premiered. However, the character has a longer pedigree than that. The medieval MORALITY PLAY featured a villain figure, the VICE, whose resem-blance to characters in Shakespeare and Marlowe is not coincidental; both writers must have been familiar with the Vice since childhood. But Richard also incorporates a more modern archetype, the MACHIAVEL, a calculating politician whose mis-deeds are directed toward particular ends. The

Vice's lewd jests and common horseplay give way to a grave assessment of political interest, although verbal wit is part of the Machiavel's character. The Machiavel is a naturalistic figure—a human being, if a depraved one—while the Vice is more allegorical in nature. Thus Richard's personality has a humanly believable quality that is lacking in the criminal-king of traditional history.

It is plain that Shakespeare's character bears very little resemblance to the actual King Richard III, who ruled only briefly. Surviving accounts of his times were written largely by his enemies, and modern scholarship has discovered that the reality of his reign bore little resemblance to the version Shakespeare received and popularized.

Richard has long been envisioned as the physically repellent hunchback of legend. Thomas MORE first wrote of Richard's physical deformity, and Shakespeare followed suit. However, at his coronation Richard was stripped to the waist for anointing, in accordance with tradition, and this exposure seems to have provoked no comment. In fact, a hunched back is nowhere evident in contemporary portraits or accounts of the man. It appears to have been a malicious fiction, although Shakespeare surely believed it to be true.

More interesting are the playwright's purposeful alterations of the historical record as he had it. As was his usual practice, Shakespeare took many liberties with his already unreliable sources. For instance, at the end of *2 Henry VI*, Richard is made to participate in a battle that occurred when he was only three years old. Richard actually lived in exile until after Edward was crowned. His part in history did not begin until the battle of BARNET, enacted in Act 5 of *3 Henry VI*. Shakespeare wrote him into the action earlier, in order to begin to approach the grand denouement in *Richard III*, which he must have foreseen as he wrote the *Henry VI* plays. Richard also provides an interesting foil for Edward's tenderer character.

This premature introduction is magnified by giving Richard the desire to rule long before the question arises in the sources. Shakespeare's Richard begins to think, "How sweet a thing it is to wear a crown" (*3 Henry VI*, 1.2.29), fully 23 years before he comes to put one on. Not only does this generate a long, slow rise in tension, but it also empha-

Richard III (played here by Laurence Olivier) was Shakespeare's first great creation. A dazzlingly evil villain, he is as dramatically rich as many of the heroes of later plays. *(Courtesy of Culver Pictures, Inc.)*

sizes Richard's nefarious ambition early. Thus, when he is finally brought down, the resolution of England's predicament is a clear one: Richard's career has been so strikingly criminal that his death stimulates no further fighting in revenge.

The historical Richard was a very different man, innocent of most, if not all, of the crimes imputed to him. Shakespeare's sources attributed the murder of Henry VI to Richard, and the playwright added urgency to his villain's action by inventing an impetuous journey to London for the purpose. Modern scholars hold that Edward gave the order for the ex-king's death; Richard, as Constable of England, would have been responsible for seeing the order carried out. Henry's son, the Prince of Wales, murdered by Richard and his brothers in 5.5 of *3 Henry VI*, actually died in battle. Richard appears to have opposed the execution of Clarence, which was definitely Edward's doing, historically. Richard's wife, Lady Anne, died naturally.

That Richard did seize the throne is indisputable; that he had long plotted to that end seems unlikely. He could not have anticipated Edward's death at 40, and he seems to have been committed to a career as a ranking prince. He was clearly a trusted and reliable subordinate to his brother, governing the difficult northern provinces with marked success for 12 years. Edward had named Richard, the obvious choice, to serve as Protector after his death, ruling for his son, the Prince of Wales. But when Edward died, Queen Elizabeth and her relatives attempted a coup, keeping the news of the king's death from his brother, assembling military forces, and arranging for the Prince's hasty coronation. However, Richard overcame these maneuvers and assumed his role as Protector. He apparently had plans for parliamentary confirmation of this arrangement, along with the boy's later coronation, when another coup was attempted. Richard crushed this plot, but he now decided to forestall a third coup by taking the crown himself. It is impossible, with the evidence that is known today, to reconstruct the events of June 1483 precisely, but as far as history indicates, this marks the beginning of the process that Shakespeare presents as starting two decades earlier. Also, *Richard III* compresses Richard's two-year reign into a few frantic weeks. He seems to have been a quite competent king, though the shortness of his troubled reign makes judgment difficult. Shakespeare was unconcerned with the strengths or weaknesses of Richard as ruler; he simply wanted to introduce Richard's splendid crash immediately after his seeming success.

Richard may or may not have murdered Edward's two sons. Once presumed guilty—at least in good part on the strength of Shakespeare's evidence—Richard has attracted defenders in recent years. It has been observed that, once securely in power, he did not need to have them killed; that the Duke of Buckingham, thought to have coveted the crown himself, had a better motive; that Richmond, as Henry VII, might well have killed them, as he did a number of other possible pretenders to the crown. However, the two youths were never seen again after entering the TOWER OF LONDON in 1483, and responsibility must lie with Richard.

This does not make him the fierce killer of the plays, of course; if he did have the princes murdered, he was simply following a fairly ordinary political convention of the day. However, what Shakespeare's rendering of Richard's career lacks in historical validity, it more than makes up for in theatrical success. Richard as a magnificent evildoer has entered our cultural consciousness, and there he remains; we can hardly wish it otherwise.

Richmond, Earl of (Henry Tudor, later King Henry VII) (1457–1509) Historical figure and character in *3 Henry VI* and *Richard III*, the victor over King Richard III at the battle of BOSWORTH FIELD and his successor on the throne, as Henry VII. In *3 Henry VI* Richmond plays a very minor but significant role. In 4.6 he appears as a child before the newly reinstated King Henry VI, who predicts that the boy will become a ruler and the salvation of England. This entirely fictitious episode, which Shakespeare took from his sources, reveals the extreme pro-Tudor bias (see TUDOR DYNASTY) of Elizabethan historiography and therefore of the HISTORY PLAYS.

In *Richard III* Richmond's appearance in Act 5 is prepared for by Richard's panic in Act 4 at messages announcing his approach. Richmond himself arrives in 5.2; in 5.3 he is addressed by the spirits that appear to Richard on the night before the battle. In 5.5 he kills Richard in hand-to-hand combat, and in the final episode he pronounces an end to the WARS OF THE ROSES, which had beleaguered England for a generation. He is a somewhat bloodless if energetic leader, pious and filled with an awareness of his own high mission. In addressing his troops, he can claim as allies, "The prayers of holy saints and wronged souls" (5.3.242). He closes the play with a speech declaring a new era of peace and prosperity for England, ending with the sentiment, ". . . peace lives again. / That she may long live here, God say Amen."

Richmond is plainly an instrument of heavenly providence rather than a three-dimensional human being, as indicated by his rather stiff bearing and stuffy diction. He must be taken at his symbolic, ritualistic value; he is the antithesis of the ambitious nobility, exemplified by Richard, that has plagued England throughout the reign of Henry VI. He brings redemption for the crimes and sins that have been committed in the names of YORK and LAN-CASTER. In a confrontation reminiscent of a medieval MORALITY PLAY, whose traditions still lived in Shakespeare's time, Richmond represents Good, winning a classic showdown against Evil.

The historical Richmond was descended, through his maternal grandfather, from John of Gaunt, the original head of the Lancaster family, and he attracted the support of such former followers of Henry VI as John de Vere, Duke of Oxford. He was the last surviving Lancastrian male and therefore fled England in 1471, after the battle of TEWKESBURY, and lived in Brittany and FRANCE. His mother, Margaret Beaufort, Countess of Richmond, remained in England, married Lord Stanley, and conspired against the Yorkist kings. She is mentioned in 1.3.20–29 of *Richard III*. She negotiated her son's marriage, announced by him in the final speech of the play, to the daughter of Elizabeth, thus uniting the York and Lancaster branches of the PLANTAGENET FAMILY.

Richmond's other grandfather was Owen Tudor, a minor Welsh nobleman who had married the widow of Henry V, the Princess Katharine of France who appears in Shakespeare's *Henry V*. Richmond inherited from his father both his title and his descent from the kings of France.

After the time of *Richard III*, Richmond was to rule as Henry VII, the first monarch of the Tudor dynasty. He was a highly capable ruler, sometimes called England's greatest. He restored order following the wars and administered soundly, eventually leaving a large financial surplus to his heir, Henry VIII. Unhinted at in Shakespeare is the historical reality that Henry VII was every bit as ruthless as the Richard of the plays. While he adopted reconciliation as a general policy, he killed troublesome people when he saw fit. In fact, Shakespeare's Richard is saddled with several reprehensible deeds that Henry actually committed. For example, Richard says that he has imprisoned Edward of Warwick, the Boy of *Richard III*, at 4.3.36. But Henry incarcerated him because he was a potential claimant to the throne. After a number of people attempted to impersonate Warwick and seize power, Henry finally executed him in 1499. Shakespeare has Richard manipulate the life of Warwick's sister as well, marrying the Girl to a low-ranking man who cannot claim the crown. This, too, was actually Henry's doing.

Henry also sought to ensure the popularity of his usurpation by blackening the reputation of his predecessor, Richard. He encouraged the writing of vicious biographies that contributed to the legend embodied in Shakespeare's character. He also commissioned an official history of England from the Italian humanist Polydore VERGIL; this work, published in 1534, helped create the understanding of the English past that was available to Shakespeare when he wrote his history plays.

Rivers, Anthony Woodville, Earl of (ca. 1442–1483)   Historical figure and character in *3 Henry VI* and *Richard III*, the brother of Queen Elizabeth and one of the victims of Richard III. He is the son of Richard Woodville, who appears in *1 Henry VI*. Rivers plays a very minor role in *3 Henry VI*; in *Richard III* he is a pawn in a political game, being executed for no other offense than being the queen's brother and so a presumptive defender of her son, the Prince of Wales, who stands in the way of Richard III's climb to power. As he is led to his death with Grey and Vaughan in 3.3, Rivers functions as a sort of CHORUS, referring to POMFRET CASTLE, scene of many such events, and recollecting the curses of Queen Margaret, who had foretold his end in 1.3.

The historical Rivers served King Edward IV as a viceroy, governing rebellious WALES with great success. After the king's death, Richard assumed the office of Protector, ruling for the new heir, as Edward had stipulated. Rivers participated in an attempt to unseat the Protector; he was imprisoned and later, after a second coup failed, was executed.

Scrivener   Minor character in *Richard III*, a clerk who learns of a crime committed by Richard III. In 3.6 the Scrivener, whose job is to make formal written copies of documents, knows that a certain indictment he has copied is false. Supposedly the record of a proceeding justifying the hasty execution of Lord Hastings, it was actually written before Hastings had even been accused of any misdeed. The Scrivener realizes that Richard has arranged for the death of an innocent man through legal means, and he grieves that the state of public affairs permits such a ploy to succeed.

This incident, like one in 2.3, serves to emphasize that corruption can never be secret. The common people become aware of such cynical machinations, and society comes closer to political chaos as its leaders seem increasingly untrustworthy. This pattern grows more evident as Richard's ambitions come to dominate public life.

Second Murderer   Character in *Richard III*, one of the two assassins hired by Richard III to kill his brother the Duke of Clarence. The Second Murderer has an attack of conscience as the two approach their victim in 1.4, but the First Murderer reminds him of the money they are to receive, and he recovers. Their short exchange provides the only real comic relief in the play. Later in this scene, in an entirely serious vein, the Second Murderer shows an inclination to grant Clarence the mercy he pleads for. The First Murderer thereupon finishes off the duke, and the Second declares that he is too remorseful to accept payment and leaves the reward to his colleague.

Shaa, Ralph (John Shaa, Ralph Shaw) (d. 1484)   Historical figure and minor character in *Richard III*, one of two clergymen who, disguised as Bishops, accompany Richard III as he receives the Mayor in 3.7. This imposture is intended to create an air of religiosity about the would-be usurper. Shaa and Friar Penker were summoned by Richard in 3.5. The historical Shaa, sometimes thought to have been named John, was a minor clergyman. He is known to have been a brother of the Mayor.

Sheriff   Minor character in *Richard III*, the officer who escorts the Duke of Buckingham to his execution in 5.1. In the QUARTO editions, this part is assigned to Ratcliffe, apparently reflecting an economy measure in some early productions.

Stanley, Sir Thomas (ca. 1435–1504)   Historical figure and character in *Richard III*, a nobleman who betrays Richard III. Richard, suspecting a defection to the Earl of Richmond, requires Stanley's son as a hostage. Stanley allies himself with Richmond: at

the battle of BOSWORTH FIELD, he refuses to march with his forces, to Richmond's advantage, but Richard's order to kill the hostage son is not carried out. After Richmond kills Richard in combat, Stanley places Richard's crown on the victor's head.

Shakespeare's Stanley is a judicious, if not a very bold, politician. The career of the historical Stanley was rather less honorable, if similarly successful. He held a powerful position in the north of England, but he was difficult to trust. During the WARS OF THE ROSES, he fought—and on occasion refused to fight—for both sides, as he strove to ally himself with the winning faction at any point. He accordingly ended up with high office under King Edward IV, and then under Richard. His wife, Richmond's mother, was implicated in the revolt of Buckingham, but Stanley maintained his position by turning against her, receiving custody of her estates. However, it is clear that he knew of Richmond's invasion before it happened. As a result, Richard took George Stanley hostage. George, who was an adult, not the boy spoken of in the play, was captured while attempting to escape; he saved his life by incriminating his uncle, William Stanley. Thomas Stanley did indeed withhold his troops at Bosworth, as Shakespeare reports, and Richard did order George killed but was ignored. Stanley was amply rewarded with high offices under Henry VII.

In some editions, Stanley is designated Derby, for Shakespeare used that title in introducing him in 1.3. However, he is Stanley in all dialogue thereafter. The use of the title in the play is an anachronism, for Stanley only received it after the accession of Henry VII. Most editors have made the correction in the dialogue headings and stage directions.

Surrey, Thomas Howard, Earl of (1443–1524)   Historical figure and minor character in *Richard III*, a general under Richard III at the battle of BOSWORTH FIELD. Surrey, second in command to his father, the Duke of Norfolk, appears briefly in 5.3. He seems despondent just before the fighting, but, when questioned by Richard, he assures the king that his heart is lighter than his looks.

The historical Surrey was restored to his father's titles by King Henry VII, the Richmond of the play, following a period of disgrace. He appears in *Henry*

VIII as the Duke of Norfolk. He was the father of another Earl of Surrey, who also appears in that play, and he was the grandfather of the poet Henry Howard, Earl of SURREY.

Tressel Minor character in *Richard III*, one of two named gentlemen among the group accompanying Lady Anne and the corpse of Henry VI in 1.2.

Tyrell, Sir James (Sir James Tirell) (ca. 1450–1502) Historical figure and character in *Richard III*, an unscrupulous and ambitious nobleman who agrees to arrange the murder of the Prince of Wales and his brother the Duke of York. Richard III, directed to Tyrell by a Page, commissions the killings in 4.2. At the beginning of 4.3, Tyrell returns to report that the deed has been accomplished by his hired ruffians.

The historical Tyrell was not the unknown minor aristocrat depicted by Shakespeare. He had served the Yorkist cause and been knighted at the battle of TEWKESBURY, and, at the time the princes were imprisoned, he was Richard's Master of Horse. After the accession of Henry VII, Tyrell continued to hold military posts until he was executed on unrelated charges, in 1502. He was reported to have admitted at that time to arranging the murders of the princes, and Shakespeare follows Thomas MORE's account of his alleged confession. Modern scholars generally find the story unconvincing, however, and the mystery of the princes' disappearance (and probable death) remains unsolved.

Urswick, Sir Christopher See Christopher.

Vaughan, Sir Thomas (d. 1483) Historical figure and minor character in *Richard III*, an ally of Queen Elizabeth. Vaughan appears only to be executed by Richard (Richard III) in 3.3. In going to his death, he speaks one line.

The historical Thomas Vaughan was a member of the official household of the Prince of Wales, son of Elizabeth and King Edward IV. The dying king had stipulated that Richard should rule for the boy when he inherited the crown, but Vaughan participated in an attempt to unseat Richard as Protector. He was executed as a result, although the play makes his condemnation seem arbitrary.

York, Richard, Duke of (1473–ca. 1483) Historical figure and character in *Richard III*, the murdered nephew of Richard III. The younger brother of Edward, Prince of Wales, and his successor to the throne, York is a flippant youngster, given to ill-considered jokes about Richard's deformity. He appears with his mother, Queen Elizabeth, and grandmother, the Duchess of York, in 2.4 and with his brother and others in 3.1. In the latter scene, he jests about Richard's dagger, in an ominous foreshadowing of his fate. At the end of the scene, the two young brothers are escorted to the TOWER OF LONDON, from which they will never emerge. Although their murder is commonly attributed to Richard, modern scholarship finds the fate of the princes to be impenetrably obscure, barring the unlikely emergence of new evidence (see TYRELL, SIR JAMES).

Romeo and Juliet

SYNOPSIS

Act 1, Prologue

The Chorus tells, in a SONNET, that the play will concern a pair of lovers whose deaths shall end the conflict between their feuding families.

Act 1, Scene 1

Sampson and Gregory, servants of the Capulet family, encounter Abram and Balthasar, of the Montague household, in a street in VERONA. They fight; Benvolio appears and tries to stop them, but Tybalt enters and insists on dueling with him. Some Citizens attempt to break up the brawl, as Capulet and Montague join in, to the dismay of their wives, Lady Capulet and Lady Montague. The Prince of Verona arrives and chastises both families. He declares that any further fighting will be punished with death. The Prince and the Capulets depart, and the Montagues discuss with their nephew Benvolio the mysterious melancholy that afflicts their son Romeo. As Romeo approaches, his parents leave Benvolio to interrogate him. Benvolio learns that Romeo is in love with a woman who is sworn to chastity and ignores him. Benvolio recommends that his cousin consider other women, but Romeo declares that his love's beauty will eclipse all others.

Act 1, Scene 2

Paris seeks Capulet's permission to marry his daughter Juliet. Capulet argues that Juliet is too young, but he says that, if Paris can win Juliet's affections at the banquet planned for the coming night, he will give his consent. He gives a Servant a list of guests with instructions to deliver invitations, and he and Paris depart. Romeo and Benvolio pass by, and the Servant seeks their assistance, for he is illiterate. Romeo reads the list of guests, which includes the name of his beloved, Rosaline. He and Benvolio decide to attend the banquet in disguise, Romeo wishing to see Rosaline and Benvolio hoping that the sight of many beautiful women will cure his friend's lovesickness.

Act 1, Scene 3

The Nurse reminisces at length about Juliet's childhood. Lady Capulet tells Juliet about her father's plans for her marriage, and Juliet coolly agrees to consider Paris out of filial duty.

Act 1, Scene 4

Romeo, Benvolio, and Mercutio arrive at the banquet. Romeo asserts that he will not dance, due to his melancholy, and he is teased by Mercutio, who humorously enlarges on his probable enchantment by Queen Mab. The group proceeds to the party, although Romeo expresses darkly ominous feelings.

Act 1, Scene 5

Four servants joke among themselves as they clear away the dinner. While the guests dance, Romeo first notices Juliet and is enthralled by her beauty. Tybalt recognizes him and rages against his presence. Capulet orders him to be peaceful, and he leaves in disgust. Romeo addresses Juliet, and their love immediately blossoms as they kiss. Juliet is called to her mother, and Romeo learns who she is from the Nurse. He is dismayed to learn that her family is his family's rival, and she, when learning his identity from the Nurse, is similarly distressed.

Act 2, Prologue

The Chorus recounts, in another sonnet, that Romeo and Juliet cannot easily meet, their families being enemies, but their passion enables them to find a way.

Act 2, Scene 1

Romeo separates himself from his friends as they leave the party. Assuming he has gone in search of Rosaline, they depart.

Act 2, Scene 2

Juliet appears at a high window, and Romeo, in the garden below, admires her beauty. Believing herself to be alone, she soliloquizes about her love for Romeo, regretting that he is a Montague. He reveals himself, and they speak of their love and exchange vows. Juliet is called away by the Nurse, but she returns to say that she will send a messenger to Romeo the next day, to whom he can convey a plan for them to marry. She leaves but returns once more, and they exchange loving farewells.

Act 2, Scene 3

Friar Laurence, picking herbs, muses on their capacity to kill or cure. Romeo arrives and tells him of his new love and asks his help in marrying her. The Friar agrees, hoping that their alliance will end their families' feuding.

Act 2, Scene 4

Benvolio and Mercutio discuss Tybalt, who has challenged Romeo to a duel. Tybalt is well known for his skill with the sword, and Romeo's friends wonder whether the lovesick youth is up to the challenge. Meeting their friend, they banter with him about his love. The Nurse appears; Romeo's friends depart. Romeo gives the Nurse a message for Juliet: she is to go to Friar Laurence that afternoon, and they shall be married. He arranges for the Nurse to receive a rope-ladder for Juliet to lower for him that night.

Act 2, Scene 5

The Nurse returns to an impatient Juliet. She teases her charge by withholding the message briefly; when she delivers it, Juliet departs at once.

Act 2, Scene 6

Juliet comes to Romeo in Friar Laurence's cell, and they greet each other joyfully. The Friar prepares to marry them.

Act 3, Scene 1

Benvolio and Mercutio encounter Tybalt, and Mercutio begins to pick a fight. Romeo appears and is immediately insulted by Tybalt, who wishes to challenge him to a duel. Romeo excuses himself, citing mysterious reasons why he and Tybalt should be friends, but Mercutio cannot tolerate such conciliatory behavior and draws his sword on Tybalt. Romeo attempts to separate the combatants, and Mercutio is mortally wounded by Tybalt, who flees. Mercutio, after bravely jesting about his wound and cursing both Montagues and Capulets for their feuding, is carried away by Benvolio, who returns to report his death. Tybalt returns, and Romeo fights and kills him. At Benvolio's urging, Romeo flees. The Prince appears and interrogates Benvolio. Judging Tybalt to be guiltier than Romeo, he spares the latter the death sentence but banishes him from Verona.

Act 3, Scene 2
Juliet longs for night, when Romeo is to come. The Nurse brings her word of Tybalt's death and Romeo's banishment. Doubly grieved, Juliet speaks of suicide, and the Nurse volunteers to bring Romeo to her.

Act 3, Scene 3
Romeo, in hiding with Friar Laurence, learns of the Prince's edict and raves that death would be more merciful than life without Juliet. The Nurse arrives with word of Juliet's distress, and Romeo's grief reaches new heights; he too speaks of suicide. The Friar chastises him for his weakness and proposes that, after a night with Juliet, Romeo should flee to MANTUA, where he can live until his marriage becomes known, the families reconciled, and he pardoned. Romeo recovers his spirits and leaves to go to Juliet.

Act 3, Scene 4
Capulet ordains that Juliet, whose grief he finds excessive, shall be married to Paris in three days.

Act 3, Scene 5
Romeo and Juliet reluctantly bid farewell, regretting that dawn is near. The Nurse warns that Lady Capulet is coming, and Romeo departs for Mantua. Her mother tells Juliet of the proposed marriage, and Juliet refuses, objecting to the hastiness of the plan. Her father enters and flies into a rage on hearing of her refusal. Her parents leave angrily, and the Nurse advises that Juliet ignore her marriage to Romeo, which no one else knows about,

and marry Paris. Juliet resolves to seek aid from Friar Laurence.

Act 4, Scene 1
Paris confers with a reluctant Friar Laurence about his coming wedding. Juliet arrives and coolly deflects Paris's courtesies. Once alone with the Friar, she desperately craves assistance. Her talk of suicide suggests a plan to him: He will provide her with a potion that will make her seem to be dead. She will be placed in the family crypt, where Romeo will meet her so that they can flee together.

Act 4, Scene 2
As the Capulet household is busy with her wedding arrangements, Juliet appears and apologizes to her father, promising to obey him and marry Paris. Capulet moves the wedding up a day to the next morning.

Act 4, Scene 3
Juliet, alone in her bedroom, is afraid that the Friar's potion may actually kill her. She is also filled with revulsion at the prospect of awakening in the vault, perhaps to encounter the spirits of the dead and with the certain company of Tybalt's fresh corpse. But she steels herself and drinks the potion.

Act 4, Scene 4
The next morning, the wedding day, the Capulet household is astir with last-minute preparations. Capulet sends the Nurse to awaken Juliet.

Act 4, Scene 5
The Nurse, unable to rouse Juliet, raises the alarm that she is dead. Her parents and Paris—who arrives with Friar Laurence and the Musicians intended for the wedding festivities—grieve for her. Friar Laurence counsels acceptance of God's will and ordains her solemn interment in the family vault. Peter then engages the Musicians in a bit of humorous byplay.

Act 5, Scene 1
Balthasar arrives at Romeo's refuge in Mantua with the news that Juliet has died. Romeo immediately plans to return to Verona and join his beloved in death; he buys a fast-acting poison from an Apothecary.

Act 5, Scene 2

Friar John reports to Friar Laurence that he has been unable to deliver Laurence's letter to Romeo. Laurence sends John to fetch a crowbar, planning to open the vault and take Juliet into hiding in his own cell until Romeo can be summoned.

Act 5, Scene 3

Paris visits Juliet's tomb at night. His Page (2), posted as a lookout, whistles a warning that someone is coming, and Paris hides. Romeo appears with Balthasar, whom he sends away with a letter to Montague. Balthasar leaves but hides nearby to observe. Romeo breaks into the tomb, and Paris steps forth to challenge him. They fight, as the Page leaves to call the Watchmen, and Romeo kills Paris. He addresses Juliet, whom he believes to be dead, saying that he will remain with her forever. He drinks the poison and dies. Friar Laurence arrives and views the carnage just as Juliet awakens. He tells Juliet what has happened and begs her to flee, for he can hear the Watchmen coming. She refuses and stays. She kisses her dead lover and stabs herself with his dagger, as the Watchmen appear. They arrest Balthasar and the Friar as the Prince arrives, followed by Juliet's parents and Romeo's father, all of them drawn by the news of the tragedy. The Friar gives an account of Juliet's feigned death and Romeo's misinformation. His tale is confirmed by Balthasar and by Romeo's letter to his father. The Prince points out that the feud between the two families has led to this moment, and Montague and Capulet forswear their hostility and vow to erect golden statues of the two lovers.

George Cukor's 1935 film version of *Romeo and Juliet*. In 5.3 Friar Laurence arrives in the vault to find Juliet (Norma Shearer) awakening to the sight of her dead lover, Romeo (Leslie Howard). *(Courtesy of Culver Pictures, Inc.)*

COMMENTARY

Romeo and Juliet is justly famed for the quality of its lyric poetry, but it is no less extraordinary for its sophisticated organizational devices, which enhance its vivid evocation of a world of love and death. Shakespeare compressed the elapsed time of the story from more than nine months in his source (see "Sources of the Play") to less than five days: Romeo and Juliet meet on a Sunday, marry the next day, and die in the predawn hours on the following Friday. The progression of the days is clearly marked by a succession of dramatic daybreaks: Before he appears, Romeo is described as wandering at dawn (1.1.116–121); the next sunrise finds him below Juliet's window in the famous "balcony" scene (2.2), and the following morning he leaves by that window after the couple's surreptitious wedding night. The Nurse finds Juliet's drugged body at sunrise on Thursday, and at the play's end, a gloomy daybreak accompanies the discovery of the tragedy by the Prince and the couple's parents. The playwright uses a virtuoso display of techniques to heighten the explosive speed of the plot development.

The many symmetries of the play strengthen the spectator's sense of exorably passing time. The Prince appears on three carefully spaced occasions: In 1.1 he describes the Montague-Capulet feud; in 3.1, the pivotal scene in which Tybalt is killed, he banishes Romeo and triggers the tragic conclusion; and in 5.3 he summarizes the play's course. Other matching scenes link the events of the tragedy, as when the Nurse delivers a message to Juliet, delaying its contents each time, in 2.5 and in 3.1. The first message is a happy one: Romeo has summoned Juliet to their marriage; the second instead reveals Romeo's disastrous duel with Tybalt.

Telling juxtapositions also catch our attention, perhaps most strikingly when the fury and desolation of the duel scene is immediately followed by the lyrical brilliance of Juliet's soliloquy that opens 3.2. Moreover, the duel itself follows Romeo and Juliet's marriage; Romeo falls into the depths of the feud just as he ascends to seeming bliss. His very effort to effect a reconciliation with Juliet's kinsman leads to the death of Mercutio, which in turn requires vengeance. These connections do not occur in his source; Shakespeare added them to heighten the dramatic tension. In another such alteration, the playwright has Romeo first encounter Juliet before his presence at the Capulet feast is discovered, rather than afterward, as in the source. In this way, Romeo's ecstatic expression of love (1.5.43–52) itself provokes Tybalt's wrath, sparking the violent chain of events that follows.

An effective contrast in 4.4 emphasizes a basic opposition between the lovers and the world, while also conveying the sense of hastening hours. In this scene the Capulet household hums with prenuptial excitement, completely unaware that Juliet lies in fateful slumber under the same roof. In another striking juxtaposition of scenes, Romeo, having learned of his bride's apparent death, exits with his newly purchased poison at the end of 5.1; at the beginning of 5.2, Friar John immediately enters to explain why he could not inform Romeo of the truth.

The repeated use of certain motifs also unites the events of the play. One such motif is the passage of time. Initially, time passes slowly. Romeo, lost in his infatuation with Rosaline, moans that "sad hours seem long" (1.1.159). But the tempo quickens: Mercutio complains of wasted time as he and Romeo approach the Capulets' feast, and just before Romeo first sees Juliet, Capulet complains to an aged relative, Cousin Capulet, that the years fly by too rapidly. As Romeo leaves the party, now in love, Capulet remarks with surprise that it has grown late. As Romeo spies Juliet at her window, he compares her with the sun and with "a winged messenger of heaven" (2.2.28). However, the accelerating passage of events begins to take on an ominous tone. Juliet, after she and Romeo have first acknowledged their love, says fearfully: ". . . Although I joy in thee, / I have no joy of this contract tonight: / It is too rash, too unadvis'd, too sudden, / Too like the lightning, which doth cease to be / Ere one can say 'It lightens'" (2.2.116–120). Hearing of Romeo's love for Juliet, the Friar warns, "Too swift arrives as tardy as too slow" (2.6.15). From this point, the pressures of time only intensify: Romeo and Juliet must end their wedding night suddenly; Capulet impulsively moves the wedding date forward a day; Friar John's delay deprives Romeo of the truth about Juliet's apparent death; Friar Laurence arrives only seconds too late to prevent the fatal denouement.

Several times feverish haste is described as resembling the flash of lightning or gunpowder, combining the image of fleeting seconds with that of light, the second major motif in the play. When Romeo first encounters Juliet, he compares her to the brilliant light of torches, and in the balcony scene he associates her with sunlight (2.2.3), starlight (2.2.15–17), daylight (2.2.20–22) and the brightness of an angel (2.2.26). Juliet proposes that Romeo, if she "cut him out in little stars" (3.2.22), could fill the sky and cause the night to outshine the day. But light, with time, comes to work against the lovers. As dawn arrives to end their wedding night and signal the beginning of Romeo's exile, he moans, "More light and light; more dark and dark our woes" (3.5.36).

Images of contrasting light and darkness color the play's tragic climax. The Friar describes the action of the potion he gives the desperate Juliet as "Like death when he shuts up the day of life" (4.1.101), but when Romeo opens the tomb he calls it a "lantern" lit by Juliet's beauty, making "This vault a feasting presence, full of light" (5.3.86). Finally, the Prince's closing speech in 5.3 begins with the observation that "A glooming peace this morning with it brings; / The sun for sorrow will not show his head" (5.3.304–305).

As the prominence of darkness and light suggests, *Romeo and Juliet* is a play about extremes and oppositions: the union of the lovers versus the feud between their families; age against youth; the weight of the past versus the promise of the future. Most important, the lovers themselves stand in opposition to the rest of the world—Juliet's irritable father, her matchmaking mother, the bawdy Nurse, the volatile Mercutio, and the self-righteous Friar, all of whom are content to enact the roles required by their places in society. The lovers, however, experience another, private world in which they feel a finer degree of responsibility to each other and to their love. Their isolation gives their dying a sacrificial quality, atoning for the sins of their families and of Verona at large.

The lovers are especially distinguished from their fellow citizens by their speech. Their expressions of love are filled with the intense language of lyric poetry: striking images, exaggerated comparisons, and the use of rhetorical figures traditionally associated with love. Among these is the use of the sonnet, whose formal organization and lyrical fervor suggest the nature of the play itself: rigorously paced and emotionally high-pitched. Acts 1 and 2 are each introduced by a sonnet, spoken by the Chorus, suggesting to the audience (which in Shakespeare's day, more than now, will have been likely to recognize the form on hearing it) that they will witness a structured presentation of emotion. Following a number of sonnet fragments (as in the exchange between Romeo and Benvolio at the end of 1.2), Romeo and Juliet's first encounter takes the form of a sonnet (1.5.92–105) that they deliver jointly. Their subsequent dialogue is in blank verse, less stylized and more dramatically powerful, but the use of the sonnet form in the opening scenes suggests the poet's private recollection of emotion. This permits an exhibition of the lovers' intimate experience, inexpressible in ordinary speech. Shakespeare was writing his early *Sonnets* while he was composing *Romeo and Juliet;* the idea of integrating love lyrics within his romantic love story must have seemed delightful.

As a tragedy of love, ultimately derived from the prose fiction of RENAISSANCE Italy, *Romeo and Juliet* was a novelty in its day; Elizabethan audiences expected to find lovers in COMEDY, whose complicated plots led to happy endings in marriage. Although the tale of *Romeo and Juliet* was well known in prose versions (see "Sources of the Play"), tragic destinies in the theater were customarily reserved for ancient rulers and quasi-mythical figures, in dramas (such as Shakespeare's own *Titus Andronicus*) that imitated those of the Roman playwright SENECA. However, despite its unusual protagonists, *Romeo and Juliet* also reflects the traditional values of medieval melodramas of the Wheel of Fortune and, like them, carries catharsis with its load of woe. Fortune, to the medieval mind, brought down the mighty and thus demonstrated that humanity was subject to forces beyond its control, but this was not necessarily a pessimistic notion, for it expressed the certainty of a world of fate beyond human suffering. This ancient tradition was strongly reinforced by the Christian concept of heaven, which was still a vital force in Shakespeare's day. *Romeo and Juliet* concerned the destiny of two young people—not that of, say, an emperor—but it demonstrated the turnings of the Wheel of Fortune equally well. Thus the play was both conventional and novel.

Romeo and Juliet seems somewhat out of place in the line of Shakespeare's development as a writer of tragedy. Shakespeare's extraordinary later tragedies, such as *Hamlet, Othello,* and *King Lear,* are centered on magnificent but flawed individuals whose personalities lead them to attempt to control their destiny and thereby succumb to an inevitable downfall. Romeo and Juliet bear no resemblance to these mighty protagonists; although they have faults, it is not their weaknesses that bring them to their unhappy end but their "inauspicious stars" (5.3.111). The young lovers are victims of fate. Thus the play does not belong in the continuum of works, from *Titus Andronicus* to *Macbeth,* that concern themselves with the relationship of evil and personal character. Rather, in its emphasis on fulfillment, its final reconciliation, and its celebration of the power of love, *Romeo and Juliet* anticipates the ROMANCES, Shakespeare's strange and great last plays.

SOURCES OF THE PLAY

The tale of *Romeo and Juliet* had been popular in the literatures of England and the Continent before Shakespeare adapted it. His chief source was *The Tragicall Historye of Romeus and Iuliet,* a poem by Arthur BROOKE (1562). He also knew the story from *Palace of Pleasure,* by William PAINTER, which appeared in several editions prior to 1580. In addition, George GASCOIGNE had made the tale the subject of a MASQUE in 1575, and Brooke mentions in his preface a play of the 1550s.

Brooke's poem is a free translation of a French prose work by Pierre Boaistuau (d. 1566), published in Paris in 1559. This in turn was derived from a story (1554) by the Italian writer Mateo BANDELLO, who had adapted the work of another Italian, Luigi Da Porto, whose version was published in 1530. Several variations of the tale existed before that (elements of the plot appear in Latin literature as early as the third century A.D.), but Da Porto was the first author to name the lovers Romeo and

Giulietta and to set the action in Verona in the midst of a feud between the Montagues and Capulets. He was also the first to assert that the tale was historical, a belief that persisted into modern times. Bandello, Boaistuau, and Brooke all added elements of plot and character, whereas Shakespeare simply rearranged the material, changed the pace considerably (see "Commentary") and expanded the roles of several characters, notably Mercutio and the Nurse.

Brooke's chief contribution to the tale was to emphasize the role of fate. In this he was influenced by CHAUCER's *Troilus and Creseyde,* which was then the most famous of English love stories. Shakespeare, perhaps influenced by Brooke, was also affected by this work; he took from it the use of recurrent motifs that is so strong an element in *Romeo and Juliet.* Also, Chaucer's *Parliament of Fowles* was the source for part of Mercutio's "Queen Mab" speech (1.4.53–95).

Various other sources include Samuel DANIEL's *Complaint of Rosamund* (1592), from which Shakespeare derived Romeo's description of Juliet's body in the tomb (5.3.92–96), as well as several minor ideas and images. The well-known French poet Guillaume DU BARTAS, in a 1593 translation by John ELIOT, influenced the lovers' debate on bird song in 3.5. It is also likely that the playwright was inspired by Sir Philip SIDNEY's great sonnet sequence *Astrophel and Stella* (1591) in seeing the lovers as maturing in isolation through awareness of the power of their love. And the setting of the "balcony" scene (2.2) may derive from a similar situation in Sidney's work.

TEXT OF THE PLAY

We can deduce that Shakespeare wrote *Romeo and Juliet* after 1593, when the latest of its sources was published, and before 1596, since the first edition of the play appeared in early 1597, bearing on its title page the boast that the play was already popular on stage (see "Theatrical History of the Play"). *A Midsummer Night's Dream* contains numerous phrases and ideas that resemble material in *Romeo and Juliet;* since these passages are scattered throughout *Romeo and Juliet* but mostly appear early in the *Dream,* it is assumed that Shakespeare began his comedy with the newly completed tragedy in mind. A *Midsummer Night's Dream* is dated to 1595 or early 1596; *Romeo and Juliet* is therefore thought to have been written in 1594 or early 1595.

The first edition of the play, the QUARTO of 1597, known as Q1, was a pirated edition produced by John DANTER and Edward ALLDE. It is a BAD QUARTO; that is, it was transcribed from the recollections of actors who had performed in it. It is thought that this text was originally prepared for an acting company's provincial tour, for which the play was shortened. Q1 was superseded in 1599 by a second edition (Q2), published by Cuthbert BURBY and printed by Thomas CREEDE. It is nearly 50 percent longer and includes numerous corrected passages. Q3 (1609) was a reprint of Q2, and Q4 (1622) reprinted Q3, although Q1 was also used in places. The FIRST FOLIO edition of 1623 was based on Q3 and Q4. A fifth Quarto edition, Q5, a reprint of Q4, appeared in 1637.

Q2 was probably printed from Shakespeare's FOUL PAPERS, as is indicated by its many inconsistent stage directions and other peculiarities. Therefore it is generally regarded as the most authoritative text and is the basis for most modern editions, although Q1, which clearly reflects early performances, is often consulted, especially with reference to its more elaborate stage directions.

THEATRICAL HISTORY OF THE PLAY

Romeo and Juliet has always been among the most popular of Shakespeare's plays. The title page of the first Quarto edition asserted (in 1597) that the play had "been often (with great applause) plaid publiquely" by HUNSDON'S MEN, and its frequent publication testifies to its continued popularity well into the 17th century. However, the earliest surviving record of a particular performance is from 1662, when William DAVENANT revived the play in an adaptation now lost. Later 17th-century productions altered Shakespeare's play greatly; for instance, in the 1670s an adaptation that preserved the lives of the lovers played in a London theater on every other night, alternating with another version in which they died. Thomas OTWAY's *Caius Marius* (1680), a version that was staged regularly for 70 years, was set in ancient Rome. In the mid-18th

century, rival adaptations by Colley CIBBER and David GARRICK, both somewhat truer to the original, were extremely popular. They played London at the same time in 1750—starring Spranger BARRY and Garrick, respectively—in the notorious "*Romeo and Juliet* War." Shakespeare's text was reestablished on the stage in the 1840s, and it has continued to be performed frequently. In 1845 Charlotte CUSHMAN played Romeo opposite the Juliet of her sister Susan. Henry IRVING's production of the 1880s, John GIELGUD's of 1935 (in which he and Laurence OLIVIER played Romeo and Mercutio, changing roles on alternating nights), and Franco ZEFFIRELLI's of 1960 were particularly notable. More recently, Mark RYLANCE starred in the 1989 production directed by Terry HANDS, and in 2003, as Artistic Director of the Shakespeare's Globe Theatre (see WANAMAKER, SAM), he produced an avant-garde Brazilian version.

Romeo and Juliet has been very popular with moviemakers. At least 17 FILM versions have been made (only *Hamlet* has been filmed more often), in six languages, including Arabic and Hindi, by directors such as Francis X. Bushman (1916), George Cukor (1936), Paul CZINNER (1965), and Franco Zeffirelli (1968). In 1996 director Baz Luhrmann (b. 1962) startled audiences with his *Romeo + Juliet*, set in a fictional contemporary city, "Verona Beach" (actually Mexico City and Veracruz), and starring Leonardo DiCaprio as a pistol-wielding Romeo. *Romeo and Juliet* has also been produced for TELEVISION six times, beginning as long ago as 1947.

Vincenzo BELLINI's *I Capuleti e I Montecchi* (1830) and Charles GOUNOD's *Roméo et Juliette* (1867), two of the several 19th-century OPERAs derived from Shakespeare's play, are occasionally performed today. In addition, *West Side Story*, the popular American musical drama of stage (1958) and screen (1961), is an adaptation of *Romeo and Juliet*, set among street gangs in modern New York City. Shakespeare's play has also inspired classical composers, including Hector BERLIOZ, who created a "dramatic symphony" with voices (1838), and Pyotr Ilich TCHAIKOVSKY, who composed a symphonic fantasy (1864), both entitled *Romeo and Juliet*. The ballet (1936) by Serge Prokofiev (1891–1953) is a staple of modern classical dance.

CHARACTERS

Abram (Abraham) Minor character in *Romeo and Juliet*, a servant of the Montague family. In 1.1 Abram and Balthasar brawl with servants of the Capulet household. This episode illustrates the extent to which the feud between the two families has upset the civic life of VERONA.

Anthony Minor character in *Romeo and Juliet*, a Serving-man who helps clear tables in 1.5.

Apothecary Minor character in *Romeo and Juliet*, the druggist from whom, in 5.1, Romeo buys a poison with which to kill himself, believing Juliet to be dead. Romeo believes that the poverty-stricken Apothecary can be bribed to break the law and defy common moral sense by selling him this drug. The young hero veers between contempt for the Apothecary and sympathy for another victim in a world of misery.

Balthasar Minor character in *Romeo and Juliet*, servant of Romeo. In 5.1 Balthasar brings Romeo the erroneous news that Juliet is dead, triggering the last phase of the tragedy. In 5.3 Balthasar accompanies Romeo to Juliet's tomb. Romeo sends him away with a letter to Montague, but, concerned about his master, he stays to observe him. At the end of the play he gives the Prince of Verona the letter, which helps to explain the tragedy to the lovers' parents.

Balthasar is the only servant of the Montagues in the play except for Abram and a nameless companion, who participate in the brawl in 1.1. Accordingly, Balthasar is conventionally designated as the companion, who neither speaks nor is named in early texts of the play.

Benvolio Character in *Romeo and Juliet*, friend and cousin of Romeo. Benvolio's good sense and calm temperament are contrasted with the belligerence of Romeo's other friend, Mercutio. In 2.1, knowing that Romeo wishes to be alone, Benvolio draws Mercutio away. He attempts to prevent the brawl among the servants in 1.1 and the fight between Mercutio and Tybalt in 3.1; in both cases he is ineffectual. This courteous and gentle character (whose apt name means "good will") appropriately disappears from the play as the tragedy unfolds.

Capulet Character in *Romeo and Juliet*, the father of Juliet and the head of the family bearing his name, rivals to the Montague clan. Though short-tempered, Capulet at first seems benevolent: He resists the marriage proposal by Paris in 1.2, observing that Juliet is too young, and in 1.5 he orders Tybalt to leave the banquet rather than fight Romeo. However, in 3.4 he suddenly decides to give Juliet, by now secretly married to Romeo, to Paris and rages furiously at his daughter when she resists; he belongs to the conventional, unfeeling world that opposes the lovers. When he impulsively moves the wedding date up by a day (4.2), Capulet becomes an agent of fate, hastening the play's tragic climax. His humorous involvement in the wedding preparations does not restore him to our affections, nor does his cursory and somewhat stilted mourning when he believes the drugged Juliet to be dead. Only at the end of the play, when his daughter's actual death impels him to seek a reconciliation with Montague, can we again find him humanly sympathetic.

The feud between the Capulets and the Montagues did not in fact occur, although Shakespeare and his sources believed it to have been real. (See VERONA.)

Capulet, Cousin (Old Man) Minor character in *Romeo and Juliet*, an aged relative of Capulet. Cousin Capulet (called "Old Man" in some editions) speaks only two lines in a brief conversation, at the feast in 1.5, on the rapid flight of the years. This episode, occurring just as Romeo and Juliet are about to meet, is one instance of the motif of time's passage, which recurs throughout the tragedy.

Catling, Simon See Musicians.

Chorus Minor character in *Romeo and Juliet*, the nondramatic figure who comments on the play in each PROLOGUE, preceding Acts 1 and 2, respectively. In the manner of an ancient Greek CHORUS, this character comments on the drama from outside it, displaying a knowledge that no character could have. In the Prologue to Act 1, the Chorus not only provides a terse account of the tragedy's course but suggests a response to it, pointing out that the feud between families "makes civil hands unclean" (Prologue.4) and that the "fearful passage" (Prologue.9) of the love affair will provide the only resolution of the conflict. Prior to Act 2, the Chorus extols the two lovers while outlining the difficulties that the feud will cause them. Each prologue takes the form of a SONNET, traditionally reserved for romantic poetry, preparing the audience (which in Shakespeare's day will have been likely to recognize the form on hearing it) for a love story. This treatment reflects the fact that a tragic love story was a novelty in the 1590s. TRAGEDY ordinarily concerned warriors and kings; lovers were expected to appear in COMEDY, where they would find a happy ending in marriage.

Citizens   Several minor characters in *Romeo and Juliet*, townspeople of VERONA who attempt to halt the street fighting between the feuding Montague and Capulet families in 1.1 and 3.1. Their presence reflects the importance Shakespeare placed on civil disorder—one of his favorite themes—as an element in his tragedy of young lovers.

Friar John   Minor character in *Romeo and Juliet*, an unsuccessful emissary between Friar Laurence and the exiled Romeo. In 5.2 Friar John reports that he has been unable to deliver Laurence's letter to Romeo, having been quarantined as a suspected plague carrier. Thus Romeo remains unaware that the death of Juliet is feigned, and the tragic denouement is launched.

Friar Laurence (Friar Lawrence)   Character in *Romeo and Juliet*, the clergyman who assists Romeo and Juliet. Although presented as a respectable, well-meaning old gentleman given to platitudes, the Friar serves as an agent of malevolent fate. In his first speech (2.3.1–26) a sententious bouquet of rhymed observations on plant lore, he demonstrates the conventionality of thought that will lead him to proceed recklessly—to the lovers' destruction—while maintaining an air of caution. Moreover, his remarks on good and bad uses for herbs foreshadow the role of potions and poisons later in the play. He warns Romeo against haste in such passages as 2.6.9–15, but nonetheless agrees to perform the

secret marriage of the young lovers. The Friar's flimsy morality is evident when he advises the distraught Juliet in 4.1. Accepting a bigamous marriage as an alternative, though not an ideal one, he proposes a devious capitulation to her parents' wishes, accompanied by the desperate expedient of the sleeping potion. In the final scene, his lack of character is richly demonstrated as he abandons Juliet in the predicament his rash plans have brought about.

Gregory   Minor character in *Romeo and Juliet*, a servant of the Capulet household. Gregory and his fellow servant Sampson brawl with servants of the Montague family in 1.1, after opening the play with a pun-filled comic dialogue in which Gregory taunts his companion for being a coward. The brawl is purely verbal until Tybalt appears and the rival households come to blows. The episode illustrates the lengths to which the feud between the families has gone, with their servants pursuing the quarrel in the streets.

Juliet   One of the title characters in *Romeo and Juliet*, the lover of Romeo. Juliet first appears as a conventional upper-class daughter, affectionately dependent on her Nurse and accepting of the marriage to Paris that is planned for her. However, when she is gripped by passion for Romeo, she displays a heroic capacity to resist her world, despite the dangers of her love. She accepts death no less readily than Romeo when destiny has destroyed their lives.

When she first meets Romeo, she shows herself to be intelligent and perceptive. She matches wits with him in improvising their joint SONNET (1.5.92–105), and she recognizes in him traces of the bookish, artificial lover he has been earlier, remarking that he kisses "by th'book" (1.5.109). While no less enraptured than her lover during the subsequent "balcony" scene (2.2), she is nonetheless more aware than he of their danger, as in 2.2.116–120, and it is she who sees that they must commit themselves to marriage if their plight is to be overcome. Although her response to the onset of passion is mature, she does not lose her appeal as a blooming young lover. Her soliloquy at the opening of 3.2, before she learns of Romeo's banishment, is a brilliant and utterly endearing expression of the impatience of the lover looking forward to a tryst.

When faced with Romeo's banishment and the prospect of an enforced marriage to Paris, Juliet agrees to take the sleeping potion offered by Friar Laurence. In 4.3.15–58, she reviews a roster of possible terrors she faces in a frightening speech that underlines the courage with which she must and does proceed. She is no less resolute at the tragic climax of the play. Waking to find that mischance has overwhelmed her efforts, she does not hesitate to join her lover in death rather than continue living in a world that lacks their love.

It has often been thought that Juliet's age, 14, represents a typical marriage age for English women of Shakespeare's day, but historians believe that the normal age was the late teens or early 20s. In any case, Shakespeare lowered Juliet's age from that given in his source, 16, and lines such as 1.2.8–13 suggest that she is supposed to be thought of as quite young for marriage, perhaps to emphasize her vulnerability. On the other hand, Lady Capulet states explicitly that Veronese girls younger than Juliet were mothers (1.3.69–71). The question remains puzzling.

Lady Capulet   Character in *Romeo and Juliet,* mother of Juliet and wife of Capulet. Desiring the marriage of Juliet to Paris, Lady Capulet is curt, imperious, and coldly unsympathetic to her daughter's qualms, even without knowing that they stem from her passion for Romeo; she is a representative of the conventional world that opposes the young lovers. Her grief in 4.5, when she believes the drugged Juliet is dead, elicits our sympathy, but we may remember her enraged demands for revenge on Tybalt's murderer in 3.1. She does not speak in the final scene of reconciliation.

Lady Montague   Minor character in *Romeo and Juliet,* mother of Romeo and wife of Montague. Lady Montague appears only twice, beside her husband, and speaks only one line. In 5.3 she is said to have died of grief following Romeo's banishment.

Mab   Fairy queen referred to in *Romeo and Juliet.* Mercutio delivers an elaborate jesting speech (1.4.53–95) describing Queen Mab as a bringer of dreams to humans in a variety of social situations. The passage, a montage of fairy lore, country superstition, and humorous character types, has the chaotic energy that characterizes both Mercutio and the violent world that opposes the private universe of the young lovers, Romeo and Juliet. Parts of the speech have literary antecedents—notably in *The Parliament of Fowles,* by CHAUCER—but Queen Mab as "midwife" (1.4.54) of dreams is known only in this passage and is probably Shakespeare's invention.

The name Mab is associated with fairies; there was a Queen Mabh in Irish fairy lore, and in the dialect of Shakespeare's native WARWICKSHIRE the word *Mabled* was once current, meaning "led astray by fairies or elves." Also, Mab is expressly tiny, and the word *mab* means "small child" in Cymric, the language of WALES. Shakespeare's interest in Wales and its language at the period when *Romeo and Juliet* was written, and its importance as the origin of many elements of Warwickshire folklore, make it a possible source for the name.

Masquers   Group of nonspeaking characters in *Romeo and Juliet,* the men who accompany Romeo to the banquet held by Capulet. In the 16th-century courtly entertainment that evolved into the formal MASQUE, guests often costumed themselves, as Romeo and his friends do in 1.4, and were known as masquers. Arriving in groups and often dressed thematically, the masquers declared themselves to be party crashers and demanded to dance. Uproarious flirtation was expected to follow. Named characters sometimes appear as masquers elsewhere in Shakespeare's plays (e.g., in *Much Ado About Nothing,* 2.1.78, and *Henry VIII,* 1.4.64–87).

Mercutio   Character in *Romeo and Juliet,* Romeo's friend who is killed by Tybalt. Mercutio, a buoyantly ribald and belligerent young gallant, serves as a foil for the maturing Romeo, who is discovering that love offers a more profound world than that of gentlemanly pleasures and enmities. Named for Mercury, the impudent god of thievery, Mercutio embodies an instability inherent in the noble society of Verona. His brilliant comedic monologue on Queen Mab (1.4.53–95) builds to a chaotic crescendo that suggests the violence that is lurking just beneath the surface of Veronese life. He is one of Shakespeare's bawdiest characters; in a mock incantation in 2.1.16–38, in which he lists the anatomical parts of Romeo's supposed beloved, Rosaline, he deflates the rhetoric of romance. His unabashedly carnal approach to love contrasts with the pure devotion that Romeo learns, and his belligerence is compared with Romeo's intention to make peace with Tybalt after his marriage to Juliet.

Mercutio ultimately belongs to the conventional world that opposes the young lovers. He blindly fulfills his role in that world by pointlessly insisting on fighting Tybalt, thereby launching the tragic complications of the play. While we can admire his wit, his loyalty to Romeo, and his courage in death, we also see that Mercutio has little business declaring "a plague o'both your houses" (3.1.92, 100, 108) when he has himself contributed so dramatically to the final catastrophe.

Montague   Character in *Romeo and Juliet*, Romeo's father and the head of the family bearing his name, rivals to the Capulet clan. Montague appears only briefly, in the three scenes in which the feud with the Capulets erupts into violence (1.1; 3.1; 5.3), and on the first two occasions he accepts in conventional terms the objections of the Prince of Verona to the fighting. In the final episode of reconciliation (5.3.295–309), he offers to commission a golden statue of Juliet as a public memorial to the love that the feud has doomed.

Although Shakespeare believed the Montague-Capulet conflict was a historical reality, in fact it never occurred. (See VERONA.)

Musicians   Minor characters in *Romeo and Juliet*, three players hired by Paris to provide music at his wedding to Juliet. However, Juliet is found apparently dead, and they are not needed. They are then accosted by the servant Peter, who demands free music and engages them in a comic exchange (4.5.100–141). Their names, Simon Catling, Hugh Rebeck, and James Soundpost, indicate the instruments they play. A catling is a small, lutelike string instrument; a rebec, an early violin; a soundpost,

for the singer in the group, is an internal component of a string instrument.

Nurse   Character in *Romeo and Juliet*, a servant in the Capulet household, the nanny and former wet-nurse of Juliet. The longwinded Nurse, a broadly comical figure who repeatedly resorts to the low humor of sexual innuendo, functions as a foil for Juliet's delicacy and openness; in 1.3 the anecdote she relates from Juliet's childhood illuminates the heroine's background. But as the tragedy deepens, the Nurse loses her humorous qualities and becomes a symbol of the conventional world that opposes the private realm of the lovers. Further, her crass recommendation that Juliet simply ignore her union to the banished Romeo (3.5.212–225) serves to isolate the heroine at a crucial moment. In her last appearance the Nurse cackles mindlessly about

Juliet's Nurse (played by Edna May Oliver in the 1936 film of *Romeo and Juliet*) is one of the most famous comedy roles in all of Shakespeare. A perfect foil for Juliet's idealism, the Nurse represents the crassness of the conventional world. *(Courtesy of Culver Pictures, Inc.)*

sex as she attempts to wake the drugged Juliet, and she echoes the uncomprehending grief of the family when it appears that the girl is dead.

Page (1) Minor character in *Romeo and Juliet*, a young servant of Mercutio. Mortally wounded in 3.1, Mercutio sends the Page, who does not speak, to summon a surgeon.

Page (2) Minor character in *Romeo and Juliet*, a servant of Paris. The Page accompanies his master on his nocturnal visit to the grave of Juliet in 5.3; when Romeo arrives and fights with Paris, the Page summons the Watchman and later testifies to the Prince.

Paris Character in *Romeo and Juliet*, a nobleman who wishes to marry Juliet. Paris, who is forced on Juliet by her parents, confidently assumes that he will wed her. He is closely juxtaposed with Romeo throughout the play. Though no villain, Paris is nonetheless an agent of the world that opposes the private universe of the lovers, and this is indicated by his staid and predictable behavior and speech. His sentiments are those of the conventionally poetic lover, the type of lover Romeo was before he met Juliet. Lady Capulet even compares him to a book in 1.3.81–88. His smug exchange with Juliet in 4.1 can only stiffly approximate the brilliant poetry of her dialogue with Romeo. In his final appearance—at Juliet's tomb in 5.3—this well-meaning but vapid gentleman declares his grief in a formal sestet that is reminiscent of Romeo's word-play in Act 1; the contrast is completed when the mature Romeo arrives, desperate and resolute. Paris honorably opposes the man whom he believes is desecrating Juliet's tomb, but he dies without comprehending, or even seeing, his rival's passion.

Peter Minor character in *Romeo and Juliet*, a servant in the Capulet household, the assistant of the Nurse. In 2.4.154–157 Peter makes a brief speech that both furthers a sexual innuendo and displays comical cowardice. His principal appearance, however, is in 4.5.100–138. When the Musicians hired for the wedding of Juliet are dismissed because she is believed to have died, Peter accosts them. He demands free music and then engages them in a comic exchange, insulting them and playing on their names. A stage direction in the Q2 edition of the play (see *Romeo and Juliet*, "Text of the Play") indicates that Peter was portrayed by Will KEMPE, a famous comic of the day.

Petruchio GHOST CHARACTER in *Romeo and Juliet*, a follower of Tybalt. Petruchio appears only in a stage direction at 3.1.34, though he is also mentioned as a guest at the Capulet banquet (1.5.130). Shakespeare presumably intended to develop Petruchio as he wrote 3.1, but he did not in fact do so. Then, with his typical inattention to details, the playwright let the stage direction stand. A ghost character is taken as evidence that the published text in which he first appears—in this case Q2 (1599) of *Romeo and Juliet*—was printed from Shakespeare's own manuscript, or FOUL PAPERS, and is thus especially authoritative.

Potpan See Serving-man.

Prince of Verona (Prince Escalus) Character in *Romeo and Juliet*, the ruler of VERONA, where the play is set. The Prince is a representative of civil order, an important ideal for Shakespeare. The Prince appears three times in the play. First, in 1.1 he describes the feud between Montague and Capulet. In 3.1 he banishes Romeo and precipitates the climax of the tragedy; rather too late, he states a principle of statecraft that has been too little observed in Verona: "Mercy but murders, pardoning those that kill" (3.1.199). At the close he summarizes the fateful resolution of the feud, accepting blame "for winking at . . . discords" (5.3.293). This acknowledgment of the state's responsibility for order was not present in Shakespeare's sources; it reflects the playwright's interest in the civic as well as the purely personal ramifications of tragedy. This theme recurs throughout Shakespeare's work in dramas ranging from *Richard II* to *King Lear* to *The Tempest*.

In the stage direction that introduces him at 1.1.79, and nowhere else, the Prince is given a name, Escalus. This is a Latinization of Della Scala, the name of the princely family that ruled Verona in the late Middle Ages.

Rebeck, Hugh   See Musicians.

Romeo   One of the title characters in *Romeo and Juliet*, the lover of Juliet. Romeo progresses from posing as the melancholy lover of Rosaline to a more mature stance as Juliet's devoted husband, committed to her despite the world's displeasure. Romeo's early speeches declaiming his affection for Rosaline are parodies of conventional courtship; preposterously bookish and artificial, they emphasize by contrast the depth of his later love for Juliet. And Romeo undergoes another maturation as well: From helpless hysteria in 3.3, after his banishment, he comes in 5.3 to a resolute acceptance of what he sees as his only choice—death with Juliet.

Romeo's growth is clearly brought about by his love. When he and Juliet first meet, he has not yet found a stronger mode of expression than the conventional SONNET, as she recognizes when she observes, "You kiss by th'book" (1.5.109). In their mutual ecstasy in the "balcony" scene (2.2), it is Juliet who, though no less enraptured, is the more aware of the likely consequences of their love. Further, we recognize the impulsive boy in Romeo as he urges Friar Laurence to haste in 2.3. Once married, however, Romeo begins his transformation: In his attempt to make peace with Tybalt, he wishes all the world to love as he does, although to no avail. As he departs from Juliet into banishment after their abbreviated wedding night, he offers hope to his despairing bride and displays a true maturity in sharing the mutual consolation necessary in their seemingly hopeless situation. At the end of the play, he has achieved the capacity to stand alone in the face of tragedy, as is demonstrated in the contrast between himself and Paris. Paris contents himself with formal rhymed verses reminiscent of Romeo's speeches in Act 1, whereas Romeo himself burns brightly with desperate determination.

Rosaline   Character who is mentioned but does not appear in *Romeo and Juliet*, the object of Romeo's infatuation before he meets Juliet. Early in the play, Romeo asserts his love for the apparently indifferent Rosaline in immature, self-consciously poetic terms. The episode emphasizes by contrast the depth of his passion for Juliet when it develops.

Sampson   Minor character in *Romeo and Juliet*, a servant of the Capulet household. Sampson and Gregory brawl with servants of the Montague family in 1.1, after opening the play with a pun-filled dialogue in which Sampson boasts of his bold fighting spirit, while Gregory taunts him for being a coward. They both content themselves with verbal battle until Tybalt inspires them to bring matters to blows. Shakespeare presumably gave Sampson a heroic name to add another touch of humor to his role, but the thought went undeveloped; the name is not spoken in the dialogue.

Servant   Minor character in *Romeo and Juliet*, a worker in the Capulet household. In 1.2 the Servant is given a list of guests to Capulet's banquet and instructed to deliver invitations. However, he is illiterate and seeks the help of Romeo, who happens to be passing by. Thus Romeo learns of the banquet, which he will attend in search of Rosaline but where he will meet Juliet. At the banquet the Servant (or perhaps another one) is unable to identify Juliet in 1.5.42.

Serving-man   Any of several minor characters in *Romeo and Juliet*, members of the staff of the Capulet household. A Serving-man summons Lady Capulet to dinner in 1.3. In 1.5 four Serving-men, one of whom is comically named Potpan, jestingly clear away the banquet while preparing for a backstairs party of their own. In 4.2 and 4.4 Serving-men joke with Capulet as they assist in his preparations for the wedding of Juliet. These mellow and humorous domestics serve to suggest an atmosphere of bourgeois solidity to the Capulet household.

Soundpost, James   See Musicians.

Torchbearers   Group of nonspeaking characters in *Romeo and Juliet*, men who accompany Romeo and the Masquers to the banquet given by Capulet. Romeo, mooning over Rosaline, says he wishes to join the Torchbearers (1.4.11–12) because they were expected to watch from the sidelines and not participate in the dancing.

Tybalt   Character in *Romeo and Juliet*, a cousin of Juliet. The belligerent Tybalt insists on fighting for the Capulet family against the Montague clan on any occasion. His arrival turns the humorous verbal confrontation between servants in 1.1 into a violent brawl. When he recognizes Romeo at the feast in 1.5, he wants to duel with him on the spot. The next day he fights and kills Mercutio, thus inciting Romeo to slay Tybalt in revenge, the act for which he is banished. In Shakespeare's source, Tybalt is merely a name, appearing only to be killed by Romeo in a street fight. The playwright elaborates the character to generate dramatic tension in the first half of the play; Tybalt serves to emphasize the potential for violence that accompanies the developing love between hero and heroine.

Watchmen Minor characters in *Romeo and Juliet*, guards who patrol the streets of VERONA at night. In 5.3 the Watchmen are summoned to the tomb of Juliet by the Page, who has seen his master, Paris, fighting with Romeo. They find the bodies of Paris and the two lovers and arrest the witnesses, Friar Laurence and Balthasar. The Watchmen represent the general population of Verona in opposing the bloody feuding of the Montague and Capulet families.

Sir Thomas More

Play attributed in part to Shakespeare. *Sir Thomas More* presents episodes from the life of Thomas MORE, a Catholic martyr who was executed by King Henry VIII for his refusal to accept the English Reformation. It was probably written around 1593 or 1600 (scholarly opinions differ) for the ADMIRAL'S MEN. The manuscript of *Sir Thomas More,* which was assembled around 1595 (or 1603), is mostly in the handwriting of Anthony MUNDAY but with additions in five different hands, one of which—known as "Hand D"—is generally accepted as Shakespeare's. If so, this is the only surviving sample of the playwright's handwriting, aside from six signatures on legal documents. For *Sir Thomas More,* he wrote three pages of script comprising one scene of 147 lines, in which More subdues a riot with a moving oration.

That this is Shakespeare's composition is demonstrated through several lines of evidence. First, the handwriting is very like that of the playwright's six known signatures. Further, peculiar spellings—such as *scilens* for *silence*—occur both in Hand D's pages and in editions of Shakespeare's plays that are known to derive from the author's FOUL PAPERS. Perhaps most tellingly, the imagery used in Hand D's text resembles Shakespeare's, especially in lines that are very similar to passages in both *Coriolanus* and *Troilus and Cressida.* Lastly, the political ideas expressed in Hand D's scene agree with what we know of Shakespeare's thinking, for they demonstrate a respect for social hierarchy combined with sympathy for the common people and stress the malleability of the commoners through oratory.

The odd manuscript of *Sir Thomas More* was the result of government CENSORSHIP; apparently the play was originally submitted to Edmund Tilney, the MASTER OF REVELS, who refused to permit its performance without major revisions. Accordingly, several pages were torn from the original manuscript and replaced with others. Scholars believe that the six hands that recorded the text were those of the three collaborators on the original play plus two revisers and a professional scribe. It is generally held that the original text was written by Munday, Henry CHETTLE, and possibly Thomas HEYWOOD, while the revisions were written by Chettle, Thomas DEKKER, and Shakespeare. The revisions did not have their intended effect; Tilney was not moved, and *Sir Thomas More* was not performed until 1964, when it was staged in Nottingham, England.

Sonnets

Body of 154 poems, each a SONNET, written by Shakespeare over an unknown period of time, probably around 1592 to 1598. The *Sonnets* are love poems. They describe aspects of two different loves experienced by the poet, one for a young man and the other for a woman. Some of the *Sonnets* are great poems (Sonnets 18, 29, 55, 116, and 130 are among the most praised), while a few are poor, but it is as a sonnet sequence—a new genre at the time—that they are particularly fascinating, offering an extraordinary range of love poems. They encompass several distinct points of view on love, unified by a series of delightful observations on the power of poetry to record them.

The *Sonnets* comprise two groups of poems: the larger group (Sonnets 1–126) is addressed to the young man, the other (127–154) to the woman. (Although the sex of the addressee is unspecified in most of the *Sonnets*, all those that do address a man precede Sonnet 126, which as the only 12-line variation on the sonnet form seems to close the initial group. Similarly, all of the *Sonnets* that explicitly address a woman fall in the second group.)

In the first group, the poet manifests his love for the young man in a variety of ways. In Sonnets 1–17 he speaks of his friend's beauty and insists that he should marry and have children in order to perpetuate that beauty beyond his eventual death. In the next group of poems (and in many of the others), the poet describes his love in brilliant variations on traditional love poetry, often referring to the poetry love stimulates. However, as the sequence progresses, the poet speaks of his disappointment that his friend has left him, or at least does not love him in return. In 40–42 it appears that the friend has even stolen the poet's (female) lover. In 78–86 the poet fears that his place in his friend's affections (and perhaps in his literary patronage) has been taken by another, superior poet. In 110–111 the poet worries that his friend resents his public displays (probably a reference to Shakespeare's career as an actor). Gradually, however, over the course of the last several dozen poems of this group, the spirit of love returns, apparently reflecting a reconciliation between the friends. Sonnet 126 closes the series with a return to the subject of the young man's beauty and mortality.

Sonnets 127–154 address a woman of dark complexion and metaphorically dark morals (often referred to as Shakespeare's "Dark Lady"), who has betrayed the poet's love by loving other men. She may be married, in which case the love she *has* given the poet also constitutes betrayal. In 133–134 the poet complains that not only has she been

unfaithful to him, she has done so with his friend, thereby leaving him abandoned by both of his loves. Apparently the situation in Sonnets 40–42 is seen here from another angle. The "Dark Lady" sonnets bemoan the poet's plight as an unrequited lover, and they often rail against the woman and against love in general. These poems are sometimes called the "vituperative sonnets."

In these two sets of poems, a love triangle is compellingly, if only implicitly, portrayed. There is no actual evidence that the situation was not simply a literary creation, but many of the poems are so convincingly delighted or aggrieved with love that most readers find themselves assuming that the *Sonnets* are autobiographical, or at least based on personal experience, and that the young man, the "dark lady," and the "rival poet" are representations of real people. Despite the lack of evidence, a wide range of suppositions about Shakespeare's life have been engendered by the *Sonnets*.

The most contentious conclusion that has been drawn from the *Sonnets* is that Shakespeare was homosexual. However, the poems offer no unambiguous evidence on the subject. The poet refers to and addresses his friend as his "lover," but in Shakespeare's day the word had many nonsexual connotations, and its meaning varied greatly with context. It could mean sexual partner, but it could also be used in the formal close of a letter—"Thy lover" was as common and as sexually neutral as "Sincerely yours" (it is so used in *Julius Caesar* 2.3.7). Moreover, in the context of friendship, the word *lover* was synonymous with the word *friend*. Shakespeare often used it as such in the plays (e.g., in *The Merchant of Venice* 3.4.7; *2 Henry IV* 4.3.13; *Coriolanus* 3.3.213). Sexual puns and innuendos of all sorts, indiscriminate in their references to male and female genitals, are common throughout the *Sonnets*—as they are throughout Elizabethan secular literature in general—but they serve chiefly to promote an atmosphere of licentiousness rather than to suggest particular acts or attitudes. Sonnet 20 is frequently cited as evidence of Shakespeare's homosexuality, because in it the poet ascribes many feminine attributes to his friend, plays with clever references to his penis, and calls him "the master mistress of my passion" (20.2). However, in this poem the poet actually disclaims a sexual relation with his friend—whose penis is said to be "to my purpose nothing" (20.12)—and willingly surrenders sex with him to women. While scholarly opinion remains varied, it is safe to say that the *Sonnets* do not clearly demonstrate homosexuality in its lovers, quite apart from the likelihood that Shakespeare, like other sonneteers of the day, wrote of an invented relationship.

In any case, the identity of the young man intrigues those who read the *Sonnets* as autobiographical. The assumption is generally drawn that he is identical with the mysterious "Mr. W. H." described as the "onlie begetter" of the *Sonnets* in the dedication to the first edition (see below). The two models most frequently suggested have been Henry Wriothesley (W. H. reversed), Earl of SOUTHAMPTON, and William Herbert, Earl of PEMBROKE. Each was a literary patron connected with Shakespeare: *Venus and Adonis* and *The Rape of Lucrece* are dedicated to Southampton and the FIRST FOLIO to Pembroke, who was also a son of the patron of PEMBROKE'S MEN, a theatrical company with which Shakespeare may have acted. Thus, they suit the implied references to patronage in several of the *Sonnets*. Also, each declined to marry a proposed bride—Southampton in 1590, Pembroke in 1595—making him suitable for the pleas of Sonnets 1–17. However, various commentators point to disqualifying attributes of each. In any case, the point cannot be proved, and so there have been many more nominees. Almost any near-contemporary of Shakespeare with the initials W. H. or H. W. has been proposed. A William Hughes—supposedly the object of a pun in Sonnet 20 but otherwise unrecorded—has been hypothesized (that he should be named William is suggested by the "Will sonnets" [135–136], where the word *will* appears 19 times, possibly echoing the names of the poet and his rival for the Dark Lady's love—the young man). Other possibilities emerge if the young man of the *Sonnets* is not considered identical with Mr. W. H.; among the nominees have been the poet's son Hamnet SHAKESPEARE, Robert Devereux, Earl of ESSEX, and Queen Elizabeth I (heavily disguised).

Many proposals have been also made for the identity of the "Dark Lady." However, none has even the superficial credibility of Southampton and Pembroke, and scholars often simply ignore the question. The most frequently named Dark Ladies are Mary FITTON and Emilia LANIER. Others include Lucy Morgan (active 1579–1600), a onetime lady-in-waiting to Queen Elizabeth who became a brothel keeper; Penelope Rich (1563–1607), the sister of the Earl of Essex; and William DAVENANT's mother (chiefly because Davenant claimed to be Shakespeare's illegitimate son).

Speculation has similarly surrounded the "rival poet" of Sonnets 78–86. Most poets of the period have been named: George CHAPMAN and Christopher MARLOWE most often, with honorable mention to Barnabe BARNES and Gervase MARKHAM. However, none of these questions can be profitably pursued; not only is evidence entirely lacking, it is not even clear that Shakespeare had any real people in mind. All three figures function well as literary constructs—characters placed in a quasi narrative, such as appear in many other sonnet sequences of the day.

The dates of the *Sonnets* are undetermined and are the subject of continuing scholarly debate. Though the only certainty is their existence before 1609, when they were published, a generally accepted view holds that they were probably all written between 1592 and 1598. These years saw a vogue for sonnet sequences—at least 20 were published—stimulated by Sir Philip SIDNEY's *Astrophel and Stella* (1591), and Shakespeare's poems were apparently part of this trend. In 1598 Francis MERES mentioned that Shakespeare had written sonnets, and versions of two of them (138 and 144) were published in 1599 as part of THE PASSIONATE PILGRIM. Of course, it is not known that all of them had been written by then. Nevertheless, parallels to the *Sonnets* in Shakespeare's other works are most frequent in *Venus and Adonis* (1592–93), *The Rape of Lucrece* (1593–94), *Love's Labour's Lost* (ca. 1593), *Romeo and Juliet* (1594–95), and *Richard II* (1595), so the years of the sonnet craze seem the likeliest period of composition for the entire group of poems.

Commentators occasionally doubt the authorship of a few of the sonnets, especially 145, which is a poor poem and the only sonnet written in tetrameter (see METER), as well as 153 and 154, which seemingly have little to do with the others and are the only ones that derive from a specific source (see below). However, each of these poems bears some relationship to its neighbors, and most scholars accept them as genuine.

The collected *Sonnets* were first published in 1609 by Thomas THORPE in a QUARTO edition (printed by George ELD) known as Q. They were printed in the order described above, which has subsequently been considered standard (though various editors have altered it) and followed by *A Lover's Complaint*. An introductory page reads: "TO THE ONLIE BEGETTER OF THESE INSVING SONNETS MR. W.H. ALL HAPPINESSE AND THAT ETERNITIE PROMISED BY OUR EVER-LIVING POET WISHETH THE WELL-WISHING ADVENTVRER IN SETTING FORTH." This enigmatic message, signed "T. T.," is unpunctuated (in that there is a period after every word), ungrammatical, and generally difficult to interpret. The term *onlie begetter* may signify the inspirer of the *Sonnets* (presumably the young man of 1–126), or it may simply refer to the procurer of the manuscripts from which they were printed; some commentators find other, more arcane possibilities. In any case, the dedication has been subjected to great scholarly scrutiny, but in the absence of further evidence, it must remain intractably obscure.

As noted above, only Sonnets 153 and 154 have a clear source: They are variations on a well-known classical epigram dating to at least the first century A.D. (this epigram was variously rendered in several languages, and Shakespeare's immediate source is not known). OVID's *Metamorphoses*, a favorite Shakespearean source, is echoed in wordings and conceits here and there throughout the *Sonnets*, but the overall scheme of the group as a whole—the accounts of the poet's two loves—has no literary source. However, that Shakespeare wrote a sequence of sonnets can be attributed to the influence of Sidney's *Astrophel and Stella*. Also, an earlier convention required that sonnets be devoted to love, and Shakespeare followed this tradition, though he approaches the subject in an unconventional manner. The love relationships of the *Sonnets* are reconfigurations of the courtly love usually depicted in love sonnets: The object of the poet's love is addressed in the formal terms of the tradition and is beautiful and virtuous, as expected, but he is, unconventionally, a man; the expected woman is present, but she is neither beautiful nor virtuous. Each sonnet is concerned with love, as is the collection as a whole, but the points of view taken and the aspects of love dealt with vary greatly, sometimes even within an individual poem. Shakespeare's characteristic recognition that life is complicated and that contradictory ideas and impulses often coexist is very well demonstrated in these works. The *Sonnets*, like the best of Shakespeare's dramas, offer an experience that transcends both scholarly disputes and the differences between the poet's world and our own.